JAPAN

GUIDE

BE A TRAVELER - NOT A TOURIST!

OPEN ROAD TRAVEL GUIDES SHOW YOU
HOW TO BE A TRAVELER – NOT A TOURIST!

Whether you're going abroad or planning a trip in the United States, take Open Road along on your journey. Our books have been praised by **Travel & Leisure, The Los Angeles Times, Newsday, Booklist, US News & World Report, Endless Vacation, American Bookseller, Coast to Coast,** *and many other magazines and newspapers!*

Don't just see the world – experience it with Open Road!

ABOUT THE AUTHORS

Patrice Fusillo has spent more than 20 years working in international exchange, including The Asia Society, The Institute of Foreign Bankers, and The Japan Society. An 11-year Tokyo resident, Patrice now makes her home in Oakland, California, where she is a cross-cultural consultant.

Noriko Araki, a lifelong Tokyo resident, is a freelance writer. Trained as an anthropologist, Noriko enjoys looking at her culture and society from both inside and out. Both avid travelers, Noriko and Patrice have written monographs on Japanese culture, and are co-authors of Open Road Publishing's *Tokyo Guide*.

BE A TRAVELER, NOT A TOURIST - WITH OPEN ROAD TRAVEL GUIDES!

Open Road Publishing has guide books to exciting, fun destinations on four continents. As veteran travelers, our goal is to bring you the best travel guides available anywhere!

No small task, but here's what we offer:

• All Open Road travel guides are written by authors with a distinct, opinionated point of view – not some sterile committee or team of writers. Our authors are experts in the areas covered and are polished writers.

• Our guides are geared to people who want to make their own travel choices. We'll show you how to discover the real destination – not just see some place from a tour bus window.

• We're strong on the basics, but we also provide terrific choices for those looking to get off the beaten path and experience the country or city – not just see it or pass through it.

• We give you the best, but we also tell you about the worst and what to avoid. Nobody should waste their time and money on their hard-earned vacation because of bad or inadequate travel advice.

• Our guides assume nothing. We tell you everything you need to know to have the trip of a lifetime – presented in a fun, literate, no-nonsense style.

• And, above all, we welcome your input, ideas, and suggestions to help us put out the best travel guides possible.

JAPAN

GUIDE

BE A TRAVELER - NOT A TOURIST!

Patrice Fusillo & Noriko Araki

OPEN ROAD PUBLISHING

2nd Edition

ACKNOWLEDGEMENTS

We thank the many people who helped us capture the energy and vitality of Japan. Many of the maps appear courtesy of the Japan National Tourist Organization and we thank JNTO's Isao Yoshiike, Kaneyuki Ono and Marian Goldberg for their assistance. Judith T. Smith tirelessly assisted with editing. Akiko Yamaguchi drew the many illustrations that grace these pages. Big thanks to our publisher, Jonathan Stein, for giving us the opportunity to write this book.

Thanks also go to Nancy Berry, Sandy Berry, Rosemary and Glen Bonderud, Jane Faller, Takeshi Hasegawa, Nagako Hiyoshi, Steve and Chikako Hytha, Takashi Katano, Pat Langan, Milagros Louise, Yin-wah Ma, Jane Singer Mizuguchi, Cesare Monti, Sue Muroga, Shigeko Nishiyama, Hideko Sakurai, Keiko Sakurai, Anne Torige, Yumi Yamazaki, Jan Wessel, Patty Goodman, Reiko Kuribayashi, Namiko Sakamoto, and Nancy Wilson. Last, but not least, we thank our husbands, Tadashi Araki and David Hytha, and our children, Naoko and Nobuyuki Araki and Renee and Allison Hytha.

In revising the book, I am grateful for the assistance of Yoshimi Mizuno, Mariko Tatsumi, Toyokazu Okada, Tomoko Inuishi and Marian Goldberg, all with the Japan National Tourist Organization, and am also indebted to Rose Eng Lee, Steve Butler, Chikako Takezawa Hytha, Patricia A. Langan, Bill and Nada Finan and Jane Singer Mizuguchi.

Cover photos by Donald Nausbaum, Carib Photo, Toronto, Canada. Maps by James Ramage, except those indicated as courtesy of Japan National Tourist Organization. The authors have made every effort to be as accurate as possible, but neither they nor the publisher assume responsibility for the services provided by any business listed in this guide; for any errors or omissions; or any loss, damage, or disruptions in your travels for any reason.

TABLE OF CONTENTS

26. GLOSSARY   874

INDEX   876

SIDEBARS

SIDEBARS

1. INTRODUCTION

Japan is an extraordinary place, one of the world's most exotic, intriguing, puzzling and enticing destinations anywhere in the world.

Already anchored firmly in the 21st century, Japan still reveres its age-old traditions. Craftsmen spend months creating a perfect lacquer bowl while hundreds of Walkmen roll off a production line every hour. High atop a 50-storied steel and glass skyscraper, a small wooden Shinto shrine receives daily offerings of rice and *sake*. Japan has been more successful than most countries at maintaining a balance between old and new.

Some people avoid Japan, assuming it's not exotic enough – they picture only skyscrapers and men dressed in dark suits. Others avoid it because they have heard stories of $150 melons and $300-a-pound beef and assume the entire country is way over budget for them. Still others fear traveling in a country where they can't read signs.

Set aside these worries and get ready for the trip of a lifetime. Castles, temples, virtual reality game centers, quiet hot spring resorts, glittering urban centers, dramatic *kabuki* dance, Zen meditation, state-of-the-art factories, volcanoes belching smoke, serene rock gardens, 1000-year-old shrines, postmodern architecture and much more await you. We detail highlights of the best-known sights, but also recommend off-the-beaten-path alternatives.

Afraid you won't know how to act at a Japanese inn? We explain the etiquette from the time you arrive till the time you leave, including when to remove your shoes and how to use a Japanese bath. Are you worried about going outside your hotel to try other restaurants? We'll get you into restaurants where locals go and prepare you to order like a pro in no time. Not sure what temples and shrines are all about? We give you enough background information to help you understand what you see and, more importantly, how to enjoy it.

Afraid of the high cost of travel? We tell you how to find the best prices on international tickets and how to travel economically within Japan. Yes, we detail Japanese inns and hotels where you'll be pampered in a style to which you'd like to become accustomed, but we also tell you about places where two meals are included for less than it costs to stay at a Holiday Inn.

So pack your bag, get set, and come visit one of the most enchanting countries in the world – Japan!

2. OVERVIEW

Japan might be the most overanalyzed country in the world. Entire forests have been sacrificed to produce books explaining Japan to Westerners. So it's no surprise that everyone visits Japan with expectations. Some people romantically picture Japan as the *Teahouse of the August Moon,* a nation where the entire population dresses in kimono and lives a rarefied life in quaint buildings, writing *haiku* poetry and performing tea ceremony as delicate *koto* melodies waft through the air.

Others see Japan as a vision of the future, out of control: huge faceless sprawling cities with millions of people crowding into subways, living in cramped apartments, racing to keep up with the pace of robots next to them on the assembly line.

A third group, the road warriors who fill the business class seats of planes crossing the Pacific, interact with aggressive businessmen driving hard bargains around the world and see Japan as just plain hard work.

In reality Japan contains aspects of all three, but much more. The country of 125 million people working hard and playing hard also offers beautiful scenery, exceptional monuments, a fascinating history and an endless numbers of unique experiences:

• Stand in Shinjuku Station, the world's busiest train station.
• Climb to an isolated mountain temple in a dense forest an hour away from the same train station.
• Marvel at a sea of neon signs so dense you can read a newspaper at night on the street.
• Visit a war museum perennially at the center of controversy over Japan's past.
• Bathe in a steaming outdoor hot spring bath catching snowflakes on your tongue.
• Watch your car, TV or Walkman come off its production line.
• Join an entire nation in celebrating cherry blossoms.
• See meditative tea ceremonies performed in rustic huts.
• Exchange toasts with fun-loving Japanese in a raucous bar under the railway tracks.

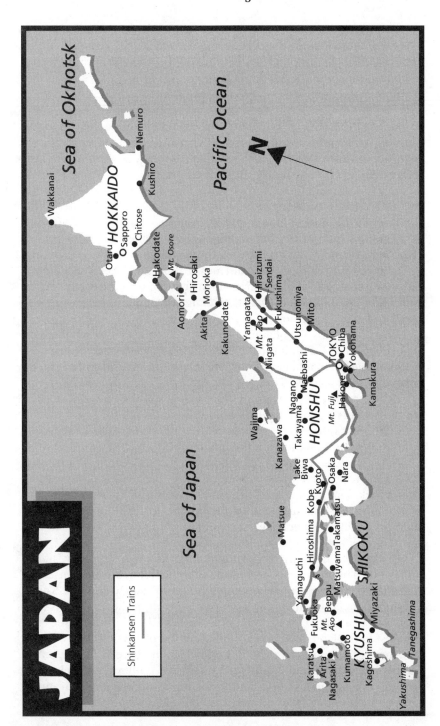

• Enjoy some of the finest cooking in the world, some of it uncooked.
• Ski on an indoor slope on a sweltering 90° day.
• Marvel at unbelievably high prices — but then go to a discount store and
    buy a camera that's still unavailable overseas.
• Gaze in awe at the world's largest bronze Buddha.

Japan offers soaring castles and 1000-year-old temples, legacies of the country's long and colorful history. Its virtual reality game centers and factories, manned only by robots, deliver you squarely into the 21st century. Japan offers so much; the greatest difficulty is deciding what to see with your limited time. Don't fret, we offer lots of suggestions in the next chapter, *Suggested Itineraries*.

Tokyo is the pulse of modern Japan. Seat of the national government, the city isn't a stodgy place inhabited only by bureaucrats. It's the center of the fashion and retailing industries, the big trading houses, the banking and financial industries, the arts and music. Home to 150,000 restaurants and bars, people crowd the entertainment areas into the wee hours of the morning. Once the castle town of the Tokugawa shoguns, some neighborhoods still evoke a memory of the feudal past.

Near Tokyo lies **Yokohama**, a cosmopolitan port city; **Kamakura**, a former capital with a multitude of temples in a quiet seaside setting; and **Nikko**, home of an unbelievably ornate shrine, the mausoleum of one of Japan's greatest leaders, Tokugawa Ieyasu.

Kyoto, capital of Japan for 1100 years, is still the nation's cultural capital. Masters carry on centuries-old refined traditions. Hundreds of tranquil temples and serene gardens dot the city and the surrounding hills — the traditional co-exists with the modern.

Nara, Kyoto's neighbor, ruled Japan in the 8th century. A fantastic collection of ancient temples containing masterpieces of sculpture sits in a quiet park. This tranquil city is the unlikely home of the world's largest bronze Buddha that happens to live in the world's largest wooden building. Slightly farther afield is one of Japan's oldest Buddhist temples where 8th century wooden buildings still stand.

Osaka, a thoroughly modern and sprawling industrial city, holds gems of turn-of-the-century and postmodern architecture. An outstanding aquarium and a fascinating puppet theater will add to any visit. **Kobe**, a cosmopolitan port city hit by a devastating earthquake in 1995, is well on its way to a full recovery. West of Kobe lies **Himeji** whose castle, the grandest in the land, towers gracefully over the plains.

Among the industrial cities in western Japan, there are some gems: **Kurashiki's** magnificently preserved district of traditional storehouses provides one of Japan's most picturesque urban landscapes; **Okayama's** garden ranks among Japan's finest; and **Hiroshima's** poignant A-Bomb memorials plead for world peace. Across the narrow Inland Sea, the island of **Shikoku** offers breathtaking scenery and Japan's most famous 88-temple pilgrimage.

On western Japan's isolated Japan Sea coast, the small cities and towns of **Matsue**, **Hagi**, and **Tsuwano** preserve remnants of Japan's samurai past. The Shinto shrine of **Izumo** ranks among Japan's most revered. The island of **Kyushu** features thoroughly modern large cities like **Fukuoka**, **Kumamoto**, and **Kagoshima** plus small villages where artisans have carried on pottery and textile traditions for generations.

Skipping to the opposite end of Japan, **Hokkaido**, the sparsely populated northern island, features beautiful mountain scenery, world-class hiking and skiing, an outstanding winter snow festival and the rare opportunity to see Japanese cranes perform mating dances in their natural habitat.

South of Hokkaido lies **Tohoku**, the northeastern part of Japan's main island. The rugged mountainous area offers spectacular scenery, mountain getaways, hiking and skiing, quiet hot spring inns and rustic crafts.

Nagano in Japan's mountainous interior, host of the 1998 Winter Olympics, features towering mountains, clear rivers, great hiking and skiing and a handful of picturesque towns that once served as way stations for travelers. **Matsumoto City** features Japan's oldest castle keep.

Kanazawa, a city on the Japan Sea, is home to one of Japan's most magnificent gardens. Thriving craft traditions date back to the days when it was a wealthy feudal domain. The well-preserved merchant quarter of **Takayama**, a small city nestled in the mountains, transports you back to feudal era. Remote villages still maintain picturesque thatched-roof buildings where farmers have lived for centuries. The city of **Nagoya**, home to an excellent museum of Japanese art, provides easy access to Japan's most sacred Shinto shrine at Ise. Two small but lovely castles lie within an hour of Nagoya at **Inuyama** and **Hikone**.

Fascinating places match fascinating experiences. Sports lovers can revel in *sumo*, baseball, soccer and a host of martial arts. Crafts aficionados can choose from ceramics, weaving, dyeing, papermaking and woodworking to name just a few.

Experience Japanese hospitality by staying at a traditional inn. Bathe at a hot spring resort. Try a variety of Japanese cuisine from *sushi* bars to noodles to *kaiseki*, elaborate haute cuisine. Sing your heart out at a karaoke bar. Browse through temple flea markets and antique stores.

Take the plunge. Japan awaits you.

3. SUGGESTED ITINERARIES

Travelers from North America cross the international date line and arrive in Japan the following day — don't forget to factor this into your travel schedule. We do not include the day of arrival in our itineraries.

To avoid back-tracking, investigate flying into **Narita Airport** in Tokyo and leaving from **Kansai International Airport** in Osaka or vice versa. When you return to North America, you arrive on the same day you leave Japan.

SEVEN-DAY ITINERARY FOR A FIRST-TIME VISITOR TO JAPAN

Day 1 – Tokyo
Day 2 – Tokyo
Day 3 – Morning: Travel to Hakone by train. Overnight at Hakone.
Day 4 – Morning: Travel from Hakone to Kyoto by train. Overnight at Kyoto.
Day 5 – Kyoto
Day 6 – Day trip to Nara or Himeji Castle by train. Overnight at Kyoto.
Day 7 – Morning: Kyoto. Late afternoon: Depart from Kansai airport or return to Tokyo.

Three-day extension to Kanazawa & Takayama

Days 1-6 as in the seven-day itinerary,
Day 7 – Morning: Kyoto. Afternoon: Travel to Kanazawa by train. Overnight at Kanazawa.
Day 8 – Kanazawa
Day 9 – Morning: Travel to Takayama by train (via Toyama). Overnight at Takayama.
Day 10 – Morning: Takayama. Afternoon: Return to Tokyo by train (via Nagoya).

TEN-DAY ITINERARY: TOKYO, KYOTO, & ALONG THE INLAND SEA

Day 1 – Tokyo

Day 2 – Tokyo

Day 3 – Morning: Travel to Hakone by train. Overnight at Hakone.

Day 4 – Morning: Travel from Hakone to Kyoto by train. Overnight at Kyoto.

Day 5 – Kyoto

Day 6 – Kyoto

Day 7 – Morning: Travel to Himeji by train. Late Afternoon: Travel to Kurashiki by train. Overnight at Kurashiki.

Day 8 – Morning: Kurashiki. Afternoon: Travel to Hiroshima by train. Overnight at Hiroshima.

Day 9 – Morning: Travel to Miyajima. Overnight at Miyajima.

Day 10 – Travel to Tokyo or Osaka by train (via Hiroshima).

Four-day extension to the remote Japan Sea area

Day 10 – Morning: Travel from Miyajima to Tsuwano (via Hiroshima and Ogori). Overnight at Tsuwano.

Day 11 – Morning: Tsuwano. Afternoon: Travel from Tsuwano to Hagi by train. Overnight at Hagi.

Day 12 – Afternoon: Travel from Hagi to Izumo by train. Stay at Yakumo Honjin near Izumo.

Day 13 – Morning: Izumo. Afternoon: Matsue. Overnight at Matsue.

Day 14 – Travel to Tokyo or Osaka by air or rail.

SEVEN-DAY ITINERARY TO TOHOKU IN NORTHERN JAPAN

Day 1 – Morning: Travel to Kakunodate by train. Overnight at Kakunodate.

Day 2 – Afternoon: Travel to Nyuto Onsen area by trains and bus (via Lake Tazawa). Overnight at a hot spring inn at Nyuto Onsen.

Day 3 – Morning: Travel to Tono by train (via Morioka). Overnight at Tono.

Day 4 – Morning: Travel to Hiraizumi by train (via Hanamaki). Late afternoon: Travel to Sendai by train. Overnight at Sendai.

Day 5 – Day trip to Yamadera or Matsushima. Overnight at Sendai.

Day 6 – Morning: Travel to Nikko by train (via Utsunomiya). Overnight at Nikko.

Day 7 – Afternoon: Late afternoon: Return to Tokyo by train.

TEN-DAY ITINERARY TO KYUSHU

Day 1 – Travel to Fukuoka by air or rail. Overnight at Fukuoka.

Day 2 – Day trip to Karatsu, Arita or Yanagawa

Day 3 – Morning: Fukuoka. Afternoon: Travel to Nagasaki by train. Overnight at Nagasaki.

Day 4 – Nagasaki

Day 5 – Morning: Travel to Kumamoto by train (via Tosu). Overnight at Kumamoto.

Day 6 – Morning: Travel to Kagoshima by train. Overnight at Kagoshima.

Day 7 – Morning: Travel to Chiran. Afternoon: Travel to Ibusuki. Overnight at Ibusuki.

Day 8 – Morning: Travel to Miyazaki. Overnight at Miyazaki.

Day 9 – Morning: Travel to Yufuin. Overnight at Yufuin.

Day 10 – Travel to Tokyo or Osaka by air or rail.

BEST OF JAPAN

Tailor your trip to fit your interests. Here are our top picks:

Castles

Hikone

Himeji

Inuyama

Kumamoto

Matsue

Matsumoto

Well-preserved historic districts

Hagi

Kakunodate

Kanazawa

Kurashiki

Matsue

Takayama

Tsumago and Magome

Ceramics

Arita

Ashikaga

Hagi

Imbe

Kanazawa

Karatsu

Kyoto
Onta

Traditional Crafts
Kanazawa
Kyoto
Takayama

Hot Springs
Hakone
Lake Towada area
Nyuto Onsen
Nikko area
Yufuin

Temples & Shrines
Dewa Sanzan
Ise
Izumo
Kamakura
Kyoto
Nikko
Osorezan

Nature
Izumi
Kamikochi
Kushiro
Lake Towada and Oirase Gorge
Nikko area
Yakushima

Gardens
Chiran
Kagoshima
Kanazawa
Kyoto

Volcanoes
Mt. Aso
Mt. Fuji
Sakurajima

Contemporary Architecture
Fukuoka
Osaka
Tokyo

Festivals
Akita
Aomori
Hirosaki
Kyoto
Nagasaki
Sapporo
Sendai
Takayama
Yamagata

Museums
Arita
Ashikaga
Atami
Kanazawa
Kurashiki
Kyoto
Osaka
Tokyo

World War II History
Chiran
Hiroshima
Nagasaki

Performing Arts
Kyoto
Osaka
Takarazuka
Tokyo

4. LAND & PEOPLE

Japan perches on the ring of fire encircling the Pacific Ocean. The crush of plates formed dramatic mountains and enormous volcanoes. The resulting four main islands — **Hokkaido**, **Honshu**, **Shikoku** and **Kyushu** — and over one thousand smaller islands stretch 1200 kilometers.

Mountains define Japan. They created the archipelago by rising from the floor of the Pacific Ocean to form its backbone. Mountains cover the interior of the four main islands and often run down to the water's edge. Venerated **Mount Fuji** at 3776 meters is Japan's tallest, but the **Japan Alps**, named after their European cousins, have more than 20 peaks over 3000 meters. Volcanoes — 188 in all — dot Japan. More than 40 are still active, but eruptions are hardly daily events.

The island chain is crescent shaped; Tokyo and Kyoto are actually east/west of each other, rather than north/south. Tokyo shares the same latitude as Los Angeles and Raleigh, North Carolina. Sendai is even with New York and Wakkanai, the northern tip of Hokkaido, with Montreal.

Japan's forests cover 67% of the country compared to only 10% of Great Britain. Why does everyone think of Great Britain as a green nation and Japan as an overpopulated megalopolis? Japan has very little flat land. Most of the narrow country's interior is mountainous and offers great off-the-beaten track getaways — you are never more than 100 kilometers from the sea in any point in Japan.

The islands of Japan are at the meeting point of major geological plates — this means lots of seismic activity. They average about 7500 earthquakes a year — that's 20 a day — but before you scratch Japan off the visit list, know that the vast majority are too weak to be felt except by sensitive seismographs. The big ones come along only once every 70 to 100 years.

The few plains support the vast majority of Japan's population. While Japan's overall population density is only 331 per square kilometer, the greater Tokyo area and the Kobe-Osaka-Kyoto region crowd in over 10,000 people per square kilometer. And the Tokyo-Yokohama area supports 25 million people, the largest urban center in the world. But take an hour-long train ride to the mountains and you're hard pressed to find a soul. Japan is about the same size as California but if you take the amount of habitable land and subtract the amount used for agriculture and industry, the entire country, all 125 million people, ends up living in a space the size of Connecticut. Seventy percent of the population lives along the Pacific coast from Tokyo to northern Kyushu.

Although the sea surrounds Japan, it has used the seas to keep the world at arms' length for most of its history. Japan was not a major ocean-going nation. The oceans served as Japan's defense against invasion; other than a disastrous attempt to conquer Korea in the late 16th century and the expansionism in Asia leading to World War II, Japan focused inward.

FUN FACTS

California is larger than the whole of Japan.

Japan's land is 1/25 the size of the US. The population is 1/2 of the US.

Japan's gross domestic product (GDP) is over 60% of the size of the US GDP. Per person GDP is $32,654 versus $27,799 for the US.

Japan's economy is nine times larger than China's.

About 14% of Japan is agricultural land; 67% is forest and woodland.

Population density per square kilometer: 331. How does this compare? Hong Kong: 5481; Singapore: 4741; Bangladesh: 818; India: 279; Germany: 228; China: 124; US: 28; Russia: 9; Canada: 3; Australia: 2.

Japanese have the world's longest life expectancy: 83.59 years for women, 77.01 years for men. US life expectancy: 79.1 for women and 72.3 for men.

WEATHER

Extending over twenty degrees of latitude from the chilly northern tip of Hokkaido to subtropical Okinawa, Japan has many different climatic zones. Hokkaido is very cold in winter and cool in summer. Northern Honshu has a cold winter and a hot summer. Tokyo, Kyoto and western Japan have fairly mild winters and hot, steamy summers. The Japan Sea coast gets harsh and snowy winters. Okinawa is subtropical. All of Japan except Hokkaido experiences a month-long rainy season early June to mid-July.

We feel sorry for Japanese weather forecasters. Because islands comprise the country, the weather patterns are unstable, so the day to day weather is unpredictable. It's not unusual for tomorrow's weather to be opposite of this morning's newspaper report.

All of Japan, except Okinawa, supports four distinct seasons. Japanese culture exalts in celebrating the seasons. Cherry blossoms in spring, foliage in autumn, the heat of summer and snowfall in winter mark major milestones of the year.

Geography and climate patterns have blessed Japan with copious amounts of usable water from rain, melting snowcaps and large lakes. The climate lent itself to rice cultivation. Rice growing demands cooperation among farmers to distribute water. Some argue this fact is the basis for the emphasis on cooperation in Japanese society and culture.

SOCIETY & PEOPLE

Japan is almost always characterized as a society where social harmony is valued higher than individuality. In a country of 125 million people, the reality is much more complex.

Certainly Japan has a strong group orientation. At any tourist sight around the world, bus loads of Japanese travelers follow flag toting guides. Pins with company logos adorn employees' lapels as if they were Gucci jewelry. From a young age, children in both public and private schools wear military-looking uniforms.

But many don't fit the mold. Japan has more than its share of eccentrics from computer designers to novelists, from craftsmen devoting their lives to reviving a dying art to corporate executives writing poetry in their leisure time.

But the average Japanese also doesn't fit this mold. People assert their individuality although it may be in different and less dramatic ways than in the West. More Japanese than ever opt to travel individually. Children who have lived overseas were once shunned when they returned to Japan; now special schools and programs help them maintain their second language proficiency and cross-cultural skills. Company employees bail out to run a new venture or a bed and breakfast in a ski resort or climb the world's great peaks.

Many people assume that the large corporations, which produce the cars, electronics, steel and toys known around the world, employ the vast majority of Japanese workers, but it is not true. More people work for small companies and mom-and-pop operations that do not provide the cradle-to-grave safety nets. But not all large companies are lean manufacturing machines. Banks and financial institutions still operate as if they were in the stone age. Cashing a simple traveler's check can take 20 minutes and involve a half-dozen bank clerks.

The company has assumed many of the functions once provided by the extended family. While lifetime employment is no longer an undeniable right in the large corporations (and it never was in smaller companies), the company often provides housing, commuting passes, vacation hostels and even matchmaking services. Companies function hierarchically. Salaries and promotion are based on age, not skills. Workers endure more than many of their counterparts in the West: two hour commutes on packed trains, cramped living conditions and long hours in the office. Employees often arrive home late in the evening following after-hours socializing with colleagues and customers. The subways and commuter trains are as crowded at 10pm as they are at 6pm. Wives almost never participate in business entertainment.

Although contemporary society developed from a feudal system, Japan is remarkably egalitarian. World War II effectively destroyed most of the wealth of the old families; postwar land reform finished the process. Aristocratic titles were abolished after the war. The imperial family lineage is restricted to a small group; princes marry commoners and princesses born into the imperial family lose their titles upon marriage.

Education defines Japan's elite today. Graduates of top universities enter the prestigious government ministries and large corporations. Scions of aristocratic families figure prominently among the elite, but so do people from average families.

Japan is overwhelmingly middle class. One amazing fact about Japanese corporations is the range in salary between the company president and the lowest paid employee is among the lowest in the world.

The countryside has emptied out as people migrated to urban centers for good jobs. Farmers are fairly affluent today thanks to generous government subsidies. But the sons who stay behind to work the family farm are hard-pressed to find Japanese women willing to marry into the hardworking lifestyle. Some marry Philippinas and Thai women.

The Role of Women

The role of women is a highly complex subject. Until the mid-1980s, most women worked only in clerical positions (called OLs for Office Ladies). Then a labor shortage and an equal opportunity employment law strengthened women's positions in the workplace. This law has no teeth; it doesn't carry penalties for companies who did not comply. Companies have established a professional track for women, but many women have been disappointed by the limited opportunities; only 1.5% of senior managers and just over 7% of lower level managers are female.

Being a housewife and a mother still carry a lot of respect in Japan. Women often quit their jobs either when they marry or when they give birth to their first child. But to maintain a high standard of living, many will work part-time. Women run the household, handle the finances and take chief responsibility for the children and their education. With many husbands away until late in the evening, they live fairly independent lives. Despite the reputation for fathers being absent, you will see lots of families together on weekend excursions from zoos to ski slopes.

Japanese women are quite picky about whom they marry. Their social status is largely dependent on their husband's employment. If they do not find someone with the right credentials, they prefer to remain unmarried, a path taken by an estimated 14% of young women today. Many live with their parents and spend their considerable income on clothing, entertainment and travel. Women who did not marry by the age of 25 used to be branded "Christmas cakes," out of date after the 25th. Now the average age of marriage is in the late 20s.

Weddings

Weddings are large, formal and expensive affairs, usually taking place at hotels. Traditionally, wedding ceremonies were Shinto and held at shrines or hotels, attended only by immediate family members, and followed by a large reception. More people now opt for Christian weddings so their friends can attend the ceremony itself, and in Japan you don't have to be a Christian to have a church wedding. On weekends, the lobbies of large hotels see an endless parade of wedding parties dressed in kimono and other finery.

Most people find their own mates (80% marry for love) or friends and family may introduce them to appropriate partners. No matter how they meet, brides and grooms usually ask an older couple to serve as their ceremonial "go-between" at the wedding ceremony. At the reception, the go-betweens sit with the couple on the dais while the parents sit at the back of the hall.

Speeches by bosses, colleagues and friends punctuate wedding receptions. The bride, queen for a day, starts off wearing a traditional wedding kimono or a white wedding gown and changes into one or two other Western-style ball gowns during the reception. As a counter to this formal affair, a second, more informal party for friends at a restaurant or disco usually follows the main reception. Most Japanese travel overseas on honeymoons. Hawaii and Australia are two popular destinations.

All of this does not come cheap. The average marriage in Tokyo, including reception, honeymoon and finding a new apartment, costs ¥6.5 million (roughly $60,000). The reception expenses average ¥2.7 million (about $20,000) although gifts of money offset about half that expense.

The groom bears the greatest expense, then the bride, the parents of the bride and the parents of the groom.

Japan has one of the lowest divorce rates among developed nations. Laws discourage divorce, but social pressure plays an equally large role. Divorce has become more common in the last few years and remarriage has also increased.

Kids & School

Japan's birthrate has hit an all time low of 1.43 births per woman, not enough to sustain the current population levels. Women rarely bear more than two children. Cramped living conditions and the expense of a first-class education deter most from having larger families.

Since college education is the greatest determinant of a child's career success, education competition begins in preschool, and even before. Upwardly mobile parents press their children to get into the "right" kindergartens so they are on track for admission to the top universities. Some three and four year olds even go to cram school to prepare for admission to kindergarten.

Cram schools supplement the normal education to get an edge in taking exams. Japanese school children go through examination hell to get into the better middle and high schools as well as into universities. If a student fails to gain admission to a good university, rather than attending a second-rate one, he or she may choose to spend a year of intensive study at a test preparation school and retake the exams the following year.

There are some cries to change the entrance exam system, but little reform appears forthcoming. About 40% of high school graduates go on to colleges, universities and junior colleges. While it's very difficult to gain admission to top Japanese universities, once admitted, most Japanese say that university life is considerably less rigorous than high school. Many students consider the four years a respite between examination hell and a lifetime of work.

The Security Net

The government and Japanese pundits worry about who will support an increasingly aging population. In 1997, for the first time the number of people over age 65 exceeded the number of children under 14. Retirement age is between 57 and 60, but many workers take on a new job and work another five to ten years usually at reduced pay. Most security guards appear to be over 60. For many, retirement means time for a more active cultural life and travel.

Most people retire with a pension equal to two years' salary, woefully inadequate to support themselves. Thus in the postwar period, Japanese have salted away 15 to 20% of their annual income in preparation for old age. Health care is from cradle to grave, but with some twists. In many hospitals, you must provide your own meals and linens. Traditionally, aging parents lived with the oldest son, but with small urban apartments, longer life spans and smaller families, this custom has changed too.

Government

Japan is a democratic country with a two-house parliament called the **Diet** that's led by a prime minister elected by the majority party. The emperor comes from the longest continuously reigning dynasty in the world but today has only ceremonial duties. Japan is divided into 47 **prefectures**, each with its own governor and assembly. Each city, town and village also has its own government.

Politics in the postwar period has been dominated by one party, the conservative **Liberal Democratic Party** (LDP) — the joke is that it's neither liberal nor democratic. However, the last several years have witnessed major political upheaval with the LDP dividing into several conservative parties; the main opposition, the Socialists, self-destructing; and a host of political finance scandals. Most of the recent political divisions are based on personality, not on ideology.

Different from US politics, the national bureaucracy wields enormous power by writing as well as implementing the laws the Diet passes. Japan's best and brightest go into an alphabet soup of ministries. The country runs on the often touted "Iron Triangle" of the LDP, the bureaucracy and industry. Although some change is afoot, political stability has fostered the economic growth of postwar Japan.

The postwar Constitution renounces war. Japan's commitment of troops to United Nations' peacekeeping efforts is a constant source of debate in the government. Japan's armed forces, named the Self-Defense Forces, receive the third largest defense budget in the world.

THE JAPANESE YEAR

While modern Japan seems high tech and urbanized, by and large the Japanese year still revolves around the traditional agrarian calendar. Here are the highlights of the year:

New Year's Day is January 1. Japan switched from the Chinese lunar calendar to the Western calendar in the late 19th century, but until after World War II family holidays revolved around the old calendar.

The New Year's celebration, the most important holiday in the year, spreads over several days. Everything stops. Offices close December 28 or 29 until January 3 or 4. Although museums and even some temples close, it's one of the best times of the year to get a sense of traditional culture.

Preparations for New Year's holiday begin right after Christmas. Houses are decorated with pine, bamboo and plum — all auspicious symbols. Just as Christmas decorations in the West stay up for some time, Japanese keep their New Year's decorations up until January 7.

The New Year's holiday is a family time. They gather together to eat special meals and spend the time playing traditional games such as guessing poems, spinning tops and flying kites. Before midnight, people begin to visit Shinto shrines to pray for prosperity in the coming year. It's called *hatsumode*, first visit of the year. Some of the most popular shrines have several million visitors during the first few days of January. If you happen to be in Japan during the New Year's celebrations, go to a Shinto shrine to share the excitement and enthusiasm of people optimistically welcoming the new year.

NEW YEAR'S DECORATIONS

*Shimekazari (Shinto Straw Festoons) are made with rope, string and folded **washi** paper, and placed at the front entrance, tokonoma alcove and other locations at New Year's to keep evil spirits from entering the home. Some people also adorn the fronts of their cars with them during the New Year's season.*

*Kadomatsu are pine branches and bamboo arranged in a stand and placed at either side of the entrance. They welcome the good spirits. People also put pounded rice cakes in the tokonoma and cook **oseichi**, special food to welcome the gods.*

Coming of Age Day is the second Monday in January. All those who turn twenty between January 16 of the previous year and January 15 of the new year become adults. They then can vote and buy alcohol and tobacco. Many of these new adults go to Shinto shrines to pray for good fortune — on auspicious occasions, Japanese pray to Shinto gods — and throw parties to celebrate. The young women and a few young men dress in formal kimono, so remember to take your camera to the shrines.

Setsubun, February 3, marks the passing of winter although we think it is more wishful thinking than anything else. Japanese buy special soy beans at supermarkets and throw them in every room of the house declaring: "Luck come in, devils go out!" Some Shinto shrines perform dances where beans are thrown to expel the demons in the coming year.

Valentine's Day, February 14, was a cultural transplant during the Occupation after World War II. It's widely celebrated by young people, but there's a twist. We don't know if the Allied Powers were trying to be

SCHOOL STARTS WHEN?

Japan is one of the few developed countries where the school year starts in April. Recently some people have begun to advocate starting the school year in September to bring it in line with international practice. Believe it or not, one of the main reasons it hasn't changed is the emotional tie with cherry blossoms. Most Japanese associate the first day at school with seeing cherry blossoms in full bloom.

funny or the soldiers wanted to receive lots of sweets, but from the beginning, women gave chocolate to men. Today, they give chocolate not only to their special honeys, but to all the men at their offices. Men are supposed to give a return gift on March 14, White Day.

Girls' Day (Hina Matsuri) is celebrated on March 3. The tradition started with families going on outings to view peach blossoms. Girls would throw paper dolls into the river to cast off illness and misfortune. Eventually, the dolls became more elegant and elaborate and no one threw them into the water any more. Instead these dolls came to represent the imperial court and were set up on stands. Today, maternal grandparents usually give a set of dolls for a child's first girls' day. Set up about a month before the actual day and taken down on March 3rd, superstition says if the dolls aren't taken down on Girls' Day, the girl won't get married.

White Day, March 14. This holiday dates back only to the 1980s. Men are supposed to give white chocolate to women as repayment for Valentine's chocolate. To us this holiday always seems to be manufactured by the candy companies.

Vernal Equinox Day, March 20 or 21. On the first day of spring, like the first day of autumn, Japanese clean the graves of their ancestors.

Ohanami, Cherry Blossom Viewing. Late March through mid-April. Cherry blossoms are so much a part of Japanese society that the weather forecast, in what meteorologists call the "flower front," reports on cherry blossoms and estimates peak viewing times. Incredibly, the predictions are almost always correct.

Japanese love cherry blossoms, their brief bloom a simile for the impermanence of life itself. Cherry blossom viewing goes back hundreds of years. Woodblook prints and screen paintings show splendid viewing parties. A generation or two ago, families would gather under the trees with a picnic and enjoy the flowers. Today, companies plan elaborate outings, sending the newest recruits to save space in prime spots. In the evening, when everyone gathers, beer and *sake* flow freely and are consumed with large quantities of food. In the latest twist, some groups bring video monitors to view tapes of cherry blossoms. What could be more Japanese?

Beginning of School Year, April 1. There's a summer break mid-July through September 1, and a two-week break at the end of March.

Golden Week, April 29 through May 5. Within this period, there are four national holidays: April 29, May 3, 4 and 5, so many people take off the entire time. It's a really bad time to travel anywhere in Japan because everything is so jammed; *shinkansen* trains run at 160% of capacity and expressways (what a misnomer) sport 70-kilometer backups. But Golden Week is a lovely time to visit big cities; they are like ghost towns even though museums, temples, department stores and most restaurants stay open.

Children's Day, May 5. This holiday used to be called Boys' Day, but after World War II, in the spirit of equality, it changed to Children's Day. But to this day, it's mainly families with sons who fly *koinobori*, large carp streamers. Just as carp swim upstream, children are urged to work hard, hard enough to go against the currents to achieve success.

O-chugen Gift Giving Season. Gifts are exchanged in June and early July.

GIFT GIVING SEASONS

Gift giving is an important custom in Japan. There are two formal gift-giving seasons, at the end of the first half of the year and at year's end. Japanese love to give presents. The gesture is more important than the present itself. Japanese are almost obsessed with the idea that if they don't give presents, they have not expressed their gratitude, pleasure or other feelings. So gift giving helps society function smoothly.

Most people give practical presents such as food items, fruit or whiskey. We love to go to department stores to check out the elaborate gift displays; seeing ten cans of Budweiser beer or fruit cocktail expensively packaged in a box cracks us up. Presents do get recycled, but most people won't admit it.

Japanese also take time and pride in gift wrapping – the form is often more important than the substance. Formal calligraphy announces the gift giver's name on special paper on top of the glossy wrapping paper.

Foreign visitors are usually exempt from this gift-giving frenzy, but bring a small present from your country if you are going to visit a Japanese home.

Summer Fireworks *(hanabi)* displays have been held in July since the Edo period as a psychological relief from summer's oppressive heat and humidity.

O-Bon, August 13 to 16, is the Buddhist festival of the dead. During this time, spirits of the deceased return to their hometowns. City dwellers also return to their hometowns to visit their ancestors' graveyards. Nowadays, most people go as an excuse to see family, or travel elsewhere. There are a lot of summer festivals around this time. People dress in cotton *yukata* robes, eat at open air stalls and perform *bon odori* dances. If you are traveling in Japan during this period, be sure you make reservations well in advance – because trains, airplanes and highways are crowded. We like to stay in the cities because they empty out but museums, department stores and most restaurants remain open.

Autumnal Equinox, September 23 or 24, the first day of autumn. Traditionally this day is the one when Japanese clean the graves of their ancestors. Lots of Shinto shrines have harvest festivals, and local shrines have children parade *mikoshi* (portable shrines) around the neighborhood.

Autumn Foliage Viewing takes place in October and November. Like cherry blossom viewing, it has taken on almost cult status. Famous viewing sites such as Nikko and Kyoto become impossibly crowded.

Shichi-go-san Festival (Seven-Five-Three), November 15, is one of the most photogenic events of the year. Bring lots of film when you visit shrines. Girls age seven and three and boys age five go to a shrine to pray for good health. In the old days, these ages were considered to be dangerous years for children. Most of the girls dress in fancy kimono and some boys wear the traditional *hakama* outfit. Families celebrate the festival anytime during the week or two around November 15, not only on that one day.

Christmas, December 25. Japan is not a Christian country; only a minuscule portion of the population is Christian, but you would never know it looking at department stores. On November 1, as soon as the Halloween decorations are put away, Christmas decorations appear. Many Japanese exchange Christmas presents with family members or close friends, but there is no element of religion involved. Christmas cakes with white frosting are eaten on Christmas day. Christmas Eve, incidentally, is the year's biggest date night, similar to New Year's Eve in the US.

End of Year Preparations. The end of the year is so busy, it is called *shiwasu*, "even the master teacher runs," because the usually sedate teacher must also run to finish all the chores. Houses must be cleaned, all debts must be settled and any outstanding matters taken care of so that you can start the new year with a clean slate. Japanese give end-of-year presents called *oseibo* to anyone for whom they feel obligation such as doctors, companies and individuals. Companies hold *Bonenkai* "let's forget the bad luck in the year" parties. On New Year's Eve, Japanese eat *soba* noodles — the length of the noodles suggests longevity.

Matsuri Festivals

The roots of Japan's many festivals lay in the agrarian nature of society. Many of the festivals occur in the spring when farmers would pray for successful harvests and in the autumn to give thanks to the gods. At Shinto festivals, *mikoshi* (portable shrines) parade through the streets, pulled or carried by eager townspeople.

The **Gion Festival** in Kyoto in July, Takayama's spring and autumn festivals and the big summer festivals in Akita, Aomori and Hirosaki in northern Honshu rank among Japan's most popular.

JAPANESE RELIGION

Ask most Japanese whether or not they are believers in Shintoism or Buddhism and the answer is "Yes." Many small Shinto shrines are found on Buddhist temple grounds. The tolerance and symbiotic relationship between the two religions in Japan often bewilder Westerners.

Unlike Christianity or Islam, in Japan religion is not exclusive. Most Japanese have Shinto marriages, birth and coming-of-age celebrations. They go to Shinto shrines at New Year's to pray for prosperity and before examinations to pray for success. But Shintoism doesn't do well with death, which is considered polluting, so Japanese turn to Buddhism for funerals and the afterlife.

Shinto

The original Japanese religion is Shinto, an animist religion. Shintoists worship natural objects such as mountains, the sun and animals for their supernatural powers. The most important aspect of Shintoism is that ancestors are also worshipped. Lively legends set forth the origins of Japan. The Yamato clan, from whom the current imperial line traces its heritage, claims to have descended from the Sun Goddess, Amaterasu. Shinto gods, called *kami,* number in the thousands.

Most Shinto shrines are simple wooden structures with little adornment. Representing the sacred space inhabited by *kami,* shrines aren't cluttered with statues. A simple *torii* gate, traditionally made of wood but sometimes constructed of cement or metal, marks the entrance. Near the gate there is a basin of water to cleanse your hands and mouth as ritual purification before entering the precincts.

The main hall contains a small area where believers sit while rites are performed. In front of the main building sits a money box. Japanese throw some coins in the box, clap two times, bow and pray. Some shrines have a gong or bell on a long rope; pulling the rope helps get the gods' attention. Sacred dances called *kagura* are performed on the small covered platforms in front of the main hall of some shrines. The shrine sells amulets and fortunes.

You may notice strips of white paper tied to trees and fences. These are *omikuji*, fortunes which you can purchase for ¥100. When the fortune is very good, Japanese post it to make sure the gods take note; when it's very bad, they post it to pray for the gods to change it. If it's okay, they take it home. The fortunes are almost always in Japanese, but a few shrines, such as Kasuga Shrine in Nara, have ones in English.

You may also notice small wooden plaques hanging on posts on the shrine's grounds. These plaques are called *ema*, literally horse pictures. In ancient days, people donated horses to the shrine, but when it became too expensive, not to mention cumbersome, they donated pictures of horses. This custom evolved into a shrine producing small plaques usually with pictures of the shrine or the year's zodiac animal. Japanese purchase these plaques, write their prayers on the back and hang them so the gods can help them achieve their goals. Our highly unofficial survey reveals most have to do with passing entrance exams, having luck in love or recovering from an illness.

Buddhism

In the 5th and 6th centuries, Buddhism was introduced to Japan by Koreans. Prince Shotoku adopted Buddhism as a state religion for the ruling class, but the religion did not supplant Shintoism; the two existed side by side.

Prince Shotoku set up a system of building a Buddhist temple in each of the 64 provinces with Todai-ji Temple in Nara as the head. The close relationship between Buddhism and the state placed too much political power in the hands of the monks. This meddling became so annoying that in the late 8th century, Emperor Kammu moved the capital from Nara to Kyoto.

The early days of the Kyoto Heian period saw new forms of Buddhism. The priest Kukai (Kobo Daishi) went to China to study Buddhism and established esoteric Shingon Buddhism, centered at Mt. Koya outside of Osaka. The esoteric sect relied on ritual and mystic experiences to achieve enlightenment, and their temples were located in mountain settings. Enryaku-ji Temple on Mt. Hiei, under the priest Saicho, became the center for the Tendai sect that emphasized the belief in Amida, a benevolent intermediary to the Buddha.

Pure Land Buddhism decreed that anyone could gain salvation by sincere chanting of the Amida Buddha's name. This belief had enormous

WHICH ANIMAL ARE YOU?

Just as Zodiac signs in the West symbolize particular traits of those people who were born under a particular sign, the animal of the year, eto in Japanese, has meanings in Japanese culture. Twelve animals make a twelve-year cycle. The original concept must have come from ancient China like so many other things in Japan.

Japanese legend goes something like this. In the old days, a god or a Buddha wanted to test the loyalty of the animals, so he sent a quick message to each to visit him ASAP. As soon as the message arrived, the Ox began its trek, knowing he wasn't a fast mover. Amazingly, he thought he'd made the trip in record time. But, lo and behold, just as the Ox arrived, a smart Mouse jumped off his back, and voila, the mouse was first to greet the god! So the Mouse is first and then the Ox followed by Tiger, Rabbit, Dragon (the only imaginary animal), Snake, Horse, Sheep, Monkey, Chicken, Dog and Wild Boar.

Japanese enjoy associating various personal characteristics of those born in a certain animal's year – a Mouse is known to be hard working; an Ox, patient; a Tiger, short tempered. Knowing a person's animal gives a good hint a person's age without being too direct. Perhaps, you can deceive another's eyes by six years, but to look 12 years younger or older than you actually are needs more than a special technique!

Toward the end of each year, many varieties of the animal of the next year begin to appear in craft shops and department stores. Made from Japanese paper or from clay, people display their animals for fun and possibly for protection. The year of the Dragon, 2000, will be followed by the year of the Snake, 2001. We find the animal of the year makes a special present at baby showers. By the way, a cat chose to enjoy a nap rather than going to greet a god, so we don't have anyone officially born in the year of Cat. Interestingly in Vietnam there's a Cat instead of a Rabbit.

Which animal are you?

appeal to aristocrats who saw chaos and collapse of social order everywhere. It also made Buddhism accessible to the masses; up to this point, Buddhism was the domain of the aristocratic upper classes only.

In the Kamakura period (12th to 14th century), Buddhism brought from China became more Japanized. The priest Shinran founded the populist True Pure Land Sect. The charismatic priest Nichiren founded a Buddhist sect bearing his name in the 13th century. His nationalistic ideology derided other sects for being foreign.

Zen Buddhism also caught hold in Japan in the early years of the Kamakura period. Zen relied on *zazen* (meditation) and *koan* (philosophical riddles) to achieve enlightenment. A believer would constantly think of the riddle until all other thoughts left his head. Only then could he achieve enlightenment. These self-discipline aspects made Zen popular with the warrior class.

During the Edo period, the Tokugawa shogunate regulated nearly every aspect of life, including the freedom to travel. Going on a pilgrimage was one of the few legitimate excuses to hit the road. People traveled great distances to visit temples and shrines. Naturally when they got there, they also wanted to enjoy themselves. Small towns and entertainment districts grew up around the temples' gates.

When you visit a Buddhist temple, the first thing you'll notice is a large free-standing wooden entrance gate, frequently a two-storied affair. *Nio* (fierce guardian statues) often stand watch inside the gate, ready to repel evil spirits. Buddhist temples have no standard configuration. The main hall, usually called *hondo* or *kondo*, will have a Buddha figure of worship, but it may not be visible. There's often a lecture hall called *kodo*, a bell tower, sometimes a multistoried pagoda and usually the abbot's quarters. Zen temples have *shukubo* (dormitories) and kitchens since their priests live communally. If the kitchen is open to the public, be sure you go in to see the huge stoves where priests prepare vegetarian meals for hundreds of monks.

At the main hall, believers put money in a box and bow and say their prayers. You can buy incense and candles and offer them with a prayer, quite similar to the Roman Catholic Church. At some temples you'll see people waving incense smoke over their bodies, believing that the incense will heal their ailments and protect them from illness.

Christianity

St. Francis Xavier brought Christianity to Japan in 1549 when he landed in Kyushu. Some feudal lords were converted but the religion never made major inroads. In 1597 the ruler Hideyoshi ordered the death of 26 priests and converts, ushering in an era of persecution. The Shimabara Rebellion in 1637 was the last stand of the Christians who gathered in a castle outside of Nagasaki. Over 37,000 Christians were killed in the siege. The remaining Christians went underground and were called Hidden Christians.

In the late 19th century when Japan ended its long period of isolation, Western missionaries came and started churches and schools. But Christianity has never attracted more than a small percentage of the Japanese population.

Religion in the Modern Period

Until the beginning of the Meiji period (1868), respect for Shinto *kami*, adoration of Buddha, and the practice of ancestor worship all existed side by side. To accompany the "restoration" of imperial power, the Meiji government found moral justification in "State Shintoism." Buddhism, branded as a foreign religion that subverted Japanese Shintoism, was persecuted and many temples and treasures destroyed. The emperor, as a descendant of the Sun Goddess, provided the link between the gods and the state.

The new Constitution, written during the Occupation following World War II, guarantees religious freedom. New religions as well as Christianity have their adherents. **Soka Gakkai**, derived from Nichiren Buddhism, appeals to the disaffected lower middle class and formed a political party called Komeito. **Aum**, a fringe cult-religion, catapulted into the headlines with its deadly sarin gas attack in the Tokyo subways in 1995. Most people remain with Shintoism and Buddhism for their daily lives.

Are Japanese religious? Each year more than half the Japanese population go to a Shinto shrine at New Year's to pray for prosperity, but just as many Westerners go to church on Christmas, it doesn't necessarily indicate a high degree of religious involvement. Many people maintain altars in their homes to pray for their ancestors. Some people have Buddhist altars, some have Shinto and some have both. In this way, religion is part of Japan's cultural life.

JAPANESE ARCHITECTURE

Traditional Japanese houses emphasize a harmony with nature much more than their Western counterparts. Wood is the main building material and the rooms are designed to look out onto gardens. The entire side of the house opens to become part of the natural environment. To Japanese, staying cool during the sizzling hot and humid summer has been more important than keeping warm in the cold winter. While traditional houses are still built in rural areas, in the cities new houses are overwhelmingly Western style, but most have at least one Japanese room.

What is a Japanese room? *Tatami* straw mats cover the floor and a *tokonoma* alcove displays art and flower arrangements. *Shoji*, sliding doors with paper panels, divide the room from a veranda that overlooks a garden. Diffused light coming through the *shoji* adds a wonderful softness to the interior. *Fusuma*, heavy sliding doors often decorated with paintings, divide rooms. Wooden sliding doors on the exterior of the building protect the veranda and room. Natural wooden beams, posts and ceilings are complemented by plaster or earthen walls.

The history of Japanese architecture as we know it begins in the 6th and 7th centuries, when court buildings and temples imitated Chinese and Korean forms. Today, **Horyu-ji Temple** in Nara, built in 607, contains the world's oldest wooden building.

Gradually, the Japanese changed the Chinese architectural forms to a more indigenous residential architecture for the aristocracy called *shinden-zukuri*. Japanese elements were incorporated into Chinese layout and construction techniques: using unfinished wood, putting in gravel gardens and raising the floor. *Shinden* is the main hall of the complex. Partitions, not walls, divided rooms. Buildings connected to each other by covered walkways. A large pond reached by a covered walkway was nearby. The best example of *shinden* architecture is the **Kyoto Imperial Palace**, a faithful 1800s reproduction.

By the Momoyama period, *shoin* architecture developed, evolving from Zen priests' studies that looked out onto a garden. The style eventually became the audience halls for feudal lords. Much of what we think of as traditional Japanese: *tatami* mats, *tokonoma* alcoves, *shoji* screens, and decorative door paintings came from this style. The grandest *shoin* is Ninomaru Palace of **Nijo Castle** in Kyoto.

The simplicity of tea ceremony influenced Japanese architecture beyond the rustic tea hut; it led to the development of a more natural style of *shoin* called *sukiya* architecture. It is airy, less ornate and doesn't have boldly decorated door panels. *Sukiya* uses only the best natural materials. The understated architecture fits in with the garden surrounding it. **Katsura Imperial Villa** in Kyoto is a prime *sukiya* building.

The Momoyama period was also the golden age of castle building. The new style of gun warfare necessitated defensive castles. The prototype built by Oda Nobunaga at Azuchi on the shores of Lake Biwa was destroyed just a few years after completion. Castles had massive stone walls and were often surrounded by moats. Plaster covers the wooden structure and the remaining exposed wood was lacquered for fire resistance. Castles had windows designed for firing muskets and shooting arrows as well as openings for dropping stones and hot oil on invaders. Warriors did not live in the multistoried castle keeps but rather in residences on the grounds. **Himeji Castle** is Japan's grandest existing castle.

Commoners, of course, did not live on a grand scale. They had modest wooden dwellings called *minka* (people's houses). Many different styles of *minka* reflect climatic conditions. In the snowy mountains of central Japan, farmers built structures with steep thatched roofs so the snow would slide off. Other areas used tile roofs. **Minka-en**, an open air museum near Tokyo, features about twenty farmhouses moved from all over Japan. Visit the preserved sections of **Kyoto** to see the wooden urban architecture of merchants and townspeople. **Kanazawa, Matsue**, and the small town of **Kakunodate** have exceptionally well-preserved samurai districts.

In the Meiji period, Western architecture became very fashionable, as did buildings combining Western and Japanese styles. Western architects like British Josiah Condor came to Japan to design monumental buildings and train Japanese. **Tokyo Station** and the **Bank of Japan Building** are outstanding examples.

Today, Japan has an active contemporary architecture scene. Architect Tange Kenzo brought modern Japanese architecture into the international limelight with the **National Gymnasiums** in Yoyogi Park in Tokyo, built for the 1964 Olympics. Today Ando Tadao and Isozaki Arata are two of the most prominent names among the considerable number of innovative architects transforming Japanese and foreign cities with their postmodern architecture. Tokyo, Osaka and Fukuoka sport large numbers of postmodern structures.

JAPANESE GARDENS

Gardens with bushes pruned to strange shapes, gardens of only rock, moss and gravel, gardens the size of postage stamps, plants hundreds of years old, but Lilliputian sized. What are these Japanese gardens all about?

Japanese gardens are carefully designed and cultivated works of art. But there is little that's natural about them except the materials. Over the course of Japan's history, the garden has gone through several transformations.

Heian Period *(8th to 12th century)*

The aristocracy of the Heian period built gardens with large ponds for boating. Designed to be viewed from the water or from the adjacent buildings, these gardens were not meant for strolling. Aristocrats held poetry and music parties in these natural landscapes. In the later part of the Heian period, many aristocrats turned to faith in the Amida Buddha who promised a peaceful heaven to all believers.

This Western Paradise was often depicted in gardens filled with flowering trees and plants. **Byodo-in Temple**, near Kyoto, is the finest example.

Kamakura Period *(12th to mid-14th century)*

In medieval times, gardens became places to stroll. Walking along the path, each step brought a new view in the exploration of the garden. Dry landscapes appeared as parts of the larger garden: large rocks were used to represent mountain scenery, waterfalls and streams. **Tenryu-ji Temple's** garden in Kyoto is a renowned garden of this era.

Muromachi Period *(mid-14th to mid-16th century)*
 Zen Buddhism took hold in the turbulent times of the medieval period when central authority collapsed. Zen gardens took the dry landscape design, which was one element of the larger gardens, and used it to build small gardens. These gardens usually surrounded the priests' quarters and were used for meditation. The rocks, gravel, moss and small bushes are abstracts. Maintenance of a garden — raking gravel, removing falling leaves — became a religious exercise for Zen priests. **Ryoan-ji Temple** has the most famous Zen garden, but there are many others, including **Nanzen-ji Temple** and **Daisen-in**, a subtemple of Daitoku-ji Temple, all in Kyoto.

Momoyama Period *(late 16th century)*
 Japan was unified under three successive warlords and an era of prosperity began. These warlords' gardens, like their castles and residences, were designed to impress. Momoyama gardens had lots of rocks and exotic plants brought by Portuguese traders from Southeast Asia, and were masculine symbols of authority. The gardens were designed to be viewed from the veranda so most did not have paths for strolling.
 Two great Momoyama gardens still in existence today are **Sambo-in** at Daigo-ji Temple, southeast of Kyoto and **Kokei Garden** at Nishi Hongan-ji Temple in Kyoto. The latter is open to the public only sporadically.

Tea Gardens
 The cult of tea ceremony, which took off in the Momoyama period, led to a very different type of garden. The tea garden transports the visitor from the mundane outside world to the ethereal environment of the teahouse. Walking along the dewy path, a visitor makes a transition, setting aside all earthly cares and getting into a serene state. The goal is to create a walk in the woods but does not mean the garden is wild. The carefully groomed garden has local species of plants and trees, but not flowering trees or flowers. Tea gardens use stepping stones, stone lanterns and stone water basins. Water basins placed near the ground mean visitors have to crouch to use them, putting them closer to nature.
 Tea gardens came to have inner and outer areas, divided by a gate. In the outer, the visitor could change clothes in a small shed and wait on a bench for the host. The inner garden contains a covered bench, a water basin and the teahouse itself. Since tea gardens were usually designed into existing space in urban areas, they are quite small. A famous tea garden is **Uraku-en** at Inuyama near Nagoya.

Edo & Meiji Eras

By the Edo period (17th to 19th century), large gardens were built for aristocrats and warriors. Used for strolling, these gardens had a variety of vistas you would notice as you walked along a path. Many gardens used "borrowed scenery," incorporating the vista of a distant mountain or another scene into the garden itself. The **Katsura Imperial Villa's** garden is one of the most magnificent in Japan. In Kagoshima, **Iso Garden** brilliantly incorporates Sakurajima's volcano into its design.

In the Meiji era, Japanese landscape designers began incorporating Western design. **Shinjuku Gyoen Garden** and **Furukawa Garden**, both in Tokyo, combine Japanese and European garden design.

TEA CEREMONY

Tea ceremony isn't just having a cup of tea in the afternoon. Amazingly, much of what the world associates with Japanese aesthetics derives from the tea ceremony.

Tea, originally used as a medicine, came from China and became popular among Zen Buddhists in the 12th and 13th centuries. Tea drinking gradually evolved into a formal and ritualistic aesthetic experience. Tea ceremony came to be conducted in a rustic tea hut set in a small garden. Tea ceremony became an art form.

Today, the highly stylized tea ceremony is still practiced by men and women. Hot water is added to powdered green tea and whipped until it's frothy. Before you drink your tea, you must admire not only the setting of the room, but also your tea bowl, the flowers in the *tokonoma* alcove and the tea itself. A small sweet is served to counter the tea's bitter taste.

Experience a tea ceremony at one of the special schools for tea ceremony or at a large hotel.

FLOWER ARRANGING

Japanese flower arranging is the antithesis of Western arranging where every space is filled. The Japanese asymmetrical and often sparse arrangement dates back to the medieval Muromachi period. Flowers, arranged in a variety of containers, are placed in the *tokonoma* alcove of homes, inns and temples. There are many different schools of flower arranging, some very classical like Ikenobo and Koryu while others like Sogetsu are quite avant-garde. Many of the larger schools offer instruction in English, and visitors are welcome.

JAPANESE ART

Utilitarian pottery and ritual clay objects, made during the **Jomon Period** (10,000 B.C.–300 B.C.) comprise the earliest Japanese art. In the subsequent **Yayoi Period** (300 B.C.–A.D. 300) pottery thrown on a wheel and bronze ritual objects such as mirrors and bells appeared. The **Kofun Period** (A.D. 300–700) produced elaborate *haniwa,* clay figures of people and animals that were placed on the large keyhole-shaped burial mounds.

Religious art flourished in Japan after the introduction of Buddhism in the 6th century. Originally the art copied Korean and Chinese objects, but developed a Japanese style within a short period of time. Most Japanese art in the Heian period was religious art, with the exception of handscrolls called *Yamato-e* (literally Japanese paintings), an indigenous style of painting.

For all its political chaos, the Kamakura era was a dynamic time for sculpture. The sculptors Kokei, Unkei and Kaikei made dramatic and realistic sculptures. The **Nio guardians** at **Todai-ji Temple** in Nara are excellent examples of this style.

TREASURING NATIONAL TREASURES

*Japan takes great pride in its history and traditions. Early in this century it enacted laws protecting works of art and other cultural assets. The most important buildings and works of art were designated **National Treasures** and those less important but also worthy of preservation were named **Important Cultural Properties**. About 1000 objects and buildings are National Treasures; some 11,000 are Important Cultural Properties. The government provides financial assistance to museums, temples and other owners for the preservation of these valuable assets.*

*After World War II, the Japanese government recognized endangered traditions also needed preservation. Craftsmen, artisans and performing artists who have reached the pinnacles of their fields are designated **Intangible Cultural Assets**, but are more commonly called **Living National Treasures**. About 150 people currently hold Living National Treasure status, masters in fields as divergent as ceramics and weaving, swordmaking and noh chanting. Japan is the only country that so honors the people who preserve traditional culture.*

Strongly influenced by Chinese Sung Dynasty landscape paintings, Zen ink paintings dominated the arts during the Muromachi period. While the early works by Zen monks imitated the Chinese, the great monk-artist Sesshu changed all that by putting his personal imprint on monochrome landscape painting.

The brief **Momoyama Period** saw an explosion in the arts. The great age of castle building led to dramatic screen paintings on gold leaf to embellish the dark castles and the residences. The Kano school painters were commissioned to make bold, larger-than-life compositions to glorify the military leaders. Genre painting also came into its own during the Momoyama period. The merchant class amassed wealth and wanted paintings of everyday life. Other paintings depicted Portuguese who came to Japan and were called *Nanban* (Southern Barbarian) paintings, so named because the Portuguese sailed into Japan from the south. These paintings illustrate the Japanese fascination with the exotic foreigners.

The **Kano School** became the official painters to the Tokugawa shogunate, and Kano Tanyu moved to Edo with the shogun. The Kano School looked to China for inspiration. A more indigenous school of painting was the **Rimpa School**, which took inspiration from the Japanese Yamato-e paintings. Their works were decorative and abstract and have enormous appeal even today.

In the Edo Period Japan entered a long period of isolation. Cut off from other cultures, it looked inward. Feudal lords had to make periodic trips to Edo, the seat of the Tokugawa shogunate, and needed to present gifts. Each province worked hard to develop unique high quality art. The Nabeshima domain in Kyushu produced exquisite porcelain exclusively used as gifts to the shogun and other feudal lords.

For wealthy merchants at the other end of the social spectrum, *ukiyo-e*, pictures of the floating world, caught their fancy. The early paintings gave way to woodblock prints by the early 18th century. These prints used courtesans and *kabuki* actors as their themes and were distributed widely at low cost. Frowned upon by the Edo elite, *ukiyo-e* received little attention until the paintings reached Europe where they had a profound effect upon the Impressionists including Van Gogh and Cezanne.

With the Meiji Restoration in 1868, Japan began incorporating Western perspective in a type of painting called *nihon-ga*. Many Japanese went to Paris to study and painted totally in the Western style.

Today, we find that traditional Japanese aesthetics are expressed best not in contemporary art but in the fashion designs of Issey Miyake and Yohji Yamamoto and architectural accomplishments of Ando Tadao and Isozaki Arata.

TRADITIONAL CRAFTS

Japan's craft movement thrives today. Unlike many other countries, Japan continues to appreciate its crafts traditions even in the face of modern industrialization. Japanese relish their products and have the money and willingness to pay the high cost of these labor intensive objects.

Part of the credit for maintaining craft traditions goes to the "Mingei Movement" of the 1920s and 1930s. A dedicated band of artisans including Yanagi Soetsu, Yamada Shoji and Kawai Kanjiro along with the British potter Bernard Leach, saw beauty in the everyday objects made by unknown craftsmen. This influential group of people saved many a craft from extinction.

For a good overview of Japanese crafts, visit the **Japan Traditional Crafts Center** in Tokyo. While they sell all the objects they display, the center also functions like a museum and has video tapes demonstrating the processes. A few of the major crafts follow.

Ceramics

Few countries have Japan's reverence and love of pottery. We are sure one of the reasons Japanese serve food on individual plates is to have an excuse to surround themselves with beautiful ceramic dishes. Pottery making goes back to prehistoric times, but in the 16th century Momoyama period, rustic local pottery got a big boost when it became the favored choice for tea ceremony. In the 17th century, porcelain production burgeoned in Kyushu and Kyoto. Today, some artisans continue producing pottery based on traditional techniques and patterns while others are making innovative contemporary ware, more an art than a craft.

Some of the major pottery production centers are **Arita**, **Echizen**, **Imbe**, **Kagoshima**, **Kanazawa**, **Karatsu**, **Kyoto**, **Mashiko**, **Seto**, **Shigaraki**, **Tajimi** and **Tokoname**.

Textiles

Japan's textile traditions stretch from the banana fiber fabrics of Okinawa to the heavy fibers of northern Japan. Cotton, silk and linen are the most commonly used fibers. In the Edo era, the shogunate prohibited the merchant class from wearing silk, so to subvert this rule they wore subdued cotton kimono lined with silk. Indigo-dyed cotton was the uniform for the peasant while the upper classes luxuriated in silk.

Kimono are no longer worn daily and are mostly worn at formal occasions, similar to Westerners wearing evening gowns. Some women are willing to pay huge sums of money for hand-dyed kimono. Young women take courses to learn how to wear a kimono.

Among the many different textile designs is *yuzen*, painting designs on silk, a process popular in **Kanazawa** and **Kyoto**. *Shibori* is a tie-dying technique, but nothing like the tee shirts popular in the US in the 1970s. *Kasuri*, or ikat, dyes patterns on the threads before weaving them to create a design. Elaborately woven brocades are made in **Kyoto**. Other kimono have stenciled or embroidered designs. **Okinawa** produces brightly colored *bingata* fabrics, some stenciled while others are painted freehand.

Old kimono and other textiles are some of the great bargains in Japan. Go to a shrine flea market for a wide selection.

Lacquer

Japan produces so much lacquer ware that in Europe the term "japan" means lacquer, just like "china" means ceramics. The sap of the lacquer tree is applied again and again over a wooden base to create a lacquered object. Sometimes the natural grain of the wood shows through while other times the lacquer forms an opaque surface. Lacquer should be kept in a humid environment to prevent the wood from cracking, so it may not be the ideal gift to take home. Less expensive lacquer pieces may have a core made of composite wood or plastic.

Sometimes Westerners have a difficult time telling the difference between real lacquer and plastic, but after picking up a few pieces the differences are apparent.

The main lacquer producing areas are **Aizu Wakamatsu**, **Hirosaki**, **Kamakura**, **Kyoto**, **Wajima**, **Takayama**, the **Kiso district** (**Hirasawa** and **Narai**) and **Yamanaka** near Kanazawa.

Wood & Bamboo

Japan's abundant forests means lots of wood is available for furniture making. *Tansu*, Japanese chests, are used for storage in traditional Japanese houses. Mountainous areas such as **northern Honshu**, **Matsumoto**, **Takayama** and **Niigata** excel in furniture making. Bamboo baskets are found throughout Japan but the **Okayama** and **Beppu** areas are particularly famous production sites still utilizing traditional weaving patterns.

Metalwork

Iwate Prefecture in northern Honshu is known especially for cast iron tea kettles called *nambu tetsubin*.

Washi Paper

Japanese *washi* paper, often called rice paper in the West, has nothing to do with rice. Paper is made from the fibers of the mulberry plant. Some *washi* paper has large fibers with attractive textured patterns while other paper is painted or stenciled. Many different objects are made from *washi* paper: lampshades, screens, luncheon mats, wallets, umbrellas and, naturally, stationery. **Mino** and **Echizen** are two of the largest *washi* production centers.

PERFORMING ARTS

Japanese traditional performing arts, although holdovers from the Edo Period, find large and appreciative audiences throughout the country. *Kabuki*, *bunraku* and *noh* are the big three.

Kabuki

Kabuki is the most accessible of traditional Japan's performing arts for non-Japanese and Japanese. We urge you to make time to see *kabuki* not only to enjoy the highly stylized performance but also to take in the festive ambiance. The brief English synopsis will give you the plot, but just like Shakespearean plays, the plot is only one aspect of the entire experience: you can't help but be dazzled by the sumptuous costumes, the acting, the music and the stylized movements. Each time we go, we notice something we haven't found before. *Kabuki* is for entertainment, so enjoy.

Okuni, a female dancer from Izumo Grand Shrine, started *kabuki* when she went to Kyoto to raise funds for the shrine in the early 16th century. She led a troupe of dancers who performed spirited and lusty dances on the banks of the Kamo River in Kyoto. Screen paintings show the excitement people felt watching these women dance in striking costumes. Okuni soon incorporated plots in her dances and used *noh* drums and flutes. *Kabuki's* popularity grew.

Many of the dancers were prostitutes; and some brothel owners would have women dance *kabuki* to entice customers. Because of this lewd image, the Tokugawa shogunate banned women from dancing *kabuki* in 1629. Young boys then played the women's roles, but eventually they were also prohibited from dancing. By mid-Edo period all the parts were played by adult men.

The merchant class in Edo took to *kabuki*. It had almost everything the merchant class, the lowest social class, yet the wealthiest, enjoyed most — beautiful "women," tales of love, vengeance, adultery, war, ghosts and death.

Kabuki actors specialize in male or female roles. Watch carefully how the *onnagata* (the male actors who play female roles) conveys femininity through the movements of his hands, eyes and hips.

The musicians are off to the side of the stage, behind a curtain. Dramatic music indicates an actor is about to appear on the stage via the *hanamichi*, literally the "flower path," the long entrance walkway through the audience to the left side of the stage.

Feel the excitement of the audience as the plot reaches its climax. At a most untimely moment, you may suddenly notice your neighbor is eating oranges or chocolate right in middle of the climax. Don't let it bother you. In the old days people went to *kabuki* theater the same way they went for a picnic, carrying lunch, supper, tea and snacks. It's not considered rude to eat and drink your way through a *kabuki* performance although the rustling of papers and *bento* boxes can get annoying. Since performances last several hours, you are welcome to come and go as you please. You can take your own meal or buy a *bento* box or sandwich in the theater.

In *kabuki* there's a real intimacy between the actors and the audience. You might be surprised to suddenly hear a member of the audience shout out something incomprehensible. He is probably screaming the actor's name. It's like saying "Bravo," but is usually done by a member of the actor's fan club.

The major theaters are **Kabuki-za** and the **National Theater** in Tokyo, **Minami-za** in Kyoto and **Shochiku-za** in Osaka. There are two programs a day each lasting about four hours; the first begins at around 11am and the second at 4:30pm. In Tokyo *kabuki* is performed every month from the 1st until the 26th; the schedule varies in Kyoto and Osaka. Get the English guidephones, it really helps you understand what is going on.

To be on the safe side you should reserve your seats in advance. If you only want to see *kabuki* for a short time, Kabuki-za in Tokyo offers one-act tickets called *makumi-seki*. Buy them 15 minutes before the act begins. These are nose-bleed seats, high up in the back of the theater, and although you can't rent English earphones, you still can have a delightful introduction to *kabuki*.

Bunraku

Japan's traditional **puppet theater** evolved into popular entertainment for all classes, but especially for the common people, at roughly the same time as *kabuki* — in the early 17th century. *Bunraku* combines three elements — texts narrated by the chanters, the *shamisen* music introduced to Japan around 1570 from the Ryukyu Islands (Okinawa), and three-quarter size puppets — which make *bunraku* so intriguing. The great playwright **Chikamatsu Monzaemon** authored 130 plays in the 17th century. One of his most famous works, *Love Suicide of Sonezaki* (Sonezaki is now in central Osaka) was made into a *bunraku* play just a few weeks after the true love tragedy occurred.

When we first start watching *bunraku*, it's hard to ignore the three puppeteers dressed in black manipulating each puppet. As the plot gets more and more complex we cease noticing these men and simply enjoy watching the dolls come alive.

Hand-made, the puppet's head is an art itself. Special craftsmen produce these dolls using techniques handed down from generation to generation. We love to watch the facial expressions of the puppets, changing delicately by the puppeteer's manipulation. Watch the master puppeteer (who usually appears unmasked in formal kimono) as he takes on the puppet's persona while simultaneously keeping his distance. Also enjoy the puppets' strikingly colorful and elegant costumes.

Pay attention to the narrator who sits next to the *shamisen* musician. Watching him narrate the story exhausts us. Listen to the deep piercing notes of *shamisen*. The music, the chanting and the puppets themselves combine to provide a riveting theatrical experience.

Bunraku is based in Osaka but performs several months a year in Tokyo. If you are near either city, do your best to see it. The English language earphones are worth their small rental price.

Noh

Unlike *kabuki* and *bunraku*, *noh* never had mass appeal. It's the art for cultured individuals, not unlike opera in the West. *Noh* originated with the Shinto religion when priests danced at shrines to ensure a good harvest. Later troupes of roaming actors performed on behalf of the priests.

During the Muromachi period (14th to 15th century), under the patronage of the shogun, *noh's* distinctive drama form developed. **Ze-ami Motokiyo** (1363–1443) not only wrote most of the major plays but also established the aesthetic of *yugen*, the elegant, the profound and the mysterious, which *noh* expresses. Ze-ami also established the stage, costumes, masks and acting conventions.

Noh is a masked dance drama performed by men dressed in sumptuous costumes of elaborate silk brocade. The costumes are works of art by themselves and are often displayed in museums.

Musicians, playing drums and flutes, and the chorus sit on the stage, a smallish square with an entrance passageway at the left. There's little movement in *noh*. Actors take slow steps and their voices are garbled by the masks. Most plays express psychological tension between the main actor *(shite)* and a bystander *(waki)* and usually involve spirits and demons interacting with mortals.

Noh is a beautiful art form but is difficult to appreciate. If you go expecting understatement, you won't be disappointed. Some plays have been translated in English and it helps if you know the play before you attend the performance. Occasionally, a *noh* theater will have a performance with an English introduction. Jump at the chance to attend it.

Kyogen

Kyogen is a comic interlude performed between *noh* plays to give the audience time to relax (apart from sleeping during the *noh* performance). This farcical theater deals with every day human relationships. The major characters are feudal lords, servants, priests, novices, farmers and merchants, all who want to enjoy the good life. Kyogen is light and accessible and is increasingly performed on its own. Occasionally *kyogen* plays are performed in English.

Japanese Traditional Music

Hogaku, traditional Japanese music, came from China and Korea. Traditional instruments are used in *kabuki, noh* and *bunraku* theaters, but the music is also performed for music's sake. *Gagaku* is the court music from the Heian times and is sometimes still performed, either to accompany dance or songs or solely as instrumental music.

The main instruments in the Japanese classical repertory are drums, *shakuhachi* and other flutes, *koto* (zither), *biwa* (lute) and *shamisen* (stringed instrument).

Classical performances are common in the large cities. The Nihon Ongaku Shudan (Pro Musica Nipponica) plays modern music using Japanese instruments.

Buyoh

Buyoh is classical Japanese dance derived from *kabuki* but performed for dance's sake, not as part of a dance drama. Unlike *kabuki,* both women and men participate in performing abstract and narrative dances.

Butoh

Butoh is avant-garde dance, popularized by the Sankai Juku troupe in the 1970s. The stark dance from usually features nearly naked performers with shaven heads and bodies painted white.

Taiko

Taiko, drumming on instruments of many different sizes, derived from Shinto festival drumming. Several troupes including Kodo and Za Ondekoza raised it to an art form and have gained world-wide attention for their creative and expressive use of percussion. Kodo holds a big "Earth Celebration" every August on Sado Island. If there's a *taiko* performance when you're in Japan, by all means attend.

LANGUAGE

Japanese don't widely speak English, but don't let the language barrier deter you from traveling in Japan. People are friendly and will go out of their way to make sure you are okay.

Although Japanese study English in junior high school, high school and college, the emphasis is on passing exams, not on comprehension and speaking. Say "hello" to high school students and it's unlikely that they can carry the conversation any further. But in the big cities, a surprising number of people speak English, especially people who work in the tourist trade.

Prepare to be illiterate. Japanese does not use the Western alphabet. Unlike traveling in Europe, you won't be able to read signs. But don't be shy about asking people to help you. Speak slowly and clearly.

In the big cities, lots of signs are in English including in subway and train stations. Although it's fashionable for beauty shops, restaurants, bars, bakeries and boutiques to have signs in English, it doesn't mean there is an English-speaking staff inside.

Should you take a Japanese language course before coming to Japan? If you are spending one week in Tokyo or Kyoto, don't bother. If you are going to be spending an extended period in remote rural areas, then it's worth the effort. But make sure you take a Japanese-for-Travelers course rather than an introductory class in Japanese.

We find that a good phrase book goes a long way. We like Berlitz' *Japanese for Travelers* because you can point to the written Japanese.

Japanese didn't have a written language so around the 6th century they adopted Chinese characters called *kanji*. Since these characters didn't mesh well with spoken Japanese, they developed two syllabic alphabets to use with the *kanji*.

The vowels in Japanese are very clear (like Italian) and always pronounced the same way:

a as in father
e as in red
i as in police
o as in more
u as in food

If you learn only one word in Japanese, the most useful word is *sumimasen*. It technically means "I'm sorry" and "excuse me." You can use it to get someone's attention, to request a favor and to say thank you.

Here are some basic phrases to get you on your way.

O-hayo gozaimasu	Good Morning (use until mid-morning)
Kon-nichi wa	Good Day (use mid-morning until evening)
Konban wa	Good Evening
O-yasumi nasai	Good Night (use before going to bed)
Sayonara	Good-bye
Domo arigato	Thank you
Doo Itashimashite	You are welcome
Sumimasen	I am sorry, Excuse me
Wakarimasen	I don't understand
Hai	Yes
Iie	No

Moshi-moshi	Hello (on telephone)
Hajime mashite	How do you do? (When first meeting someone)
O-genki desu ka?	How are you?
Hai, okagesama de	Fine, thank you.
Chotto matte kudasai	Please wait a minute.
Onegai shimasu	Please (said when requesting a favor or service)
Tasukete!	Help!
Kaji	Fire
Nan desu ka?	What is it?
Nanji desu ka?	What time is it?
Doko desu ka?	Where is it?
Dare desu ka?	Who is it?
Ikura desu ka?	How much does it cost?
Yasui	Inexpensive
Takai	Expensive
Migi	Right
Hidari	Left
Massugu	Straight
Tomatte	Stop
Ichi	One
Ni	Two
San	Three
Shi (Yon)	Four
Go	Five
Roku	Six
Shichi (Nana)	Seven
Hachi	Eight
Kyu	Nine
Ju	Ten
Hyaku	Hundred
Sen	Thousand
Man	Ten Thousand

Form 10s by putting *ju* after the number: 20 = *ni-ju*

Form teens by putting the number after *ju* (10): 15 = *ju-go*

Form hundreds by putting the number before *hyaku* (100): 500 = *go-hyaku*

Form thousands by putting the number before *sen* (1000): 2000 = *ni-sen*

Form ten thousands by putting the number before *man* (10,000): 30,000 = *san-man*

TWO COUNTRIES DIVIDED
BY A COMMON LANGUAGE

Japan uses a lot of English loan words, pronouncing them in a Japanese way. Bus is basu, taxi is takushi, computer is compuuta, television is terebi, all fairly straightforward. But some loan words in Japanese do not relate to their English primary meaning and sometimes they are shortened so they are unrecognizable. A native speaker could be completely confused. Here's a sampling:

Smart *(sumaatto) – Stylish*

Family con *(fami con) – Computer games played on TV (short for family computer)*

Wa-pro *– Word processor*

Body con *(bodi con) – A short, form fitting dress (short for body conform)*

Creap *– A brand name for non-dairy coffee creamer*

Salaryman *(sarariman) – A male company employee*

OL *or* **Office Lady** *(Ofisu redii) – A female clerical worker*

Skin *(sukin) – A condom*

Seku hara *– Sexual harassment*

Wet *(wetto) – Emotional*

Dry *(dorai) – Unemotional, realistic*

Talent *(tarento) – Television personality*

Trainer *(toraina) – Sweatshirt*

Mansion *(manshon) – Apartment building*

Depaato *– Department Store*

Free size *(furi saizu) – One size fits all*

ETIQUETTE

Here are a few points of Japanese etiquette that will make your trip go more smoothly. For etiquette in Japanese restaurants, inns and baths, see the Food & Drink and Planning Your Trip chapters.

Bowing: Japanese don't shake hands, they bow. The angle of the bow depends on the relationship between the two people. Friends may merely nod their heads while greeting the emperor necessitates a deep bow with your head down to your knees. Unless you plan to have an audience with the emperor, don't worry about it too much. Japanese who have some knowledge of the West will often put out their hands to shake. The best advice is to follow the lead of the person you are greeting.

Name Cards: Everyone in Japan has a name card called *meishi* and business people exchange them as soon as they meet. You won't need them while traveling for pleasure but they are mandatory for business.

However, if you plan on meeting a lot of people, for instance, if you're a member of an exchange program, have a card made up with your home address.

Names: Japanese traditionally write the family name first, followed by the given name. We have used this same order for names in this book. Usually Japanese are addressed by their family name, followed by *san*, an all-purpose honorific meaning Mr., Mrs., or Ms. Don't call Japanese by their given names unless they specifically request you to.

Footwear: Japanese exchange shoes for slippers when they enter houses and remove the slippers when walking on *tatami* (straw) mats. Workers often wear slippers in offices, but guests do not. You also have to remove your footwear when entering a Buddhist temple. Wearing slip-on shoes will make your life easier.

5. A SHORT HISTORY

THE EARLIEST YEARS

Archaeological finds show there have been people hanging around Japan for a long time, maybe more than 30,000 years. Apparently, hunters crossed land bridges that once connected Japan with the Asian continent. Archaeologists have found remains of their early stone tools.

JOMON PERIOD
(ca. 10,000–300 B.C.)

At the end of the ice age, global warming melted ice caps, and the rising sea level cut Japan off from the continent. The period takes its name from earthenware decorated with *jomon* (cord marking). People used earthenware and lacquered containers, so lacquering — "japanning" — is a very old process. By the end of the era, villagers had extensive contact with neighboring areas as well as with the Korean peninsula.

The Japanese diet today is healthy provided you avoid fast food, but in Jomon times, it was even better balanced. People ate the meat of animals hunted in the forest and gathered roots, nuts and saltwater shellfish. The semipermanent villages had huts with thatched roofs sunken into the earth. Jomon settlements have been found throughout the Japanese islands. **Sannai-Maruyama**, a Jomon village near Aomori City in northern Honshu, is one of the largest and best excavations to visit.

The Japanese language, which most linguists connect to Korean and other Altaic (Turkic and Mongolian) languages, developed during the Jomon period.

YAYOI PERIOD
(ca. 300 B.C.–A.D. 300)

During the Yayoi period, Japanese learned rice cultivation, metal-working, pottery making and textile weaving from the Asian continent. The actual name, Yayoi, comes from an area in Tokyo where advanced earthenware was discovered.

IN THE BEGINNING...

*In the beginning were two deities, **Izanagi** and **Izanami**, an exceedingly fertile couple who were brother and sister. They gave birth to the islands of Japan as well as to other gods. Izanami died while giving birth to the God of Fire. Izanagi tried to follow her to the land of the dead but couldn't stand the putrid smell. He continued to give birth to deities including **Amaterasu**, the Sun Goddess, and her brother **Susa-no-o**, the God of Storms.*

Susa-no-o angered Amaterasu by destroying her palace and rice fields so she retreated to a cave, which plunged the world into darkness. To lure her out, one god performed a lewd dance. As she listened to other gods howling with laughter, Amaterasu's curiosity was aroused and she asked what was going on. The gods told her the most powerful god had appeared. Amaterasu stuck her head out to see who it could possibly be and saw her own reflection in a mirror. The gods took advantage of this opportunity to pull her from the cave. Susa-no-o was exiled and eventually ended up in Izumo, near present-day Matsue.

*Amaterasu sent her grandson, Ninigi, to earth to rule over Japan. He arrived in southern Kyushu with imperial regalia: a mirror, a sword and a jewel. Ninigi's grandson, **Emperor Jimmu**, fought his way east conquering his enemies, including the gods at Izumo, and became the first emperor of Japan thus establishing the imperial line.*

Wet-rice cultivation was introduced into Kyushu from the Korean peninsula and spread rapidly throughout western Japan and then to northern Japan. Becoming a rice-growing culture meant villagers had to cooperate closely to irrigate rice paddies, leading to the development of a more sophisticated social organization. Villagers cultivated fields with iron implements.

While iron was used for utilitarian objects, bronze was the metal of choice for rituals and rulers. Elaborately decorated ceremonial bronze mirrors, bells, swords and spears were also produced.

Towards the latter part of the Yayoi period, loosely organized political entities emerged. The first written account of Japan appears in Chinese chronicles around A.D. 57 and refers to the "Land of Wa," composed of several small states. *Wa* meant petty, but over time the Japanese changed it to a homonym meaning harmony.

Himiko, a shaman queen, ruled an area that scholars believe was in northern Kyushu. In A.D. 237, Himiko sent an envoy to the Kingdom of Wei (China). Yes, it's hard to believe it in Japan's male-dominated political world today, but a woman is the first ruler of Japan mentioned in a written history.

KOFUN PERIOD
(ca. A.D. 300–593)

By the mid-4th century, the **Yamato** clan had increased its power until it controlled most of the central regions and established the Yamato court. Its base was the Yamato plain in present-day Nara Prefecture. Although the first 15 emperors of Japan are shrouded in myth and legend, the Yamato rulers were the first emperors of Japan and set up a colony in Korea.

This age is known for its large *kofun* — keyhole shaped burial mounds — built for the emperors and other members of the imperial family. Many of the tombs were ringed with *haniwa*, clay figures and objects that might have been substitutes for live burials. The largest *kofun* is **Emperor Nintoku's** (early 5th century) in Osaka Prefecture. Located on an 80-acre site, it is 500 meters long, 35 meters high and surrounded by three moats; it rivals the pyramids in size. **Emperor Suinin's** burial mound in the Nishi-no-Kyo area, near Nara city, is one of the most convenient to see.

As Buddhism was introduced from the Asian continent by mid-6th century, the ruling class devoted its wealth to the creation of temples, thus ending the Kofun period.

ASUKA PERIOD
(593–710)

The Asuka Period is generally regarded as the beginning of the historic era in Japan. The **Empress Suiko** was crowned in 593 and designated Asuka, in present-day Nara Prefecture, as the capital of Yamato.

This era was strongly influenced by Buddhism, which arrived from China via Korean immigrants. They also brought the Chinese writing system and Chinese Confucian principles. During roughly the same period that Christianity transported Mediterranean culture to northern Europe, Buddhism served as the vehicle to carry Chinese culture from the mainland to Japan. By the end of the 6th century, Buddhism was firmly established as the religion of the ruling classes.

In 604, the Seventeen Article Constitution was set forth by **Prince Shotoku**, a devout Buddhist and regent for Empress Suiko, his aunt. The constitution established Buddhism as the state religion and strengthened the unity of the state, using the Chinese administrative system as a model. Prince Shotoku founded **Horyu-ji Temple** in 607 and encouraged scholars to spread Buddhism among the ruling class. He sent a series of diplomatic missions to China. In a letter from the emperor of China written in 607, Japan was referred to as the Land of the Rising Sun for the first time. Missions to China continued for the next 200 years despite the great expense and dangers of crossing the treacherous South China Sea.

After Prince Shotoku's death in 622, the Soga clan assassinated Shotoku's son and usurped power. In 645 a coup d'etat deposed the empress who was succeeded by her younger brother. **Prince Naka-no-Oe**, who led the coup with **Nakatomi-no-Kamatari**, became the crown prince and later ruled under the name of **Emperor Tenchi**. Given the name Fujiwara as a reward, the Nakatomi clan remained powerful regents to emperors for the next 500 years.

In 645 Emperor Tenchi instituted the **Taika Reforms**. Based on Tang China, the reforms abolished private land ownership, placing all land under imperial control; rival clans were stripped of their land but, in return, were given aristocratic titles. The reforms also established the principle of a permanent capital. Prior to these reforms, the capital moved every time a new emperor or empress came to power.

Most of Asuka period art relates to Buddhism. Examples include the Buddha of the Future at **Chugu-ji Temple** and the Shaka Triad at **Horyu-ji Temple** in Nara.

PRINCE SHOTOKU

Prince Shotoku (574-622) figures prominently in any Who's Who of Japanese history. He set in motion the changes that would lead to the Taika Reforms which altered Japan's political landscape. Born into the Soga clan, the ruling family of the time, he became regent for his aunt Empress Suiko. A devout Buddhist, he founded Horyu-ji and many other temples. At the same time, he recognized the political impact of Buddhism, setting up a hierarchy under central control. In 604 the Seventeen Article Constitution, which established Confucian ethical and political principles, was proclaimed to the people. The first article, "Harmony is to be valued," shows the concept of harmony has been central to Japanese society for a long time.

NARA PERIOD
(710–794)

Heijo-kyo, present-day Nara, was designated as the permanent capital by the emperor in 710. Its layout was based on the grid system of Tang China's capital city Chang-an, now known as Xian. In present-day Nara the actual site is a park on the outskirts of the city.

PILLOW TALK

During the Asuka and Nara periods, Japan imported Chinese culture in a big way. But in the Heian period, it slowly digested and transformed these imports until they became uniquely Japanese.

*The most notable example is the writing system. Since Japan didn't have its own written language, it borrowed Chinese ideographs in the 6th century. Grafting onto a written language was cumbersome, so in the early Heian period, the Japanese introduced two **kana** alphabets spelling out Japanese words. Formal documents were written in Chinese characters, but private letters, including love letters, were written in the new kana. Aristocratic women learned to write; until this era, only men learned to read and write. Although men continued to use Chinese ideographs, women were free to write in kana.*

*Two of Japan's most well-known works of literature are "The Tale of Genji" by **Murasaki Shikibu** and "The Pillow Book" by **Sei Shonagon**. Written by court women in the Heian period, they give riveting insights to the intrigue, love and politics of court life.*

The Nara court was closely modeled after the Chinese system and included a central bureaucracy. Buddhism prospered. This golden age of temple building resulted in 361 new temples including **Kofuku-ji** and **Todai-ji**, which houses an immense bronze Buddha in the world's largest wooden building.

The court at Nara spent such large amounts of money that it found itself in dire financial straits. The Buddhist monks became so powerful that they began to undermine the power of the emperor. During the last 10 years of the period, the capital moved to Nagaoka replacing Heijo-kyo as the permanent capital. In 794 the capital moved again — this time to Kyoto.

Japanese began using Chinese ideographs in the 6th century. In 712 the *Kojiki*, the oldest Japanese record of ancient Japan, was compiled, and in 720 the *Nihon Shoki*, Chronicles of Japan, were completed. Up to that time, Japan had neither a written record of its history nor a written language of its own. The two chronicles are heavily based on the mythological origins of Japan and use these myths to firmly establish the emperor as a descendent of the Sun Goddess, Amaterasu.

HEIAN PERIOD

(A.D. 794–1185)

In 794 **Emperor Kammu** established the capital called Heian-kyo, Capital of Peace, in present-day Kyoto. He desperately wanted to get away from the powerful Buddhist temples in Nara that undermined his authority. Like Nara's Heijo-kyo, the city layout copied China's capital, Chang-an.

Emperor Kammu allowed only two temples within the city's precincts, Sai-ji and To-ji, both at Kyoto's southern perimeter. Enryaku-ji Temple was built on Mt. Hiei, northeast of the city, to protect it from the evil spirits residing in that direction. Kammu had hoped to limit the power of the Buddhist temples, but within a few generations, they were firmly enmeshed in the ruling structure.

The Heian period was the golden age of Japan's aristocratic culture. Under the emperor, the nobility lived a life of leisure indulging in poetry, music and other cultural pastimes. Art and architecture flourished and Japanese artistry came into its own, breaking free from the Chinese dominated aesthetic of the earlier ages. By the middle of the Heian period, the court stopped sending embassies to China, and Japan became isolated from the Asian continent. Unfortunately, few monuments of the Heian period remain. The one outstanding example is **Byodo-in Temple**, outside of Kyoto.

For a while the emperors kept control of the government and the land. But in time, their functions became more centered on ritual and culture. The **Fujiwara** family gained strength as regents, the highest ranking ministers who ran the state. The Fujiwara married their daughters to emperors so their grandsons would be emperors. The emperors retired early, sometimes after reigning just a few years.

In the 11th century, the Fujiwara women stopped producing heirs. Emperor Go-sanjo (reigned 1069-1072) was the first emperor in a hundred years who did not have a Fujiwara mother. Political power passed to retired emperors, called cloistered emperors, who competed with the Fujiwara for the acquisition of land. The aristocrats and monks appointed local families to administer their land, greatly increasing the power of these provincial officers.

The aristocracy was having too good a time to notice that trouble was brewing in the provinces. Law and order broke down; provincial families started small armies that gave birth to the *samurai* (warrior) class. Soon there were two powerful regional warlords. The emperor used one of these clans, the **Taira** (also known as the Heike clan), to rid himself of the Fujiwara regents.

But the Taira were soon enmeshed in a power struggle with their rivals, the **Minamoto** (also known as the Genji clan), and a struggle over imperial succession ushered in a period of civil war. The Taira imprisoned the emperor and put the emperor's grandson, whose mother was a Taira, on the throne. The Minamoto fought back and, in the sea battle of Dan-

HISTORIC COMPARISONS

In Japan & Asia	*In Europe & America*
794: *Capital of Japan established at Kyoto*	**800**: *Charlemagne crowned emperor of Holy Roman Empire*
1069-1072: *Reign of Emperor Go-sanjo*	**1066**: *William the Conqueror crowned king of England*
1185: *Establishment of the first shogunate(government by warriors) in Japan.*	**1215**: *King John of England issues Magna Carta.*
1271: *Marco Polo begins his journey to the court of Kublai Khan in China.*	
1274: *Kublai Khan invades Japan for the first time.*	
1281: *Second invasion of Japan by Kublai Khan.*	
1333: *Ashikaga Shogunate established in Japan.*	**1337**: *One hundred years of war begins between England and France.*
1467: *Onin War begins in Japan, ushering in one hundred years of war and chaos.*	**1492**: *Columbus lands in America*
1639: *Japan begins 200 year period of isolation.*	**1620**: *The Mayflower lands at Plymouth Rock*
	1776: *US Declaration of Independence*
	1789: *French Revolution.*
	1804: *Napoleon crowns himself emperor of France.*
	1837: *Victoria becomes the queen of England, ruling until 1901.*
1839–42: *Opium Wars in China.*	
1853: *Commodore Perry sails his black ships into Tokyo Bay*	**1861–65**: *Civil War in the US.*
1867: *Tokugawa shogun is overthrown.*	

no-ura in 1185, annihilated the Taira. The Heian era, the "era of peace" went down in flames.

KAMAKURA PERIOD
(1185-1333)

When the Minamoto defeated the Taira, **Minamoto Yoritomo** established a military government centered at **Kamakura**, close to present-day Tokyo. He wanted to get away from the intrigues of the court and shelter his warriors from the easy life of Kyoto. Yoritomo asked the emperor to name him shogun; reluctantly he complied in 1192. For the first time political power shifted into the hands of the warrior class where basically it remained until 1868.

The emperor and his court remained in Kyoto but were powerless. The court allowed the shogun to appoint vassals to run the provincial estates, which led to the establishment of a feudal system. The samurai code solidified, stressing loyalty and obedience to their superiors above all else.

After only three generations, there was no heir to the Minamoto shogun and power shifted to the Hojo clan, the family of the first shogun Yoritomo's powerful wife, **Hojo Masako**.

Under **Kublai Khan**, the Mongols invaded Kyushu in 1274 and 1281 in attempts to control Japan. On both occasions, the Mongol fleets were damaged by mighty typhoons while the whole country could do nothing but pray frantically for victory. That's why the Japanese called these typhoons *kamikaze* – divine wind. No foreign force ever occupied Japan until the end of World War II in 1945.

While the Mongol invasions brought national unity against an external threat, it also planted the seeds for decline. Resentment grew from the other samurai: the Hojo, who monopolized the top positions, did not adequately reward the samurai who fought the Mongols. **Emperor Godaigo**, with the support of disaffected warriors, overthrew the shogunate in 1333.

Despite all the turbulence, the Kamakura era was one of great artistic flowering. A dynamic style of sculpture blossomed under priest-artists such as **Unkei** and **Kaikei**. Zen Buddhism, with its tenets of strict mental discipline and meditation, appealed to the warrior class and also found favor with emperors and aristocrats.

MUROMACHI PERIOD
(1333- 1573)

Emperor Godaigo's success in returning power to the throne was short-lived. **Ashikaga Takauji**, the samurai leader who helped Godaigo overthrow the Kamakura shogun, turned against the emperor, attacked Kyoto, and forced Godaigo to retreat to **Yoshino**. Takauji installed another emperor and had himself appointed shogun, ruling from Kyoto.

In the meantime, Godaigo set up a separate, competing court in Yoshino in 1333. This dual system meant the emperors lost the last vestiges of power and the government was firmly in the hands of the shogun.

The Ashikaga shogunate could never control Japan. The regional warlords increased their power, fighting among themselves and sometimes even taking on the central government. The **Onin War** broke out in Kyoto in 1467; what began as a battle for shogun succession lasted for ten years and destroyed Kyoto in the process. When the Onin War was over, there was no clear winner, just weaker armies. Law and order had broken down completely and the **Warring States** era began. The shogun, who was the central authority, had no power over the regional *daimyo* (feudal lords) who constantly battled with each other. As *daimyo* were able to expand the territory under their control, regional political and economic centers emerged. One *daimyo* could not unify the country. Instead, chaos reigned.

In 1543 a Portuguese ship, blown off course, landed on the small island of Tanegashima, just south of Kyushu. This seemingly insignificant event was to change the course of Japanese history: the Portuguese had firearms. Japan mastered this new technology and was soon producing its own guns. The feudal lords who mastered gun warfare suddenly had the upper hand. Christianity was also introduced; **St. Francis Xavier** landed in Kyushu in 1549. Although he was allowed to spread his good tidings, Christianity never became a major force in Japanese spiritual life.

The Ashikaga shoguns were more interested in the arts than governing. During the Muromachi Period, the **Golden Pavilion** and the **Silver Pavilion** were built in Kyoto. Much of what we think of as traditional Japanese culture has its roots in this era: *noh* theater, tea ceremony, flower arranging and brush painting.

MOMOYAMA PERIOD
(1573-1603)

Through a brilliant strategy of firearm warfare, **Oda Nobunaga**, the feudal lord of an area near Nagoya, gained control of large sections of Japan. He was absolutely brutal, destroying all that stood in his way. His troops overran the temple-fortress of Mt. Hiei, northeast of Kyoto, killing thousands of monks and leaving nothing standing. It wasn't as though he had slain passive monks deep in meditation; they, too, were a heavily armed force. In 1573, Nobunaga deposed the last Ashikaga shogun and continued to unify the country. While attending a tea ceremony in Kyoto, Nobunaga was assassinated by one of his vassals.

Toyotomi Hideyoshi, Nobunaga's most trusted general, and, incidentally, a person who rose from the lowly position of foot soldier, continued Nobunaga's campaign. By 1590, the seemingly impossible happened: Japan was united. Hideyoshi then turned outward and attacked Korea, but these campaigns ultimately ended in failure.

After unifying Japan, Hideyoshi did much to centralize power. He ordered a census and froze movement between the warrior and farmer classes. Until then, the lines between lower-ranking samurai and farmer had been fluid. Hideyoshi conducted a sword hunt, confiscating swords from the farmers and monks; only samurai could be armed. Taxes had to be paid in rice. Hideyoshi began moving the feudal lords to different fiefdoms to reward or punish them, in effect making the *daimyo* regional administrative officials.

Hideyoshi was brilliant at all things except one: producing an heir. Late in his life, his favored consort gave birth to two sons, but one died as an infant. When Hideyoshi died in 1598, his only son was still young. Hideyoshi set up a group of five councilors, the most powerful feudal lords, to oversee the affairs of state, hoping that they would keep each other in check. But before long, **Tokugawa Ieyasu** saw his opportunity. Ieyasu's dramatic victory at the **Battle of Sekigahara**, fought in 1600 on the plains outside of Nagoya, ensured his dominance by defeating the feudal lords loyal to Hideyoshi's heir. In 1603, Ieyasu had the emperor name him shogun.

This short-lived era was one of the most dynamic in Japan's history, not only militarily but also in art and architecture. Feudal lords built huge castles to protect their fiefdoms against the new forms of firearm warfare. They stood as tangible symbols of power and authority.

With peace came prosperity, and the feudal lords sumptuously decorated their castles and residences with golden screens, paintings and gardens. Nobunaga's Azuchi Castle set the standard although it was destroyed only a few years after its completion. Hideyoshi built dazzling castles in Fushimi (south of Kyoto) and Osaka. **Himeji Castle** in Himeji City and **Nijo Castle** (Nijo is actually a palace) in Kyoto are the best surviving examples of the grand architectural style of the Momoyama era.

The tea ceremony came into its own and elevated Japanese ceramics to an art. Tea ceremony also popularized more rustic forms of architecture since the ideal place to perform the ceremony is in a simple hut. New kinds of performing arts, *kabuki* and *bunraku* puppet theater, began during this time.

JAPAN'S RULING PERSONALITIES

A famous poem illustrates the different personalities of the three successive unifiers – Oda Nobunaga, Toyotomi Hideyoshi and Tokugawa Ieyasu. Imagine each man's reaction as he is given a nightingale or cuckoo bird.

Nobunaga says ruthlessly: "If the cuckoo will not sing, I will kill it."

Hideyoshi shows his ingenuity: "If the cuckoo will not sing, I will make it sing.

And Ieyasu shows his patience: "If the cuckoo will not sing, I will wait for it."

A famous anecdote tells how the three men made an omelet together: Nobunaga broke the eggs, Hideyoshi beat them, and Ieyasu ate the omelet.

TOKUGAWA (EDO) PERIOD
(1603-1868)

Tokugawa Ieyasu's rule ushered in a long period of peace and prosperity; Tokugawa shoguns ruled for the next 15 generations. Ieyasu moved his administration to a small castle town called **Edo** (present-day Tokyo). Using Hideyoshi's social system as a foundation, he created four classes: warrior, farmer, artisan and merchant. Controls were put into effect on all aspects of life but, within the framework, townspeople prospered and cities grew. In the 18th century, Edo had one million residents and may have been the largest city in the world.

The Tokugawa shogunate viewed the spread of Christianity as a threat. In the 1630s, the shogunate expelled all foreigners and banned Christianity. Japan closed its ports; foreigners could not enter and Japanese could not leave. The only exceptions were two small enclaves that remained in Nagasaki — one for Chinese and one for Dutch.

In order to control the feudal lords, their families were obligated to reside in Edo when the lords were in their own domains. Through a system called *sankin kotai*, the shogunate required the feudal lords to come to Edo every year. Naturally, they didn't travel alone but were accompanied by retainers and servants, often numbering hundreds of people. Such massive endeavors siphoned off a lot of funds; even if they'd wanted to revolt, feudal lords couldn't have afforded it. To accommodate these feudal entourages, small post towns and roads developed to Edo from all corners of the country. The same transportation network was used for the distribution of goods.

Merchants were on the lowest rung of society. Consumption laws restricted almost every aspect of their lives from what clothes they could wear to how many stories high their houses could be. But they flourished under the burgeoning commercial system. They amassed commercial wealth and become the moneylenders to the increasingly impoverished feudal lords and samurai, who were forbidden to engage in commercial activity. Some of the merchant families have gone on to create large corporations with names that are familiar today: Mitsui, Sumitomo and Yasuda. Mitsukoshi, Japan's oldest department store, started as a kimono shop during the Edo period.

As the commoners prospered, so did their arts. *Kabuki* theater flourished as did *ukiyo-e*, woodblock prints. Licensed by the shogunate, large pleasure quarters appeared where music, dance and poetry became intertwined with the skin trade.

But in time, cracks appeared in the system. The shogunate and feudal lords raised their rice taxes to cover growing expenditures. The gap widened between merchant/landowners and peasants, and the peasants began to revolt.

On the international front in the 19th century, Western powers were colonizing China and demanded Japan reopen its borders. In 1853 **Commodore Matthew Perry's** black ships sailed to Tokyo Bay and forced the government to accept a friendship treaty. Soon trade treaties were signed with the US and other Western powers. But the Tokugawa shogunate was ill equipped to handle these crises, and lower ranking samurai toppled the shogun in 1867. The movement solidified over returning the emperor to power. In 1868, the **Meiji Restoration** installed the **Meiji Emperor** as head of government.

MEIJI PERIOD THROUGH WORLD WAR II
(1868-45)

For the next few decades, massive changes swept the country. The capital and the emperor moved to Edo, renamed **Tokyo**.

When the Meiji era started, Japan was a weak, undeveloped country emerging from more than two hundred years of isolation. Suddenly it was exposed to the international stage. By the end of Meiji, less than fifty years later, Japan had made major changes in its social, economic and political systems to catch up with the West, and had become a military power by defeating China and Russia.

The new constitutional government consisted of parliament (called the Diet) and an executive branch. The dismantled feudal domains gave way to a system of prefectures, and feudal lords assumed titles based on European peerage systems. The government, modeled after the West, established banking, rail and ship networks, and communication, legal and educational systems. Government and private companies worked together to build a strong industrial base.

Urban Japanese had a love affair with all things Western. People donned Western clothing, began to eat meat and foods favored in the West, and built Western-style buildings. Not too many of these buildings are still around but **Meiji Mura**, an open-air museum near Nagoya, has lots of examples.

JAPAN'S GREAT LEAP FORWARD

*In the middle of the 19th century when Japan opened to the rest of the world, Japanese were shocked to discover how over two centuries of isolation left them ignorant of Western developments in science, medicine and engineering. So one of the first things the Meiji government decided was to bring in, at substantial cost, the leading overseas experts. Over 4000 **oyatoi** (literally honorable employees) came to advise the government on the construction of the new state and to educate the next generation of leaders. The Japanese government considered this a temporary measure to make up for lost time. By the mid-1870s the government began to cut back on the number of oyatoi because of the huge expense and because the quality of the advisors varied widely.*

More then half of these advisors were British. They concentrated on public works – construction of the railways and shipping industry. The French were bureaucrats, the Germans doctors and policemen and the Americans teachers and agricultural specialists. All left an impact on the Japanese society, some which are still seen today in ways big and small: the genesis of today's excellent rail system, the uniforms schoolchildren still wear, the legacy of beer making.

But learning wasn't only one way. Some of the foreign experts became fascinated by traditional Japanese art and culture and made efforts to preserve the traditional artifacts of Japanese society just when Japan wanted to throw it all away. Ernest Fenollosa, an American professor of philosophy and art played an important role saving from destruction traditional Japanese Buddhist artifacts and art; his collection is in the Museum of Fine Arts in Boston.

The government began to assert itself on the international scene, trying to revise the unequal treaties the Tokugawa shogunate signed. Japan went to war with China in 1894–95; the victorious Japan received Taiwan as a colony. In 1904–5, Japan challenged and defeated Russia, which was the first time an Asian nation defeated a European power. The defeat gave a strong boost to the Japanese military. In 1910, Japan annexed Korea, the trophy Hideyoshi wanted three hundred years earlier.

During World War I, Japan sided with the Allied Powers of Britain and France and attacked German territories in China. After the war, some of these colonies came under Japanese control.

Industrial growth led to the increasing polarization of Japanese society. Large numbers of people flocked to the cities to work in factories. Poor working conditions led to dissent and Marxist labor movements took hold. At the same time, ultranationalists demanded territorial expansion. The worldwide panic of 1929 led to fewer markets for Japan's exports.

The feeble government could not cope with all these problems and became dominated by military extremists. Japan annexed Manchuria in 1932 and invaded Beijing in 1937. Britain, Holland and the US responded to Japanese expansion in China by imposing a series of economic sanctions including an oil embargo. Negotiations between Japan and America to settle the dispute were inconclusive.

In December 1941, the Japanese military attacked Pearl Harbor in a preemptive strike to break the embargo and eliminate US naval forces from blocking its expansion in Asia. The US immediately declared war on Japan. Japan was initially successful in gaining control of much of Asia, including Southeast Asia and the lion's share of China, but the tide turned against the Japanese military as early as June 1942. By mid-1943, Japan was losing the war.

By the end of the war, Allied bombing had reduced almost every city in Japan to rubble. Dropping the atomic bombs on **Hiroshima** and **Nagasaki** in early August 1945 led to the Japanese surrender on August 15. **Emperor Hirohito**, who ruled from 1926–89, addressed the Japanese people by radio for the first time in history. He urged Japanese to "Endure the unendurable and suffer what is insufferable," a famous line indelibly etched in the memory of all Japanese born before the war.

POSTWAR PERIOD
(1945-Present)

Under the command of **General Douglas MacArthur**, American Allied Forces occupied Japan for six and a half years after the end of World War II. The Japanese government, put in power by MacArthur and the Occupation forces, restructured Japanese society. A new constitution drafted in 1947 renounced war and gave broad civil rights such as freedom of speech and religion. Women received the vote. Land reform was carried out and the *zaibatsu*, large industrial conglomerates (the original military industrial complexes), were broken up. The new government was based on a parliamentary system. The emperor remained as the symbol of the state and implicitly relinquished any divine right to rule.

In September 1951, Japan signed the **San Francisco Treaty**, which allowed Japan to conduct foreign policy. Economic development became the government's top priority. The Korean War in the 1950s gave Japan the impetus to reconstruct its economy and by the 1960s, Japan was competing in the world market. Hosting the Olympics in 1964 was Japan's coming-out party.

The postwar government has been overwhelmingly dominated by the Liberal Democratic Party (LDP). With the triangle of a strong party, strong bureaucracy and strong industry, the LDP shepherded Japan through its economic redevelopment. Japan's well-educated and hard-working population rose to the challenge at great personal sacrifice. Often overlooked is the role of women, so-called shadow workers, who contributed to economic growth by freeing men from all domestic responsibility. Japan now has the world's highest per capita income and is the second largest economy on the planet.

In the late 1980s, protracted economic growth and cheap credit led to frenzied increases in the price of land, in the stock market and in other valuations. The cost of land in major cities skyrocketed and middle class families found themselves shut out of the real estate market like never before. Japanese companies were so flush with cash, they bought up large chunks of Hawaii and other prime US properties at highly inflated prices. All of this came crashing down in 1992 with a recession that stymied the Japanese economy for the next half-dozen years.

Rapid economic development has come at a high price. A growth policy based on exports causes friction with Japan's trading partners. Rapid redevelopment at any cost means high levels of pollution and environmental damage. Urban dwellers sacrifice high standards of living and a rapidly aging population is increasingly expensive to support. Prohibited by the Constitution from maintaining an army, the Japanese "Self-defense Force" actually constitutes one of the 9th or 10th largest military forces in the world and is under pressure to participate in peacekeeping missions around the globe. The Japanese government is under pressure to play a role in international affairs commensurate with its economic power. All these issues pose challenges in the coming decades.

When Emperor Hirohito died in January 1989, his son **Akihito** ascended the throne ending 63 years known as the Showa era and ushering in the current **Heisei** period.

THE ROLE OF THE JAPANESE EMPEROR

The **imperial family** is a source of fascination to the Japanese public and many regard its members as celebrities. Nearly every week women's magazines feature imperial family members in color photographs. But the imperial family lives privately behind the "chrysanthemum curtain" (the 16-petal chrysanthemum is the imperial symbol). This distance only makes the media and the public clamor for more information.

The Japanese emperor descends from one of the world's longest continuing lineages. The first written histories of Japan, compiled under the auspices of the emperor in the 8th century, take great pains to trace the roots of the ruling family to the Shinto Sun Goddess **Amaterasu**. Some of the earliest emperors actually practiced a dual system: the celibate older brother took care of Shinto religious rituals while the younger brother had political control and produced heirs to continue the line.

Soon after the introduction of Buddhism in the 6th century, the emperors realized the powerful centralizing force of the religion and became avid believers. Shintoism and Buddhism existed side by side. More often than not, emperors became Buddhist monks after they abdicated. And abdicate they did. Perhaps it was the stress of the office, but few emperors spent more than a handful of years in the top position. Emperors came to have little political power, either forceful regents or shoguns ruled in their behalf from the 10th century on.

This system continued until 1868. Low-ranking samurai, who master-minded the overthrow of the Tokugawa shogunate, coalesced around "returning" the emperor to power. The Meiji Emperor moved from Kyoto to Tokyo and the capital moved with him — powerful symbols that he was head of the nation. Even so, the emperor had little real political power; the constitutional government ruled in his name.

The fledgling government found it convenient to push the concept of "State Shinto," a national religion, with the emperor at its head. This idea provided the basic symbol for continuity of the imperial lineage, which was needed by the new government to achieve modernization with the least resistance. After all, who could be against the emperor? The emperor, as the connection between the gods and the state, was beyond reproach. Although historically many emperors built magnificent Bud-dhist temples and became monks after abdication, Buddhism was now discredited and many temples were destroyed. There was a frenzy of Shinto shrine building including a national system of state shrines headed by Yasukuni Shrine in Tokyo.

During the Meiji period, the emperor system changed in important ways. The emperor now ruled for life and could only be succeeded by a male heir, (although previously there had been female emperors — empress is a title reserved for the wife of the emperor.) The Meiji Emperor fathered 14 children before one male lived. This system has meant great stability; since 1868 Japan has only had four emperors.

Elements of the extreme loyalty and fealty of the warrior class transferred to the emperor: when Emperor Meiji died in 1912, General Nogi, a hero of the 1905 Russo-Japanese War, committed suicide. **Meiji Shrine**, deifying the emperor and empress, was built in Tokyo with funds collected from citizens all over Japan. The right wing militarism of the 1930s and 1940s, which culminated in Japan's involvement in World War II, was carried out in the name of Emperor Hirohito. How much he really knew and approved is a hotly debated topic among historians.

After the end of the World War II, American experts on Japanese culture and language convinced General Douglas MacArthur the emperor was a valuable asset in maintaining control of the Japanese. If the emperor proclaimed Japan would be a democracy, people would follow. MacArthur realized that trying the emperor as a war criminal would make the maintenance of law and order almost impossible, and he didn't want to lose lives of American soldiers keeping peace in occupied Japan.

The first chapter of the Constitution, which came into effect on May 3, 1947, proclaims "sovereignty resides in the people" and "the emperor is the symbol of the state and of the unity of the people."

The emperor lost his divine status. The aristocratic classes lost their titles; titled royalty became restricted to the immediate male family members of the emperor. The current empress, **Michiko**, is the first commoner to marry into the imperial line; she has been joined by Princess Masako, wife of the crown prince; Princess Kiko, wife of the emperor's second son, and the wives of other princes. Female members of the imperial family lose their imperial status when they marry, which is why some speculate that Princess Nori, the only daughter of the current emperor, isn't in any rush to find a mate.

JAPAN'S HISTORICAL PERIODS

Jomon Period: ca. 10,000–300 BC
Yayoi Period: ca. 300 BC–AD 300
Kofun Period: ca. AD 300–593
Asuka Period: 593–710
Nara Period: 710–794
Heian Period: 794–1185
Kamakura Period: 1185–1333
Muromachi Period: 1333–1573
Momoyama Period: 1573–1603
Edo Period: 1603–1868
Meiji Period: 1868–1912
Taisho Period: 1912–1926
Showa Period: 1926–1989
Heisei Period: 1989–present

6. PLANNING YOUR TRIP

WHEN TO VISIT - CLIMATE

Japan has four distinct seasons offering travelers a range of choices. For us, autumn is the best time to visit, although the Japanese autumn begins later than Europe's or North America's. For Japan's coastal cities, autumn starts in late September and lasts until the end of November. Fall foliage is spectacular in many parts of the country, adding natural color to your trip.

Noriko loves to travel on the Pacific side of Honshu from late November through January when the weather is sunny and crisp. Winter begins in mid-December and lasts until early March.

Spring is another popular travel time. Cherry blossoms are spectacular in late March and early April, but the weather is usually unstable. A glorious spring day can be followed by several cold and rainy ones. From the end of April until early June, the weather is clear and sunny, and many flowers are in bloom.

Rainy season begins in early June. Starting in Kyushu, it moves northeast and lasts a little over a month. The season is unpredictable — some years it rains heavily and other years there's almost none. But the weather is always cloudy and humid with fairly large variations in temperature. Hokkaido doesn't get the seasonal rains so Japanese flock to the northern island this time of year.

About mid-July, the hot, steamy summer follows the rainy season. Usually, there are about two months of high temperatures and humidity, making touring almost unbearable. If you have to travel in the summer, we recommend you choose the rainy season over the muggy summer months. Typhoons are in-season during August and September; the summer heat finally dissipates in mid-September when there's a little rain, and the air is crisp and clear.

Kyoto, Osaka and northern Kyushu have colder winters and warmer summers than Tokyo.

Tips for Winter Travel

When you travel in Japan's mountains in the winter, you need to dress as warmly as you would in mountains anywhere during the winter. But in Japan's coastal cities, where there are great temperature variations, even from day to day, here are some tips to help you enjoy winter touring.

• Layer your clothing. Scarves are good for regulating your body temperature. Over your street clothes, wear a sweater and a jacket, preferably windproof. It's much more practical than wearing one heavy coat. Make sure you have gloves and a hat.

• Bring heavy socks or bootie-type slippers. Since you must remove your shoes to enter most temples, feet freeze rapidly without an extra layer.

• Buy hot packs, *hokaron,* at any drug store. There's a brand called Mycoal that has its name in English. Some types come with adhesive backing to stick on clothes. They stay warm for hours and are great to put in your pockets and at the back of your neck. For your own protection, never put a hot pack directly on your skin. We'd never survive winter without hot packs.

• Most vending machines sell warm drinks including canned coffee, tea, cocoa, corn soup and Japanese tea. The cans are so hot when they come out of the machine that they can double as good hand warmers.

When to Travel — Avoiding Peak Times

Most Japanese tend to travel at the same time because it's the only time they can get time off from work without feeling guilty. Try to avoid traveling in Japan during these peak times although it's a good time to be in Tokyo, Osaka and other large cities. They empty out. If you do travel

TOKYO'S AVERAGE TEMPERATURE & RAIN

	Jan	Feb	Mar	Apr	May	June
Temp °C	3	4	7	13	17	21
Temp °F	37	39	45	54	62	70
Rain, inches	4.3	6.1	9	10	9.6	12

	July	Aug	Sept	Oct	Nov	Dec
Temp °C	25	26	23	17	11	5
Temp °F	77	79	73	62	51	41
Rain, inches	10	8	11	9	6.4	3.8

during these peak times, be sure to make your reservations well in advance. The newspapers often report 70 kilometer tie-ups on the expressways, and *shinkansen* trains run at 150% of capacity.

Some peak periods:
• **New Year's**, *December 27 through January 4*
• **Golden Week**, *April 29 through May 5*
• **O-Bon Holiday**, *August 13-16*

Other busy times are April-May and October-November. Make your reservations in advance.

WHAT TO PACK

First of all, what not to pack. Pack lightly!!! Taxis from the international airports are expensive. In most train stations, porters are scarce as are escalators and elevators. You'll have to struggle with your luggage up and down steps. Coin lockers big enough for large suitcases are difficult to come by and only the largest train stations will have baggage storerooms. The less you have with you, the easier your trip will be.

For touring, pack comfortable clothes. Japanese tend to dress quite well so you'll probably feel out-of-place in sloppy jeans. That doesn't mean you have to dress up for sightseeing, but you don't want to look sloppy.

We find it best to layer clothing. Except in the heat of August, when it's always hot and muggy, the temperature is unpredictable. In spring and fall, you'll need a jacket or sweater. In the June-July rainy season, it can be cool and rainy or warm and rainy, so make sure you have a light jacket and a folding umbrella. Summer is hot and humid, but you may need a light jacket to prevent yourself from freezing in air-conditioned hotels and restaurants. You'll need a fairly heavy coat in winter since it can snow in Tokyo, Osaka or Fukuoka. Of course, if you are going to the mountains or to Hokkaido, you'll need very heavy winter clothing.

Comfortable walking shoes are a must. Japan is a country best discovered on foot. Most likely, you'll be using mass transportation a lot and that means going up and down a lot of stairs. Our friends visiting from overseas tell us they have never walked so much in their lives.

Don't forget your slip-on shoes. Shoes come off when you enter Japanese houses and restaurants with *tatami* mats. Shoes come off when you enter most temples. They even come off at many museums. So shoes come off and on a lot. And you'll be glad when you don't have to stop to untie and tie them time and again. Reminder: to avoid embarrassment, make sure your socks don't have holes.

Hotels and inns nearly always supply *yukata* (cotton kimono robes), tooth brushes and hair dryers, so lighten your bag by a few ounces. If you are staying at inexpensive accommodations, bring a towel.

You should also always carry pocket tissues and/or a handkerchief to use as a hand towel or napkin. Public toilets usually do not have hand towels, but most have toilet paper.

A small folding umbrella is essential. It can rain any time of the year. Make sure you have one extra pair of shoes and socks in case your feet get soaked. During the rainy season, take waterproof shoes and a light raincoat.

Make sure you pack drugs, both prescription and over-the-counter. You won't find many familiar brand names such as Tylenol, and it will be difficult, if not impossible, to fill your medical prescriptions. If you wear glasses, have a copy of your prescription in case you lose or break your glasses.

North American appliances generally work in Japan without a converter or adapter so you can leave the extra equipment at home.

While you can generally buy almost anything you need in Japan, you may not like the price. Double the US price is average, sometimes it's more. And worse yet, clothes are styled for petite Japanese — a sweater sleeve might be halfway up your arm or pants may fit more like shorts. If you are a large person or wear large shoes, you could have real difficulties. So it's best to be self-sufficient.

Camera film purchased at a discount electronics shop is one of the few things cheaper in Tokyo than New York. But film at tourist sights is expensive. Throw away cameras are readily available.

COST OF TRAVEL

Japan always heads the list of the most expensive travel destinations. And there's good reason. At a deluxe hotel, room rates start at ¥20,000 (about $175-200 at today's exchange rate, but check the paper – recent rates have fluctuated between ¥100 and ¥130 to the dollar) and are often twice as much for two. Hotel food is expensive. Breakfast can cost ¥3000 — imagine freshly squeezed orange juice for ¥1500, lunch for ¥6000 and dinner ¥10,000 and up. If you stay at a deluxe *ryokan* (Japanese inn), dinner and breakfast are included although the rate can be ¥30,000 per person or higher. Expenses of ¥50,000 per day are common for top-of-the-line travel.

These costs are comparable to staying in similar accommodations in European capitals. These expenses may be okay for the businessman on expense accounts or for the traveler who's willing to pay for the best accommodations; for the average traveler, Japan can cost quite a bit less.

A rail pass, which is bought in your home country and validated after arrival, and advance-purchase domestic air tickets minimize transportation costs. The Welcome Inn Reservation Center and Japan Inn Group can arrange accommodations for you at between ¥4000 and ¥8000 per person. At rock bottom; youth hostels are ¥3000 or under per night.

Frugal travelers should plan on spending about ¥10,000 per person per day excluding transportation — this includes hotel, meals, subways and admission charges. A moderate budget is about ¥20,000 a day. Top-of-the-line can cost from ¥30,000 per person.

If you budget about ¥1000 for breakfast, ¥700 to ¥3000 for lunch — lunchtime specials are one of Japan's best kept secrets — and ¥3000 to ¥5000 for dinner, you'll eat quite well. Dinner and breakfast are included in the cost of most Japanese inns.

Temple and museum admissions are extremely reasonable — ¥300 to ¥1000 — but can add up when you are visiting several a day.

PASSPORTS & VISAS

Yes, you must have a valid passport to travel to Japan. Americans can apply for one at regional post offices or go directly to a district office. But don't procrastinate because sometimes it can take several months to work its way through the passport agency.

Visas depend on your nationality. Currently, citizens of the United States, Canada, Australia, New Zealand, France, Italy and a host of other countries need not apply for a visa in advance if they are staying in Japan for less than three months for business or leisure. To be sure, check with the Japanese Embassy in your country. You can come for business meetings but can't draw salary from a company in Japan. The Japanese government does not allow you to extend your stay. To do so, you must leave the country and return. Hint: if you are desperate, you can fly to a nearby foreign city such as Seoul, return immediately and stay another three months. But if you do this more than twice in a row, immigration may give you a hard time. If you want to change from a temporary visitor visa to a working visa, the immigration bureau requires you to leave the country to obtain the new visa. Again, Seoul is the closest place.

Citizens of Austria, Germany, Ireland, Liechtenstein, Mexico, Switzerland and the United Kingdom can stay for six months without applying for a visa in advance.

If you will be earning money in Japan or want to stay for a longer period, you have to get a visa before you travel.

In the US, the Japanese Government maintains visa sections in Consulate Generals in Atlanta, Anchorage, Boston, Chicago, Detroit, Denver, Honolulu, Houston, Kansas City, Los Angeles, Miami, New Orleans, New York, Portland, San Francisco and Seattle.

•**New York**: *Consulate General of Japan, 299 Park Avenue, New York, NY 10171. Tel. 212/888-0889*

• **Washington, DC**: *Embassy of Japan, 2520 Massachusetts Avenue, Washington, DC 20008. Tel. 202/238-6700*
• **San Francisco**: *Consulate General of Japan, 50 Fremont Street, San Francisco, CA 94104. Tel. 415/777-3533*

Be sure you call to check their hours before you go; these guys make bankers' hours look like overtime.

CUSTOMS & HEALTH
Arriving
On the airplane you will be given an immigration form and a customs declaration. You need not fill out the customs declaration unless you are over the allowances; see below.

If your plane arrives from a third-world country, you may have to fill out a yellow health form reporting your whereabouts for the last 14 days and informing the health authorities if you have symptoms such as diarrhea, vomiting or fever. If you come from the US or Western Europe, you just walk through the barrier without turning in a form. We had friends who marked "yes" to one of the symptoms; the next day the Health Service came to their house to quarantine them and spray everything with antiseptic.

You shouldn't have much problem clearing customs. The Japanese government allows you to bring reasonable amounts of personal effects and equipment. You can also bring in duty-free gifts totaling ¥200,000, three bottles of liquor, 400 cigarettes, and 2 ounces of perfume. Persons 19 and under cannot bring in liquor or cigarettes. If you don't exceed the allowances, go to a counter marked Duty Free. If you're over, go to a counter marked Dutiable Goods. When you are carrying fruit, fresh flowers or other agricultural products, you need to stop at the quarantine desk for an inspection before you clear customs; there are restrictions on some items.

If you arrive from a country known for drug trafficking, Customs might give your bags more than a once-over. Sometimes they x-ray sealed boxes. Naturally, drugs and firearms are a no-no. Customs agents may actually ask you if you are carrying drugs or guns.

Returning to America
On your return trip to the US, the airline will give you a US customs declaration form. You need to fill out one per family. The US allows you to bring in one liter of alcohol and 200 cigarettes duty free. US residents can take in $400 of goods duty-free per person; nonresidents are allowed $100. On amounts over $400, Customs assesses a flat-rate duty of 10% on

the next $1000. Above that, the duty varies with each item. Also, be sure to declare it if you are carrying more than $10,000 in currency.

If you are traveling with high-priced foreign-made goods like fur coats or expensive jewelry, register them with the US Customs at the airport in the US before you depart to ensure there is no question of being charged duty on your return. You shouldn't have any problem with a laptop computer.

TOURS & TRAVEL AGENTS

Large operators offer tours as well as package deals that include airfare and hotels, but your time is your own. Unless it is a special-interest one, we don't recommend tours; tour operators tend to take people to standard sights only. But you might find it economical to use some of the package tours the large operators organize. Their buying power can get you air and hotel rates you cannot get on your own. Here are a few operators that offer tours, package deals, discount air tickets, discount hotel rates and the Japan Rail Pass.

- **Japan Travel Bureau** (JTB). Japan's largest travel agency. The New York office is at *810 7th Avenue, 34th floor, New York, NY, 10019. Tel. 212/698-4900, Fax 212/586-9686; www.jtbusa.com.* JTB has offices all over the world.
- **Kintetsu International Express**. *1325 Avenue of the Americas, Suite 2001, New York, NY, 10019. Tel. 212/259-9510, Fax 212/259-9505; www.kintetsu.com.*
- **Tokyu Travel America**. *21221 S. Western Avenue, Torrance, CA, 90501. Tel. 310/783-6560, Fax 310/782-7347; www.tokyutravel.com.*
- **Airport Travel**. *5959 W. Century Boulevard, Suite 1407, Los Angeles, CA, 90045. Tel. 310/410-0656; 800/310/5549, Fax 310/410-1954; www.airporttravel.com.* They offer low-cost packages and homestays.
- **Singapore Airlines** offers a one-week package of air fare from Los Angeles, five nights at the Tokyo Hilton Hotel, airport transfers and a half-day city tour for $999. Travel agents can book it or contact Singapore Airlines *Tel. 800/742-3333; www.singaporeair.com/americas.*

Consolidators

Travel agents who issue consolidator or other low-cost tickets advertise in the Sunday travel sections of the *New York Times*, the *Los Angeles Times* and other major newspapers. Several that we have used are:

- **Japan Budget Travel**, *9 East 38th Street, New York, NY. Tel. 212/686-8855*
- **Euro-Asia Holidays**, *47 West 34th Street, New York, NY. Tel. 212/279-8528, Fax 212/279-8539*
- **Express Fun Travel Service**, *330 Tenth Street, San Francisco, CA 94103. Tel. 415/864-8005; 800/722-0872, Fax 415/863-9523*

CYBERTRAVEL

You can practically travel to Japan without leaving your computer chair. Here are some favorite web sites:

Japan National Tourist Organization. *www.jnto.go.jp. Should be everyone's first cyber-stop. The newly-expanded site has enough information to keep you busy for several lifetimes. Look here for event calendars, regional travel information, hotel listings, bookings for the Welcome Inn Reservation System and much more. Also www.japantravelinfo.com.*

Railway Information. *JR East's web site is www.jreast.co.jp; JR West's: www.westjr.co.jp.*

Japan's English Language Newspapers:
Japan Times: www.japantimes.co.jp
Asahi Evening News: www.asahi.com/english
Daily Yomiuri: www.yomiuri.co.jp/index-e.htm
Mainichi Daily News: www.mainichi.co.jp/english/index.html
Nikkei Weekly: www.nni.nikkei.co.jp. Business and financial news.

Japan Information Network. *www.jinjapan.org. Extensive information on government, business, culture as well as great links.*

Kids Web Japan. *www.jinjapan.org/kidswebjapan. An excellent source of information on Japan for children.*

Maps and Yellow Pages. *www.mixpizza.omron.co.jp. A business directory with excellent maps.*

Train and Air Information and Fares. *www.bijapan.com. Click on the Travel Expert icon. Put in your destination and the Travel Expert will give you routes and fares.*

Currrency Converter. *www.bloomberg.com/markets. What's the yen worth today? The answer is just a few clicks away.*

Sake. *www.sake-world.com. Interested in Japanese rice wine? Check out sake guru John Gauntner's comprehensive site.*

Japanese Cuisine. *www.bento.com. Tokyo Food Pages has extensive listings of Japanese food sites.*

Museums: *www.dnp.co.jp/museum/icc-e.html.*

Special Tours & Opportunities

Several companies offer tours with a different twist:

- **Walking Tours of Japan** (they aren't all walking tours) has to be one of the best-kept tour secrets. Run by Steve Beimel and Michael Kuranoff who know Japan inside and out; their tours give you an insider's perspective at a moderate price. *Espirit Travel, 2101 Wilshire Boulevard, Suite 101, Santa Monica, CA, 90403. Tel. 800/377-7481; 310/829-6060; www.espirittravel.com.*

- **Journeys East's** tours emphasize experiencing Japanese culture. Participants stay in traditional inns and meet local people. *Journeys East, PO Box 1161, Middletown, CA, 95461. Tel. 800/527-2612; 707/987-4531, Fax 707/987-4831. Email: JEinUSA@aol.com; www.journeyseast.com.*
- **Seniors Abroad** runs homestay trips for persons over 50. *Seniors Abroad, 12533 Pacato Circle North, San Diego, CA, 92128. Tel. 858/485-1696, Fax 858/487-1492. Email: haev@pacbell.net.*
- **Elderhostel** runs trips to Japan for the over 55 set. *Elderhostel, 75 Federal Street, Boston, MA, 02110. Tel. 877/426-8056; www.elderhostel.com.*
- **Interhostel**, at the University of New Hampshire, is organizing a family travel program staying at universities and taking short (one to three week) courses. *Interhostel, University of New Hampshire, 6 Garrison Avenue, Durham, NH, 03284. Tel. 800/733-9753; 603/862-1147, Fax 603/862-1113; www.learn.unh.edu.*

Art Tours of Japan, led by artist Karyn Young, focuses on exploring traditional arts and crafts and visiting contemporary artists' studios, museums and galleries. *126 Frustuck Avenue, Fairfax, CA 94930. Tel. 415/454-0389, Fax 415/455-0702. Email: kyst@msn.com.*

Absolute Asia's tours are all private and custom-designed to fit the traveler's interests, schedule and budget. Special interest trips include traditional crafts, culinary tours, gardens, ceramics and architecture. *180 Varick Street, New York, NY 10014. Tel. 800/736-8187, 212/6271950, Fax 212/627-4090; www.absoluteasia.com.*

Adventure Travel Tours

Tour companies run adventure trips around the world. When it comes to Japan, they tend to emphasize Japanese culture rather than hiking and outdoor experiences. In this way, they are quite similar to the high-quality tours mentioned above rather than safaris and trekking that we usually find with adventure travel.

- **Wilderness Travel** offers a Temples, Treasures & Teahouses tour. *1102 Ninth St., Berkeley, CA, 94710. Tel. 800/368-2794; Tel/Fax 510/558-2488. Email: info@wildernesstravel.com; www.wildnernestravel.com.*
- **Geographic Expeditions** runs a Country Inns from Tokyo to Kyoto tour. *2627 Lombard Street, San Francisco, CA, 94123. Tel. 800/777-8183, 415/922-0448, Fax 415/346-5535. Email: info@geoex.com; www.geoex.com.*
- **At Last the Best!** tours include Ascent of Mt. Fuji and The Alps of Japan. *10989 Dorchester Way, Truckee, CA 96161. Tel. 888/445-8857; www.atlastthebest.com.*
- **Butterfield and Robinson**, a tour operator specializing in luxury bicycling, has an eight-night Japan Bike and Walk tour. *70 Bond Street,*

Toronto. ON, Canada M5B 1X3. Tel. 800/678-1147, 416/864-1354, Fax 416/864-0541; www.butterfieldandrobinson.com.

Betchart Expeditions runs a "Wild Heritage Expedition," one of the few tours to Japan which focuses on native plants and animals and natural landscapes. *17050 Montebello Road, Cupertino, CA 95014. Tel: 800/252-4910, 408/252-4910. Fax: 408/252-1444. Email: Betchartex@aol.com.*

Hands-on Experiences

As a nation with so many craft and art traditions, a trip to Japan can be highlighted by participating in some of the many workshops introducing you to a particular art.

• **Papermaking Workshop**. A three-day workshop is held monthly in a traditional farmhouse in the countryside near Mino, a papermaking town in Gifu Prefecture, near Nagoya. Run by a group of foreigners interested in preserving this dying art, the workshop is a hands-on introduction to Japanese papermaking. The workshop is run in English, Japanese and other languages as needed. *Washi Survival School, 2485 Warabi Yatsubo, Mino-shi, Gifu, 501. Tel. (0575)34-8335, Fax (0575)34-8355.*

• **Ceramic Workshop and Homestay**. A five-week workshop is held each summer for ceramic artists to work with the potters of Tokoname, a ceramic center with a 900-year heritage. Apply by February 28. *International Workshop of Ceramic Art in Tokoname (IWCAT), c/o Tokoname Chamber of Commerce and Industry, 5-58 Shinkai-cho, Tokoname, Aichi, 479-0837, Fax (0569)34-3223. Email iwcat@japan-net.ne.jp; www.japan-net.ne.jp/~iwcat.*

• **Niijima International Glass Art Festival** is held every November at Niijima, a small island 10 hours by boat from Tokyo. International glass artists participate in the nine-day workshop. *Niijima Glass Art Center, Mamashita Kaigan Street, Niijima-mura, Tokyo, 100-0402. Tel. (04992)5-1540, Fax (04992)5-1240; www.guild.ne.jp/niijima.*

• **International Zen Center**, near Kyoto, welcomes international visitors who would like to experience Zen meditation and temple life. Stays can be as short as one day or several months. *Kyoto International Zen Center (Rinzai sect), Jotoku-ji, Inukai Sogabe-cho, Kameoka, Kyoto, 621. Tel. (0771)24-0152, Fax: (0771)24-0378, e-mail: kyotozen@zen.or.jp.*

• **Earth Celebration** is organized by the world famous Kodo Drummers. The festival on Sado Island in late August features percussion artists from all over the world. *148-1 Kaneda Shinden, Ogimachi, Sado-gun, Niigata, 952-0611. Tel. (0259)86-3630, Fax (0259)86-3631; www.kodo.or.jp.*

• **Toga International Arts Festival** draws drama lovers from all over the world to its traditional and avant-garde performances. The 10-day festival is held in early August in Toga, a small mountain village near

Toyama. The renowned architect Isozaki Arata designed the festival's amphitheater. *2-14-19-302 Shimoochiai, Shinjuku-ku, Tokyo, 161. Tel. (03)3951-4843 or (0763)68-2216.*

- **Taiko Drumming Weekends** are organized periodically by Wanderlust Adventures. *Contact Cathy Bernatt at cbernatt@gol.com.*
- **Home Visit System.** In about a dozen cities, the Japan National Tourist Office (JNTO) has established a program to visit a Japanese family in their home. There's no charge and you can spend a few hours, usually in the evening, talking with the family. Be sure to take a small gift such as flowers, cookies or something from your home country. Telephone contact numbers are given either in the home visit system or practical information section of the cities where it operates.
- **Goodwill Guides.** There is a network of Goodwill Guide clubs made up of volunteers who will guide you around their city. Many Japanese do this in order to meet foreign travelers and have an opportunity to speak English. There is no charge for this service. Since these are volunteer organizations, their contact phone numbers are always changing. Rather than publish obsolete numbers, we recommend that you contact the JNTO Travel Information Center, *Tel. (03)3201-3331 or 0088-22-4800,* or the local tourist office for the current number.

Further Information

For other opportunities from study tours to cooking schools, the **Shaw Guides** are an excellent source of information. Access them at *www.shawguides.com.*

The **National Registration Center for Study Abroad** (NRCSA), a consortium of universities and language schools, has information on language and cultural programs. *P.O. Box 1393, Milwaukee, WI, 53201. Tel. 414/278-7410 or 278-0631; www.nrcsa.com.*

TRAVEL FOR THE DISABLED

Traveling with disabilities is a challenge in Japan. Superficially, it appears that Japan has done so much. Subways and many thoroughfares have sidewalks with raised lines and dots ("street Braille" a friend calls them) to guide the blind. Many traffic lights chirp to assist them. Trains and buses have "Silver Seats" for the disabled and the elderly. But when we look around, we realize it's rare to see a blind person or someone in a wheelchair.

Japan tends to keep its disabled hidden in institutions and behind walls. Sometimes you'll see physically or mentally handicapped people on an outing to a zoo or park, but most of the time they are out of view.

It's almost impossible to get from the street to a train platform without climbing stairs. A few stations have wheelchair lifts on the stairs, and the number will probably increase. Elevators in train stations are practically unheard of. Train companies protest it's too expensive to build elevators for so few people. Their position is that they will provide personnel to carry people in wheelchairs up and down stairs as long as they know in advance. To demonstrate the indignity of such a system, activists occasionally organize a protest by having 20 or 30 wheelchairs converge on a station at the same time.

We're not trying to discourage disabled people from visiting Japan. Just be prepared and remember that it's not easy to get around.

The Japan Red Cross has put out a bilingual book called *Accessible Tokyo*; it's a must for the disabled traveler. The book gives detailed information on facilities at hotels, shopping areas, museums, theaters, parks and zoos.

• **The Japanese Red Cross Language Service Volunteers**, *c/o Volunteers Division, Japanese Red Cross Society, 1-1-3 Shiba-daimon, Minato-ku, Tokyo, 105, Tel. (03) 3438-1311.*
• **Accessible Tokyo**, *www.jwindow.net/LWT/Toyko/Redcross/redcross.index.htm.*

The lion's share of international flights arrive at **Narita Airport** (NRT), officially the New Tokyo International Airport, outside Tokyo or at **Kansai International Airport** (KIX), near Osaka. There are some international flights into regional airports such as Sapporo, Nagoya and Fukuoka, but they are almost exclusively intra-Asia flights. If you are heading to the Osaka/Kyoto/Kobe area or points west, investigate flying into Kansai International Airport. It will save you the hassle of getting there from Narita.

China Airlines, the Taiwan airline, flies into Haneda Airport, which is otherwise used for domestic flights. Haneda is more convenient to Tokyo than Narita. You can fly China Airlines from Taipei and from Honolulu to Haneda.

AIRLINES

Traveling from North America, American Airlines, ANA (All Nippon Airways), Canadian Airlines, Continental, Delta Air Lines , Japan Airlines, Korean Air, Malaysia Airlines, Northwest Airlines, Singapore Airlines and United Airlines provide direct service. The major gateway cities are

Atlanta, Chicago, Dallas, Detroit, Honolulu, Los Angeles, Minneapolis, New York, Portland (Oregon), San Francisco, San Jose (California), Seattle, Toronto, Vancouver, and Washington DC. Since the flight is so long, do yourself a favor and choose a flight with an easy connection.

All major European carriers serve Japan from their countries.

Most airlines offer three classes of service: First, Business and Coach. So many business people travel to Japan that on some flights business class takes up most of the plane. Most airlines have nonsmoking flights to Japan. Japanese airlines no longer have smoking on international flights.

Making Air Reservations

Any travel agent can issue tickets to Japan. Ticket prices are all over the map. In coach, it's possible a passenger could pay three or four times more than the person sitting next to him. If you phone the airline asking for fares, they will have a standard fare and some lower APEX (advance purchase) fares. But you can get less-expensive fares by going through travel agents who deal with consolidators — the airlines' way of selling wholesale seats. Our advice is to shop around and decide whether it's worth the savings to have more restrictions. Actually, consolidator tickets often have fewer restrictions than APEX tickets. We list several consolidators above under *Tours & Travel Agents*.

If you are planning to travel elsewhere in Asia, it's almost always less expensive to have the destination included in your ticket rather than buying a separate ticket in Japan. You can get some fairly cheap discount tickets in Japan, but they give you little flexibility.

The big Japanese travel agencies such as Japan Travel Bureau, Kintetsu Travel, and Tokyu Travel offer discount tickets as well as packages. See their addresses above under *Tours & Travel Agents*.

Surviving the Flight

No matter how you look at it, the flight is going to be long. Flying time is 13 1/2 hours from New York, 13 from Chicago and 10 1/2 from San Francisco. Because you cross the international date line traveling from North America, you arrive the day following your departure. Returning to North America, you arrive the same day you leave Japan. Flying west actually takes longer than flying east because the Pacific jet stream runs west to east.

There is almost no way to make the trip bearable. Some friends knock themselves out; others sleep naturally. We just endure. Good books — occasionally a good movie, but don't count on it — help pass the time. A friend uses this time to catch up on her letter writing.

JET LAG

Unless you are coming from Asia or Australia, jet lag is an inescapable part of traveling to Japan. There are jet-lag diets, but we've never had the discipline to follow them – who wants to drink coffee only at strange times? To minimize jet lag, eat lightly on the plane, avoid alcoholic beverages, drink plenty of water and walk around to keep your blood flowing. When traveling west from the US, Patrice's husband, who's flown enough miles on airplanes to be awarded a free trip to the moon, swears by sleeping for several hours immediately after take-off and then staying awake for the rest of the flight. This system puts him closer to the Japanese schedule. Easy to say, but since flights leave North America around noon, how can we sleep then?

After arriving in Japan, go to your hotel, have dinner and stay up as late as you can, 9 or 10pm if you can manage it. We find taking melatonin or Tylenol PM helps before going to bed; we still wake up at 2am but can get back to sleep fairly easily. And if you are wide awake at 5am, rather than grumbling, get an early start on the day by going to the fish market or checking your e-mail.

The day after your arrival, try to spend some time outdoors because sunshine helps your body reset its clock. Late afternoon, around 4 or 5pm, is usually the worst time; you can hardly keep your eyes open. Rather than giving in, take a walk or do exercises to wake yourself up.

It will take a few days to get over jet lag. If your trip is for just a few days, it may not be worth the effort to try. We have come to the conclusion that the more exhausted we are before a trip, the easier it is to get over jet lag.

Not eating airline food helps; request fruit plates and other special meals in advance. We find heavy airline food tends to make us feel worse, so we bring fruit and snacks. Drink lots of liquids – about one cup of water an hour; the airline cabin is almost humidity free. Avoid alcoholic drinks because they lead to further dehydration. Don't be tempted just because they're free. If you get up periodically and walk around the cabin, you can improve your circulation as well as your state of mind.

On most airlines, once the plane's door is locked, you are free to change seats within your class. If you see several unoccupied seats, move immediately before some savvier traveler takes them. It helps to stretch out if you have extra seats, but be careful about the bulkhead seats – you can't raise the armrests. The same applies to some three-in-a-row business class seats.

Be sure to ask for a seat assignment when you make your reservations or else you might find yourself right next to the bathroom or wedged in a center seat. If smoke bothers you, ask for a seat as far away from the smoking section as possible; it won't help you if the smoking section starts in the row behind you.

Some airlines do not assign seats in the exit rows until the day of the flight. If you'd like extra leg-room, inquire when you check in.

People have individual preferences about window or aisle seats. You can lean against windows to rest and won't have people climbing over you to get to the aisle. But then, it's troublesome to get up and out. Aisles offer stretching room and easy access to bathrooms, but you have to put up with people climbing over you. It's up to you.

If two people are traveling together, some airlines will allow you to reserve a window and an aisle seat with an empty seat in-between. If the flight is full and someone is assigned that seat, that passenger is almost always grateful to trade for an aisle or window.

Don't get discouraged. It's a long flight, but it's well worth it.

FROM THE AIRPORT TO THE CITY
NARITA AIRPORT (NRT)

When you arrive at **Narita Airport**, dog-tired after umpteen hours on the road, don't be surprised to find that you still have a 60-kilometer trek into Tokyo! Don't despair, train service makes it almost bearable.

Who knows why the airport is so far away from the city? It's something to do with noise and land rights, and since the government is still fighting with radical farmers over land, great big Narita has only one runway, although a second runway may be completed by 2002.

Narita is officially known as New Tokyo International Airport (as opposed to Haneda, Tokyo International Airport). Haneda handles domestic flights almost exclusively.

Narita has two terminals imaginatively named Terminal 1 and Terminal 2. Terminal 2 opened several years ago and has helped ease the severe congestion, but it does not make using the airport a pleasure. A free shuttle bus connects the terminals: at Terminal 1, use bus stop 5; at Terminal 2, use bus stops 8 and 18.

Between 2 and 6pm, the peak arrival time, foreigners may stand in line for an hour at the Immigration counters. If you are a non-Japanese resident of Japan, use the Japanese lines; if you are a visitor, you have to wait. Congestion continues into the baggage area: the carousels, even in Terminal 2, are quite close together. The good news is there are usually plenty of free baggage carts, and you can use them on the escalators.

As you exit the baggage and customs area, there are counters for money exchange, hotel reservations, limousine bus tickets, delivery services to send suitcases, and a Japan Rail counter to validate rail passes. An airline information counter has basic tourist information and can help you with ground transportation. For info on all of Japan, go to the Tourist

Information Center on the arrival floors of both Terminal 1 and 2. Open daily 9am-8pm.

Domestic transfers: Narita has only a few domestic flights. To connect with domestic flights, you'll probably have to trek to Haneda Airport, nearly two hours away by train or bus. Keikyu line tram takes 1 hour and 45 minutes and costs ¥1560. The bus averages two hours and runs ¥3000.

Money Exchange

Money exchange counters are in the arrival area. They are open from 6:30am to 11pm in Terminal 1 and 7am to 10pm in Terminal 2. They stay open until the last flight arrives. The Bank of Tokyo-Mitsubishi has full banking services in both terminals between 9am and 3pm, Monday through Friday.

Amenities

Both terminals offer children's playrooms, Terminal 1 on the third floor, Central Building; Terminal 2 on the third floor. On the 3rd floor, Terminal 2 also has day rooms, showers, a business center and a video room. There are a number of stores in each terminal, but most are outside the transit area. Duty free shops are inside the transit areas. The selection in the Duty Free shop in Terminal 1 is limited mainly to alcoholic drinks and cosmetics so don't wait until the last moment to do your shopping. Terminal 2's Duty Free shops have a more extensive selection.

Delivery Services

Send your luggage to your hotel and travel unencumbered. Go to the ABC counter outside customs. Charge is ¥1860 per bag for the greater Tokyo area, and luggage is delivered the next day. You can also send luggage anywhere else in Japan.

When returning to Narita, you can send your bag ahead. Several days ahead of your departure, call **Sky Partners**, *Tel. (03)3545-1131*, to arrange pick-up or ask your hotel to arrange it for you. Sending bags to Narita costs ¥2100 each. You travel hassle-free to Narita by train and pick up your luggage at the ABC counter at the airport.

GROUND TRANSPORTATION FROM NARITA

There's no end to the number of ways you can get into Tokyo from Narita. Which one you choose depends on your budget, the amount of luggage and time you want to spend.

Taxi

If money is no object, taxi is the easiest way to get to Tokyo although it's not always the fastest. The fare to central Tokyo averages about

¥25,000, including expressway tolls. The drawback is that if the express-way traffic is moving at a snail's pace, so are you. Taxi trunks house a large LP gas tank, which means you can't put in as many suitcases in there as you think, but station wagon taxis and mini-vans are often available at the airport.

Trains

The most dependable way into Tokyo is by train. By connecting to the subway and/or other travel lines, you can get practically anywhere. The shortcoming is that trains are difficult to navigate with heavy luggage. It's not too bad at Narita where you can take your luggage cart almost to the train. At the other end, you have to carry everything up and down stairs to get to a taxi or connect to another train, and porters are rare. An alternative is to send your luggage from the airport to your downtown hotel (see Delivery Services above); it will arrive the following day. That way, all you'll have to worry about is your carry-on bag. We love the train if we're traveling light or have sent our bags ahead.

Narita Express (NEX): JR runs this comfortable, reserved-seat express train several times an hour to Tokyo Station (¥2940) with some trains continuing on to Shinjuku (¥3110), Ikebukuro (¥3110), Shinagawa (¥3110) and Yokohama stations (¥4180). NEX takes 55 minutes to Tokyo Station. The spacious seats offer ample leg room, and each car has a large luggage storage place. During peak travel times, the trains fill up, but standing is allowed. You can buy your tickets at the JR booth on the first floor or on the basement level near the train platforms.

A less-expensive alternative is to take the regular **JR express train** on the same line. It's an ordinary train without reserved seating or special luggage areas; it takes about 90 minutes to reach Tokyo Station. The fare is ¥1280.

Keisei Railway Skyliner: Fares are cheaper than NEX, but Ueno, the terminal station, is not as central as Tokyo Station. The Skyliner is an all reserved-seat train that stops at Nishi Nippori and Ueno Stations — either station ¥1920. The trip takes just under one hour. Note: Nishi Nippori is the more convenient transfer point to the JR Yamanote line, Tokyo's loop line. The Skyliner is not as popular as NEX and usually has seats available when NEX is sold out.

Keisei offers the cheapest fare to Tokyo via its limited express train *(tokkyu)*. For ¥1000, the train takes about 70 minutes to Nishi Nippori and a few minutes more to Ueno.

Limousine Bus

Limo buses have the advantage of whisking you away from terminal exit to hotels and other points around Tokyo. If they do not stop at the hotel where you are staying, you can take a short taxi ride to your final destination. They accept two pieces of luggage per person, and their personnel load and unload your baggage. Sounds great? Here's the bad news: Tokyo traffic can be pretty horrendous, and the trip can take more than two hours at peak times. We take the bus when we want to have our luggage with us and want a fairly hassle-free ride.

The Limousine Bus counter — you can't miss its big orange sign — has a bilingual computer screen that lists departure times. Select your destination and buy a ticket for the appropriate bus; be aware of your departure time and go outside to wait at the location number marked on your ticket and on a sign outside the terminal. The bus company accepts credit card payments at its Tokyo City Air Terminal (TCAT), Shinjuku Station, Yokohama City Air Terminal (YCAT) and Narita Airport counters. If you board a bus at a hotel to return to Narita Airport, you'll have to pay cash for your ticket.

If we have a lot of luggage and don't want to risk spending time sitting in traffic, we take a bus to TCAT on the eastern side of the city which avoids downtown traffic. Usually the trip doesn't take more than an hour. At TCAT, we pick up a taxi, either a normal one or a station wagon taxi. A fairly efficient way to get into the city, this way is much cheaper than taking a taxi all the way from Narita to center city.

To return to Narita Airport by limo bus, it's best to have a reservation made at least one day in advance. Hotels can make it for you or call *Tel. (03)3665-7220.*

Buses run to and from the areas listed below. The times are best-case scenarios; during rush hours, it could take much longer. The limo bus counter staff should be able to give you fairly accurate running times.
• Tokyo City Air Terminal: ¥2900, 55 minutes
• Tokyo Station, Yaesu Exit: ¥3000, 70 minutes
• Haneda Airport: ¥2900, 75 minutes
• Shinjuku Station and Hotels: ¥3000, 85 minutes
• Ginza Area Hotels: ¥3000, 80 minutes
• Akasaka Area Hotels: ¥3000, 85 minutes
• Shinagawa and Ebisu Area Hotels: ¥3000, 85 minutes
• Shiba Park Area Hotels: ¥3000, 80 minutes
• Kudanshita Area Hotels: ¥3000, 90 minutes
• Maihama Hotels and Disneyland: ¥2400, 60 minutes

Car Rental
Toyota, Nippon and Nissan have counters at both Terminal 1 and 2, but do yourself a favor and let someone else get you into Tokyo.

Tokyo City Air Terminal (TCAT)

Departing passengers should know about TCAT at Hakozaki, which is at the Suitengu-mae subway stop on the Hanzomon line. From TCAT, you can get on a limo bus to Narita. Because the bus doesn't need to go through the most congested sections of Tokyo, it usually takes under one hour to reach the airport.

Ask your airline whether or not you can check in at TCAT and find out the minimum check-in time. Several airlines have check-in counters where you can get your boarding pass, check your luggage, and, best of all, clear immigration.

During peak travel times at the airport, you may wait more than 30 minutes in immigration lines, but at TCAT you rarely wait more than five. Immigration authorities give you a pass that allows you to bypass the Narita airport immigration counter altogether. Just surrender your pass at the glass window along the wall of Narita's immigration area.

Departure Tax

The departure tax for Narita is no longer collected separately. It is now included in your airline ticket price.

Security

When we enter Narita Airport, we always feel that there must be a war going on that we don't know about. Security is very tight and guards in battlewagons hang around looking serious. You'll need to show your passport to enter the airport. What's this all about? Militant farmers blew up part of the airport when it first opened in 1978.

Contact Numbers

Reminder: if you are calling Tokyo from Narita, you must use the (03) area code.
· **Flight information**: *Tel. (0476)34-5000*
· **Narita Customs**: *Tel. (0476)34-2128*
· **Tokyo City Air Terminal**: *Tel. (03)3665-7111*
· **Tourist Information Center**: *Tel. (0476)34-6253*
· **Web site**: *www.narita-airport.or.jp/airport*

Layover Suggestions

You have a five-hour layover at Narita Airport. "Great," you think, "I'll go into Tokyo for a meal." Think again. Narita is in the boondocks so don't even consider going into Tokyo unless you have at least a 9- or 10-hour layover.

There are a handful of short excursions you can take to see a little of the "real Japan," both old and new.

Narita City, home of Narita-san Shinsho-ji Temple, a huge complex visited by millions of Japanese each year. It's one of the most popular temples to visit during New Year's. From JR Airport Station, take the local train to JR Narita Station (¥230, 10 minutes). Walk the kilometer down **Omotesando**, Pilgrim's Path; it takes about 15 minutes if you don't stop, but how can anyone not stop?

On the right side of Omotesando, close to the station, is Ramen Bayashi, an inexpensive Chinese noodle shop with large portions. Lion's Den, a little further down on the left, serves Western-style food. The proprietor speaks fluent English. Fujikura Shoten, two blocks further down on the left, is a wonderful bamboo shop selling all sorts of goods: their bamboo radish grater is famous. Just past the bamboo shop is **Narita Tourist Pavilion** (Narita Kankokan). Open 9am to 5pm. Closed Monday and December 29-31. Free admission. The Pavilion gives a good history of the temple and displays some of its festival floats and woodblock prints of Narita in the Edo Period. On Thursday mornings, the hall welcomes you to participate in Japan's meditative tea ceremony.

Continue down Omotesando until you enter **Shinsho-ji Temple**. The temple was founded in 940. It's difficult not to be impressed with the imposing gate and buildings. You'll see many amulets for sale. Narita-san, as the Japanese affectionately call the temple, is willing to be responsible for your traffic safety. Buy one of the charms and you'll be protected against traffic accidents. When you're in a taxi, look for a synthetic brocade square hanging from the side of the front window — the traffic safety charm. We bet more than half come from Narita-san.

Narita Koen Park, a lovely strolling garden, is behind the main temple buildings. All in all, a few relaxing hours spent in Narita City should help you cope with your airport experience.

National Museum of Japanese History, **Sakura** (Kokuritsu Rekishi Minzoku Hakubutsukan, "Reki-haku"). This huge museum — 35,000 square meters of floor space — has excellent exhibits using both artifacts and excellent replicas covering Japanese history and culture including archaeology, folklore and history. It's a good introduction to Japan's traditional society and culture. English earphones are available. The museum is located in Sakura Park, which was once the castle grounds of a powerful feudal lord. *Take the Keisei local train from Keisei Airport Station to Keisei Sakura Station (¥420, 20 minutes). From the station, it's a 20-minute walk or 7-minute taxi ride. Open 9:30am to 4:30pm. Closed Monday (Tuesday if Monday is a holiday) and December 27 through January 4. ¥420.*

Tokyo Disneyland. If the kids are with you, what better way to entertain them than at Mickey's Kingdom? Airport limo bus takes one hour. *Adults: ¥3670 general admission, ¥5200 for unlimited rides. Children age*

4-11, ¥3570; children age 12 through 17, ¥4590. Tel. (047)354-0001; www.tokyodisneyland.co.jp.

KANSAI INTERNATIONAL AIRPORT (KIX)

This airport is five kilometers offshore on a man-made island in Osaka Bay; it's connected to the mainland by an access bridge. Opened in 1995, the huge glass and steel structure looks like it's built with an erector set — the building is 1.6 kilometers long. The island is still settling and to prevent the building ending up as a pile of shards, each pillar has a hydraulic jack that is adjusted daily. When it opened, the landing rights were the highest in the world but have been reduced to match Narita's. Kansai is Japan's first and only 24-hour airport, but there are few late night flights.

If you are going to Western Japan, it's easiest to fly into Kansai and bypass Tokyo all together. This suggestion may be easier said than done because Narita gets the lion's share of international flights. Kansai has some domestic flights so you can connect to another Japanese city. Transferring is a cinch — instead of shuffling over to a domestic terminal, you just go to the second floor of the airport.

And the airport was designed with passengers in mind. The transit area has a children's play room plus a shower and rest area. You can use the baggage carts on the escalators, and the Wing Shuttle whisks you from the central check-in area to your gate.

The **Kansai Tourist Information Center**, on the first floor, has extensive information in English. Open daily 9am to 9pm, *Tel. (0724)56-6025*. The 24-hour telephone number for airport information, including flights and ground transportation, is *Tel. (0724)55-2500*; it can handle inquiries in English.

Baggage storage is available on the first, second and fourth floors and is open from 6am to 11pm. **Money exchange** counters are inside the customs area and a Bank of Tokyo-Mitsubishi is on the second floor. For those with time to spare, the 3rd floor has restaurants and a shopping arcade. And the Aeroplaza Shopping Center is reached via the airport's covered walkway.

Departing passengers must pay a Passenger Service Facilities Charge of ¥2650 for adults and ¥1330 for children ages 2 through 11.

Ground Transportation

An extensive network of trains, buses and boats can get you anywhere in the Kansai area. Trains are faster than buses because they don't get caught in traffic. But the bus may be a better choice if you have cumbersome luggage. Since porters are nearly nonexistent, lugging it through a train station can be a real pain.

GETTING TO OSAKA FROM KIX
By Train
Osaka Station: JR Kansai Airport Rapid WING takes 55 minutes and costs ¥1160; the regular Rapid train takes 10 minutes longer but costs the same. **JR Kansai Airport Rapid Trains** (*Kaisoku*) take 70 minutes and cost ¥1160, stopping at about 12 stations en route.

Shin Osaka Station (for shinkansen trains): The JR Kansai Airport Express Haruka takes 45 minutes and costs ¥2980.

Tennoji Station (southeast Osaka): The JR Kansai Airport Express Haruka takes 29 minutes and costs ¥2270.

Namba Station (southwest Osaka): JR Kansai Airport Rapid Trains (*kaisoku*) to JR Namba Station take 53 minutes and cost ¥1030.

The private **Nankai Train** has limited express service called Rapid (but written "Rapi:t") to Namba Station (¥1400) that takes 28 to 34 minutes depending on the stops. The regular Nankai Express *kaisoku* takes 41 minutes and costs ¥890; it makes about nine stops.

By Bus
Buses to central Osaka cost ¥1300: **JR Osaka Station**, 60 minutes; **Kintetsu Uehonmachi Station**, 56 minutes; **Nakanoshima**, 70 minutes; **OAP** (Osaka Amenity Park) **and Honmachi**, 75 minutes. **OBP** (Osaka Business Park), **Shinsaibashi and Uehonmachi**, 50 minutes; **O-CAT**, at JR Namba Station, 45 minutes, ¥880; **Nanko South Port**, 45 minutes.

Osaka International Airport (Itami): 80 minutes, ¥1,700.

By Boat
Tempozan Harbor: 38 minutes, ¥1650. Tempozan Harbor is away from Osaka's center, and you'll have about a 7-minute walk from the dock to the subway.

GETTING TO KYOTO FROM KIX
Train: Kyoto Station: JR Kansai Airport Express Haruka takes 75 minutes and costs ¥3490 reserved seat, ¥2980 unreserved.

Bus: Kyoto Station: 105 minutes, ¥2300. Reservation recommended. *Tel. (075)682-4400.*

GETTING TO KOBE FROM KIX
Train: Take any of the trains to Osaka Station and change to the JR line to Sannomiya Station.

Bus: JR Sannomiya Station: 70 minutes, ¥2200.

Boat (Jet Foil): Kobe City Air Terminal (K-CAT) on Port Island: 30 minutes, ¥2650.

GETTING TO NARA FROM KIX

Train: Take the limited express or express train (see Osaka for options) to Tennoji and transfer to the JR Kansai Honsen line to JR Nara Station: 30 minutes.

Bus: 95 minutes, ¥1800; reservation required from Nara to the airport, but not vice versa.

DEPARTING FROM KIX

If you are departing from KIX, the **City Airline Terminals** (CAT) may make your life easier. You can check in baggage and get your boarding pass if you are flying on JAL and some other airlines. JAL is an agent for some airlines, so ask your airline if you can use a CAT. Also ask about the minimum check-in time. You don't want to get to the city terminal and find out you haven't left yourself enough time.
• **Kyoto CAT**: B1, JR Kyoto Station. Open 6am to 5pm.
• **Namba CAT**: 2F, Nankai Namba Station. Open 6am to 6pm.
• **Osaka CAT**: JR Namba Station, Osaka City Air Terminal Building. 6:30am to 6pm. In addition to ANA and JAL, Air France, Asiana, Austrian Airlines, Korean and United maintain counters.
• **K-CAT Kobe** (Port Island): JAL: 7am to 3pm; JAS: 7:30am to 6pm; ANA: 7:30am to 7pm.

Contact Numbers
• **Airport Bus** (KATE Airport Limousine Bus): *Tel. (0724)61-1374*
• **Nankai Train** (English phone): *Tel. (06)643-1005*
• **JR West Train**: *Tel. (06)345-8001*
• **Kansai Airport**: *www.kansai-airport.or.jp*

GETTING AROUND JAPAN

AIR VS. RAIL

There's no way to get around it; transportation in Japan is expensive. But with a little forethought and planning, you can minimize the cost. One way is to buy a Japan Rail Pass, but you must do so before arriving in Japan. Another way is to include domestic flights on your international ticket, but you can't do that if you have a special discount ticket. The third way is to buy an advance-purchase air ticket, but you have to buy it 28 days in advance to get the least expensive fares.

Regular air fares and *shinkansen* (high-speed) train fares are about the same. If you aren't going too great a distance, for example between Osaka and Tokyo, when you factor in time getting to and from the airports, door-to-door is pretty much the same time. And, it's easier to take the train than to fly.

But if you are going a greater distance, say Tokyo to Sapporo or Tokyo to Kagoshima, although the cost is about the same, the train takes much longer, so most people prefer to fly. As a matter of fact, Tokyo to Sapporo is the busiest air route in the world.

When you're trying to decide whether to travel by air or train, look at your itinerary as well as the different costs. The rail pass makes train travel less costly. So does buying advance-purchase air tickets or including domestic flights on your international ticket, but you can't do so with all tickets. Next, factor in your personal preferences; some people love the efficiency of airplanes while others relish time on the rails.

If you want to comparison shop, call the JNTO's overseas branches for more information. The offices are listed at the end of this chapter. Or click on the travel expert icon at *www.bijapan.com* for fares and times.

AIR TRAVEL INSIDE JAPAN

Japan has an extensive domestic air network serviced by three major carriers: **All Nippon Airways** (ANA), **Japan Airlines** (JAL) and **Japan Air System** (JAS). We haven't found much difference between them although their marketers must spend millions to prove otherwise. Choose whichever has the best schedule for you. Since Japan is a fairly compact country, most flights are between one and two hours in duration.

We're sure you've heard a lot about the high standards of Japanese service, but it isn't true on the domestic airlines. They are just cattle cars by another name. Most planes have only one class of service, but some are now putting on a super-seat section for a small additional charge — between ¥3000 and ¥4000. Regular seats are small and jammed together. The airlines use a lot of 747s for short hauls on popular routes because they can pack in so many people; it's not unusual to have more than 500 seats.

Even on a two-hour flight, you may not be served more than a cup of coffee, tea or consommé. If you do get one, snacks are hardly a gastronomic feast. If you are traveling over mealtime and cannot wait until you get to your destination, pick up something at the airport.

Pilots make announcements in English as well as Japanese. Flight attendants speak some English and usually go out of their way to make sure foreign travelers are comfortable, bringing English magazines and newspapers. They also may try to protect you from yourself. Once Noriko was knitting on a plane, and the flight attendant told her to stop because it was too dangerous.

Some airplanes have cameras in their underbelly so you can watch the take-off and landing if that's what you like — actually we don't like it. And for your inflight entertainment, you can watch Japanese television or some short film. Good language practice.

TRANSPORTATION ABC's

Traveling in Japan means wading through an alphabet soup:
ANA, *All Nippon Airways (pronounced Zen-nikku)*
ANK, *Air Nippon*
JAC, *Nihon Air Commuter*
JAIR, *J-air*
JAL, *Japan Air Lines*
JAS, *Japan Air System*
JNTO, *Japan National Tourist Organization*
JR, *Japan Railways*
NAL, *Naka-Nihon Airline*

Airfares

Note: airlines have just deregulated so there may be changes. The airlines have three levels of regular fares depending on the season: regular, off peak (December and January except for New Year's) and peak (Golden Week, most of August and New Year's). The fares increase or decrease by several thousand yen.

Domestic carriers have a fare system offering deep discounts to travelers who book their flights in advance. Seats are limited and you can't change the reservation once you buy the ticket. If you cancel, you get only 50% back. You need to pick up the ticket within several days of making the reservation. You can save 20 to 50% by booking 14 days to two months in advance on most flights, but discounted seats are limited.

Savings can be substantial. Tokyo-Fukuoka discount fare is ¥16,000 vs. ¥27,500 regular fare vs. ¥21,720 *shinkansen* train. These fares are not available during Golden Week, mid-August and New Year's. In addition to these advance-purchase fares, here are some other discounts:
• **Series Tickets** (*Kaisuken*). 15% discount on a series of 4 or 6 tickets (one way) to the same destination; some have to be used by the same person, others don't.
• **Welcome to Japan fares**: JAL offers special discounted fares to international passengers who enter Japan on JAL. Savings can be substantial.
• **Visit Japan fare**: ANA offers a fare of ¥12,600 per domestic flight. Must be purchased outside of Japan, but you don't have to fly ANA to Japan to be eligible.

Making Reservations

Your travel agent can make reservations or you can make them directly with the airline. ANA, JAL and JAS all have English-speaking reservations agents. Call their reservation number and ask to speak to an English speaker. Actually, when the agent picks up the phone, you don't have to say anything more than "Hello" to be connected to an English-speaking staff member.

You can use these toll free reservation numbers from anywhere in Japan:
• **ANA**: *Tel. 0120-029-222*
• **JAL**: *Tel. 0120-25-5971*
• **JAS**: *Tel. 0120-51-1283*

All three airlines' web sites are quite thorough, accessing flight schedules, seat availability, arrival and departure schedules, fares, and airport information. JAS' web site is *www.jas.co.jp*; ANA's is *www.ana.co.jp* or *www.fly-ana.com*; JAL's is *www.japanair.com*.

TRANSPORTATION INFORMATION

*The best source for train information is the **JR English Information Line**, open Monday through Friday, 10am to 6pm, Tel. (03)3423-0111. Or call the **Japan Travel Phone** toll free between 9am and 5pm daily: 0088-22-4800. These numbers don't work in Tokyo or Kyoto. In Tokyo call (03)3201-3331 and in Kyoto (075)371-5649.*

TRAINS

Japan is a train-lover's dream. Rail lines connect the far corners of the four main islands. You can find steam engines as well as some of the fastest trains in the world. Millions of Japanese ride trains every day. Japan is ninth in the world in total rail mileage but is first in actual passenger miles — no easy feat given countries like India and China have more than ten times Japan's population.

In 1889, a train from Osaka to Tokyo took 19 hours; today it takes 2 1/2 on the super express *Nozomi shinkansen*. **JR – Japan Rail** – is currently experimenting with mag-lev trains, but don't expect to ride above the rails for a while.

At the center of all this activity is a handful of companies called Japan Rail Group, more commonly known as JR. Spun off from the government-operated Japan National Railways in the 1980s, companies known as JR East, JR Central, JR West, JR Kyushu, JR Hokkaido, et al., work together to provide seamless service so you probably won't realize as you travel around the country that these are different companies. In addition to JR, private companies provide train service, usually in the larger cities and usually at lower cost than JR. The JR web site provides schedules and fares: *www.japanrail.com.*

Shinkansen Trains

Coming on the scene in 1964 and signaling the end of the postwar period with Japan achieving the state-of-the-art high-speed service, the *shinkansen* (high-speed) train is still a symbol of Japanese technology. Today, France's TGV is faster. English speakers call Japan's *shinkansen* trains **bullet trains**, but since Japanese don't know that term, we use *shinkansen*. If you ask a conductor how to get to a bullet train, he'd just scratch his head.

Japan has a network of *shinkansen* lines. The **Tokaido-Sanyo line** runs from Tokyo through Yokohama, Nagoya, Kyoto, Osaka, Kobe, Hiroshima and terminates in Fukuoka at Hakata Station. The **Joetsu line** runs from Tokyo to Niigata on the Japan Sea. The **Tohoku line** runs from Tokyo via Sendai to Morioka. The **Akita line** runs from Tokyo to Akita City; **Yamagata line** from Tokyo to Yamagata City; **Nagano line** from Tokyo to Nagano City. If you immediately notice a common thread, it is that they all start or end in Tokyo — a dramatic example of what being the center of power means.

In Tokyo, the *shinkansen* trains all depart and arrive at **Tokyo Station**, with the exception of the Tohoku *shinkansen* that departs from both Tokyo and Ueno Stations. *Shinkansen* stations often have "Shin" in their name, such as Shin-Osaka or Shin-Yokohama. Shin means new and these stations were newly built for the *shinkansen* and are usually away from the center of the city.

Shinkansen have two classes of service, **ordinary** *(futsu-sha)* and **superior** (Green Car — *guriin sha*). For most people, ordinary class is, well, ordinary but adequate. If you are very large, the seats might be tight. Green Car offers larger seats, more leg room and a more exclusive environment. Usually, Japanese corporations only provide Green Car for their top executives.

Shinkansen trains usually run like clockwork, but nature can wreak havoc with their schedules. Snow slows them down as does the flooding that accompanies typhoons. And if there's an earthquake, service is at a standstill until the entire track is checked for damage. If your train is more than two hours late without notice when you boarded it, you are entitled to a refund upon your arrival. The refund consists of the express surcharge, but not the basic fare.

Reserved *(shitei seki)* and unreserved *(jiyu seki)* seats are available. Reservations cost ¥500 and are worthwhile for your peace of mind. If you have a rail pass, there is no additional charge for a reservation. During peak travel seasons and heavy travel times like Friday evening, if you don't have a reservation, you may end up standing for the better part of the trip. About one-half of the train is reserved. The platform signs, in English, will tell you which cars are which. If you are traveling without reservations, line up as soon as you can at the place marked on the platform; it may make the difference between sitting and standing. On a mid-day train mid-week, you can usually get a seat in the unreserved section.

SHINKANSEN TRAVEL

Travel by **shinkansen**, *zinging along the rails at 200 kilometers an hour, is an experience not be missed, but most of your fellow passengers will be almost blasé. After settling in your seat, you'll notice that a lot of riders (except children) have started to nod off regardless of the time of day. For many Japanese, the shinkansen is the place to catch up on sleep.*

You'll never starve on the train. Through the aisles, attendants push carts laden with coffee, juice, beer, whiskey, sandwiches, bento box meals and ice cream. They even offer boxes of sweets for sale as souvenirs. If you can't find anything to eat on the cart, there's usually a small canteen in one of the cars; and some trains have dining cars too.

When we first used our laptop computer on the train, people would watch with curiosity, but today laptops are more common place. And in the age of the cellular phone, the train is a traveling office to many businessmen – the few who aren't napping, that is. JR requests passengers use the cellular phones only at the ends of the cars so other travelers aren't disturbed; most people comply.

If you're feeling left out because you don't have a cellular phone, you can make a call from public phones on the train. You can buy telephone cards from the vending machine next to the phone. Even telephones are hungry on a train; you'll see how quickly they eat up your card.

Stops are announced in English. Make sure you gather up your belongings and head for the exit before the train pulls into the station. Stops are brief and you don't want to get stuck on the train. If you don't get to the exit quickly, you may end up at the next station. Believe it or not, it happened to a friend of ours.

Also, remember to keep your ticket; you'll have to surrender it at the station.

Speed has its price. *Shinkansen* trains have a substantial surcharge over the basic fare. To gain access to the trains, you must cross an additional ticket barrier inside the JR station. You must show your ticket at the *shinkansen* gate and when exiting give the agent your surcharge ticket or seat reservation ticket (but not the main ticket). It's quite confusing.

Sometimes a *shinkansen* ticket is in two parts, one for the regular fare and one for the surcharge or the seat reservation. If you have two tickets, you surrender the surcharge ticket at the *shinkansen* barrier and the other one as you exit the station. If you only have one, hold on to it; show it at the *shinkansen* barrier but do not surrender it until you reach the second barrier.

If you are utterly confused, just show your tickets to the person at the gate; he will take the correct one. Just be careful not to give your entire ticket away at the *shinkansen* barrier because you'll have to do some explaining at the main station barrier. If this happens, just say *"shinkansen"* and the staff person will probably figure it out.

Limited Express, Express, & Local Trains

Limited express *(tokubetsu kyuko)* trains are the fastest next to the *shinkansen*. Yes, we know that limited express sounds slower than express. But in this case, a limited express makes a more limited number of stops than an express train. Confused? Just remember that limited express is faster than express. They run on normal tracks and don't make as many stops, so they get there faster than express trains.

You must pay a limited-express surcharge *(tokkyu ken)*. There are reserved and unreserved seats and, just like the *shinkansen*, reservations cost ¥500. You are allowed to change the reservation once at no charge. Most limited express trains have Green Cars for an additional fee.

Express *(kyuko)* trains stop at only at the larger stations. You pay a surcharge, but not as high as the limited express fee. Express trains have reserved and unreserved cars.

Rapid *(kaisoku)* trains make more stops than express. You do not pay a surcharge, and they do not have reserved seats.

Local *(kaku eki teisha)* are the slowest trains and stop at every station. They do not have reserved seats.

Purchasing Tickets

You can buy JR tickets at any JR train station. Limited express and *shinkansen* tickets are sold at the *midori no madoguchi* (Green Window) sales counter. At smaller stations, they may not have a *midori no madoguchi;* then the clerk in the office can sell you a ticket. At very small stations in rural areas, *shinkansen* tickets are unavailable.

You can buy local and express tickets from **vending machines**. The fares are shown on a chart above the machines. In big cities, the larger JR stations will have a fare map in English. If you don't know the fare, you can go to the ticket window and tell the staff person your destination or buy a ticket for the minimum fare and pay the rest on the train or when you get off. If you buy a regular ticket, but end up on a limited express, you can pay the surcharge on the train. Some of the vending machines will take ¥1000, ¥5000 and ¥10,000 notes. Look for the symbol on the top of the machine. Generally you can buy a ticket at a vending machine up to about ¥1800. After that, you have to buy it at a counter.

Even though the ticket you buy may cost the equivalent of the average annual income in many a third-world country, JR deals almost exclusively in cash. If you want to pay by **credit card**, in Tokyo you have to go to the Tokyo Station's Travel Service Center near the Yaesu central exit or to Shinjuku Station's Travel Service Centers; one is near the South exit, another near the East exit. There are other JR Travel Service Centers, but these are the only three that accept credit cards. In Osaka Station, the Travel Service Center will accept credit cards. Another way to pay by plastic is to buy your JR ticket from one of the large travel agencies such as JTB. They usually accept credit cards.

The trains fares we list under *Arrivals & Departures* for each city are one-way fares.

Making Reservations

JR's ticketing staff speak very little English — what were they doing in school during their six years of English classes? To make it easier, write down the date, your destination, the number of tickets and the time of the train you want. Also write down if you want smoking or nonsmoking. If you know the specific train number and/or time, write it down too. Show this information to the ticket agent. It's much easier to have it all in front of you than to try to communicate orally. Seat reservations cost ¥510, but are free with a rail pass.

The JNTO puts out a booklet in English called *Railway Time Table* listing schedules of the *shinkansen* trains and other popular routes and the fine points of train fares. You can obtain a copy at any JNTO office. See *For More Information* at the end of this chapter.

If you want to do some investigative work, JR publishes a comprehensive **train schedule** as big as a telephone book and entirely in Japanese. A copy is usually near station ticket counters. If you have a good bilingual map, you can decipher the schedule. This process is cumbersome and time consuming, but at least you can get some information. In the front of the book are full-color maps of Japan. Use your bilingual map to match up the Japanese names of cities. You'll notice there's a number next to the train line on the map. That's the page number of the schedule. Turn to that page and try to match up the Japanese writing of your points of departure and arrival to figure out the train times. One drawback is not all the trains listed run daily; some run only on holidays or weekends.

Japan Rail Pass

The **Japan Rail Pass** is an economical way for you to travel on JR trains, buses and ferries if you are doing a lot of moving around. If you are simply traveling round-trip from Tokyo to Kyoto, it is less expensive to buy an individual ticket. Generally, if you start in Tokyo and are going beyond the Kyoto/Osaka/Kobe area, it's cost effective to buy a 7-day pass.

The catch is that rail passes can be used only by foreign visitors who are here on short-term visits for sightseeing. You must have "temporary visitor" stamped into your passport. If you've come for business, you can use it as long as you are listed as a temporary visitor. If you are traveling under any other kind of visa such as an entertainment visa, you are ineligible. Foreigners living and working in Japan are ineligible. JR is strict and will not issue a rail pass if they deem you are ineligible.

You must purchase your rail pass exchange order outside Japan. Most travel agencies can obtain one, but if you have difficulty, contact an overseas JNTO office for names of agencies. You have to present the exchange order to a JR office in Japan to receive the actual rail pass, and you must show your passport. If you validate your rail pass at Narita or Kansai International airports, you can use it to take a JR train to the city. You can also wait and validate it at a JR Travel Service Center in any major city. You'll receive a list of places with your exchange order. When you validate your pass, specify the date you wish to begin travel. It does not have to begin on the day you validate your pass.

Should you get a rail pass? It depends on your itinerary. Yes, if you will travel a lot in a short time. It may be cheaper to buy point-to-point tickets if you plan to spend longer periods in a limited number of places. This decision is something you make ahead of time because it is absolutely impossible to buy the exchange order in Japan.

One nice thing about the rail pass is it saves a lot of the hassle of buying tickets at the train station. You have absolute flexibility, jumping on and off trains whenever you want. And if you want seat reservations, you can get them at no extra charge. We recommend that you get seat reservations so you don't have to worry about standing.

The fine print: The rail pass is not valid for travel on the *Nozomi shinkansen*, the fastest train between Tokyo and Fukuoka. And it's good on JR trains, buses and ferries, but not on private train lines or any other buses or ferries. If you want to take an overnight train, you have to pay a supplemental charge. And take good care of your pass; if you loose it, you're out of luck.

You can buy more than one rail pass; they do not need to run consecutively. For instance, if you are staying in Japan for two months, you can get one for the first part of the trip, and another for the latter part.

JAPAN RAIL PASS FARES, IN YEN

	Ordinary Class		Green (First) Class	
	Adult	Child (6-11)	Adult	Child (6-11)
7-day pass	28,300	14,150	37,800	18,900
14-day pass	45,100	22,550	61,200	30,600
21-day pass	57,700	29,850	79,600	39,800

Several of the JR companies have special regional rail passes which you may want to consider if you are traveling extensively in one area:

JR East Pass

JR East, the rail company which serves a large area from the northern tip of Honshu Island, Japan's main island, to Nagano in central Japan, recently introduced the JR East Pass. If you are heading north or east from Tokyo, it may save you money. The pass is limited to JR East's service areas and to people who have short-term tourist visas.

The pass offers two features which the JR Rail Pass doesn't: a discounted fare for "youths" aged 12 through 25 (in ordinary class only), and a flexible four-day pass which can be used on any four days within a 30 day period. In addition to the flexible four-day pass, JR East offers passes for five and ten consecutive days.

You must buy an Exchange Order before traveling to Japan; present the order in Japan to receive the actual pass. Most travel agents can issue exchange orders; if you have difficulty, try the overseas offices of Japanese airlines or of the large Japanese travel agents such as JTB, or contact the Japan National Tourist Organization.

The price of a **five-consecutive-day pass** in ordinary class is ¥20,000 for adults (above age 25), ¥16,000 for youths (age 12-25) and ¥10,000 for children (age 6-11). The fare for green car (first class) is ¥28,000 for people age 12 and over and ¥14,000 for children age six through 11. Children under six travel free but do not get their own seat.

A **ten-consecutive-day pass** in ordinary class runs ¥32,000 for adults, ¥25,000 for youths and ¥16,000 for children. The fares for green car run ¥44,800 for adults and ¥22,400 for children.

The **flexible four day pass** in ordinary class costs ¥20,000 for adults, ¥16,000 for youths and ¥10,000 for children. For green car, ¥28,000 for adults and ¥14,000 for children.

The JR East web site can give further information at *www.jreast.co.jp* (click on the English icon) or you can phone the JR East Infoline in English, *Tel. (03)3423-0111.*

JR West Rail Pass

JR West serves the area Kyoto to the western tip of Honshu island, along the Inland Sea. JR offers two types of passes, the **Kansai Area Pass** for travel along the Kyoto to Himeji corridor which includes Osaka, Kobe and the Kansai Airport and the **Sanyo Area Pass** for travel along the Osaka to Hakata (Fukuoka) corridor, including Kobe, Himeji, Okayama, Kurashiki and Hiroshima.

The one-day **Kansai Area Pass** costs ¥2000 for adults and ¥1000 for children ages 6-11; the four-day pass runs ¥6000 for adults, ¥3000 for children. It is good for all non-reserved seats on local and rapid-service trains; if you use limited express trains you must pay a surcharge. It does not work on shinkansen trains. The pass is a great deal if you doing a good bit of travel around the area. For instance, the regular Kyoto to Himeji one-way fare is ¥2210 on the rapid-service train.

The **Sanyo Area Pass** runs ¥20,000 for four consecutive days and ¥30,000 for eight consecutive days (children 6-11 are half-price). This pass is good on all JR West trains including the Nozumi shinkansen in the Osaka-Hakata corridor. You can get reserved seats at no extra charge. Again, the pass is worthwhile if you plan on moving around a lot. To compare, the Osaka to Hakata (Fukuoka) shinkansen fare is ¥14,590.

JR West Rail Passes can be purchased in Japan at a JR West ticket office. To be eligible, you must be a non-Japanese visitor who has a "temporary visitor" stamp in your passport. Only one pass can be purchased per trip. You can also purchase the pass overseas through most travel agents.

For more information, consult JR West's web site at *www.westjr.co.jp* and click on the English icon.

JR Kyushu Rail Pass

Travelers spending time in Kyushu might want to consider the JR Kyushu Rail Pass for travel all over the island on local, express and limited express trains. A five-day pass costs ¥15,000 and seven-day pass ¥20,000. The pass entitles you to reserved seats.

Purchasing the pass makes sense if you are traveling extensively around Kyushu in a brief period of time. To compare, one way Hakata to Kagoshima fare on limited express trains is ¥14,070.

An exchange order for the pass must be purchased abroad before you enter Japan. Most travel agents can issue it, or through Japan Air Lines or All Nippon Airways.

Special Fares

JR runs some special fares that you may want to consider. Note: Most of these discount tickets are not valid during Golden Week, the mid-August Obon season and New Year's.

Full Moon Pass. Isn't it a great name? This pass gives unlimited travel by Green Car on all JR trains except *Nozomi* (superfast *shinkansen*) to a couple whose combined ages are 88 and over. You're also eligible for a 20% car discount by Eki Rent-a-car. The cost is ¥79,000 for a 5-day pass, ¥98,000 for 7-day pass and ¥122,000 for 12-day pass; these prices are for two people. This pass can be worthwhile if you do a lot of traveling, not just round-trip to one city or if you are traveling to a distant city, e.g. Tokyo to Fukuoka. But when you compare this cost with the cost of a Green Car rail pass, it shows what a good deal the rail pass is.

Nice Middy Pass. Who makes up these names up? This pass is for two or more women over 30 traveling together. It's available only in the spring and autumn. Three days unlimited travel in ordinary class costs ¥56,000 for two women and ¥84,000 for three.

JR Shuyuken (Area pass). The area passes include train fare from a major city to the destination area plus unlimited travel within the zone. They are usually valid from 8 to 14 days. The drawbacks are you still have to pay an additional *shinkansen* or limited express surcharge and unless you are doing extensive traveling within the zone for a long period of time, you can usually do better with a regular ticket. Wide Shuyuken is for a large area such as Hokkaido or Kyushu while Mini Shuyuken is for a smaller area.

Series Ticket (Kaisuken) on the shinkansen. This set of six one-way tickets carries you between two points. The tickets must be used within three months but not necessarily by the same person. It's worthwhile if you are three or more or need to make repeat trips. You don't realize great savings, but every little bit helps. For instance, Tokyo-Kyoto *kaisuken* costs ¥73,260 or ¥12,210 each way. The regular *shinkansen* fare is ¥13,240.

Q Kippu. These tickets are discounted round-trip tickets good on limited express trains and some *shinkansen* trains. They are good for unreserved seats only.

JR Rent-a-car. JR offers train and car rental combination tickets, 20% off train fare and 20% off car rental. Most large stations have JR's Eki Rent-a-car. JR usually has a special deal: if you travel more than 200 kilometers on a JR ticket, you receive specially reduced prices for car rental.

Travel Agents

Some of the large travel agents such as JTB issue JR train tickets and make *shinkansen* and limited express train reservations. Look for the JR symbol outside. Many of the larger agencies accept credit cards.

ESSENTIAL TRAIN VOCABULARY

eki	train station
kisha	long distance train
densha	regional train
shinkansen	bullet train
tokkyu	limited express train
kyuko	express train
futsu sha	local train
jiyu seki	unreserved seat
shitei seki	reserved seat
kin'en seki	nonsmoking
kippu	ticket
katamichi	one way
ofuku	round trip
ichi mai	one ticket
ni mai	two tickets
san mai	three tickets
yon mai	four tickets
kodomo ichi mai	one child's ticket (age 6-11)
kodomo ni mai	two child's tickets (age 6-11)
josha ken	basic ticket
tokkyu ken	limited express surcharge
guriin sha	green car (premium class)
guriin sha ken	green car surcharge
tsugi no densha	next train
(place) ma-de no kippu	ticket to (place)

Useful Questions:

ikura desu ka?	What's the fare?
(place) ma-de nan ban homu desu ka?	The train to (place) leaves from what platform?
kono densha wa (place) ma-de ikimasu ka?	Does this train go to (place)?

Children

JR and other train companies are kind to parents. Children under six ride free although they don't get their own seat. If you want to guarantee a seat, you have to buy a child's ticket. Children ages six through eleven pay half-fare, rounded off to the higher ¥10. Twelve and over pay the full adult fare. On JR ticket machines, there's a button for children's tickets. Press this button and the children's price is displayed.

English Information

JR Information Line can give you information in English on schedules, fares, best routings, discount tickets, etc. The staff is really excellent. They're open Monday through Friday, 10am to 6pm, *Tel. (03)3423-0111.*

LONG DISTANCE BUSES

Japan has an extensive network of long distance buses, especially night buses that are popular with college students. The buses are large and comfortable, and the fares are lower than the train fares. They almost always take longer than trains; do you really want to spend your night on a bus? But they are a budget alternative. We've listed long distance buses under each city.

CAR RENTALS

You may not be able to live without your car back home, but you really do not want to drive in Japan. Train and air transportation are fast and efficient. Urban traffic is a nightmare; car rentals, parking and gas are exorbitant and the highway tolls between cities often are as much as the train fare. And, Japan drives on the left side of the road, opposite the US, Canada and continental Europe. British and Australian drivers can breathe one sigh of relief.

But there is one exception. If you are traveling in rural areas and want to see remote places or pack a lot into a short time, drive. But pick up your rental car at the local airport or train station, rather than try to drive from a big city.

All airports have car rental counters. The large train stations have them as do the larger towns and cities. The main car rental companies are: **Nippon Rent-a-Car**, **Toyota Rent-a-Car**, **Mazda Rent-a-Car**, **Japaren** and **Eki Rent-a-Car**. Hertz also has operations here, but doesn't have as many outlets as the others. The advantage with Hertz is it's easy to make reservations in North America. Nippon Rent-a-Car has a relationship with National Car Rental so you can book through them in North America.

The car rental companies have nearly identical rates. For ¥300 you can get a "Member's Card" that gives you 20% discounts on all but the smallest car. It's worthwhile getting one.

Car rentals for the first 24-hour period run from ¥8800 for a subcompact to ¥28,000 for a luxury sedan. Prices for subsequent days decrease about 30%. You can rent a car for as short as 6 hours. You will need an international divers license; get one before you leave your home country. Your local automobile association can give you details.

Reservations numbers:
- **Japaren**: *Tel. (03)5397-8911*
- **Mazda**: *toll free: Tel. 0120-17-5656*

- **Nissan**: *Tel. (03)5424-4123*
- **Toyota**: *Tel. (03)3264-0100*
- **Nippon**: *Tel. (03)3469-0910*
- **Hertz**: *toll free: Tel. 0120-38-8002*
- **Eki Rent-a-Car**: *make reservations through Japan Rail*

DRIVING IN JAPAN

*To rent a car, you must have an **international driver's license**. In the US, get it at the American Automobile Association. If you are going to drive, a good bilingual road map is essential. We like **Road Atlas Japan** published by Shobunsha and available in English language book stores. Its maps have helpful information such as "this road closed in winter" or "this road extremely congested in fall." These are the things you really need to know.*

The main roads in rural areas are remarkably well marked in English. The expressways have bilingual signs as do many of the national and prefectural roads. If the signs aren't in English, these roads have route numbers that are posted fairly regularly.

Alcohol and driving do not mix. Japanese law does not allow any alcohol in the blood so you can't even have one drink and drive. The police routinely stop cars for breath tests. Penalties for drinking while intoxicated are high.

The stop sign is a red triangular sign pointing downwards. Japan uses international traffic signs.

The Japan Auto Federation has a reciprocal relationship with the American Automobile Association and other auto associations. If you are a member, you can use their services.

Remember, Japan drives on the left side of the road.

INTRACITY TRANSPORTATION

You are most likely to use subway, buses, and taxis to get around cities.

Subways

The major cities — Fukuoka, Kobe, Kyoto, Nagoya, Sapporo, Sendai, Tokyo and Yokohama — all have subways. We generally prefer to take subways in cities because they are fast and inexpensive. Even though traffic is crawling at the street level, the subways whisk you to your destination underground.

Subways work on a zone system. Purchase a ticket from the vending machine before boarding the train; most of the stations have a fare map in English. If you can't figure out the fare, buy a ticket for the minimum amount and pay the rest when exit. Some machines accept ¥1000 bills and a few will take ¥5000 and ¥10,000 bills. If you don't have change and the machine doesn't take bills, ask the station clerk. If you make an error, the station clerk will refund your money if you haven't used the ticket. Make sure you keep your ticket in a safe place; you'll have to surrender it upon exiting. Most subway systems now also have stored-value cards.

To enter the train platform, put the ticket through the mechanized gate or have the attendant punch it. The train platforms are marked with the names of the major stations on the line. The sign on the wall gives the station name and the names of the previous and next stations. Some subways have one sign only in Japanese and the next sign in English. Walk down the platform to find the English sign.

The horror stories about rush-hour crowding are true. The Japanese use the expression "Packed like *sushi*" because a *sushi* chef slaps the fish against the rice, leaving no room for air. This expression is much more accurate than English's, "packed like sardines" because sardines, at least, have a little wiggle room. Avoid taking subways between 8am and 9:30am especially if you have luggage or small children. On the plus side, the Japanese commuters tend to be so polite that they will move if there's any space at all even though there's little room to maneuver. And just when you think it's physically impossible for one more person to get in the car, another half-dozen will squeeze in.

The evening rush hour isn't as bad as the morning's because people leave the office at different times and usually go out to dinner. The trains are as busy at 10pm as they are at 6pm.

Subway trains have "Silver Seats" for the elderly and disabled. If you fit either category, look for them.

Buses

In the larger cities, we prefer subways over buses because bus routes are complicated and buses can get stuck in traffic. Kyoto is the exception — it has a terrific bus system. In some cities you pay the fare as you get on and others you pay as you get off. If you don't have exact change, you can get change from the fare box for ¥1000 bills and coins.

Buses that go outside the center of the city work on the zone system. As you board the bus, take a small ticket that has the zone number. When you get off of the bus, pay the amount for the zone listed on the chart at the front of the bus. If you don't have a zone ticket, you may have to pay the highest fare. When you get on at the beginning of the line, there may not be a zone ticket because you automatically have to pay the highest fare.

Taxis

Taking a taxi is a convenient way to go a short distance but can be pricey for a longer trip. The drop-of-the-flag meter cost takes you two kilometers and is between ¥580 and ¥660. A few taxi companies have initiated a system of paying ¥340 for one kilometer to encourage passengers for very short trips.

ESSENTIAL TAXI JAPANESE

(place) ma-de onegai shimasu	*Please take me to (place)*
Tomatte kudasai	*Stop*
Migi magatte	*Turn right*
Hidari magatte	*Turn left*
Massugu	*Go straight*
Reshito onegai shimasu	*Please give me a receipt*

New Yorkers will be shocked by the pristine state of Japanese taxis. The cars are all late models and the seats have spotless white slipcovers. The drivers wear ties and white gloves and are generally pretty gentle drivers. The driver opens and closes the door automatically with a lever, so don't close the door behind you. We are so used to this system that we've left the door open in New York cabs. Naturally, the drivers weren't amused.

Available taxis have a sign in red lights on the passenger side of the windshield. At night, the light on the top of the roof is lit when the taxi is available.

Taxis are all metered. You'll pay highway tolls in addition to the meter amount. If you would like a receipt, say, "*reshito.*" It's best to have some small bills because occasionally a taxi driver can't change a ¥10,000 note.

Don't get in a taxi armed only with an address. In most cities it's not sufficient to find the place — Kyoto is the exception. Give the driver a map. Ask the hotel clerk to draw a map or have one faxed to you. More than once, we have gotten in a taxi and told the driver to take us to a major landmark, but the taxi driver had no idea where it was. It turned out the driver had just arrived from a rural area.

Taxi drivers usually do not speak English. Have the hotel doorman discuss any complicated instructions with the driver.

ACCOMMODATIONS

Japan has a wide range of accommodations from deluxe hotels to small family-run inns. Picking the right place goes a long way toward making or breaking your trip. It depends on your pocketbook and what type of accommodation you feel comfortable with. In large cities, accommodations are almost exclusively Western hotels while in remote villages, there may be nothing but small Japanese inns.

JAPANESE INNS

Staying in a Japanese inn is one of the best ways to experience Japanese culture. We recommend you do it at least once during your trip. The inns are keepers of a tradition that has all but disappeared from the daily lives of Japanese. Perhaps that's why Japanese enjoy staying at **ryokan**, traditional Japanese inns. They take great pride in their food, their personal service, their facilities and gardens, however small, and their interior design.

There are many types of *ryokan*, from small wooden inns to large cement buildings with hundreds of rooms. We prefer the smaller inns. Most inns with over 30 or 40 rooms give you cookie-cutter service. The rate for most *ryokan* includes two meals, dinner and breakfast.

Your room will be a sparsely furnished traditional Japanese room with *tatami* mats on the floor, a *tokonoma* alcove where flower arrangements and art are displayed and sliding *shoji* doors with paper panels. If it isn't a multistoried building, your room will probably look out on a small garden. In older inns, there may not be a private toilet, which, we must complain, is a pain in the middle of the night. Larger inns may have a communal bath in addition to the private bath. Don't be shy. Enjoy this opportunity to take a bath in a spacious tub looking out at nature.

Dinner will most likely be served in your room. As a matter of fact, your room is all-purpose: living room, dining room and bedroom. As you enter the room, you'll notice a low table with cushions where you sit to drink tea. The maid sets up your dinner on this table. After dinner, the maid moves the table and sets up *futon* bedding on the floor. In the morning, the maid returns to fold up the bedding and set up breakfast on the table. In larger inns, breakfast may be served in a communal dining hall, often as a buffet. In this case, there will probably be some Japanized Western food items such as ham, bread and coffee.

There are some drawbacks to Japanese inns. They are fairly rigid in their meal times, and you are often out of luck if you want to have a late dinner, say anything after 7pm. They also have rigid check-in and out times, usually check-in is from 3pm and check-out at 10am. Often the maid will be knocking on the door at five after ten if you are still in the room. The inns, however, are happy to hold your luggage.

Another drawback is the attendant frequently comes in and out of your room, bringing tea and meals, and clearing dishes. She does leave you alone after she sets up the *futon* bedding after dinner, but if you want a high level of privacy, the whole procedure is intrusive. And some inns wake you up in the morning with music over the loudspeakers.

In *ryokan*, the price is based per person. If there are more than two people in your group, you may get a slightly lower price. Japanese inns prefer to have a party of four stay in the same room. *Ryokan* prices begin at about ¥8000 per person with two meals and can go as high as ¥70,000 for a deluxe room in a top inn. The average rate is about ¥15,000 per person.

How to Behave at a Japanese Inn

Staying at a Japanese inn is a unique experience. Don't be surprised if you feel like a VIP. At the front door, the staff is usually waiting to greet you and give you your slippers. Take off your shoes and leave them at the entrance. In some larger inns, you'll wear your shoes to your own room. You may be asked to fill out a registration card in the lobby, but often you complete it in your own room. The staff will accompany you to your room and help you to get settled. Be sure to remove your slippers before entering the *tatami* mat room.

You'll get a lot of personal attention from your room attendant; probably she'll only be taking care of two or three rooms in total. She will serve you Japanese tea and sweets in your room, and, while you have tea, will explain the inn's facilities and arrange a time for your dinner and breakfast — it sounds flexible, but your choice is usually within fairly narrow parameters. She may ask if you would like to order beer or *sake* (rice wine) with dinner.

Japanese think it's a luxury to take a bath before dinner and will usually indulge themselves at a *ryokan*, either in the communal bath or a private bath. After a bath, Japanese don a *yukata* (cotton robe) provided by the inn and may stroll around garden before dinner. They will wear their *yukata* until they dress in the morning. It's okay to wear them to eat dinner and to walk outside in a small resort town, but not in a large city.

Yukata come in several sizes and if you are tall, the room attendant may automatically bring you a larger one so you don't have to go around with your knees showing. If she doesn't, ask for XL. Make sure you wear the *yukata* with the left side over the right, and tied with the belt provided. The deceased are dressed in kimono with the right over the left, so make sure everyone knows you're still alive and kicking. Sometimes *yukata* have so much starch, they practically stand up by themselves.

You'll find special slippers in the toilet room. It's a real no-no to wear them out of that room because they are considered unclean.

Ryokan serve dinner on the early side, about 6pm, and it can be a drawn-out affair with a procession of courses. If you're going to arrive after 6pm, make sure the inn knows ahead of time. You may not be able to get dinner after a certain time unless prior arrangements have been made. Some inns will allow you to stay without eating dinner. After dinner, the maid clears away your dishes and sets up the *futon* bedding. We often enjoy a walk while she tidies up the room for the night. At the entrance, inns have *geta* (wooden sandals) so you won't have to put your street shoes back on; if you wear a size 13, you may have to reclaim your own shoes.

Ryokan may lock their doors at a certain hour, such as 11pm. Check with the inn if you plan to stay out late.

In the morning, the maid will put away your bedding and set up your breakfast. If breakfast is in a communal room, the bedding will disappear while you're out of the room. Check-out is quite early, usually 10am, and you are expected to clear your room by that time.

You don't need to tip a maid unless she provides you with exceptional service such as washing your clothes or making special arrangements. If you would like to tip her, wrap the money in paper or an envelope and slip it to her after she serves tea or after picking up the breakfast dishes. ¥1000 to ¥2000 is sufficient.

Japanese *onsen* inns (hot springs) basically operate the same way except guests take a lot of baths.

A few tips:
- If sitting on the floor is painful, pile up several seat cushions to make a modified chair if your room doesn't have a chair and table — usually there's a small Western-style seating area next to the window.
- If you can't live without coffee or English tea, take instant with you. Boiling water is always available.
- Japanese pillows can be a pain in the neck. Traditional pillows are filled with barley and sometimes are really hard. If it's too uncomfortable to sleep on, we put our pillows under the *futon*. If that's still too hard, we give it up all together and use a towel or sweater.
- If the idea of eating fish and rice in the morning sends your stomach into tailspins, ask if they will prepare a Western breakfast: *"yoshoku."*

Onsen

Onsen are hot spring areas. Japanese go to get away, and take baths for therapeutic purposes or for relaxation. They have become extremely popular in the last decade or so with all segments of society: families, young singles and senior citizens.

Onsen inns run the same way a *ryokan* runs, but *onsen* will have large communal indoor baths (divided by sex) and often outdoor baths, *rotemburo,* where you may bathe among rocks and lush greenery. In remote areas, some inns have mixed bathing.

BATHING ETIQUETTE

Over the centuries, Japanese have developed a deep love of bathing and a unique way of enjoying it. A bathtub is used only for soaking, never for cleaning. Before you get into the tub, wash yourself. Small stools and basins are provided: sit down, lather up and then rinse thoroughly. Only then are you ready to enter the bath.

Warning! Be extremely careful; the water may be scalding. You can cool down a small bath by adding some cold water, but there's little you can do to cool down a large one. If there's an outdoor bath, its temperature is almost always lower than an indoor bath's.

Don't pull the plug when you finish.

Japanese use small white towels that they sometimes put on their heads when they sit in the tub. They are not washcloths, and Japanese are horrified if you dip them in the bath water.

Minshuku

Minshuku are small family-run inns, usually less expensive than *ryokan.* You do not have the high level of service of a *ryokan* but it is replaced by the personal attention of the proprietor. The two meals are home-cooked fare and are usually served in a communal dining room.

As a *minshuku* guest you will have to make up your *futon* bedding and put it away. The mattresses are stacked in the closet. To make the bed, first put down the foam mattress and then the cotton mattress. If there isn't a foam mattress, you can put down two cotton mattresses. Next, put the sheet on the mattress and tuck it in. The quilt and top sheet are together as one unit, and you place it on top of the bottom sheet. In the morning, fold everything and put it away except for the dirty sheets and *yukata* robes. Towels may not be provided at *minshuku* so it's best to take one. Toilets and baths are usually down the hall.

In rural areas, *minshuku* may have only space heaters and can get quite cold at night. At some places in the mountains, the proprietor will give you a little charcoal warmer to put in bed to keep your feet warm.

Minshuku run between ¥5000 and ¥9000 per person with two meals.

PUBLIC LODGES & PUBLIC VACATION VILLAGES

Kokumin shukusha, public lodges, and *Kokumin kyukamura*, public vacation villages, are run by local governments to provide low-cost accommodations in parks and vacation areas. They are inexpensive, functional and clean. The rooms, usually Japanese style, are comfortable although architecturally unexciting. The lodges have a lounge area for coffee and a choice of meals. Public lodges are popular in season, so you may need to make reservations well in advance. Most lodges are equipped with heating and air-conditioning systems.

With two meals, public lodges cost between ¥7000 and ¥12,000 per person.

WESTERN-STYLE HOTELS

Western hotels are a good choice for someone on business who needs all the services as well as travelers in large cities who want the comforts, service and flexibility of a Western hotel.

Deluxe: The top deluxe hotels compare with the best worldwide. They provide all the comforts you expect: a high level of service, a choice of restaurants, 24-hour room service, a concierge to help you with any request, business centers, shopping arcades, health centers and travel service. They are very similar to their cousins in the US or Europe except that the rooms may be smaller than comparable ones in an American hotel. The international chains like Hilton and Hyatt have hotels in Japan, but there are also some excellent hotels that are independent or part of a Japanese chain. Within the rarefied top class of hotels, there is little to differentiate them except for location. Expect to pay ¥20,000 and up for a single in a deluxe hotel in a large city.

Next come the medium-priced Western hotels. They are not as flashy as the deluxe and may not offer all the services; for example, there may be only one or two restaurants. Although the rooms are usually smaller and their carpets not as new, they do have private baths. Medium priced hotels start at about ¥10,000 for a single.

Business Hotels offer Western-style accommodations and are geared to the Japanese businessman on a limited expense account. The rooms are small, functional and almost always have a small bathroom attached. They offer limited services — no room service and sometimes no restaurant, but most will serve breakfast for a modest additional charge, usually between ¥700 and ¥1000. Business hotels sell drinks and cigarettes from vending machines.

The rooms can be very small, but business hotels are good choices for inexpensive accommodations in convenient locations — often close to the train station. Just remember they're not the Ritz. Business hotels vary in price from about ¥6000 to ¥12,000 for a single.

Pensions are usually small, Western-style accommodations in resort areas, especially in the mountains. They often pride themselves on their Western cuisine. Prices at pensions vary from ¥6000 to ¥15,000 and usually include two meals.

Youth Hostels are inexpensive accommodations open to people of any age. You do not need to be a member of the International Youth Hostel Federation. Service and facilities have been improving in recent years as the hostels have been trying to attract families and adult groups.

Youth hostels cost between ¥1500 and ¥4000 per person per night; meals are extra.

UNIQUE EXPERIENCES

Love Hotels

Eminently practical, the Japanese designed love hotels for private time. You'll spot them by their whimsical design, lots of neon, small or no windows and names like Hotel Princess and Hotel Charming. Built to ensure privacy, the entrances have gates where the couple is out-of-sight immediately after entering, and covers are provided for automobile license plates. The check-in process is completely impersonalized: choose a room from the pictures on the wall and pay a cashier who is behind a screen.

They say the majority of people who use love hotels are married – to each other. Couples lack privacy in a small apartment where children tend to sleep with their parents and grandma may be just a paper wall away. We're still skeptical. Can you imagine exiting a love hotel and someone sticking a clipboard in your face and asking "Are you two married?" What would you say?

You can rent a love hotel room for two hours ("Rest") or overnight ("Stay"). They are cheaper than staying at a business hotel, and the beds are bigger, but the drawback is you can't check in for the night until about 9pm. But the rooms are clean and they all have private baths. And where else could you sleep in a Tarzan room? You must be a hetero couple to stay at love hotels. A two-hour "rest" costs about ¥4000; and it's ¥8000 for an overnight "stay." Prices are clearly posted outside and you'll often find weekday afternoon specials.

Love hotels tend to be clustered in districts, not only in large cities but also in rural areas and around expressway interchanges. If you are stuck at Narita Airport, there's a group of love hotels at Tomisato, a small town about 10 kilometers from the airport.

Capsule Hotels

Only in Japan where land is so valuable and drinking so widespread, would capsule hotels develop. They cater to businessmen who are out working or drinking past the last train. It's cheaper to spend the night at a capsule hotel than take a taxi home.

Capsule hotels give you a space similar to a train berth – about the size of a coffin – with a *futon* mattress and television. Baths are communal. Most capsule hotels are open only to men and cost about ¥4000 per person to stay overnight.

MAKING HOTEL RESERVATIONS

Travel agents can make hotel reservations at hotels and larger inns. If you book through the overseas offices of the large Japanese travel agencies (JTB, Kintetsu, etc.), the rate is often cheaper than the full-price rack rate that we list. Contact numbers for these agencies are under organized tours. Ask for the seasonal specials when you use large travel agencies in Japan.

There are also several services to assist the individual traveler:

Welcome Inn Reservation Center

This service, organized by the International Tourism Center of Japan, makes reservations for overseas visitors at small inns and inexpensive hotels throughout Japan. Usually you can get lower rates through the Welcome Inn Reservation Center than if you contact the hotel directly.

Obtain a brochure from JNTO overseas offices. From outside Japan, you can request reservations by mail, fax or email: *Welcome Inn Reservation Center, c/o International Tourism Center of Japan, B1. Tokyo International Forum, 3-5-1 Marunouchi, Chiyoda-ku, Tokyo, 100. Tel. (03)3211-4201, Fax (03)3211-9009. Email: wirc@www.jnto.go.jp.* You can also access information and make reservations through the JNTO home page: *www.jnto.go.jp.*

Once you arrive in Japan, you can go in person to their reservations counter at the Tourist Information Center in Tokyo or Kyoto and at Narita and Kansai airports to book rooms:

• **Tokyo Tourist Information Center**: *B1, Tokyo International Forum, 3-5-1 Marunouchi, Chiyoda-ku, Tokyo, 100-0005. Welcome Inn hours are 9:15am to 11:30am, and 1pm-4:45pm, Monday through Friday.*

• **Kyoto Tourist Information Center**: *1st floor, Kyoto Tower Building, Higashi-Shiokoji-cho, Shimogyo-ku, Kyoto, 600-8216. Welcome Inn hours are 9am to 11:30am, and 1pm-4:30pm, Monday through Friday.*

• **Narita Airport Tourist Information Center**: Main office: *Terminal 2, Arrival Floor. Tel: (0476)-34-6251. Branch: Terminal 1, Arrival Floor (1st Floor). Tel. (0476)30-3383. Reservations made 9am to 7:30pm daily.*

• **Kansai International Airport Tourist Information Center**: *Arrival Floor, Passenger Terminal Building. Tel. (0724-56-6024. Reservations made 9am to 7:30pm daily.*

Japanese Inn Group

This association of inexpensive small inns and *minshuku* goes out of its way to welcome foreign tourists. The association issues a brochure that is available at overseas JNTO offices or from the association itself. The brochure has a photo and map for each inn and lists its facilities. You are not required to eat meals at the inn. You can book a room by mailing or faxing the reservation form directly to the inn; you'll receive a confirmation. These accommodations tend to be basic but friendly, clean and comfortable.

Write to or call: **Japanese Inn Group Head Office**, *c/o Ryokan Asakusa Shigetsu, 1-31-11 Asakusa, Taito-ku, Tokyo, 111-0032. Tel. (03)3843-2345, Fax (03)3843-2348*. JNTO has information on the Japanese Inn Group on its home page: *www.jnto.go.jp*. You can make reservations online through the Japanese Inn Group's web site: *members.aol.com/jinngroup*.

Japan Minshuku Center

They book reservations for *minshuku* throughout Japan, but you can also make reservations directly with the inn. *B1, Tokyo Kotsu Kaikan Building, 2-10-1 Yurakucho, Chiyoda-ku, Tokyo. Tel. (03)3216-6556. English is spoken. Open 10am to 7pm. Closed Sunday.*

Youth Hostels

National Office: *Suidobashi Nishiguchi Kaikan, 2-20-7 Misaki-cho, Chiyoda-ku, Tokyo 101. Tel. (03)3288-1417.*

Reservations can be made on the internet: *www.znet.or.jp/~jyh*. Scroll down until you reach the English icon.

FOR MORE INFORMATION

JNTO – the **Japan National Tourist Organization** – has offices throughout the world. They have brochures and maps and are helpful in answering your questions. The JNTO web sites, *www.jnto.go.jp* and *www.japantravelinfo.com*, provide extensive information.

The North American offices are:
- **New York**: *One Rockefeller Plaza, Suite 1250, New York, NY 10020. Tel. 212/757-5640, Fax 212/307-6754*
- **Chicago**: *401 N. Michigan Avenue, Suite 770, Chicago, IL 60611. Tel. 312/222-0874, Fax 312/222-0876*
- **San Francisco**: *360 Post Street, Suite 601, San Francisco, CA 94108. Tel. 415/989-7140, Fax 415/398-5461*
- **Los Angeles**: *515 S. Figueroa St., Suite 1470, Los Angeles, CA 90071. Tel. 213/623-1952, Fax 213/623-6301*
- **Toronto**: *165 University Avenue, Toronto, Ont. M5H 3B8. Tel. 416/366-7140, Fax 416/366-4530*

JNTO also maintains offices in Sao Paolo, London, Paris, Beijing, Frankfurt, Bangkok, Hong Kong, Seoul and Sydney.

JNTO runs Tourist Information Centers in Tokyo and Kyoto:

- **Tokyo**: *B1 Floor, Tokyo International Forum, 3-5-1 Marunouchi, Chiyoda-ku, Tokyo 100-0005. Tel. (03)3201-3331*
- **Kyoto**: *1st Floor, Kyoto Tower Building, Shichijo-Karasuma sagaru, Shimogyo-ku, Kyoto 600-8216. Tel. (075)371-5649*

Both offices are open 9am to 5pm Monday through Friday, 9am to 12 noon Saturday, closed Sunday, national holidays and December 29-January 3. The helpful staff has extensive English-language information and can make reservations for low-cost accommodation through the Welcome Inn Reservation system.

7. BASIC INFORMATION

BUSINESS HOURS

Standard business hours are 9am to 5pm, Monday through Friday. Banks are open 9am to 3pm. Department stores are open 10am to 7 or 8pm. Most department stores close one weekday, but all are open on Saturday and Sunday.

CLOTHING SIZES

You'll notice immediately that Japanese are smaller than Americans or Europeans, so buying clothes may be a problem. Even if you are slender, garments, even Western designer labels, are designed to fit the shorter limbs of the Japanese.

Japan has a unique sizing system:

Women's Clothing

Japanese	9	11	13	15	17
American	6	8	10	12	14
English	8	10	12	14	16
Continental	34	36	38	40	42

Men's Clothing

Japanese	S	M	L	LL	LLL
American	34	36	38	40, 42	44, 46
English	34	36	38	40, 42	44, 46
Continental	44	46	48	50, 52	54, 56

Men's Shirts

Japanese	36	37	38	39, 40	41, 42
American	14	14 1/2	15	15 1/2, 16	16 1/2, 17
English	14	14 1/2	15	15 1/2, 16	16 1/2, 17
Continental	36	37	38	39, 40	41, 42

Women's Shoes

Japanese	23	23 1/2	24	24 1/2	25	25 1/2	26
American	6	6 1/2	7	7 1/2	8	8 1/2	9
English	4 1/2	5	5 1/2	6	6 1/2	7	7 1/2
Continental	36	37	38	39	40	41	42

Men's Shoes

Japanese	25	25.5	26	26.5	27.5	27.5	28	29
American	6	6 1/2	7 1/2	8	9	9 1/2	10	11
English	5	6	7	8	9	9 1/2	10	11
Con'l	39	40	41	42	42 1/2	43	44	45

Children's Clothing

Japanese size	Height/Inches	Weight/Kilos	Weight/Lb.
60 cm	to 26"	to 7 kg	to 16 lb.
70 cm	26 - 30"	6 - 9 kg	14 - 21 lb.
80 cm	30 - 34"	9 - 12 kg	20 - 28 lb.
90 cm	34 - 38"	12 - 15 kg	26 - 33 lb.
100 cm	38 - 42"	14 - 18 kg	31 - 40 lb.
110 cm	42 - 46"	17 - 21 kg	37 - 48 lb.
120 cm	46 - 50"	20 - 24 kg	44 - 55 lb.
130 cm	50 - 53"	23 - 29 kg	52 - 64 lb.
140 cm	53 - 57"	28 - 36 kg	62 - 80 lb.
150 cm	57 - 61"	57 - 61 kg	75 - 95 lb.

DELIVERY SERVICES

Japan has private package delivery services called *takkyubin*. Parcels are sent from one part of Japan to another quickly and efficiently. These services are great and make traveling in Japan easier. Japanese usually ship their skis, golf clubs, and suitcases to their destinations ahead of time so they can travel unencumbered. We send our suitcases ahead to Narita Airport to avoid the hassle of carrying them. Cost varies by weight and destination but usually runs between ¥1000 and ¥2000.

Take advantage of this system by shipping your purchases and unneeded items to the hotel at your final destination in Japan so you don't have to carry everything with you. Hotels can provide boxes and arrange the delivery service, or you can take your parcel to practically any convenience store. There are several delivery companies, each recognizable by its logo displayed in front of stores: cat, pelican, kangaroo, etc.

Some of the big companies offering international courier services are **United Parcel Service**, *Tel. (03)3639-5441;* **Federal Express**, *Tel. toll free 0120-003-200;* and **DHL**, *Tel. (03)5479-2580.* The post office's international express mail is called **EMS**; it's less expensive than the courier services but does not guarantee a delivery date.

ELECTRICITY

Japan's electricity is 100 volts. Eastern Japan is 50 cycles while western Japan is 60. In the late 19th century, Germans engineered the western electrical system while Americans designed the eastern; the result is this schizophrenic system.

Since 100 volts is so close to America's 120, appliances run without converters although they run more slowly. American plugs (two vertical prongs) are standard in Japan. Electric clocks and other very sensitive machinery go out of kilter because they run more slowly, but there's no problem with computers and most electronic equipment. American hair dryers work but run slightly slower.

You'll need plug adapters as well as converters for any 220 volt appliances. Top hotels will provide them upon request.

EMBASSIES

- **Australia**: *2-1-14 Mita, Minato-ku, Tokyo. Tel. (03)5232-4111*
- **Canada**: *7-3-38 Akasaka, Minato-ku, Tokyo. Tel. (03)3408-2101*
- **New Zealand**: *20-40 Kamiyama-cho, Shibuya-ku, Tokyo. Tel. (03)3467-2271*
- **United Kingdom**: *1 Ichibancho, Chiyoda-ku, Tokyo. Tel. (03)3265-5511*
- **United States**: *1-10-15 Akasaka, Minato-ku, Tokyo. Tel. (03)3224-5000*

EMERGENCY TELEPHONE NUMBERS

To report a fire or call an ambulance, dial 119. Large cities have English-speaking personnel. Remember to speak slowly. On a pay phone, press the red button and dial 119. No money is needed. Ambulance is *kyukyu sha;* fire is *kaji*.

To call the Police, dial 110; use these three digits anywhere in Japan. On a pay phone, press the red button and then dial 110. No money is needed.

- **Japan Helpline**: *24-hour assistance with any matter. Toll free: 0120-461-997.*
- **Tokyo English Lifeline (TELL)**: *Tel. (03)3968-4099. 9am to 4pm; 7pm to 11pm. If you are having a personal crisis, this free service will help.*

ENGLISH LANGUAGE PUBLICATIONS

Japan has four English-language newspapers. None rivals *The New York Times*, but there is a lot of emphasis on international news using wire service stories. The *Japan Times* has the largest circulation and is the only one of the four that is not published by a vernacular Japanese newspaper.

The *Japan Times, Mainichi Daily News* and *Daily Yomiuri* are morning papers while the *Asahi Evening News* comes out in the afternoon.

The *Nikkei Weekly*, the English edition of the *Nikkei Shimbun*, Japan's *Wall Street Journal*, gives a good summary of business news and trends.

The *International Herald Tribune* and *Asian Wall Street Journal* are widely available at hotel shops.

International editions of *Time, Newsweek, Business Week, Fortune*, and other publications are available at hotel shops and bookstores with English-language sections.

MEDICAL FACILITIES

Japan's national health insurance system does not cover visitors. Make sure your insurance covers you in Japan. If it doesn't, take out an overseas travel policy in your own country.

In an emergency, ask hotel personnel to phone for a doctor or an ambulance. If you are not at your hotel, dial 119 for an ambulance (*kyukyu sha*). The operator will ask your address. Remember to speak slowly. The ambulance staff provides little assistance other than transportation. They are not paramedics and may have only oxygen. The ambulance will take you to the closest hospital that has space and can treat you for your ailment. They do their best to take foreigners to an international hospital.

Emergency rooms in Japanese hospitals do not run the same way as in American hospitals. If there isn't a bed, you may not be accepted. It's best to have a doctor make arrangements or the ambulance will find you a hospital. In a medical emergency, the **Japan Helpline** can assist you by finding the closest English-speaking doctor or hospital. Call toll free, 24 hours a day, *Tel. 0120-461-997.*

Most doctors work on a clinic system: you go in and wait your turn. Japanese doctors tend to prescribe a lot of drugs and are their own pharmacists. They also tend to give you only enough medication for a few days so you have to come back. (National health reimburses doctors by the number of visits, therefore they try to stretch them out.) Japanese doctors tend to give their patients little information about their conditions; there's a feeling that it's a "burden" on a patient. If this information is not volunteered, you may need to ask a lot of questions, especially about what kind of medication or treatment you are given. Doctors in international clinics and hospitals work in a more international style.

In Tokyo the largest international clinic is **Tokyo Medical and Surgical Clinic**, *Mori #32 Building, 3-4-30 Shiba Koen, Minato-ku, Tokyo. (Across from Tokyo Tower). Tel. (03)3436-3028. Hours are 9am to 5pm Monday through Friday and 9am to 12 noon Saturday.* A doctor is on call 24 hours.

St. Luke's International Hospital, located in the Tsukiji area of Tokyo, has a long history of experience with international patients. Its

Japanese name is Sei Roka Byoin. *9-1 Akashi-cho, Chuo-ku, Tokyo. Tel. (03)3541-5151.*

Oriental Medicine is popular in Japan. Based on Chinese medical theories, acupuncture, moxibustion and acupressure *(shiatsu)* are used to treat various conditions. If you would like to try it, **Edward Acupuncture Clinic** in Tokyo is run by a Japan-trained British doctor, Edward Obaidley. *Coop Sangenjaya 301, 2-17-12 Sangenjaya, Setagaya-ku. Tel. (03)3418-8989.*

MONEY & BANKING

The dollar-yen exchange rate fluctuates daily. In the last several years, **the rate for US dollars has varied between ¥100 and ¥130.** Check the business page of your newspaper for current rates or find it online at *www.bloomberg.com/markets.*

Japanese currency is called **yen** (¥). Coins come in denominations of 1, 5, 10, 50, 100 and 500 yen. The one-yen coin is small, lightweight and silver colored; it feels about as insignificant as it is. The 5-yen coin is copper colored with a hole in the center. It's unique as it's the one coin that has its denomination written only in Japanese. The 10-yen coin is copper colored and is slightly larger than the 5. The 50-yen coin is silver with a center hole. The 100-yen coin is silver, slightly larger than the 50-yen piece and has no hole. The 500-yen coin, incidentally the most valuable coin in general circulation in the world, can really weigh you down. These large silver-colored coins are as substantial as they are valuable.

Bank notes come in ¥1000, ¥5000 and ¥10,000 varieties and are all clearly marked. A ¥2000 note will be introduced shortly.

Don't underestimate your cash needs. Japan is an expensive country and money goes quickly. It's also a cash-based country. Credit cards are accepted at more and more places in cities but not in rural areas. You'll be fine using credit cards if you stick to large hotels, the larger Japanese inns, and some of the more expensive restaurants, but you don't want to be held hostage by your credit card. Sometimes we find a place that says it accepts Visa or MasterCard but will only honor cards issued by Japanese financial institutions.

Foreign currency is not accepted. You can purchase yen-denominated traveler's checks overseas, but we don't think it's worth the effort; most establishments won't accept them so you have to cash them at banks or hotels anyway. US-dollar traveler's checks are the most convenient. Members of the American Automobile Association can buy traveler's checks without charge, and even if you pay a 1% fee, it's offset by the more favorable exchange rate.

WHO ARE THESE GUYS ON THE MONEY?

When you pull out the bills in your pocket, don't expect to find Emperor Akihito. Who are these guys adorning your paper money? Japan is one of the few countries that doesn't put portraits of the emperor or politicians on its notes.

Natsume Soseki (1869-1916) graces the ¥1000 note. Japanese consider him one of the greatest writers of the modern era and his books, "Botchan" and "I am a Cat," are translated into English.

Nitobe Inazo (1862-1933) embellishes the ¥5000 note. He was one of Japan's most international statesmen. In late 19th century Nitobe studied in the US and in Germany. He married an American woman, wrote "Bushido (The Way of the Samurai)," served as the first president of Tokyo Women's Christian College, a prestigious women's college, and was Assistant General Secretary of the League of Nations.

Fukuzawa Yukichi (1835-1901) is pictured on ¥10,000 note. Fukuzawa went to the US on the first ship to cross the Pacific in 1860 after the long period of isolation. He is best known as the founder of Tokyo's Keio University, the oldest private university in Japan. Fukuzawa strongly advocated equality between social classes and between the sexes.

Changing Money

Money can be changed at the airport after you clear customs formalities at international arrivals. The exchange counters stay open until the last flight arrives. Most banks exchange money during operating hours from 9am to 3pm, Monday through Friday (a few small ones may not have facilities). Banks close on holidays. You can exchange cash or traveler's checks for Japanese currency, but you must show your passport.

Some travelers buy foreign currency in their home countries before going abroad. The exchange rate isn't usually that good and money exchange is fairly painless at Japanese airports. If you want to buy some yen for your peace of mind, purchase just enough for the first few days.

At the bank or money exchange counter, you'll notice several different rates posted. Some are for buying yen, others for selling. Remember, if you are changing dollars, you look under the buying column, because you are buying yen. Traveler's checks have a more favorable rate of exchange than cash, usually about one yen difference. This difference often compensates for the 1% fee you may have paid for traveler's checks.

The myth of Japanese efficiency evaporates at the foreign exchange counter of a bank. After you fill in the form and hand over your funds, the transaction goes through about a half-dozen hands as everyone checks to make sure no mistakes have been made. The entire procedure often takes 10 or 15 minutes or even longer. Airport counters are much more efficient.

Hotels and department stores also exchange money although the rate is not as favorable as a bank offers.

Citibank is our bank of choice for exchanging money. The staff speaks English; the rate is good, and business is conducted efficiently. Naturally, the branch network is not as extensive as Japanese banks, but there are several branches in Tokyo as well as in Yokohama, Osaka and Kobe. Some branches are open Saturday from 10am to 2pm. Call their toll free, 24-hour information line: *Tel. 0120-50-4189.* Citibank's ATMs are open 24 hours and accept Plus and Cirrus system cards.

Cash, ATM, & Credit Cards

Japanese carry a lot of cash. In Japan, with crime low, theft isn't a major concern, but being careful goes without saying. Even if you use credit cards for most of your hotels and meals, you'll need cash for transportation, lunches and small purchases. Personal checks are not widely used.

If you need cash:

Get cash from an ATM either as an advance against a credit card (you must have a PIN number) or directly from your bank account with an ATM card. This process looks easy since ATM machines are everywhere. But ATMs run by Japanese banks do not accept credit cards issued in foreign countries. You have to use an ATM run by a nonbank finance company that accepts foreign credit cards. But beware, your bank or company may have a limit as low as $250, which isn't a lot of yen.

Citibank, DC and Mullion ATMs will accept international Visa and MasterCard that are Plus System or Cirrus. JCB ATMs will accept Plus System bank cards. UC ATMs accept Cirrus MasterCards. To take out the guesswork, call your credit card company (they all have English speaking personnel) for the closest machine or office:
- **Visa**: *(toll free) Tel. 0120-133-173.* Visa card holders can also get cash advances at branches of Sumitomo Bank. Go to *www.visa.com/pd/atm/main.html* for their ATM locator.
- **MasterCard**: *Tel. (03)5350-8051 or 0031-11-3886.* Go to *www.mastercard.com* for their ATM locator.
- **American Express**: *(toll free) Tel. 0120-376-199*
- **Citibank**: *(toll free) Tel. 0120-50-4189*

American Express has closed its central Tokyo office. For check cashing service for its card holders you have to go to Ogikubo, a 15-minute train ride from Shinjuku Station, *4-30-16 Ogikubo, Suginami-ku, Tokyo, Tel. (03)3220-6250.*

NATIONAL HOLIDAYS

Banks, post offices, schools, government and private offices are all closed on national holidays. Stores are generally open although mom and pop shops will probably close. Museums and restaurants are usually open. If a holiday falls on a Monday, many museums, which are ordinarily closed, will open and take the following day as a holiday. When a holiday falls on a Sunday, Monday is a holiday.

Japanese travel on holidays so train, air and hotel reservations need to be made well in advance, especially if the holiday forms a long weekend. The peak travel times are around the New Year (December 27 through January 4), Golden Week (April 29 through May 5) and August 13-16.

Holidays include:

• January 1	New Year's Day (banks and post offices usually close until Jan. 4)
• Second Monday of January	Coming of Age Day
• February 11	National Foundation Day
• March 20 or 21	Vernal Equinox Day
• April 29	Greenery Day
• May 3	Constitution Day
• May 4	Additional holiday between two holidays
• May 5	Children's Day
• July 20	Marine Day
• September 15	Respect for the Aged Day
• Sept. 23 or 24	Autumnal Equinox Day
• Second Monday of October	Health Sports Day
• November 3	Culture Day
• November 23	Labor Thanksgiving Day
• December 23	Emperor's Birthday

NATURAL DISASTERS

Earthquakes

Japan has some of the shakiest real estate on earth. Most of the quakes are too small to be felt, and a "big one" comes along only every 80 years or so. Japan has some of the strongest building codes in the world. If you do experience an earthquake, here are a few basic precautions:

• Stay inside. Unless you are in a rural area, it is safer to be indoors than outside where falling glass and debris can injure.

- If you are in an apartment or house, turn off the gas on the stove.
- Open a door or window so you have an escape route should the shifting building jam an exit.
- Get under a table or desk. If you don't have one, stand under the doorway.
- If you are on the street, stay away from any high walls; take cover in the nearest building.
- Elevators are equipped with seismic detectors and will stop at the nearest floor. Do not stay in the elevator.
- Every neighborhood has a designated evacuation point, usually a park or school. Do not evacuate unless the building is unstable or threatened by fire.
- In an emergency, NHK radio and television and FEN radio (US military radio, 810 AM) will broadcast reports in English.

Tidal Waves

Tsunami, or tidal waves, can strike the coast after an earthquake. Low-lying areas have warning sirens. If you are on the seacoast and feel an earthquake or hear the sirens, immediately head for higher land.

Typhoons

Typhoons are generally more an annoyance than anything else. During the August-to-October season, Japan may experience a half-dozen typhoons, but they are fairly localized. A typhoon that hits Kyushu usually does not have any effect on Tokyo. They are not as strong as the ones that hit the more tropical countries and usually bring only heavy rain and wind, sometimes causing landslides in mountainous areas.

Typhoons do create uncomfortable sightseeing, and the heavy rains can cause air, train and bus delays. Usually a typhoon will blow over within a day.

PERSONAL SAFETY

Japan is one of the safest countries in the world. There's very little violent crime (in 1996 only 17 people were killed by firearms — sounds like a bad weekend in New York). Don't let this low crime rate fool you. That suitcase you leave alone at a train station will probably be there when you return in five minutes, but then again, what if it isn't? Petty crimes such as pick-pocketing and purse-snatching occur, so keep your eyes open and be careful.

People love to tell amazing stories of how taxi drivers tracked them down to return forgotten items. We don't want to pooh-pooh them because it does happens, but you can't count on it. Patrice left a camera (with her name and address on it) in a taxi and never saw it again. We know a foreign resident who was upset because the camera he left in the lobby of his own apartment building was gone when he returned 30 minutes later. "I thought it would be safe; this is Japan," he said. Don't take any chances.

In most places, it's safe for a woman to walk alone at night although we avoid some of the sleazier entertainment districts. Taking trains and buses alone are no problem.

YOUR LOCAL NEIGHBORHOOD POLICE BOX

The police in Japan have a system of neighborhood police boxes, called **koban**. *They're staffed by a few policemen who use the box as a center. From it, they ride around the neighborhood on bicycles and get to know the residents and merchants.*

Since Japan has a fairly low crime rate, the police aren't very busy catching criminals. Their main task, at least in urban areas, is to give directions to bewildered souls who can't find their destinations. The police boxes are equipped with excellent maps showing the area building by building; stop in if you ever get lost. The police seldom speak more than a few words of English, but they can point out things on a map.

If you lose your wallet and don't have any money to get to your hotel, the police can lend you the funds. If you lose anything, report it; the police will do their best to track it down.

POST OFFICES

Post offices are distinguished by a red symbol that resembles a T with an extra horizontal line on top. Post offices offer both postal and banking services, so there are two sets of counters. In urban post offices, the postage counter is usually marked in English. If it isn't, the staff will direct you to the right place.

Post offices are open 9am to 5pm, Monday through Friday. Major post offices in large cities will also have Saturday and sometimes Sunday hours, and the biggest will have a 24-hour counter.

Sending a letter under 25 grams within Japan costs ¥80; ¥90 for up to 50 grams. If it's over 12 x 23.5 cm (slightly smaller than an American business envelope), the cost is ¥120 for up to 50 grams. Postcards sent within Japan cost ¥50.

Postcards sent by airmail anywhere in the world cost ¥70 and aerograms are ¥90. Letters sent within Asia cost ¥90 for the first 25 grams and ¥50 for each additional 25 grams. Letters to North America, Europe, Middle East and Oceania cost ¥110 for the first 25 grams and ¥80 for each additional 25. Mail to Africa and South America costs ¥130 for the first 25 grams and ¥100 for each additional 25.

The post office staff automatically shows you the cost on a calculator, so communication is rarely a problem. Even the post office has an English-language web site. Access it at *www.postal.mpt.go.jp/new-eng*.

The post office has an international express service called **EMS**. It is less expensive than using international delivery services such as Federal Express and DHL although it may not be quite as fast.

Inexpensive boxes are sold at post offices. You can mail boxes overseas if they weigh under 20 kilos (44 lb.).

Japanese addresses have a three digit postal code, followed by a dash and four more digits.

Convenience and other stores displaying the postal T sign sell stamps as do larger hotels. Postal boxes, usually red, are in front of post offices and at many other locations on the sidewalk. You cannot mail a letter by putting it in a residential mailbox; they are for delivery only.

Stamp collectors should ask for commemorative stamps, *kinen kitte*. The Tokyo Central Post Office at Tokyo Station has a large philatelic section.

ESSENTIAL POSTAL VOCABULARY

kitte	*stamp*
kookuu fusho	*aerogram*
hagaki	*postcard*
kookuu bin	*air mail*
funa bin	*sea or surface mail*
futoo	*envelope*
hako	*box*

SMOKING

Depending on your perspective, Japan is either a smoker's paradise or a nonsmoker's hell. As the only developed country where the number of smokers is increasing, Japan is a tobacco company's dream come true. More than 50% of Japanese men smoke, and women in their twenties are the fastest growing segment of the market. Popular American brands are readily available; cigarettes cost about ¥250 a pack, and vending machines are on nearly every street corner.

If you arrive armed with nonsmoker's rights, you will have to make some adjustments. Don't expect Japanese to be apologetic or polite about their smoking—people feel free to light up almost everywhere. Some taxis are so smoke filled that you can't see through the windows, and the driver keeps on puffing. On the plus side, cigars and pipe smoking are a rarity.

Nonsmoking sections are unavailable in most restaurants, and those that have them tend to be in hotels or Western-style places. You can ask for nonsmoking (both "nonsmoking" and *kin'en seki* are used), but most traditional Japanese restaurants simply aren't familiar with the concept. If cigarette smoke really bothers you, avoid bars and *izakaya* drinking establishments where the air is often blue with smoke.

Smoking is prohibited on commuter trains and subways although train platforms may have designated smoking areas. Long distance trains have cars designated smoking and nonsmoking in both reserved and unreserved cars. If smoke bothers you, be sure you request *"kin'en seki"* when you make your seat reservation. Just walking through some smoking cars on *shinkansen* trains makes us wish we had our aqua lungs.

Occasionally, in fairly remote areas, a limited express train may consist of three cars only: one reserved for smoking and two unreserved, one for smoking and one for nonsmoking. In this situation, we usually make reservations in the smoking car but check for available seats in the nonsmoking, unreserved car. If there aren't any seats in the smokefree atmosphere, our logic is that a smoky seat is better than no seat at all.

TAXES

Japan has a 5% consumption tax added to the price of all goods and services. On some things such as taxi fares and newspapers, the tax is included in the price. But on most items, the tax is added at the cash register. We are forever walking around with pockets full of change; nothing ever costs an even amount.

If your meal in a restaurant costs over ¥7500 per person, an additional tax of 3% is added. And if your accommodations are over ¥15,000 per person per night, there's an additional 3% local tax.

TELEPHONES

You are never far from a telephone in Japan. Public phones are everywhere: in restaurants, hotel lobbies, coffee shops, on the street, in the subway station and on *shinkansen* trains. Some are simple, oversized dial phones that accept only ¥10 coins; others are state-of-the-art public phones with ISDN lines and digital displays.

Calling Japan from Overseas

Japan's country code is **81**, which means when calling Japan from overseas you must dial 81 before the area code. Then you must drop the first (0) of the area code. When we give you phone numbers, the area codes is in parentheses. Area codes are a series of numbers ranging from 2 digits to 6, but they all begin with 0. So if a Tokyo number is listed as (03)1234-5678, from overseas you dial your country's international access number, then 81, then 3: the (03) area code with the initial 0 dropped, then the number 1234-5678. The most frequent mistake is people forget to drop the 0 of the area code.

Calling within Japan

Long distance within Japan: When you call long distance within Japan, you must use the complete area code. Long distance may not be as far as you think. Even if you're calling the next town, if its area code is different, you must dial it. If you are calling Tokyo from Narita Airport or Osaka from Kansai International Airport, you must dial the area code.

Local calls in Japan: Dialing local calls, omit the area code and dial the number. Local numbers are not standard; they can have anywhere from 5 to 8 digits.

Toll free is called Free Dial. These numbers usually begin with 0120 or 0088. To call from a pay phone, insert ¥10 to make the call; it will be returned.

Old Tokyo numbers. Several year ago, all Tokyo numbers within the (03) area code went to 8 digits. If you have an old number that only has 7 digits, add a 3 between the area code and the 7-digit number.

Osaka numbers. Osaka numbers have gone to 8 digits. For a 7-digit number, add a 6 between the area code and the 7-digit number.

Using Pay Phones

Some public telephones accept only coins, others only telephone cards and others take both. A local call costs ¥10 for 90 seconds and will disconnect if you don't deposit more money. You can put in ¥10 and ¥100 coins; unused coins are returned, but the machine doesn't give change. If you insert a ¥100 coin and only talk ¥20 worth, you will not get a refund.

Telephone cards are convenient because you don't have to worry about having change. Cards come in denominations of ¥500 and ¥1000 and are sold nearly everywhere: at hotels, convenience stores, subway kiosks, vending machines, etc. Insert the card, dial the number and the cost of the call is deducted. Cards have message units worth ¥10 each; units are displayed in a window on the phone. If you finish one card, insert another without interrupting your call. Telephone cards are especially convenient when making long distance calls as the units click by at a quick pace.

Calling Overseas from Japan

International telephone calls from Japan are expensive. Hotels are notorious for jacking up charges for international calls, so it's usually in your interest to bypass the hotel switchboard whenever you can. One way is to use the Home Country Direct systems. You dial an access number and then either dial the telephone number or talk to your home country operator. Americans can use AT&T, MCI and Sprint calling cards.

Access numbers:

• **AT&T**: *Tel. 00539-111*
• **MCI**: *Tel. 00539-121*
• **Sprint**: *Tel. 00539-131*

For other home country direct access codes, dial 0051.

Telephone booths marked international will allow you to make overseas calls using telephone cards. Seven-Eleven and other convenience stores sell international telephone cards that can be used at any telephone booth (one is called the "Love Home Card"). AT&T's card, available only at Lawson's Convenience Stores, is one of the least expensive international telephone cards.

KDD is the largest international operator. You can reach their bilingual operators at 0051.

TIME DIFFERENCE

The entire country of Japan is within one time zone, 9 hours ahead of Greenwich Mean Time, and 14 hours ahead of New York (Eastern Standard Time). Japan doesn't use daylight saving time; subtract one hour when figuring the time difference from a country that does have daylight saving time.

TIPPING

Tipping has never caught on in Japan and we hope it never does. We save so much brainpower by not having to figure out correct percentages. You do not tip waiters, taxi drivers, hairdressers, bell boys, bathroom attendants — no one (there's one exception, so keep on reading). We have offered tips for exceptional service only to have them refused. If you leave money on a restaurant table, it's likely the staff will chase after you to give it back, presuming you forgot it.

Large hotels and restaurants will add a 10% service charge to your bill, but most eateries do not.

The one exception is that some people tip when they stay at an expensive Japanese inn, giving ¥1000 or ¥2000 to the room attendant. They tip either after the attendant has poured tea and given an introduction to the inn or in the morning after breakfast. The money can't just be handed over openly, it's considered too crass. It's put in a small envelope and presented surreptitiously.

A highly unofficial survey of our friends found about half tip at Japanese inns. Our recommendation is not to tip unless you want something special such as laundry washed. (In high-class inns, the staff will wash your clothes without an additional charge).

TOILETS

You'll come across two types of toilets in Japan, traditional squat types and Western toilets. To use the squat type, face the hooded side of the toilet and give your leg muscles a good workout. Make sure your clothing doesn't touch the ground.

There are a lot of public bathrooms. Those in department stores, hotels, fast-food shops and restaurants are usually well maintained, but facilities in public parks and subways leave something to be desired; they are not unsafe, just smelly. Toilet paper is usually provided, but paper hand towels are not, so make sure you have tissues or a handkerchief.

Most often, signs for appropriate toilets are indicated by female and male figures. If not, you can ask "*onna?*" for women and "*otoko?*" for men. To ask where the toilet is, say "*toi-re*" or "*o-te-arai*" with a rising intonation.

Toilet seats have gone high tech. In department stores you may encounter a toilet seat that has a control panel resembling a 747's. In reality, it's a built-in electronic bidet with buttons controlling water temperature, strength and aim of stream and air dryer. Actually, it's best to ignore the whole thing and look for the flusher on the tank of the toilet. If you can't find a flusher at the usual place, look around. Sometimes it's on the floor or wall. It may even be activated by an electric eye.

WHEN HIGH TECH MEETS TOILETS IN JAPAN

We were at a party when an American woman came out of the bathroom laughing hysterically. A broad wet stripe was splashed across her dress and face. She had turned around to flush the toilet and hit the bidet button instead giving herself an instant shower.

A British friend lives in an apartment with a state-of-the-art bathroom. Everything has a button, even one to raise and lower the toilet seat. Noriko tried unsuccessfully to lower it manually. "Why can't I move it by hand?" she asked. "Japanese don't want to contaminate themselves by touching toilet seat germs, even in a private residence," was the reply. The door to this same bathroom opens and closes by remote control buttons.

The latest toilets will actually analyze your urine. What's next? Pregnancy tests?

Sometimes small restaurants have only unisex bathrooms. Walking through to the toilet stall, there may be a urinal in the sink area. A woman is supposed to just walk past a man using it as if he isn't there. Often in park facilities, the urinals are visible to people outside.

Recently built rest rooms have wheelchair access stalls.

For some inexplicable reason, certain segments of the Japanese male population, including taxi drivers and those under the influence of alcohol, think the closest wall is their urinal. There's nothing you can do except ignore it.

Many young Japanese women have decided that they do not want anyone to hear their sounds of elimination and flush the toilet to mask the noise. To counter this waste of water, some buildings have installed buttons which when pressed, sound like flushing water. Only in Japan...

TOURIST OFFICES

The Japan National Tourist Office runs **Tourist Information Centers** specially for foreigners at Narita and Kansai International Airports and in Tokyo and Kyoto. Stop by for brochures, maps, travel advice and general information. The Tokyo and Kyoto offices have Welcome Inn Reservation Centers that will book rooms at reasonably priced hotels and inns.

Tokyo
Tokyo International Forum, B1F, 3-5-1 Marunouchi, Chiyoda-ku, Tokyo, 100-0005. Tel. (03)3201-3331. Open 9am to 5pm, Monday through Friday; 9am to 12 noon Saturday. Closed Sunday, holidays and December 29-January 3.

Narita Airport
Terminal 2, 1st floor (Arrival Floor). Tel. (0476)34-6251. Open daily 9am to 8pm.
Terminal 1, 1st floor (Arrival Floor). Tel. (0476)30-3383. Open daily 9am to 8pm.

Kyoto
Kyoto Tower Building, 1F, Higashi-Shiokoji-cho, Shimogyo-ku, Kyoto, 600-8216. Tel. (075)371-5649. Open 9am to 5pm, Monday through Friday; 9am to 12 noon Saturday. Closed Sunday, holidays and December 29-January 3.

Kansai International Airport
Passenger Terminal Building, 1st floor (Arrival Floor). Tel. (0724)56-6025. Open daily 9am to 9pm.

Japan National Tourist Organization Web Site

The JNTO web site addresses are *www.jnto.go.jp* and *www.japantravelinfo.com*. Extensive information on traveling in Japan and good links.

Prefecture Information

Tokyo has tourist and promotion offices for most prefectures where you can pick up brochures and even buy some local products, but don't expect to find English-speaking staff. The offices are concentrated in two places at Tokyo Station: the 9th floor of the Daimaru Department Store at the station's Yaesu exit and at the Kokusai Kanko Kaikan, to the left of the Yaesu exit. Most are open 9am to 5pm, Monday through Friday.

Japan Travel Phone

For travel information and language assistance call the Japan Travel Phone daily between 9am and 5pm. Outside Tokyo and Kyoto, call toll free: *Tel. 0088-22-4800*. Within Tokyo, call *Tel. (03)3201-3331*. Within Kyoto, the number is *Tel. (075)371-5649*. The Tokyo and Kyoto numbers are not available Saturday afternoon and Sunday; at these times you should use the toll-free number.

Local Tourist Bureaus

Almost every town or city which gets tourists will have a travel information center at the train station. You can usually get an English map and some basic information and have an agent book a hotel or inn for you. You'll need to give your price range. Larger cities will have English speaking staff, but in smaller places, you'll have to communicate at some basic level. Tourist offices which are part of the "i" tourist information system should have English speakers available. These offices use a logo with a question mark and "information" printed below. Tourist offices are called *kanko annai-sho*.

WATER

Yes, you can drink the water. You may not like the chloride taste of city water, but it's potable. If you prefer, you can find both imported and domestic mineral water in supermarkets and convenience stores. For a while it was chic to hang around with a bottle of Volvic water, but that fad seems to have passed.

WEIGHTS & MEASURES

Japan is on the metric system. On the following page are some useful tables for you:

Weight

1 gram	0.035 ounces
1 kilogram	35.27 ounces
	2.2 lb.
1 ounce	28 grams
1 pound	454 grams
	0.454 kilograms

Kilograms to pounds: multiply kilograms by 2.2
Pounds to kilograms: multiply pounds by 0.45

Length

1 centimeter	0.39 inch
1 meter	39 inches
1 kilometer	0.62 miles
1 inch	2.5 centimeters
1 foot	30 centimeters
	0.3 meters
1 mile	1.6 kilometers

Kilometers to miles: multiply kilometers by 0.62
Miles to kilometers: multiply miles by 1.61

Volume

1 liter	1.06 quarts
	0.26 US gallon
1 gallon	3.78 liters

Liters to US gallon: multiply liters by 0.26
US Gallon to liters: multiply gallons by 3.78

Temperature

0°C	32°F
20°C	68°F
100°C	212°F

An easy way to convert roughly from **Celsius to Fahrenheit** is to double the Celsius temperature and add 30. For example: 20°C x 2 + 30 = 70°F. For an exact amount, take 9/5 of the Celsius temperature and add 32.

Fahrenheit to Celsius: subtract 32 from Fahrenheit temperature, multiply by 5 and divide by 9.

8. SPORTS & RECREATION

Since Japan perfected the art of making TVs, VCRs and other tools for couch potatoes, you may not think it would be a good place for live sports. But spectator sports like sumo, baseball, soccer, karate and judo, are thriving in Japan.

Do you find doing more exciting that watching? Hiking, skiing, cycling and mountain and rock climbing all beckon. And if it's martial arts that interest you, there could be a *dojo* in your future.

Searching for some mindless entertainment? *Pachinko* is sure to fit the bill or why not croon your heart out in a karaoke pub or box?

On your mark, get set, go.

SUMO

Sumo wrestling, the Japanese national sport, involves wrestling matches between huge, nearly naked men who can weigh as much as 500 pounds. The sport itself is very simple, but its rituals together with its simplicity make sumo a fascinating sport to watch. We know many foreigners living in Japan who are glued to the tube during an entire tournament.

SUMO LEGENDS

One former grand champion polished off six dozen bowls of noodles in one sitting.

Another once wolfed down 36 box lunches.

A champion consumed three bottles of whiskey during a night of drinking.

And then there's the story about a 440-pound wrestler who drank 38 quart bottles of beer during an all-night drinking session with his stablemates.

Sumo goes back 2000 years and is tied to Shinto religion: matches at shrines were offerings to the gods for a good harvest. To this day, bouts take place in a ring, *dohyo*, under a thatched roof resembling a shrine.

So what is sumo all about?

Before an actual bout begins, wrestlers go through a series of rituals that include throwing salt to purify the ring and staring each other down. Then they begin. The first man who steps out of the ring or touches the ground with any part of his body other than the soles of his feet, loses. If two wrestlers fall simultaneously, the first one to touch the ground loses. The *gyoji* (referee), wearing traditional, colorful robes and a tall hat, makes the final judgment and announces his decision by pointing his fan toward the winner.

Wrestlers can use any or all of more than 48 different techniques including pushing, pulling, lifting, tripping and slapping. But there are limits: for example, they cannot pull off each other's topnots or punch. Most bouts are over within a minute or so.

Known as *rikishi* (strong men), sumo wrestlers live communally in *heya* (stables). In this hierarchical arrangement, younger wrestlers defer to the upper-ranked *rikishi,* and perform menial tasks such as cleaning in addition to training. Wrestlers train from early morning until about 11am. Next they have their first of two meals of the day, gaining bulk by eating huge quantities of *chanko nabe,* a stew with meat, fish, tofu, *udon* noodles and vegetables. If you would like to visit a sumo stable to watch a training session, check for telephone numbers under Sports in the Tokyo chapter.

Tournaments last 15 days and are held six times a year: three in Tokyo and one each in Osaka, Nagoya and Fukuoka. The wrestler who wins the most bouts is the champion for that tournament.

The best seats, boxes with *tatami* mats and near the ring, are almost impossible to obtain. Companies and individuals renew their subscriptions year after year. It's easier to obtain chair seats, especially the least expensive advance sale seats at ¥3000 and the unreserved seats at ¥2100, sold each morning of a tournament. The daily seats go on sale at 8am at the box office. On weekends, holidays and during the last week of the tournament, you must go early to be assured of a ticket; on weekdays, especially early in the tournament, you can sometimes get to the box office as late as 9am or 10am and still get a ticket.

A tournament begins each day at 10am, and the lowest-ranking *rikishi* wrestle first. The really good guys don't go on until about 4pm, and the last bout always ends by 6pm. If you have an inexpensive ticket, it's perfectly acceptable to sit closer to the ring in the reserved seats until the rightful owner shows up — usually about 3pm.

NHK, the national television station, broadcasts the bouts from 3:30pm. The satellite channel, which your hotel may carry, provides English commentary. So if you are in Japan during a tournament, make sure you catch at least a couple bouts on TV.

The **Annual Sumo Tournament** schedule is:

• **Tokyo**: held in Kokugikan Hall – January: 1st or 2nd Sunday through 3rd or 4th Sunday; May: 1st or 2nd Sunday through 3rd or 4th Sunday; September: 1st Sunday through 3rd Sunday
• **Osaka**: held in Osaka Furitsu Taiiku Kaikan – March: 2nd Sunday through 4th Sunday
• **Nagoya**: Aichi Ken Taiiku-kan – July: 1st Sunday through 3rd Sunday
• **Fukuoka**: held in Fukuoka Kokusai Center Sogo Hall – November: 2nd Sunday through 4th Sunday

You can follow Sumo on the official web site: *www.sumo.or.jp/index_e.html*, and on the Sumoweb: *www.sumoweb.com.*

MARTIAL ARTS

In addition to extreme physical fitness, all the martial arts involve and emphasize rigorous mental training and discipline. For devotees, visiting Japan provides an opportunity to see some of the top black-belt experts. You can actually participate at some of the *dojo* (training centers). For information, refer to the sports section of the Tokyo chapter. If you are in another part of the country, contact the appropriate federation for local places. Take along your training uniform, remember your techniques and try not to break any bones.

Karate originated in China, developed in Okinawa and arrived in mainland Japan in the early 20th century. Karate (empty hand) is primarily a means of self-defense. Although the empty hands are considered as weapons themselves, no other weapons are allowed. Kicking is permitted and that empty hand is used for lots of punching.

For more information, contact **The Japan Karate-do Federation**, *6F, No. 2 Sempaku Shinkokai Building, 1-11-2 Toranomon, Minato-ku, Tokyo. Tel. (03)3503-6640* or the **International Headquarters of the Japan Karate Association**, *Room 408, 29-3 Sakuragaoka, Shibuya-ku, Tokyo. Tel. (03)5459-6226.*

Judo, another form of self-defense, is native to Japan and was developed from battlefield techniques — participants learn to dodge and toss their opponents. Police men and women often end up as national champions so be careful who you challenge. A trip to the **Kodokan**, judo headquarters, in Tokyo is a must for judo enthusiasts. For more information, contact **All Japan Judo Federation**, *c/o Kodokan, 1-16-30 Kasuga, Bunkyo-ku, Tokyo. Tel. (03)3818-4199.*

Kendo, Japan's traditional form of fencing, evolved from medieval swordsmanship. *Kendo* probably has the widest participation of any sport among Japanese school children. You'll see children on the train toting their bamboo swords to class. The All Japan Championships are held in Tokyo each December. For more information, contact **All-Japan Kendo Federation**, *c/o Nippon Budokan, 2-3 Kitanomaru-koen, Chiyoda-ku, Tokyo. Tel. (03)3211-5804.*

Aikido is a 20th century blend of karate, judo and *kendo*. The attackee uses the movements of the attacker to thwart the attacker himself. For more information, contact **International Aikido Federation**, *17-18 Wakamatsu-cho, Shinjuku-ku, Tokyo. Tel. (03)3203-9236.*

BASEBALL

America's favorite pastime is also Japan's. One of the few Western sports to catch on really big, Japan is baseball crazy. While professional baseball is popular, the summertime high school championships take on almost mythical proportions.

If you are in Japan between early April and late September, attend a baseball game for an exhilarating experience. If you buy a ticket in the bleachers, you'll quickly be caught up in the local crowd's enthusiasm.

Japan has two leagues. **Central** and **Pacific**; each has six teams. The pennant winners slug it out in the Japan Series every autumn. Baseball fields are smaller than their American cousins and except for four domed stadiums at Tokyo, Nagoya, Osaka and Fukuoka, most games are played outdoors.

JAPANESE BASEBALL TEAMS

Pacific League Teams
Chiba Lotte Marines, Chiba Marine Stadium
Fukuoka Daiei Hawks, Fukuoka Dome
Kintetsu Buffaloes, Osaka Dome
Nippon Ham Fighters, Tokyo Dome
Orix Bluewave, Green Stadium Kobe
Seibu Lions, Seibu Stadium, Tokorozawa (Tokyo outskirts)

Central League Teams
Chunichi Dragons, Nagoya Dome
Hanshin Tigers, Koshien Stadium
Hiroshima Toyo Carp, Hiroshima Stadium
Yakult Swallows, Jingu Stadium, Tokyo
Yokohama Baystars, Yokohama Stadium
Yomiuri Giants, Tokyo Dome

Teams are allowed three foreign players on their rosters — usually imports from the American baseball leagues.

Most of the teams are named after corporations, not after a town. The first time Patrice went to a game, she thought the team was named the Nippon Hams, not the Nippon Ham Fighters. The Yomiuri Giants, based in Tokyo, are everyone's favorite team and tickets are hard to get on short notice. Unless they are really hot, getting tickets for other teams is not usually a problem. Tickets are available at the stadium either in advance or at the game or through computerized ticket vendors such as Ticket Pia.

Want to keep up to date on Japanese baseball? Check out the official baseball home page at *www.inter.co.jp/baseball.*

SOCCER

Soccer hit Japan big time in 1993 when the professional J. League was launched. While the initial ardor has dimmed somewhat, soccer is still popular among young people. Be ready to jump up and cheer along with the other enthusiastic fans. Japan and Korea will co-host the World Cup in 2002.

The 16 teams have both international and Japanese players. The season runs in two stages: March through May and August through November with the championship games in early December.

The sixteen teams hail from all over Japan, but every year two teams rotate between the top and second tier.
Avispa Fukuoka
Sanfrecce Hiroshima
JEF United Ichihara
Jubilo Iwata
Kashima Antlers
Kashiwa Reysol
Kawasaki Frontale
Verdy Kawasaki
Vissel Kobe
Kyoto Purple Sanga
Nagoya Grampus Eight
Cerezo Osaka
Gamba Osaka
Shimizu S-Pulse
FC Tokyo
Yokohama Marinos

SKIING & SNOWBOARDING

Japan hosted the **Winter Olympics 1998** in **Nagano** and the 1972 Winter Olympics in Sapporo, so the skiing is unquestionably world class.

Although international skiers don't flock to Japan the same way they do to Switzerland or Austria, don't misinterpret that to mean that the slopes are empty. Skiing is a national passion, especially among younger Japanese.

The prime skiing areas are in Hokkaido, Tohoku and the Alps of central Japan. Most skiers favor Hokkaido's powdery snow, but the easy proximity of Tohoku and the Japan Alps ensures their popularity also. And if you don't want to bother to travel to the mountains, the world's first indoor ski slope provides year-round skiing without leaving the Tokyo area.

Snowboarding has become popular in the last few years much to the consternation of diehard skiers. Some places restrict snowboarding.

When you arrive at the slopes, you may be bowled over by skiers donning state-of-the-art equipment and ski wear, but their skills aren't necessarily commensurate. People skiing on trails beyond their ability is a major problem; for accomplished skiers, the best way to avoid this problem is to quickly hit the most advanced trails where fewer people ski.

Just about every ski area rents equipment. But before you go, if your shoe size is above 26.5 (about a US men's 8 1/2 or 9), call ahead to make sure they have boots to fit you. One-day rental of skis, poles and boots usually runs between ¥3000 and ¥4000.

Lift passes average ¥3500 a day; half-day and night passes are usually also available. Some ski slopes allow you to pay for each ride on the lift.

Most ski areas offer a full range of accommodations from simple ski lodges to elegant hotels and Japanese-style inns. Prices for accommodations can start as low as ¥5000 per person and go as high as ¥20,000 or more. Travel agents have a full range of package tours; this is the most economical way to ski in Hokkaido. For not much more than the price of airfare, you can get a three-day ski package to Hokkaido. Beltop Travel specializes in ski tours to Hokkaido for the international community. *BPS Square 6F, 2-10-6 Tsukiji, Chuo-ku, Tokyo 104-0045. Tel. (03)3544-0939, Fax (03)2544-0955; www.beltop.com.*

On the main island, if your budget is really tight, join the thousands of young Japanese and take the overnight buses to the ski areas.

For serious skiers, pick up a copy of *Ski Japan!* by T.R. Reid and published by Kodansha in 1994. Also check out *www.skijapanguide.com* for extensive information.

BICYCLING

If you are prepared for hilly and mountainous terrain, Japan's underpopulated rural areas beckon you. Japan has some bicycling trails, but touring for any distance means you will be on public roads. Whatever you do, avoid bicycling in the large metropolitan areas like Tokyo and Osaka.

Cycling terminals located all over the country cater to bicyclists and offer inexpensive accommodations (about ¥5000 per person with two meals).

Serious bicyclists should contact the **Bicycle Culture Center** for information in English at *Jitenshakai Kaikan, No. 3 Building, 1-9-3 Akasaka, Minato-ku, Tokyo, 107. Tel. (03)3584-4530. Open 10am to 4pm. Closed Sunday and public holidays.* The Bicycle Culture Center publishes several detailed maps, but only the city names are marked in English. Make sure you have a good bilingual map before you start out. The best source is **Buyodo**, *3-8-6 Nihonbashi, Chuo-ku, Tokyo, 103. Tel. (03)3271-2451.*

Most cyclists find it best to take their own bikes with them to Japan. While you can purchase bikes, touring bikes have given way to mountain bikes and frames tend to be in the 37-47 centimeter range, too small for tall bikers. And you may not like the price tag.

To transport your bike on JR trains, you must disassemble it and put it in a bike bag (called *rinko bukuro*). You may need to pay an additional luggage fee of ¥270; it's called a *temawari-hin kippu*. Flying domestically, you also must disassemble your bike and put it in a bike bag; it is counted as part of your baggage allowance. Traveling by ferry, merely roll your bike on board; you might have to pay a small extra charge.

One more thing to remember: most of Japan is pretty hot and steamy in summer, and cold and icy in winter. Spring and autumn are prime cycling times. But if you want to cycle in summer, Hokkaido's mild climate and no rainy season make it a good bet.

For more information on biking in Japan, consult *Cycling Japan: A Personal Guide to Exploring Japan by Bicycle* by Bryan Harrell, Kodansha, 1993. Also check out the Japan Cycling Navigator at *www.t3.rim.or. jp/~sayori*, and *www.tokyocycling.com*.

HIKING

With its many mountains, Japan offers hikers and mountain climbers a full range of opportunities from simple day hikes to scaling 3000-meter peaks. As close as one hour outside the main cities of Tokyo and Osaka, trails await you. And in winter, ice climbing on frozen waterfalls is popular. The mountains have huts for hikers; some provide meals and a futon and others just cabins where hikers can spend the night.

For more information, consult *Hiking in Japan: An Adventurer's Guide to 35 Routes* by Paul Hunt, Kodansha, 1988.

GOLF

Golf is a luxury sport in Japan, a country where land close to urban centers is at a premium. Memberships at the top clubs can run into tens of millions of yen.

The sport has become a form of corporate entertainment, and countless deals have been closed on the golf course. If you happen to play, pray you don't make a hole-in-one or you'll be expected to buy drinks and presents for club members and friends. There's actually hole-in-one insurance to guard against such financial disasters.

When Japanese travel overseas, they are astounded how inexpensive the game can be. So leave your clubs at home unless you receive an invitation from a corporate friend.

PACHINKO

A hybrid between one armed bandits and pinball, *pachinko* mesmerizes hundreds of thousands of Japanese every day. You can't miss *pachinko* parlors; they are everywhere — all 18,000 strong. In cities you usually find them near train stations. You'll recognize them by their flashing neon lights and their gaudy, plastic flower arrangements. When you walk by, the ringing noise is almost deafening and you'll notice that cigarette smoke clouds the room. In rural areas, *pachinko* parlors' signs light up an area for blocks like a mini-Las Vegas.

While technically not considered a form of gambling, players earn small prizes like lighter fluid flints or a certificate in exchange for *pachinko* balls. To collect their winnings, players go around the corner to a small window, which looks like a drug drop-point, and exchange these certificates for cash.

Until recently, the game, patronized mainly by students and housewives who "should" be spending their time elsewhere, had an unsavory image. Many of the parlors are owned by second or third generation Koreans resident in Japan, whose donations are one of North Korea's main sources of foreign currency. *Pachinko* parlor owners always turn up on the list of the country's biggest tax dodgers. But in the last year or two, the industry has tried to change its image. New, upscale parlors have marble floors, coffee bars and nonsmoking sections. Although still outside, their exchange windows resemble movie theater ticket windows.

Unlike pinball, there's very little skill involved other than choosing a machine that is set for a larger payoff. *Pachinko* mavens line up before a shop opens to have first choice. How do you tell which machines are best? Look for the machines that have the widest space between the pins around the big payoff hole.

So if you have an hour to kill waiting for a train, pop into a *pachinko* parlor. But keep your eye on the clock.

KARAOKE

Put a microphone in front of a normally reserved Japanese, and a transformation occurs. Soon he (or she) is belting out tunes in Japanese and often in a foreign language also.

Japan has melded technology with music to produce karaoke, a product they now export all around the world. Laser discs or the latest satellite-provided karaoke libraries provide the music and display the words on a video screen while you do the singing. Anyone can be an instant Frank Sinatra or Barbra Streisand.

In the last few years, a major transformation has occurred: karaoke bars have given way to karaoke boxes. Rather than singing in front of strangers at a pub, now you can rent a room that will seat anywhere from 2 to 50 and enjoy your own private karaoke session.

Most machines usually have a few songs in English. You have no excuse not to belt out *My Way*, *I Left My Heart in San Francisco*, *Country Road* and a sampling of Beatles tunes.

9. TAKING THE KIDS

Traveling with kids can be a lot of fun in Japan. Even hard-to-please teenagers love castles and ninja stories. These combined with the Japanese natural affinity for children make for a great family trip.

Naturally, you have to plan and pace your trip specially. Most of our friends who have toured as families have balanced their sightseeing; they don't rush from temple to temple because, basically, the kids won't stand for it. For most families, one major activity a day is enough. Some of the major activities can be aquariums, zoos, science museums and other sights, the same places Japanese families go.

Kids are a great icebreaker. Japanese love children and will go out of their way for them and for you. Since they don't often see very many foreign kids, especially outside the big cities, they quickly drop their normal reserve to make a big fuss of them. Over and over again, Japanese will say of your children *Kawaii, kawaii! (cute)*. Patrice's daughters began to think *kawaii* was their name.

We've divided our suggestions by age to give you some ideas how to make the best of a family trip.

A few advance preparations will get your trip off to a good start:
• Children need passports (and if adults need visas, children do also).
• Shoes that slip on and off greatly simplify touring with children (and adults!).
• To give a sense of adventure, have the children practice using chopsticks at home.
• Teach the children a few simple words of Japanese: *domo* (thank you), *hai* (yes) and *sayonara* (good-bye).
• Get an English translation of Japanese fairy tales.
• Have older children look at the web site "Kids Web Japan" to learn about the country: *www.jinjapan.org/kidsweb*.

BABIES

Traveling with babies takes surprisingly little adjustment. With a baby backpack or stroller, you can go about your day. Most train and subway stations don't have elevators so be prepared to lug a stroller up and down the stairs.

No need to carry all your supplies from home. Disposable diapers are available everywhere. You'll find the familiar Pampers name as well as an assortment of Japanese diapers equally as good. Drug stores and department stores carry powdered baby formula. SMA by Wyeth is one common brand name but there are several others. Soy-based formula is also easy to find. Buy diaper wipes and jars of baby food as well as freeze-dried baby food in drugstores, supermarkets and department stores.

Department stores provide special rooms with cribs and nursing areas near the children's department. Many rest rooms have changing tables.

Health concerns shouldn't be a major worry. You can drink the water anywhere in the country. High standards of hygiene mean there's little fear of catching exotic diseases.

Make sure you have children's medicine such as pain relievers and cold and cough medications because the Japanese brands will be unfamiliar. Japan has good medical care and in an emergency ask your hotel to call a doctor. (See the Medical Emergency section of Basic Information.) If the child has special medication, make sure you bring it with you. Americans should have a thermometer with them because Japanese ones register in Celsius.

Babysitting

Large hotels can arrange baby-sitting for you, but it may be a problem at smaller inns. The Japanese generally do not use baby-sitters and rely on family members.

TODDLERS & YOUNG CHILDREN

Parents must be creative in planning interesting schedules for young children. Sandwich your sightseeing with stops in parks, playgrounds and other kid-friendly places. Every sizable city sports a zoo and natural history and science museums. Aquariums are commonplace as are theme and amusement parks. Department store toy sections usually have some samples on display to amuse children and most department store rooftops have play equipment to keep the kids occupied. And if all else fails, there's Tokyo Disneyland.

If your child will only eat hamburgers, you are in luck. The ubiquitous fast food restaurants provide inexpensive meals. But you should be able to find food for finicky eaters in other restaurants also. Most children will eat fried chicken chunks *(kara-age)*, noodles, and deep fried shrimp *tempura*. So try to branch out. And plain white rice is available everywhere.

SURVIVING THE FLIGHT WITH KIDS

No matter what you do, the international flight is going to be long. And traveling with children you probably won't have the luxury of immersing yourself in a good book to help the time pass quickly. But with some preparation, the flight doesn't have to be an ordeal.

While many people hesitate to travel with infants, we find that traveling long distances with babies under the age of one is easier than with slightly older children. Children between one and three are mobile and difficult to keep occupied on a long flight. Steel yourselves for countless trips up and down the aisles. By age three, most children are able to sit still, look at books and entertain themselves, at least for part of the trip.

On international flights, children under two can travel free but are not entitled to a seat. This isn't a problem with an infant, but a long trip in economy class with a nearly two-year-old on a lap is our idea of hell on earth. Ask the airline how full the plane is and consider springing for a ticket if you have little hope of getting an extra seat. Airlines generally charge two-thirds of an adult fare for children age two through eleven.

Get your seat assignments when you make your reservations; you don't want to get to the airport and discover you can't sit together (or do you?). For babies, you want to be in the bulkhead seats where bassinets fasten, but with older children the bulkhead seats are a hindrance. They're right under the movie screen, a distraction for children trying to sleep. The armrests of bulkhead seats don't raise, so a child can't stretch out on your lap. And since you cannot put your carry-on luggage under the seats in front of you, it's a nuisance to get toys and snacks.

With smaller children, make sure you pack in your carry-on baggage at least two changes of clothes (and one for yourself). Dress your children in layers so you can adjust for temperature changes on and off the aircraft. Bring a variety of toys and games to keep them entertained. We buy something new and surprise the children with it on the airplane; the novelty keeps them occupied for a while.

Make sure you have enough diapers to see you through the flight and to your destination. Airplanes usually supply diapers, but you don't want to count on it and sometimes they have only one size. Bring a cup with a cap for small children to prevent spills.

Take along healthy snacks for the flight. Look into children's meals, which must be ordered in advance. On some airlines this means hamburgers, which may not be appealing to your child. The regular meal or another type of special meal may be a better choice. But we find it's best not to rely on the airline for meals. Taking some of your children's favorite foods can make the dining experience more pleasant. Make sure the children drink plenty of liquids to avoid dehydration.

For older children, a selection of books and a gameboy helps the time pass faster.

Traveling with younger children means paying closer attention to your travel schedule. You want to avoid being on subway and commuter trains at rush hour, usually 8 to 9:30am. Be careful boarding the train; sometimes there's a large gap between the train and the platform. You may want to consider using a stroller for a child as old as age four or five because chances are you'll do a lot of walking. You can rent strollers at zoos and amusement parks or take your own.

You'll need to carry baby wipes *(wetto tissue)* for hands and faces, if not bottoms, and a package of tissues for bathrooms. Japanese drugstores sell *benza kurina* to sanitize toilet seats.

OLDER CHILDREN & TEENAGERS

Older children and teenagers have a higher tolerance for sightseeing, but you still need to customize the schedule. Make sure you visit at least one castle. Break up sightseeing days with amusement parks, theme parks, zoos, aquariums, and science and natural history museums. Don't overlook the video arcades and the virtual reality arcades.

TRAVEL COSTS

Traveling by train, subway and buses, children under six years old ride free and six through eleven pay half fare. On a long distance train, a child under six is not entitled to a seat, so if it's crowded, the child will have to sit on your lap. If this would be a problem, buy a child's ticket. The Japan Rail Pass is available for children six through eleven at one-half the adult cost. On domestic airplane flights, children under three fly free but do not get their own seat. Children three through eleven are half price.

At hotels and Japanese inns, the tariff for children gets tricky. Many Western hotels don't have rooms with two double beds because the rooms are small. Many charge per person, even if the person is a child. The large American chains like Hyatt, Hilton and Holiday Inn are a plus here because they generally have a policy of no extra charge for children in the room with their parents. At Japanese inns, if the child is under three or four, you can request a *futon* only (no meals for the child) and usually will be charged a few thousand yen. (Don't worry about not having a meal for a small child, there will be more than enough food on your plate to share.) For an older child, the tariff is usually half the adult price. But there is no standard policy and it has to be negotiated with the inn.

Most temples, amusement parks and other attractions have reduced prices for children, often one price for elementary school children, another for junior and senior high school and a third for college students. Usually children under six are admitted free to museums and temples, but amusement parks and zoos generally charge admission for children three and older.

GREAT PLACES TO TAKE THE KIDS IN TOKYO

National Children's Land (Kodomo no Kuni) is a large hilly park popular with families. It used to be an ammunition depot so there still are cement bunkers in the hills; hopefully, they're empty but we didn't get close enough to check. The verdant park geared to children is refreshingly noncommercial. Activities include a cycling course, boating, pony rides, swimming pools in summer, ice skating in winter, a dairy farm complete with homemade ice cream, a small zoo, a nature study center, a plum garden, a swan pond, and a playground with unusual climbing structures and sculptures. The food sold on the grounds leaves a lot to be desired, so it's best to take a picnic lunch. *Tel. (045-961-2111. Open 9:30am to 4:30pm; 5pm July and August. Closed Monday and December 31 and January 1. ¥600. From Shibuya take the Shintamagawa line to Nagatsuda and change for the shuttle train to Kodomo no Kuni, about 45 minutes from Shibuya.*

Tokyo Sesame Place. Unlike most amusement parks, this one doesn't have rides; children have to participate actively. The climbing apparatus is first rate, and all the favorite Sesame Street characters perform live in a studio. The whole place is in a green area on top of a mountain. Small children love it. *403 Ajiro, Itsukaichi-machi, Nishitama-gun, Tokyo. Tel. (0425)96-5811. Open 9am to 5pm. Closed Thursday. Children ages 3 to 12 ¥1000, adults ¥2000. From Shinjuku Station take the JR Chuo line to Hachioji Station and then 30 minutes by bus.*

Sanrio Puroland. If you have a small child who loves Hello Kitty, put Puroland on your itinerary. It's an indoor amusement park where the terminally cute cat holds court. There are rides and shows. After 4pm, ticket prices drop; we find three hours is enough, so this is a cheaper alternative. *Tel. (0423)72-6500. Open 10am to 7pm. Closed Tuesday. ¥4400 adults, ¥4000 children. Take the Odakyu or Keio line from Shinjuku Station to Tama Center Station, about 45 minutes.*

Tama Zoo (Tama Dobutsu Koen). The zoo is in the hills of suburban Tokyo, and it's worth the trip to enjoy the park-like atmosphere. You can ride a special bus through a large lion pen. The insectarium has a fantastic conservatory filled with lush plants, butterflies and other insects. *7-1-1 Hodokubo, Hino-shi, Tokyo. Tel. (0425)91-1611. Open 9:30am to 5pm (enter by 4pm). Closed Monday and December 29 through January 3. ¥500. Keio Line express train to Takahata-Fudo Station, change for shuttle train to Keio Dobutsu Koen Station. Entrance is across the street from the station.*

Tokyo Disneyland. You didn't travel all the way to Japan to see Mickey and his friends. But, if you have kids, Disneyland is sure to keep them amused for a day. It's also an interesting sociological study to see Japanese and other Asian people enjoying themselves in such an over-whelmingly American experience. Tokyo Disneyland has been a big hit since it opened in 1983 and boasts that it has had more than 190 million visitors. Unless you're a masochist, avoid going on weekends or during Japanese school holidays; it may seem that all 190 million are there at one time. *1-1 Maihama, Urayasu. Tel. (0473)54-0001; www.tokyodisneyland.co.jp. General admission ¥3670. Tickets with admission to unlimited attractions are ¥5200 for 18 and over, ¥4590 children 12 through 17 and ¥3570 children 4 through 11. Opening hours vary with the season and day, but at a minimum: 9am until 7:30pm. The easiest way to get there is to take the JR Keiyo line from Tokyo Station to Maihama Station.*

Shinagawa Aquarium. This aquarium is one of the best in Tokyo. Our kids can't get enough of the dolphin and sea lion shows and the underwater tunnel with fish swimming all around you. *Tel. (03)3762-3431. Open 10am to 4:30pm. Closed Tuesday (open daily July 23 through September 2) and December 29 through January 1. ¥900. 5-minute walk from Omori Kaigan Station on the Keihin Kyuko line – board train at Shinagawa Station.*

10. FOOD & DRINK

THE BASICS

The Japanese love to eat out. The country has literally hundreds of thousands of restaurants from hole-in-the-wall places to elegant tea houses, boisterous beer halls, exclusive bars and much, much more. Prices vary from a few hundred yen for noodles at a stand-up counter to ¥40,000 or ¥50,000 for rarefied *kaiseki*. Restaurants are more than eateries; people go to bond with their colleagues, to relieve the stress of corporate life, to date, and to cement relationships and business deals.

Japanese food is more than raw fish and rice. Noodles in soup or plain; grilled, boiled and stewed meat and fish; deep fried vegetables and fish; curry rice; fried pork cutlets — all are now Japanese. When you add readily available Western food from spaghetti to hamburgers, Southeast Asian and other ethnic food, the culinary choices are nearly limitless.

To entice you out of your hotel, we've compiled lists of the major types of restaurants and the most common menu items to help you decide where and what to eat. As a non-Japanese-speaking visitor, it's really easy to eat only in hotel restaurants, but on the whole, most are overpriced and geared to visitors on expense accounts. Aren't you here to explore Japan? Be adventuresome and eat where Japanese eat. It's a great way to get a glimpse of everyday life and sample all kinds of different food.

Right away, you'll notice plastic food models that are outside many restaurants to tempt prospective diners. These miniature works of art are useful for ordering; beckon to a staff member to accompany you and point to your choice. You might have to swallow your pride, but you'll get the meal you think you want.

If you are counting pennies, and even if you aren't, lunch nearly always costs less than dinner. Restaurants have lunch specials often for a fraction of the nighttime cost. It's a great way to try an expensive restaurant and stretch your travel dollars.

Restaurants often have set fixed meals, *setto* and *teishoku*, and course meals, *kosu*. With set meals or *teishoku*, the entire meal usually comes at the same time, often on a tray. A *teishoku* will usually have the main course plus rice, soup and pickles. A course is similar to a set, but food is served one course after the other. A meal served in courses will always finish with rice, pickles and soup.

Japanese food is traditionally served in individual dishes. We'd hate to be dishwashers since even the simplest meal can generate at least a half-dozen dishes.

Your hotel may advertise a Viking breakfast. Don't be alarmed; Erik the Red is not joining you. Viking simply indicates the meal is a buffet; the term is used to describe any buffet meal — breakfast, lunch and dinner.

We divided restaurants into four categories:
- **Inexpensive**, *Under ¥3000*
- **Moderate**, *¥3000 to ¥6000*
- **Expensive**, *¥6000 to ¥12,000*
- **Very Expensive**, *Over ¥12,000*

RESTAURANT ETIQUETTE

When you walk into a restaurant, a staff member will greet you, *"Irrashaimase"* (welcome). You don't need to answer, just smile. You may be asked how many are in your party: *"Nanme sama...?"* Holding up the correct number of fingers is appropriate. If you are shown to a seat on a *tatami* mat, be sure you remove your shoes before stepping on the straw mat. If you are allergic to smoke, ask for no smoking, *kin'en seki;* no smoking sections are new to Japan and limited almost exclusively to hotel and Western restaurants, but there's no harm in asking.

Japanese have a wonderful custom of providing wet towels, *oshibori*, that are usually hot, but sometimes are chilled in summer. Use the towel to wipe your hands. In most restaurants you keep it for your napkin. If the *oshibori* is taken away, use a handkerchief or tissue instead. Using napkins is not a Japanese custom, which means they aren't usually provided; when you find them, they can be small, waxy and pretty useless.

Japanese eat Japanese food with chopsticks so give it your best try. If you are absolutely unable to get food to your mouth, ask for a fork. Most restaurants have them. When you are not using your chopsticks, lean them on the chopstick rest or put them across your plate. Never leave them sticking out of food. It reminds Japanese of the bowls of rice offered to the deceased at their graves.

It's impolite to use your own chopsticks to pick up food from a communal dish unless you have turned them end-for-end and use the clean part. The exception is with *nabe* stew pots. Never pass food from one set of chopsticks to another. It reminds Japanese of funerals where cremated bones are removed by family members.

The Japanese like to use appropriate tableware. Japanese food is eaten with chopsticks; Western food with a knife and fork; curry rice with a spoon and fork; and *ramen* noodles with a Chinese ceramic spoon. Fingers are okay for *sushi* at a *sushi* bar, but at a table, use chopsticks. Use chopsticks to eat Japanese noodles (*soba* and *udon*) and drink the broth straight from the bowl. Mom may have scolded you for doing it at home, but here it's the custom. Also, remember it's okay to slurp your noodles — sorry, Mom. Notice the Japanese at the next table; obviously, at least among men, slurping is perfectly acceptable. It's supposed to enhance the flavor.

Most of the time, you pay after your meal. But, at cheap stand-up noodle shops, museum canteens and other public places, you may have to buy a ticket for your food up front. Sometimes tickets are sold by vending machines and other times at the cash register.

Japanese don't usually mix food and money. You'll almost never be asked to pay at the table. (The exceptions are the Parisian cafes and some trendy California-Asian restaurants.) Money is handled at the cash register near the exit. If your bill is presented to your table after you're served, take it to the cash register to pay. If it is not presented to your table, don't worry, it will appear magically when you get to the cash register. At the register you'll usually find a small tray, put your money in this tray, rather than handing it directly to the cashier. Your change will be returned on the same tray. Of course, at fast food shops, pay at the counter when served. In cities more and more restaurants accept credit cards, but small noodle shops and mom and pop places do not.

Best of all, there's never any tipping — no, not ever. Hotels and some upscale restaurants will add a service charge. You will have to pay the 5% consumption tax and, if the bill is over ¥7500 per person, an additional 3% local tax will be added. What a relief not to worry about how much to tip.

Japanese do not eat food on the street, and it's considered in bad form to do so. No one will reprimand you for an occasional ice cream cone, but you'll notice most Japanese hang around the ice cream parlor until they finish.

ALCOHOLIC DRINKS

Japanese usually drink beer or *sake* with their meals. When they go out with colleagues after work, drinking is usually more important than eating. Restaurants serving traditional Japanese food will have beer, *sake*, whiskey and perhaps *shochu* (a sweet potato liquor) on hand. For other alcoholic beverages, you have to go to a bar.

When you go out for drinks, try following the Japanese custom of pouring drinks for your companions and they, in turn, will pour yours. It's

ESSENTIAL FOOD & DRINK VOCABULARY

Here are a few words you might need in a restaurant:

yoshoku	Western cuisine
washoku	Japanese cuisine
Oyu	hot water
Omizu	cold water
Ocha	Japanese tea
Fooku	fork
Supuun	spoon
Naifu	knife
Ohashi	chopsticks
Osara	plate
Chawan	rice bowl
Gohan	rice
Choshoku	breakfast
Chushoku	lunch
Yushoku	dinner
Okanjo	bill, check
Biru	beer
O bin	large bottle of beer
Chu bin	smaller bottle of beer
Nama biru	draft beer (sometimes served in bottles)
Durafuto biru	draft beer, always from a keg
Sake	Japanese rice wine
Atsukan	hot sake
Hiya	chilled sake
Mizu wari	whiskey and water
Shochu	spirits usually made from sweet potato
Oyu wari	shochu with hot water
Ume sawa	shochu with soda and a plum
Uron tii (uron cha)	oolong tea (popular with people who don't want alcohol)
Koka kora	Coke

If you say "Oishikatta" (it was delicious) and "Gochiso sama" (thank you for the meal) as you finish paying the bill, the Japanese will be impressed with your language ability.

considered gauche to pour your own drink, so hold your glass while it is being filled, and when everyone has a full glass, toast with a rousing "Kampai!"

SAKE - THE DRINK OF THE GODS

Sake, rice wine, was first brewed more than a thousand years ago as an offering to the gods. Signifying purity, even today small cups of sake are placed on Shinto altars in homes and shrines. When you go to a Shinto shrine, look for casks of sake piled at the entrance. People donate sake to the shrine as a way of requesting the good graces of the gods. Sake is used to toast weddings, births, and just about any celebration. Remember the word **Kampai**, *literally "bottom's up," you can use it to toast any occasion.*

You can drink sake warm or cold. When served chilled, it is often poured into a small square wooden box where there's a little salt in one corner. The texture of the wood gives the sake a real earthy taste. When served warm, sake is poured into tiny ceramic cups that are good for just one or two sips.

Sake is made from rice that is polished to remove all the outer layers. Good quality water and rice are essential for the production of superior sake. That's why Fushimi in Kyoto and Nada in Kobe are famous for their sake. Most rice wine is still produced by local breweries, just like wineries in the European countryside

You can enjoy drinking sake at any time, not only with food. Traditionally, Japanese drink sake when admiring cherry blossoms and autumn foliage, when moon viewing and snow viewing, and merely for sake's sake.

NOODLES - SOBA & UDON

Noodles, along with rice, are a staple of the Japanese diet. It is said that Japanese living overseas often miss their noodles more than anything else.

The history of noodles spans centuries and continents. The noodles Marco Polo brought back to Europe from China have evolved into pasta, a not-so-distant cousin to Japanese *soba* and *udon*. Developed in the kitchens of Zen temples, *soba* appealed to all classes during the Edo period.

Today noodles are available everywhere from cheap stand-up train station shops to rustically decorated restaurants; they're an inexpensive and filling casual meal. Most noodles are machine made today, but some shops still take great pride in making their own noodles by hand. Often a window on the street provides a perfect viewing place for passersby. One afternoon we spent a good half-hour watching the chef kneading *soba* dough and cutting it into thin strips with a huge cleaver. His work-of-art was delicious.

Most noodle shops serve both *soba* and *udon*. *Soba* is a thin, long noodle made of buckwheat flour. Until this century, it was the staple food for people living in mountainous areas where rice couldn't be cultivated. *Udon* is a thicker, white noodle made of wheat flour. *Udon* and *soba* are prepared in similar ways; be sure to tell the restaurant staff which one you want.

Cold noodles are served plain on a straw mat along with a dipping sauce in a cup and a small dish containing leeks and *wasabi* (grated horseradish). Place the leeks and horseradish in the sauce; then put a chopstick's worth of noodles in the sauce and eat them from the cup. When you've finished your noodles, the staff may offer you a pot of milky water in which the noodles were boiled. If you feel adventuresome, pour this water into the dipping-sauce cup and drink it as soup.

Hot noodles are served in a fish-based broth that can include vegetables, seaweed, or meat. If you like spicy food, sprinkle your noodles with *shichimi* (hot red pepper flakes), found on the table and not fiery hot. Eat the noodles with chopsticks and drink the broth directly from the bowl. It's polite to slurp as you eat the noodles, but it's an art we're still striving to perfect. If you down a whole bowl of broth, you'll undoubtedly develop an unquenchable thirst that will last all afternoon. There's no need to drink it all; just take a sip.

Each region prepares broth in a slightly different way. Tokyo's broth is dark and quite salty while Kyoto's is lighter. Regions also have their special noodles: Nagoya prides itself on *kishimen*, a white wheat noodle cut flat, resembling fettuccini.

When you order, specify *soba* or *udon*. If you want an extra large portion, tell the staff *"omori,"* which will cost one or two hundred yen more.

Soba is supposed to be good for your health and helps lower blood pressure. Japanese must eat *soba* on New Year's Eve because the long noodles symbolize longevity and long lasting good luck.

Cold noodles:

Mori soba (udon)	plain cold *soba (udon)* noodles
Zaru soba (udon)	cold *soba (udon)* with dried seaweed sprinkled on top
Tenzaru soba (udon)	cold *soba (udon)* with *tempura* on the side
Hiya mugi	thin white noodles served chilled (only in summer)
Somen	a very thin noodle served in chilled water (only in summer)

Hot noodles:

Kake soba (udon)	soba *(udon)* in broth with green onions
Sansai soba (udon)	soba *(udon)* in broth with mountain vegetables
Nameko soba (udon)	soba *(udon)* in broth with small, slippery mushrooms
Kitsune soba (udon)	soba *(udon)* in broth with fried thin tofu
Tempura soba (udon)	soba *(udon)* in broth with a deep fried shrimp
Tororo soba (udon)	soba *(udon)* in broth with grated mountain potato
Tsukimi soba (udon)	soba *(udon)* in broth with a raw quail egg
Namban soba (udon)	soba *(udon)* in broth with duck or chicken
Tanuki soba (udon)	soba *(udon)* in broth with little fried bits of *tempura* batter
Nabeyaki udon	udon cooked in a ceramic casserole in broth with vegetables, chicken, fried shrimp and fish cake

RAMEN

Ramen, long, thin Chinese-style egg noodles, are served in pork or chicken broth with bean sprouts and a thin slice of pork. *Ramen* shops almost always serve *gyoza*, fragrant Chinese dumplings filled with minced pork, cabbage, ginger and onion. Standard condiments are soy sauce, chili oil, vinegar and white pepper. Concoct your own mixture as a dipping sauce.

Often brightly lit and decorated with Chinese motifs, *ramen* shops provide a place for cheap and fast food and are popular with students. Usually you'll find a counter and a few small tables where you can enjoy your noodles.

The basic *ramen* menu is:

Miso ramen	noodles in fermented bean paste broth
Shoyu ramen	noodles in soy sauce flavored broth
Shio-aji ramen	noodles in salt flavored broth
Gyoza	sautéed pork dumplings, a serving is usually about six dumplings
Yakisoba	sautéed noodles with meat, fish and vegetables

SUSHI

Just say "Japanese food" to most foreigners and they immediately think of *sushi*. Nothing could be more quintessentially Japanese than *sushi* chefs wearing pristine white jackets and *hachimaki*, rolled towels wrapped around the head, solemnly slicing fish behind untarnished wooden counters. *Sushi* has a 400-year history.

Sushi basically refers to anything served with vinegared rice; it doesn't have to be raw fish only. Patrice was in a *sushi* bar when a German tourist sat next to her. This man was a vegetarian but wanted to try *sushi*. It turns out that he could easily fill up on nonfish *sushi*.

Sushi and *sashimi* are both served in *sushi* bars. *Sashimi* is plain slices of raw (and occasionally cooked) fish. (*Sashimi* is also served as a starter as a part of a larger meal in other restaurants.) *Sushi* is fish served on top of a rice patty or rolled in rice and is eaten with thin slices of pink pickled ginger called *gari* and dipped in soy sauce called *murasaki*. (*Sushi* has its own parlance). *Gari* and a cup of piping hot tea are served to refresh your palate so you can appreciate the different flavors.

You can put some horseradish (*wasabi*) in the soy sauce. Some purists prefer to put tiny amounts on the fish instead. Either way is okay. *Sushi* has the horseradish already in the center. If you'd like yours made without horseradish, just say *"sabi nuki"*.

Big hint: Learn from our experience. When dipping your *sushi* in soy sauce, make sure you dip the fish side; if you dip the rice side, the rice patty disintegrates before your eyes.

Sushi comes in two ways, *nigiri* and *chirashi*. *Nigiri* is fish on an individual cake of rice. *Chirashi* is an assortment of fish placed on top of rice in a bowl.

In a *sushi* bar, you can order a la carte just by pointing. Many places offer set menus at lunch, but not too many do in the evening. Set menus usually come in three grades: *nami* or *ume* is regular; *jo* or *take* is special; and *tokujo* or *matsu* is premium. The difference is more in the type of fish rather than quantity. Sometimes the set is only an assortment of *sushi*, other times it includes soup and pickles.

We usually drink beer or *sake* with *sushi* and finish off with tea. We also like to end our feast with a bowl of *miso* soup, *aka dashi*.

One type of inexpensive *sushi* shop is called *kaiten zushi*, revolving *sushi* bar. The guests sit at a circular counter with a conveyor belt running around it. The chefs assemble the *sushi* and put it on the belt. You help yourself to whatever comes around. If you don't see what you want, ask the chef to make it. At the end of the meal, the clerk counts your plates. Different color plates signify different prices, but conveyor belt *sushi* is always cheap, with most dishes going for ¥120 to ¥200. *Sushi* purists turn up their noses, but it's a lot of fun.

You're most likely to find the following items at a *sushi* shop:

Akagai	red clam
Ama-ebi	raw shrimp
Anago	cooked eel with thick sauce
Awabi	abalone (expensive)
Buri	yellowtail, in season in autumn and winter

Ebi	cooked shrimp
Hirame	flounder
Hotate	scallop
Ika	squid
Ikura	salmon roe (expensive)
Katsuo	bonito, in season April through June
Maguro	tuna
Toro	premium cut of tuna, fattier than *maguro*
Chu toro	premium cut of tuna, fattier than *toro*
O toro	most fatty cut of tuna and most expensive
Saba	mackerel
Sake	salmon
Shiromi	white fish, such as flounder and sea bass
Tai	sea bream, in season in spring
Tako	cooked octopus
Uni	sea urchin roe (expensive)
Nori tama	sweet sliced omelet
Maki	generic name for fish or veggies rolled with rice and thin seaweed
Kappa maki	cucumber roll
Tekka maki	tuna *(maguro)* roll
Oshinko maki	pickle roll
Natto maki	fermented soy bean roll
Negi toro maki	leek and fatty tuna roll
Ume shiso maki	pickled plum and beefsteak leaf roll

YAKITORI

Yakitori (literally, grilled chicken) shops are usually casual, neighborhood places where the beer and *sake* flows freely and morsels of chicken and other food are skewered and grilled over a charcoal fire. There are often big red-paper lanterns out front and counters inside where you can sit and watch your food prepared. You may smell a *yakitori-ya* before you see it; the fragrance of grilled charcoal escapes with smoke into the street. Most *yakitori-ya* are open only in the evening. There is a genre of new, upscale *yakitori* restaurants, but most are down home cheap eats. Legend has it a Dutch man in Nagasaki during the Edo period secretly whet the appetite of the Japanese by introducing them to grilled chicken. A well-known *yakitori* restaurant chain in Tokyo has taken its name, Nanbantei (Southern Barbarians, which means any Europeans) from this folklore.

Most *yakitori* costs ¥150 to several hundred yen a stick. In addition to ordering a la carte, many places offer a set, usually about five to seven sticks, all different. *Yakitori* isn't only chicken; vegetables, pork and other foods are also grilled.

Some of the most common types are:

Momo	dark chicken meat
Sasami	white chicken fillet without skin
Tebasaki	chicken wings
Tsukune	chicken meatballs
Shoniku	chicken with skin
Kawa	chicken skin
Reba	liver
Motsu	giblets
Negima	leeks
Ginnan	ginko nuts
Piiman	small green peppers
Negi maki	pork rolled around leeks
Shiso maki	shiso mint rolled with pork
Aspara maki	pork rolled around asparagus

KUSHIAGE

Kushiage is skewered morsels of food similar to *yakitori*, but dipped in batter and deep fried rather than grilled. Usually you order by the set with a certain number of sticks. Some places keep bringing you different sticks until you ask them to stop.

TONKATSU

Tonkatsu is pork breaded and deep fried. Inside the crunchy thick crust, the meat is soft and tender. *Tonkatsu* is always served with a mound of shredded cabbage, to help you digest the oil, and a thick soy sauce. It's a popular lunch for office workers as well as a casual dinner out. Some restaurants will give unlimited servings of cabbage and rice and may come around asking *"Okawari?"* ("refills?"). Say *"Hai"* for yes and *"Ii desu"* for no.

Tonkatsu is one of the first Western style foods to become popular in the late 19th century when Japan ended its period of isolation. The government, trying to reduce the influence of Buddhism, lifted the ban on eating meat. *Tonkatsu* comes in two main forms: *hire* (fillet) and *rosu* (chop). The fillet uses the tenderloin and is soft and nearly fat free. The *rosu* is what we know as pork chops and has a layer of fat around the edge. Purists prefer the *rosu* because the meat is more flavorful. The fillet costs more because it's a premium meat.

The *teishoku* (set meal) comes with soup, rice and pickles. Just add *teishoku* to the end of the following to order:

Hire katsu	pork fillet cutlet
Rosu katsu	pork chop cutlet

Ebi furai	prawns breaded and fried
Kaki furai	oysters breaded and fried (usually available only in winter)
Shogayaki	sauté of thin slices of pork, ginger and onions

TEMPURA

Tempura, fish and vegetables dipped in batter and quickly fried, is popular with foreigners. Japanese learned the cooking technique from the Portuguese when they came to Japan in the 16th century. The shogun Tokugawa Ieyasu loved *tempura* so much that legend says he died at age 74 from overeating it.

Along with *tempura* you're served *tentsuyu,* dipping sauce in a bowl, and a small mound of grated *daikon,* radish. Plop the radish into the sauce and dip the *tempura.* Purists like to sit at the counter of *tempura* shops so the food can go directly from the frying pan to the clean sheet of white paper on the plate. They are right; it tastes better hot. The paper helps to drain any excess oil. We love to watch chefs make ice cream *tempura* for dessert.

Tempura is often served as a set meal, *teishoku,* with rice, soup and pickles but you can also order it a la carte (*ippin*). *Tempura* shops sometimes also sell *tendon,* shrimp *tempura* in a bowl of rice topped with a sauce. Usually sitting at the counter and ordering a la carte is more expensive than ordering a set.

Tempura teishoku	*Tempura* set with a variety of fried fish and vegetables and rice, pickles and soup
Tendon	Fried shrimp on a bowl of rice
Kakiage	*Tempura* cutlet made with shrimp, scallops and vegetables

EVERYTHING IS NOT ALWAYS WHAT IT APPEARS TO BE/#1

One of our favorite remarks from a visiting friend goes something like this: "If you want my honest opinion, Japanese have a lot to learn about making pickles." Heinz or Vlasic they're not, but Japanese pickles have their own unique taste and charm. Japanese always serve pickles and rice at the end of a meal. Give them a try and you may never eat kosher dills again.

YAKINIKU

Yakiniku (grilled meat) is a Japanese version of Korean food. Meat is marinated in a soy-garlic, hot-pepper mixture and grilled at the table.

Some shops still use charcoal braziers, but most use high-tech, built-in gas grills with an internal fan to whisk away the smoke.

Yakiniku is spicier than Japanese food and has a big following among young people. *Yakiniku* restaurants also serve Korean vegetables and sometimes Korean soups. Some *yakiniku* restaurants offer *teishoku*, especially at lunch. The *teishoku* includes rice, soup, vegetables, and pickles. But usually in the evening you order a la carte. Make sure you order vegetables as well as meat and rice to eat with it.

After you order, the staff will turn on your grill and bring plates of raw food. You can control the temperature of a gas grill, with charcoal you are out of luck. When the food is cooked, put it in the plate of dipping sauce. We like to put the meat and vegetables on top of our rice and eat the two together.

Food for grilling:

Karubi	beef from the rib
Rosu	lean beef
Hire	beef fillet
Reba	beef liver
Tan	beef tongue
Buta rosu	lean pork
Chikin	chicken
Nasu	eggplant
Shiitake	mushrooms
Yasai moriawase	assorted vegetables
Yakiniku teishoku	set meal

Other:

Kimuchi	kimchi, spicy pickled cabbage
Namuru	marinated vegetables such as sprouts and spinach
Kuppa	meat and vegetables in a rice and egg drop broth
Wakame soup	seaweed soup

COFFEE SHOPS & CAFES

For a tea-drinking country, the Japanese love their coffee. Coffee houses are everywhere; many serve an expensive cup of coffee in smoky surroundings, but for the price of one cup, you can spend the entire day; no one will ask you to leave. Some people use coffee shops as their offices and classrooms, conducting business and giving lessons. Coffee shops are warm in winter and cool in summer while people's apartments may not be.

In a classic coffee shop, coffee is expensive, running between ¥400 and ¥800, and there are no refills. Some places have elevated the coffee making process to an art and produce a superb cup. Others are fairly mediocre. There's a new breed of inexpensive coffee-shop chains (Pronto, Veloce) that produce a decent cup of coffee at a reasonable price (about ¥180). It's fast-food coffee, you order at a counter; there's also a self-serve baked-goods counter. Starbucks has arrived, but it doesn't look like traditional coffee establishments are going out of business.

Most coffee shops serve some food, usually toast, sandwiches, pilaf and curry rice. Coffee shops are a great place to eat breakfast with their **morning service**. No, it has nothing to do with church. In the morning from about 8am until 11am, there's a special deal when you get coffee or tea, toast and salad, and sometimes a hard-boiled egg, all for around ¥500.

Here's some basic coffee shop vocabulary:

Kohi	generic coffee
Burendo kohi	blended coffee, usually the standard
Amerikan kohi	American coffee, usually weaker
Uinnaa kohi	Viennese coffee (with whipped cream)
Moka kohi	Mocha coffee
Kafe ore	cafe au lait
Aisu kohi	iced coffee
Esupuresso	espresso
Kapuchino	cappuccino
Kocha or *tii*	tea such as Lipton's
Miruku tii	tea with milk
Remon tii	tea with lemon
Aisu tii	iced tea
Miruku	milk
Kokoa (hotto, aisu)	cocoa (hot, iced)
Remon sukkashu	lemon squash
Orenji jusu	orange juice
Koka kora	coca cola

Coffe shop food:

Pirafu	pilaf
Kare raisu	curry rice
Hamu sando	ham sandwich
Yasai sando	vegetable sandwich
Mikkusu sando	mixed sandwich: ham, tuna, cucumber, lettuce
Tosuto	toast (often about three slices thick)

NABE, SHABU-SHABU & SUKIYAKI

Nabe is a one-pot stew cooked at your table, usually in a ceramic pot. This winter fare is often eaten at home but available in restaurants also. It's different from a stew in Western cooking because *nabe* uses a thin broth and the food cooks quickly. The simmering broth is brought to the table along with fish or meat and vegetables, tofu and clear noodles. You cook your own food. At the end of the meal, noodles or rice cakes are put into the flavorful broth which you drink as a soup.

Yose-nabe	stew with vegetables and fish or chicken
Dote-nabe	oyster stew
Ishikari-nabe	salmon stew, a Hokkaido specialty
Udon-suki	*udon* noodles stew

Shabu-shabu is a *nabe* variation very popular with foreigners. You cook razor thin slices of beef, vegetables and tofu in a broth in a copper pot and then dip them in a sesame or soy sauce. Many restaurants serve an all-you-can-eat menu *(tabe hodai)* that satisfies the meat cravings of many an international visitor. *Shabu-shabu* is relatively expensive because beef isn't cheap. The price depends on the type of beef: American is cheapest; then generic Japanese beef; then Matsuzaka; then Kobe; the latter two are premium beefs.

Sukiyaki is another beef dish popular with international visitors. *Sukiyaki* evolved as a Japanese dish after eating beef was introduced at the end of the 19th century.

Thin slices of beef, vegetables and tofu are sautéed with a sweet soy sauce in an iron skillet at the table. The waitress cooks *sukiyaki* for you. At Japanese homes, cooking *sukiyaki* is invariably the father's duty.

Chanko-nabe is stew eaten by sumo wrestlers and is also available in special restaurants. Sumo wrestlers eat large quantities to give themselves bulk, but in small servings the food is certainly not fattening. Traditionally the meat of four legged animals like beef or pork wasn't used to make *chanko-nabe* — it reminded the wrestlers of being on their hands and knees, that is, losing a bout.

Sakana-chanko	stew with fish
Toriniku-chanko	stew with chicken

TEPPANYAKI

Teppanyaki is food cooked on a steel grill. It can be very downscale where you cook it yourself (usually at a *okonomiyaki* restaurant) or upscale where chefs cook the meal before your eyes. Benihana of New York raised *teppanyaki* to a theatrical art, but in Japan, it's usually a fairly subdued dining experience. Because *teppanyaki* generally involves beef, it's a fairly expensive meal and can be exorbitant at hotel and other top restaurants.

The chef will usually ask you if you want your meat *wafu* style (soy sauce flavored) or *miso* sauce flavored.

Teppanyaki	usually comes as a set and includes meat and vegetables, rice, soup and pickles and sometimes grilled ice cream.
Saaroin suteiki	sirloin steak
Tendaroin suteiki	tenderloin steak
Hire suteiki	fillet

CURRY

Lovers of Indian curry will not recognize the Japanese version, a thick mild curry sauce with a few specks of meat served with rice and red ginger pickles. It's copied from English curry, which is more sweet than spicy, which fits the Japanese palate. Curry is fast food and a favorite among students looking for a cheap, filling meal. Actually, we have to admit that it grows on you.

Chikin kare	chicken curry
Bifu kare	beef curry
Pooku kare	pork curry
Hayashi kare	hashed beef curry

ODEN

Oden, skewers of fish and vegetables stewed in a broth, is winter fare and a favorite of *yatai*, the night stalls set up in cities. Even convenience stores have pots of *oden* on their counters in winter — it's the ultimate Japanese fast food.

There is some regional variation in ingredients but the main ones are:

Atsu age	blocks of deep fried tofu
Fukuro	fried tofu pouch filled with vegetables
Ganmodoki	tofu patty with bits of vegetables
Konbu	kelp seaweed
Daikon	giant radish
Konnyaku	gelatinous cake made from a tuber
Shirataki	white noodles made from a tuber
Tamago	hard boiled egg
Tsukune	chicken meat balls
Gobo	burdock root
Dango	fish cake in a ball
Satsuma age	fried fish cake, sometimes with bits of vegetables
Hanpen	a white, spongy fish cake
Tako	octopus

UNAGI

Unagi is freshwater eel and the dish is especially popular in the heat of summer because it's supposed to give stamina. Usually the eel is dipped in a heavy soy sauce, barbecued on charcoal and served over rice. Tradition has it that to promote his friend's business, Hiraga Gennai, a weird Edo period scholar, promoted the idea that *unagi* should be eaten on the day of the ox in summer (around July 20) to combat the heat. It's also supposed to improve virility so you may find more men than women eating it.

Una don	Grilled eel served over rice in a bowl
Unaju	Grilled eel grilled served over rice in a lacquer box
Unagi teishoku	Eel over rice, soup and pickles
Unagi no kabayaki	Eel grilled on skewers
Shira yaki	Eel grilled without the thick sauce

DONBURI

Donburi is Japanese fast food eaten by people in a hurry. It's cooked and served over rice in a large bowl. Its low price makes it popular with students. A number of chains, such as Yoshinoya with its bright orange signs, sell it along with some noodle shops and other inexpensive eateries.

Gyu-don	Sautéed beef and onions over rice
Oyako-donburi	Sautéed chicken with a soft omelet and onions over rice
Katsu-don	Breaded and fried pork cutlet on rice with a soft omelet on top
Tendon	Fried shrimp over rice with sweetened soy sauce

YOSHOKU - WESTERN FOOD, JAPANESE STYLE

Yoshoku is Japanized Western food that developed after the Meiji Restoration in 1868 when Japan was fascinated with anything Western, including food. This hybrid cuisine is rather strange to Western visitors. Some of the classic dishes are omelets filled with rice and served with ketchup and gratins that are mostly cream sauce. As a cuisine, *yoshoku* is fading fast, being eclipsed by more authentic Western food. While young people now flock to Italian trattorias and French bistros, older folks still enjoy eating this comfort food.

Some of the offerings are:

Omuraisu	omelet wrapped around rice
Korokke	croquettes

OKONOMIYAKI

Okonomiyaki is often called pizza, but the only thing in common is a round shape. *Okonomiyaki* is most popular in the Osaka to Hiroshima corridor, although restaurants can be found all over Japan. The name literally means "cooked as you like it." You usually cook it on a grill at your table, cooking the bits of meat, seafood and vegetables held together with a thin pancake batter. You can season the finished product with green seaweed powder, bonito flakes, red pickled ginger or mayonnaise. *Okonomiyaki* restaurants usually also serve *yakisoba*, grilled noodles, which you also cook yourself. It's almost always an inexpensive meal, costing around ¥1000.

You order your meal by choosing the ingredients you want:

Gyuniku	beef
Buta	pork
Ika	squid
Tako	octopus
Yasai	vegetables
Mikkusu	mixed (usually all of the above)
Yakisoba	stir fried *soba* noodles (can choose above ingredients)
Yaki-udon	stir fried *udon* noodles (can choose above ingredients)

ROBATAYAKI

Robatayaki restaurants are casual and lively places where guests sit at a counter and the cooks, kneeling in front of a charcoal grill surrounded by platters of vegetables, fish and meat, prepare food as you watch. Ordering is easy – simply point at the food you want and about five minutes later, it will come to you freshly grilled. The waitresses and cooks will shout out your order so the whole experience is noisy and cheerful.

Drinking beer and *sake* are as much of the experience as eating the food. While *robatayaki* restaurants seem like they should be fairly inexpensive, some are very pricey.

KAMAMESHI

On the plastic food displays, you may notice rice cooked in an iron kettle set into a wooden box. This is a *kamameshi* restaurant. Rice is topped with meat, vegetables and/or seafood and steamed until cooked. When you are served, stir the ingredients into the rice until it resembles stir-fried rice.

Gomoku meshi	five ingredients, usually vegetables, shrimp and chicken
Tori meshi	chicken

Sake meshi	salmon
Ebi meshi	shrimp
Takenoko	bamboo

VEGETARIAN CUISINE

Until the mid-19th century, Buddhism prohibited eating meat so the traditional Japanese diet consisted of fish, vegetables and grains. Even today, vegetarians can easily find something to eat in most Japanese restaurants.

Zen Buddhist temples raised vegetarian fare to an art. Called *shojin ryori*, it relies primarily on vegetables, tofu, *miso* bean paste and wheat gluten. Since it's a lot of work to prepare, *shojin ryori* tends to be expensive. One variation is *fucha ryori*, vegetarian temple food with a Chinese influence. Heavier sauces are used and food is served from large platters, rather than in individual portions. Kyoto and Mt. Koya are good places to sample vegetarian temple food although restaurants can be found in Tokyo and other large cities.

KAISEKI

Formal Japanese cuisine served at important occasions is known as *kaiseki*. Originally it was a meal served after the tea ceremony, which helps explain why quantity has never been of prime importance. The emphasis is on using seasonal foods and the freshest ingredients available. Beautifully arranged on individual ceramic dishes that are chosen to reflect the nature of the food, the meal is as much a feast for the eyes as it is for the stomach. Eating *kaiseki* is similar to eating one appetizer after another. Although the amounts are small, you realize how full you are by the 8th or 9th course. *Kaiseki* tends to be expensive because of its labor-intensive preparation and the high cost of ingredients. Try it at lunchtime when it costs less or better yet, stay at a Japanese inn, *ryokan*, where dinner is included in the room rate. The best *ryokan* stand as excellent restaurants in their own right.

There is no standard *kaiseki* menu. The set meals are named individually by restaurants, but you choose by price. A typical meal consists of a starter, *sashimi,* a dish of grilled food, *nimono* (steamed vegetables), a vinegared dish, clear soup (to cleanse the palate), fried food such as *tempura,* rice and pickles.

IZAKAYA - DRINKING PLACES

Izakaya are casual pubs popular for after-work get-togethers. They serve beer, *sake* and usually whiskey and *shochu,* a strong liquor usually made from sweet potatoes, as well as a variety of foods to accompany the beverages. Not potato chips, but substantial food to make a dinner of it. Usually you order a number of dishes and share with your group. *Izakaya* tend to be fairly inexpensive.

Many are chains with branches all over the country, such as Tengu (logo is red mask with long nose), Tsubohachi and Murasaki. While *izakaya* menus are almost always written in Japanese, the chains have menus with a lot of pictures. If they don't, use our food guide.

Remember, if your neighbor is eating something interesting, point discreetly to his food and tell the waiter *"Onaji no onegai shimasu."*

Important note: If you see a sign for a place that says pub but looks unwelcoming, don't go in. Many small, exclusive Mama-san bars call themselves pubs.

Yakitori	grilled chicken on skewers
Tsukune	chicken meat balls on skewers
Niku jaga	potatoes stewed with bits of meat and onions
Hiya yakko	cold tofu
Age dashi tofu	fried tofu in a sauce
Tofu suteiki	grilled block of tofu
Guriin sarada	green salad
Tsuna sarada	tuna salad
Wakame su	vinegared seaweed
Harumaki	spring rolls
Eda mame	young boiled soy beans, don't eat the pod; especially good with beer
Kara age	deep fried morsels of chicken
Yaki nasu	grilled eggplant
Yose nabe	one pot stew: fish, seafood, chicken, vegetables (winter only)
Ika somen	thin strips of raw squid
Sashimi moriawase	assorted *sashimi* (slices of raw fish)
Miso shiru	*miso* (fermented bean paste) soup
Onigiri	rice balls filled with pickled plum *(ume)*, salmon *(shake)* or cod roe *(tarako)*
Yaki onigiri	grilled rice balls, outside is crunchy like rice crispies
Ochazuke	rice with tea poured over it and flavored with plum *(ume)*, salmon *(shake)*, seaweed *(nori)*, or cod roe *(tarako)*
Zosui	thick rice soup flavored with egg *(tamago)* or chicken *(tori)*

FAMILY RESTAURANTS

Names like Denny's and Royal Host may sound familiar, but did you think you could ever order *miso* soup or *tonkatsu* in one? The family restaurants are all over Japan and while the atmosphere is similar to their American cousins, both Japanese and Western food are served.

The food is predictable and uninspired but will do in a pinch. These casual eateries are good for kids because they offer a wide variety of food and have high chairs and a large dessert menu with a lot of dressed-up ice cream. No one minds if your kids are a little noisy; Japanese kids are noisy too.

Western food in family restaurants leans towards spaghetti, hamburger steak, pilaf and salads. Japanese food is heavy on the cutlets and noodles. Prices are reasonable; coffee has unlimited refills; and there are usually smoking and nonsmoking sections. The menu may be written in Japanese only, but pictures of everything make ordering a cinch.

WESTERN & ETHNIC RESTAURANTS

In addition to the many types of Japanese food, cities have many foreign restaurants serving French, Italian, German, American, Mexican, Chinese, Thai, South Asian and other types of food. Some of the top French and Italian restaurants can hold their own against any in the world. The recent popularity of Italian food has put a trattoria on almost every city street corner.

Over the last few years, there has been a boom of restaurants serving ethnic food sometimes devoted to one cuisine, but more often having a cross section of South and Southeast Asian food. The spiciness of these other cuisines is often toned down for the Japanese palate.

JAPANESE SWEETS

In urban areas you'll see patisseries selling beautiful cakes and pastries. Then you'll pass a Japanese sweet shop and everything looks so unusual. Since the procedure for making sweets is so complicated, Japanese do not make them at home. Instead Japanese buy them in shops, preferably in a nice old shop that has been producing sweets for generations.

Japanese sweets don't use butter or flour; most use sweetened beans and rice pounded into a dough. Yes, they are virtually fat free, but not low calorie.

Sweets are eaten in the afternoon with green tea. Japanese do not eat sweets for dessert; if they have anything at all, it will be a small piece of fruit. Don't be disappointed when you are served three strawberries or a thin slice of melon on a lacquer dish. Chocolate cake after a Japanese dinner is unheard of.

We like to pick up some sweets and have a snack when we get back to our hotel room. Although you may think it's strange to eat beans as a sweet, give it a try. They grow on you.

Yokan	a gelatin made from beans and served in slices
Mitsumame	cubes made from agar-agar, and mixed with fruit and beans
Anmitsu	agar-agar cubes, sweet bean paste, fruit and beans
Gyuhi	sweetened *omochi*, pounded rice cakes
Zenzai	warm sweetened beans with pounded rice cakes
Warabimochi	jellied cube made from *kuzu* root and coated with bean flour
Higashi	a dried sweet made of sugar taken with bitter green tea
Namagashi	bean paste sweets shaped into flowers in season, often eaten as a second "course" at tea ceremony

TEA

Foreigners may think that all Japanese tea is the same, but there are many different varieties. Restaurants usually serve complimentary *o-cha*. In Japanese restaurants, you'll have to ask for water: "*Mizu o kudasai.*"

O-cha	Generic name for Japanese tea
Hoji cha	Roasted tea, brown color, no caffeine
Mugi cha	Barley tea, served chilled in summer
Matcha	Powdered green tea, used in tea ceremony
Genmai cha	Tea made from tea leaves and roasted brown rice

BARS

Most Japanese eateries have a limited drink menu (but not a limited supply!). Beer, *sake*, whiskey and sometimes *shochu* are standard. If you would like something more exotic, you'll have to go to a bar.

There shouldn't be any trouble finding one in entertainment districts and hotels in large cities. In rural areas, you're out of luck.

Japanese love the bottle-keep system. In Japanese society, everyone (well, almost everyone) wants to belong to a group and what better way than having your own bottle at a bar. In most bars you'll see bottles lined up on shelves on the walls. If you'd like to do the same, here's how the system works. You purchase a bottle the first time and, at the larger bars, receive a membership card. At the small places, they just know you. Then, when you come back, you pay a small set-up charge for ice and soda water.

In bars, they will have the mixed drinks you're familiar with at home. You can order in English but put a Japanese spin to it so the bartender will understand. For instance, gin and tonic becomes "jin tonikku."

One word of warning: drinking can be expensive in Japan. Even in average bars, mixed drinks run ¥1000 and up and more in hotel bars.

BENTO SHOPS

Bento, literally meaning lunch box, is the Japanese answer to sandwiches. They are the ultimate fast food and are popular at lunchtime as well as for an inexpensive dinner. Usually included are rice, meat or fish, vegetables, salad and pickles. At *bento* shops you can often buy instant soup as well as small portions of salad. They're also available at many chain stores such as Hoka Hoka, but usually mom and pop operations – often part of a meat store – have better food. It isn't gourmet cuisine, but it's good and the price is right.

Bento are popular to eat when traveling, and stations on long-distance train lines will have at least one stand selling *bento* with regional specialties. The prepackaged boxes are even stamped with their assembly time. It's unlikely they are more than a few hours old. For health reasons, *sushi* with raw fish is not sold.

Some popular *bento* are:

Katsu	bento with *tonkatsu,* breaded and fried pork cutlet
Shogayaki	sautéed slices of pork, ginger and onion
Kara-age	morsels of chicken dipped in batter and deep fried
Hanbaagaa	hamburger
Chikin teriyaki	chicken sautéed in a sweet soy sauce

FAST FOOD

Western fast food is everywhere. McDonalds, Burger King, Wendy's and Arby's are around as are homegrown versions like Lotteria and First Kitchen. But none is a carbon copy of their American cousins. You can find familiar Big Macs, but they have also tailored their offerings to suit the Japanese palate. When was the last time you ordered a *matcha* (green tea) shake or a *teriyaki* burger at a McDonalds? How about a soy burger at Mos Burgers or a grilled rice ball at KFC (Kentucky Fried Chicken)? Where else could you buy a squid and corn pizza at Dominos?

Fast-food outlets run pretty much the same way they do in America. You order at the counter, pay, and take your food either to a table or outside. When you belly up to the counter, the staff person mumbles something quickly to you in Japanese. They are most likely asking *"Kochira de meshi agarimasu ka?"* meaning "Are you going to eat here?" Say *"Hai"* for yes or, if you want to take out, say *"Motte kaerimasu."*

The menu posted over the counter will most likely be in Japanese, but don't let it intimidate you. On the counter itself are menus with pictures. Fast-food joints like to package sets: you get a hamburger or some other item with french fries and a drink for a slightly cheaper price than buying them separately. Morning set is about ¥390 and includes burger, fries and drink.

If all else fails, remember fast food has English names, so just say hamburger, fries and coke with a Japanese accent, and you'll be understood.

DEPARTMENT STORES

In your quest for good food, don't overlook the department stores. Almost all have a variety of restaurants selling reasonably priced food on the top floor. These restaurants are nothing like the greasy spoons some department stores have back home. Many are branches of well-known restaurants. Department store eateries tend to have generous plastic food displays, making ordering a cinch. Be forewarned that they tend to be crowded at lunch time, so lines are not uncommon. Most restaurants in department stores stay open past the store's closing hour, so you don't have to eat an early supper. If you are unsure of where to eat, you can always find a good place in a department store.

You must go down to the food floors in the basements of department stores. You'll find counters selling baked goods, bread, meat, fish, *bento*, Chinese, Japanese, Western and South Asian prepared food, *yakitori*, *tempura*, *sushi*, *tonkatsu*, *oden* stew, fruit, Japanese and Western sweets, tea and pickles. It's a feast for the eye and great entertainment. You can buy prepared food and take it back to your hotel or eat it outside. Many stalls also give samples. Unless you're shameless, you probably can't make a meal of the samples, but it will take the edge off your hunger.

One warning: while the *tempura* and fried cutlets look great, if they aren't eaten piping hot, they tend to be greasy.

BAKERIES

Many bakeries produce high-quality bread far superior to anything you find in an American supermarket. In addition to plain bread, they make bread filled with cheese, bacon and other fillings suitable for lunch. Every department store has a bakery on its food floor. In rural areas, the offerings may be limited to prepackaged items.

Bakeries are always self-service. As you enter, take a tray and tongs, make your selections, and carry them to the cash register. You will probably find bread stuffed with potato, cheese, or bacon. Many bakeries sell sandwiches, usually on soft, crust-free white bread, but occasionally on rolls or brown bread. Japanese love mayo-laden sandwiches with unlikely ingredients such as potato salad, macaroni salad or strawberries. The possibilities are endless.

Bakeries also sell donuts, but beware, many an unsuspecting foreigner has bought a jelly donut only to bite in and find curried tuna or bean paste. If an object appearing to be a jelly donut has fried crumbs on the surface, it's probably a curry donut. If not, it's probably filled with bean paste.

You'll find drinks and individually portioned salads in a refrigerator case, so it's easy to find an entire and inexpensive meal in a bakery.

If you have a yearning for a jelly donut, Mr. Donut seems to have branches near the train station of every sizable city.

EVERYTHING IS NOT ALWAYS WHAT IT APPEARS TO BE/#2

A recently arrived American friend prepared her husband's lunch as she'd always done in the US. He hungrily opened his bag and was thrilled to see what he assumed was his favorite – a peanut butter and jelly sandwich. From his first big bite, he knew something was really wrong and spit it out immediately. It looked like peanut butter, but what had happened to its taste? He carefully wrapped his sandwich and took it home for further investigation.

When he presented it to his wife, she was rather surprised to see it again and to hear his tale of woe. Trying to figure out what was wrong, together they carefully examined the peanut butter in a plastic container that she bought at a local grocery. The following day, a Japanese friend solved the mystery – what they both thought was peanut butter was, in fact, light miso paste!

CONVENIENCE STORES

Seven-Eleven, Lawsons, AM-PM and other convenience stores are nearly everywhere except in remote villages. You can get an inexpensive meal here. Amongst the wide array of products are *bento* meals, sandwiches, hard-boiled eggs and instant noodles. Most have Chinese buns called *man* warming on the counter. Meat-filled dumplings are called *niku-man;* sweet bean-paste filled are *an-man*. In winter they may have a pot of *oden*: fish cakes and vegetables simmering in broth. All you need to do is point to what you want and the clerk will pack up everything to go.

When you buy a *bento* at a convenience store, the cashier will ask you *"Atatame masu ka?,"* "Do you want it heated?" Say *"Hai"* for yes, *"Ii desu"* for no. Somewhere on the counter, there's usually a thermos of hot water for making instant noodles. If you don't see it, ask *"Oyu?"*

Convenience stores sell instant coffee; one kind is packaged with a cup, creamer, sugar and a stirrer. Great coffee it isn't, but if you're desperate for coffee after a night in a Japanese inn, it will do the trick.

In addition to food, convenience stores are mini community centers. They have copy machines, fax machines (usually you can send only domestically), delivery service pick-up, and sell telephone cards and stamps. They're open until late in the evening or 24 hours.

EVERYTHING IS NOT ALWAYS WHAT IT APPEARS TO BE/#3

Another newly arrived friend was making pastry early on a Thanksgiving morning. How early was it? Too early to disturb a neighbor to borrow a couple of eggs to finish her pies. Undaunted, our heroine jumped on her Japanese housewife's bicycle and raced to a nearby convenience store where she bought two neatly-wrapped plastic containers holding two eggs each. "Only in Japan," she thought.

Back again in her kitchen and ready for anything, she gently tapped the first egg on the edge of the counter; nothing happened. She tapped a little harder; again nothing happened. Finally she banged the egg as hard as she could only to discover she'd bought hard-boiled eggs. "Only in Japan," ran through her mind again and again as she giggled about the experience while finishing her early morning project about noon.

VENDING MACHINES

It seems there are more vending machines than people in Japan. They are everywhere, often two or three side by side, across the street from another half-dozen. The good news is there's no reason to go thirsty. The bad news is they add nothing to the decor.

The majority of vending machines sell soft drinks, but you can also find ones purveying cigarettes, batteries, fast food (complete with microwave), rice, snacks, film, disposable cameras, condoms, movies tickets, beer, whiskey and *sake*.

Drink machines sell hot and cold canned juice, soda, coffee, tea, Japanese tea, and sometimes soup. The standard price is ¥120, but it is higher in hotels and resort areas. Sometimes "hot" and "cold" are written in English on the vending machine. When the signs are in Japanese only, heated drinks will have a red stripe under them and chilled drinks will have a blue one. With typical Japanese efficiency, in winter half a vending machine sells heated drinks while in summer the machines are adjusted so nearly all drinks are chilled.

Japanese are addicted to canned coffee and a single vending machine may stock as many as 10 different varieties from black to cafe-au-lait. You'll also find cocoa and a number of teas, including English tea, green tea, barley tea and oolong tea. Sports drinks, with names like Pokari Sweat and Aquarius vie with soda, juice, yogurt drinks (our favorite brand name is Calpis) and other concoctions. On most cans, there's something in English to identify its contents but, if you can't find anything, chances are the drink is either Japanese or Chinese tea.

PLASTIC FOOD

Japan has so many different kinds of restaurants and many have menus written only in Japanese. This could mean that you'd either have to do a lot of pointing at other diner's meals (hoping that they are eating something appealing) or you'd be stuck eating at hotels or tourist restaurants. But fortunately, Japanese invented plastic food. Lots of restaurants have colorful displays in their windows. Just a glance will tell you what type of food the restaurant serves and usually the price. Gesture for the waiter or waitress to come to the display to order your meal.

Several words of warning:

• Displays of stew-pot type meals such as shabu-shabu and nabe will often show the quantity of food served to two people, but the price listed is per person.

• Avoid eating in restaurants where the plastic food is dirty and faded. If the restaurant doesn't care how it looks to the public, chances are the kitchen doesn't care either.

Making plastic food is an art perfected in the postwar era. At first the models were made of wax, but they melted in the hot sun. Now made of molded plastic, they are remarkably realistic representations. You can buy some to take home, but they are not cheap. Pieces of sushi cost about ¥500 each; a bowl of noodles is ¥4000; and a complicated food display can run in the tens of thousands. Several shops in the Kappabashi district in Tokyo sell them. We have a friend who puts a sunny-side-up egg on her living room carpet to see guest's reactions. Actually, not all the food on display is plastic. A friend, telling his visiting girlfriend about plastic food, touched the daily special on display outside a restaurant to illustrate his point. Turns out it was real food. What a surprise! And he was trying to impress his girlfriend with his knowledge of the local culture.

11. JAPAN'S BEST PLACES TO STAY

Japan's wide range of hotels, inns and lodges adds to the allure of any trip. As in most countries, you'll find the full spectrum of accommodations from deluxe international hotels to youth hostels. But in Japan, traditional inns provide another layer. They range from ¥100,000 per person a night for luxury accommodations with personal service to small family-run inns at about ¥4500 per person where you put out your own bedding. To enjoy your stay at a Japanese inn, you will need to shift from Western cultural expectations of hospitality, fine dining and accommodations to those of the Japanese. Staying at a traditional inn adds a uniquely Japanese dimension to your trip.

Of all the different places we stayed, we'll always cherish the memory of our unique experiences at this handful of inns and hotels.

ATARASHIYA, *Yuwaku Onsen, Kanazawa, 920-1122. Tel. (076)235-1011, Fax (076)235-1024. ¥18,000 per person with two meals. Credit cards only with prior arrangement.*

There is nothing intrinsically special about Atarashiya. It's located on the Japan Sea about 30 minutes outside the city of Kanazawa in a hot spring area. Constructed of freshly cut blonde wood, the fairly casual building belongs to the architectural style inspired by teahouses. Although the building itself is new, the inn has a 250-year history. The setting isn't particularly grand. Although foothills are nearby; the inn is in a flat valley, near rice fields and next to a barn where mushrooms grow.

But everything combined to make a most memorable stay for us. We were caught in Kanazawa traffic and wouldn't arrive until 7pm. We called to let them know we indeed were on our way. You have to know that most Japanese inn owners start biting their nails if you haven't checked in by 5pm — after all, dinner is waiting. No problem, we were relieved to hear. When we arrived and were shown our room, the proprietress suggested we soak in a hot spring bath before dinner, which meant she knew we wouldn't eat dinner until 8pm. And the staff was cheerful about it. In most inns, the kitchen help has gone home by 8pm.

Served in a wing of private dining rooms, dinner was divine. Course after course arrived with cold foods ice cold and warm foods piping hot: seasonal appetizers, fresh *sashimi* from the nearby Japan Sea, delicate *chawan mushi* custard, crispy *tempura*. Each course was beautifully served on ceramic and lacquer plates. Our waitress informed us that the owner's first love is cooking. As if we couldn't guess.

The building's architecture adds to the feeling of serenity. The simple yet tasteful hallway makes a few turns as you walk to your room; the soft glow of lanterns lights the small indoor rock gardens and your path. Simple Japanese-style guest rooms, with sliding *shoji* doors, provide an oasis of peacefulness, and at bed time, the staff prepares each room for the night by laying out *futon* and warm fluffy quilts.

Atarashiya's two hot spring baths, one for each sex, hold about ten people each, but we had one to ourselves. From the bath, the large picture window overlooks trees backed by a bamboo fence.

Now we are looking for an excuse to return to Atarashiya.

CHUJIKAN, *2036 Fuegashima, Miyagi-mura, Seta-gun, Gunma, 371-1100. Tel. (0272)83-3015, Fax (0272)83-7522. From ¥10,000 per person with two meals. Credit cards.*

For a great getaway from Tokyo, Chujikan can't be beat. The small rural inn features outdoor hot spring baths overlooking a deep ravine and waterfall and serves delicious country fare. Chujikan takes its name from an Edo period Robin Hood who hailed from this area. Kunisada Chuji robbed the rich and shared his booty with the poor. Each of the inn's 13 guest rooms bears the name of one of Chuji's followers.

Chujikan was recently rebuilt in a traditional rural style. The result is the best of both worlds, an authentic building containing amenities you would expect to forego: central heating and air conditioning plus private toilets. Attention was paid to the authenticity of every detail of this farmhouse-style building including the long sloping roof, which resembles its thatched relatives. Beams crisscross the high ceiling of the corridor leading to the guest rooms. Dark wood is used throughout, giving a much more rustic feel than the blonde wood usually favored in Japanese buildings. The hallway's dark wooden floors glisten. Throughout the stucco walls are a light cream color, and farm implements decorate the entryway.

Unlike most Japanese inns, you do not wear slippers in Chujikan. Instead guests are provided with soft white *tabi* socks to wear with a cotton *yukata* robe.

Meals are served in a Japanese-style central dining room where guests sit at low tables. Before dinner, the cheerful cook explains what she has prepared. Her love of food is obvious and shows in her eyes when she appears to serve her finished products. Dinner is good mountain fare including *sashimi* of river fish, mountain vegetables, *tempura* and locally raised steak you grill at your table. The day we were there, the cook served special fern fritters which she made from perfect tender ferns she found in her garden.

Another highlight at Chujikan is the outdoor hot spring baths, one for men and one for women, side by side but separated by a bamboo fence. The stone baths have stunning views of the deeply wooded ravine and waterfall. At night basket torches light the baths and powerful lamps illuminate the waterfall. But this being Japan, the men's bath affords a better view of the waterfall.

HOTEL IL PALAZZO, *3-13-1 Haruyoshi, Chuo-ku, Fukuoka, 810-0003. Tel. (092)716-3333, Fax (092)724-3330. Singles from ¥13,000. Doubles from ¥22,000. Credit cards.*

Il Palazzo, designed by Italian architect Aldo Rossi and five other architects, breaks the mold for Western-style hotels. Situated in the heart of a love hotel district, Il Palazzo provides the ultimate in high-Milan style. The design has nothing to do with Japan, but is a fabulous monument to postmodern architecture.

The building's windowless facade, with its accentuated horizontal steel beams and marble pillars, resembles a warehouse in New York city's Soho. But the real treat awaits you inside the lobby. Featuring a red mahogany ceiling, it's a delightful place to sit and watch people as they come and go. The light smell of garlic wafting through the air is from the adjacent Ristorante and entices you to eat Italian fare, which was marvelous.

Four theme bars flank the hotel, each done in a unique and brazen design. Be sure to check out the decor in each one, but go into the one with the unpronounceable Russian name, Oblomov, to see roses encased in lucite pillars and enjoy a drink.

The hotel offers seven floors of guest rooms with only 12 rooms per floor. The modest size rooms are done in striking mahogany and an almost spartan-like Milan style. And, the windows open all the way .

HORAI, *750 Izusan, Atami, Shizuoka, 413-0002. Tel. (0557)80-5151, Fax (0557)80-0205. From ¥41,000 per person with two meals. Credit cards.*

Mt. Horai is the Buddhist depiction of heaven. Its namesake's inn recreates an idyllic paradise on earth. Situated high on a hill above Sagami Bay in Atami on the Izu Peninsula, Horai's superb location sets it apart from other deluxe Japanese inns. Each of the 16 rooms of this elegant Japanese inn features an entire wall of *shoji* screens that open to offer stunning views of the bay.

Stay at Horai for a delightful retreat. Take time to appreciate the simplicity, beauty and attention to detail found not only in the physical surroundings, but also in the meals served in your room, your personal attendant's thoughtful service and the pervasive presence of mother nature.

The experience of staying at Horai is heightened by journeying down the many steps and corridors to the open air hot spring bath located much closer to the water. With so few guest rooms, you can find a time to relax in total privacy surrounded by views of nature.

Horai awaits you less than an hour from Tokyo on the *shinkansen* train. While it is pricey, splurge for an experience you will remember for a long time.

PARK HYATT HOTEL, *3-7-1-2 Nishi Shinjuku, Shinjuku-ku, Tokyo, 163-1055. Tel. (03)5322-1234, Fax (03)5322-1288. US and Canada toll free: 800/233-1234. Rooms from ¥48,000. Credit cards.*

Perched high atop the 52-storied Shinjuku Park Building, high tech meets high hospitality. The architecturally stunning hotel floats above Tokyo, setting a new standard for luxury hotels.

The Park Hyatt creates a warm, small-hotel atmosphere in a postmodern skyscraper by successfully dividing the grand public spaces and restaurants from the guest rooms. Guests use a private internal elevator to reach their floors and check in and out in a small, living room-like area. The 178 guest rooms, the largest in Tokyo, sport contemporary furniture and large windows to maximize the stunning views. The oversized, opulent bathrooms feature both a tub and a shower. Equipped with two telephone lines, a fax machine, dataport and voice mail, the guest rooms readily double as offices.

The public areas are equally grand. Three glass pyramids top the skyscraper. The elevator whisking you to the 41st floor opens onto the four-storied glass pyramid of the Peak Lounge and Bar; the view is incredible. During the day, enjoy tea and light meals overlooking the sprawling city. When the sun goes down, the lounge transforms itself into a glittering candle-lit space with the lights of Tokyo forming a nightscape.

The second glass pyramid provides one of the most magnificent settings for a health club anywhere. Swim in the 20-meter pool and work out on the exercise equipment under the glass dome with Tokyo spread out in front of you.

The third and largest pyramid houses the chic New York Bar and Grill, one of Tokyo's most popular restaurants. In the evening, enjoy live jazz in the bar. The restaurant, serving continental fare, pulsates with the excitement of the Big Apple.

The two-storied Kozue Restaurant serves refined Japanese cuisine in a contemporary setting. The wooden decor provides a warm ambiance, and all tables have a view of Mt. Fuji — at least on the days when Mt. Fuji allows itself to be seen.

The Park Hyatt provides an oasis high above the hustle and bustle of Tokyo.

TAMANOYU, *Yufuin Onsen, Oita-gun, Oita, 879-5197. Tel. (0977)84-2158, Fax (0977)85-3541. From ¥35,000 per person with two meals. Credit cards.*

Set in the woods, Tamanoyu is one of the most delightful inns we have encountered. Innovative architecture and Japanese folk art combine to provide a refined and elegant retreat. The main building is a low structure with a long, sloping tiled roof and glass doors — a successful mixture of California and Japanese architecture. The extensive use of wood brings the outdoors inside. The 18 guests cottages are connected by a wooden covered walkway.

Ironically, folk art adds a sophisticated touch in both the public spaces and the guest rooms. Bed quilts made from *kasuri,* an indigo and white ikat weave, grace the rooms. The same fabric, under glass, covers the bathroom countertops where fluffy towels are piled high in round, hand-woven bamboo baskets. Japanese *washi* paper covers delicate light fixtures. The guest rooms are Japanese style although some have an additional room with Western beds.

Dinner is served on blue and white and other folk art plates. Our dinner included grilled chicken, a medley of seasonal vegetables and *miso* soup. The sherbet for dessert was delicately flavored with *yuzu,* a Japanese citrus. Upon request, Tamanoyu will serve a Western breakfast, complete with homemade jam.

Yufuin is a hot spring resort town and Tamanoyu takes great pride in its baths. Each cottage has a wooden tub and the room has large windows looking into the woods. But if you really want to get even closer to nature, the communal baths, one for women and one for men, await you outdoors.

Tamanoyu is pricey but cannot be beat for a complete getaway.

YOSHIKAWA INN, *Tominokoji, Oike sagaru, Nakagyo-ku, Kyoto, 604-8093. Tel. (075)221-5544, Fax (075)221-6805. 13 rooms. From ¥30,000 per person with two meals. Credit cards.*

A night at Yoshikawa caps off any trip to Kyoto. This traditional wooden inn in central Kyoto provides warm hospitality and enables you to experience the refined Kyoto lifestyle.

Constructed in *sukiya* style, the low building evolved from tea ceremony architecture and emphasizes unity with nature. The small lobby has a hearth and is decorated with two antique *bunraku* puppets. Many of the rooms look out at the large, well-kept garden. The rooms themselves are simple Japanese style with wooden ceilings, plaster walls, sliding *shoji* screens covering the windows and woven *tatami* mats on the floor. Yoshikawa is an island of tranquillity in the middle of Kyoto.

Yoshikawa distinguishes itself by its personalized service. The *kaiseki* dinner is served in your room, and the attendant brings course after course made with the freshest seasonal ingredients. Since Yoshikawa is also a *tempura* restaurant, dinner climaxes with crisp *tempura* just plucked from the frying pan. Yoshikawa also offers *shabu-shabu* for dinner.

For a relaxing bathing experience, the bathrooms feature wooden tubs made from cypress.

YOYOKAKU, *2-4-40 Higashi Karatsu, Karatsu, 847-0017. Tel. (0955)72-7181, Fax (0955)73-0604. Rates from ¥15,000 per person with two meals. Credit cards.*

Staying at Yoyokaku is one of the delights of visiting the small town of Karatsu, a pottery-making center by the sea. Yoyokaku is a stone's throw from the water's edge, but don't visit this exquisite Japanese inn expecting to find a beach resort. Its focus is inward to provide a memorable retreat featuring traditional Japanese hospitality.

Yoyokaku's street face is a simple Japanese building with deep eaves and a lattice wooden front. This urban streetscape belies the rambling inn and spacious garden on the inside. The large hanging lantern in the entryway casts a soft glow over the roughly paved stone floor that leads to the quiet reception area. Covered walkways connect the lobby with the guest rooms. Each room offers a different vista of a garden filled with delicately pruned pine trees that are left in a more natural state than in a typical Japanese garden. Sago palms add a tropical feel.

Dinner is served in your room, and you have a choice of either *kaiseki* or *shabu-shabu*. Unless you can't live without meat, we urge you to order *kaiseki*, a delightful profusion of seasonal dishes arranged on beautiful plates and bowls. Although we were there in autumn, a green maple leaf decorated our freshly grilled fish and a lid with the pattern of red maple leaves covered a delicate fish stew. Breakfast is served in a communal dining room; you have the choice of traditional Japanese fare or coffee, toast and eggs.

Mr. Okouchi, the proprietor, speaks English. He has a small gallery at the inn where he displays and sells the works of Nakazato Takashi, a potter who may have made the dishes you used at dinner. Yoyokaku provides warm hospitality in a friendly environment.

12. TOKYO

Tokyo, as electric as the neon that lights up Ginza, Shinjuku and Shibuya, is filled with energy and excitement. We find it one of the most dynamic and exhilarating cities in the world.

Today, Tokyo has 12 million inhabitants but that tells only a part of the story. Right next door is Yokohama, Japan's second most populous city. The metro area has a combined population of 25 million people, one of the largest on the planet. It's no wonder we feel as though the entire populace is trying to get on the same train during the rush hour.

Although Tokyo is a huge, crowded place, it's a city of neighborhoods. Most people live in low-rise housing, shop near their homes and know their neighbors and merchants. We've divided Tokyo by districts and urge you to choose several different areas to spend your time in rather than rushing from sight to sight. You'll come away with a better feeling for the city as a whole.

Tokyo is perpetually in a state of flux. Buildings constructed a mere twenty years ago are demolished to make way for something newer, bigger, better. One of Tokyo's great strengths is its willingness to innovate, whether it be in food, fashion or architecture. New restaurants seem to spring up overnight. French cafes, Italian trattorias, California Asian cuisine and Southeast Asian food have been part of the last few waves, but something new is always around the corner. Architectural experiments abound and many are even sponsored by the city government.

The young are walking monuments to the latest trend, be it brown hair, green hair, bell bottoms, slouch socks or platform shoes. Well-dressed middle-aged Japanese women, the new leisure class, spend their days eating lunch with their friends, going to museum exhibitions, department stores and concerts. And we can't forget the legions of Japanese businessmen, wearing the mandatory gray or blue suits, always off to their next appointment.

Tokyo steamrolls over its past to come to something new. It is not a museum town like Kyoto. When Tokyo set out to build a museum to

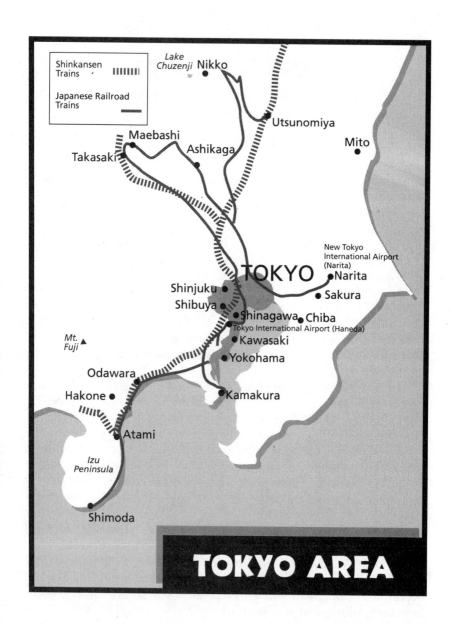

Shinkansen
Trains

Japanese Railroad
Trains

Lake
Chuzenji Nikko

Utsunomiya

Mito

Maebashi

Ashikaga

Takasaki

New Tokyo
International Airport
(Narita)

TOKYO

Narita

Shinjuku

Sakura

Shibuya

Shinagawa Chiba
Tokyo International Airport (Haneda)

Mt.
Fuji

Kawasaki

Yokohama

Odawara

Hakone

Kamakura

Atami

Izu
Peninsula

Shimoda

TOKYO AREA

immortalize its past, it built a high tech building resembling something from *Star Wars*. Most buildings are Western style; most people wear Western dress; and coffee houses are filled with people drinking cafe au lait.

But despite the city's Western facade, people still retain an essential core of Japaneseness. Wearing Western clothing, living in Western-style buildings and eating Western food does not mean Japanese are just like Americans or Europeans. Traditional aesthetic sensibilities still abound: traditional Japanese restaurants are constructed in modern office buildings; *ikebana* flower arrangements adorn hotels, restaurants and private homes; and small Shinto shrines are built on the rooftops of office towers. People take time to go to gardens and temples simply to view whatever flower is in season.

Tokyo is a gourmet's dream. Among the thousands of restaurants from stand-up noodle shops to exclusive *ryotei*, where dinners may cost ¥50,000 per person, is something for every palate and every pocketbook.

Tokyo doesn't have world-class sightseeing attractions like the Tower of London or the Louvre. Amazingly, its two most popular destinations are Disneyland and Tokyo Tower, an imitation Eiffel Tower. You didn't come all this way to see either one.

Instead, Tokyo is a city to be experienced: visit the fish market at 6am to see the tuna auction; spend a couple of hours in a department store watching people as they go about their daily lives; and be part of the swirling mass of commuters in Shinjuku or Tokyo stations during rush hour. The avant-garde thrives alongside traditional performing arts like *kabuki* and *bunraku*. And top orchestras, opera companies, rock stars, jazz musicians and dancers all put Tokyo on their itineraries today.

Tokyo's charms are not immediately apparent when you approach the city by bus or train from Narita Airport or arrive on the *shinkansen* train. The city is built on a large, flat plain that is covered with nondescript, gray buildings as far as the eye can see.

But don't be put off by the vast expanse of gray buildings or the idea that sometimes the sidewalks are so crowded that an ant wouldn't have a chance. Tokyo is unique. Seek out the special places: a tiny museum with exquisite works of art, a quirky music club, a *yakitori* bar under the tracks and a three year-old dressed in formal kimono at a temple.

With little violent crime, Tokyo has to be one of the safest cities in the world. We walk without concern any time of the day or night.

Get ready to explore of one of the world's most unusual cities.

History

Tokyo began as **Edo**, a fishing village where the *daimyo* (feudal lord) **Ota Dokan** built his castle in the 15th century. It remained a backwater until 1590 when Toyotomi Hideyoshi awarded the fiefdom to **Tokugawa Ieyasu**. After Hideyoshi's death, Ieyasu consolidated power and had himself named shogun in 1603. He found Edo to be the perfect place to rule Japan — far from Kyoto, home of the imperial court, and on the large and fertile Kanto plain. Ieyasu built his castle on the site of Ota's.

In the Tokugawa era, Japan closed its doors to the outside world. Edo grew rapidly in this peaceful and prosperous milieu. As a means of control, all of Tokugawa's samurai lived in Edo as did the families of the feudal lords. The feudal lords themselves alternated between their domains and Edo. When you include the retainers of the feudal lords, some half-a-million samurai spent at least a part of the year in Edo. Naturally, the number of merchants, artisans and laborers grew in order to provide services for the population. By the 18th century, Edo had over one million residents and ranked among the largest cities in the world.

The Tokugawa's castle was the grandest in Japan. The city itself is set up as a typical castle town. The labyrinth of dead end roads was designed to confuse an attacking army. Unfortunately, to this day, it confuses residents and visitors alike. The residences of the feudal lords and samurai were to the northwest, west and south of the castle in a belt ringing the hills called **Yamanote**. The commoners lived on reclaimed land east of the castle that became known as *shitamachi,* literally, low city.

As the Edo period went on, the samurai class grew more and more impoverished and dependent on the increasingly wealthy, but still bottom-of-the-social-ladder, merchants. Although the Tokugawa shogunate issued many decrees in an effort to control the merchant class, ways were found around them. For instance, merchants were forbidden to wear silk so they wore clothing with rough cotton on the outside but lined with fine silk. Merchants had restrictions on the number of stories in their houses, but the interior didn't always match the exterior. Because of these restrictions, the aesthetic that blossomed had a veneer of restraint.

Perhaps because of the restrictions, an exuberant popular culture flourished and people flocked to *kabuki* theater and the pleasure quarters where they were entertained by *geisha* trained in music and dance as well as worldly pleasures. Woodblock prints, *ukiyo-e,* literally pictures of the floating world, captured the excitement of the scene.

By the middle of the 19th century, the Tokugawa shogunate had run out of steam. **Commodore Matthew Perry** sailed his black ships into Tokyo Bay and demanded that Japan open its doors. The shogunate eventually complied but couldn't take the stress of the new era. A movement of lower-ranking samurai from far-off western Honshu and Kyushu toppled the government; and in 1868 the Meiji Emperor was restored to power. The new capital, renamed Tokyo (Eastern Capital), became the residence of the emperor ending Kyoto's 1100 year tenure as the capital.

Rapid modernization and industrialization followed. New Western-style buildings became fashionable — some wooden, others brick. One particularly famous building, the Rokumeikan, was the scene of many balls where Japanese dressed in formal Western attire. At this time, *haikara* (high collar) came to mean anything Western and intellectual — Western shirts with high collars were such a contrast to open-collared kimono. People poured in from the countryside to work in the new factories, and Tokyo's population grew.

But there were setbacks along the way. The **Great Kanto Earthquake** in 1923 struck at mid-day while lunch was being cooked on charcoal braziers. Huge conflagrations destroyed neighborhoods of dense wooden houses, and when the smoke cleared, 140,000 people had perished and half the city was in ruins. Tokyo rebuilt and within a decade was back to its prequake levels. Again, during World War II, Tokyo was nearly flattened by American air raids. In one night over 100,000 people died. After the war, the city sprang up again.

Tokyo is the pulse of modern Japan. Not only are the Diet and government ministries based here, but it's also the center for the banking and financial industry, the big trading houses, the fashion and retailing industry, music and the arts and on and on. Because the government plays a central role in industrial planning, even corporations based in Osaka and Kyushu feel the necessity to maintain large offices in Tokyo. Rural Japanese have gravitated to the cities in search of a better life.

As the population has increased, Tokyoites have been forced to live further and further from the city center. Many have long commutes on packed trains; one and a half hours each way is not uncommon. The national government continues to discuss decentralization and moving all or part of its offices to another city, but we'll believe it when we see it.

The emperor lives on the Tokugawa's castle grounds in what is now called the Imperial Palace. While Tokyo is no longer a castle town, it has some remnants. Tokyo's convoluted road system, a holdover from the castle era, makes the city difficult to navigate. One of the major Japanese newspapers, the *Asahi Shimbun*, divides its metro news coverage into Jonan, Johoku, Josai and Joto — literally, south, north, west and east of the castle.

Planning Your Stay - Tokyo Itineraries

We recommend that you wander through Tokyo's many neighborhoods to get the most from the city. We've structured Seeing the Sights to assist you in each area. Before you set off, look at the current *Tokyo Journal* or a newspaper that lists the wide variety of cultural and art

TOKYO HIGHLIGHTS

• *Viewing the city from the top of the Metropolitan Government Building in Shinjuku*
• *The walls and moats of the Imperial Palace*
• *A stroll through Korakuen Garden or Rikugien Garden*
• *The electronics stores in Akihabara*
• *The neon signs lighting up Ginza, Shibuya and Shinjuku*
• *Eating yakitori under the tracks near Yurakucho Station*
• *Seeing the tuna auction at dawn at Tsukiji Market*
• *The postmodern buildings especially the Tokyo International Forum and Opera City*
• *Serene Meiji Shrine*
• *Stopping in for a one-act kabuki performance at Kabuki-za*
• *Asakusa, a lively area which still retains some of old Edo's atmosphere*

offerings available. It might help you to determine which area you choose to visit.

We have divided Tokyo into 18 areas:
1. Around the Imperial Palace
2. From Ginza to Nihonbashi
3. From Tsukiji to Roppongi
4. Asakusa
5. Ueno
6. Yanaka
7. Akihabara and Kanda
8. Asakusabashi, Ryogoku, Fukagawa and Kiba
9. Shinagawa and Meguro
10. Ebisu
11. Shibuya
12. Harajuku and Omotesando
13. Aoyama and Akasaka
14. Shinjuku
15. North of the Imperial Palace
16. Ikebukuro
17. Tokyo Waterfront
18. Outskirts

If your stay in Tokyo is really limited, we've drawn up a couple of itineraries to help you enjoy your visit.

HANGING OUT AT NARITA?

Unless you have at least an eight-hour layover between flights at Narita Airport, don't come into the city. See the Narita Airport section in Chapter 6, Planning Your Trip, for close-to-the-airport suggestions.

For a daytime layover, take the Keisei train to Ueno Station and visit Ueno Park. To see three different aspects of Tokyo that are all located in the park, stop at the National Museum, the Shitamachi Museum and Toshogu Shrine. Then walk through the Ameyoko market, south of the park, for a view of everyday life.

For an evening layover, take the Narita Express train (NEX) to Tokyo Station. At Tokyo Station, change for the JR Yamanote line and go one stop south to Yurakucho Station. Under the tracks a few blocks south of the station are the hole-in-the-wall yakitori restaurants where you can eat some grilled chicken, drink some beer and sit shoulder to shoulder with half of Tokyo's work force. Then walk east and see the glitzy Ginza area all decked out in lights.

One (Very Full) Day

If you only have one day in Tokyo, it's really a shame, but here's how we would spend one very full day.

If you are jet lagged and wake up early, go to the Fish Market in Tsukiji where the tuna auction begins around 5am. Explore the retail shops outside the market itself. Have *sushi* for breakfast at one of the many shops in the area or hop a taxi to a Ginza hotel — the Ginza Tokyu has a nice café for a Western breakfast if raw fish doesn't do it for you in the morning. Walk through the Ginza district, but not too early because most of the shops don't open until 10am. Make sure you go into one of the big department stores such as Mitsukoshi or Matsuya.

Take a taxi to Hama Rikyu Garden (except on Monday when it's closed) for a stroll in one of Tokyo's best gardens and jump on the ferry up the Sumida River to Asakusa. Have a late lunch in the Asakusa area; see the Asakusa Kannon Temple and buy your souvenirs from the shops along the Nakamise arcade. Eat dinner at Nanbantei or Honmura-an in Roppongi. If you can still keep your eyes open, go to Roppongi, Shibuya or Shinjuku to see the lights and the nightlife.

Two Days

Day 1: Go to Asakusa to see the Kannon Temple and the shops in the area. Take the ferry to Hama Rikyu Garden. Then walk over to Ginza, taking in one act at the Kabuki-za. Explore Ginza and walk west to the Imperial Palace and go into the East Garden.

Day 2: Start your day at Meiji Shrine; then walk around Harajuku stopping at the tiny Ota Museum to view its woodblock print collection. Walk along Omotesando and stop at the nearby Nezu Museum and garden. If you still have energy, walk to Shibuya.

ARRIVALS & DEPARTURES

By Air

Narita Airport: Arriving from overseas, you're almost sure to land at Narita Airport, an inconvenient 60 kilometers outside central Tokyo. See Chapter 6, Planning Your Trip, for airport and ground transportation information.

Haneda Airport: Almost all domestic flights arrive at Haneda Airport, technically called Tokyo International Airport. Haneda is on Tokyo Bay, between Tokyo and Yokohama, and offers convenient connections via monorail to central Tokyo. The recently built terminal is spacious and airy.

Direct train service is now available from Haneda to Shinagawa Station on the Keihin Kyuko line. Fare ¥400.

The Tokyo Monorail takes 23 minutes from Haneda to Hamamatsucho Station where you can connect to Japan Rail (JR) Yamanote loop line and the JR Keihin line. Fare ¥470.

Limousine bus connects Haneda Airport with Akasaka area hotels (45 minutes, ¥1000); Ikebukuro area hotels (60 minutes, ¥1100); Narita Airport (75 minutes, ¥3000); the Rinkai Fukutoshin area hotels (15 minutes, ¥500); Shinjuku Station and area hotels (50 minutes, ¥1200); Tokyo City Air Terminal (25 minutes, ¥700); and Tokyo Station (40 minutes, ¥900). If you have a lot of luggage, it's easier to take the bus than to carry your luggage on the train.

Car rentals are available from the major companies at Haneda Airport, but don't even think of driving in Tokyo.

By Train

All the Tokaido shinkansen trains arriving from western Japan terminate at Tokyo Station. Some shinkansen trains heading north terminate at Ueno Station while others continue on to Tokyo Station. Unless you are going to be staying in the Ueno area, take a train that stops at Tokyo Station; it's more central and has many train lines to make connections. Your shinkansen ticket can be used to travel to any JR station within the JR Yamanote loop.

Long-distance express trains (not shinkansen) terminate at Tokyo, Ueno and Shinjuku stations. All are stops on the JR Yamanote loop line, so you can easily get to all parts of the city from any of these stations.

Local commuter lines terminate at the following stations on the JR Yamanote loop line: Gotanda, Ikebukuro, Meguro, Shibuya, Shinagawa, Shinjuku, Tokyo and Ueno.

By Bus

A series of highway buses, including overnight buses, connect Tokyo with other cities. Buses are almost always cheaper than trains but can be much slower. For instance, the shinkansen train takes you to Kyoto in 2 hours 45 minutes and costs ¥13,220. The bus takes 7 hours and costs ¥8180.

The main long-distance bus stations are at Tokyo Station (Yaesu exit), Shinjuku Station (West exit), Ikebukuro Station and Shinagawa Station. JR Pass holders can use JR buses, but the vast majority of the highway buses are run by private companies.

By Car

Arriving in Tokyo, you'll use one of the expressways that converges at a ring road called the Shuto Expressway. At this point all traffic comes to a grinding halt if it hasn't already done so about 20 or 30 kilometers outside the city. Traffic is so bad that it's sheer madness for visitors to drive into Tokyo.

ORIENTATION

Tokyo is a large, sprawling city on **Tokyo Bay**. With the exception of some new waterfront developments, Tokyo turns its back to the bay. The city of 12 million stretches out further than the eye can see and connects to neighboring cities and towns forming one great big urban sprawl.

Fortunately, Tokyo has an efficient subway and train system. The roads are particularly difficult to figure out; only the large thoroughfares have names. The Japanese word *dori* means street or avenue.

There are many busy commercial districts. The **Imperial Palace** is in the center and lends some greenery to a city that doesn't have a lot of park space. The business and financial districts of Marunouchi and Otemachi are east of the palace as is **Ginza**, the famous shopping area. Government ministries are concentrated in Kasumigaseki, due south of the palace. Major commercial centers have developed in Shinjuku, Ikebukuro and Shibuya, all on the JR Yamanote train line that loops around the central city. Asakusa and Ueno, northeast of the palace, are areas that retain some of the traditional aspects of old Tokyo, Edo.

Addresses are a world unto themselves and maps are an absolute necessity. Tokyo has 23 wards called *ku*. The wards are divided into districts. Large districts are divided into two or more sections called *chome*. Blocks each have a number and buildings within the block have a number.

Addresses are written 4-3-2 Roppongi or 3-2 Roppongi, 4-chome. What this means is the building is in the 4th *chome* of Roppongi, on block three and in building two. Good luck finding it. Even cab drivers have difficulty finding places. Always ask your host or a restaurant to fax a map to you at your hotel or else you may wander indefinitely. Ask for a landmark building. If you are really desperate, go to the closest police box. Neighborhoods often have maps posted showing every block in the district.

HOW'S THE WEATHER?

The average year in Tokyo has 180 days of fair weather, 102 cloudy days, 80 rainy days, and 3 snowy days. Tokyo and Washington, D.C. enjoy similar climates and seasonal changes. Autumn begins in late September and lasts until early December; the weather is crisp and dry. Winter is pleasantly sunny with brilliantly clear skies and mild temperatures. Spring starts in March with rain and sometimes wet snow as well as gusty winds from the Asian continent. Humidity rises as spring turns into summer. Rainy season runs from early June through mid-July. It's called tsuyu or plum rain because the plums ripen with the rain. High humidity and high temperatures make Tokyo almost unbearable in late July and August. Just when we think we'll never be cool again, the autumn breezes begin in September. July through October is the typhoon season; Tokyo usually experiences two or three a year.

What about Mt. Fuji? In an average year, the elusive mountain is clearly visible from Tokyo 54 days and faintly visible 25 days. You have a better chance of seeing Japan's highest peak in the winter when the skies are clearer.

GETTING AROUND TOWN

Subways and trains are the most efficient ways of getting around town because you don't get stuck in traffic. A good map is essential, and the one put out by the **Japan National Tourist Organization** (JNTO) is one of the best. In addition to covering the central city, there is a subway map and a suburban train map.

For more detail, *Tokyo: A Bilingual Atlas,* is excellent and available in hotel bookstores and stores stocking English books.

On Foot

Tokyo is best seen on foot. If you race from place to place, it's really difficult to get a good feel for the city. Instead, choose a specific area, take the subway to it and explore on foot to your heart's content. Just make sure your shoes are comfortable.

Subway & Trains

A great rail system whisks you around town. The trains and subways are clean, fast, inexpensive, run every few minutes and are unbelievably reliable. It's true that you can practically set your watch by them, and, incredibly, the transit authority even posts a schedule. Trains start running about 5:30am and continue till around midnight. You'll find the times of the first and last trains posted outside entrances to the stations.

Tokyo subways and trains are a source of disbelief to jaded New Yorkers. Upholstered seats, overhead racks for packages, signs alerting you the train is arriving, markers on the platform floor indicating where the doors will open, arrival announcements, and graffiti-free trains and stations are taken for granted by the Japanese. On the other hand, the crowded rush-hour trains, especially between 8 and 9:30am, can really get your day off to a miserable start.

Subway maps and information are on the internet at *www.tokyometro.go.jp*.

PACKED LIKE SARDINES

The Japanese expression **sushi zume**, *the equivalent of "packed like sardines," means made like sushi. A sushi chef slaps rice and fish together without a millimeter of air between them. To a passenger aboard a packed rush-hour train, a can of sardines looks positively spacious. Men have been known to arrive at their offices with lipstick stains on their suit jackets – souvenirs from poor female commuters pushed up against their backs.*

Each subway line has an identifying color; it's painted as a stripe on the train and the signs have a circle of that color. By following these colors, it's easy to make connections.

Several different transit systems serve Tokyo. The subway itself, called *chikatetsu* (literally underground train), has two systems: **Eidan** and **Toei**. You can ride within each system on one ticket, but you must pay a double fare to connect. You can buy a special ticket that allows you to transfer between the two systems for a slight savings. At the ticket machine counter, there's a fare map for these connections, but it is almost never translated into English.

Then there are JR trains that run above ground. The **JR Yamanote** is a loop line that circles central Tokyo. Other JR lines run east/west, radiating out of central Tokyo like spokes of a wheel. Subways and JR lines require two different fares.

Additionally, there are private lines that run from the suburbs to Tokyo. They usually terminate at a station on the Yamanote line but, to make things really confusing, sometimes they continue into Tokyo as subways. If you connect from private lines to subways or JR, you must pay two fares but the fares can be put together on the same ticket.

All the trains run on a zone system and fares are based on distance. For the subway, ¥160 is the minimum fare and will usually carry you four or five stops. The fare rises to ¥190 for five to about nine stops and ¥230 for ten to about 15 stops.

Purchase your ticket at the ticket machines. Both subways and JR trains have two kinds of machines; the older machines flat against the wall, and the new machines that protrude at an angle. The angled machines are bilingual, so it's easier to use them. They accept ¥1000, ¥5000 and ¥10,000 bills. If the station has only the older machines, look at the top to see if they take large bills. The station attendant will break a large bill.

A fare map in Japanese is posted on the wall above the machines. Most of the subway stations and some of the JR stations have English-language fare maps, usually beside the machines. If you cannot figure out the fare, buy a ticket for the minimum amount and pay the difference to the clerk at the gate when you get off.

Before you go onto the platform, insert your ticket in a computerized gate; make sure you remember to pick up your ticket; keep it in a safe place because you have to present it when you exit.

The subway sells a stored-value card called **SF Metro Card** that is available in denominations of ¥1000, ¥3000 and ¥5000. JR has a similar card called IO (pronounced e-o) for ¥3000 and ¥5000. Make sure you don't buy a JR Orange Card — they are good only for buying tickets from a machine.

The stored-value cards are really handy for visitors because you don't have to figure the fare; you just put the card in the ticket gate machines both entering and exiting, and the correct fare is automatically deducted. If you forget to take your ticket out of the machine, a bell will ring to remind you. You can also use these stored-value cards to buy individual tickets from the machines.

There are also passes for unlimited travel, but unless you are going to do a lot of moving around Tokyo in one day on the trains, it's less expensive to buy point-to-point tickets. The different plans are as follows:

· **Tokyo Free Kippu Ticket**. ¥1580. Good for one-day travel on the JR trains, Toei subway trains, Toei buses and Eidan subway trains. Buy the pass at JR stations and major subway stations. You can't use it on JR express trains. You must buy the pass at a ticket booth.

- **Tokunai Free Kippu Ticket**. ¥730. Good for one-day travel on the JR trains within Tokyo's 23 wards — generally within the JR Yamanote line loop and a few stations farther out.
- **Toei One-day Economy Pass** *(Ichi nichi joshaken)*. ¥700. Good for one-day travel on the Toei subway line, Toei buses and Toei streetcar. Available at subway stations. The Toei subway has only a few lines, so this pass isn't useful to most visitors.
- **TRTA (Eidan) Subway One-day Open Ticket** *(Ichi nichi joshaken)*. ¥710. Good for one-day travel on TRTA subways. Buy the pass at subway vending machines that accept the Metro card. If it's one of the machines that's angled out from the wall, the button for the pass is marked in English.

Private lines tend not to have fare maps in English, so buy the minimum fare and pay the difference when you exit. Even though most stations are computerized, there's always an attendant.

Children under six ride the trains free of charge; ages six through eleven are half-price, rounded up to the nearest ¥10. Some fare machines have a button marked *kodomo* and "children," others have the half-price buttons below in red, behind a clear plastic protector. Lift the plastic to buy a ticket.

LOOPING AROUND TOKYO

*The **JR Yamanote** line circles central Tokyo. A complete loop takes one hour. There are two lines – one running clockwise, the other counterclockwise. Eventually you'll arrive at your destination even if you get on the wrong one.*

The Yamanote is not the fastest way around town. It makes 29 stops, but it is convenient because every station except three connects with at least one subway or train line. Since the Yamanote runs above ground, some suggest taking it all the way around to get a feel for the city. But, frankly, you won't see much of the city because of all the buildings near the tracks.

You'll rarely wait more than a few minutes for a train. Cars get so crowded during the rush hour that some trains have cars with folding seats. During the morning rush hour, you're not allowed to sit, which makes it easier to pack in more people.

Buses

Tokyo's extensive bus network is not very user friendly. The routes are pretty convoluted and traffic conditions can make the ride slow going.

Route maps are almost never in English. Generally we recommend that you stick to trains and subways.

But if you do take a bus, the fare costs ¥200 – deposit your money in the clear plastic fare box as you enter. The fare machine gives change for ¥500 coins and ¥1000 bills if you put your money in the appropriate slots, not in the plastic box.

Taxis

Getting around Tokyo by taxi is convenient for relatively short trips, but it's much faster to take a train to get across town. The meter usually starts at ¥660 for two kilometers, but with recent deregulation, companies offer slightly different fares. A small number of taxis offer a fare of ¥320 to ¥340 for one kilometer to entice customers who are going only a short distance. There's no additional fee for luggage. Between 11pm and 5am, you pay a 30% surcharge that is reflected in the meter. Remember, no tipping.

Most taxis will take a maximum of four passengers; they'll take five if they don't have bucket seats in the front. Japanese taxi drivers are about as honest as you can get, but they speak almost no English. They turn on the meter automatically, and if they take a roundabout route, it's usually out of ignorance.

Taxis cruise so you only have to raise your arm to hail one. Empty taxis have red lights on the passenger side of the dashboard and at night a roof light is lit. Technically, you are not supposed to hail taxis in crosswalks, but they will stop. Hotels and train stations have taxi queues. If you're having difficulty getting a taxi, go to the nearest large hotel.

Given Tokyo's traffic congestion, most drivers are fairly considerate, so we don't have the cacophony of horns you hear New York. And, you don't have to fear for your life when you step into a taxi.

Make sure you have a map to your destination to give the driver unless you are going to a very famous landmark like Wako Department Store in Ginza for example. And make sure you have your hotel's address card for your return trip. Usually the name of the hotel is the same in Japanese and English, but there are exceptions. If you say, "Imperial Hotel," to a taxi driver, most likely you'll get a blank stare; Japanese call it, *"Teikoku Hoteru."*

Tourist Information

• **Tourist Information Center (TIC):** *B1, Tokyo International Forum near Yurakucho Station, 3-5-1 Marunouchi, Chiyoda-ku, 100-0005. Open 9am to 5pm, Monday through Friday; 9am to 12 noon Saturday. Closed December 29 through January 3. Tel. (03)3201-3331.* Make sure you pick up TIC's excellent map of Tokyo; you have to ask for it. The office has extensive travel information on all of Japan. They tend to give out standard brochures, but if you ask them specific questions, they'll get the information for you. TIC has a Welcome Inn Reservation Center where, once in Japan, you can go in person to request reservations at moderately priced accommodations all over Japan. The reservation center doesn't operate on Saturday mornings.

• **Tokyo Welcome Card**. Check with the Tourist Information Office if there currently are any Tokyo Welcome Card programs. The cards, available free of charge to foreign tourists, offer discounts at hotels, museums, tourist sights and amusement facilities.

• **Teletourist Service**: 24-hour tape recording in English of events in Tokyo: *Tel. (03)3201-2911.*

• **Shinjuku Station**: Information Bureau of Tokyo is located near the East Exit and another one is near the West Exit "i" Tourist Office. *Open 9am to 6pm. Closed Sunday.*

• **Tokyo Station**: Information Bureau of Tokyo is near the Yaesu Exit "i" Tourist Office. *Open 9am to 6pm. Closed Sunday.*

• **Home Visit System**: Call the Tourist Information Center. *Tel. (03)3201-3331.*

• **Goodwill Guides**: Tokyo Metropolitan SGG Club. Contact JNTO Tourist Information, *Tel. (03)3201-3331.*

WHERE TO STAY

Tokyo is chock full of hotels: deluxe hotels, moderately priced hotels, business hotels and budget Japanese inns. No matter what kind you choose, look for a hotel convenient to train or subway lines; otherwise you can spend a lot of time stuck in traffic.

Tokyo's top-of-the-line **deluxe hotels** are on a par with the best worldwide. The international groups — Hilton, Intercontinental, Hyatt, Four Seasons, Westin — are joined by top Japanese names — Okura, Imperial, New Otani— to provide a standard of service for which Japan is famous. Notoriously expensive Tokyo real estate means rooms are often smaller than at similar hotels overseas. This trend is changing because the newer deluxe hotels like the Park Hyatt and Westin Tokyo have larger rooms.

Deluxe hotels offer all the services business travelers expect — translators, secretarial assistance, meeting rooms, shopping arcades and travel agencies. You'll also find standard cable television with CNN and BBC, concierges to assist you, a plethora of restaurants and bars, 24-hour room service, and a pool and sports facilities. One quibble is many of the these hotels charge an additional fee for the sports club and pool.

If you are searching for a deluxe hotel, our advice is to choose one based on location. Frankly, the decor may vary, but they all offer top service and amenities. A deluxe hotel will cost ¥25,000 and up plus a 10% or higher service charge and 8% tax. In this bracket, there's only a minor differential between a single and double room.

Moderately priced hotels are a good option for those who don't need all the amenities of a deluxe hotel. They have at least one or two restaurants on the premises and room service although it probably won't be 24-hour. The room will be equipped with a hair dryer, cotton *yukata* robe, shampoo and toothbrush. Since these hotels tend to be smaller, the atmosphere is more personal. Often in moderately priced hotels, double or twin rooms cost nearly twice as much as a single.

Plan to spend ¥12,000 to ¥25,000 for a twin room in a moderately priced hotel. Expect a 10% service charge and 5% tax, 8% if the room rate is over ¥15,000.

Business hotels cater to Japanese road warriors. Japanese corporations are notoriously cheap so the staff travels on limited budgets. Business hotels offer no-frills accommodations. The rooms are minuscule — we have been in some singles where we could spread our arms and touch both walls — but the rooms are clean and they have private baths though you may have to use a shoehorn to get in. Service is minimal; most serve a breakfast for ¥1000 or under, but there may not be a regular restaurant. Forget about room service; the best you can do is a vending machine for drinks and snacks. Business hotels tend to be in central locations close to train stations. If you view a hotel only as a place to spend the night, staying at business hotels stretches your travel dollar.

Business hotels run between ¥7000 and ¥12,000, and do not add a service charge.

Japanese Budget inns are another alternative. They are simple places providing basic Japanese-style accommodation. The inns are usually small and run by friendly people. Often you won't have a private bath. You tend to find Japanese budget inns in interesting old neighborhoods like Asakusa and Ueno. They are a little far from central Tokyo, but people who choose to stay at them usually find that the atmosphere makes up for the inconvenience. Budget inns cost between ¥4500 and ¥7000 per person, less for two in a room, and do not add a service charge. The doors are usually locked at 11pm or 12 midnight.

No matter what sort of accommodation you wish to stay in, do yourself a favor and make reservations before you arrive Tokyo. You don't want to have the task of finding a place after a long trans-Pacific flight. Tokyo hotels do fill up at times you would never anticipate such as when a large convention is in town. In February, students and their mothers come from all over Japan for university entrance exams, and hotel rooms can be almost impossible to find even in the top price range.

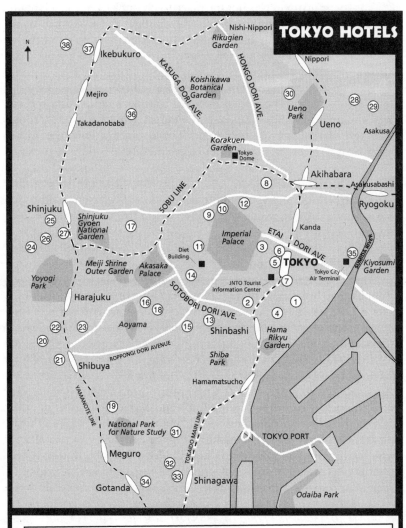

Tokyo Hotels

1. Hotel Seiyo Ginza
2. Imperial Hotel
3. Palace Hotel
4. Ginza Tobu Hotel
5. Tokyo Station Hotel
6. Tokyo Marunouchi Hotel
7. Yaesu Fujiya Hotel
8. Yamanoue Hotel (Hilltop Hotel)
9. Hotel Kayu Kaikan
10. Fairmont Hotel
11. Tokyo Diamond Hotel
12. Kudan Kaikan
13. Hotel Okura

14. Capitol Tokyu Hotel
15. Roppongi Prince Hotel
16. President Hotel
17. Hotel JAL City
18. Asia Center of Japan
19. The Westin Tokyo
20. Creston Hotel
21. Hillport Hotel
22. Shibuya Tobu Hotel
23. Kodomo no Shiro Hotel
24. Park Hyatt Hotel
25. Keio Plaza Hotel
26. Shinjuku Washington Hotel

27. Hotel Century Southern Tower
28. Asakusa View Hotel
29. Ryokan Shigetsu
30. Sawanoya Ryokan
31. Miyako Hotel
32. Tobu Takanawa Hotel
33. Shinagawa Prince Hotel
34. Ryokan Sansuiso
35. Royal Park Hotel
36. Four Seasons Hotel
37. Hotel Metropolitan
38. Kimi Ryokan

Tokyo unfortunately is not the place to try out a traditional Japanese inn. The few Japanese inns in Tokyo are budget accommodations and although acceptable as such, do not have the service, standards and charm of traditional Japanese *ryokan* inns. Save the *ryokan* experience for an out of town trip.

Also missing from the Tokyo scene are intimate, reasonably priced small hotels. Perhaps because the cost of land is so high, most hotels are large and impersonal or small and impersonal with cookie-cutter rooms. Although service may be excellent, Tokyo doesn't have the quirky, eccentric inns found in many other large cities. It doesn't have the grand old hotels either. They were bulldozed long ago in Tokyo's quest for newer, bigger and better.

To help you orient yourself, we list the convenient sightseeing areas to each hotel district, which you'll find later in this chapter in the *Seeing the Sights* section.

Ginza, Hibiya & Marunouchi

The centrally located area east of the Imperial Palace is convenient to shopping and business centers. Transportation is excellent with a slew of subway lines serving the area. This district is convenient to our Seeing the Sights area 1, *Around the Imperial Palace*; and area 2, *From Ginza to Nihonbashi*.

1. HOTEL SEIYO GINZA, *1-11-2 Ginza, Chuo-ku, Tokyo, 104-0061. Tel. (03)3535-1111, Fax (03)3535-1110. US toll free: 800/44-SEIYO; www.seiyo-ginza.com. Doubles from ¥48,000. Credit cards. Ginza Itchome Station.*

If money is no object and privacy and service are your priorities, choose the Hotel Seiyo. This small, luxurious hotel offers a nearly unparalleled level of service including being assigned a personal secretary. The hotel has only 200 rooms and, in place of a lobby, there is a small, tastefully decorated reception room. Hotel Seiyo takes great pride in its opulent and spacious bathrooms that have separate tubs and showers.

2. IMPERIAL HOTEL, *1-1-1 Uchisaiwai-cho, Chiyoda-ku, Tokyo, 100-8558. Tel. (03)3504-1111, Fax (03)3581-9146. Toll free in USA and Canada: 800/223-6800; www.imperialhotel.co.jp. Singles from ¥30,000. Twins from ¥35,000. Credit cards. Hibiya Station or JR Yurakucho Station.*

Legendary service and a great central location make the Imperial a top choice for businessmen or tourists willing to pay the price. Some of the rooms overlook Hibiya Park and the Imperial Palace. Their concierges go to extraordinary lengths to assist you, be it to send flowers to Aunt Mabel in Kansas or track down that Hiroshige woodblock print you can't live without. The business center provides computers and secretarial service; every room has a fax machine. The large lounge in the lobby is filled with businessmen from around the world making deals. One piece of advice: taxi drivers do not know the name Imperial Hotel; you have to tell them *Teikoku Hotel,* its name in Japanese.

The present hotel, which opened in the late 1960s, is on the site of the Frank Lloyd Wright-designed Imperial Hotel. Step into the Old Imperial Bar on the mezzanine floor of the main building for a glimpse of the old masterpiece; the interior was moved from the old hotel. The original lobby has been preserved at Meiji Mura, an open air museum near Nagoya.

3. PALACE HOTEL, *1-1-1 Marunouchi, Chiyoda-ku, Tokyo, 100-0005. Tel. (03)3211-5211, Fax (03)3211-6987; www.palacehotel.co.jp. 393 rooms. Singles from ¥24,000. Doubles and twins from ¥29,000. Credit cards. Otemachi Station.*

The Palace Hotel is a good deluxe hotel in the Marunouchi business district. Relatively small for a luxury hotel, and only ten stories tall, it's an oasis in a district of high-rise office buildings. Located across the street from the Imperial Palace moats, the Palace Hotel has great views of the verdant grounds. Ask for a room facing the palace. Their 10th floor French restaurant, Crown, is one of the best in the city and has panoramic views, but isn't for those on limited budgets.

4. TOKYO RENAISSANCE GINZA TOBU HOTEL, *6-14-10 Ginza, Chuo-ku, Tokyo, 104-0061. Tel. (03)3546-0111, Fax (03)3546-8990; www.tobu.co.jp. 206 rooms. Singles from ¥17,000. Doubles from ¥23,000. Credit cards. Ginza or Higashi Ginza Station.*

We recommend this hotel not only for its great location but also for its personalized service. The room size is larger than most in this class. The restaurants are good but with so many eateries within walking distance, there's no need to eat in. The hotel offers good value.

5. TOKYO STATION HOTEL, *1-9-1 Marunouchi, Chiyoda-ku, Tokyo, 100-0005. Tel. (03)3231-2511, Fax (03)3231-3513. Singles from ¥13,000. Doubles from ¥19,000. Credit cards. Tokyo Station.*

This old-fashioned Western hotel in the station in the heart of Tokyo is often overlooked, but its faded grandeur is perfect for travelers looking for the offbeat. The hotel opened in 1914, the same year as Tokyo Station. The rooms have high ceilings and the tile bathrooms are charming. The long narrow Georgian windows are double sealed so the rooms are quiet. The main dining room's French food is good and offers great station views. And just think, you can leave the hotel just a few minutes before your train's departure.

6. TOKYO MARUNOUCHI HOTEL, *1-6-3 Marunouchi, Chiyoda-ku, Tokyo, 100-0005. Tel. (03)3215-2151, Fax (03)3215-8036. Singles from ¥13,000. Twins from ¥24,000. Credit cards. Tokyo Station, Yaesu exit.*

Marunouchi Hotel is one of the oldest hotels in Tokyo. It has an excellent location in the heart of the Marunouchi business district and is only minutes away from Tokyo Station and a number of subway stations. The old-fashioned hotel is fairly intimate yet offers a variety of restaurants: a French restaurant called The Bamboo, a *sushi* bar, a Kyoto-style Japanese restaurant and a Chinese restaurant. The lobby is on the small side but has a comfortable café called Samurai.

7. YAESU FUJIYA HOTEL, *2-9-1 Yaesu, Chuo-ku, Tokyo, 104-0028. Tel. (03)3273-2111, Fax (03)3273-2180. Singles from ¥14,850. Doubles from ¥17,000. Twins from ¥24,200. Credit cards. Tokyo Station, Yaesu exit.*

Yaesu Fujiya Hotel is just a few minutes walk away from Tokyo Station and a number of subway stations, so it's conveniently located for business and sightseeing. The rooms are on the small side and the decor is nothing to write home about, but it has all the basics.

North of the Imperial Palace

The hotels located close to the Imperial Palace offer pleasant walks around the moat, which doubles as Tokyo's most popular jogging route. The area is convenient to Seeing the Sights areas 1, *Around the Imperial Palace*; area 2, *From Ginza to Nihonbashi*; and area 15, *North of the Palace*.

8. YAMANO-UE HOTEL (HILLTOP HOTEL), *1-1 Kanda Surugadai, Chiyoda-ku, Tokyo, 101-0062. Tel. (03)3293-2311, Fax (03)3233-4567. Singles from ¥15,000. Doubles from ¥22,000. Twins from ¥26,000. Credit cards. Jimbocho Station.*

Built in 1937, Yamano-ue Hotel is one of Tokyo's older hotels and still has a very old-fashioned air. The hotel is on a hill in a district filled with universities, so the atmosphere is very different from the chic veneer of Ginza or Shinjuku. Yamano-ue was a favorite haunt of novelists including Mishima Yukio, who wanted to finish work undisturbed. Rooms with old style wooden furniture are like stepping back into your grandmother's house. On clear winter days, you may be able to see Mt. Fuji and the surrounding mountains. Transportation is convenient: Tokyo Station, Ginza, Ikebukuro, Shinjuku, and Akasaka are within a 10-minute train ride away.

9. HOTEL KAYU KAIKAN, *8-1 Sanban-cho, Chiyoda-ku, Tokyo, 102-0075. Tel. (03)3230-1111, Fax (03)3230-2529. US toll free: 800/421-0000. Singles from ¥14,000. Doubles from ¥21,000. Twins ¥22,000. Credit cards. Hanzomon Station.*

Managed by the Hotel Okura, Kayu Kaikan is a quiet hotel offering good service and food. Known for catered affairs given by government ministries, not many Japanese realize it is actually a hotel. Located only a few minutes walk from Marunouchi, a major business area, we find it convenient for business as well as touring around the city.

10. FAIRMONT HOTEL, *2-1-17 Kudan Minami, Chiyoda-ku, Tokyo, 102-0072. Tel. (03)3262-1151, Fax (03)3264-2476. Singles from ¥11,000. Doubles from ¥20,000. Credit cards. Kudanshita Station.*

This smallish hotel is one of our favorites. It's location, on the north side of the Imperial Palace, is reasonably central yet offers tranquillity and tree-top views. Facing the Imperial Palace's Chidorigafuchi Moat, the rooms look out on cherry blossoms during their short spring season and offer lush greenery at other times. Rumor has it if you want to stay here during the cherry blossom season, you need to make reservations one year in advance! With or without the cherry blossoms, the hotel is cozy yet elegant. Beautiful fresh flower arrangements always adorn the lobby.

11. TOKYO DIAMOND HOTEL, *25 Ichiban-cho, Chiyoda-ku, Tokyo, 102-0082. Tel. (03)3263-2211, Fax (03)3263-2222. Singles from ¥12,000. Doubles from ¥20,000. Twins from ¥24,000. Credit cards. Hanzomon Station.*

Located just one minute from Hanzomon subway station, the hotel is a stone's throw from the Chidorigafuchi Moat, one of the all-too-few open green areas in Tokyo. Their twin rooms are reasonably spacious for the price. Restaurants include Chinese, Japanese, *sushi* bar, coffee bar and a Western main dining room.

12. KUDAN KAIKAN, *1-6-5 Kudan Minami, Chiyoda-ku, Tokyo, 102-0074. Tel. (03)3261-5521, Fax (03)3221-7238. Singles from ¥8500. Twins from ¥15,000. Doubles from ¥16,500. Credit cards. Kudanshita Station.*

One of the few Meiji era hotels remaining in Tokyo, Kudan Kaikan overlooks the Imperial Palace moat. It is a tranquil and cozy medium-sized hotel with basic comforts. Although nothing fancy, the rooms are well kept and the staff is very friendly and helpful. It's close to Kudanshita Station on the Tozai, Shinjuku and Hanzomon subway lines and only a 10-minute taxi ride from Tokyo City Air Terminal.

Akasaka & Roppongi

The districts of Akasaka and Roppongi are centrally located and are filled with restaurants, bars and clubs. This district is convenient to Seeing the Sights areas 3, *Tsukiji to Roppongi*; and 13, *Aoyama and Akasaka*.

13. HOTEL OKURA, *2-10-4 Toranomon, Minato-ku, Tokyo, 105-8416 Tel. (03)3582-0111, Fax (03)3582-3707; www.okura.com. Singles from ¥28,500. Twins from ¥32,000. Doubles from ¥36,000. Credit cards. Kamiyacho Station.*

The Okura is one of Tokyo's best hotels. American presidents and other dignitaries use it as their Tokyo base. The hotel opened in the early 1960s and the lobby has a sort of 1950's Eisenhower charm, low ceilings, retro chairs and soft light filtering in through *shoji* screens. The rooms are fairly standard and are on the small side, given the price. The hotel is enlarging some of its rooms to stay competitive with the newer luxury hotels. Service is extraordinary; the staff jumps through hoops to accommodate the guests. Slightly away from central Tokyo, the closest subway stop, Kamiyacho Station, is about a five-minute walk down the hill.

14. CAPITOL TOKYU HOTEL, *2-10-3 Nagata-cho, Chiyoda-ku, Tokyo, 100-0014. Tel. (03)3581-4511, Fax (03)3581-5822. Singles from ¥23,000. Doubles from ¥30,500. Credit cards. Akasaka Mitsuke Station or Kokkaigijido-mae Station.*

The Capitol Tokyu, one of our favorite hotels, has all the services of a big hotel, but is intimate enough that the doormen know your name by your second day. The hotel used to be a Hilton, but in the 1980s, Hilton moved to a new site in Shinjuku and Tokyu management took over. The understated lobby is always decorated with a huge seasonal floral arrangement; in spring, you find fully opened cherry branches arranged in an enormous bamboo basket; and in autumn, red maple branches mixed with green pines are on display. The lobby looks out on a small, peaceful garden. Located at the top of a hill adjacent to Tokyo's popular Hie Jinja Shrine, it is a superb place to stay for business as well as sightseeing. The good-sized rooms have some Japanese touches such as *shoji* paper screens that give a special softness to the atmosphere.

15. ROPPONGI PRINCE HOTEL, *3-2-7 Roppongi, Minato-ku, Tokyo, 106-0032. Tel. (03)3587-1111, Fax (03)3587-0770. US Toll free: 800/542-8686; www.princehotels.co.jp. Singles from ¥19,500. Doubles and twins from ¥23,000. Credit cards. Roppongi Station.*

Designed by Kurokawa Kisho, an internationally known architect, the Roppongi Prince Hotel is built around an inner court with an open air sky-blue swimming pool in the center. The sides of the pool are transparent so coffee shop patrons have the weird experience of having a fish-eye view of the swimmers — reason enough to make sure we're in shape before swimming here. The hotel has a very postmodern feel with its bright colors and contemporary furniture. It has only 216 rooms. Located just off noisy Roppongi Dori, the hotel is a quiet oasis. It's an especially good choice for someone interested in Roppongi's nightlife since it's an easy walk downhill from the entertainment district.

16. PRESIDENT HOTEL, *2-2-3 Minami Aoyama, Minato-ku, Tokyo, 107-8545. Tel. (03)3497-0111, Fax (03)3401-4816. Singles ¥12,000. Doubles ¥17,000. Credit cards. Aoyama Itchome Station.*

The President offers some of the best, moderately priced accommodations in Tokyo. The hotel has a comfortable, casual feel. All our friends who have stayed liked it and many are repeat customers. The rooms are on the small side; but its good location, around the corner from the Aoyama Itchome subway stop, more than compensates.

17. HOTEL JAL CITY, *3-14-1 Yotsuya, Shinjuku-ku, Tokyo, 160-0004. Tel. (03)5360-2580, Fax (03)5360-2582. Singles from ¥11,000. Doubles from ¥17,000. Twins from ¥18,000. Credit cards. Yotsuya san-chome Station.*

JAL City is a new, moderately priced hotel, a step up from a business hotel. The attractive rooms are larger than in a business hotel and are equipped with trouser presses and hair dryers. Yotsuya san-chome, a stop on the Marunouchi subway line, is only one minute away.

18. ASIA CENTER OF JAPAN, *8-10-32 Akasaka, Minato-ku, Tokyo, 107-0052. Tel. (03)3402-6111, Fax (03)3402-0738. Singles with bath from ¥7500. Twins with bath from ¥10,500. Member of Welcome Inn Reservation Center. Aoyama Itchome Station.*

Asia Center is one of Tokyo's best inexpensive hostels. Located in a quiet area near Akasaka and Roppongi, the Asia Center is convenient to transportation and for sightseeing and shopping. The simple rooms are almost like college dorms, but clean. The atmosphere is very international, and the staff is friendly and helpful. Make sure you book here far in advance because it fills up.

Aoyama, Shibuya & Ebisu

The Shibuya-Ebisu-Aoyama area didn't have many hotels, but this situation has changed with the opening of the Westin Tokyo and a number of smaller hotels. This area is convenient for sightseeing, shopping, eating and entertainment. Seeing the Sights areas 10, *Ebisu*; 11, *Shibuya*; 12, *Harajuku and Omotesando*; and 13, *Aoyama and Akasaka* are close by.

19. THE WESTIN TOKYO, *1-4-1 Mita, Meguro-ku, Tokyo, 153-0062. Tel. (03)5423-7000, Fax (03)5423-7600. Singles from ¥30,000. Twins and doubles from ¥33,000. Credit cards. Ebisu Station.*

Opened in 1994 in the new Yebisu Garden Place, Westin Tokyo offers generous-sized rooms with opulent European-style decor. All the rooms have large desks, and fax machines are available upon request. The hotel exudes a feeling of spaciousness; even the restaurants have lots of elbow room. The many shops and restaurants of Ebisu Garden Place are outside the front door, and Ebisu Station is a five-minute, moving-sidewalk ride away.

20. CRESTON HOTEL, *10-8 Kamiyama-cho, Shibuya-ku, Tokyo, 150-0047. Tel. (03)3481-5800, Fax (03)3481-5515. Singles from ¥13,000. Doubles from ¥19,000. Twins from ¥20,000. Credit cards. Shibuya Station.*

Creston Hotel is a pleasant, tranquil place to stay in the Shibuya area. Although located just a few blocks from the energetic shopping and nightlife center, the streets around the hotel are quiet. The interior is done in soothing, subdued colors. The rooms and bathrooms are relatively spacious for the price. Each room is equipped with an outlet for a fax machine, which you can rent at the front desk. The basement houses a delicious, popular and reasonably priced *shabu-shabu* restaurant called Shabuzen.

21. HILLPORT HOTEL, *23-19 Sakuragaoka, Shibuya-ku, Tokyo, 150-0031. Tel. (03)3462-5171, Fax (03)3496-2066. Singles from ¥11,000. Twins from ¥20,000. Credit cards. Member of Welcome Inn Reservation Center. Shibuya Station.*

Located just a few minutes walk from the south exit of JR Shibuya Station, Hillport Hotel is a reasonably priced family hotel one step up from a business hotel. The work of architect Hara Hiroshi, the stylish marble lobby is especially attractive, and the hotel is artfully designed. The rooms are on the small side, but adequate. The hotel has several "function rooms" with beds that fold into the wall so you can hold meetings during the day.

22. SHIBUYA TOBU HOTEL, *3-1 Udagawa-cho, Shibuya-ku, Tokyo, 150-0042. Tel. (03)3476-0111, Fax (03)3476-0903; www.tobu.co.jp. Singles from ¥12,000. Doubles from ¥16,400. Twins from ¥20,000. Credit cards. Shibuya Station.*

The Tobu Hotel is in the middle of Shibuya's shopping and entertainment district; by walking outside, you have instant entertainment. The rooms are small but cheerfully decorated in pastel colors. Twin rooms are much larger than doubles. It's a good choice for a moderate hotel in an excellent location.

23. KODOMO NO SHIRO HOTEL (CHILDREN'S CASTLE), *5-53-1 Jingumae, Shibuya-ku, Tokyo, 150-0001. Tel. (03)3797-5677, Fax (03)3406-7805. Singles ¥6720. Twins ¥14,280. Credit cards. Member of Welcome Inn Reservation Center. Shibuya or Omotesando Station.*

Children's Castle, an activity center for children from toddlers to high school age, houses a hotel. It's an ideal place to stay with the kids; most guests also have the kids with them. Reservations can be made six months in advance, and it fills up. The hotel is conveniently located close to Shibuya and Omotesando. Stay away from the single rooms because they don't have windows. They also have a few Japanese-style rooms, which kids usually enjoy.

Shinjuku

Shinjuku is home to at least a half-dozen high-rise deluxe hotels that all provide first-rate service and accommodations. Shinjuku is a busy commercial and business center with lots of department stores, restaurants and bars. A dozen train lines go through Shinjuku so transportation is excellent. For sightseeing, refer to Seeing the Sights areas 14, *Shinjuku* and 16, *Ikebukuro*.

24. PARK HYATT HOTEL, *3-7-1-2 Nishi Shinjuku, Shinjuku-ku, Tokyo, 163-1055. Tel. (03)5322-1234, Fax (03)5322-1288. US and Canada toll free: 800/233-1234. Rooms from ¥48,000. Credit cards. Hatsudai or Shinjuku Station, south exit.*

Perched on floors 39 to 52 of the Shinjuku Park Tower Building, the Park Hyatt is an architecturally stunning hotel that seems to float above the city. The three towers of the building have glass atriums and provide incredible panoramic views from the hotel's lounge, swimming pool and New York Grill restaurant. Despite its location, the hotel has only 178 rooms and provides personalized service. The rooms are the largest in Tokyo and come equipped with fax, video and laser disc machines. The large, opulent bathrooms have separate baths and showers.

Selected as one of our Best Places to Stay; see Chapter 11 for more details.

25. KEIO PLAZA HOTEL, *2-2-1 Nishi Shinjuku, Shinjuku-ku, Tokyo, 160-8330. Tel. (03)3344-0111, Fax (03)3344-0247. US toll free: 800/222-KEIO. Singles from ¥16,000. Doubles and twins from ¥24,000. Credit cards. Shinjuku Station, west exit.*

The Keio Plaza was the first high-rise hotel in west Shinjuku. From the upper floors, you're ensured spectacular views through the hotel's large windows. Only a few minutes from Shinjuku Station, it's the closest of the area's hotels. The Lo Spazio restaurant has a stunning, high-Milan interior and serves delicious Italian food. Be sure you have a drink in the Polestar bar on the top floor bar where you'll enjoy a memorable panoramic view.

26. SHINJUKU WASHINGTON HOTEL, *3-2-9 Nishi Shinjuku, Shinjuku-ku, Tokyo, 160-8336. Tel. (03)3343-3111, Fax (03)3342-2575. Singles from ¥13,650. Doubles from ¥17,850. Twins from ¥18,300. Credit cards. Shinjuku Station, west exit.*

This large (1600 rooms) hotel has ship-like portholes for windows. Check-in is completely computerized although there are real people to assist you. Rooms are small, but adequate. Service is minimal: no bellboys and no room service. There are, however, more than a dozen restaurants in the complex. Choose the Washington Hotel for a no-frills stay in Shinjuku.

27. HOTEL CENTURY SOUTHERN TOWER. *2-2-1 Yoyogi, Shibuya-ku, Tokyo 151-8583. Tel. (03)5354-0111. Fax. (03)5354-0100. Singles from ¥16,000. Doubles and Twins from ¥22,000. Credit cards. Shinjuku Station South Exit.*

This new hotel, occupying the 19th to 35th floors of a skyscraper, is a welcome moderate-price addition to the Shinjuku hotel scene. The lobby is a stunningly sleek combination of wood and floor-to-ceiling vistas. The stylish rooms are designed for comfort and feature two-line phones with data ports. Best of all, you are only a few minutes away from Shinjuku Station, but are above the hustle and bustle.

Asakusa & Ueno

Stay in Asakusa if you want a nostalgic journey to old Tokyo. It's not that the district is perfectly preserved, but the atmosphere takes you back to bygone days even though very few wooden buildings remain. The downside is Asakusa is fairly inconvenient to western Tokyo; just keep in mind that it's a 35-minute subway ride to Shibuya.

Seeing the Sights areas 4, *Asakusa*; 5, *Ueno*; 6, *Yanaka*; 7, *Akihabara*; and 8, *Asakusabashi, Ryogoku, Fukagawa and Kiba* are close by.

28. ASAKUSA VIEW HOTEL, *3-17-1 Nishi Asakusa, Taito-ku, 111-0035. Tel. (03)3847-1111, Fax (03)3842-2117. Singles from ¥15,000. Doubles from ¥21,000. Twins from ¥28,000. Credit cards. Asakusa Station.*

We find it jarring to see the Asakusa View Hotel, a 28-storied, modern concrete complex that towers over Asakusa, Tokyo's center of traditional culture where most buildings don't top three stories. Yet, it is an option if you want to be in Asakusa but don't want to stay at small, Japanese budget inn. The marble lobby as well as the rooms are faux art-deco style. Inside the hotel, you feel a million miles away from the commotion of Tokyo. On the 6th floor, the Japanese rooms face a Japanese garden; they start at ¥40,000 for two people. The swimming pool is covered by a roof that is open in good weather.

29. RYOKAN ASAKUSA SHIGETSU, *1-31-11 Asakusa, Taito-ku, Tokyo, 111-0032. Tel. (03)3843-2345, Fax (03)3843-2348. Singles from ¥8000. Twins from ¥15,000. Japanese or Western Breakfast, ¥1200; Japanese dinner ¥2000. Credit cards. Part of the Japanese Inn Group and Welcome Inn Reservation Center. Asakusa Station.*

This inn is our budget choice in Asakusa. The small inn, recently reconstructed, has 10 Japanese rooms and 14 Western rooms, all with private baths. Located only a stone's throw from Asakusa Kannon Temple, traditional downtown Tokyo is all around you. On the top floor, there's a spacious Japanese-style bath with a grand view. The clientele is overwhelmingly foreign.

30. SAWANOYA RYOKAN, *2-3-11 Yanaka, Taito-ku, Tokyo, 110-0001. Tel. (03)3822-2251, Fax (03)3822-2252. ¥4700 for one person without meals. ¥8800 without bath, ¥9400 with bath for two persons without meals. Credit cards. Member of the Japanese Inn Group and Welcome Inn Reservation Center. Nezu Station.*

This small economical inn is located in Yanaka, an old downtown area that has retained its old-Tokyo feeling. It's a good budget choice if you're looking for Japanese accommodations in a traditional district. The building itself is nondescript, but the rooms are all Japanese style and comfortable. The inn is convenient to Ueno and is just a few minutes by taxi from the Keisei Ueno Station for Narita Airport trains. The friendly owner is one of the organizers behind the Japan Inn Group.

Shinagawa area

The large concentration of hotels in this area goes back to feudal times when Shinagawa was the first stop on the road from Edo to Kyoto. Today Shinagawa is nine minutes from central Tokyo. Shinagawa doesn't have major sightseeing spots but is on the Yamanote line, which means you can easily reach any part of Tokyo. Seeing the Sights area 9 is really convenient from hotels in this district.

31. MIYAKO HOTEL, *1-1-50 Shiroganedai, Minato-ku, Tokyo, 108-8640. Tel. (03)3447-3111, Fax (03)3447-3133; www.radisson.com. Singles from ¥18,000. Doubles from ¥30,000. Twins from ¥22,000. Credit cards. Meguro Station.*

Built on the estate of a prominent businessman and politician, the Miyako Hotel has a quiet atmosphere surrounded by lush greenery. The Japanese garden, seen through the huge glass windows of the cafe, gives the impression of looking at an eight-panel screen. The rooms are a good size and have large windows. They have a swimming pool and sports club for guests for a ¥2000 fee. The hotel is fairly far from train stations but runs a shuttle bus to Meguro Station. This situation will improve drastically once the new subway line opens sometime around the year 2000.

32. TOBU TAKANAWA HOTEL, *4-7-6 Takanawa, Minato-ku, Tokyo, 108-0074. Tel. (03)3447-0111, Fax (03)3447-0117; www.tobu.co.jp. Singles from ¥13,000. Twins ¥20,000. Doubles from ¥25,000. All include Western or Japanese breakfast. Credit cards. JR Shinagawa Station.*

Tobu Takanawa is a lovely small hotel in a very convenient location and offers personalized service. Three minutes walk from Shinagawa Station, the neighborhood is surprisingly quiet. The lobby faces a small inner court, so the atmosphere is especially tranquil. The business corner offers translation and other services.

33. SHINAGAWA PRINCE HOTEL, *4-10-30 Takanawa, Minato-ku, Tokyo, 108-8611. Tel. (03)3440-1111, Fax (03)3441-7092; www.princehotels.co.jp. Singles from ¥10,900 (main building), ¥14,000 (annex) and ¥18,000 (new wing). Twins from ¥14,400. Credit cards. JR Shinagawa Station.*

The Shinagawa Prince Hotel consists of three different buildings, each with varying room sizes, and is a good choice for a moderately priced hotel. To us, the singles in the main building are absolutely claustrophobic. Instead, we prefer the new wing because the high rise puts you above everything making the rooms appear light and airy. The hotel's many restaurants include a food court, Aji Kaido Gojusantsugi, on the 38th floor: the *sushi, tempura, yakitori, kushiage* and *teppanyaki* areas all have a grand view.

34. RYOKAN SANSUISO, *2-9-5 Higashi Gotanda, Shinagawa-ku, Tokyo, 141-0022. Tel. (03)3441-7475, Fax (03)3449-1944. Singles without bath from ¥4900. Twins with bath ¥9000. Credit cards. Part of the Japanese Inn Group and Welcome Inn Reservation Center. Gotanda Station.*

For the budget traveler who wants Japanese-style accommodations in a central location, Sansuiso may be for you. Still, we have to be honest about the accommodations. The location is convenient, the price is reasonable, and the atmosphere is Japanese. But the slightly run-down inn is on small street, surrounded by office buildings — most of the rooms don't get sunshine. But it is quiet. The owner is hospitable, friendly and caters to foreigners. The inn doesn't serve meals, but there are tons of restaurants in the neighborhood. Try Tokyu Supermarket next to Gotanda Station for a wide variety of take-out foods on the first floor — *sushi* to sandwiches.

Tokyo City Air Terminal (TCAT) Hakozaki area

If you are staying in Tokyo for a very short time, you might want to consider the TCAT area. You won't waste time getting from airport to the hotel, and it's built above a subway station. Seeing the Sights area 2, *From Ginza to Nihonbashi* is most convenient.

35. ROYAL PARK HOTEL, *2-1-1 Nihonbashi Kakigara-cho, Chuo-ku, Tokyo, 103-8520 Tel. (03)3667-1111, Fax (03)3667-1115. US and Canada toll free: 800/448-8355. Singles from ¥22,000. Doubles from ¥30,000. Twins from ¥30,000. Credit cards. Suitengu-mae Station.*

If you take a limousine bus from Narita Airport to TCAT, you'll be relaxing in your room before your fellow passengers reach their hotels. Located literally next to TCAT, the hotel is popular with airline crews. Although it's a little far from the center of things, being right above Suitengu-mae subway station means you can get anywhere in Tokyo easily. The hotel is equipped with a good business center and a fitness club as well as a variety of restaurants including 20th-floor eateries with good views. You can even watch CNN. When it's time to leave Tokyo, you won't even have to drag your suitcase next door to TCAT to catch the airport bus — the bellman will roll it over for you.

Mejiro & Ikebukuro

Mejiro is a fairly quiet residential area. Ikebukuro, a busy commercial center in the northwest corner of Tokyo, is loaded with stores, restaurants and bars. It's far from the downtown business centers, but being on the JR Yamanote loop line as well as several subway lines, it offers good transportation.

Seeing the Sights areas 14, *Shinjuku*; 15, *North of the Palace*; and 16, *Ikebukuro* are the most convenient.

36. FOUR SEASONS HOTEL, *2-10-8 Sekiguchi, Bunkyo-ku, Tokyo, 112-8667. Tel. (03)3943-2222, Fax (03)3943-2300. Toll Free in the US: 800/ 332-3442. Doubles from ¥37,000. Credit cards. Mejiro Station.*

Located on the grounds of a large Japanese garden, the Four Seasons has one of the best settings in Tokyo. Lush greenery surrounds you and since the hotel is not high rise, you feel part of the garden. The spacious feeling carries over into the large lobby that's attractively decorated with Asian objects. Also on the grounds is one of Tokyo's most well-known wedding reception halls, Chinzanso; you may see many beaming couples gathered with their families. The guest rooms are large by Tokyo standards and well appointed. Bice, the elegant main restaurant, serves delicious Italian food — it's the first major hotel in Tokyo not to have French cuisine in the main dining room. Four Seasons' only drawback is its poor location relative to a train station; the hotel runs a shuttle to Mejiro Station.

37. HOTEL METROPOLITAN, *1-6-1 Nishi Ikebukuro, Toshima-ku, Tokyo, 171-8505. Tel. (03)3980-1111, Fax (03)3980-5600. Toll free from US and Canada: 800/465-4329. Singles from ¥16,500. Doubles and twins from ¥22,000. Credit cards. Ikebukuro Station, west exit.*

The hotel is also called Crowne Plaza Metropolitan, part of the Holiday Inn group. It's an 814-room new hotel that has a half-dozen restaurants, an outdoor swimming pool (open July to September) and business amenities. Located a few minutes walk from Ikebukuro Station and next to the Tokyo Metropolitan Art Space, you have easy access to transportation and the shopping and restaurants of Ikebukuro. Removed from the commotion of Ikebukuro's streets, the hotel is quiet and less expensive than the top deluxe hotels. The Metropolitan is good value for a full-service hotel.

38. KIMI RYOKAN, *2-36-8 Ikebukuro, Toshima-ku, Tokyo, 171-0014. Tel. (03)3971-3766. No fax. Single ¥4,500. Twin from ¥7,500. No credit cards. Ikebukuro Station, west exit.*

This inn is legendary among budget travelers, and the guests are almost exclusively foreigners. The 37 Japanese-style rooms are very clean; none has a private bath. The singles and regular twins are very small; we suggest you spring for the larger twin that costs ¥7500. The brothers who own the inn backpacked extensively in Europe in the 1970s and realized Japan lacked inexpensive pension-style accommodations, so they decided to open the inn. The place is very popular, especially on weekends, so book in advance. The police box at the west exit of Ikebukuro Station has maps to Kimi Ryokan.

WHERE TO EAT

No doubt about it, Tokyoites are obsessed with eating. The city has over 150,000 restaurants and bars. It's a shame we can only eat three meals a day. At that rate, it would take us about 137 years to try them all.

If you think restaurants are nearly always found at street level, you're in for a surprise in Tokyo. Six- and eight-storied buildings sometimes house dozens of restaurants. You find them in basements, on penthouse floors, and scattered throughout department stores. And as if there weren't enough, when darkness falls, wooden carts drop down their sides and become portable restaurants.

Japanese cuisine is varied and restaurants tend to specialize. You won't be able to get *tempura* in a *sushi* bar, nor *sushi* in a *tempura* restaurant. But sometimes, especially in areas frequented by tourists, you'll find restaurants serving a wide variety of Japanese food. But why limit yourself to Japanese food? Tokyo has excellent French, Italian, Indian, Thai and other cuisines. So when you tire of soy sauce, branch out.

Tokyo has restaurants to suit all budgets. Inexpensive noodles, the original Japanese fast food, compete with Western fast food and revolving *sushi* bars to fill the bellies of budget travelers. At the other end of the spectrum, posh restaurants serve top-of-the-line fare to the well heeled and those on expense accounts. Fortunately, most restaurants fall between the two, providing tasty food and reasonable value.

Tokyo goes through food fads. When a particular cuisine becomes the rage, restaurants multiply with alarming speed until a new trend replaces it. Generic ethnic and Thai have peaked, but Italian trattorias, Parisian cafes and California Asian eateries are still on the rise. Restaurants appear and disappear almost overnight and then, they sometimes reappear. More than once we've gone and have found a construction site where there once was a restaurant; in six months, the same restaurant is ensconced in shiny new digs. But to be on the safe side, call before you go far out of your way.

Successful restaurants often open branches. Although the name is the same, sometimes the menu is different. For instance, many famous

RESTAURANT PRICE CATEGORIES
A word on how we have categorized the restaurants:
- *inexpensive is under ¥3000 per person*
- *moderate is ¥3000 to ¥6000*
- *expensive is between ¥6000 and ¥12,000*
- *very expensive is over ¥12,000*

restaurants have branches in department stores, but the menu in the department store is usually less expensive than at the main shop.

Japanese restaurants tend to serve fixed meals called sets, courses or *teishoku*. In some places you cannot order a la carte, while others will offer both. A typical Japanese course includes a starter, main dish, rice, pickles and soup. But with *kaiseki*, Japanese haute cuisine, the entire meal seems in search of a main dish; you are served small dish after small dish.

Restaurants have wide variations in price. A restaurant expensive in the evening can easily have a ¥1500 lunch special. Or a restaurant may have a ¥7000 set dinner, but if you only want one or two courses, your bill can be less. It's a sweeping generalization, but we'll say it anyway: in Western restaurants, the set meals can be boring, and you may have a better meal by ordering a la carte. Alcoholic beverages, especially wine, can add substantially to the cost of a meal — even beer or *sake* (rice wine) adds up.

Lunch is Tokyo's big bargain. Even very expensive restaurants have a more reasonably priced menu at noontime. If you want to try a specific restaurant but don't want to pay the high price, look into eating your mid-day meal there. For office workers, 12 noon is the universal lunch hour, so expect restaurants in business areas to be packed at this time. Eat before noon or after 1pm to avoid the crowds. But don't wait too late because most restaurants stop serving lunch by 2pm. Tokyoites also eat dinner on the early side, around 6:30 to 7pm. Many restaurants stop serving by 8:30pm or 9pm.

Restaurants have a last-order time, but you usually have about an hour after that time to eat. The closing time we list is actually the last-order time. If you arrive later, you will almost always be refused; restaurants take their hours seriously.

There's a 5% tax added. Sometimes it's included in the menu price, but usually it is additional, and if your meal is over ¥7500, an another 3% tax is charged. Hotel and high-end restaurants usually add a 10% service charge. Do not tip, ever, even if there is no service charge. Usually you settle the bill at the counter near the exit, not at the table.

If you can't figure out where to eat, head to the closest department store or to the basement of a large office building. Both will have a number of reasonably priced restaurants usually with lots of plastic food samples outside their doors. And department store restaurant floors stay open later than the store itself.

Do yourself a favor, and slip out of your hotel to try some of Tokyo's many restaurants. If the menu posted is only in Japanese, look at it as an adventure. Use the extensive menu listings in Chapter 10, *Food & Drink*, to order any type of Japanese food. Eating in Tokyo is a great cultural and culinary experience. *Bon Appetit*, or, as the Japanese say, *Itadakimasu*.

We have divided Tokyo restaurants into the following dining areas:

Akasaka

MIMIU *(Udon-suki, moderate). 3-12-13 Akasaka, Minato-ku. Tel. (03)3505-3366. Open 11:30am to 8:30pm. Closed Sunday. Akasaka Mitsuke Station.*

A branch of the well-known Osaka restaurant, Mimiu serves *udon-suki*, a one-pot dish with *udon* noodles, chicken, fish and vegetables cooked in broth. Special noodles that stay firm when cooked and the nearly clear, tasty broth are the secrets to success. We really feel warmed up eating here on cold wintry days. *Udon-suki* costs ¥3500.

ROSSO E NERO *(Italian, moderate). 2-A Kioi-cho Building, Chiyoda-ku. Tel. (03)3237-5888. Open 11:30am to 2pm; 5:30pm to 10pm. Closed Sundays and holidays. Akasaka Mitsuke Station.*

True to its name, the interior decor is red and black with lots of plants creating a cozy atmosphere. Although the selection of Italian wine is fine, Noriko adores their orange juice. Its color is almost as red as tomato juice and the taste is superb. Some of our favorites are *bruschetta del conte* (garlic toast topped with perfectly ripened diced fresh tomatoes, basil and olive oil); *vitello tonnato* (thin slices of veal in tuna and anchovy sauce); and *gnocchi* in pesto sauce. The homemade pastas are served perfectly al dente.

GRANATA *(Italian, inexpensive to moderate). B1, TBS Kaikan, 5-3-3 Akasaka, Minato-ku. Tel. (03)3582-3241. Open daily 11am to 10pm. Akasaka Station.*

Granata is a Tokyo institution. Located in the basement of a local landmark, the TBS building, it's easy to find. We suspect it's popular with Tokyoites because it is authentic Roman style rather than adjusted to local taste. Platters of antipasto sit on a table in the center of the room so you have a sense of what's to come. The restaurant is divided into several semiprivate corners, giving an intimate feeling. Pastas are delicious and fish and meat are cooked well: the chicken a la Roma is our favorite. They offer lunchtime service ranging from ¥1100 to ¥3800. Dinner courses are ¥4800 and ¥8800 and include two starters, fish, meat, dessert and coffee. A la carte is also available.

HINAZUSHI *(Sushi, inexpensive to moderate). B1, Nambu Building, 3-3 Kioi-cho. Chiyoda-ku. Tel. (03)3230-1884. Open weekdays 11:30am to 2:30pm; 5pm to 11pm. Saturday, 12 noon to 10:30pm, Sunday and national holidays, 12 noon to 10pm. Akasaka Mitsuke Station.*

From the exterior, Hinazushi looks rather exclusive so you may wonder if this is the right place. But as you enter, a friendly, kimono-clad hostess greets you. The interior is contemporary Japanese — long paper lanterns and fresh flower arrangements placed on a beautiful stone floor. The lunchtime set consist of nine kinds of *sushi* and one *temaki* roll for ¥1000. If you want to choose your *sushi*, ask for the *okonomi nigiri:* you select 12 pieces for ¥2300. At dinner an all-you-can-eat course costs ¥4300. Hinazushi has an English menu; you merely write down your order. It's a perfect place to eat *sushi* to your heart's content. Juni-an, the adjacent restaurant sharing the same entrance, is a *kaiseki* restaurant managed by the same company. If you'd prefer, *kaiseki* meals cost ¥4300 (lunchtime only), ¥5300, and two different courses for ¥7300.

TAJ *(Indian, inexpensive to moderate). 3-2-7 Akasaka, Minato-ku. Tel. (03)3586-6606. Open 11am to 2pm; 5pm to 10pm; 11am to 3pm; 5pm to 9:30pm Sundays and national holidays. Akasaka Mitsuke Station.*

Conveniently located near the Akasaka Mitsuke subway station, Taj has been serving authentic Indian food in Tokyo for quite sometime. It's a popular restaurant with Indian expatriates. Lunchtime specials start from ¥830 and lunchtime *tabe hodai* (all you can eat) costs only ¥1200. Noriko loves their Masala Dosa, a South Indian dish, which costs ¥1300.

SUSHI SEI *(Sushi, inexpensive to moderate). 3-7-12 Akasaka, Minato-ku. Tel. (03)3584-2552. Open weekdays 11:45am to 2pm, 5pm to 10:30pm; Saturday 11:30am to 2pm, 4:30pm to 10pm. Closed Sunday and national holidays. Akasaka Mitsuke Station.*

One of the many branches of the reasonably priced Sushi Sei, we love this shop with its immaculate *sushi* bar and friendly staff. Lunch *nigiri sushi* sets cost ¥850-1500; dinner will cost under ¥5000 per person.

TORAYA *(Japanese sweets, tea room). 4-9-22 Akasaka, Minato-ku. Tel. (03)3408-4121. Open 8:30am to 8pm, until 6pm Sunday; tea room in the basement open 11am to 6:30pm; to 5pm weekends. Akasaka Mitsuke Station.*

When the emperor moved from Kyoto to Tokyo in 1868, Toraya moved with him. The Kurokawa family has been making Japanese sweets since the 10th century and enjoys the connoisseurship of the Imperial family. The shop faces busy Aoyama Dori; its traditional Japanese gray and white stucco walls make it easy to find. Toraya sells freshly made bean paste sweets in seasonal flowers shapes for ¥370. It's rather expensive for a small sweet, but it's a piece of art. In the basement is a contemporary tea room where you can enjoy tea and sweets in a relaxed atmosphere. Toraya even has a branch in New York City.

HYOTAN *(Japanese, moderate to expensive). 1F Harashima Bldg, 6 San'ei-cho, Shinjuku-ku. Tel. (03)3225-7060. Open 11am to 10pm Monday through Saturday, 12 noon to 9pm Sunday and holidays. Reservations recommended. Yotsuya Station.*

In an unlikely location on the first floor of an undistinguished apartment building lies this gem of an eatery. The design is sleek, contemporary Japanese with lots of wood, understated lighting and seating at chairs and tables. The decor includes several gourds, the restaurant's namesake. The food is *kaiseki*, a delight for the eye and the palate. All meals end with Hyotan's signature homemade noodles, *udon* or *soba*, your choice. Lunch courses are ¥3500 and 5000; dinner ¥3500 to ¥10,000.

Asakusa

BON *(Japanese temple vegetarian, expensive). 1-2-11 Ryusen, Taito-ku. Tel. (03)3872-0375. Weekdays lunch at 12 noon, dinner at 5pm; weekends: 12 noon, 3pm and 5pm. Closed Tuesday. Iriya Station.*

Fucha-ryori is a special Zen Buddhist vegetarian cuisine introduced by a Chinese monk who founded Mampuku-ji Temple at Uji, near Kyoto, in the 17th century. Tucked away among the low houses in a quiet residential area of old downtown Tokyo, Bon is an oasis of serenity. The moment you see the entrance, you know that even the smallest details have not been neglected — the paving stones have been sprinkled with water as a symbol of purification. Note the flower arrangement at the front desk, the dynamic calligraphy of the character for Bon (meaning Buddhist devotee), and the well-polished cobblestone entrance where you remove your shoes. Bon has eight private *tatami* mat rooms with under-the-table pits so you can stretch your legs. Your meal consists of dish after dish of delectable tidbits served on beautiful plates. The set meals, consisting of 12 courses, cost ¥6000-10,000 at lunchtime on weekdays, and ¥7000-10,000 on weekends and evenings. Reservations necessary.

KUREMUTSU *(Japanese, expensive). 2-2-13 Asakusa, Taito-ku. Tel. (03)3842-0906. Open 4pm to 10pm. Closed Thursday. Asakusa Station.*

Set in a small traditional house, Kuremutsu's interior is filled with farmhouse furniture and implements. The food is cooked Kaga style from Kanazawa; there's lots of fresh fish. Their specialty is steamed red snapper stuffed with *okara* (the chaff left from making tofu); it can serve three people. Courses cost ¥5000, ¥8000 and ¥10,000.

ICHIMON *(Japanese, moderate). 3-12-6 Asakusa, Taito-ku. Tel. (03)3875-6800. Open 6pm to 11pm. Iriya or Asakusa Station.*

When you are in Asakusa at the end of the day, stop here for dinner. Ichimon is a drinking establishment so the beer and *sake* rice wine flows freely, and the atmosphere is lively. When you enter, purchase ¥5000 worth of *mon*, a now extinct small coin, which you use to pay for drinks and food. When you leave, return any remaining coins. Ichimon is old farmhouse style with tables as well as *tatami* mats. There are lots of different types of *sake*. The food is simple fare that goes with drinking: *nabe* stews in winter and *takebue tofu* in summer are two favorites.

ASAKUSA IMAHAN *(Sukiyaki, inexpensive to expensive). 3-1-12 Nishi Asakusa, Taito-ku. Tel. (03)3841-1114. Open daily 11:30am to 9:30pm. Asakusa Station.*

Imahan is justifiably the most well-known *sukiyaki* restaurant in Tokyo. The secrets are using marbled beef from Omi province (present Shiga prefecture) and a sugarfree sauce. At lunch Imahan serves *sukiyaki* sets for ¥2000 and ¥3500. Dinner *sukiyaki* courses cost ¥6000, ¥8000 and ¥10,000. The difference in the price depends on the cut of meat. Try it for a change from fish and vegetables.

SANSADA *(Tempura, inexpensive to expensive). 2-2-1 Asakusa, Taito-ku. Tel. (03)3841-3400. Open 11:30am to 9pm. Asakusa Station.*

"First Asakusa, second Kannon (Buddha of Mercy) and third Sansada's *tempura*," is an old expression. Known for its crispy, honey-colored Edo-style *tempura* (versus Kansai style that is a lighter color), the Sansada family has been frying *tempura* for seven generations — 160 years at the same site. It is located by Kaminarimon Gate that leads to the temple. At lunch they serve a *tendon* set for ¥1200 and a variety of set menus including *tempura*, soup, rice and pickles starting at ¥2000. The annex has *tatami* mat rooms with views of the garden and has sets consisting of *sashimi*, vinegared vegetables, soup, rice, pickles and their special *tempura* ranging from ¥4100 to ¥8000. The shop is large enough that you don't need to make reservations unless it's imperative you eat at a certain time. They charge an additional 10% if you make a reservation.

KAWAMATSU *(Japanese, moderate). 1-4-1 Asakusa, Taito-ku. Tel. (03)3841-1234. Open 11:30am to 9pm. Closed Monday. Asakusa Station.*

A Japanese restaurant with efficient service and good food on a busy street just a stone's throw from the Kaminarimon Gate, Kawamatsu offers Edo-style Japanese meals at comparatively reasonable prices. The friendly kimono-clad owner of the shop speaks English and is always happy to explain the shop's history to customers. She will probably recommend you try *Kawamatsu-zen*, a lunch box filled with lots of different food cooked in a variety of ways, ¥3200; *tempura teishoku* (starter, *tempura*, rice,

---

TEMPURA

Do you wonder why we've listed so many tempura shops in Asakusa? Asakusa Kannon Temple was a major pilgrimage site – a beacon for people all over Japan. Once they arrived, they looked for more than religious salvation; they wanted to have a good time and eat good food. Japan adopted tempura from the Portuguese who arrived in the 16th century, so it was exotic and trendy.

Asakusa is on the Sumida River, so the shops were always able to get fresh tempura ingredients including fish and shrimp. The tradition has survived although, fortunately, today the fish and shrimp don't come directly from Tokyo Bay.

---

soup, pickles and ice cream) for ¥2300, *sashimi teishoku* for ¥2800, or *unagi teishoku* at ¥2700. They also offer *kaiseki* meals for ¥7000.

AOIMARUSHIN *(Tempura, inexpensive to moderate). 1-4-4 Asakusa, Taito-ku. Tel. (03)3841-0110. Open daily 11am to 9pm, until 8pm Sundays and holidays. Asakusa Station.*

Aoimarushin is famous for crispy Edo-style *tempura* served with a sweet and sour sauce. You'll love it. The house specialty is *kakiage tempura*, mixed vegetables and seafood all mixed together. The *kakiage* course costs ¥2300. *Tendon* is also good at ¥1200.

OWARIYA *(Soba, inexpensive). 1-1-3 Asakusa, Taito-ku. Tel. (03)3841-8780. Open daily 11:30am to 8:30pm. Asakusa Station.*

This *soba* noodle shop has been around more than 100 years. The specialty, *tempura soba* at ¥1300, is famous for its monster shrimp that are larger than the bowl. Frying in sesame oil makes the *tempura* very light.

LA FLAMME D'OR *(Beer hall, inexpensive). 1-23-1 Azumabashi, Sumida-ku. Tel. (03)5608-5381. Open daily 11:30am to 11pm (April through September), 11:30am to 10pm (October through March). Asakusa Station.*

Everyone who goes to Asakusa looks across the Sumida River and says "What's that strange building with a gold curlicue on top?" The answer is the Asahi Beer Company's headquarters. According to designer Philippe Starck, the golden object symbolizes beer froth — use your imagination. The contemporary interior decor gives a sense of spaciousness. You definitely feel you're going through a time warp as you cross the bridge from the traditional atmosphere of Asakusa to the 21st century. Along with cold, frothy beer, the hall serves inexpensive food such as sausages and noodles. Budget ¥1500 for lunch and ¥3500 for dinner.

TOWADA *(Soba, inexpensive). 1-33-5 Asakusa, Taito-ku. Tel. (03)3841-8270. Open 11:30am to 8pm. Closed Monday. Asakusa Station.*

Towada is known for its special *soba* noodles made of 100% buckwheat flour. Standard *soba* is made with a combination of buckwheat and wheat flour; the latter is needed to make a smooth dough. Towada prides itself on a secret recipe that eliminates the need for wheat flour. This is the place to try genuine *soba*. *Zaru* (plain *soba* with dipping sauce) costs ¥750 and *tempura soba* is ¥1350.

Ebisu

CHATEAU RESTAURANT TAILLEVENT ROBUCHON *(French, very expensive). 1-13-1 Mita, Meguro-ku. Tel. (03)5424-1338. Main restaurant open daily 12 noon to 1:30pm; 6pm to 8:30pm. Cafe open daily 11:30am to 2:30pm; 5:30pm to 8:30pm. Ebisu Station.*

Taillevent Robuchon is a collaborative effort of two Parisian rivals. The original plans called for moving a French chateau to Tokyo stone by stone, but building codes became too cumbersome — instead they built a new one. The chef, Bernard Clays, is Belgium born and trained with one of France's top chefs. When the restaurant opened, it was booked solid for months, but reservations are much easier to come by today. The set dinners cost ¥15,000-25,000. If the main restaurant is too pricey, try the more casual Cafe Français that serves lunch sets for ¥2800-4800 and dinner sets for ¥4000, ¥4800 and ¥7500.

IL BOCCALONE *(Italian, moderate). 1F, Silk Ebisu Building, 1-15-9 Ebisu, Shibuya-ku. Tel. (03)3449-1430. Open 6pm to 11pm. Closed Sunday. Ebisu Station.*

For a change from Japanese food, Il Boccalone is an ideal place. One of the most popular Italian restaurants in Tokyo, Il Boccalone is always crowded with people of all ages who enjoy eating and love a festive atmosphere. The staff is Italian. The open kitchen area gives a very up-to-date touch to the place, and the large fresco paintings make you think you might be in Rome. The pastas are delicious, but their real specialty is charcoal grilled fish and meat. We recommend you make reservations as far in advance as possible because the restaurant fills up.

Ginza, Hibiya, Marunouchi & Tsukiji

KAMOGAWA *(Japanese, moderate to expensive). B1F, Okura Bekkan Building, 3-4-1 Ginza, Chuo-ku. Tel. (03)3561-0550. Open 11:30am to 4pm; 5:30pm to 10pm. Sundays and national holidays 11:30am to 4pm. Ginza Station.*

Special gardeners and carpenters came from Kyoto to build this elegant traditional restaurant in the midst of bustling Ginza. Indeed, as you go down the stairs, you enter a serene and peaceful world. Attention has been paid to the most minute details: stepping stones, dimly lit lanterns and bamboo hedges that separate the private rooms. The fresh fish comes directly from Kamogawa in Chiba Prefecture where the owner has a hotel. The vegetables are always the freshest of the season. What amazes us most is how the food is presented. Kamogawa has such a variety of plates and lacquer bowls and dishes that it is a delight to see the innovative serving. If you don't have time to go to Kyoto, Kamogawa is a good place to experience *kaiseki* in a traditional Japanese atmosphere. At lunchtime *kaiseki* courses run from ¥5000 to ¥30,000; dinner *kaiseki* courses are ¥5800-30,000.

ZAKURO *(Japanese, inexpensive to expensive). B1, Sanwa Building, 4-6-1 Ginza, Chuo-ku. Tel. (03)3535-4421. Open daily 11am to 9:30pm. Ginza Station.*

This Ginza shop is a branch of a famous Japanese restaurant. We like it because of the high quality of the food and the reasonable price. (The main shop, located in Akasaka across from the American Embassy, is rather expensive — the *shabu-shabu* set meals run ¥11,000, ¥13,000 and ¥16,000.) The staff, dressed in kimono, are friendly and efficient, bringing hot towels and tea as soon as you sit down. At lunchtime there's a special set menu called *wa-teishoku A* for ¥2500; it consists of small starters, *sashimi* and a main course (meat or fish), rice, *miso* soup, pickles and dessert. *Tempura teishoku* costs ¥2500. Fresh hot tea is served frequently, usually just when our current cup cools down enough to drink.

At dinnertime the menu moves to the higher side, but their seasonal *wa-teishoku*, a type of *kaiseki* course, is worth the ¥6500. For an appetizer, enjoy seasonal vegetables that are followed by *sashimi*, grilled fish, vinegared vegetables, steamed vegetables and mixed rice. Noriko loves a refreshing special dessert, cooked plums in syrup. It's best to make reservations for dinner.

KOOMIYA *(Taiwan-style shabu-shabu, inexpensive to moderate). B1, Nakaya Ginza Building, 5-8-16 Ginza, Chuo-ku. Tel. (03)3573-3540. Open daily 11:30am to 2pm; 5pm to 10:30pm. Ginza Station.*

This small restaurant serves *shabu-shabu* Taiwan style. Just like Japanese *shabu-shabu*, thin strips of beef and vegetables are cooked in broth at the table, but the dipping sauce is richer. Lunch courses for ¥1000 and ¥1200 do not include *shabu-shabu*, but you can have it if you order in advance. *Shabu-shabu* course, ¥2600, includes dessert. Koomiya is next to Matsuzakaya Department Store.

SUSHI SEI *(Sushi, inexpensive to moderate). Dai Nana Kanai Building B1, 8-2-13 Ginza, Chuo-ku. Tel. (03)3571-2772. Open weekdays 11:30am to 2pm, 5pm to 10:40pm. Saturday 11:45am to 2pm, 4:30pm to 10pm. Closed Sunday and holidays. Ginza Station.*

There are more than one hundred *sushi* shops in the area, including six Sushi Sei branches. No doubt this is really the land of *sushi* and with good reason — Tsukiji fish market, the source for all, is close by. We like this shop for its beautifully presented fresh fish, contemporary Japanese decor, quiet ambiance, friendly staff and high-tech toilet. The lunchtime *sushi* set includes a tiny starter, *sushi* for the main course, and soup; it costs only ¥850. You can also order *omakase* (the customers let the chef choose the best of the day), which costs ¥1850 and ¥2300 at lunch; ¥2300 and ¥2500 at dinner. Or you can sit at the counter and point to whatever you fancy. Remember the price of fish varies according to the season and the weather (if the seas are rough or calm). An average bill is ¥2500 per person.

BUONO BUONO *(Italian, inexpensive to moderate). 2F, Nishi Ginza Department Store, 4-1-2 Ginza, Chuo-ku. Tel. (03)3566-4031. Open daily 11:30am to 11pm. Yurakucho Station.*

Located just two minutes from Yurakucho Station on the Yamanote line, Buono Buono is a favorite for Milan-style Italian cuisine. Choose from three set lunch menus ranging from ¥1600-3500. The ¥1600 offers great value: antipasto, pasta, dessert and coffee. The atmosphere is bright and cheerful; watch the passersby through the large glass windows. One warning: at lunchtime, plan to arrive before 12 noon or after 1pm because Buono Buono is popular with area office workers. Set dinners cost ¥6000 and ¥8000; you can also order a la carte.

EDOGIN *(Sushi, inexpensive to expensive). 4-5-1 Tsukiji, Chuo-ku. Tel. (03)3543-4401. Open 11am to 9:30pm. Closed Sunday. Tsukiji Station.*

Edogin serves some of the best *sushi* in Tsukiji, which is why there will often be a line of people waiting. *Nigiri sushi* sets start at ¥1000 and include soup. Have lunch here after tramping around the fish market.

SUSHI KO *(Sushi, inexpensive to moderate). 6-5-8 Ginza, Chuo-ku. Tel. (03)5568-0505. Open daily 11:30am to 2pm; 5pm to 4am. Ginza Station.*

The chef of this reasonably priced *sushi* shop spent 10 years in California and will happily tell you everything about his fish in fluent English. *Nigiri sushi* sets run ¥700 to ¥3000; you can also order a la carte.

TOUTOUKYO *(Chinese dim sum, inexpensive to moderate). B1, Ginza World Town, 5-8-17 Ginza, Chuo-ku. Tel. (3)3572-5666. Open 11:30am to 11pm. Ginza Station.*

This restaurant makes 84 different kinds of *dim sum* by hand. We love to come here with a large group and choose food from wagons wheeled around the restaurant. The lunch sets start at ¥700 — choice of noodles, Chinese dumpling, vegetable and dessert.

FARM GRILL *(American, inexpensive). 2F, Ginza Nine Sango-kan, 8-5 Ginza, Chuo-ku. Tel. (03)5568-6156. Open 11:30am to 11pm. Shimbashi Station.*

Farm Grill serves all-American buffet fare like chicken, steak and ribs at very reasonable prices. The lunch buffet, from 11:30am to 5pm, is ¥1500; dinner buffet is ¥1900 for women, ¥2300 for men.

YAKITORI UNDER THE TRACKS, *Yurakucho Station.*

One of our favorite inexpensive places to eat dinner is at one of the many *yakitori* pubs under the tracks south of Yurakucho Station. Eating here is definitely no frills. Protected from the elements by hanging plastic sheets, most shops are half-indoors and half-outdoors. Weekday evenings the places are crowded with office workers from the nearby areas. Beer, *sake* and whiskey flow freely, so the atmosphere is lively and noisy. The food is basic *yakitori* and other Japanese pub fare. From Ginza 4-chome crossing, walk in the direction of the Imperial Palace. Just after you walk under the expressway, turn left after the New Tokyo building; you can't miss the dozen or so eateries.

Harajuku & Aoyama

FUJIMAMAS *(Japanese, moderate). 6-3-2 Jingumae, Shibuya-ku. Tel: (03)5485-2262. Just off of Omotesando near Kiddyland, turn at the small street with Swatch on the corner and it's on the right. Lunch 12 noon to 3 pm, to 4pm on weekends; dinner 6pm to 11pm. Harajuku or Jingumae Station.*

Fujimamas is our top choice for dining in the area. The inviting, rustic decor is matched by delightful Japanese food with a touch of fusion thrown in and artfully served on handmade plates. Lunch is limited to three sets a day ranging from ¥1000 to ¥1400 and dinner averages ¥3000. Bi-lingual staff is a plus.

ASADA *(Japanese, moderate to expensive). B1, 2-7-13 Kita Aoyama, Minato-ku. Tel. (03)5411-0171. Open daily 11:30am to 2:30pm; 5pm to 10pm. Gaien-mae Station.*

This restaurant is a branch of the famous Asadaya in Kanazawa on the Japan Sea. During the 17th-19th centuries, under the connoisseurship of the Maeda feudal lords, a special cuisine called *Kaga ryori* developed. Asada uses fresh ingredients sent directly from Kanazawa and the food reflects the seasons. At lunch the *Godan Bento* (a five-layer lunch box) costs ¥4000 and *kaiseki* course is ¥7500. At dinner the *Kaga kaiseki* course is served at tables (¥12,000) and *Tateyama* course (¥16,000) is served in private Japanese-style rooms. The special seasonal weekend *kaiseki* course costs ¥10,000. The serene atmosphere of this restaurant is a treat at any time.

KIHACHI *(Nouvelle French, moderate to expensive). 4-18-10 Minami Aoyama, Shibuya-ku. Tel. (03)3403-7477. Open 12 noon to 2:30pm; 6pm to 9:30pm. Sunday 12 noon to 8pm. Omotesando Station.*

Kihachi is the perfect place to have lunch after browsing around the designer boutiques of Aoyama; it is a continuation of contemporary Japan. Fashionable Japanese women fill the restaurant at lunchtime. At dinner time, the mood changes and the clientele includes more couples. Kihachi serves French cuisine using Japanese ingredients — especially lots of fresh fish. The chef's salad, which is to die for, includes fresh raw fish and lots of herbs; it's topped with roasted almond slivers. The lunch sets include appetizer, fish or meat, authentic French dessert and coffee and cost ¥2500 to ¥6000. Set dinners cost ¥8000 and ¥10,000, but the chef encourages customers to order a la carte at dinner for maximum appreciation of his inventive culinary talent. The decor is bright and open, and the staff is friendly.

LUNCHAN *(American, moderate). 1-2-5 Shibuya, Shibuya-ku. Tel. (03)5466-1398. Open daily 11:30am to 11pm. Omotesando Station.*

Bright and airy, Lunchan serves upscale American home cooking. Meat loaf is on the menu, but so are pastas and duck. The decor is open and bright, and you can see the chefs at work in the open kitchen. Sunday brunch is a treat. So are the desserts —they're American sized. Entrees run from ¥1500 to ¥2600.

BARBACOA GRILL AOYAMA *(Brazilian, inexpensive to moderate). B1, Evergreen Building, 4-3-24 Jingumae, Shibuya-ku. Tel. (03)3796-0571. Open 11:30am to 3pm; 5:30pm to 11pm. Omotesando Station.*

This basement restaurant serves an enormous lunch for ¥950 and a lunch buffet for ¥1430. At dinner they have Brazilian all-you-can-eat for ¥3300; it's heavy on barbecued beef. The dinner salad bar course is ¥2800. Come here if you need a meat fix at a reasonable price.

IL FORNO *(Italian cafe and pizzeria, inexpensive to moderate). 2F, La Mia Building, 5-1-3 Minami Aoyama. Tel. (03)3400-0517. Open daily 11:30am to 3pm; 5:30pm to 10:30pm. Omotesando Station.*

For a real cross-cultural experience, try Il Forno for California-Italian food in the heart of Tokyo. A branch of the Santa Monica eatery, the atmosphere is more California than Japan. The menu includes pasta, pizza, meat and fish, and there's a spa section for calorie counters — we said it was California, didn't we? The pizza has a delicious thin crust; you can choose from 15 different toppings. Tea and coffee refills are free, a rarity in Japan. The young waiters and waitresses, sporting T-shirts and black pants, are friendly. Lunchtime specials cost ¥1000-1200.

LAS CHICAS *(Eclectic, inexpensive to moderate). 5-47-6 Jingumae, Shibuya-ku. Tel. (03)3407-6865. Open daily 11am to 11pm. Omotesando Station.*

Tucked away on a back street off Aoyama Dori — turn at Citibank — funky Las Chicas is popular with Tokyo's young expats. The restaurant has a front garden terrace and several rooms inside. The food is eclectic combining American, Continental and Asian. Service is irregular, but everyone is having too good a time to notice. You can even play on the internet. Entrees average ¥1400.

MAISEN *(Japanese tonkatsu, inexpensive). 4-8-5 Jingumae, Shibuya-ku. Tel. (03)3470-0071. Open daily 11am to 10pm. Omotesando Station.*

There are thousands of *tonkatsu* shops in Tokyo, but Maisen stands out. The deep-fried pork cutlet is so tender you can cut it with your chopsticks (if you can manipulate them, that is). Maisen serves *tempura* and *sashimi* in addition to *tonkatsu,* but we recommend you stick with what they do best — *tonkatsu.* Maisen serves an inexpensive lunch until 5pm. The *katsu* set (*tonkatsu,* rice, soup and pickles) costs ¥820; *hitokuchi-katsu teishoku* (bite-sized pieces of *tonkatsu* with rice, soup and pickles) costs ¥800. No item on the menu costs more than ¥3500. Considering Maisen's location in pricey Omotesando, it is a bargain.

BINDI *(Indian, inexpensive to moderate). 7-10-10 Minami Aoyama, Minato-ku. Tel. (03)3409-8755. Open daily 11:30am to 2pm; 6pm to 9:30pm. Omotesando Station or Hiroo Station.*

Tokyo has many Indian restaurants, but tiny Bindi offers one of the most versatile menus. The Mehtas serve delicious home cooking at incredible prices. *Sag* chicken (chicken and spinach) costs ¥1100; *boti kabab* (three pieces of grilled lamb) ¥1000; fish *tikka* (four pieces of swordfish) ¥1300. If you are craving a certain Indian dish, call Mr. Mehta and he'll do his best to accommodate your request.

Kanda

YABU SOBA *(Soba, inexpensive). 2-10 Awaji-cho Kanda, Chuo-ku. Tel. (03)3251-0287. Open 11:30am to 7:30pm. Ogawamachi Station.*

Yabu Soba is a classic noodle shop known all over Japan; for more than 100 years, it's served *soba* noodles in the same place. It's worth a detour to visit. The setting is like a movie: a traditional wooden two-storied building with a garden and a small pond in front. Patrons sit at tables as well as on *tatami* mats. The waiters announce your order to the kitchen in voices so resonant, some claim to come only to hear them. But it would be a shame not to order the wonderful noodles with their out-of-this-world broth. *Seiro soba* costs ¥600; *tempura soba* is ¥1500. Best picks include *kamo-nanban* (*soba* with duck), ¥1500, and *anago-nanban* (*soba* with freshly cooked sea eel), ¥1700.

Odaiba

ODAIBA CAFE *(Continental, moderate). 1-3-5 Daiba, Minato-ku. Tel. (03)5531-2771. Open daily 11:30am to 11pm Sunday through Thursday; 11:30am to 5am Friday and Saturday. Odaiba Kaihin Koen Station.*

Odaiba, part of the new waterfront development, is the hottest area in Tokyo. Odaiba Cafe is on Sunset Restaurant Row, a string of a half-dozen restaurants that all have terraces to see the beach across the street. We like Odaiba Cafe's food and atmosphere, which is both casual and romantic. The succulent grilled salmon for ¥2400 is a favorite; the portions are large by Japanese standards. Every evening they have live jazz. And if you want to stay up late, they don't close until 5am on weekends. Figure on ¥5000 per person. Make reservations to avoid disappointment.

SAM CHOY *(Hawaiian, moderate). 1-3-5 Daiba, Minato-ku. Tel. (03)5531-5036. Open 5:30pm to 9:30pm weekdays; 11am to 9:30pm weekends. Odaiba Kaihin Koen Station.*

This sister restaurant of Sam Choy at Hawaii's Diamond Head is one of Tokyo Bay's hot spots. Sam Choy, the celebrity-chef, is a Chinese-American born to a family that loves good food. Choy excels at combining the best ingredients of the East and the West. Mahi mahi, steamed white fish wrapped in leaves, is a signature dish. Costing ¥2500, it's large enough to share. He also has a slew of mouth-watering appetizers. Reservations are a must.

Roppongi, Hiroo & Nishi Azabu

TAKAMURA *(Japanese kaiseki, very expensive). 3-4-27 Roppongi, Minato-ku. Tel. (03)3585-6600. Open 12 noon to 3:30pm; 5pm to 10:30pm. Closed Sunday and national holidays. Roppongi Station.*

Surrounding this quaint and tranquil restaurant in a private house, a bamboo grove insulates you from the commotion of Roppongi. The restaurant has eight private *tatami* mat rooms, all different but charming. One has a pit under the table, so specify it if you'd like to stretch your legs. The *robata* room has a rustic open hearth. *Sake* rice wine is served in freshly cut bamboo containers. Using the freshest seasonal ingredients course after course, the *kaiseki* is a visual treat. Lunchtime set meals cost ¥15,000 -25,000 including a flask of *sake* and service charge. Dinner sets cost ¥17,000, ¥20,000 and ¥25,000 plus a ¥2000 room charge, 15% service charge and 8% tax. So unless someone else is picking up the tab, lunch is the time to enjoy one of Tokyo's most exquisite dining experiences.

INAKAYA *(Robata-yaki, expensive). East branch: 1F, Reine Building, 5-3-4 Roppongi, Minato-ku. Tel. (03)3408-5040. West branch: 7-8-4 Roppongi, Minato-ku. Tel. (03)3405-9866. Open daily 5pm to 5am. Roppongi Station.*

Inakaya is a boisterous restaurant popular with tourists. It's a country-style *robata-yaki* restaurant with a folk art ambiance. All the patrons sit at a large u-shaped counter. Chefs dressed in traditional garb sit behind charcoal grills surrounded by baskets filled with ingredients waiting to be cooked. You merely point at what you want to eat, and it will be cooked for you. The staff shouts out your order, so it's a noisy, festive place. Our biggest complaint is the restaurant is too expensive. By the time you have a beer or two, *sake* and a few dishes, your bill is over ¥10,000.

KISSO *(Japanese kaiseki, inexpensive to moderate). 1B, Axis Building, 5-17-1 Roppongi, Minato-ku. Tel. (03)3582-4191. Open 11:30am to 2pm; 5:30pm to 9pm. Closed Sunday and national holidays. Roppongi Station.*

Located in the basement of the Axis Building, a center of contemporary design, Kisso fits right in. The ambiance is modern Japanese, accented with paper lanterns and artfully arranged fresh flowers. The food is presented on a black lacquered tray and contemporary Japanese dishes. The food emphasizes what's in season, and the fresh citrus-fruit sherbet is to die for. Lunch set costs ¥1200; it changes every day depending what the chef finds at the morning market. *Donburi* is available at ¥1200. *Kaiseki* courses are ¥3800 and ¥5000. Dinner sets begin at ¥8000. After your meal, browse in a corner section where they sell dishes like the ones used to serve you.

ERAWAN *(Thai food, inexpensive to moderate). 13F, Roi Building, 5-5-1 Roppongi, Minato-ku. Tel. (03)3404-5741. Open daily 5pm to 11:30pm. Roppongi Station.*

Erawan, a Thai restaurant with a view, ranks among our favorite Tokyo eateries. On the 13th floor of the Roi Building, it offers fantastic views of Tokyo. The teak wood decor makes you think you're in Bangkok. The food is authentic and the price reasonable. Unlike many Thai restaurants, they don't tone down the spices for the Japanese palate. Each dish costs between ¥1200 and ¥2000; we always order several dishes and share. Some of our favorites are spicy fish cake (¥2000); *mee krob*, crispy vermicelli (¥1200); spicy eggplant salad (¥1200); fried rice served in a fresh pineapple half (¥1500); and *pad thai* noodles (¥1200). The menu indicates how spicy the food is.

NANBAN-TEI *(Japanese yakitori, inexpensive to moderate). 4-5-6-Roppongi, Minato-ku. Tel. (03)3402-0606. Open 5pm to 10:30pm. Roppongi Station.*

Nanban-tei serves inventive *yakitori*. In addition to the usual array of chicken and vegetables, you can have pork with asparagus, beef with Japanese basil leaves, and other tantalizing combinations. The dinner course, ¥3500, comes with 14 different sticks including raw vegetables you dip in a thick *miso* sauce; *omakase* course, ¥3000, has 10 different sticks. You can also order a la carte. The friendly staff speak English, and there is an English menu. Nanban-tei is popular with locals as well as with foreign residents, so it is best to make reservations. There are several branches around central Tokyo.

MIKASA *(Continental, inexpensive to moderate). Arisugawa West, 1F, 5-14 Minami Azabu, Minato-ku. Tel. (03)3448-8924. Open 11:30am to 10pm; 11am to 10pm Sundays and national holidays. Hiroo Station.*

Mikasa is a light and airy place for a casual lunch in the Hiroo area. In fair weather, you can eat on the patio under large cloth umbrellas. The menu is heavy on Italian, but they also serve fish cooked in nouvelle French style. Mikasa emphasizes using fresh, local seasonal ingredients. Also, unlike many Tokyo restaurants that serve an assortment of bite-size portions for dessert, Mikasa lets you choose from among its tantalizing desserts. The lunch menu starts at ¥1200.

NEW HOKKAIEN *(Chinese, inexpensive to moderate). 2F, No. 23 Togensha Building, 3-16-15 Roppongi, Minato-ku. Tel.(03)3505-7881. Open daily 10:30am to 2pm; 5pm to 10pm. Roppongi Station.*

As a long-standing Beijing-style Chinese restaurant, New Hokkaien is always crowded with young and old, Japanese and foreigners. It's one of Tokyo's few Chinese restaurants that hasn't adjusted its recipes to suit the Japanese palate. In addition to standard and authentic Chinese dishes, you can choose delicate and tasty dim sum.

KITCHEN 5 *(Southern European and Middle Eastern, moderate). 4-2-15 Nishi Azabu, Minato-ku. Tel. (03)3409-8835. Open from 6pm to 9:45pm. Closed Sunday, Monday and holidays. Also closed for five weeks late July to August and four weeks around New Year's. Hiroo Station.*

Kobayashi-san, the female chef, closes the restaurant for extended periods several times a year when she travels to Europe and the Middle East to try out new cuisines. She returns and incorporates what she has learned to make delicious, eclectic fare. There is no menu; Kobayashi-san goes to the market every morning, chooses the freshest food and cooks it. The offerings are placed on the counter and you tell her your choices. While you never know what you'll find, we adore her spicy chicken, ratatouille, and pasta in fresh tomato and basil sauce. The restaurant is tiny—there's only a small counter and one table. Come before 7pm or you may have to wait. Dishes cost about ¥1800 each; ¥5000 should buy enough for an average appetite.

LA TERRE *(French, inexpensive to moderate). 1-9-20 Azabudai, Minato-ku. Tel. (03)3583-9682. Open 11:30am to 2pm; 6pm to 8:30pm. Closed Sunday and national holidays. Kamiyacho Station.*

Tucked away on a little alley across from the Russian Embassy, La Terre is a cozy and romantic French bistro. When the weather is good, there are a few tables outside. La Terre is especially popular in the spring when cherry trees blossom and new leaves sprout; reservations are a must. The cherry trees are right outside the restaurant; even if you are facing the back, you can see them reflected in the mirror. The food is French but on the light side. The lunchtime sets cost ¥2000, ¥2500 and ¥4000. Dinner courses are ¥6000, ¥8000 and ¥10,000. You can also order a la carte.

LE FRICOTEUR *(French bistro, inexpensive to moderate). 4-11-28 Nishi Azabu, Minato-ku. Tel. (03)3498-4508. Open 12 noon to 2pm; 6pm to 12 midnight. Closed Sunday. Hiroo Station.*

This intimate French bistro has a friendly chef and staff and serves good, honest fare. The specialty is red wine beef stew, which melts in your mouth (¥3400 for two). The lunchtime set menus from ¥850 are a bargain: appetizer, main dish and coffee. Evening set meals cost ¥6000.

KUSHIHACHI *(Yakitori, expensive). 3F, Seshido Building, 3-10-9 Roppongi, Minato-ku. Tel. (03)3403-3060. Open 5:30pm to 11pm. Closed Sunday and national holidays. Roppongi Station.*

It's pricey but a lively traditional Japanese dining experience. The ¥7000 basic set includes 10 kinds of *yakitori* and other delicacies on skewers plus four side dishes.

HONMURA-AN *(Soba, inexpensive). 7-14-18 Roppongi, Minato-ku. Tel. (03)3401-0844. Open 11:30am to 9pm. Closed Tuesday. Roppongi Station.*

Located behind Hotel Ibis, Honmura-an dishes up some of Tokyo's best *soba* noodles. Walk up the few steps to reach this lively shop always crowded with aficionados. *Soba* can cost more here than at average shops, but it's worth every yen. The house specialties are *tempura seiro,* cold *soba* with *tempura* on the side (¥1700) and *kamo seiro,* cold *soba* you dip in duck broth (¥1300). *Tempura soba,* (the *tempura* shrimp floats in the hot broth on top of noodles) is ¥2100. *Sansai* (mountain vegetable) *soba* costs ¥900. After you finish eating cold *soba,* the staff brings hot water in a square lacquer container. Mix this water with your remaining dipping sauce and drink as a soup.

JOHNNY ROCKETS *(American, inexpensive). 2F, Coco Roppongi Building, 3-11-10 Roppongi, Minato-ku. Tel. (03)3423-1955. Open 11am to 11pm Monday to Thursday; 11am Friday to 11pm Sunday. Roppongi Station.*

For that hamburger craving, bypass McDonalds. Johnny Rockets is a retro American diner serving burgers, fries and shakes. Most of the fun-loving staff are foreigners. The shop's most popular "original hamburger" costs ¥900, soft drinks are ¥500. Yes, it's more expensive than fast food, but worth it. Weekend evenings Johnny stays open all night so you can fill up after dancing nearby.

KAOTAN RAMEN *(Ramen, inexpensive). 2-34-30 Minami Aoyama, Minato-ku. Tel. (03)3475-6337. Open 12 noon to 5am; closed Sundays. Roppongi Station.*

Located at the foot of Aoyama Cemetery, it is hard to miss this shack that serves legendary *ramen.* Their Benzes parked nearby, people queue up to eat the ¥650 bowl of noodles.

MONSEN *(yakitori, expensive). 2-13-8 Azabu Juban, Minato-ku. Tel: (03)3452-2327. Open 6pm to 10pm. Closed Sunday. Reservations necessary. Roppongi Station.*

Monsen features some of the best yakitori in town. The chef-owner, Kazuhiro Iwamoto is a genius with his dishes, using the freshest seasonal ingredients. Each glory has its price and Monsen is no exception – dinner will set you back ¥10,000 plus drinks.

Ryogoku

CHANKO DOJI *(Chanko nabe, inexpensive to moderate)*. *1-28-4 Midori-cho, Sumida-ku. Tel. (03) 3635-5347. Open daily 11:30am to 2pm; 5pm to 10:30pm. Ryogoku Station.*

Chanko Doji serves *chanko nabe*, the stew that sumo wrestlers eat: vegetables, tofu, *udon* noodles, chicken and fish are cooked together in a broth. Don't worry, it's not fattening, sumo wrestlers just eat a lot of it. At lunchtime, the *nabe* is ¥1800-2800 and *kamo chanko* (duck chanko) is ¥2300. Dinnertime, *tori chanko* (chicken chanko) is ¥4000, *yokozuna chanko* (champion chanko) is ¥5000.

MOMOJIYA *(Japanese, inexpensive to moderate)*. *1-10-2 Ryogoku, Sumida-ku. Tel. (03)3631-5596. Open 5pm to 9pm. Closed Sunday. Ryogoku Station.*

Momojiya serves venison and boar dishes and badger soup. The *inoshishi* (boar meat) *nabe* is ¥4000. *Inoshishi teishoku* (¥4500) includes boar meat, rice, pickles and mushroom soup. Ask them to substitute badger soup if you prefer.

Shibuya & Daikanyama

HASSAN *(Shabu-shabu, moderate)*. *B1F, Junikagetsu Building, 1-18-7 Jinnan, Shibuya-ku. Tel. (03)3464-8883. Open daily 11:30am to 10pm. Shibuya Station.*

The restaurant is known for its special ceramic plates, *Takatori-yaki* ware, introduced to Japan by a Korean potter named Hassan during the 17th century. Located in the basement of the Junikagetsu Building, Hassan has a quiet, traditional air; the windows look out on bamboo trees. Lunchtime menus consist of two *shabu-shabu* sets: ¥1500 for imported beef and ¥2500 for Japanese beef. All you can eat *shabu-shabu (tabehodai)* costs ¥3900 and ¥4500 at lunchtime, and ¥4500 and ¥5900 at night. After 4:30pm they add a 10% service charge.

SHABU ZEN *(Shabu-shabu, sukiyaki, and kaiseki, moderate)*. *B1, Shibuya Creston Hotel, 10-20 Kamiyama-cho, Shibuya-ku. Tel. (03)3485-0800. Open 5pm to 11pm weekdays; 5pm to 10pm weekends. Shibuya Station.*

Shabu Zen serves *shabu-shabu* at a very reasonable price. You can order a *tabehodai*, all you can eat for ¥3800-5800. The least expensive set uses US beef, the next up (¥4500) uses Japanese beef and the highest (¥5800) uses Kobe beef, raised where the animals are drinking beer and listening to Mozart and Bach. They also serve *sukiyaki* and *kaiseki*. The basement has high ceilings and a contemporary Japanese ambiance. Most customers sit at tables but there are *tatami* mat rooms along one side.

TABLEAUX *(Continental/American, moderate)*. *B1, Sunrise Daikanyama Building, 11-6 Sarugaku-cho, Shibuya-ku. Tel. (03)5489-2201. Open daily 5:30pm to 11pm. Daikanyama Station.*

Popular with models and expats, this restaurant has a richly textured decor of deep red brocades and velvets; in other words, early bordello. The food is eclectic and good — surprisingly inexpensive given the surroundings and clientele. Their pasta is delicious as is the seafood. Tableaux is in Daikanyama, an area known for fashionable boutiques and eateries. The American manager is very friendly and will be more than happy to assist you with choosing your food and wine.

KAIKA-YA (*Japanese home-style cooking, moderate*). *23-7 Maruyama-cho, Shibuya-ku. Tel. (03)3770-0878. Open 11:30am to 2pm weekdays; 6pm to 10:30pm daily. Shibuya Station.*

This tiny Japanese bistro ranks among our favorite places for original and inventive Japanese home-style cooking. The lunch menu has only a few offerings all priced around ¥1000, decided by the chef after he goes to the morning market. We recommend that you tell the chef "*omakase course,*" ¥3000, and the chef will give you a sampling of the best dishes of the day. One specialty is tuna ribs, tuna cooked on the bone in a thick soy sauce. The sign for the restaurant is in Japanese, but you'll see "By the Sea" in English.

RAJ MAHAL (*Indian, inexpensive to moderate*). *5F, JOW Building, 30-5 Udagawa-cho, Shibuya-ku. Tel. (03)3770-7680. Open daily 11:30am to 10pm. Shibuya Station.*

Raj Mahal is an excellent Indian restaurant. The decor is suitably Indian without being over the top and the *tandoori* oven, visible through the kitchen's glass window, lends an air of authenticity. The *tandoori* meats, fish and *nan* bread are wonderful as are the curries. Fortunately, the flavors haven't been toned down for the Japanese palate. Raj Mahal's manager, Mr. Panda, is always very helpful with dining suggestions. The menu is both in English and Japanese. Lunchtime specials range from ¥950 to ¥1800 and most entrees are in the ¥1500 range.

SAMRAT (*Indian, inexpensive to moderate*). *Koyas One Building, 6F, 13-7 Udagawa-cho, Shibuya-ku. Tel. (03)3770-7275. Open daily 11am to 5am. Shibuya Station. Samrat has other shops in Roppongi (Shojikiya Building 2F, 4-10-10 Roppongi, Minato-ku. Tel.(03)3478-5877); in Ueno (OAK Building 2F, 4-8-9 Ueno, Taito-ku. Tel.(03)5688-3226); and in Shinjuku (Seno Building 7F, 3-18-4 Shinjuku, Shinjuku-ku. Tel.(03)3355-1771).*

One of several Indian chain restaurants in Shibuya, Samrat serves good food at reasonable prices. The chef and most of the staff are Indian so communication in English is no problem. Curries are good as is the *nan* bread. The lunchtime menu is served until 4pm, a real plus. For ¥890 you can have two kinds of curry, a drink, and all the rice and *nan* you can eat. Since Samrat is one of the few restaurants open until the wee hours of the morning, stop in for late night dining.

ANATOLIA *(Turkish, moderate). B1, Miyamasuzaka Building, 2-19-20 Shibuya, Shibuya-ku. Tel. (03)3486-7449. Open daily 11am to 11pm; 3pm to 11am Sunday. Shibuya Station.*

Anatolia is a small basement restaurant serving hearty Turkish food. The picture menu is in English as well as in Japanese. They have three set courses costing ¥3300 to ¥4400, but we prefer to order a la carte. Our favorite is the *iskender* kebobs.

SUSHI SEI *(Sushi, inexpensive). B2, Shibuto Cine Building, 2-6-17 Dogenzaka, Shibuya-ku. Open 11:30am to 2pm, 5pm to 10pm weekdays, 11:30am to 9:30pm weekends and national holidays. Closed the 3rd Monday of the month. Shibuya Station.*

This *sushi* bar in the basement of the Shibuto Cine Building, right across the street from the Shibuya 109 Building, is popular for its fresh and reasonably priced *sushi*. It gets crowded, so come for dinner before 7pm or else you'll have to wait. We usually go with the chef's course, an assortment of *nigiri sushi*, for ¥2500. You can also order a la carte.

KABALA *(Thai, moderate). B1F, Pink Dragon Building, 1-23-23 Shibuya, Shibuya-ku. Tel. (03)3498-0699. Open 11:30am-2pm; 5:30pm-10:30pm. Closed Sunday. Shibuya Station.*

As you go down the stairs, you'll notice that the owner's taste is most peculiar. Kabala has more to offer than the delicious Thai food it serves. The interior decor is closer to continental Europe, and the cutlery is decorated with unusual heavy patterns without a Thai connection. The Thai food is out of this world; two of our favorites are *pad thai*, a translucent noodle dish, and minced pork with basil leaves. Entrees run about ¥1600.

IROHANIHOHETO *(Japanese/Western, inexpensive). 1-19-3 Jinnan, Shibuya-ku. Tel. (03)3476-1682. Open daily 5pm to 3am. Shibuya Station.*

This large and noisy drinking establishment is popular with young people on limited budgets. The decor is country, with farm implements and other stuff decorating the interior. The food is inexpensive and the menu extensive; ordering is easy because the menu has pictures. The food is a combination of Japanese and Western. It's not haute cuisine, but then again, neither are the prices. Try the *ika somen* (thin strips of raw squid on ice), fried noodles and Hokkaido potatoes.

MELA *(Indian, inexpensive). 3F, Kasumi Building, 2-25-17 Dogenzaka, Shibuya-ku. Tel. (03) 3770-0120. Open daily 5pm to 2am. Shibuya Station.*

There are a zillion Indian restaurants in Shibuya, but this ranks among the best. Tucked away in a small alley, it's popular with shoppers and people working in the area. The decor tries to copy a village hut. The waitresses speak a bit of English.

COCINA MEXICANA LACASITA *(Mexican, moderate). 3F, 13-4 Daikanyama, Shibuya-ku. Tel. (03)3496-1850. Open daily 12 noon to 10pm. Daikanyama or Shibuya Station.*

One of the few Mexican restaurants around where, if you close your eyes, the food is actually on par with the real stuff in Mexico. Lunch sets are around ¥1000, dinner for under ¥4000.

MOMO PARADISE *(Shabu-shabu, inexpensive). 6F, Shibuya Beam, 38-3 Udagawa-cho, Shibuya-ku. Tel: (03)3461-2941. Open daily 11:30am to 2pm, 5pm to 10pm. Shibuya Station.*

Inexpensive *shabu-shabu* and *sukiyaki* is the name of the game at Shibuya's Momo Paradise, one in a chain of about a half-dozen restaurants around the Tokyo area. The meat is imported, and while it could never be mistaken for Kobe beef, it's perfect for the meat-starved traveler on a budget. All-you-can-eat *shabu-shabu* or *sukiyaki* is an incredible ¥1000 for lunch and ¥1500 for dinner; for ¥3500 you can gorge on all-you-can-eat-and-drink *shabu-shabu* and *sukiyaki*.

Shinagawa, Takanawa & Gotanda

AJIKAIDO GOJUSANTSUGI *(Japanese, inexpensive to moderate). 38F, Shinagawa Prince Hotel. 4-10-30 Takanawa, Minato-ku. Tel. (03)3440-1111. Open 11:30am to 2pm; 5:30pm to 10pm. Shinagawa Station.*

The top floor of the newest wing of the Shinagawa Prince Hotel offers a slew of casual Japanese eateries gathered together. Shinagawa was the second of 53 stations on the Tokaido Road between old Tokyo and Kyoto. This floor features the foods that feudal era travelers enjoyed on their way. You can choose from *yakitori, sushi, oden, teppanyaki, tempura* and *shabu-shabu*. The views are spectacular.

CACCIANI *(Italian, inexpensive to moderate). 1F, 3-11-3 Takanawa, Minato-ku. Tel. (03)3473-3939. Open daily 11am to 2:30pm; 5pm to 10pm. Takanawadai Station.*

If you are staying at one of the Shinagawa/Takanawa hotels, try this lovely neighborhood Italian restaurant for a good change. Cacciani offers light and tasty Italian cuisine. Pizza is thin and crusty — the house special is Pizza Bianca with mozzarella cheese and homemade ham for ¥1900. The *antipasti misti* always includes a variety of local mushrooms and eggplant marinated in a herb vinaigrette. We have friends who come all the way across town to eat chicken *diavola*— a small tasty chicken slowly grilled until it's golden (¥2200). It is big enough for two people. Lunch set starts from ¥850.

SHER, *in the tennis court building behind the Shinagawa Prince Hotel. Open daily 11am to 9:30pm. Shinagawa Station.*

This unlikely site houses a surprisingly good, Japanese-style curry shop. Chicken curry costs ¥850; mushroom curry, ¥850, dry chicken curry with five small pieces of chicken on top of curried rice, ¥1000. You can specify if you want your curry medium, hot or very hot.

NE QUITTEZ PAS *(French, expensive). 3-15-19 Higashi Gotanda, Shinagawa-ku. Tel. (03)3442-2382. 12 noon to 2pm; 6pm to 9:30pm. Closed Monday. Gotanda Station.*

Outstanding French cuisine at this quiet, neighborhood restaurant with a small garden offering al fresco dining in warmer weather. The chef, a former boxer, spent three years in France and returned as a masterful chef. The menu is fixed and always centers around fish. One favorite is a large clam char-cooked in its shell. It's totally blackened when you get it and pops open with the twist of the fork. Inside is a succulent clam cooked in its own juice. The menu is prix fixe, lunch is ¥6500, dinner ¥6500, ¥10,000 and ¥12,000.

IL CAVALLO *(Italian, moderate). 3F, 5-25-19 Higashi Gotanda, Shinjuku-ku. Tel. (03)5420-2223. 11:30am to 2pm; 6pm to 9:30pm. Closed holidays. Gotanda Station.*

Located on the third floor of the Tokyo Design Center, this stylish Italian eatery serves excellent Italian food. Lunch courses range from ¥1500 to ¥3500; dinner ¥4500 and ¥7000.

Shinjuku

NEW YORK GRILL *(American Continental, moderate to expensive). Park Hyatt Tokyo, 3-7-1-2 Nishi Shinjuku, Shinjuku-ku. Tel. (03)5323-3458. Open daily 11:30am to 2:30pm; 5:30am to 10:30pm. Shinjuku or Hatsudai Station.*

One of Tokyo's hottest restaurants sits on the 52nd floor of the Park Hyatt Hotel. The New York Grill's views are spectacular. The weekday lunchtime buffet offers an appetizer, salad and dessert buffet, and you order the main course from the menu (¥4400). On weekends, the system is the same but includes champagne, and the cost is ¥5800. Dinner set menus cost ¥10,000 and ¥15,000. We prefer lunch because the daytime views of Tokyo are more interesting than nighttime. Four large murals are reminiscent of New York, but if you look closely, a little of Japan slips in. The adjacent bar has live jazz music in the evenings. Try to avoid coming on a cloudy day. Be sure you make reservations.

KOZUE *(Japanese, moderate to expensive). Park Hyatt Tokyo, 3-7-1-2 Nishi Shinjuku, Shinjuku-ku. Tel. (03)5323-3460. Open daily 11:30am to 2:30pm; 5:30pm to 10pm. Shinjuku or Hatsudai Station.*

We love the open, spacious feeling Kozue exudes: the large glass windows, high ceiling and wide tables. High up in the Park Tower Building, the huge glass windows afford a bird's-eye view of western Tokyo and on a clear day, a glimpse of Mt. Fuji. The lunch box set menus are ¥3900 and ¥4800, and *tendon* set costs ¥2800. *Tendon* set includes beautifully presented *sashimi* as a starter, *tendon*, clear soup and pickles. On weekdays they have a special bento course that ends with dessert and coffee served in the adjacent lounge (¥5000). Dinner *kaiseki* courses start at ¥12,000, *shabu-shabu* at ¥15,000. Kozue is a lovely place for a special Japanese meal.

CARMINE EDOCHIANO *(Italian, moderate). 9-13 Arakicho, Shinjuku-ku. Tel. (03)3225-6767. Open 12 noon to 2pm; 6pm to 10pm. Yotsuya Station.*

This is a sister restaurant to Carmine and it's in an out-of-the-way place. But we think it is worth a visit to enjoy authentic Italian food in a very Japanese atmosphere, a fascinating combination. Located in a Taisho-era wooden house, the small reception hall is like entering a friend's home. But you are requested not to take your shoes off. Most of the tables are upstairs although the Japanese room downstairs also beckons invitingly. The waiters wear navy blue monk's working outfits.

Each room is small because they have converted a small private house into a restaurant. And yet the kitchen in this very Japanese environment produces delicious Italian food. The ¥2500 lunch sets includes antipasto, pasta, dessert and coffee; the ¥3500 set adds a fish or meat dish. The set dinner is ¥6000. Pasta a la carte runs ¥1600 to ¥2000.

TSUNAHACHI-KADOHAZU-AN *(Tempura, inexpensive to expensive). 3-28-4 Shinjuku, Shinjuku-ku. Tel. (03)3358-2788. Open daily 11am to 3pm; 5pm to 9:30pm. Shinjuku Station.*

Tsunahachi-Kadohazu-an ranks among Tokyo's top *tempura* shops. Located a few minutes east of Shinjuku Station, the entire six-storied building is dedicated to serving *tempura*. The automatic glass door leads you to a reception desk where you are directed to a floor. The elevator's door is lacquered. Each floor is decorated differently: one floor is modern Japanese with black, gray and white colors and another has an ancient Heian soft pastel color scheme. You can either sit at a table or on *tatami* mats. The business lunch consists of *tempura*, appetizer, cooked vegetable, rice, soup and pickles and costs ¥1200. The lunch set runs ¥1800-3800.

We like the special salad; the marinated tuna makes an unusual combination with tomato and minced leek in a soy-based dressing. The *tempura* is fried crispy and the vegetables and fish are tender. At dinner you can sit at the counter and enjoy *tempura* cooked right in front of you, these sets start at ¥5000. You can also order a la carte.

CARMINE *(Italian, moderate). 1-19 Saiku-machi, Shinjuku-ku. Tel. (03)3260-5066. Open 11:30am to 2pm; 6pm to 9:30pm. Ichigaya Station.*

Though located in an inconvenient place, a 15-minute walk from Ichigaya Station, Carmine serves delicious and authentic Italian food. The small restaurant has a casual atmosphere. The *penne al gorgonzola* alone is worth the trek. Lunch sets start at ¥1800. The special course A at dinner is a great deal for ¥3800; it includes antipasto, pasta, main dish, dessert and coffee. Don't go without a reservation.

AGIO *(Italian, inexpensive). 7F, Isetan Department Store, 3-14-1 Shinjuku, Shinjuku-ku. Tel. (03)3354-6720. Open 11am to 9pm. Closed Wednesday. Shinjuku Station.*

Agio, a cozy Italian restaurant, serves delicious pasta and pizza. It almost always has people waiting outside, but they provide chairs so the usually brief wait is comfortable. From the entrance you see fresh tomatoes, colorful peppers, garlic, zucchini and a chef kneading pizza dough. The atmosphere is casual and the staff attentive.

Shirogane & Meguro

KASHO *(Teppanyaki, moderate to expensive). Gajo-en Hotel, 1-1-8 Shimo Meguro, Meguro-ku. Tel. (03)5434-3978. Open 11:30am to 2:30pm; 5:30pm to 9:30pm weekdays. 11:30am to 9:30pm weekends. Meguro Station.*

Kasho is one of the many restaurants at Meguro Gajo-en Hotel, which we think is an incredible example of Japanese aesthetics with a twist of Chinese style. The hotel personifies the Japan-Fujiyama-Geisha style: gaudy, kitschy, inscrutable, static and strange. Don't miss the lacquered bathroom that you reach by crossing a small red-lacquered drum-shaped bridge. Now, about the food — Kasho serves delicious *teppanyaki* in this fascinating environment. Food is served on plates too tasteful for the rest of the hotel. Once seated, you receive a napkin-apron lest you get splattered by the food that's grilled in front of you. Lunch courses start at ¥3000; they include a starter, vegetables, small salad, fish or meat. Watching the chef at work with his knife cutting meat and vegetables is a treat, but don't expect Benihana theatrics. A small Japanese sweet and coffee are served at lounge tables away from the grill. At dinner time courses range from ¥6000 to ¥15,000.

SHIROGANE *(Japanese, moderate). 3F, Ritz Shirogane, 6-16-28 Shirogane, Minato-ku. Tel. (03)3449-0033. Open daily 11:30am to 2pm; 5:30pm to 9pm. Meguro Station.*

A very contemporary Japanese restaurant, Shirogane is located in a chic contemporary concrete building. Its interior combines the modern with traditional touches like bamboo branches covering the ceiling. The thick wooden tables are comfortable for a long, leisurely meal. The lunchtime *shokado bento* (¥3000) is an elegant lunch. It includes an appetizer, a variety of vegetables, fish and meat tidbits served in a lacquered box and either *tempura* or steak with a Japanese sauce, rice, soup, and dessert. When we want a quiet lunch and a place where we can talk, we go here. Set dinners are ¥6000, ¥9000 and ¥15,000. Unlike most Japanese restaurants, Shirogane ends its meals with dessert and coffee.

DAIGO (*Japanese tonkatsu, inexpensive*). *1-25-21 Shirogane, Minato-ku. Tel. (03)3444-2941. Open 12 noon to 2pm; 6pm to 9pm. Closed Monday and 3rd Tuesday. Meguro or Ebisu Station.*

Daigo is located in the middle of nowhere from the tourist's point of view, but we love this tiny *tonkatsu* shop so we often go out of our way to have lunch here. The delicious and tender *tonkatsu* is accompanied by lots of shredded fresh cabbage and a tasty thick sauce. The special tofu salad is sublime (¥600). *Hire katsu* set costs ¥1800 and *rosu katsu* set ¥1500. They even have an English menu.

TONKI (*Japanese tonkatsu, inexpensive*). *1-1-2 Shimo Meguro, Meguro-ku. Tel. (03)3491-9928. Open 4pm to 10:45pm. Closed Tuesday and 3rd Monday. Meguro Station.*

Tonki raises cooking *tonkatsu* to an art form. A special formula dips the pork cutlets in batter three times for a thick crust and tender meat. Tonki is popular and you may have to wait; opt for a seat at the counter instead of upstairs. When you enter you'll be asked to choose either *hire* (fillet) or *rosu* (chop). While you are waiting for a seat, your dinner is being prepared, so by the time you sit down, your food is almost ready. *Hire teishoku* and *rosu teishoku* each cost ¥1650.

TOSHI-AN (*Soba, inexpensive*). *5-17-2 Shiroganedai, Minato-ku. Tel. (03)3444-1741. Open 11:30am to 7:30pm. Closed Monday and Tuesday. Meguro Station.*

It's not unusual to see people standing in line waiting, not so patiently, to get into Toshi-an. Homemade *soba* is the specialty here. The dipping sauce and broth is real Edo-style dark brown. The decor includes beautiful *tansu* chests and broad wooden tables with matching chairs. Plates are selected to match the rustic folk art decor.

Ueno

HANTEI (*Japanese kushi-age, moderate to expensive*). *2-12-15 Nezu, Bunkyo-ku. Tel. (03)3828-1440. Open 12 noon to 2pm; 5pm to 9:30pm. Sundays 4pm to 8:30pm. Nezu Station.*

We love to take visitors to this restaurant in a charming old wooden building. Our favorite is to eat in the cozy, thick-walled storehouse, but there's also a room with tables and *tatami* mat rooms are upstairs. Ask for the *kura* (storehouse) when making a reservation. *Kushi-age* are deep fried morsels on sticks. You don't order, they just start bringing you sticks. After twelve, they'll ask if you want to continue. Just tell them when you don't want any more. Twelve sticks cost ¥4000.

SASA-NO-YUKI (*Tofu, inexpensive to moderate*). *2-15-10 Negishi, Taito-ku. Tel. (03)3873-1145. Open 11am to 9pm. Closed Monday. Uguisudani Station.*

As vegetarian food becomes more popular, Sasa-no-yuki's popularity grows. Make a reservation to eat here the day you decide to wander around the old traditional downtown areas. Sasa-no-yuki, which literally means "snow on the bamboo leaves," has been producing tofu for nearly 300 years. Only Japanese soy beans and fresh well water are used, so the tofu is sublime. An American friend who tasted its tofu for the first time described it as "cool, clean, slightly sweet, with an almost buttery texture." The restaurant knows how to cook tofu 300 different ways, but don't worry about having to slog through a fat menu. There are several courses: from three different dishes of tofu for ¥1500 to eight dishes for ¥4200. There's even an English menu. The seating is all on *tatami* mats looking out over a lovely garden — come dressed to sit on the floor.

HONTE PONTA. *3-23-3 Ueno, Taito-ku. Tel. (03)3831-2351. Open 11:30am to 2pm; 4:30pm to 8pm. Closed Monday. Ueno or Okachimachi Station.*

This old-fashioned shop serves *yoshoku,* Japanized Western food. The ¥2500 *tonkatsu* is popular; it includes pork cutlet and *miso* soup.

Outskirts of Tokyo

UKAI TORIYAMA *(Japanese, moderate to expensive). Minami Asakawa-machi, Hachioji-shi. Tel. (0426)61-0739. Open 11am to 8pm weekdays, 11am to 7pm Sunday and national holidays. Takao-san guchi Station.*

Mt. Takao is a popular destination for Tokyoites fleeing urban congestion. Only 55 minutes from Shinjuku, suddenly you are in a heavily wooded cedar forest. Ukai Toriyama is the perfect escape for lunch or dinner. The restaurant, on a river ravine, is a collection of farm and teahouses moved from all over Japan. Dine in a thatched roof farmhouse or in a teahouse that once belonged to the powerful Maeda feudal lord. The setting personifies the Japanese ideal many Western tourists seek.

You'll have the choice of several different set meals; all include charcoal grilled *ayu* river fish, our favorite. The chicken course includes an appetizer, *sashimi,* soup, grilled *ayu,* chicken you grill over charcoal, special rice and pickles for ¥4500. The beef course, which uses Hida beef from the Takayama area in central Japan, costs ¥7500. *Sake* rice wine is served from fresh bamboo containers.

It is hard to believe that Ukai Toriyama is so close to Tokyo. From Shinjuku Station take the Keio express train to Takao-san-guchi Station, the end of the line (55 minutes). The restaurant runs a complimentary shuttle bus from the station. If it doesn't come within a few minutes, call to request one.

SEEING THE SIGHTS

Each of Tokyo's many districts has its own special character. The best way to get a feel for Tokyo is to explore it on foot: wander along busy shopping streets, down little alleys and meander through temple compounds. Tokyo still has small neighborhoods with tiny specialized shops where local residents buy tofu, fish, vegetables and other daily necessities. Merchants are friendly and life is at a pace more akin to small villages. There are also business districts like Marunouchi and Shinjuku where Japan's office workers spend most of their waking hours. Finally, there are the glittering shopping and entertainment areas like Ginza, Shinjuku, Shibuya and Harajuku where Japanese relax and play.

We divide Tokyo into 18 areas and give directions for informal walking tours. Be aware of two different Tokyo's existing side by side – the contemporary and the traditional. Some remnants of old Japan still exist in Asakusa and Ueno, but the up-to-the-moment places are Shibuya, Harajuku and Shinjuku.

And take your time to sit in a cafe and watch the world go by. Spend a few hours in a museum savoring its art. Participate in a tea ceremony or take a flower arranging class. Have a traditional *shiatsu* massage. Explore a flea market.

Area 1: Around the Imperial Palace, pages 240-245
Area 2: From Ginza to Nihonbashi, pages 245-252
Area 3: From Tsukiji to Roppongi, pages 252-257
Area 4: Asakusa, pages 257-262
Area 5: Ueno, pages 262-266
Area 6: Yanaka, pages 266-268
Area 7: Akihabara and Kanda, pages 268-271
Area 8: Asakusabashi, Ryogoku, Fukagawa and Kiba, pages 271-275
Area 9: Shinagawa and Meguro, pages 275-277
Area 10: Ebisu, page 277
Area 11: Shibuya, pages 277-284
Area 12: Harajuku and Omotesando, pages 286-291
Area 13: Aoyama and Akasaka, pages 291-295
Area 14: Shinjuku, pages 295-299
Area 15: North of the Imperial Palace, pages 300-301
Area 16: Ikebukuro, pages 301-302
Area 17: Tokyo Waterfront, pages 302-307
Area 18: Outskirts, pages 307-309

Area 1: Around the Imperial Palace
Time for the walk: about 1/2 day and longer if you visit all the museums. The closest subway station is Nijubashi-mae on the Chiyoda line.

We'll start at the **Imperial Palace**. Although it sounds like it is an important sight, in reality, there's no Buckingham Palace-type mansion to gaze upon and no stately imperial guard standing watch. The emperor lives in a low residence not visible from the street, but the formidable castle walls and moats are beautiful.

HOPELESSLY LOST?

Tokyo began as a castle town, and castle towns are notoriously difficult to navigate. Designed to confuse the enemy, roads that start out parallel to each other suddenly end up perpendicular. And you can go into a maze of tiny alleys and find that the only way out may be the way you came in. Tokyo not only confounded invading armies, it still confounds residents and visitors alike. But don't let that get in your way. Wander around. What's the worst that could happen?

*If you become hopelessly lost, here's our foolproof method for getting yourself where you want to be: Hail a taxi and tell the driver: "**Ichi ban chikai eki ma-de**," and he'll take you to the closest subway station or JR train station. From there you can get anywhere in the city. Another way, but not as foolproof, is to jump on the nearest city bus. Buses usually begin and end their routes at train or subway stations. Although this approach is a little more risky, you'll eventually end up at a train station having seen another part of Tokyo.*

The palace grounds are an oasis of green in the center of the city. The five-kilometer sidewalk around the perimeter of the palace is a popular place to jog although we find the car exhaust makes it less than perfect. On Sundays from 10am to 4pm, the roads on the eastern and northern sides are closed to cars; bicycles are available free of charge from the Babasakimon Police Station.

On the east side of the palace along Hibiya Dori, there's a wide open area called Kokyo-mae Hiroba, graced by many pruned pine trees. **Nijubashi Bridge**, a double-arched iron bridge designed by a German architect in the 19th century, is now the main entrance to the palace. It's nearly mandatory for Japanese tourists to be photographed in front of this bridge. Walk north parallel to **Uchibori Dori** (literally Inner Moat Avenue) until you reach the **Otemon Gate** (literally Principal Gate) across from the Palace Hotel.

If you are dying to go into the inner grounds of the palace other than on January 2 and December 23 when the emperor gives audiences, take a tour in Japanese given by the Imperial Household Agency. Apart from the idea that you have entered the palace's inner sanctum, we don't think it's worth the trouble, but here's the information: *90-minute tour leaves from the Kikyo-mon gate, across from the Palace Hotel, at 10am and 1:30pm weekdays. You must call the Imperial Household Agency, Tel. (03)3213-1111, ext. 485, to make an appointment and then go to the Sankan-gakari Visitor's Office to pick up your permit card at least one day in advance of the tour. The office is open 9am to 4:30pm weekdays, closed for lunch from noon to 1pm. It's best to have a Japanese speaker make the phone call.*

Imperial Palace and Kitanomaru Park

⛩ Yasukuni Shrine

? Tourist Information
▭ Japan Railways
- - - Subway Lines
▨ Moats

National Theatre

Diamond Hotel
British Embassy
Fairmont Hotel
千鳥が淵
Tayasumon Gate

Hanzomon Gate

Chidorigafuchi Park
Nippon Budokan Hall
Crafts Museum
Kudanshita
九段下駅

Imperial Palace

Kitanomaru Park
北ノ丸公園

Science Museum

Kita-Hanebashimon Gate
National Museum of Modern Art

桜田門駅
Sakuradamon
Imperial Household
Agency
Takebashi
竹橋駅

Metropolitan
Police Board
Sakuradamon Gate
Higashi Gyoen Garden
東御苑

Nijubashi Bridge
Mainichi Newspapers

Hirakawamon Gate

N

Hibiya
Park

Imperial
Palace Plaza
Otemon Gate

Statue of Kusunoki

Palace
Hotel

Hibiya
日比谷駅
Nijubashi-mae
二重橋前駅
Otemachi

Otemachi 大手町駅

Yurakucho
Otemachi

JR Yurakucho Station
有楽町駅
Central Post
Office
Tokyo

JR Tokyo Station
東京駅

?

There are three ways to enter the **East Garden** (Higashi Gyoen); the most common way is through the Otemon Gate. The powerful feudal lord Date, from the Sendai area, built it in the early 17th century to show his loyalty to the Tokugawa shogun. The present gate is a replica built in 1967; the tall wooden gate is imposing with its heavy doors and fine metalwork.

The garden is open from 9am to 4pm (until 3:30pm November through February), but you must enter at least one hour before closing (that is, by 3pm). Closed Monday, Friday and December 25 through January 3. Admission is free. Pick up a plastic tag at the office just past the gate and surrender it when leaving. You do not have to leave by the same gate.

The peaceful garden is psychologically far removed from the bustle of Tokyo that's outside the gates. Inside are more castle walls, lots of trees and bushes and a few buildings. The **Imperial Court Museum** (Sanno-maru Shozokan), a tiny museum, displays pieces of the imperial family's collection of Japanese art. *Tel. (03)3213-1177. Open 9:15am to 4pm. Closed*

Monday and Friday. No admission fee. The **Fujimi Turret** and **Fujimi Armory** are the only two Tokugawa-era buildings remaining. As their names suggest, they were prime places for viewing Mt. Fuji as well as important places for castle defense.

Inside the East Garden lies a small but exquisite Japanese garden that has beautiful iris flowers in June. This was the garden of the private residence of the Tokugawa shoguns. A stone foundation marks the site of the Tokugawa's castle keep that was destroyed by fire in 1657.

From a steep slope called Shiomizaka, you could see the tides on Tokyo bay 130 years ago, but today it only offers views of the concrete and steel buildings of Hibiya. The weird looking octagonal building, with its mosaic walls, is the **Togaku-do**, a concert hall built for the (then) empress in 1969.

Exit the East Garden on the north side to enter **Kitanomaru Park** that was once the home of the imperial guard and is now the abode of a number of cultural institutions. The heavily wooded park even has nature trails.

Just across from the gate is the **National Museum of Modern Art** (Tokyo Kokuritsu Kindai Bijutsukan). This museum houses a large collection of modern Japanese art — from the Meiji Period onward. If you've seen traditional Japanese art, a stop here will fill you in on what happened after the floodgates to the West opened in the late 19th century. Note: closed until Autumn 2001. *3-1 Kitano-maru Koen. Tel. (03)3214-2561. Hours 10am to 5pm. Closed Monday. ¥420.*

A few minutes walk from the museum takes you to **The Crafts Gallery** (Kogeikan). The museum, exhibiting contemporary renderings of traditional crafts such as pottery, lacquer and weaving, is housed in a 1910 red brick building, the former headquarters of the old Imperial Palace Guard. We like to visit to get a sense of what's happening in the contemporary craft scene. *Tel. (03)3211-7781. Open 10am to 5pm. ¥420.*

Turn left as you leave the Crafts Gallery and the **Japan Science Museum** (Kagaku Gijutsukan) will be on your right. Despite its austere, institutional facade, the museum is a great place to take the kids — lots of hands-on exhibits related to robots, electronics, technology and space exploration. *Tel. (03)3212-8471. Open daily 9:30am to 4:50pm, enter by 4pm. Closed Monday and December 29-January 3. ¥600.*

At the northern tip of Kitanomaru Park is the **Budokan**, built for martial arts for the 1964 Olympics. Until Tokyo Dome was built in the late 1980s, the Budokan was a favored venue for rock concerts — the Beatles played there in 1966. From the Budokan, exit over the moat. The area along the moat is **Chidorigafuchi Park**; its hundreds of cherry trees ensure a spectacular sight in the spring, but it's pretty any time of year. You can rent boats and row along the moat. The main street is Yasukuni Dori.

CASTLES & PALACES

When Tokyo became the capital of Japan in 1868, stripping Kyoto of this status, the emperor made the bold decision to move to Tokyo. He needed somewhere to live and what better place than the castle grounds that the Tokugawa shoguns vacated – they were sent packing to the Shizuoka area. In its heyday, the castle's area was 608 acres, and the outer walls formed a 16-kilometer circle. Today the inner area is a mere 28 acres, but the names of some of Tokyo's streets show how large the castle grounds were: half of central Tokyo is inside Sotobori Dori, which means Outer Moat Avenue.

The Tokugawa built a large castle keep and a splendid residence, but fire destroyed the keep in 1657. Their power was so secure they didn't bother to rebuild it. When the Meiji Emperor moved to Tokyo, he built a Western-style palace in 1889; it was destroyed in an air raid during World War II. The current palace is a low structure built for Emperor Akihito after his father's death. If you want to take a peek, the upper floors of office buildings along Hibiya Dori look down on the palace grounds; we find the most convenient place is from the Idemitsu Museum. The place's green copper roof is in the middle of so many trees. Don't bother to go too far out of your way; there's not much to see.

The outer precincts of the palace – the East Garden, Kitanomaru Park and Chidorigafuchi Park – are accessible to the public. The inner part, containing the emperor's residence, is open to the public only two days a year when the emperor greets his people: January 2 to celebrate New Year's and December 23, the emperor's birthday. It's a pretty subdued affair, but go if you happen to be in Japan. Most likely, it will be your only chance to see the emperor.

As you wait to enter the inner precincts, you are given a Japanese paper flag. Then you walk over Nijubashi Bridge with about 2000 other people and end up in a plaza in front of one of the palace buildings. With his family members beside him, the emperor stands on a glass-enclosed balcony. He says a few words of welcome and people wave their flags. Some people seem to get carried away by the mere sight of the emperor, but to most it's just another event. The newspapers report how many people went to visit the emperor. Now it's usually between 30,000 and 50,000; when the emperor's father, the Showa Emperor, was alive, many more people attended.

Walk up Yasukuni Dori for about five minutes or until you see the bronze *torii* gate on the right, which is the entrance to **Yasukuni Shrine**. Yasukuni, founded in 1869, is a controversial Shinto shrine because it enshrines soldiers killed in war. Every year some Cabinet members participate in a special ceremony on August 15 to mark the end of World

War II. The cabinet members are asked if they visit Yasukuni as public figures or as private individuals. It's not a moot question. Leftists accuse the ministers of violating the Constitution that separates state and religion by honoring convicted war criminals. Right wingers denounce the ministers as unpatriotic if they don't show up. The only way to avoid the entire controversy is not to be a cabinet minister.

Politics aside, the buildings themselves are very low key; hundreds of cherry trees on the premises make it one of Tokyo's prettiest places to see cherry blossoms. Actually, the Meteorological Agency uses two trees at Yasukuni as the standard to predict Tokyo's blossom season. When those trees bloom, the cherry blossom season begins officially.

While you are there, stop at the **Yushukan**, the yellow building to the right of the shrine, Japan's war museum. Inside you will find war memorabilia from samurai costumes to a *kamikaze* torpedo and glider planes. Unfortunately there isn't much description written in English, but the graphic exhibits need little explanation. *3-1-1 Kudankita, Chiyoda-ku. Tel. (03)3261-8326. Open daily 9am to 5pm. ¥300.*

Area 2: From Ginza to Nihonbashi
This walk takes the better part of a day, less if you don't do too much window shopping or don't stop in museums. The streets in this area are laid out in a grid, so it's easy to find your way.

This area, east of the Imperial Palace, contains some of Tokyo's most famous shopping districts and office centers, art galleries and a handful of excellent museums. You can combine this area with the Imperial Palace (see above).

This walk can start with an early morning visit to the Tsukiji Fish Market (see its description under Tsukiji). From the fish market, walk north along Shin Ohashi Dori and turn left on Harumi Dori. The Kabuki-za will be several blocks down on the right. If you sleep late and skip the fish market, take the Hibiya subway line to Higashi Ginza Station and get off at the central exit. The Kabuki-za will be in front of you.

You can't miss the **Kabuki-za**. Built in 1924, the gaudy building exudes the brashness of *kabuki* theater itself. You can buy a one-act ticket to get a glimpse of this vibrant art form that combines music, dance and singing (see Performing Arts later in this chapter for ticket information).

Return to Harumi Dori and continue walking down toward the center of Ginza. Across the first large intersection after the Kabuki-za, there's a small wooden building at an angle on the far side. This tiny shop sells *tabi* (Japanese socks), small towels and other cotton goods. We often pick up some inexpensive gifts there. Continue walking on the left side of Harumi Dori. If you feel like resting your feet or having breakfast, turn left after

Togeki, a movie theater, and you'll find the Ginza Tokyu Hotel. The cafe is a pleasant place to have a cup of tea or a bite to eat.

Return to Harumi Dori. Just before you reach Chuo Dori, the **Nihonshu Center**, the Japanese Sake Center, is on the left. It offers tastes of four different types of Japanese rice wine for ¥300 — one of the best deals in town. They have *sake* from all over Japan so it's a good place to figure out which type you like best.

Continue walking down Harumi Dori to the heart of Ginza, the 4-chome intersection where Harumi Dori and Chuo Dori meet. At night, the neon lights on this corner are so bright you can easily read a newspaper. On the corner are two of Japan's most exclusive department stores: **Mitsukoshi** where the prices are merely high and **Wako**, where they are astronomical. Make sure you go inside Wako; the ground floor has some of the most expensive watches on this planet. The basement has a corner featuring Japanese goods where you can find some reasonably

GINZA

*The mention of **Ginza** to Japanese conjures up visions of high society and shopping. This idea goes back a hundred years to a time when Ginza came to stand for all that was fashionable. Ginza was the site of the Tokugawa government's silver mint, established in 1612, and many silversmiths had their workshops here. They gave the area its name: Ginza means "silver guild."*

Fire destroyed Ginza in 1872 so the Meiji government, in the early days of its rapid Westernization program, had British architect Josiah Conder design a Western-style center. Hundreds of brick buildings were built and sidewalks were planted with willow trees and lit by gas lights. People turned out to see the development and soon a thriving commercial center was born. They flocked to see Western products like men's suits and women's dresses. Department stores opened branches here. Woodblock prints depict large-nosed foreigners wearing frock coats accompanied by women wearing hoop skirts. They strolled in Ginza under cherry trees and gas lights, and horse-drawn carriages were in the street.

World War II air raids flattened Ginza; the Wako Department Store building is one of the few structures that survived. Ginza recovered quickly and resumed its position as the country's foremost retail area.

Today, Ginza attracts a sophisticated, middle-aged crowd to its expensive shops and art galleries. The name Ginza has become synonymous with the best, and we find it used everywhere we travel in Japan: Ginza bar in Kumamoto, Ginza Dining Hall in Hokkaido, Ginza shopping mall in Hiroshima and Ginza Dori in small towns in the middle of nowhere.

priced items. Wako's clientele tends toward old-fashioned women from good families. This Mitsukoshi is a branch of the Nihonbashi store; the ground floor Tiffany Boutique is popular with the twenty-something set. With a 300-year history, Mitsukoshi knows how to make money on some of the most expensive real estate on this globe.

From Harumi Dori, turn left onto Chuo Dori. On the corner is the **Ginza Core Building**; it's basement restaurant, **Shabuzen**, has some of the least expensive *shabu-shabu* in town. We don't know how it survives because during the peak of the economic bubble in the late 1980s, this property was so expensive that a two *tatami* mat (6 feet by 6 feet) piece of land cost more than one million U.S. dollars. One block further along, you'll come to **Matsuzakaya**, another of Ginza's large department stores; this one is especially famous for its kimono, and **Familiar**, exclusive children's fashions. Walking along the same street you reach the **Lion Sapporo Beer Hall** with good beer and neat mosaic walls. Soon after is **Ginza Pocket Park**, which, despite its name, is a building, an amazingly small one that houses an architectural studio run by Tokyo Gas. Next to it is **Yamaha Hall**, a music store selling Japanese as well as Western sheet music, hot-off-the-design-table electones and Yamaha's latest models.

On the other side of Chuo Dori, just before the expressway, is **Hakuhinkan Toy Park**, one of Tokyo's largest toy stores. Walking back toward the Ginza 4-chome intersection, you'll come to **Shiseido**, where the cosmetics' manufacturer started in 1872. The cafe is a pleasant place to stop for a cup of coffee. At Shiseido, turn left and walk down five short blocks to Sotobori Dori, turn left and you'll find **Takumi**, a great folk craft shop. The area between Sotobori Dori and Chuo Dori is filled with art galleries, boutiques and bars with Ginza in their names.

Retrace your steps to Chuo Dori and be sure you stop at **Kyukyodo** where incense, paper, tea ceremony utensils, fancy greeting cards, brushes and other calligraphy equipment have been sold for 300 years. Kyukyodo is next to the bright San-ai Building at the Ginza 4-chome crossing. Crossing Harumi Dori, you'll see **Mikimoto Pearls** on the left. Mikimoto invented the culturing process and is the name-brand place to buy pearls. The quality is excellent and some goods are priced low enough so you may not have to mortgage your house. On the right is **Matsuya** Department Store and **Itoya**, a great shop for stationery and paper goods, where half the goods are imported and half are Japanese.

Return to the Ginza 4-chome crossing and turn right on Harumi Dori, heading in the direction of the Imperial Palace. **Jena Books** on the left has a cramped but good selection of English-language books. Farther down on the left is the **Sony Building**, with electronic showrooms and the exclusive Maxim's and Sabatini's restaurants. On the other side of the street, after you walk under the expressway, are the twin department stores, **Hankyu** and **Seibu**. In a novel design, they connect on each floor. The clock in the plaza comes alive with a miniconcert every hour; it is one of the area's most popular meeting places.

When Harumi Dori meets Hibiya Dori — the green trees and open spaces of Hibiya Park and the Imperial Palace are on the far side — turn left and walk a few short blocks to the **Imperial Hotel**, one of Tokyo's most famous. This was the site of the Frank Lloyd Wright-designed hotel that opened in 1923 but succumbed to the wrecking ball in 1968. Actually, the Wright low-style lobby has been reassembled in Meiji Mura, an open air park outside of Nagoya. The current Imperial Hotel's bar, on the second floor, has some of the fittings of Wright's original bar.

Across the street on the northern side of the hotel is the **Tokyo Takarazuka Theater** where the all-female revue performs. The performances are really kitschy, but great fun — a cross between Las Vegas and *kabuki*.

Keep walking down this road; under the railroad tracks, you'll find the **International Arcade**, a slightly run-down shopping arcade catering to foreign tourists. You can get export model electronics, old kimono, jewelry and souvenirs. Despite the surroundings, it's not a bad place to shop for souvenirs. **Hayashi Kimono** has an especially good selection of old kimono.

In this same area, under the railroad tracks, there are some good hole-in-the-wall *yakitori* restaurants. Most are closed during the day but come alive in the evening when office workers are looking for cheap beer and eats.

The front of the Imperial Hotel faces **Hibiya Park**, the first Western-style park in Tokyo; while it's filled with office workers searching for some greenery and fresh air at lunchtime, it has little to recommend it to a visitor. Behind Hibiya Park is **Kasumigaseki**, a ghetto of government ministry buildings. Unless you want to see institutional architecture, there's no reason to spend any time there.

From the front of the Imperial Hotel, walk north on Hibiya Dori, in the direction of the Imperial Palace. Soon after crossing Harumi Dori, the **Daiichi Mutual Life Insurance Building** is on your right. Built in 1938, it was one of the few buildings that survived the bombing of World War II. General Douglas MacArthur used it to as headquarters for the Occupation forces; his office is preserved today.

One block further takes you to the **Idemitsu Museum of Arts**, one of our favorite museums in Tokyo. It's funded by the Idemitsu Oil Company so clearly it has the resources to continue adding to its superb collection of Oriental art. Located on the 9th floor of an uninspired office building, the display space is divided into three main rooms. It's not too large so we find we can look at the objects with appreciation. This museum is where you can admire monk Sesshu's 15th-century monochrome paintings, Momoyama and early Edo lively, gold-leafed genre paintings and the exquisite colors of Ninsei's world famous vase. The temporary exhibitions are top notch. After viewing a show, sit and enjoy a complimentary cup of tea overlooking the verdant Imperial Palace grounds. *Imperial Theater Building, 9F, 3-1-1 Marunouchi, Chiyoda-ku. Tel. (03)3213-9404. Open 10am to 5pm. Closed Monday. ¥500.*

From the Idemitsu Museum you can cross Hibiya Dori and enter the palace grounds and pick up our tour under Imperial Palace. But we are going to walk east, away from the palace. You'll run into the massive **Tokyo International Forum** complex. One of the most recent offerings on the cultural scene, this building finally gives Tokyo the grand architectural statement it has long wanted. Designed by New York-based architect Rafael Vinoly, the glass, steel and stone structure houses performance halls for concerts, dance and theater as well as a conference center, restaurants and the **Tourist Information Office**, an excellent source of information. The soaring 60-meter-high, all glass atrium is a sight to behold. Even if you are not going to a concert here, stop by to see what ¥1.65 billion, not including the price of the land, will buy.

After leaving the Forum, follow the train tracks north a few blocks to **Tokyo Station**. Designed by Tatsuno Kingo, a leading turn-of-the-century Japanese architect, the western facade of the station was built in 1914. Tatsuno built the station in Queen Anne style with red brick. Today Japanese traveling to Amsterdam always say, "There's Tokyo Station" when they see Central Station. The entrance facing west was used exclusively by the imperial family, but is now used by mere mortals, and plenty of them. Over 2500 trains pass through the station every day. The Tokyo Station Hotel, part of the station, is a convenient and pleasant place to stay.

The district around Tokyo Station is **Marunouchi**, literally "within the citadel." During the Edo period, feudal lords had their official residences in this area. But at the end of the era, in the mid-19th century, they packed up and went back home. By the late 19th century, the district was so deserted that foxes and badgers lived side by side. The savvy Mitsubishi family bought the land for next to nothing and constructed Western-style buildings designed by Josiah Conder. Now, in the mid-1990s, Mitsubishi has decided to move south of Shinagawa Station to develop a new business center, but Marunouchi remains one of the most prestigious office districts.

North of the station is Eitai Dori; turn right to head east on this major thoroughfare. This area is called Otemachi and is a banking and business center. Soon you will reach the intersection of Eitai Dori and Chuo Dori. This area is Nihonbashi. A turn to the right will take you to the famous and

TOKYO'S RAIL STATIONS

Tokyo Station was not Tokyo's first train station; that honor falls to **Shimbashi Station***. Built with the technical assistance of British engineers – employed by the Meiji government at an outrageous cost – the first railway opened between Shimbashi and Yokohama in 1872. At that time Shimbashi was on the waterfront. The train took 53 minutes and stopped at four stations en route. The excitement of this engineering feat came just four short years after the overthrow of the feudal Tokugawa government and can be seen in ukiyo-e woodblock prints. In 1879, a railway between* **Ueno Station** *and Aomori, in northern Japan, commenced operations; and in 1889, service began on the Tokaido railway between Shimbashi and Kobe. Ueno wasn't connected to Shimbashi until Tokyo Station opened in 1914.*

Shimbashi remained Tokyo's major railway station until the government commissioned Tatsuno Kingo to design a new station to commemorate Japan's victory in the Russo-Japanese War. Tatsuno studied in Europe and designed a red-brick, three-storied building. The roof and interior were heavily damaged by bombing during World War II and after the war, the station was rebuilt as a two-storied building. With the construction of the shinkansen line in the 1960s, the eastern side of the station now shows no traces of the original building, but the western side still maintains its graceful facade.

The skyrocketing cost of land in the 1980s tempted JR to raze the building, but the outcry was so strong that the building was spared.

now, unfortunately, totally unremarkable **Nihonbashi Bridge**, literally the Bridge of Japan, that's half swallowed by an overhead expressway. The bridge is considered the center of Japan and distances are measured from here. During the Edo period, Nihonbashi was the intersection for the five roads that connected Edo to the provinces. Once the bridge was a beautiful, curved wooden structure (see a reconstruction in the Edo Tokyo Museum), but today it's cement.

Cross the Nihonbashi Bridge and continue on Chuo Dori. You'll come to **Mitsukoshi**, the prestigious department store's main store. Some purists insist on buying their goods at Mitsukoshi's main store, not at the newer Ginza or Shinjuku or other branches. Mitsukoshi developed into a department store from a kimono shop in the Edo period and was the first shop to display its goods in glass cases at the turn of the century. Before that, goods were brought from the storage areas at the customer's request.

From Chuo Dori, turn left right after Mitsukoshi. Incidentally, Kiya, Tokyo's most famous knife store, is on the right of this intersection. The

Bank of Japan Building, built in 1898, was Japan's first major Western-style building designed by a Japanese — in this case by Tatsuno Kingo who also designed Tokyo Station.

NIHONBASHI

*Located along the canals, **Nihonbashi** was the heart of the downtown area in the Edo Period. Boats carrying goods from all over Japan flocked to the docks. Apparently, Nihonbashi was cursed because five, large, ruinous fires started there.*

*During the Meiji period, Nihonbashi was a district that exemplified the drive to Westernize. At the turn of the century, **Maruzen Book Store**, a center for the intelligentsia, became the first in Japan to sell foreign books and luxury goods. **Takashimaya** was one of the first Japanese department stores. Across the Renaissance-style Nihonbashi Bridge stands the **Bank of Japan**, the centerpiece of the modern banking system. Nihonbashi was one of the trendy places of that time as Omotesando is now.*

After a long period of neglect and construction of an overhead expressway that bisects the district, Nihonbashi is being resurrected as an area that, ironically, has retained its Japaneseness.

Retrace your steps and cross back over the Nihonbashi Bridge and walk to the Tokyu Department Store. Behind Tokyu is a tiny **Kite Museum** that's jam packed with Japanese and foreign kites. These aren't your run-of-the-mill diamond-shaped kites; some resemble birds, warriors and squid. The collection belongs to the owner of the first floor restaurant, Taimei Ken. *Tel. (03)3275-2704. ¥200. Open 11am to 5pm. Closed Sunday and holidays.*

Walk back to Chuo Dori. Two blocks past the Eitai Dori intersection is **Takashimaya**, an old-time department store. Across the street is **Maruzen** that has been selling foreign language books and goods since the turn of the century. The selection of Japanese novels translated into English is especially good. Maruzen also has an area with an excellent selection of Japanese crafts.

Walk south about four blocks on Chuo Dori to Yaesu Dori. On the far corner is the Bridgestone Building, which houses the **Bridgestone Museum of Art** (Bridgestone Bijutsukan). This museum has one of Japan's best collections of modern European art and focuses especially on the Impressionists and Western-style works by Japanese artists. The Japanese works incorporate some elements of Japanese aesthetics into their works. *2F, Bridgestone Building, 1-10-1 Kyobashi, Chuo-ku. Tokyo. Tel. (03)3563-0241. Open 10am to 6pm. Closed Monday. ¥500.*

Retrace your steps along Chuo Dori and turn right on Eitai Dori. On the right is a well-known paper goods shop called **Haibara** that sells Japanese *washi* paper, stationery and other goods made from the paper. We like to buy lightweight gifts here.

Continue down Eitai Dori and cross under the expressway. The **Yamatane Museum** is on the left corner of the next major intersection near the Kayabacho subway station. The museum has a strong collection of modern Japanese art. Surrounded by securities dealers, this site is an unlikely spot for an art museum, but the collection belonged to the head of Yamatane Securities. *7-12, Nihonbashi-Kabutocho, Chuo-ku, Tokyo. Tel. (03)3669-4056. Open 10am to 6pm. Closed Monday and New Year's. ¥700.*

Walk along the small street where Yamatane Museum is located. Several blocks down on the left, you'll find the **Tokyo Securities Exchange**, the stock market. The exchange's glassed-in area provides an excellent view of the trading floor. To teach you about the market, the extensive Exhibition Plaza features many interactive displays in English as well as Japanese.

Visitors are welcome Monday through Friday, 9am to 4pm and an English tour is given at 1:30pm. It's best to telephone to reserve a spot on the hour-long tour. 2-1 Nihonbashi-Kabutocho, Chuo-ku. Tel. (03)3666-0141. Free admission.

SENIOR PRIVILEGE

Senior Citizens 65 and over are admitted free to the following museums. You'll need to present your passport for admission.
- *National Science Museum, Ueno*
- *National Museum of Modern Art, Kitanomaru Park*
- *Crafts Gallery, Kitanomaru Park*
- *Tokyo Metropolitan Teien Museum, Meguro*
- *Tokyo Metroplitan Art Museum, Ueno*
- *Tokyo National Museum, Ueno*
- *Edo Tokyo Museum, Ryogoku*
- *Tokyo Metropolitan Museum of Photography, Ebisu*
- *Silk Museum, Yokohama*
- *Kanagawa Museum of Modern Art, Kamakura*
- *Japan Open Air Folk House Museum, Kawasaki*

Area 3: From Tsukiji to Roppongi
A walk from Tsukiji to Roppongi takes the better part of a day.

When Japan opened to the West in the middle of the 19th century, the government assigned Tsukiji as a foreign settlement. When restrictions were lifted around the turn of the century, most foreigners didn't stick around; many moved to Yokohama. Today, Roppongi is an international district filled with restaurants, discos, bars, clubs and shops.

Tokyo Central Wholesale Market /Tsukiji Market (Tsukiji Shijo). *5-2-1 Tsukiji, Chuo-ku. Tel. (03)3542-1111. 10-minute walk from Tsukiji Station of Hibiya Subway Line; use exit 1, walk down Shin Ohashi Dori, cross Harumi Dori and turn left at the next corner. Turn right at the small shrine and go over the bridge. The fish market is in front of you. Alternatively take bus #1 from Shimbashi Station's east exit to Tsukiji Chuo Shijo stop (5 minutes). Open 5am to 3pm. Fish auction is 5:10am to 5:50am. The fruit and vegetable auction is at 6:30am to 7:30am. Closed Sunday, holidays and some Wednesdays. Have your hotel call the market or check with the Tourist Information Office before setting out on Wednesday morning.*

Fishermen all over the world are early risers, and Japan's are no exception. When you wake up jet lagged at 4am, jump out of bed and head for Tsukiji market, Japan's largest fish market. See the huge frozen hulks lined up on the floor for the 5am tuna auction's high-speed drama — it's great fun to watch. If you prefer to sleep later than 4am, there's still lots of activity afterwards.

The fish market moved from Nihonbashi after the 1923 earthquake. Today there are over a thousand wholesalers, and no one minds if you wander up and down the aisles as long as you stay out of the way of the carts that whiz by — they stop for no one. Make sure your shoes can survive a good soaking as the floor is wet and slippery. If you feel like having an escorted tour in Japanese, phone for reservations for a 9:30am tour. There's really no need to bother — it's more fun to wander around on your own.

The back streets around the intersection of Harumi Dori and Shin Ohashi Dori are filled with retail shops catering to the chefs. You'll find the most amazing kinds of kitchenware, knives and dry goods at reasonable prices.

Finish off your morning with a breakfast or lunch of *sushi*. **Tsukiji Sushi Sei**, founded in the Edo period, is really popular; people line up even before it opens at 8am. *4-13-9 Tsukiji, Chuo-ku. Tel. (03)3541-7720.* Sushi Sei even has a branch in New York. If you don't feel like eating raw fish, we suggest you go to Uogashi Ramen that faces Shin-Ohashi Dori. Once again you'll find many people waiting in line to be served delicious Chinese noodles in broth with sliced roasted pork for only ¥500.

Across Harumi Dori is **Tsukiji Hongan-ji Temple** originally built in Nihonbashi in 1617. The current building, constructed in 1934, is based on an Indian temple design and is one of the most unusual temple buildings in Japan.

From the fish market, it's a short walk to Hama Rikyu Garden. From the market, continue walking south on Shin Ohashi Dori, staying on the left side of the road. After the road curves right, the entrance to the garden is on the left.

Hama Rikyu Garden. *1-1 Hamarikyu Tei-en, Chuo-ku. Tel. (03)3541-0200. Open 9am to 4:30pm. ¥300. Free to seniors over 65 and juniors under 12. Closed Monday and at New Year's.* This large, Japanese-style strolling garden was once the private duck-hunting preserve of the Matsudaira, a branch of the Tokugawa family. The Imperial Household took it over in the late 19th century and entertained foreign dignitaries on the grounds. U.S. President Ulysses S. Grant was feted at one of the teahouses. The salt water pond rises and falls with the tides of the Sumida River inlet and is the home of many ducks; none is hunted today. The low, zigzagged wooden bridge over the pond offers changing views of the garden around you. Since the garden is on the water, it gives you a feeling of space as it is much more open than the usual, meticulously calculated Japanese garden.

EARLY MORNING ACTIVITIES IN TOKYO

- *Jog around the Imperial Palace: traffic is light, so car exhaust isn't bad*
- *Tsukiji Fish Market*
- *Asakusa Kannon Temple*
- *Shrine flea markets on Sunday mornings*

From the Hama Rikyu Garden's pier, one alternative is to take the ferry up the Sumida River to Asakusa — see the Asakusa write-up. Boats leave every 40 minutes.

If you prefer to stay on land, walk south alongside the expressway for about 10 minutes to reach **Kyu-Shiba Rikyu Garden**. Although fairly small and now surrounded by tall buildings, it's one of our favorite gardens in Tokyo. This strolling garden was once at the water's edge; the sand at the pond's edge maintains a little of the waterfront feeling. The pond's water level, connected with the sea, rises and falls with the tide. In mid-May, the wisteria and azaleas are in full bloom. *1-4-1 Kaigan, Minato-ku. Tel. (03)3434-4029. Open 9am to 4:30pm. Closed Monday and December 29 through January 3. ¥100. 1-minute walk east of JR Hamamatsucho Station.*

The area east of the garden, **Takebashi**, has recently undergone redevelopment and offers a pleasant stroll along the waterfront. The new Intercontinental Hotel's Asian Tables restaurant has good Asian food and a spectacular view of the Rainbow Bridge. Walk to Hamamatsucho Station, just west of the Shiba Rikyu Garden. The street just north of the station leads west to **Zojo-ji**, a temple in Shiba Park. Several blocks before the park you'll see a wooden gate in the middle of the road. **Daimon** (literally big gate) is the outer gate for Zojo-ji; all the land inside the gate used to belong to the temple.

Near the gate, turn left onto a tiny road sandwiched between Sanwa Bank and Yoshinoya fast food. On the left, in a beautifully restored former *geisha* house, is the **Tolman Collection**. Run by Americans Norman and Mary Tolman, long-term residents, the gallery sells contemporary Japanese prints. *2-2-18 Shiba Daimon, Minato-ku. Tel. (03)3434-1300. Open 11am to 7pm. Closed Tuesday.*

Tokyo doesn't have grand temples like Kyoto — most have only pocket-sized lots. **Zojo-ji**, established by the Tokugawa shogunate is the exception. This temple, along with Kan'ei-ji in the northern part of the city, was one of the Tokugawa's family temples and could have been used as a fortress to protect the castle against an invasion from the south. The buildings, rebuilt in the 1970s, are unremarkable, but the impressive main gate has stood since 1605.

From Zojo-ji, fans of Asian art can take a detour to the **Matsuoka Museum of Art** — walk north on Hibiya Dori until the 7th block on the right. In an old building, this small museum houses a superb collection of Chinese ceramics and other Oriental art. *5-22-10 Shimbashi, Minato-ku. Tel. (03)3431-8284. Open 10am to 5pm. Closed Monday and at New Year's. ¥550. 3-minute walk from the A4 exit of Onarimon Station on the Toei Mita subway line.*

Behind Zojo-ji, you can't help but notice a transplanted Eiffel Tower — **Tokyo Tower**. Built in 1958, the 333-meter structure is the tallest stand-alone steel structure in the world. Unlike Paris' Eiffel Tower that sits gracefully in a large park, Tokyo's is plopped on top of a concrete building in the middle of an urban neighborhood. Some 3.7 million people visit the tower each year; it's a sightseeing destination second only to Disneyland. But we don't recommend that you join the long queue. Tokyo Tower is tacky, rundown, and overpriced; you can get as good a view from the Tokyo Metropolitan Government Building in Shinjuku without paying an admission charge. We really hate how the down elevator deposits you on the fourth floor of the building and forces you to walk down the stairs past an aquarium, a wax museum, a chamber of horrors, a trick art gallery and whatever else the owners think will get you to part with your yen. *Open daily 9am to 8pm mid-March to mid-November; until 6pm mid-November through mid-March. ¥270 to the main observatory; an additional ¥520 to the higher special observatory.*

The road that goes past the main entrance to Tokyo Tower leads you to a large intersection on Sakurada Dori. On the far right side, behind some buildings, is a huge Darth Vadar-like building that is the temple of the **Reiyukai**, one of the new Buddhist sects. Go inside for a closer look at the neo-Buddhist architecture.

Return to the intersection and walk up the hill on Gaien Higashi Dori, past the Russian Embassy and the Azabu Post Office and walk under the expressway. Continue on the same road; you are deep in the heart of **Roppongi**, a nightlife area filled with restaurants, discos and bars. The area is fairly quiet in the daytime, but when the sun goes down, it's all-night party time.

EDOKKO

*Old time Tokyoites love to use the term **Edokko**. In the strictest sense Edokko (literally a child of Edo) is a person who is at least the third generation born in Edo (or Tokyo). In other words, if your grandparents were born in Tokyo, you are full-fledged Edokko. But in feudal times, Edokko meant more than just genealogy. An Edokko had to live in **shitamachi**, the crowded area the Tokugawa shogunate designated for merchants, entertainers, apprentices and traders. In the Edo period, 70% of the population lived in shitamachi whereas 70% of land in Edo was occupied by the warrior class.*

Edokko were fun-loving people, who could cry easily over sentimental stories; were contemptuous of the snobbish high-class warriors whom they felt didn't know how to enjoy life; and were very proud of being Edokko. Their distinctive language can be compared to Cockney in London – it's hard to imitate unless you are born to it.

Edokko took great joy in the pleasures of everyday life. The Tokugawa shogunate restricted every aspect of their lives from the types and colors of their clothes to the materials they could use to build their houses. Although people quickly learned to circumvent these rules, conspicuous consumption was out. As a result, people spent their money on enjoying life; an old expression says that if they had extra, they would spend it in a night. Pleasure quarters flourished throughout shitamachi and samurai, barred from mingling, would often disguise themselves so they could get in. To capture the fleeting moment, people took great delight in fireworks and cherry blossoms.

Roppongi has a few daytime attractions. One of our favorite places is the **Axis Building** on the left side of Gaien Higashi Dori about two blocks past the expressway as you walk away from Tokyo Tower. The building is devoted to modern design. The street floor has a **Living Motif** store, which reminds us of Pottery Barn in the U.S. Downstairs, **Nuno** is a fabulous textile store that supplies Issey Miyake with his raw material.

There's also a selection of clothes of their own design. **Kisso**, on the same floor, sells pottery and is a *kaiseki* restaurant that serves its food on its own plates. **Bushy** has beautiful contemporary lacquer ware from small bowls to furniture and matching lamps.

Continue walking in the same direction and in a few blocks, you'll reach another large intersection under the expressway. This is **Roppongi Crossing** and is known to nearly every taxi driver in town. The **Almond coffee shop**, on the corner, is THE place to meet. Virtually every set of directions for anything in Roppongi starts at Almond. Incidentally, Almond is famous as a landmark, but not for its coffee.

Walk under the expressway, and continue north on Gaien Higashi Dori. Take the 3rd right to reach the **Azabu Museum of Arts** (Azabu Bijutsu Kogeikan), a contemporary concrete structure, where you may find an excellent exhibition of Japanese crafts. *4-6-9 Roppongi, Minato-ku. Tel. (03)5474-1371. Open 10am to 6pm. Closed Monday. ¥800. 3-minute walk from Roppongi Station of Hibiya subway line.*

The Hibiya subway line's Roppongi Station is near Roppongi Crossing or if it's close to dinner time, why not try one of Roppongi's many restaurants.

Areas 4, 5, 6, 7, 8: Shitamachi — Tokyo's Old Downtown

The walking tours listed below —Akihabara, Asakusa, Asakusabashi, Fukagawa, Kanda, Kiba, Ryogoku, Yanaka, and Ueno — are all part of old *shitamachi*, commoners' districts in the feudal days. To this day there are vestiges of old Edo.

Shitamachi (low city) was Edo's eastern edge along the Sumida River where merchants and artisans resided. Even today, people are more friendly to each other than in other areas. It was the tradition that the *shitamachi* people supported each other in every aspect of life — from sharing food they cooked in their small kitchens to sharing money. Inevitably such close contact has diminished and relationships have become more impersonal. Today Japanese talk nostalgically about the good old days. Keep this in mind as you explore Tokyo's *shitamachi*.

Area 4: Asakusa

You can reach Asakusa by boat from Hama Rikyu Garden or Hinode Pier at Hamamatsucho. Boats depart every 40 minutes to cruise up the Sumida River. ¥660 to Hinode, ¥620 to Hama Rikyu. To reach by subway, take the Ginza subway line to Asakusa Station; use the stairway in the middle of the train platform and go out exit 1.

Asakusa is one of the few areas in Tokyo that retains the earthy *shitamachi* atmosphere of old Edo. Although most buildings are postwar constructions, the low-rise buildings, shops selling crafts and kimono, and traditional restaurants evoke the memory of an age that has all but disappeared from most Tokyo neighborhoods. Asakusa is definitely not glitzy and the contrast with contemporary Tokyo makes a visit a must. Plan to spend at least a half-day; longer if you want to explore lots of shops.

While the Sumida is a rather plebeian river with undistinguished low bridges, the boat ride is fun and a change from the usual subways and trains. At the Asakusa boat pier, cross Edo Dori and walk on the wide street, Kaminarimon Dori, until the gate with the large red lantern is on your right.

If you've come by subway, you will be on Kaminarimon Dori. Walk west, away from the river, for one block to reach **Kaminarimon Gate**, the large red gate with a huge red paper lantern. Every group of Japanese tourists must have its picture taken under the lantern. Across the street is a **Tourist Information Office**, which has maps and information in English. Ask for the map of Kappabashi, the restaurant supply district. This map lists every store and the goods it sells. *Open daily 10am to 5pm.*

The Kaminarimon Gate has large statues of the guardian gods of thunder and wind, Raijin and Fujin. Pass through the gate and you enter the lively world of the **Nakamise** (literally inner shops) with its bazaar atmosphere and crowded with people and tiny shops selling everything

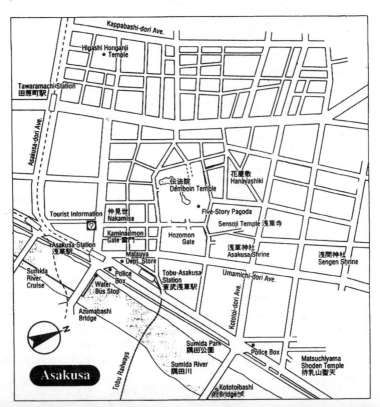

Courtesy of Japan National Tourist Organization

from cheap trinkets to expensive kimono, wigs and hair ornaments, traditional toys, Japanese paper umbrellas, exquisite origami paper, swords, sweets and freshly grilled rice crackers. You'll see shops grilling rice crackers over charcoal and others making bean-filled cakes so you know they are fresh. You may think it's a special festival, but it's like this every day.

Although the buildings are postwar, this area has been a thriving souvenir center for hundreds of years catering to the pilgrims who came to the temple area in search of salvation and entertainment. Many of the stores have been run by the same family for generations.

We especially like **Bairindo**, the first store on the left selling sugar-covered beans; **Okadaya**, in the last block on the left, sells traditional Japanese umbrellas; and in the last block on the right before reaching the inner gate, you find **Tsuruya** selling tortoise shell crafts; **Sukeroku** selling miniature wooden toys complete in every detail; and **Kimuraya** selling *ningyo-yaki*, molded cakes filled with sweet bean paste.

At the end of the long promenade is a second gate, the Hozomon Gate, that leads to the precincts of **Senso-ji Temple**, also called Asakusa Kannon Temple. The Main Hall, Kannondo, is straight ahead. *Open daily 6am to 5pm, April through September and 6:30am to 5pm, October through March.* The temple's history dates to the 7th century when fishermen found a tiny golden statue of Kannon, the Bodhisattva of Mercy, in their nets. In the 16th century, the Tokugawa shogun donated the land on which the temple now stands. Senso-ji was one of the most important temples in the Edo period. World War II air raids destroyed the temple buildings; the present concrete main hall was constructed in 1958. People don't visit Senso-ji to admire architectural relics; they go for the overall atmosphere and, to be fair, some people pray for salvation.

There's a bronze incense stand in front of the main hall; you'll notice people directing the smoke to parts of their bodies. Believers feel the smoke will cure ailments and protect from illness. To the left of the main hall is **Asakusa Jinja**, a Shinto shrine that honors the three fishermen who found the Kannon image. This building is one of the few in the area that dates from the 17th century as does the Nitenmon Gate, which is to the right as you face the shrine. The fishermen who found the golden Kannon statue in the 7th century are not honored in the Buddhist temple; instead, they have their own Shinto shrine. This is a good example of the long and (generally) harmonious relationship between Shintoism and Buddhism.

On the third Sunday of May, the shrine runs the **Sanja Festival**, one of Tokyo's largest festivals. Large *mikoshi* (portable shrines) are carried through the neighborhood to commemorate the fishermen finding the golden Kannon statue. Lots of *sake* and beer ensure that everyone has a good time and that the bearers feel no pain.

The **pagoda** to the left of the main hall was originally built at the command of the third Tokugawa shogun. The present structure was built in 1973. Behind the pagoda is the **Hanayashiki Amusement Park**, Tokyo's oldest. Unless you have kids with you, it's definitely skippable.

South of the pagoda is **Dempoin Garden**, Senso-ji's chief abbot's residence. The beautiful, peaceful strolling garden is attributed to the 17th century master Kobori Enshu. You can enter the garden if the temple doesn't have any religious events planned. It's best to make a reservation – have a Japanese speaker call *(03) 3842-0181;* if you don't have a reservation, go to the temple's administrative office at the left side of the pagoda. Go into the *Shomuka* office (third door on the left), sign a book and receive a ticket. The garden closes at 3pm and is closed on Sunday and holidays.

To enter the garden, you must return to Nakamise and turn right at the first street, Dempoin Dori. The entrance to the garden is on the right. There are some wonderful shops along the way: **Yonoya**, a comb shop; an abacus shop; kimono shops; and **Daikokuya**, a good *tempura* restaurant with *tendon* as its specialty. If you go past the garden's entrance gate, on the left is **Nakasei**, another good *tempura* restaurant that has a nice garden, and **Yoshikami** that serves Japanized Western fare such as steaks and fried shrimp.

Entering the garden, you leave behind all the bustle of the streets outside and take a step back in time. The strolling garden has a large pond, Japan's oldest temple bell, cast in 1387, and a teahouse. There are wonderful views of the pagoda from around the pond.

Turn left as you leave the garden; cross over the busy Nakamise arcade and turn left – not at the back of the Nakamise stores, but on the next street. On the left is **Fujiya**, a shop selling *tenugui*, small cotton towels printed with beautiful traditional Japanese designs – dragonflies, plum blossoms, thunder, water wheels, snow and cloud patterns to name just a few. These reasonably priced items make great gifts. A little further down is **Hyakusuke**, a shop that sells traditional Japanese cosmetics such as safflower lipstick and **Kuremutsu**, a delicious country-style restaurant. On the right is a bell tower that used to ring on the hour to tell time in old Edo.

Then turn around and retrace you steps on the same street. After Fujiya, on the left is a noodle shop easily recognized by the counter for rolling noodles that's behind a glass window. The tasty noodles make it a good place for lunch. In an old wooden building next door is **Tatsumiya** Restaurant, chocked full of antiques. Its food is reasonably priced. And on the right side, in the last block before the main street, is a wonderful little paper crafts shop called **Kurodaya**. This area has an extensive maze of covered streets with stores selling inexpensive clothing and traditional crafts. It's a fun place to wander, especially on a rainy day.

Return to the main road, Kaminarimon Dori. If you want to call it quits, turn left. You'll go past **Kamiya**, Japan's oldest bar, established in the 1880s and known for its *denki* brandy (electric brandy) drink. The Ginza subway station is there or you can cross Edo Dori. To the left of the Azumabashi Bridge is the pier where you board the **Sumida River Cruise** boats that can take you down the river to Hama Rikyu Garden and Hinode Pier at Hamamatsucho. One more travel alternative is to catch the **double-decker bus** to Ueno from in front of Kaminarimon Gate. It leaves a few times an hour and costs ¥200.

Across the Sumida River is an unusual contemporary building: a black box topped with a golden curlicue. This building is Asahi Beer headquarters and has a beer hall inside.

Unless you are ready for a drink, turn right on Kaminarimon Dori, and go away from the river. Several blocks down on the right is a wonderful shop, **Tachikichi**, selling a wide range of Japanese ceramics.

Continue walking on the same road until it ends at Kokusai Dori. Across the street to the right is the **Drum Museum** (Taikokan). The shop downstairs sells drums and festival instruments, but upstairs is where the real fun begins. The museum has drums from all over the world, and you can play them — except for a few of the rarest ones. There's even a large Japanese *taiko* that's 3 feet in diameter. Our kids love this place. *Miyamoto Unosuke Store, 4F, Kokusai Dori, 2-1-1 Nishi Asakusa, Taito-ku. Tel. (03)3842-5622. Closed Monday and Tuesday. Open 10am to 5pm. ¥300.*

Turn right as you exit the Drum Museum and walk a few short blocks to a main street, Asakusa Dori. Turn right on Asakusa Dori. The south side of the street is lined with shops selling Buddhist altars and other religious goods.

IF YOU'RE ON A BUDGET...

Maybe not all the best things in life are free, but these are:
· *East Garden of Imperial Palace*
· *Meiji Shrine*
· *Asakusa Kannon Temple*
· *Kappabashi*
· *Tokyo Metropolitan Building Observatory in Shinjuku*
· *Flea markets at shrines on Sunday mornings*
· *Department Stores: the merchandise may be expensive, but there is enough to entertain you for hours – from craft galleries on the top floors to food samples in the basement – without ever dipping into your pockets.*

Several blocks further along, you'll easily see a building on the far right corner with a giant chef's head on the roof. This landmark announces your arrival at **Kappabashi**, the restaurant supply district. Turn right; shops on both sides of the street sell dishes, pots and pans, knives, signs, uniforms for chefs, waiters and waitresses and anything else the restaurant trade could possibly use. We love **Biken** and **Maizuru**, both in the first block on the right, selling brightly colored plastic display food that looks good enough to eat. Bring home some *sushi* that will never spoil. About two blocks down on the left, there's a shop selling *noren*, the curtains that hang in a doorway to identify a shop, at a fraction of department store prices. Don't worry if you don't want to buy things by the case; small quantities are okay. Ironically, there are few restaurants in the area.

From Kappabashi, return to Asakusa Dori; turn left, the Ginza subway station is a few blocks down. Ueno is just two stops away.

Area 5: Ueno

To reach Ueno, take the JR Yamanote line to Ueno Station. Use the park exit on the west side.

Ueno is a mixture of people and cultures: well-dressed women who go to museums and concert halls mix with wide-eyed tourists from the Japanese provinces; children of all ages on school excursions; shoppers

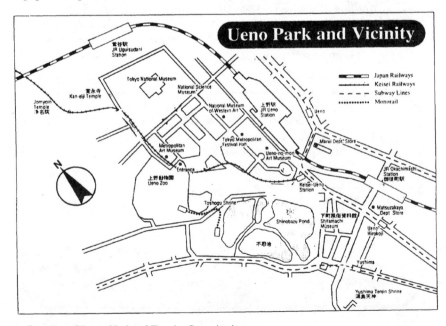

Courtesy of Japan National Tourist Organization

seeking the bargains of Ameyoko; illegal aliens, many of whom work in areas served by trains from Ueno Station; and the homeless.

Back in the days of Edo, Ueno was a major commercial center for the merchant and artisan classes. The large Ueno Park, now the home of a half-dozen cultural institutions and countless cherry trees and pigeons, is on the grounds of the once powerful **Kan'ei-ji Temple**, the Tokugawa's family temple. This temple, along with Zojo-ji in the south, was designed to act as a first fortress against attacks on the castle as well as offer protection from the evil spirits who dwelled in the northeast.

After the surrender of the Edo Castle in 1868, some of the Tokugawa's warriors retreated to Kan'ei-ji Temple. Their fighting with supporters of the emperor destroyed the temple's main buildings. The temple never recovered. Eager to cut the influence of the temple, in 1878 the new Meiji government converted the area into a park that contained Japan's first zoo and museums. Inside Ueno Zoo, a **five-storied pagoda** built in 1631, is all that remains of Kan'ei-ji within the park's boundaries.

When you arrive by subway and depart Ueno Station, the building in front of you is **Tokyo Metropolitan Festival Hall** (Tokyo Bunka Kaikan). Built in 1961, the hall was one of Japan's first postwar structures to receive international acclaim. For two decades it remained Tokyo's main concert hall; now there are over twenty.

Follow the wide path to the right of the hall; the **National Museum of Western Art** (Kokuritsu Seiyo Bijutsukan) is on the right. Le Corbusier designed this three-storied building that houses the Matsukata collection of Western art. It won't give New York's Museum of Modern Art a run for its money, but the museum has an extensive Rodin sculpture collection and often offers outstanding traveling exhibitions. The museum was recently renovated. *Tel. (03)3828-5131. Open 9:30am-5pm. Closed Mondays and December 25-January 4. ¥420.*

Continuing along the same path, you'll reach a large plaza filled with pigeons. Straight ahead is the **Ueno Zoo**; on the right is the **Science Museum**, and the **Tokyo National Museum** is at the end of the plaza on the right.

Ueno Zoo (Ueno Dobutsu Koen), Japan's first zoo (dating from 1882), is a pleasant urban zoo and the only place where pandas live in Japan. If all you want to do is see pandas and leave, enter by the main gate near Ueno Park's central plaza; the panda house is just a few minutes walk to the right. You can then duck back out. Pandas sleep in the afternoon, but you can still see them in their air-conditioned comfort. The zoo also sports a new vivarium. A monorail connects the two parts of the zoo. The western part is around Shinobazu pond and has a nice petting zoo for children. Shinobazu Pond is the home to many ducks and other water birds. *9-83 Ueno Koen, Taito-ku. Tel. (03)3828-5171. Open daily 9:30am to 5pm (enter by 4pm). Closed Monday and December 29 through January 3. ¥500.*

National Science Museum (Kokuritsu Kagaku Hakubutsukan). This museum is a favorite of our kids. There are exhibitions on physics, chemistry, zoology and botany, astronomy and oceanography. The dinosaur exhibition is a big hit. *Tel. (03)3822-0111. Open 9am to 4:30pm. Closed Monday and December 26 through January 3. ¥420.*

Tokyo National Museum (Tokyo Kokuritsu Hakubutsukan). The National Museum holds Japan's largest collection of art — over 88,000 objects. Only a fraction is on display at any time, but a stroll through the galleries will give you an excellent overview of Japanese and Asian art. The National Museum is not an exhaustive (or exhausting) museum like the Louvre or British Museum. You don't have to devote a lifetime to see it; a few hours is enough. The temporary exhibitions are often very crowded, but the regular galleries rarely are. And if you don't want to see the temporary exhibition, purchase a ticket for the permanent collection only (*josetsu-ken*).

The museum is a complex of buildings. The large main building, straight ahead as you enter, houses Japanese art. Completed in 1937, the building has concrete walls and Japanese-style roofs, representing a synthesis of East and West. This hall houses Japanese art and temporary exhibitions. On the first floor are sculpture, arms and armor, textiles and ceramics while paintings, lacquer ware and calligraphy are on the second. A few of our favorites from the permanent collection are Hasegawa Tohaku's superb early 17th century brush painting of a pine forest — we can almost hear the wind rustling through the pines; the lively and humorous masks used for the court dances in the Nara period; and a Muromachi period six-panel screen, *Pine Trees on the Beach,* painted on gold leaf.

The building to the left of the main gallery, the Hyokeikan, is a faithful imitation of Western architecture constructed at the turn of the century. The Asian art collection is in the gallery to the right of the main building; it contains Chinese, Korean, South Asian and Middle Eastern art. No visit to the National Museum is complete without a stop at the Horyu-ji **Homotsukan**. The stunning, modern building houses the treasures of Nara's Horyu-ji Temple in state-of-the-art displays. Check out the computer database containing English-language information on the collection. Another new building is the **Heisei-kan**, built to commemorate the marriage of the current crown prince. The building holds temporary exhibitions and Japanese archaeology. *13-9 Ueno Koen, Taito-ku. Tel. (03)3822-1111. Open 9am to 5pm. Closed Monday and December 26 through January 3. ¥420, additional for special exhibitions.*

Tokyo Metropolitan Art Museum (Tokyo-to Bijutsukan) exhibits mainly modern Japanese art. There's no standing exhibition so check to see what is on display. *8-36 Ueno Koen, Taito-ku. Tel. (03)3823-6921. Open 9am to 5pm. Closed Monday and New Year's. Admission fee varies.*

Just south of Ueno Zoo is **Toshogu Shrine** that was built in 1651 to honor the first Tokugawa shogun. Like the Toshogu Shrine in Nikko, the style is very ornate; if you don't have a chance to get to Nikko, you can get some idea from this shrine. The stone and bronze lanterns that line the approach were donated by the feudal lords. The descending dragons of the Karamon (Chinese Gate) were carved by Hidari Jingoro, the same sculptor who worked on Nikko's famous, ornate Yomeimon Gate. The dragons are so vividly portrayed it was believed they would drink water from Shinobazu Pond at night. The shrine is designated a National Treasure. *Open 9am to 4:30pm or 6pm, depending on the season. ¥200.*

TOKYO UNIVERSITY

*Nicknamed **Todai**, Tokyo University is at the pinnacle of Japan's higher education system – the dream of tens of thousands of ambitious students. Founded in 1877, Todai was the first imperial university and was built on the estate of the Maeda family. The Maeda feudal lords' domain was second only to the shogun's. When the Tokugawa shogunate collapsed in 1868, the Maeda packed up and returned home to Kanazawa.*

The main gate, Akamon (literally the red gate), was built to commemorate the wedding between a Maeda and the daughter of Shogun Ienari. She was above him in the social hierarchy and apparently she never let her hapless husband forget it. Tales abound about how she always seated herself in a higher position and how her husband talked to her in public using honorific language suited to a daughter of the shogun rather than the way a normal husband would speak to his wife.

The university's campus spans 124 acres and includes a garden belonging to the Maeda estate. To visit, take the Marunouchi subway line to Hongo-san-chome Station.

Benzaiten Shrine is on an island in the middle of the Shinobazu Pond, the southwest part of Ueno Park, and is dedicated to the only female among the seven deities of good fortune. Benten is a patron of music, beauty and the arts and is often depicted playing a lute near the water, which explains why Benzaiten shrines are often found on islands.

At the southern tip of Ueno Park, east of Shinobazu Pond, is the **Shitamachi Museum**. This small museum displays a reproduction of a downtown merchant's area in old Edo. The district was a center for commoner's culture. The second floor houses exhibits of goods and toys used in everyday life. It's quite a charming museum and is a nice break from the high culture of Ueno's other museums. *2-1 Ueno Koen, Taito-ku. Tel. (03)3823-7451. Open 9:30am to 4:30pm. Closed Monday. December 29 through January 3. ¥200.*

From the Shitamachi Museum, walk south until you reach Kasuga Dori. Turn right. About two blocks after the Yushima subway station, **Yushima Tenjin Shrine** is on the left. This small shrine is dedicated to Sugawara Michizane, a 9th century scholar who has been deified as the god of scholarly achievement. In February, when the universities have entrance exams, it is crowded with students praying to pass their entrance exams. On the grounds there's a small grove of plum trees, Michizane's favorite blossom.

Walk back east along Kasuga Dori until you reach Okachimachi Station of the elevated JR Yamanote line. The area north from Okachimachi to Ueno Station is **Ameyoko Market**, a free-wheeling, boisterous place where bargains abound. Ameyoko started as a black market after World War II. Ame is short for America; originally goods pilfered from the Occupation army were the main commodities.

The outdoor market that runs alongside the train line has fishmongers, green grocers and dry goods sales people all barking out their specials to passersby. What a small world we live in: fresh Maine lobsters, Norwegian salmon, smoked salmon, Southeast Asian spices, imported coffee and tea are just a few of the items available in a few short blocks.

The shops, in a warren under and east of the tracks, sell mostly imported clothing, cosmetics, suitcases, shoes and whatever else is popular at the moment. Recently some fairly glitzy buildings have gone up in the Ameyoko area.

From Ueno, the Yanaka and Akihabara/Kanda areas are convenient.

Area 6: Yanaka

To reach Yanaka, take the JR Yamanote line to Nippori.

Yanaka is a quiet backwater with lots of narrow roads with old temples, residences and shops recalling the Tokyo of 100 years ago. Yanaka has alleys where small houses, with lots of potted plants placed outside, stand so close to one another that they practically touch. We enjoy the quiet atmosphere of the district conveniently located north of Ueno Park. You can easily spend two or three hours wandering around, but avoid Mondays when many museums are closed.

The Tokugawa shogunate ordered temples to move to Yanaka as a first wall of defense against invasion. The area was spared major fires and bombing so many of these temples still remain although on much smaller plots of land than in the Edo period.

Don't think of Yanaka as a perfectly preserved district of wooden houses. Most people prefer modern houses over drafty and damp wooden ones, which means that if they have enough money, they usually rebuild. Since most of Yanaka's residents are of modest means, they haven't rebuilt quite to the same extent as in other areas.

When you arrive at Nippori station, walk to the north exit at the very end of the platform, go up the stairs and take the west exit. Stairs to the left lead to Yanaka Cemetery; this detour is lovely during cherry blossom season. Instead, take the road heading away from the station and turn left at the third street where there's a bright orange post box on the corner. The **Asakura Sculpture Gallery** (Asakura Chosokan) is on the left. This museum was the studio-residence of Asakura Fumio (1883-1964) who's considered to be the father of modern Japanese sculpture. You'll recognize it by the ragged cement pillars making a wall around the residence. Asakura designed his house without any angular forms, even to the point of using round cypress poles. His lovely, albeit small, water garden has a pond that occupies most of the space and an assortment of plants that bloom in white all year round — only one has red flowers. Asakura's teahouse is elegant and rustic. *7-18-10 Yanaka, Taito-ku. Tel. (03)3821-4549. Open 9:30am to 4:30pm. Closed Monday and Friday and New Year's. ¥300.*

Turn left as you exit the sculpture gallery. On your left a few buildings down is **Sandara Kogei**, a craft store with ceramics, baskets, textiles and lacquer. A little further down on your left you'll pass **Saboh Hanahenro**, a small restaurant serving seasonal food and coffee, tea and sweets. Continue along this street and on the left you'll come to **Art Iroiro Space Ogura-ya**, a 150-year-old traditional wooden building formerly a pawnshop, now exhibiting art. *7-6-8 Yanaka. Tel. (03)3826-0562. Open 11am to 6pm. Closed Monday.*

You will eventually come to an intersection with a stop light and a Sun Royal Star store on the left. Turn right at this intersection. The road leads downhill past many temples. On the right in the block before the station, you'll find **Kikumi Sembei**, a charming rice cracker shop. Turn around, retrace your steps, and a block or so down on the opposite side of the road is **Isetatsu**. Located in a traditional wooden house with a large picture of a *kabuki* actor above the door, this shop has an excellent assortment of Japanese handprinted paper and crafts. You'll find paper with unusual patterns like *kabuki* actors' make-up styles and feudal lords' family crests. Isetatsu also has beautifully printed cotton cloth with traditional patterns. *2-18-9 Yanaka, Taito-ku. Tel. (03)3823-1453. Open daily 10am to 6pm.*

As you exit Isetatsu, turn right on the street to the right of the store. **Gallery Fukufuku Neko**, a small folk craft shop, is on the left. Turn left at the first street and bear to the right when the street ends — about a five minute walk. On the right is the **Daimyo Clock Museum** (Daimyo Dokei Hakubutsukan). This museum displays Japanese clocks made during the Edo period. These clocks are unique: time was geared to sunrise and sunset, and the length of the hours varied depending on the season. In summer, one daylight hour could last almost twice as long as a nighttime hour. This extremely complicated system meant clocks had to be reset twice a day. Only *daimyo* (feudal lords) could afford such an luxury; hence, the name, *daimyo* clocks. Two of our favorites are the pillow clock used in the bedroom and a tiny clock made into an *inro*, a tiny decorative medicine bottle. *2-1-27 Yanaka, Taito-ku. Tel. (03)3821-6913. Open 10am to 5pm. Closed Monday, July through September and December 25 through January 15. ¥300.*

Turn left as you exit the museum gate and follow the small alley down the steps, turn left at the base of the steps. This road leads downhill to Shinobazu Dori, a main thoroughfare. On the way you will pass on the left Sawanoya Ryokan, a small inn popular with foreigners, and **Imojin**, a Japanese sweets shop, selling bean paste pancakes outside. Step inside for a more relaxing cup of tea and traditional sweets. Cross Shinobazu Dori to reach **Nezu Shrine**, a Shinto shrine famous for its azaleas blooming in the spring. After visiting the shrine, return to Shinobazu Dori, turn right and Nezu Station on the Chiyoda line is several blocks down. From here you are also near the Ueno Park area.

Area 7: Akihabara/Kanda

To reach Akihabara, take the JR Yamanote line to Akihabara Station, one stop from Okachimachi Station or two stops from Ueno Station. Or you can walk south from Ueno, parallel to the Yamanote train tracks, for about 15 minutes.

Akihabara is a high-tech shopper's paradise. Dubbed "Electric Town" by JR's sign makers, the area is enveloped in a neon glow. Shop after shop has its goods spilling onto the street. Figure on spending a half-day in this area.

Akihabara began its electronic reputation after World War II by selling black market goods. Later it began to stock household appliances and became the place Tokyoites went to buy their televisions, washing machines and transistor radios. Now, while you can still buy household appliances, computers and software overwhelm the visitor. The area's many alleyways have booths selling semiconductors and all sorts of parts that require a Ph.D. to identify.

One of the largest shops is **Laox**, pronounced "Raokkusu," which has eight shops within a two or three block area. They and other large shops have duty free departments that specialize in export goods in 120 and 240 volts and have an English-speaking staff. Take your passport to be exempt from paying the 5% consumption tax.

Unlike most shops in Japan, you can usually bargain for a slightly cheaper price at Akihabara's shops as well as at discount electronic shops in other areas. Or in lieu of a cheaper price, you can negotiate some freebies such as extra batteries. So don't be shy about asking for a discount.

You may find that goods are cheaper in New York than they are in Akihabara, but you're sure to find the latest or fully loaded models that have not yet left Japan's shores. We don't know a capacitor from a widget, but we love to browse around Akihabara. There's still a free-wheeling, black market atmosphere even though highly sophisticated goods are now for sale.

Electronic junkie friends have told us that recently Akihabara has lost some of its competitive edge to other big discount shops like Bic Camera, Sakuraya and Yodobashi Camera in Shibuya and Shinjuku. For the foreign visitor, these shops are fine for cameras and video cameras, but they don't have the selection of overseas models for electronic appliances

If you want to have a peek in a traditional Chinese (Oriental) herb medicine shop on Chuo Dori, the main road of Akihabara, turn right at Ishimaru Denki, just before the bridge over the Kanda River. On the right is **Kinokuniya Kan Yakkyoku**, *1-2-14 Soto Kanda, Chiyoda-ku*. This old shop is still flourishing and sells authentic Chinese medicines at reasonable prices, reasonable, that is, as long as you aren't looking for rare items like powdered antlers of a young deer, ¥100,000 for a one month supply.

If you're interested in seeing a few temples, continue along this road for several blocks until **Yushima Confucian Shrine** (Yushima Seido) is on your right. This shrine was affiliated with the Tokugawa shogunate's top samurai school. The Chinese-style building was rebuilt in 1934 after the 1923 earthquake. The main temple building houses a statue of Confucius and is open on Saturday, Sunday and holidays — the grounds are a good escape from the city.

Across Hongo Dori, the street at the back of the shrine, is the entrance to **Kanda Myojin Shrine**, a Shinto shrine with history that goes back to the 8th century. The Tokugawa Shogunate designated it Edo's guardian shrine. While the building was reconstructed in the 1930s, it's faithful to earlier architectural styles. Kanda Myojin holds one of Tokyo's largest and noisiest festivals every other year on May 15. On the shrine's grounds, the Mikoshi-den houses the ornate *mikoshi* (portable shrines) that men, decked out in festival gear, carry through the streets. Fortified with plenty of *sake* and beer, they feel very little pain.

Walk back along the Kanda River to the Akihabara area. Turn right on Chuo Dori and cross over the Mansei Bridge. The **Transportation Museum** (Kotsu Hakubutsukan) is on the right at a fork in the road just past the bridge. The building is old and has a run down feeling, but its heart is in the right place. What a great place to take kids! You can't miss it because a *shinkansen* train is on display at the side of the building. The first floor has trains; cars and ships are on the second; and aviation is on the third. The first steam locomotive used in Japan, which began service between Shimbashi in Tokyo and Yokohama in 1872, is on display. You can sit in the driver's seat of a Yamanote car while a film takes you on the loop all around Tokyo. The model train panorama has about 20 trains, and there's a demonstration of them a few times each hour. We loved the 1938 Datsun car and the primitive stop lights, but our kids loved driving the trains. *25 Kanda Sudacho, 1-chome, Chiyoda-ku. Tel. (03)3251-8481. Akihabara Station on JR Yamanote line. Open 9:30am to 5pm. Closed Monday and December 29 through January 3. ¥310.*

The small road forking off from Chuo Dori at the Transportation Museum leads to Yasukuni Dori, a major thoroughfare. Walk along Yasukuni Dori to reach the heart of Kanda Jimbocho — about 20 minutes. First you'll walk through a **sporting goods** district with nearly 100 shops that sell discounted skiing equipment and ski ware as well as paraphernalia for other sports. The biggest shops are Victoria Sports and Minami Sports. Discounts can reach 80% for last year's goods. *If you want to bypass sporting goods, hop on the Toei Shinjuku subway line at Ogawamachi Station on Yasukuni Dori; and take it one stop to Jimbocho. Use the A-6 exit and you'll come out on the corner of Yasukuni Dori and Hakusan Dori.*

WHERE CAN YOU GO ON MONDAYS WHEN ALMOST EVERY MUSEUM IS CLOSED?

- *MOA Museum in Atami*
- *Kamakura*
- *Meiji Shrine, Omotesando and Harajuku*
- *Asakusa Kannon Temple*
- *Japan Traditional Craft Center in Aoyama*

Jimbocho is Tokyo's book store center with lots of shops selling new, used and rare books in Japanese and English and sometimes other languages, and maps and woodblock prints. The concentration of universities in this area during the Meiji era made it a natural. Rumor has it that the area wasn't bombed during World War II because of the precious antique books in the old shops, but we're skeptical that anyone's aim could be so accurate.

Many of the shops are on Yasukuni Dori on one side of the street. A few of our favorites are **Ohya Shobo** *(1-1 Kanda Jimbocho, Chiyoda-ku, Tel. (03) 3291-0062)* for a good collection of woodblock prints, illustrated books and maps; **Hara Shobo** for woodblock prints *(2-3 Kanda Jimbocho, Chiyoda-ku, Tel. (03) 3261-7444);* and **Kitazawa Books** for an excellent selection of used and rare books in English *(2-5 Kanda Jimbocho, Chiyoda-ku, Tel. (03) 3263-0011).*

Area 8: Asakusabashi/Ryogoku/Fukagawa/Kiba

Allow the better part of a day for this tour. To reach Asakusabashi, take the JR Sobu line to Asakusabashi Station.

Asakusabashi is a bustling wholesale and retail shopping district. Across the Sumida River, Ryogoku is the center of sumo wrestling, Japan's national sport, and is known for a large fireworks display every summer. The sumo stadium is there as well as most of the sumo stables where wrestlers live and train. The large wrestlers, dressed in cotton *yukata* robes, are often on the streets. But sumo isn't the only act in town. Near the stadium are the Edo Tokyo Museum, a small strolling garden and an earthquake memorial; all are worth seeing.

The Asakusabashi Station exit lets you out on Edo Dori, a main road lined with doll and paper goods shops. For paper products, we love to browse in **Shimojima**, there are a half-dozen stores in the area, each selling different products. **Sakura Horikiri**, located on the road along the south side of the train tracks east of the station, sells craft kits using Japanese paper. You have the option of assembling your kit under expert instruction. Shimojima has so many kinds of reasonably priced wrapping paper, both Japanese and Western, that we find it difficult to choose and always come home with more than we need. Also on Edo Dori are several large stores selling elegant dolls in glass cases. Year round you can find dolls for Girls' Day, March 3, and Boys' Day, May 5.

Walk north on Edo Dori and turn right on Kuramae Dori, crossing over the Sumida River. On the right one block after the bridge is the Earthquake Memorial Park. The architecturally eclectic **Centotaph Hall** memorializes the victims of World War II bombing raids as well as the 40,000 people who perished on this site in the fire storm after the 1923 earthquake.

Exit the park from the rear of the hall; across the street is the **Kyu Yasuda Garden**. The quiet park preserves the spirit of Edo gardens. This strolling garden was constructed about 300 years ago; the pond's water level used to rise and fall with the tide of the nearby Sumida River, but today it's controlled artificially. Like the residences of so many other feudal lords, the garden was purchased by a wealthy businessman — in this case the founder of Yasuda Bank, today's Fuji Bank — in the late 19th century. *1-12 Yokoami, Sumida-ku. Open 9am to 4:30pm. Closed at New Year's. Free admission.*

Just south of the park is the **Sumo Stadium** (Kokugikan), home of three sumo tournaments each year. In the building is the small **Sumo Museum** (Sumo Hakubutsukan). The museum is not worth a trek across town, but if you are at the Edo Tokyo Museum, stop in. It has sumo paraphernalia. The trophies aren't very interesting, but some of the old photos are fun. During sumo tournaments, the museum is open only to ticket holders. For information on sumo tickets, see the "Sports & Recreation" chapter. *To go directly to the Sumo Stadium, use the Ryogoku Station of the JR Sobu line. 1-3-28 Yokoami, Sumida-ku, Tokyo. Tel. (03)3622-0366. Free admission to museum.*

Next to the stadium is the **Edo Tokyo Museum** (Edo Tokyo Hakubutsukan). *1-4-1 Yokoami, Sumida-ku, Tokyo. Tel. (03)3626-9974. Ryogoku Station on the JR Sobu line. Open 10am to 6pm; until 8pm Thursday and Friday. Closed Monday and December 28 through January 4. ¥600, additional admission fee for special exhibitions.*

Flush with cash in the middle of the bubble economy of the 1980s, Tokyo decided to build a museum to immortalize its past. It's a Darth Vadar-like building – a silvery steel raised platform with a long escalator taking you from street level into the guts of the building. Designers say the building imitates a rice storehouse that sits on stilts to prevent rodents from eating the grain; the only similarity we see is tall pillars. Instead of the earthy organic feeling of a wooden rice storehouse, the building reminds us of an overgrown robot.

Half the museum is dedicated to Edo, as Tokyo was known during the Tokugawa shogunate (1603-1868), and begins with a reconstruction of the gracefully arched wooden Nihonbashi Bridge, the place from which all distances were measured and where all roads began. Crossing the bridge, imagine how an Edo-period traveler in straw sandals and straw hat must have felt beginning his journey. The museum depends heavily on reconstructions but succeeds in vividly displaying Edo. The other half of the museum displays Tokyo from 1868 onward, through the Meiji craze for all things Western, the 1923 earthquake, the destruction of World War II and the reconstruction in the postwar period. A gallery in the basement has special exhibitions.

Earphones with an English tape are available free of charge at the ticket booths at street level; you pay a refundable deposit. We think they're unnecessary because the text is the same as the English panels in the museum. The museum shop in the basement has an excellent selection of traditional crafts, some of which you find only in the Shitamachi area.

Kiyosumi Dori is the main road running along the eastern side of the Edo Tokyo Museum. Walk south on Kiyosumi Dori one block to the intersection of Keiyo Dori. Here is **Lion-do**, a clothing store that caters to sumo sizes. Stock up on your sumo sized T-shirts here. *Tel. (03)631-0650.* Also near this intersection is **Chanko Doji**, which serves *chanko nabe* sumo fare: raw vegetables, tofu, *udon,* chicken and fish cooked together in a broth. *Tel. (03) 3635-5347.*

Two short blocks south of Keiyo Dori on the left side of Kiyosumi Dori is **Kikuya**, a shop specializing in *tabi,* one-toed socks. *1-9-3 Midori, Sumida-ku. Tel. (03)3631-0092. Closed Sunday and holidays.*

Another good place to eat in the Ryogoku area is **Momojiya** (see *Where to Eat),* which serves venison, boar dishes and badger soup. *1-10-2 Ryogoku, Sumida-ku. Tel. (03)3631-5596.*

Fukagawa is fairly close to Ryogoku. Continue walking along Kiyosumi Dori for about 20 minutes until the Kiyosumi Garden is on your right or hop in a taxi since it's not a particularly pleasant walk. **Kiyosumi Garden** (Kiyosumi Tei-en). This beautiful and peaceful garden was the site of the villa of feudal lord Kuze Yamato-no-kami. Iwasaki Yataro, founder of the Mitsubishi empire, purchased the estate in the late 19th century and seriously upgraded the garden by adding lots of rare rocks from all over Japan. Its large pond is home to thousands of carp. *3-3-9 Kiyosumi, Koto-ku. Tel. (03)3641-5892. Open daily 9am to 4:30pm. Closed December 28 through January 4. ¥150.*

Return to Kiyosumi Dori and turn on to Moto Kuyakusho Dori, across the street from the park. Down several blocks on the left is the **Fukagawa Edo Museum** (Fukagawa Edo Shiryokan). This small museum has 11 buildings all moved from the Fukagawa area. They've been reconstructed to show a working class neighborhood during feudal times and include stores, warehouses, merchants' houses and tenements. It's smaller and less pretentious than the Edo Tokyo Museum. When we were here, some older Japanese touring the museum kept saying, *"Natsukashii,"* — "I'm nostalgic for the good old days." *1-3-28 Shirakawa, Koto-ku. Tel. (03)3630-8625. Open daily 9:30am to 5pm; closed December 28 through January 5. ¥300.*

From the museum, turn left on Kiyosumi Dori and walk about 15 minutes to the Monzen Nakacho Station on the Tozai subway line. You can also take #33 bus to the station. To visit one of the premier alternative art spaces in Tokyo, turn right onto Eitai Dori , the main road where the subway station is, and make the first right after the canal. Turn right at the first corner to reach the **Sagacho Exhibit Space**. This gallery, housed in a refurbished art deco building, formerly the laboratory of the All-Japan Rice Market, is one of the best venues in Tokyo to see the work of up-and-coming artists. The gallery reminds us of New York's Soho galleries. *3F, Shokuryo Building, 1-8-3 Saga, Koto-ku. Tel. (03)3630-3243. Open 11am to 6pm. Closed Sunday and holidays.*

At Monzen Nakacho Station, take the subway one stop to **Kiba**, which literally means timber place. In the Edo period, logs were carried by boats to the canals of the district. To get from the Fukagawa Edo Museum or Sagacho Exhibit Space to the Museum of Contemporary Art (next stop below), it's actually much more efficient to take a taxi.

The only reason to go to Kiba is the **Museum of Contemporary Art, Tokyo** (Tokyo-to Gendai Bijutsukan), with the self-proclaimed nickname "MOT." This museum opened in 1995, and is another large public project planned during the heyday of the bubble economy. The large postmodern stone and glass complex has a zillion little nooks and pathways. It seems as though more thought was put into creating a signature piece of

THE TALE OF THE 47 RONIN

This tale of samurai loyalty has captured the imagination of the Japanese even 400 years after it occurred. The story begins when Asano Takuminokami, a young feudal lord head of a small domain west of Himeji, arrives in Edo. A country bumpkin, he didn't follow common practice and go to see Kira Kozuke-no-suke, the shogun's head of protocol, to present a gift and ask for his guidance. Asano expected to be informed of the protocol of an engagement at the shogun's castle. But the head of protocol, miffed over the breach of etiquette, refused to coach Asano, so he wound up wearing the wrong clothes to the castle.

*Humiliated, Asano angrily drew his sword against Kira, but others stopped Asano from killing him. As a result, Asano committed ritual suicide since samurai were prohibited from drawing their swords within the castle grounds. After Asano's death the shogun confiscated his domain and divided it among other feudal lords. Asano's retainers became **ronin** (masterless samurai). The ronin were so incensed they vowed to do what their lord could not – kill Kira – even though they knew that they themselves would have to commit suicide for this action.*

The ronin planned meticulously – the leader left his wife to live a dissolute life in brothels to make sure no one was suspicious of the plan. Forty-seven of Asano's retainers broke into Kira's residence on a snowy evening, December 14, 1702, and killed him. They then killed themselves.

The pathos of this feat has been immortalized in kabuki, bunraku, movies, TV dramas and even in contemporary opera. Naturally, some take artistic license with the facts. While only about a year elapsed between Asano's suicide and Kira's death, in many plays it stretches out to a decade. Something in the Japanese psyche has great empathy towards tragedy and glorifies the losers; the tale of the 47 ronin pulls all the right strings to make it a classic.

architecture than a working museum. However, the museum holds excellent exhibitions of contemporary art by both Japanese and international artists and, if there's a good exhibition, it's worth the trek even though it's located in the middle of nowhere. We find the practice of charging separate admission fees for each exhibition annoying. Usually several exhibitions run simultaneously and charge anywhere from ¥500 to ¥1000 each. *4-1-1 Miyoshi, Koto-ku. Tel. (03)5245-4111. Open 10am to 6pm, until 9pm Friday. Closed Monday and December 20 through January 4.*

Area 9: Shinagawa & Meguro

On the southern part of the Yamanote loop, the sights in the Shinagawa and Meguro areas are spread out. Rather than walking long distances, we recommend that you take a taxi from one to another.

Sengaku-ji. From Shinagawa Station, walk about 10 minutes north on Hibiya Dori. An otherwise ordinary temple, Sengaku-ji is famous because the 47 *ronin* (masterless samurai) are buried here. This story is one of Japan's favorites about samurai loyalty — the revenge by the retainers of a feudal lord who was forced to commit suicide. People come and pray for the *ronin*, putting one stick of incense on each grave. By the 47th, we were pretty dizzy from breathing the incense.

A five-minute walk will take you to **Tozen-ji** Temple. From Sengaku-ji, walk back towards Shinagawa Station and turn to the right after you pass the pedestrian overpass. Tucked away on a quiet, small alley lined with willow trees, Tozen-ji's simple and austere Zen atmosphere is impressive. The temple was used as the British Legation between 1859 and 1873. It's a shame that the part the British used is not accessible to the public. Still it's a lovely small temple, so drop in when you are in the neighborhood.

From Sengaku-ji, it's a 25-minute walk or 5-minute taxi ride to the **Hara Museum of Contemporary Art** (Hara Bijutsukan). *4-7-25 Kita Shinagawa, Shinagawa-ku. Tel. (03)3445-0651. Open 11am to 8pm weekdays, 11am to 5pm weekends and holidays. Closed Monday. ¥700. 15-minute walk from JR Shinagawa Station or from Shinagawa Station Takanawa exit, take bus #90 to Gotenyama stop. Web site: www.haramuseum.or.jp.*

The Hara Museum is one of the best places to see the cutting edge of contemporary art in Tokyo. Housed in a 1930s Bauhaus-style residence, the museum features Japanese and international artists. The prominent Hara family produced a free-thinking mayor of Tokyo in the early part of this century. His grandson is one of Japan's biggest collectors of contemporary art. The museum has a cafe serving good food, a rarity among Tokyo's museums. In summer you can dine in the garden, a truly delightful experience.

Turn right as you leave the grounds of the Hara Museum and at the large intersection with Yatsuyama Dori, cross the street and continue walking on the narrow road. On the right is **Kaitokaku**, the estate of Baron Iwasaki, the founder of the Mitsubishi empire. The grounds are not open to the public, but today Mitsubishi uses the turn-of-the-century robber baron's mansion for entertaining. Kaitokaku is one of the few large estates left intact in Tokyo.

After about a seven-minute walk, the street merges into a larger road and the Takanawa Prince Hotel is on the right. Continue walking straight; just past the end of the hotel's property is a street light. There's always a police guard at this intersection. Turn left. In one block, you'll come to a large intersection. Cross Sakurada Dori and on the other side the road forks into two small streets. Take the one on the right. Several blocks down, past a playground, is a big red sign that says **Han-nya-en**. Turn left and follow the road as it curves around to the right. Turn left at another red sign; the Hatakeyama Collection and Han-nya-en are just past the parking lot. The walk takes about 20 minutes; if you want to save your time and energy, take a cab.

The **Hatakeyama Collection** has one of the best museum settings in Tokyo and is a must-see for anyone with a serious interest in the tea ceremony and its arts. The museum is tucked away on a quiet side street in a verdant compound of gardens, teahouses and an elegant residence. Hatakeyama Issei, a successful machine industry businessman and a tea ceremony connoisseur, collected tea utensils, hanging scrolls and ceramics. Hatakeyama himself designed the gallery that includes three tea ceremony rooms. The famous collection includes a beautiful handscroll that is the result of the collaboration between two of the most versatile artists in the Edo period: Hon'ami Koetsu and Tawaraya Sotatsu. There are also dynamic tea bowls and square plates by Ogata Kenzan. The museum exhibits about 50 objects at a time, changing shows with the seasons. *2-20-12 Shiroganedai, Minato-ku. Tel. (03)3447-5787. Open 10am to 5pm. ¥500.*

The museum shares a garden with Han-nya-en, an elegant, traditional building, the former Hatakeyama residence. Today it is an extremely pricey restaurant, dinner runs about ¥50,000 per person. Mishima Yukio used Han-nya-en as the setting for his novel *After the Banquet.*

From the museum, walk back to Sakurada Dori, turn right and walk about five minutes down the hill to Gotanda Station. Take the JR Yamanote line one stop to **Meguro Station**. Come out the east exit of the station and walk east along Meguro Dori for five minutes. Just after you pass under the expressway, you'll come to the **Tei-en Museum** (Tokyo-to Tei-en Bijutsukan) on the left. The only remaining Art Deco building in Tokyo, the Tei-en Museum is the former residence of Prince Asaka. Built in 1933, Henri Rapin designed the building, and much of the glasswork is by Rene Lalique. The museum does not have a permanent collection but often has exhibits relating to Art Deco. We love to bring a picnic lunch and eat in the museum's French and Japanese gardens — admission to the garden only is ¥200. *5-21-9 Shiroganedai, Minato-ku. Tel. (03)3443-8500. Open 10am to 5pm. Closed 2nd and 4th Wednesday. Admission varies with the exhibition.*

Just beyond the Tei-en Museum is the **Nature Study Park** (Shizen Kyoiku-en), a heavily wooded area with educational programs to teach Tokyoites about nature because they see little of it in their real lives. It's a good place to surround yourself with some trees. This park is one of the few original forests of the Musashino plain and is left in an authentic state. Don't get disgusted by the crows that have decided to move in; the Tokyo government would like to move them out, but hasn't discovered how.

Continue walking down Meguro Dori for another five minutes. Just after the pedestrian overpass, on the right corner is **Happo-en**, a catering hall that is popular for weddings. The complex has a lovely strolling garden that once belonged to the Okubo family, chief retainers to the Tokugawa shoguns. You can have a nice meal here or just enjoy the garden.

Walk back to the west side of Meguro Station. On the southeast side is a small road coming off to the left of Sakura Bank at an angle. Walk down this road about five minutes until you come to Meguro Gajoen.

Meguro Gajoen is a wedding palace and hotel, and even though you have no intention of getting married, you must stop in. The place was an early 20th century building that was completely rebuilt a few years ago, and some of the art has been incorporated into the new structure. An outrageous project undertaken at the height of the economic bubble, it's as "bubbly" as you can get — a real tribute to the crazy 1980s when cost was no object for anything. It is so way out, we love to show it off to visitors.

The hotel really functions as a wedding palace with rooms on the side. The large contemporary structure has a tall atrium overlooking a Japanese garden. There are several restaurants, including a good *teppanyaki* restaurant, Kasho, where lunch courses begin at ¥3000.

The long hallway has huge paintings of Japanese women; be sure to look up at the ceiling where fan-shaped paintings look down on you. Sneak a peek into the *tatami* mat lobby of the Japanese-style banquet room. It's Japanese rococo with paintings moved from the original building. And don't forget to go into the rest rooms in the lobby; they, too, are works of art.

You can walk back up the hill to Meguro Station for the JR Yamanote line.

Area 10: Ebisu

On the western side of Tokyo, one stop south of Shibuya on the JR Yamanote line.

Ebisu was a quiet and nearly forgotten neighborhood until **Yebisu Garden Place** opened. It's one of Tokyo's few urban complexes incorporating offices, commercial and residential space, a luxury hotel, and numerous restaurants. Until the late 1980s, the site was Yebisu's beer brewery. The moving sidewalk at the south exit of Ebisu Station delivers you to the complex. The plaza has lots of open space, but unfortunately most is bricked over — more grass would have been nice. The area is packed with young people, especially dating couples, on evenings and weekends.

The Westin Tokyo Hotel is there as is a small branch of Mitsukoshi Department Store. The site used to house the Yebisu beer factory, so naturally there is a beer hall and a beer museum. The upscale French restaurant, Taillevent Robuchon, is in a faux chateau; plans to move a real one from France were nixed because of building codes. Dinner is pricey; lunch is less so or why not try the basement cafe. A host of other restaurants serve everything from *sushi* and *tonkatsu* to spaghetti.

The **Tokyo Metropolitan Museum of Photography** (Tokyo-to Shashin Bijutsukan) alone is worth the trip to Yebisu Garden Place. The museum is the premier place to view photography and video art in Tokyo. *Yebisu Garden Place, 1-13-3 Mita, Meguro-ku. Tel. (03)3280-0031. Open 10am to 6pm, Thursday and Friday until 8pm. Closed Monday. ¥1000. Web site: www.tokyo-photo-museum.or.jp.*

The commercial area around the northern exit of Ebisu Station has lots of shops catering to area residents and makes for some interesting strolling.

Area 11: Shibuya

Shibuya is three stops on the Yamanote line from Shinjuku.

Shibuya has an entirely different feel than most other districts of Tokyo. The Shibuya area is one of Tokyo's trendiest areas; it's always crowded with people and exudes energy and excitement. Filled with shops and restaurants, it caters to a young crowd dressed from head to toe in the latest fashions. It's much smaller and doesn't have the same massive office buildings and hotels. People come to Shibuya to play, not work. Even if you are over 25, don't stay away from Shibuya. There are enough "establishment" places so you won't feel out of place.

The area was once the boondocks, far removed from the population center around and east of the castle. After the 1923 earthquake, people started moving west, searching for open space, and Shibuya's prosperity began. For the last two decades, two parvenu department store compa-

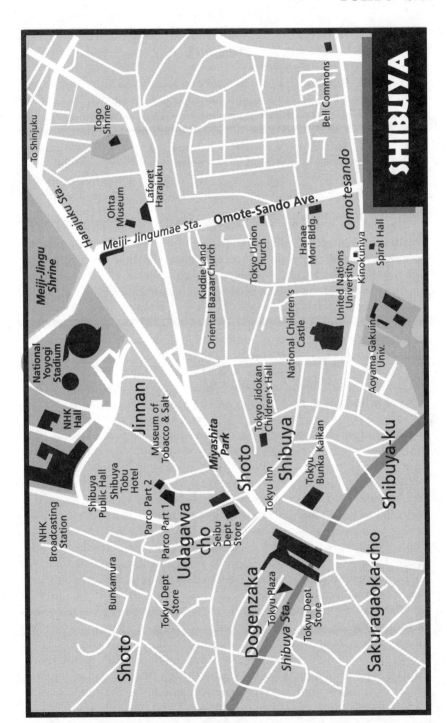

SHIBUYA

To Shinjuku

Harajuku Sta.

Togo Shrine

Bell Commons

Laforet Harajuku

Ohta Museum

Meiji-Jingumae Sta.   Omote-Sando Ave.

Meiji-Jingu Shrine

Omotesando

Kiddie Land

Oriental Bazaar

Tokyo Union Church

Hanae Mori Bldg.

United Nations University

Kinokuniya

Spiral Hall

National Yoyogi Stadium

National Children's Castle

Aoyama Gakuin Univ.

NHK Hall

Jinnan

Museum of Tobacco & Salt

Tokyo Jidokan Children's Hall

Shibuya-ku

Shibuya Public Hall

Shibuya Tobu Hotel

Miyashita Park

Shoto

Shibuya

NHK Broadcasting Station

Parco Part 2

Parco Part 1

Tokyu Inn

Tokyu Bunka Kaikan

Bunkamura

Seibu Dept. Store

Udagawa cho

Shoto

Tokyu Dept Store

Dogenzaka

Tokyu Plaza

Shibuya Sta.

Tokyu Dept Store

Sakuragaoka-cho

nies, Tokyu and Seibu, have been competing to build the best department stores and fashion buildings; in the process, they've put Shibuya on the map.

This walk through Shibuya can take one hour if you don't stop or all day for shopaholics. Begin at Shibuya Station, a fairly small place when compared to Shinjuku or Ikebukuro but served by six train and subway lines. There's a small plaza at the northwest quadrant of the station, with a statue called **Hachiko**, named after a famous dog, where friends wait to meet each other (see above sidebar). On evenings and weekends the area is so crowded it's almost impossible to find someone unless he or she has pink hair. Actually, being blonde is a plus. There's a small police box in **Hachiko Plaza**.

The buildings around Hachiko Plaza have bright neon lights, billboards and video screens that light up the evening sky. The noise level can be unbearable when people concerned about the future —politicians, right wingers, left wingers, you name it — park their sound trucks next to the plaza and blast out speeches no one wants to hear.

The large intersection has to be one of Tokyo's most crowded; literally a thousand or more people cross at the same time and, naturally, all go in different directions. Sometimes it feels like all of Tokyo's 12 million residents have converged on the intersection at the same time. The experience can be disconcerting when you're not used to crowds; instead of letting it overwhelm you, follow the person in front of you by looking at his or her shoes. People will try to avoid bumping into you.

From Hachiko Plaza, locate and walk towards the **Shibuya 109** building; it has a big silver silo; be careful because there are several 109 Buildings. In the time you walk the block, you will probably receive at least three packets of tissues advertising all sorts of services imaginable. On the left you'll see a discount electronics store with its goods spilling out onto the sidewalk and hear its advertising jingle blasting over loudspeakers. Welcome to **Bic Camera**. Despite its name, Bic sells computers, household appliances, stereos and nearly anything else electronic. Where else would you find small foot warmers in winter and ice sherbet makers in the shape of a penguin in summer? The prices are comparable to Akihabara's, but export models aren't stocked. Next to Bic is **Kobe-ya**, a bakery that has delicious bread and sandwiches.

Shibuya 109 was one of the first "fashion buildings" — basically vertical malls chocked with small stores and restaurants. At the Y intersection in front of the 109 building, bear to the right. Along the right side of the building is a traditional-looking restaurant with plastic food displays. This restaurant is **Kujira**, one of the few places in Japan serving whale meat. Leave your Greenpeace membership card at home if you want to give it a try.

HACHIKO, MAN'S BEST FRIEND

*Shibuya would not be complete without an explanation of **Hachiko**, the famous dog statue that has to be Tokyo's most famous meeting place. Who is this dog? Hachiko, an Akita (a Japanese species which is almost extinct today), was born in Akita Prefecture in 1923. His master was a professor at Tokyo Imperial University. Hachiko always accompanied his master to the train station and would return to the station in the afternoon to meet him coming home.*

In 1925, when Hachiko was only two years old, his master died while teaching a class. Even though the gardener, who lived in Asakusa, adopted Hachiko, the faithful dog walked across Tokyo everyday to wait at Shibuya Station for his master to return. Commuters came to know Hachiko. In 1932 he was featured in the Asahi Shimbun newspaper and became an instant celebrity. The dog died at the age of 13. Every year on April 8, a special commemorative festival is held in front of the bronze statue at Shibuya Station. Such dogged loyalty has won the hearts of the Japanese.

As you continue along the road, a *pachinko* parlor, **Maruhan**, is on your right. Japan's largest, this parlor was one of the first of the new upscale breed. To get first shot at the best machines, people line up long before the 10am opening. Next to Maruhan is a money exchange office run by Bank of Tokyo-Mitsubishi that is open from 12 noon to 6pm.

The road leads to Tokyu Department Store's main store. Around the back of the department store is **Bunkamura**, literally Culture Village. Under one roof, you'll find Orchard Hall, the home of the Tokyo Symphony; smaller halls; art movie theaters; Bunkamura Museum, home to high-quality traveling exhibitions; gallery space and restaurants.

The main entrance of Tokyu Department store is a Y intersection; walk along the left side of the Y. Turn right at the next traffic light; Shibuya City Hotel will be on the left. Follow this road along the perimeter of Tokyu Department Store and up the hill. The road ends at the **Kanze Noh Theater**. Turn left and follow the red brick sidewalk for a block. On the right, in a yellow brick building, is the **Toguri Museum of Art** (Toguri Bijutsukan). The building is architecturally undistinguished, but this small museum is one of our favorites and is a must for anyone seriously interested in ceramics. The 2000-piece collection of Chinese, Korean and Japanese ceramics belonged to a businessman; only a small portion is on display at a time. The Imari and Nabeshima pieces are outstanding. The museum organizes four exhibitions a year. *Tel. (03)3465-0070. Open 10am to 5:30pm. Closed Monday. ¥1030.*

Continue along the red sidewalk. Shoto Park will be on your left. Just past the park, at the intersection with the traffic light, in a contemporary concrete building is **Gallery TOM**, a unique gallery where you can touch the art as well as see it. Bronze, stone and wooden sculptures are on display including works by Rodin. *Tel. (03)3467-8102. Open 10:30am to 5:30pm. Closed on Sunday, Monday and national holidays. ¥600 (¥300 for visually handicapped).*

Retrace your steps; pass the Toguri Museum and turn right when the Kanze Noh Theater is on your left. Go down the hill. At the traffic light where Shibuya City Hotel is on your right, continue up a narrow road. This is Rambling Road, which will take you up the hill to the heart of **Maruyama-cho**. Once the exclusive preserve of love hotels and sleazy bars, these have now been joined by legitimate establishments, making it one of Shibuya's main entertainment areas. There must be more love hotels per square meter here than anywhere else in Japan. Their rates are listed outside; "rest" is for two or three hours, and "stay" is for overnight. On the legitimate side, **On Air East** and **On Air West** have live music performances; **Club Asia** is a restaurant and disco; and **Dr. Jeekans** is a virtual reality amusement parlor. Its first floor bar, **Wood and Stone**, features inexpensive food and drinks.

Continue rambling along Rambling Road until it descends slightly. At this intersection is a traffic light. Turn left on to Dogenzaka, another of Shibuya's main roads. A few blocks on the left is the **Prime Building**; on the second floor there's a food court serving all sorts of cuisines at reasonable prices. Dogenzaka leads you back to Shibuya Station. Just before the station, turn left, 109 Part 2 building will be on the far corner. **Seibu Department Store**, one of Tokyo's most trendy, is on the left and offers an especially good selection of Japanese designer wear. Seibu's Loft Building is a rival to Tokyu Hands (see below) and its SEED building has avant-garde clothing, gallery space and a performance hall. A little further down the road is **Tower Records**, the world's largest CD and tape store. The book store has an excellent selection of English-language books, magazines and newspapers from all over the world and some of the lowest prices in Japan.

Walk back to Seibu; turn onto the street between the two Seibu buildings and follow it for several blocks. Stay on the road while it curves to the right. Just past McDonalds is the back entrance to **Tokyu Hands**. Tokyu Hands invented the "Do-it-yourself" genre of stores. It has everything you could ever think you need or want for your hobby or leisure time. We recommend you take the elevator to the top floor and walk down. You go past sections for bicycles, automotive supplies, hardware, cooking, sewing, art supplies, party supplies, outdoor equipment, paper goods, lumber, posters, frames and more. Even if you aren't interested in

SHIBUYA WITH CHILDREN

Shibuya has lots of great places for children:
• *TEPCO Electric Energy Museum. Run by the Tokyo Electric Power Company, this eight-storied building is filled with hands-on displays – everything you always wanted to know about electricity. Kids love it. Tel. (03)3477-1191. Open 10:30am to 6:30pm. Closed Wednesday. Admission free. From Hachiko Plaza, take the road to the left of the 109 Part 2 building running parallel to the tracks. When the road curves to the right, the glass and steel museum building with a domed roof is on the right.*
• *Tokyo Metropolitan Children's Hall (Tokyo-to Jido Kaikan). This hall entertains children from toddlers through junior high students. It has climbing equipment, computers, crafts, music room and a lot more to keep children and their parents occupied for the better part of the day. 1-18-24 Shibuya, Shibuya-ku. Tel. (03)3409-6361. Open 9am to 5pm. Closed usually the 2nd and 4th Mondays and around New Year's. No admission fee. From Hachiko Plaza at Shibuya Station, walk under the train tracks and turn left at the major road, Meiji Dori. At the first traffic light, turn right and the hall is on the left, one block in.*
• *Children's Castle (Kodomo no Shiro). Kids are definitely kings and queens in this castle. There is everything to entertain them on a rainy day and on sunny days too. Younger children love the climbing equipment, crafts and story book areas. View videos in the audio-visual room – they have a fair number in English. Older children enjoy the more extensive craft program, music room, performances and more. Don't overlook the roof garden with bicycles and a jumping-on-balls area. Children's Castle even has a hotel on the premises – an ideal place to stay with children. 5-53-1 Jingumae, Shibuya-ku. Tel. (03)3797-5666. Open 12:30pm to 5:30pm, weekdays; 10am to 5:30pm weekends, holidays and school holidays. Closed Monday. ¥500. From Hachiko Plaza at Shibuya Station, walk under the train tracks and continue on that street up the hill. You'll pass the large post office. When the road ends, bear left onto wide Aoyama Dori. Children's Castle is two blocks on the left. You can't miss the unusual sculpture out front.*

buying anything, it's a major cultural experience just to see what the store offers. One of our favorite, truly original souvenirs is a clock made with plastic *sushi*. One warning: avoid this cultural experience on Sunday afternoons. There may be as many people as there are items in the shop.

Exit Tokyu Hands from the main exit on the first floor; turn right as you leave the store and walk about two short blocks to a traffic light. This street is Koen Dori. At the intersection are several buildings called **Parco**, one of the best "fashion buildings." There's an especially good selection of Japanese and Japan-inspired designers such as Issey Miyake, Yohji Yamamoto and Jurgen Lehl.

Turn left onto Koen Dori. The **Tobacco and Salt Museum** is in a red brick building one block up on the right. Tobacco may not be politically correct, but no one has told this museum. Tobacco and salt were government monopolies, which is why this unlikely combination exists. The museum displays pipes, Edo period woodblock prints depicting smoking and antique cigarette manufacturing equipment. Salt production equipment is also on display. The museum puts on temporary exhibitions on a wide range of themes. *1-16-8 Jinnan, Shibuya-ku. Tel. (03)3476-2041. Open 10am to 6pm. Closed Monday and December 29-January 3. ¥100.*

Continue along the same road until it opens into a large intersection. Yoyogi Park is straight ahead; NHK, the public television station, is to the right. **NHK Studio Park** is on the 3rd and 4th floors of the NHK Broadcasting Center. You can see the stage sets of popular TV dramas. *Open 10am to 6pm. Closed 2nd Monday. ¥200.*

Across a wide brick walkway from NHK is the **National Gymnasium**, two distinctive buildings designed by Tange Kenzo for the 1964 Olympic Games. The smaller one, with a seashell spiral roof, is for basketball, and the larger one is for swimming and diving, but other events are also held. These buildings look so contemporary that they belie their age.

Yoyogi Park is an oasis of green in the city. The wide open area is great for running around, playing frisbee or having a picnic lunch. The park has a bicycle course; children under 15 can borrow bicycles at no charge between 9am and 4pm, except Monday.

Adjacent to Yoyogi Park is **Meiji Shrine**, which is the first stop in our Harajuku tour (see next sights section, area 12, below). Harajuku Station is one minute away from the entrance to the shrine.

Side trip from Shibuya: Japan Folk Craft Museum (Nihon Mingei-kan). The museum is a little out of the way, but worth the effort. Housed in a folk-style building, itself a piece of art, the museum has a collection of folk art gathered together by Yanagi Soetsu, a pioneer in the *mingei* (folk art) movement of the 1930s. On top of Yanagi's collections, the museum has an extensive assortment of earthy Japanese ceramics, dynamic woodblock prints by Munakata Shiko and country-style furniture.

We enjoy seeing the sunlight streaming through the paper windows of the *shoji* screens. Temporary exhibitions change with the seasons. The museum's charming and tiny shop is well stocked with folk craft items. *From Shibuya Station, take the Inokashira line train two stops to Komaba Todai-mae. At the station, cross the tracks and take the road parallel to the tracks up the hill. 4-3-33 Komaba, Meguro-ku. Tel. (03)3467-4527. Open 10am to 5pm. Closed Monday and at New Year's. ¥1000.*

Area 12: Harajuku & Omotesando

To reach Harajuku, take the JR Yamanote line to Harajuku Station or the Chiyoda subway line to Meiji Jingumae Station.

Harajuku offers a contrast between the traditional and the contemporary. The staid and solemn Meiji Shrine, hidden deep inside a forest, is only a few hundred meters away from the trendy shops of Takeshita Dori and Omotesando. This sums up the dichotomy of modern Japan.

Harajuku is an area for the young and the young at heart. Students throng the streets to see the latest teen fashions and to be seen. Some come to this mecca from as far away as Osaka and Sendai. The age of Harajuku's customers has been getting younger and younger. Once the haunt of high school students, the streets are now crowded with junior high students.

Omotesando (literally pilgrim's main path) is the fashionable area along the approach road to Meiji Shrine. This wide avenue is often called Tokyo's Champs Elysees. Both are lined with tall trees and have some cafes and McDonalds on them, but the similarity doesn't go much beyond that.

Built in 1924, Harajuku Station is one of the few in Tokyo that has retained its original architecture, a European half-timbered look. Head for the green trees across the bridge spanning the Yamanote line's tracks. The plaza gives way to a dense forest beyond a wooden *torii* gate. It's about a 10-minute walk through the woods to **Meiji Shrine** (Meiji Jingu). The woods were designed as part of the shrine and contain trees and plants gathered from every Japanese prefecture. It's almost impossible to believe you're in the center of Tokyo.

Meiji Shrine was built to deify the Meiji Emperor who died in 1912. He was restored to power at the end of the Tokugawa era (1868) and helped Japan usher in the modern era. With the exception of the Treasure House, the original buildings were destroyed in World War II. The present shrine was built in 1958.

The understated plain buildings made of cypress wood have long, sloping copper roofs. Maiden priestesses wearing white kimono over orange *hakama* pants sell amulets and other good luck items at the stalls on the side. On weekends, Shinto priests formally dressed in pale blue costumes perform weddings, bless newborn babies and conduct other ceremonies. We love to see couples dressed in wedding kimono or a baby, dressed in a formal kimono, held by a mother in traditional dress – fathers almost always dress in Western attire; all look delighted to be there.

Meiji Shrine is one of the most popular places to visit at New Year's to welcome the gods and pray for good luck; several million people crowd the shrine during the first days of the year. Look closely at the pillars of the main hall – the exterior sides have lots of dents from being hit by flying coins.

Behind the shrine is the **Treasure House** that displays artifacts belonging to the Meiji Emperor and Empress. The 1921 building is a good example of the religious revival architecture of the time. *Treasure House is open 9am to 4pm, November through February, and 9am to 4:30pm, March through October. Closed 3rd Friday. ¥400.*

Also on the grounds of the shrine is the peaceful **Inner Garden**, built by the Meiji Emperor for his wife whose favorite flower was the iris. The iris garden is beautiful in June; we are always amazed by the many hues of the purple iris. The garden also has a lovely teahouse overlooking a water lily pond; we find it more dramatic to see the water lily pond before approaching the irises. *¥300.*

Meiji Shrine is open from dawn until sunset, making it a good place to go for an early morning stroll; guards do not permit jogging.

Return to Harajuku Station; walk along the station's side, parallel to the train tracks. There's a traffic light at the back exit; turn right at this light and you are on **Takeshita Dori**. You'll immediately notice that the average age of the people around you is about 15. Takeshita Dori used to be a hangout for high school students, but now junior high students have taken over. The stores sell inexpensive clothes and jewelry. You'll also find a number of stores selling crepes, a popular snack with this age group.

Walk down Takeshita Dori until you reach Meiji Dori. If you turn left, you'll come to **Togo Shrine**; its lively antique and junk market will captivate you the first and fourth Sundays of the month.

Rather than going to Togo Shrine, on Meiji Dori turn right and walk to the next major intersection, where Meiji Dori meets Omotesando. Turn right and then right again at the first little street. You'll come to the **Ota Memorial Ukiyo-e Museum** (Ukiyo-e Ota Kinen Bijutsukan). Exchange your shoes for slippers before entering this tiny museum. The museum has an exhaustive *ukiyo-e* collection put together by a businessman in the insurance field; it includes woodblock prints by Hokusai, Utamaro, Hiroshige and other famous artists of the Edo period. Only a small portion is shown at a time. Exhibitions change every month. You need to step onto *tatami* mats to see some of the works. Exhibitions change every month. *Tel. (03)3403-0880. Open 10:30am to 5:30pm. Closed Monday and the last few days of every month to change the installation. ¥500.*

Near the Ota Museum is the unusually named **Do! Family Museum of Art** that features exhibitions for the whole family. *1-12-4 Jingumae, Shibuya-ku. Tel. (03)3470-4540. Open 11am to 6pm. Closed Monday. ¥300.*

OUR FAVORITE TOKYO MUSEUMS
- *Idemitsu Art Museum, Hibiya*
- *Nezu Institute of Art, Omotesando*
- *Toguri Art Museum, Shibuya*
- *Japan Folk Craft Museum, Komaba, near Shibuya*
- *Sagacho Exhibit Space, Fukagawa*
- *Taiko Drum Museum, Asakusa*
- *Suntory Museum of Art, Akasaka*
- *Ota Memorial Museum of Art, Harajuku*

Return to Omotesando. On the far side of the road is a shop called **Chicago**. Most of the store sells recycled clothing from America, but there's also a good used kimono section.

As you exit Chicago, turn right. Just before you cross Meiji Dori, a small shop called **Condomania** is on the right. It caused a small stir when it opened several years ago.

The boulevard of Omotesando is lined with shops, boutiques and restaurants. The many cafes and bakeries will surely tempt you. **Peltier** and **Cafe de Rope**, both on the right, have tasty pastries. Make a detour for an excellent restaurant: across from the Vivre 21 building is a police box. Go down the steps to the left of the box and walk along the little alley; just before the barrier, in a traditional building on your left, you'll find the restaurant **Kiku**, featuring homestyle Japanese cooking. The interior decor is Japanese modern.

Return to Omotesando. On the far side of Omotesando is **Kiddyland**, a large toy store popular with children of all ages. Next door is **Fuji Tori**, which has both new and antique ceramics, screens and other traditional goods. In the next block is **Oriental Bazaar**, stocking new and antique items and catering to foreigners.

Across the street, you'll notice some old brown buildings. The Dojunkai Apartments were built in 1925 after the big earthquake and look slightly out of place. These were among the first apartments built in Japan. Today, many of the ones that line Omotesando have been turned into charming shops and galleries taking advantage of the old-time atmosphere.

Under the coffee shop named **Chat Noir**, is one of Tokyo's best known revolving *sushi* restaurants. This restaurant is very popular and its high turnover ensures that the *sushi* hasn't spent the afternoon going around and around on the conveyor belt. You'll also pass **Cafe de Flore**, a cousin to the shop in Paris, a trendy French-style cafe serving espresso for ¥600 and hot chocolate for ¥900. Further along is the boutique of

TWO DIFFERENT MUSEUMS

Burned out on museums? Does the idea of visiting just one more make you catatonic? Here are a few that are sure to whet your appetite.

Meguro Parasitological Museum (Meguro Kiseichukan). 4-1-1 Shimo Meguro, Meguro-ku. Tel. (03)3716-1264. Open 10am to 5pm. Closed Monday and holidays. Free admission. This museum is the only one in the world devoted to parasites. Is it a coincidence that a country that has raised eating raw fish to an art form should have this museum? Parasites of all shapes and forms are cheerfully presented in glass jars. The museum's prized possession is a tapeworm 9 meters long – they even have a tape measure that you can pull out to get an idea how long 9 meters really is. Their T-shirts with the museum's theme, "the wonderful world of worms," make great presents. And, unlike most museums, you can photograph to your heart's content. Just make sure you go after lunch or you may never eat again.

Bicycle Culture Center (Jitensha Culture Center). 1-9-3 Akasaka, Minato-ku. Tel. (03)3584-4530. Open 10am to 4pm. Closed weekends. Free admission. Located across the street from the American Embassy, you have to go through the building's parking garage to reach the center. It's a well-done display on biking and includes some of the earliest bikes produced.

Hanae Mori, the first Japanese fashion designer to make it big on the international scene. The basement has small shops selling Japanese and Western antiques, and on the fifth floor, **L'Orangerie** serves a delicious Sunday brunch. Across the street is **Asahi Gallery**, an antique shop with absolutely beautiful works. The collection of screens on the second floor is excellent.

As you continue along Omotesando, you'll come to McDonalds; turn left at the small road before it. The road ends in one block; turn left and then immediately right. On the right is **Gallery Kawano** that sells vintage textiles. Continue down the road and the large building on the left is **Maisen**, a popular *tonkatsu* restaurant — lunch specials are a bargain.

Retrace your steps to Omotesando and go to the large intersection where Aoyama Dori and Omotesando meet. Cross Aoyama Dori and continue straight ahead. The road narrows substantially. On the left corner is an old shop that sells flower arrangement supplies. You are sure to find vases unlike anything in the West. You'll also find *kenzan* (iron flower holders) and special scissors. Make a slight detour onto Aoyama Dori for a good bakery, **Andersen's**. They have deli-style sandwiches in the basement and slightly more upscale restaurant on the second floor.

The narrow road, the continuation of Omotesando, has boutiques of many of Japan's best-known contemporary fashion designers as well as international designers—Issey Miyake, Yohji Yamamoto, Kawakubo Rei's Comme des Garçons and Jurgen Lehl. A ten-minute walk will show you the latest in men's and women's fashion design. Even if you are not interested in buying clothes, we are sure you'll enjoy seeing the conspicuously creative contemporary designs as well as the simple and subdued interior decorations. Make sure you stop in the From First and Collezione buildings, on the right just before the Nezu Museum.

Before you reach these two buildings, on the right will be the **Tessenkai Noh Institute**, a most unlikely contemporary concrete building with a steel door. Inside is an authentic *noh* stage where *noh* is performed several times a month.

The road leads to a large intersection. Cross the main road, and you'll be standing in front of a stucco wall on the far right side. This wall surrounds the grounds of the **Nezu Institute of Fine Arts** (Nezu Bijutsukan); the entrance is about a half-block down the road. This small gem of a museum is tucked away behind high walls, possibly to keep trendy Aoyama at arms length. The museum houses the collection of Nezu Kaichiro, founder of the Tobu Railway Company. During the early part of this century, he assembled a first-rate art collection, especially strong in tea ceremony utensils. The museum has Ogata Korin's *Irises*, a masterpiece screen painting, and the *Nanchi Waterfall* scroll painting from the Kamakura era. The Nezu Institute has two galleries: one displays temporary exhibitions – not always from the museum's collections – and the second has a permanent display of the museum's holdings. The museum's collection is so extensive that only a small portion is on view at any one time. The Iris screen, for instance, is shown every spring in late April and early May.

The Institute has a large strolling garden open to the public at no charge. It's a serene place that we love to visit to escape from the overload of all the shops in Aoyama. *6-5-1 Minami Aoyama, Minato-ku. Tel. (03)3400-2536. Open 9:30am to 4:30pm. Closed Mondays and around New Year's. ¥1000.*

Across the street from the museum is a small art gallery, **Honjo**, which carries new and antique items. As you exit Honjo, turn right. On the right you'll come to **Zero First Design**, a store selling contemporary Japanese furniture and crafts. Across from Zero First is a small alley. At the end of the alley is the **Ishii Collection**, a tiny antique shop. Return to the main road.

When the road ends at Kotto Dori, literally Antique Street, turn right (many of the antique shops have been forced out by high rents). The ones remaining make for fun browsing. This road ends at Aoyama Dori. Turn right and a few blocks down is the Omotesando subway station served by the Ginza, Hanzomon and Chiyoda lines. If you continue walking down Aoyama Dori , you'll tour Aoyama and Akasaka Mitsuke.

Area 13: Aoyama & Akasaka

From the Omotesando Station on the Ginza, Hanzomon and Chiyoda subway lines, exit onto Aoyama Dori. If you come out at Fuji Bank, cross Omotesando, the road with stone lanterns at the entrance, going in the direction of the police box.

These two districts are fashionable areas lined with elegant boutiques and restaurants.

As you walk along Aoyama Dori, you'll pass premier retailers. Brooks Brothers looks so authentic you may think you are on Madison Avenue. Several blocks down, on the right is the **Japan Traditional Craft Center** (Zenkoku Dentoteki Kogeihin Senta). It's on the second floor and can be difficult to locate: look for Haagen Dazs ice cream parlor. This gallery has an excellent selection of crafts from all over Japan. Although you can purchase anything in the shop, it feels like a museum. The center also has video tapes showing different Japanese crafts; many are in English. There is no charge to view the videos. *2F, Plaza 246 Building, 3-1-1-Minami Aoyama, Minato-ku. Tel. (03)3403-2460. Open 10am to 6pm. Closed Thursday and December 29 through January 4.*

The Traditional Craft Center is at the intersection of Killer Dori, a street known for its fashion and other boutiques, and Aoyama Dori. Heading south, the road leads to Aoyama Cemetery. North leads to the National Stadium. On the corner diagonally across from the Craft Center is **Bell Commons**, a "fashion building" with stores and restaurants. It has a branch of the good and reasonably priced *sushi* shop, **Sushi Sei**. The north side is more interesting for it has **Watari-um**, an art space showing avant-garde international and Japanese artists *(3-7-6 Jingumae, Shibuya-ku. Tel. (03)3402-3001).* **On Sundays**, a great art book shop, in the same building and run by the same people, has one of the world's most extensive selection of postcards.

Return to Aoyama Dori and continue walking in the same direction. On the left is Meiji Outer Garden that has several stadiums, the **Meiji Memorial Picture Gallery** (Kaigakan) and **Meiji Jingu Outer Garden Children's Park** (Meiji Jingu Gaien Jido Koen). The Picture Gallery is housed in a large, turn-of-the-century Western building. Inside it has an 80-panel mural illustrating Japan's history which is of interest only to Japanese history buffs.

This Children's Park, in the Meiji Outer Garden, is to the right as you face the Picture Gallery. Young children cannot get enough of this place; it's one of the nicest playgrounds in Tokyo. The extensive climbing structures keep the kids amused for hours. In the summer months, a beer

FLOWERS, FLOWERS EVERYWHERE

Japanese adore cherry blossoms and also enjoy other flowers. Flower viewing seems to be a major preoccupation for large segments of the population. Here are a couple of favorite places to view flowers in season. But beware, you will not be viewing them in solitary splendor.

Plum *(mid-February to mid-March)*
Yushima Tenjin Shrine. Yushima Station on Chiyoda subway line.
Shinjuku Gyoen Garden. Shinjuku san-chome on Marunouchi subway line.

Peonies *(May)*
Nishi Arai Taishi. Nishi Arai Station on the Hibiya line – transfer to a special train that takes a few minutes to the temple.

Wisteria *(May)*
Kameido Tenjin Shrine. Kameido Station on the JR Sobu line. Follow the crowds for the 10-minute walk. The garden was destroyed in the World War II firebombing, but the roots survived and the plants grew again.

Azaleas *(May)*
Nezu Shrine. Nezu Station on Chiyoda Subway line.

Iris *(mid-June)*
Meiji Shrine Garden. Harajuku Station on the JR Yamanote line.
Koishikawa Korakuen Garden. Iidabashi Station on JR Sobu line.
Yasukuni Shrine. Kudanshita Station on Tozai, Hanzomon and Shinjuku subway lines.
East Garden of the Imperial Palace. Otemachi Station for five subway lines.

Hydrangeas *(early June to early July)*
Hakusan Shrine. Hakusan Station on Toei Mita subway line.
Meigetsuin. Kita Kamakura Station on JR Yokosuka line.

garden which also serves noodles and barbecue is set up next to the park. *9 Kasumigaoka, Shinjuku-ku. Tel. (03)3478-0550. Open daily 9:30am to 4pm. ¥150 adults, ¥50 children.*

Continuing on Aoyama Dori, on the left is a long wall with lots of trees behind it. Behind the wall is the **Akasaka Detached Palace**, which holds the residences of the imperial princes and princesses.

Across the street is the **Canadian Embassy**; its gallery often has excellent exhibitions. A block further along is the **Sogetsu Kaikan**; designed by Tange Kenzo, it is the contemporary hall of the Sogetsu flower arranging school. Stunning displays decorate the lobby; the stones there were sculpted by Isamu Noguchi and symbolize flowers, stone and water. Flower arranging classes in English are held regularly (see *Flower Arranging* later in this chapter).

Two blocks along on the right is a modern building; the ground floor has an old Japanese motif of blocks placed at an angle. This building houses **Toraya**, one of Japan's most famous confectioners. The main shop used to be based in Kyoto where it served the imperial family, but it moved to Tokyo with the emperor. The treats are a feast for the eyes. The shop has a tea room as well as a small exhibition space.

For a short detour to see Japan's imitation of European court architecture, turn left at the edge of the Akasaka Detached Palace grounds and follow the road that runs next to the palace walls. You'll be parallel to the expressway for a short time. On the left is the **Akasaka Detached Palace** (Geihinkan), which was built in 1909. Designed by architect Katayama Tokuma as the residence of the Taisho Emperor when he was crown prince, the prince found it too luxurious to live in. Today it is the official guest house for heads of state. The palace is probably the greatest Western-style architectural work of the Meiji period.

Retrace your steps to Aoyama Dori. On the left, just before the expressway, is the Suntory Building, home of the **Suntory Museum of Art**. The museum has a strong collection of traditional Japanese art including paintings, ceramics, lacquer ware and textiles. The permanent collection is supplemented with borrowed art works to organize excellent exhibitions. *Suntory Building, 11th floor, 1-2-3 Moto Akasaka, Minato-ku. Open 10am to 5pm. Until 7pm on Friday. Closed Monday. ¥700.*

The large intersection with the overhead highway is Akasaka Mitsuke, a business and entertainment center. During the day, restaurants are filled with businessman enjoying inexpensive lunch specials. At night it's still a businessmen's haunt, but the atmosphere changes and they crowd into dimly lit, sophisticated restaurants and private clubs. This area has several large hotels that are popular with foreign business executives (See *Where To Stay*).

As you reach the intersection just beyond the Suntory Museum, you'll see the **New Otani**, a large hotel on the left across the moat. Open to the public, it has a beautiful Japanese garden that you enter by going through a building that adjoins the hotel's main building and tower. Across the street, the **Akasaka Prince Hotel**, is a stark, modern hotel designed by Tange Kenzo. You can't help noticing the **Akasaka Tokyu Hotel**, nicknamed the pajama hotel because of its stripes.

Walk on Sotobori Dori, in front of the Akasaka Tokyu Hotel. This is the heart of **Akasaka Mitsuke**, a commercial area filled with restaurants and bars. Most of the establishments are on the roads running parallel to Sotobori Dori. Several blocks down Sotobori Dori on the left is a large *torii* gate. Pass through the gate and follow the road around to enter the quiet compound of **Hie Jinja Shrine**. The shrine was founded by the first feudal lord of Edo, Ota Dokan, and became Edo's most popular shrine during the Tokugawa era. Held every other year in June, the shrine's Sanno Festival is one of Tokyo's largest.

Walk back down the hill and continue on Sotobori Dori. At the overhead expressway, turn left. This road will take you to the **Japanese Diet Building** (Kokkai Gijido) where parliament meets. The building took 18 years to build and was completed in 1936. The Kokkai Gijido-mae Station of the Chiyoda line is located at the Diet Building.

Area 14: Shinjuku

The JR Yamanote, Chuo, Sobu, and Saikyo lines; the Marunouchi and Toei Shinjuku subway lines; and the private Odakyu and Keio train lines all serve Shinjuku Station.

Shinjuku is really two cities, one east and one west of the station. Nishi (West) Shinjuku is a forest of high-rise buildings. When seen from a distance, it looks like the city of Oz rising from the plains. East of the station, there's a jumble of stores, restaurants, bars and raucous nightlife spots. You can party there all night long. Dividing the two is **Shinjuku Station**, Japan's and maybe the world's busiest — over two million people pass through each weekday.

Shinjuku epitomizes all that is Tokyo — masses of people, a railway system that runs with amazing precision, bombardment by street noises, high-rise architecture, myriad department stores, infinite small shops and boutiques, discount shops, and a maze of alleys filled with entertainment of all sorts.

Begin at Shinjuku Station, but not during the morning rush hour. At the west exit of the station are two large department stores, Keio and Odakyu. West of these department stores, one block from the station, is a small area of discount electronic stores, *pachinko* parlors and cheap eateries. **Yodobashi Camera** has an excellent selection of cameras and other electronic gear, all at discount prices.

Walk back to the main plaza of the west exit of the station. Across from **Odakyu Halc**, a store selling furniture and interior goods, is the Shinjuku L Building. **Toto** and **Inax**, bathroom equipment manufacturers, have showrooms on the 26-27th floors and 20-21st floors respectively. Stop in for an amazing view of the bathroom of tomorrow that's available today. Both showrooms are open daily from 10am to 6pm.

Behind the Shinjuku L Building is the Yasuda Kasai Kaijo Building. The 42nd floor **Seiji Togo Memorial Yasuda Kasai Museum of Art** (Yasuda Kasai Togo Seiji Bijutsukan) displays van Gogh's *Sunflowers*, bought a dozen years ago by a Japanese for a mere ¥5.3 billion. Other than the van Gogh, a few Cezannes and Renoirs and works by surrealist Togo

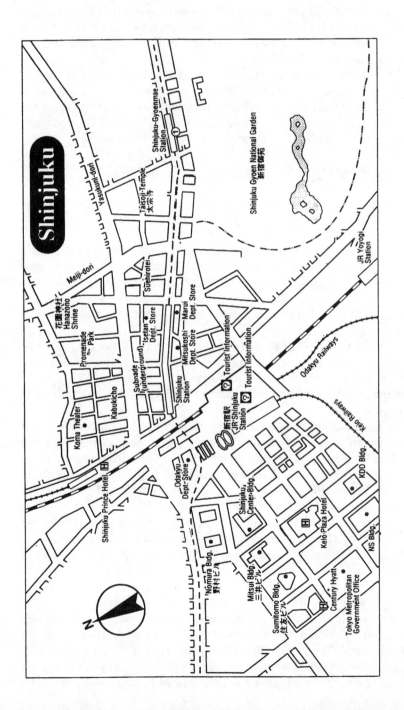

Shinjuku

Yasukuni-dori

Shinjuku-Gyoenmae Station

Taisoji Temple 太宗寺

Shinjuku Gyoen National Garden 新宿御苑

Meiji-dori

Suehirotei

Hanazono Shrine 花園神社

Isetan Dept. Store

Marui Dept. Store

Promenade Park

Subnade (underground)

Mitsukoshi Dept. Store

JR Yoyogi Station

Koma Theater

Kabukicho

Shinjuku Station

Tourist Information

Tourist Information

Odakyu Railways

Shinjuku 新宿駅 Station

Keio Railways

JR Shinjuku Station

Shinjuku Prince Hotel

Odakyu Dept. Store

Shinjuku Center Bldg.

KDD Bldg.

Nomura Bldg. 野村ビル

Mitsui Bldg. 三井ビル

Keio Plaza Hotel

NS Bldg.

Sumitomo Bldg. 住友ビル

Century Hyatt

Tokyo Metropolitan Government Office

N

Courtesy of Japan National Tourist Organization

Seiji, the museum is unremarkable, but it has a spectacular view. *Yasuda Kasai Kaijo (Yasuda Fire and Marine) Head Office Building, 1-26-1 Nishi Shinjuku, Shinjuku-ku. Tel. (03)3349-3081. Open 9:30am to 5pm. Closed Monday and New Year's. ¥500.*

The skyscrapers in this area are lined up like dominoes – atriums and plazas make the area one of the most open of Tokyo's commercial districts. The Keio Plaza Hotel was the first high rise, but now there are more than a dozen others. We like the Shinjuku Sumitomo Building's inner triangular courtyard that's open all the way to the sky.

The **Tokyo Metropolitan Government Building** (Tocho), designed by Tange Kenzo, has such an interplay between the different textures and colors of the stones and windows that we get vertigo looking at it. Tange said his inspiration came from Paris' Notre Dame Cathedral. The government complex has three towers and a low assembly building. The twin towers have observatories on their 45th floors. This view is the best in town, and the price is right – free. On a clear day you can see Mt. Fuji and all Tokyo's grayness sprawled out in front of you. We like to have coffee in the open cafe, but don't bother on a cloudy day – you may not see beyond the windows. *Open 9:30am to 5:30pm weekdays; 9:30am to 7:30pm weekends and holidays. Closed Monday. Free admission.*

West of the municipal building is **Shinjuku Central Park**. While its name may conjure up images of skating rinks and hansom carriages, the reality is far different. This park has more cement than trees, but is a respite from the city.

South of the park, on Koshu Kaido, is the **Shinjuku Park Tower**. Run by Tokyo Gas, architect Tange Kenzo designed the 52-storied postmodern structure. A number of floors are devoted to architectural and interior design. **Conrans**, the British store, has a shop there. The top floors house the **Park Hyatt Hotel**, which has some of the best views in the city; its restaurant, the **New York Grill**, is one of Tokyo's most popular. Stop and have a drink in the 52nd-floor lounge.

Just beyond Park Tower is another high-rise complex, **Tokyo Opera City**. It's at Hatsudai Station on the Keio train line or about a 20-minute walk from Shinjuku Station; use the south exit and walk left along Koshu Kaido. One of Tokyo's newest office and cultural complexes, the center has a wide array of cultural offerings. The 4th to 6th floor **NTT InterCommunication Center** (ICC) has state-of-the-art multimedia technology and puts on exhibitions, film and video showings, workshops and provides electronic information. The **New National Theater** has an opera house plus a medium and a small theater. The 200-meter-long glass-roofed Galleria runs the length of the complex. And there are enough stores and restaurants in the complex to keep you busy and well-fed for a long time.

CHERRY BLOSSOMS IN TOKYO

The whole city goes cherry crazy at the end of March and in early April. One of the first official duties of new corporate recruits is to spend the day sitting on blue tarps to safeguard prized prime space under the cherry trees. The rest of the office troops down after work for an evening of booze, food and song under the cherry blossoms. As a foreigner, groups will ask you to join them for a drink.

Some of the favored viewing spots follow:

Ueno Park *has over one thousand trees. Unfortunately, Ueno is one of the most popular party places and gets pretty messy by the end of the evening.*

Chidorigafuchi Park, *along the northern perimeter of the Imperial Palace, is a beautiful place; some of the trees lean into the castle moat.*

Yasukuni Shrine, *just up the street from Chidorigafuchi Park, has about a thousand trees, two of which the Meteorological Agency uses as the measure to determine Tokyo's official cherry blossom season.*

Yoyogi Park *is technically only open from 5am to 5pm so you don't get the drunken rowdiness that mars other sites.*

Aoyama Cemetery *is one of our favorite viewing sites. The trees form a archway over the road.*

Shinjuku Gyoen Garden *has 1500 trees.*

Koishikawa Korakuen, *a lovely Japanese garden, is a good place to see cherries in a serene and traditional setting.*

Sumida River *near Asakusa Station has 1100 trees lining the river.*

From Opera City, walk east along Koshu Kaido, and cross over the train tracks at Shinjuku Station. The east side of the station has an entirely different feel. In contrast to the high rises with large plazas, east Shinjuku is a warren of tiny streets and a million little shops, restaurants and bars.

After you cross the train tracks, turn right at the Shin Minami-guchi building of Shinjuku Station. Alongside this building is a path leading to **Shinjuku Times Square**, the new building that houses a branch of Takashimaya Department Store; Kinokuniya, Tokyo's best selection of English books; Sega Joyopolis, a virtual reality arcade; lots of other shops; restaurants and movie theaters.

Continue along Koshu Kaido until it meets Meiji Dori in a large, triangular intersection. Bear to the left and in one block you'll be at the large Shinjuku san (3)-chome intersection where Meiji Dori and Shinjuku Dori meet. **Isetan**, one of Japan's premier department stores is on the far left corner and is the only major prewar building left in Shinjuku. The large store has an especially good selection of clothes by young Japanese designers. The store also has a foreign customer service desk where a bilingual staff can assist you with your shopping.

Across the street from Isetan is **Marui Fashion Kan**, a store popular with young women. Behind it is **Tsunahachi**, an excellent *tempura* restaurant serving reasonably priced set meals.

Next to Marui is **Mitsukoshi Department Store**. Continue along Shinjuku Dori past Mitsukoshi and the many discount electronic shops that blare theme songs to sidewalk strollers. You'll come to the **Studio Alta** building with its large video screen; it's one of the most popular meeting places in Shinjuku because it is close to the east exit of Shinjuku Station. Walk down one of the narrow roads on either side of Studio Alta, and you'll come to Yasukuni Dori, a wide street.

The small streets on the other side of Yasukuni Dori put you in the heart of **Kabuki-cho**, one of Tokyo's entertainment districts where legitimate and raunchy establishments exist side by side. During the day, it's a pretty tame place. Kabuki-cho has legitimate inexpensive restaurants, bars, taverns, movie theaters, *pachinko* parlors, and video arcades as well as peep shows, strip shows, massage parlors, soaplands (full service baths), porno shops and girlie shows of every kind. Kabuki-cho parties till dawn. Unlike the sleazy entertainment districts in most cities around the world, women are rarely threatened physically even at night; but drunken men may make rude comments. It's best for women to stick to the main alleys. A word of warning: don't go by the prices posted outside establishments; they may be only the admission charge. Make sure you know the real costs up front, and don't be shy about asking.

To continue our exploration of Shinjuku, return to Yasukuni Dori and turn left, walking east. After Isetan Department Store, turn left onto Meiji Dori, a large thoroughfare. Two blocks down is a small shrine called **Hanazono** where there's a good flea market on the 2nd and 3rd Sunday of each month. This shrine has existed for a long time and is a popular place to pray for commercial success.

Retrace your steps along Meiji Dori and turn left on Yasukuni Dori. At the next large intersection, turn right onto Gyoen Dori. The area on the left between Yasukuni Dori and Shinjuku Dori is **Shinjuku ni (2)-chome** and has Tokyo's largest concentration of gay bars.

Gyoen Dori leads you to **Shinjuku Gyoen Park**. The garden was once the site of the feudal lord Naito's mansion and became an imperial garden after the emperor moved to Tokyo in 1868. It has Japanese and Western-style gardens, including a formal French garden and English landscape gardens and is a popular place to view cherry blossoms in the spring. *Open 9am to 4:30pm. Closed Monday. ¥200.*

Area 15: North of the Imperial Palace

These places are most easily reached by subway or JR train. Take the JR Yamanote line to Mejiro Station; board the #60 bus in front of Sakura Bank and get off at Chinzan-so stop. Alternatively, take the Yurakucho subway line to Edogawabashi Station.

Here are a handful of our favorite places fairly close together and north of the Imperial Palace:

Formerly the estate of Yamagata Aritomo, a Meiji Restoration leader and founder of the Japanese army, **Chizanso** is a wedding palace with one of Tokyo's prettiest gardens. The Four Seasons hotel is on the grounds. Chizanso's garden restaurant serves Genghis Khan barbecue.

Across the street from Chizanso is **St. Mary's Cathedral**. A study in steel and concrete, this contemporary church was designed by Tange Kenzo and built in 1966 to commemorate the 100th year anniversary of Japan lifting its ban on Christianity.

Take the Yurakucho subway line two stops to Ichigaya Station to reach the **Takagi Bonsai Museum**. It's just a one-minute walk from exit #3. The JR Sobu line's Ichigaya station is also close. Walk along Nittere Dori, away from the moat, and turn left at the Bank of Yokohama. The museum is just past the bank. You'll know the building by the statues of two guard dogs.

Bonsai are trees that may be hundreds of years old, but because of special pruning, they are only one or two feet tall. This little gem of a museum exhibits *bonsai* trees and changes the display weekly to show trees at the peak of their seasons. An elevator whisks you to the 9th floor roof where trees are displayed around a spring-fed pond. The white clay walls provide a lovely backdrop to view the dwarfed plants. The museum has an audio tape in English. On the 8th floor, *ukiyo-e* woodblock prints show that *bonsai* have been part of Japanese life for a long time. Also, seasonal *bonsai* and antique pots are on display.

If you notify the museum one week in advance, an English-speaking person will be available to guide you. Included with the price of admission is coffee or tea so you can sit and contemplate *bonsai*. *1-1 Goban-cho, Chiyoda-ku. Tel. (03)3221-0006. Open daily 10am to 5pm. ¥800. On the 8th and 9th floors of the Meiko Shokai Building.*

From Ichigaya Station, take JR Sobu line two stops to Suidobashi where **Koishikawa Korakuen Garden**, a traditional Japanese garden, is located behind Tokyo Dome. It's also convenient to Korakuen Station on the Marunouchi and Nanboku subway lines. Koishikawa Korakuen is a lovely place that was the strolling garden of the Mito branch of the Tokugawa family. First constructed in 1629, Chinese influence is evident in the bridges and design. The Naitei area, near the east gate, has changed little from the Edo times. The contrast between this quiet, peaceful garden and the hustle-bustle of the Tokyo Dome area couldn't be greater. *1-6-6 Koraku, Bunkyo-ku. Tel. (03)3811-3015. Open daily 9am to 4:30pm. Closed Monday and December 29 through January 3. ¥330.*

Tokyo Dome, the Big Egg, is at Korakuen and Suidobashi stations. It's Japan's first huge, domed stadium and hosts everything from baseball and rock concerts to flower shows. The Yomiuri Giants and Nippon Ham Fighters baseball teams play there. The Baseball Hall of Fame Museum is located just outside the dome.

Hop on the Nanboku subway line at the Tokyo Dome and go four stops north to Komagome Station. **Rikugi-en Garden** is a seven-minute walk away. The JR Yamanote line also goes to Komagome Station. Anyone seriously interested in Japanese gardens can't miss this garden that dates from 1695 when it was built by Yanagisawa Yoshiyasu, an aid to the fifth Tokugawa shogun. The garden, deserted after Yoshiyasu's death in 1714, saw new life in 1879 when Iwasaki Yataro, the founder of the Mitsubishi industrial empire, bought it and restored it. The park is filled with scenes alluding to masterpieces of literature and was designed so strollers walk clockwise around the large pond; be sure you go in the right direction.

There are several teahouses in the park, including Takimi-no-Chaya and Tsutsuji Chaya. Fujishiro-toge, an artificial hill constructed to view Mt. Fuji, provides the best vantage point. *6-16-3 Hon-Komagome, Bunkyoku. Tel. (03)3941-2222. Open daily 9am to 5pm. Closed Monday and December 29 through January 3. ¥300.*

Area 16: Ikebukuro

The JR Yamanote and Saikyo lines; the Marunouchi and Yurakucho subway lines; and the private Seibu and Tobu train lines all serve Ikebukuro Station.

Ikebukuro has metamorphosed over the last decade or so from a nondescript suburban neighborhood to a major transportation, commercial and cultural nexus. Everything in Ikebukuro seems to take on gigantic proportions: some of Japan's largest department stores — Sunshine 60 was Japan's tallest building for a while — and a zillion clothing, record and electronic stores. Nothing is in moderation.

Ikebukuro Station itself is a study in chaos. There are two huge department stores in the station, **Seibu** on the eastern side and **Tobu** on the western. Between the two, you'll find everything you could ever want. Tobu's restaurant "floor" spans six stories — from the 11th to 17th. The central building's 9th floor has an extensive variety of Japanese goods. The Tobu Museum has first-rate exhibitions. On the other side of the station, equally gigantic Seibu is home to lots of restaurants. The basement, filled with edibles from all over Japan and the world, is a sight to behold. The amount and variety is incredible; if it's not in Seibu's basement, it may not exist. Seibu's Sezon Museum of Art has excellent traveling exhibitions. Two blocks west of Ikebukuro Station is **Tokyo Metropolitan Art Space**. The 28-meter atrium houses a three-storied waterfall and lush green trees that certainly create a different atmosphere from what is outside. The complex has theaters, concert halls and exhibition space. Long escalators lead to a huge concert hall; its acoustics are excellent for a full scale orchestra, but the hall is too big for a chamber orchestra. The Tokyo Metropolitan government spent lavishly by inviting first-rate orchestras from all over the world. We have to admit that we find it quite jarring to leave the serenity of the hall to go out into the noise, chaos and crowds of Ikebukuro.

Sunshine City is Ikebukuro's other famous complex. Use the east exit of Ikebukuro Station, walk along Green Dori, which is perpendicular to the station, and turn left onto Sunshine 60 Dori. After crossing the expressway, the **Amlux building** is on your right. Run by Toyota, the large, neon-lit building is a motor enthusiast's dream and includes a massive display of cars, a simulated factory, a 3-D theater and a computer-equipped studio where you design your own car. If you get lost at night, the brightly lit building will help you get your bearings.

Just beyond Amlux is Sunshine City. Sunshine 60, as its name implies, is a 60-storied tower. The **World Import Mart** has merchandise from all over the globe and its 10th floor houses the **Sunshine International Aquarium**. Our recommendation — save the ¥1600 cost of admission and visit Shinagawa Aquarium or Tokyo Water Life Park. *Tel. (03)3989-3467.*

Sunshine City's Bunka Kaikan has the **Ancient Orient Museum** on its 7th floor. It displays pottery and other antiquities from the Middle East to Japan. *Tel. (03)3989-3491. Open 10am to 4:30pm. Closed Monday. ¥400.*

Area 17: Tokyo Waterfront (Ariake/Rinkai Fukutoshin)

A new monorail, Yurikamome, named after a type of seagull alluded to in historic poetry, connects Shimbashi Station with Ariake. You can also get there by ferry from Hamamatsucho – 20 minutes, ¥350. One word of warning: the Yurikamome monorail can be incredibly crowded over the weekend. The whole area is new and Tokyoites find it fashionable to visit. There are sometimes long lines to board the monorail even though it departs every ten minutes. We've heard horror stories of people waiting more than two hours when there's been a big convention. The alternative is to take the Yurakucho subway line or JR Keiyo line to Shin Kiba Station and change for the Rinkai Fukutoshin line. Take it three stops to Tokyo Teleport Station.

When a city like Tokyo runs out of space, it turns to the water. Landfill has been going on at least 400 years — the Ginza was once a marsh. The latest development is the Tokyo Waterfront Project, a landfill island called **Rinkai Fukutoshin**. It's the brainchild of a long-term governor of

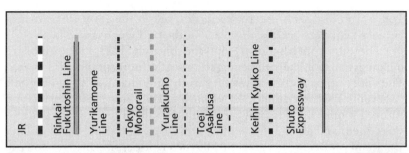

JR

Rinkai Fukutoshin Line

Yurikamome Line

Tokyo Monorail

Yurakucho Line

Toei Asakusa Line

Keihin Kyuko Line

Shuto Expressway

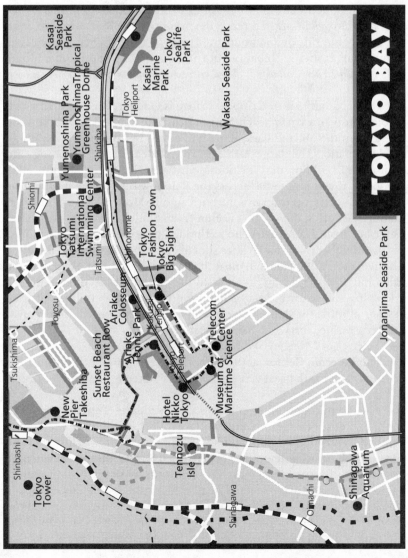

TOKYO BAY

Tokyo who lost his fifth-term reelection bid in the early 1990s mainly because taxpayers became disgusted at the outrageous price tag.

The waterfront has a lot of empty lots, but it also has some postmodern buildings that look like the opening scenes of the futuristic film *Bladerunner*. The entire scene is surreal with futuristic buildings like Tokyo Big Site (Convention Center), the Hotel Nikko, Fuji Television Headquarters and Ariake Frontier Building just a few minutes walk from the water's edge — sand, shells and all.

Rainbow Bridge is a graceful 800-meter suspension bridge. You can cross on foot between *9am and 7pm April through October and 9am to 6pm November through March.* To reach the bridge on the Shibaura side, it's a ten-minute bus ride or 25-minute walk from JR Tamachi Station, or a five-minute walk from the Shibaura Futo Station on the Yurikamome Monorail. *The pedestrian walkway is closed every 3rd Monday and December 29-31. ¥300.*

On the other side of Rainbow Bridge is **Odaiba Marine Park**, which is complete with a sandy beach. **Sunset Beach Restaurant Row**, across the street from the Marine Park, has a half-dozen restaurants each with an outdoor patio. The large **DECKS Tokyo Beach** is a shopping and amusement building that includes a virtual reality game arcade called Joyopolis. If you don't walk across the Rainbow Bridge, the most convenient mode of transportation is the Yurikamome Monorail from Shimbashi Station. Get off at the Odaiba Kaihin Koen Station. You can also take a water bus from Hamamatsucho's Hinode Pier to Odaiba Keihin Koen.

Landlubbers and sailors alike should enjoy the **Museum of Maritime Science** (Fune no Kagakukan) near the Fune no Kagakukan Station on the monorail. Shaped like an ocean liner, the museum is devoted to the sea and ships and features lots of hands-on boat stuff as well as intricate models of different ships. You can visit an Antarctic observation ship as well as a former ferry, the Yotei Maru. *Open 10am to 5pm (until 6pm on weekends). Closed Monday and New Year's. ¥1000.*

The **Telecom Center**, at the monorail's Telecom Center Station, has an observatory with great views of the entire waterfront area. *Open 11am to 8pm. ¥600.*

The Aomi monorail stop brings you to **Palette Town**, yet another shopping/entertainment complex. **Venus Fort** is hailed as a shopping center designed for women (aren't all shopping centers?). The ploy must not be working because on the very crowded Sunday afternoon when we visited, lots of men were in sight. From the outside Venus Fort resembles a warehouse made of corrugated steel, on the inside it's all faux European classic architecture. Next to Venus is **Mega Web**, a huge Toyota showroom cum amusement park. You can ride in an electric car around the building or, if that is too slow, check out the simulation driving. And if that is not enough, mosey on over to **NeoGeoWorld**, an amusement complex complete with Hyper Bowling, karaoke, and thrilling rides. Outside is the world's tallest (at least for the moment) ferris wheel, Giant Sky Wheel, from which on a clear day you can see Mt. Fuji. Next door are the HyperShoot and HyperDrop, two gut-wrenching rides.

At the next monorail stop, Kokusai Tenjijo Seimon, looms **Tokyo Big Sight**, the huge new convention center. The signature building resembles four upended pyramids supported by a tinker-toy structure. It's worth a stop to check out the architecture of this futuristic building; the large atriums that let the sun shine in. The Observation Bar Lounge on the 8th floor has great sea views. *Tel. (03)5530-1115.* On the other side of the station is Tokyo Fashion Town, which would like to become center of the fashion industry; there are also some retail shops.

The Hotel Intercontinental Tokyo Bay is on the mainland side of the waterfront development at Takeshiba at the Takeshiba Station of the Yurikamome monorail or JR Hamamatsucho station. A free observatory on the 24th floor of South Tower has wonderful views of Rainbow Bridge and the entire waterfront area.

Tokyo Sea Life Park is only a subway ride away. *6-2-3 Rinkai-cho, Edogawa-ku. Tel. (03)3869-5152. Open 9:30am to 5pm (enter by 4pm). Closed Monday and December 29 through January 3. ¥700. Kasai Rinkan Koen Station on JR Keiyo line or ferry from Hinode Pier at Hamamatsucho (55 minutes, ¥800).* This fabulous aquarium is on the waterfront in the newly developed Kasai Rinkan Park. Most of the structure is below ground. You enter through a large glass dome that's similar to an upside-down goldfish bowl, and you descend into the body of the building – goldfish never had it so good. The aquarium has a huge donut-shaped tank filled with tuna and other fish. Walking through the center, you have a great view of the tuna that are so silvery they look like they've been spray painted. The aquarium opens out onto the sea, and has an artificial beach where children can pick up shellfish and other shore creatures. The penguin area is out on the patio overlooking the sea. The way the pen is constructed, we can look longingly at the open seas, but the penguins can't.

Tokyo Sea Life Park is located inside Kasai Seaside Park, a large park that is reclaiming Tokyo's beachfront. Crystal View, a wonderful postmodern, glass observation building near the aquarium, is a popular place for couples to enjoy the sunset.

Nearby Tokyo Sea Life Park is a botanical garden called **Yumenoshima Tropical Plant Dome**. *3-2 Yumenoshima, Koto-ku. Tel. (03)3522-0281. Open 9:30am to 4:30pm. Closed Monday and December 29 through January 3. ¥300. 15-minute walk from Shinkiba Station on the Yurakucho subway line and JR Keiyo line.* This botanical garden is constructed in an attractive greenhouse dome.

ENJOY THE NEW YEAR JAPANESE STYLE!

The biggest holiday is New Year's – a special festive season and a highlight of the year. Japanese start preparations several weeks in advance just as Westerners start enjoying Christmas weeks in advance. The end of the year is regarded as the time to settle all financial transactions and unfinished business. Museums close from about December 27 through January 3. Department stores stay open through December 31; usually they're packed the morning of the 31st as people buy last minute items, but all close January 1, and many stay closed on January 2.

So what's there to do at year's end?

· Go to Tsukiji Outer Market. You don't have to go early in the morning. December 28-31 it's thronged with people buying food and decorations for New Year's.

· Eat soba noodles the night of December 31st; they symbolize longevity.

· Go to a Buddhist temple at midnight December 31st to ring the bells to repent and get rid of the sins of the past year. Buddhist temples ring their bells 108 times, once for each type of sin according to Buddhist belief. At Kan'ei-ji in Ueno, pay ¥3000 to ring the bell; at Enkaku-ji 100 pairs of people can ring the large bell, a National Treasure, for free. At Tokei-ji in Kamakura, you can ring the bell for ¥100; you must be in line by 11:40pm, and the bell is rung 108 times.

· Watch TV. Kohaku Uta Gassen is a New Year's Eve program as classic as Guy Lombardo and the Times Square ball. More than half the population has the TV tuned to NHK, the national television station. Japanese popular singers divide into two teams, red (women) and white (men) who compete by singing songs.

· Go to a concert. Many orchestras have programs beginning at 10pm so you can welcome in the New Year with music.

· Trains run all night long on December 31.

· During New Year's, go to a Shinto shrine with millions of Japanese to welcome in the gods. If you really want to get fancy, do a pilgrimage circuit of seven shrines representing the seven lucky gods.

· Go to the Imperial Palace on January 2 to see and hear the emperor give his New Year's greetings.

· Chinese restaurants open on January 2; go to Yokohama's Chinatown.

· Go for a hike. Mt. Takao is close, and you're rewarded with a temple at the top.

· Kabuki begins the year on January 3. All month, some people attend wearing formal kimono and the atmosphere is festive.

Tokyo is lovely during the New Year's holidays. Best of all, the streets are empty. Almost all restaurants, except in hotels, are closed January 1; but shopping areas like Shibuya and Shinjuku are bustling on January 2. Convenience stores stay open throughout the holiday so you can always get basic commodities.

The **Tokyo Port Wild Bird Park** (Tokyo-ko Yacho Koen) is in the waterfront area, but you approach it using the Tokyo Monorail from Hamamatsucho Station, heading toward Haneda Airport. Get off at the second stop, Ryutsu Senta Station. You'll be sure we sent you to the wrong place because all you'll see are large, ugly warehouses. But walk east toward the water, and you'll reach a large water bird reserve, divided into sea and freshwater bird reserves. The reserve has an observatory with telescopes. *Open 9am to 5pm, until 4:30pm November through January. Closed Monday. ¥200.*

Area 18: Outskirts

Tokyo has lots of great spots to visit outside the city center. When you factor in transportation time, each place listed takes the better part of the day to visit.

Gotoh Museum (Gotoh Bijutsukan) and Seikado Bunko Library (Seikado Bunko) are both located in suburban Tokyo. Both museums are surrounded by greenery and are fairly close together; a visit makes a good outing to see art and culture and gives you a break from downtown Tokyo.

Seikado Bunko Library. Seikado Bunko's collection once belonged to the famous businessman Iwasaki Yataro who started the Mitsubishi empire at the end of 19th century. The outstanding collection includes Japanese, Korean and Chinese art. The display of about 40-50 items changes quarterly. Some of the masterpieces include the illustrated diary of Lady Murasaki, the author of the *Tale of Genji;* Edo-period artist Sotatsu's famous screen painting of the *Tale of Genji*; and a world famous black *temmoku* (oil spot) tea bowl. *2-23-1 Okamoto, Setagaya-ku. Tel. (03)3700-2250. Open 10am to 4pm. Closed Monday. ¥800. Take the Shin Tamagawa line from Shibuya Station. Get off at Futako Tamagawa Station. Take bus # 4 and get off at Seikado Bunko-mae.*

To go to the Gotoh Museum, return to Futako Tamagawa Station, and take the Tokyu Oimachi line one stop to Kaminoge.

The **Gotoh Museum** houses the collection of Gotoh Keita, the founder of the Tokyu rail, real estate and retail empire. The museum has masterpiece scroll paintings of the *Tale of Genji* from the 12th century; because of their fragility, they are only shown during a brief period each spring. Gotoh's fine collection also includes Chinese and Japanese paintings, calligraphy and ceramics – there's always something to see. Behind the museum is a peaceful hillside garden with two tea huts. *9-25-3 Kaminoge, Setagaya-ku. Tel. (03)3703-0662. Open 9:30am to 4:30pm. Closed Monday. ¥700. To return to Shibuya Station, take the Tokyu Oimachi line one stop to Futago Tamagawa Station and change to the Shin Tamagawa line to Shibuya Station.*

Edo-Tokyo Open Air Architectural Museum (Edo-Tokyo Tatemono-en). The city of Tokyo established this branch of the Edo-Tokyo Museum, to preserve historical architecture. Both traditional Japanese and Western-influenced buildings are represented, over 20 structures in all. The visitors hall presents an overview of Tokyo's architectural history. The museum makes a fun outing from central Tokyo. *3-7-1 Sakura-cho, Koganei-shi, Tokyo. Tel. (042)388-3300. ¥300. Open 9:30am to 5:30pm (until 4:30pm October through March). Musashi Koganei Station on JR Chuo line, at gate 4 on north side of station take bus heading to Mitaka, get off at Edo-Tokyo Tatemono-en Mae stop*

Jindai-ji Temple and **Jindai-ji Botanical Park** (Jindai-ji Shokubutsukan). If the city is closing in on you but you don't want to go too far, take this day trip. Less than an hour from Shinjuku Station, the area is an oasis of calm. *From Shinjuku Station, take the JR Chuo line to Mitaka and board the #56 bus heading to Chofu.*

Jindai-ji Temple goes back a thousand years. The thatched-roof entrance gate and meditation center, located in a large building to the right of the entrance, are two of the few thatched-roof structures left in Tokyo. Most temple buildings were rebuilt in the Edo era after a disastrous fire. The temple has lots of statues, but the most famous is the Hakuhobutsu, which was carved around 700 and discovered under a temple building in 1909. The statue is displayed under glass in the Shaka-do, a modern building.

Take the cobblestone path at the left of the temple. You climb up a wooded hill to reach a tall spire with a building encircling it. This pet cemetery makes sure that Fido also attains everlasting peace. When you get hungry, head for one of the many *soba* stands all over the temple precincts. The local specialty is Jindai-ji *soba*, eaten by the Tokugawa shogun. Supposedly, the fresh spring water makes the *soba* noodles special; whatever the reason, they sure are tasty.

Behind Jindai-ji is the **Jindai-ji Botanical Park**, Tokyo's largest botanical garden that was once part of the temple complex. The garden has many different trees and plants including dogwoods given to the Japanese government by the US government in exchange for the cherry trees that grace Washington, D.C. Ask at the entrance gate for a strolling map in English. *Jindai-ji Botanical Garden. Tel. (0424)83-2300. Open 9:30am to 4pm. Closed Mondays. ¥400.*

Japan Open Air Folk House Museum (Nihon Minka-en).This place is one of our favorites to take guests to soak up some greenery and history. It's an easy trip out of central Tokyo and gives you a glimpse of how people lived in the countryside. Until about 100 years ago, Japan was primarily an agricultural country — yes, it's difficult to believe when you see metropolitan Tokyo. From all different areas of   Japan, 20 old farmhouses were reassembled in this hilly and heavily wooded park. The buildings have been meticulously restored and furnished. Wooden chests, storage bins for rice, *sake* and soy sauce, clay cooking stoves and cooking utensils and other objects give some sense of how people lived.

We find the variety of buildings amazing – some have thatched roofs, others tile or shingle. Some from very snowy areas needed steep roofs so the snow wouldn't accumulate while others have flat ones. One farmhouse has a noodle shop or you can pick up something to eat near the station and have a picnic in the large park. *7-1-1 Masugata, Tama-ku, Kawasaki. Tel. (044)922-2181. Open 9:30am to 4pm. Closed Monday and December 27 through January 4. ¥300. From Shinjuku Station take the Odakyu train (local or express) to Mukogaoka-yuen. It's about a 15-minute walk alongside the monorail until the monorail veers to the left at a small river, you continue straight ahead on a fairly narrow street until you reach the parking lot. If you don't want to walk, it's less than 5 minutes by taxi.*

Mt. Takao (Takao-san). When Tokyo starts closing in around us, we head for our favorite, easy getaway. Mt. Takao is a mere 55 minutes from Shinjuku Station, but it could be another planet. After traveling through a seemingly endless urban mass, the green hills suddenly open up and the air becomes fresher.

Take the Keio line from Shinjuku Station to Takao-san guchi. Make sure you take an express and that your car says Takao-san guchi. Some trains split at Hachioji Station. If in doubt, ask. And the stop before Takao-san guchi is Takao, so don't get off too early. At Takao-san guchi Station, turn right as you exit and walk along the path to the cable car station. Along this path are some *soba* noodle shops. The local specialty is *tororo*

TAKAO'S HIWATARI FESTIVAL

*Mt. Takao is one of the mountains where **yamabushi** (ascetic priests) go for rigorous training to attain salvation and enlightenment. Two of the other mountains are Dewa Sanzan in Yamagata Prefecture and Mt. Yoshino in Nara Prefecture.*

*On the second Sunday in March, priests dressed in brilliant orange and yellow robes participate in **Hiwatari**, a walking-on-fire ritual, to complete their annual training. A monstrous bonfire, as big as the buildings around, is built in front of the Museum of Natural History, not far from the train station. After the flames are extinguished and the coals are still smoldering, the chief priest chants sutras and walks barefooted on the ashes as if he were walking on velvet lawn. Other priests follow him across the coals.*

Spectators are invited to join and many, including children, follow. No one seems to get burned. We were really tempted to join in the fun, but foolishly wore panty hose. The moral: wear socks if you feel like experiencing foot toasting.

soba, buckwheat noodles with grated mountain potatoes, but you'll find other varieties of noodles also.

From the cable car station, you can board a cable car or ski lift chair to the top of Mt. Takao. The fare for either is ¥470 one way; ¥900 round trip. The cable car is faster but if you factor in waiting time, you arrive at the top at about the same time. Service begins as early as 8am during the summer. There are also several hiking trails up, and since we've seen women hike in high heels, you know the mountain isn't too challenging. We usually take a lift up and walk down. The walk up takes about 90 minutes; the mountain is about 600 meters high.

At the top of the lift, you walk another 10 minutes or so to **Yakuo-in Temple**, which has a history spanning 1200 years. Belonging to the esoteric Shingon sect, Yakuo-in has statues and masks of long-nosed spirits called Tengu. These are beings who live deep in the mountains and help fulfill the wishes of believers.

Continue up the mountain to the peak. On clear days you have a nice view of Mt. Fuji. There's also a small nature museum at the top. Go down the mountain by cable car, chair lift or on your own two feet.

The area has a charming restaurant that we highly recommend: **Ukai Toriyama**. It's a short ride from the Takao-san guchi Station. A complimentary shuttle bus operates between the restaurant and the station, but if it's an off-hour, you might have to call and ask for a pick-up.

Ukai Toriyama is nestled deep in the mountains along a small river gorge. The restaurant consists of about a dozen teahouses; some are several hundred years old and others are more recent constructions. There is also a large farmhouse for big groups. If you are a group of four or more, you will be seated in your own teahouse. Several different set menus are offered; you'll grill the main course on a charcoal hibachi. The food is good and the mood is peaceful. When we eat there, we feel we're a million miles away from Tokyo.

Reservations are recommended, especially on weekends. The staff speaks some English, and there is an English menu. *Set menus begin at ¥4500. Tel. (0426)61-0739.*

Ski Dome (SSAWS Gelande). On the trip in from Narita Airport, you may have noticed a huge, sloping building with steel girders for legs. This is the Ski Dome, Japan's first and largest indoor ski slope. Want to go skiing on a sweltering August day? No problem. The dome is open all year round and, ironically, is most crowded in winter. Here, high-tech meets snow. When you enter, you receive a computer card that keeps track of your expenses including food, ski and clothes rental and how much time on the snow. The snow making itself is computer controlled. In only two minutes, two high-speed ski lifts whisk you to the top of the 500-meter slope. And there's a tow rope for beginners. It's one of those experiences that only the Japanese could have invented.

After skiing, dip in the heated pool for ¥500. Or shop in the many stores selling pricey ski gear. *2-3-1 Hamacho, Funabashi, Chiba. Tel. (0474)32-7000. Admission: all day pass (ichi-nichi ken) ¥5400 or by the hour (jikan ken) ¥2200 plus ¥1000 per hour; ski equipment: ¥1800, ski wear: ¥1800. Generally open from 10am to 10pm but varies with the day and season. Take the JR Keiyo line to Minami Funabashi Station.*

NIGHTLIFE, ENTERTAINMENT & CULTURE

In the evening, Tokyo transforms itself from a monotonous city into a glittering entertainment center. *Salariman* (Japanese-English for male, white-collar workers) and office ladies (Japanese-English for female clerical workers) escape from their concrete office buildings and head to bars, restaurants and clubs to eat and drink with their friends and colleagues or to continue business discussions with their customers. It's an essential part of the bonding process.

Friday night is date night and the party goes on late into the evening. In Roppongi, Shibuya and Shinjuku, the sidewalks are as crowded at midnight as they are at 7pm.

Each entertainment district has it's own feel. **Ginza** is very establishment, popular with middle-aged businessmen and up. **Akasaka** is a real hodgepodge: *geisha* houses catering to titans of industry and politics are side by side with inexpensive bars. **Roppongi** is popular with foreigners and Japanese who want a slightly more international atmosphere. **Shibuya** attracts a young crowd. Shinjuku's **Kabuki-cho** is a raucous, anything-goes area.

Tokyo's music scene is lively. International names come through, playing at the Tokyo Dome, clubs called "live houses" or intimate jazz joints. Discos rock until the wee hours of the morning. Cover charges usually run between ¥1500 and ¥5000. Sometimes drinks are included; sometimes they are extra.

Bars and clubs come and go with alarming speed. Here are a few that have some staying power, but to be on the safe side, check before you trek across town. The *Tokyo Journal* has listings in English.

LIVE HOUSES & DISCOS
Roppongi

BIRDLAND (jazz), *Basement of the Square Building. 3-10-3 Roppongi, Minato-ku. Tel. (03)3478-3456.*

There are a bunch of discos in the building, but you would never know it in Birdland. The intimate jazz club is far removed from all the craziness outside.

DESPERADO TOKYO, *B1F, Elsa Building, 3-13-12 Roppongi, Minato-ku. Tel. (03)3475-6969.*

Live 70s and 80s rock. ¥1500 cover; none if you sit in the bar.

ROPPONGI PIT INN (jazz and soul), *3-17-7 Roppongi, Minato-ku. Tel. (03)3585-1063.*

A Roppongi institution that features acts by top-notch Japanese and international musicians.

BODY AND SOUL (jazz), *6-13-9 Minami Aoyama, Minato-ku. Tel. (03)5466-3348.*

This really relaxed club features jazz usually played by Japanese musicians.

CAVERN CLUB, *5-3-2 Roppongi, Minato-ku. Tel. (03)3405-5207.*

Live Beatles music by sound-alike bands. You don't have to close your eyes to think the Fab Four have returned; even though the musicians are Japanese, they look like the Beatles. Alas, dancing is not allowed. Cover ¥1400.

KENTOS, *5-3-1 Roppongi, Minato-ku. Tel. (03)3401-5755.*

Next to and under the same management as the Cavern Club. Kentos has live 1950s and 1960s music and the tiny dance floor is packed. Cover ¥1400.

LEXINGTON QUEEN, *3-13-14 Roppongi, Minato-ku. Tel. (03)3401-1661.*

Granddaddy of Tokyo's discos, it's still going strong. It's a favorite drop-in place for movie stars when they're in town.

VELFARRE, *7-14-22 Roppongi, Minato-ku. Tel. (03)3402-8000.*

Tokyo's largest disco — the entrance is a spectacular staircase. Open only until midnight.

TATOU TOKYO, *7-6-2 Roppongi, Minato-ku. Tel. (03)5411-4433.*

Live music at this large and popular club.

YELLOW, *1-10-11 Nishi Azabu, Minato-ku. Tel. (03)3479-0690.*

Huge, trendy disco with lots of events.

Aoyama

BLUE NOTE TOKYO (jazz), *FIK Minami Aoyama Building, B1, 5-13-3 Minami Aoyama, Minato-ku. Tel. (03)3407-5781.*

A sister of New York's legendary Blue Note; top international musicians perform at top prices.

Shinjuku

SHINJUKU PIT INN, *3-16-4 Shinjuku. Tel. (03)3354-2024.*

Jazz and rock.

LIQUID ROOM, *Shinjuku Humax Pavilion, 7th floor, 1-20-1 Kabuki-cho, Shinjuku-ku. Tel. (03)3200-6831.*

Usually has live music, but sometimes djs.

CODE, *4F, Shinjuku Toho Kaikan, 1-19-2 Kabuki-cho, Shinjuku-ku. Tel. (03)3209-0702.*
Huge, allegedly Asia's largest club. Three dance floors so something for everyone.

Shinjuku-ni (2) chome is Tokyo's gay district and home to several hundred bars. A few that are welcoming to non-gays are: **Fuji** (*2-12-16 Shinjuku, Tel. (03)3354-2707);* **Kinsmen** *(2-18-5, 2F, Shinjuku, Tel. (03)3354-4949);* **Kinswomyn** for women only, *Daiichi Tenka Building, 2-15-10 Shinjuku, 3F, Tel. (03)3354-8720);* **Delight** for dancing (*Dai-ni Hayakawaya Building, B1, 2-14-6 Shinjuku, Tel. (03)3352-6297).*

Shibuya
ON AIR WEST, *2-3 Maruyama-cho, Shibuya-ku. Tel. (03)5458-4646.*
"Live house" with mostly rock performers. Cover varies with the musicians.
CLUB QUATTRO, *5F, Quattro Building, 32-13 Udagawa-cho, Shibuya-ku. Tel. (03)3477-8750.*
A popular live house with a rock focus. Cover varies with the musicians.
CLUB ASIA, *1-8 Maruyama-cho, Shibuya-ku. Tel. (03)5458-5963.*
Asian pop music.

Meguro
BLUES ALLEY JAPAN, *Meguro Station Hotel, B1, 1-3-14 Meguro, Meguro-ku. Tel. (03)5496-4381.*
A branch of the Washington, D.C. blues club, Blues Alley serves French and Italian food and has live music on Fridays.

KARAOKE
Karaoke, a peculiarly Japanese invention now spread worldwide, has people crooning out songs in bad voices in bars and pubs. A recent addition is karaoke boxes, private rooms that mercifully save the ears of strangers. Most karaoke bars have only a small selection of songs in English — *My Way* and *Diana* are the favorites. An exception is **Keets** in Roppongi; they have over 3000 English songs, so you are sure to find your favorites. And it won't blow the bank: ¥2000 cover charge includes two drinks. *Dai-ju Togensha Building, 4F, 2-4-9 Roppongi, Minato-ku. Tel. (03)3584-3262.*
The classiest karaoke bar is **Festa,** just north of the Russian Embassy on Gaien Higashi Dori, where you can eat gourmet fare and sing your heart out in private rooms. The best deal is the ¥5000 package that includes the room charge, three hours of karaoke and Japanese food. *3-5-7 Azabudai, Minato-ku. Tel. (03)5570-1500. Open 5pm to 5am. Closed Sunday and holidays.*

CULTURAL PERFORMANCES

The *Tokyo Journal*, a monthly magazine, is an excellent source of information on performing arts events. The English language newspapers also have listings.

Kabuki

KABUKI-ZA THEATER, *on Harumi Dori, just past Showa Dori. Higashi Ginza Station on the Hibiya subway line is the closest stop, but it's only about a 5-minute walk from the Ginza Station on the Ginza subway line. Ticket prices ¥2500 to ¥16,500. One act tickets ¥600 to ¥1000, depending on the length of the act. Matinee begins at 11am; evening performance at around 4:30pm. For reservations, call (03)5565-6000 at least one day in advance.*

You'll be given a reservation number; armed with your reservation number, go to the ticket office to the right of the main entrance on the day of the performance. For one-act tickets, there's a ticket window to the left of the main entrance. Tickets go on sale 15 minutes before the act begins. If you see one act and decide you want to stay for the next one, you have to go back downstairs to buy another ticket. Call the Tourist Information Office for one act schedule times.

We highly recommend that you rent earphones with English commentary that are available in the lobby. They cost ¥600 plus a ¥1000 deposit, which is refunded when you return the headset. Unfortunately, you can't get earphones with a one-act ticket. *Kabuki* is performed every month from the 1st through the 25th.

NATIONAL THEATER (Kokuritsu Gekijo), *near the Hanzomon station of the Hanzomon subway line. Tickets are ¥1500 to ¥9000. Earphones with English commentary available. 4-1 Hayabusa-cho, Chiyoda-ku. Tel. (03)3265-7411.*

The National Theater features *kabuki* performances on a regular basis. *Kabuki* there doesn't have the "downtown, down home" atmosphere of the Kabuki-za; the focus is more educational. A small gallery on the second floor displays *ukiyo-e* woodblock prints and documents pertaining to the current performance. The theater's summertime classroom series is a short lecture on *kabuki* followed by a performance. It's geared to high school students, but don't let that put you off — it's an excellent introduction to *kabuki*.

Noh

Unlike *kabuki* and *bunraku, noh* plays are staged only once with the same cast. A *noh* theater has only a handful of productions every month and tickets tend to sell out quickly.

NATIONAL NOH THEATER (Kokuritsu Noh-gakudo). *4-18-1 Sendagaya, Shibuya-ku. Tel. (03)3423-1331. Tickets generally range from ¥2100 to ¥3800.*

Tickets available at the box office and Ticket Pia and Ticket Saison agencies. Usually there are a half-dozen productions a month.

HOSHO NOH THEATER (Hosho Noh-gakudo). *1-5-9 Hongo, Bunkyo-ku. Tel. (03)3811-4843. Suidobashi Station on JR Sobu or Mita subway line. Tickets range from ¥3500 to ¥6500.*

An English summary of the play is usually available..

TESSENKAI NOH THEATER (Tessenkai Noh Gakudo Kenshujo). *4-21-29 Minami Aoyama, Minato-ku. Tel. (03)3401-2285. Exit B4 of Omotesando Station on Chiyoda, Ginza and Hanzomon subway lines.*

Turn left at top of exit. Theater is on the left, about two blocks down.

KANZE NOH THEATER (Kanze Noh Gakudo). *1-16-4 Shoto, Shibuya-ku. Tel. (03)3469-5241. 10 minute walk from Shibuya Station.*

Head to Tokyu Department Store; take the road going uphill by the entrance of Orchard Hall, around the back of the department store.

Bunraku

Bunraku Puppet Theater is performed in the small hall of the National Theater (Kokuritsu Gekijo, Shogekijo) several months a year (see Kabuki, above). The hall was specially designed for *bunraku*. If it's in town when you are, we urge you to go. Rent the English earphones.

Western Classical & Popular Music, Dance & Theater

Tokyo is on the touring map for world class artists and the listings are a virtual *Who's Who* of the music world. Japan has a great interest in Western music; Tokyo alone boasts ten resident symphony orchestras.

In the late 1980s, at the height of the bubble economy, some people went to concerts night after night paying ¥30,000 a ticket without thinking twice. Fortunately those days are long gone, but the plethora of concert halls constructed during that frenzy still remains. Now tickets are more reasonably priced. You still will have to pay top dollar for superstars. Tickets for a recent tour of New York's Metropolitan Opera featuring Luciano Pavarotti and Placido Domingo, for example, sold for ¥14,000 to ¥62,000. You won't have to fork over that much for most performances. Tickets for piano, violin or chamber music range from ¥3000 to ¥8000.

The *Tokyo Journal's* listings are the best source of information in English. You can go to a Ticket PIA or Ticket Saison counter for information, but most is printed in Japanese. Some major halls are:

ORCHARD HALL, *use the Hachiko exit of Shibuya Station. Tel. (03)3477-3244.*

This is part of the Bunkamura complex, attached to Tokyu Honten

Department Store in Shibuya. The hall is the home of the Tokyo Philharmonic.

SUNTORY HALL, *part of the Ark Hills complex near Roppongi. The closest subway is Kokkai Gijido-mae on the Chiyoda subway line or take bus # 1 from Shibuya Station's east side to the Ark Hills stop. Tel. (03)3584-9999.*

There are two concert halls; the acoustics in the main hall are excellent. You can buy drinks and sandwiches at the bar if you can't wait until after the concert. If we are not seeing a vocal recital, we like to sit on the seats behind the stage so we can see the conductor's facial expressions; these tickets happen to be the cheapest.

TOKYO METROPOLITAN FESTIVAL HALL (Tokyo Bunka Kaikan), *at Ueno Park; use Ueno Station, Koen (park) exit. Tel. (03) 3828-2111.*

There are two halls; the small concert hall is one of the best in Tokyo for chamber music.

NHK HALL, *use Harajuku or Shibuya Station. Tel. (03)3465-1751.*

NHK Hall accommodates over 4000 people, making it one of the Tokyo's largest halls. The acoustics are good, but we find the building uninspired.

TOKYO OPERA CITY AND NEW NATIONAL THEATRE, *Hatsudai Station on Keio line or Shinjuku Station. Tel. (03)5353-9999.*

The long-awaited opera house and theater is part of a high-rise complex.

HAMA RIKYU ASAHI HALL, *adjacent to Asahi Shimbun (Newspaper) Building, use Shimbashi or Tsukiji Stations. Tel. (03)3351-4043.*

Good acoustics.

TOKYO GEIJUTSU GEKIJO, *part of the Tokyo Metropolitan Art Space. Use Ikebukuro Station, exit 2b. Tel. (03)5391-2111.*

TOKYO INTERNATIONAL FORUM (Tokyo Kokusai Forum), *use Yurakucho Station on the JR Yamanote line. Tel. (03)5221-9000.*

One of Tokyo's newest, has four halls in the sleek post-modern building.

CASALS HALL, *use Ochanomizu Station on JR Sobu line or Shin Ochanomizu on Chiyoda subway line. Tel. (03)3291-2525.*

Named to honor cellist Pablo Casals, this hall was built for chamber music concerts. The balcony seats are excellent.

KIOI-CHO HALL, *use Akasaka Mitsuke or Yotsuya Stations. Tel. (03)3237-0061.*

Built at the time of the bubble economy, the hall is over the top — marble floors and a much-too-big chandelier; the acoustics are excellent.

OJI HALL, *use Ginza Station. Tel. (03)3567-9990.*

Relatively small but perfect for piano concerts.

TSUDA HALL, *use Sendagaya Station. Tel. (03)3402-1851.*
Like Oji Hall, this is also an excellent venue for piano concerts.
KAN-I HOKEN HALL, *use Gotanda Station, located on the west side. Tel. (03)3490-5111.*
Not acoustically perfect, but offers excellent ballet, modern dance, musicals and foreign stage plays.
ART HALL AFFINIS, *use Toranomon Station on Ginza subway line, exit 3. Tel. (03)5572-4945.*
This is one of Tokyo's newest chamber music halls.

Theaters
Panasonic Globe Theater, *3-1-2 Hyakunin-cho, Shinjuku-ku. Tel. (03)3360-1151. Use Shin-Okubo Station on the JR Yamanote line.*
A copy of the English original – it's twice the size – usually presents Shakespearean plays performed by Japanese and foreign companies.
Ginza Saison Gekijo, *1-11-1 Ginza, Chuo-ku. Tel. (03)3535-0555. Use Ginza Itchome subway station.*
Come here to see Japanese and foreign stage plays.

Popular Music
Superstars like the Rolling Stones and Michael Jackson perform at the Tokyo Dome. Artists who might not attract 50,000 fans appear at the many concert halls, clubs and "live houses" that dot Tokyo. In addition to the halls listed above and Blue Note Tokyo, the following clubs are popular venues:
CLUB CITTA KAWASAKI, *use Kawasaki Station on the JR Keihin Tohoku line. Tel. (044)244-7888.*
CLUB QUATTRO, *5F, Quattro Building, 32-13 Udagawa-cho, Shibuya-ku. Tel. (03)3477-8750. From Shibuya Station's Hachiko Plaza, walk down the brick road at the huge Shibuya Hachiko crossing.*
ON AIR WEST, *on Rambling Road in Shibuya's Maruyama-cho. 2-3 Maruyama-cho, Shibuya-ku. Tel. (03)5458-4646. From Shibuya Station's Hachiko Plaza walk to Tokyu Honten Department Store and bear to the left. Turn left at Shibuya City Hotel.*

Ticket Agencies
You can reserve tickets by calling or going to a ticket agency. When making a telephone reservation, take the confirmation number to a ticket counter by the date the agent tells you. Tokyo is sprinkled with ticket counters; the agent can tell you the closest one. Ticket Pia and Ticket Saison accept credit cards.
Ticket agencies will not accept reservations on the day of a performance. You'll need to call the hall to reserve tickets and pick them up at

the box office before the performance. Box offices do not accept credit cards.
• **Ticket Pia**, *Tel. (03)5237-9999*
• **Ticket Saison**, *Tel. (03)5990-9999*
• **CN Playguide**, *Tel. (03)5802-9990*

COOKING CLASSES
While in Tokyo, hone your culinary talents at the following places:

A Taste of Culture, run by an American, Elizabeth Ando, who is a trained Japanese chef, offers cooking classes, tasting programs, market tours and other field trips. *1-22-18 Seta, 401, Setagaya-ku, Tokyo 158-0095. Tel. (03)5716-5751, Email: aeli@gol.com.*

Konishi Japanese Cooking Class offers a variety of sessions in English led by culinary professional Kiyoko Konishi. *3-1-7-1405 Meguro, Minato-ku, Tokyo 153-0063. Tel/Fax (03)3714-8859.*

FLOWER ARRANGING
Classes are all in English at the following places:

OHARA SCHOOL, *5-7-17 Minami Aoyama, Minato-ku. Tel. (03)3499-1200. Three-minute walk from Omotesando Station on Ginza, Hanzomon and Chiyoda subway lines.*

Classes 10am to 12 noon, Wednesday and Thursday; 1:30-3:30pm Tuesday. ¥2000 plus about ¥2000 for flowers. Reservations required.

SOGETSU SCHOOL, *7-2-21 Akasaka, Minato-ku. Tel. (03)3408-1151. 5-minute walk from No. 4 exit Aoyama Itchome exit of Ginza and Hanzomon subway lines. Closed August.*

Classes 10am to 12 noon Monday. ¥4850 including flowers. Reservations required.

IKENOBO OCHANOMIZU GAKUIN, *2-3 Kanda Surugadai, Chiyoda-ku. Tel. (03)3292-3071. 3-minute walk from Ochanomizu Station on JR Chuo and Sobu lines and Chiyoda subway line.*

Classes on Wednesday at 11am, 2pm and 4pm. ¥3700 fee includes flowers. Reservations required.

TEA CEREMONY
You can participate in a traditional Japanese tea ceremony, which is more like a meditative ritual than having tea in the Western sense.

TOKO-AN (IMPERIAL HOTEL), *4F, Main Building, 1-1-1 Uchisaiwai-cho, Chiyoda-ku. Tel. (03)3504-1111. Hibiya Station of Hibiya, Chiyoda and Toei Mita subway lines.*

Tea ceremony performed between 10am and 6pm except Sunday and holidays. Reservation required. Tea ceremony takes about 20 minutes. ¥1500.

CHOSHO-AN (HOTEL OKURA), *7F, Main Building, 2-10-4 Toranomon, Minato-ku. Tel. (03)3582-0111. Toranomon Station of Ginza subway line or Kamiyacho Station of Hibiya subway line.*

Tea ceremony performed between 11am to 4pm except Sundays and national holidays. Reservations required. Tea ceremony takes about 30 minutes. ¥1050.

SEISEI-AN (HOTEL NEW OTANI), *7F, Tower, 4-1 Kioi-cho, Chiyoda-ku, Tokyo. Tel. (03)3265-1111. Near Akasaka Mitsuke Station of Ginza and Marunouchi subway lines and Nagatacho Station of Yurakucho and Hanzomon subway lines.*

Tea ceremony performed 11am to 12 noon and 1pm to 4pm Thursday, Friday and Saturday. Reservations required for groups of five or more. Tea ceremony takes about 20 minutes. ¥1050.

CHADO KAIKAN HALL, *3-39-17 Takadanobaba, Shinjuku-ku. Tel. (03)3361-2446. From Takadanobaba Station on JR Yamanote line, walk 15 minutes or take a bus heading toward Otakibashi-shako and get off at the Takadanobaba yon(4)-chome stop.*

Tea ceremony is performed between 10:30am and 2:30pm, Monday through Thursday, but only three weeks of every month. Tea ceremony takes about one hour. ¥2000.

HAPPO-EN, *1-1-6 Shiroganedai, Minato-ku. Tel. (03)3443-2446. 15 minute walk from Meguro Station on JR Yamanote line.*

Tea ceremony is performed between 11am and 5pm daily. Reservations required. ¥2000 for tea ceremony, ¥800 for tea and sweets without tea ceremony.

PUBLIC BATHS & HOT SPRINGS

The *sento* or public bath is a Tokyo institution that is fast disappearing. In 1968, Tokyo had 2687 public baths that served 6 million people a day, but today the number has dwindled to 1500. Many Japanese houses and apartments did not have baths, but over 90% do today. Most *sento* are local neighborhood institutions where you see people, mostly students and old people, enter carrying a plastic bucket with their soap and toiletries. For basic bath etiquette, see the sidebar on Bathing Etiquette in Chapter 6, *Planning Your Trip*.

In *shitamachi* (the old commoner's area), even today the tradition of relaxing with your neighbors is still alive. In Yanaka, for example, more than 10 *sento* (public baths) are located within a small radius.

Volcanoes and hot springs go together, so even Tokyo has hot springs called *onsen*. After all, Mt. Fuji is only an hour away by train. It last erupted in 1701, and although it is now dormant, it could erupt again.

The following are a few *sento* worth trying:

KOSHI NO YU and **AZABU JUBAN ONSEN**, *1-5-22 Azabu Juban, Minato-ku. Tel. (03)3401-8324. Open 3pm to 9pm. Closed Tuesday. Ground floor: ¥370; 3rd floor: ¥1300.*

On the first floor, you can soak in the same hot spring water as the *onsen* on the third floor. The old style bath has a two-story high ceiling and a mural painting. The Azabu Juban area has a lot of foreign residents so it's not unusual to see non-Japanese bathing here.

DAI NI SAKURA YU, *6-6-2 Jingu-mae, Shibuya-ku. Tel. (03)3400-5680. Open 3:30pm to 11pm. Closed Monday. Jingumae Station on the Chiyoda subway line. Use exit 4, turn around at the top of the stairs and cross Meiji Dori, take the second right (it's a narrow road). Before the road forks, turn right at the coin laundry. Turn right again. The bath is the building that looks like a temple. ¥385.*

This 40-year-old building resembles a temple and is a wonderfully old-fashioned bathing experience in the midst of trendy Harajuku.

PUBLIC BATHING THE JAPANESE WAY

Public bathhouses, **sento***, have a long history in Japan – back to the 8th century. Much more than a place to clean your body, they are community centers. Neighbors exchange news and gossip and bond with each other. Certain bath houses have been associated with the sex trade. They were called "Toruko" after the Turkish bath, but after the Turkish Embassy complained, they began to be called "Soaplands." Public baths however are legitimate, family-oriented places. Since most homes and apartments now have private baths, the remaining sento are struggling to survive in an environment of decreasing use and increasing costs. Most now have electronic massage chairs, and some have coffee bars. Soon we expect a Starbucks. You may even find a diaper changing table in the men's changing room.*

SPORTS & RECREATION

SPORTS

Sumo

Tokyo hosts three, 15-day **sumo tournaments** every year in January, May and September. NHK (Channel 1) televises the bouts every day from 4 to 6pm. NHK satellite broadcasts sumo with English explanations, but not every hotel provides satellite service. If you are in Tokyo, don't settle for watching a bout on television when you could see it live.

Sumo tournaments take place at the Sumo Stadium, formally known as the Kokugikan at Ryogoku Station of JR Sobu line. Advance tickets go on sale at the stadium as well as at Play Guides Ticket Bureaus – branches at Isetan Department Store in Shinjuku, Seibu Department Store in Shibuya and Ikebukuro, and Kyukyodo in Ginza. The most expensive seating is on *tatami* mats near the ring. These seats come with food and souvenirs, but are almost impossible to obtain. Further back are chair seats. They cost ¥8100, ¥6100, ¥3600 and ¥2100. Standing-room tickets for ¥2100 go on sale at 8am each day of the tournament.

Weekends sell out quickly and the second week sells out before the first. Sometimes it's fairly easy to get tickets on weekdays during the first week. But if you want standing-room tickets on weekends, you have to be in line at least an hour or two before tickets go on sale.

The sumo tournament runs from 10am until 6pm; the lowest ranking wrestlers go first. The good guys don't wrestle until about 3:30pm, and most ticket holders don't come until then. You can buy an inexpensive ticket and sit down near the ring until the rightful owner of the seat claims his seat. You don't have to be embarrassed because everybody does this.

Sumo wrestlers live communally in **stables** and practice from about 6am to 11am. Some stables allow visitors to watch the practice, but you must make an appointment in advance. Try:
• **Azumazeki Beya**, *Tel. (03)3625-0033*. This stable has a lot of Hawaiian-born wrestlers. It's near the Honjo Azumabashi Station of the Toei Asakusa subway line.
• **Tatsunami Beya**, *Tel. (03)3631-2424*. Near Ryogoku Station on the JR Sobu line.
• **Kasugano Beya**, *Tel. (03)3631-1871*. Near Ryogoku Station on the JR Sobu line.
• **Tokitsukaze Beya**, *Tel. (03)3624-8549, 3-15-3 Ryogoku, Sumida-ku*. Near Ryogoku Station on the JR Sobu line.

Baseball (Yakyu)

Six professional baseball teams call the metro Tokyo area home. Baseball has two leagues: the Pacific and the Central. The baseball season begins in mid-April and ends with the Japan Series in October. Tickets are usually pretty easy to obtain at the stadium or through ticket agencies except for the Yomiuri Giants, nearly everyone's favorite team. Their seats sell out well in advance. Most teams have inexpensive outfield seats for children, usually about ¥500; bleacher tickets for their mommies and daddies cost about double.

Baseball fans may want to stop at the **Baseball Hall of Fame Museum** (Yakyu Taiiku Hakubutsukan) at Tokyo Dome. ¥350. *Tel. (03)3811-3600*.

For the **Central League**:

Yomiuri Giants play at Tokyo Dome, a covered stadium, so games are never rained out. Tickets range from ¥1200 for nonreserved outfield bleachers to ¥5900 for the best seats. Tokyo Dome is a one-minute walk from Korakuen Station on the Marunouchi subway line and three-minute walk from Suidobashi Station on the JR Sobu, JR Chuo and Mita subway line. *Tel. (03)3811-2111.*

Yakult Swallows play at Jingu Stadium in Meiji Outer Garden in central Tokyo. Tickets cost between ¥1500 and ¥3900. Jingu Stadium is a five-minute walk from Gaien-mae Station on the Ginza subway line. *Tel. (03)3236-8000.*

Yokohama BayStars play at Yokohama Stadium. Tickets range from ¥1500 to ¥5000. Yokohama Stadium is near Kan-nai Station on the JR Negishi line. *Tel. (045)661-1251.*

For the **Pacific League**:

Nippon Ham Fighters play at Tokyo Dome. The first time Patrice went to a game, she thought the team was named the Nippon Hams, but that's the name of the company that owns them. Tickets cost ¥1500 to ¥5100. See the Yomiuri Giants listing above for transportation information. *Tel. (03)3811-2111.*

Seibu Lions play at Seibu Lions Stadium. Tickets cost ¥1500 to ¥3200. When the Lions win the pennant or the Japan Series, Seibu Department Store has a huge sale to celebrate. The stadium is at Seibu Kyujomae Station on the Seibu Ikebukuro line. *Tel. (0429)25-1151.*

Chiba Lotte Marines play at Chiba Marine Stadium. Tickets cost ¥1300 to ¥4000. The stadium is a 15-minute walk from the Kaihin Makuhari Station on the JR Keiyo line. *Tel. (043)296-8900.*

Soccer

J League is Japan's popular professional soccer league. The season runs from March through May, then takes a break and resumes in August. The championship playoffs occur in early December. The Tokyo metro area has several soccer teams. Most of the time, teams play their home games at their stadiums, but occasionally they play at the National Stadium (Kokuritsu Stadium) near Sendagaya Station on the JR Sobu line in central Tokyo. Ticket prices run between ¥2000 and ¥5000.

The teams are as follows:

JEF United Ichihara play at Ichihara Stadium in Chiba Prefecture. 20-minute walk from the west exit of Goi Station on the JR Uchibo line. *Tel. (0436)21-4441.*

Kashiwa Reysol play at Kashiwa Stadium in Kashiwa City. 20-minute walk from the east exit of Kashiwa Station on the Chiyoda subway line. *Tel. (0471)62-2201.*

Verdy Kawasaki play at Todoroki Stadium in Kawasaki. From Musashi Kosugi Station on the Tokyu Toyoko line or JR Nambu line, take a bus from #1 or #2 bus stand heading toward Mizonokuchi and get off at Todoroki Ground Iriguchi stop. *Tel. (044)722-0303.*

Yokohama Marinos play at International Stadium in Yokohama. Near Shin Yokohama Station.

Martial Arts

Each martial art has a federation that can give you information on the sport and places of instruction throughout Japan.

Aikido

International Aikido Federation (Kokusai Aikido Renmei). *17-18 Wakamatsu-cho, Shinjuku-ku. Tel. (03)3203-9236.* At the same address is the **Aikido Hombu Dojo,** the gym that offers lessons on a monthly basis. Visitors are welcome to observe practice sessions.

Judo

All Japan Judo Federation (Zen Nihon Judo Renmei). *c/o Kodokan, 1-16-30 Kasuga, Bunkyo-ku. Tel. (03)3818-4199.* The Kodokan offers monthly instruction and has a spectators gallery to view practice sessions. Classes run 6pm to 7:30pm Monday through Saturday.

Nihon Budokan Budo Gakuen holds classes at the Nihon Budokan in Kitanomaru Park, 6:30pm to 7:30pm Monday, Wednesday and Friday. Spectators are welcome to watch practice sessions in this hall built for martial arts competitions in the 1964 Olympics.

Karate

Japan Karatedo Federation (Nihon Karatedo Renmei). *No. 2 Sempaku Shinkokai Building, 1-11-2 Toranomon, Minato-ku. Tel. (03)3503-6640.* There's no gym here, only offices.

Japan Karate Association/International Headquarters JKA (Nihon Karate Kyokai). *Room 408, 29-3 Sakuragaoka, Shibuya-ku, Tel. (03)5459-6226. Dojo: 3-15-9 Nishi Azabu, Minato-ku.* Take a trial class for ¥1000 but spectators aren't allowed.

Goju-ryu Yoyogi Ryushinkan. *4-30-3 Sendagaya, Shibuya-ku. Tel. (03)3402-0123.* Near Yoyogi Station on JR Yamanote line. This school offers monthly instruction and allows spectators. Classes 3 to 5pm; 7 to 9pm Monday, Wednesday and Friday.

Kendo

All Japan Kendo Federation (Nihon Kendo Renmei), *c/o Nippon Budokan, 2-3 Kitanomaru-koen, Chiyoda-ku. Tel. (03)3211-5804.*

Nippon Budokan Budo Gakuen at the Budokan (address above). *Tel. (03)3216-5143.* Classes are on an annual basis.

Kyudo (Japanese archery)

All Nippon Kyudo Federation (Zen Nihon Kyudo Renmei). *4F, Kishi Memorial Hall, 1-1-1 Jinnan, Shibuya-ku. Tel. (03)3481-2387.* Maybe it's because of stray arrows, but spectators aren't allowed at any of the schools.

Swimming Pools

Tokyo Gymnasium Indoor Swimming Pool. *1-17-1 Sendagaya, Shibuya-ku. Tel. (03)5474-2111.* Sendagaya Station on JR Sobu line. Open 9:30am to 9pm. ¥450. Has 50 meter and 25 meter pools.

Tokyo Tatsumi International Swimming Pool. *Tel. (03)5569-5061.* 10-minute walk from Tatsumi Station on Yurakucho subway line. Open 9am to 9pm. Closed 3rd Monday. ¥450.

National Olympic Memorial Youth Center (Kokuritsu Orimpikku Kinen Shonen Senta). *3-1 Yoyogi Jingu-en-cho, Shibuya-ku. Tel. (03)3467-7201.* On the Yoyogi side of Yoyogi Park, a new building in the center houses a great pool with a retractable roof. Despite its name, the pool is open to everyone. Open daily 10am to 8pm. ¥260.

SHOPPING

Tokyo is a shopper's dream. Are you interested in state-of-the-art electronics, the latest international fashions, age-old traditional crafts? All are available. Some of our favorite places to shop are described in the following pages.

Japan's **department stores** are cultural institutions. In addition to every conceivable style of clothing, the stores have extensive basement food floors where they sell prepared gourmet treats in addition to staples, meat, fish and vegetables. Most have galleries where exhibitions rival top museums. The kimono department usually has other, more affordable items like *yukata* (cotton robes), which are good mementos of Japan.

Department stores usually close about twice a month — always on the same day of the week. There isn't any pattern to their closing, and they stay open all week during the gift-giving seasons in June and December. We list the closed day after each department store, but remember, it isn't every week.

The standard opening time for department stores is 10am; they close between 7 and 8pm. Other stores usually open around the same time, sometimes 11am. Tokyo is not an early morning city. Arriving at a department store right as it opens is an unbelievable experience. Uniformed staff members stand at the entrance and bow to the first customers of the day.

Large stores will usually refund the 5% consumption tax to foreign visitors if you purchase goods over ¥10,000. Keep your passport handy; you'll need to show it.

MORE THAN JUST SHOPPING: JAPANESE DEPARTMENT STORES

When friends visit from abroad, we always start one day by going to a department store for its official opening ceremony, which begins at 10am sharp. Don't be late or you'll miss it! At the main entrance, you'll hear soft music playing over the loudspeaker system. Uniformed employees line up inside the entrance to the store, smiling in welcome and bowing politely. They make you feel like a VIP, which is great fun for a little while!

Japan's department stores pride themselves on being cultural as well as shopping centers. You would never expect to find an exhibition of Japanese masterpieces from the Tokyo National Museum at Macy's. But in Japan, you might find an exhibition of French Impressionists from a top museum displayed in a special gallery. Be sure to visit these galleries usually located on a top floor of most department stores; there's almost always an admission charge.

And don't miss the basement food floor! Wander around sampling delicacies to your heart's content; some stores are so generous with their free tastes that you can even forego lunch. Make sure you go to the fruit section to see ¥15,000 melons and ¥10,000 packages of cherries. Before you faint, be aware that most are bought by companies as gifts. Then go to the meat department and check out the Kobe and other premium beef selling for ¥50,000 a kilo, a mere $250 a pound. The more expensive the meat, the more marbled it is with fat. We still don't know who buys it.

Some department stores have Japanese souvenirs in a special section catering to tourists; if you are in a store that doesn't, go to the kimono department where a variety of traditional items like noren curtains or scarves are for sale – either one makes a great gift.

FLEA MARKETS

We love to browse in the **flea markets**. Held at shrines, they're usually open from dawn until about 3pm. You'll find inexpensive second-hand kimono, vintage porcelain, ceramic dishes, lacquer ware, clocks, movie posters, dolls, toys and just plain junk; go early for the best selection. Antiques can be pricey, but the markets offer goods for every budget. Used silk kimono are real bargains, costing as little as ¥1000. If a kimono smells musty, one trick is to put it in a clothes dryer with a sheet of fabric softener and run it on low for a few minutes. Dealers speak a little English; some post prices and others don't. You can always ask for a discount, and you can often get a 10% reduction — sometimes more. Rain cancels flea markets.

Some good flea markets for you to visit include:
- **Togo Shrine**, 1st and 4th Sundays. Harajuku Station on Yamanote Line or Meiji Jingumae Station on Chiyoda subway line.
- **Nogi Shrine**, 2nd Sunday. Nogizaka Station on Chiyoda subway line.
- **Hanazono Shrine**, 2nd and 3rd Sundays; Shinjuku san-chome Station on Marunouchi subway line.
- **Roi Building**, 4th Thursday and Friday, Roppongi Station on Hibiya subway line.
- **Tomioka Shrine**, 1st of month and 1st Sunday. Monzen Naka-cho Station on Tozai subway line; walk east on Eitai Dori for about 3 minutes, shrine is on left.
- **Heiwajima Antique Fair** (Zenkoku Kotto Matsuri), *2F, Heiwajima Tokyo Ryutsu Center. Tel. (03)3980-8228.* Tokyo Monorail from JR Hamamatsucho Station to Ryutsu Center stop. The three-day sale is held in March, May, June, September and December and has over 200 dealers from all parts of Japan. If you can't find it here, it probably doesn't exist.

SHOPPING IN GINZA & NEIGHBORING DISTRICTS
Department Stores
- **Mitsukoshi**, *Ginza 4-chome intersection. Closed some Mondays. Tel. (03)3562-1111.*
- **Wako**, *Ginza 4-chome intersection. Closed Sunday. Tel. (03)3562-2111.*
- **Matsuya**, *One block down from Mitsukoshi. Closed some Tuesdays. Tel. (03)3567-1211.*
- **Matsuzakaya**, *South of Ginza 4-chome intersection. Closed some Wednesdays. Tel. (03)3572-1111.*
- **Hankyu**, *Near Yurakucho Station on Harumi Dori. Closed some Thursdays. Tel. (03)3575-2233.*
- **Seibu**, *Next to Hankyu. Closed some Wednesdays. Tel. (03)3286-0111.*

Other Stores
- **Takumi**, *8-4-2 Ginza, Chuo-ku. Tel. (03)3571-2017. Open 11am to 7pm. Closed Sunday.* Japanese folk crafts.
- **Kyukyodo**, *5-7-4 Ginza, Chuo-ku. Tel. (03)3571-4429. Open 10am to 7:30pm; 11am to 7pm on Sunday and holidays.* Sells incense, Japanese *washi* paper, tea ceremony utensils, cards and calligraphy supplies.
- **Mikimoto Pearls**, *4-5-5 Ginza, Chuo-ku. Tel. (03)3535-4611. Open 10am to 6pm. Closed Wednesday.* Japan's premier pearl shop of the company who invented the culturing process.
- **Itoya**, *2-7-15 Ginza, Chuo-ku. Tel. (03)3561-8311. Open 10am to 7pm; 10:30am to 6pm Sunday and holidays.* A large, well-stocked stationery and paper goods store — a delight for browsing.

•**Jena,** *5-6-1 Ginza, Chuo-ku. Tel. (03)3571-2980. Open 10:30am to 7:50pm; 12 noon to 6pm Sunday. Closed holidays.* A large selection of foreign books.

•**Tenshodo,** *4-3-9 Ginza, Chuo-ku. Tel. (03)3561-0021.* With a 120-year history, this shop sells the unlikely combination of toys and jewelry. Japanese women didn't wear jewelry with kimono, only hair ornaments, so this shop was one of Japan's first to sell Western-style jewelry.

•**Yoseido Gallery,** *5-5-15 Ginza, Chuo-ku. Tel. (03)3571-1312. Open 10am to 6:30pm. Closed Sunday and holidays.* Carries a large selection of contemporary prints by Japanese artists.

•**Hayashi Kimono,** *International Arcade, 2-1-1 Yurakucho, Chiyoda-ku. Tel. (03)3501-4012. Open daily 9:30am to 6:30pm.* Hayashi has a good selection of used kimono, *happi* coats, cotton *yukata*, T-shirts and other souvenir items. It's in the International Arcade, which is under the tracks on the road on the north side of the Imperial Hotel.

SHOPPING IN NIHONBASHI
Department Stores
•**Mitsukoshi,** Mitsukoshi-mae Station on Ginza subway line. *Closed some Mondays. Tel. (03)3241-3311.*

•**Takashimaya,** At Nihonbashi Station on Ginza and Tozai subway lines. *Closed some Wednesdays. Tel. (03)3211-4111.*

•**Tokyu,** At Nihonbashi Station on Ginza and Tozai subway lines. *Closed some Thursdays. Tel. (03)3273-3111.*

Other Stores
•**Ozu Washi,** *2-6-3 Nihonbashi Honcho, Chuo-ku. Tel. (03)3663-8788. Open 10am to 6pm. Closed Sunday.* Ozu is a calligrapher's paradise with hundreds of papers to choose from. It also sells stationery and small paper gift items.

•**Haibara,** *2-7-6 Nihonbashi, Chuo-ku. Tel. (03)3272-3801. Open 9:30am to 5pm. Closed Sunday and holidays.* A good selection of Japanese paper craft items and stationery.

•**Heiando,** *3-10-11 Nihonbashi, Chuo-ku. Tel. (03)3770-3641. Open 10am to 6pm. Closed Sunday and holidays.* Exquisite lacquer ware.

SHOPPING IN ROPPONGI & NEIGHBORING DISTRICTS
•**Kurofune,** *7-7-4 Roppongi, Minato-ku. Tel. (03)3479-1552. Open 10am to 6pm. Closed Sunday.* Kurofune (Black Ship), run by American John Adair, has an impeccable collection of antique *tansu* chests and ceramic hibachi – many museum-quality.

- **Art Plaza Magatani**, *5-10-13 Toranomon, Minato-ku. Tel. (03)3433-6321. Open 10am to 6pm. Closed Sunday and holidays.* Magatani resembles a junk store with goods cluttering every surface, but there's a wide variety of Japanese antiques, including dolls.
- **Japan Sword**, *3-8-1 Toranomon, Minato-ku. Tel. (03)3434-4321. Open 9:30am to 6pm weekdays, 9:30am to 5pm Saturday. Closed Sunday and holidays.* This shop is more like a museum of traditional Japanese swords.
- **Axis Building**, *5-17-1 Roppongi, Minato-ku. Tel. (03)3587-2781. Most shops are closed Sunday.* This building has shops with modern designs including **Living Motif**, selling housewares; **Nuno**, selling contemporary Japanese textiles and clothes; **Kisso**, contemporary ceramics and **Bushy**, modern lacquer ware.
- **Boutique Yuya**, *6-15-2 Roppongi, Minato-ku. Tel. (03)5474-2097. Open 12 noon to 5pm or by appointment. Closed Sunday and holidays.* Stunning, one-of-a-kind contemporary clothing made from vintage kimono.
- **Blue and White**, *2-9-2 Azabu Juban, Minato-ku. Tel. (03)3451-0537. Open 10am to 6pm. Closed holidays.* Almost everything is this shop is blue and white: textiles, ceramics, paper, original clothing and other articles; you'll find some of the most creative items with a traditional feel that are available in Tokyo.
- **Hasebeya**, *1-5-24 Azabu Juban, Minato-ku. Tel. (03)3401-9998.* Carries high caliber antique *tansu* chests and decorative items.
- **Okura Oriental Art**, *3-3-14 Azabudai, Minato-ku. Tel. (03)3585-5309. Open 10am to 6pm. Closed Monday.* A good selection of *tansu* chests, porcelain and other Japanese antiques is available.
- **Kathryn Milan**, *3-1-14 Nishi Azabu, Minato-ku. Tel. (03)3408-1532. Open 10am to 6pm weekends and holidays, by appointment at other times.* Antique *tansu* chests and other items are beautifully displayed in an early 20th century house.
- **Wally Yonamine Pearls**, *4-11-8 Roppongi, Minato-ku, Tokyo. Tel. (03)3402-4001. Open 9:30am to 5:30pm. Closed Sunday and holidays.* This pearl shop is a favorite of the expat community.
- **Washikobo**, *1-8-10 Nishi-Azabu, Minato-ku. Tel. (03)3405-1841. Open 10am to 6pm. Closed Sunday and national holidays.* Filled with all kinds of Japanese paper, crafts and traditional toys from all over Japan. We can easily spend an hour browsing in this small shop. It's a great place to buy lightweight souvenirs.
- **Tolman Collection**, *2-2-18 Shiba Daimon, Minato-ku, 105. Tel. (03)3434-1300. Open 11am to 7pm. Closed Tuesday.* Housed in a former *geisha* residence, the gallery sells contemporary Japanese prints.
- **Tsukamoto**, *4-1-9 Roppongi, Minato-ku. Tel. (03)3403-3747.* An excellent selection of folk art pottery from Mashiko.

• **Tomoyo**, *Gody Building, 1F, 6-8-8 Roppongi, Minato-ku. Tel. (03)3479-1176. Open 9:30am to 6pm; until 4pm Saturday. Closed Sunday.* Original clothes and decorative items using traditional Japanese textiles.

SHOPPING IN SHIBUYA

Shibuya is actually wall-to-wall stores. There are lots of "fashion buildings" filled with small stores, an urban Japanese answer to shopping malls. Stop in Tokyu Plaza, 109 and Parco to see what they're all about.

Department Stores

• **Seibu**, North of Shibuya Station Hachiko Plaza. *Closed some Wednesdays. Tel. (03)3462-0111.*
• **Tokyu Toyoko**, At Shibuya Station. *Closed some Thursdays. Tel. (03)3477-3111.*
• **Tokyu Honten**, 10-minute walk west of Shibuya Station. *Closed some Tuesdays. Tel. (03)3477-3111.*
• **Marui**, One block down from Seibu. *Closed some Wednesdays. Tel. (03)3464-0101.*

Other Stores

• **Parco**, *15-1 Udagawa-cho, Shibuya-ku. Tel. (03)3464-5111. Open daily 10am to 8:30pm.* Chic fashion building.
• **Tokyu Hands**, *12-18 Udagawa-cho, Shibuya-ku. Tel. (03)5489-5111. Open 10am to 8pm. Closed some Wednesdays.* Don't miss the ultimate do-it-yourself shop.
• **Tower Records**, *1-22-14 Jinnan, Shibuya-ku. Tel. (03)3496-3661. Open daily 10am to 10pm.* World's largest record shop — actually, it only has CDs and tapes. The bookstore has an excellent selection of English-language books, magazines and newspapers from around the world at Tokyo's best prices.
• **Beniya**, *2-16-8 Shibuya, Shibuya-ku. Tel. (03)3400-8084. Open 10am to 7pm. Closed Thursday.* Has a good selection of Japanese and Southeast Asian folk crafts.
• **Kuroda Toen**, *B1, Metro Plaza Building. Tel. (03)3499-3225. Open 11am to 7pm. Closed Sunday and holidays.* This shop has a good selection of unusual ceramic ware.
• **Marunan**, *2-5-1 Dogenzaka, Shibuya-ku. Tel. (03)3461-2325. Open daily 10am to 8:30pm.* Large fabric store that has a good selection of Japanese fabrics in the basement.
• **Uematsu**, *2-19-15 Shibuya, Shibuya-ku. Tel. (03)3400-5556. Open 10am to 7pm. Closed 1st and 3rd Sundays.* Across the bus plaza on the east side of Shibuya Station, Uematsu carries art supplies including special brushes and inks for Japanese calligraphy and *sumi-e* painting.

SHOPPING IN HARAJUKU, OMOTESANDO & AOYAMA

Takeshita Dori caters to junior high and high school students. The shops are filled with inexpensive clothing and jewelry.

Omotesando, a wide, tree lined boulevard, was made for browsing. Cafes, fashionable clothing stores and antique shops all vie for your attention.

The extension of Omotesando south of Aoyama Dori has a high concentration of fashion-designer boutiques. The From First Building on the right side, just before the Nezu Institute of Arts, has Issey Miyake, Jurgen Lehl and Masuda (Nicole) boutiques.

Kotto Dori is the street running from Kinokuniya Supermarket to the Fuji Film Building. Although many are being run out by fashion designers' shops, there are still some art dealers along this road, including **Morita Antiques** and **Karakusa**.

Some notable stores in these districts include:

- **Oriental Bazaar**, *5-9-13 Jingumae, on Omotesando. Tel. (03)3400-3933. Open 9:30am to 6:30pm. Closed Thursday.* It's touristy, but is the best place in town for one-stop souvenir shopping. Oriental Bazaar sells antiques and new items. Look for cotton *yukata* robes, vintage kimono, ceramics, *ukiyo-e* prints and much more. Mori Silver on the second floor has some of the most reasonable prices in town for pearls.
- **Fuji Torii Co**, *6-1-10 Jingumae, Shibuya-ku. Tel. (03)3400-2777. Open 11am to 6pm, Closed Thursday.* Sells antiques, screens, scrolls, lacquer, ceramics, lamps, furniture, woodblock prints, paper crafts and traditional stationery. Next to Kiddyland on Omotesando.
- **Kiddyland**, *6-1-9 Jingumae, Shibuya-ku. Tel. (03)3409-3431. Open 10am to 8pm. Closed 3rd Tuesday.* Five floors of toys for kids of all ages. Packed on weekends.
- **Ishii Collection**, *6-3-15 Minami Aoyama, Minato-ku. Tel. (03)3468-6683. Open 10:30am to 6:30pm.* Ishii is a tiny store with antique *tansu* chests.
- **Honjo Gallery**, *Palace Aoyama Building, 6-l-6 Minami Aoyama, Minato-ku. Tel. (03)3400-0277. Open 10:30am to 5pm; 12 noon to 4pm Sunday. Closed Monday.* Honjo sells *ukiyo-e* woodblock prints and contemporary and traditional art objects.
- **Japan Traditional Craft Center**, *Plaza 246 Building, 2F, 3-1-1-Minami Aoyama, Minato-ku. Tel. (03)3403-2460. Open 10am to 6pm. Closed Thursday and December 29 through January 4.* An excellent selection of crafts from all over Japan.

The basement of the Hanae Mori Building is a center for antiques. Small shops sell Western and Japanese antiques. **Beniya** (different from the Shibuya craft shop) has a good selection of *ukiyo-e* woodblock prints;

Kikori has antique *tansu* chests. Look also for the corner shop, **Komon Aizome Sei**, selling blue and white traditional textiles and clothing.

SHOPPING IN SHINJUKU
Shinjuku is one large shopping center with a half-dozen department stores and countless smaller shops.

Department Stores
• **Keio**, At Shinjuku Station's west exit. *Closed some Thursdays. Tel. (03)3342-2111.*
• **Odakyu**, At Shinjuku Station's west exit. *Closed some Tuesdays. Tel. (03)3342-1111.* Odakyu Halc has an excellent selection of furniture.
• **Mitsukoshi**, On Shinjuku Dori, east of Shinjuku Station. *Closed some Mondays. Tel. (03)3354-1111.*
• **Isetan**, On Shinjuku Dori, east of Shinjuku Station. *Closed some Wednesdays. Tel. (03)3352-1111.* Foreign Customer Service: (03)3225-2514.
• **Marui**, On Shinjuku Dori, east of Shinjuku Station. *Closed some Wednesdays. Tel. (03)3354-0101.*
• **Takashimaya**, In Times Square Building, south exit of Shinjuku Station. *Closed some Wednesdays. Tel. (03)5361-1111.*

Other Stores
Times Square Building, *Shinjuku South, 5-24-2 Sendagaya, Shibuya-ku.* We don't know where its name came from, but it has nothing to do with New York. It's a shopper's paradise containing Takashimaya Department Store, Kinokuniya Book Store, Tokyu Hands do-it-yourself shop, HMV Record Shop, game arcade Joyopolis, an IMAX theater, and 28 restaurants.

Discount electronic shops are **Yodobashi Camera** at Shinjuku Station west exit and **Sakuraya** on Shinjuku Dori east of Shinjuku Station.

Bingoya, *10-6 Wakamatsu-cho Shinjuku-ku. Tel. (03)3202-8778. Open 10am to 7pm. Closed Monday.* Take bus #74 towards Tokyo Joshidai from Shinjuku Station's west exit. Get off at the 8th stop, Kawada-cho. For the Japan folk craft lover, Bingoya is a dream come true. Though located at an odd place, it's worth the detour. The five-storied small building is packed with folk crafts: natural color hemp cloth, blue and white fabrics, hand-woven material from all over Japan, delicate bamboo baskets, intriguing straw work, ceramics for daily use, fascinating folk toys, handmade paper, beautiful paper lanterns, and folk style furniture. It's easy to spend money and time. And, if you find you bought too much to carry, ship your purchases directly abroad.

TOKYO'S SPECIALIZED MARKETS

Tokyo's shops believe in the motto "birds of a feather flock together." Here are some of the areas where similar shops cluster.

Akihabara. *Dizzying array of discount electronics, computers and household appliances. Akihabara Station on JR Yamanote and JR Sobu lines.*

Asakusabashi. *Wrapping paper, boxes, artificial flowers, toys and Japanese dolls. Asakusabashi Station on the JR Sobu line.*

Hanakawado. *Shoes, shoes and more shoes. The district started by selling traditional footwear like geta and zori, but has branched out. On Edo Dori near Asakusa. Asakusa Station on Ginza subway line.*

Jimbocho. *New, secondhand and rare books, prints and maps. Jimbocho Station on Tozai subway line.*

Kappabashi. *Restaurant supply district. Come here for plastic food models, tableware, kitchen utensils, pots, uniforms and anything else the restaurant trade desires. Tawaramachi Station on the Ginza subway line.*

Musashi Koyama. *Covered shopping street selling inexpensive clothes, household items, toys and secondhand furniture. Musashi Koyama Station on the Mekama line – two stops from Meguro.*

Nippori. *Everything for sewing: fabric, notions and patterns. On Nippori Chuo Dori. Nippori Station on JR Yamanote line.*

Okachimachi. *Jewelry in all price ranges, including small diamond, emerald and pearl districts. Under and west of the tracks heading south from Okachimachi Station on the JR Yamanote line*

Togoshi Ginza. *Sells inexpensive toys, clothes and household articles. Japanese go there for bargain shopping. Togoshi Ginza Station on the Ikegami line – two stops from Gotanda Station.*

Tsukiji Outer Market. *Sells kitchen utensils, knives, dishes, and anything else chefs may need. Tsukiji Station on Hibiya subway line.*

SHOPPING IN ASAKUSABASHI-RYOGOKU

Asakusabashi's shops sell wrapping paper and other paper goods, Japanese dolls, toys and seasonal decorations at incredibly cheap prices. **Shimojima** is the largest paper goods shop and has several stores along Edo Dori. Japanese dolls in cases for Girls' and Children's Days are the specialty of a half-dozen stores on Edo Dori including **Kyugetsu**, **Yoshitoku**, **Shugetsu** and **Kuramae Ningyo-sha**.

Some notable stores in this district include:

• **Sakura Horikiri**, *1-25-3 Yanagibashi. Taito-ku. Tel. (03)3864-1773. Open 9:30am to 5:30pm. Closed Sunday and holidays.* The shop is stocked with paper kits and paper to make attractive craft items such as sets of drawers. You can choose among 800 different papers and, if you wish, assemble the kit in the store. The staff speaks some English and there are English instructions to take home. This activity is great for a rainy day. From Asakusabashi Station, walk north on Edo Dori; turn right after Kyugetsu Doll Store and it's on far left corner of second block.

· **Glass Land Tokyo**, *3-27-8 Asakusabashi, Taito-ku. Tel. (03)5821-5115. Open 10am to 6pm.* From Asakusabashi Station, walk north on Edo Dori and turn left onto Kuramae Bashi Dori. It's three blocks down on the left. This outlet store for Sasaki Crystal offers some of the best deals in town on stemware and other glass items.

· **Ryogoku Takahashi Company**, *4-31-15 Ryogoku, Sumida-ku. Tel. (03)3631-2420.* This shop is loaded with inexpensive sumo wrestling souvenirs.

SHOPPING IN ASAKUSA

Asakusa has many shops selling traditional Japanese goods; we've listed them above under the Asakusa section in *Seeing the Sights*.

SHOPPING IN OCHANOMIZU

· **Origami Kaikan**, *1-7-14 Yushima, Taito-ku. Tel. (03)3811-4025. Open 9am to 5pm. Closed Sunday and holidays.* One of the best places for Japanese *washi* paper, Origami Kaikan sells *yuzen* paper (patterns printed on paper). It also has paper for calling cards, stationery and origami. Make sure you see the second showroom that's downstairs from the main room.

PRACTICAL INFORMATION

Places of Worship

All of the following churches have services in English:

· **Franciscan Chapel Center** (Catholic), *4-2-37 Roppongi, Minato-ku. Tel. (03)3401-2141*

· **St. Alban's Church** (Anglican/Episcopal), *3-6-25 Shiba Koen, Minato-ku. Tel. (03)3431-8534*

· **St. Anselm's Benedictine Church** (Roman Catholic), *4-6-22 Kamiosaki, Shinagawa-ku. Tel. (03)3491-6966*

· **St. Paul's International Lutheran Church**, *1-2-32 Fujimi, Chiyoda-ku. Tel. (03)3261-3740*

· **Tokyo Baptist Church**, *9-2 Hachiyama-cho, Shibuya-ku. Tel. (03)3461-8425.*

· **Tokyo Union Church** (Interdenominational), *5-7-7 Jingumae, Shibuya-ku. Tel. (03)3400-0047*

· **Jewish Community Center**, *3-8-8 Hiroo, Shibuya-ku. Tel. (03)3400-2559*

Essential Phone Numbers
- **Tourist Information Center**, *Tel. (03)3201-3331.*
- **JR East InfoLine**, *Tel. (03)3423-0111.* 10am to 6pm weekdays. Information on JR trains all over Japan.
- **Tokyo English Life Line**, *Tel. (03)3968-4099.* 9am to 4pm; 7pm to 11pm daily. Personal crisis counseling.
- **Japan Helpline**, toll free *Tel. 0120-461-997.* 24 hours. Offers advice and assistance.
- **Police**, *Tel. 110*
- **Fire & Ambulance**, *Tel. 119*

Health

There are doctors who serve the English-speaking community. In an medical emergency, it's best to contact the front desk of your hotel. Call 119 for an ambulance.
- **Tokyo Medical and Surgical Clinic**, *No. 32 Mori Building, 3-4-30 Shiba Koen, Minato-ku. Tel. (03)3436-3028.* Across from Tokyo Tower. All doctors are English speaking. Clinic has a doctor on call 24 hours for emergencies.
- **St. Luke's Hospital**, *9-1 Akashicho, Chuo-ku. Tel. (03)3541-5151.* Has a long history of serving the foreign community.
- **Japan Helpline** is a 24-hour toll free service. They will assist you to find a doctor or hospital in a medical emergency. *Tel. 0120-461-997.*
- Pharmacies with English-speaking staff: **American Pharmacy**, *Hibiya Park Building, 1-8-1 Yurakucho, Chiyoda-ku, Tokyo. Tel. (03)3271-4034.* Open daily 9:30am to 7pm; **Tokyo Medical and Surgical Clinic Pharmacy**, *No. 32 Mori Building, 3-4-30 Shiba Koen, Minato-ku. Tel. (03)3434-5817.* Open 9am to 5:30pm, until 1pm on Saturday. Closed Sunday; **National Supermarket Pharmacy**, *4-5-2 Minami Azabu, Minato-ku. Tel. (03)3442-3181.* Open daily 9:30am to 6:30pm.
- For a Shiatsu massage, try: **Namikoshi Shiatsu**, *3F, Dai Nana Seiko Building, 5-5-9 Akasaka, Minato-ku.* ¥6500 for a one-hour massage. Basic English spoken; popular with foreigners.
- For acupuncture, try: **Edward Acupuncture Clinic**, *Coop Sangenjaya 301, 2-17-12 Sangenjaya, Setagaya-ku. Tel. (03)3418-8989.* Englishman Edward Obaidley trained in Japan; and **Baba Kaiseido Acupuncture Office**, *2-4-5-305 Shiba Daimon, Minato-ku. Tel. (03)3432-0260.* English spoken.

Libraries
- **National Diet Library**, *1-10-1 Nagatacho, Chiyoda-ku. Tel. (03)3581-2331.* The largest collection of books in Japan, the Diet Library is open to anyone over 20 years old. Books may not be checked out.

- **Tokyo Metropolitan Central Library**, *5-7-13 Minami Azabu, Minato-ku. Tel. (03)3442-8451*. A research library (books may not be checked out).
- **JETRO Library**, *2-2-5 Toranomon, Minato-ku. Tel. (03)3582-5549. Open 9:30am to 4:30pm, Monday through Friday. Closed 3rd Tuesday*. Focuses on economic and trade publications.
- **Japan Foundation Library**, *20F, Ark Mori Building, 1-12-32 Akasaka, Minato-ku. Tel. (03)5562-3527*. This library has an extensive collection of English-language books on Japan. Only non-Japanese residents may borrow books.
- **American Center Library**, *11F, ABC Building, 2-6-3 Shiba Koen, Minato-ku. Tel. (03)3436-0901*. Run by the US Government, the collection focuses on the US and has a large selection of American magazines. Only Japanese may borrow books.
- **British Council Library**, *1-2 Kagurazaka, Shinjuku-ku. Tel. (03)3235-8031*. Publications on the UK are the focus. Annual membership fee ¥3500.
- **World Magazine Gallery**, *3-13-10 Ginza, Chuo-ku. Tel. (03)3545-7227. Open 10am to 7pm. Closed Monday*. You'll find over 100 magazines that you can read on the premises or in the adjacent coffee shop. You can't borrow them, but they have copy machines. Walk down the street to the right of Kabuki-za Theater for two blocks. Magazine House is on the 2nd floor of the eight-storied pink and gray striped building.

Post Offices
- **Central Post Office**, *just south of Tokyo Station*, has a 24-hour counter.

FAVORITE STOPS WITH KIDS

Here are some fun stops if you're traveling with kid in this and other chapters:
- *National Children's Castle, page 151*
- *Tama Zoo, page 151*
- *Tokyo Disneyland, page 151*
- *Shinagawa Aquarium, page 152*
- *Tokyo Sea Life Park, page 304*
- *Ski Dome, page 310*
- *Tokyo Sesame Place, page 151*
- *Sanrio Puroland page, page 151*
- *Museum of Maritime Science, page 304*
- *Zoorasia, page 342*

13. SIDE TRIPS FROM TOKYO

Sharing space with 25 million people in the greater Tokyo area makes even the most avid urbanite itch to get out of town. Fortunately, within an hour or two are charming places where you can take in gorgeous scenery, breathe fresh air and rejuvenate yourself.

While we do list some hotels and inns, most of these trips assume that your home base will be Tokyo, so refer to Chapter 12 for places to stay. To locate the destinations in this chapter, see the map on page 186.

SIDE TRIPS FROM TOKYO HIGHLIGHTS

- *The cosmopolitan, international city of Yokohama*
- *The Great Buddha at Kamakura*
- *Hakone's hot springs and Open Air Museum*
- *MOA Museum of Art in Atami, one of Japan's finest*
- *The quiet port town of Shimoda*
- *Nikko's ornate Toshogu Shrine*
- *The quiet hot spring resort and unique "exiles cuisine" of Yunishigawa*
- *The splendid ceramics museum in Ashikaga*
- *The studio of a charming ambassador of indigo dyeing near Ashikaga*

YOKOHAMA

Just 18 kilometers south of Tokyo, **Yokohama**, Japan's second largest city, is often overlooked next to high-profile Tokyo. The delightful cosmopolitan city faces the waterfront. And, as one of the first ports to reopen to foreigners (1859) after the long period of isolation, Yokohama's engaging history begs for further exploration.

American Commodore Mathew Perry landed with his Black Ships in Yokohama in 1854, one year after he demanded the Tokugawa shogunate open up Japan to trade. The shogunate complied. Yokohama soon grew into one of the largest ports in Asia and had a wild-west atmosphere. As port-of-call for American, European and Chinese ships, Yokohama soon became a very international city and remains so today.

ARRIVALS & DEPARTURES

Accessible by train from Tokyo, the trip takes a mere 30 minutes. You have the choice of the JR Keihin Tohoku line, JR Yokosuka line, JR Tokaido line, Tokyu Toyoko line and Keihin Kyuko line.

GETTING AROUND TOWN

Yokohama has excellent mass transit systems. There's a municipal subway, numerous train lines, buses and ferries.

The Blue Line, a double-decker bus system, provides convenient service for sightseeing. The route is Yokohama Station, Yokohama Museum of Art, Sakuragicho Station, City Hall, Chinatown, Harbor View Park and Bay Bridge. The return route is Bay Bridge, MYCAL Honmoku, Motomachi, Yokohama Doll Museum, Yamashita Park, Sakuragicho Station and Yokohama Station. The fare is ¥270 and a one-day pass costs ¥600.

A shuttle boat, Sea Bass, runs every 15 minutes between Yokohama Station and Yamashita Park. 10am to 6pm. ¥600.

Tourist Information

Yokohama has been an international city for so long that there is excellent information available in English. The tourist offices are at **Yokohama Station, Shin Yokohama Station** and Sakuragicho Station open daily from 10am to 6pm.

The **Central Information Office** is on the first floor of the Silk Center Building, a 15-minute walk from Kannai Station. Open 8:45am to 5pm weekdays and 8:45am to 1pm Saturdays, *Tel. (045)641-5824.*

All are "i" Tourist Information offices.

Home Visit

Contact the Tourist Information Offices listed above to arrange a visit to a Japanese home.

WHERE TO EAT
Chinatown
   MANCHINRO TENSHINPO *(Chinese dim sum, moderate). 156 Yamashita-cho. Tel. (045)664-4004. Open daily 10 am to 10pm.*
   Manchinro has to be one of the most popular dim sum restaurants in Chinatown. Even with a reservation, you'll probably end up waiting 15 to 30 minutes. Still, it's worth the hassle for the tasty dim sum. Manchinro serves more than 70 dishes: some of our favorites are shark fin *gyoza* dumplings, scallop *gyoza*, steamed shrimp dumplings, steamed tofu with shrimp and spring rolls. For ¥3500 to ¥4000, you'll have plenty to eat.
   SAIKO SHINKAN *(Chinese dim sum, inexpensive). 192 Yamashita-cho. Tel. (045)664-3155. Open 11:30am to 9pm. Closed 3rd Thursday.*
   This dim sum restaurant is another favorite. We especially like mixed rice wrapped and steamed in leaves and crab meat *gyoza*. You can order a dim sum set for ¥3000.

Minato Mirai
   LA VELA *(Italian, moderate). 2F, Intercontinental Hotel, 1-1-1 Minato Mirai, Nishi-ku. Tel. (045)223-2222. Open 11:30am to 2:30pm, until 5:30pm weekends; 5:30pm to 9:30pm.*
   This is a wonderful place to eat and take in the exhilarating views of Yokohama Bay through the large picture windows. The food is authentic Italian fare. The lunchtime set (¥3200) has a salad and appetizer buffet and a dessert buffet; you select your entree.

SEEING THE SIGHTS
Negishi Station Area
   Sankeien Garden. *Open daily 9am to 5pm. Closed December 29-31. ¥300 for outer garden and ¥300 for inner garden. From JR Negishi Station, take a bus 10 minutes to Honmoku stop. 6-minute walk. Or from JR Negishi Station, 7-minute taxi ride. Or from Yokohama Station's east exit, take bus #2 or #125 to Honmoku Sankeien mae (about 35 minutes).*
   Located in a highly industrialized area, Sankeien is an oasis of rolling green hills, ponds, bridges and traditional Japanese buildings. The wealthy silk merchant Hara Tomitaro founded Sankeien in 1906. The inner garden houses an excellent collection of historic buildings moved from all over Japan. Since Japanese houses are constructed of wood without using nails, they are easily moved from place to place. The Rinshunkaku is a villa of the Tokugawa shogun. The Juto Oido is one of the few buildings remaining from Tenzui-ji Temple in Kyoto, built by Hideyoshi in 1591. At the direction of the second Tokugawa shogun, the Choshukaku was constructed in 1623 for Fushimi castle. The Yanohara

house is an extremely well-preserved farmhouse. Sankeien is also famous for its flowering plants: plum, cherry, iris and water lilies and for colorful autumn foliage.

Sakuragicho Station Area

Minato Mirai 21 is a large, new futuristic development on the water complete with hotels, shopping, museums and an amusement park. A moving sidewalk whisks you — well, actually, crawls is more accurate — from JR Sakuragicho Station.

Among the park's attractions are:

Nippon Maru is a 29-sail tall ship constructed in 1930 as a training vessel. The graceful ship, as tall as a 12-storied building, is nicknamed the Swan of the Pacific. Now retired, it sits in dry dock and is open to the public. *Open 9am to 5pm. Closed Mondays and December 29-31. ¥600 (combined admission with Yokohama Maritime Museum).*

Next to the Nippon Maru is the **Yokohama Maritime Museum**, a beautifully laid-out underground museum that shows the history of the port of Yokohama from the time when Commodore Perry sailed his Black Ships and demanded Japan open trade. *Open 10am to 5pm; until 6:30 in July and August; until 4:30 in November and December. Closed Monday and December 29-31. ¥600 (combined admission with Nippon Maru).*

Yokohama Museum of Art (Yokohama Bijutsukan) houses art and photography from this century. *Tel. (045)221-0300. Open 10am to 6pm. Closed Thursday. ¥500 for permanent collection, additional charge for temporary exhibitions.*

Landmark Tower, a 70-storied skyscraper, is currently Asia's tallest building. The futuristic building looks like something from Sci-Fi movies. The 68th-floor Japanese restaurant Shikitei and Chinese restaurant Kouen both have fantastic nighttime views of the city and bay.

Cosmo World has some amusement rides left behind from the 1989 exposition. **Yokohama Gulliver Land**, under the world's largest wooden dome, sports a model of Yokohama in the 1960s and a futuristic view of the Minato Mirai project in 2010. The huge **Ferris wheel**, once the world's tallest, is here also. The 105-meter high wheel takes 15 minutes to go around once and offers great views from the top.

Kannai Station Area

Kanagawa Prefecture Museum of Cultural History (Kanagawa Kenritsu Rekishi Hakubutsukan). *5-60 Minaminaka Dori, Naka-ku. Tel. (045)201-0926. Open 9:30am to 5pm. Closed Monday, last Tuesday of the month and New Year's. Free. 8-minute walk from JR Kannai Station.*

It's a worthwhile stop just to see the fantastic 1904 Beaux Arts-style building — the oldest building extant in Yokohama, and there's an added bonus of the recently renovated museum that has excellent displays covering prehistory, the Kamakura period (the region's heyday), Edo culture, the Meiji era and modern Japan.

Yokohama Archives of History (Yokohama Kaiko Shiryokan). *3 Nihon Odori, Naka-ku. Tel. (045)201-2100. Open 9:30am to 5pm. Closed Monday and December 28 through January 4. ¥200.*

The archives, located at the site of the signing of the first friendship treaty between Japan and the US, is filled with exhibits showing Japan's encounter with the West during Yokohama's early days, the second half of the 19th century. History buffs will love it; all others should skip it.

Silk Center and Silk Museum. *1 Yamashita-cho, Naka-ku. Tel. (045)641-0841. Open 9am to 4:30pm. Closed Monday, last day of the month and New Year's. ¥300.*

Yokohama thrived on its silk industry at the turn of the century. There's a tourist information center on the first floor and a museum showing how to make silk is on the second and third floors. Buy your silk in the basement arcade.

Ishikawacho Station Area

Motomachi, accessible to Ishigawa-cho Station, catered to the foreign residents restricted to living in this area during Yokohama's early days. Today it is the city's toniest shopping district filled with boutiques, restaurants and bars. You can climb up the Bluff to **French Hill** (Furansu zaka) and **Harbor View Park** (Minato no Mieru Oka) for great views. The **Foreigner's Cemetery** (Gaijin Bochi) is a great place to wander and look at the tombstone inscriptions. *Open only Friday through Sunday in April and November, and Sunday and national holidays May through October.* The entire area has a very Western feel.

Yokohama Doll Museum (Yokohama Ningyo no Ie). *18 Yamashita-cho, Naka-ku. Tel. (045)671-9361. Open 10am to 5pm; until 6:30pm in July and August. Closed Monday and December 29 through January 1. ¥300. 13-minute walk from Ishikawacho Station.*

The museum features an excellent collection of dolls from all over the world. One room displays international dolls, another room Japanese. It's a delightful place for children or fans of dolls.

Yamashita Park, running along the waterfront for about one kilometer, is a great place for a stroll and some fresh sea air.

Chinatown is between Yamashita Park and Ishikawacho Station. The area is small but is packed with restaurants and shops selling Chinese goods. We've listed a couple of good restaurants under *Where to Eat*, but the best rule is to go to a place where people are standing in line.

YOKOHAMA'S THEME PARKS

Yokohama isn't all museums and parks – check out these theme parks:
WILD BLUE YOKOHAMA. *Tel. (045)511-2323. Open 10am to 9pm. ¥2900. From Tsurumi Station on JR Keihin Tohoku line, take a taxi for the 10-minute ride or the #16 bus from bus platform #5 to Heian Koko-mae bus stop.*

This indoor water park is great for older kids. Home to the longest indoor wave pool in the world, the waves change – some are good for boarding, others for swimming. The fan-shaped artificial beach even has lounge chairs. In addition to the standard beach, you'll find a waterway – a circular pool with constant current; a kiddies' lagoon – a shallow pool for infants; and a party lagoon – an outdoor pool with waterfall and water slides. And, because most of the park is under cover, you never have to worry about being rained out or sunburned. Try it on weekdays because weekends are crowded. And avoid the Japanese school holidays.

YOKOHAMA HAKKEIJIMA SEA PARADISE. Hakkeijima, Kanazawa-ku. Tel. (045)788-8888. Open daily 10am to 9pm but varies with the season. Aqua Museum: ¥2400. Rides: ¥300 to ¥1000. No admission charge to enter the island. Take the Keihin Kyuko line to Yokohama and change for the Seaside line to Hakkeijima. (55 minutes from Shinagawa Station).

A new theme park on a reclaimed island, Sea Paradise has a large aquarium with dolphin, seal and sea lion shows. Their signature Sea Tube has an escalator that forms a tunnel to travel through the huge fish tank. As you ascend, fish swim all around you. For an additional fee, the island also features amusement rides. There're lots of stores and a variety of restaurants. In case you have your yacht with you, there's even a marina.

Elsewhere in Yokohama

The **Skywalk** under the Yokohama Bay Bridge is not for the faint-hearted. An elevator carries you up to the observation deck where you walk along the Skywalk that's suspended under the bridge. At the end is the Sky Lounge where you can take in the spectacular panoramic view. When the weather is clear, you can see Mt. Fuji lording over the metropolitan area. *Tel. (045)506-0500. Open 9am to 8pm; 10am to 6pm November through March. Closed Tuesday. ¥600. The Blue Line double-decker bus stops here; from JR Sakuragicho Station, it's the last stop on the Skywalk bus.*

Yokohama Children's Science Center (Yokohama Kodomo Kagakukan). *5-2-1 Yokodai, Isogo-ku. Tel. (045)832-1166. Open 9:30am to 5pm. Closed Monday and December 28 through January 1. ¥400. Planetarium* *and Omnimax are each ¥600 extra. From Yokohama Station, take the JR Negishi line to Yokodai Station. 3-minute walk.*

The center puts science on a level that children can understand, and there're lots of hands-on exhibits and demonstrations about science and space. The space gym teaches about astronaut training, and the planetarium about space itself. Enjoy incredible films at the domed Omnimax theater where the seats are tilted at a 30° angle for maximum viewing pleasure.

Zoorasia, *1175-1 Kamishirane-cho, Asahi-ku. Tel: (045)959-1000. Open 9:30am to 4:30pm, until 6pm in summer. Closed Tuesday. ¥600. Take a bus from Tsurugamine or Mitsukyo stations on the Sotetsu line.*

Kids will love this new, wide-open zoo where the animals aren't kept in cages.

KAMAKURA

Kamakura was the shogun's capital from 1192 to 1333 and gave its name to the epoch. This small town, just a one-hour train ride south of central Tokyo, is the perfect place for a side trip. Surrounded on three sides by low mountains and on the fourth by the sea, verdant Kamakura feels a million miles from Tokyo. Most of Kamakura's residents commute to Tokyo, but the town is much more than just a suburb. It has an air of quiet greatness — over 100 temples, built in its heyday, still remain. Kamakura's most famous landmark is the **Daibutsu**, the Great Buddha, which stands 13 meters tall.

If you have at least three days in Tokyo, make sure you spend one of them in Kamakura. For those looking to stretch their legs, hiking trails in the hills link temples together. But there's also plenty to see in the flatlands.

ARRIVALS & DEPARTURES

The JR Yokosuka line leaves from Tokyo Station every 15 minutes. You can also board it at Shimbashi, Shinagawa and Yokohama Stations. The train takes about an hour from central Tokyo. Get off at Kamakura Station or Kita Kamakura Station.

Tourist Information

The **Tourist Information Office** ("i" Tourist Information) is located in Kamakura Station and has maps and brochures in English. Open daily 9am to 6pm, *Tel. (0467)22-3350.*

Goodwill Guide: To arrange a volunteer guide from the Kanagawa Student Guide Federation, in advance contact the Tokyo Tourist Information Center, *Tel. (03)3201-1331.* Available only on weekends.

WHERE TO EAT

Kamakura, a center for Zen Buddhism for hundreds of years, has many restaurants that serve vegetarian Buddhist food, *shojin ryori*. Try it in a peaceful setting. You don't have to eat only temple food. Restaurants dish up everything from French and Italian to Indian. Although most visitors to Kamakura come for the day and leave before eating dinner, some places require dinner reservations.

HISAGOTEI *(Tofu cuisine, moderate), 3-8-7 Komachi. Tel. (0467)24-1882. Open daily 11:30am to 4:30pm, 5:30pm-8pm. 15-minute walk from Kamakura Station.*

The chef, a tofu lover, prides himself on serving excellent tofu. You can get it here in every conceivable form: steamed, jellied, pureed and cooked with fish and seasonal vegetables. Located in a quiet area off Wakamiya-oji, the main drag, Hisagotei is a lovely restaurant where you can enjoy a relaxing meal while overlooking a green garden with many hydrangeas. The *Hagi-zen*, a seven course set, costs ¥5000.

MONZEN *(Buddhist vegetarian, moderate), 407 Yamanouchi. Tel. (0467)25-1121. Open daily 11am to 7:30pm.*

Monzen caters *shojin ryori* at Kencho-ji Temple for large annual religious rituals, so there's no question about its authenticity. A set meal consists of nine different dishes, rice and soup and costs ¥5000. We're always amazed how many different ingredients are used to create the famous Zen five tastes — sweet, sour, salty, hot and bitter; five different cooking methods — raw, simmer, fry, grill and steam; and five different colors — yellow, blue, red, white and black. Monzen serves you at tables or in Japanese rooms. No need to make a reservation.

SA-AMI *(Buddhist vegetarian, moderate), 2-4-4 Jomyoji. Tel. (0467)24-9420 Open 11am to 4pm. You can make reservations for dinner. Closed Thursday.*

Sa-ami is on the right as you approach Hokoku-ji, the Zen temple where the chef learned to prepare special Buddhist vegetarian cuisine. He selects each vegetable and carefully cuts, cooks and serves it. He uses time-consuming procedures to produce high-quality fare; it takes one night to make perfect *goma dofu* (sesame tofu). The seven course *Honzen* costs ¥4000. Order the *tenshin* set for vegetarian dim sum for ¥2000. The food is so healthy, we can't help but feel virtuous after eating here. It's best to make lunch reservations because Sa-ami is popular.

HACHINOKI *(Buddhist vegetarian, moderate), 7 Yamanouchi. Tel. (0467)22-8719. Open 11am to 2pm. Closed Monday.*

Hachinoki, which opened in the early 1960s, is one of the oldest *shojin ryori* restaurants in Kita Kamakura. The mother of the current owner was very creative with her vegetarian menus and the tradition continues.

Specialties include tofu with nuts and bamboo shoots cooked in an original sauce. The restaurant has a lovely garden setting. The set course, which changes monthly, offers seven different dishes, rice and soup for ¥3000. As it tends to sell out quickly, it's best to arrive before noon. Reservations accepted only from groups of ten or more. There's also a branch just a few minutes walk from Kita Kamakura station at *350 Yamanouchi, Kamakura.*

A RICCIONE *(Italian, inexpensive to moderate), B1, Komachi Building, 2-12-30 Komachi. Tel. (0467)24-5491. Open 11am to 3pm; 5:30pm-9:30pm. Closed Tuesdays.*

A branch of the Milan restaurant, A Riccione has delicious home-made pasta and lots of seafood. The wine list is quite extensive. Set meals run ¥1300-2500 and ¥4500 at dinner.

MONTE COSTA *(Italian, inexpensive to moderate), 1-5-7 Yukinoshita. Tel. (0467)23-0808. Open 11am to 8pm. Closed Monday and 3rd Tuesday.*

This older house combines traditional Japanese and Western architecture, creating a unique ambiance. All rooms look out onto a small garden. The chef goes to the market every morning to select the freshest seafood; he recommends patrons order a la carte. We love the herb marinated seafood, ¥1500. Italian *kaiseki* course costs ¥5000. Monte Costa is rather crowded at lunchtime; it is advisable to make a reservation. The restaurant is located just off Komachi Dori.

MIYOKAWA *(Kaiseki, inexpensive), 1-16-17 Hase, Kamakura. Tel. (0467)25-5556. Open daily 11am to 9pm.*

This elegant restaurant has surprisingly inexpensive lunch fare. The most popular set meal is *Hyotan Bento* at ¥2300, a lunch presented in a lacquered, gourd-shaped container. It's a treat for the eyes. You can eat at tables or in *tatami* mat rooms. Since Miyokawa is close to the Great Buddha, it is always crowded, so it's best to make reservations.

SEEING THE SIGHTS

A First-Trip Itinerary

Kamakura has 69 temples and 20 shrines, but for a first-time visit, we think it's best to limit yourself to just a few. One itinerary is to see the **Great Buddha**, **Hase Temple** and **Tsurugaoka Hachimangu Shrine**, leaving time to walk to the water's edge as well as browse in Kamakura's many antique and craft shops.

At Kamakura Station, you can either take a taxi (about a 10-minute ride; tell the driver "Daibutsu" — Die-boot-su) or a tram. To go by tram, do not leave Kamakura Station when you get off the train. Take the Enoden tram — you'll have to turn in your train tickets at a little window and buy a new ticket to Hase Station. Take the tram three stops to Hase

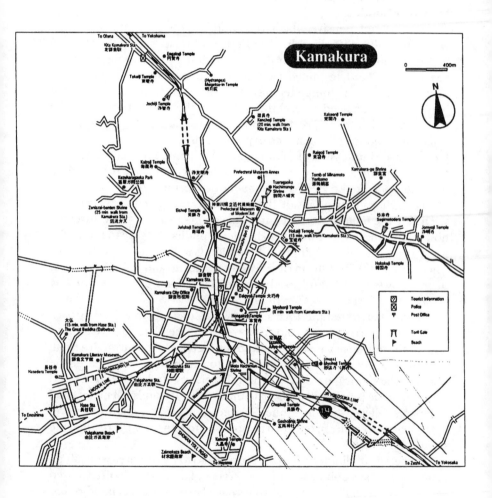

Kamakura

Station, about five minutes. We love this little tram that practically runs through the backyards of houses along the tracks.

At Hase Station, turn in your ticket and walk along the road towards the right for about four blocks until the souvenir shops end and a wooden gate is on your right. This gate is the entrance to **Kotoku-in**, which houses the **Great Buddha**.

Serene and pensive, the Great Buddha sits surrounded by the Kamakura hills. With the help of a priest, a court lady raised the funds to make a Buddha. Completed in 1243, it was destroyed in a storm not five years later. The determined lady once again raised funds and a new bronze Buddha was completed inside a large wooden hall in 1252. That building was damaged several times. Clearly the Buddha wanted to be outdoors, and in 1495 a great tidal wave swept away the wooden building. The Great Buddha has remained exposed to the elements ever since. His face gives the impression of calmness and discipline. You may notice that the statue seems ill proportioned from a distance, which is true because it was designed to be viewed from about five feet in front.

For ¥20, you can go inside the Buddha. There actually isn't much to see inside the hollow bronze figure, but you may want to try it. After all, how many other times can you go inside a Buddha? Be sure to notice the giant straw sandals hanging on the building wall next to the Buddha. These are for the Buddha in case he wants to get up and walk. To the best of our knowledge, he hasn't used them yet. *The temple is open daily from 7am to 6pm; until 5pm October through March. ¥200.*

As you exit the temple, turn left and walk along the street leading back to the tram. Turn right two blocks down; after one block, this road dead ends at the entrance gate of **Hase Kannon Temple**. Pass through a small garden with pond and climb the stairs to reach the main area of the temple. Hase's origins date to the 8th century and the eleven-faced Kannon statue is believed to predate the temple. It stands 9.3 meters and is Japan's tallest wooden statue. To the right of the main hall is an octagonal prayer wheel; one turn is supposed to be as good as reading the sutras in the hall.

Since you've climbed up all the stairs, walk over to the area with tables. From this vantage point you have a good view of the sea that's often dotted with windsurfers. There's a small snack bar where you can get noodles and sweets.

On the grounds of the temple you can't help noticing hundreds and hundreds of small statues, many with small bibs, toys and pinwheels. These are Jizo, the guardian of children, and are placed to pacify the spirits of children never born because of miscarriage and abortion. *Hase Kannon Temple is open 8am to 5pm. ¥300.*

Leave the temple and walk back to the main street; turn right and you will reach the Enoden tram that will take you back to Kamakura. If you want to see the beach, the same street will lead you toward Yuigahama Beach. Waikiki it isn't, but being one of the closest beaches to Tokyo means it's unbearably crowded with sunseekers and windsurfers in summer, especially on weekends. On sunny winter days, it's a lovely place to feel the warmth of the sun.

Retrace your steps to the tram to Kamakura Station.

At Kamakura station, use the east exit, the one on the right side of the station. As you exit to a large plaza with lots of buses, on the left there's a small street called **Komachi Dori**. Just before you come to Komachi Dori is **Toshimaya**, a shop usually crowded with Japanese buying their famous dove-shaped cookies, a mandatory souvenir from Kamakura. The smallest packet costs ¥450. Walk along Komachi Dori past antique and craft stores, tucked among other shops. It's also packed with restaurants, both traditional and modern, and lots of coffee shops where you can rest your tired feet.

Along this road, on the left is **Mon**, a comfortable coffee shop displaying works by local artists; **Yamago** selling bamboo craft items; and **Shato**, a tiny store stuffed with colorful Japanese *washi* paper and crafts. On the right past Shato is **Takahashi**, which sells bamboo baskets, garden gates and wooden garden tools.

When the stores along the road give way to greenery, turn right and you will reach the entrance to **Tsurugaoka Hachimangu Shrine**, founded by the Minamoto clan in 1063. Pass through the vermilion gate and you will reach a red drum-shaped bridge. In the old days, only the shogun was allowed to cross it. But you don't have to try negotiating the bridge's steep slopes because it's flanked by two flat bridges — how did the shogun do it?

When shogun Minamoto Yoritomo's wife, Hojo Masako, was pregnant, he ordered a grand boulevard constructed so the new prince could arrive in style for his blessing at the shrine. The large avenue, **Wakamiya Oji** (Young Prince Avenue), leads from the sea to the shrine. The median is planted with cherry trees and azaleas and is a favorite flower viewing place for Japanese.

Yoritomo's wife Masako was one of the most powerful women in Japanese history. Her husband and two sons died before her, so she and her father ran the country.

IN THE QUIET COURTYARD OF
TSURUGAOKA HACHIMANGU SHRINE

*Dramatic events in Japanese history occurred in the shrine's courtyard
– the area where there's a covered dance platform and steep, stone steps
leading to Tsurugaoka Hachimangu Shrine's main buildings. The shogun
Minamoto Yoritomo turned against his half-brother Yoshitsune, who
wasted no time fleeing. Yoritomo captured his brother's lover, Shizuka, a
beauty famed for her dancing. He ordered her to dance for him, and she
defiantly performed a dance praising her lover. Yoritomo was so angered
that he ordered her killed, but his wife Masako interceded to spare Shizuka's
life.*

*As you climb the steps, on your left is a huge ginko tree that also played
an important role in history. In 1219 the third Kamakura shogun was
assassinated there by a disgruntled nephew who was hiding behind the tree.
There were no heirs; the Kamakura shogunate ended! Power passed from
the Minamoto to the Hojo clan and Kamakura remained the capital. In the
autumn the tree's golden colors brighten up the area.*

In contrast to the spacious lower grounds, the actual shrine buildings
at the top of the steps are crowded together and not worth much time.
However, there are two museums on the shrine's lower grounds worth
visiting.

The first is the **Kanagawa Museum of Modern Art** (Kanagawa
Kenritsu Kindai Bijutsukan), which was designed by a Japanese disciple
of Le Corbusier. The museum holds Japanese and international contemporary art exhibits. *Tel. (0467)22-5000. Open 9:30am to 5pm. Closed
Monday. ¥800.*

The **Treasure House** (Kokuhokan) is on the opposite side of the
shrine's grounds. A stop here is a must for anyone interested in Kamakura-
era art; it houses sculptures and paintings, many belonging to the temples
scattered around Kamakura. The sculpture of this era was dynamic and
vigorous. *Tel. (0467)22-0753. Open 9am to 4pm. Closed Monday. ¥150.*

As you walk down Wakamiya Oji, stop to browse in the shops selling
the local specialty, Kamakura *bori* (carved lacquer ware). Turn right at
Kamakura Station to catch the train to Tokyo.

Overachiever's Itinerary – An Alternative Walking Tour

If you are filled with energy and want to see lots of temples, get an
early start and take the JR Yokosuka train to Kita Kamakura Station, one
stop before Kamakura. Near the station are three quiet temples:

Engaku-ji Temple is one of Kamakura's five great Zen temples. It goes back to 1282 and was built for the souls of the soldiers killed during Kublai Khan's invasion. Today it is only a shadow of its former self and most of the buildings are recent reconstructions. The large wooden gate, built in 1780, gives some hint of its former grandeur. The grounds are large with many subtemples, so allow yourself 30 to 60 minutes if you want to get a good feel for a Zen temple. The tiny Chinese-style Sharidan was built in 1285 and houses a relic from the Buddha. The wood joinery is simply fantastic. *Open 8am to 5:30pm; until 4pm in winter. ¥200.*

Tokei-ji Temple, founded in the 13th century, was known as the divorce temple. It was a Buddhist nunnery where women could seek refuge from abusive husbands. A man could divorce his wife by just writing a letter to her, but a woman did not have a similar right. After residing at Tokei-ji for three years, a woman was divorced. It was a sanctuary until the end of the Edo period. The narrow, stone steps leading to the temple gate lead to a small quiet garden. We can't ever visit without imagining those women who must have run up those steps knowing they would be safe if they reached the top. Today, women visit to pray to rid themselves of persistent unsuitable suitors and to find Mr. Right. *Open 8:30 daily am to 5pm; until 4pm November through February. ¥100 for the garden, ¥300 for the Treasure House.*

Meigetsu-in is also known as the Hydrangea temple because there are thousands of flowers that bloom in June. Masses of pink, blue, purple and white hydrangeas line the stone steps leading to the gate and to the garden. The bamboo groves accentuate the beauty of the flowers in the garden. There are also thousands of people who come to see them. If you want to see the temple at the height of its beauty, try to arrive early in the morning. At other times of the year, the temple is practically deserted. *Open daily 9 am to 4:30pm. ¥300.*

Walk along the main road for about 15 minutes from Kita Kamakura Station and you'll reach **Kencho-ji Temple**, the first and grandest of Kamakura's five great Zen temples and founded in 1253. The extensive grounds have many subtemples scattered about. To enjoy a lovely Japanese garden, go to Hojo, the abbot's quarters, which is the last of the main buildings in a straight line from the main gate, itself the finest wooden structure in Kamakura. Take off your shoes and walk along the wooden balcony that leads to the garden; its design is attributed to the priest Muso Kokushi who designed Tenryu-ji Temple in Kyoto. This garden incorporates bushes and trees and a pond. If you are full of energy, climb up the narrow, 245 steps and walk until you reach the peak of the hill. It's an exercise that Zen priests must have done for centuries; the breezes at the top feel so refreshing. *Open 8:30am to 4:30pm. ¥300.*

Leave Kencho-ji and continue to walk along the main road — it's busy and noisy, but there is no other way. In about 10 minutes you'll reach the upper part of **Tsurugaoka Hachimangu Shrine**, which is described in our first walking tour.

From the shrine, walk down wide Wakamiya Oji or Komachi Dori, which runs parallel and is the road to the right. When you reach Kamakura Station, catch the Enoden tram or take a taxi to the Great Buddha, following the course set out in the first walking tour.

Zeni-arai Benten & Hokoku-ji Temple

A couple of other favorite places in Kamakura are the following:

In the hills to the west of Hachimangu Shrine lies **Zeni-arai Benten**, a small, colorful shrine tucked in a mountain grotto. It's very popular with Japanese because it's believed that money washed there will double in value. There are even baskets to make the process easier. Yen or foreign money can be washed; next time we're going to try credit cards.

Hokoku-ji Temple was built at the end of the Kamakura period. The temple's bamboo garden, the ground covered by fallen bamboo leaves, is a little off-the-beaten path but a beautiful place to visit. We love to watch the rays of sunlight streaming through the thick foliage. You can sit and have a cup of tea in the serene setting. *From Kamakura Station take the #4 Keihin Kyuko bus. Get off at Jomyo-ji and walk for about five minutes. Open 9am to 4pm. ¥200.*

SHOPPING

Komachi Dori and **Wakamiya Oji** have shops selling antiques, bamboo crafts, Japanese paper and Kamakura *bori*, local lacquer ware.

Serious collectors of Japanese art should make an appointment to visit **House of Antiques**, a beautifully converted farmhouse, which is a store selling screens, furniture and other Japanese antiques. *Phone Mr. Takishita at (0467)43-1441. 5-15-5 Kajiwara, Kamakura.*

HAKONE & MT. FUJI

A mere hour southwest of Tokyo, **Hakone** is the city's playground. Tokyo's urban sprawl suddenly stops at the mountains. Tokyoites go there to breathe clean air and get back in touch with nature. The resort area has something for everyone: hiking, boating, hot springs, golfing, art museums and splendid views of **Mt. Fuji**.

You can make Hakone a one-day trip, but start early to get the most out of your day. If you can spare the time, Hakone is a good place to stay overnight to see what a Japanese hot spring area is all about.

Odakyu Sightseeing Service Center. Odakyu Railway Company has set up a special information desk catering to foreign travelers. Here you can get assistance in English, buy rail tickets and Free Passes to Hakone and other destinations, book hotels, inns and Odakyu tours. Okakyu has developed several tours geared to foreign travelers: one and two day self-guided trips to Hakone and Kamakura with detailed information in English. *The Center is on the ground floor of the West Exit of Shinjuku Station, near the ticket barrier for the Okakyu trains. Tel: (03)5321-7887, Fax. (03)5321-7886. www.odakyu-group.co.jp/english. Open daily 8am to 6pm.*

ARRIVALS & DEPARTURES

Hakone is a large area covering many mountains and towns. The most convenient gateway is the town of **Hakone Yumoto**.

The fastest way to get to Hakone, and the recommended route for rail pass holders, is to take the JR *Kodama* (local) shinkansen train from Tokyo Station to Odawara, about 30 minutes, and change for the Odakyu private rail line to Hakone Yumoto, 10 minutes. The less expensive Tokaido local train takes 1 hour and 30 minutes from Tokyo Station to Odawara.

If you aren't using a rail pass, the best way to Hakone is to take the private Odakyu train line from Shinjuku Station to Hakone Yumoto. The Romance Car (their name, not ours) is an all-reserved-seat express that takes 1 hour 25 minutes to Hakone Yumoto. The Odakyu express to Odawara takes 90 minutes; then it's another 10 minutes to Hakone Yumoto; some of the trains go all the way through to Hakone Yumoto.

One word of warning: Traffic on Hakone's narrow mountain roads often backs up on weekends and holidays. If you have the choice of taking a bus or train, opt for the train. We have inched along in buses for hours; it sure is frustrating. If you have the option, go midweek.

Hakone Free Pass

If you plan to travel around the Hakone area, purchase the **Hakone Free Pass** or the **Hakone Weekday Pass** available at Odakyu train ticket offices and through travel agents. (See Odakyu Sightseeing Service Center above.) Even if you are going to Hakone for only one day, you won't have to buy separate tickets for all the different conveyances. If you plan to go to Hakone and only spend time at Hakone Yumoto, you don't need to buy the pass.

The Free Pass is good for travel for three days on Odakyu trains, the Hakone Tozan Railway, the Sounzan cable car, the Hakone Ropeway, the boat on Lake Ashinoko and Hakone Tozan buses. The Weekday Pass is good for two days of travel Monday through Friday on these same modes of transportation. JR rail pass holders should buy the Hakone pass to start in Odawara: the Free Pass costs ¥4130 and the Weekday Pass ¥3410. If you are starting your travel from Shinjuku Station, the Free Pass costs ¥5500 and the Weekday Pass ¥4700; each includes round-trip transportation on the Odakyu line from Shinjuku Station. The Odakyu's Romance Car surcharge is an additional ¥850 each way. Free Pass and Weekday Pass holders are entitled to small admission discounts at many museums.

Tourist Information

The **Hakone Tourist Information Office** is about one block from Hakone Yumoto Station. Go out the exit onto the plaza and walk up the main road; Tourist Information is on the left, next to the Fire Station. Open daily 9am to 5pm, *Tel. (0460)5-5700*. They have a lot of information in English and have English-speaking staff members ("i" Tourist Information Office).

Goodwill Guides: Contact the Tourist Information Office listed above for the current contact number to arrange a volunteer goodwill guide.

WHERE TO STAY

Virtually all hotels and inns in the Hakone area have hot springs. Hakone's terrain was created by volcanic eruptions and hot spring villages are scattered around a fairly large area. To really enjoy the place, try to stay at one that has a *rotemburo* open air bath.

NARAYA RYOKAN, *162 Miyanoshita, Hakone, Ashigarashimo-gun, Kanagawa, 250-0404. Tel. (0460)2-2411, Fax (0460)7-6231. Rates from ¥25,000 per person with two meals. Credit cards.*

This elegant Japanese *ryokan* in a beautiful and spacious garden setting is in perfect harmony with the surrounding mountains. And if that wasn't enough, the *kaiseki* food is a real treat. The 20-room inn goes back several hundred years, but the current buildings were built about a century ago. The hotel has a loyal following of dignitaries and ordinary people who come back again and again.

FUJIYA HOTEL, *359 Miyanoshita, Hakone, Ashigarashimo-gun, Kanagawa, 250-0404. Tel. (0460)2-2211, Fax (0460)2-2210. Singles from ¥12,000. Twins from ¥20,000. Ask for their special rate for foreigners, currently a twin is $121. Credit cards.*

The Fujiya was the first Western-style hotel built in Japan and is a hybrid of Japanese and Western architectural styles. If you like faded glory, Fujiya is for you. The hotel shows its age, which is what we find charming about it. The dining room is from the 1930s and is a pleasant place to have lunch or dinner. The rooms have Japanese details like coffered ceilings and *shoji* screens; the old fashioned furniture may remind you of your grandmother's. We find Fujiya, nestled in the side of a mountain, a pleasant getaway.

ICHINOYU, *90 Tonosawa, Hakone, Ashigarashimo-gun, Kanagawa, 250-0315. Tel. (0460)5-5331, Fax (0460)5-5335. From ¥9800 per person with two meals. Credit cards.*

Ichinoyu is a rambling wooden inn along the river's edge. The current buildings are about 100 years old but the inn itself, Hakone's oldest, goes back over 350 years. They are very proud that the shogun paid them a visit. It's a delightful, unpretentious old inn.

TAMAKI, *1300 Gora, Hakone, Ashigarashimo-gun, Kanagawa, 250-0408. Tel. (0460)2-3103, Fax (0460)2-3104. From ¥13,000 per person with two meals. Credit cards. 4-minute walk from Gora Station.*

A large red Japanese umbrella greets you at the entrance, rain or shine. Tamaki is a small Japanese inn with only 12 rooms. The proprietress gives her personal attention to the guests. The garden has huge mountain cherry trees. The inn pays attention to small details: at the outdoor bath, the bamboo baskets for clothes match the bamboo roof. The homestyle *kaiseki* cooking tops off your stay.

MOTO HAKONE GUEST HOUSE, *103 Moto-Hakone, Hakone, Ashigarashimo-gun, Kanagawa, 250-0522. Tel. (0460)3-7880, Fax (0460)4-6578. Singles ¥5000. Twins ¥10,000. Member of the Japanese Inn Group and Welcome Inn Reservation Center.*

This centrally located small inn is close to Lake Ashinoko in Moto Hakone. With only five rooms, it's like staying in someone's home. The Japanese-style accommodations are simple, but good value for the economy-minded traveler.

FUJI HAKONE GUEST HOUSE, *912 Sengokuhara, Hakone, Ashigarashimo, Kanagawa, 250-0631. Tel. (0460)4-6577, Fax (0460)4-6578. Singles from ¥5000. Twins from ¥10,000. Credit cards. Member of Japanese Inn Group and Welcome Inn Reservation Center.*

The Fuji Hakone Guest House is a little far off-the-beaten track, but is a comfortable Japanese-style inn. It's a small house set back from the road and is a good budget choice.

WHERE TO EAT

HATSUHANA *(Noodles, inexpensive), Yumoto. Tel. (0460)5-8287. Open 10am to 7pm. Closed Tuesday.*

Located at the foot of Yumoto Bridge, Hatsuhana is one of Hakone's most famous *soba* shops. The specialty is *soba* with grated mountain potatoes. It's so popular that 20 kilos of mountain potatoes are used each day. *Seiro soba* costs ¥900; *yamakake soba* ¥950.

SHIKAJAYA *(Tofu cuisine. inexpensive), 6-minute walk from Yumoto Station. Tel. (0460)5-5751. Open 11am to 2:30pm. Closed Thursday.*

Shikajaya's specialty is tofu, and it's so good, they serve Soun-ji Temple monks. All food is freshly cooked after you order. *Shika-tenshin,* the most popular set, consists of tofu steak with *miso* sauce, rice and soup, ¥2300; a set with more dishes is ¥3200.

JURAKU *(Tempura, inexpensive), Miyanoshita. Tel. (0460)2-2318. Open 11am to 3pm; 5pm-8pm. Closed 1st and 3rd Mondays.*

Juraku, a Miyanoshita *tempura* shop, is close to Hakone Shrine and the Fujiya Hotel. *Tendon* costs ¥1300, *Tempura teishoku* set is ¥2500.

PICKOT *(Bakery, inexpensive), Miyanoshita. Tel. (0460) 2-2211. Open daily 10:30am to 5:30pm.*

This bakery is located just in front of Fujiya Hotel and sells the Fujiya Hotel's famous bread. Pick up some bread and sandwiches for a quick lunch.

SEEING THE SIGHTS

Hakone's transportation system lends itself to taking a circular route that covers a number of terrains and sights as well as lots of different modes of transportation: train, cable car, ropeway, boat and bus. You can do this route in one day if you leave Tokyo by 8am, but you will not have time to see all the museums listed.

From Hakone Yumoto, take the **Hakone Tozan Railway**. This little train has switchbacks to negotiate the steep mountain slopes; it takes 50 minutes to go 15 kilometers. The motorman runs from one end of the train to the other every time there's a switchback. As the train passes through the deeply forested areas, it almost touches hydrangeas, azaleas and other flowering bushes along the tracks.

The Hakone Tozan Railway's Miyanoshita Station is convenient to the **Fujiya Hotel**, Japan's first Western-style hotel and built in 1878. You can eat lunch in the wood-paneled, 1930s dining room; it's like stepping back in time. Across the street from the hotel are several Japanese antique shops, a holdover from the days when most of the visitors were foreigners. One is S.M. Shiba; it's been serving foreign visitors for over 100 years.

Miyanoshita also offers a wonderful outdoor hot spring bath, **Shizenkan**, where you soak on the side of a hill in a heavily wooded area overlooking the river gorge. It's a little difficult to locate. As you come out the driveway of the Fujiya Hotel, turn left onto the main road. Just after the road forks you stay to the right; the entrance path is beyond a small parking lot. *Tel. (0460)2-0265. Open 10am to 8pm. ¥2500. Since they limit the number of bathers, you must make a reservation on weekends, and it's advised on weekdays.*

Continue on the train to the Chokoku no Mori stop. Slightly up the hill to the left of the station is the **Hakone Open Air Museum** (Chokoku no Mori) — a wonderful mountaintop site that blends beautiful natural scenery with modern sculpture. This museum alone is worth a trip to Hakone. Works by Rodin, Moore, Miro, Calder, Debuffet, Brancusi and other 20th century masters grace the lawns, and there's an entire Henry Moore area. Pavilions house sculptures not suited for outdoor exposure, and there's a playground where kids can touch and play on sculptures. The Picasso pavilion displays oil paintings, sculptures, tiles and plates, demonstrating Picasso's versatility and energy. *Tel. (0460)2-1161. Open 9am to 5pm, March through October; until 4pm November through February. ¥1600.*

Return to the train station and ride one stop to Gora, the end of the line. Take the cable car to Koen-kami Station. The **Hakone Art Museum** is just a two-minute walk. This museum, a sister to the MOA Museum in Atami, is devoted to Japanese ceramics and tea ceremony wares. The collections of prehistoric Jomon pottery as well as Bizen pottery are impressive. Although small, the beautifully landscaped Japanese-style Shinsenkyo Garden has maple trees, a bamboo grove and a teahouse. The garden's ground is covered with soft moss. *Tel. (0460)2-2623. Open 9am to 4pm. Closed Thursday. ¥900.*

Take the cable car to the top of the mountain, Sounzan. The nearby **Hakone Sounzan Art Museum** houses the unlikely combination of Henry Moore prints and Chinese porcelain. *Open 9am to 5pm; until 4pm November through March. Closed Tuesday. ¥1000.*

At Sounzan, board the Hakone Ropeway for a tummy-wrenching ride over a large gorge. It's not for those who have a fear of heights. Get off at **Owakudani**, literally "large boiling hell," where the terrain resembles a moonscape. Hakone has a long history of volcanic eruptions and the last eruption occurred here. The air is heavy with the sulfuric stench that's reminiscent of rotten eggs, and you'll wonder what suddenly happened to the verdant forest. There's a short, walking trail through the surreal landscape. You can also buy eggs that have been boiled in the gurgling hot spring water. Local lore says eating one will extend your life for seven years. The **Natural Science Museum** is a good place to take the kids; you can see a volcanic eruption on film. *Tel. (0460)4-9149. Open 9am to 4pm; until 4pm December through February. ¥400.*

Continue on the ropeway down the mountain to **Lake Ashinoko**. If you're lucky, you'll be able to see the elusive Mt. Fuji from the gondola as you come down the mountain. At the lake, board the tacky faux pirate ship. Despite the touristy kitsch of your conveyance, it's a lovely cruise across the large Lake Ashinoko, which is surrounded by mountains. On the left shore of the lake, the red *torii* gate in the water belongs to Hakone Shrine. This gate is one of the most photographed sights in Hakone; don't be surprised when the cameras start clicking. Get off the boat at Hakone Machi.

Near Hakone Machi is the **Hakone Checkpoint** (Hakone Sekisho), a replica of the building that stood there during the Edo period when

HOT SPRING BATHING IN HAKONE YUMOTO

Even if you come to Yumoto just for the day, top off your trip with an outdoor hot spring bath; Yumoto offers several open to the public. It's best to bring your own towel, but if you don't have one, you can buy a small, thin one similar to a kitchen towel, at the front desk for about ¥200.

Kappa Tengoku is on the hill above Hakone Yumoto Station. Exit into the small plaza where taxis line up and take the small road under the tracks. Immediately turn right and walk up the steep hill; Kappa is on the left. Kappa Tengoku is an older place with a stone outdoor bath set among trees. Tel. (0460)5-6121. Open 10am to 10pm. ¥700.

Yuzo has a large indoor bath and a small outdoor bath. It's pleasant but since it's on the main drag, the outdoor bath doesn't have views of nature. From Hakone Yumoto Station, walk up the main street. Yuzo is several blocks up on the right; the Ebisu bridge bears off to the left and in front of Yuzo, a small street comes out at a sharp angle on the right. Yuzo does not have a sign marked in English. The building is white stucco and has diagonal tiles on the ground floor. Its restaurant serves reasonably priced Japanese meals. You can also stay there; rooms cost ¥15,000 per person with two meals. The bath is open 10am to 9pm. Closed Wednesday. ¥1300.

Tenzan has two separate baths; to the right is a newer wooden bath that's half indoors and half outdoors, and to the left is a rock bath entirely outdoors plus four other baths. Tenzan is very popular on weekends so it's best to come first thing in the morning. Tenzan's restaurant serves shabu-shabu for ¥2300 and tenzanyaki (teppanyaki) for ¥1800 on the first floor. The second floor has less expensive noodles and snack foods. Tenzan is about a 15-minute walk from Hakone Yumoto Station, near the Oku Yumoto Iriguchi bus stop. Tel. (0460)5-7446. Open daily 9am to 11pm. The admission policy is a little tricky. It costs ¥900 to enter either the baths on the right or the ones on the left. If you want to try them both, pay an additional ¥200.

people's right to travel was severely restricted by the shogunate. This spot was a major barrier on the Tokaido Road that linked Edo (Tokyo) to Kyoto. Since mountains were on all sides, it was difficult and dangerous to get off the road. The shogunate especially wanted to be sure that wives and children of feudal lords required to live in Edo, essentially as hostages, didn't sneak home. The checkpoint dates to 1619. The adjacent exhibition hall shows the history of the Tokaido Road. *Open 9am to 4:30pm; until 4pm December through February. ¥300.*

Along the lake beyond the checkpoint are several hundred cryptomeria trees planted by the shogunate in 1618. If the weather cooperates, this is one of the best places to photograph Mt. Fuji.

From Moto Hakone, take the Tozan bus back to Hakone Yumoto. The main road in town is lined with shops selling crafts, sweets and pickles.

Other Sights

Hatajuku Yosegi Hall (Hatajuku Yosegi Kaikan). A specialty of Hakone is *yosegi*, a wood inlaid mosaic made into all sorts of objects like boxes, chests and bookmarks. Every shop in Hakone sells them, but at Yosegi Hall you can see the process. *Yosegi* make an unusual souvenir. *Tel. (0460)5-8170. Open 9am to 5pm. Closed at New Year's. Free admission. Hatajuku bus stop.*

Amazake Jaya, near Yosegi Hall, is a rustic country-style place good for a drink and rest. The specialty is *amazake*, a nonalcoholic offshoot of *sake* rice wine.

Yutopia. The name is a play on words. *Yu* is Japanese for hot water. And it does provide the ultimate bathing experience. Yutopia is a bathing theme park. There's an herb bath, a coffee bath, a waterfall bath, a foot-massage bath, a *sake* rice wine bath, a lavender-scented bath, and a large swimming pool filled with hot spring water. Altogether, there are twenty different baths and pools. Wear a bathing suit. Rent a bath towel for ¥200. *Tel. (0460)2-4111. Open 9am to 6:30pm. ¥2600. From Hakone Yumoto take the Tozan train to Kowakudani or bus to Kowaki-en.*

SHOPPING

Hakone is filled with shops selling *yosegi* inlaid wooden boxes and other crafts. One especially nice shop is **Taichido** in Hakone Yumoto; it sells wooden *daruma* dolls, the roly-poly dolls that evolved from a priest who meditated so long his legs and arms atrophied. *Tel. (0460)5-7051. Open 9am to 5pm.*

EXCURSIONS & DAY TRIPS
CLIMBING MOUNT FUJI

The Japanese have an expression: Everyone must climb **Mt. Fuji** once, but only a fool would do it twice.

Long the symbol of Japan, the 3,776 meter Mt. Fuji is the country's tallest peak. A Shinto shrine graces the summit of the dormant volcano. Mt. Fuji, or *Fuji-san* as the Japanese call it, first erupted 8,000 years ago. The most recent eruption was in the early 18th century.

The graceful mountain, beautiful to view from afar, changes with the seasons and may be one reason why the Japanese glory in seasonal variety. Fuji in winter is blanketed with snow, and in summer, the mountain takes on a bluish hue. The date of the first snowfall in September is an eagerly waited event reported on TV and in newspapers.

Mt. Fuji has different profiles. The view from the Pacific Ocean is considered the front. This view is the one you see from the *shinkansen* train from Tokyo to Kyoto. Some people prefer the opposite view.

Despite Fuji-san's distant beauty, the climb up it isn't at all attractive. Volcanic ash covers much of the terrain. But it's worth the climb for the spectacular view from the summit. The mountain isn't an especially difficult climb — every year some octogenarians do it — but you need to be physically fit.

The mountain has rest areas called stations, and today a road goes up to the fifth station. After that, you're on your own. The most popular hiking trail leaves from the fifth station and takes from five to seven hours to reach the peak.

Many people try to reach the peak in the early morning to see the breathtaking sunrise. One way to do this is to climb most of the way early in the day and spend the night at a mountain hut. Then you get up at about 3am to finish the climb. An alternative is to start your climb at around 9pm and climb all night. You should reach the peak before sunrise.

The climbing season runs from July 1 to August 31. The 25 mountain huts are open only during this period. Before and after, the danger of a heavy snowfall is too great although, out of season, some hearty types do climb up with skis attached to their backs. Make sure you have good hiking boots, a long-sleeved shirt and pants, rain gear, a flashlight, plenty of water and warm clothing including a jacket — even if it's warm at the fifth station, you still can get snow at the top.

A favorite souvenir is a walking stick bought at the fifth station for ¥1000 and stamped at every station on your way up. Another is to buy a can of Mt. Fuji summit air.

A few words of warning: the mountain huts are simple with *futon* mattresses placed on the floor. No one is turned away, so you may have less than one *futon* to yourself. Also, Mt. Fuji is very crowded, especially on weekends. Be prepared to be part of an endless line snaking its way toward the summit.

Getting to Fuji

By bus: Kawaguchiko is the jumping off place to reach Mt. Fuji's fifth station. Buses to Kawaguchiko run frequently from platform #50 at the Shinjuku Highway Bus Terminal across the street from Keio Department Store at the west exit of Shinjuku Station. Fare ¥1700 one way.

By train: Take the JR Chuo line to Otsuki where you change to the Fuji Kyuko line. The trip takes 2 hours to 2 hours 30 minutes, depending on which train you are on. The fare is ¥4000 for limited express trains and ¥2370 for rapid trains. If you have a rail pass, you have to pay the fare on the private Fuji Kyuko line: ¥1110.

From Kawaguchiko to the fifth station, called Fuji-san gogome, there are six buses a day and more on weekends. Fare ¥1700 one way.

Direct bus from Tokyo's Shinjuku Station to the fifth station operates daily between July 10 and August 31 and on weekends and holidays from September 1 through November 23. The trip takes 2 hours 30 minutes; there are only three buses a day. Reservations are required. Contact Fuji Kyuko Reservation Center, *Tel. (03)3374-2221.* Travel agents can also book seats. ¥2600.

ATAMI

A hot spring seaside resort town on the Izu Peninsula, **Atami** is only 45 minutes south of Tokyo Station by *shinkansen* train. It has an excellent museum of Japanese art, the MOA Museum, and a fantastic Japanese inn, Horai. But besides these, the city is entirely skippable.

Tokyoites used to visit a once quiet Atami for the mild winter weather. But, in the late 1950s, large nondescript hotels and condos began to be built, ruining the natural beauty of the area. You'll find *pachinko* parlors, bars and red-light districts. Many of the numerous inns and hotels cater to the peculiarly Japanese practice of company overnight outings when all the employees eat, drink and sing karaoke as part of the bonding ritual. These outings are regarded as one of the required annual events, like Christmas parties in America.

ARRIVALS & DEPARTURES

The *Kodama* (local) shinkansen train runs from Tokyo Station to Atami and takes 45 minutes. If you are using a rail pass, this train is the best way. The *Odoriko* and Super View *Odoriko* limited expresses from Tokyo or Shinjuku Stations cost nearly the same as the shinkansen but take 1 hour 15 minutes. The Super View trains have extra large windows on the side facing the sea. The least expensive alternative is the Acty train that runs from Tokyo or Shinagawa Stations and takes 1 hour 30 minutes.

Tourist Information

The "i" Tourist Information Office is at Atami Station View Plaza, *Tel. (0557)81-6002.*

WHERE TO STAY

Atami has a fabulous top-of-the-line Japanese inn, Horai. If this isn't what you are looking for, we recommend that you don't spend the night in Atami. The hotels are right on top of each other, huge concrete boxes with little to recommend them. Hakone is not far away or you can head for Shimoda, at the tip of the Izu peninsula.

HORAI, *750 Izusan, Atami, Shizuoka, 413-0002. Tel. (0557)80-5151, Fax (0557)80-0205. From ¥41,000 per person with two meals. Credit cards.*

Horai is an elegant Japanese inn on a hill overlooking Sagami Bay. With only 16 rooms, including five separate cottages, guests are pampered in fine style. The outdoor hot spring bath, protected by a wooden roof, offers a wonderful view of the sea. For more information, see Horai in Chapter 11, our Best Places to Stay.

SEEING THE SIGHTS

The main reason to visit Atami is to see the **MOA Museum of Art** (MOA Bijutsukan). It's a monument to an egomaniac, Okada Mokichi, who founded a religion based on the premise that man can best discover his spiritual self when surrounded by beautiful objects. And surround himself he did. In the 1940s, Okada bought up masterpieces of Japanese and Chinese art and later built a monument to house them that combines technology and art. MOA stands for Mokichi Okada Association (Okada is the family name). The whole thing sounds like a great tax dodge, but the collection and setting are superb.

From Atami Station, take a bus from platform #4 or taxi to the museum; either will take under 10 minutes. Built on a hillside, you enter the museum from the lowest level. Humongously long escalators, actually 203 meters long, take you up the mountain until you reach a strange circular hall where a laser show is seen periodically throughout the day.

Continue up another escalator until you reach the Henry Moore Plaza where the outdoor Moore statue is on a bluff; take in the great views of the sea. The beautifully designed main hall of the museum has floor-to-ceiling windows designed to take in the exhilarating view.

The museum itself has many superb works of Japanese art including the Rimpa school artist Ogata Korin's 18th century *Red and White Plum Blossoms*. To preserve the delicate screen, it is only on display from the end of January until the end of February, the same time the plum trees blossom. On display year round is Nonomura Ninsei's elegant *Wisteria Design Tea Jar*. The extensive collection also has paintings, calligraphy and sculpture and exquisite Chinese Sung Dynasty celadon ceramics. The museum also has a small collection of Western paintings that includes a Rembrandt and a few Monets.

Okada was a tea connoisseur and the museum has lots of tea utensils as well as a replica of Hideyoshi's gaudy, golden teahouse. On the extensive museum grounds is a replica of Ogata Korin's Kyoto home and teahouse and a restaurant serving *kaiseki* cuisine using food grown on the MOA's organic farm. *Tel. (0557)84-2511. Open 9am to 5pm. Closed Thursday and at New Year's. ¥1500.*

If you visit the museum in February and are inspired by Korin's magnificent Plum Blossom screen, you can go to **Atami Plum Garden** (Atami Baien), on a nearby hill, to see hundreds of plum blossoms. Atami's mild climate means plums start blooming as early as December.

SHIMODA

South of Tokyo, near the tip of the Izu Peninsula is the historic town of **Shimoda**. It's of special interest to Western visitors because in 1854, **Commodore Matthew Perry** arrived with his American Black Ships and negotiated with Japanese officials to open Japan to trade after a two-hundred year period of isolation. Shimoda was one of the first two ports open to foreigners. The first American consul, Townsend Harris, established his residence here in 1856.

Shimoda also has hot springs and many buildings with an attractive old style of architecture called *namako-kabe,* diamond shaped black tiles outlined with white plaster.

ARRIVALS & DEPARTURES

The JR limited express *Odoriko* train and the Super View *Odoriko* train take 2 hours 25 minutes to reach Shimoda from Tokyo or Shinjuku Station. The Super View has large windows and costs more; it is an all-reserved-seat train. You can also take the Izu Kyuko Railway from Atami and Ito City.

Tourist Information

Near Izukyu Shimoda Station, Shimoda's **tourist information office** has lots of information in English. *Tel. (0558)22-1531.*

Goodwill Guides: Contact the Tokyo Tourist Information Center, *Tel. (03)3201-3331,* for the current contact number to arrange a volunteer goodwill guide.

WHERE TO STAY

KOMURASAKI, *1-5-30 Nishi Hongo, Shimoda, Shizuoka, 415-0036. Tel. (0558)22-2126, Fax (0558)22-2127. ¥35,000 per person with two meals. Diners Club and Amex.*

Our friends who recommended this tiny charming inn wanted to keep it a secret. Komurasaki has only five rooms all facing the well-kept Japanese garden. Each room has a *rotemburo* (an outdoor hot spring bath) on the balcony for private bathing. In the bathroom there's also a wooden bath tub from which you can admire the garden through the large windows. The owner, a charming and friendly woman, is attentive to the needs of her guests. It's only three minutes from Shimoda Station, but the owner is happy to pick you up if you telephone.

ISHIBASHI RYOKAN, *185-1 Rendai-ji, Shimoda, Shizuoka, 415-0031. Tel. (0558)22-2222, Fax (0558)22-2121. From ¥15,000 per person with two meals. Credit cards.*

Ishibashi Ryokan has spa facilities such as whirlpool and steam baths plus an outdoor bath.

KANAYA RYOKAN, *114-2 Kouchi, Shimoda, Shizuoka, 415-0011. Tel. (0558)22-0325, Fax (0558)23-6078. From ¥15,000 per person with two meals; ¥7000 without meals. No credit cards.*

Kanaya has the largest bath tub in the Izu Peninsula, and there are a lot of bath tubs in Izu! The wooden tub is 15 meters by 5 meters.

MINSHUKU HAJI, *708 Sotoura, Shimoda, Shizuoka, 415-0013. Tel. (0558)22-2597, Fax (0558)23-1064. From ¥5000 per person with two meals. No credit cards. Member of Welcome Inn Reservation Center.*

Haji, a simple inn located in a beach area called Sotoura, is run by a man who speaks English. It's a ten-minute bus ride from Shimoda Station.

WHERE TO EAT

Fish is what you eat in Shimoda, fish so fresh it probably was swimming in the morning.

NAKAGAWA *(Japanese, inexpensive,. 1-12-17 Shimoda. Tel. (0558)22-0310. Open 11am to 9pm. 10-minute walk from Shimoda Station.*

This restaurant, decorated with rustic folk art, has a very friendly staff. Fish is the specialty. The *tempura teishoku* (¥1500) is delicious as is the deep fried *kinmedai karaage* (tasty red snapper), ¥1300.

KIYUU *(Japanese, inexpensive), Renjaku-cho Dori. Tel. (0558)22-8698. Open 11am to 9pm. 5-minute walk from the station.*

The proprietors tell us that their fish is the freshest in Shimoda, but we are wondering who is counting the nano-seconds. The *sashimi teishoku* sets cost ¥1300 and ¥1600, and yes, the fish is delicious. If you want your fish cooked, try the *tempura teishoku,* ¥1500. *Omakase* set (chef's special) is ¥3000.

SEEING THE SIGHTS

Shimoda is a small town where most of the sights can be reached on foot.

To see what these feared Black Ships are all about, you can take a 20-minute ride on a replica of Perry's boat, the **Susquehanna**. Given the size of today's aircraft carriers, it's hard to believe that this ship could have evoked such panic. *Boats depart between 9:30am and 3:30pm. ¥920.*

Gyokusen-ji Temple is where American consul Townsend Harris and his translator Henry Heusken lived in 1856–7. The site reverted to a Zen temple after Harris left. A hall on the temple's grounds displays documents in English and Japanese. You'll also find a sign erected in Japanese and English to commemorate the first cow killed to be eaten in Japan; it was for Harris' consumption.

Ryosen-ji Temple is where Commodore Perry negotiated with officials of the Tokugawa shogunate to arrange the US Peace Treaty signed in 1854. The treasure hall houses documents about this period. Nearby Choraku-ji Temple is where the Japan-America Peace Treaty ratifications were exchanged and the Japan-Russia Peace Treaty was signed in 1854.

Hofuku-ji Temple is where the courtesan Tojin Okichi is buried. Assigned to be Harris' attendant in 1857, she was dismissed after three days because of a skin ailment. Chastised for being rejected by a foreign barbarian, she lived out her days in shame. Okichi committed suicide in 1890. The temple displays Okichi's personal effects. *Open daily 8am to 5pm. ¥300.*

Anchokuro is the restaurant Okichi established in 1882; it is in business today as a *sushi* shop. The second floor rooms are preserved and some of Okichi's belongings are on display. *Open 10am to 10pm. ¥200.*

Zushu Shimoda History Museum is a well-designed museum with attractive exhibits chronicling Shimoda's past. It's a must for history buffs. *Tel. (0558)23-2500. Open 8:30am to 5pm. ¥1000.*

For a change of pace from all this history, head to the **Shimoda Floating Aquarium** (Shimoda Kaichu Suizokkan), a ten-minute bus ride from Shimoda Station. The aquarium floats so you can see fish swimming in their native habitats. The aquarium also features dolphin shows and feeding sessions. A limited number of people can touch or swim with the dolphins and pilot whales. *Tel. (0558)22-3567. Open daily 9am to 5pm. Closed December 6-10. ¥1700.*

NIKKO

One of Japan's most famous architectural monuments, **Toshogu Shrine**, is in **Nikko**, a small town in the mountains that's a two-hour train ride northwest of Tokyo. The shrine, so ornate you think it can't be possibly be Japanese, is the mausoleum of Tokugawa Ieyasu, the 16th century unifier who founded the Tokugawa shogunate that ruled for 260 years. Nikko was recently declared a UNESCO World Heritage Site.

But Nikko offers much more than just this shrine. The surrounding mountains offer walking and hiking; Lake Chuzenji is popular for water sports; and Yumoto has hot springs and skiing. Nikko is a popular summer retreat with temperatures lower than Tokyo's. Emperor Taisho, the grandfather of the present emperor, had a villa in Nikko.

If you get an early start and only visit the Toshogu Shrine area, you can make a day trip to Nikko. But if you want to go up into the mountains, you need to stay overnight.

ARRIVALS & DEPARTURES

The easiest and least expensive way to Nikko is via the private Tobu line from Asakusa Station in northeastern Tokyo. The limited express trains take 1 hour 55 minutes; all seats are reserved (¥2740). For half the price, you can take the *Kaisoku* (express) train that takes 15 minutes longer (¥1320). The only catch on the express is you have to make sure you sit in the front two cars because some trains divide at Shimo Imaichi Station, the stop before Nikko Station.

To take advantage of your JR rail pass, take the Tohoku shinkansen train from Tokyo or Ueno Station to Utsunomiya (50 minutes). Change for the Nikko line for the 45 minute ride to JR Nikko Station. Note that JR and Nikko Tobu Stations are a few minutes walk from each other.

Tourist Information

Stop at the "i" tourist information window in the Nikko Tobu Station to pick up maps and English-language brochures, *Tel. (0288)53-4511.* Open daily 8:30am-5pm.

Goodwill Guides: Contact the Nikko Tourist Information Office listed above for the current contact number to arrange a volunteer goodwill guide.

WHERE TO STAY

KANAYA HOTEL, *1300 Kami-hatsuishi-machi, Nikko, Tochigi, 321-1401. Tel. (0288)54-0001, Fax (0288)53-2487. Twins from ¥18,000. Doubles from ¥22,000. Credit cards.*

This classic hotel was one of the first Western hotels in Japan. The rooms blend Japanese and Western architecture. While it is showing its age, Kanaya is a good choice if you want to stay in a hotel with a lot of character. Perched up on a hill above the Shinkyo Sacred Bridge, Kanaya has fantastic views of the mountains.

MORI-NO-HOTEL, *2551 Yumoto, Nikko. Tochigi, 321-1662. Tel. (0288)62-2338, Fax (0288)62-2477. ¥13,000 per person with two meals. Credit cards.*

Located in the midst of a forest, Mori-no-Hotel is an ideal place to relax after a busy day in Nikko. It's 50 minutes by bus from Nikko but worth the trip for a quiet getaway. A fire is lit in the lobby fireplace every evening; even in summer Oku-Nikko (Inner Nikko) becomes cool in the evening. The rooms are Japanese-style.

NIKKO ASTRAEA HOTEL, *Kotoku Onsen Nikko, Tochigi, 321-1400. Tel. (0288)55-0585, Fax (0288)55-0731. From ¥14,000 per person with two meals. Credit cards.*

This hotel is a favorite retreat when we feel the need to escape from Tokyo. We like to come here any time of year: when the new leaves turn the hills bright green; when the mountains provide welcome relief from the summer heat; when autumn colors brighten the forest and when snow falls on us in the outdoor bath after a day of cross-country skiing. The wooden lodge's open lobby with floor-to-ceiling windows offers great views of the mountains. The staff is friendly and helpful, and meals are served in the first floor dining room. Choose between Japanese- and Western-style accommodations. The hotel has a large indoor hot spring bath and a wonderful stone outdoor bath.

TURTLE INN NIKKO, *2-16 Takumi-cho, Nikko, Tochigi, 321-1433. Tel. (0288)53-3168, Fax (0288)53-3883. From ¥4200 per person without meals. Credit cards. Member of Japanese Inn Group and Welcome Inn Reservation Center.*

HOTORI-AN, *8-28 Takumi-cho, Nikko, Tochigi, 321-1433. Tel. (0288)53-3663, Fax (0288)53-3883. From ¥5800 per person without meals. Credit cards. Member of Japanese Inn Group and Welcome Inn Reservation Center.*

Turtle Inn and Hotori-an, just down the street from each other, are run by the same friendly people and either is a good budget inn choice. Opened in 1994, Hotori-an is newer and all 11 rooms have private baths. One room is Western style, and the rest are Japanese style. Turtle Inn also has 11 rooms: five Japanese style and six Western style. Only three rooms here have private baths. You can have Japanese or Western dinner and breakfast served on Mashiko folk pottery. Hotori-an also has a small gallery of Mashiko pottery. The inns are only a 10-minute walk from Toshogu Shrine. Nearby is a wonderful walk along a path lined with Jizo statues.

WHERE TO EAT

GYOSHINTEI *(Buddhist vegetarian, moderate), 2339-1 Sannai, Nikko. Tel. (0288)53-3751. Open 11:30am to 7pm. Closed Thursday.*

Housed in a simple Japanese building behind the stone building

Meiji no Yakata restaurant, Gyoshintei serves Buddhist vegetarian food. The main dining room, where you sit on *tatami* mats, looks out over the garden. The specialty is *yuba* (soy milk skin), a delicate food cooked in broth, with fresh vegetables. Sets cost ¥3500 and ¥5000. *Kaiseki* meals are available for ¥5000 and ¥8000. The restaurant is rather small so it's best to make reservations.

NIKKO KANAYA HOTEL *(Western, moderate), 1300 Kami-hatsuishi, Nikko. Tel. (0288)54-0001. Open 12 noon to 3pm; 6pm to 8pm.*

The main dining room of the Kanaya Hotel is a charming old-fashioned room. The house specialty is trout, but other Western dishes are also served. Located on the hill behind Shinkyo Bridge, it's a convenient lunch place. The lunch set costs ¥3500 and consists of an appetizer, grilled rainbow trout — a Nikko specialty — dessert and coffee.

MASUDAYA *(Japanese, moderate), 439 Ichiyamachi, Nikko. Tel. (0288)54-2151. Open 11am to 2pm, or earlier if they run out of the day's food. Closed Thursday.*

Masudaya specializes in *yuba,* the curd that collects on the top of boiling soy milk. The delicate food is much more delicious than it sounds. Masudaya serves some of the best *yuba* in Nikko. The lunch set (¥4100 at a Western table) includes *yuba* soup, *yuba sashimi,* fried fish and other *yuba* dishes. If you sit on *tatami* mats, the set costs ¥5500 and includes dessert. Masudaya is open only for lunch and reservations are a necessity. It's located on the left side of the main road, about half way between Nikko Tobu Station and Shinkyo Bridge.

SEEING THE SIGHTS

As you exit Nikko Tobu train station, either take a bus from platform 1, 2 or 3 in front of Nikko Tobu Station to the Shinkyo Bridge stop or walk up the main road (toward the right as you exit the station) for about 20 minutes until you reach the Shinkyo Bridge.

Shinkyo Bridge is a gently arched, red wooden bridge over the Daiya River; it marks the entrance to the shrine's grounds. In the old days, only shoguns and imperial messengers crossed the bridge.

Follow the long sloping walkway called Omotesando, and you'll soon reach a large courtyard with temple buildings. Here you can buy a set of tickets for ¥900 for admission to Toshogu Shrine, Rinno-ji Temple and Futarasan Shrine.

The first temple you see is **Rinno-ji**, a Buddhist temple with a long history that stretches back to 766. The main hall is called the Sanbutsudo (Three Buddha Hall) and houses three huge gilded statues of Buddhist deities. The hall's architecture is unusual in that the low stone floor in front of the statues allows visitors to stand right in front of them. You need to walk around to the right side of the building to go down the stairs for a close-up view.

The close proximity of Rinno-ji, a Buddhist temple, and Toshogu, a Shinto shrine, illustrates that the two religions have had a long and close relationship over the past thousand years. When Buddhism was persecuted in the late 19th century, special dispensation was given to Nikko so the temples there did not experience anywhere near the destruction of many others.

Continue up Omotesando and you'll reach the Sennin Ichidan (1000 people stone stairs); these ten broad steps were as far as commoners could venture. The over 8-meter granite *torii* gate is Japan's largest stone *torii*. You have arrived at Toshogu Shrine.

Toshogu Shrine has put Nikko on the map. Tokugawa Iemitsu, the third shogun, built the Shinto shrine in 1636 to deify his grandfather, Ieyasu, founder of the shogunate that ruled Japan from 1603 until 1868. The arts favored by the 16th century great unifiers and 17th century shoguns were bold and brash, a big change from the monochrome Zen Buddhist art that preceded it. These guys had power and money and used it to create huge monuments. Iemitsu brought together the best artists and craftsmen in the land to create the flamboyant shrine.

To the left of the *torii* gate is a five-storied pagoda. Wait, you may be thinking, this is a Shinto shrine and pagodas belong in Buddhist temples. Well, this pagoda shows how intertwined the two religions were. After you enter the gate, this area contains the **Sacred Storehouses**. The **Sacred Stable** is on the left; it has the famous carving of monkeys: hear no evil, speak no evil, see no evil.

Climb up the steps to the next terrace; the many stone lanterns you see were donated by feudal lords all over Japan. The huge revolving bronze lantern is from Holland, the only European country with which Japan maintained diplomatic relations. The Tokugawa family crest is upside down, but being foreigners, they got away with that error. If a feudal lord had made that mistake, it might have cost him his life. All the way on the left is the **Honjido**, dedicated to the 12 gods of war. On the ceiling is an enormous painting of a dragon. If you clap your hands at the marked spot, you can hear the dragon roar.

At the top of the stairs to the upper terrace is the famed **Yomei Mon Gate**. Lavishly decorated with over 400 carvings, no place on the entire surface is unadorned. The gate's nickname is Higurashi no Mon, Sunset Gate, because you can become so engrossed in looking at it, the whole day will pass. You'll find birds, flowers, dragons, Chinese sages and so much more.

TOO PERFECT?

The artisans who made the Yomei Mon Gate were so impressed with their work that they thought if they made the gate too perfect, the gods would be jealous. So they made one flaw: the geometrical pattern is upside down on the far left pillar. It's called the evil-averting pillar. It must have worked because the shrine has stood for 350 years.

A small **Karamon** (Chinese gate) leads to the inner courtyard. You can remove your shoes and enter the **Honden**, main hall. You pass through the **Haiden** where a mirror represents the deity of Tokugawa, then through a passageway called Ishi-no-ma to enter the main hall.

The eastern side of the inner courtyard has the **Sakashita-mon Gate**, beyond which are the stairs leading to Ieyasu's tomb. On the lintel is the famous statue of the **Nemuri Neko**, the sleeping cat. She is sleeping so peacefully even the steady click of cameras doesn't awaken her. It's rumored that she comes down at night to rid the shrine of mice.

Climb the simple stone stairs to the top of the hill to **Ieyasu's tomb**. All around the tall cryptomeria trees lend a sacred air to the site. The unadorned tomb is such a contrast to all the ornateness down below; we really get the impression that Ieyasu is in a truly peaceful state. And well he should be. When he died at the age of 74, he had accomplished what he set out to do. Not only did he manage to rule Japan, but he also put in place an administrative structure that enabled his heirs to rule for 260 years.

You need to go back down all the steps and retrace your path to the exit of Toshogu Shrine. Rather than walking down the broad Omotesando, turn right and walk along the path lined with stone lanterns. You'll come to **Futarasan Shrine**, constructed by Ieyasu's son, Hidetada. To the left of the main hall is a pleasant garden; its simplicity is a respite from the highly decorated Toshogu Shrine.

Beyond Futarasan Shrine is **Daiyuin**, the mausoleum of Iemitsu, the third Tokugawa shogun and Toshogu's builder. Unlike the Shinto shrine built for his grandfather, Iemitsu's own tomb is purely Buddhist.

From there you can return to the main street and either catch a bus to go into the mountains or return to the train station.

Lake Chuzenji, Kotoku & Yumoto

The road from Nikko to Lake Chuzenji is called Iroha Slope — the equivalent of ABC slope because each hairpin turn is named after one of the 48 sounds in the old Japanese alphabet. You can catch a bus from

Nikko Tobu Station or on the main road that runs in front of Toshogu Shrine.

The lakeside area is a popular place for Japanese to vacation, and the Kegon waterfall is on the itinerary of every tour group. We honestly don't think it's worth the effort. The streets around the lake are filled with tacky souvenir stands and the waterfall is modest; you can take an elevator to its base if you feel like it. Unless you cannot survive without pedaling a swan boat around the lake, continue on to **Kotoku** and **Yumoto**.

Yumoto and Kotoku are on a plateau surrounded by mountains. The small hot spring town of Yumoto has lots of inns. It also has the honor of having Japan's first ski slope; the hill is modest but popular with people looking for a convenient ski slope. Walk around the small **Lake Yunoko**, which means hot water lake — you can feel the warmth of the lake fed by hot springs. It's especially pleasant in autumn when the foliage puts on a show.

Kotoku, one of our favorite Tokyo getaways, features meadows framed by mountains and peaceful birch forests. During the winter, cross-country ski trails criss cross the terrain. The Astraea Hotel is a comfortable lodge.

The surrounding mountains and plains have lots of hiking trails, something for every level. **Senjogahara** is a marsh where you can saunter along on wooden walkways. Surrounded by volcanic mountains, it was once a lake. During the summer the marsh is filled with wildflowers.

YUNISHIGAWA ONSEN

Deep in the mountains, this unassuming remote hot spring village northwest of Nikko has a surprising history.

In 1185, the Genji clan annihilated its rivals, the **Heike**, but some Heike managed to flee. The victorious Genji went on to establish the Kamakura shogunate, but their need for vengeance was so strong, they searched to eradicate the surviving Heike, some of whom fled to the Nikko area. The Heike felt they were safe — this was 500 years before Toshogu Shrine was built and Nikko was like being in remote Alaska — nothing was there.

But, when a son was born to the leader of the Heike, the group celebrated by using a kimono to make a carp banner, long a boy's symbol. The noise of the chickens the Heike kept also gave away their positions. Genji warriors discovered and killed about half the exiles. The surviving Heike fled farther north and ended up in Yunishigawa. To this day residents of Yunishigawa neither raise chickens nor fly the carp banner on Boys' Day.

The Heike had lived the high life in Kyoto and even married into the imperial family, so primitive living in a harsh mountain hamlet was a major step down. To bolster their spirits, the young Heike women prepared feasts of mountain vegetable stew, grilled deer, bear meat and river fish. Yunishigawa is today famous for its "exiles cuisine" cooked over an open hearth.

Four hundred years ago, the discovery of hot springs in Yunishigawa put the village on the map. The Heike have been hoteliers ever since. Yunishigawa is famous for its outdoor baths along the banks of the river. You can soak year round, looking at snow, brilliant red autumn foliage, or green hillsides. When we visited Yunishigawa in February, the snow was piled ten feet high.

ARRIVALS & DEPARTURES

Yunishigawa can be combined with a trip to Nikko. Spend the morning at Toshogu Shrine in Nikko. After lunch take the Tobu train from Nikko to Kinugawa Onsen. You will have to change trains in Shimo Imaichi Station, the first stop. At Kinugawa Onsen Station, switch to the train to Yunishigawa Station. Board the Tobu bus to Yunishigawa. 25 minutes, ¥880. The buses meet the train.

To travel to Yunishigawa directly from Tokyo's Asakusa Station, take the Tobu line express train to Yunishigawa Onsen, about three hours. There are eight trains a day. Board the Tobu bus for the 25-minute ride to Yunishigawa.

WHERE TO STAY

HONKE BANKYU RYOKAN, *Yunishigawa Onsen, Tochigi, 321-2601. Tel. (0288)98-0011, Fax (0288)98-0666. Rates from ¥18,000 per person with two meals. Credit cards.*

This older inn is a real treat. Each of the 30 Japanese-style guest rooms is decorated in a rustic fashion; some of the rooms have their own hearth for cooking Heike cuisine and all have wooden bath tubs. They also have a large outdoor wooden bath overlooking the river. Honke Bankyu is famous for its food. With a family descended from the original group of exiles, they should know what Yunishigawa cuisine is all about.

YAMASHIROYA GRAND HOTEL, *Yunishigawa Onsen, Tochigi, 321-2601. Tel. (0288)98-0311, Fax (0288)98-0733. Rates from ¥10,000 per person with two meals. Credit cards.*

This simple hotel on the water in the central part of the village is a good choice; it recently underwent a renovation. The outdoor bath overlooks the river.

SEEING THE SIGHTS

Yunishigawa is easily seen on foot. The real attractions are the baths, the unusual food, the terrific scenery and the good hiking, but you can get a dose of history at the following places:

In the center of town is the **Exiles Folklore Museum**, a tiny, one-room place that resembles a cluttered attic. It's easy to dismiss it entirely until you realize that many of the objects are over one thousand years old. *Tel. (0288)98-0432. ¥300.*

Up the road is **Heike Village** (Heike no Sato), a group of seven traditional thatched-roof buildings with displays of how the Heike lived. Craftsmen demonstrate carving bowls and ladles, one way the Heike supported themselves. Other buildings have Heike costumes and furnishings. *Tel. (0288)98-0126. Open 8:30am to 5pm; 9am to 4:30 December through March. ¥500.*

ASHIKAGA

Ashikaga, north of Tokyo, has a fabulous museum of Japanese porcelain, a must for ceramics aficionados. It also has a wonderful indigo dyer who welcomes visitors and gladly gives explanations in English. These two attributes alone make for a worthwhile getaway. But we have more for you. One of the most charming country hot spring inns is about an hour and a half from Ashikaga. All three combine to make a memorable off-the-beaten-path side trip.

ARRIVALS & DEPARTURES

The Tobu train Isezaki line provides service to Ashikaga from Tokyo's Asakusa Station. The limited express takes 70 minutes, costs ¥2100 and runs every hour. The semiexpress takes almost two hours and costs ¥940.

WHERE TO STAY

CHUJIKAN, *2036 Fuegashima, Miyagi-mura, Seta-gun, Gunma, 371-1100. Tel. (0272)83-3015, Fax (0272)83-7522. From ¥10,000 per person with two meals. Credit cards.*

We enjoyed our stay at Chujikan so much that we've included it in our Best Places to Stay in Chapter 11. The inn was recently reconstructed in a traditional Japanese rural style. The lobby is like a farmhouse; you step up from the entrance area into a small, sunny room with an *irori* hearth. All 13 rooms are Japanese style and have private toilets and sinks. But the real winner is the stone outdoor bath that overlooks a river ravine and waterfall. The men's and women's baths are side by side, separated by a bamboo fence. In the evening, the waterfall is illuminated. The food is country-style home cooking served in a Japanese-style central dining room. The cheerful cook explains each dish she is serving. Staying at Chujikan is like taking a step back in time.

From Ashikaga Station (or Omata Station if you are coming from Sei Ai Kobo), take the JR Ryomo line to Maebashi, about 45 minutes. Take a shuttle bus from Maebashi Station to Chuo Maebashi Station and take the Jomo Dentetsu train to Ogo Station (15 minutes). From there catch a bus to Akagi Jinja Shrine (25 minutes). As you get off, call the hotel from the public phone and you'll be picked up. Taxi from Maebashi Station takes 45 minutes and costs about ¥5000. A taxi from Ogo Station takes 20 minutes and costs ¥3000.

SEEING THE SIGHTS

Kurita Museum, *1542 Komaba-cho, Ashikaga, Tochigi. Tel. (0284)91-1026. Open daily 9:30am to 5pm; until 6pm on Sunday and holidays. Closed December 29-31. ¥1550. 15- minute taxi ride from Tobu Ashikaga Station, fare is ¥2500 to ¥3000. From JR Tomita Station on JR Ryomo line, 10-minute walk. On the way back you can wait for a bus to the station or ask the information desk to call a taxi.*

Located on a hilly 660 acres of pine woods, the dozen buildings were designed by architect Taniguchi Yoshiro and reflect the traditional Japanese aesthetic of subdued beauty. The collection of Imari and Nabeshima ceramics is the largest in the world. Nabeshima ware is unequaled for its subtle colors; Imari's designs are famous the world over. One building houses the highly prized, ornately embellished porcelains that decorate European castles and manor houses. Another has the more subdued Nabeshima and Imari ware made for Japanese feudal lords and other wealthy individuals. Every time we go back, they seem to have added a new building.

The museum's works were collected by a businessman, Kurita Hideo. As the hometown boy who made good, he decided to establish the museum in Ashikaga. Our only gripe is every building has a gift shop, and the one at the entrance is probably half the length of a football field.

Sei Ai Kobo, *897-1 Omata-cho, Ashikaga, Tochigi. Tel. (0284)62-1531.*

This workshop is the showroom of Mr. Okawa, an energetic seventy-something man who has to be Japan's best ambassador for indigo dyeing. Mr. Okawa is happy to demonstrate the natural dyeing process, and he does so in good English learned at technical school. For ¥1000 you can dye a handkerchief: by folding and tying it, you can make an original design. You'll wash out your creation in the small stream running behind Mr. Okawa's workshop, the same place where he rinses all his works. The showroom is filled with his handiwork: scarves, shawls, *noren* curtains, clothing and more, all deep blue indigo color. Our favorite are indigo silk socks with five toes that are supposed to prevent athlete's foot. Unfortunately, the one-sized socks were too small for our husbands, so we are now their proud owners.

From the Tobu Ashikaga and JR Ashikaga train stations, a taxi to Mr. Okawa's workshop costs about ¥4500. A less expensive way is to take the bus from Tobu Ashikaga Station heading to Kiryu Tenjin machi and get off at Omata Station. From there it's a few minutes by taxi or a 10-minute walk.

If you use JR trains, take the JR Tohoku Honsen line from Ueno Station to Oyama Station — rapid trains take about one hour; and switch to the JR Ryomo line to Omata Station — a 45-minute ride. It's a few minutes by taxi or a 10-minute walk.

INDIGO BLUES

The all-natural **indigo dyeing process** *is disappearing in Japan. Fortunately, dedicated dyers like Mr. Okawa work hard to preserve the art.*

Indigo is a bush grown in Shikoku, an island in Western Japan. In the autumn, the leaves are picked and placed in a jar to decompose for several months. Then sake rice wine and sugar are added to start the long fermentation process. The dye is a living organism and needs to be fed sake and stirred daily to keep it alive.

The pot of dye doesn't look like much — a green, oozy liquid. Indigo needs oxygen to bring out the color, so when cloth comes out of the pot it looks greenish, but within a few seconds, exposure to air changes the color to its characteristic blue color.

14. HOKKAIDO

Hokkaido, Japan's northernmost large island, is not on many international tours of Japan, but we have had some of our best experiences there. Its spaciousness and frontier spirit create a different atmosphere from the rest of Japan. Hokkaido has fewer cultural treats than other parts of Japan, but the wintertime events are just plain wonderful.

Even today, the island feels spacious and underpopulated with one fifth of Japan's land, but only 5% of its population – about 5 1/2 million. It's a different Japan. People have room to spread out, and large national parks with soaring mountains, deep gorges and hot springs take up a large part of the land. More than 50% of the island is mountains and forests. Actually, Hokkaido feels like the state of Maine in the US; it's about the same size and has similar terrain if you discount the volcanoes.

The climate is pleasantly cool in summer. Since there's no rainy season, it's deluged with Japanese visitors seeking greener pastures for hiking and walking in June and July. In winter, Hokkaido transforms itself into a wonderland and becomes a mecca for cold-weather sports. Purists say the dry powdery snow makes for much better skiing than the snow on Honshu island. **Sapporo** hosted the Winter Olympics in 1972.

And Hokkaido excels at **winter festivals**. Two million visitors flock to Sapporo's snow festival each February to see the spectacular snow sculptures, some several stories high. Hokkaido is also hot spring heaven – many volcanoes ensure a supply of bubbling hot mineral water in most of the island.

And we can't forget the food. All the agricultural development paid off. Hokkaido is famous for its fresh fish and seafood, wonderful dairy products like milk, butter and ice cream, and delicious vegetables like asparagus and potatoes. The *sushi* is some of the best in the country, and Sapporo's *ramen* noodles are known all over Japan.

Up until the end of the 19th century, most of Hokkaido (then called Ezo) was the domain of the **Ainu**, Japan's aboriginal people who were chased north off Honshu Island.

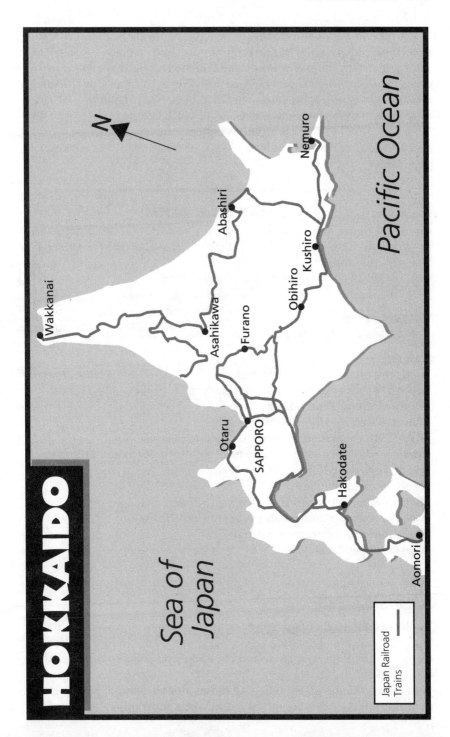

After the fall of the Tokugawa shogunate in 1868, the new Meiji government aggressively pushed colonization and changed the name of the island to Hokkaido. The government invited foreign experts to advise on its agricultural development. American Edwin Dun came in 1873 and established livestock breeding. In 1876 American William S. Clark established Sapporo Agricultural College, which later became Hokkaido University, one of the six prestigious imperial universities before World War II. His advice to the students, "Boys, be ambitious," was taken very seriously.

HOKKAIDO HIGHLIGHTS

* *Sapporo's magnificent snow festival*
* *Eating Genghis Khan barbecue with 3000 of your closest friends in a beer hall in Sapporo*
* *The turn-of-the-century atmosphere in Otaru*
* *The panoramic view of Hakodate from Mt Hakodate*
* *The graceful mating dance of Japan's native cranes near Kushiro*

Planning Your Stay

Spend two days in Sapporo, and one day each in Otaru, Hakodate and Kushiro. Tailor your trip to fit your interests with these suggestions:
• **Fantastic Snow Festival**: Sapporo
• **Crane watching all year round**: Kushiro
• **Early 20th century port towns**: Otaru and Hakodate
• **Meiji era Western-style architecture**: Sapporo, Otaru and Hakodate
• **First Western-style fortress**: Hakodate
• **Fresh crabs**: Hakodate
• **Great sushi**: Otaru and Hakodate
• **Cool summer without a rainy season**: all of Hokkaido
• **Postmodern architecture**: Kushiro
• **Glassblowing**: Otaru

SAPPORO

It seems that all of Japan turns up in **Sapporo** for the **Snow Festival**. For one week every February, around the 5th to 11th, the city becomes a frozen wonderland with snow and ice sculptures gracing its parks and boulevards.

Sapporo shines all winter. With mountains all around, people grab their downhill or cross-country skis and take a short train ride for a few hours of skiing. But winter isn't the only time to visit. Sapporo still has some reminders of its 19th century frontier days. Built at the turn of the century, Western-influenced Meiji period buildings give the city an exotic flavor. And when the snow melts, hiking trails abound.

The name "Sapporo" comes from an Ainu word meaning "the river which runs along the reed-filled plains." Well, there aren't many reeds left. The city was set up in a modern, grid plan based on the best of 19th century US urban planning. Parks and open green land dot the city; an excellent subway system runs under the wide boulevards.

With about 1.7 million residents, about a third of Hokkaido's population, people live a relaxed life that is the envy of many other Japanese urban dwellers. Like most of Hokkaido's people, Sapporo-ites have a practical, down-to-earth spirit that is a legacy of the frontier days a mere century ago.

ARRIVALS & DEPARTURES
By Air
Sapporo is served by Chitose Airport, which is fairly distant from the city center. The Tokyo to Sapporo air corridor is the busiest in the world.

To/from Tokyo Haneda: over 30 flights/day (ANA, JAL, JAS. ¥24,700)

To/from Osaka Itami: 3 flights/day; **Kansai:** 9 flights/day (ANA, JAL, JAS. ¥30,850)

To/from Nagoya: 12/flights/day (ANA, JAL, JAS. ¥27,650)

To/from Fukuoka: 4 flights/day (ANA, JAL, JAS. ¥38,400)

Service to/from Akita, Aomori, Fukushima, Hanamaki, Hiroshima, Izumo, Kagoshima, Kochi, Komatsu, Kumamoto, Matsumoto, Matsuyama, Misawa, Miyazaki, Nagasaki, Naha, Niigata, Oita, Okayama, Sendai, Shonai, Takamatsu, Tokushima, Toyama, and Yamagata airports as well as to the local airports within Hokkaido.

For Ground Transportation:
Bus: to Sapporo Station (65 minutes, ¥820)
Taxi: to Sapporo Station (50 minutes, ¥12,000)
Train: to Sapporo Station (36 minutes, ¥1040)
We recommend taking the train, especially in winter. It's quick, easy and the most dependable route in snow.

By Train
To/from Tokyo: Take the Tohoku shinkansen from Tokyo or Ueno Station to Morioka. Change for a limited express train to Hakodate — on some trains you'll have to switch at Aomori; and at Hakodate change for

a limited express to Sapporo. All in all, the trip takes about 11 hours and costs ¥22,330. Now you know why the air corridor between Tokyo and Sapporo is so crowded.

Several overnight trains depart daily from Ueno Station and arrive in Sapporo about 15 hours later. Fares run about ¥23,000. The new double-decker "Cassiopeia" runs three or four times a week depending on the season. ¥30,750 sleeping car, each room with private bath.

To/from Hakodate: Sapporo is about 3 1/2 hours by limited express train from Hakodate. ¥8590

ORIENTATION

Sapporo is one of the few Japanese cities set up on a grid pattern, making navigating easy.

GETTING AROUND TOWN

Sapporo has an excellent mass transit system, which includes three subway lines, one streetcar and an extensive bus network. A one-day pass *(ichi nichi joshaken)*, good on all three means of transport, costs ¥950.

Tourist Information

Sapporo Tourist Information Center is at the Odori Station of the subway. Staff members speak English, and there is a wide range of English-language information. Open daily 10am to 6pm. Closed December 30 through January 3, *Tel. (011)232-7712.*

JR Sapporo Station has the **Lilac Paseo International Information Corner. Sapporo Communication Plaza**, in the *Sapporo MN Building, Nishi 3-chome, Kita i-jo, Chuo-ku. Tel. (011)211-3678.* Open 9am to 5:30pm. Closed December 28 to January 3.

WHERE TO STAY

Sapporo has mostly Western-style accommodations and many of the hotels are very large.

SAPPORO RENAISSANCE HOTEL, *1-1-1 Toyohira-4, Toyohira-ku, Sapporo, 062-0904. Tel. (011)821-1111, Fax (011)842-6191. Doubles from ¥33,000. Credit cards.*

One of Sapporo's newest hotels, the Renaissance is an elegant hotel on the river about a 10-minute taxi ride from Sapporo Station. The health club is excellent, but even better is the great jogging right from the hotel. The rooms are large; it's easy to forget that you're in Japan. The wide range of restaurants includes Chinese, Japanese, Italian and American fare.

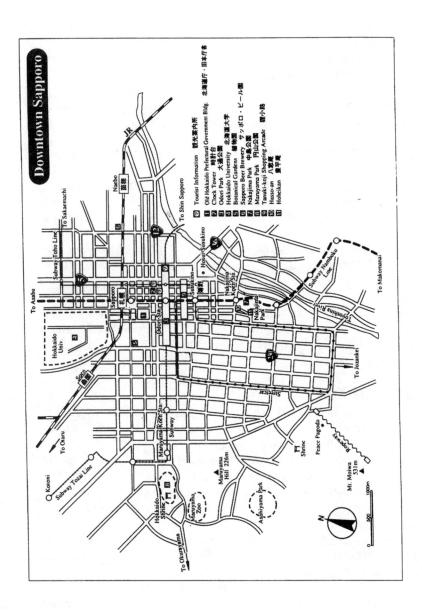

Downtown Sapporo

2 Tourist Information 観光案内所
1 Old Hokkaido Prefectural Government Bldg. 北海道庁・旧本庁舎
2 Clock Tower 時計台
3 Odori Park 大通公園
4 Hokkaido University 北海道大学
5 Botanical Gardens 植物園
6 Sapporo Beer Brewery サッポロ・ビール園
7 Nakajima Park 中島公園
8 Maruyama Park 円山公園
9 Tanuki-koji Shopping Arcade 狸小路
10 Hasso-an 八窓庵
11 Hoheikan 豊平館

HOTEL ALPHA SAPPORO, *5-9-1 Nishi, Minami-1, Chuo-ku, Sapporo, 060-0061. Tel. (011)221-2333, Fax (011)221-0819. Twins from ¥19,000. Credit cards.*

This 145-room hotel, just two minutes from the Odori subway station, has an excellent location and is part of the Hotel Okura group.

HOTEL NEW OTANI SAPPORO, *1-1 Nishi, Kita-2, Chuo-ku, Sapporo, 060-0002. Tel. (011)222-1111, Fax (011)222-5521. Singles from ¥14,000. Twins from ¥25,000. Credit cards.*

Part of the New Otani chain, the 338-room hotel is about a 10-minute walk from Sapporo Station. The least expensive rooms are so tiny, they are business hotel size.

KEIO PLAZA HOTEL SAPPORO, *7-2-1 Nishi, Kita-5, Chuo-ku, Sapporo, 060-0005. Tel. (011)271-0111, Fax (011)221-5450. Singles from ¥13,000. Twins from ¥23,000. Credit cards.*

Only a five-minute walk from Sapporo Station, the hotel's location is hard to beat. With 521 rooms, it's a large hotel with ten restaurants and bars. The hotel has a nice indoor pool and a well-equipped sports center.

NAKAMURAYA RYOKAN, *Nishi 7, Kita 3, Chuo-ku, Sapporo, 060-0003. Tel. (011)241-2111, Fax (011)241-2118. Singles ¥7000. Doubles ¥13,000. Credit cards. Member of Japanese Inn Group and Welcome Inn Reservation Center.*

A good budget choice, this 29 room, Japanese-style inn is a seven-minute walk from Sapporo Station. Dwarfed by larger office buildings around it, the inn is across the street from the Botanical Garden. Breakfast and dinner are available.

WHERE TO EAT

Sapporo is known for its fresh seafood, for *ramen* noodles, for *Ishikari nabe* (a stew pot with salmon, tofu and vegetables) and for Genghis Khan barbecue, lamb grilled on a steel plate.

HYOSETSU-NO-MON *(Seafood, expensive). Minami 5, Nishi 2. Tel. (011)521-3046. Open 11am to 11pm.*

A kitschy, touristy place serving king crab, it's really a lot of fun. Folk dancers entertain you while you nibble away on crab and other delicacies. Set menus run from ¥5000.

SAPPORO BIER GARTEN *(Beer garden, inexpensive to moderate). Kita 6, Higashi 9, Higashi-ku. Tel. (011)742-1531. Open daily 11:30am to 9pm. Closed December 31 through January 2.*

You can't visit Sapporo without eating at the brewery. The first beer brewery in Japan now has a huge (seats 3500), lively beer hall in an old brick warehouse. The specialty is *jingisukan*, Genghis Khan barbecue, slices of lamb and vegetables grilled at your table on a steel plate. The Viking for ¥3400 offers all you can eat and all the beer you can drink for

1 hour 40 minutes. When we arrived, we were a little surprised when the staff gave us large plastic bags and told us to seal our coats inside. We left reeking of grilled lamb and realized the bags saved us some dry cleaning bills. There is a beer garden on the premises.

SUGINOME (*Japanese, expensive*). *Minami 5, Nishi 5, Chuo-ku. Tel. (011)521-0888. Open 5pm to 10pm. Closed Sunday and holidays. Reservations a must.*

This restaurant, in a brick building, serves traditional Hokkaido cuisine including fresh fish grilled over an open hearth. The set menus run ¥6000, ¥8000, ¥10,000 and ¥12,000.

YAGUMO (*Noodles, inexpensive*). *Odori, Minami 1, Nishi 4. Tel. (011)231-0789. Open 10:30am to 8:30pm. Occasionally closed on Mondays.*

Conveniently located in the center of Sapporo, Yagumo is a special noodle shop. In a traditional setting decorated with folk art, you'll sit on *tatami* mats and eat delicious noodles. The *goma soba* (sesame *soba*) is sublime. ¥450.

AJANTA (*Indian, inexpensive*). *1-10 Minami 22-Jo Nishi 7-chome, Chuo-ku. Tel. (011)521-7040. Open 11am to 3pm. Closed Monday and Friday. One-minute walk from streetcar Honan Shogako-mae stop.*

This funky little restaurant is a bit out of the way but worth it for one of those only-in-Japan experiences. Run by a couple who love Indian food, for 25 years they have been cooking their versions of Indian curries (not Japanese curry rice), which includes chicken, lamb and vegetable curry; it's served until the day's portions run out. Each curry costs ¥980.

SEEING THE SIGHTS

Clock Tower (Tokeidai) was the drill hall for the Sapporo Agricultural College built in 1878; the clock has chimed on the hour since 1881. An American professor designed the wooden structure. *Open 9am to 6pm. Closed Monday and December 29 through January 3.*

A five-minute walk away is the **Old Hokkaido Government Building** (Kyu Hokkaido-cho), an 1888 red Victorian structure designated an Important Cultural Property. The building, based on the Massachusetts State House, is an excellent example of eclectic Western-style Meiji architecture. *Open weekdays 9am to 5pm and Saturdays 9am-1pm. Closed Sundays, holidays and December 29 through January 3.*

Nakajima Park, south of Susukino, has the **Hoheikan**, an eclectic Western-style building built in 1880 as a hotel. The architects had no training in Western architecture so they used Japanese construction techniques. The Meiji Emperor stayed there when he visited Sapporo soon after its construction. *Open daily from 9am to 5pm.* Also in the park is **Hasso-an**, a teahouse built in the early Edo period and set in a Japanese garden. *Open daily 9am to 6pm. Closed mid-November through April.*

SNOW, SNOW & MORE SNOW

Sapporo's **Snow Festival** *is a dazzling world-class show. Block after block of beautiful snow sculptures, many three-stories high, and hundreds of ice sculptures make this the world's best snow festival. Huge sculptures boggle your mind: cartoon characters, rock stars, five-storied pagodas, antebellum mansions straight from Gone with the Wind, and much much more. Forget about cold toes and the two million visitors; it's a delight to behold.*

It's almost impossible to get a hotel room in Sapporo during the February 5–11 festival. Tour agents book all the rooms well in advance, which means that you have little choice but to buy an expensive package tour. To avoid this, arrive one or two days before the festival opens. You can see the snow sculptures being made and won't have to put up with the throngs. The only disadvantage is the Makomanai Military Camp, which has sculptures kids can climb on, does not open to the public until the festival itself opens.

The main site is central Sapporo's **Odori Park**, *but it has been joined by a winter wonderland for children at Makomanai Military Camp and an ice sculpture promenade along Susukino. The huge snow sculptures at Odori Park are towering structures made with bull-dozed snow that is carefully chiseled into buildings, characters and nearly anything else you can imagine.*

The **Hokkaido Museum of Modern Art** (Hokkaido Kindai Bijutsukan) features a collection of modern glass art and works by Hokkaido-born artists, by other Japanese artists and by foreign artists. *Open 10am to 5pm. Closed Monday and December 27 through January 4. ¥250 for special exhibitions.*

On the outskirts of Sapporo is the huge **Nopporo Forest Park** (Nopporo Shinrin Koen). *To reach the park, take the JR Hakodate line to Shin Sapporo Station, then from platform #10, take the bus to Shinrin Koen.*

The park is home to the **Historical Museum of Hokkaido**, detailing Hokkaido's relatively brief history. *Tel. (011)898-0456. Open 9:30am to 4:30pm. Closed Monday, some holidays and December 29 through January 3. ¥610.*

The **Historical Village of Hokkaido** is also in the park. This excellent open-air museum features restored historic buildings. *Tel. (011)898-2692. Open 9:30am to 4:30pm. Closed Monday and December 29 through January 3.*

NIGHTLIFE & ENTERTAINMENT

Susukino, the nightlife and entertainment area, is packed with 6000 bars, restaurants, porn shows and more. Crowded with all different kinds of people, it's fun to wander around Susukino.

SHOPPING

Perhaps because of its long, cold winter, Sapporo has lots of arcades and underground shopping malls. **JR Sapporo Station** has a shopping mall, and **Aurora Town** and **Pole Town**, two large malls, are under Odori Park. If that isn't enough, try **Sapporo Factory** under a huge glass atrium; the covered **Tanuki Koji Shopping Arcade**; and across the river from Tanuki Koji, the **Nijo Ichiba Fish Market**.

EXCURSIONS & DAY TRIPS
OTARU

A mere 30 minutes by train from Sapporo is the port city of **Otaru** with an historic district that looks like time passed it by. And in a sense it has. At the turn of the century, Otaru was a major port and commercial center of Hokkaido; in 1880, it was connected to Sapporo by Hokkaido's first train. Gradually, Otaru lost its position to ports further south and better connected with Honshu. While the glory days are long gone, the canal and warehouse district, with its gaslights and brick and stone buildings, is from another era. The city is also a center for glassmaking.

Getting to Otaru

To/from JR Sapporo Station: Otaru is 30 minutes by express train, 50 minutes by local on the Hakodate Honsen Line. ¥620.

Tourist Information

The **Tourist Information Center** is at the entrance of the JR Otaru Station. English language maps and brochures are available. *Tel. (0134)29-1333.* Open 10am to 6pm weekdays and 9:30am to 5:30pm weekends.

Where to Stay

While there are hotels in Otaru, we recommend you make a side trip from Sapporo.

Where to Eat

NIHONBASHI *(Sushi, inexpensive to moderate). 1-1-4 Inaho. Tel. (0134)33 3773. Open 11am to 9pm.*

Located at the street called Sushi-ya Dori *(sushi* shop street), Nihonbashi is the most famous shop. You may have to line up, but the outstanding *sushi* makes the wait worthwhile. *Sushi* sets start at ¥1200; for a splurge, the most expensive set costs ¥4800. In between, there are about 10 different set meals so no matter what your budget, you can enjoy some of the freshest *sushi* in Japan.

BOSHOKU *(Japanese and Western, inexpensive). 1-3-7 Ironai. Tel. (0134)22-2131. Open 11:30am to 9pm. Closed Sunday.*

This casual restaurant serves both Japanese and Western food and is a good place to stop while browsing along the canal.

Seeing the Sights

From the station, walk down Chuo Dori towards the water. Running parallel to the canal is Shikinai Hondori. In this area are many buildings from the turn of the century: the **Bank of Japan** building designed by Tatsuno Kingo, the architect of Tokyo Station and Tokyo's Bank of Japan building; **Mitsui Bank** building, now called Sakura Bank; the **NYK Shipping Line** Branch office; **Tomioka Catholic Church** and the **Otaru Grand Hotel Classic**, originally called the Etchuya Hotel.

The **canal**, built during the Meiji period, still has a turn-of-the-century feel. It is lined with stone and brick warehouses; many are turned into restaurants, bars, museums and shops. Check out the granite patterns of the walkway.

Train enthusiasts will want to walk 15 minutes from the north end of the canal to the **Hokkaido Train Museum** (Hokkaido Tetsudo Kinenkan) where Japan's first steam locomotives are displayed. The building itself was constructed in 1885. *Open 9:30am to 4pm May through October. Closed Monday and holidays. Free admission.*

Otaru is home to the world's largest music box store: **Otaru Orugooru-do** sells 3000 different music boxes. *Tel. (0134)22-1108. Open daily 9am to 6pm.* Next door, the **Antique Museum** has music boxes on display. *Open daily 9:30am to 6pm. ¥500.*

Otaru has become a major glass-producing center. The **Kitaichi Glass Sangyo-kan**, in a series of renovated warehouses built in 1892, displays and sells thousands of glass objects from around the world. Stop for a cup of tea at the adjacent **Kitaichi Hall**, which is lit by oil lamps. *Tel. (0134)33-1993. Open daily 9am to 6pm.* If visiting Kitaichi leaves you wanting to see more glass, go to the nearby **Otaru Venezia Art Museum** for a reproduction of rooms in Venice's Glace Palace. Incredibly, over 20,000 pieces of glassware are exhibited. *Tel. (0134)33-1717. Open daily 9am to 6pm. ¥700.*

To finish off the glass extravaganza, take the bus about 15 minutes to Tenguyama. At the **Glass Studio** you'll see glass being made; it's home to about a dozen artists. *Tel. (0134)33-9390.*

For a panoramic view of Otaru, take the ropeway up to the peak of **Tenguyama** (Mt. Tengu). *Open 9:20am-4pm. Round trip ¥1000.* At the top is a restaurant called **House of Tengu**, which has lots of *tengu* masks on display. *Tengu* are gods who live deep in the mountains and are always portrayed with long noses.

HAKODATE

Hakodate, a city of 300,000 in southern Hokkaido, makes a good first stop in Hokkaido on your way north. The 54-kilometer **Seikan tunnel** now connects the islands of Honshu and Hokkaido.

One of the first three ports in Japan opened to foreigners in the late 1850s, Hakodate has wonderful turn-of-the-century, Western-inspired architecture. Overnight here for an intriguing glimpse of what happened when East met West 140 years ago. Much of the commerce was with Russia and remnants of Russian influence remain. Older than most of Hokkaido's cities, the Matsumae feudal lords ruled Hakodate for the better part of the Tokugawa period.

ARRIVALS & DEPARTURES

By Air

Hakodate Airport is 20 minutes from the city.

To/from Tokyo Haneda: 8 flights/day (ANA, JAL. ¥22,900)
To/from Nagoya: 2 flights/day (ANA. ¥25,550)
To/from Osaka Kansai: 4 flights/day (ANA, JAL. ¥28,600)
To/from Fukuoka: 1 flight/day (JAL. ¥36,650)
Service to/from Fukushima, Niigata, Sapporo, Sendai and Toyama and other airports in Hokkaido.

For Ground Transportation:
Bus: to Hakodate Station (20 minutes, ¥300)
Taxi: to Hakodate Station (20 minutes, ¥2000)

By Train

To/from Tokyo: take the Tohoku shinkansen train to Morioka and change to a limited express train to Hakodate. You may have to change trains at Aomori Station. The trip takes about 7 hours and costs ¥18,000.

To/from Sapporo: the *Hokuto* limited express train (3 hours 50 minutes, ¥8390)

By Bus

To/from Sapporo: 3 buses/day (5 hours, ¥4680)

GETTING AROUND TOWN

Hakodate fans out from Mt. Hakodate. Buses and trams are your best bet for getting around town.

Tourist Information

The "i" Tourist Information Center is at JR Hakodate Station. *Tel. (0138)23-5440. Open 9am to 7pm.*

WHERE TO STAY

HAKODATE-ONUMA PRINCE HOTEL, *Nishi Onuma Onsen, Nanae-cho, Kameda-gun, Hokkaido. Tel. (0138)67-1111, Fax (0138)67-1117. Twins ¥27,000. No singles or doubles. Credit cards.*

About 50 minutes outside Hakodate and 10 minutes from JR Onuma Koen Station, the Prince Hotel has hotel rooms and log cabins brought from Finland. The extensive facilities include a golf course, swimming pools, hiking trails and hot spring baths. In winter, it transforms itself into a cross-country ski center.

HOTEL JAL CITY, *22-15 Horaimachi, Hakodate, Hokkaido, 040-0043. Tel. (0138)24-2580, Fax (0138)27-2581. Singles from ¥8000. Doubles from ¥16,000. Credit cards.*

This pleasant and moderately priced hotel is just five minutes by taxi from JR Hakodate Station and 20 minutes from Hakodate Airport. The two restaurants, Italian and a pub-style cafe, are known for using the freshest ingredients. Enjoy a view of Hakodate Bay from the rooms on the higher floors of the 12-storied building.

PENSION HAKODATEMURA, *16-12 Suehiro-cho, Hakodate, Hokkaido, 040-0053. Tel. (0138)22-8105, Fax (0138)22-8925. Singles ¥5800. Doubles ¥10,600. Credit cards. Member of the Japanese Inn Group and Welcome Inn Reservation Center.*

This simple pension is centrally located. Fifteen rooms are Western style; two are Japanese style. Breakfast and dinner are available for an extra charge.

WHERE TO EAT

KANIKKO *(Crab, expensive). 4-5 Matsukaze-cho. Open 5pm to 10:30pm. Closed Monday.*

Kani means crab and Kanikko's specialty is just that. They steam, boil, or grill depending on the kind of crabs available. And the price varies with the market. A soft shell crab large enough to feed two to three people costs ¥8000.

TAROZUSHI *(Sushi, inexpensive). 32-8 Motomachi. Tel. (0138)22-0310. Open 11:30am to 9pm. Closed Monday.*

Near the British Consulate, Tarozushi has some of the best *sushi* in town. It also has great views of Hakodate Bay, the source of all the fish and seafood served. Set meals, all served with the special house soup, run ¥1400, ¥1900 and ¥2600.

SEEING THE SIGHTS

Start your day at the Asaichi (morning market) near Hakodate Station. To get a good sense of Hakodate's history, start at **Motomachi Park** at the foot of Mt. Hakodate, a short walk from the Suehiro-cho tram stop. Be prepared for some huffing and puffing as you climb the hills, but at least you will be rewarded with some great views.

The **Former Hakodate Ward Meeting Hall** (Kyu Hakodate-ku Kokaido) was built in 1910. You can't help but notice the bright blue and yellow building. Make sure you see the sumptuous interiors, including a marble reception room. A local millionaire funded the building. Today the Great Hall is frequently used for concerts. *Tel. (0138)22-1001. Open daily 9am to 7pm; until 5pm in winter. ¥500.* The nearby **Hakodate Municipal Photo History Museum** exhibits fascinating photos of Hakodate's early days. *Tel. (0138)27-3333. Open daily 9am to 7pm; until 5pm in winter. ¥200.*

Stop in for tea and scones at the **Former British Consulate**. Rebuilt after a fire in 1913, you can see models of Commodore Matthew Perry's black ships. *Open 9am to 7pm; until 5pm in winter.*

Enough on how the privileged lived. To get a sense of the life of commoners, go to the **Hakodate Municipal Local History Museum** (Shiritsu Hakodate Hakubutsukan Kyodo Shiryokan). Everyday objects like clothing and furniture are on display. *Open 9am to 4:30pm; until 4pm in winter. Closed Monday, holidays and the last Friday of the month.*

A Russian priest originally built the **Russian Orthodox Church** in 1859. The church was later rebuilt after a fire in 1916. The Byzantine structure is sure to make you think you're on the wrong continent.

Head down to the water to see the brick **Kanamori Storehouses**, today converted into **Hakodate History Plaza**, complete with shops, beer hall and photo exhibition hall. *Open daily 9:30am to 7pm.*

Then take a bus or streetcar to Goryokaku Koen-mae, site of the star-shaped **Goryokaku Fort**. Constructed in 1864 by the Tokugawa shogunate in its waning days, Goryokaku is Japan's first Western-style fort. Designed to protect against foreign invaders, especially Russians, the only action it saw was from Japanese. After the fall of the shogun in 1868, Tokugawa loyalists fled to Hakodate and established an independent government. Meiji government troops attacked them in the fort. Only by building the nearby **Shiryokaku Fort** were the government troops able to displace the renegades. The park has thousands of cherry trees, which make it popular in springtime. For a bird's-eye view, climb the ugly but functional Goryokaku Tower: *open 8am to 5:45pm; from 9am to 5:45pm October through April. ¥630.*

Top off your visit at the top of **Mt. Hakodate**, but do so at twilight or in the evening for a splendid view of the city's lights spread out before you. *The ropeway is open 10am to 9:50pm; until 8:50pm November through April. The panorama is called the "million-dollar view," but you can have it for a mere ¥620 one way or ¥1130 round trip on the ropeway.*

KUSHIRO

Kushiro is famous for cranes—beautiful, red-crested, four-to-five-feet tall, Japanese cranes. Even if you are not a bird watcher, it's worth a stop to marvel at these magnificent birds. A trip to Kushiro is a complete contrast to urban Japan.

ARRIVALS & DEPARTURES

By Air
   To/from Sapporo: 3 flights/day (JAS. ¥14,250)
   To/from Tokyo Haneda: 5 flights/day (ANA, JAS. ¥28,550)
   To/from Osaka Kansai: 1 flight/day (JAS. ¥34,050)

For Ground Transportation:
Bus: to JR Kushiro Station (40 minutes, ¥910)
Taxi: to JR Kushiro Station (35 minutes, about ¥5000)

By Train
   To/from Sapporo: JR limited express to JR Kushiro Station. (3 hours 50 minutes, ¥8920)

By Ferry
   Ferry from Tokyo takes about 30 hours and costs from ¥13,100 to ¥31,500, depending on how luxurious you want your accommodations.

Tourist Information
   Tourist information is available at JR Kushiro Station. *Tel. (0154)23-5151.* Open 9am to 5:30pm. You can call the **Tourist Association**, *Tel. (0154)31-1993* from 9am to 9pm; there are English-speaking staff members.

WHERE TO STAY

CASTLE HOTEL, *2-5 Okawa-cho, Kushiro, Hokkaido, 085-0837. Tel. (0154)43-2111, Fax (0154)42-0318. Singles ¥6000. Twins ¥12,000. Credit cards.*

Designed by Mozuna Kiko, a well-known modern architect, the hotel is a four-minute walk from Fisherman's Wharf. You certainly can't miss the contemporary building; the small towers give you the feeling that you're aboard a ship.

TOKYU INN, *13-1-14 Kita Odori, Kushiro, Hokkaido, 085-0015. Tel. (0154)22-0109, Fax (0154)24-5498. Singles ¥6800. Twins from ¥12,200. Credit cards.*

Across from the JR Kushiro Station, the inn is convenient and clean.

SEEING THE SIGHTS

Kushiro is a large port city but for a visitor, the cranes are the biggest attraction. The tall and graceful Japanese cranes, *tancho,* do not migrate — they stick around eastern Hokkaido. In winter, the monogamous birds perform a graceful courting dance no human can match. The birds faced extinction, but now numbers are increasing and have doubled to 400 in the last decade.

In the 1950s, Kushiro had two harsh winters back-to-back, and the cranes nearly starved to death. One man, a Mr. Itoh, began to feed them. Being extremely cautious creatures, they began accepting food from this man and this man only. For years he fed them every winter out of his own expenses. Now several environmental groups give financial support to Mr. Itoh's son, who took over the task.

The cranes are easy to see in winter, but in the summer they go deep into the marshy areas and it's difficult to see them.

Kushiro Shitsugen National Park encompasses the vast marshes the cranes call home. To see the birds, go to **Tanchozuru Shizen Koen**, *112 Tsuruoka, Kushiro, five minutes by taxi from the airport. Open daily 9am to 4pm. ¥300.* Here you can see some cranes all year round. In winter, head to the **Marshland Museum and Observatory** (Kushiro Shitsugen Tenbodai) to see the birds in heated comfort. The birds are in this area only in winter; in summer, you can take in the marshland flora. *The marshes are 35 minutes by bus from JR Kushiro Station to Kushiro Shitsugen Tenbodai Bus stop. ¥360.*

To see the cranes' courting rituals, some of the most ostentatious in the animal world, take a bus from JR Kushiro Station toward either Tsurui-mura or Kawayu Onsen. Get off at Tsurumidai (45 minutes) or Itoh Sanctuary (60 minutes) where Mr. Itoh, whose father started feeding the cranes in the 1950s, maintains a sanctuary. The birds are usually in a courting-dance mood in February.

Another plus for visiting Kushiro is it's the hometown of a well-known modern architect, Mozuna Kiko, who designed some neat contemporary buildings. Check out the surreal **Kushiro City Museum** (Kushiro Shiritsu Hakubutsukan), which sits on a hill in Harutori Park *(by bus from the JR Kushiro Station to Kagakukan Dori stop)*. The stunning **Fisherman's Wharf Moo**, built in 1989, houses stores and restaurants. The huge greenhouse atrium with an indoor park serves as a recreation center during the long winter. The entire colorful structure really picks up the waterfront.

To skip back in time from the postmodern to the ancient, Kushiro also has two Ainu forts, **Moshiriya** and **Charanke**.

15. TOHOKU

Tohoku literally means "northeast" and encompasses the six north-ernmost prefectures in Honshu, Japan's main island. Visit Tohoku for gorgeous natural scenery, towering mountains, rugged cliffs plunging into the sea, wild festivals, hiking, skiing, local crafts and friendly people.

Spectacular summer festivals in early August in Akita, Aomori, Hirosaki, Yamagata and Sendai lure millions from all over Japan. Tohoku has visitors all year round: to ski in winter (and in some places actually into the summer); to take in the shockingly bright greens of spring leaves; to enjoy the cool mountains in summer and the colorful red and yellow autumn foliage amid the evergreens.

Historically Tohoku was the boondocks — far, far away from the capital city of Kyoto. Even when Tokyo became the capital, Tohoku remained on the fringe and was considered Japan's far north. The area's old name, Michinoku, means "the end of the road." The good news is even though Tohoku seems remote, excellent transportation systems provide easy access. The *shinkansen* train extends from Tokyo to Akita, Morioka and Yamagata. Airports located in Akita, Aomori, Hanamaki, Misawa, Sendai and Yamagata link Tohoku to the rest of the country. A series of long distance bus lines also connects the cities.

Planning Your Stay

Unless skiing is your objective, stay away from Tohoku in winter. Not only are many sights and mountain roads closed, but the severe cold makes traveling unpleasant. Spring brings the brilliant greens of new leaves and autumn's colorful foliage is famous throughout Japan; those are prime travel periods. Tohoku's mountains are popular in summer with urbanites fleeing the heat. The summer festivals in early August attract millions of spectators; be sure to make your hotel reservations well in advance.

Tohoku is relatively spread out. Here's how much time you should allow in each place: Hirosaki, 1 day; Shimokita Peninsula, 2 days; Towada-ko, 1 day; Tazawa-ko and Kakunodate, 2 days; Yamadera, 1 day; Dewa

TOHOKU

HOKKAIDO

Shinkansen Trains ‖‖‖

Japanese Railroad Trains ▬

Sea of Japan

Hirosaki

Aomori
Mt.Hakkoda ▲
Oirase Valley
Ninokuchi

Towadako

Akita

Tazawako

Morioka

Kakunodate

Hanamaki

Tono

Sakata

Hiraizumi

Tsuruoka

Mt.Gassan ▲

Matsushima

Yamagata

Sendai

Niigata

Yonezawa

Kitakata

Fukushima

N

Aizu-Wakamatsu

Koriyama

Pacific Ocean

TOHOKU HIGHLIGHTS

- *Hirosaki's handsome castle keep set amid cherry trees*
- *The beautiful natural scenery of Oirase Gorge*
- *Summer skiing and hiking on Mt. Hakkoda*
- *Mt. Osore, the sacred Buddhist mountain*
- *Samurai residences of Kakunodate*
- *Soaking in a hot spring bath at a rustic inn*
- *The mummified Buddhas and ascetic mountain priests of Dewa Sanzan*
- *Thatched-roof L-shaped farmhouses at Tono*
- *Hiraizumi's 12th century temple*
- *Climbing the mountain to Yamadera Temple*

Sanzan, 2 days; Hiraizumi, 1 day; Aizu Wakamatsu, 1 day. Tailor your trip to fit your interests:

- **Archaeology**: Sannai-Maruyama
- **Castles and Feudal History**: Hirosaki, Aizu Wakamatsu
- **Uniquely Japanese religious experiences**: Osorezan, Dewa Sanzan, Yamadera
- **Hot springs**: Tsuta Onsen, Yachi Onsen, Nyuto Onsen, Tamagawa Onsen, Atsumi Onsen
- **Preserved samurai district**: Kakunodate
- **Skiing**: Mt. Hakkoda, Zao
- **Hiking**: Oirase Gorge, Mt. Hakkoda, Lake Towada-ko, Lake Tazawa-ko
- **Festivals**: Nebuta at Aomori and Hirosaki, Kanto at Akita, Tanabata at Sendai, Yamagasa at Yamagata
- **Crafts**: Aizu Wakamatsu, Hirosaki, Kahoku near Yamagata City
- **Shrines and Temples**: Zuiho-ji at Matsushima, Yamadera, Dewa Sanzan

AOMORI CITY

A convenient gateway to Hirosaki, Lake Towada-ko, Shimokita Peninsula and Hokkaido, **Aomori**, a sprawling port and prefectural capital, has little to offer for any substantial amount of time. But if you find yourself there with time to kill, there are a few good museums.

ARRIVALS & DEPARTURES

By Air – Aomori Airport

To/from Tokyo Haneda: 4 flights/day (JAS. ¥21,850)

To/from Osaka Itami: 2 flights/day; **from Kansai**: 1 flight/day (JAS. ¥26,850)

To/from Nagoya: 1 flight/day (JAS. ¥23,650)

To/from Sapporo Chitose: 2 flights/day (JAS. ¥15,500)

To/from Fukuoka: 1 flight/day (JAS. ¥34,400)

The airport is too small to get lost. There is a tourist information counter in the lobby, which has English brochures and sells bus tickets to Hirosaki and Aomori.

For Ground Transportation:

By bus: Board the buses outside the airport lobby exit; signs are in English. Departures are timed with plane arrivals. The bus to Aomori Station takes 35 minutes and costs ¥560.

By taxi: Taxi takes 30 minutes to Aomori Station and runs about ¥3600.

By Train

To/from Tokyo: JR Tohoku shinkansen train to Morioka (2 1/2 to 3 hours) and transfer to JR *Hatsukari* limited express train (2 hours 20 minutes, ¥17,040).

To/from Hirosaki and Akita: JR Ohu line has limited-express trains *Inaho* and *Tazawa* running between Akita to Aomori via Hirosaki. Hirosaki to Aomori (30 minutes, ¥650), and Akita to Aomori (2 hours 45 minutes, ¥5450).

To/from Hokkaido (Hakodate): The JR Tsugaru Kaikyo line runs from Aomori to Hokkaido through the 54 kilometer Seikan tunnel. *Hatsukari* limited express train (1 hour 55 minutes, ¥5340). *Kaisoku* (express) trains (2 hours 20 minutes, ¥3150).

By Long Distance Bus

To/from Tokyo: Overnight JR Bus departs Tokyo Station (10 1/2 hours, ¥10,190)

To/from Morioka: 5 buses daily between Morioka Station and Aomori (3 1/4 hours, ¥3100) One is a JR bus.

To/from Sendai: 4 buses daily between Sendai and Aomori including one JR bus. (4 1/2 hours, ¥5600)

By Ferry

Ferry runs 12 times a day from Aomori to Hakodate (3 1/2 hours. ¥1400). Higashi Nihon Ferry, *Tel. (0177)82-3631.*

GETTING AROUND TOWN

Buses and taxis are the best way to get around Aomori. City buses run on a zone system; you pay when exiting. If you do not get on at the beginning of line, take a small ticket listing the zone when you board; the chart above the driver indicates your fare.

Tourist Information

The tourist information booth at JR Aomori Station is straight ahead as you exit through the ticket wickets by the entrance to Lovina Department Store, *Tel. (0177)34-2500.* Open 9am to 6pm. Closed December 31, January 1 and the 4th Monday through Wednesday in January.

Eight minutes walk from the station is **ASPAM**; no, not a type of canned meat, but a prefectural tourism building. The prefecture has poured a lot of money into it in hopes of boosting tourism. The triangular structure has tourist information, displays of local crafts and, naturally, gives you an opportunity to buy souvenirs. The 13th floor observation lounge (¥600) has panoramic views of downtown Aomori and the harbor and a tourist film is shown on the 2nd floor (¥400). The address is: *1-1-40 Yasukata, Tel. (0177)35-5311.* Open 9am to 6pm. Restaurants and Observation Lounge open until 10pm. Closed December 31 and January 1. ASPAM is a "I" Tourist Information Center.

Aomori Welcome Card

Travelers to Aomori Prefecture can obtain an **Aomori Welcome Card** which offers discounts at hotels, stores and cultural sites. Get yours at JNTO's Tokyo Tourist Information Center or at tourist information centers in Aomori City (see above), Aomori Airport, Hirosaki City, Misawa Airport, Masakari Plaza Tourist Information in Mutsu and Lake Towada Tourist Information Center. Only travelers whose visa is for a stay of one year or less are eligible. You need to have your passport to apply.

WHERE TO STAY

CENTRAL HOTEL AOMORI, *1-11-2 Yasukata, Aomori City, 030-0803. Tel. (0177)22-1100, Fax (0177)22-1250. Singles ¥5800. Twins ¥11,000 with breakfast. Credit cards.*

A new hotel where most of the rooms have a view of the Aomori Bay and bridge.

SAKAMOTO, *3-3-12 Honcho, Aomori City, 030-0802. Tel. (0177)76-1481. No fax. From ¥7000 per person with two meals. Credit cards. 15-minute walk from Aomori station.*

This small and quiet Japanese inn serves a six-course family-style dinner.

WHERE TO EAT

JINTAKO *(Regional cuisine and live music, moderate to expensive). 1-6-16 Yasukata. Tel. (0177)22-7727. Open 6pm to 10:30pm. Closed 1st and 3rd Sunday.*

A restaurant to enjoy local flavor in every sense! Fresh fish as well as live music featuring Tsugaru *jamisen* (a three-stringed instrument) and local folk songs, played by the lively sisters who run the place. A set meal costs ¥5000.

SEEING THE SIGHTS

If you are in Aomori June through early August, stop at **Nebuta Rasseland** and see the fantastic *nebuta* festival floats being made. It is located on the far side of Aoi Umi Park, a few minutes from ASPAM. *Open June 1 through August 8, 10am to 5pm, longer hours closer to the festival. Free admission.*

The **market district**, just one minute from JR Station, has lots of fresh fish and seafood and a real local flavor. *Open 5am to 6:30pm. Closed Sunday.*

Munakata Memorial Museum (Munakata Shiko Kinenkan). *Tel. (0177)77-4567. Open 9:30am to 4:30pm; closes at 4pm December through March. Closed Monday, public holidays in winter and December 27 through January 4. ¥300. From JR Aomori Station take the bus towards Nakatsutsui or Kohato Danchi, and get off at Munakata Shikokan Dori. ¥190.*

This museum houses a collection of works by one of Japan's most celebrated modern woodblock print artists, the late Munakata Shiko, who was designated a National Living Treasure in 1970. Known for his dynamic and almost primitive wild-looking figures, Munakata would sometimes cut a woodblock without first sketching it. The traditional building has a lovely Japanese garden.

Sannai-Maruyama. *Open 9am to 6pm, May through August; until 4pm September through April. Free admission. From Aomori Station bus stop #2, 30 minutes by bus to Sannai-Maruyama Iseki Mae (8 to 9 buses/day).*

This stop is a must for anyone interested in Japanese archaeology. This site is the largest and oldest Jomon village excavated until now and has made archaeologists rethink their theories of life 4000 to 5500 years ago. The size of the village and its ritual decorations assume a higher level of technological advancement. Evidence points to the cultivation of vegetables. The *shiryokan* (museum) houses the objects unearthed; the excavations continue.

Aomori Prefectural Museum (Aomori Kenritsu Kyodokan). *Open 9:30am to 5pm; until 4pm October through March. Closed Monday, public holidays, last day of the month and December 28 through January 4. ¥310. Take bus at gate 8 of JR Aomori Station toward Aoyagi Keiyu Tobu Eigyosho and get off at Honcho go-chome (10 minutes). 5 minutes by taxi.* This museum exhibits the history of the prefecture, which is more interesting than it might sound since it covers prehistoric relics and more recent folk craft.

Asamushi Aquarium (Asamushi Suizokukan). *Open 9am to 6pm, until 5pm Nov. and Dec.; until 4:30pm Dec. through April. Closed December 30-31. ¥1580. 40 minutes by bus from Aomori Station, platform 1, get off at terminal, Asamushi Suizokukan. ¥750; or a 10-minute walk from Asamushi Onsen station on JR line.* This popular aquarium features a tunnel through the large fish tank and dolphin shows.

THE WILD NEBUTA FESTIVAL

*Aomori's **Nebuta festival**, August 2-7, is one of Japan's wildest.*

The fantastic three-dimensional nebuta floats of warriors and demons are pulled through the streets of Aomori by thousands of haneto (costumed attendants). Anyone can be one of the haneto; simply go to a department store and buy or rent a costume. Of course, a lot of energy is needed. You must shout "rasera, rasera," jump up and down and dance with abandon. Alcohol aids the process.

It takes about three months to make a float. Bent metal wire is attached to a wooden frame to create the form. Washi paper is attached to this frame and the design is painted on the surface.

Illuminated from the inside, the floats literally float along the road. They can be as big as 9 meters wide and 5 meters tall and weigh as much as four tons. Each float costs about ¥10 million: ¥4 million for labor and the rest for materials.

The festival's origins are obscure, and there are several conflicting legends. One says it's related to the Tanabata Festival, a summer festival when children carried lanterns and other decorations. A variation says the festival was to lull the farmers out of their winter sleepiness. The word "nebuta" could have come from nembute, which in Aomori dialect means "sleepy." A further similarity is both Tanabata and Nebuta decorations are thrown into the sea on the last day.

Another theory puts the origin in the 800s when a general was sent to subdue the local Ezo people. The general built a large lantern and the Ezo were so curious they came out of hiding and were then captured.

Whatever its beginnings, it's a great festival to see.

HIROSAKI

A small city once the castle town of the Tsugaru feudal lords, **Hirosaki** retains some elements of its glorious past. Although no longer the capital of the region (that honor falls to bland Aomori City), Hirosaki proudly remains the region's center of culture and education.

Lord Tsugaru built his castle in Hirosaki in the early 1600s — a few of the original buildings still stand. The castle grounds are now lined with thousands of cherry trees. Framed with cherry blossoms, photographs of the tiny castle grace zillions of calendars all across Japan.

The first Tsugaru lord sided with Tokugawa Ieyasu in 1600 and, as a member of the winning side, he received a larger domain. He must have done something really right because his son married one of Ieyasu's daughters, the ultimate trophy wife. Christian missionaries from the West flocked to Hirosaki in the 1870s. We don't know how many souls they saved, but one living legacy is the many Western-style buildings constructed at that time.

You may be startled to find swastika-like symbols on manhole covers and in other places around town. Long before Hitler perverted their use, the Tsugaru family adopted the swastika, an ancient Buddhist symbol, as its emblem. The city continued the tradition after the end of the feudal period.

ARRIVALS & DEPARTURES

By Air

Aomori is the closest airport. See Aomori Arrivals and Departures for flight information.

For Ground Transportation:

By bus: The Konan Bus to Hirosaki departs after the arrival of each plane and takes one hour to Hirosaki. Buy a ticket at the airport information counter or pay as you get off the bus. Fare ¥750. The bus deposits you at the Hirosaki Bus Terminal, behind Ito Yokado Department Store, about a five minute walk from JR Hirosaki Station.

By taxi: 50 minutes to JR Hirosaki Station, ¥5600.

By Train

Hirosaki is on the JR Ohu line that connects Aomori and Akita.

To/from Akita: JR *Tazawa* and *Inaho* limited express trains (2 hours, ¥4400)

To/from Aomori: JR *Tazawa* and *Inaho* limited express trains (30 minutes, ¥1790). Local (50 minutes, ¥650)

To/from Morioka: JR *Hatsukari* limited express (2 hours 20 minutes) and switch to the JR Ohu line, 30 minutes on the *Tazawa* and *Inaho* limited express trains. ¥7850.

By Bus

To/from Tokyo: Overnight bus from Shinagawa and Hamamatsucho (9 1/2 hours, ¥10,050)

To/from Morioka: 15 buses/day (2 hours 20 minutes, ¥2930). Several are JR buses.

To/from Sendai: 3 buses/day (4 hours 20 minutes, ¥5090). Some are JR buses.

ORIENTATION

The area around the JR Hirosaki Station is run down and you may wonder if you are in the right place. Don't despair; the historic districts have maintained more of the atmosphere of Lord Tsugaru's age. Hirosaki is small enough to cover on foot, and most sights can be seen in one day.

GETTING AROUND TOWN

Local buses work on a zone system; unless you board at the terminal, pick up a ticket with the zone number as you enter the bus and refer to the fare chart above the driver when you get off.

Bicycle Rentals: Hirosaki would be a perfect city to explore by bicycle, but the closest rental place is a 20-minute walk in the opposite direction. **BH Rental Lease**, *3-1-19 Joto Chuo, Tel. (0172)28-2242*, will deliver bikes to the station if you arrange it in advance.

Tourist Information

The **Tourist Information Office** at JR Hirosaki Station is on your right as you exit the station. *Tel. (0172)32-0524*. Open 8:45am to 6pm; until 5pm January through March. They have brochures and maps in English and can assist you with hotel reservations, but little English is spoken.

The **Hirosaki Sightseeing Information Center**, *Tel. (0172)37-5501*, is located across from Hirosaki Park. See the Seeing the Sights information below.

Both centers are "i" Tourist Information Offices.

WHERE TO STAY

Hirosaki isn't a great place to spend the night. The Japanese-style accommodations are worn and although perfectly acceptable, the Western hotels are nothing special.

HOTEL NEW CASTLE, *24-1 Kamisayashi-machi, Hirosaki, 036-8354. Tel. (0172)36-1211, Fax (0172)36-1210. Singles ¥7900. Twins ¥11,000. Credit cards. 15-minute walk from JR Hirosaki Station, 5-minutes by taxi.*

The New Castle Hotel is close to Hirosaki Park so it's very convenient for seeing the sights.

CITY HIROSAKI HOTEL, *1-1-2 Omachi, Hirosaki, 036-8004. Tel. (0172)37-0109, Fax (0172)37-1610. Singles ¥7800. Twins ¥11,500. Credit cards.*

A modern Western-style hotel located close to the train station, rooms have a view of the surrounding mountains. An Italian restaurant at the top of building serves lunch for ¥2500 and dinner for ¥5000. Guests can use the swimming pool and fitness club for a ¥3000 fee.

ISHIBA RYOKAN, *55 Moto Teramachi, Hirosaki, 036. Tel. (0172)32-9118, Fax (0172)32-5630. ¥10,000 per person with two meals. No credit cards.*

One of the oldest Japanese inns in the area, Ishiba was founded 120 years ago and has seen better days. All 18 rooms are Japanese style.

WHERE TO EAT

TAKASAGO *(Noodles, inexpensive). 1-2 Oyakata-cho. Tel. (0172)32-8025. Open 11am to 6pm. Closed Monday.*

Located in an older traditional house on the block behind the Aomori Bank Building, Takasago has an old-fashioned noodle shop. The *soba* noodles are thinner than most. Noodles cost ¥700 to ¥1500.

FUJIDANA *(Japanese, inexpensive). 20-1 Moto Nagacho. Around the corner from the Aomori Bank Building. Tel. (0172)37-3700. Open 11:30am to 3pm; 5pm to 9:30pm. Closed Sunday.*

Fujidana serves *tempura* set lunches for ¥1000. A special *bento* lunch costs ¥2000 and requires an advance reservation.

SUIMEISO *(Japanese, moderate to expensive). 69 Moto Teramachi. Tel. (0172)32-8281. Open 11am to 1:30pm, 5pm to 8:30pm. Closed Monday. Located on the same street as Hirosaki church.*

The elegant building, a villa belonging to the chairman of Aomori Bank, was constructed at the turn of the century. No expense was spared. Gold leaf covers the ceiling of one room and a famous Toyama artisan carved the transoms. A Kyoto designer built the dry-landscape garden. Lunchtime service is *tsuki gawari zen* (set menu) changes every month, ¥3000. The *Shirakami* set meal for dinner is ¥17,000.

SUZUME NO OYADO *(Japanese, inexpensive to moderate). 55-4 Okeya-machi. Tel. (0172)35-8584. Open 12 noon to 2pm; 5pm-9pm.*

There is no set menu; the food served changes daily depending on which ingredients the owner found freshest at the market that morning. *Teishoku* lunch is ¥2000 and *kaiseki* lunch runs from ¥3000. Dinner courses range from ¥4000 to ¥7000.

LIVE HOUSE YAMAUTA *(Live music and regional cuisine, moderate). 1-2-7 Omachi. Tel. (0172)36-1835. Open 5 to 11pm.*

If you are in Hirosaki during the evening, go to Yamauta. The region is famous for *Tsugaru jamisen*, a stringed musical instrument reminiscent of a banjo. The folk music is masculine and dynamic. During the seventies, some Japanese popular musicians incorporated the music into their songs, not unlike the way the Beatles experimented with the sitar. Run by a well-known performer, Yamada Chisato, Yamauta lives up to its name and has nightly *Tsugaru jamisen* performances. It also serves inexpensive regional cuisine.

You can even find **fast food** in Hirosaki. Check out the Dotemachi shopping street for Mr. Donut and Kentucky Fried Chicken.

SEEING THE SIGHTS

From JR Hirosaki Station, take a taxi for about ¥1000 or bus #51 or #61 from platform 3 to Shiyakusho-mae Koen Iriguchi. The **Hirosaki Sightseeing Information Center**, a modern brick and glass structure in a wide plaza, is a logical place to start your touring. *Open 9am to 6pm; until 5pm December through March. Closed December 29 through January 3.*

The tourist desk has English brochures and maps and computerized hotel information. The same building has an excellent exhibition of Hirosaki crafts, including a step-by-step display of Tsugaru lacquer — all 48 steps. It's called fool's lacquer — only a fool would go through so much trouble.

Next store, the **Float Pavilion** (Dashi Tenjikan) displays the elaborate carts pulled at festivals. Also in the square is the former **City Library** (Kyu Hirosaki Shiritsu Toshokan), a Renaissance-style building constructed in 1906 and moved to its present site in 1987. Since it houses a library museum, a look from the outside is enough. The plaza also holds the **To-o Gijuku Missionaries Home**, built in 1904 for Western teachers. *Open daily 9am to 4:30pm. Closed December 29 through January 3. Admission to library and home ¥300.*

Continue along the perimeter of the park to the **Fujita Memorial Japanese Garden** (Fujita Kinen Tei-en). Built in 1919 by a businessman, the garden incorporates the distant Mt. Iwaki into its landscape. *Open 9am to 5pm. Closed Mondays and November 23 until mid-April. ¥300.*

Across the street is **Hirosaki Park**, the grounds of the castle. Enter the park and wind your way around the three moats to the central keep. Before you cross a bright red bridge over the last moat, you reach an open area called **Ninomaru**, where the Tsugaru family residence once stood.

The castle was completed in 1611, but 15 years later lightening destroyed the five-storied keep and for nearly 200 years, there wasn't one. In 1810, the Tsugaru domain produced 100,000 *koku* of rice and to celebrate, the feudal lord moved one of the original guard towers to the long vacant site of the castle keep. It's really quite tiny and doesn't have the majestic feel associated with most Japanese castle keeps, but the building's scale underlines the modest size of this domain. Inside the keep

SHIRAKAMI MOUNTAINS

Shirakami Sanchi Mountains, the world's largest virgin forest of Japanese beech trees, are a UNESCO World Heritage Site. Despite this designation, the hiking trails are relatively untrodden. The waterfalls freeze in winter and are popular with ice climbers. During the Edo period, locals would predict the harvest based on the thickness of the ice.

The easiest way to get to Shirakami is by a guided tour (in Japanese) from Hirosaki. The Konan Bus runs a tour Sundays and holidays from late June through mid-October. The bus leaves Hirosaki at 8:30am for the hour-long trip to the forest. You walk along the Anmon Falls Hiking Trail, roughly a three-hour hike. The bus leaves to return to Hirosaki at 2:30pm. ¥2500. Information: Konan Bus, Tel. (0172)36-5061. Other trails in Shirakami Sanchi are more difficult to reach as you have to approach them from the Japan Sea side.

is a museum that displays samurai armor and belongings of feudal lords. *Open daily 9am to 5pm. Closed November 24 through March 31. ¥300.*

Hirosaki Park, home of 5000 weeping cherry trees, celebrates the blossoms each year with a festival from April 23 through May 5. Awash in pale pink, the castle looks really beautiful. One warning: avoid the festival if you have a fear of crowds. *¥300 admission fee to enter the park's inner areas during the festival.*

Continue through the park to exit at the **Kamenoko Mon** or north gate, the only gate built when the castle was originally constructed. Directly across the street is a wooden building housing a liquor store, **Ishiba House** (Ishiba-ke). Enter the shop and pay ¥100 to look at the living areas of this prosperous merchant's house. Check out the high-gloss polish of the wooden floor, which is maintained by cleaning daily with a simple cloth. *Open 9am to 5pm. Closed Thursday.*

The Ishiba shop is in an Historic House Preservation District where a few samurai houses and some handsome walls and gates remain. The **Ito, Iwate** and **Umeda** samurai houses are open to the public free of charge. *Open 9am to 4pm, April through October; Ito and Umeda closed Tuesday and Friday. Iwate closed Monday and Thursday. November through March all houses open only on Saturday and Sunday.*

TOHOKU'S TRADITIONAL CRAFTS

HIROSAKI CRAFTS

Tsugaru Kogin Zashi. Cotton couldn't be grown in Hirosaki's severe climate, so the fabric was an expensive imported item. The feudal lords prohibited commoners from wearing cotton; they had no choice but to wear a very rough hemp. Women embroidered geometric patterns on the hemp to strengthen it and make it heavier, which kept people warmer through the cold winter. Today Hirosaki's citizens can wear anything they like, but you still find small souvenir items like wallets and coasters made of embroidered hemp .

Tsugaru tako-e kite paintings were originally made to be flown, but today you don't see many kites over Hirosaki. The craft developed as another way for lower-ranking samurai to support themselves. The kite's ribs are made of cypress wood native to the area; most Japanese kites use bamboo supports. The washi paper surface is adorned with paintings of famous samurai warriors.

Tsugaru lacquer is also called "fool's lacquer" because only a fool would go through the zillion steps to make it. The rough surface of a lacquer piece is covered with many different colors and then sanded in a way that results in a multicolored surface. Stop at the Tourist Information Center near Hirosaki Park to see the step-by-step process.

At the edge of the historic district and facing the castle moat is **Kawasaki Indigo Dyeing Workshop** (Kawasaki Some Koujou), which features indigo-dyed crafts in an Edo-era building. The shop has an excellent selection of indigo products from handkerchiefs to clothes. Admission to a small museum and workshop is ¥200. Try your hand at dyeing a handkerchief in indigo for ¥1100. *Open 9am to 5pm. Closed Thursday.*

On the corner facing Kawasaki Dyeing Workshop is **Nebuta Village** (Nebuta Mura). Hirosaki's **Nebuta festival**, held August 1-7, is one of the largest and most famous of Tohoku's summer festivals. This festival is more subdued than its neighbor Aomori's.

Hirosaki's nebuta floats are two dimensional: huge fan-shaped frames are decorated with bright paintings. Illuminated from the inside, wax highlights the paintings and gives them greater translucence. Unless you are in Hirosaki for the festival, stop in at the village. You might wonder whether or not you should have bothered as you walk down the long hallway past tacky souvenir shops. But, hang on. Soon you'll enter a large, darkened room with an illuminated float in the center and smaller floats lining its perimeter. A drummer and flutist play, giving a sense of the excitement of the festival's music. Then try your own hand at drumming. The village also has a garden with some of the most exquisitely pruned pine trees we've ever seen. You'll also find craftsmen demonstrating pottery, kite painting, *kokeshi* doll making and paper crafts. For a fee you can try them yourself. *Open daily 9am to 5pm; until 4pm December through March. Closed December 31. ¥500.*

To see turn-of-the-century Western architecture, walk alongside the moat and turn left after the high school. Turn right at the next street and you will come to **Hirosaki Church**, a Gothic building built by Methodists in 1907. Continue along this road until the Aomori Bank Building is on the right corner. Turn right and you see the **Aomori Bank Memorial Hall** (Aomori Ginko Kinen-kan), a splendidly restored Renaissance-style building constructed in 1906. *Open 9:30am to 4:30pm April through November. Closed Tuesday and in winter. ¥200.*

Saishoin Temple, a 15-minute walk or short taxi ride, is the home of a five-storied pagoda built in 1667 for the souls of the Tsugaru warriors killed in battle.

Chosho-ji Temple, the Tsugaru family temple, is a taxi ride or a long walk away. Lord Tsugaru ordered the Zen temples in his territory to relocate to this area. The broad avenue is lined with 33 temples. Chosho-ji's two-storied gate, built in 1629, is designated an Important Cultural Property. All the Tsugaru lords are buried at this temple, including one who is a local legend because his body mummified rather than decomposed. *Open 8am to 5pm; until 4pm November through March. ¥300.*

Nakano Nebuta Tako Seisaku-sho is a must for people interested in the bright kites for which Hirosaki is famous. Samurai began to paint famous warriors' faces on kites to supplement their meager income. Mr. Nakano, the area's foremost kite painter, welcomes visitors to try painting a kite or a nebuta figure. Reservations are necessary; plan on spending two hours. *Tel. (0172)32-7033. Open 9 to 5pm. 20 minutes on foot from station, ¥1000.*

SHOPPING

Founded in 1897, **Tanakaya** has thick black pillars and white walls. For sale is an excellent assortment of Tsugaru crafts including lacquer ware. Small *sake* cups start at ¥500 and Tsugaru lacquer chopsticks are ¥1000. Paintings and prints by local artists cover the second floor walls. *Ichiban-cho Kado. Tel. (0172)33-6666. Open daily 10am to 7pm.*

SHIMOKITA PENINSULA

The tip of this peninsula is the northernmost point of Honshu Island. It's the home of **Osorezan**, one of the three mountains in Japan that Buddhists believe are inhabited by the spirits of the deceased. It truly is a vision of another world.

The **Shimokita Peninsula** itself is underpopulated, mountainous and heavily forested. On the western shore fantastic cliffs drop to the sea. Getting to the mountainous interior means traversing the peninsula's long, thin neck (about an hour by train or car), an uninteresting trip unless you get a charge out of the nuclear power plant at Rokkasho.

It is possible to travel from Aomori, see Osorezan and return in the same day. If you have an extra day, try to see more of the peninsula. And if you're looking for quaint, thatched-roof farmhouses or historic edifices, don't visit Shimokita; the buildings are more utilitarian than attractive.

ARRIVALS & DEPARTURES

Mutsu is the largest city, but no train station bears that name. The JR Ominato line ends at Ominato Station. The main bus station is at Tanabu. To reach Tanabu, use the private Shimokita Kotsu line from JR Shimokita Station to Tanabu Station.

By Train

To/from Aomori or Misawa: JR Ominato line starts in Noheji and terminates at Ominato Station (about one hour, ¥1100). Noheji Station is 40 minutes from Aomori, 20 to 30 minutes from Misawa and 1 hour 50 minutes from Morioka on the Tohoku Honsen Line.

A private train line, Shimokita Kotsu, connects with the JR Ominato Line at Shimokita Station. It stops at Tanabu (¥200), the major bus hub, and terminates at Ohata on the northern coast (30 minutes, ¥410).

By Bus

To/from Aomori: 8 buses/day from ASPAM building to Mutsu Bus Terminal near Tanabu Station. (2 hours 40 minutes, ¥2520).

Buses from Mutsu Bus Terminal go to all parts of the peninsula, but some routes have fairly infrequent service.

By Car

It takes about one hour to drive from Noheji to Mutsu. The main roads are well marked in English all over the peninsula, which makes driving a good choice. Car rental is available in Noheji (Nippon Rent a Car) and Mutsu.

By Ferry

Ferry service between Oma, on the tip of the Shimokita Peninsula, and Hakodate in Hokkaido. 3 to 4 ferries/day (1 hour 40 minutes, ¥1000).

GETTING AROUND

The private Shimokita Kotsu train and buses are the mass transportation choices. If you are pressed for time, rent a car at Aomori or Noheji.

WHERE TO STAY

HOTEL NEW YAGEN, *6-10 Aza Yagen, Shimokita-gun, Aomori, 039-4400. Tel. (0175)34-3311, Fax (0175)34-2364. Rates ¥10,000 per person with two meals. Credit cards.*

We wish the architect had constructed a building in harmony with the beautiful mountains rather than this white elephant, a five-storied cement structure with a bright red roof. Never mind — the hotel is well situated facing the river and mountains; once you are inside, you can forget about its exterior. The outdoor hot spring baths overlook the river and are reached via a wooden corridor that has a scent of freshly cut wood. Soak yourself in the hot spring and forget about the rest of the world. The New Yagen, the best hotel in Shimokita, is deep in the forest, so it's easy to forget you are only about 10 kilometers from the sea. The dinner is heavy on seafood, especially sea urchin and tender fresh squid.

FURUHATA, *1 Ohata Aza Yagen, Shimokita-gun, Aomori, 039-4401. Tel. (0175)34-2763, Fax (0175)34-6315. From ¥11,000 per person with two meals. Credit cards.*

This small and simple inn at Yagen Onsen is on the bank of the river. The hot spring bath is made of wood.

KAKUCHO HASE RYOKAN, *75 Shimofuro Onsen, Kazamaura-mura, Shimokita-gun, Aomori, 039. Tel. (0175)36-2221, Fax (0175)36-2668. Rates from ¥9000 per person with two meals. Credit cards.*

Inspired by the ships' lights on the bay, the noted author Inoue Yasushi wrote a novel at this inn, which made it famous with Japanese. Located on the northern coast of Shimokita, all the rooms look out over the Tsugaru Straits where you, too, can see the lights of the fishing boats twinkling on the water. The hotel has its own hot springs.

WHERE TO EAT

NANKO *(Japanese, inexpensive). 2-5 Tanabu-machi, Mutsu. Tel. (0175)22-7377. Open 11:30am to 9pm. Walking distance from Tanabu Station, close to Tanabu Shrine.*

Located in a building constructed of *hiba* (a type of cedar) wood, Nanko specializes in seafood caught in local waters. Their *sanshoku kamameshi* features clams, scallops and sea urchin cooked on top of rice, ¥1500. The Shimokita *teishoku* includes *toban-yaki* (grilled seafood and vegetables), *sashimi* and salad for ¥2500.

SHIN WAFU IZAKAYA *(Japanese, moderate). Suzusei Honcho Building, Hon-cho, Mutsu. Tel. (0175)22-6001. Open 5pm to 12 midnight.*

This lively pub-restaurant has a large red lantern hanging at the entrance. It serves seafood sets and *nabe* stews priced from ¥3000.

MARUMI-YA *(Noodles, inexpensive). 105-60 Nakajima-cho, Ohata. Tel. (0175)34-2433. Open 10am to 7pm. Closed 1st and 3rd Sundays.*

Just as pasta made with squid ink is popular in Italy, this restaurant serves *ramen* noodles made of squid ink and flour for ¥800.

SEEING THE SIGHTS

Osorezan

Translated into English as Mt. Terror, Mt. Dread or Mt. Fear, you immediately get the idea that **Osorezan** is not a place for a picnic. But it is certainly not to be missed if you want both an unusual and a uniquely Japanese experience.

Located in a volcano's crater, the surrounding forested peaks are verdant and peaceful. But inside the crater is a vision of hell. There is no growth or vegetation. Ash-colored rocks, pools of green sulfuric water, steam rising from deep within the earth, bright yellow sulfur deposits and the aroma of rotten eggs combine to resemble a moonscape. Originally a shamanistic folk religion developed there and then Buddhists claimed it as their own. The traditional wooden buildings of Bodai-ji Temple look as if they have been plopped down on the lunar surface.

At the entrance to the complex, there is a red wooden bridge over the Sanzu River that represents the bridge the deceased must cross to enter the other world. If you feel like it, the bridge is open for mere mortals to use (for practice). After the bridge, you pass some temple buildings and a few small wooden huts containing hot spring baths. These primitive tubs contain the sulfuric water gurgling up in the area; anyone can use these baths, but you need your own towel. The idea is to purify yourself before you enter the sacred area.

After the baths, a small fence opens onto a desolate wasteland with several small pavilions. Some are dedicated to Jizo, the Buddha who helps people cross into heaven. Small Jizo statues are clothed in red bibs and hold toys for the spirits of deceased children — those who were never born because of miscarriage and abortion.

The paths are lined with small piles of stones. These piles symbolize the plight of people in hell. Every night, the demons knock down the piles. Every day representatives of the living build them up again. By rebuilding these piles, the living release people from hell, and prayers from family and friends can quiet the demons.

Osoresan has *itako,* blind shamanesses, who communicate with the spirits. They undergo rigorous training and enter a trance to communicate with the deceased. The *itako* come from all over the Tohoku region and make contact with the other world during festivals held July 20–24 and October 9–11. Although *itako* receive messages from departed loved ones that they deliver to the living, they cannot deliver messages from the living to the departed, a frustrating and costly exercise for the practical minded. While we tend to be skeptical of the entire exercise, believers have no doubt that they are communicating with their loved ones. And at the very least, some sociologists feel the process can be therapeutic for the living. The cost is ¥3000 to contact each deceased person. *The temple is open 6am to 6pm and closed from the end of October until May 1. ¥500. Bus from Tanabu Station or Mutsu Bus Terminal takes 35 minutes and costs ¥730.*

If you are driving, there is an excellent mountain road from Osorezan to Yagen Onsen, a good place to spend the night. By bus you must return to Mutsu Bus Station; take a bus or train to Ohata (30 minutes) where you catch a bus for the 20-minute ride to Yagen Onsen.

Yagen Onsen

Yagen Onsen, a tiny hot spring area deep in the mountains, is so remote it feels about a million miles from civilization. And it is. A feudal lord who sided with Hideyoshi's forces at the siege of Osaka Castle in 1614 settled in the Yagen area. He was on the losing side, but he was so far away, no one bothered him.

Yagen Onsen is a great area to visit for walking and relaxing. Paths run along the river and in the mountains deeply forested with beech trees. We love the walk along the river.

Several kilometers down the road is **Oku Yagen Onsen** where **Meoto Kappa no Yu** offers free outdoor hot spring baths in a peaceful setting on the banks of the river. The new log cabin rest house opens onto two open air baths along the side of the river. It's an inviting place to stop and soak yourself in the clear hot spring water, which makes your skin feel silky. There is even a children's bath complete with slide and a rest house with simple and inexpensive food.

Hotokegaura

The remote cliffs of **Hotokegaura** offer some of Japan's most spectacular scenery. Giant rocks, sculpted by nature, rise from the sea amidst a backdrop of green mountains. The name means Buddha's Bay — mysterious, just like the Buddha.

The cliffs can only be seen by boats, which leave from Sai. You can also take a ferry to Aomori City from Sai; the trip takes 2 1/2 hours. It's easiest to reach Sai by car although it can be done by mass transit. Be sure you get current bus and ferry information from the tourist office because service is limited.

SHOPPING

Mutsu Local Products Hall (Mutsu Shimokita Kanko Bussan-kan Masakari Plaza). *1-10-25 Yanagi-machi, Mutsu. Tel. (0175)22-0909. Open 10am to 6pm. Closed on Tuesdays in winter.* A typical tourist-oriented shop, it's a good place to find many Shimokita products under one roof. Try soap made from *hiba* (cedar) wood.

Masakari, the attached restaurant, serves *miso kaiyaki*, a traditional Aomori dish of scallops grilled in the shell with *miso* sauce. ¥1000.

LAKE TOWADA-KO & OIRASE GORGE AREA

Lake Towada-ko and **Mt. Hakkoda** have quiet mountain hot springs and lots of natural beauty. Your image of Japan as only a high tech center with endless urban sprawl will change after seeing this area. Among the many places noted for autumnal beauty, Lake Towada-ko is prime for viewing brilliant red leaves. Japanese make a lot of fuss about autumn foliage — the weather report includes the peak time in each area. Normally unvisited areas are deluged with people when the leaves change. Countless poems about autumn foliage have been written since the *Manyo-shu*, the earliest anthology of poetry, recorded poetry in the 8th century.

Mountain peaks ring Towada-ko, a beautiful crater lake. The **Oirase River**, running north from the lake, presents postcard-perfect scenery. While a few towns, especially Yasumiya on the lake, lack any character and are best avoided, the entire area, part of Towada Hachimantai National Park, is surprisingly undeveloped. If you plan to seek inspiration to compose a poem about autumn foliage, avoid weekends in mid-October when tour groups and crowds obscure your vision.

ARRIVALS & DEPARTURES

By Bus

To/from Aomori City: JR buses leave from JR Aomori Station. 8 buses/day. (3 hours to Lake Towada-ko, ¥3000; 1 1/2 hours to points north of lake). There is infrequent bus service as far as Mt. Hakkoda from November through March.

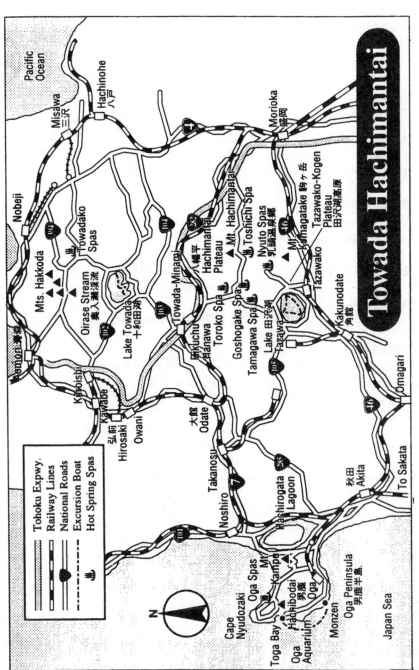

Courtesy of Japan National Tourist Organization

To/from Hirosaki: Konan Bus runs to Lake Towada-ko from April 1 though November 3, 3 buses/day; two additional buses during brief peak seasons (2 hours, ¥2310).

To/from Morioka: depart Morioka Station. 4-9 buses/day between April and mid-November (2 1/4 hours, ¥2420). JR runs a few of these buses.

By Car

Main roads in this area are well marked in English even in this remote area, so driving is fairly stress free. Traveling by car allows you the most flexibility. Car rentals are available in Aomori and Hirosaki.

WHERE TO STAY

We recommend staying north of Oirase Gorge where the hot spring inns are smaller and more individualistic. The hotels nearer to Lake Towada-ko are large and cater to tour groups.

HAKKODA HOTEL, *1 Hakkoda, Aomori City, 030-0111. Tel. (0177)28-2000, Fax (0177)28-1800. From ¥23,000 per person with two meals or doubles at ¥32,000 without meals. Credit cards.*

This hotel is for people who want to be in the mountains but also want all the conveniences of a luxury hotel. Constructed in a log-cabin style, the hotel exudes rustic elegance. There are both Japanese- and Western-style rooms; all look out onto the wooded countryside. French food, using local ingredients, is served in the dining room, which has a high ceiling criss crossed with wooden beams.

TSUTA ONSEN, *Tsuta Onsen, Towada-ko-machi, Kamikita-gun, Aomori, 034-0301. Tel. (0176)74-2311, Fax (0176)74-2244. From ¥10,000 per person with two meals in the old wing; from ¥17,000 per person in the new wing.*

Tsuta is our first choice in the area. The traditional original wooden building has been joined by a tastefully constructed new wing, which gives you the choice between an older, more rustic room and a newer room with a private toilet. Recently reconstructed, the wooden hot spring bathhouse is charming. Purists love the bath because it's located directly above the source of the water. It's the earth's natural force that causes it to bubble up. Visitors can take a bath between 8am and 8pm for a fee of ¥400.

SUKAYU ONSEN, *Sukayu, Yamanaka, Hakkoda, Aomori City, 030-0111. Tel. (0177)38-6400, Fax (0177)38-6677. From ¥10,000 per person with two meals. Credit cards.*

In 1684 a hunter injured a deer and pursued it, intending to finish the job. He found it three days later nursing its wounds in the hot spring water at Sukayu, literally "deer's bath" in local dialect. For over 400 years, people have soaked themselves there to treat muscle pains. During the Edo period, the bathers wore special white kimono to protect their skin from the snow and the harsh sunshine.

Today, this charming old inn's the bath is inside a wooden building and is a famous *sennin-buro,* thousand-person bath. Many tour buses stop every day, but the bath is hardly ever full. The bathhouse, the size of an Olympic swimming pool, contains several baths. All are open to both sexes, but between 10 and 11pm access is restricted to women only. This inn is especially popular with the older set. You can drop in to take a bath for ¥400, and the restaurant is open to the public. The inn is well known for its *soba* noodles and river fish. Bring your own towel.

YACHI ONSEN, *Yachi Onsen, Minami Hakkoda, Towada-ko-machi, Aomori, 034. Tel. (0176)74-1161, Fax (0176)74-1168. ¥9000 per person with two meals. No credit cards.*

Located in a marsh at an altitude of 800 meters, skunk cabbage blooms in the spring. Many of the guests come to this simple, slightly ramshackle mountain inn for its therapeutic hot spring. The staff is very friendly and the cuisine features river fish and mountain vegetables. The inn is well located for climbing Mt. Hakkoda, and the manager knows the trails well. Visitors can use the hot bath for ¥400 between 6am and 7pm.

HAKKODA LODGE, *1 Hakkoda-san, Aomori City, 030. Tel. (0177)38-5030. No Fax. ¥8000 per person with two meals. Open March 20 through October 31. No credit cards.*

A cozy wooden mountain lodge with an outdoor hot spring bath, it reminds us of an inn or bed and breakfast that we might find in New England. It's close to Mt. Hakkoda's ski ropeway, which runs year round making hiking on Mt. Hakkoda a cinch even for couch potatoes. The restaurant, open to the public, features mountain vegetables and river fish.

SEEING THE SIGHTS

We recommend the area north of Lake Towada-ko primarily to experience remote hot springs and enjoy the serenity of the mountains far away from the hustle of the urban areas. **Mt. Hakkoda** is well known to the Japanese for its tragic history. In 1902, Japan was preparing for war with Russia and sent an army contingency on a hike across the mountain. The hike was supposed to train them for fighting in Siberia, but a sudden blizzard killed all but ten of the 210 hapless participants who weren't even issued heavy coats.

Today the mountain is known for skiing and hiking; the ski lift also operates in the summer so not-so-energetic hikers can start walking a mere two hours from the summit. The mountain is famed for its **snow monsters** — trees transformed into weird creatures by special snow conditions.

Heading south toward Lake Towada-ko, next you'll arrive at **Oirase Gorge**. The rock-strewn stream rambles through thick woods creating idyllic scenery. Some spots are calendar quality and, not surprisingly, you may run across many photographers using their professional-looking equipment.

You can drive, take a bus, cycle, or walk along the river; if you have time, walking or biking are the best ways to enjoy the scenery. Rent bicycles at the JR bus stop at Yakeyama (¥620); it takes about two hours to reach Nenokuchi. From the same place, you can also send your luggage ahead to Nenokuchi for ¥400 per bag. If you choose to walk along the gorge, it will take 3 3/4 hours from Yakeyama. To shorten this walk to 2 1/2 hours (9 kilometers) and still see the most picturesque sections, begin your walk at Ishigedo. If you are on the JR bus, jump off at the Yakeyama stop; send your luggage on ahead and quickly reboard the same bus for the short ride to Ishigedo. If you are coming from Lake Towada-ko, rent bikes and send luggage from the JR station in Nenokuchi; and reclaim your luggage at Yakeyama.

From Nenokuchi, you can board a boat for an hour-long cruise along the lake to Yasumiya, but be prepared for obnoxious loud-speaker narration. Boats depart every 30 minutes and cost ¥1320. The mountain peaks along the perimeter of the crater lake create a beautiful natural environment. In Yasumiya you can catch a bus to Morioka.

Kosaka

If you are driving, you can detour through Kosaka and visit Japan's oldest wooden *kabuki* theater. From Lake Towada-ko, take Rt. 103 west. As you climb into the mountains, a road marked for **Kosaka** will turn to the right. Follow this road to Kosaka, a town time passed by.

Korakukan, *Kosaka-machi. Tel. 0186)29-3732. ¥1500 for performance and guided tour. ¥500 for tour.* Kosaka was once a major copper producing area and Korakukan theater was built to entertain the workers. Constructed in 1910, Korakukan is Japan's oldest wooden *kabuki* theater extant. The exterior is Western style, but inside it is a typical *kabuki* theater including the *hanamichi*, a walkway through the audience from which where actors enter; *tatami* mat seating for the audience; and a rotating stage. During a backstage tour you'll get an opportunity to see how the rotating stage works. Performances are held daily.

From Kosaka, you take Rt. 282 south to Rt. 341 to get to Tamagawa Onsen, Lake Tazawa-ko and Kakunodate; or pick up the Tohoku Expressway to Morioka. You can also go north on Route 282 or the Tohoku Expressway to Hirosaki or Aomori.

Tamagawa Onsen

Located off the beaten path in the mountains, **Tamagawa Onsen** is famous for its curative powers. Unlike many *onsen* hot springs where young people flock for a weekend getaway, Tamagawa is filled with people trying to cure illnesses. While its effectiveness has not been proven scientifically, stories abound of terminally ill cancer patients who survived more years than expected.

The water is heavy with sulfur, radium, other minerals and acid. This hot spring holds Japan's record for the highest output of water: 9000 liters/minute. That's the equivalent of filling 45 oil drums a minute. This rushing water creates a hot water river three meters wide.

The large indoor bath has mixed-sex bathing. Because of the strength of water, you should only bathe for a short time and then rinse off. In addition to soaking in baths, many people sit on straw mats in tented areas to absorb the steam. *Kazuno, Hachimantai, Akita, 014-1201. Tel. (0187)49-2352. No fax. From ¥5000 per person with two meals. No credit cards. Accessible by bus from Lake Tazawa-ko or by car driving between Lake Towada-ko to Lake Tazawa-ko on Rt. 341.*

KAKUNODATE

Kakunodate's samurai district, one of the best preserved in Japan, has a quiet, rural and almost austere atmosphere that sets it apart from other samurai districts in larger places like Matsue and Kanazawa. Dark wooden walls line the quiet streets that are overgrown with tall trees, including many weeping cherries. A half-dozen samurai homes are open to the public. Being able to see the difference between the styles of living of upper- and lower-ranking samurai makes a visit to Kakunodate absolutely fascinating.

This small town began to flourish in 1620 when the Satake family of Akita built a secondary castle here. The first Lord Satake married a member of a prominent Kyoto aristocratic family. In her luggage were the accouterments of refined Kyoto culture – kimono and dolls and three weeping cherry trees. Soon Kakunodate's samurai began planting weeping cherry trees. Because of these connections with the capital city, Kakunodate earned the nickname "Little Kyoto of Tohoku."

The structure of the town hasn't changed much over the years. There are two samurai districts: **Uchimachi**, the larger one, and **Tamachi**, a smaller one closer to the station. Uchimachi was populated by warriors who served the feudal lord. Tamachi's inhabitants were a branch of the family and took care of the temples and shrines. The Uchimachi samurai district and the merchant district were separated by an open area of land called the *hiyoke*. In addition to clearly demarcating the boundary, this space served as a fire break. The merchant quarter is still a bustling commercial area although few of the original buildings remain.

ARRIVALS & DEPARTURES
By Air
Akita Airport is 50 minutes (¥890) by bus to Akita City; then take the train from Akita to Kakunodate. The shinkansen takes 50 minutes, ¥2950.

By Train
To/from Morioka: Akita shinkansen train from JR Morioka Station to JR Kakunodate Station (55 minutes, ¥2770). Make sure your train stops at Kakunodate; two trains don't. Local service on JR (90 minutes, ¥1110).
To/from Akita: Akita shinkansen train (50 minutes, ¥2950)

By Bus
To/from Akita: from Akita Station. 7 buses/day (1 1/2 hours, ¥1300)
To/from Lake Tazawa: from Tazawa-ko Station. 7 buses/day (40 minutes, ¥480)
To/from Tokyo: Odakyu overnight bus departs Shinjuku West Exit Bus Station (8 1/2 hours, ¥8870)

By Car
To/from Akita City: 60 minutes by car. Rt. 13 to Rt. 46.
To/from Morioka: 90 minutes by car. Rt. 46.

ORIENTATION
Much of Kakunodate shuts down from December through March. The weeping cherry trees bloom in late April/early May. They are beautiful and attract large numbers of visitors. If possible, avoid weekends during cherry blossom season, and don't expect to admire the blossoms in solitary splendor.

GETTING AROUND TOWN
Kakunodate is small enough you can cover it on foot. Bicycles are also convenient and available for rent at Hanaba Taxi in front of the train station. *Tel. (0187)53-2131*. ¥200/hour or ¥1200/day.

Tourist Information
The **Tourist Information office** is close to the station and has a good English map and brochure. *Tel. (0187)54-2995*. Open 9am to 5pm.

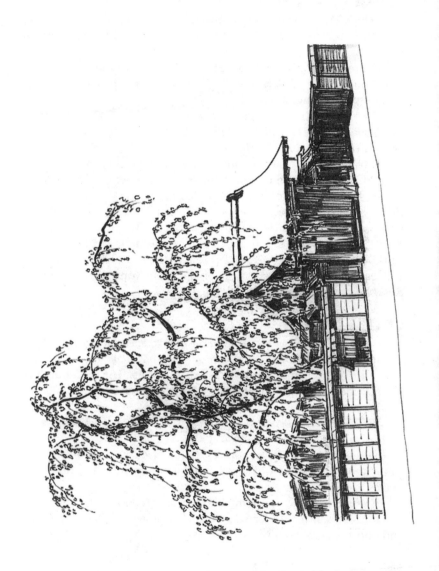

WHERE TO STAY

ISHIKAWA RYOKAN, *32 Iwase-machi, Kakunodate-machi, Senhoku-gun, Akita, 014-0316. Tel. (0187)54-2030, Fax (0187)54-2031. From ¥9800 per person with two meals. No credit cards.*

For ten generations the same family has been running this inn that is now housed in a modern building. They are very proud of their local home-style cooking.

HYAKU SUIEN, *31 Shimonaka-machi, Kakunodate-machi, Senhoku-gun, Akita, 014-0317. Tel. (0187)55-5715, Fax (0187)54-3195. ¥9800 per person with two meals. No credit cards.*

A friendly and charming inn with a 140-year old history, this inn is housed in a traditional building, the former residence of a doctor. The sliding doors are decorated with bold calligraphy. Chock-a-block with memorabilia, the inn even has a small museum. Meals are served around the *irori* hearth. The inn is open to the public for lunch from 11am to 3pm. *Kuri-okowa* set costs ¥2100 and includes chestnuts steamed with rice. Another house specialty is *Hyakusui nabe* (from ¥2000): mountain vegetables, shellfish and bear meat or beef that you cook at your table. Reservations necessary for *Hyakusui nabe*.

WHERE TO EAT

PARIYA *(Japanese–Western, inexpensive to moderate). 8 Hanaba-shita. Tel. (0187)54-4147. Open 12 noon to 1:30pm; 6-7:30pm. Closed Monday.*

Both Western and Japanese dishes are served. The restaurant prides itself on mountain vegetables, *sansai*. Lunch ¥2000; dinner ¥3000. Reservations necessary.

ENJU-AN *(Noodles, inexpensive). Inside Aoyagi House complex. Tel. (0187)54-3773. Open 9am to 3pm.*

This attractive noodle shop serves *Inaniwa tenobe udon*, a long, thin white noodle, a specialty of southern Akita Prefecture. The photo menu makes ordering easy.

HYAKU SUIEN, listed under *Where to Stay* above, also serves lunch

ISAMIYA, listed under *Shopping* below, is a good place for green tea and unusual Japanese sweets.

SEEING THE SIGHTS

Before you start touring, stop at **Nishinomiya Kura Storehouse**. Built in 1919 as a rice storehouse, it has been converted to a tourist information center and rest place. You can see a video of Kakunodate. On the second floor, you'll find displays of antique dishes and other ceramic objects from families in the area. *11 Tamachi Kami-cho. Tel. (0187)54-1558. Open 9am to 5pm. Closed mid-November until mid-April. 10-minute walk from the station.*

Take the road that dead ends into the JR station, make your third left and the building is on the right a little bit in.

Uchimachi, the former samurai district, maintains some flavor of the feudal period. The dark wooden walls and ornate gates hide the residences and gardens of Kakunodate's feudal elite. Today, although only a few of the original houses remain, a walk through the district returns you to bygone days.

Aoyagi House. Built in 1680, the gate is designated an Important Cultural Property. This high-ranking samurai house has a formal entrance for distinguished visitors and one for the family. A mini-museum complex houses exhibits of samurai armor and swords; Western objects collected by the master; a festival float and everyday household objects such as ceramics, dolls, lacquer ware and other memorabilia. The pride of the garden is a 280-year old weeping cherry. A noodle restaurant is also on the premises (see Enjo-an, Where to Eat). *Tel. (0187)54-3257. Open 9am to 5pm, winter until 4pm. ¥500.*

Ishiguro House. The Ishiguro family, noted doctors and scholars, moved to this elegant thatched-roof house in 1853. It is simpler than the Aoyagi house but is also famous for its weeping cherry. The feudal lord even regulated the style of entrance gates — Ishiguro's indicates the medical profession. *Tel. (0187)55-1496. Open 9am to 5pm. Closed December until mid-April. ¥300.*

CHERRY TREES EVERYWHERE

In the early 17th century, the first Lord Satake married a woman from a prominent Kyoto family; in her dowry were three weeping cherry trees. The trees flourished in Kakunodate's climate, and the samurai copied the feudal lord by planting their own weeping cherries, which transform the samurai district into a cascade of pink every April. Some 400 trees remain today; over 150 have been designated National Natural Treasures.

Three samurai houses in a row, **Iwahashi**, **Kawarada** and **Odano**, all belonged to middle-ranking samurai and are open free of charge.

Matsumoto House. Located off the main road, behind the Denshokan. This house belonged to the lowest-ranking samurai — a footman. The humble dwelling underscores that the lower samurai lived very modest lives. Usually a craftsman is present, weaving baskets with strips of young maple. *Free admission.*

Kakunodate has a few small museums: Kakunodate History and Folklore Hall and Kakunodate Samurai Hall; you are much better off spending your time in the samurai houses.

Cherry Bark Craft Hall (Kabazaiku Denshokan) is located on the main street among the samurai houses. This museum and training center is for *kabazaiku*, cherry bark craft, historically made by lower-ranking samurai to supplement their income. In addition to demonstrating and displaying goods made of cherry bark, the hall has kimono and dolls brought from Kyoto, samurai armor, maple-bark crafts and Shiroiwa ceramics. With prior reservations, you can make your own cherry-bark object for ¥1300. *Open 9am to 5pm: until 4:30pm December through March. Closed Thursdays December through March and December 28 through January 4. ¥300.*

Ando Brewery (Ando Jozo Moto). Located in the merchant section of Kakunodate, this *sake* brewery and soy sauce manufacturer has maintained the traditional building. *Tel. (0187)53-2008.*

To commemorate to birth of the current emperor, the town of Kakunodate planted two kilometers of cherry trees along the Hinokinai River in 1933. At long last, many Japanese rejoiced at the birth of the crown prince after the birth of several older sisters; Kakunodate expressed its delight by planting cherry trees.

KABAZAIKU CHERRY BARK CRAFT

During the feudal era, samurai were barred from farming. Lower-ranking samurai had few ways to support themselves. In the 1780s, Lord Satake encouraged them to use the bark of mountain cherry trees to make decorative but utilitarian objects such as tea canisters, trays, saucers, chests of drawers, etc. Today the stores of Kakunodate are filled with these rustic handmade objects.

SHOPPING

Isamiya, *Next to Iwahashi House. Tel. (0187)54-3108. Open 9am to 5pm.* Housed in a samurai residence, Isamiya makes and sells *nama-morokoshi*, a sweet made from roasted beans. Stop in to sample or sit down for a leisurely snack and tea.

Kakunodate Sakura Kabazaiku Dai-ni Center, *Across the street from Ishiguro House. Tel. (0187)55-5631.* A small shop selling cherry bark goods at a discount.

Fujiki Denshiro Shoten, *45 Shimo Shinmachi. Tel. (0187)54-1151.* In this large showroom, the major distributor of cherry bark products displays a wide range of goods — furniture, trays and saucers, toothpick holders, handbags and cosmetic cases. Try a cherry-bark telephone card for a change. Be sure to take a minute to look at the baskets and local products in the two small shops across the street.

MORIOKA

The former castle town of **Morioka** is a pleasant medium-sized city of 260,000. The castle is gone, and from the train station the city looks like any other modern urban area, but Morioka has pockets of traditional architecture and culture, excellent craft shops and good restaurants. And the physical setting is awesome. Snow-clad most of the year, Mt. Iwate is visible in the distance towering over rice fields and orchards.

The castle, built by the ruling Nambu family in 1597, was torn down in 1874 after the end of the feudal period. The only remnants are graceful stone walls in a park in the center of the city.

ARRIVALS & DEPARTURES

By Air

Hanamaki Airport serves Morioka.

To/from Osaka Itami: 3 flights/day (JAS. ¥25,700)

To/from Sapporo Chitose: 2 flights/day (JAS. ¥18,300)

To/from Nagoya: 2 flights/day (JAS. ¥22,500)

To/from Fukuoka: 3 flights/week (JAS. ¥33,350)

For Ground Transportation:

By bus: Take a bus from the airport to JR Morioka Station (50 minutes, ¥1260).

By taxi: 40 minutes to JR Morioka Station, about ¥9000.

By Train

To/from Tokyo: JR Tohoku shinkansen train *Yamabiko* from either Ueno or Tokyo station (between 2 1/2 and 3 hours, ¥13,840)

To/from Aomori: JR *Hatsukari* limited express train (2 hours 20 minutes, ¥5970)

To/from Sendai: JR Tohoku shinkansen trains (1 1/4 hours, ¥6290)

To/from Akita: The new JR Akita shinkansen train (1 3/4 hours, ¥4500)

By Bus

To/from Hirosaki: 15 buses/day (3 hours 20 minutes, ¥2930). Several are JR Buses.

To/from Aomori: 6 buses/day (3 hours 25 minutes, ¥3160). One run daily by JR Bus.

To/from Sendai: 14 buses/day (2 hours 40 minutes, ¥2850). Several buses a day run by JR Bus.

To/from Lake Tazawa-ko. April 25 through October 3: 5 buses/day
(1 1/2 hours, ¥1390).

Tourist Information

The **Tourist Information Office** is on the second floor of the JR
Morioka Train Station. It has information on the entire region plus
English-speaking staff. *Tel. (0196)25-2090.* Open 8:30am to 7:30pm.
Closed December 31 through January 2.

WHERE TO STAY

KITA HOTEL, *17-45 Uchimaru, Morioka, Iwate, 020-0023. Tel. (0196)25-2711, Fax (0196)25-2714. Singles from ¥5500. Twins from ¥11,000. Credit Cards.*

This small comfortable hotel is centrally located. The dining room
serves both Japanese and Western breakfasts for ¥1100.

MORIOKA GRAND HOTEL ANNEX, *1-9-16 Chuo-dori, Morioka, Iwate, 020-0021. Tel. (0196)25-5111, Fax (0196)22-3527. Singles from ¥7000. Twins from ¥14,000. Doubles from ¥15,000. Credit Cards.*

Located in the center of Morioka City, the hotel is convenient for
sightseeing as well as for business. The steak house restaurant, serving
local Iwate beef, is a Morioka institution.

WHERE TO EAT

TAKUBOKU-AN *(Noodles, inexpensive). 1F, Morioka City Hotel, 8-14 Morioka Ekimae Dori. Tel. (0196)51-3030. Open daily 11am to 3pm, 5pm to 10pm.*

This restaurant is a good place to try *wanko-soba*, a local specialty. Bite-
sized amounts of noodles are spread flat in round bamboo plates.
Reservations are a must. Set menu is ¥2300.

AZUMAYA *(Noodles, inexpensive). 1-8-3 Nakanohashi Dori. Tel. (0196)22-2252. Branch across from JR Morioka Station: 2F, 8-11 Ekimae Dori. Tel. (0196)22-2233.*

One of Morioka's best known *wanko soba* shops. The main restaurant
is in a traditional wooden building in an older section of town. If you don't
have time to go so far, there's a branch across the street from the train
station on the second floor. The atmosphere is completely different, but
the noodles are the same. If you don't feel like downing plate after plate
of noodles, order the *nambu soba kaiseki* meal for ¥2500. It includes soup,
noodles in broth with mushrooms, cold noodles and tempura.

NAMBU ROBATA *(Japanese, moderate). 3 Hachiman-cho. Tel. (0196)22-5082. Open for dinner only.*

The interior of this restaurant is a real farmhouse. You sit around on
raised hearths where food is grilled. The *Nambu robata* set, ¥4200, includes
fish, seafood, vegetables and tofu.

WANKO SOBA

Wanko soba is always associated with soba eating competitions. You are given stacks of small plates, each containing bite-sized portions of noodles. As soon as you finish eating the noodles on the plate, the waitress, standing behind you, replaces it with a full one. You use matchsticks to keep track of how much you have eaten. Finish as many as hundred plates and you receive a certificate! Bon appetit.

SEEING THE SIGHTS

Morioka is a pleasant city to wander around for a half-day. The area along the Nakatsugawa River around the Naka-no-hashi Bridge is a great place for strolling. The **Iwate Bank Building** is a Renaissance-style structure. **Gozaku** has traditional shops.

Hashimoto Art Museum (Hashimoto Bijutsukan). *10 Sai no Kami. Tel. (0196)52-5002. Open daily 10am to 5pm. Closed December 29 through January 3. ¥700. About 25 minutes by #8 bus from Morioka Station.*

Make sure you stop here when you're in Morioka. Slightly out of the way, on a hill outside the center of the city, the museum is constructed in the style of a *magariya*, a traditional, L-shaped, thatched-roof farmhouse popular in the region. Built by artist Hashimoto Yaoji (1903–1979), the museum houses his works as well as European paintings. More than the paintings, we enjoyed the excellent displays of Japanese folk crafts including *tansu* chests, textiles and lacquer ware.

SHOPPING

Morioka has distinctive craft traditions including iron tea kettles called *nambu tetsubin*. Even though they weigh a ton, don't be put off; if you are charmed by the kettle's simple beauty, ship one home, and get a dose of iron every time you use it.

From JR Morioka Station, cross the Asahi Bridge and turn left. The area is called **Zaimoku-cho** and it's a wonderful shopping street. In the late afternoon, vegetables and other goods are for sale on the street. **Kogensha**, a fabulous craft shop, sells regional crafts as well as those from all over Japan. The store actually has three buildings: two are traditional white stucco storehouses, and the third is a modern building across the street. Another good shop is **Ono Sensaisho** that sells stencil-dyed textiles. Zaimoku-cho also has shops selling sweets, crackers and other local delicacies.

The **Konya-cho** district retains some of the old time flavor of Morioka. A few fun shops are **Kamasada Kobo**, *2-6 Konya-cho,* for iron tea kettles; **Moriku Shoten** for bamboo baskets; and **Shirasawa Sembei-ten**, *2-16 Konya-cho,* for Morioka-style crackers. There's even a *sake* brewery.

TONO

A small village deep in the hills, **Tono's** folk tales have put it on the map. It is also noted for farmhouses called *magariya,* (distinctive L-shaped buildings). The bottom of the L is a stable for horses so, without separate heating, they stay warm during the long winter. Tono (pronounced Toh-no) is a popular stop for Japanese urban dwellers nostalgic for village life.

In 1910, Yanagida Kunio, a major mover and shaker in the folklore movement, collected first-hand folk tales. This book has become required reading for many Japanese school children. To get the most out of your visit to Tono, pick up a copy of *Tales of Tono,* a translation by Ronald Morse. You can buy it at Tono Furusato Kosha, near the Tourist Information Office. Then, armed with the book, rent bicycles to explore the region.

ARRIVALS & DEPARTURES

From JR Hanamaki Station (south of Morioka) take the JR Kamaishi line express train 40 minutes to JR Tono Station.

Tourist Information

The **Tourist Information Office** is located close to JR Tono Station and has English-language brochures and maps. *Tel. (0198)62-4244.* Rent bicycles there or from several shops near the station.

WHERE TO STAY

MAGARIYA, *30-58-3 Niizato, Ayaori-machi, Tono, Iwate, 028-0531. Tel. (0198)62-4564. No fax. Rates from ¥9800 per person with two meals. No credit cards.*

This small family-run inn is an old restored *magariya* farmhouse and the perfect place to catch the mood of the rustic village.

FOLKLORO TONO, *5-7 Shinkoku-cho, Tono, Iwate, 028-0522. Tel. (0198)62-0700, Fax (0198)62-0800. Singles ¥7000; Twins ¥10,000 with breakfast. No credit cards.*

This new Western-style bed and breakfast-type establishment is on the second floor of the JR Tono Station; a Western continental breakfast is served.

WHERE TO EAT

Tono's specialty is *hitsuko soba*. Noodles served in circular containers are stacked in three layers; the fourth layer contains various condiments.

YOSHINOYA *(Noodles, inexpensive)*. *18-98-1 Shiroiwa Matsuzaki-machi. Tel. (0198)62-5172. Open daily 10am to 8pm.*

Hitsuko soba is the shop's most popular dish. In winter people come from far-away cities to eat *nabeyaki-udon, udon* noodles cooked in a casserole, ¥820.

ICHIRIKI *(Regional Japanese, inexpensive)*. *5-27 Chuo Dori. Tel. (0198)62-2008. Open 11am to 8pm. Closed irregularly.*

Ichiriki has been serving delicious regional cooking for three generations. The special sauce for eel has put it on the map. The cooking uses only ingredients from the Tono area. *Teishoku* set meal costs ¥1350.

SEEING THE SIGHTS

Your visit to Tono must include the **Chiba family house** (Chiba-ke), a 200-year old thatched-roofed *magariya* farm house. Tokyo University, citing it as one of the top-ten private houses in Japan, did a splendid job of restoration.

Stop by the **Tono City Museum** (Tono Shiritsu Hakubutsukan) for information on the village and a multimedia presentation of its folk tales. *Tel. (0198)62-2340. Open 9am to 5pm. Closed last Monday of the month and Mondays in winter. ¥500.*

If you haven't overloaded on folk tales, head to the nearby **Tono Folk Village** where local storytellers recite Tono's famous tales. Be warned, however, the narrator's speak in such a strong local dialect even most Japanese don't understand what they say.

To see more restored farmhouses, stop at **Denshoen**, an open-air museum.

LAKE TAZAWA-KO & NYUTO ONSEN

This volcanic crater lake is surrounded by low mountains; with a depth of 423 meters, it's Japan's deepest. Since the lake is spring fed, it never freezes. In the mountains east of the lake, **Tazawa-ko Kogen Plateau** has great rustic hot spring inns. It's also a ski center with many small hotels and pensions.

ARRIVALS & DEPARTURES

By Train

To/from Akita: JR Akita shinkansen train (60 minutes, ¥3280). JR local train (115 minutes, ¥1620)

To/from Morioka: JR Akita shinkansen train (30 minutes, ¥1980). JR local train (50 minutes, ¥740)

To/from Kakunodate: JR Akita shinkansen train (13 minutes, ¥1560). JR local train (20 minutes, ¥320)

By Bus

To/from Akita: From Akita Station. 6 buses/day (2 hours 10 minutes, ¥1680)

To/from Kakunodate: 7 buses/day (40 minutes, ¥620)

Tourist Information

The **Tourist Information Office** is an "i" Tourist Information Office, at Tazawa-ko Station. *Tel. (0187)43-1111.*

THE LEGEND OF LAKE TAZAWA-KO

*Lake Tazawa-ko never freezes. Japanese legend explains this phenomenon with the tale of **Tatsuko Hime**, a beauty who was afraid of losing her looks and youth. She prayed and prayed and received a message to drink some water from the lake. Suddenly, she was a water dragon.*

Tatsuko Hime married Hachiro-taro. After eating a fish that made him very thirsty, he too, drank water from Lake Towada-ko and turned into a water dragon. Hachiro-taro lives in Hachiro-gata on Oga Peninsula in Akita Prefecture. For conjugal visits, he spends the winter with Tatsuko Hime. Their passionate lovemaking prevents Lake Tazawa from freezing while Hachiro-gata freezes.

Tatsuko's golden statue is on the south shore of the lake. The colorful water dragon festival is held the 4th weekend in July. Young people carry 50-meter long dragon floats in the lake.

SEEING THE SIGHTS

Lake Tazawa-ko is popular with young Japanese vacationers. We use it as a gateway to the Nyuto Onsen. If you want to tour the lake, there's a 40 minute boat tour four times a day from late April to early November. ¥1150.

There are many hotels along the edge of the lake. Our recommendation is to bypass these places and stay in the Nyuto Onsen area, about 30 minutes from Lake Tazawa-ko.

Nyuto Onsen area is popular all year: hiking in the spring, summer and fall and skiing in winter. You can ski from November until May. In spring, the skunkweed flowers bloom in the marshes. The many hot springs draw visitors all year long. Nyuto Onsen is made of seven different *onsen* (hot springs) spread out in a five-kilometer area. Each hot spring has only one or two inns and is tucked away in a valley. Buses run six times a day from Tazawa-ko Station to Nyuto Onsen. The 55-minute trip costs ¥740.

WHERE TO STAY

YAMA NO YADO, *Tazawako-machi, Senhoku-gun, Akita, 014-1204. Tel. (0187)46-2100, Fax (0187)46-2800. From ¥13,000 per person with two meals. Visa Card.*

Actually a branch of Tsuru-no-yu, this recently built inn is a good choice for a small, up-to-date hot spring hidden deep in the woods. The traditional Japanese building has lovely, open wooden beams. You'll eat your dinner around *irori* hearths, sitting on pillows on a wide-planked floor. The natural beams and the *shoji* paper doors give a rustic yet elegant atmosphere. The inn's specialty is a stew called *yama no imo nabe*, consisting of mountain potatoes and vegetables seasoned with *miso* paste. The inn has only nine rooms, each with private bath and toilet. Open year round.

TSURU-NO-YU, *Tazawako-machi, Senhoku-gun, Akita, 014-1204. Tel. (0187)46-2139, Fax (0187)46-2761. From ¥8000 per person with two meals. Visa Card.*

The Akita feudal lord came to use the baths in 1661. A hunter discovered the hot springs when he saw an injured crane bathing in the water; *tsuru no yu* means crane's hot water. The inn began in 1701, and the current innkeeper is 14th generation. The rustic thatched-roof inn, deep in the woods, has several different baths, including a white water bath, a black water bath, a waterfall bath, an outdoor bath for woman only and a mixed bath. You can get off the bus at Tazawa-kogen and call the inn. Someone will pick you up. Open year round. Visitors can use the baths between 8am and 5pm, ¥400.

TAZAWA-KO KOGEN KYUKA-MURA, *Komagatake, Tazawako-machi, Senhoku-gun, Akita, 014-1201. Tel. (0187)46-2244, Fax (0187)46-2700. From ¥6500 to ¥10,000 per person with two meals depending on room and dinner. No credit cards.*

This modest building has comfortable rooms and good food. It is located in the center of the Nyuto Onsen district and is convenient for hiking. The hot spring bath includes a small outdoor bath. The coffee shop is handy for a morning caffeine fix.

To avoid: **KUROYU INN** in the Nyuto Onsen area. The thatched-roof buildings were all in a state of disrepair. The food is mediocre; the staff is surly; the *rotemburo* outdoor bath is minuscule, and the indoor bath is scalding hot. The literally paper-thin walls means we heard our neighbor's 5am conversation (they were four rooms away). It was just as well that breakfast was served at 7am because we didn't want to linger.

AKITA

Today **Akita**, an industrial city with oil refineries, has little to interest the tourist except for the Kanto Festival, one of Japan's most famous. You can also use Akita as the gateway to Kakunodate and Lake Tazawa.

ARRIVALS & DEPARTURES

By Air

To/from Tokyo Haneda: 6 flights/day (JAL, ANA. ¥17,400)

To/from Nagoya: 1 flight/day (ANA. ¥20,650)

To/from Osaka: 1 flight/day each from **Itami** and **Kansai** airports (JAS. ¥24,300)

To/from Sapporo Chitose: 2 flights/day (JAS. ¥17,900)

To/from Fukuoka: 3 flights/week (ANA. ¥31,950)

For Ground Transportation:

By bus: to JR Akita Station,50 minutes, ¥890.

By taxi: to JR Akita Station, 40 minutes, about ¥7000.

By Train

To/from Tokyo: JR Akita shinkansen train (4 hours 20 minutes, ¥16,810). Overnight train from Tokyo's Ueno Station (9 1/2 hours, ¥11,860)

By Bus

To/from Tokyo: Odakyu overnight bus from Shinjuku West Exit Bus Station (10 hours, ¥9450)

To/from Sendai: 3 buses/day including one overnight bus (4 hours 40 minutes, ¥4000)

To/from Lake Tazawa-ko and Kakunodate: 6 buses/day (1 hour 50 minutes from Tazawa-ko, ¥1680); (1 hour 30 minutes from Kakunodate, ¥1330)

WHERE TO STAY

EITARO RYOKAN, *6-15 Senshu Yadome-machi, Akita City, 010-0877. Tel. (018)833-4151, Fax (0188)32-2090. From ¥14,000 per person with two meals. Credit cards.*

The exterior of the building looks Western style but inside it's pure Japanese. The specialty of this quiet inn is the *obako nabe* stew with fish and vegetables served with *ponzu*, a citrus-flavored sauce.

KANTO FESTIVAL

*Every year from August 4–7, the normally sleepy city of Akita is wide awake for the **Kanto Festival**. The festival's parade features 160 men balancing 10-meter bamboo poles that are strung with lanterns, which glow against the dark summer sky. The bearers move the poles from one part of their bodies to another, balancing them on their foreheads, shoulders, hips and in the palms of their hands. Even children, wearing cotton yukata robes, participate in the festival; they have special lanterns shaped like red goldfish.*

The festival's history goes back 360 years to a ritual performed during the summer's Obon Festival, the Buddhist festival for the dead. Residents decorated their gates with lanterns to help returning spirits find their own homes more easily. This practice was expanded to have movable lights so that the returning souls could see the entire town.

The festival is also a time to pray for a good harvest; the position of the lanterns on the pole symbolizes the rice grains on the tip of a branch.

Over one million spectators attend the festival each summer, so make your hotel reservations far in advance.

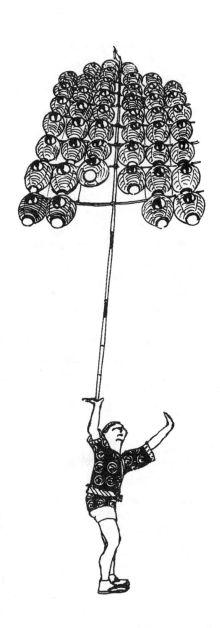

AKITA CASTLE HOTEL, *1-3-5 Naka Dori, Akita City, 010. Tel. (018)834-1141, Fax (0188)34-5588. Singles from ¥9000. Twins from ¥16,000. Credit cards.*

This hotel, part of a chain, is a comfortable place to stay.

AKITA WASHINGTON HOTEL, *2-2 Omachi, Akita City, 010-0921. Tel. (0188)65-7111, Fax (0188)23-8133. Singles from ¥8000. Twins from ¥15,000. Credit cards.*

For a simple business hotel, this centrally located lodging is a good choice. The 11th floor restaurant, Ginza, serves a special *nabe* stew.

WHERE TO EAT

SUGINOYA *(Japanese, moderate). 4-1-15 Naka Dori. Tel. (0188)35-5111. Open 11am to 9pm.*

A seafood restaurant where you can choose your swimming fish, and it will be prepared according to your wishes. You can have *kamakura otsukuri sashimi* for ¥1500; the fish is placed in its own little igloo. For fans of sea bream, for ¥4500, you can eat the entire fish prepared several different ways.

SEEING THE SIGHTS

Today, **Senshu Park**, the site of Akita's castle, has a replica. *Open to the public 9am to 4:30pm. ¥100. Closed late December through late March.*

Neburi Nagashikan opened in 1992 to preserve the area's traditional ethnological art and culture. If you are not in Akita when the Kanto Festival is on, you can see the large lanterns on display at this place. *Tel. (0188)660-7091. Open 9:30am to 4:30pm. ¥100. Take a bus heading toward Shinya, get off at Torii-machi.*

HIRAIZUMI

Incredibly, tiny provincial **Hiraizumi** once rivaled Kyoto in its cultural glory; it was the center of the region 850 years ago. When you discover Hiraizumi's charms, you can imagine how glorious it must have been in its heyday. Today, it is one of the best places in Japan to see Heian architecture.

Hiraizumi was the capital of Michinoku, the old name for Tohoku. We love this name because it means "End of the Road," and really describes how Kyoto-ites saw this part of Japan. And end of the road it was. From 1090 to 1189, the waning days of the Heian era, a warrior clan called the **Northern Fujiwara** ruled virtually all of Tohoku. The Fujiwara consciously designed the city to emulate Kyoto. The first ruler, **Fujiwara no Kiyohira**, rebuilt **Chuson-ji Temple** with over 40 splendid buildings.

The Fujiwara ruled Hiraizumi for only three generations; they became entangled in a controversy that was the clan's undoing. A Kamakura shogun, Minamoto Yoritomo, ordered the death of his half brother Yoshitsune. The third Fujiwara lord sheltered Yoshitsune but, under pressure from the shogun, attacked Yoshitsune, who committed suicide. The shogun still sent a large force to attack Hiraizumi and the last Fujiwara ruler perished.

Hiraizumi saw glory for such a short period of time, so people mull over the ephemeral nature of life and the rise and fall of power. The Edo era poet Basho wrote: "The summer grass, 'Tis all that's left, Of ancient warriors' dreams."

ARRIVALS & DEPARTURES

By train: At JR Ichinoseki Station (where the Tohoku shinkansen stops), take the Tohoku Honsen line to JR Hiraizumi Station (10 minutes, ¥330).

By bus: At Ichinoseki Station, take the Iwate Bus to Hiraizumi Station (25 minutes, ¥310). The same bus continues on to Chuson-ji Temple (10 minutes, ¥310).

GETTING AROUND TOWN

Hiraizumi is a small town. Chuson-ji is about a half-hour walk from the station or you can take the bus. Bicycles are ideal for getting around; rentals are available near Hiraizumi Station.

Tourist Information

The **Tourist Information Office** is at JR Hiraizumi Station. Open daily 8:30am to 5pm. Closed December 29 through January 3. *Tel. (0191)46-2111.*

WHERE TO STAY

HIRAIZUMI-SO, *Aza-Miyama, Nagashima, Hiraizumi-cho, Nishi-Iwai-gun, Iwate, 029-4101. Tel. (0191)46-2131. Fax (0191)46-2131. Rates from ¥6800 per person with two meals. No credit cards.*

A simple public lodge that offers Japanese-style accommodation.

WHERE TO EAT

HIRAIZUMI RESUTO HAUSU *(Japanese, inexpensive). 10-7 Hiraizumi Sakashita. Tel. (0191)46-2011. Open daily 9am to 4pm.*

Located across from the Hiraizumi bus stop, this spacious restaurant serves local specialties. The popular *Benkei-no chikaramochi* includes five different kinds of rice cakes known as a source of energy. ¥1200.

SEEING THE SIGHTS

Chuson-ji Temple was founded about 850 by the famous priest En-nin. From 1105 to 1126, the first Fujiwara ruler rebuilt the temple to appease the souls of warriors killed in battle. He built over 40 buildings in the Heian architectural style. A fire in 1337 destroyed most of the temple and in the 17th century, a powerful feudal lord from the Date clan rebuilt much of it.

Today, two original buildings remain and they are well worth a visit. The **Golden Hall** (Konjikido) dates from 1124. A tiny building, it is only five square meters, and its black lacquer walls are decorated with gold leaf. This building is so famous that most scholars think Marco Polo was referring to it when he mentioned in *Tales of the Orient* that in Zipang (Japan), buildings have roofs of gold. The interior is inlaid with precious stones and mother of pearl. The hall was built to house the mummified bodies of the Fujiwara rulers. Unfortunately, for protection, a larger cement building covers the Golden Hall.

The other original building is a sutra hall called **Kyozo**. Its octagonal dais is decorated with wonderful inlaid motifs.

While at the temple, stop in the **Treasure Hall** (Sankozo). It contains temple treasures including sutras written in gold ink on indigo paper, a thousand-armed Kannon statue, Fujiwara swords and the lacquer box used to transport the head of the last Fujiwara ruler to the Kamakura shogun. *Chuson-ji Temple is open 8am to 5pm; 8:30am to 4:30pm November through February. ¥800.*

About a five-minute walk from the JR Hiraizumi Station is **Motsu-ji Temple**. The priest En-nin, founder of Chuson-ji, established Motsu-ji for protection of the country. The second Fujiwara ruler restored the temple in the mid-12th century. At its height, the temple had 40 pagodas and 500 monasteries. There are no buildings today, but the peaceful Jodo garden, which was a representation of Buddha's paradise on earth, is well worth a stroll. *Open 8am to 5pm; 8:30am to 4:30pm September through April. ¥500.*

YAMAGATA

Yamagata is a former castle town; the ruins can be seen in the park. It is not a great sightseeing city and usually is not a destination in itself, but Yamagata makes a good gateway for visiting Yamadera and the three sacred mountains of Dewa Sanzan. Since Yamagata Prefecture is famous for beef, you'll have no problem finding steak restaurants.

Yamagata's **Hanagasa Festival** is one of Tohoku's big four. Held every year from August 6–8, over 900,000 visitors arrive to watch folk dancers wearing hats elaborately decorated with flowers

ARRIVALS & DEPARTURES

By Air

Yamagata Airport
To/from Tokyo Haneda: 3 flights/day (ANA. ¥13,100)
To/from Nagoya: 1 flight/day (JAL. ¥19,600)
To/from Osaka Itami: 2 flights/day; **Kansai**: 1 flight/day (JAS. ¥23,050)
To/from Sapporo Chitose: 2 flights/day (JAS. ¥20,090)

For Ground Transportation:
Bus: to Yamagata City (40 minutes, ¥710)
Taxi: to Yamagata City (40 minutes, about ¥6900)

By Train

To/from Tokyo: The Yamagata shinkansen runs from Tokyo (both Tokyo and Ueno Stations) to Yamagata. Some of the Tohoku and Yamagata shinkansen trains run together until Fukushima where they divide; if you are in nonreserved seating, make sure you are in the appropriate half of the train. The Yamagata shinkansen trains, called *Tsubasa,* take about 3 hours to reach Yamagata from Tokyo. ¥11,030.

To/from Sendai: The JR Senzan line express train (1 hour 10 minutes, ¥1100). Yamadera Station is on this line.

By Bus

To/from Tsuruoka: Buses run between Yamagata Sanko Building Bus Terminal to Tsuruoka Bus Terminal passing through Gassan and Yudono-san. 10 buses/day (2 hours 15 minutes, ¥2000).

To/from Tokyo: 2 buses/day Tokyo Station to Yamagata Station, including one overnight bus. (Daytime 5 1/2 hours; overnight 7 1/2 hours, ¥6420).

Tourist Information

The **Yamagata Tourist Office**, an "i" Tourist Information Office, is in front of JR Yamagata Station. Open daily 10am to 6pm. The English information telephone line is *(0236)31-7865.*

WHERE TO STAY

HOTEL METROPOLITAN YAMAGATA, *1-1-1 Kasumi-cho, Yamagata City, 990-0039. Tel. (0236)28-1111, Fax (0236)28-1166. Singles from ¥9500. Twins from ¥17,000. Credit cards.*

A new hotel located close to the JR Yamagata Station, the Metropolitan has fairly spacious rooms and a Japanese and a Western cafe restaurant.

HOTEL LIMOGE, *1-35 Tokamachi, Yamagata City, 990-0031. Tel. (0236)25-1133, Fax (0236)25-1099. Singles from ¥6000. Twins from ¥11,000. Credit cards.*

Located in the central part of the city, the quiet rooms face the garden.

WHERE TO EAT

SHABUKIN NIKU NO KANAZAWAYA *(Japanese, moderate). 1-4-6 Kasumi-cho. Tel. (0236)42-4417. Open 6pm to 10pm. Closed Sunday.*

This restaurant's sister shop is a butcher store, so it serves high-quality Yonezawa beef. Only two minutes from JR Yamagata Station, the restaurant is on a busy street but has a quiet atmosphere. The *shabu-shabu* sets run from ¥3500 to ¥6000. The citrus-flavored *ponzu* dipping sauce is a house specialty. Try the Ginjo *sake* with your meal.

SAGORO *(Steak and beef, moderate). 1-6-10 Kasumi-cho. Tel. (0236)31-3560. Open 11:30am to 9pm. Closed Sunday.*

Established in 1910, Sagoro is one of the oldest beef restaurants in Yamagata. *Sukiyaki teishoku* costs ¥3500, steak *teishoku* ¥4000.

UZENYA *(Noodles, inexpensive). 1-18-11 Hatago-machi. Tel. (0236)22-5702. Open 11am to 7:30pm. Closed Monday.*

This shop has been selling handmade *soba* since 1916. The *uzenmori* (cold *soba*) costs ¥700 and is more than enough for one person.

AJI-NO-MATABE *(Regional cooking, inexpensive to moderate). 2-2-30 Hatago-machi. Tel. (0236)22-0357. Open 11:30am to 2pm; 5:30pm to 9pm. Closed Sunday.*

This quiet restaurant serves local vegetables in season. The *Matabe-zen* costs ¥2000 at lunch and ¥3000 at dinner. Reservations recommended.

SEEING THE SIGHTS

The **Kyodo-kan** is a three-storied Western-style building the likes of which may never have been seen. The first floor has 14 sides, the second 16, and between the 2nd and 3rd there are eight sides and a veranda. It is designated an Important Cultural Property. The museum houses documents related to medicine in the 19th century, so the real fun is seeing the outside. *Tel. (0236)44-0253. Closed Monday, 3rd Sunday and holidays. ¥200.*

Yamagata Museum. On a rainy day, you can always visit this museum, which has paintings by Chagall, Picasso, Renoir and others purchased during the 1980s bubble economy, and works by Yamagata artists. *Tel. (0236)22-3090. Open 10am to 5pm. Closed Monday. ¥500.*

Yamagata produces pottery called **Hirashimizu**. Six kilns are clustered at the outskirts of Yamagata. To try your hand at pottery, make a reservation at Heikichi kiln. *Tel. (0236)22-4801. Open daily 9:30am to*

2:30pm. ¥2000 includes instruction and enough clay to make three mugs or two plates. Reservations necessary.

SHOPPING

Yamagata Prefectural Products Hall (Yamagata-ken Bussanten). *Tel. (0236)22-3485. Open 9:30am to 5:30pm. Closed Monday November through March.* The place is geared to snag Japanese tourists but is convenient for gathering diverse products under one roof. The hall sells Hirashimizu ceramics, *benihana* (safflower) dyed goods, dolls, *kokeshi* dolls, crafts, sweets, noodles, pickles, local *sake* and more.

EXCURSIONS & DAY TRIPS
KAHOKU

If you are interested in crafts, stop at **Kahoku**, an easy side trip from Yamagata City. During Yamagata's castle town days, the area was a main producer of safflower, a valuable commodity used to dye fabric crimson red and to make traditional lipstick. The district grew more than 50% of Japan's safflower. It was shipped down the Mogami River to Sakata where boats carried the flower to Fukui on the Japan Sea. Then it was packed on horses and carried to Lake Biwa; once again it was taken by boat across the lake to Otsu and then transported on horses to Kyoto where finally it was used to dye silk for the ruling classes. After all this trouble, no wonder it was worth more than gold.

Kahoku was a wholesale center for the trade. But trade worked both ways. The Kahoku merchants, who went to Kyoto, were rich enough to return with Kyoto kimono, works of art, furniture and *hina* dolls for Girls Day. Every year in early April several families open their homes to the public to show their magnificent dolls. At the end of the Tokugawa era, demand for safflower stopped and many of the farmers switched to other crops. Recently, the popularity of safflower oil among the health conscious and a revival of craft techniques have increased demand, and large areas are once again under cultivation. In early summer, the fields are awash with the small red flower.

The estate of the Horigome family, one of Kahoku's prosperous merchants, is now the **Safflower Museum** complex (Kahoku Benibana Shiryokan). Several of the traditional buildings have been restored and, across the bridge, a new hall displays safflower-dyed kimono and other items related to the safflower trade. *You can also try your hand at dyeing with safflower for ¥1030. The museum is open daily 9am to 5pm; until 4pm November through February. ¥300. Tel. (0237)73-3500.*

You can also dye your own hanky with safflower by visiting a highly respected expert, Suzuki Takao. *Make an appointment: Tel. (0237)73-4454. Dyeing a handkerchief costs ¥1000.*

Getting to Kahoku

Kahoku is about 15-minute taxi ride from Yamagata Airport. The closest train station is Jinmachi, a local stop on the JR Ohu line running from Yamagata; it's a 20-minute taxi ride from the station.

ZAO

The resort area of **Zao** is one of the largest ski areas in Tohoku and is also a popular hiking area when the snow melts. Only 50 minutes by bus from Yamagata City, visitors use the hot springs all year long. There are 35 lifts, one gondola and several cable cars spread out over a large area. Ski trails cater to all abilities. But if you want to ski with **snow monsters**, take the Zangesaka or Juhyogen courses. Snow monsters? Fierce winds blowing over the Sea of Japan from Siberia deposit ice droplets on the forest of fir trees near the top of the mountains, which turns them into spectacular ice sculptures. February is the peak time for snow monsters.

After a long day of skiing or hiking, relax in a hot spring tub at Zao Onsen. The entire area is volcanic and dotted with hot springs. Make sure you take off all jewelry before bathing because the water is acidic.

ARRIVALS & DEPARTURES

From Yamagata Station, take a bus (about 45 minutes, ¥780) or taxi (40 minutes, about ¥4500) to Zao Onsen.

Tourist Information

The **Tourist Information Office** telephone number is *(0236)94-9328.*

WHERE TO STAY

ASTOREA HOTEL, *Yokokura, Zao Onsen, Yamagata City, 990-2301. Tel. (0236)94-9603, Fax (0236)94-9181. Rates from ¥22,000 for two people with two meals. Credit cards.*

Located at the base of the mountain, you can ski to and from this hotel that serves French food.

ZAO ONSEN ECHO HOTEL, *1117 Zao Onsen, Yamagata City, 990-2301. Tel. (0236)94-9533, Fax (0236)94-9234. Rates from ¥12,000 for two people with two meals. No credit cards.*

The hotel has a large outdoor hot spring bath that's popular with skiers and hikers.

YAMADERA

Risshaku-ji, popularly known as **Yamadera**, is a fantastic temple perched on the side of the mountain. Founded in 860 by the famous priest En-nin, Yamadera literally means "mountain temple." The main hall, **Kompon Chudo**, in the lower part of the complex, dates from the 14th century. Most of the other buildings are from the 16th century. Pass through the Sanmon gate and start climbing the 1015 stone steps — even octogenarians do it. The path leads through an ancient cedar forest. On the way up, visit the observation point on the left; the view is stunning. At the top is the **Oku-no-in**, the inner shrine. Plan on spending about two hours all together.

For a change from temple viewing, go to **Ishiyama Kokeshi**, just a two-minute walk from the station. Yamadera *kokeshi* dolls, the round wooden dolls, are famous and you can paint your own. *Tel. (0236)95-2947. Takes 30 minutes and costs ¥500.*

ARRIVALS & DEPARTURES

Yamadera is a station on the JR Senzan line between Sendai and Yamagata. Rapid train (45 minutes from Sendai, ¥740); local train (65 minutes) and 20 minutes from Yamagata, ¥230.

WHERE TO STAY

If you want to spend the night in Yamadera, the small **YAMADERA PENSION** is a comfortable inn across from the station. *Tel. (0236)95-2240. 4274 Yamadera, Yamagata City, 999-3301. From ¥8350 per person with two meals and private bath. No credit cards.*

THE NARROW ROAD OF OKU

*The poet **Basho** (1644–1694) produced his famous work **The Narrow Road of Oku** while visiting Tohoku in the late 17th century. He begins the volume with "The months and days are the passing guests of a hundred generations; the years that come and go are also travelers." Basho wrote one of his most famous haiku poems while visiting Yamadera; it describes how the sudden trill of a cicada intensifies the silence. "How still it is! Stinging into the stones, The locust's trill." (Translation by Donald Keene).*

TSURUOKA

Tsuruoka doesn't have much to interest the foreign visitor except as the gateway to the **Dewa Sanzan** mountains. If you have some extra time, stop at the Chido Museum on the west side of Tsuruoka Park where rural houses, Western-style buildings and Sakai clan (the area's feudal lords) treasures are on display.

ARRIVALS & DEPARTURES
By Air
Shonai Airport serves the area.
To/from Tokyo Haneda: 3 flights/day (ANA. ¥14,900)
To/from Osaka Kansai: 1 flight/day (ANA. ¥22,600)
To/from Sapporo Chitose: 1 flight/day (ANA. ¥19,350)

For Ground Transportation:
Bus: to Tsuruoka (35 minutes, ¥790)
Taxi: to Tsuruoka (25 minutes, ¥3800)

By Train
To/from Niigata: JR Uetsu Honsen line by limited express (2 hours 10 minutes, ¥4400)

By Bus
To/from Yamagata: 10 buses/day (2 hours 15 minutes, ¥2000)
To/from Tokyo: overnight bus from Shibuya and Ikebukuro (9 hours, ¥7870)

WHERE TO STAY
Rather than stay in the city itself, it's more interesting to stay in one of the nearby hot spring areas such as Yunohama, Atsumi or at one of the temple lodges of Dewa Sanzan.
HOTEL SANNO PLAZA, *608 Sanno-machi, Tsuruoka, 997-0028. Tel. (0235)22-6501, Fax (0235)24-4396. Singles from ¥5000. Doubles from ¥8000. Credit cards.*
A seven-storied business hotel, most of the rooms are singles. The popular restaurant on the first floor serves a *sashimi teishoku* for ¥2000.

WHERE TO EAT
KYOZUSHI *(Japanese, inexpensive). Honcho 1-chome, Showa Dori. Tel. (0235)22-4704. Open 11am to 2pm; 5pm to 9:30pm. Closed Tuesday.*
Kyozushi serves only fresh fish from the Japan Sea. If good fresh fish is unavailable, rumor is that the restaurant closes. Naturally, the place is crowded. The *nigiri-jo sushi* set costs ¥1500, *nabe* stews run from ¥2000. From JR Tsuruoka Station, take a bus toward Yudagawa Onsen; get off at Ginza Dori, and it's a three-minute walk to the restaurant.

BENIYA *(Japanese, expensive)*. *7-35 Izumi-cho. Tel. (0235)24-8222. Open 5pm to 10pm. Closed irregularly.*
Serves *kaiseki* cuisine made with local ingredients. Set meals run from ¥6000. Reservations recommended.

KANAZAWAYA *(Noodles, inexpensive)*. *3-48 Daihoji-machi. Tel. (0235)24-7208. Open 11am to 3pm; 5pm to 8pm. Closed Wednesday and 3rd Thursday.*
Kanazawaya specializes in *soba* noodles served with their own sauce. The *wafu* course *nagomi* includes *tempura* and *soba* for ¥2300.

SEEING THE SIGHTS

Chido Hakubutsukan. The museum has several Western-style buildings, rural farm buildings and collections of armor and other paraphernalia of the warrior class as well as folk artifacts. It's a good place to get a glimpse of life during the feudal era. The Japanese garden is lovely. *Tel. (0235)22-1199. Open 9am to 5pm. ¥620. Take the Shonai Kotsu bus toward Yunohama or Atsumi Onsen. Get off at Hakubutsukan-mae (10 minutes).*

Taihokan. This Dutch Baroque building has some Renaissance features and is a good example of how Japanese interpreted Western architecture at the end of the 19th century. The small museum displays letters and local historic documents. *Tel. (0235)24-3266. Open 9am to 4:30pm. Closed Monday. Free admission. Close to city center; take the bus to Shiyakusho-mae.*

Dewa Yuki Shuzo Shiryokan. Visit this *sake* brewery turned into museum and enjoy a taste of *sake* rice wine. *From JR Station take Shonai Kotsu bus toward Yunohama Onsen, get off at Oyama Komisen Mae (25 minutes). Tel. (0235)33-3262. Open daily 8:45am to 4:30pm. ¥100.*

EXCURSIONS & DAY TRIPS
YUNOHAMA ONSEN

Yunohama Onsen is the last stop on the Shonai Kotsu bus from JR Tsuruoka Station (40 minutes). It is a large hot spring resort facing the Japan Sea; unfortunately most of the hotels are large cement structures with few redeeming qualities. For tourist information, *Tel. (0235)75-2258.*

One small hotel that breaks away from the norm is **UMIBE NO OYADO IKKYU**, *1-9-25 Yunohama, Tsuruoka 997-1201. Tel. (0235)75-2031, Fax (0235)75-2040. From ¥12,300 per person with two meals. Credit cards.* This Japanese-style inn has only 17 rooms. Every room has a view of the setting sun over the Japan sea. The chef emphasizes that he serves only the freshest seasonal food. Try the *sake* called Hatsumago — first grandchild.

ATSUMI ONSEN

This is a hot springs resort on the shores of the Japan Sea, with a history going back one thousand years. It is reached by JR train on the Uetsu Honsen line, 40 minutes to Atsumi Onsen Station from Tsuruoka. You can also take the Shonai Kotsu Bus from JR station to Atsumi Onsen, 50 minutes. By car take Route 7; it's 30 kilometers from Tsuruoka. Tourist information: *Tel. (0235)43-3547.*

BANKOKUYA, *Yuami, Atsumi-cho, Nishi Tagawa-gun, Yamagata, 999-9201. Tel. (0235)43-3333, Fax (0235)43-2277. ¥18,000 per person with two meals. Credit cards.*

Located at the foot of Mt. Atsumi, the back of the hotel overlooks the Atsumi River. The newly rebuilt outdoor bath is a superb place to relax and enjoy the verdant garden. In spring, the grounds are covered with cherry blossoms. The 300-year old establishment is known for its seafood cuisine.

TACHIBANAYA, *Yuami, Atsumi-cho, Nishi Tagawa-gun, Yamagata, 999-7201. Tel. (0235)43-2211, Fax (0235)43-3681. From ¥15,000 per person with two meals. Credit cards.*

Another inn with a 300-year history, Tachibanaya has a well-kept Japanese garden with a large pond that's home to lots of carp. The annex, an authentic Japanese wooden structure, overlooks the garden. If you stay in the main building, you can still enjoy their garden. Three generations of imperial family members have stayed at Tachibanaya.

DEWA SANZAN

Three sacred mountains in western Yamagata prefecture, **Haguro-san**, **Yudono-san** and **Gassan**, make up remote Dewa Sanzan. All three are closely tied with *yamabushi,* ascetic priests who undergo rigorous mental and physical training to attain enlightenment. If you have time to see only one mountain, we recommend Haguro-san — it's the easiest to access and the most sacred.

Tourist Information

See **Tsuruoka** above for arrivals and departures.

You can get information on all three mountains at the **Tourist Information Office** in Haguro, which is located in the ward office. Open 8:30am to 5pm. Closed weekends and holidays. *Tel. (0235)62-2111.*

WHERE TO STAY

KAMBAYASHI-BO, *Temple lodgings at top of Haguro-san. Tel. (0235)62-2273. No fax. ¥8000 per person with two meals. No credit cards. Call Ideha Kaikan to make a reservation: (0235)62-4727.*

Experience a pure Buddhist setting complete with religious training and Buddhist vegetarian food. Take Shonai Kotsu bus toward Haguro-sancho; get off at Haguro Center, then it's a two minute walk.

MINSHUKU KAYABUKIYA, *Tamugimata, Ashi-mura, Higashitagawa-gun, Yamagata, 997-0532. Tel. (0235)54-6103. No fax. ¥7800 per person with two meals. No credit cards. From Tsuruoka city take a bus toward Yudonosan. Get off at the Tamugimata stop, one before the last stop. About one hour.*

This small inn is one of the few remaining inns built in the "samurai helmet" style. The thatched-roof buildings have second floor entrances for use during the winter, and the gables on the second floor resemble a helmet.

HAGURO KOKUMIN KYUKAMURA, *8 Aza Haguroyama, Haguro-machi, Higashi Tagawa-gun, Yamagata, 997-0211. Tel. (0235)62-4270, Fax (0235)62-4271. From ¥6000 per person with two meals. Credit cards.*

A recreation center featuring tennis and camping in summer and skiing in winter.

SEEING THE SIGHTS

Haguro-san

In addition to *yamabushi,* **Haguro-san** has lots of religious monuments. You can reach the top of the mountain by bus or car from Tsuruoka; but for an authentic experience, get off at the village of Toge (about 40 minutes from Tsuruoka) and walk up. Stop at **Kogane-do,** built by the first shogun, Minamoto Yoritomo, in the early 13th century. You'll pass a **five-storied pagoda,** a National Treasure over 600 years old, and begin the ascent of 2446 stone steps, about one hour of huffing and puffing to the top. Going up and down these steps is part of the *yamabushi's* rigorous training. While one trip up probably isn't enough to ensure enlightenment, the view is nothing short of superb.

Near the top is the **History Museum** (Rekishi Hakubutsukan) that houses a collection of religious objects relating to Dewa Sanzan. Especially famous is a copper mirror found in a pond.

Ideha Cultural Hall (Ideha Bunka Kinenkan) is at Haguro Center. The museum shows the training undertaken by *yamabushi. Open 9am to 5pm. Closed Tuesday. ¥400.*

Gassan

Gassan is the most beautiful of the three mountains to look at, and its volcanic peak is also the highest at 1984 meters. Although you may see Buddhist monks, clad in white, undergoing severe physical training on the sacred mountain, Gassan is more popular for its secular aspects: climbing season runs from July 1 to September 30. View alpine flowers at the Midagahara plateau near the eighth station rest house. Choose among

THE MUMMY OF DAINICHI-BO TEMPLE

To see a mummy, stop at **Dainichi-bo Temple**. *According to legend, the famous priest Kobo Daishi threw three objects from his ship when he was returning from China in the 9th century. The spot on the ground where each fell was to become the site of a temple. Dainichi-bo is where one coin landed. The temple prospered, especially with the support of the third Tokugawa shogun's wet nurse, who prayed that Iemitsu, her charge, would be selected as shogun. We'll never know whether or not her prayers did the trick, but Iemitsu did become shogun. Over the years, the temple received support from the Tokugawa family. With the Meiji Restoration in 1868, the government pressured the temple to change into a Shinto shrine. When it did not, most of the buildings were burned.*

Dainichi-bo houses a rather unusual mummified priest, which was a relatively popular practice in this area. Actually the priest who showed us around took great pains to explain that the mummified priest is not a mummy in the traditional Egyptian style in which the internal organs are removed and the body preserved. These mummies' bodies are still intact, and they haven't been embalmed.

Dainichi-bo's mummy was a priest who died at age 96. You can see him shriveled up, clad in a brilliant yellow monk's robe. The priest slowly decreased his intake of food to the point where he drank only small amounts of water. He sat in a casket so he would be ready to leave the world at any time. He then drank lacquer to clean his organs and asked that he be buried alive and that his casket not be opened for 1000 days. When the time was up, his mummified body was found. This practice was banned long ago, so you don't find any recent nonmummified mummies around.

Dainichibo is about a 20-minute walk from Oami bus stop on the bus running between Yamagata and Tsuruoka.

seven different routes from the rest house to the peak; the rocky slope is not so steep, and the peak is a mere two hours away. In addition to **Gassan Jinja Shrine**, the peak has magnificent panoramic views. The shrine is open July 15 to September 15. ¥300 for purification to enter the sacred shrine.

Gassan is one of the few places in Japan that boasts summer skiing, which is available from May until end of July. *From Tsuruoka take the Shonai Kotsu bus to Gassan Hachigome, 90 minutes.*

Yudono-san

Yudono-san is famous for **Yudono-san Jinja Shrine**, but it isn't at the top of the mountain. The center of the shrine is a sacred rock under which lies the source of hot spring water. In the old days, the shrine didn't have even a *torii* gate, only the rock. *Yamabushi* trained on Gassan and Haguro-san but found enlightenment at Yudono Jinja. *Open June 1 through November 1. By bus from Tsuruoka, take the Shonai Kotsu bus toward Yudono-san and get off at the last stop, 90 minutes. From there, it's a 20-minute walk to the shrine.*

SAKATA

Sakata, on the Japan Sea, flourished during the Tokugawa era by shipping rice, safflower and other commodities. It is the home of the Honma family, once Japan's largest landowners. They were so wealthy, they had more economic power than many feudal lords. An old saying goes: "Maybe it is impossible for me to become a member of the Honma family to enjoy a life of luxury; I have a better chance of becoming a feudal lord."

Today a Honma residence is open as a museum. Nearby, another museum displays photographs taken by a native son.

ARRIVALS & DEPARTURES

Sakata is on the JR Hakushin line; 30 minutes north of Tsuruoka by limited express trains, ¥1620; 46 minutes by express trains, ¥480.

Tourist Information

At JR Sakata Station. *Tel. (0234)24-2233.*

WHERE TO EAT

LE POT AU FEU *(French, moderate). 1-10-20 Saiwaicho. Tel. (0234)26-2218. Open 11:30am-2pm; 5:30-8pm. Closed Wednesday. Reservations necessary.*

For a change from Japanese fare, try some authentic French food. Lunch sets ¥1000-2500; dinner from ¥3000.

SENRYU *(Noodles, inexpensive). 2-6-9 Nakamachi. Tel. (0234)22-1188. Open 11:30am to 7:30pm. Closed Wednesday.*

Senryu serves lots of different kinds of homemade noodles. The most popular dish is *ushio ramen* for ¥700; its broth is fish flavored.

SEEING THE SIGHTS

Honma Residence (Honma-ke Kyu Hontei). This house was used by the outrageously wealthy Honma family until the end of World War II. Never damaged by fire or earthquakes, the 200-year old home is one of the finest landowners' residences you can visit today — no expense was spared in its construction. A new wing was built when a member of the Sakai (feudal lord) family visited. *Tel. (0234)22-3562. Open 9:30am to 4:30pm; until 4pm December through March. ¥600. From Sakata Station take the Shonai Kotsu bus toward Tsuruoka, get off at Honcho stop (8 minutes).*

Honma Art Museum (Honma Bijutsukan). An annex of the Honma residence has been converted into a museum that displays the family collection. The wonderful 23-room villa has a display of fine Kyoto *hina* dolls every spring. Also there's a garden where the Honma received a mission from the shogun in 1768. *Tel. (0234)24-4311. Open daily 9am to 5pm. ¥700. 5-minute walk from Sakata Station.*

Domon Ken Kinenkan. Make every attempt to fit in a stop at this lovely museum. Located in a beautiful wooded area at the foot of Mt. Iimori, the strikingly contemporary building was designed by Taniguchi Yoshio, a famous architect. American Isamu Noguchi's sculpture graces the museum, and Teshigahara Hiroshi designed the garden; each is a famous name in contemporary Japanese design. The museum houses the photographic collection of Domon Ken; Sakata was his hometown. His work includes photographs of historic Japanese buildings as well as contemporary scenes. *Tel. (0234)31-0028. Open 9am to 4:30pm. Closed Monday but open daily in July and August. ¥420. From JR Sakata Station, take the Shonai Kotsu bus toward Jurizuka, get off at Domon Ken Kinenkan (15 minutes).*

YONEZAWA

A small, quiet castle town, **Yonezawa** was ruled by the illustrious Uesugi family from 1598 to 1867. The family produced one of Japan's most famous warriors, Uesugi Kenshin, but when the family made a tactical error by siding against Tokugawa Ieyasu, they found themselves banished to the backwater of Yonezawa.

The town is famous for its weaving, done by lower-ranking samurai to supplement their income. Its beef is known throughout Japan. Yonezawa also has small, quiet hot springs scattered about.

ARRIVALS & DEPARTURES

Yonezawa is 40 minutes by express train from Yamagata City. From Tokyo, Yonezawa is 2 hours 10 minutes by Tohoku shinkansen.

GETTING AROUND TOWN

Yonezawa is a small town easily accessible by bicycle. Bicycle rental is available at the JR Yonezawa Station and at Uesugi Kinenkan.

Tourist Information

It's located at JR Yonezawa Station, on the left as you exit. Open daily 8:30am to 6pm. *Tel. (0238)24-2965.*

WHERE TO STAY

Rather than staying in Yonezawa, go to rustic **Shirabu Onsen**, 50 minutes by bus.

NISHIYA, *Shirabu Onsen, Seki, Yonezawa, Yamagata, 992-1472. Tel. (0238)55-2480, Fax (0238)55-2212. From ¥10,000 per person with two meals. No credit cards.*

A quaint old inn with a thatched-roof main building; the hot spring baths even include a waterfall.

SEEING THE SIGHTS

Uesugi Memorial Hall (Uesugi Kinenkan). Built on the sight of the Uesugi family residence in Yonezawa castle, the 14th generation descendant still lives in part of the building. The garden is a copy Hamarikyu Garden in Tokyo. On display are Uesugi treasures and area crafts. The hall also has a restaurant where you can eat Yonezawa specialties including beef and carp. Set meals start at ¥2500. *Tel. (0238)21-5121. ¥300. Open 9am to 5pm; until 4pm December through March. Restaurant is open 11am to 3pm; 5pm to 8pm. Reservations necessary for dinner. Closed Tuesday. Within walking distance from Uesugi Jinja-mae bus stop from JR Yonezawa Station.*

Keisho-den is the treasure house of Uesugi Jinja and has the famous screen painting of Kyoto by Kano Eitoku, which Oda Nobunaga gave to Uesugi Kenshin. A visit is worthwhile just to see the screen; the collection also includes costumes, samurai armor and Kenshin's helmet. *Open 9am to 4pm. Closed December through March.*

SHOPPING

Yonezawa is famous for its woven *tsumugi* silk. A kimono made of this silk is too casual to wear to a wedding; it is more appropriate for tea ceremony, so it's a real luxury. To supplement their meager incomes, the silk was woven by lower-ranking samurai in the feudal era. Go to the **Weaving History Hall** (Orimono Rekishi Shiryokan) near Uesugi Jinja to see examples of this beautiful and intricate weaving. *Open 9am to 5pm. Closed December 29 through January 1.*

SENDAI

A city of about one million, **Sendai** is large and modern — during World War II, bombing flattened the city. It is easy to get around having been rebuilt based on a grid. A few monuments still remain from its glorious past as the castle town of the illustrious Date family. Sendai is the jumping off point to see Matsushima, a group of islands named one of the three most beautiful places in Japan.

Sendai's famous **Tanabata Festival** every August 6–8 sees the city decked out with thousands of bamboo poles festooned with bright streamers.

ARRIVALS & DEPARTURES

By Air

To/from **Nagoya**: 4 flights/day (ANA, JAS. ¥20,000)

To/from **Osaka Itami**: 6 flights/day; **Kansai**: 3 flights/day (ANA, JAL, JAS. ¥22,800)

To/from **Sapporo Chitose**: 5 flights/day (ANA, JAL, JAS. ¥20,800)

To/from **Hiroshima**: 2 flights/day. (ANA. ¥27,300)

To/from **Fukuoka**: 2 flights/day (JAS, ANK. ¥32,150)

Service to Komatsu and Matsuyama 1 flight/day on ANA and 1 flight/day service to Asahikawa, Hakodate and Kagoshima on Air Nippon (ANK)

For Ground Transportation:

By bus: to JR Sendai Station Nishi Guchi (West Exit) (40 minutes, ¥910)

By taxi: 40 minutes to JR Sendai Station, about ¥5500.

By Train

To/from **Tokyo**: Tohoku shinkansen train from Tokyo or Ueno Stations (2 hours, ¥10,590)

To/from **Morioka**: Tohoku shinkansen train (1 hour 20 minutes, ¥6290)

To/from **Yamagata**: JR Senzan line express (1 hour, ¥1110)

By Bus

To/from **Morioka**: 15 buses/day (2 hours 40 minutes, ¥2850). Some are JR buses.

To/from **Aomori**: 4 buses/day (4 hours 50 minutes, ¥5700). Some are JR buses.

To/from **Hirosaki**: 3 buses/day (4 hours 20 minutes, ¥5090). One a day is a JR Bus.

To/from **Tokyo** 3 buses/day from Shinjuku Station (5 hours, ¥6210).

GETTING AROUND TOWN

Sendai's subway system and extensive bus network radiates from the JR Sendai train station.

Tourist Information

The "i" **Tourist Information Office** is on the second floor of JR Sendai Station. *Tel. (022)222-3269.* Open daily 8:30am to 8pm. Closed December 31 through January 3. English-speaking staff members are available.

The Sendai International Association runs an English hot line 9am to 8pm daily. *Tel. (022)224-1919.*

Goodwill Guides: Miyagi Goodwill Guide Club provides English-speaking guides for Sendai. Contact the tourist office or Sendai International Association (above) for the current contact number.

WHERE TO STAY

SENDAI HOTEL, *1-10-25 Chuo, Aoba-ku, Sendai, 980-0021. Tel. (022)225-5171, Fax (022)268-9325. Twins from ¥12,000. Doubles from ¥16,500. Credit cards.*

The Sendai Hotel has a 150-year history although the building is modern. It features eight different restaurants, and the fifth floor has well-kept Japanese gardens. You can't believe you're in the middle of the city, just across the street from JR Sendai Station.

JAL CITY HOTEL, *1-2-12 Kakyoin, Aoba-ku, Sendai, 980-0013. Tel. (022)711-2580, Fax (022)221-5533. Singles from ¥8800. Twins from ¥15,000. Credit cards.*

A big step up from the average business hotel, the staff is friendly and efficient. This choice is good for a moderately priced hotel.

WHERE TO EAT

Sendai is noted for fresh oysters from its bay.

SENDAI KAKI TOKU *(Oysters, inexpensive). 4-9-1 Ichibancho, Aoba-ku. Tel. (022)222-0785. Open 11am to 9pm; weekends and holidays from 12 noon. Closed Monday.*

This place is for oyster-holics — everything served has oysters. During the summer try the oyster tofu for ¥1000. In winter, have the oyster stew with *miso* sauce *(dotenabe)* from ¥2000. Fresh oysters in vinegar cost ¥1200; set menus start at ¥4000.

DATE YASHIKI *(Regional cuisine, inexpensive). 3-4 Kokubun-cho, Aoba-ku. Tel. (022)261-2071. Open from 11:30am-2pm; 5pm-8:30pm, earlier if they finish their daily supply of food. Closed Sunday.*

The specialty of the house is *seiro meshi,* rice steamed in a square box. *Gomoku* has shrimp, crab, salmon and oysters steamed on top of rice, ¥800.

SEEING THE SIGHTS

Zuihoden Hall is the mausoleum of feudal lord Date Masamune. The 17th century building was destroyed during World War II, but the replica is faithful to the ornate Momoyama style of the original. *Tel. (022)262-6250. Open daily 9am to 4:30pm; until 4pm in winter. ¥550. From Sendai Station platform #11, take the bus toward Otamaya-bashi, get off at Otamaya-bashi (20 minutes). It's a 10-minute walk.*

Near Zuihoden are the ruins of Sendai's castle, **Aoba-jo**. High up on the hill, the park has great views of the sea and the city. Steep stone walls and one watch tower remain. *From Sendai Station platform #9, take the bus to Aoba-joshi.*

Toshogu Shrine was built by the second Date feudal lord in 1654. The building still retains the magnificent architectural style of the Momoyama period. The main hall and Chinese-style gate are designated Important Cultural Properties. *No admission charge. From Sendai Station, take the Shiei bus toward Nankodai, get off at Miyamachi go-chome (15 minutes).*

Osaki Hachiman Jinja Shrine. This shrine has an illustrious history. Founded in the 12th century, Date Masamune moved it to Sendai in 1602. The Momoyama-style black lacquered hall built in 1607 is designated a National Treasure. *Admission free. 20 minutes by bus from JR Sendai Station (platform # 25 or 29) to Hachiman Jinja-mae.*

Sendai Ciy Museum (Sendai-shi Hakubutsukan) exhibits the history of the prefecture, emphasizing Date Masamune's glory days. *Open 9am-4:45pm. Closed Mondays. ¥400.*

SHOPPING

The largest shopping center in all of Tohoku is at **Ichiban-cho Shopping Mall**, a covered arcade about ten minutes walk from Sendai Station. It has department stores, small shops and restaurants.

Katsuyama Shuzo is an interesting *sake* brewery that served as *sake* purveyors to the Date family for 300 years. The shop, in a traditional wooden building, sells a variety of high-quality rice wine, including the best-selling Kenshozan, a dry *sake*. *Open 9am to 6pm. Closed Sunday and holidays. Tel. (022)222-4451. 2-10-57 Uesugi, Aoba-ku.*

Sendai is noted for its *kokeshi*, slender painted wooden dolls, distinct from other Tohoku *kokeshi*. Stop by **Gangu-an Kokeshiya** for an excellent selection. *1-chome Kokubun-cho. Tel. (022)222-5889. Open daily 8am to 6pm.*

MATSUSHIMA

Matsushima, an area with hundreds of islands covered with pine trees, is called one of the three most scenic places in Japan. This designation is more of a curse than a blessing and is living proof that in Japan, a place is preserved in inverse proportion to the number of people who know about it. Since Matsushima is so well known, the streets are crowded with tacky souvenir shops and bus loads of tourists following their flag-waving guides. The boats you take to see the beautiful islands have loud speaker systems blaring out the nuances of each island.

Personally, we prefer to stay at home and look at a single *bonsai* pine tree or at a picture of Sotatsu's screen painting of Matsushima in the Freer Gallery of Art in Washington, D.C. The screen's pine islands are scattered over the blue water and the red trunks of the trees contrast with the green needles. But back to reality...

If you can put up with the crowds and the noise, the reward in Matsushima is the beautiful Zen temple, **Zuigan-ji**. Built in the Momoyama period, it's a National Treasure.

ARRIVALS & DEPARTURES

Take the JR Senseki train from JR Sendai Station to Matsushima Kaigan Station or Hon-Shiogama Station. Our preference is to get off at Hon-Shiogama Station (about 25 minutes).

Tourist Information

A **Tourist Information booth** is near Matsushima pier. They have maps and information in English. *Tel. (022)354-2618*. Open daily 8:30am to 5pm and until 4:30pm in winter. There's another information center near Matsushima Kaigan Station.

Goodwill Guides: The Matsushima Goodwill Guides offer English-speaking guides for Matsushima. Contact the Sendai International Association (9am to 8pm daily), *Tel. (022)224-1919*, for the current number.

SEEING THE SIGHTS

Our preference is to take the train to Hon-Shiogama Station. As you exit the station, walk toward the right, alongside the water, and turn right onto the road that leads to the pier. Take the **sightseeing boat** for Matsushima, passing by many of the area's famous islands. Try not to be too put off by the loud narration.

After you are deposited at Matsushima pier, walk for about five minutes to **Zuigan-ji Temple**. Tucked into the mountainside, you'll pass many shallow, moss-covered caves where monks used to meditate. The temple's history goes back a long way. The famous priest En-nin founded it in the 9th century, and it's had many powerful patrons: the first Kamakura shogun turned it into a Zen temple in the 12th century, and four hundred years later, the feudal lord Date Masamune rebuilt it in splendid Momoyama style. The National Treasures are the **main hall**, the **gate** and the **kitchen**, all date from that time. The main hall has splendid screen paintings of peacocks. The **Treasure House** (Seiryuden), a modern building, houses the temple's treasures including Kano Eitoku's magnificent screen paintings of hawks and European objects brought back by Masamune's envoys to Rome. *Open 8am to 5pm, April through September; closes at 4pm or 4:30pm other months. ¥700.*

As you leave the temple, turn right onto to the main road that parallels the water. When this road jogs right, turn left to reach **Kanrantei**, a tea pavilion on the top of Cape Tsukumi. Toyotomi Hideyoshi gave this simple building from his Fushimi Castle to Date Masamune in the late 1500s. The screen paintings were done by Kano Sanraku. *Open 8am to 5pm; 8:30am to 4:30pm November through March. ¥200.*

As you walk towards Matsushima Kaigan Station, rather than turning right to enter the station, turn left and you will reach the picturesque vermilion Togetsukyo Bridge leading to Oshima Island. In the old days, the island was used by priests for meditation and was off limits to women.

AIZU WAKAMATSU

The former castle town of **Aizu Wakamatsu** is a picturesque city today. The reconstructed castle keep is in a large park that graces the center of the city. A number of historic buildings remain from Aizu's feudal era, and the city is a center for crafts including lacquer, ceramics and folk arts. Aizu is close enough to Tokyo for an easy overnight trip or it can be part of a longer Tohoku itinerary.

Aizu Wakamatsu earned its place in the sun in 1868 when the feudal lord, a descendant of the first Tokugawa shogun, opposed the overthrow of the Tokugawa shogun and the return of power to the emperor. The ensuing battle destroyed large parts of the city.

The people still have proud memories of the warriors and their families who committed suicide rather than risking capture. One of the most famous incidents involves twenty samurai boys, all in their teens, who tragically committed suicide when they mistakenly thought Aizu castle had fallen.

ARRIVALS & DEPARTURES
By train

To/from Tokyo: take the Tohoku shinkansen train to Koriyama (1 1/2 hours) and change to the JR Ban-etsu Saisen line. The express takes 1 hour 10 minutes to Aizu. ¥9750.

To/from Sendai: take the Tohoku shinkansen train to Koriyama (48 minutes); change to the JR Ban-etsu Saisen line, 1 hour 10 minutes to Aizu. ¥7020.

GETTING AROUND TOWN

The main sights are clustered in two areas: around the castle and on Mt. Iimoriyama. Use buses or taxis to get from one to the other.

Tourist Information

A **Tourist Information Center** is located in View Plaza at the JR Aizu Wakamatsu Station. Open 9:30am to 5:30pm; 10am to 5pm on Sunday and holidays. Closed December 31 through January 2. *Tel. (0242)32-0688*. Another Tourist Information Center is on the grounds of the castle and is open daily 8:30am to 5pm. *Tel. (0242)29-1151*. Both are "i" Tourist Information Offices.

WHERE TO STAY

TAGOTO, *5-15 Johoku-machi, Aizu Wakamatsu, Fukushima, 965-0042. Tel. (0242)24-7500, Fax (0242)24-9182. From ¥10,000 per person with two meals. No credit cards.*

The family business began as a Japanese restaurant serving fresh fish from the river. The tradition for delicious food still continues. The well-polished cypress hallways and wooden bath give the ten-room inn a relaxing ambiance.

SHIBUKAWA TONYA BEKKAN, *3-28 Nanoka-machi, Aizu Wakamatsu, Fukushima, 965-0044. Tel. (0242)28-4000, Fax (0242)26-6464. From ¥10,000 per person with two meals. No credit cards.*

The buildings were used as storehouses during the Meiji period but are now converted into a lovely contemporary Japanese inn.

WHERE TO EAT

MITSUTAYA *(Tofu, inexpensive). 1-1-25 Omachi. Tel. (0242)27-1345. Open 10am to 5pm. Closed 3rd Wednesday; January through March closed every Wednesday.*

This restaurant is famous for its *dengaku*, skewered *tofu*, potatoes and other foods charcoal grilled with a thick *miso* sauce. Set menus run from ¥1500. They also have a shop adjacent to the restaurant where you can pick up dried *tofu* to take home.

TAKINO *(Japanese regional cuisine, inexpensive). 5-31 Sakae-machi. Tel. (0242)25-0808. Open daily 11am to 9pm.*

This restaurant is known for its *wappa meshi*, fragrant rice steamed and served in a wooden box topped with mountain vegetables, mushrooms, crab and seafood. The building itself once belonged to the shogunate, so the atmosphere is laden with history.

KIRIYA (*Noodles, inexpensive*). *2034 Aizu Wakamatsu-shi. Tel. (0242)25-3851. Open 11am to 9pm. Sunday 11am to 7pm. Closed Wednesday.*

The buckwheat used to make *soba* comes from an area known for its high quality. *Gongen soba* uses buckwheat from this area, ¥1420. There are only 30 portions available each day. Another specialty is *Aizu ganko soba,* which costs ¥1200.

SEEING THE SIGHTS

Aizu's sights are fairly spread out. We suggest you first see the area around the castle, then go up Iimoriyama Hill, and finally to the samurai village.

Tsuruga-jo, Aizu's castle, is in a large park in the center of the city. While the castle keep itself is a reconstruction, the walls and moats of the once great fortress are original. In spring, over a thousand cherry trees turn the area into a pale pink paradise. The castle keep looks authentic from the outside, but the inside has broad staircases and linoleum floors and houses a museum of local history. *Open daily 8:30am to 5pm. But it is closed the first Monday through Thursday in July and the first Tuesday through Thursday in December. ¥400. Arrange for a goodwill guide by calling (0242)29-1151.*

Aizu Sake Historical Museum (Aizu Shuzo Rekishikan) is near the castle in an authentic *sake* brewery, which shows the process of making rice wine and displays historic objects. *Open 8:30am to 5pm; until 4:30pm in winter. ¥300.*

Fukushima Prefectural Museum (Fukushima Kenritsu Hakubutsukan). Just across the street from the castle is a modern museum with excellent displays of the area's history and culture. *Open 9:30am to 5pm. Closed Monday and December 28 through January 4. ¥250 plus additional fee for special exhibitions.*

About a 10-minute walk from the museum is **Oyakuen**, a beautiful Japanese garden where the Matsudaira clan once had their villa. The garden has a large pond and is perfect for strolling; in summer, the lotus flowers are splendid. There's a medicinal herb garden also, which gives the garden its name (literally "medicinal herb garden"). *Open daily 8:30am to 5pm except the first Monday through Thursday of July and first Tuesday through Thursday of December. ¥300.*

From Oyakuen, take a taxi to Iimoriyama. You'll be at the base of the mountain, which you can't miss for all the souvenir shops. If you don't want to walk up the mountain, you can glide up on an outdoor escalator for a small fee.

Mt. Iimoriyama is the site of a tragic incident in Aizu's history. During the civil war in 1868, Aizu was fighting to preserve the position of the Tokugawa shogun. Opposing forces attacked the city. A group of young samurai called Byakkotai (White Tiger Brigade) returned to Aizu and saw smoke engulfing the castle. They thought all was lost so they committed *harakiri,* ritual suicide. In fact, the smoke was some outhouses that went up in flames, and the battle continued for another month before the Aizu forces were defeated. To this day, Japanese come by bus loads to view the scene of this tragedy. We have to admit we find it hard to understand the glorification of such a senseless act — perhaps it's because they were so young. The graves of the boys are on the mountain as are two monuments from the fascist governments of Germany and Italy that commemorate the boys' actions.

Mt. Iimoriyama is also home to an ingenious marvel of Japanese architecture, a temple called **Sazae-do.** The tower built in 1796 is a hexagonal structure that represents 33 pilgrimage temples. The building is constructed in such a way that you go to all 33 areas without being at the same spot twice. *Open 8:15am to sunset. ¥300.*

From Mt. Iimoriyama, take a taxi to Bukeyashiki-mae or take the bus, get off at Yaroga-mae and walk about 10 minutes. **Aizu Samurai Residences** (Aizu Buke Yashiki) are a collection of samurai homes showing what life was like for the warriors during the feudal era. *Open daily 8:30am to 5pm; until 4:30pm December through March. ¥850.*

SHOPPING

Aizu's has a rich tradition of crafts including lacquer ware, folk pottery called Hongo-yaki, indigo-dyed cloth and paper mache oxen called *akabeko.* Many shops near the station sell a variety of goods.

For a demonstration of how Aizu lacquer is made, go to the **Yamada Lacquer Ware Exhibition Hall** (Yamada Shikki Kaikan), about 10-minute walk from the station. You can also buy lacquer ware there. *Open daily 8:45am to 5:30pm; until 5pm December through March.*

EXCURSIONS & DAY TRIPS
KITAKATA

This small town is famous for its many well-preserved storehouses and for its *ramen* noodles. The town was a production center for rice, *miso* bean paste and soy sauce so many warehouses were built to store the goods. A fire in the late 1800s destroyed the town, but the locals were astounded that the warehouses still standing. So, they decided to build all their buildings in warehouse style. At least 2500 today.

It's fun to wander around Kitakata's streets. They are lined with storehouse-type architecture housing shops, restaurants, warehouses, homes and temples. Also, make the trip to **Kumano Jinja Shrine**, about a ten-minute taxi ride from the station. The simple Shinto shrine is a long hall with a thatched roof supported by fifty pillars; there are no walls. The building dates from 1085 and is designated an Important Cultural Property.

When in Kitakata, you must eat *ramen;* the area's famous for its noodles and 150 ramen restaurants dot the town. You'll notice every store in town has souvenir packages for visitors to take home. The best shop in town is **MAKOTO SHOKUDO**, *7116 Tsukimi-cho. Tel. (0241)22-0232. Open 7:30am to 7pm. Closed first and third Mondays.* The special *ramen* costs ¥550.

Getting to Kitakata

Kitakata is 30 minutes from Aizu Wakamatsu on the JR Ban-etsu Saisen line.

OUCHIJUKU

Feudal lords stayed at this small town on their annual jaunts to Edo (Tokyo). It's a quaint little place with just one main road, closed to traffic, with about 20 thatched-roof buildings. Many today have been turned into small inns. Almost every building has a small store out front. During the day, the town is filled with tourist buses making brief stops; at night it's a quiet and wonderfully charming village and a good place to overnight. Although we stayed there on a Saturday night in summer, we had the village practically to ourselves.

We stayed at **YAMATOYA MINSHUKU**, *6 Yamamoto, Ouchi, Shimogo-cho, Minami Aizu-gun, Fukushima, 969. Tel. (02416)8-2911. Rate ¥7000 per person with two meals. No credit cards.* The thatched-roof inn is simple, and the country fare is delicious.

Getting to Ouchijuku

From Aizu Wakamatsu, take the Aizu line from Nishi Aizu Station to Yunokami Onsen (45 minutes, ¥600). From there it's a 20-minute taxi ride. Or one hour by bus from Aizu Wakamatsu Station to Yunokami Station. (6 buses/day, ¥1090).

16. NAGANO PREFECTURE

Nagano Prefecture is the heart of the **Japan Alps**, a snowbound wonderland in winter and a great hiking and mountain climbing center in summer. For rural Japan close to Tokyo and Nagoya, it's hard to beat Nagano.

Hosting the **1998 Winter Olympics** catapulted Nagano to center stage and brought a slew of new developments including a *shinkansen* train that whisks you from Tokyo to Nagano City in one and a half hours. As one of Japan's few landlocked prefectures, this mountainous area, known as "the roof of Japan," offers a distinct blend of historic sights and natural beauty — spectacular mountain views.

Several spots are well worth the trip.

The city of **Matsumoto** is home to one of Japan's oldest castles and a top woodblock print museum. The **Nakasendo Road**, one of the main thoroughfares between Kyoto and Tokyo during the feudal age, literally transports you to several feudal-era post towns: **Narai**, **Tsumago** and **Magome**. The city of **Nagano** has one of Japan's most sacred Buddhist pilgrimages to **Zenko-ji Temple**, in a lovely setting overlooking the city. Nagano Prefecture is great for hiking and mountain climbing in summer and skiing in winter. Because of road and rail improvements for the Olympics, Nagano is more accessible than it has ever been.

The large prefecture of Nagano is bisected by two major JR rail lines. We cover the eastern portion first and then the western portion.

Planning Your Stay

Spend at least a few days in the Nagano area: Spend one night in Matsumoto or Nagano City as a jumping off point. Then spend one to two nights in Kamikochi in the Japan Alps and, for a more historic bent, one to two nights in one of the lovely preserved post towns of Tsumago, Magome or Narai. Nagano offers a variety of experiences:

• **Castles**: Matsumoto Castle, known as the "blackbird" castle
• **Folk art Museums**: Matsumoto Folk Craft Museum, Japan Folklore Museum

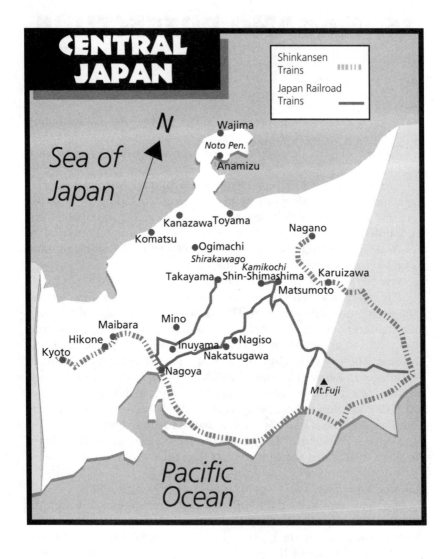

NAGANO HIGHLIGHTS
- *Make a pilgrimage to Zenko-ji Temple in the city of Nagano*
- *Climb to the top of Matsumoto Castle*
- *Visit the Hokusai museum in Obuse*
- *Bathe with wild monkeys at Korakukan*
- *Admire a 13th century pagoda at Bessho Onsen*
- *Hike high in the mountains of Kamikochi*
- *Overnight in an old-style inn at Narai, Tsumago or Magome*

- **Art Museums**: Japan Ukiyo-e Museum, Matsumoto; Hokusai Museum, Obuse
- **Temples**: Zenko-ji, according to Buddhist belief, everyone ought to visit once in a life time
- **Preserved Post Towns**: Narai, Tsumago, Magome
- **Crafts**: Narai, Kiso Hirasawa, Tsumago, Magome
- **Hiking**: Kamikochi, Karuizawa
- **Wild Monkeys**: Korakukan near Kanbayashi Onsen
- **Turn-of-the-century Western-style Architecture**: Karuizawa, Kaichi Gakko School Building, Matsumoto

NAGANO CITY

Until recently, **Nagano** was a small and unassuming mountain city. But, as the home to **Zenko-ji**, one of Japan's most famous Buddhist temples in a lovely setting overlooking the city, pilgrims have been tramping to Nagano for centuries. The Nagano JR Station is actually a copy of Zenko-ji's main hall.

Other than the temple and the **Olympics**, the city has little of interest to the international traveler. But favorite side trips are to the small town of **Obuse** where the woodblock artist Hokusai spent some time, to **Bessho Onsen**, a hot spring town brimming with temples, and to a remote mountain inn near Kanbayashi Onsen where monkeys bathe in hot spring waters.

ARRIVALS & DEPARTURES

By Air
   Matsumoto is the closest airport.

   For Ground Transportation:
   Bus: to Nagano Bus Terminal (70 minutes, ¥1430)

By Train

To/from Tokyo: The new Asama shinkansen train connects Tokyo Station with Nagano (1 1/2 hours. ¥7970).

To/from Nagoya: the JR *Shinano* limited express trains take 3 hours. ¥7130.

By Bus

To/from Tokyo: From Ikebukuro Station 4 buses/day (3 3/4 hours, ¥4000); from Shinjuku Station 4 buses/day (3 hours 40 minutes, ¥4000).

To/from Osaka: Overnight bus (7 hours, ¥6930)

To/from Matsumoto: 16 buses/day (1 hour 20 minutes, ¥920)

Tourist Information

The **Tourist Information Booth** is in the plaza in front of JR Nagano Station. *Tel. (026)226-5626.*

WHERE TO STAY

NAGANO DAIICHI HOTEL, *1-16 Minami Chitose, Nagano City, 380-0823. Tel. (026)228-1211, Fax (026)224-2188. Singles from ¥6000. Twins from ¥11,000. Credit cards.*

Nagano Daiichi Hotel's central location makes it convenient for seeing the sights. Breakfast costs ¥1000.

FUJIYA RYOKAN, *80 Daimon-cho, Nagano City, 380-0841. Tel. (026)232-1241, Fax (026)232-1243. From ¥9000 per person with two meals. Credit cards.*

On the main road leading to Zenko-ji, Fujiya has catered to pilgrims for generations. The inn is like a museum. The turn-of-the-century building is Western style but the rooms themselves are Japanese style. The entire place has an old-fashioned atmosphere. The inner garden is lovely, and the inn's best room overlooks the garden and costs ¥25,000.

SAIHOKUKAN, *528-1 Agata-cho, Nagano City, 380-0838. Tel. (026)235-3333, Fax (026)235-3365. Singles from ¥8000 with breakfast. Twins from ¥14,000. Credit cards.*

One of the oldest hotels in Nagano City, its located only five minutes by taxi from the station; Saihokukan has friendly staff and offers good value.

TEMPLE LODGINGS: ZENKO-JI SHUKUBO, *Tel. (026)234-3591. Fax:(026)235-2151. From ¥7000. No credit cards.*

Most of the pilgrims to Zenko-ji stay in temple lodgings. Spending a night at a temple lodging is an unforgettable experience, so go for the adventure. Apart from the fact that pilgrims tend to start rather early in the morning, temple lodges operate pretty much the same as Japanese inns. You can contact the above numbers directly with the dates and number of people, and they will book you in the best temple lodging available. But remember rooms fill well in advance around Japanese holidays.

Among the 39 temple inns in Nagano, we recommend the following two:

GENSHO-IN, *Motoyoshi-cho. Tel. (026)232-3685.*
ZUIJOBO, *Motoyoshi-cho. Tel. (026)232-3667.*

WHERE TO EAT

TOKUGYOBO *(Buddhist vegetarian fare, moderate to expensive). Motoyoshi. Tel. (026)232-0264. Open 11am to 2pm; 5pm to 8pm.*

Try authentic Buddhist vegetarian cuisine like the monks have been making for hundreds of years at Zenko-ji. Set meals start at ¥1000. Reservations are required; the staff speaks some English.

DAIMARU *(Noodles, inexpensive). 504 Zenko-ji Daimon-cho. Tel. (0262)32-2502. Open daily 9am to 6:30pm.*

Daimaru, located on Nagano Chuo Dori, the road leading from the Nagano Station to Zenko-ji Temple, is on the left just before the temple buildings begin. You can't miss the large glass window where the chef rolls out *soba* noodles — you know your noodles are fresh. They even serve *soba* (buckwheat) tea; we couldn't help buying a package to bring home. Noodles begin at ¥500.

PETER'S BISTRO *(Western, inexpensive). 3-16-22 Yoshida. Tel. (026)241-3235. Open 11:30am to 9:30pm. Near the Yoshida stop on the Nagano Dentetsu line, 4th stop from Nagano Station.*

Run by American expats, the restaurant is popular with Westerners craving pizza (from ¥600), Mexican fare and bagels.

SEEING THE SIGHTS

The magnificent temple of **Zenko-ji** is a 25-minute walk from JR Nagano Station along Nagano Chuo Dori. If you don't feel like walking the entire distance, take a bus or taxi to Daimon. Many of the shops along the road have been catering to pilgrims for a long time. Stores selling Buddhist goods such as prayer beads, special pilgrim hats, incense and household altars, as well as toys and dried *soba* noodles line the path between the Niomon and Sanmon gates.

Pilgrims have flocked to Zenko-ji for centuries. Folklore says you must visit the temple at least once in your life in order to enter paradise. And rather than take chances, millions visit every year.

The temple's origins are obscure but probably go back to the 7th century. In 552, the king of Korea gave the emperor the statue that is now Zenko-ji's main Buddhist image. But don't expect to see this Buddha today; legend says it's so sacred that even glancing at it can cause blindness. A copy is displayed only once every seven years.

At the center of the large courtyard is a huge metal incense burner shaped like a lion's mouth. The incense people have burned over the years has made the lion's mouth appear to drool with tar. In front is the **Hondo** (main hall), a large two-storied thatched-roof building, was rebuilt in 1707 and restored in 1989. Inside, make sure you walk through the pitch black corridor around the Kaidan platform. Legend has it that if you touch the key on the wall, you're assured of entering paradise. The hall also has an Obinzurusama statue. If you touch the part of the statue where you ail, it's believed you will be cured. *Open daily 4:40am to 4:30pm; winter 6am to 4pm.*

Zenko-ji is not affiliated with any Buddhist sect, but the Jodo and Tendai groups rotate leadership. The **Daihogan**, a convent on the left before you reach the Niomon Gate, belongs to the Jodo sect. By tradition a female member of the imperial family heads the convent. Zenko-ji always remained opened to women, a rarity among Buddhist temples. Daihogan's treasure hall contains a well-known statue of the Nehanzo Buddha, the image of him entering Nirvana. *Open daily 5:30am to 4pm. ¥200.*

The treasure house of the **Daikanjin**, belonging to the Tendai sect, houses a noted *Tale of Genji* scroll. The garden is one of Japan's loveliest. *Open daily 6am to 3pm. ¥200.*

SHOPPING

The main shopping district, near JR Nagano Station, is where you'll find department stores and arcades. Stores selling interesting crafts line Nagano Chuo Dori, the approach to the temple. Nagano area crafts include ceramics, bamboo items, pongee silk textiles, straw horses and clay dolls.

EXCURSIONS & DAY TRIPS
OBUSE

A mere 30 minutes from Nagano, the small town of **Obuse** makes a good half-day trip. Once a bustling commercial center, today the town is restoring its Edo-period buildings. Home of Takai Kozan, an important patron of the famous woodblock artist and painter **Katsushika Hokusai** (1760–1849), Hokusai spent some time here.

Getting to Obuse
To/from Nagano: take the Nagano Dentetsu train (from the west exit of JR Nagano Station). Local train (29 minutes, ¥650).

Where to Eat
Chestnuts are the specialty here; they seem to grace every meal. Lots of restaurants serve chestnuts but we especially enjoyed our meal at:

SUZUKI KADAN *(Japanese, inexpensive). Located on the far side of the parking lot next to the Hokusai Museum. Tel. (026)247-5656. Open 10am to 4pm. Closed Tuesday.*

The restaurant is in an old farm building moved from Niigata. The high ceilings expose rough wooden rafters. Because there was a lot of snow in Niigata, the windows are high. Sit either at tables or on *tatami* mats. The specialty is chestnuts; lunch consists of rice steamed with chestnuts and three side dishes for ¥1000 or with five side dishes for ¥1500.

SAN POO LOH *(Western and Japanese, inexpensive). Across from the entrance to the Hokusai Museum. Tel. (026)247-5433. Open 10am to 9pm. Closed Tuesday.*

Enjoy Western food in this bright, contemporary Japanese building. The pasta set (¥1500) includes a starter of pate and smoked salmon, spaghetti *carbonara*, a small steak with french fries and mushroom and scallop sauté. The portions aren't large but this should be enough to keep you going all afternoon. San Poo Loh also serves *yakiniku* and curry rice.

Seeing the Sights

The historic area of Obuse is about a seven-minute walk from the station. Bicycles, available for rent at the station, are convenient for getting around the area.

The high point is the **Hokusai Museum** (Hokusai-kan), featuring paintings, sketches and two fantastic festival floats decorated by the master artist. *Open daily 8am to 5pm; 9:30am to 4:30pm November through March. Closed December 31 and January 1. ¥500.*

Takai Kozan Hall (Takai Kozan Kinenkan). Across the small road from the Hokusai Museum, this small storehouse displays the art work of Kozan, Hokusai's patron.

Japan Lantern Museum (Nihon Akari Hakubutsukan). Across the main road, about a five-minute walk from the Hokusai Museum, this museum exhibits all sorts of paper lanterns and lights used in Japan. Although the descriptions are only in Japanese, the variety of lanterns is still fun to see. *Open 9:30am to 5pm; until 4:30pm November 21 through March 20. Closed Wednesday and December 30 through January 2. ¥300.*

About two kilometers away and best reached by taxi or bicycle, **Gansho-in** is the temple where Hokusai painted his fantastic phoenix mural on the ceiling. Hokusai fans shouldn't miss it.

BESSHO ONSEN

Well off-the-beaten path, this small town makes a nice getaway from Nagano City. The hot spring town actually dates back to the 9th century and was even mentioned in the 11th century *Pillow Book* by court lady Sei

Shonagon. It wasn't until the succeeding Kamakura period that Bessho came into its own. A provincial governor, related to the Kamakura shoguns, imported grand temples to this remote outpost, earning it the name "Nagano's Little Kamakura."

In spring the many cherry trees add a pale pink glow to the town and in autumn the maples turn crimson red. But anytime of year, Bessho Onsen is an enjoyable place to wander, taking in the temples and soaking in the hot spring baths.

Getting to Bessho Onsen

Limited express train from Nagano to Ueda takes between 20 and 25 minutes; 13 minutes on the Asama shinkansen. Local trains take 35 minutes. From Ueda, take the private Ueda Kotsu train (30 minutes, ¥570).

Where to Stay

TAMAYA, *227 Bessho Onsen, Ueda, Nagano, 386-1431. Tel. (0268)38-3015, Fax (0268)38-3027. From ¥15,000 per person with two meals. Credit cards.*

Tamaya has large outdoor baths and is conveniently located in the center of Bessho Onsen.

HANAYA HOTEL, *169 Bessho Onsen, Ueda, Nagano, 386-1431. Tel. (0268)38-3131, Fax (0268)38-7923. From ¥15,000 per person with two meals. Credit cards.*

Hanaya is just a five minute walk from the train station yet is really quiet. It's one of the oldest inns in town and has spacious outdoor baths.

Seeing the Sights

The highlight is **Anraku-ji Temple**, which has an exquisite octagonal pagoda built in the Kamakura era and based on Chinese Sung Dynasty architecture. Nestled against the hill, imagine how impressive and imposing the pagoda must have looked when it was built in the 13th century in this small village in the middle of nowhere. The only Chinese-style three-storied pagoda in Japan, it is designated a National Treasure.

Pagodas are the name of the game in Bessho Onsen. **Joraku-ji Temple** has a Kamakura period stone pagoda, covered with moss. **Zenzan-ji's** later Muromachi period pagoda has three stories.

Make sure you also stop at **Chuzen-ji Temple** to see a lovely thatched-roof Yakushi-do hall.

JIGOKUDANI: MONKEYING AROUND IN HELL VALLEY

*Did you ever think you would see wild monkeys in a hot spring bath? This is the name of the game in **Jigokudani**, literally Hell Valley. But we have to warn you, Hell Valley is remote. It's not that Jigokudani is so far from Nagano – an hour-long train ride and a 15-minute bus ride – but the last 1.6 kilometers (one mile) are on foot.*

While you can make a day trip of it, we recommend staying overnight at a simple mountain inn called Koraku-kan. It's a little bit rickety and if you can't exist without central heating, go elsewhere. But the old wooden inn with 12 rooms is about as off the beaten path as you can get. The hospitality of the Takefushi family and the inn's five baths will warm you up enough to survive the cold winter nights. And in the summer you'll revel in the cool mountain air. Dinner, served at 5pm (probably because there's nothing else to do), consists of grilled ayu fish, tempura of mountain vegetables, carp sashimi, a duck stew and homemade pickles.

The real heroes of Jigokudani are monkeys, technically macaques but often called snow monkeys. Their mountain habitats were disappearing, so the monkeys began encroaching on the area's apple orchards. Farmers knew they had to do something. So they built a monkey park behind Koraku-kan to feed them daily. And the monkeys also got their own hot spring bath, which they use all year round. Morning is the best time to see the monkeys bathe. Occasionally the monkeys wander over to Koraku-kan's tubs, so you may not be bathing alone. Monkey Park open daily 8am to 5pm. ¥360.

*You can stay at: **KORAKU-KAN**, Jigokudani, Yamanouchi, Shimotakai, Nagano, 381-0401. Tel. (0269)33-4376, Fax (0269)33-3244. Rates from ¥9000 per person with two meals. No credit cards. Daytime visitors are welcome to use the baths from 8am to 9:30am and 12 noon to 3pm, ¥400.*

Getting to Jigokudani: *From Nagano, take the private Nagano Dentetsu train to Yudanaka, (about one hour, ¥1130). Board a bus there for Kanbayashi Onsen (15 minutes, ¥220) and get off at the last stop. From there walk about 30 minutes (1.6 kilometers) to Koraku-kan.*

KARUIZAWA

This hill station, today a playground for well-heeled Tokyoites, got its start from Westerners in Japan at the turn of the century. The area was a post town until the end of the Edo period (1868) and stagnated when the road bypassed the town. A British missionary, Archdeacon Alexander

Shaw, fell in love with the area in 1886 and brought his family to summer here. Other missionaries and Western businessmen followed and then wealthy Japanese jumped on the band wagon. In 1899 a railroad connected Karuizawa with Tokyo and the resort flourished. Western-style hotels, summer homes, golf courses and tennis courts appeared.

Now connected by *shinkansen* train to Tokyo, Karuizawa's easy access makes it a popular getaway for golf, hiking and breathing fresh air. Young Japanese women, attracted to the Western-style shops and restaurants, flock to the cute European-style pensions. Beautiful scenery, good hiking and interesting Western-style architecture combine to make Karuizawa an attractive stop to travelers weary of temples and large cities. One warning: Don't go to Karuizawa during July and August. In the center of the town it will seem like Tokyo's Ginza, Shibuya and Harajuku's shopping crowds all rolled into one.

ARRIVALS & DEPARTURES

To/from Tokyo: The new Asama shinkansen train from Tokyo takes one hour and 15 minutes, ¥5750. JR limited express trains from Tokyo's Ueno Station take 1 hour 55 minutes. Many, but not all of the limited express trains also stop at Naka-Karuizawa Station.

To/from Nagano: About 30 minutes by shinkansen, ¥3580.

Tourist Information

The **Tourist Information Offices** have extensive literature in English. Ask for copies of their *Karuizawa Tourist Handbook* and *The Highlands of Japan: 3000 Feet High in Karuizawa.*

Karuizawa Station: *Tel. (0267)42-2491*. Open 8:30am to 5:15pm. Open mid-June through November.

Naka-Karuizawa Station: *Tel. (0267)45-6050*. Open 8:30am to 5:15pm. Open mid-June through November.

WHERE TO STAY

KARUIZAWA MAMPEI HOTEL, *925 Karuizawa, Karuizawa-machi, Kitasaku-gun, Nagano, 389-0102. Tel. (0267)42-1234, Fax (0267)42-7766. No singles. Twins from ¥23,000. Credit cards.*

Built in 1894, this elegant yet rustic mountain hotel has been providing excellent accommodations and service for over 100 years.

HOTEL KASHIMA NO MORI, *1373-6 Karuizawa, Karuizawa-machi, Kitasaku-gun, Nagano, 389-0102. Tel. (0267)42-3535, Fax (0267)42-5335. Rooms from ¥15,000. Credit cards.*

Kashima no Mori Hotel is a low-rise hotel built along a trout stream. The hotel, which only has fifty rooms, blends in with nature and is a comfortable and relaxing place to stay. Breakfast costs ¥2100.

SEEING THE SIGHTS

In order to enjoy your stay in Karuizawa, quickly get beyond all the tacky souvenir stores and fast food restaurants. Either rent a bicycle — shops are everywhere — or set off on your own two feet. Leave the station area for Kyu-Karuizawa, two kilometers north of Karuizawa, where houses and lodges blend in with the woods. Stop and see **St. Paul's Catholic Church**, designed by an American architect and the old **Mikasa Hotel**, Japan's oldest wooden Western-style hotel, built in 1905 and retired in 1970. It is now a museum. *Closed December through March. ¥200.*

Climb up the Usui Pass to the **Usui Pass Observation Platform** for an outstanding view of volcanic Mt. Asama and the surrounding mountains. Climbing the active volcano is prohibited. From the Nite Bridge at the end of Karuizawa Ginza, the walk takes about 1 1/2 hours.

Bird lovers should flock to **Wild Bird Wood** because this area is home to about 130 species of birds. The park has a 2 1/2 kilometer trail through the forest and two observation huts. From Naka-Karuizawa Station, take a bus five minutes to Nishiku-Iriguchi stop and walk about 10 minutes.

For a moonscape on earth, see the Onioshidashi Rocks, a lava bed from Mt. Asama. The **Onioshidashi Rock Garden** offers great views of the rocks. *Open 7am to 6pm May through September; 8am to 5pm October through April. ¥300.*

For a relaxing bath, head to **Sengataki Onsen** which sports good-sized indoor and outdoor baths. *Tel. (0267)46-1111. Open 1pm to 9pm; 11am to 10pm on Saturdays. ¥1100; ¥1500 mid-July through August and New Year's.* The onsen is located within the **Karuizawa Skating Center**, a complex which offers ice skating all year round and in spring, summer and autumn tennis, roller skating and cycling; also an outdoor pool filled with hot spring water in summer. The center is five minutes by taxi from Naka Karuizawa Station.

MATSUMOTO

Although Nagano City is the prefectural seat, **Matsumoto** is the cultural capital. The large, well preserved castle in an impressive setting in the center of the city, has Japan's oldest existing keep. The city has several small but outstanding museums including a woodblock print museum and two folk art museums and some antiques shops which are great for browsing.

Sitting on a broad plateau, Matsumoto has good views of the mountains and is a gateway to the Japan Alps.

ARRIVALS & DEPARTURES

By Air

Matsumoto Airport flights serve:

To/from Sapporo Chitose: one flight/day (JAS. ¥25,750)

To/from Osaka: one flight/day from Itami airport (JAS. ¥16,600)

To/from Fukuoka: one flight/day (JAS. ¥26,050)

For Ground Transportation:

Bus: to Matsumoto Station (30 minutes, ¥540)

Taxi: to Matsumoto Station (about 30 minutes, ¥3500)

By Train

To/from Tokyo: The *Super Azusa* limited express from Shinjuku Station (2 1/2 hours, ¥6710).

To/from Nagoya: The *Shinano* limited express, JR Chuo Honsen line (2 hours, ¥5870).

By Bus

To/from Tokyo: Highway buses from Shinjuku Station. 12 buses/day, 3 hours, ¥3400.

To/from Nagoya: 10 buses/day, 3 1/2 hours, ¥3260.

To/from Osaka: 2 buses/day, 5 1/2 hours, ¥5710.

To/from Nagano: 16 buses/day, 1 hour 20 minutes, ¥920.

Planning Your Stay

One day in Matsumoto is sufficient to cover the main sights. Highlights are the castle and the Japan *Ukiyo-e* Museum.

GETTING AROUND TOWN

Matsumoto is a fairly compact town and sights tend to be clustered. The castle is about a 15 minute walk from the train station.

Tourist Information

Matsumoto Station has an "i" Tourist Information Office. *Tel. (0263)32-2814.* Open 9:30am to 6pm; 9am to 5:30pm November through March. Closed December 29 through January 3.

Goodwill Guides: The Alps Language Service Association and the Matsumoto SGG Club provide English-speaking guides for Matsumoto. Contact the tourist office (above) or the Japan Travel-Phone, *Tel. 0088-22-4800,* for the current contact number.

WHERE TO STAY

The advantage of being in Matsumoto is lots of hot springs ring the city . So unless you are in a rush you don't need to stay in the city itself.

ENSHO, *Yunohara, Satoyamanobe, Matsumoto, 390-0221. Tel. (0263)33-1235, Fax (0263)35-3367. From ¥12,000 with two meals. No credit cards.*

During the Edo period, feudal lords came to Utsukushigahara Onsen to relax and Ensho was a popular place for feudal lords to stay. The inn has three different styles of building — the main building is a large formal Japanese building with a huge roof; the new *sukiya* annex is built in a lighter, more casual Japanese style; and the newest addition is a 250-year-old farmhouse moved from Niigata Prefecture that's converted into spacious guest rooms. The meals feature lots of delicately cooked mountain vegetables. Take a bus from Matsumoto Station to Utsukushigahara Onsen, about 20 minutes; walk about 100 meters from the bus stop.

HOTEL BUENA VISTA, *1-2-1 Honjo, Matsumoto, 390-0828. Tel. (0263)37-0111, Fax (0263)37-0666. Singles from ¥7500. Twins from ¥15,000. Credit cards.*

Matsumoto's glitziest hotel is just a few minutes from Matsumoto Station. The 200-room Buena Vista has all the amenities including five restaurants, a business center and a conference hall.

HOTEL YAKUSHIDAIRA, *Yakushidaira Onsen, Matsumoto, 399-0023. Tel. (0263)58-2141, Fax (0263)86-5868. From ¥10,000 per person with two meals. No credit cards.*

In the hills, this folk art style inn offers great views of Matsumoto and the surrounding mountains. Even the hot spring baths (both indoor and outdoor) have panoramic views. The food is delectable homestyle fare. The only drawback is the inn is a 25-minute taxi ride from Matsumoto Station, about ¥4000. To avoid this, take the #2 bus going to Matsudaisen; there are only two a day, at 2:40pm and 4:10pm. Get off at Chushin Matsumoto Byoin stop. Call the inn before you get on the bus and someone will meet you at the bus stop.

ENJYOH BEKKAN, *110 Utsukushigahara-onsen, Matsumoto, 390-0221. Tel. (0263)33-7233, Fax (0263)36-2084. Singles from ¥5300. Twins from ¥9800. Credit cards. Member of Japanese Inn Group and Welcome Inn Reservation Center.*

Located on the outskirts of Matsumoto in a hot spring area, this inn offers very reasonably priced Japanese-style accommodation without meals. Breakfast and dinner are available for an additional charge. The inn even has great views of the Japan Alps. At Matsumoto Station, take the bus for Utsukushigahara Onsen and get off at the last stop (20 minutes).

WHERE TO EAT

Noodles are the name of the game in this neck of the woods.

SOBASHO *(Noodles, inexpensive).* 2-3-11 Shiro-nishi. Tel. (0263)36-3003. *Open 11am to 6pm. Closed Wednesdays.*

Located right behind Matsumoto Castle, this bright restaurant serves *soba* noodles made on the premises. *Sansai soba* costs ¥1000.

AGATANO-MORI DANWASHITSU *(Coffee, inexpensive).* 3-1-1 Agata. Tel. (0263)36-7654. *Open 10am to 6pm. Closed Mondays.*

Located in Agata Park area near the former Matsumoto High School, this quiet tea room is a favorite place to rest our feet. The cake set, coffee or tea with your choice of cake, costs ¥650.

SEEING THE SIGHTS

Matsumoto Castle (Matsumoto-jo), the hallmark of the city, sits on a plain in the center of the city. The imposing five-storied keep is one of the few originals left in Japan. The surrounding moat and the stone walls date from 1504. Around the castle the moat is so wide that the castle looks like an island in a pond. The wooden walls of the castle were painted in black lacquer in contrast to the white plaster and the gray-tiled roof. Against the snow covered Japan Alps, the scene is spectacular. Matsumoto's castle's nickname is "blackbird castle." Climb up to the top floor for an excellent view of the city and surrounding snow-covered mountains. One distinctive feature is the castle's "Moon Viewing" annex, added to enjoy the moon viewing parties. *Open daily 8:30am to 5pm. Closed December 29 through January 3. ¥520.*

Next to the castle is the **Japan Folklore Museum** (Nihon Minzoku Shiryokan), which displays a collection of archaeology, history and folk art from the region. *Tel. (0263)33-1569. Open daily 8:30am to 5pm. Closed December 29 through January 3. Admission included in Matsumoto Castle ticket.*

Fans of Western-style Japanese architecture should walk about 10 minutes north of Matsumoto Castle to the **Kaichi Gakko School Building**. Constructed in 1874, the former school is Japan's oldest Western-style school building. Nagano Prefecture has been interested in children's education and has produced many teachers. The school's architect had no experience with Western construction so he went to Tokyo to see what was being built. He returned and built the school, using Japanese storehouse construction techniques. The result is a delightfully eclectic building, complete with a Chinese-style roof over the entrance. The colorful school today is a museum; while educational materials are on display, it was the playful architectural detail that mesmerized us. *Open daily 8:30am to 5pm; December through February closed Sundays and national holidays. Closed December 29 to January 3. ¥310.*

Japan Ukiyo-e Museum (Nihon Ukiyo-e Hakubutsukan) houses one of the most extensive collections of woodblock prints and includes rare works by Hokusai, Hiroshige and other masters collected by the Sakai family. The contemporary concrete and glass structure provides a great venue for viewing the Edo period prints. *Tel. (0263)47-4440. Open 10am to 5pm. Closed Monday and December 26 through January 3. ¥900. Take either a taxi from Matsumoto Station (about 8 minutes) or take the Matsumoto Dentetsu train two stops to Oniwa Station; from there it's a 15 minute walk.*

Matsumoto Folk Craft Museum (Matsumoto Mingeikan) has an excellent collection of folk artifacts from all over the world. The building is a traditional Matsumoto storehouse built in the 1830s. The drawback is the museum is a little bit out of the way, but fans of folk art will find it worth the trouble. *Tel. (0263)33-1569. Open 9am to 5pm. Closed Monday and December 29 through January 3. ¥210. From Matsumoto Station, take the bus 15 minutes to Shimo-Kanai Mingeikan-guchi stop.*

KAMIKOCHI

Kamikochi, 1500 meters high and the center of **Chubu Sangaku National Park**, offers spectacular views of the peaks of the Japan Alps. Perched along a fast-flowing river, this superb mountain resort is a great getaway from busy city life. Serious mountain climbers begin their climbs there, but the area is also filled with couch potatoes seeking solace from the heat of the cities. Kamikochi is relatively easy to reach and offers peaceful and fairly flat hiking trails along the Azusa River, so hiking doesn't have to entail a commitment to climb the 3000-meter mountains. Fancy mountain lodges cater to the well heeled, but simpler accommodations also exist.

The Reverend Walter Weston, a British missionary, climbed many mountains in the late 19th century and gave the "Japan Alps" their name. A small monument is dedicated to him. A festival in his honor occurs on the first Sunday in June, a time of year when the lush new leaves paint a stunning scene against the snow-covered Hotaka mountains. On a clear day you can see smoke from Yakedake, an active volcano.

You can get to Kamikochi only when the snow melts enough to make the roads passable; the roads are open only early April to mid-November. The best time is in the autumn when the trees turn scarlet red and golden yellow. But the spring foliage, which begins to pop out in late May, is also beautiful and the area is not as crowded.

Tourist Information

The Tourist Information Office is at the bus station, *Tel. (0263)95-2405.*

ARRIVALS & DEPARTURES

By train

To/from Matsumoto: take the Matsumoto Dentetsu train to Shin-Shimashima Station (30 minutes, ¥680) and then bus to Kamikochi (1 hour 15 minutes, ¥2050).

By bus

To/from Takayama: to Hirayu Onsen, 55 minutes, ¥1530. Transfer to a bus from Hirayu Onsen to Kamikochi, 65 minutes, ¥1550. The latter bus operates only late April through late November, depending on snow conditions.

By car

Take Route 158 from Matsumoto to Nakanoyu for the approach road to Kamikochi. Cars are not allowed on the approach road during peak times: weekends and national holidays, late April to early August, late July through late August and most of October. During these times, park your car at Nakanoyu and take a bus or taxi.

Parties of four will find a taxi more economical than the bus. The road is open late April through early November.

WHERE TO STAY

KAMIKOCHI IMPERIAL HOTEL, *4468 Kamikochi, Azumi-mura, Minami Azumi-gun, Nagano, 390-1516. Tel. (0263)95-2006, Fax (0263)95-2412. Doubles from ¥26,300. Credit cards.*

A branch of the well-known Tokyo Imperial Hotel, this rustic mountain lodge caters to travelers who want all the amenities even in the mountains. The original (1907) building was the first Western-style resort hotel built; but the current one, rebuilt in the early 1960s, is based on the original. It's a luxurious log cabin facing the river. In the lobby is a huge fireplace that is lit even in midsummer. The spacious rooms all have a balcony. A drawback is meals are as expensive. Western breakfast costs ¥2400, Japanese ¥2500, and dinners are also high. And apart from *ramen* shops, there's not much around open in the evening.

KAMIKOCHI ONSEN HOTEL, *Kamikochi, Azumi-mura, Minami Azumi-gun, Nagano, 390-1516. Tel. (0264)95-2311, Fax (0264)95-2639. From ¥23,000 per person with two meals. JCB card only.*

This inn is one of the two in Kamikochi that have hot spring baths.

NISHIITOYA SANSO, *Kamikochi, Azumi-mura, Minami Azumi-gun, Nagano, 390. Tel. (9263)95-2206, Fax (0246)95-2208. From ¥13,000 with two meals. No credit cards.*

Located 100 meters from the Kappa Bridge, this is a convenient place to start your hiking. The rooms facing the back are very quiet.

SEEING THE SIGHTS

Mountain walks are the name of the game here.

The **Kappa Bridge** offers scenic views of Mt. Oku Hotaka. Two kilometers downstream is the **Taisho Pond**, formed by a volcanic eruption in 1915 (during the Taisho period).

We recommend you don't spend much time in this central area because it gets crowded. Head up river in the direction of Tokusawa; the walk from Kappa Bridge to Tokusawa, along the Azusa River, takes about two hours each way. Amazingly, once you leave the Kappa Bashi area, you have the trail practically to yourselves. Enjoy the tranquillity, the birds, and the fresh air as you walk along the fast-running Azusa River. And even though mountains surround you, the path is pretty flat.

NARAI

An excellently preserved post town (see sidebar below), the main road is lined with two-storied wooden buildings, some with shops selling crafts and lacquer ware. But the good news is **Narai** isn't overrun with tourists the same way as its more popular cousins, Tsumago and Magome.

When you get off the train, you may feel as thought you've been plunked down in the middle of nowhere. Turn left as you exit the station, and soon you are in the middle of this historic town. Pinch yourself because you could be on a samurai movie set. Don't worry about getting lost, Narai has only one main road.

Wander the streets, browsing in the craft shops filled with many lacquer and wood items. Stop in the **Tokuriya Local History Museum** (Tokuriya Kyodokan), *open 9am-4:30pm; until 4pm December through March, ¥200; closed Mondays and holidays*. The former inn has been converted into an engaging museum. **Kamidonya Hall** (Kamidonya Shiryokan), a nearly 300-year-old building, is now also a museum, *open 8am-5pm, ¥300; closed January and February*. Narai has several picturesque *sake* breweries including **Hiranoya**. Look for the ball of cedar leaves over the door.

The two towns on either side of Narai also excel at crafts. **Kiso-Hirasawa**, one stop north of Narai, is the center of the area's lacquer production. While the town isn't picturesque like Narai, lots of shops sell reasonably priced Kiso lacquer. Stop in the **Kiso Lacquer Museum** (Kiso Shikkikan) for an historic overview, *open 9am-5pm; until 4pm December to March; closed Mondays, ¥300*. Every year on the first Friday through Sunday of June, Kiso-Hirasawa holds a large lacquer festival where you may find lots of bargains.

Yabuhara, the town south of Narai, specializes in wooden combs. Watch them being made at several workshops.

ARRIVALS & DEPARTURES

By Train

To/from Matsumoto: Local train to Narai takes 45 minutes. Trains run only about every two hours. ¥570.

To/from Tokyo: take the Matsumoto train Super Azusa but get off at Shiojiri, about 10 minutes before Matsumoto Station. Change for a JR Chuo Honsen line local train, about 20 minutes. ¥7130.

To/from Nagoya: Take the *Shinano* limited express train to Kiso Fukushima Station, 1 hour 20 minutes, and change for the local train to Narai, 20 minutes. ¥4810.

THREE NAGANO POST TOWNS

*The **Nakasendo Road**, one of the few roads connecting Edo (present-day Tokyo) and Kyoto during the feudal period, runs through the heavily wooded Kiso valley. Isolated from the rest of Japan, the Central Alps to the east and the North Alps to the west create a deep valley. Eleven **post towns** catered to the needs of travelers.*

Feudal lords were among their most important and frequent guests. The shogun required each lord to travel to Edo every year. In addition to using physical presence as a way of control, traveling annually with a large entourage kept the lords from amassing enough wealth to challenge the shogun. The lavish spending of the feudal lords enriched the innkeepers and merchants.

*Today, three former post towns are excellently preserved: **Narai**, **Tsumago** and **Magome**. The trains and main roads of the 20th century bypassed all three. If the towns had become part of the national rail system, they would have modernized. Instead, they stand as architectural examples of an earlier age.*

You don't need to see all three post towns; choose either Narai, Tsumago or Magome. Travelers pressed for time can make an easy side trip from Matsumoto to Narai. But if you can swing it, we recommend spending an overnight at Tsumago or Magome, two post towns just a few kilometers from each other: it's possible to hike from one to the other (eight kilometers). Tsumago and Magome are also easily reached from Nagoya.

WHERE TO STAY

Many of Narai's buildings are family-run inns.

ECHIGOYA RYOKAN, *Narai, Nakagawa-mura, Kiso-gun, Nagano, 399-6303. Tel. (0264)34-3011. No fax. From ¥13,000 per person with two meals. No credit cards.*

For over 200 years, Echigoya has served as a travelers' inn. The atmosphere transports you back to the feudal era. Service is excellent. Be forewarned: they accept only six guests a day, so make your reservation well in advance.

ISEYA MINSHUKU, *Narai, Nakagawa-mura, Kiso-gun, Nagano, 399-6303. Tel. (0264)34-3051, Fax (0264)34-3156. Rates from ¥8000 per person with two meals. No credit cards.*

Housed in a lovely wooden building, this comfortable family-run inn has a great location in the center of Narai. They use lots of mountain vegetables in the home-cooked meals.

NARAISO, *Narai, Nakagawa-mura, Kiso-gun, Nagano, 399-6303. Tel. (0264)34-3660, Fax (0264)34-2095. ¥8500 with two meals. No credit cards.*

Located at the top of the hill above Narai, this newer inn will pick you up when you call from Narai Station. The rooms are clean and quiet.

TSUMAGO & MAGOME

These twin historic towns, Japan's answer to Williamsburg, are some of the best preserved towns in Japan. Lovely wooden buildings, stone covered main streets barred to traffic and serene mountain settings combine to make these post towns one of our favorite country stops in Japan. They are popular tourist sights but they have one other special feature — you can get away from the crowds by hiking from Magome to Tsumago. It's an easy eight kilometer (five mile) hike and pleasant summer, spring and fall. Our advice: see the towns in the early morning and late afternoon so you are not competing for space with the bus loads of visitors.

Tsumago's tale falls into the "every-cloud-has-a-silver-lining" category. The post town prospered during the Edo era (1603-1868) when it catered to travelers heading back and forth to Edo. But when the Tokugawa shogunate collapsed, so did Tsumago's reason for existing. The new railroads carried people and goods. To add insult to injury, both the highway and the train bypassed Tsumago. And the area had a particularly greedy landlord who taxed the people so heavily they couldn't afford to modernize.

By the 1960s, the townspeople desperately needed to do something to rejuvenate the town. Stepping back, they realized their jewel was their preserved post town. So they set about to make it attractive to tourists by burying telephone and electric lines, passing laws forbidding modern construction and opening inns and shops. The plan worked; tourists arrived and today Tsumago is one of Japan's most authentic post towns.

ARRIVALS & DEPARTURES

To/from Matsumoto or Nagano: Take the JR *Shinano* limited express train to Nakatsugawa Station (1 hour 15 minutes from Matsumoto, ¥4180; 2 hours from Nagano, ¥5550). Board the bus to Magome. 12 buses/day, 30 minutes, ¥540. From Magome to Tsumago buses take 30 minutes, ¥650; check the schedule because there are only about five buses a day.

An alternative is to get off at Nagiso, one express stop before Nakatsugawa, and take a bus to Tsumago (7 minutes, ¥270) and Magome (35 minutes, ¥810). This gets tricky: only a few limited express trains a day stop at Nagiso. You can get off at Kiso Fukushima Station and change for a local train, but don't do it without checking the schedule – you could sit for as long as two hours waiting for the local train.

To/from Tokyo: From Shinjuku Station take the JR *Azusa* limited express train to Shiojiri (2 hours 30 minutes). Change for the *Shinano* limited express train to Nakatsugawa (1 hour 5 minutes, ¥9730). Follow directions above for buses from Nakatsugawa.

For JR rail pass holders, it may be slightly quicker to take the shinkansen from Tokyo to Nagoya (2 hours) and take the JR *Shinano* limited express train to Nakatsugawa (1 hour 10 minutes). ¥12,150.

To/from Nagoya: Take the JR *Shinano* limited express train to Nakatsugawa (1 hour 10 minutes, ¥2940) and follow the directions above for buses from Nakatsugawa.

Tourist Information

In **Tsumago**, the tourist information office is in the center of town. *Tel. (0264)57-3123.* Open 9am to 5pm. Closed December 29 through January 3. Will make reservations for inns.

In **Magome**, it's halfway up the slope in a small courtyard across from the entrance to the Toson Memorial Hall. *Tel. (0264)59-2336.* Closed December 29 through January 5. Will make reservations for inns.

WHERE TO STAY

One of the pleasures of visiting this area is staying in quaint old inns. Warning! They are not luxurious, and you probably won't have a private toilet; meals are usually served in communal dining rooms, and there may not be central heating or air conditioning. But we found the unique experience made up for any discomfort.

Tsumago

MATSUSHIROYA RYOKAN, *Terashita, Tsumago, Nagiso-machi, Kiso-gun, Nagano, 399-5302. Tel. (0264)57-3022, Fax (0264)57-3356. From ¥10,000 per person with two meals. No credit cards.*

A traditional inn with a long history, Matsushiroya is in the heart of Tsumago.

FIJI-OTO RYOKAN, *Tsumago, Nagiso-machi, Kiso-gun, Nagano, 399-5302. Tel. (0264)57-3009, Fax (0264)57-2595. From ¥10,000 per person with two meals. No credit cards.*

Located in the central part of the town, this inn is one of two inns that have survived since the Edo period.

AGEHAYA, *Tsumago, Nagiso-machi, Kiso-gun, Nagano, 399-5302. Tel. (0264)57-2508. No fax. ¥7000 per person with two meals. No credit cards.*

There are 21 family-run inns in the Tsumago area. Agehaya is one of the best and has a particularly friendly proprietor. It's located about a five-minute walk from the center of Tsumago — the locals consider that "far."

DAIKICHI, *Tsumago, Nagiso-machi, Kiso-gun, Nagano, 399-5302. Tel. (0264)57-2595. No fax. ¥7500 per person with two meals. No credit cards.*

Friends enjoyed their stay at this family-run inn.

Otsumago

About a 15-minute walk from Tsumago lies Otsumago, a small hamlet with a few farmhouses and fish ponds. We prefer to stay here for its serene mountain atmosphere.

HAGATO TSUTAMURAYA, *1479-1 Azuma, Nagiso-machi, Kiso-gun, Nagano, 399-5302. Tel. (0264)57-3235, Fax (0264)57-3765. From ¥7000 per person with two meals. No credit cards. Member of Welcome Inn Reservation Center.*

A wonderful family-run inn in Otsumago serves delicious mountain vegetables and river fish, raised in their own ponds.

MINSHUKU HANAYA, *Tsumago, Nagiso-cho, Kiso-gun, Nagano, 399-5302. Tel. (0264)57-3106, Fax (0264)57-4084. From ¥7000 per person with two meals. No credit cards.*

This inn in Otsumago has so many plants you can hardly see the entrance. The accommodations are very simple, and the staff is friendly and the mountain fare tasty.

Magome

Magome also offers a number of traditional inns. Tajimaya, near the bottom of the slope, offers clean accommodations, good food and a friendly staff:

TAJIMAYA, *Magome, Yamaguchi-mura, Kiso-gun, Nagano, 399-5102. Tel. (0264)59-2048. No fax. From ¥9000 per person with two meals. No credit cards.*

SEEING THE SIGHTS

Spend time wandering along the main road lined with two-storied houses constructed of wood and plaster, the windows covered with lattice. The first floors of many have been converted to shops selling local crafts like items made of wood, woven straw hats and folk toys. At one point the road makes a sharp bend, a defensive technique designed to slow the enemy in the event of an attack.

Even post towns were divided into areas according to class: Terashita's houses and inns were for commoners while Nakamachi was for samurai.

Make sure you go into the **Waki-Honjin Okuya**, an official inn of the Edo period that served high-ranking officials. A *honjin* was the highest ranking inn, the place where feudal lords would stay. The *waki-honjin* was second best, housing the feudal lord's top retainers. And, if more than one feudal lord passed through at the same time, the *waki-honjin* hosted the second lord. At the end of the feudal period the master of the Waki-Honjin Okuya decided to rebuild the inn using cypress wood that previously was off-limits to commoners. So the 1877 building has sumptuous wood used throughout. The Meiji Emperor stayed here in 1881. Behind the Waki-Honjin is a folk museum. *Open 9am to 5pm. Closed December 29 through January 1. ¥300, or ¥900 which includes admission to the Nagiso Historical Museum (Rekishi Shiryokan) and Tsumago Juku Honjin.*

Walking up the hill on the path through the center of town takes you to **Kotoku-ji Temple**, where the main building dates to 1725.

Magome, another post town about eight kilometers south of Tsumago, conveys a completely different ambiance. While Tsumago lies in a valley, Magome clings to the side of a hill and offers great views of Mt. Ena. The entire town was rebuilt after a disastrous fire in 1895; it doesn't feel as old as Tsumago. Many of the old buildings are now inns and shops.

Shimazaki Toson, a well-known Meiji period author who wrote about the area, is Magome's hometown boy made good. Halfway up the slope, his birthplace is now the Toson Memorial Hall (Toson Kinenkan), which occupies the site of the old inn for feudal lords. While the complex is of little interest to visitors not familiar with Toson's work, one of the buildings predates the 1895 fire.

To reach Magome from Tsumago, either take a bus (30 minutes, ¥650) or walk along the old Nakasendo Road (3 hours).

HIKING THE OLD NAKASENDO ROAD

Get a feel for what it must have been like for Edo period travelers by walking the short stretch of the Nakasendo Road between Magome and Tsumago. Although it is called a road, trail is more appropriate. The Tokugawa shogunate strictly controlled the movement of people. Only special messengers could travel by horse; everyone else was on foot. Well, not always on foot. High ranking officials, such as feudal lords, traveled by palanquin, carried on the shoulders of several men. Donkeys carried goods. Everything moved in slow motion, the way the shogunate wanted it.

While you can walk the trail in either direction, we prefer to start in Magome, which is downhill most of the way. Allow three hours to reach Tsumago. From Magome, walk north, uphill, first on a path and then on a paved road. The path veers off from the road at a pass, Magome Toge. From here it is more or less downhill all the way. You'll go through thick forests, past two waterfalls, one "male" and one "female," and through a small farming hamlet. You may take a slight detour through Otsumago, an area with farmhouses and fish ponds, before finally reaching Tsumago.

You don't want to hike lugging your suitcase? The Tourist Information Offices run a luggage transportation service. Both the Tsumago and Magome Tourist Information Offices accept bags between 8:30am and 11:30am for afternoon delivery. Note the dates: this service runs daily from July 20 through August 31 and on weekends and national holidays March 20 through July 20 and September 1 through November 23. ¥500 per bag.

Buses between the two towns take about 30 minutes and cost ¥650. But check the schedule; other than the summer peak travel time (late July through August), only about a half-dozen buses run a day.

17. TAKAYAMA & ENVIRONS

For us, **Takayama**, a little patch of old Japan, is a destination that never disappoints. We can't imagine an itinerary without it. Historic buildings in actual, functioning communities convey a sense for life during bygone days, but are still actively used today. Takayama is surrounded by mountains, and has great views of the Japan Alps. Takayama's craftsmen are renowned for their furniture, *ichi-i itto-bori* sculpture, lacquer and woodblock prints.

Although the small city lies deep in the mountains of central Japan, Takayama is surprisingly convenient: only two hours and 20 minutes from Nagoya by train. Fit in a stop when traveling between Tokyo and Kyoto.

From Takayama you can jump further into the country to the isolated mountain villages of **Shirakawago** and **Gokayama**, designated World Heritage Sites by UNESCO for their unique steep thatched-roof architecture. If you are searching for old country Japan, this is the area to see.

TAKAYAMA AREA HIGHLIGHTS
• *The well-preserved merchant districts of Takayama*
• *Stay at an old thatched-roof farmhouse in Shirakawago or Gokayama*
• *The all-night bon odori dances in Gujo Hachiman*
• *Make your own Japanese washi paper in Mino*
• *Delicious mountain vegetables, river fish and Hida beef*

Planning Your Stay

Try to stay two days in Takayama. For the lucky souls who have more time, you can easily spend it in Takayama or you can go to Shirakawago or Gokayama for a more rural setting; spend one day in each. In the summer, spend one day at Gujo Hachiman for its famous dancing. The old papermaking town of Mino offers excellent multiday workshops for the ultimate hands-on experience.

TAKAYAMA

With a population of 65,000, **Takayama** is small enough to walk nearly everywhere. Since the city is set up on a grid system, finding your way is easy. The local cuisine, especially Hida beef, *ayu* (a small river trout), mountain vegetables and *hoba miso* (fermented bean paste grilled on a magnolia leaf) will have you regretting you can only eat three meals a day.

In the late 1500s, Lord Kanamori, a general under the great unifier Toyotomi Hideyoshi, built a castle on the hill above Takayama. Kanamori built the town, introduced the refined Kyoto culture and even copied Kyoto's grid pattern. The Kanamori family ruled the area for 107 years until the Tokugawa shogunate took over. The castle was dismantled and without a feudal lord (the shogun sent governors) merchant culture became paramount. Commodities like timber and lead plus local industries such as making soy sauce, *miso* (fermented bean paste) and *sake* (rice wine) flourished, and tradesmen got rich.

But the problem was they couldn't show off their wealth. The shogunate strictly regulated consumption so that merchants, being at the bottom of the social ladder, were forbidden to own what they could easily afford. They used their wealth to develop discriminating craft traditions such as delicate wood carving, and poured their energies into creating sumptuous festival floats.

When the shogunate collapsed in 1868, the merchants were finally able to purchase what they wanted. In 1875 a disastrous fire destroyed most of the business quarter. The silver lining was the wealthy merchants could now rebuild unencumbered by restrictions. These were conservative people: they chose to rebuild in the same traditional style rather than the new Western style sweeping Japan's cities. And they went wild, using rare woods and exquisite craftsmanship. The result is the Sanmachi Suji district that today gives Takayama its distinctive character.

Planning Your Stay

If you have only one day, our recommended itinerary follows:

Morning: Go to the morning market at Takayama Jinya; visit Takayama Jinya. Browse the streets of Sanmachi Suji and walk along the Miyagawa River to Kusakabe and Yoshijima houses.

Afternoon: Option 1: Go to the Hida Folk Village (if Gokayama or Shirakawago is on your itinerary, skip it). Option 2: Visit Takayama

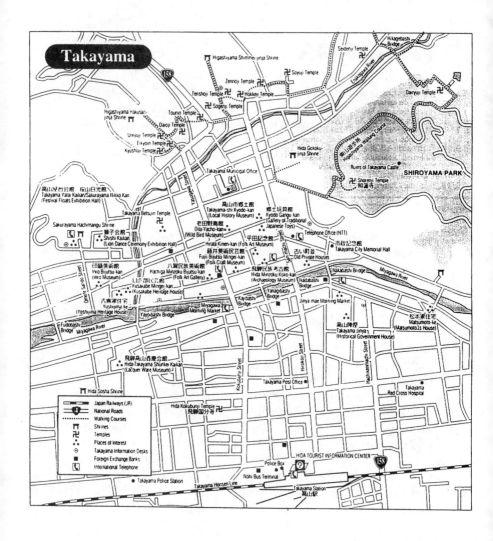

Festival Floats Exhibition Hall, Lion Dance Ceremony Exhibition Hall, Inro Museum and Hida Takayama Lacquer Ware Museum.

If you have two days, take both options and follow the same basic plan at a more leisurely pace, stop for coffee in a quaint shop, splurge on a *shojin ryori* (Buddhist vegetarian cuisine) lunch, and explore the many folk art and antique shops in Sanmachi Suji.

Dates To Remember

• **April 14-15: Spring Festival**
• **October 9-10: Autumn Festival**. The Spring and Autumn Festivals are are considered one of Japan's three most beautiful. Make sure you make hotel reservations far in advance at these times, or commute from a nearby city such as Furukawa.
• **7th of each month May through October: Garakuta Antique Market**, on Sanmachi Dori.
• **August 1-15: Ema-Ichi** (Ema Market). Held at Yamazakura Jinja every year. Wealthy patrons used to make offerings of horses to temples, but this evolved into offering pictures of horses, usually painted on plaques of wood. Here *ema* are hand painted on *washi* paper. At this lively festival that runs from morning into the evening, you can buy *ema* for ¥2000 and up. Pasting it on the gate or entrance of your home brings good luck.

ARRIVALS & DEPARTURES

By Train

To/from Nagoya: *Hida* limited express trains on the JR Takayama Honsen line take 2 hours 20 minutes. ¥5870. Nine departures daily. Shinkansen train from Tokyo to Nagoya takes 2 hours, 1 hour from Osaka and 45 minutes from Kyoto.

To/from Osaka-Kyoto area, a direct limited express train leaves Osaka at 7:58am, Kyoto at 8:30am and arrives Takayama 1:06pm. ¥6510 from Osaka, ¥5880 from Kyoto. The return train leaves Takayama at 3:25pm. You save time, but not money, if you take the shinkansen train from Osaka/Kyoto to Nagoya and change to the *Hida* limited express.

To/from Kanazawa, take train to Toyama, 40 minutes. From Toyama, the *Hida* limited express takes 1 hour 20 minutes. ¥3220.

By Bus

To/from Matsumoto: You can do this but it gets complicated. Buses run May through November through the mountains, but you have to change three times. From Matsumoto take the Matsumoto Dentetsu train to Shin Shimashima (30 minutes), then the Kita bus towards Kamikochi getting off at Nakanoyu (1 hour), change to the Nohi bus to Hirayu (1 hour) and again change to the Nohi bus to Takayama (1 hour). Check the connection schedule with the tourist office in Matsumoto or Takayama to make sure you don't get stranded.

GETTING AROUND TOWN

Takayama is a fairly small city easy to navigate because it is built on a grid. Sights tend to be fairly close to each other; you can take a bus or taxi to one area and go on foot from there. Bicycle is a great way to get around, the central area of town is flat and is easy biking even for sedentary types.

Bicycle Rentals are available at Takayama JR Station, on the right as you exit the ticket wicket. ¥300 per hour; ¥1300 per day. Some hotels offer bike rentals as do bicycle shops.

Tourist Information

Hida Takayama Tourist Information Office, 1 Showa-machi, Takayama, 506. *Tel. (0577)32-5328.* Open 8:30am to 6:30pm; November through March 8:30am to 5pm. Located in front of the JR Takayama Station. They have maps and brochures in English, speak English and are extremely helpful with information on Takayama and surrounding areas.

WHERE TO STAY

NAGASE RYOKAN, *Kami-ninomachi, Takayama, 506-0845. Tel. (0577)32-0068, Fax (0577)32-1068. From ¥15,000 per person with two meals. Credit cards.*

Nagase's excellent location in the heart of the Sanmachi historic district makes it an ideal choice for a traveler wanting a centrally located traditional inn. The 200-year-old inn has spacious rooms with garden views. The bath is fragrant with the scent of cypress wood. Dinner is formal *kaiseki* style served in your room.

HOTEL TAKAYAMA HOSHOKAKU, *1 Baba-machi, Takayama, 506-0838. Tel. (0577)34-0700, Fax (0577)35-0717. From ¥14,000 per person with two meals. Credit cards. Member of Welcome Inn Reservation Center.*

On the hill above the Sanmachi area, the rooms have a good view of Takayama. The hotel features a *rotemburo*, one of the few outdoor hot spring baths in Takayama City. All rooms have a private bath and toilet. The hotel is walking distance to Takayama Jinya, the morning market and Sanmachi Suji, but we found the hotel too large and impersonal.

RYOKAN YAMAKI, *1 Baba-machi, Takayama, 506-0838. Tel. (0577)33-8554, Fax (0577)33-3709. From ¥10,000 per person with two meals. American Express only.*

Located on the hill above the Sanmachi area and decorated in a tasteful Japanese style, this small inn has delicious food. They serve meals on exquisite Shibukusa ceramic plates, the work of Takayama's potters.

RYOKAN HIDA GASSHOEN, *3-chome, Nishinoishiki-machi, Takayama, 506-0031. Tel. (0577)33-4531, Fax (0577)32-9022. From ¥11,000 per person with two meals. No credit cards. On the outskirts of town close to the Hida Folk Village and about 10-minute bus or 5-minute taxi ride from Takayama Station.*

The entrance path winds through an imposing stone garden on a hill. The inn features two 200 year old *gassho zukuri* farmhouse buildings moved from the Gokayama area and a newer building in the same style. You eat your meals around an *irori* open hearth. Stay here to experience the *gassho zukuri* style of living of the villages of Shirakawago and Gokayama. Because the historic atmosphere is preserved, rooms are on the small side.

MURASAKI RYOKAN, *Nanoka-machi, Takayama, 506-0005. Next to Shunkei Nuri Lacquer Ware Museum. Tel. (0577)32-1724. Fax (0577)33-7512. From ¥7500 with two meals. No credit cards.*

In summer Murasaki Ryokan is instantly recognizable by the hundreds of flowering plants covering the facade. Run by a family that's been in the hotel business for 300 years, many customers keep coming back to Murasaki for its *nabe* stew in winter.

MINSHUKU YAMAKYU, *58 Tenshouji-machi, Takayama, 506-0832. Tel. (0577)32-3756, Fax (0577)35-2350. ¥7000 per person with two meals. No credit cards. Member of Welcome Inn Reservation Center.*

Yamakyu is a real find. In the hills above central Takayama, this inn offers hospitality and delicious meals that would cost twice the price in most places. The proprietors don't speak English but that doesn't dampen their warm welcome.

MINSHUKU SOSUKE, *1-64 Okamoto, Takayama, 506-0054. Tel. (0577)32-0818, Fax (0577)33-5570. From ¥7500 per person with two meals. No credit cards. Member of Welcome Inn Reservation Center.*

This *minshuku* is a renovated, 150-year-old farmhouse located across the street from the hideous looking Takayama Green Hotel. This unpretentious inn has tiny rooms but offers a very friendly environment where you meet people from all over Japan and the world at meals.

MINSHUKU UENOYA, *95 Kami-ninomachi, Takayama, 506-0845. Tel. (0577)32-3919, Fax (0577)36-3332. From ¥7000 per person with two meals. No credit cards. Member of Welcome Inn Reservation Center.*

A small, comfortable inn fabulously located in the Sanmachi Suji historic district. Housed in an older building, meals are served in a communal dining room on the first floor.

TAKAYAMA CITY HOTEL FOUR SEASONS, *1 Kanda-machi, Takayama, 506-0006. Tel. (0577)36-0088, Fax (0577)36-0080. Singles from ¥6930. Twins from ¥13,200. Credit cards.*

This business hotel bends over backwards to accommodate women. The sixth floor is restricted to women and is decorated in soft, feminine colors. The hotel has a large bath and a sauna; it's located close to the Shunkei Nuri Lacquer Ware Museum.

WHERE TO EAT

KAKUSHO *(Buddhist vegetarian, expensive). 2-98 Baba-cho. Tel. (0577)32-0174. Lunch: 11:30am and 1:30pm seatings; 5pm-7:30pm.*

Kakusho is a well-known *shojin ryori* (Buddhist vegetarian cuisine) restaurant. Situated in a 250-year-old traditional wooden building, guests eat in small private *tatami* mat rooms overlooking the garden. You have your choice of *shojin kaiseki* from ¥10,000 or a more modest *shojin tenshin* (small amounts of 10 different dishes) from ¥5500. At these prices, we wanted our meal to be memorable, and we weren't disappointed. Reservations required. English is spoken.

HATOYA *(Japanese beef, moderate to expensive). 3-110 Ojinmachi. Tel. (0577)32-0255. Open 11:30am to 2pm: 5pm to 6:30pm. Closed Tuesday.*

The building was constructed in 1876 and much of the original architectural detail remains. Try the delicious *sukiyaki* made with Hida beef for ¥4000, Japanese-style steak from ¥5000. Order wine to accompany the beef. Every room is private and advance reservations are necessary. Hatoya is located on the same road as the Inro Museum, three blocks to the north.

SUZUYA *(Regional Japanese, inexpensive). 24 Hanakawa-cho. Tel. (0577)32-2484. Open 11am to 3pm; 5pm to 8pm. Closed Tuesday.*

This restaurant in an old traditional house is well known to locals for its reasonably priced food. The mountain vegetables and Hida beef are especially good. Try the *Hoba yaki:* beef, tofu, vegetables and *miso* grilled on a magnolia leaf at your table. ¥1300. Order rice at ¥500 to complete meal. The English menu, with photographs, makes ordering a cinch.

EBISU *(Soba noodles, inexpensive). Kami-ninomachi. Tel. (0577)32-0209. 10am to 6pm. Closed Tuesday.*

A noodle shop in a beautiful old building has been serving *soba* since the turn of the century. The present owner is from the third generation. They offer a range of *soba* at moderate prices. We enjoyed their *sansai soba. Two other branches: Hanakawa-cho, Tel. (0577)33-3366, close to Kokubun-ji; and Shinmeicho, Tel. (0577)35-0555, across the river from Takayama Jinya.*

HISADAYA *(Regional Japanese, inexpensive). Kami-sannomachi. Tel. (0577)32-0216. Open 10am to 3pm. Closed Wednesday.*

This former traveler's inn has turned out consistently good cooking for 100 years. Decorated with Edo period furniture and art, it's an option for lunch while in the area. Try the *Hisadaya bento*, which has ten different items prepared using locally grown fresh ingredients, ¥1800.

WHAT'S COOKING IN TAKAYAMA?

Hoba miso, *a thick fermented soy bean paste on a large magnolia leaf cooked at your table over a brazier. Often meat and vegetables are mixed with the miso and eaten with rice. It is incredibly delicious or, as the Japanese say, "Oishii..."*

Hida beef is locally raised and cooked with miso or sukiyaki style.

Ayu, *a small river fish, which survives only in the cleanest water is a summer specialty. Try it grilled with salt or pickled.*

Sansai, *mountain vegetables, are plentiful given the geography of the area. No meal in this area is complete without a few bites of sansai. You can dine on a meal consisting almost exclusively of healthy mountain vegetables or have it in soup with noodles (sansai soba).*

Mitarashi-dango *are balls of pounded rice with a soy based sauce. You'll see sidewalk stands selling this not-so-sweet sweet.*

ENOTECA *(Italian, inexpensive). Hirokoji Dori, across the street from Gelateria on the second floor. Tel. (0577)33-0414. Open 6pm-10:30pm. Closed Sunday and third Monday.*

Try this casual Italian restaurant for a change from Japanese food. Spaghetti *pomodoro* is ¥1100 and spaghetti *carbonara*, ¥1300.

HAIKARA *(Coffee, inexpensive). 1-45 Sanmachi, close to Takayama Jinya. Tel. (0577)33-3531. Open 8am to 5pm. Closed Wednesday.*

The name Haikara is from the English "high collar," a term used in the Meiji period to describe Japanese who took to Western ways including wearing shirts with high collars as compared with the low necklines of kimono. This coffee house is furnished with antiques and features homemade pizza. Margherita pizza costs ¥1100.

BAREN *(Coffee, inexpensive). Kami-sannomachi. Tel. (0577)33-9201. Open 9am to 5pm. Closed Thursday.*

A *baren*, a small bamboo disc covered with leather, is used by woodblock print artists to rub the paper against the wood, creating the print. This shop, in an 1830s commoner's house, is a combination coffee and print shop and the atmosphere matches the prints displayed. Try the coffee and green tea pie set for ¥700.

RANKA *(Coffee, inexpensive). Kami-sannomachi. Tel. (0577)32-3887. Open 8am to 6pm. Closed Thursday.*

Located in a white stucco *kura* storehouse, this coffee shop is an eclectic blend of English country and antique Takayama. It's a favorite shop of ours for a respite from sightseeing.

GELATERIA *(Ice cream, inexpensive). Hirokoji Dori, one block from Takayama Station. Tel. (0577)34-3434. Open 9:30am to 8pm, until 6pm on Sunday. Closed Tuesday.*

Gelateria sells low calorie *gelato* using fresh local fruit. You can choose *sakura* (cherry blossom) gelato in April, and sweet potato in autumn. Single ¥280, double ¥350.

SEEING THE SIGHTS

Early risers take note: most of Takayama's museums open a half-hour earlier during the summer months.

Sanmachi Suji

An excellently preserved merchant quarter, the area is a must-see. Constructed mostly in the late 1800s after the fire, picturesque wooden buildings are on both sides of the narrow roads. The small ditches alongside the road are an instant source of water for fire extinguishing and also came in handy for snow removal.

While there are many museums in the district, do not attempt to see all of them; your time is better spent browsing around the neighborhood, stopping in the antique and crafts shops and the *sake* breweries, and having a leisurely coffee in a cafe.

TAKAYAMA'S HISTORIC MERCHANT DISTRICT

*Walking the streets of **Sanmachi Suji**, you'll notice many shops selling art prints, especially **woodblock prints**. Takayama's love affair with the art form began in the 1910s and 20s when farmers were looking for something to do during the long winters when snow covered the ground. Having had a long tradition as carpenters and wood carvers, woodblock printmaking took hold and has been popular ever since.*

*In Sanmachi Suji, you'll probably notice large brown balls hanging over some doorways – these buildings are **sake breweries**. The large ball of cedar leaves outside an entrance is decoration as well as a sign that new sake is being made; when the green leaves turn brown, the sake is done. Takayama's pure mountain water makes the sake a favorite among connoisseurs. Many breweries offer tastings of the new sake in January and February.*

Kami-Sannomachi in the Sanmachi Suji district is one of our favorite streets. All the buildings on the narrow street are made of wood and many have intricate lattice facades. On one side of the street is a *miso* (fermented bean paste) shop, a *keyaki* wood crafts shop, a *sake* brewery, a shop selling stenciled folk toys and other objects, and an indigo-dyed fabric shop. The other side of the street has two art print shops including Baren, a cafe and print store. On the corner in a white storehouse is a coffee shop, Ranka.

Hirata Collection (Hirata Kinenkan). *Kami-ninomachi. Tel. (0577)33-1354. Open 9am to 5pm. ¥300.* The Hirata family was one of Takayama's wealthiest merchants purveying candles and hair oil. Their shop name, Utsuboya, is written on a beautiful indigo-dyed *noren* curtain hanging outside the door. Displayed inside the merchant's house are lanterns, lighting fixtures and furniture as well as cosmetics and mirrors giving you a glimpse of a woman's possessions.

Takayama Museum of Local History (Takayama-shi Kyodokan). *75 Kamichino-machi. Tel. (0577)32-1205. Open 8:30am to 5pm; December through February 9am to 4:30pm. Closed Monday except July through October and closed December 29-31.* Housed in a 100-year-old storehouse, you'll see archaeological finds from Takayama, items from the time of the Kanamori family in the 16th century and objects relating to the Takayama festival.

There are several other museums, mostly private collections, in the Sanmachi Suji area: the **Hida Archaeology Museum** (Hida Minzoku Koko-kan), the **Fujii Folk Craft Museum** (Fujii Bijutsu Mingei-kan), **Gallery of Traditional Japanese Toys** (Kyodo Gangu-an), **Oita Wild Bird Museum** (Oita Yacho-kan) and the **Hachiga Folk Art Gallery** (Hachiga Minzoku Bijutsukan). It is absolute overkill to go into all the museums in Takayama; we guarantee you will be a walking zombie. Instead, definitely see the Kusakabe and Yoshijima Houses and perhaps one of the other folk craft museums — we like the toy museum because it's different from the others.

Jinrikisha. *Sanmachi Suji. For reservation call (0577)32-1430. Open 10am to 4pm; 9am to 5pm in summer. No rides on rainy days.* Turn back the clock, have a ride on a rickshaw. A man dressed in period costume pulls the two wheeled carriage. Pay ¥1000 for a photo session, ¥3000 for a 15-minute stroll for two around the Sanmachi area and ¥5000 for a 30-minute ride.

Sakurayama Hachimangu Shrine Area

Inro Museum (Inro Bijutsukan). *1-98 Dai Shinmachi. Tel. (0577)32-8500. Open 9am to 5pm, April through November. Closed Tuesday. ¥500.* This small museum housed in a white stucco storehouse has a superb collection of *inro*, the small, delicately decorated lacquered containers hung from the man's *obi* belt, and *netsuke*, the tiny sculptured objects that secured the *inro*.

Until the middle of the Edo period, only the highest aristocrats were allowed to wear them. The *inro* on display highlight the craftsmanship of wood carving and lacquer decoration and the fashionable side of Edo men.

TAKAYAMA'S FESTIVALS

Takayama dresses up twice a year – for its Spring and Autumn festivals. They began in 1652 when Takayama was a small provincial town and have grown as the town has become wealthier. The elaborate festival floats, built by communities, were one of the few outlets the wealthy merchants had to flaunt their wealth. Each float is different.

The Spring Festival takes place April 14–15, usually coinciding with cherry blossoms. Dedicated to Hie Jinja Shrine, the festivities begin with a parade and performances by intricate mechanical puppets. During the evening, the floats are lit with paper lanterns and paraded through the streets. The 15th, the main day of the festival, sees more parades. Hundreds of costumed people accompany the floats, some are escort samurai, some perform lion dances and others play traditional music.

The Autumn Festival, October 9–10, begins at Sakura-yama Hachiman Shrine and for two days parade around the city. The evening parade begins at 6pm on the 9th. The floats, as with the Spring Festival, are accompanied by costumed samurai, musicians and dancers.

Some of the floats have the famous karakuri mechanical dolls that date back several hundred years. These puppets, manipulated by strings requiring as many as eight puppeteers, come alive before your very eyes. You can see them demonstrated at the Lion Dance Ceremony Exhibition Hall all year round.

Takayama's festivals are not for those who fear crowds. Over two million spectators take over this small city and, needless to say, accommodations are sold out months in advance. If you cannot get reservations, stay in a nearby town such as Furukawa or Gero.

Festival Floats Exhibition Hall (Yatai Kaikan) and **Sakurayama Nikko Kan**. *178 Sakura-machi. Tel. (0577)32-5100. Open 8:30am to 5pm; December through February 9am to 4:30pm. ¥820.* If you are not visiting Takayama during the Spring or Autumn festival, stop by to see some of the elaborate festival carts at rest until their next outing. They also have a great scale model of Toshogu, the grand shrine located in Nikko outside of Tokyo. During the feudal period, Takayama remained under the direct rule of the Tokugawa shogun and Takayama maintained a special relationship with the shrine, built to deify Tokugawa Ieyasu.

Lion Dance Ceremony Exhibition Hall (Shishi Kaikan). *53-1 Sakura-machi. Tel. (0577)32-0881. Open 9am to 5pm. ¥600.* Stop here to see displays of the masks for the lion dance performed at Takayama's festivals and also for performances of the *karakuri*, the fabulous mechanical dolls which perform atop some of the festival floats.

Kusakabe House (Kusakabe Mingeikan). *1-52 Ojin-machi. Tel. (0577)32-0072. Open 8:30am to 5pm; December through February closes 4:30pm. Closed December 29 through January 1. ¥500.* Put Kusakabe House on your list of must-sees. The Kusakabe family were wealthy merchants and purveyors to the Tokugawa family. The current building, the first merchant house built in Takayama after the disastrous fire in 1875, dates from 1879. True to its original style, the Kusakabe house is a typical Edo period affluent merchant's house with incredible beam construction. Free tea and *osembei* rice crackers are served in the courtyard.

Yoshijima House (Yoshijima-ke). *1-51 Ojin-machi. Tel. (0577)32-0038. Open 9am to 5pm; December through February closes at 4:30pm and on Tuesday. Closed December 28 through January 1. ¥500.* Another merchant house located next to Kusakabe, Yoshijima is more intimate and has more delicate wooden lattice work. The Yoshijima family, major landlords and *sake* brewers, knew how to live well.

Hida Takayama Lacquer Museum (Hida Takayama Shunkei-kan). *1 Kanda-machi. Tel. (0577)32-3373. Open 8am to 5:30pm; November through March 9am to 5pm. Closed December 31 and January 1. ¥300.* Shunkei nuri lacquer's color is unique to the region; it ranges from light brown to dark reddish brown. The grain of the wood shows through the semitransparent lacquer. This museum attractively displays about 1000 pieces of *shunkei nuri* ware, ranging from large *tansu* chests to small incense burners, and the stages of construction. Stop in the attractive gift shop adjacent to museum for reasonably priced goods.

TAKAYAMA EXPERIENCES

- *Wander the streets of Sanmachi Suji*
- *Eat a lunch of shojin-ryori, Buddhist vegetarian cuisine*
- *Visit a Williamsburg-like re-creation of rural Japan at Hida Folk Village.*
- *Shop till you drop for antiques and folk crafts in countless stores*
- *See the spring or autumn festival with its floats and mechanical dolls*
- *Try Takayama's famous sake, Kusudama.*
- *Enjoy the morning market at Takayama Jinya*

Takayama Jinya Area

Takayama Jinya. *Tel. (0577)32-0643. Open 8:45am to 5pm; until 4:30pm December through March. Closed December 27 through January 4. ¥420.* The Jinya was a villa of the ruling Kanamori family until it was taken over as an administrative center by officials sent from the Tokugawa shogunate in 1692. Eventually they built their residences within the compound.

These well-preserved rooms are some of Japan's finest examples of the austere architecture of the warrior class. The large rice storehouses display artifacts and documents from the Tokugawa era. There is even a room with some strange equipment where prisoners were interrogated and tortured. The Jinya is the only extant Tokugawa administrative building in Japan and is one of the most interesting stops in Takayama.

Matsumoto House. *125 Kamikawa Hara-machi. About a 10 minute walk from Takayama Jinya. Tel. (0577)36-5600. Open 9am to 4:30pm. Open only on Saturdays and Sundays. Free admission.* Matsumoto house is the oldest merchant house in Takayama; being away from the center of town it survived the huge fire in 1875. Stop here to see the Omoya main building, the *kura* for rice storage and the pickles storehouse built in 1826.

Morning Market (Asaichi). *Actually there are two markets, one at Takayama Jinya compound and a second along the Miyagawa River. 6am to 12 noon; 7am to 12 noon November through March.*

The market's history goes back to the 1600s when Lord Kanamori ruled over the area, and farmers sold mulberry leaves for silkworms at an evening market. Gradually other farmers joined them and switched the market to the morning. Given the number of tourists who visit, the market remains remarkably untouched — local women sell fruit, vegetables, flowers, homemade pickles, *miso*, pounded rice sweets and a few local crafts. Noriko's cat said the catnip was the best she's ever tasted.

Takayama Station Area

Kokubun-ji Temple. *Tel. (0577)32-1395.* Although the temple is located in a busy area, inside the compound it is very quiet. The temple was established in 746 and has huge ginko trees over one thousand years old. The three-storied pagoda was built in 1821 after the seven-storied one collapsed. The compound is open all the time but to enter the hall, the fee is ¥300.

Shiroyama Area

Shiroyama Koen Park, on the hill above the Sanmachi area, contains remnants of Takayama castle, the seat of power for Lord Kanamori until the late 1600s. The pleasant walking path offers good views of Takayama City and the snow-covered Japan Alps. The cherry blossoms in spring and the brilliant autumn foliage make these times especially beautiful.

Shoren-ji Temple, *at the gate of Shiroyama Park. Tel. (0577)32-2052. Open 8am to 6pm; November through March 8:30am to 5pm. ¥200.* This old temple was moved from Shokawa-mura in Shirakawago in 1959 when the Miboro dam was built. The temple's history goes back to 1253, but most of buildings date from 1504 and are in the typical Muromachi style; the bell tower is the oldest in the area.

Takayama Outskirts

Hida Folk Village (Hida Minzokumura). *Tel. (0577)33-4714. Open 8:30am to 5pm. Closed December 30 through January 2. ¥700. About 10 minutes by bus from the Takayama Bus Center platform #2 to Hida no Sato. Taxi from JR Station is about ¥1000.* About 30 houses were moved to this open air museum from all over the Hida area. There are descriptive signs in English and a taped guide system. Some of the houses have craft demonstrations, although the demonstrations in the traditional folk craft and arts section were very difficult to see. The village has two separate sections, about a ten-minute walk apart: the Old House Reservation and the Hida Folk Museum. Go to the Reservation first and then walk down the hill to the Hida Folk Museum. If your itinerary includes Shirakawago or Gokayama and your time is limited, you don't need to stop here.

SHOPPING

Takayama's antique and folk art shops are legendary. The area around Kami-ichinomachi has the greatest concentration of antique shops, many with goods stuffed from floor to ceiling. Sometimes antiques are not available anywhere else in the country so if you see something you really like, buy it; you may never find it again.

Usagiya Shop. *Close to Jinrikisha stop. Tel. (0577)34-6611.* The proprietress designs all the goods, mostly around a rabbit theme. And we don't mean stuffed bunnies. The crafts are of the highest quality and include handmade paper, indigo-dyed fabric and lanterns. A fabulous shop for browsing even if bunnies are not your thing. *Open 8:30am to 6:30pm; 9:30am to 5:30pm November through March.*

Kusakabe Miso Shoyu Tsukuri. *Tel. (0577)32-0122.* Miso (fermented soy beans) was the biggest source of protein for Takayama citizens during the long winter. The salt content of Takayama *miso* is lower than most other Japanese *miso* so you can eat it alone. Perhaps that explains why *hoba miso* (grilled on a magnolia leaf), either alone or with meat and vegetables, is the area's most popular dish. This shop has been selling *miso* for hundreds of years. Go in just to check out the building — this typical merchant's house has a low front and opens up to an atrium-like structure that's crisscrossed with massive wooden beams.

Ema-sho, *across from the Takayama Kyodokan. Tel. (0577)33-3116.* This shop sells antiquities from the Edo period to the early 20th century.

Momoyama Shop. *Kami-ichinomachi. Tel. (0577)36-5509. Open 9am to 6pm. Closed 17th and 18th of each month.* Momoyama specializes in beautiful old textiles and sells sets of small pieces for a quilter.

Hokokusha. *Kami-ninomachi. Tel. (0577)34-0504. Open 8am to 8:30pm.* Since 1841 Hokokusha sells Shibukusa ceramic ware, which is made with a special clay found near Takayama. The pottery has an off-white base color and is decorated with bright colors. Prices start at ¥900.

Komingei Kura Tsubo. *8 Kami-ichinomachi. Tel. (0577)33-1437. Open 8:30am to 5pm.* This excellent folk art shop sells trays, baskets, *tansu* chests, lacquer ware and ceramics.

Ichiyu Shop, *across the street from the Takayama Lacquer Ware Museum. Tel. (0577)32-3373. Open 9am to 5pm.* This small shop carries the three major types of pottery made in Takayama: Shibukusa, Yamada and Koito wares. Prices are reasonable, from ¥800.

SHOP TILL YOU DROP IN TAKAYAMA

Takayama, filled with stores selling everything from antiques to sweets, is a shopper's dream. Known for its craft traditions and surrounded by forest, wood is the predominant material in the stores.

Shunkei Lacquer Ware: The local lacquer has a distinctive yellow-brown tone and is semitransparent so you can see the grain of the wood.

Ichii Itto-bori: Decorative figures such as Buddhas, folk gods, etc. are carved from one piece of yew wood.

Ceramics: There are three major kinds. Shibukusa is a delicately decorative ware, influenced by Kutani ware. Koito, the oldest kiln, has an understated, mostly earth-tone glaze. Yamada also uses an earthen-colored glaze and is more for daily use.

Furniture: Since wood craftsmanship plays such a large role in Takayama, it's not surprising that it is a furniture center also. Artisans make both Western-style and Japanese furniture.

Woodblock prints: A natural art form given the area's affinity to wood, you'll find lots of local prints.

FURUKAWA

Furukawa, a small former castle town, is an easy half-day side trip from Takayama. It had its brief moment in the sun, flourishing as a castle town between 1573–92, but has been pretty much a backwater ever since. Usually much quieter than Takayama, Furukawa comes alive during the wild "naked" festival April 19–20. From 10pm in the evening of the 19th, bands of scantily clad men struggle to place individual drums on the top of the drum float. A procession of festival floats follows on the 20th.

ARRIVALS & DEPARTURES

Furukawa is easily reached by JR train from Takayama (17 minutes); make sure you take a local train that costs ¥280. The limited express saves four minutes but costs an additional ¥1000. Note the train station is called "Hida Furukawa."

GETTING AROUND TOWN

Furukawa is a small town easily accessible on foot, but bicycles are also convenient and rentals are available at the station.

Tourist Information

Kita Hida (North Hida) **Tourist Information** is located outside Hida Furukawa Station, Kanamori, Furukawa-cho. *Tel. (0577)73-3180.* Open 9am to 5:30pm.

WHERE TO STAY

Stay in Furukawa when Takayama's rooms are all booked. Frequent buses and trains connect the two places and even a ride back by taxi won't break the bank.

BUSUITEI, *3-8-1 Furukawa-cho, Mukai-machi, Yoshima-gun, Gifu, 509-4241. Tel. (0577)73-2531, Fax (0577)73-4623. From ¥13,000 per person with two meals. No credit cards.*

On the banks of the Miyakawa River, the inn started as a restaurant in 1869 and is still noted for its good food. Rooms are traditional style.

WHERE TO EAT

SEIYO ZEN DOKORO MAEDA *(Beef, moderate). Next to the Post Office, a 5-minute walk from the station. Tel. (0577)73-2852. Open 11:30am to 2pm; 5pm to 8:30pm. Closed Thursday and May 10 through June 10.*

This family-run casual restaurant specializes in Hida steak. Try the *amiyaki* steak, grilled with a special sauce for ¥2800.

LA MUSASHI *(French, inexpensive to moderate). Tel. (0577)73-6661. Open 10am to 9pm. Closed Thursday.*

A French restaurant next to Hida Furukawa Matsuri Hall uses local ingredients in the cooking. *Muniere* set lunch ¥1200. Have tea and sweets between 3pm and 5pm.

SEEING THE SIGHTS

Along the Seto River (actually more like a stream) are picturesque warehouses with white stucco walls decorated with wooden lattice work. Willow trees line the narrow pathway.

Furukawa Festival Hall. *14-5 Ichi-no-machi. Tel. (0577)73-3511. Open 9am to 5pm; until 4:30pm December through March. Closed Thursday December through March. ¥800.* A modern building housing several festival floats; a film shows all the action of the Furukawa festival.

Mishimaya Candle Shop. *Tel. (0577)73-4109. Open 9am to 6pm. Closed Wednesday.* Stop here to see Mr. Mishima make vegetable wax candles; he is the sixth generation master of the 230-year-old shop. This classic Japanese candle has a concave shape and is red or white; some now have painted decorations. Candles begin at ¥75.

GOKAYAMA & SHIRAKAWAGO

Located in the mountains, **Gokayama** is a series of villages and hamlets long isolated from the rest of the country. They were so secluded that in the Edo period, Lord Maeda, ruler of the Kaga domain centered in Kanazawa, secretly produced gunpowder here. Before the road was constructed in 1925, it was almost impossible to access the area even though the mountains aren't particularly high. Today you can easily drive through it in an hour.

Gokayama, along with its neighboring area **Shirakawago**, developed an unusual style of farmhouse architecture called *gassho zukuri* or praying hands. The name comes from the steep angle of the thatched roofs, which resemble the letter A or hands in prayer and are designed to accommodate a heavy snowfall. Under the eaves there is room for several floors used for silkworm cultivation. UNESCO designated Shirakawago and several hamlets of Gokayama as a World Heritage Site in 1995.

SPEND THE NIGHT IN A WORLD HERITAGE SITE

Staying in a **gassho zukuri** *inn is an unforgettable experience not to be missed. The accommodations are not luxurious: inns don't have private baths, and meals are eaten communally, similar to country bed and breakfasts in the West. In many inns, the walls don't go to the ceiling and only sliding doors may separate you from the next room, so your privacy is limited. At the same time, the distinguished architecture and the genuine hospitality of the innkeeper more than compensate for the lack of amenities.*

Gokayama and Shirakawago seem so similar today, but during the Edo period they hardly interacted at all. Gokayama belonged to the Kaga domain, which governed from Kanazawa. The ruling Maeda family kept it isolated by setting up check points on the river. The only mountain pass was 700 meters high. Shirakawago, as part of the Takayama area, fell under the direct rule of the shogun.

Even today, the two areas belong to different prefectures. As you drive along Route 156 between Shirakawago and Gokayama, you criss-cross the river more than a half-dozen times; the steep ravines leave little space for the road highlighting how isolated the two were.

Planning Your Trip

Stay one day in Shirakawago and one in Gokayama. If you need to choose between the two, we recommend Gokayama even though it is more difficult to reach. Ogimachi, the center of the Shirakawago district, has increasingly become more of a tourist center while the tiny hamlets of Gokayama work hard to preserve their way of life.

Many places shut down during the winter so spring through autumn are the best times to visit.

SHIRAKAWAGO

Ogimachi is the most important village in the fairly large district of Shirakawago, home to some 80 *gassho zukuri* buildings, many now family-run inns. It is a pleasure to wandering among the rustic buildings, rice paddies and flower and vegetable gardens.

ARRIVALS & DEPARTURES

Car and bus are the two ways to reach the Shirakawago area. The two main bus stops servicing Ogimachi are Ogimachi Jinja Mae and Ogimachi Gassho Shuraku.

By Bus

To/from Kanazawa/Takaoka: The Kaetsu no Tetsudo bus company operates four buses a day from Takaoka to Ogimachi, passing through Gokayama. Takaoka is about 40 minutes by JR train from Kanazawa. Takaoka to Ogimachi takes 2 hours 20 minutes and costs ¥2350.

To/from Kanazawa and Nagoya: The Meitetsu bus company provides service from Kanazawa through Gokayama and Ogimachi to Nagoya, departing Nagoya 8:40am; arriving Ogimachi 2pm; arriving Kanazawa 5pm. The return service departs Kanazawa 9:40am, arrives Ogimachi 12 noon and arrives Nagoya 6pm. This bus usually runs only between mid-July and mid-November. Fare ¥4760 Nagoya to Ogimachi; ¥2730 Ogimachi to Kanazawa. This bus can also be used to reach the Gokayama area.

To/from Takayama: From Takayama Bus Center at the JR station, take Nobi bus from platform 5 to Makido (3 buses/day, 1 hour 20 minutes, ¥1930). Change for the JR Bus for Hatogaya (4 buses/day, 50 minutes, ¥1430). Make sure that you check the current schedule with the Tourist Information Office at the JR Takayama Station to be sure the buses have convenient connections.

To/from Nagoya: JR runs a bus from Nagoya to Ogimachi at peak tourist times, departing Nagoya 8:05 am and arriving Ogimachi 1:08pm. The return leaves Ogimachi 12:38pm, arriving Nagoya 5:34pm. Fare ¥4670. This bus runs during the Golden Week holidays, mid-July through November 10 and the New Year holiday period.

By Car

To/from Kanazawa/Toyama: take the Hokuriku Expressway to Tonami interchange then Route 156 south. Ogimachi in Shirakawago is about 2 hours from Kanazawa or Toyama.

To/from Takayama: Take Route 41 north from Takayama. At Noguchi, Route 41 turns to the right but you continue straight until you reach Route 360 west leading to Ogimachi.

An alternate route from Takayama is Route 158 west to Route 156 north to Ogimachi. This way takes you past the Miboro dam and its large lake.

Both routes are well marked and should take about 1 1/2 hours to Ogimachi.

Bus Tour from Takayama

You can take a Japanese bus tour from Takayama to Ogimachi; some tours will allow you to only go one way and stay in Ogimachi. Tours run on weekends and holidays April through November and daily during the peak travel times of late July through August and early October. Check with the Takayama Tourist Information Office for tour information.

OGIMACHI

Ogimachi is totally accessible on foot; 15 minutes gets you from one end of town to the other.

Tourist Information

The **Tourist Information Office** is located in the center of town close to the Gassho Shuraku bus stop. Open 8:30am to 5pm. Closed Wednesday. *Tel. (05769)6-1751 or 6-1013.* Limited English is spoken but pick up map in English. Staff members will assist you with reservations at inns.

DOBUROKU FESTIVAL

*Every October 14 to 19 Ogimachi comes alive with its **Doburoku Festival**. Doburoku is a milky unrefined sake rice wine made by nearly every household in this area prior to the Meiji period (1868). Then the government banned the individual production of sake. Five shrines in the Shirakawago area protested on the grounds that they needed to make their own sake to offer to the gods. The officials relented and allowed these five to continue the tradition.*

The festival takes place on the grounds of Shirakawago Hachimangu Shrine. The shrines parade special floats, the villagers dress in traditional costume and dedicate lion dances and folk songs to the gods. Doburoku sake, freely offered to all in the shrine compound, ensures the festival is a very spirited affair (no pun intended).

Where to Stay

The Tourist Information Office in the center of Ogimachi can book lodgings but only basic English is spoken. The Tourist Information Office at Takayama Station can also assist you.

The following *minshuku* are all *gassho zukuri* buildings and share the same address: Shirakawa Ogimachi, Ono-gun, Gifu, 501-0627:

FURUSATO, *Tel. (05769)6-1033. No fax. From ¥7700 per person with two meals. No credit cards.*

The head Shinto priest at Shirakawa Hachimangu Shrine next door runs Furusato; his wife is a noted cook. Furusato's claim to fame is the Crown Prince stayed here when he came through a few years ago.

RIHEI, *Tel. (05769)6-1552, Fax (05769)6-1758. From ¥7700 per person with two meals. No credit cards.*

Rihei is the oldest building in Ogimachi. The mother and daughter-in-law who run it are extremely knowledgeable about herbs and mountain vegetables and cook wonderful vegetable *tempura*. They recently renovated their bathrooms. The *minshuku* is on a main thoroughfare so it's a bit noisy.

ITCHA, *Tel. (05769)6-1422, Fax (05769)6-1233. From ¥7700 per person with two meals. No credit cards.*

Itcha serves vegetables grown in their owns fields and their friendly atmosphere has earned them many loyal customers.

JUEMON, *Tel. (05769)6-1053. No fax. From ¥7700 per person with two meals. No credit cards.*

Located slightly on the southern outskirts of town, but still less than a 10-minute walk from the center of Ogimachi, Juemon is run by a very friendly woman, Sakai-san, who plays the *shamisen*, sings folk songs and shows you how to accompany her on the *sasara*, an unusual wooden instrument you snap to create music.

Where to Eat

CHAYA CHUBEI *(Regional Japanese, moderate). Tel. (05769)6-1818. Open 8am to 5pm. Closed December until mid-March.*

Chaya Chubei is the oldest restaurant in Ogimachi. The *Chubei teishoku*, ¥3000, includes Hida steak, tofu and mountain vegetables, 15 dishes in all.

HAKUSUIEN *(Regional Japanese, inexpensive). Located on the main road heading toward Route 360, across from the gas station. Tel. (05769)6-1511. Open 9am to 4pm. Closed December to March.*

The chef-owner goes up in the mountains to pick wild vegetables. The *wa-teishoku* set meal (¥1650) features grilled *iwana* trout, *soba* noodles and mountain vegetables.

MASUEN BUNSUKE *(Regional Japanese, inexpensive). Located a little out of town, on Route 360, about 1/2 kilometer up the hill on the right, but is still reachable on foot. Tel. (05769)6-1268. Open 8am to 9pm.*

The family cultivates trout and proudly serves its produce in a *gassho zukuri* farmhouse. You eat the set meal (¥1600) on *tatami* mats around *irori* hearths. The sound of water running from one pond to another is a delightful accompaniment to the meal.

SHIRAOGI *(Japanese, inexpensive). Located across the parking lot from the Tourist Information Office, the open porch makes it easy to find. Open 9am to 6pm.*

Shiraogi serves inexpensive Japanese fare such as noodles and curry rice and has an English menu.

KITANOSHO *(Regional Japanese, inexpensive). Tel. (05769)6-1506. Open 10am to 5pm. Closed December through March.*

Located across the street from the inn Juemon in the southern part of town, Kitanosho's dining room looks out over the river. The varied menu is in English with pictures and includes noodles, mountain vegetables and fish. Noodles cost ¥600 to ¥800; set meals ¥1100 to ¥1600.

Seeing the Sights

While there are sights to see, some of our best memories are relaxing and enjoying the ambiance of the rural town. Patrice once spent a warm summer afternoon with friends at the banks of the river, building a makeshift dam with rocks and cooling off in the water.

Shirakawa Folk Village (Gassho Zukuri Minka-en). *Tel. (05769)6-1231. Open 8:40am to 5pm April through November; until 6pm in August; 9am to 4pm December through March. Closed Thursday except during the peak periods: April 29 to May 5, August and October 10 through November 3. Closed December 30 through January 1. ¥700.* A spacious open air museum in a park-like setting features 25 *gassho zukuri* buildings including a shrine, farmhouses and storage huts. Craft demonstrations give you a feel of life in the old days. In the Taikenkan learn how to make *soba* noodles for a fee of ¥1800, reservations are required.

Doburoku Hall (Doburoku Matsuri no Yakata). *Tel. (05769)6-1655. Open 8:30am to 4:30pm April through November; 9am to 4pm December through March. ¥300.* A small hall on the grounds of Shirakawa Shrine which displays the Doburoku Festival costumes and gives you a taste of the special *sake*. You can see a lengthy video of the festival held October 14 to 19.

Daily Life Hall (Seikatsu Shiryokan). *Tel. (05769)6-1818. Open 8am to 5pm April through November, closed in winter. ¥200.* A small museum on the southern outskirts (next to Juemon Minshuku); Seikatsu Shiryokan displays lots of folk implements used in farming and within the house.

Myozenji Kyodokan. Myozenji Temple's main hall is a beautiful thatched-roof building with ornate wood work over 200 years old. The Myozenji House, the head priest's residence, is the grandest *gassho zukuri* building in Ogimachi and is open to the public. *Tel. (05769)6-1009. Open 7:30am to 5pm April through November; 8am to 5pm in winter. ¥200.*

Tenbodai Lookout Point. About 20-minute walk from the center of Ogimachi, Tenbodai is on a bluff. Once the sight of a castle built strictly for defense in the Muromachi age (1400s), it has great views of Ogimachi and is worth the walk up. Test your photographic skills with panoramic shots of Ogimachi. The nearby restaurant/shop, Tenshu Kaku (Castle

Keep) is not the least bit attractive but go in to see the photo display of four seasons in Ogimachi.

ARRIVALS & DEPARTURES

Gokayama's inaccessibility adds to its appeal. Since the area is difficult to reach, it's not overrun with sightseers. The hamlets of Ainokura and Suganuma retain a quiet atmosphere with few gift shops or other by-products of tourism.

Gokayama's layout, a series of villages spread out over 15 kilometers, makes it impossible to see it all without a car. Buses are infrequent so you can't hop on and off at each village. Your choices are to see only one or two areas, to walk between the closest villages, to use taxis (they have to be called) or to see the area by rental car.

By Bus

To/from Kanazawa: The Kaetsu no Tetsudo bus company operates four buses a day from Takaoka to the Gokayama and Shirakawago areas. Takaoka is about 40 minutes by JR train from Kanazawa, making easy access from that city. Takaoka to Shimonashi village in Gokayama takes 1 hour 40 minutes, ¥1140.

To/from Kanazawa and Nagoya: The Meitetsu Bus has service from Kanazawa through Gokayama and Ogimachi to Nagoya, departing Kanazawa 9:40am, arriving Shimonashi (Gokayama) 11:04, Ogimachi 12 noon and Nagoya 5:52pm. The return service departs Nagoya 8:40am; arrives Ogimachi 1:50pm, Shimonashi (Gokayama) 3:36pm, and Kanazawa 5pm. This bus usually runs only between mid-July 1 and early November.

To/from Takayama: If you are coming from Takayama, you have to go through Shirakawago and take a bus from there to Gokayama (see Shirakawago's *Arrivals & Departures*).

By Tour Bus

One convenient way to see the Gokayama area is by Japanese tour bus which runs from the end of April through early November only on Saturdays, Sundays and holidays. The bus leaves Takaoka Station at 9am and stops at Gokayama Washi no Sato, Nishi Akao, Suganuma, Kaminashi and Ainokura and arriving back at Takaoka Station at 5:15pm. ¥6500. You can also take the tour bus one way, either from Takaoka to Ainokura

¥3800 (includes lunch and admission fees) or back from Ainokura to Takaoka ¥3000 (transportation only). *Tel. (0766)25-2356.*

By Car

To/from Kanazawa and Toyama: A car gives you greater flexibility. From Toyama City, Toyama airport or from Kanazawa, take the Hokuriku Expressway to Tonami interchange and then Route 156 south. Gokayama is about 1 1/2 hours from Toyama or Kanazawa. Route 156, which passes endlessly through tunnels and mountain underpasses, is well marked in English.

To/from Takayama: Take Route 41 north. At Noguchi, Route 41 turns to the right, but you continue straight ahead until you reach Route 360 west to Ogimachi. At Ogimachi take Route 158 north to continue on to Gokayama.

An alternate route from Takayama is Route 158 west to Route 156 north to Ogimachi and Gokayama. This way takes you past the Miboro dam and its large lake.

Both routes are well marked and should take about 2 hours to the southern part of Gokayama.

THE VILLAGES

Gokayama's villages are listed from north to south along Route 156. If you are traveling from Takayama, you will reach these places in reverse order.

Many small museums are scattered around Gokayama; go into one or two of them but it's unnecessary to go into every one. Our favorites are the Murakami and Iwase Houses.

TAIRA-MACHI

Back in the 11th century the Genji and the Taira clans slugged it out for military control of the country. The Taira lost and some of the banished clan fled to this remote and mountainous area where detection was almost impossible.

Heading south on Route 156, **Gokoyama Washi village** (Washi no Sato) features three museums clustered together about five kilometers before you reach Route 304. They are the **Taira Village Folklore Museum** (Taira Kyodokan), **Taira Village Paper Craft Center** (Taira Washi Kogei Kenkyukan) and **Mountain Collection Hall** (Yama tono Taiwakan) and a ¥300 pass will admit you to all.

We find the Taira Village Paper Craft Center with its papermaking demonstrations the most interesting of the three; for ¥500 you can make a sheet of paper. The shop is stocked with delicate dolls, stationery, masks, jewelry, Noguchi-style paper lanterns and other objects made of paper.

The second floor has a small display of Japanese paper and examples of handmade paper from around the world. *Open daily 8:30am to 5pm.*

The Folklore Museum on the hill overlooking the road has dioramas of early life as well as folk craft objects and gunpowder paraphernalia. The Mountain Collection Hall tells about the area's natural habitat. *Open daily 8:30am to 5pm; Folklore Museum closed late April to late December.*

We recommend you stop in the Paper Craft Center and skip the other two. If traveling by bus, by-pass them all.

AINOKURA

At Shimonashi, turn onto Route 304. You'll pass the **Gokayama Paper Cooperative** where you can see Japanese paper being made and for ¥500 make a sheet yourself. As we watched the laborious process of steaming the mulberry wood, separating it from the bark, washing it, taking out the brown parts, mixing the mulberry pulp with water, sifting it onto sheets and drying the sheets, we marveled the cost wasn't greater. The shop has attractive goods from Zodiac figures to stationery. *Open 8:15am to 5pm May through November; closed Tuesday; December through April closed Sundays and holidays. ¥100.*

Continue up the hill to Ainokura, a picturesque hamlet of some 30 farmhouses, 20 in the *gassho zukuri* style, set among the rice paddies. With luck, the tour buses won't be there for the small village is easily overrun. Ainokura sprung up 450 years ago around the temple; papermaking and silk cultivation were its primary sources of income. It still retains a tranquil feeling and a simpler way of life. Housewives sell their produce and fresh flowers from their houses. The UNESCO World Heritage Site designation for Ainokura includes the surrounding rice paddies as well as the nearby forests that protect the town from landslides and avalanches. The **Ainokura Folklore Museum** (Minzoku-kan) is housed in a *gassho zukuri* house. *Open 8:30am to 5pm daily. ¥200.*

Where to Stay

Ainokura has 10 *minshuku*, including seven in *gassho zukuri* buildings. All cost from ¥7500 per person with two meals and share the following address: Ainokura, Tairamachi, Higashi Tonami-gun, Toyama, 939. The following are all *gassho zukuri* buildings:

YUSUKE, *Tel. (0763)66-2555, Fax (0763)66-2578*, is the residence of the chairman of the village preservation committee and is one of the larger houses.

GOEMON, located at the center of the village, also has camping. *Tel. (0763)66-2154.*

SHOSHICHI, *Tel. (0763)66-2206.*

NAGAEMON, *Tel. (0763)66-2755.*

KAMINASHI

Route 156 runs right through the center of **Kaminashi** so the village could not maintain its pristine condition like Ainokura or Suganuma. However, there are some worthwhile sights.

Murakami-ke House is a large *gassho zukuri* house built 400 years ago in the Momoyama period. The present owner likes to sit by the hearth, serve tea and regale his guests with the history of the area. He may even honor you with his rendition of a local folk song. The building is a little more upscale than your typical farmhouse and contains several guest rooms, a mezzanine and a work area for manufacturing gunpowder. *Open daily 8:30am to 5pm. ¥350.*

Kokiriko Utanokan, several buildings down from the Murakami House, is a small museum dedicated to folk music and papermaking. *Open 10am to 4pm. Closed December through early April. ¥200.*

Exiles Hut (Rukei-goya). Take the street that dead ends at Murakami House; cross the river and you'll find a small hut on the hill on the right. Lord Maeda, head of the Kaga domain, used to exile political prisoners, like farmers who complained about heavy taxes, to the right bank of the Sho River. There were several types of exile huts: some where the prisoners could walk around and others where they could not. Believe it or not, this hut was the luxury model.

Hakusan-gu Shrine, up from the parking lot next to Murakami House, has a Honden main hall that dates from 1502 and is the oldest wooden building in Toyama Prefecture. Make sure you walk up close to it because the Honden is hidden behind a hall that's similarly sized, but much newer.

Near Hakusan-gu Shrine you can see an unusual thatched-roof bell tower belonging to Enjo-ji Temple. This simple tower is an example of the interrelationship between Shintoism and Buddhism — thatch is usually used in Shinto shrine construction, not in Buddhist temples.

Where to Eat

Shokuro restaurant is in a *gassho zukuri* building to the left of Murakami House's parking lot. The specialty *sansai teishoku* (mountain vegetable set) for ¥1300 includes a variety of mountain vegetables, *soba* noodles, tasty Gokayama tofu, rice, and pickles. They also serve *soba* and *udon* noodles from ¥400 to ¥600. *Tempura soba* costs ¥550.

Around Kaminashi area, there are several other places serving local Japanese food as well as coffee houses for a caffeine fix.

GASSHO ZUKURI, PRAYING HANDS

The mountainous areas of Gokayama and Shirakawago are known for the farmhouse style called **gassho zukuri***. The buildings have very steep thatched roofs to bear the heavy snowfall. The deepest on record recorded in the area is 9 meters – 27 feet! The term gassho zukuri means "praying hands," which the roof resembles. An angle of 45° is more aesthetically pleasing than the sharper 60° angle, but the steeper angle leaks less so most farmers chose practicality over beauty.*

The sharp angle of the eaves leaves room for several stories in the attic, primarily used for storage. With the development of sericulture (silk production) in the area in the late 1800s, these extra stories became perfect spots to cultivate silkworms. There were no windows in the thatch so the only light on the upper floors came from windows in the side walls. The silkworms, munching away on their mulberry leaves, gravitated to the available light.

The buildings are constructed without nails; the wooden beams fit together and are secured with rope. Wooden panels form the walls; this style is different from most Japanese farmhouses that have mud walls. The one or more irori hearths on the ground floor provided heat and were used for cooking. There were no chimneys because the roof leaked around them. The billowing smoke covered the ropes and wood with soot, preserving them and acting as an insecticide to kill the bugs in the thatch. Since most residents no longer put fires in their hearths every day, the roofs have to be changed more frequently.

Shirakawago and Gokayama use different types of thatch. The Gokayama type is thinner and the roofs have to be changed every 20-25 years. Shirakawago thatch is thicker and used to last for up to 50 years. Because their thatch is changed more frequently, Gokayama houses have a more manicured appearance while Shirakawago's seem shaggy.

Thatching was a community affair involving as many as 200 people. Each family had its own field and would store its produce each year until there was enough for a roof. Today, grass is grown communally. Until the 1920s, virtually all the houses in the Gokayama and Shirakawago areas were gassho zukuri style but since then simpler and easier to maintain buildings have been constructed. Today there are about 80 gassho zukuri buildings in Shirakawago; in the early 1950s there were 275. Many were destroyed during the postwar dam building boom and those not destroyed were considered dinosaurs. In 1958 a confectioner from Kawasaki, a city next to Tokyo, offered to buy a gassho zukuri house for ¥200,000. Since the roof needed changing, the owner readily agreed and the building was moved to Kawasaki. The original owner long forgot about the house until one day the phone rang and he was told his house had been declared an Important Cultural Property. Today you can see the Yamashita House at Minka-en, an open air museum in Kawasaki.

Some gassho zukuri houses were disassembled by their owners who left the wood piled up along the road, free for the taking. One such building was brought to the Kabuki-cho district of Tokyo and is now a restaurant serving country fare.

SUGANUMA

This tiny hamlet, located down the hill off of Route 156, is designated a National Historical Site and UNESCO World Heritage Site. The ten *gassho zukuri* farmhouses are scattered around the rice fields; two are small museums: **Gokayama Folklore Museum** (Gokayama Minzoku-kan) and **Gunpowder Museum** (Ensho no Yakata). *Both are open from 9am to 4pm. Closed December 29 through January 3. ¥300 admits you to both.*

Where to Stay

GOROBE MINSHUKU, *Suganuma, Kami Tairamura, Higashi Tonami-gun, Toyama, 939-1919. Tel. (0763)67-3502.* From ¥8000 per person with two meals. *No credit cards.*

Nicely renovated, Gorobe is one of the most attractive *gassho zukuri minshuku* in Gokayama and Shirakawago. House specialties include pheasant *nabe*, a stew which is cooked at your table, *iwana* river trout and mountain vegetables, all served around an *irori* hearth. Be forewarned that Suganuma is a small village with few diversions; you are really in the sticks. Plan on taking walks and reading.

Where to Eat

YOHACHI, a restaurant in a *gassho zukuri* building next to the parking lot, serves *tempura teishoku* set ¥1000, *tendon* ¥900, *sansai* (mountain vegetable) *soba* ¥600, as well as other soba and *udon* dishes. Closed Thursday. It's basically the only act in this small hamlet.

NISHI AKAO

Nishi Akao, like Kaminashi, is a village on Route 156 with modern buildings interspersed with traditional ones.

Iwase-ke House, built in 1727, is the largest in Gokayama and is designated an Important Cultural Property. Its owners used to produce gunpowder in summer and make paper and grow silkworms in winter. During its prime in the Edo era, about 35 people lived here; today there are three.

When we visited the house, the 89-year-old owner, Mr. Kato, invited visitors to sit at the hearth and hear the residence's history. Iwase House is a rare example of combining farmhouse architecture with *shoin zukuri*, which was popular with samurai; in the living room there is an alcove and carved transom panels called *ranma*. You can't help noticing the large black lacquer and gold leaf Buddhist altar, the largest in a residence in the area, according to Mr. Kato. We give it high marks for gaudiness. The formal entrance at the far end of the house was only used by the representative of Lord Maeda, who came to pick up the gunpowder; the Iwase family was responsible for selling the village's gunpowder to the feudal lord. The house even has a small closet where guards could hide to protect the feudal lord's representative. The attic floor was not completely closed in so the hearth's warm air heated the upper floors. *Open daily 8am to 5pm. ¥300.*

Next to Iwase House is a small temple, **Gyotoku-ji**. The thatched-roof entrance gate doubles as the bell tower. If you look closely at the pillars, you will see some cut marks. During a fire in the mid-1800s, the villagers began to cut down the gate fearing it would set the temple on fire. It proved unnecessary but the saw marks remain.

SEX & THE ART OF LIVING IN THE COUNTRY

The large gassho zukuri houses could accommodate an extended family; often 30 people lived under one roof. The patriarch's immediate family slept in a private room, but others including unmarried sons and servants slept on the mezzanine or second floor. This arrangement obviously didn't encourage intimacy, so most couples would go to the forest for privacy. Not surprisingly, the birth rate was lowest nine months after the winter.

Where to Eat

When in Nishi Akao, check out the **KISSA SHIMIZU** which specializes in bear meat. Kissa actually means coffee shop — an unlikely venue for bear meat. In the old days, when villagers found bears hibernating in the early spring, they became the meat for festivals. Even today the bear meat served here is caught locally. It's tough, but tasty. Try the *kuma udon* (noodles with bear meat) for ¥750 or *kumajiru* (bear soup) for ¥400. *Tel. (0763)67-3647. Open 10am to 6pm.*

GUJO HACHIMAN

Gujo Hachiman, a small castle town in Gifu Prefecture with a population of 18,000, is famous for its **Bon Odori dances** held on 29 nights between mid-July and early September. You can literally dance the night away. For the four-day period from August 13 to 16, the height of O-bon, the dancing begins at 8pm and lasts until dawn.

Gujo Hachiman is not the sort of place you should make a major detour to visit, but make a stop if you are in the area and if it is a summer night with dancing scheduled.

ARRIVALS & DEPARTURES

To/from Nagoya: take the Meitetsu train line to Shin Gifu (30 minutes, ¥530). From Shin Gifu take the Gifu Bus towards Gujo Shirotori, which stops at Gujo Hachiman (90 minutes to 2 hours, ¥1480).

GETTING AROUND TOWN

The small town is easy to get around on foot. You can take a taxi up to the castle if a 25-minute walk up sounds too tiring.

Tourist Information

Gujo Hachiman Tourist Association is located across from the former Gujo Hachiman Town Hall. *Tel. (05756)7-0002.* English maps are unavailable, and little English is spoken.

WHERE TO STAY

MIFUKU, *808 Shimatani, Hachiman-cho, Gujo-gun, Gifu, 501-4222. Tel. (05756)7-0329, Fax (05756)5-2146. From ¥13,000 per person with two meals. No credit cards.*

Conveniently located in the merchant section of town, Mifuku is an older traditional Japanese inn with architectural details from the early 1900s. Its old-fashioned feeling is the equivalent of visiting your Grandmother's house. Rooms are relatively small but overlook the river. Summer dinners include *ayu* river trout, caught in the river just outside your room and prepared four different ways.

BIZEN-YA RYOKAN, *264 Shimo-yanagi-machi, Gujo Hachiman, Gifu, 501-4214. Close to Shimbashi. Tel. (05756)5-2068, Fax (05756)7-0007. From ¥10,000 per person with two meals. No credit cards.*

The oldest *ryokan* in Gujo Hachiman is located in the town center but is very quiet once you enter the gate. The garden has beautiful bamboo and a Japanese pond. The friendly staff serves fresh *ayu* fish in summer and boar *nabe* stew in winter.

SEEING THE SIGHTS

Gujo Hachiman Castle. *Located on a bluff across the Yoshida river, about a 20-minute walk uphill from the Hachiman Honcho bus stop. Tel. (05756)5-5839. Open 9am to 5pm. Closed December 20 through January 10. ¥300.* This side of town was the domain of the samurai class and the feudal lord, whose residence was at the base of the castle hill. A fire in the early part of this century destroyed most of the samurai district. The castle was built in 1559, disassembled in the 1870s and reconstructed in 1933. The Tokugawa shogunate changed the ruling family five times; the Aoyama, the last family appointed, governed for seven generations.

WE COULD HAVE DANCED ALL NIGHT...

Bon Odori dancing is a popular summer pastime throughout all of Japan, but Gujo Hachiman has to be the Bon Odori capital. On the prime nights in August, up to 100,000 people take to the streets.

Bon (or O-bon), the Buddhist festival takes place every August when spirits of the deceased return to their home villages. Japanese who have left the rural areas to work in the city also return home during this time to welcome back and pay respect to their deceased relatives. Actually, many Japanese now go overseas in August, but the traditionally minded return home. Folk dancing, called Bon Odori, is a popular diversion in many villages.

In Gujo Hachiman, the feudal lord wanted to plan entertainment for his people over the summer and instituted a mass Bon Odori dance. All citizens could participate, which meant that classes could mix – farmers danced next to samurai. The tradition continued and still thrives today.

The town takes on a festive atmosphere. Vendors sell food and drinks and set up game booths. Several hundred lanterns are placed on the banks of the river. The musicians sit on a wooden festival cart that moves to a different section of town every evening.

The dances themselves are slow, rhythmic and repetitive. Dancers of all ages with most dressed in yukata, a casual cotton summer kimono, make a large chain. While the local residents know the dances by heart, as neophytes you only have to position yourself next to an experienced dancer and copy the motions; within a few minutes you'll dance with confidence.

Coffee shops stay open, offering a place to rest and get a dose of caffeine to help you through the night. Musicians drink raw egg yolks to give them the energy to make it through the night. But the dancing lasts all night only from August 13 to 16; otherwise it ends at 11pm on Saturdays and 10:30pm on weekdays and Sundays.

Honcho district

The Honcho district, the samurai residential area, has a few blocks of traditional homes remaining. They have an architectural feature called *sode-kabe*, literally "kimono sleeve walls." A second floor wall juts out about one meter and offers some protection against the spread of fire as well as jumping rodents. You'll note that many of the buildings have a fire bucket hanging on the side of the house, which indicates they store water on site.

Hashimoto-cho district

This area, designated the merchant area in feudal times, remains the commercial center of town. Many of the buildings, some sporting modern facades, date back several hundred years.

A trio of museums is within a stone's throw of each other; a combination ticket for ¥700 admits you to all three; ask for a *sankan-ken*.

Folk Life Museum (Omodakaya Mingeikan). *Shin-machi. Tel. (05756)5-3332. 9am to 7pm daily. ¥250.* This museum is the residence of a well-known painter whose works are mostly of fish. Visit here to see a typical wealthy merchant's house complete with storehouses, gardens, residential areas and the shop up front that still operates. Inside the compound is a well still used for washing clothes. Looking at the facade from the street, you would never imagine that there was so much under one roof.

Directly to the left of the Omodakaya Folk Life Museum is a small path next to a running stream. The lane has been paved with small stones. The path leads you to the front door of the **Yudo-kan**, a small and whimsical gallery run by a local artist who is a genius for creating animals and other creatures using paper and scissors. Incredibly, before your eyes, a flat piece of paper suddenly turns into a fish. If you are lucky, Mr. Mizuno will be there, sitting at the table demonstrating his craft. Buy one of the how-to books to try it at home. Even though the books are in Japanese, the diagrams are easy to follow. *Inari-cho. Tel (05756)5-3274. Open 9am to 5pm. Closed Thursday except in July and August. ¥300.*

Across the street from the Yudo-kan is the **Saito Art Museum** (Saito Bijutsukan). *Shin-machi. Tel. (05756)5-3539. Open 9am to 5pm; July and August open until 6pm. Closed Thursday except in July and August. ¥300.* The owners of this private museum have been involved in tea ceremony for 270 years and display beautifully an impressive collection of refined tea bowls and other tea utensils. The museum is in a storehouse-style building that has thick white stucco walls. Behind is a small garden with a *suikinkutsu* fountain. Under the stone basin below the ground is a small cave with a shallow puddle of water. As the water drips from the basin into the puddle, the splashing echoes in the cave creating a distinctive, peaceful sound. When it is absolutely quiet, the sound is heard even inside the house; given the normal hustle and bustle of life, you'll have to put your ear next to a bamboo pole by the fountain to hear it.

This unique fountain is one small way the merchant class circumvented the luxury law during the Edo era. A small shop in the museum connects to a larger folk arts shop that carries a tasteful selection of locally made crafts including indigo-dyed fabrics, ceramics and paper goods.

SHOPPING

Sampuru Kobo Kaneyama, *Tokiwa-cho. Located between the Tourist Information Center and Hachiman Elementary School. Tel. (05756)7-1870.* This is the shop that invented food samples, those tantalizing specimens seen outside restaurants all over Japan. They still produce more than half of the country's output. Plastic has replaced candle wax as the medium but perfecting a sample is still a laborious process. You can see these artistic specimens being crafted and buy some fruit, parfaits, pizza or grilled fish for your personal collection.

Tanizawa. *839 Honcho, a few doors down from the bus terminal. Tel (05756)5-2074.* This shop sells traditional fabrics and fabric items such slippers, purses, hats, blouses and toiletry bags. You'll also find kimono fabric in Gujo Hachiman's famous Tsumugi weaving style. Each thread is dyed prior to weaving.

Wa and Bi. *Across from the post office on Sakyo-machi street. Tel. (05756)5-3664.* This shop as an attractive assortment of gift items — ceramics, handkerchiefs and stationery.

MINO

Although **Mino** has been a Japanese papermaking center for 1300 years, today the overwhelmingly industrial town has little to offer the foreign visitor. To us, Mino represents the worst of contemporary Japan, building only for economic expediency and turning its back on centuries' old traditions. Mino remains a paper production center but most is manufactured by machine; a small and dedicated group of artisans continues to make paper by hand. Mino's small preserved merchant district is known for its *utatsu* (distinctive ornate fire walls).

The real reason you might want to come to Mino is to participate in a papermaking workshop run by CraftsLinks, an organization founded by several foreigners to introduce papermaking to an international audience.

ARRIVALS & DEPARTURES

· **To/from Nagoya:** Take the Meitetsu train to Shin Gifu, a shinkansen train stop, (30 minutes), change to a little trolley on the Meitetsu Tagami line to Mino, which runs once an hour (1 hour, ¥650). If you are on a JR rail pass, you can take JR from Nagoya to Shin Gifu, but you will only save about ¥100.

To/from Shin Gifu and Gujo Hachiman: Gifu Bus company runs buses from Shin Gifu to Gujo Hachiman, which stop at Mino (40 minutes to 1 hour, ¥850).

SEEING THE SIGHTS

Imai House (Imai-ke Jutaku). *Tel. (0575)33-0021. Open 9am to 4:30pm; until 4pm October through March. Closed Tuesday. ¥300.* Located in the center of the preservation section, this house belonged to a paper merchant. The building still has a traditional tile roof, *utatsu* walls and a lovely garden.

CraftsLinks, an organization founded by a dedicated group of foreigners, organizes three day workshops to introduce Japanese paper-making techniques. CraftsLinks offers participants the rare opportunity to work with Japanese master papermakers and English speaking assistants to learn the history and basics of papermaking. The workshop takes place in a restored traditional papermaker's house in a rural valley outside Mino. The workshop's tuition of ¥55,000 covers accommodations, meals and materials. Contact: **The CraftsLinks Washi Survival School**, *2485 Yatsubo-Warabi, Mino-shi, Gifu, 501. Tel. (0575)35-2504, Fax (0575)46-2739.*

UTATSU FIRE WALLS

*Mino's merchant houses have second floor fire walls called **utatsu**. While they began simply as a protection against spreading fire, increasingly ornate tile-roof structures capped the walls. Before long, only the well-to-do could afford to build them and they became an ostentatious show of wealth. The Japanese expression "Utatsu ga agaru," literally "He has built a utatsu," means he is doing very well financially.*

Mino Paper Village Hall (Mino Washi no Sato Kaikan). *Tel. (0575)34-8111. Open 9am to 5pm. Closed Tuesday, December 29 through January 3 and the day after a holiday. ¥500.* A gleaming concrete and glass structure erected in honor of paper, the hall is located 10 kilometers out of town necessitating a ¥3000 taxi or a 25 minute ride on an infrequent bus. The hall's dioramas show the stages of making *washi* paper by hand and displays show a small number of paper objects.

A child's craft section can keep your kids occupied, at least for a short while. And, in the basement, you can make your own paper. The good news is the signs are bilingual; the bad news is the place is too manicured and polished to convey the earthiness of making paper.

SHOPPING

Washi no mise, *Next to Imai House. Tel. (0575)35-1282. Open 10am to 6pm.* The shop sells Mino paper and lots of things made from it: five postcards for ¥400, Noguchi lampshades from ¥1000, magnificent *yuzen* patterned *washi* paper ¥1500. Stock up here on lightweight souvenirs.

18. KANAZAWA & NOTO PENINSULA

On the surface, **Kanazawa** looks just like any another medium-sized Japanese city. But its beautiful gardens, feudal-era buildings, excellent museums, delicious cuisine and thriving arts and crafts scene combine to make it one of our top destinations. Kanazawa also serves as the gateway to the **Noto Peninsula**. The rugged, wind-swept peninsula features remote fishing and farming villages and one of Japan's centers of lacquer production .

Planning Your Stay

Try to spend at least two days in Kanazawa. If you have the time, we highly recommend an overnight trip to the Noto Peninsula.

When to Go: Kanazawa is notorious for bad winter weather. When Siberian winds swoop down, you really don't want to tramp around gardens. From mid-June to mid-July is the rainy season. Summer heat rules out June through August. Prime times are April–May when lots of flowers are in bloom, and September–November when the autumn foliage is gorgeous. Bring your umbrella; it could rain any time of year.

KANAZAWA & NOTO PENINSULA HIGHLIGHTS
· *Strolling through Kenrokuen Garden*
· *Secret passages and intriguing devices at Ninja Dera*
· *Thriving craft traditions: gold leaf, ceramics, lacquer and yuzen dyeing*
· *Savoring a meal of Kaga ryori at Sugi no I or Otomoro*
· *Eating seafood just pulled from the Japan Sea*
· *Noto's windswept beaches and cliffs*
· *Browsing through Wajima's morning market*

KANAZAWA

Kanazawa, located on the Japan Sea coast, was home to the castle of the powerful Maeda feudal lords. This domain was called Kaga, a name you will hear again and again.

With all their wealth, the Maeda built a splendid city. Look at Ishikawa Mon, the solitary remaining castle gate, and the moat walls around it to get an idea of the scale of the castle. Kenrokuen, the garden built outside the castle walls, is one of the three finest in Japan according to the people who chronicle such things.

While Kanazawa had the good fortune to escape bombing during World War II, don't expect a perfectly preserved castle town. The modern parts of the city are not particularly distinguished. But historic areas of town lie in the shadows of up-to-date commercial centers, a pairing seen over and over in contemporary Japan. Kanazawa is a city where you can spend only one day, hit the highlights and still go away with a sense of its history or where you can spend a week savoring its offerings without getting bored. For the busy traveler, try to spend at least two days here.

Kanazawa still has a strong sense of history and culture which has been lost in many other cities. The artisans and craftsmen Lord Maeda imported from Kyoto created elegant and unique traditions in ceramics, textiles, lacquer, cuisine and gold leaf that still thrive. The appreciation of *noh* theater by common people is so strong that it is rare to attend a wedding in Kanazawa today where there isn't at least one relative regaling the happy couple with a *noh* chant.

Planning Your Stay

Try to spend at least two days in Kanazawa. If you have only one day in Kanazawa, here is our recommended route. Make sure you wear comfortable walking shoes and get an early start.

Morning: Ishikawa Mon Castle Gate, Kenrokuen Garden and Seisonkaku, Ishikawa Traditional Craft Museum, taxi or 20-minute walk to Sugi no I Restaurant for lunch.

Afternoon: Myoryu-ji Ninja Temple and Teramachi Temple District, Nishi Geisha District, Kutani Kosen Kiln. If you still have time and energy, see the Nagamachi Samurai District including Nomura Samurai House and Saihitsu-an Yuzen Dyeing Center.

If you have more than one day, here are some half-day itineraries that you can mix and match, depending on your interests and the weather:
• Ishikawa Mon Castle Gate, Kenrokuen Garden, Seisonkaku, Kanazawa Shrine, Ishikawa Prefectural Museum of Traditional Products and Crafts or Ishikawa Prefectural Art Museum.

- Myoryu-ji Ninja Temple, Teramachi Temple District, Kutani Kosen Kiln, Nishi Geisha District.
- Nagamachi Samurai District including Nomura House, Saihitsu-an Yuzen Dyeing Center and Kanazawa Shinise Kinen Kaikan, Oyama Jinja, Kanko Bussankan (Ishikawa Products Center) and Korimbo for shopping.
- Ohi Ceramic Museum, Terajima Samurai House, Higashi Geisha District, Utatsuyama.
- Yuwaku Onsen on the outskirts of Kanazawa for Edo Mura and Danpu-en. You can easily make this an all-day excursion.
- When the weather is perfectly awful or when museum fever strikes go to Ishikawa Prefectural Museum of Traditional Products and Crafts, Ishikawa Prefectural Art Museum, Ishikawa Prefectural History Museum, Honda Museum.

When you are in a shopping frenzy visit Kanko Bussankan (Ishikawa Products Center), Uesaka, then to Korimbo for contemporary shopping or to Omicho Market for local produce. Many of the shops listed below in *Shopping* are charming and have been in business for generations. See *Seeing the Sights* for detailed information on these places.

Dates to Remember
- **January 6: Kagatobi Dezomeshiki.** Men wearing only white loincloths and twisted white bands perform a special ceremony to begin the fire-fighting year. In the old days, the only way to prevent major fires was to pull down buildings to stop the fire from spreading. The *tobi's* job was dangerous — pulling down the highest part of the building. Today, the *tobi* is the star of the festival. He climbs high up on a pole doing acrobatics and splashing water. While *dezomeshiki* is performed all over the country, Kanazawa's is famous for its large scale. But remember, January is cold!
- **Mid-June: Hyakuman Goku Festival.** This festival celebrates Lord Maeda's entrance into Kanazawa on June 14, 1583. In addition to a large samurai parade with a TV personality dressed as Lord Maeda. other features include a grand tea ceremony party at Seisonkaku, free admission to Kenrokuen Garden and a torch-lit *takigi noh* performance in the park — the traditional equivalent of summer theater at Regents Park or a concert at Tanglewood.
- **Early November: Yukitsuri.** To protect them from wet, heavy snow, gardeners build rope and straw umbrellas over the pine trees in Kenrokuen Garden.

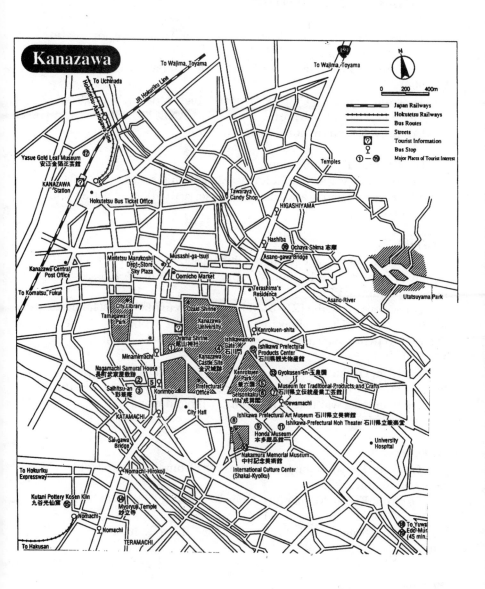

Kanazawa

ARRIVALS & DEPARTURES

By Air

Komatsu Airport is the closest airport, but Toyama airport is also convenient if you can't get a flight into Komatsu.

To/from Tokyo's Haneda Airport: 8 flights/day (ANA, JAL, JAS. ¥16,000)

To/from Sapporo's Chitose Airport: 2 flights/day (ANA. ¥26,900)

To/from Fukuoka Airport: 2 flights/day (ANK. ¥24,150)

JAL provides international service to Seoul.

For Ground Transportation:

Airport to City: Buses to JR Kanazawa Station meet every arrival (40 minutes, ¥1100). There is also frequent bus service to JR Komatsu Station (12 minutes, ¥260).

By Train

To/from Tokyo: take JR Joetsu shinkansen to Nagaoka (1 hour 40 minutes); transfer to a JR limited express *tokkyu* train to Kanazawa (2 hours 30 minutes, ¥13,470).

You can also take the JR Tokaido shinkansen to Maibara (2 hours 20 minutes). Not all *Hikari* shinkansen trains stop at Maibara, so inquire. Transfer to JR *Shirasagi* limited express to Kanazawa (1 hour 50 minutes, ¥15,270).

To/from Osaka and **Kyoto**: take JR Super *Raicho* limited express (2 hours 40 minutes; 2 hours 10 minutes respectively; ¥7240 and ¥6510).

To/from Nagoya: take a JR *Shirasagi* limited express (2 hours 55 minutes, ¥6930).

By Express Bus

To/from Tokyo: Seibu Bus, 4 buses/day from Ikebukuro Station (7 hours 30 minutes, ¥7840)

To/from Kyoto: Keihan Bus, 5 buses/day to Kanazawa (4 hours 20 minutes, ¥4060)

To/from Nagoya: Meitetsu Bus, 10 buses/day to Kanazawa (4 hours, ¥4060)

By Car

Kanazawa is located on the Hokuriku Expressway. We do not recommend that you drive in the city. The roads are crowded, difficult to navigate, not well marked in English and parking is expensive. You may wish to rent a car in Kanazawa and drive to the Noto Peninsula.

• **Nippon Rent-a-Car**: *JR Station. Tel. (076)263-0919*

• **Toyota Rent-a-Lease**: *1-3-10 Kanda. Tel. (076)241-0100*

GETTING AROUND TOWN

Kanazawa has an extensive bus system and a good bus map in English at the tourist office. Buses leave from the east exit of Kanazawa station. As you board a bus at the rear, take a paper ticket that designates your boarding zone; when you disembark at the front, pay the amount listed on a chart near the exit.

For ¥900 you can get a daily pass that entitles you to unlimited bus travel within the city; it isn't cost effective unless you use the bus frequently. If you plan on a lot of hopping around, purchase the pass on the bus or at the Hokuriku Bus Counter near the bus platforms at the east exit of JR Station. Ask for Kanazawa Free *Josha Ken*, which means you can get on and off freely at any stop! A loop bus called Kanazawa Historical Trail leaves from gate 10 and hits many of the sights. ¥200. Buses to Kenrokuen Garden leave from gate 11.

Taxis are plentiful and not too expensive since Kanazawa is fairly compact.

You can also rent bicycles; when the weather is good this is an ideal way to get around. Rent bicycles at the JR Station, both from **JR Rent-a-Cycle**, *Tel. (076)231-5075*, and **Hokutetsu Rent-a-Cycle**, *Tel. (076)263-0919*.

Tourist Information

A **tourist information desk** is located at Kanazawa JR Station next to JR's Green Window. An English speaker is on duty from 10am to 6pm to assist you and to make hotel reservations. *Tel. (076)232-6200*. Open 9am to 6pm. Excellent English maps and brochures are available.

Another tourist information desk is located on the first floor of the Kanko Bussankan (Ishikawa Products Center) near Kenrokuen Garden (see *Shopping*). Only Japanese is spoken, but English brochures and maps are available.

Goodwill Guides: The Kanazawa Goodwill Guide Network will provide English-speaking volunteer guides. Contact the Kanazawa Tourist Information Office at Kanazawa Station, *Tel. (076)232-6200*, or the JNTO Tourist Information Center in Tokyo, *Tel. (03)3201-3331, toll free 0088-22-4800*.

Bus Tours

There are bus tours in Japanese, but you are better off on your own unless you want practice in Japanese comprehension. If your time is extremely limited, you might consider a tour because you'll see a lot in a half-day. Tours leave from the Hokutetsu Teiki Kanko Bus Center close to the Kanazawa Miyako Hotel at the east exit of JR station, *Tel. (076)221-5011*.

Two of the more interesting offerings are:

The Kenrokuen Circuit: In four hours you see Oyama Jinja Shrine, Seisonkaku, Kutani ceramics, Nagamachi Samurai District and Kenrokuen Garden. Daily tours at 8:40am and 1:25pm except Dec. 28 to Jan. 3. ¥3000.

The Jokamachi B Circuit: you'll see Utatsuyama, Kenrokuen Garden, Ishikawa Prefectural Art Museum, Ninja Dera Temple and Ace Kanazawa in 3 hours, 50 minutes. Daily from March 20 through November 30. Tours at 1:55pm. ¥2600.

WHERE TO STAY

Numerous hotels, including some of the newest, are located in the station area. Although we have listed several, we prefer to stay closer to the center of town. While the Japanese-style inns are comfortable and lend a suitable atmosphere to your visit, we usually stay at a Western-style hotel so we can eat at some of Kanazawa's many restaurants.

ANA HOTEL KANAZAWA, *16-3 Showa-machi, Kanazawa, 920-8518. Tel. (076)224-6111, Fax (076)224-6100. 255 rooms. Singles from ¥9000. Doubles from ¥21,000. Credit cards.*

This large hotel located near the station has a high atrium lobby complete with fountains. The 19th-floor bar has great views of the city.

HOLIDAY INN KANAZAWA, *1-10 Horikawa-cho, Kanazawa, 920-0847. Tel. (076)223-1111, Fax (076)223-1110. Doubles from ¥16,000. Credit cards.*

The Holiday Inn is also close to the station. With all the comforts of home, it's like being transported to America. Frequent flier coupons from some airlines are accepted, and there's no additional charge for children in the same room as their parents.

HOTEL NIKKO KANAZAWA, *2-15-1 Hon-cho, Kanazawa, 920-0853. Tel. (076)234-1111, Fax (076)234-8802. Singles from ¥13,000. Doubles from ¥24,000. Credit cards.*

Kanazawa's newest hotel is near the station and part of JAL's luxury chain.

KANAZAWA NEW GRAND HOTEL, *1-50 Takaoka-machi, Kanazawa, 920-0864. Tel. (076)233-1311, Fax (076)233-1591. Singles from ¥8000. Doubles from ¥16,000. Credit cards.*

This comfortable hotel is centrally located — close to Oyama Shrine, Korimbo shopping area and walking distance to many sights. The 12th-floor restaurant is a fun place to have a drink and take in the views of the city around you.

RYOKAN MIYABO, *3 Shimo Kakinokibatake, Kanazawa, 920. Tel. (076)231-4228, Fax (076)232-0608. From ¥13,000 per person with two meals. Credit cards.*

Miyabo is an oasis of tranquillity in the center of the city. It has a beautiful Japanese garden and is noted for its Kaga cuisine served on lacquer dishes. Most of the buildings are from the Meiji era. Ask for a room in the older wing; they have more character.

KANAZAWA CITYMONDE HOTEL, *2-10 Hashiba-cho, Kanazawa, 920-0911. Tel. (076)224-5555, Fax (076)224-5554. Singles ¥9240. Doubles from ¥13,000. Credit cards.*

Situated close to Kenrokuen Garden, this hotel is a great value and is our first choice for a Western-style hotel in Kanazawa. The lobby overlooks a tea garden and the bright and airy rooms are reasonably spacious. The Ohi Ceramics Museum is next door.

NEW GRAND INN KANAZAWA, *3-7 Kenroku Moto-machi, Kanazawa, 920-0931. Tel. (076)222-1211, Fax (076)222-1591. Singles ¥6500. Doubles from ¥10,500. Credit cards.*

This well-situated, red-brick business hotel, a stone's throw from Kenrokuen Garden, is on a quiet side street. Its eclectic restaurant serves Japanese, Chinese and French fare.

RAPORTO KANAZAWA, *2-5 Kanazawa-machi, Kanazawa, 920-0936. Tel. (076)231-2000, Fax (076)231-2100. Western style: Singles ¥6930. Twins ¥11,550. Japanese style: ¥10,000 for two people without meals. Credit cards.*

This new hotel, run by Nippon Telephone and Telegraph, is tucked away behind the souvenir shops of Kenrokuen slope. With only 24 rooms, it is very quiet and the room size is adequate. The casual restaurant is good and reasonably priced. This is a good choice for an inexpensive, clean hotel in a excellent location, but be prepared for minimal English from the staff.

HOTEL ACTY KANAZAWA, *1-2-44 Katamachi, Kanazawa, 920-0981. Tel. (076)233-3900, Fax (076)233-3005. Singles ¥5800. Twins ¥12,000. Credit cards.*

Located behind the busy Korimbo crossing, this business hotel has the distinction of being well located and quiet. The rooms are fairly spacious. Friends who stayed here loved it. Hotel Acty is a good choice for the economy-minded traveler.

PENSION RASPBERRY, *22-24 Takaoka-machi, Kanazawa, 920. Tel. and Fax (076)223-0757. ¥5000 per person without meals. Dinner ¥3000; breakfast ¥500. Notify about meals when you make a reservation. Credit cards.*

The owners of this pension have spent a lot of time in Europe, and the place is popular with foreigners. A European home-style dinner costs ¥3000. The pension is conveniently located for an after-dinner stroll to the Nagamachi samurai district.

YOGETSU, *1-13-22 Higashiyama, Kanazawa, 920-0831. Tel. (076)252-0497. No fax. ¥6500 per person with two meals. ¥4500 per person without meals. No credit cards.*

Here is your opportunity to stay in a 100-year old *geisha* house. This small inn, located in the Higashi Geisha Quarters, has only five simple, but comfortable, rooms.

RYOKAN MURATAYA, *1-4-2 Katamachi, Kanazawa, 920-0981. Tel. (076)263-0455, Fax (076)263-0456. ¥4500 per person without meals. Member Welcome Inn Reservation Center and Japanese Inn Group. Credit cards.*

Centrally located in the busy Katamachi area, this inn is surprisingly quiet and comfortable. A member of the Japanese Inn Group, it goes out of its way to welcome foreigners. All the rooms are Japanese style. None of the 11 rooms has a private bath, but the shared facility is okay.

Yuwaku Onsen

About a 20-minute bus ride from Kenrokuen Shita bus stop is Yuwaku Onsen, a small, quiet hot spring village in the mountains. If we are staying in Kanazawa for several days, we enjoy a break from the hustle and bustle of the city for at least one night.

ATARASHIYA, *Yuwaku Onsen, Kanazawa, 920-1122. Tel. (076)235-1011, Fax (076)235-1024. From ¥18,000 per person with two meals. Credit cards only with prior arrangement.*

With its 250-year history, this quintessential Japanese-style inn is a real find. It was recently rebuilt, and the current structure is a low-lying building made of pale wood; it has only eight guest rooms. The staff is exceptionally accommodating and the food, served on a variety of beautiful ceramic plates, is expertly prepared by the owner-chef. This inn is one of the few we've stayed where they actually serve hot food piping hot and cold food well chilled. We enjoyed our stay here so much we've included it in Chapter 11, most memorable stays.

WHERE TO EAT

JR Kanazawa Station Area

HYAKUMAN GAI, *Kanazawa JR Station. Tel. (076)260-3700. Open 10am to 9pm.*

During the recent renovation of Kanazawa Station, an attractive two-part shopping arcade was added. Kanazawa-kan features restaurants, local crafts and food, and Trend-kan has clothing and accessories. There are 15 inexpensive restaurants where you can get lunch or dinner for ¥1000 — lots of plastic samples help with your selection.

DAIMYO CHAYA *(Regional Japanese, inexpensive to moderate). 7-5 Konohana-machi. Tel. (076)231-5121. Open 11:30pm to 2pm; 4pm to 10pm. Close to the Chuo exit of JR station, behind the Kanazawa Miyako Hotel.*

This popular and lively restaurant serves local Kaga specialties. Eat among displays of samurai armor, guns and swords. At lunch they have a samurai set for ¥1500 and at dinner a *karo* set for ¥4000.

WHAT'S COOKING IN KANAZAWA?

With its appreciation of the finer things in life, the Maeda clan did not neglect cuisine. The local cooking, called Kaga ryori (cuisine), relies heavily on fresh seafood and mountain vegetables. Kaga kaiseki, or formal dining, is not as delicate as its Kyoto cousin but is still beautifully arranged. By all means try Kaga fare; if you stay at a Japanese inn you will almost always get it for dinner. Located so close to the sea, Kanazawa also excels at sushi. Some regional specialties are

Jibuni stew: Duck or chicken is coated with flour, stewed with seasonal vegetables such as mushrooms, bamboo shoots and lotus root, and wheat gluten, soy sauce, sake and broth. The thick stew is served with wasabi horseradish.

Kabutoni: A healthy dish, red snapper fish is stuffed with okara (made from soy beans) and vegetables and then steamed. The shape of this dish resembles a kabuto, a samurai helmet. Traditionally it was served on Boys' Day, May 5, but now it is eaten on any auspicious occasion.

Kuzu kiri: The thin noodle is made from arrowroot and served with a sweet, molasses-like sauce.

Katamachi & Korimbo Areas

Katamachi is Kanazawa's dining and nightlife center. Some say it has the highest concentration of restaurants in Japan, which probably means in the world. Try anything from fast food to refined *kaiseki* and everything in-between. The department stores of Korimbo offer food floors where you can buy or sample just about anything; there's also a bevy of restaurants; many are inexpensive. Check out Korimbo 109 and Daiwa Department Store.

KABURAGI *(French–Japanese, inexpensive to moderate). 2-6-8 Katamachi. Tel. (076)233-2002. Open 11:30am to 2pm and 5pm to 10:30pm.*

East meets West in Kanazawa. French food (Japanized, of course) is served on Kutani ceramic plates. The lunch set is ¥1500 and dinner is from ¥3500.

CAPPRICIOSA *(Italian, inexpensive). B1, Toku Katamachi Building, 1-4-18 Katamachi. Tel. (076)260-8855. Open 11:30am to 9:30pm.*

When you tire of seafood and soy sauce, take a break with pizza or pasta. Part of a nationwide chain, Cappriciosa serves large portions; one bowl of pasta can easily serve two or even three people. Pasta costs about ¥1500 per bowl.

HANANURI *(Coffee, inexpensive). 1-1-51 Hirosaka. Tel. (076)231-6300. Open 10am to 6pm. Closed Wednesday. Close to the Korimbo intersection.*

In a modern setting, drink coffee and tea from elegant Wajima lacquer cups that sell for ¥25,000 and up in Tokyo department stores. It's a good place to come to revitalize yourself after a day of sightseeing.

Kenrokuen Garden Area

MIYOSHIAN *(Regional Japanese, inexpensive to moderate for lunch, very expensive for dinner). 1-11 Kenroku-machi. Tel. (076)221-0127. Open 10:30am to 2pm; 4:30pm to 8:30pm. Closed Wednesday.*

Miyoshian, a traditional wooden building in Kenrokuen Garden, overlooks a pond and is a glorious setting for lunch. Order a *Kaga obento* (box) lunch (¥1500 to ¥3000) or *jibuni* stew and other local favorites a la carte. Dinner, a much more expensive affair, requires a reservation and is limited to groups of eight or more, ¥15,000.

KENKEN OCHIN *(Regional Japanese, inexpensive to moderate). 2-37 Higashi Kenroku-machi. Tel. (076)222-1600. Open daily 11am to 9:30pm.*

Located at the top of the Kenrokuen slope and overlooking the city, this restaurant features Kaga cuisine. It serves a special box meal *(ochinhako bento)* in a three-layered lacquer set inspired by the Maeda's picnic lunches. Both the quality and quantity of food are good. Try the *yuzen* for ¥2500.

KINJORO KENROKUEN *(Regional Japanese, inexpensive to moderate). 2F. Kanko Bussankan, 2-20 Kenroku-machi. Tel. (076)222-5188. Open 11am to 6pm. Closed Tuesdays.*

A branch of a famous and very expensive Kaga-style restaurant, this shop in the Kanko Bussankan (Ishikawa Products Center) is reasonably priced and conveniently located. The plastic food displays make your selection easy. Set meals start at ¥1800.

HYOTEI *(Japanese-Western, inexpensive to moderate). 1F, Hokuriku Hoso Kaikan, 3-2-1 Honda-cho. Tel. (076)261-8788. Open 11:30am to 9pm. Closed Tuesday.*

This restaurant has large glass windows and gives you a bird's-eye view of the Honda family garden, which is closed to the public. It serves Western-style Kaga cuisine — eat special Noto beef with chopsticks. Set meals are from ¥2500.

KIKKO TEI *(Japanese, inexpensive). 2-5 Kenroku-machi. Tel. (076)231-2000. Open 11am to 3pm; 3pm to 5pm tea; 5pm to 9pm dinner.*

Tucked away behind the souvenir shops on Kenrokuen slope, we came upon this quiet, casual Japanese restaurant that's located in a small hotel, Rapporto Kenroku, run by Nippon Telephone (see *Where to Stay*). After many days of seafood, we found a welcome relief in the steak and tofu set (¥1900) and *toban* steak (¥2500). *Tempura, sashimi* and other Japanese fare are also served. Lunch starts at ¥750.

Musashi, Oyama-cho, Owari-cho Areas

OTOMORO *(Regional Japanese, expensive to very expensive). 2-27 Oyama-cho. Tel. (076)221-0305. Open 11am to 9pm. Reservations required.*

The chef, a descendant of Lord Maeda's cooks, takes great pride in preparing food the same way it was once cooked for the feudal lord. The restaurant is in a beautiful Japanese building; the handsomely displayed furniture has been in his family for generations. Using delicacies from the mountains and the Japan sea, Kaga cuisine is a treat that shouldn't be missed. Lunch is from ¥10,000 and dinner from ¥13,000.

KOTOBUKIYA *(Japanese vegetarian, expensive to very expensive). 2-4-13 Owari-cho. Tel. (076)231-6245. Open 12 noon to 2pm; 5pm to 8pm. Closed Tuesday. Reservations required one day in advance.*

Situated in the midst of the merchant area of this castle town, Kotobukiya is housed in an Edo-era wooden building that was once a kimono shop. In the 1920s, the founder, who apprenticed at a famous restaurant, decided to serve vegetarian Buddhist food so he wouldn't compete with his mentor. The chef prides himself on using as many as 50 different ingredients in a meal. Courses from ¥7000 to ¥12,000.

OMICHO SHOKUDO *(Japanese, inexpensive). Omicho Ichiba Market. Tel. (076)221-5377. Open 7:30am to 4:30pm.*

Located in the market, this place is a popular dining spot where rice is cooked on a traditional stove and fish is grilled over charcoal. For ¥1500 the Omicho *teishoku* gives you *sashimi*, vinegared vegetables, stewed vegetables, rice and *miso* soup.

SUSHI GEMPEI *(Sushi, inexpensive to moderate). Omicho Ichiba Market. Tel. (076)263-4349. 10:30am to 8pm. Closed Sunday and holidays.*

With only 11 chairs, this tiny shop almost always has a line because it serves some of the best *sushi* in town at reasonable prices. There are some unique rules: one bottle of beer or two flasks of *sake* per customer and no children allowed. The marks on the plate indicate the amounts per item that are tallied when you finish.

YAYOI SUSHI *(Sushi, inexpensive). Omicho Ichiba Market. Tel. (076)224-0841. Open 11am to 3pm; 5pm to 8pm, holidays 11am to 3pm. Closed Sunday.*

Some Kanazawa residents tell us Yayoi has the best *sushi* in Kanazawa. Our guess is that Gempei and Yayoi, both within the Omicho Market, will just have to slug it out. At lunchtime Yayoi serves *daimyo-don* (tuna and other fish on a bowl of rice) for ¥1500 and *ikura-don* (salmon roe on a bowl of rice) for ¥1200.

Teramachi Area

SUGI NO I *(Regional Japanese, moderate for lunch, very expensive for dinner). 3-11 Kyokawa Machi, between Sakura and Ohashi Bridges. Tel. (076)243-2288. Open from 11am to 2pm; 4pm to 10pm. Reservations necessary.*

If you're looking for a pleasant respite from touring the city, lunch here is a must. Located in a traditional wooden building, you can dine either on the first floor in a private room for ¥500 additional per person or on the second floor in a large *tatami* mat room that overlooks a private garden and the Sai River. We urge you to splurge; you'll feel like you're dining in your own private garden. Kaga cuisine is exquisitely presented on beautiful lacquer and ceramic dishes. A "Ladies Lunch" costs ¥3000 and a *bento,* with slightly larger portions, is ¥3500. Dinner runs ¥15,000.

Utatsuyama Area

ROKKAKUDO *(Japanese, inexpensive to moderate). 1-38-27 Higashiyama. Tel. 0120-005-115 (toll free). Open 11am to 10pm.*

This restaurant, high on a hill, has large windows overlooking the area's greenery. Steak set costs ¥1600, *Utatsuyama teishoku* ¥1900.

KANAZAWA'S ONE-MINUTE HISTORY

Kanazawa's history highlights its fierce local pride. During the Warring States period of the 15th century, farmers joined the militant Ikko (single-minded) sect of Buddhism and were ruled by priests for one hundred years around the time Columbus discovered America. This farmers' kingdom had low taxes and, as one of the few areas not under warrior control, escaped the great devastation of the era. Oda Nobunaga, the first of the three great unifiers, sent his best generals to subdue the area. One of his trusted assistants, Maeda Toshiie, was granted land on the Noto Peninsula. He went on to serve Oda's successor, Toyotomi Hideyoshi, who awarded him Kanazawa and the surrounding land. The Maeda's land holdings were increased after Sekigahara, the battle in 1600 that divided the feudal lords into winners and losers. Although Maeda forces did not participate in the battle, they ended up on the right side by supporting the Tokugawa. The Maeda clan ruled the area until the end of the feudal era in 1868.

The Kaga region, with Kanazawa as its capital, proved to be a fertile area, producing over one million koku (hyakuman goku) of rice annually. A koku is about five bushels of rice and is enough to feed one man for a year. After the city of Edo (Tokyo) – the Tokugawa shogun's home turf – Kaga was the richest domain in Japan. Kanazawa constantly reminds you of this proud fact – there is a Hyakuman Goku Street and a Hyakuman shopping arcade and a Hyakuman Goku Festival and on and on.

SEEING THE SIGHTS

Kanazawa has excellent museums, gardens, preserved districts and crafts. It is a city best seen on foot or by bicycle; walk the back streets and discover small alleys, earthen walls with lattice windows, intriguing shops and restaurants, quaint buildings and scenes of daily life.

Kenrokuen Area

Kenrokuen Garden. *Open 7am to 6pm March 1 to October 15; 8am to 4pm October 16 to February 28. Admission ¥300, free for seniors over 65. Kenrokuen-shita bus stop.* This large garden, Kanazawa's most famous sight, succeeds in attracting many visitors, so try to avoid a mid-day visit when the weather is nice. It's remarkable that the same place can look so different — peaceful and almost quiet — in early morning or late afternoon. These times are best unless you want to be with the throngs following their flag-carrying, megaphone-blaring guides. Despite this, Kenrokuen is a beautiful garden. Don't miss it.

Kenrokuen served as a garden outside the castle walls for the Maeda family, but it did not take its present form until the early 19th century. The fifth Lord Maeda built a villa on the grounds, but it burned down in 1759. The 11th Lord began to redevelop the area in 1774 and created the first waterfalls. His successor constructed a retirement residence in the southern part of the garden and asked a feudal lord from Tohoku to name it. This lord chose the name Kenrokuen after a Chinese poem that listed six attributes of a perfect garden: size, seclusion, technology, antiquity, fresh water and panoramic views.

There are some 5000 trees and who knows how many rocks; each one seems to have a history. The major points of interest are **Kotoji Lantern**, an unusual two-legged stone lantern that is the famous symbol of the garden and the city that you see on every poster; the **Korean Lantern**, a pagoda-like structure brought back from Korea during the 1590s invasion; and **Yugao-tei**, a thatched-roof teahouse with a red lacquered interior. The garden's most popular tree is *kiku zakura* or chrysanthemum cherry — one flower has several hundred petals — that is in full bloom in late April and early May. In winter, the pine trees are protected against the heavy wet snow by bamboo and rope supports called *yukitsuri*. They resemble straw Christmas trees.

There are six entrances to the park: Ishikawa Gate entrance is usually the preferred one, but it really depends on your itinerary.

Seisonkaku. *Open 8:30am to 4:30pm. Closed Wednesday, June 14 and December 29 through January 2. ¥600. Dewa Kokuritsu Byoin mae or Honda-machi bus stops.* Seisonkaku, located on the edge of Kenrokuen Garden, is a splendid villa in the *shoin zukuri* style that was built in 1863 by Lord Maeda for his mother. Sit in the reception room and imagine what a son

TECHNOLOGY & THE ART OF GARDEN BUILDING

*Although **Kenrokuen Garden** is situated on the top of a hill, running water for its ponds and streams is never a problem. The endless supply comes from a system established in 1632. A tunnel, bored through rock 10 kilometers up the Sai River, carries water to Kanazawa castle. The water made the castle relatively siege-proof, and it also helped increase the region's rice production – its basis of wealth – and offered some protection against major fires although you have to wonder how effective it was since there were seven major fires in the castle alone.*

Kenrokuen used this water system to fill ponds and create waterfalls, fountains and streams. The original pipe system, made of rocks with hollowed out centers, still supplies water to the garden. You can see some excavated stone pipes inside the gate of Oyama Jinja and outside the Ishikawa Prefectural History Museum.

he must have been. Obviously, no expense was spared for mama and although the building is no longer as large as it once was, it is it still very grand. The use of Dutch glass in some of the sliding doors is a fine example of the fascination for anything Western. Works of art collected by the Maeda family are on display.

Kanazawa Jinja Shrine is next to Seisonkaku. This small Shinto shrine was built by the 11th Lord Maeda and is dedicated to the god of education. At the shrine is a pond where, according to legend, a farmer saw gold floating in the water when he was washing potatoes. This tale has given Kanazawa its name meaning marsh of gold. Close by is the Plum Garden where 280 trees bloom in March.

Ishikawa Prefectural Museum for Traditional Products and Crafts. (Ishikawa Kenritsu Dento Sangyo Kogeikan). *1-1 Kenrokuen-machi. Tel. (076)262-2020. Open 9am to 5pm. April to November: closed 3rd Thursday; December to March: closed every Thursday; closed December 29 through January 3. ¥250 or a special bargain: admission to Kenrokuen and the Museum for ¥300. Dewa-machi Kokuritsu Byoin-mae bus stop.* Located on the border of Kenrokuen Garden, this museum has an excellent presentation of the area's crafts. And what crafts they are — refined and elegant lacquer, Kutani pottery, gold leaf, *yuzen* dyeing and on and on. Even giant Japanese fireworks are available but, unfortunately, there is no legal way to carry them back home. The museum's English brochure is a comprehensive introduction to the collection.

The museum lists a purchase price for each object on display although it does not sell it. Items are available in local stores and, you may be relieved to know that they are often at a more reasonable price than the one listed. You may also contact the appropriate craft guild to buy the desired objects — the museum has a list of the guilds.

Ishikawa Prefectural Art Museum (Ishikawa Kenritsu Bijutsukan). *2-1 Dewa-machi. Tel. (076)231-7580. Open 9:30am to 5pm. Closed December 24 through January 3. ¥350; an additional charge for special exhibitions. Dewa Kokuritsu Byoin mae or Honda-machi bus stops.* The museum houses an excellent collection of Kutani ceramics, samurai armor and art objects — many belonged to the Maeda. A pheasant-shaped ceramic incense burner, a National Treasure by a famous 18th century potter Nonomura Ninsei, is proudly displayed in a room by itself. Works by local artists are also shown. Each year the museum mounts several temporary exhibitions of both Western and Japanese art.

Ishikawa Prefectural Noh Theater (Ishikawa Kenritsu Noh Gakudo). *4-18-13 Ishibiki. Tel. (076)264-2598. Open 9am to 5pm. Closed Monday, holidays, and December 29 through January 3. Free admission. Dewa Kokuritsu Byoin mae or Honda-machi bus stops.* Lord Maeda's appreciation of *noh* was passed down to his minions, and Kanazawa's citizens have deep respect for the art form even today. This theater is the first built by a prefectural government, and the stage itself was moved from another site in Ishikawa. About one production a week is staged, but the theater is open for viewing at other times. Use the office entrance to the left of the main door when there isn't a performance. There's a small display of *noh* robes and masks. On Saturday evenings from June to September, the theater stages *noh* performances for ¥1000.

Honda Museum (Hanro Honda Zohinkan). *3-1 Dewa-machi. Tel. (076)261-0500. Open 9am to 5pm. Closed Thursday November through February and closed December 29 through January 2. ¥500. Honda-machi bus stop.* The Honda family had close connections to the Tokugawa shogunate and served as high-level advisors to the Maeda; the family's income was greater than many feudal lords'. This museum features their collection of samurai armor, firemen's clothing, bridal trousseaux and art works plus gifts from the Tokugawa.

Ishikawa Prefectural History Museum (Ishikawa Kenritsu Rekishi Hakubutsukan). *3-1 Dewa-machi. Tel. (076)262-3236. Open 9am to 5pm. Closed May 22 to 28 and at New Year's. ¥250. Dewa Kokuritsu Byoin mae or Honda-machi bus stop.* This museum, located in a distinctive Meiji-era red-brick building that was once an ammunition depot, features archeological as well as feudal-era objects and everyday items. Think of it as the prefecture's attic. You can even try on samurai armor.

Ishikawa Mon Gate. *Kenrokuen-shita bus stop.* The only castle gate extant is one of a few buildings of Kanazawa castle not destroyed by fire. The castle, one of the finest in Japan, looked invulnerable but it wasn't — there were seven major fires, none caused by war. The silver-painted roof tiles were made of lead so they could be melted down for ammunition. After destruction by fire earlier in the century, the gate itself was rebuilt in 1788. A long barracks for lower-ranking samurai also remains as do some impressive stone walls that hint at the grandeur of the original edifice.

Gyokusen-en Garden. *8-3 Kosho-machi. Tel. (076)221-0181. Open 9am to 4pm. Closed December 11 until early March. ¥700. Kenrokuen-shita bus stop.* Located down the hill from Kenrokuen Garden, Gyokusen-en is a good antidote for the crowds of its well-known neighbor. The small and tranquil strolling tea garden uses water from Kenrokuen and also borrows the larger park's scenery making it appear larger. For ¥500, you can enjoy green tea that's served to you while you enjoy a view of the garden.

Kaga Yuzen Industry Hall (Kaga Yuzen Dento Sangyo Kaikan). *8-8 Kosho-machi. Tel. (076)224-5511. Open 8:30am to 5:30pm. Closed Thursdays November 21 to March 20 and at New Year's. ¥370. Kenrokuen-shita bus stop.* Next to Gyokusen-en is a hall dedicated to *yuzen* dyeing. The first floor holds exhibits of *yuzen* fabrics, and craftsmen demonstrate how it's made. In the basement is a workshop where you can try your hand at the delicate painting.

Nagamachi Area

Nagamachi Samurai District features walls made of earth and stone topped with roof tiles. The tranquil atmosphere transports you back to the Kanazawa of 150 years ago. To confuse unwanted visitors, the streets don't run parallel. Although few of the homes are original, they do not detract from your walk along the old narrow roads and canals. By the end of the feudal period, the samurai were destitute and had no choice but to sell their land holdings. The Nomura family was no exception and sold the last of its land to a merchant in the late 1800s. He moved a house to the site that is now open to the public. The **Nomura Samurai House** is a typical samurai residence with a lovely garden. *Open daily, April to September 8:30am to 5:30pm; winter until 4:30pm. ¥500. Korimbo bus stop.*

Saihitsu-an Yuzen Silk Center. *1-3-16 Nagamachi. Tel. (076)264-2811. Open 9am to 12 noon, 1pm to 4:30pm. Closed Thursday and around New Year's. ¥500. Korimbo bus stop.* Close to Nomura Samurai House, Saihitsu-an demonstrates the *yuzen* dyeing process. The complex patterns, usually of flowers, birds and other natural designs, are hand painted on silk fabric. Children under 10 are not welcome.

Kanazawa Shinise Kinen Kaikan (Old Merchant House). *2-2-45 Nagamachi. Tel. (076)220-2524. Open 9:30am to 5pm. Closed Wednesdays and December 29 through January 3. Free Admission. Korimbo bus stop.* This recreated building is a merchant's shop and residence.

Oyama Jinja enshrines the first Lord Maeda, and the Hyakuman Goku festival parade begins here every June 14. Originally built on Mount Utatsu at the outskirts of the city, in 1873 it was moved to its present site. The peaceful garden is in the style favored by the famous early 17th century tea master, Kobori Enshu. The unusual Western-inspired front gate was originally a lighthouse and features five-colored stained glass designed with the assistance of two Dutch medical instructors in 1875. At the back of the shrine you'll find the east gate, originally from Kanazawa castle and dating from 1662. *Open 9am to 5pm. Minami-cho or Korimbo bus stop.*

Teramachi Area

Myoryu-ji Temple. *1-2-12 Nomachi. Tel. (076)241-0888. Open 9am to 4:30pm, until 4pm December through February. ¥700. Closed December 28 through January 2. Telephone reservations are required to tour the temple; if you come without one, ring the intercom to the left of the main building and if there is space they will fit you in. Tours are every half-hour and are only in Japanese. Korimbo bus stop.*

Although Myoryu-ji is nominally a temple, the third Lord Maeda, fearing an attack by the Tokugawa, really built it as a fortress, thus earning it the nickname Ninja-Dera. Myoryu-ji has nothing to do with ninja. It is an incredibly complicated structure with 29 stairways and four stories within a building that appears to have only two from the outside. At the time it was built, the Tokugawa shogun prohibited buildings taller than three stories. The top floor was a lookout tower and legend has it that the well had a tunnel connected to Kanazawa castle. There's a four-*tatami* mat room (an unlucky number) with a door that couldn't be opened from the inside; it was designed for Lord Maeda to commit suicide if all else failed — luckily it wasn't used. The Tokugawa never attacked the Maeda, but this temple shows how paranoid the Maeda were. Unfortunately, the tour is given in Japanese and the English pamphlet is very general, but you can still enjoy seeing the place and figure out most of the devices. For example, behind the altar there is a sliding door that leads to a hidden staircase. When the sliding door is closed, it locks the floor board so that you cannot gain access to the staircase. To avoid the hordes of tourists, either go early in the morning or late in the afternoon on weekdays.

Myoryu-ji is located in the **Teramachi Temple District**, one of two areas (along with Utatsuyama) where Lord Maeda ordered all non-Ikko temples to locate. Not only did this clustering protect against an Ikko revolt, but the temples also served as lines of defense against invading armies. Today, Teramachi is a quiet area with lots of old walls and gates, making for fun strolling. It is also very well marked with bilingual signs.

A few minutes walk away from Teramachi is **Kutani Kosen Pottery**, *5-3-3 Nomachi. Tel. (076)241-0902. Open daily 9am to 4:30pm. Closed New Years. Free admission. Nomachi bus stop.* This kiln is the only Kutani kiln in Kanazawa city; the others have relocated to Teraimachi in the suburbs. Observe craftsmen working on all aspects of Kutani pottery and, for a fee, you can paint your own. Your finished work is sent to you within a week. The shop has good quality work and some seconds are available at reduced prices. Kutani is too gaudy for us, but here they have some attractive simpler patterns of birds and flowers.

The **Nishi Geisha District** today is much smaller than its sister, the Higashi Geisha District, but some attractive two-storied wooden buildings are still actively used.

Nishi Chaya Shiryokan. *2-25-28 Nomachi. Tel. (076)247-8110. Open 9:30am to 5pm. Closed Wednesday and December 29 through January 3. Free admission. Korimbo bus stop.* The first floor features memorabilia of a local author and is of little interest to non-Japanese. But go inside to view the second floor's tea room with its elegant dark red walls and lacquered wooden beams. Surrounded by musical instruments, you may imagine a *geisha* entertaining customers even today.

Hashiba-cho

Omicho Ichiba Market, which dates back to the feudal period, prides itself on being the kitchen of Kanazawa. It's a great old-fashioned market; walk among the 200 shops selling tiny live eels, whole salmon, and assorted other fish, seafood, seaweed, vegetables, pickled radishes, tofu and local *sake*. Shopkeepers and chefs shop in the morning while locals and tourists arrive in the afternoon. If you get hungry, stop at Omicho Shokudo, Sushi Gempei or Yayoi Sushi (see Where to Eat.). *Open from early morning to evening. Musashi-ga-tsuji bus stop.*

Ohi Museum (Ohi Bijutsukan). *2-17 Hashiba-cho. Tel. (076)221-2397. Open 9am to 5pm. Closed at New Year's. ¥700. Hashiba-cho bus stop.* In the 1600s, Lord Maeda invited the tea master Sen Soshitsu to Kanazawa. Ohi Chozaemon, a Raku-style potter from Kyoto, accompanied him. Ohi began using a local clay and an amber glaze that is prized by tea connoisseurs. The tenth generation master, Chozaemon Toshiro Ohi, continues the tradition today. The museum, located in a contemporary building designed by avant-garde architect and film maker Teshigahara Hiroshi, lies beyond a traditional wooden building and a magnificently pruned old pine tree.

Terajima Samurai House (Terajima Oyutei). *10-3 Otemachi. Tel. (076)224-2789. Open 9am to 4pm. Closed Thursday, day after a national holiday and December 29 through January 3. ¥300. Hashiba-cho bus stop.* The well-preserved house and garden of a middle-ranking samurai gives you a sense of their life. Drink green tea overlooking the garden for ¥300.

Higashi Geisha District & Utatsuyama

Higashi Geisha District was a pleasure quarter licensed by Lord Maeda. Although some of the buildings are still used as *geisha* houses, don't expect neon lights and the garish atmosphere associated with modern entertainment districts. If that's what you're looking for, go to Katamachi. Higashi Geisha District is a quiet area with many old wooden buildings with lattice fronts. To see the interior of a teahouse, see the **Shima Geisha House.** *1-13-21 Higashiyama, Tel. (076)252-5675. Open 9am to 6pm. Closed Mondays and December 15 to February 28. ¥400. Hashiba-cho bus stop.* The inn Yogetsu is a former teahouse (see Where to Stay). Stop at **Sangen no Fukushima**, a *shamisen* shop where musical instruments used by *geisha* are made. *1-1-8 Higashiyama. Tel. (076)252-3705. Open 10am to 4pm. Closed Friday.*

On the hills of **Utatsuyama** are some 50 Buddhist temples, mostly of the Nichiren sect. They were moved here around 1600 at the request of Lord Maeda and, along with the temple community at Teramachi, served as a first line of defense against invasion. The area is a pleasant place to stroll or have a picnic lunch. Some of the notable temples include **Ryukoku-ji** where Miyazaki Yuzensai, the father of *yuzen* dyeing, is buried and **Zensho-ji**, the grave site of Shisetsu, the founder of the Kaga Hosho school of *noh*. Zensho-ji's gate was painted red, a color used only with the Maeda feudal lord's permission, because of Shisetsu's close association with the feudal lord. **Shinrensha** and **Kokaku-ji** have appealing gardens. Also on Utatsuyama is the **Utatsuyama Craft Workshop** where you can watch artisans at work as well as participate in one-day workshops. *Tel. (076)251-7286. Open 9am to 4:30pm. Closed Tuesday. Utatsuyama bus stop.*

JR Kanazawa Station Area

Kanazawa Yasue Gold Leaf Museum. *31-4 Kita-yasue. Tel. (076)233-1502. Open 9:30am to 5pm. Closed Tuesday, the day after a national holiday and December 29 through January 3. ¥300. Short walk from the Nishiguchi (West Exit) of JR Kanazawa Station.* This small museum, founded by a well-known gold-leaf craftsman, Koumei Yasue, shows the process of making gold leaf and displays objects made with gold leaf including screens, Buddhist altars, lacquer ware and ceramics. Enjoy a complimentary cup of tea with gold floating in it; we're told it's good for digestion.

KANAZAWA OUTSKIRTS

Edo Mura. *25 Yuwaku Onsen. Tel. (076)235-1111. Open 8am to 6pm April to October; 8am to 5pm November to March. ¥1100. Bus to Yuwaku Onsen* *from gate 10, JR Kanazawa station (¥550) and from Kenrokuen Shita stop. Get off at Hakuunro Hotel. Short walk up the hill.*

If you have more than a day or two in Kanazawa, take a bus out to Yuwaku Onsen; it is only a 20-minute ride from Kenrokuen Shita bus stop. You can stay the night at this hot spring village (see *Where to Stay*) or spend as little as a half-day visiting Edo Mura. The twenty structures of this open air museum were moved to the site and show the lifestyles of different social classes during the Edo period. As well as an inn that catered to traveling feudal lords, there is a house of a poor farmer and a merchant's house with a hidden second floor which was forbidden. Your admission fee also entitles you to enter **Danpu-en**, the sister museum of Edo Mura, which features traditional crafts in authentic buildings. A free shuttle bus transports you.

Teraimachi

Teraimachi, a town on the outskirts of Kanazawa, is the place to visit if you have a serious interest in Kutani ceramics. *A bus from Kanazawa JR Station takes one hour; and a bus from Komatsu JR Station takes 15 minutes.*

Teraimachi Kutani Ceramics Museum (Teraimachi Kutani Yaki Shiryokan) and **Teraimachi Kutani Ceramics Center** (Teraimachi Kutani Yaki Togeikan). *Open 10am to 5pm. Closed Monday and December 29 through January 3. ¥300 fee admits you to both.* The museum has an excellent collection of Kutani ware from early pieces to contemporary. At the nearby Ceramics Center, for a fee, you can paint your own Kutani piece that will be mailed to you after it's fired.

Kutani-yaki Danchi Kyodo Kumiai. *22 Izumidai Minami. Tel. (0761)58-6102.* Located nearby is a wholesale district that also sells to individuals. Prices of Kutani ware are usually lower than in Kanazawa.

SHOPPING

Ishikawa-ken Kanko Bussankan (Ishikawa Prefectural Products Center). *2-20 Kenroku-machi. Tel. (076)222-7788. Open 9am to 6pm. (Winter from 10am). Closed every other Thursday.*

This center is a good place to shop especially if your time is limited. Gathered under one roof are lacquer, gold leaf, Kutani from different kilns, *yuzen* fabric, baskets, paulownia wood crafts, sweets, *sake* and prepared seafood. Many of Kanazawa's well-known shops sell their products here. The second floor has an inexpensive restaurant, Kinjoro, serving Kaga cuisine (see Where to Eat). The center is located at the bottom of Kenrokuen slope; the area around it is crowded with souvenir shops.

Erihana. *34 Katamachi. Tel. (076)261-9188. Open 10am to 7pm. Closed Wednesday.*

Erihana features colorful *yuzen* fabrics. You probably won't spring for a kimono — prices begin at ¥1 million — but the small purses, handkerchiefs and quilting material won't break your bank and make nice gifts.

Moroeya. *1-3-22 Katamachi. Tel. (076)263-7331. Closed Wednesday. Open 9am to 8pm.*

A shop with a long history, Moroeya specializes in Kutani pottery and carries a range of styles from traditional to modern. The second floor has Kutani produced by well-known artists while the basement has Arita and Kiyomizu ceramics.

Kokuryudo. *1-4-10 Honcho. Tel. (076)221-2039. Open 9am to 8pm. Closed Tuesday.*

This shop, close to the JR station, sells a variety of Kutani ware, including works by young artists, and has reasonably priced small items like chopstick rests and teacups. Prices are relatively low since they buy directly from kilns.

Iwamoto Kobo. *15-43 Yasue-cho. Tel. (076)231-3627. Open 9:30am to 7pm. Closed Tuesday.*

Iwamoto Kobo sells saucers, hibachi braziers, vases and other objects made of paulownia wood. Families used to plant a paulownia tree when a daughter was born, and when she got married, made a charcoal brazier using the wood. Delicate designs are painted with lacquer on the surface. The family has been engaged in this traditional Kaga craft for four generations.

Sakuda Gold and Silver Leaf Shop. *1-3-27 Higashiyama. Tel. (076)251-6777. 9am to 6pm. Open daily.* A well-known shop for gold and silver leaf. They also have a small display in the Ishikawa Products Center.

Uesaka. *5-10 Kosho-machi. Tel. (076)264-1511. Open 9am to 6:30pm.*

Like Iwamoto Kobo, Uesaka sells paulownia wood crafts such as small chests and vases. Uesaka is close to the Ishikawa Products Center where it also maintains a small display.

Matsumoto Kamiten. *1-8-21 Katamachi. Tel. (076)262-8517. Open 9am to 6pm. Closed Sunday.*

This shop, which has been selling Japanese paper for 100 years, is a feast for the eyes. The colorful paper will remind you of kimono fabric. In addition to sheets of paper and stationery, they sell wallets and a variety of attractive items made from *washi* paper.

Tawaraya. *2-4 Kobashi. Tel. (076)252-2079. Open 9am to 6pm. Closed Sunday.*

Even if you are not interested in tasting the barley sweets sold here, stop in to see this old-fashioned shop. You can't miss the wonderfully photogenic indigo banner hanging outside the entrance; *ame* is written on it. *Ame* means sweets.

Tsuda Ume Mizuhiki Tokabo. *1-1-36 Nomachi. Tel. (076)244-0432. Open 9am to 6pm. Closed Sunday and holidays.*

The art of package wrapping is practiced seriously in Kanazawa. This shop makes the elaborate decorations that adorn presents, especially the auspicious gifts exchanged at betrothal ceremonies. Although we visit here to watch the staff adeptly make decorations, we usually end up buying special paper and silver and gold cords.

A NOTE ON KAGA CRAFTS

The wealth of the Kaga domain, ruled by the Maeda, was second only to the Tokugawa shogun's. The Maeda family passed down its strong interest in the arts from generation to generation and used its considerable fortune to introduce and nurture fine arts, performing arts and education. During the Edo period, Kanazawa, a regional city, was on a par with Kyoto in many artistic endeavors.

At the invitation of Lord Maeda, connoisseurs of tea ceremony, ceramics, kimono design, *noh* and other art forms came to Kanazawa; individual styles flourished. Originally, the Maeda controlled the production and distribution of some crafts such as ceramics and gold leaf, but they were to become the basis of local industry at the end of 19th century.

Kutani Ceramics

The origin of Kutani ceramics is shrouded in mystery. Local lore has it that Gojo Saijiro was sent by Lord Maeda to learn porcelain-making at Arita in Kyushu. In order to gain access, he married a local woman. After ten years he abandoned wife and child, returned to Kaga and established a kiln at Kutani, a small village outside of present-day Yamanaka Onsen. Today only the excavated kiln site remains at Kutani. The ware produced at Kutani, known as Ko-kutani (old Kutani), resemble Arita's. Despite this legend of Gojo Saijiro, there's a lot of speculation that early Kutani was really made in Arita because the shards excavated at the Kutani kiln don't resemble Ko-kutani ware.

The designs were mostly floral and bird patterns, often with geometrical borders. The kiln died out around 1700, coinciding with the death of Gojo Saijiro and financial difficulties the Maeda family faced at that time.

In 1806, Lord Maeda invited the well-known Kyoto potter Aoki Mokubei to reestablish a kiln. Aoki was expert in a number of different ceramic styles including blue and white, celadon, polychrome overglaze and gold enamel ware. A number of kilns sprang up at this time, but by mid-century they were again in decline. Then, toward the end of the 19th century, the opening of international trade revitalized the ceramics industry, which led to the wide popularity of a garish and ornately

decorated red and gold pottery in the West. This look became synonymous with Kutani.

Today, Kutani pottery production, centered in the suburban town of
Teraimachi, encompasses many different styles, much of it geared to the
mass market.

Yuzen Dyeing

Miyazaki Yuzensai, a Kyoto fan painter renowned for painting his
designs on fabric, was invited to Kaga by Lord Maeda. Yuzensai popularized the style named after him, but it's unlikely that he created the yuzen
dyeing process. These highly decorative silk kimono appealed to aristocratic taste.

An outline is drawn on silk fabric with washable blue ink. These lines
are covered with starch paste to keep them separated; next, dye is painted
inside the marked borders. The entire fabric is washed to get rid of the
starch paste and excess dye. In the old days the fabric was always rinsed
in the river, but today it happens infrequently; when it does, a crowd of
spectators gathers. Kaga yuzen uses deep colors and designs of flowers,
birds and other natural scenes realistically depicted — for instance, insect
holes are sometimes painted. Less expensive yuzen is stenciled, rather
than hand painted.

Gold Leaf

Today Kanazawa produces 99% of Japan's gold leaf. During feudal
times, the shogun restricted production to Kyoto and Edo (Tokyo). After
a major fire at Kanazawa castle, Lord Maeda secretly brought in artisans
to make the gold leaf needed for its reconstruction. Production remained
a secret until 1868, but, when the economy opened, gold leaf developed
into a vigorous local industry.

Making gold leaf is an eight-staged process that begins by mixing
silver and copper into the gold. The metal is rolled thinly, cut into small
pieces and beaten. Small squares are then placed between special sheets
of paper. A bundle of 1800 sheets is wrapped in leather and beaten with
a mechanical hammer. The resulting gold leaf, 1/10,000 millimeters
thick, is cut with an ingenious bamboo tool and is then ready to be used.
The gold is applied to screens, Buddhist altars, lacquer ware and ceramics.
Incredibly, one ounce of gold is pounded to the size of a tatami mat (90
centimeters x 1.80 meters or about 3 feet by 6 feet), but during the feudal
era when gold was even more valuable, it was pounded to the size of two
tatami mats.

NOTO PENINSULA

Jutting out into the Japan Sea northeast of Kanazawa, this large, windswept peninsula does a better job than most places of retaining a traditional way of life. Fishing, farming and lacquer-making are the main occupations. The rugged, wind-beaten western and northern coasts are sparsely populated while the calmer inner coast is home to more people as well as to built-up hot spring resorts.

You can make a long day trip from Kanazawa or spend a night or two rambling around the many villages, mountains and beaches. Spend most of your time in the smaller towns on the western and northern coasts and stay away from built-up areas like Wakura Onsen.

ARRIVALS & DEPARTURES

By Train

To/from Wajima: From JR Kanazawa Station take the JR Nanao Line to Wakura Onsen (55–100 minutes depending on the train, ¥1260 to ¥2710). Transfer to the private Noto Tetsudo Line to Wajima (64 minutes, ¥1120).

By Bus

To/from Wajima: From JR Kanazawa Station. 10 buses/day (2 hours, ¥2,100). Local bus service connects to towns on the peninsula.

By Tour Bus

Hokuriku Tetsudo, Tel. (076)221-5011, runs the Noto Hanto Teiki Kanko Bus (sightseeing bus) with a Japanese tour guide. If you can stand the tour guide's banter and being herded behind a flag, it is an easy way to see the area. The tourist office inside JR Kanazawa Station has an English speaker who can assist you with arrangements. Among the many options are

To/from Kanazawa: Express to Wajima for morning market, Wajima Lacquer Art Museum, Wajima Lacquer Center, Soji-ji Temple, Ganmon, Chirihama Beach. Depart Kanazawa 7:20am; return 3:30pm. ¥7200.

To/from Kanazawa: Chirihama Beach, Myojo-ji Temple, Ganmon, and Wajima. Depart Kanazawa 9:10am; return 6:10pm. ¥7400.

One-way tours

From Kanazawa to Wajima or Maura on Sosogi Coast: depart Kanazawa 9:10am; arrive Wajima 3:05pm (¥5400) and arrive Maura 4:05pm (¥6400).

From Wajima to Kanazawa: Several tours leave in the morning; taking different routes, they arrive in Kanazawa around 3pm.

By Car

Rent-a-car gives you the most flexibility in getting around the Noto Peninsula. Car rentals are available in Kanazawa and in Wajima. It takes about 2 to 3 hours to drive to Wajima. The Noto Hanto Yuryo Doro (Noto Toll Road) is fast and well marked in English, but we like to take smaller roads along the western coast. Follow the coastline, seek out small villages and partake of the essence of rural Japan.

Many of the smaller roads aren't well marked so a good bilingual map is indispensable. We recommend *Road Atlas Japan* available in English-language book stores.

SEEING THE SIGHTS

From Kanazawa to Wajima

Chirihama Nagisa Beach Drive: For seven kilometers between Imahama and Chirihama, enjoy the thrill of driving on the hard sand at the water's edge. Driving from Kanazawa, exit the Noto Yuryo (Toll Road) at Imahama. Turn left at the foot of the expressway, then left again when the road ends and right at the end of that road. Tour buses also go along the beach drive.

Keta Taisha is a Shinto shrine that dates from the 8th century. The present main hall was built in the 1650s. The oldest structure is a gate from the Momoyama period. The weather beaten buildings are more ornate than many Shinto shrines. Dedicated to the god of marriage, there are many plaques hanging that contain people's wishes for a good mate. ¥100. *By bus from JR Hakui Station.*

Myojo-ji Temple. This temple is the center of the area's Nichiren Buddhist sect and dates to 1294. Many of the present buildings, including a five-storied pagoda and main hall, were built by the third Lord Maeda in the 1600s to honor his mother. Today, ten buildings on the grounds are designated Important Cultural Properties. The temple has restored many buildings to their original forms by replacing tile roofs with multi-layered thin cedar shingles. Wooden cloistered walkways connect many of the buildings. Make sure you visit the garden; turn left at the bottom of the covered staircase and sit on the veranda overlooking the garden and the pagoda. ¥350. *By bus from JR Hakui Station.*

Noto Kongo is an outstanding scenic area of coastline with cliffs, beaches and spectacular rock formations. Take a boat ride through the area.

Soji-ji Temple was once the seminary of the Zen Buddhist's Soto sect. A huge fire in 1898 destroyed the temple; only Dentoin, a small building on the right of the main hall survived. The seminary moved to Yokohama after the fire; the rebuilt temple has a quiet, peaceful air. The celibate Zen Buddhist priests live communally.

Kami Ozawa is a small hamlet on the sea where picturesque fences made of entire bamboo trees protect houses against the strong winter winds. Don't miss this photo opportunity.

WAJIMA

Wajima, a center of high-quality lacquer production — one third of its 33,000 citizens work in the lacquer industry — is also known for its fresh seafood. The morning market is as famous as Wajima lacquer; friendly women sell fresh produce and seafood along Asa-ichi Dori. You can easily shop and eat your way through town. Wajima is small enough to see on foot or by bicycle, and you should try to spend one day here.

See *Arrivals & Departures* above, under Noto Peninsula.

Tourist Information

Tourist Information Office (Wajima Kanko Annai Center) is on the left as you exit the station. Open 10am to 6pm. *Tel (0768)22-1503.* No English is spoken, but they do have English maps and brochures and will make hotel reservations.

Bicycle Rental

Bike rentals are available at **Okina Rent-a-Cycle** located near the train station. *Tel. (0768)22-0300.*

Dates to Remember
• **April 4-5: Hikiyama Matsuri**: A spring festival when a lacquered float adorned with flowers is pulled through the streets.
• **July 31-August 1: Gojinjyo Daiko**: Wild masked drumming and dancing.
• **August 23-25: Wajima Taisai**: A portable shrine, accompanied by many giant paper lanterns, is paraded.

WHERE TO STAY

There are about 140 inns in the area; most are *minshuku*.

VIEW SUNSET MONZEN FAMILY INN, *29-58 Aza-Sendai, Monzen-cho, Keshi-gun, Ishikawa, 927-2351. Tel. (0768)42-2050, Fax (0768)42-2080. ¥12,500 per person with two meals.*

And now, for something completely different... The Noto Peninsula has lots of traditional rural architecture, but this hotel looks like a spaceship that has landed on a hill overlooking the Japan Sea. Designed by architect Mozuna Kiko, it is a welcome futuristic addition. The imaginative use of color and whimsical and inventive use of space makes this inn a great choice. A stunning pedestrian walkway with arched beams pairs steel plates with dark wood and has a slit window to view the sea. The Japanese-style rooms have innovative alcoves and curved doors. Definitely select a Japanese room, not a Western one. The hotel even has hot spring baths, both indoors and outdoors.

The only drawback is it is about a 30-minute drive from Wajima or a 30-minute bus trip (bus toward Monzen, get off at Minami Kuroshima) from Anamizu Station on the JR Nanao/Noto Tetsudo line. You can also take an express (*tokkyu* or *kyuko*) bus from Kanazawa Station heading to Monzen and alight at Minami Kuroshima (about 2 hours).

WAJIMA-SO KOKUMIN SHUKUSHA (Wajima Public Lodge), *49-21 Mitsuura-machi, Wajima, Ishikawa, 928-0067. Tel. (0768)22-2357, Fax (0768)22-8250. ¥6800 per person with two meals.*

A comfortable no-frills public lodge located near the beach at Sodegahama; some rooms have sea views.

HEGURA, *91 Kamimachi, Fugeshimachi, Wajima, Ishikawa, 928-0077. Tel. (0768)22-1018. Fax: (0768)22-1018. ¥7000 per person with two meals.*

Located in a house that once belonged to a lacquerer, Hegura is close to Sumiyoshi Shrine and the afternoon market.

YASHIKI, *15 Kawai-cho, Wajima, Ishikawa, 928-0001. Tel. (0768)22-0138, Fax (0768)22-5729. ¥12,000 per person with two meals.*

While this inn doesn't look like much from the outside, the interior has lacquered beams and pillars. The proprietor's lacquer ware collection is on display, and meals are served on Wajima lacquer ware.

WHERE TO EAT

HANANURI (*Coffee shop and regional cooking, inexpensive). Kawai-cho on Chuo Dori. Tel. (0768)22-0521. Open 8:30am to 5pm.*

Located inside the Wajimaya Honten building, this modern coffee shop is decorated in lacquer — the furniture, bar and even the phone booth. Coffee, tea and sweets are served on lacquer ware. We marveled over the attractive design and the lightness of our lacquer tea cups and mulled over buying a few until we learned they sell for ¥30,000. Hananuri serves a full meal of regional fare, exquisitely presented on lacquer dishes, but you must give them at least one-hour's advance notice to prepare the meal, ¥2800.

NOTO KICHI (*Regional Japanese, inexpensive to moderate). Asaichi Dori. Tel. (0768)22-6636. Lunch 11am to 2pm; Dinner 5pm to 8pm. Closed Wednesday, December 31 and January 1.*

This restaurant, an old family business, serves seafood on red lacquer ware. Lunch ¥2500. Dinner ¥3000. *Ishiri kaiyaki*, a Wajima specialty of seafood and vegetables cooked in a large shell at your table, costs ¥650.

NOTO NIKO *(Bakery, inexpensive). Ekimae Dori. Tel. (0768)22-4757. Open 7am-7pm. Closed Sundays.*

Located on the main street close to the station and across from the stone lantern store, this small bakery has delicious bread and products like sausage bread that make a tasty lunch.

YABU SOBA *(Soba, inexpensive). 4-45 Kawai-cho on Asaichi Dori. Tel. (0768)22-2266. Lunch 11am to 3pm; Dinner 5pm to 8:30pm. Closed Tuesday.*

In a traditional wooden house with lacquered pillars, beams and ceilings, this noodle shop uses special buckwheat grown in Noto and stone grinds the flour. *Seiro soba* is ¥650; *wanko soba* (noodles prepared five ways) costs ¥1600.

WARASHO *(Regional Japanese, inexpensive to moderate). 2-70-5 Kawai-cho. Tel. (0768)22-1140. Lunch 11:30am to 2pm; Dinner 5pm to 8pm. Closed Thursday.*

Serves Noto beef—its distinctive taste allegedly comes from the ocean wind. Lunchtime *sawarabi bento* serves seasonal fare for ¥1000; at dinner, the *Asaichi* course includes steak and seafood for ¥3000. The sign in the window says "Coffee and Beef" in English.

SEEING THE SIGHTS

Asaichi (Morning Market). *Open daily 8am to 12 noon. Closed on the 10th and 25th of each month and January 1 to 3.* Local women, their heads covered by scarves to protect against the sun and the wind, sell fish, seafood, flowers, seaweed, vegetables, pickles, sweets and simple handicrafts. Although the market has become increasingly touristy, it keeps its local flavor and is fun to browse around. Come before 10am when the tour buses arrive from Kanazawa. The stores on the street open at 8am also.

Yuichi (Evening Market) *is held near Sumiyoshi Shrine from 3pm until sunset.* This local market sells fish, seafood and produce.

Ishikawa Wajima Lacquer Museum (Ishikawa-ken Wajima Urushi Bijutsukan). *Tel. (0768)22-9788. Open 9am to 5pm. Closed December 29 to 31. ¥600.* Designed in the style of the Shosoin, a famous imperial storehouse in Nara, the museum displays masterpieces of Wajima lacquer as well as contemporary designs and lacquer from other Asian nations.

Wajima Lacquer Center (Wajima Shikki Kaikan). *Tel. (0768)22-2155. Open 8:30am-6pm. ¥200.* Located in central Wajima, this drab building has shops on the first floor that sell lacquer. The second floor houses a museum showing the history of Wajima lacquer from the 16th to 19th centuries. Come here only if you don't get to the Ishikawa Wajima Lacquer Museum.

Kiriko Kaikan. *Tel. (0768)22-7100. Open 8am to 5pm. ¥500.* Like many other places where the summer is short but sizzling hot, the Noto

Peninsula is famous for its summer festivals. In Wajima the giant lanterns are lacquered. You can see them year round, and videos recreate the excitement of an actual festival.

Gojinjyo Daiko Drumming. Noto was one of the few areas not under feudal rule — the farmers had strong autonomy. Attacked by a warlord in the late 16th century, the relatively defenseless villagers donned ferocious masks, covered their hair with seaweed and drummed wildly, scaring away the enemy. *This dance is reenacted July 31 and August 1 at Nafune Hakusan Shrine. April through October performances are held in the Wajima Bunka Kaikan near the train station at 8:45pm, ¥600.*

Cosmopolitan Museum. As you walk along Asaichi Dori, the morning market street, you cannot help but notice a garish Georgian-style building breaking the rhythm of the sedate, mostly wooden architecture. We do not know why the town fathers allowed such an audacious monstrosity to be constructed and only assume it has to do with the power of its owner, Inachu, one of the largest lacquer companies. Inside you'll find lacquer from all over the world; we think it's skippable.

SHOPPING

Most shops in Wajima are open from 8am to 5pm. The shops of the three major lacquer companies are:

Wajimaya Honten. *Kawai-cho, Chuo Dori. Tel. (0768)22-0521. Open 8am to 5pm.*

Traditional and modern designs including contemporary coffee cups at prices to knock your socks off — how about one cup and saucer for ¥32,000?

Omukai Koshudo. *6-45 Futatsuya-cho. Tel. (0768)23-1315. Open 8am to 5pm.*

On the outskirts of town, this large and bright showroom features both contemporary and traditional designs. Observe the craftsmen at work on the second floor. Cross the Futatsuya Bashi Bridge, turn left and the showroom is on your left.

Inachu. *2-245 Kawai-cho. Tel. (0768)22-2300. Open 8am to 5pm (summer until 6pm).*

Located in a traditional building at the center of town, most of the ware is tourist oriented. You can view craftsmen at work. Inachu has another shop next to Kiriko Kaikan Hall.

Washi no Hanaya. *Asaichi Dori. Tel. (0768)22-8409.*

This shop features handmade Japanese *washi* paper, masks and other objects made from paper. We couldn't resist buying lamps and vases made from *washi* paper embedded with flowers.

WAJIMA LACQUER WARE

Lacquer ware has been so closely associated with Japan that another name for it is Japanning. In this sense, Wajima is the center of Japan for it has been producing high-quality lacquer ware for over 500 years. Wajima lacquer's reputation is matched by its prices – this is not the place to pick up cheap souvenirs to take home.

Lacquer, the sap from the urushi or lacquer tree, is adhesive, yet provides a durable surface when dried.

Making lacquer ware is a highly cooperative process involving many artisans. First the wood core is shaped, usually on a lathe. Less expensive lacquer has a compressed wood or even plastic base. A ribbon of linen glued with lacquer reinforces the brittle edges. An undercoating is applied to the base and then layer upon layer of lacquer – as many as 150. Finally, the piece may be decorated using the maki-e or chinkin technique.

For maki-e, a design on the surface of the object is painted with lacquer and then gold or silver dust is sprinkled on it. For chinkin, a design is etched in lacquer that is covered with gold leaf.

Wajima is a very traditional place; most of the objects follow classic designs although a small but growing number of artisans are experimenting with contemporary design. They must be doing something right because young people are flocking to learn the craft, a rarity in contemporary Japan.

Don't leave Wajima without seeing lacquer ware being made. Actually, it is hard to avoid. The big stores such as Inachu and Omukai Koshudo have their craftsmen working behind glass so you can observe the entire process.

Quai. *1-7-13 Kawai-cho. Tel. (0768)22-8685. Open 9am-5:30pm.*

A wonderful shop featuring beautiful contemporary lacquer ware and ceramics made according to traditional techniques. The stark displays made us think we were in a tiny art gallery. Make sure you see some of the best of modern Wajima ware as well as rustic Suzu pottery made further up the Noto Peninsula. Prices for their exquisite pieces are high — chopsticks start at ¥7000.

Tefu Tefu. *Asaichi Dori. Tel. (0768)22-6304. Open 8am-5pm.*

Run by the same people as Quai, we really enjoy browsing in this cluttered folk art shop. Tefu Tefu carries its own line of lacquer ware as well as textiles, baskets and ceramics.

Okuda Shikki Ten. *1-28 Kawai-cho. Tel. (0768)22-0770.*

Across from Quai, this shop looks like many of the lacquer retail shops in town, but it has a tasteful selection at reasonable prices. We bought so many things here, we had to ship them back to Tokyo.

EXCURSIONS & DAY TRIPS
HEGURA-JIMA

If Noto isn't remote enough for you, take the 1 hour 50 minute ferry ride to **Hegura-jima** (Hegura Island), an island where female divers collect abalone and migratory birds gather. There are modest *minshuku* on the island if you wish to stay over night. *The ferry leaves Wajima at 8:30am and departs Hegura at 2:30pm; 1pm November through March; ¥3040 round trip. Hegura Line Co. Tel. (0768)22-4381.*

FARTHER ALONG THE NOTO PENINSULA

Continuing from Wajima along Outer Noto, the following are our recommended stops:

Mii. Several kilometers south of Wajima on the road to Anamizu and a stop on the Noto Tetsudo Train is a small town called Mii. One section is a hamlet of many thatched-roof houses. While it looks like it came out of a movie set, this is really an active, living community.

Senmaida. Between Wajima and Sosogi is Senmaida, the site of the famous 1000 terraced rice paddies. They cascade down the mountain to the water's edge and are reminiscent of Bali. For all the talk of the scarcity of land, Senmaida is one of the few places in Japan where farmers terrace rice paddies.

Sosogi. There are two distinctive houses here: Kami Tokikuni House, and Shimo Tokikuni House. They belong to descendants of the Taira clan who fled here in 1185 after a disastrous loss to the rival Genji. **Kami Tokikuni House**, *Tel. (0768)32-0171. Open 8:30am to 5pm; until 6pm April through September. ¥400.* **Shimo Tokikuni House**, *Tel. (0768)32-0075. Open 8:30am to 5pm. ¥400.* Shimo Tokikuni House, the oldest building on the Noto Peninsula, is designated an Important Cultural Property.

Suzu. Around the point of the peninsula is the home of Suzu ceramics, a rustic-looking unglazed pottery. A dedicated group of potters is reviving this tradition. The **Suzuyaki Shiryo-kan** (Suzu Pottery Museum) is a small pottery gallery; next door is a pottery studio and showroom. If you want to stay overnight here, try **SAKAMOTO RYOKAN**, *Uedo Machi, Jisha, Suzu, Ishikawa 927-1216. Tel. (0768)82-0584. No fax. ¥13,000 per person with two meals. Between October 1 and November 10, the inn serves a special local matsutake mushroom dinner that raises the rate to ¥23,000. No credit cards.* This small inn only has two rooms and a wide reputation for excellent food prepared by the chef-owner. You can have lunch and dinner without spending the night, but you must make reservations.

Suzu is the terminus of the Noto Tetsudo train to Wakura Onsen from where you can catch a JR train back to Kanazawa.

19. NAGOYA & ENVIRONS

NAGOYA

Nagoya, a city of 2 1/2 million, claims the title of Japan's fourth largest city and has been the crossroads between eastern and western Japan for centuries. Like many Japanese industrial centers, the city itself isn't of prime interest to the casual visitor. But the **Tokugawa Museum** features one of the best art collections in the country and the revitalized port is home to an excellent aquarium.

Nagoya provides a gateway to **Inuyama**, site of one of Japan's few original castles and home to an outstanding open air museum featuring Meiji era architecture; **Ise**, home of Japan's most sacred Shinto shrine; and **Hikone**, another original castle. You'll find good food in Nagoya, especially local chicken, *kishimen* noodles and *sukiyaki,* using premium Matsuzaka beef raised nearby.

Nagoya borders Japan's two large plains: Kanto, with Tokyo as its center, and Kansai, with Osaka/Kyoto as its center. Always caught between the two, Nagoya people have developed a reputation for keeping their thoughts to themselves and for being ruthless in business. Other Japanese consider Nagoya folk ostentatious, symbolized by the gold dolphins on the top of the castle.

The three great leaders of the 16th century, who unified Japan after centuries of chaos, all came from this area. The first Tokugawa shogun,

NAGOYA AREA HIGHLIGHTS
· *Nagoya, home to the Tokugawa Museum*
· *Japan's 1200 year old sacred shrine, Ise*
· *Graceful Hikone Castle overlooking Lake Biwa.*
· *Inuyama Castle, the only privately owned castle in Japan*
· *The Western-style buildings in Meiji Mura, an open air museum*

Ieyasu, built a castle in Nagoya for his seventh son. Tokugawa descendants ruled the area until the end of the feudal era, 1868.

Planning Your Stay

One day in Nagoya is enough for most people. Castle aficionados should make time to see Inuyama and Hikone, a half-day each. Meiji Mura takes a full day to see. Ise, the most sacred Shinto shrine in Japan, is an hour and a half from Nagoya — you will need one day to see it.

Tailor your trip around your interests as follows:
- **Castles**: Inuyama, Hikone, and Nagoya
- **Shrines**: Ise Grand Shrines
- **Crafts**: Indigo tie-dyed textiles at Arimatsu
- **What Happened when East met West?**: Meiji Mura Open Air Museum
- **Art**: Tokugawa Museum.
- **Industrial Japan**: Toyota Museum, Toyota Commemorative Museum of History and Technology, Noritake China Center
- **Good eats**: Chicken and *kishimen* noodles in Nagoya, Matsuzaka beef

ARRIVALS & DEPARTURES

Nagoya Airport offers flights to and from all over Japan. From the Osaka or Tokyo regions, the shinkansen train service is the best bet.

By Air

Service to/from Akita, Aomori, Fukuoka, Fukushima, Hakodate, Hanamaki, Kagoshima, Kumamoto, Kushiro, Matsumoto, Miyazaki, Nagasaki, Naha, Niigata, Oita, Sapporo, Sendai, Takamatsu, Tokushima, Toyama, Yonago and Yamagata.

For Ground Transportation:
Bus: to Nagoya Station (30 minutes, ¥870)
Taxi: to Nagoya Station (25 minutes, ¥4500)

By Train

To/from Tokyo: shinkansen train (2 hours, ¥10,380)
To/from Osaka: shinkansen train (1 hour, ¥6180)
To/from Takayama: limited express train on the Takayama Honsen line (2 1/2 hours, ¥5670)

By Bus

To/from Tokyo: frequent buses from Tokyo Station (6 hours, ¥5100)
To/from Kyoto: frequent buses from Kyoto Station (2 1/2 hours, ¥2500)
To/from Osaka: frequent buses from Osaka Station (3 hours, ¥2900)

GETTING AROUND TOWN

You'll find Nagoya fairly easy to navigate. The streets form a grid pattern, and the subway is fast and efficient. In addition to JR, the extensive Meitetsu train and bus system also serve the greater Nagoya area.

Meitetsu Nice Day Pass

The Meitetsu Company issues a two-day pass for their train, Nagoya Railroad, and six bus companies. Costing ¥3000, the pass is convenient for seeing Nagoya-area sites such as Inuyama, Gujo Hachiman and Toyoto City. The pass is not convenient for getting around Nagoya itself and is not good on the JR, Kintetsu and subway trains. Only foreign passport holders are eligible. Purchase the pass at Nagoya Airport and the Meitetsu Travel Centers at Nagoya Station and Shin Nagoya Station. You need your passport to obtain the pass. The pass also entitles you to discounts at some hotels and tourist attractions.

Tourist Information

JR Nagoya Station Tourist Information Office, an "i" information office, is in the central concourse. *Tel. (052)541-4301.* Open 9am to 7pm. Closed December 29 through January 1.

The **Nagoya International Center** also has tourist information on the 3rd floor, Nagoya Kokusai Center Building, 1-chome, Nagono, Nakamura-ku, Nagoya. *Tel. (052)581-5678.* Open 9am to 8:30pm. Closed December 29 through January 3.

Home Visit: Contact the **Nagoya International Center**, *Tel. (052)581-5689*, between 9am and 5pm except Monday to arrange a visit to a Japanese home.

WHERE TO STAY

NAGOYA HILTON, *1-3-3 Sakae, Naka-ku, Nagoya, 460-0008. Tel. (052)212-1111, Fax (052)212-1225. Singles from ¥19,000. Twins from ¥28,000. Credit cards.*

The centrally located Hilton is a full-service, top-of-the-line hotel catering to business executives. You'll find a good health club and lots of restaurants.

MARRIOTT ASSOCIA HOTEL. *1-1-4 Meieki, Nakamura-cho, Nagoya 450-6002. Tel. (052)584-1111. Fax (052)584-1114. Singles from ¥17,000. Doubles from ¥24,000. Credit cards.*

Nagoya's newest hotel towers over Nagoya Station. The 52-floor building holds 780 guest rooms, a large conference center and numerous restaurants, some with mind-boggling views. The hotel caters to business travelers with a fully equipped business center and fitness facilities.

HOTEL NAGOYA CASTLE, *3-19 Hinokuchicho, Nishi-ku, Nagoya, 451-8551. Tel. (052)521-2121, Fax (052)531-3313. Singles from ¥13,000. Twins from ¥24,000. Credit cards.*

This elegant hotel lives up to its name and has good views of Nagoya Castle. While not as centrally located as the Hilton, the subway provides convenient access.

HOTEL CASTLE PLAZA, *4-3-25 Meieki, Nakamura-ku, Nagoya, 450-0002. Tel. (052)582-2121, Fax (052)582-8666. Singles from ¥8500. Doubles from ¥15,000. Credit cards.*

Located near Nagoya Station, the Castle Plaza offers good value for a midrange hotel. The indoor pool and health club facilities make it stand out.

PETIT RYOKAN ICHIFUJI, *1-7 Saikobashi Dori, Kita-ku, Nagoya, 462-0818. Tel. (052)914-2867, Fax (052)981-6836. Singles from ¥4800. Doubles from ¥8400. Credit cards. Members of Japanese Inn Group and Welcome Inn Reservation Center.*

An enthusiastic young couple runs this small inn, which is just a three-minute walk from the Heian Dori subway station on the Meijyo line. Nine rooms are Japanese style; one is Western style. None has private baths, but the inn has nice touches like a cypress wood bath tub. They serve extremely reasonably priced breakfasts (¥500) and dinners (¥1500).

WHERE TO EAT

MISO NO SUGIMOTO *(Sukiyaki and shabu-shabu, inexpensive to moderate). 1-7-16 Sakae, Naka-ku. Tel. (052)202-1129. Open 11:30am to 2pm; 5pm to 9pm. Open only for dinner on holidays. Closed Sunday and December 29 through January 4. Fushimi subway station.*

Whenever we are in Nagoya, we try to eat the delicious *sukiyaki* that's made with premium Matsuzaka beef. Choose to sit either at tables and chairs on the first floor or on *tatami* mats on the second. The menu is less expensive on the first floor. Lunchtime *sukinabe* costs ¥1500; steak lunch is ¥2000. At dinner, *shabu-shabu* runs ¥5000 and *sukiyaki* ¥6000.

MA MAISON *(Western, inexpensive). Marunouchi branch: 3-23-31 Marunouchi, Naka-ku. Tel. (052)231-2871. Sakae branch is on Sakura Dori near Otsu Street. Tel. (052)971-2260. Open 11:30am-2pm; 5pm-10:30pm. Closed for lunch on Wednesday.*

Eat at this cozy, Western-style restaurant for a change from Japanese food. The "A" lunch set includes entree, bread or rice and coffee and costs ¥840. "B" costs ¥1260 but also includes salad and dessert. The eclectic menu has spaghetti (we like the garlic spaghetti for ¥900), pizza, gratin casseroles and a delicious beef stew for ¥1500.

KAWAIYA *(Regional noodles, inexpensive). 31 Iida-machi, Higashi-ku. Tel. (052)931-0474. Open 11am to 2:30pm; 5pm to 7:30pm. Closed Sunday and* *national holidays. Take the #8 bus from JR Nagoya Station and get off at Iida-machi.*

Try Nagoya's famous flat *kishimen* noodles that resemble *fettuccini*. Kawaiya's delicious *kishimen* is a bargain at ¥500. If you don't want your noodles plain, order the *ebi oroshi kishimen,* noodles with shrimp *tempura* and grated *daikon* radish. ¥1200.

TORIGIN (*Yakitori, inexpensive to moderate*). *1F, Miyaki Building, 3-14-22 Nishiki, Naka-ku. Tel. (052)951-1184. Open 5pm to 11pm. Closed 2nd and 3rd Sundays and national holidays.*

Torigin is an excellent place to eat Nagoya-style *yakitori,* using special chickens called Nagoya *cochin.* This restaurant serves some 30 varieties of *yakitori.* Order the *cochin zanmai* set, an extensive meal for ¥4900. A la carte, three sticks of *yakitori* cost ¥750. Even if you don't like chicken, their's is so tasty, you'll be converted.

SEEING THE SIGHTS

Nagoya Castle, the city's most famous sight, has been home to some pretty powerful people. Originally the Imagawa family built a castle in the early 16th century, but Oda Nobunaga made it his residence before building his masterpiece at Azuchi. Tokugawa Ieyasu built a castle in 1612 to protect eastern Japan from attacks by the feudal lords of Western Japan. Ieyasu gave the castle to his seventh son, Yoshinao. The massive stone walls actually have signs identifying stones "donated" by various feudal lords.

Bombing raids during World War II leveled the castle; only three turrets and the massive stone walls are original. Unfortunately, when the city of Nagoya rebuilt the keep in 1952, no attempt was made to reconstruct its interior according to the original plan. And somehow the elevator doesn't fit. The keep houses a museum with hundreds of objects from the original castle. If you haven't been in other castles, plan to visit and enjoy the fabulous view from the top floor. Nagoya adopted the huge gilded *shachi* (dolphins on the roof) as its symbol. *Tel. (052)231-1700. Open 9am to 4:30pm. ¥500. From Nagoya Station take the subway two stops to Sakae and change trains; go one stop to Shiyakusho, then walk about five minutes.*

In front of Nagoya Castle lies the new **Nagoya Noh Theater**. You can browse around 9am to 7pm. Check at the theater or with the Tourist Information Office for performance dates. *Tel. (052)231-0088.*

It's well worth a trip to Nagoya to see the **Tokugawa Art Museum's** excellent collection. The museum is on the site of the residence of the Tokugawa's chief retainer, which is where the Tokugawa family lived after the Meiji Restoration in 1868. You'll find all sorts of treasures belonging to the Tokugawa family including samurai armor, documents, lacquer ware, *noh* masks, elegant kimono, and paintings. The 12th century *Tale of*

Genji scrolls are masterpieces of Japanese art; reproductions are usually displayed because of the fragility of the originals. You get a pretty good idea of the kind of life the shogun enjoyed: the austere audience room is a big contrast to his private room decorated with lacquered furniture ornately sprinkled with gold. The museum has a *noh* stage, a replica of the one at Ninomaru, the private residence of the shogun. *Tel. (052)935-6262. Open 10am to 5pm. Closed Monday and at New Year's. ¥1200. Take bus #7 bus from JR Nagoya Station to Shindeki-machi stop (about 20 minutes), then a three-minute walk.*

One of Nagoya's newest museums is the **Nagoya/Boston Museum of Fine Arts,** displaying exhibits from the museum's sister institution, Boston's Museum of Fine Arts. *Open 10am to 5pm. Closed Monday. 1-1-1 Kanayama-cho, Naka-ku, Nagoya. Tel. (052)684-0786. Kanayama Station. ¥1200.*

Nagoya is famous for its ceramics industry. For a change of pace, visit the **Noritake China Craft Center** just a few blocks north of JR Nagoya Station. They conduct craft center tours in English weekdays at 10am and 1pm. To make reservations (English is spoken), *call (052)561-7114. 3-1-36 Noritake-Shinmachi, Nishi-ku.*

Near Noritake is Toyota's monument to manufacturing, the huge **Toyota Commemorative Museum of History and Technology**. In the early 20th century, the building served as the home of Toyota Spinning and Weaving. It's a mandatory stop for technology enthusiasts. *Open 9:30am to 5pm. Closed Monday and December 29 through January 4. ¥500. Tel. (052)551-6111. Three-minute walk from Meitetsu Sakou Station or take a bus from gate #10 at Nagoya Station and get off at Noritake Shinmachi stop.*

The **Toyota Museum** (Toyota Hakubutsukan) on the outskirts of Nagoya should satisfy the appetite of even the most enthusiastic car fans. Over 100 autos from the earliest to the futuristic are here for your inspection. *Open 9:30am to 4:30pm. Closed Monday. ¥1000. Take the Higashiyama subway line to Fujigaoka. Change for the bus to Nagakute Shako at gate #2 and get off at the last stop.*

The city of Nagoya has been working hard to revitalize its waterfront; reach it by taking the subway to Nagoyako station and walking for seven minutes. The port has the excellent, futuristic **Nagoya Public Aquarium** (Nagoyako Suizokukan). *Open 9:30am to 5:30pm; until 8pm mid-July through August; until 5pm December through February. Closed Monday. ¥1500. Tel. (052)654-7080.* If ships are your thing, you'll enjoy the **Fuji Antarctic exploration ship**. *Open 9am to 5pm. Closed Monday. ¥300.* The contemporary **Nagoya Port Building** has a towering observation deck. On a clear day, you can't quite see California, but almost. *Open 9:30am to 7pm. Closed 3rd Monday. ¥300.*

It's an easy trip from Nagoya Station to **Arimatsu**, a former post town, one of the 53 stops on the Tokaido Road connecting Edo (Tokyo) with Kyoto. The merchants made fortunes selling delicate tie-dyed textiles called *shibori* to wealthy travelers heading up and down the Tokaido Road. Along a one-kilometer stretch, many of the remaining two-storied houses have impressive stucco storehouses. The **Arimatsu Shibori Museum** (Arimatsu Narumi Shibori Kaikan) displays and gives demonstrations of *shibori* tie-dyed textiles. *Tel. (052)621-0111. Open 9am to 4pm. Closed Wednesday. ¥300.* The **Arimatsu Festival Float Hall** displays an ornate festival float with a fantastic *karakuri* mechanical doll. *Open 9:30am to 4:30pm. Closed Wednesday. ¥200. To reach Arimatsu, take the Meitetsu Nagoya Line from Meitetsu Nagoya Station to Arimatsu; 19 minutes.*

SHOPPING

Nagoya's main shopping centers are around **Nagoya train station** and the **Sakae** area. Both have underground shopping malls and enough department stores to keep you busy.

INUYAMA

Inuyama, a small castle town near Nagoya, has one of the handful of original castles remaining in Japan, and the only one still in private hands. Near the castle is Uraku-en, a traditional Japanese garden with a teahouse that's designated as a National Treasure.

The area is a mecca for theme-park type places, but only one is exceptional. **Meiji Mura**, an open air museum, has a fantastic collection of turn-of-the-century buildings.

ARRIVALS & DEPARTURES

From Shin Meitetsu Nagoya Station (next to JR Nagoya Station): take the Meitetsu Inuyama train line to Inuyama Yuen Station, the closest stop for the castle (27 minutes by limited express, ¥890; 33 minutes by express, ¥540).

For the shuttle buses to Meiji Mura, use Inuyama Station (23 minutes by limited express and 29 minutes by express).

WHERE TO STAY

MEITETSU INUYAMA HOTEL, *107-1 Kita Koken, Inuyama, Aichi, 484-0082. Tel. (0568)61-2211, Fax (0568)62-5750. Singles from ¥12,000. Twins from ¥16,000. Credit cards.*

This Western-style hotel is only a few minutes from Inuyama Castle and next to Uraku-en Garden. Ask for a room with a view of Inuyama Castle.

LAKESIDE IRUKA, *118 Kiroku-yashiki, Inuyama, Aichi, 484-0024. Tel. (0568)67-3811, Fax (0568)67-7435. Singles from ¥9800. Credit cards.*

Located on the Iruka Pond adjacent to Meiji Mura, this quiet inn is an ideal base from which to explore the open air museum. If you need to be picked up after spending the day at Meiji Mura, they suggest you telephone, and they'll pick you up within ten minutes.

SEEING THE SIGHTS

Meiji Mura tops our list of places to visit in the area. The large open air museum in a park-like setting features Meiji-era (1868-1912) buildings moved from all over Japan. Well, actually the name is a little misleading because Meiji Mura's most famous building is from Taisho, the succeeding period — Frank Lloyd Wright's lobby of the Imperial Hotel dates from 1923. Many of these buildings were moved to escape demolition; the Imperial Hotel's lobby is no exception.

Meiji Mura is a testament to the incredibly vibrant Meiji period. Japan threw off 250 years of feudal rule and isolation under the Tokugawa shoguns and absorbed Western technology and science like a sponge. The country leap-frogged into the modern era. Castles and other remnants of feudalism were destroyed en masse and new buildings emulating Western architecture were erected.

The park has forty or so buildings from this era including churches, government buildings and traditional Japanese merchant houses. You'll even find a jail, a bank and a telephone exchange building. Kyoto's first streetcar and an early steam locomotive transport you around the vast grounds on the shores of a large lake. It takes a full day to see all the buildings.

Meiji Mura isn't overly commercial. You won't find popcorn vendors on every corner. In fact, you really have to search for the few restaurants. Try Meiji-era *sukiyaki*, a novelty of the period, at Ohi Gyuniku-Tei or Meiji Mura Shokudo. You are also welcome to carry your own picnic lunch. *Open daily 9:30am to 5pm; until 4pm November through February. ¥1600. From Meitetsu Nagoya Bus Station, take bus directly to Meiji Mura (1 hour) or take the Meitetsu train to Inuyama Station and change for the Meitetsu bus to Meiji Mura.*

Inuyama Castle, Japan's oldest remaining castle, dates from 1537. The keep is small compared with Himeji Castle, but it was built in the middle of the Warring States period when no one feudal lord was able to get the upper hand. Make sure you climb up to the top for a panoramic view of the Kiso River, the rice fields and the mountains in the distance. Inuyama Castle still belongs to the Naruse family who once ruled the area; it's the only privately owned castle in Japan. *Open daily 9am to 5pm. Closed December 29-31. ¥400.*

About a 10-minute walk from the castle is **Uraku-en Garden**, a tranquil Japanese garden surrounded by bamboo hedges. Oda Nobunaga's brother, Urakusai, built the Jo-an teahouse in 1618; it's one of the three tea huts designated a National Treasure. Urakusai lived a secluded life as a priest and tea master. The tea garden has over 300 varieties of tea plants. *Open 9am to 5pm; until 4pm December through February. ¥1000.*

HIKONE

This castle town, on the shores of **Lake Biwa**, is about half-way between Nagoya and Kyoto. The quiet town is home to one of Japan's few original castle keeps.

ARRIVALS & DEPARTURES

To/from Tokyo: take *Hikari* shinkansen train to Maibara Station (2 1/2 hours); change to JR Tokaido line to JR Hikone Station (5 minutes, ¥1860).

Caution: only one *Hikari* shinkansen train an hour stops at Maibara. Taking the *kodama* (local) shinkansen will add almost an hour to the trip.

To/from Nagoya: take the shinkansen train to Maibara Station (30 minutes); change to JR Tokaido line to JR Hikone Station (5 minutes). ¥3440. Or take JR Tokaido line to JR Hikone Station (1 hour 15 minutes, ¥1450).

To/from Kyoto: shinkansen to JR Maibara Station (20 minutes); change for the JR Tokaido line to JR Hikone Station (5 minutes, ¥3280.) Or take JR Tokaido line to JR Hikone Station (47 minutes, ¥1110)

Tourist Information

Hikone Tourist Information Center, an "i" Tourist Information Office, is at JR Hikone Station. *Tel. (0749)22-2954.* Open daily 9am to 5:30pm. Closed December 29 through 31.

Goodwill Guides: Contact the Hikone Tourist Information Center, *Tel. (0749)22-2954,* to arrange a volunteer goodwill guide for the castle.

WHERE TO STAY

HAKKEITEI, *3-41 Kinkame-cho, Hikone, Shiga, 522-0061. Tel. (0749)22-3117, Fax (0749)22-3120. From ¥22,800 per person with two meals. No credit cards. Closed Monday.*

Staying in this villa gives you some sense of the pampered life of feudal lords. All five rooms overlook the well-kept Japanese garden, Genkyu-en. The exquisitely presented food is served in your private room.

SEEING THE SIGHTS

Hikone Castle, the centerpiece of the town, rises three stories on Konkizan hill. The feudal lord Ii Naokatsu built the castle in 1603. His father was one of the Tokugawa's staunchest supporters and fought at Tokugawa Ieyasu's side during the decisive Battle of Sekigahara. Ieyasu rewarded him by giving him the land controlled by Ishida Mitsunari, one of the big losers of the battle. Many of the huge stones in the fortress' walls were moved from Mitsunari's Sawayama Castle.

The 13th generation feudal lord, Ii Naosuke, was in the limelight 250 years later. Instrumental in helping open Japan to the world in the waning days of the Tokugawa shogunate by signing a trade treaty with the US, he was assassinated at a gate of Edo Castle in present-day Tokyo.

The castle itself, designated a National Treasure, offers splendid views of Lake Biwa and the surrounding area. Your castle admission ticket also allows you entry into the nearby **Genkyu-en**, the Ii family's private garden. In Genkyu-en is a villa, Rakuraku-en, that was a lovely restaurant and inn up until a few years ago. The aging owner has now turned the property over to the city. *Castle and grounds open daily 8:30am to 5pm. ¥500.*

The **Hikone Castle Museum** (Hikone-jo Hakubutsukan) exhibits Ii family treasures including samurai armor, *noh* costumes, and works of art. *Open daily 9am to 4:30pm. Closed December 25-31. ¥500.*

ISE

Japan's most sacred Shinto shrine is **Ise Grand Shrine** (Ise Jingu) dedicated to **Amaterasu**, the Sun Goddess and Shinto's supreme deity, and **Toyouke**, the Goddess of Agriculture, Harvest and Silk Cultivation. Ise Shrine is the center of the indigenous Shinto religion. Although the origins of the shrine are obscure, Ise has always been associated with the imperial family who claim descent from the Sun Goddess. To this day, members of the imperial family go to Ise to report their marriages. Although Ise Shrine is home to a private religious sect, most Japanese see it as the heart of their culture. Through the ages Ise has been an important pilgrimage site.

Located only an hour and a half from Nagoya, Ise is easy to reach. By all means visit the shrine if you are very interested in the Shinto religion or traditional Japanese architecture. But we have to warn you the main sanctuaries are off limits to mere mortals so casual visitors may be disappointed.

ARRIVALS & DEPARTURES

To/from Nagoya: Take either the private Kintetsu limited express train to Ise-shi Station (1 hour 22 minutes, ¥2690) or the JR rapid train *Mie* to JR Ise-shi Station (1 hour 36 minutes, ¥1940).

Tourist Information

The "i" Tourist Information Office in Ise City is located at Kintetsu Ujiyamada Station, *Tel. (0596)23-9655.*

WHERE TO STAY

ISE CITY HOTEL, *1-11-31 Fukiage, Ise, Mie, 516. Tel. (0596)28-2111, Fax (0596)28-1058. Singles ¥6700. Credit cards. Member of Welcome Inn Reservation Center.*

This 94-room business hotel is just a few minutes walk from Ise-shi Station.

HOSHIDE RYOKAN, *2-15-2 Kawasaki, Ise, Mie, 516-0009. Tel. (0596)28-2377, Fax (0596)27-2830. One person ¥4500; two persons ¥8000 without meals. Credit cards. Member of Japanese Inn Group and Welcome Inn Reservation Center.*

This traditional Japanese-style inn has only 13 rooms. Hoshide Ryokan is both close to Ise-shi Station and convenient for visiting Ise Grand Shrine. Breakfast and dinner are available for a modest charge.

WHERE TO EAT

IWATOYA *(Japanese, inexpensive). 58 Uji-imazaike-machi. Open daily 8:30am to 5pm.*

A good place to stop for lunch near the Naiku Shrine (see Seeing the Sights), Iwatoya serves local specialties like *tekone-zushi* (rice mixed with marinated seafood) and *udon* noodles for ¥1200 and *katsu teishoku* for ¥1400.

SEEING THE SIGHTS

Ise Shrine has two parts, a fifteen-minute bus ride apart. The shrine's halls, constructed of beautiful cypress wood, remain natural. Unlike the vermilion gates of Fushimi Shrine in Kyoto, these stark and simple wood structures convey a sense of purity and sacredness.

One of the most remarkable traditions of the shrine is that some 90 buildings and 1600 objects are reconstructed every 20 years — a practice that has been going on for 1300 years. The concept behind the rebuilding is to pay respect to the Shinto spirits through the form of architecture. On a more practical side, rebuilding eats up 12,000 cypress trees. But not all is wasted — the old buildings are distributed to Shinto shrines all over the country. Rebuilding also keeps the traditional construction techniques alive — the shrine's buildings represent some of the oldest Japanese architectural styles. The shrines were last reconstructed in 1993 and will be again in 2013.

The **Geku Outer Shrine** is a five-minute walk from Ise-shi Station. Dedicated to the goddess Toyouke, the shrine dates from 477. Twice a day, offerings of food are made from Toyouke to Amaterasu through a special ceremony off limits to the public.

Take the bus from Geku to Naiku. The **Naiku Inner Shrine** is the more important of the two. It honors goddess Amaterasu, the highest deity in the Shinto pantheon. The thick grove of cedar trees covering the area lends a sacred air. To enter the main area of the shrine, cross the Uji Bridge over the rushing Isuzu River. Crossing the bridge is an act of purification; the bridge itself is reconstructed every 20 years. After the bridge, turn to the left; after you walk a while there are steps leading down to the river where pilgrims purify themselves. Heading to the main sanctuary, you'll pass two simple *torii* gates where branches of sacred *sakaki* bushes and strips of folded paper adorn the pillars. These decorated *torii* gates symbolize entering sacred space. The branches and paper are replaced every ten days. The concept of renewal is an important aspect of the Shinto religion.

The **Goshoden** (main sanctuary) contains Amaterasu's sacred mirror, one of the three treasures of the imperial family. Four fences surround the sanctuary; pilgrims can go as far as the second fence. Behind the Goshoden are two treasuries. The pristine buildings are on white raked gravel. The structures themselves derive from early storehouses; they are raised on pillars and have thick thatched roofs.

Next to the Goshoden is an identical space where the new sanctuary will be constructed. When finished, the two sit side by side until the sacred mirror is transferred during a nighttime ceremony. Then the old building is disassembled. Since the buildings are constructed without nails, they can be moved to another shrine.

20. KYOTO

We've been to **Kyoto** countless times but, just like addicts, can't ever get enough. Kyoto, a jewel of a city, served as Japan's capital for 1100 years and is still the center of traditional Japanese culture. Kyoto is home to hundreds of temples and shrines. It's also great food, world-class museums, shops selling crafts made by local artisans and much, much more. If you schedule only a day or two, you'll barely have enough time to scratch the surface of the major attractions.

Most people arrive in Kyoto expecting to see a perfectly preserved museum city. Tourist posters portray white-faced *geisha* dressed in ornate kimono, minimalist Zen rock gardens and pagodas framed by cherry blossoms, but Kyoto is not frozen in time. When you get off the train at Kyoto Station, you are greeted by the glass and steel of the new, postmodern Kyoto Station building. The real, live city is home to 1.6 million people — roughly the size of Florence, Italy. There is more traditional culture here than in any other Japanese city, but it exists side by side with the modern. You must search for it behind walls and inside buildings. What's fun about Kyoto is the more you look, the more you see.

A nice bonus is that it's really easy to get around. The city's laid out on a grid system; the streets have names, and addresses usually include the closest intersection. The subway system is fast and buses, destinations thankfully marked in English, travel to the city's farthest corners.

Planning Your Stay

Kyoto has over 2000 temples and shrines; some take up parts of mountains and others are on postage-stamp sized lots. No matter how hard you try, it's impossible to see even the main ones. While rushing from place to place, you'll probably miss the real charm and beauty of Kyoto. For us, it is the small things that define Kyoto: a confectionery in a back alley, a carefully tended garden, a shop continuing an age-old craft tradition.

The biggies on most tourist itineraries are Kiyomizu-dera, Kinkaku-ji (Golden Pavilion), Ryoan-ji, Sanjusangen-do, Nijo Castle, Heian Shrine,

KYOTO HIGHLIGHTS

· *Visiting the Katsura and Shugakuin Imperial Villas*
· *Strolling through Sento Gosho and Katsura Gardens*
· *Meditating at the rock gardens of Ryoan-ji and Konchi-in*
· *Eating yu-dofu at Nanzen-ji*
· *Shooting the rapids down the Hozu River*
· *Viewing Kyoto from the veranda of Kiyomizu Temple*
· *Strolling along Sannenzaka and Ninenzaka*
· *Browsing in the traditional shops of Gion*
· *Wandering in the tunnels of vermilion torii gates of Fushimi Shrine*
· *Admiring the bright red autumn foliage through the Sanmon Gate of Eikando*
· *Enjoy the squeaking floors of the ornate Nijo Castle*

Ginkaku-ji and Nanzen-ji. They are all important. But we urge you not to rush from one to another. Instead, incorporate two a day into an itinerary that includes temples, gardens, lunch at a charming place and time to browse and get lost in the back alleys. If you have only one or two days, this assignment is nearly impossible. But we think it's better to leave knowing there's much more to see than to leave with your head in total confusion.

We've divided Kyoto into a number of areas; you'll need the better part of a day to see an entire area. Probably you can see two areas in one day if you shorten your tour by choosing only the places most appealing to you — our recommendations are marked with an asterisk. If you have more than two days in Kyoto, make sure you get to the outskirts for at least one of your days: Ohara, Fushimi, Arashiyama or Katsura Imperial Villa. And don't miss seeing at least one imperial villa — we like Shugakuin and Katsura so much more than the Imperial Palace; the buildings have more charm and the gardens are truly special. Remember you must go to the Imperial Household Agency to make advance reservations.

Kyoto Areas In This Chapter
1. **Kyoto Station Area**: **To-ji***, Kyoto's first temple within the city and repository of Heian Period art treasures; **Higashi and Nishi Hongan-ji***, large temple complexes of the populist Pure Land Buddhist sect; **Shimabara**, the merchants' pleasure quarters.
2. **Central Kyoto**: **Nijo Castle***, the ornate Kyoto residence of the Tokugawa Shogun; **Shinsen-en**, a garden dating from the Heian Period; **Nijo Jinya**, an inn for feudal lords; **Nishiki Ichiba**, Kyoto's food market; **Imperial Palace***, the emperor's residence until 1868.

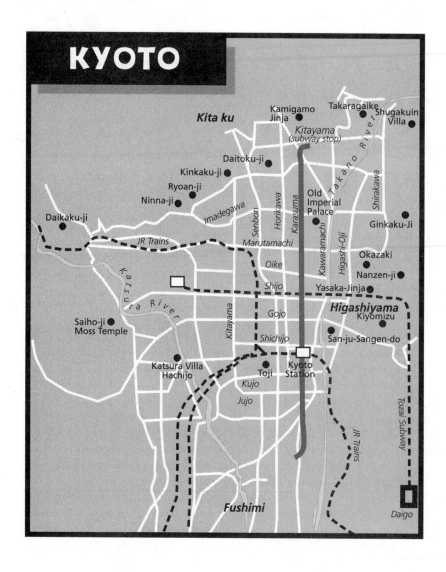

3. **Southern Higashiyama: Sanjusangen-do***, Kamakura era temple with 1001 Buddha statues; **Kyoto National Museum***, repository of Kyoto's treasures; **Chishaku-in Temple***, treasure house houses masterpieces of Momoyama art; **Kiyomizu-dera Temple***, one of Kyoto's oldest temples perched gracefully on the mountain; **Sannenzaka***, and **Ninenzaka***, historic districts preserving Edo Period merchant houses.

4. **Central Higashiyama: Yasaka Shrine***, ancient Shinto shrine; **Gion*** and **Pontocho***, *geisha* districts still active entertainment centers; **Chion-in Temple**, the huge center of Pure Land Buddhism; and **Shoren-in Temple**, a quiet imperial retreat.

5. **Northern Higashiyama: Heian Shrine***, 1890s reconstruction of the emperor's first Kyoto residence; **Okazaki Park** housing Kyoto National Museum of Modern Art, Kyoto Municipal Museum of Art, Museum of Traditional Crafts, and Kyoto Zoo; **Nanzen-ji***, a Zen temple with fine gardens and architecture; **Eikan-do**, a serene hillside temple; **Philosopher's Path**, a 2-kilometer walk; **Ginkaku-ji***, the temple of the Silver Pavilion.

6. **North-central Kyoto: Shimogamo Shrine**, one of Kyoto's first Shinto shrines; **Shokoku-ji**, a quiet Zen temple in a pine grove; **Kitano Tenmangu Shrine***, Shinto shrine dedicated to the god of learning; **Nishijin*** area, center of Kyoto's textile industry; **Urasenke**, major school of tea ceremony; **Raku Art Museum**, home of a rustic pottery tradition favored by tea ceremony connoisseurs.

7. **Northeast Kyoto** — home of some of Kyoto's best gardens and villas: **Shugakuin Imperial Villa***, emperor's retirement retreat; **Manshu-in***, a villa built by an imperial prince; **Shisen-do***, warrior-scholar's hermitage.

8. **Northern Kyoto: Kamigamo Shrine***, Shinto shrine predates Kyoto, **Entsu-ji***, small imperial retirement villa with splendid garden; **Jisso-in**, noted for door paintings; **Botanical Garden**, large park for strolling; **Garden of Fine Art**, contemporary garden with masterpieces reproduced on ceramics; **Daitoku-ji***, large Zen temple with famous rock gardens; **Koestsu-ji**, 17th century artist colony.

9. **Northwestern Kyoto: Ryoan-ji***, famous Zen rock garden; **Kinkaku-ji***, temple of the Golden Pavilion; **Nin-na-ji**, temple famous for its cherry blossoms; **Myoshin-ji**, huge Zen temple; **Kyoto Studio Park**, movie-set amusement park.

Kyoto Outskirts In This Chapter

10. **Arashiyama and Sagano areas** (northwest): Quiet area in the western hills of Kyoto. **Tenryu-ji***, temple with famous Muromachi Period garden; **Daikaku-ji***, former imperial villa with famous door paint-

ings; **Monkey Park**, climb a mountain to a monkey preserve; boating down the rapids of the **Hozu River**.

11. **Takao and Togano areas** (farther northwest): Mountainous area good for hiking; beautiful in autumn when the maples turn red. Known for its secluded mountain temples: **Kozan-ji***, **Jingo-ji** and **Saimyo-ji**.

12. **Western Kyoto**: Two famous gardens, **Saiho-ji (Kokedera)***, the moss garden, and **Katsura Villa***, the epitome of imperial rustic villas and gardens.

13. **Fushimi Area** (south): **Fushimi Inari Shrine***, thousands of red *torii* gates lining paths through hills; Fushimi **sake breweries**; **Tofuku-ji***, Zen temple with excellent gardens.

14. **Uji** (farther south): Many aristocratic villas from Heian Period; Tea growing center; **Byodo-in***, magnificent Heian era temple; **Mampuku-ji**, Chinese-style temple.

15. **Southeast**: **Daigo-ji***, the Sambo-in subtemple is the height of Momoyama architecture; **Kanju-ji** and **Zuishin-in**, Heian Period residences turned temples.

16. **Ohara**, a small rural village northeast of Kyoto: **Sanzen-in***, a mountain temple and **Jakko-in***, a Buddhist convent.

17. **Sakamoto Otsu** (further northeast): **Enryaku-ji***, once the most powerful temple in Kyoto; and **Mii-dera**, Enryaku-ji's arch enemy.

18. Side trip to **Miho Museum** in Shigaraki.

TWO DAYS IN KYOTO

Here are our suggestions for a two-day, Best-of-Kyoto tour that combines a few big sights with a glimpse of some of Kyoto's back streets:

Day 1

Sanjusangen-do, 15-*minute walk to* **Chawan-zaka** *(Tea cup slope) leading to* **Kiyomizu-dera**; *then walk through* **Sannenzaka** *and* **Ninenzaka** *areas. Lunch in this area at Okutan or Ikkyu-an. Walk to* **Yasaka Shrine** *and browse around the* **Gion** *area. Taxi or bus (#5 from Kawaramachi Shijo, the main intersection after you cross the Kamo River) to* **Heian Shrine***. Walk to* **Nanzen-ji** *and if you still have any energy, walk north on the* **Philosopher's Path***.*

Day 2

Nijo Castle. Take bus #12 in front of Nijo Castle to **Kinkaku-ji***. Walk to Gontaro for a noodle lunch then continue on to* **Ryoan-ji***. After seeing Ryoan-ji, take a taxi to* **Kitano Tenmangu Shrine** *and then walk the back streets of the Nishijin district, stopping at* **Nishijin Kaikan** *(kimono show) or the* **Orinasu-kan** *for textile displays.*

Advance Planning

If you are visiting Kyoto at a peak time such as cherry blossom time in early April, fall foliage in November, one of the major festivals or during a holiday weekend, it's imperative you have hotel reservations. All spring and fall are busy, so it's not worth risking — make reservations.

Several places require you to apply in advance. To visit the famous **Saiho-ji Moss Garden**, you must send a special return postcard, *ofuku hagaki*, available at any Japanese post office for ¥100. It must reach the temple five to ten days prior to your visit. On the blue stamp side of the post card, address it to: *Saiho-ji Temple, 56 Kamigaya-cho, Matsuo, Nishigyo-ku, Kyoto, 615*. On the green stamp side, write your name and address in Japan. On the reverse of the green stamp side, write your name(s), your address in Japan, your occupation, your age and the day you want to visit plus second and third choices. The temple will send the return portion to you confirming your appointment. When you arrive at the temple at your appointed hour you are required to do some calligraphy before viewing the garden. You must make a donation of at least ¥3000 per person.

To visit the **Katsura Imperial Villa**, **Shugakuin Imperial Villa** and **Sento Palace**, you must apply in person to the Imperial Household Agency. Apply at least one day in advance at the Agency's office on the Imperial Palace grounds. At the Imadegawa Subway station, use exit 6 and walk a short distance south on Karasuma Street. Enter the grounds at the Inui Gomon gate (you'll need to cross Karasuma Dori). It's just south of Imadegawa Dori. Make sure you take your passport. The office is open 8:45am to 12 noon and 1pm to 4pm, Monday through Friday. Also, it's closed December 25 through January 5. Tours in Japanese are conducted at Sento Palace at 11am and 1:30pm; Katsura at 10am, 11am, 2pm and 3pm; and Shugakuin at 9am, 10am, 11am, 1:30pm and 3pm. Children under 20 are not admitted.

Yes, it's a hassle, but look on the bright side: Japanese must apply by mail three months in advance.

You do not need advance reservations to tour the **Kyoto Imperial Palace** (Kyoto Gosho). English tours are given at 10am and 2pm, Monday through Friday, and you merely have to show up at the Imperial Household Agency Office (above) 20 minutes in advance to get a pass. Remember to take your passport. They also give tours on the third Saturday and on every Saturday in April, May, October and November. For Saturday tours, go to the Imperial Household Agency by Friday to get a pass. There are no tours on national holidays. **Imperial Household Agency**, *Tel. (075)211-1215*. Children must be accompanied by a grown-up (defined as someone over 20, in case you are wondering).

When to Visit

Kyoto is hot and humid in summer and cold and damp in winter. Spring and autumn are the best seasons to visit, but everyone feels the same way so you'll be in the company of thousands of others including innumerable school groups. If you can tolerate cold weather, winter is a good time to visit. Not only because you might actually see some places in near solitude, but also special pavilions and gardens normally inaccessible to the public are open to attract visitors in this off-season.

If you visit in winter, make sure you remember to pack a pair of heavy socks or bootie-type slippers so your feet won't freeze walking barefooted on the cold wooden temple floors. Special openings also occur in early April to coincide with the cherry blossom season and in early November around Culture Day, November 3.

KYOTO'S HISTORY

Kyoto was Japan's capital from 794 to 1868. This fact alone is miraculous because before that record, no capital lasted more than 75 years. Today Japanese still call Kyoto *miyako* (capital), although it hasn't been the capital for more than a century. But *miyako* means more than simply a capital city. The nuance is the place where everything is superb and elegant, the height of culture. Kyoto residents take smug delight in the fact that this term is not used to describe Tokyo.

Capital doesn't mean Kyoto was always the center of political power. For large portions of Kyoto's history, the government was in the hands of shoguns who ruled from Kamakura and Edo (Tokyo). But they had to come back to get the seal of approval from the emperor who reigned, but lacked political power.

Heian Period (794-1185) — Emperor Kammu's Heian-Kyo

Emperor Kammu set up Kyoto as the capital to escape from the powerful Buddhist temples of Nara that were undermining his authority. According to the Chinese formula, Kyoto was the perfect location for a capital surrounded on three sides by mountains. Kammu constructed the city on a north-south axis — 5.2 kilometers by 4.5 kilometers.

The present Horikawa Dori, the large road now in front of Nijo Castle, was the main north-south road and was an incredible 85 meters wide. It ran from the Imperial Palace in the north to To-ji and Sai-ji, the only Buddhist temples Kammu allowed in the city. The major east-west streets were numbered from north to south, beginning with Ichijo (First Avenue) and ending with Kujo (Ninth Avenue), south of present-day Kyoto Station. Even in the Heian times the city sprawled outside these limits. One of the delights of visiting Kyoto today is that you can still see the basic framework established 1200 years ago.

For the first hundred years or so, the emperors managed to maintain political power and authority and held on to large parcels of land. The emperors retired early, sometimes after reigning just a few years, and as part of their retirement package, they built comfortable villas and residences that often became temples upon their death. **Nin-na-ji** and **Daikaku-ji** are good examples you can visit today. As head of the Shinto religion, the emperor performed rituals but also became increasingly involved in Buddhism, often retiring as a monk.

Emperor Kammu tried to dilute the power of Buddhism by allowing only two temples in the city, **Sai-ji** and **To-ji**. These temples were to concentrate on performing rituals and stay out of the affairs of state. But within one generation, To-ji, under the priest Kukai (known posthumously as Kobo Daishi), who started the Shingon sect, convinced the emperor that the sect's sutras were vital for the continuation of the state. **Enryaku-ji**, established on Mt. Hiei to ward off the spirits of the northeast, claimed to find Shinto gods on the mountains and declared Shinto to be part of Buddhism by protecting the temple. The best laid plans of Emperor Kammu, to keep Buddhist influence out of the state, came to naught.

Chinese Tang art strongly influenced early Heian art, especially the mandalas and sculptures of esoteric Buddhism. The Buddha of Healing at **Jingo-ji** and the Mandala at **To-ji** are outstanding examples.

Fujiwara's Heian-Kyo

As they lost control of the land and people, the imperial family's functions became more centered on culture and ritual. They grew to be dependent on the support of the Fujiwara family that led to the rise of regent politics. Regents became the highest ranking ministers and ran the state. The Fujiwara married their daughters to emperors, so their grandsons would be emperors. Usually aristocratic families rejoice at the birth of a son, but in Fujiwara's case, it was the birth of a daughter that was cause for a celebration. **Fujiwara Michinaga** (966-1027) exploited this system to the extreme. Four of his daughters married emperors, which made him the father of four empresses, uncle of two emperors and grandfather of three emperors.

For Kyoto's aristocracy, life was sweet. They lived in *shinden-zukuri* style mansions that consisted of a central wooden building flanked by two wings and set in a strolling garden with a pond. They enjoyed writing poetry, playing incense games and visiting each other. They traveled in ox carts, palanquins and on horseback. This is the Kyoto of the *Tale of Genji*, the world's first novel, written by Murasaki Shikibu in the 12th century.

Narrative scrolls became important for Heian nobles who would spend hours looking at the paintings and reading the poetry.

Members of aristocracy competed with each other to build huge private temples. Temples formed monk armies to protect themselves in disputes over doctrine and land. Priests brought the Pure Land doctrine back from China; it became very popular with the nobility's increasing concern about an afterlife. Aristocrats built temples like **Byodo-in** as manifestations of the Western Paradise that awaits those who believe in the Amida Buddha.

While most of Heian-kyo no longer exists, today you can see remnants at Byodo-in and in more recent reconstructions of Heian architecture at the **Kyoto Imperial Palace** and **Heian Shrine**.

GENJI'S HEIAN-KYO

*The world's first novel, **The Tale of Genji**, was set in the Kyoto of the 10th-11th centuries. Written by court lady Murasaki Shikibu, it is our delight to confirm that the author was intimately involved with the geography of Heian-kyo, for even at the end of the 20th century, we can locate many of the places she mentions. **Nijo** is where Prince Genji's palace is located; **Nonomiya**, near Arashiyama, is where Genji bid a sad sayonara to his jealous lover, **Lady Rokujo**, whose name means Lady of Sixth Avenue. **Gojo** is where Genji's lover Yugao, literally the Evening Face, lived: "Neighborhood was a poor one, chiefly of small houses. Some were leaning precariously and there were 'evening faces' at the sagging eaves." (translated by Edward Seidensticker).*

*And then there is **Uji**, south of Kyoto, where the romance of Kaoru and Ukifune started, and **Kurama**, north of Kyoto, where Genji went to heal his malaria, and where the amorous Genji glimpsed a young Murasaki who would later become one of his favorite consorts.*

Cloistered Emperors & The Warrior Class

For some unknown reason, the Fujiwara women married to emperors stopped producing heirs. **Emperor Go-sanjo** (ruled 1069–1072) was the first emperor in a century who did not have a Fujiwara mother. Political power passed to retired emperors, called cloistered emperors, who competed with the Fujiwara for the acquisition of land, the key to their strength. As their influence in the provinces gradually decreased, land fell into the hands of powerful provincial warlords.

The emperor used one clan, the **Taira**, to dilute the power of the Fujiwara. The Taira and their rivals, the **Genji**, fought, culminating at the Battle of **Dan-no-ura** in 1185, leading to the end of the Heian Period. The influence of the Fujiwara family can be found in remote Tohoku, the northern part of Japan's main island, where a branch of Fujiwara tried to create their small *miyako* at **Hiraizumi**. The area is called Michinoku, the end of the road.

THE FALL OF THE HEIKE

*In the waning days of the Heian Period, the emperor used the Taira clan to get rid of the Fujiwara, the aristocratic family that served as regents for several hundred years. The Taira became so powerful that in 1180 its head, **Kiyomori**, imprisoned Emperor Goshirakawa and put Kiyomori's grandson, Antoku, on the throne. The Taira's rivals were the Genji clan. The brothers **Minamoto Yoritomo** and **Minamoto Yoshitsune** defeated the Taira through a series of battles that first forced them out of Kyoto and ultimately defeated them in a sea battle called Dan-no-ura in 1185.*

The hapless child emperor, Antoku (he was 7), perished at sea with his grandmother, but the Genji rescued his mother, Kenrei Monin, to prevent her from committing suicide. This wasn't as benevolent as it might appear. Vengeful spirits could wreak a lot of havoc and the Genji were not taking any chances. Kenrei Monin spent the rest of her life (roughly 30 years) at Jakko-in Temple on the outskirts of Kyoto, praying for the spirits of her family.

Kamakura Period (1185-1333)

When the Genji defeated the Taira, Minamoto Yoritomo (Minamoto is another way of reading the characters Genji) established a military government centered at Kamakura, close to present-day Tokyo. He wanted to get away from the intrigues of the court and shelter his warriors from the easy life of Kyoto. Yoritomo asked the emperor to name him shogun; reluctantly he did in 1192. This appointment marks the first time political power was in the hands of the military.

The warrior society exalted the principles of loyalty, honor and frugality, which came to be the ideals for later generations of warriors.

Zen Buddhism had great appeal to the warrior class and also found favor with emperors and aristocrats. **Nanzen-ji**, built by Emperor Kameyama in 1291, **Eikan-do** and **Myoshin-ji** were all founded in this period. The Sekisui-in hall of **Kozan-ji** is one of the few buildings extant from this time.

The turmoil of this period saw the masses flocking to Pure Land Buddhism. The priest Honen founded **Chion-in** and priest Shinran founded **Hongan-ji**. Nichiren founded the Nichiren sect, which also had broad appeal. **Sanjusangendo** is the masterpiece of the era, housing 1001 Buddhas and other dynamic sculptures. **Jingo-ji** in Takao has Kamakura period sculptures that probably would have perished if the temple had been in central Kyoto.

Muromachi Period (1333-1568)

Toward the end of the Kamakura Period, the co-existence of a nominal emperor and so many retired emperors caused problems of succession. The gentleman's agreement was that emperors would only remain on the throne for ten years and would alternate between two family lines. Emperor Godaigo refused to retire when his time was up and tried to establish direct rule; he was deposed and established his court in **Yoshino**, south of Nara, in 1333. Thus began the **Nanboku-cho**, which literally means the Northern and Southern Courts, a period of warfare that continued until 1392 when the Southern Court surrendered.

The warrior **Ashikaga Takauji** played a major role in this mess. He restored Emperor Godaigo to the throne. When the emperor called him a traitor for moving to Kamakura, an indication he was going to continue the military government, Takauji retaliated by attacking Kyoto, deposing Godaigo and installing another emperor. Takauji was then awarded the title of shogun and established his military government in Kyoto.

Ashikaga Takauji built **Tenryu-ji** in Arashiyama to appease the soul of Emperor Godaigo. The temple's garden is one of the most splendid Muromachi gardens in Kyoto.

The Ashikaga shoguns soon became more interested in the arts than in governing, and the country slid into a long civil war. The Onin War (1467–77) was a senseless 10-year battle over shogun succession and would probably have been just a footnote to history if it hadn't used Kyoto as its battlefield. In the end, one army got up and left, and the other was so weak it barely noticed. Kyoto was in ruins and no one was in real control. The next century, called the Warring States Period, saw civil war throughout the country

While Kyoto burned, the Ashikaga's Nero fiddled. Ashikaga Yoshimasa built the **Silver Pavilion** to emulate his grandfather's **Golden Pavilion**. The gardens of **Saiho-ji** and **Ryoan-ji** date from this time. **Shokoku-ji** is the Zen temple built by the Ashikaga; their priests often served as advisors. Many art forms that we consider quintessential Japanese — tea ceremony, *noh* plays, flower arrangement — were started in the Muromachi Period and blossomed in the subsequent Momoyama Period.

Momoyama Period (1568–1603)

Oda Nobunaga was finally able to unify a good part of Japan, enough so he marched on Kyoto and kicked out the Ashikaga shogunate. The Portuguese had come to Japan and brought guns. Nobunaga's brilliant use of this new weapon gave him the upper hand. He was absolutely treacherous; fearless of religion, he slaughtered thousands of monks on Mt. Hiei when they opposed him. Not one building was left by the time he got finished. It wasn't as though the monks were just reading sutras all day; they too had a highly organized army. Nobunaga's life came to a violent end in 1582 when one of his most trusted generals attacked him while he was having a tea ceremony at a Honno-ji Temple in central Kyoto.

Toyotomi Hideyoshi took over and completed the unification. Having risen from a lowly foot soldier to the pinnacle of power, Hideyoshi was denied the title of shogun because of his low birth — class still counted.

Hideyoshi's accomplishments were many. He standardized tax collection and the money, actually rice, rolled in. Rebuilding the city of Kyoto, he constructed a wall and moat for its protection, and he gave money for the reconstruction of temples. At today's Kyoto Station, platform 1 is built on Hideyoshi's wall. Most of what we consider old Kyoto today dates from Hideyoshi's reconstruction. To try to control the power of temples, he set up Teramachi (temple district) on the eastern edge so he could keep an eye on the temples.

The unifiers surrounded themselves with the best of everything: buildings were all on a grand scale; their sliding doors were covered with gold leaf and decorated by the premier Kano School of painters; the transoms were elaborately carved; and the ceilings were ornamented. The arts of tea ceremony and flower arranging as we know them today came from this time.

Tokugawa Period (1603–1868)

Hideyoshi died in 1598 when his son was still a child. To safeguard his son's succession, he set up a council of regents, his five strongest generals, with the hope they would keep each other in check. That lasted about two minutes until **Tokugawa Ieyasu**, one of the regents, saw his chance. When he won the decisive **Battle of Sekigahara** in 1600, it was clear that Ieyasu would prevail. Ieyasu brought stability and peace after a long period of chaos. Nijo Castle symbolizes his power and presence in Kyoto. He set up the administrative capital in **Edo** (Tokyo); once again political power moved from Kyoto.

Stability brought prosperity to merchants and artisans. Tokugawa instituted the *sankin kotai* system in which feudal lords had to spend alternate years in residence in Edo. This system meant that the lords spent enormous sums transporting their entourages from distant corners of the country. It also meant that transportation and communication systems were put in place and that merchants could use those systems to distribute their goods. The Tokaido Road, immortalized in Hiroshige's woodblock prints, connected Edo with Kyoto.

Tokugawa pretty much sealed off the country from the rest of world. This isolationism allowed Japanese culture to flourish without outside influences.

Kyoto yearned for the good old days of the Heian era when it was the unquestioned cultural capital of the nation. It still excelled in the arts of painting and poetry, kimono design, ceramics and other refined arts long associated with the emperor and the aristocracy. Edo, bastion of the warrior class, developed its own, more masculine culture. The ascending merchant class of Edo developed *kabuki* plays and *ukiyo-e*, pictures of the floating world of pleasure.

Towards the end of the era, the shogunate was unable to deal with the challenges of modernization especially when pressured by America's **Commodore Perry** and his black ships.

Meiji Period (1868–1912)

The Meiji Restoration of 1868 was a movement of lower-ranking samurai to bring Japan into the modern era and to restore the emperor's governing authority. In 1100 years, the emperor rarely governed. Ironically, the Tokugawa shogunate surrendered power to the emperor in 1868 at Nijo Castle, built at the height of its power. Shintoism became the national religion and the anti-Buddhist purge destroyed many temples all over the country, but especially in Kyoto.

The government moved to Tokyo and as did the emperor. This move was a blow not only to the economy of Kyoto but also to the pride of its citizens.

ARRIVALS & DEPARTURES

By Air

Kansai International Airport (KIX) and **Osaka International Airport** (Itami) serve Kyoto. If Kyoto is your main destination, explore taking an international flight to KIX rather than Narita to save yourself the hassle of traveling from Tokyo. When taking a domestic flight, Itami is closer to Kyoto than to KIX.

To/from Kansai International Airport by train: JR *Haruka* Kansai Airport Express takes 75 minutes and costs (¥3490 reserved; ¥2980 unreserved) to JR Kyoto Station; by bus to Kyoto Station: ¥2300, 135 minutes.

To/from Osaka Itami Airport by bus to JR Kyoto Station: ¥1280, 55 minutes. Taxi ¥12,000, 50 minutes.

By Train

JR Kyoto Station is on the shinkansen line and all trains, including the super-fast *Nozomi*, stop here. *Hikari* shinkansen takes 2 hours 45 minutes from Tokyo; 3 1/2 hours from Hakata (Fukuoka). Kyoto Station is also a transportation hub. You can catch trains bound for the Japan Sea coast to reach Kanazawa and Matsue; south to Nara; the Tokaido line heads east to Nagoya and, eventually, Tokyo; and to the west are Osaka, Kobe, Himeji and Hiroshima.

The mammoth postmodern station complex has a concert hall, Isetan Department Store and the Hotel Granvia in addition to JR, Hankyu and Kintetsu train lines. Shinkansen trains arrive at the south side of the station in what is called Hachijo-guchi exit; it's a hike to the main exit. But you should go to the main exit (Karasuma Central) to see the magnificent new station building. You can get taxis at the Hachijo-guchi exit and also easily connect to Kintetsu trains to Nara. If you're taking a shinkansen train from Kyoto, tell the taxi driver "Hachijo-guchi" and you'll save a lot of extra steps. The subway is accessible from either side of the station.

The main exit is called **Karasuma Central exit**, and it's on the north side of the station. From this side also you can get taxis as well as city buses. You can't help but notice the world's ugliest television tower, Kyoto Tower, across the street from the station. The Tourist Information Center is located in the Kyoto Tower Building on Karasuma Dori, the street that dead-ends into the station.

By Bus

Overnight express buses run from Kyoto to/from Tokyo Station and Shinjuku Station (8 hours, ¥8180), Hiroshima (7 hours, ¥6620), Nagasaki (11 hours, ¥11,310), Kumamoto (11 1/2 hours, ¥10,800) and Fukuoka (9 1/2 hours, ¥10,800). Express buses run from Kyoto to Kanazawa (8 buses/day, 4 1/2 hours, ¥4060).

ORIENTATION

Kyoto is in a basin with mountains encircling all but its southern side. Many temples are located in the mountains, and most are easily accessible by bus and taxi. The city itself is built on a grid system with roads running north/south and east/west. The entire basin is quite developed; there isn't a lot of open green space in the central area. The downtown commercial and shopping district is located along Shijo Dori.

Kyoto addresses usually include the closest intersection. For instance, Karasuma Shijo is the intersection of Karasuma and Shijo Streets. *Dori* means street and *koji* means alley.

GETTING AROUND TOWN

Kyoto is one of the easiest Japanese cities to get around with a good map. The Tourist Information Office has an excellent bilingual map called, *Tourist Map of Kyoto, Nara* by Japan National Tourist Organization

(JNTO), which includes a bus map. Kyoto Station's bus information counter has a transportation map in English, as does the Kyoto City Tourist Information office on the second floor of Kyoto Station.

A subway runs north/south through Kyoto Station and an east/west line runs along Oike Dori and then heads south to Daigo-ji Temple. An extensive network of buses can get you almost anywhere in the city; buses cost ¥220 and you enter by the rear door and pay your fare when you exit at the front. Buses have numbers and destinations written in English. Buses 201 to 208 are loop buses that circle sections of the city; use them to scope out the city. Buses to outlying areas work on the zone system; pick up a small ticket when you board the bus and pay the fare on the chart above the driver's head when you exit. The one-day bus pass (*shi-basu ichi-nichi joshaken*) costs ¥600; buy it at the bus terminal at Kyoto Station.

A combined one-day pass (*ichi-nichi joshaken*) costs ¥1200 and can be used on the bus and subway; but you have to really move around to make it cost-effective; a two-day pass is ¥2000. Trafica prepaid cards come in denominations of ¥1000 and ¥3000. They are good for both city buses and subways.

Taxis are plentiful and are often the fastest way for short distances; the cost is about ¥650 for the first two kilometers. If you see an MK taxi, take it. These guys try harder and their fares are slightly lower. When the driver jumped out to open the door for us we were pleasantly surprised; the company demands that its drivers give an extra degree of service.

Kyoto's once extensive tram system has been dismantled. There are still a number of train and tram lines that seem to start in the middle of nowhere; they head to outlying areas but it's as though there was a donut in the center connecting them all and now it's missing.

Kyoto is best experienced on foot although a bicycle is a great alternative especially if you want to cram in a lot in a day. Bicycle rental places are listed at the end of this chapter under *Practical Information.*

Bus Tours

Japan Travel Bureau (JTB) and **Kintetsu** run English-language bus tours. If you want to be escorted, take them, but you'll be fine getting around on your own, and it's part of the experience.

JTB Sunrise Morning Tour visits Nijo Castle, Kinkaku-ji Golden Pavilion, the Imperial Palace and the Kyoto Handicraft Center for ¥5200. JTB Sunrise Afternoon Tour visits Heian Shrine, Sanjusangendo Temple and Kiyomizu Temple for ¥5300. For ¥11,200 there's a full-day tour that combines the two and includes lunch at the Kyoto Handicraft Center. For reservations phone JTB, *Tel. (075)341-1413.*

Kintetsu Gray Line runs similar tours, *Tel. (075)691-0903.*

Garden Tours

For the garden enthusiast, an easy way to see several gardens in one day is to take a bus tour conducted in Japanese. The **Keihan Bus Company**, *Tel. (075)672-2100*, offers:

R Course departs Kyoto Station at 2pm and also at 9am on Saturdays and holidays during October/November: Tenryu-ji, Ryoan-ji and Zuihon-ji. Tour takes 3 hours and costs ¥4050.

Tourist Information

The city runs tourist information offices staffed by English speakers on both the Shinkansen and Karasuma sides of JR Kyoto Station. The main office is on the 2nd floor of the Tokyo Station building. Stop in to pick up maps and other information.

Tourist Information Center, *Kyoto Tower Building, Higashi-Shiokoji-cho, Shimogyo-ku, Kyoto. Tel. (075)371-5649.* Open 9am to 5pm Monday through Friday; 9am to 12 noon Saturday. Run by the JNTO specifically for foreign tourists, the Tourist Information Center is the best source for information and will also provide information over the phone. The Welcome Inn Reservation Center desk makes reservations at reasonably priced hotels and inns all over Japan.

Kyoto Prefectural International Center is on the 9th floor of the Kyoto Station Building, Karasuma-dori, Shiokoji sagaru, Shimogyo-ku, Kyoto 600-8216. *Tel. (075)342-5000, Fax (075)342-5050.* While geared primarily to serve foreign residents of Kyoto, they are helpful to short-term visitors also and can arrange homestays. The center has an English-language library and inexpensive internet service. *Open 10am to 6pm. Closed second and fourth Tuesdays, December 29 to January 3.*

WHERE TO STAY

Kyoto is a wonderful place to experience a Japanese inn, and there are inns to match any budget. Top-of-the-line *ryokan* can run as much as ¥70,000 per person with two meals, and you'll always remember your stay. Does spending anywhere near that amount blow your mind as well as your budget? Don't worry; there are Japanese inns that cost ¥4000 without meals, and lots in-between. Many Kyoto inns allow you to stay without dinner.

Often the less-expensive rooms do not have a toilet or bath attached although a sink is generally standard. In the smaller inns, although the bath is shared, only one person at a time uses it, so you have privacy. Also, be aware that many of the *ryokan* lock their doors around 11pm. If you plan to dance the night away, stay at a Western hotel.

We have divided Kyoto hotels into five groups:

Kyoto Station

Most of the hotels are impersonal and large, catering to tour groups. While the station's convenient to travel to Nara and Osaka, a more central location is better for touring Kyoto. It's our least favorite area to stay

KYOTO TOKYU HOTEL, not to be confused with the Tokyu Inn located on the outskirts of Kyoto. *580 Kakimoto-cho, Gojo sagaru, Horikawa Dori, Shimogyo-ku, Kyoto, 600-8519. Tel. (075)341-2411, Fax (075)341-2488. 432 rooms. Singles from ¥12,000. Twins from ¥20,000. Member of the Welcome Inn Reservation Center.*

This large, Western-style hotel has an attractive courtyard and many restaurants. It is a good choice for a top hotel located fairly close to the station.

NEW HANKYU HOTEL, *Karasuma cho-guchi shomen, Kyoto, 600-8216. Tel. (075)343-5300. 319 rooms. Singles from ¥12,000. Twins from ¥17,000. Credit cards.*

New Hankyu, just across the street from the Karasuma exit of Kyoto Station is an average hotel with undistinguished rooms. We stayed here as part of a package and it's okay, but nothing special. They have a branch of the famous Kyoto restaurant, Minokichi.

NEW MIYAKO HOTEL, *Hachijo-guchi, Kyoto, 600-8412. Tel. (075)661-7111, Fax (075)661-7135. 714 rooms. Singles from ¥9000. Twins from ¥19,000. Credit cards.*

A less expensive branch of the Miyako Hotel, it's close to the shinkansen exit (Hachijo-guchi) of Kyoto Station. With 714 rooms, it's the largest hotel in Kyoto and caters to tour groups.

Central Kyoto

Three famous inns – the first three listed below – are within one block of each other just south of Oike Dori on Tominokoji and Anenokoji. All these establishments have long traditions, elegant wooden *sukiya*-style buildings (a fairly casual, almost rustic and spartan architecture with interior gardens), impeccable service and are expensive. We found the difference between these places and ordinary *ryokan* is that when an attendant serves a dinner course and notices that you've spilled a drop of soup, the offending drop is instantly whisked away. A night in any of these three will be an experience you'll long remember.

TAWARAYA, *Anenokoji agaru, Fuya-cho, Oike Sagaru, Nakagyo-ku, Kyoto, 604-8094. Tel. (075)211-5566, Fax (075)211-2204. 19 rooms. From ¥38,000 per person with two meals. Credit cards.*

Tawaraya is Japan's oldest and most famous *ryokan*. Its graceful and subtle hospitality make staying here a relaxing experience. The rooms are almost austere in keeping with the tea ceremony aesthetic but have modern amenities such as air conditioning and television. The same family has run Tawaraya for 300 years. Dignitaries often stay here when visiting Kyoto — Tawaraya has hosted kings and queens, prime ministers and a *Who's Who* of the art, television and business worlds. The nice thing about Tawaraya is you, too, will be welcomed like a VIP.

HIIRAGIYA, *277 Nakashiroyama-machi, Anenokoji agaru, Fuya-cho, Nakagyo-ku, Kyoto, 604-8094. Tel. (075)221-1136, Fax (075)221-1139. 33 rooms. From ¥35,000 per person with two meals. Credit cards.*

Located across the street from Tawaraya, the two exteriors look similar, but the interior is a study in contrasts. Hiiragiya began in the 1800s as an inn catering to the warrior class and is more ornate than its neighbor. It has excellent food and service. For a less expensive variation, you can stay at their **annex** on Gokamachi Dori, south of Nijo, where rooms start at ¥12,000 per person with two meals. *Tel. (075)231-0151, Fax: (075)231-0153.*

YOSHIKAWA INN, *Tominokoji, Oike sagaru, Nakagyo-ku, Kyoto, 604-8093. Tel. (075)221-5544, Fax (075)221-6805. 13 rooms. From ¥30,000 per person with two meals. Credit cards.*

Yoshikawa is not as well known as Tawaraya and Hiiragiya, but it provides the same warm hospitality and ambiance. The inn tastefully incorporates the modern; for instance, television sets are hidden in cabinets with sliding doors so they don't intrude. The staff is thoughtful in undreamed of ways: because our room did not face the interior garden, our breakfast was served in a room where we could experience it. Yoshikawa is also a restaurant serving excellent *tempura* and *kaiseki* meals. You can arrange to eat *shabu-shabu* if you don't want *kaiseki*. We had such a delightful stay here, we have highlighted it in Chapter 11, our most memorable stays.

KYOTO BRIGHTON HOTEL, *Nakadachiuri, Shinmachi Dori, Kamigyo-ku, Kyoto, 602-8071. Tel. (075)441-4411, Fax (075)431-2360. 183 rooms. Singles from ¥21,000. Twins from ¥28,000.*

The Kyoto Brighton Hotel actively seeks out the foreign community and provides a higher level of service than hotels catering to Japanese tour groups. Rooms open on to a large atrium lobby and are airy and spacious. The hotel is west of the Imperial Palace and is a good choice if you're looking for Western-style accommodations. Be sure to ask about the

Brighton Benefit packages for foreigners that include room discounts, breakfast and personally-developed tours.

NEW KYOTO HOTEL, *Horikawa-Marutamachi-kado, Kamigyo-ku, Kyoto. Tel. (075)801-2111, Fax (075)801-4519. Singles from ¥8000. Twins from ¥14,000. Credit cards.*

Well located on the corner of Horikawa and Marutamachi, New Kyoto is a good choice for a moderate-priced Western-style hotel. The staff is very friendly and bends over backwards to accommodate their guests. The rooms are very clean and fairly good sized for the price.

HEARTON HOTEL, *Oike-agaru, Higashinotoin Dori, Nakagyo-ku, Kyoto, 604-0836. Tel. (075)222-1300, Fax (075)222-1313. 294 rooms. Singles from ¥8500. Doubles from ¥12,000. Credit cards. Part of Welcome Inn Reservation Center.*

This contemporary hotel is a step-up from most in its class. The marble lobby is brightly lit and the rooms attractively decorated. It's located near the Oike subway station.

COOP INN KYOTO, *Yanagibamba Dori, north of Takoyakushi, Kyoto, 604-8113. Tel. (075)256-6600, Fax (075)251-0120. Singles ¥7600. Twins ¥14,400. Credit cards.*

The Coop Inn, run by a university association but open to anyone, has moderately priced accommodations at a very central location. The Western-style rooms are small, especially the singles, but have private baths. There are also Japanese-style rooms at ¥10,000 for a single and ¥15,300 for a double. Doors close at 1am.

HOTEL MARMOL, *Gokomachi Dori and Rokkaku Dori, Nakagyo-ku, Kyoto, 604-8066. Tel. (075)213-2456, Fax (075)213-3518. Singles from ¥5900. Doubles from ¥9900. Credit cards.*

The centrally located Hotel Marmol is a cut above most business hotels. The decor is bright, welcoming and modern. Western or Japanese breakfast costs only ¥700.

HOTEL KOHRO, *Rokkahu Hokuto-kado, Sakaimachi-dori, Nakagyo-ku, Kyoto 604-8118. Tel. (075)221-7807. Fax (075)221-7649. Single ¥6000. Double ¥10,000. Rates higher during peak seasons. Credit cards.*

Hotel Kohro sports an extremely convenient location, yet is quiet. The hotel is an interesting mix of modern and traditional: an attractive building constructed of concrete with traditional Japanese roof tiles. The rooms are all Japanese style.

HIROTA GUEST HOUSE, *6-6-5 Nijo Dori, Seimei-cho, Nakagyo-ku, Kyoto, 605-8222. Tel. (075)221-2474, Fax (075)221-2627. 5 rooms. Front rooms from ¥5000 per person; storehouse suite ¥8000. No credit cards.*

This small guest house is in a quiet neighborhood south of the Imperial Palace. There are four rooms in the front and a suite in the rear. It contains a kitchen, bath and sleeping loft and is located in a stucco storehouse. The proprietor speaks fluent English and goes out of her way to make sure her guests have an enjoyable stay. She'll let you know about local events and happenings.

NASHINOKI INN, *Futasujime-agaru, Imadegawa Teramachi Nishi-iru, Kamigyo-ku, Kyoto, 602-0838 (on Nashinoki Dori, north of Imadegawa Dori). Tel. (075)241-1543, Fax (075)211-0854. 7 rooms. Single from ¥4500 per person without meals. Doubles ¥8600. Part of the Welcome Inn Reservation Center. No credit cards.*

This small budget inn is just north of the Imperial Palace grounds, two blocks east of Teramachi Dori on a quiet road. You can get a Japanese or a Western breakfast for ¥900.

RYOKAN YUHARA. *188 Kagiyacho, Shomen-agaru, Kiyamachi Dori, Shimogyo-ku, Kyoto 600-8126. Tel. and Fax (075)371-9583. ¥4000 per person with no meals. Member of the Welcome Inn Reservation Center.*

Yuhara is a top choice in the budget category. The centrally-located inn has Japanese-style rooms and a very friendly owner who speaks English.

Higashiyama — Eastern Kyoto

TAMAHAN, *477 Shimokawara, Gion, Higashiyama-ku, Kyoto, 605-0825. Tel. (075)561-3188, Fax (075)531-5128. 11 rooms. From ¥23,000 per person with two meals. Credit cards.*

This quiet inn in the Ishibe Koji area, a warren of quiet streets and picturesque buildings near Kodai-ji Temple, is everything a Japanese inn should be — understated and elegant. The *tatami* mat rooms look out over carefully tended gardens, mentally removing you from the clutter of the city. The road is so narrow that bicycles have trouble passing each other, so there isn't any distracting car noise. The inn has two buildings; the older one is our choice with its rustic rooms and wooden bathtubs. Tamahan is also a restaurant and serves delicious food: elegant *kaiseki*, a procession of artfully prepared food in exquisite dishes, or Kodai-ji *nabe*, a one-pot dish of duck, beef, pork, shrimp and vegetables cooked in a copper pot.

YOSHIIMA RYOKAN, *Hanamikoji Nishi iru, Shinmonzen, Higashiyama-ku, Kyoto, 605-0088. Tel. (075)561-2620, Fax (075)541-6493. 15 rooms. From ¥24,000 per person with two meals. Credit cards.*

Yoshiima is the inn where JTB (Japan Travel Bureau) places foreigners who ask for a Japanese inn experience in Kyoto. That's both good and bad. The inn is a well-preserved wooden structure in a good location — on Shinmonzen, the antique center — and the staff speaks English and is very experienced with dealing with foreigners. Meals are brought to the guest rooms. They serve a Western breakfast on request and for dinner they serve the types of Japanese food most foreigners will eat — *sukiyaki, shabu-shabu* and *tempura*.

On the negative side, most of the other guests will also be foreign visitors, so it's not quite a total Japanese experience. By booking through JTB overseas, you will get a rate lower than the rate above.

MIYAKO HOTEL, *Ke-age Sanjo, Higashiyama-ku, Kyoto, 605-0052. Tel. (075)771-7111, Fax (075)751-2490. 445 rooms. Singles from ¥17,000. Twins from ¥19,000. Credit cards.*

The Miyako is Kyoto's most prestigious large hotel. Its Japanese wing is truly exquisite with rustic buildings in an Japanese garden, but it's really pricey. The Western part of the hotel, white marble and pink in decor, doesn't reflect the spirit of Kyoto. The hotel is on the side of a mountain but is fairly inconvenient for touring. The hotel compensates by providing a shuttle bus to Sanjo and Kyoto Stations.

YACHIYO, *Nanzenji Bashi, Sakyo-ku, Kyoto, 606-8435. Tel. (075)771-4148, Fax (075)771-4140. 20 rooms. From ¥18,000 per person with two meals. Credit cards.*

This small inn, noted for its cuisine, has a beautiful garden. Although it's located on the approach road to Nanzen-ji, when the tourists go home in the evening, it's delightfully quiet and the back roads make good walking.

SHIRAUME, *Shirakawa-hotori, Gion-shinbashi, Higashiyama-ku, Kyoto, 605-0085. Tel. (075)561-1459, Fax (075)531-5290. From ¥18,000 per person with two meals. No credit cards.*

A delightful inn that was once a teahouse in the Shinbashi *geisha* quarter. Crossing the bridge over the small canal to reach the elegant building always makes us think we're entering a different world. The inn offers a wide range of choices for dinner or you can have breakfast only.

IWANAMI RYOKAN, *Higashioji Nishi iru, Shinmonzen, Higashiyama-ku, Kyoto, 605-0064. Tel. (075)561-7135. No fax. 6 rooms. ¥17000 per person. No credit cards.*

Iwanami is a small, charming inn located in the midst of Shinmonzen's antique shops, a perfect location for shoppers. It's also just around the corner from Shinbashi, one of Kyoto's beautifully preserved *geisha* districts. Some rooms have private toilets while others don't.

RYOKAN RIKIYA, *462-23 Shimogawara-cho, Kodaiji, Higashiyama-ku, Kyoto, 605-0825. Tel. (075)561-1300, Fax (075)561-2944. 10 rooms. ¥7000 per person without meals; breakfast ¥2000 additional. Member of the Welcome Inn Reservation Center. Credit cards.*

Rikiya is a small old wooden inn in a quiet area across the street from the entrance to Kodai-ji Temple. The Japanese breakfasts are delicious, but a Western breakfast is available upon request.

THREE SISTERS INN (RAKUTO-SO), *Okazaki, Sakyo-ku, Kyoto, 606-8321. Tel. (075)761-6336, Fax (075)761-6338. Singles from ¥8900 per person with breakfast. Doubles from ¥15,000. No credit cards.*

Three Sisters is an excellent place to stay if you'd like a small, personal Japanese inn but also want a safety net. Since 1957 the three Yamada sisters, all fluent in English, have delighted in making sure their foreign guests get the most of their Kyoto sojourns. The clientele is almost exclusively foreign, and breakfasts are Western style. The annex is block away from the main building; both are conveniently located close to the Heian Shrine.

LADIES HOTEL CHORAKUEN, *Maruyama koen-nai, Gion, Higashiyama-ku, Kyoto, 605. Tel. (075)561-0001, Fax (075)561-0006. 21 rooms. Singles from ¥5000. Twins from ¥9000. No credit cards.*

This Renaissance style former guest house has been turned into a women's hotel that's located in the quiet Maruyama Park district near Yasaka Shrine and Gion.

SAWAI RYOKAN, *4-320 Miyagawa-cho, Higashiyama-ku, Kyoto, 605-0801. Tel. (075)561-2179. No fax. 4 rooms. ¥5000 per person with no meals. No credit cards.*

Sawai Ryokan is Patrice's favorite place to stay in Kyoto. Run by Mr. Sawai who translates German art books for a living, he's a refuge from Tokyo. The street is very quiet and prohibits traffic during the day. It's lined with wooden teahouses like Mr. Sawai's and in the evening you can see *maiko* and *geisha* heading to their appointments. Ask for a front room; they are filled with antiques. The back rooms are quite plain. Mr. Sawai does not advertise and doesn't even have a permanent sign. He puts out a handwritten sign when guests are expected and removes it after they arrive. Because of the antiques, children are not accepted.

RYOKAN TERADAYA, *6-583 Gojobashi-higashi, Higashiyama-cho, Kyoto, 605-0846. Tel. (075)561-3821, Fax (075)541-8436. 5 rooms. ¥5000 per person without meals. Part of Welcome Inn Reservation Center. Credit cards.*

This small traditional wooden inn is on a small road coming off Gojozaka, one of the streets leading to Kiyomizu-dera. Despite its proximity to this major tourist center, it's quiet, used to foreigners and conveniently located for walks along Sannenzaka and Ninenzaka.

KITANOYA RYOKAN, *Sanjo, Higashi-iru-agaru, Higashiyama-ku, Kyoto, 606-8345. Tel. (075)771-1488, Fax (075)761-3386. 8 rooms. ¥4000 per person without meals. No credit cards.*

Kitanoya is a small wooden inn located on a quiet street between Sanjo Dori and the Heian Shrine. Unfortunately they've put linoleum in the hallways, but the rooms are traditional Japanese style. Kitanoya is a good budget inn.

Arashiyama — West of Kyoto

BENKEI, *34 Susukinobaba-machi, Tenryu-ji, Saga, Ukyo-ku, Kyoto, 616-8385. Tel. (075)872-3355, Fax (075)872-9310. 12 rooms. From ¥19,000 per person with two meals. Credit cards.*

Benkei is rebuilt in the traditional style and has good views of the Hozu River. The food and service are excellent. Be sure to request a room with a view; they cost the same as the others.

HOTEL RANTEI, *12 Susukinobaba-machi, Tenryu-ji, Saga, Ukyo-ku, Kyoto, 616-8385. Tel. (075)371-1119, Fax (075)881-6220. 22 rooms. From ¥17,600 per person with two meals.*

Located on the banks of a river, Rantei is a peaceful and picturesque place to stay. Tea is served in a large garden under a red umbrella.

Temple Lodgings

With over one thousand temples in Kyoto, there are many lodging facilities designed for pilgrims, but open to the public. The food is vegetarian, but beer and *sake* are often available. Some places require you to attend the early morning service; others make it optional.

HIDEN-IN, *35 San-nyu-ji, Sandai-cho, Higashiyama-ku, Kyoto, 605. Tel. (075)561-8781. No fax. ¥4500 per person with breakfast.*

This temple is popular for its views of the mountains; staff members speak English.

CHISHAKU-IN KAIKAN, *Higashiyama Nanajo, Higashiyama-ku, Kyoto, 605. Tel. (075)541-5363, Fax (075)541-4167. ¥6500 with breakfast; ¥8000 with two meals.*

This temple lodging is conveniently located, close to the Kyoto National Museum and Sanjusangendo. You'll get an early start because the temple requests you participate in the morning service at 6am (6:30am in winter). While you stay here, be sure to see the temple's excellent garden and paintings.

HIEIZAN ENRYAKUJI KAIKAN, *Hieizan, Sakamoto Hon-cho, Otsu, Shiga. Tel. (0775)78-0047, Fax (0775)79-5053. ¥12,000 per person with two meals.*

Located high up on the mountain northeast of the city, Enryaku-ji was once one of Kyoto's most powerful temples. Staying here is inconvenient for touring Kyoto but gives you some idea of the glory of a temple in its heyday. Morning service is at 6:30am (7:30am in winter); attendance is optional. It's possible to stay without meals. English spoken.

WHERE TO EAT

Kyoto restaurants are divided into the following areas:
1. Kyoto Station, page 581
2. Central Kyoto, pages 581-583

Kyoto Cooking

The Japanese have an expression that Kyoto-ites bankrupt themselves buying kimono while Osakans bankrupt themselves on eating good food. Somehow it's hard to believe that anyone could spend more time and money on food than Kyoto's denizens and the millions of out-of-towners (about 35 million) invading Kyoto every year. Kyoto is a city of restaurants. There is a whole genre called *ryori ryokan* (cuisine inns) that take the food they serve as seriously as the hospitality they provide. Back alleys, shopping districts and malls – all overflow with restaurants.

Kyoto is best known for its *kaiseki* cuisine that developed from the tea ceremony. Presentation and seasonality are most important. *Kaiseki* today means a profusion of small dishes with tidbits of food arranged impeccably on ceramic and lacquer dishes chosen to show off the food. It's really food as theater. Preparing all these labor intensive dishes and using only the finest ingredients means prices are high.

One way to have *kaiseki* without mortgaging your house is to eat it at lunchtime. Noontime *kaiseki* is usually served in a lacquer *bento* box, with tidbits of a dozen or more items plus soup and other extras on the side. It's still a feast for your eyes. A restaurant's *kaiseki* dinner might start at ¥10,000 or ¥15,000, whereas lunch is about ¥4000 or ¥5000.

Japanese do not eat *kaiseki* at home. It's saved for formal occasions such as weddings and as a treat, especially while traveling.

At home, Kyoto-ites eat *obansai ryori;* some restaurants serve this family-style cooking. Seasonality is emphasized, but it isn't as pretty or precious as *kaiseki*. Some *obansai* restaurants place large platters of food on a counter, and you choose whatever appeals to you.

Buddhism has been a major force in Kyoto almost since its establishment as the capital; so Buddhist cuisine, *shojin ryori*, is closely associated with Kyoto. This vegetarian cuisine uses fresh ingredients and tofu, *yuba* (soy milk skin) and *fu* (wheat gluten) as sources of protein. Each meal contains food with each of the five tastes: hot, sweet, sour, salty and bitter and is prepared five ways: raw, fried, boiled, grilled and steamed.

From *shojin ryori* sprang another Kyoto favorite, *yu-dofu*, which is food at its simplest. Tofu is served simmering in broth; it's eaten after dipping it in a flavorful soy-based sauce. Tofu, essentially a bland food, picks up the flavors of what is eaten with it; by the time the tofu hits your mouth, it's delicious. Restaurants pride themselves on their dipping sauces and guard their recipes like state secrets. Kyoto's tofu is famous because it's made with very pure water.

Kyoto also prides itself on its sweets. *Higashi*, made to accompany the bitter tea ceremony tea called *matcha*, are tiny and flower shaped. These dry sweets, nearly the consistency of a finely ground sugar cube, last a long time so they make unique presents to take home. Other sweets use bean paste as a filling. Many of Japan's premier confectioners are purveyors to the imperial family. Although they moved to Tokyo with the emperor in 1868, they still have shops in Kyoto.

Since Kyoto exists in the modern world, you don't have to go far without finding a McDonalds or its local equivalent.

Kyoto Station

With the opening of the new **Kyoto Station building**, the Kyoto Station area has even more places to eat. On the 11th floor, **Restaurant Gai** and Isetan's **Eat Paradise** feature over 20 restaurants with all types of food. Open daily 11am to 10pm. We especially like **Sushi Sei,** a branch of the reasonably-priced Tokyo sushi chain, *Tel. (075)352-6223*, and **Matsuyama-en,** specializing in yuba (made from tofu) and vegetables; courses start at ¥2500. *Tel. (075)342-0700.*

Another set of restaurants is called **Open View**, on the 7th through 10th floors of the station; they all provide diners with spectacular views of Kyoto and the surrounding mountains. Open 11am to 11pm. **Italia Ichiba** on the 10th floor has good pastas, pizzas and seafood at moderate prices. *Tel. (075)365-7765.* Next door, **Koke-kokko** serves yakitori and other grilled skewers in a bright and open setting. *Tel. (075)365-3390.*

IZUSEN *(Vegetarian, moderate). 2F, Surugaya Building, located near the Karasuma exit of Kyoto Station, next to JNTO Tourist Information Center. Open 11am to 4pm.*

This restaurant serves Buddhist vegetarian food; the ¥2700 set is a good deal at lunchtime.

Central Kyoto

MUKADEYA *(Japanese family cooking, moderate to expensive). On Shinmachi Dori, north of Nishikikoji, 381 Mukadeya-cho, Shin-machi, Nishikikoji* *agaru, Nakagyo-ku. Tel. (075)256-7039. Open 11am to 2pm; 5pm to 9pm. Closed Wednesday.*

Mukadeya is one of our favorite eateries in Kyoto. You eat among unpretentious antiques creatively displayed in a beautifully restored merchant's house. Even the thick-walled storehouse has been turned into a dining space. The food is Kyoto *obansai*, a home-type of cooking. At lunchtime the *Mukade bento* costs ¥3000. *Obansai* course at dinner time run ¥5000, ¥7000 and ¥10,000.

MASAGO *(Japanese, inexpensive at lunch time but expensive at dinner time). On Koromodana Dori, south of Sanjo. Ryoton Zushi-machi, Sanjo-sagaru, Koromodana Dori, Nakagyo-ku. Tel. (075)221-0211. Open 11:30am-2pm; 5:30pm-9pm.*

Masago is located in the former residence of Hirono Ryoton, one of the major domos of the tea ceremony in the late 16th century. Masago serves a delicious lunch served in a two-layered lacquer box at the bargain price of ¥700. The restaurant is in a converted storehouse; the garden is well kept and peaceful. Dinner *kaiseki* courses begin at ¥8000.

TEMPURA YOSHIKAWA INN *(Tempura, inexpensive to expensive). On Tominokoji just south of Oike Dori, Nakagyo-ku. Tel. (075)221-5544. Open 11am to 2pm; 5pm to 8:30pm. Closed Monday.*

This venerable inn is also a restaurant and serves some of Kyoto's best *tempura*. Sit at the counter in the cozy teahouse-style room and enjoy *tempura* straight from the frying pan, the way purists prefer. Lunch from ¥2000; dinner from ¥6000. You can also have *kaiseki* in a private room overlooking the garden, ¥12,000 and up.

GION HEIHACHI SHINSEN-EN *(Japanese, moderate). On Oshikoji, west of Horikawa. Tel. (075)841-0811. Open 11am to 8pm.*

In Shinsen-en Garden, there's a pleasant restaurant with large windows overlooking the pond. We had the lunchtime *udon chiri* set (¥3000). It's a stew you cook for yourself and has the fattest noodles we've ever seen. Actually they're from Akita in northern Japan, but not being authentic Kyoto fare didn't detract from them for one minute. The restaurant also serves *tempura* and *shabu-shabu*; for your convenience, there's a picture menu.

SHIRUKO *(Japanese, inexpensive to moderate). On Hitosujime east of Minamikiya, near Shijo-Kawaramachi. Minamikiya Higashi-iru, Hitosujime, Shijo-Kawaramachi, Shimogyo-ku. Tel. (075)221-3250. Open 11:30am to 8:30pm. Closed Wednesday.*

This restaurant is in a folk-art strewn traditional building and is famous for its delicious soups — *shiromiso* (white miso), *akamiso* (brown miso) and *sumashi* (clear soup). At lunchtime you'll probably have to wait in line. Soups start at ¥500; order mixed vegetable rice for ¥700 for a nice accompaniment. The *Rikyu bento* for ¥2500 is a good choice for a larger meal.

CAPRICCIOSA *(Italian, inexpensive). 2nd Floor, Vox Building, one block south of Sanjo Street, east of Kawaramachi. Tel. (075)221-7476. Open 11am to 10pm.*

This chain of Italian restaurants serves huge portions of pasta that are definitely made for sharing. They also have good pizza and salads. Pastas and pizzas run about ¥1500 each. We come here when we want a change from the dainty portions of most Kyoto restaurants.

TSUKIGASE *(Sweet shop, inexpensive). On Kawaramachi, turn right at the second block north of Shijo; it's on the south side of the street. You'll see the case with plastic sample of sweets out front. Tel. (075)221-4104. Open 12:30pm to 6pm. Closed Wednesday.*

When you feel like taking a break, this comfortable shop is a good place to try Japanese sweets. It's a popular stop for Kyoto shoppers. *Anmitsu* costs ¥630; *shiratama zenzai* is ¥650.

Central Higashiyama & Gion

OSHINBO, *(Japanese, moderate). Hanami-koji, Shijo-sagaru. Tel. (075)541-6100. From Shijo Dori, turn south on Hanami-koji, left at the second street (Junidanya is on the corner). Open 11:30am to 2:30pm; 6pm to 2am.*

Oshinbo features bansai ryori, Kyoto-style home cooking. This fun and lively place serves delicious fare around tables on tatami mats. Lunchtime *obanzai nattoku* set costs ¥1995; evening *obansai omakase nattoku* course runs ¥3885. There is also an extensive a la carte menu in English. Reservations recommended.

IKKYU-AN *(Vegetarian, moderate to expensive). Across from Kodai-ji's south gate. Kodaiji Minamimon-mae, Higashiyama-ku. Tel. (075)561-1901. Open 12 noon to 8pm. Closed Tuesday.*

The red Chinese-style gate attracts your attention. The specialty here is monks' vegetarian food, Chinese style. Lunch (12-4pm) features a *Fucha ryori* set meal for ¥3500. ¥5000 and ¥7000 sets are available at all times. After eating here, we realized what healthy and tasty foods the monks have been enjoying in Zen temples all these years!

YAGENBORI *(Japanese, moderate to expensive). On Kiritoshi Dori (north of Shijo Dori, the third block from the Kamo River) right after crossing Sueyoshicho Dori. Tel. (075)551-3331. Another branch is south of Shijo Dori on Hanamikoji. Open daily 11:30am to 2:30pm; 4pm to 10:30pm.*

Yagenbori's decor is folk-art style from Takayama, a city high in the mountains, but the food is pure Kyoto. Lunch by reservation only, ¥4500; dinner *kaiseki* courses from ¥6,000.

OKUTAN *(Tofu, moderate). Intersection of Ninenzaka and Sannenzaka. Tel. (075)525-2051.*

A branch of the famed *yu-dofu* restaurant at Nanzen-ji, this shop has a lovely garden. The *yu-dofu* course costs ¥3000.

NAKAYOSHI SHINISE *(Japanese, inexpensive)*. *5F, Emerald Building, next to Kaburenjo Theater on Ponto-cho, north of Shijo Dori. Minami, Kaburenjo, Ponto-cho, Nakagyo-ku. Tel. (075)211-4333. Open 12 noon to 3pm; 5pm to 9pm. Closed Thurssdays.*

If you plan to see *Geisha* dancing and singing at the Ponto-cho Kaburenjo, this is an ideal place to have lunch because it's in the adjacent building. The family has been serving *yuba* (soy milk skin; the texture is unusual, but delicious) in various forms for over 200 years. *Yuba tempura* is ¥2000, and a six-dish Sanjo course served only at lunch costs ¥3000.

IMOBO HIRANOYA HONTEN *(Japanese, inexpensive). Just outside Chion-in's South Gate, on the northern perimeter of Maruyama Park. Tel. (075)561-1603. Open 10:30am to 8pm.*

Along the northern perimeter of Maruyama Park is a complex of wooden buildings that makes up this one-hundred year old restaurant. Hiranoya serves *imobo*, a Kyoto specialty of stewed mountain potatoes and preserved cod. Try it for an old Kyoto experience. *Imobo* set is ¥1800.

KAPPA *(Japanese, inexpensive to moderate). On right side of Nawate Dori, north of Shijo. Tel. (075)531-2322. Open 6pm to 2am. Closed Tuesday.*

This restaurant is a casual and fun place to go; it's about as removed mentally from the sedate Kyoto *kaiseki* restaurants as you can be in the Gion district. When we want a change from serene Kyoto restaurants, we come here. It's a boisterous place where you sit at the counter and watch the cooks preparing *yakitori, sushi, tempura* and other goodies. There's an English menu, and the average tab is about ¥3000 per person although you can eat for less if you choose carefully.

KUSHIKURA HONTEN *(Kushiage, inexpensive to moderate). On Takakura Dori, north of Oike Dori. Oike agaru, Takakura Dori, Nakagyo-ku. Tel. (075)213-2211. Open 11:30am to 1:30pm; 5pm to 10pm. Dinner only Saturday and Sunday.*

You can't miss this shop because you can smell grilled chicken (free-range) the minute you step on Takakura Dori. This traditional merchant house is now a casual restaurant featuring chicken dishes and delicious *sake*. There's even a well-kept tiny garden. ¥3000 will buy a good dinner. The lunchtime sets cost ¥700-1200. Evening course of ten skewers is ¥2500.

KAGIZEN *(Japanese sweets, inexpensive). On north side of Shijo Dori, west of Hanamikoji. Tel. (075)561-1818. Open 9am to 6pm. Closed Monday.*

This sweet shop sells *kuzu kiri*, a translucent *kuzu* noodle eaten with a sweet sauce, and Kyoto sweets. We love the atmosphere of this place; it's like time stopped about 200 years ago.

RAKUSHO *(Japanese sweets, inexpensive). On Kitamon-mae Dori, north of Kodai-ji Temple. Washio-cho, Kodai-ji, Kitamon-mae Dori, Higashiyama-ku. Tel. (075)561-6892. Open 9:30am to 5:30pm. Closed Monday.*

After traipsing around the slopes of Ninenzaka and Sannenzaka, stop here for a refreshing break. This teahouse has a great garden with carp in the pond, and you can take it all in as you sit drinking green tea and eating Japanese sweets.

Northern Higashiyama

OKUTAN *(Tofu, moderate). Turn left on the small road just inside Nanzenji's first gate and follow it around, bearing to the right. Okutan is in one of the subtemples, and is next to Choshoin. 86 Fukuchi-machi, Nanzen-ji, Sakyo-ku. Tel. (075)771-8709. Open 11:30am-5pm. Closed Thursday.*

Located in a subtemple of Nanzen-ji, this venerable vegetarian restaurant has been serving *yu-dofu* for 12 generations. And the food is delicious; their ¥3000 course includes sesame tofu, grated mountain potato, *dengaku* (sticks of tofu and vegetables covered with miso sauce), vegetable *tempura*, a large pot of tofu and rice and pickles. Beer and *sake* are ¥600 extra. When the weather is good, you can eat outside under a large red umbrella on a platform covered with red felt. During the lunchtime peak, it's crowded and rushed. So try to avoid 12 noon to 1:30pm or dine at Choshoin, the subtemple next door. Okutan has a branch where Ninenzaka and Sannenzaka meet, close to Kiyomizu-dera Temple.

CHOSHOIN *(Tofu, moderate). Inside Nanzen-ji, next to Okutan. See Okutan (above) for directions. Fukuchi-machi, Nanzen-ji, Sakyo-ku. Tel. (075)761-2186. Open 11am to 3pm. Closed Wednesday and Buddhist ritual days.*

Among tofu restaurants, Choshoin is one of our favorites because of its ambiance as much as its taste. You're seated on the temple's broad

---

NANZEN-JI'S TOFU

Today Japanese immediately associate **Nanzen-ji** with **yu-dofu**; this connection began during the mid-Edo Period, 17th to 18th century. During the Edo Period, the shogunate controlled almost every aspect of people's lives, including the right to travel. Religious pilgrimages were the only legitimate way people could travel. They would go to Kyoto to visit Yasaka Shrine, Kiyomizu-dera and Nanzen-ji not only to accumulate merit but also to enjoy themselves while in the capital. Hence lots of teahouses in Gion opened to cater to those needs! Business-minded guards at Nanzen-ji started selling tofu to these pilgrims. It became famous because the clear spring water made delicious tofu. Before long, yu-dofu was served in winter.

Okay, what is yu-dofu? **Yu** means hot water. The tofu is brought to the table in simmering broth. Carefully lift it out and place it in the small dish that has dipping sauce. Tofu is bland but picks up the taste of the sauce. And the texture is sublime.

veranda that's covered with red felt and overlooks a quiet garden and pond designed in the 15th century by the famous artist Soami. Founded in 1336 as one of the subtemples of Nanzen-ji, at Choshoin you have a choice among several sets of vegetarian meals all featuring *yu-dofu*. The *matsu* course costs ¥3000.

YACHIYO *(Japanese, moderate to expensive). On the approach road to Nanzen-ji. Tel. (075)771-4148. Open 11am to 4pm; 5pm to 8pm.*

This restaurant is run by the Yachiyo Inn and serves delicious *yu-dofu* as well as a variety of *bento* box lunches. Lunch sets start at ¥2000; dinner from ¥10,000.

ROKUSEI *(Japanese, moderate). West of Heian Jingu. Nishi-yoko, Heian Jingu, Okazaki, Higashiyama-ku. Tel. (075)751-6171. Open 11:30am to 3pm; 5pm to 8:30pm. Closed Monday.*

Rokusei is known for serving Kyoto style food in wooden barrels hand made by the famous barrel shop Tarugen. The menu changes according to season. The *te-oke* (a barrel with a handle) *bento* costs ¥3000 at lunchtime and ¥4700 at dinner time.

OMEN *(Noodles, inexpensive). Tel. (075)771-8994. Open 11am to 9:30pm. Closed Thursday.*

This *udon* noodle shop, just south of Ginkaku-ji's parking lot, is decorated with folk art and makes delicious *udon* ranging in price from ¥1500 to ¥2500. We try to visit Ginkaku-ji around lunchtime as an excuse to eat here.

North Central Kyoto

NISHIJIN-UOSHIN *(Japanese, moderate to expensive). On Nakasuji Dori, south of Imadegawa Dori. Jofukuji Nishiiru, Nakasuji Dori, Kamigyo-ku. Tel. (075)441-0753. Open 11am to 3pm; 5pm-8pm.*

Since 1855, Nishijin Uoshin has been a restaurant that serves *yusoku ryori*, a cuisine based on aristocratic tradition and manners. The understated entrance gives way to a wonderful small garden and exquisite *tatami* mat rooms where food is served. Lunchtime courses begin at ¥3500; dinners are from ¥10,000.

HON-YARA DO *(Western, inexpensive). On Imadegawa Dori, west of Teramachi Dori. Teramachi Nishiiru, Imadegawa Dori, Kamigyo-ku. Tel. (075)222-1574. Open 9:30am to 9:30pm. Closed first Wednesday.*

Located at Imadegawa Dori at the north end of the Imperial Palace, it's very popular among university students and arty types, which means it's cheap and has a very friendly atmosphere. A voluminous lunch set costs ¥500 and changes every day; the dinner set is a budget-busting ¥600.

OHIRUYA TOKON *(Tofu, inexpensive). On west side of Onmae Dori, three blocks south of Kitano Shrine. 90-4 Nishimachi, Nishiiru 3, Onmae Dori, Ichijo Dori, Kamigyo-ku. Tel. (075)463-1035. Open 11am to 2pm.*

Tofu lovers, this is where you can get your fill. Only open at lunchtime, this restaurant serves nothing but tofu; it's prepared in every conceivable way including dessert. The lunch set costs ¥1800.

TSURUYA YOSHINOBU *(Japanese sweets, inexpensive). At the intersection of Horikawa and Imadegawa Dori. Horikawa Imadegawa, Kamigyo-ku. Tel. (075)441-0105. Open 9:30am to 5:30pm; Sundays and holidays 9:30am to 4:30pm.*

This family has been producing Japanese sweets since the beginning of the 19th century when Napoleon was still in Elysee Palace, and is one of the best known sweet shops in Japan. On the second floor, you can watch craftsmen decorate the sweets. Stop for a rest and enjoy green tea and sweets for ¥800.

Northeast Kyoto

BISTRO KIMURA *(French, inexpensive to moderate). On Shirakawa Dori, turn east one block south of Lawsons, then left at the next street. 33-2 Yatamachi, Ichijoji, Sakyo-ku. Tel. (075)722-6789. Open 12 noon to 2pm; 6pm to 10:30pm. Closed Monday.*

This casual French bistro serves a bargain lunch set including entree (meat and fish), salad, rice (not French bread) and soup for ¥900. If you want to have their dinner courses (from ¥3500), you need to make a reservation one day in advance; you can also order a la carte from the menu.

BENTEN CHAYA *(Noodle , inexpensive). At Manshu-in's entrance. 15 Takenouchi Ichijoji, Saikyo-ku. Tel. (075)711-5665. Open daily 10am to 5pm.*

Located across from the entrance to Manshu-in, this cozy noodle shop has delicious handmade noodles and a garden setting. We like the Monzen *soba* set, which includes mushroom *soba*, *soba* cake and green tea, for ¥1500.

TENKA IPPIN MAIN SHOP *(Ramen, inexpensive). On the west side of Shirakawa Dori about five blocks south of the road leading to Shisendo. 94 Chikuda-machi, Ichijoji, Sakyo-ku. Tel. (075)722-0955. Open 11am to 3am. Closed Thursday.*

Tenka Ippin is one of Japan's most famous *ramen* (Chinese noodle) shops, and the bright lights are about as far as you can get from the rustic charm of Shisendo. Tenka Ippin claims more than 1000 people visit this relatively small shop every day. Tenka Ippin's special broth from chicken and vegetables is a departure from *ramen's* usual pork-based broth. Once you taste it, you'll know why we can't help coming back. *Ramen* ¥550.

Rakuhoku — Northern Kyoto

DAITOKU-JI IKKYU *(Vegetarian, moderate to expensive). Daitokuji Monzen, Murasakino, Kita-ku. Tel. (075)493-0019. Open 12 noon-2pm; dinner at 5pm only.*

Set in a traditional house on a street by Daitoku-ji's East Gate, Ikkyu has been serving Buddhist vegetarian food to Daitoku-ji's priest connoisseurs for 500 years. It is famous for its Daitoku-ji style *fu* (wheat gluten — it tastes better than it sounds) and *goma-dofu* (sesame tofu). At lunchtime a *bento* is ¥3500. The dinner courses run from ¥7000 to ¥12,000. Reservations required.

IZUSEN *(Japanese, moderate). Inside grounds of Daitoku-ji Temple. 4 Daitokuji-cho, Murasakino, Kita-ku. Tel. (075)491-6665. Open 11am to 4pm.*

Daiji-in, a subtemple of Daitoku-ji, runs this restaurant that serves Kyoto-style Buddhist vegetarian food in red lacquer bowls. Eating lunch here is one of the quintessential Kyoto experiences. Lunch sets from ¥3000.

WAKUDEN *(Japanese, moderate). As you exit the East Gate of Daitoku-ji, turn right; it's on corner of Kitaoji Dori in a contemporary concrete building. 18 Yunrin-in Machi, Murasakino, Kita-ku. Tel. (075)495-5588. Open 11am to 5pm. Closed Monday.*

From the entrance, Wakuden looks more like a French bistro than a Japanese restaurant. A small restaurant with only 10 seats at a counter, it is elegantly chic and modern, yet still Japanese. The chefs assemble your meal in front of you and serve it on gorgeous ceramic and lacquer plates. The *bento* cost ¥3500 and ¥5000.

ZENRINBO *(Japanese, inexpensive to moderate). Located outside Entsu-ji Temple. 40 Kita Takagamine, Kita-ku. Tel. (075)491-2231. Open 11am to 4pm.*

This quaint thatched-roof building used to be an inn for travelers heading north. It has a wonderful *bento* lunch (¥2000) served in a box made of willow, a holdover from the days travelers would take them on the road.

LA VITA *(Italian, inexpensive). 1F Kitaoji Vivre, on the south side of Kitaoji Dori, west of Kitaoji subway station. 49-1 Kazusa-machi, Koyama, Kita-ku. Tel. (075)495-3702. Open 11am to 9pm. Lunch buffet 11am to 3pm. Closed Tuesday.*

This casual Italian restaurant is a good choice. The buffet lunch is very popular and a great value. They have salad, three kinds of pasta, and two kinds of pizza plus soft drinks for ¥1000.

TSUNAMICHI *(Noodles, inexpensive). On the north side of Kitaoji Dori east of Kitaoji Subway Station. 39-2 Kazusa-machi, Koyama, Kita-ku. Tel. (075)492-7860. Open 11am to 9pm (to 8pm Sunday and holidays). Closed Saturday and 18th-20th of each month.*

Tsunamichi's owner loves *soba* and *udon,* and you'll know why when you try his handmade noodles. His enthusiasm is infectious. *Zaru soba* costs ¥650, *torinan udon (udon* with chicken) ¥700.

AZEKURA *(Noodles, inexpensive). From Kamigamo Shrine, walk east past Ota Jinja; Azekura is on the left. 30 Okamoto-cho, Kamigamo. Tel. (075)701-0161. Open 11:30am to 5pm. Closed Monday.*

Azekura is a former *sake* warehouse that was moved from Nara by the owner to escape its destruction. In addition to a *soba* noodle restaurant, there is a bamboo garden complete with teahouse, a folk-art hall and sometimes exhibitions are held in a second floor *tatami* mat room. The entire setting transports you back in time and is a delightful respite from city life.

Rakusei — Western Kyoto

AJIRO-HONTEN *(Temple vegetarian, moderate to expensive). Located just east of the southern entrance to Myoshin-ji temple, on the south side of Myoshinji-Michi. Myoshinji Minamimon-mae, Hanazono, Sakyo-ku. Tel. (075)463-0221. Open 11am to 6:30pm. Closed Wednesday.*

Ajiro was in charge of feeding the monks of Myoshin-ji for hundreds of years and now has opened the restaurant so that laymen can also sample innovative temple vegetarian cuisine. Meals are served in private rooms on red lacquer tables. Our stomachs as well as our eyes enjoyed their lunchtime *fuchidaka bento,* served in a beautiful lacquer box for ¥3000. Dinner courses start at ¥6000. Reservations required.

WARA *(Tofu, inexpensive to moderate). As you exit Kinkaku-ji (Golden Pavilion), immediately turn right onto Kitsuji Dori and turn at the first left after Kinkaku-ji. 13-3 Somon-cho, Kinugasa, Kita-ku. Tel. (075)461-5386. Open 12 noon to 8pm. Closed Wednesday.*

Tucked in a quiet residential area near Kinkaku-ji temple, the atmosphere is as cozy as if you were visiting a Japanese friend's home. Wara specializes in *yu-dofu,* tofu simmered at your table. They serve one set which consists of vegetable *tempura,* freshly grated mountain potato, homemade sesame tofu, *yu-dofu* and rice and pickles; the cost is ¥3100 yen. Reservations necessary.

HINADORI *(French, inexpensive to moderate). On Kitsuji Dori, one block from Kinkaku-ji. 9 Somon-cho, Kinugasa, Kita-ku. Tel. (075)467-1855. Open 11:30am to 2:30pm; 5pm to 8:30pm. Closed Thursday.*

This casual French bistro is close to Wara. The chef cooked at the Kyoto Brighton Hotel for 10 years. The lunchtime set is a bargain at ¥1000. Dinner courses are from ¥3700. Reservations necessary for dinner.

GONTARO *(Noodles, inexpensive). On the left side of Kitsuji Dori, several blocks south of Kinkaku-ji. 26 Miyashiko-cho, Hirano, Kita-ku. Tel. (075)463-1039. Open 11am-10pm. Closed Wednesdays.*

The first time we walked down the road from Kinkaku-ji to Ryoan-ji, a small traditional gate with a tile roof surrounded by hedges beckoned us. Investigating further, we discovered a wonderful little noodle shop with table and chairs as well as Japanese *tatami* mat seating. It wasn't until the third visit we realized the back of the building also had tables and looked out on a little garden. Gontaro serves *soba* and *udon* noodles as well as fancier *soba kaiseki* meals.

Arashiyama

KYUGETSUEN *(Japanese, inexpensive to moderate). 7 Nakao shimo-cho, Arashiyama, Nishigyo-ku. Tel. (075)861-0429. Open 11am to 5pm. Closed Monday.*

Located close to the Nonomiya bus stop, the restaurant has a spacious garden where we enjoy relaxing as we eat sophisticated Kyoto-style cooking. *Engestu bento* costs ¥2500, *yu-dofu* costs ¥3000.

LE BRA BLUE *(French, inexpensive). 72-1 Shingucho, Saga, Ukyo-ku. Tel. (075)881-9329 Open 11:30 to 2pm; 5:30pm to 9pm. Closed Tuesday.*

If you feel like something different from Japanese cooking, stop at this small French bistro along Shin Marutamachi dori. You'll find casual Paris in Kyoto! Lunch courses from ¥1800.

Takao & Togano — Northwest of Kyoto

MOMIJI-YA BEKKAN *(Japanese, moderate). Cross over Momiji Bashi Bridge, about 500 meters down the hill from Takao Bus Stop. Takao, Umegahata, Ukyo-ku. Open daily 11am-3pm; 5pm-9:30pm. Tel. (075)871-1005.*

This quiet Japanese restaurant belongs to the famous Momiji-ya Inn (the House of the Maples). A beautifully presented *bento* box at lunch costs ¥4500.

KINSUITEI *(Japanese, inexpensive). From Togano JR Bus stop, about 200 meters on the right side going towards Jingo-ji. 1 Tohnoh-machi, Umegahata, Ukyo-ku. Tel. (075)871-6288. Open daily 9am to 5pm.*

This casual Japanese restaurant beckons you to sit under the red umbrella and enjoy *amazake* (sweet nonalcoholic *sake*) for ¥350, *yu-dofu* (boiled tofu) as a set for ¥2500, alone ¥800. We also enjoyed their *ayu*, grilled white river fish, for ¥850.

TAKAO CHAYA *(Noodles, inexpensive). Inside the Jingo-ji Temple grounds. Takao-machi, Umegahata, Ukyo-ku. Tel. (075) 872-3810. Open 9am to 5pm. Closed irregularly.*

A casual restaurant where you can rest your feet enjoying the natural surroundings and the stunning red maple foliage during the autumn (late October to early December). Try the delicious handmade *Momiji udon* (special noodles with *yuzu*, a fragrant citrus) for ¥800. A set of noodles and other dishes cost ¥1200.

Saiho-ji & Katsura — West of Kyoto

KOKE NO CHAYA *(Noodles, inexpensive). 56 Yorozuishi-machi, Matsuo, Saikyo-ku. Tel. (075)381-3191. Open 9:30am to 4:30pm. Irregularly closed.*

Located in front of Kokedera temple, this long-standing shop is a good place to eat *soba* with grated mountain potato, *tororo soba*, for ¥900. The potato has a slightly slimy consistency, but if you don't let it bother you, it's delicious.

Fushimi, Daigo-ji & Uji — South of Kyoto

In Uji, go to **Mampuku-ji Temple** and try *Fucha ryori*, Chinese vegetarian Buddhist fare. The *bento* lunch costs ¥3000; courses are from ¥5000 and require at least four people. You must make reservations one week in advance between 11am and 1pm. Lunch is served from 11:30am to 1pm. It's troublesome but worth the effort. *Tel. (0774)32-3900.*

GENYA *(Noodles, inexpensive). 698 Higashigumi-machi, Fushimi-ku. Between Fushimi Momoyama and Tamba Bashi stations, across from the Fushimi Kuyakusho Ward Office. Tel. (075)602-1492. Open 11:30am to 7pm; they close earlier if they sell out. Closed Thursday.*

We like this noodle shop for its unusual *sake kasu* ramen noodles, ¥650, using the chaff left from making local Fushimi *sake*. Genya makes a limited amount of *ramen* each day and closes when it sells out.

TORISEI *(Yakitori, inexpensive). 186 Kami Aburagake-cho, Fushimi-ku. Two blocks west of Fushimi Momoyama station. Tel. (075)622-5533. Open 11:30am to 10pm. Closed Monday.*

The owner comes from a *sake* brewery family and serves the excellent combination of good *sake* and *yakitori*. They have more than 130 kinds of chicken dishes, all made from chickens slaughtered that day. You can even try chicken *sashimi*. *Yakitori* from ¥120/stick. The restaurant is in a storehouse belonging to the Yamamoto Sake Brewery. We love the 1920's interior decoration.

Ohara — Northeast of Kyoto

GYOZAN-EN *(Japanese, moderate). Sanzen-in, Ohara, Sakyo-ku. Located across from Sanzen-in. Tel. (075)744-2321. Open daily 11am-7pm.*

Gyozan-en serves elegant Kyoto fare. Served in a three-layer *bento* box, your delicate meal includes delicious vegetables and a wheat gluten called *fu*, a favorite of Buddhist priests. Try the *Ajisai bento* (hydrangea lunch box — Sanzen-in is famous for its hydrangeas) for ¥3000.

KUMOI CHAYA *(Japanese, inexpensive). 41 Kusao-machi, Ohara, Sakyo-ku. Tel. (075)744-2240. Open daily 9am to 5pm.*

Surrounded by white walls, this rather modern looking Japanese house is near Jakko-in. They serve a delicious *miso nabe,* a chicken and vegetable stew cooked at your table over a clay hibachi. The chickens are free range and vegetables are grown locally. The homemade *miso* sauce flavors the stew. ¥2000.

TANBA CHAYA *(Japanese, inexpensive). 130 Kusao-machi, Ohara, Sakyo-ku. Tel. (075)744-2527. Open 10am-4:30pm.*

Tanba Chaya, a very casual Japanese-style lunch spot on the way to Jakko-in, serves *inaka teishoku* (country style set). It consists of *soba* with mushrooms, tofu, cooked vegetables, pickles and rice and costs only ¥1000! Who said food has to be expensive in Japan?

SEEING THE SIGHTS

We've divided Kyoto into major areas; each area takes the better part of a day to see completely, which means leaving time for lunch and for browsing around the back streets of the area. To shorten the time, we have starred the not-to-be-missed sights. Concentrating only on these, you can usually fit two districts in a day.

These are the major areas of Kyoto; page 558 lists the highlights:

1. Kyoto Station Area

To-ji*, Higashi and Nishi Hongan-ji*, Shimabara, Costume Museum and Kodai Yuzen-en Museum.

To-ji Temple is about a 10 minute walk southwest of Kyoto Station.

Every tour of the Kyoto Station area should start with the new postmodern **Kyoto Station Building**. Opened in 1998, the towering glass and steel structure features a soaring atrium and interior terracing leading to the 12th floor. The complex includes the Hotel Granvia, concert halls, Isetan Department Store and more restaurants than you can count.

To-ji Temple. *Open 9am to 4:30pm. ¥500.* One of the reasons we like To-ji so much is that when our train approaches Kyoto Station and we see the dark wooden five-storied pagoda standing out among all the concrete buildings of modern Kyoto, we know that not everything traditional has been destroyed. It's not that we think all things traditional are splendid and worth preserving, but rather that it is irresponsible not to preserve some vital parts of Japanese heritage for future generations.

Emperor Kammu established To-ji (Eastern Temple) in 796 along with Sai-ji (Western Temple) to protect the eastern and western sides of the city respectively. Fearing the power of the Buddhist temples, he allowed only these two within the city's precincts, and then only at the very edge. Incidentally, the Rashomon Gate, immortalized in Kurosawa's film *Rashomon,* was located between To-ji and Sai-ji on the southern perimeter. Stone markers are the only remains of Rashomon and Sai-ji.

In 823 the second emperor in Kyoto asked the famous priest Kukai (posthumously known as Kobo Daishi), the founder of Shingon Buddhism, to take over the temple. This sect believed in a strong role in the affairs of the state, and quickly became a powerful influence. Despite Emperor Kammu's best intentions and efforts to keep Buddhism out of the Kyoto government, it became an important force within one generation.

To-ji has been ravaged by fire many times; most of today's buildings date from the early 17th century. Inside, many of the statues are masterpieces of a much earlier era; To-ji is one of the best temples for viewing Heian sculpture.

The Main Hall (Kondo) dates from 1606 and is one of Japan's largest temple buildings built in the grand Momoyama style. In the Lecture Hall (Kodo), the statues of the Buddhas are still arranged the same way Kukai set them up: the central Buddha is surrounded by four Buddhas representing the diamond world — wisdom is as hard as a diamond so that it can smash all illusions. To the right are five bodhisattvas who help mortals find the path to enlightenment. On the left of the Buddha are five ferocious gods who can save the uneducated by frightening them. On each of the four corners is a heavenly king providing protection from evil. Even without a Ph.D. in Buddhist Studies, you'll be awed by the statues in the cool, dimly lit interior.

The five-storied pagoda, rebuilt in 1644, is the tallest in Japan.

On the 21st of each month, the date of Kobo Daishi's death, a large flea market is held on the temple grounds. We love to browse among the hundreds of vendors selling new and old antiques.

Shimabara. During the Edo Period, Shimabara was one of Kyoto's largest pleasure quarters frequented by the merchant class. Warriors had their own places. In 1617, the shogunate restricted pleasure quarters to specific areas, and Shimabara had high walls to control the patrons and prevent the women from escaping. At that time Shimabara wasn't even the suburbs; it was in the middle of rice paddies.

The women of Shimabara were well versed in the arts including poetry, music and dance. They belonged to teahouses; today only two remain: Sumiya and Wachigaiya. *Sumiya's first floor is open 10am-4pm.*

THE PLEASURE QUARTERS & THE NIGHTLESS CASTLE

*Life for the women of **Shimabara** was not a piece of cake. They were the property of the houses that purchased them. The women came from different social classes – samurai families whose head had to commit suicide, daughters of Shimabara women, and daughters of poor farmers. They went through extensive and expensive training to become well versed in music, dance, poetry and the arts. They needed to be witty and charming to their customers. While sex was part of the deal, there was more to it.*

The women of Shimabara were not free to leave the walls of the compound. They were not women of the street, but more like the window women in Amsterdam in the sense that they belonged to one house. If a man wanted to marry one, he had to pay a large fee to the house; after all, he was taking away an economic asset.

There were different ranks, and the highest was Tayu. One famous courtesan, Yoshino Tayu, married a rich merchant and was a major patron of a temple. Naturally, these women didn't have to be good at cooking, but certainly they were good at keeping the company of wealthy men, mostly merchants, who gathered there for personal pleasure as well as to talk about poetry and politics with other customers.

*Utamaro, the famous woodblock artist, spent a lot of time within Shimabara's walls. Based on his personal observations, he produced erotic art called **shunga** (literally spring pictures – what a euphemism!).*

Closed Mondays, August, and December 16-January 31. ¥1000. You can tour **Sumiya's** upstairs by applying in advance: *Tel. (075)351-0024 for a reservation. Entrance fee: ¥800.* Although the latticed wooden exterior looks severe, the interior is sumptuous. The Mother-of-Pearl Room has inlaid shell throughout. The Fan Room has fan-shaped windows and fans with poetry that adorn the ceiling. Ask the Tourist Office to arrange a volunteer guide to accompany you for a fascinating glimpse into teahouse culture.

Wachigaiya is still an active teahouse and in the evening, if you feel like hanging around, you can see *geisha* come and go. The **Omon Gate**, to the east of Wachigaiya, is all that is left of the wall that used to surround the area.

Nishi Hongan-ji Temple. *Open 5:30am to 5:30pm; May through August until 6pm; November through February until 5pm. Admission free.* Nishi Hongan-ji's history is a fascinating story of populism and the awesome power of Buddhist sects that stretched way beyond the religious realm in Japan's medieval period. It also has some of the best Momoyama Period buildings in Japan.

Nishi Hongan-ji is the head temple for the **True Pure Land Sect**, the largest of Japan's Buddhist groups. The priest Shinran (1173-1262) expounded on the teachings of his mentor, Honen, founder of the Pure Land sect, which was the antithesis of Esoteric Buddhism popular with the ruling classes. Pure Land teaches that by merely chanting a simple prayer, the Amida Buddha will grant you salvation. This approach had immediate appeal to the masses who were basically shut out of earlier forms of Buddhism. (How could a farmer give up everything to become a monk so he could reach eternal salvation? His family would starve.)

Shinran became the first Buddhist monk to marry — an act that so enraged the monks at the powerful Enryaku-ji Temple that he was exiled. Shinran's descendants continued to spread his word. In a struggle for domination, Hongan-ji moved from Kyoto. Its monk-soldiers were involved in a number of battles, and the sect eventually set up its headquarters in Osaka where it built a fortress-temple on the site of the present Osaka Castle. The monks took their populist message to the countryside and controlled huge sections of central Japan. Hongan-ji was one of Oda Nobunaga's most formidable opponents to the unification of Japan in the mid-16th century; they battled for 10 years before Nobunaga gained control of the Osaka temple.

After Osaka, the sect set up headquarters in Yamashina, today a suburb of Kyoto. Hideyoshi decided to move the temple to Kyoto where the sect could be watched. As you enter through the impressive main gate, the **Amida Hall**, open to all, is in front of you. Take off your shoes and step into the dimly lit hall where the smell of incense permeates the air. Sit down on the *tatami* mat and look around. If you are lucky, you may see a special ritual being performed for the devoted. As long as you are quiet, you are welcome to stay. While Hongan-ji's building seems very medieval, this temple still plays an active role in the everyday life of its believers.

To the left of the Amida Hall is an ornate inner gate called **Karamon** that was moved from Hideyoshi's Fushimi Castle. It's exquisite carvings were done by the same artist who designed the Tokugawa shogun's mausoleum in Nikko. The gate is called the Sunset Gate because you can be so engrossed in looking at it, you don't notice that the sun has set. It leads to the **Daishoin** and other splendid Momoyama buildings. Unfortunately, these buildings are only open at special times of the year although it's possible to make a reservation to visit them even when they are officially closed. Send a return postcard (*ofuku hagaki*) writing your name, address, telephone number, the number of people accompanying you, and your dates (give three different dates in order of preference — it's best to avoid weekends). Mail to: *Nishi Hongan-ji, Sanpai-bu, Hanayacho sagaru, Horikawa Dori, Shimogyo-ku, Kyoto, 600.* Try to come with a guide; the Tourist Information Office can arrange for a volunteer to accompany you.

It is worth the effort to see these special chambers that include a three-roomed **entrance hall**, the **Taimenjo audience hall**, the **Shiro Shoin**, believed to be Hideyoshi's private apartments, and an outdoor *noh* **stage**. The entrance hall's Tiger Room has paintings of tigers done by Kano Eitoku. Tiger skins were first brought to Japan from Korea after Hideyoshi's invasions in the 1590s; the artist had never seen a live one. The Taimenjo is a huge room with 243 *tatami* mats and 45 pillars. Ornate to an extreme — there isn't an inch of wall or ceiling space that isn't gilded or painted, the room houses Japan's first indoor *noh* stage. The **Kokei Garden** has to be the ultimate Momoyama garden. Fairly small in size and designed to be viewed from the veranda, it has literally tons of rocks that project an air of authority. It isn't a friendly garden that makes you want to take your shoes off and romp around. The outdoor *noh* stage is a National Treasure.

Walking east from Nishi Hongan-ji to Higashi Hongan-ji, you'll encounter shops that sell Buddhist artifacts such as candles, prayer beads, lacquer and gold altars. **Tanji Renshodo** is a wonderful shop that sells beeswax candles.

Detour for textile enthusiasts: On the 5th floor of the Izutsu Building on Horikawa Dori, just north of Nishi Hongan-ji, is the **Costume Museum** (Fuzoku Hakubutsukan). *Open 9am to 5pm. Closed Sunday, national holidays, June 1-19 and December 16 through January 6. ¥400.* If you'd like to see Japanese period dress, it's worth a brief stop. For more textiles, walk about 10 minutes north to the **Kodai Yuzen-en Gallery** on Takasuji, west of Horikawa Dori. *Open daily 9am to 5pm. ¥500. Yuzen* is painting on silk with dye; the technique was perfected in the early 17th century. Stop here to see displays of the colorful fabric and to try your hand at dyeing.

Higashi Hongan-ji Temple. Tying to contain the temple's power, the first Tokugawa shogun exploited a succession struggle between the abbot's sons to divide Hongan-ji into two temples in 1602. Most of the current buildings date from 1895. In the temple are large ropes made out of the hair of female believers. They donated their hair in hopes that their faith would lighten the load of the large beams that were raised to make the buildings. Inside the large **Founder's Hall** (Daishido), one of the biggest wooden buildings in the world, is a statue of Shinran, the founder of the True Pure Land Sect. The **Amida Hall**, connected by a corridor, has a statue of the Amida Buddha carved in the early 13th century by Kaikei, a famous sculptor of the Kamakura era.

Shosei-en Garden is two blocks east of Higashi Hongan-ji on Karasuma Dori. *Open 9am to 3:30pm. Admission free.* This Heian-style strolling garden, completed in 1657, includes a large pond. Stop by for a peaceful refuge from the clatter of the busy commercial area around it.

2. Central Kyoto

Nijo Castle*, Shinsen-en, Nijo Jinya, Nishiki Ichiba, Imperial Palace*.
Take bus no. 52 from Kyoto Station to Nijo-jo-mae stop for Nijo Castle.

Nijo-jo Castle (Nijo-jo). *Tel. (075)841-0096. Open 8:45am to 5pm (enter by 4pm). Closed December 26 through January 4. ¥600.*

We put up with hoards of tourists and school groups (it must be an obligatory stop for them) to see Nijo Castle, because it's one of the best examples of the **Momoyama** style of architecture, complete with sumptuous paintings and carvings. Everything is on a grand and elaborate scale, but the grandeur was carefully designed to suit the ranks of those for whom each room was intended. Try to get here when it first opens to avoid the noisy kids running on the squeaky floors.

Having won the Battle of Sekigahara in 1600, **Tokugawa Ieyasu** solidified his position and was proclaimed shogun. He then began to build Nijo Castle for his Kyoto residence, basically to humiliate the emperor by making him call upon the shogun here. From this castle in 1603, Tokugawa began his attack on the Toyotomi family, his only real obstacle to complete power. The emperor did not pay an official visit upon the shogun until 1626 after Ieyasu had died, and his grandson, Iemitsu, did the entertaining. Emperors didn't do a lot of visiting either then or now. He gave two years notice, allowing the Tokugawa time to rebuild. Iemitsu arrived from Edo (Tokyo) with 300,000 of his troops. No emperor visited Nijo Castle again until 1867 when the fifteenth Tokugawa shogun surrendered his power to the Meiji emperor.

After crossing the moat and entering the inner courtyard, you arrive at the **Karamon**, a Chinese style gate, ornate with carvings and metalwork, that was moved from Hideyoshi's Fushimi Castle. Next you enter the **Ninomaru**, not a castle at all, but a palace. Ninomaru has several buildings connected by walkways. The first is the **Tozamurai**, used for receiving imperial messengers. The paintings on the sliding doors are of leopards and tigers that must have looked most exotic and impressive to the messengers since tigers never roamed Japan's jungles. In the second building, **Shikidai-no-ma**, ministers received feudal lords. Also you'll find Kano Tanyu's famous painting of giant pine trees that's known for its bold design and unusual size — the branches span 15 meters.

The third building, **Ohiroma**, is where the emperor was entertained in 1626 and also where the "outer lords," the feudal lords on the losing side of the Battle of Sekigahara, were received. Be sure to notice the transoms between the rooms; they are decorated with carved panels featuring peonies, pine trees and imaginary birds. Some of the thick panels have different designs on each side. And, as you walk along the pathway, you'll notice the squeaking floors, designed to warn against intruders. Sometimes Nijo is referred to as the Nightingale Palace because the squeaking sounds like chirping birds.

The fourth building, **Kuroshoin** (Black Study Hall), was for the "inner lords," Tokugawa's closest allies. Paintings of cherry blossoms adorn the walls — definitely an unintimidating motif. The last building, **Shiroshoin** (White Study Hall), was the shogun's private living quarters where only women could enter. The paintings are simple Chinese scenes. In the last chamber, look for the painting of lovely sparrows sleeping in a snow-covered bamboo grove.

Enter the **Ninomaru Garden**, on the right as you exit the palace. Attributed to the famous landscape architect Kobori Enshu, the garden has lots of rocks and projects an air of authority. Originally, it didn't have any plants that might show a change of season because these were unwelcome reminders of the impermanence of life.

If you have time, cross the inner moat to the Honmaru. Today you'll see a villa built in 1847 that was moved from the Imperial Palace. Its quiet, aristocratic style is a stark contrast to the Ninomaru Palace. In this area there used to be a five-storied castle keep that was destroyed by fire in 1750. For some great views of Kyoto, climb up the southwest corner of the wall. Then you can walk through the extensive outer gardens of the castle, including the peaceful Seiryu-en Garden built by the city in 1965.

Shinsen-en Garden. *Tel. (075)821-1466. Free admission; always open.* This garden, a mere shadow of its former self, was attached to the palace **Emperor Kammu** built when he established Kyoto as the capital in 794. Built in the Chinese style, this huge strolling garden had many vermilion pavilions used by the Heian aristocracy for moon viewing, poetry writing and other noble pursuits. In 1227 fire destroyed the palace, and it was not rebuilt; the garden declined. Since the pond never went dry, To-ji Temple used it during times of drought. Eventually, through disuse and neglect, the city encroached upon the garden, and a hefty chunk went to Nijo Castle built by the Tokugawa shogun in the early 17th century. When you're in the area, stop for a brief look at one of Kyoto's earliest gardens even though there's not much to see today,

A pleasant place to have lunch in the park is **Gion Heihachi Shinsen-en**, a restaurant with large windows overlooking the pond.

On Oike Dori, between Shinsen-en and Horikawa Dori, lies a small shop, **Asakoji**, that specializes in Japanese traditional crafts made of linen,.

Nijo Jinya. *South of Nijo Castle, off Oike Dori. Tel. (075)841-0972. Admission is only by guided tour in Japanese. Be sure to make reservations in advance. Non-Japanese speakers should be accompanied by a translator; call the Tourist Information Center in advance to arrange for a volunteer. Tours at 10am, 11am, 2pm and 3pm. ¥1000. Children under 15 are not allowed.* Nijo Jinya was built in the early 17th century as an inn for feudal lords who did not have Kyoto residences. The Ogawa family, whose ancestors built the inn, live in part of it. The Ogawas were paranoid about assassins and fire so used the latest technologies to thwart both. Since Kyoto burned regularly and the inn still stands, some of the fire-fighting technology must have worked. And despite the *ninja*-type mazes, staircases, hidden rooms and guard closets, emergency exits and other tricks, there was never as much as a sword fight in the building. Next to the feudal lord's room is a small room designed for *noh* performances. As in many *noh* theaters, large ceramic urns are placed under the floor to improve the acoustics; in this case, whispering voices do not carry outside the room when the sliding doors are closed, making it perfect for secret meetings.

The Museum of Kyoto (Bunka Hakubutsukan). *Tel. (075)222-0888. Open 10am to 5:30pm. Closed third Wednesday. Permanent exhibit ¥500; additional fee for temporary exhibitions.* This wonderful museum is dedicated to presenting Kyoto's culture and crafts. The turn-of-the-century Bank of Japan Building is the annex while the main building is a contemporary granite structure. The permanent exhibit displays the history of Kyoto and its craft traditions; the museum arranges English guides upon request. This museum is one of our favorite rainy day places in Kyoto.

The first floor of the museum has a several shops selling Kyoto crafts. We stop here when we don't have much time to shop. **Sanko** sells paper, calligraphy brushes, ink and other art supplies. **Rakushi Kan** sells Japanese *washi* paper in sheets and crafts made from paper — notebooks, dolls, stationery, etc.

Nishiki Ichiba Market extends from the *torii* gate of Nishiki Temmangu Shrine to Takakura Dori. Packed within these 400 meters are tiny shops selling Kyoto specialties: sweets, *yuba* (the skin of soy milk), *fu* (wheat gluten), tea, kelp, fresh fish, at least 100 different kinds of pickles, and fresh vegetables like huge turnips and bright red carrots available only in Kyoto. Some shops sell kitchen utensils. We love to come here to see Kyoto's residents going about their daily lives; usually we stop to buy some perishables before going home.

Kyoto Imperial Park (Kyoto Gyoen). When the emperor resided in Kyoto (until 1869), the residences of aristocrats were in this area that surrounds the Imperial Palace. When the capital moved to Tokyo, these buildings were destroyed and the area turned into a park. The only buildings remaining are the Imperial Palace (Kyoto Gosho), Sento Retirement Palace (Sento Gosho) and Omiya Gosho. The latter is not open to the public. The large park (1.3 kilometers long, 700 meters wide) adds badly needed open green space to Kyoto. It has nine gates so you can enter from any side. In the center of the city, it's a great place for a jog or walk anytime of day.

Kyoto Imperial Palace (Kyoto Gosho). *Admission by guided tour only. Tours in English Monday through Friday at 10am and 2pm. Apply at the Imperial Household Agency office at least 20 minutes in advance; take your passport. Tours are also held on the 3rd Saturday of the month and every Saturday in April, May, October and November, but you must apply by Friday.*

If you see Nijo Castle before the Imperial Palace, you'll probably be disappointed or surprised by the simplicity of the buildings. We like the Imperial Palace because it shows the emperor lived (relatively) modestly compared with the shogun, but the buildings are elegant and dignified. Also keep in mind that for most of Kyoto's 1100 year stint as capital of Japan, the emperor had little political power and lived off the kindness of shoguns.

The original palace of Emperor Kammu, Kyoto's founder, was near Shinsen-en Garden (near Nijo Castle), but earthquakes and other disasters befell the city, which was a sign that the gods were not pleased. Emperors believed that the location of the palace might be contributing to the disasters so they lived in temporary quarters called *sato dairi* until Emperor Kogen built the palace on this site in 1331.

To set some idea of the earliest imperial residences, you need to look no further than Heian Shrine, a copy of Tang Chinese architecture. With successive rebuilding the bright vermilion style changed into an a more naturalistic, subdued architecture that you see at the Kyoto Imperial Palace.

The Ceremonial Hall (Shishinden) was the center of the palace. The roof is made of cypress bark, which gives it a stately yet subdued appearance. The emperor's throne sits on a dais. The throne's canopy is embroidered with a phoenix, the mythical Chinese bird used in auspicious ceremonies. Stands for the emperor's sacred treasures flank the throne and an orange tree and a cherry tree, symbols of imperial presence, grow in front of the broad veranda. The Seiryoden Hall was used for formal occasions and has paintings by Tosa school artists. The imperial crest, a 16-petal chrysanthemum, is in evidence everywhere.

The Otsune Goten was the actual residence of the emperor.

Sento Palace (Sento Gosho). *Admission by guided tour only. Tours in Japanese at 11am and 1:30pm. Be sure to apply to the Imperial Household Agency office one or two days in advance. People under age 20 not allowed.* The third Tokugawa Shogun, trying to ingratiate himself with the emperor, provided the Sento Palace as a retirement residence for Emperor Gomizuno. He's the same emperor who had Shugaku-in Villa in northeast Kyoto that was also built for him by the shogun. Gomizuno used his fat allowance from the Tokugawa shogunate to indulge himself and create this strolling garden that is completely different from the symbolic Zen rock gardens. Emperor Gomizuno lived here from 1629 until his death in 1680.

Sento Palace's garden design, attributed to the master Kobori Enshu, is superb and reveals different scenes as you walk along its paths. Black shiny pebbles cover the shore around the south pond; they were a gift from a feudal lord who is said to have delivered them individually wrapped in squares of silk. Most of the buildings perished in a fire in 1856, but it's well worth the trouble of getting permission to visit the garden.

Two short blocks west of the Imperial Palace is **Clifton Karhu's studio**. Karhu is an American artist who has lived in Kyoto since 1955. His highly acclaimed colorful woodblock prints are beautiful renditions of traditional Kyoto. *Call ahead to make an appointment to visit his studio on Tuesday, Friday and Saturday. Tel. (075)415-0606. Muromachi Dori, south of Shimochoja-machi Dori.*

3. Southern Higashiyama

Sanjusangen-do*, Kyoto National Museum*, Chishaku-in Temple, Kawai Kanjiro Memorial Hall, Kiyomizu-dera Temple, * Sannenzaka* and Ninenzaka*.

Take bus no. 206, 208 or 18 from Kyoto Station to Sanjusangen-do-mae stop for Sanjusangen-do Temple.

Sanjusangen-do. *Open 8am to 5pm; November 15 through March, 9am to 4pm. ¥600.* Sanjusangen-do translates as 33 bays — there are 33 areas between the 34 pillars in this long building. Thirty-three is also the number of incarnations of the Kannon Buddha. Originally built in 1164, destroyed by fire and reconstructed in 1266, the hall houses 1001 gilded images of **Kannon**, the Buddha of Mercy. The large gilded, 11-faced,

KYOTO'S LOCAL COLOR: CHERRY BLOSSOMS & AUTUMN FOLIAGE

Japanese delight in the change of seasons. Cherry blossoms and autumn foliage are almost revered, and people make excursions to distant places solely to view them. Cherries bloom in early to mid-April in Kyoto while autumn leaves are at their crimson best in November.

Here are a handful of favorite blossom viewing places:
- *Arashiyama Koen Park, western Kyoto*
- *Daigo-ji Temple, southeast of Kyoto Station*
- *Heian Shrine Garden, central Kyoto*
- *Kiyomizu-dera Temple, eastern Kyoto*
- *Maruyama Koen Park, central Kyoto*
- *Ninna-ji Temple, northwest Kyoto*
- *Uji Koen Park, southeast of Kyoto Station*

The wooded hills of Kyoto have many maple trees that turn the mountainsides into blazing red. The best viewing is along the hilly perimeter of the city at:
- *Eikan-do, north of Nanzen-ji, in eastern Kyoto*
- *Tofuku-ji, south of Kyoto Station*
- *Kiyomizu-dera Temple, eastern Kyoto*
- *Ginkaku-ji (Silver Pavilion), northeast Kyoto*
- *Arashiyama Area, western Kyoto*
- *Takao, north of Arashiyama,*
- *Togano area, north of Arashiyama*

1000-armed, seated Buddha in the center is a masterpiece sculpted by Tankei in 1254. It is flanked by 500 smaller, but nearly life-size statues.

The carvings of the robes, the ritual objects in their hands, and facial expressions are different in each statue. These sculptures were done at the height of Kamakura Period; in no other period in Japanese art history is there so much dynamic sculpture. Looking at these gilded statues in this dimly lit building is a really awesome experience.

In the hall behind the 1001 Buddhas, there are statues of the gods of wind and thunder as well as of the 28 attendants. These masterpieces of Kamakura artistic vigor derive from Hindu deities and have surprisingly well-preserved colors.

On the veranda of the long building, the *Hikizome* ceremony takes place every year on January 15. Archers shoot arrows the length of the building, 60 meters, to hit a target. In the Edo Period, an archer would have 24 hours to shoot as many arrows as he could. The best record was over 13,000 arrows shot with some 8000 making the mark. Notice the gashes on the pillars — not everyone hits the target.

Kyoto National Museum. *Open 9am to 4:30pm. Closed Monday and December 26 through January 3. ¥420; additional fee for temporary exhibitions.* Because it's one of the few places where you can see a large collection of Japan's cultural treasures under one roof, we love to visit here. Built in 1895 by the Imperial Household Agency, the museum preserves many of Kyoto's art works in danger of being destroyed; the original French Renaissance-style building today houses temporary exhibitions. Many of the art works actually belong to Kyoto's shrines and temples but are cared for by the museum. The permanent exhibition displays an excellent cross section of Japanese art including archaeological finds, ceramics, Buddhist sculpture, lacquer, paintings, calligraphy and textiles. Look for the brief English explanations.

Chishaku-in Temple. *Open 9am to 4:30pm. ¥350.* Hideyoshi built a temple on the site of the present Chishaku-in to enshrine his eldest son, Tsurumatsu, who died at age two. On view in a special treasure house are masterpieces of Japanese art by Hasegawa Tohaku and his school — paintings on sliding doors of cherry and maple trees. We love to come back again and again to view these paintings. The quality of the paintings is so good that they are better in person than in art books — quite a tribute to the paintings.

The temple's garden dates from 1674. Supposedly it was inspired by Lu-shan in China. It's a classic Momoyama-style garden — designed to be enjoyed and admired from the veranda of the building. Behind the pond and sloping uphill are rocks, bushes and trees. The pavilion is built over the pond. If you'd like to see well-preserved Momoyama paintings and landscape garden and your time is really limited, Chishaku-in is an excellent choice.

Kawai Kanjiro Memorial Hall. *Open 10am to 5pm. Closed Monday; August 10-20; and December 24 through January 7. ¥900.* Kawai was a potter and a leader in the *mingei* movement that popularized folk craft in the 1930s. He converted this wooden house to his residence and studio. It's a hybrid style, combining Western and Japanese, so some rooms have *tatami* mats and others have country-style tables and chairs. Many of Kawai's ceramic works are on display. Make sure you go behind the house to see Kawai's studio and his climbing kiln. The kiln is so huge we wonder how long it took Kawai and his students to make enough objects to fill it. We can't try to duplicate it today because antipollution laws prohibit firing within the city limits.

The main east-west street by the Kawai house is Gojo; the northern side is lined with shops selling Kiyomizu ceramics in all price ranges.

Kiyomizu-Dera Area

The Kiyomizu-dera area is one of the most popular places to visit in Kyoto. When we visited in February, northern Kyoto was deserted — we practically had Daitoku-ji to ourselves. But when we went to Kiyomizu, it was so crowded with tourists and school groups that we could hardly find a place to walk. Don't go to Kiyomizu just for the temple; wander around the area. We can spend hours browsing in the ceramics shops and exploring the preservation districts of Sannenzaka and Ninenzaka.

There are two approaches to Kiyomizu: one from the north along the quiet and well-preserved streets of Ninenzaka and Sannenzaka, and the other from the east coming up from Higashi Oji Dori with streets filled with ceramics shops — one street is called Chawan Zaka (Teacup Hill). The area has a Kiyomizu-yaki ceramics fair in early August. Coming from the south, you'll reach Chawan Zaka first.

Kiyomizu-dera Temple. *Open from 6am to 6pm. ¥300.* After a long trek past countless tacky souvenir stands, the entrance of Kiyomizu opens up before you. Few temples in Kyoto are so popular or have such a long history; Kiyomizu predates the founding of Kyoto. In 778, the priest Enchin traveled from Nara searching for the pure water that he dreamed about. At the spring he met a hermit; later Enchin realized that the hermit was the Kannon Buddha. Enchin carved a statue of the Buddha and established a temple.

Fire destroyed Kiyomizu several times, but the structures at the gate are the few that survived the fire of 1629. The entrance gate, **Niomon**, is one of the temple's oldest structures (1478). Its fierce guardian deities protect the temple from evil. Behind the gate is a bell tower built in 1596. The **Saimon** (West Gate) is a Momoyama era structure built about the same time as the bell tower.

The three-storied **pagoda**, one of the largest of its type in Japan, was originally built in 847; but the present structure is from 1633.

Next you pass the dragon fountain for washing and go through the middle gate to enter the inner sanctum of the temple. After passing the Asakura-do Hall housing an 11-faced Kannon Buddha, you reach the **Hon-do** (Main Hall), the most famous building of the complex. It is an elegant structure with a large wooden **veranda** protruding over the cliff; it's supported by massive wooden scaffolding. The porch is a stage designed for dancing and is flanked by two smaller porches. The roof is made of cypress shingles and blends with the forest around it. The thick maple forest in the ravines of the Higashiyama hills adds a picturesque charm to the area.

When you make an irreversible decision, the Japanese have a famous saying that's similar to "the die is cast" or "crossing the Rubicon:" you have jumped from the terrace of Kiyomizu Temple.

The Kannon statue of the Main Hall is shown only every 33 years. Mark your calendars now: the next time is 2028. Behind the Main Hall is a Shinto shrine called **Jishu Gongen** where people come to pray for luck in love. There are two large stones and if you can walk blindfolded from one to the other, you will have success in love. At the shrine you can buy amulets for any occasion: luck in love, success in exams, traffic safety, etc. This shrine is one of the few in Japan with signs in English.

After the Main Hall, there's a steep stairway going down. Rather than take it, follow the hillside path around to the right and go past the Shaka Hall, Amida Hall and Inner Hall, and then go down the hill and to the right to reach the **Otowa Waterfall**. Chances are you'll see pilgrims standing on the cement platform to purify themselves under a stream of pure water from a spring deep within the mountain. There are also ladles for the less rigorous to cleanse themselves. This waterfall is the holy and pure water that Enchin discovered.

From below you have a great view of the scaffolding of huge wooden pillars holding up the porch of the Main Hall. Kiyomizu temple is famous for being famous; the views of Kyoto from the balcony and the view of the balcony from beneath it make Kiyomizu special for us.

There's an exit in the ravine so you don't have to climb all the way back up to the Main Hall. If you take the road going down at this exit, you are on Chawan Zaka, a pleasant walk with fewer souvenir shops than on the temple's main approach. The ceramics shops are much more subdued. To get to the main street and Sannenzaka from the temple exit, walk to the right until you reach the temple's main entrance gate; then turn left to go down the hill.

Walking down the main approach, look carefully for a set of steps descending on the right. They will be right before **Shichimitogarashi**, a shop specializing in ground pepper. You've reached **Sannenzaka**, one of the most delightful walks in Kyoto. The cobblestone road is one of Kyoto's few historic preservation areas and is lined with graceful two-storied wooden buildings. Many are tastefully executed shops and restaurants that cater to the area's visitors. After a few blocks, a small road forks off to the right. This is Ninenzaka, a similar type of street. At the intersection of Ninenzaka and Sannenzaka is a branch of Okutan, a *yu-dofu* restaurant, a good lunch stop.

If you stay on Sannenzaka, you'll come to an ancient pagoda that stands alone. Yasaka Pagoda is all that's left of a temple that was destroyed by fire in the 17th century. The pagoda has stood since 1440.

Ninenzaka leads you to a fairly open plaza where you are jarred by the massive concrete Ryozen Kannon statue erected in 1955. Ikkyu-an, a Chinese Buddhist vegetarian restaurant, is on the road leading south from the Ryozen Kannon. Next to Ryozen Kannon is the peaceful **Kodai-**

ji Temple, built by Hideyoshi's wife as a memorial to him. The building has an exquisite lacquer interior, but unfortunately is only open sporadically as are the temple's two rustic teahouses that were moved from...where else but Hideyoshi's Fushimi Castle. One, Kasa-tei, has a wonderful umbrella-shaped ceiling. Definitely stop here if it's open.

As you continue in front of Kodai-ji, you'll reach Rakusho, a peaceful teahouse and garden and a good place to rest your tired feet. Wander the warren of narrow paths making up picturesque Ishibekoji, an area of traditional teahouses, inns and restaurants. Continuing north, you'll come to the east gate of Yasaka Shrine (see the following section).

KYOTO, CITY OF PEACE

*In 974, when Emperor Kammu established **Heian-kyo** (Capital of Peace), the original name of Kyoto, he modeled it after Xian, the ancient capital of China. The city was systematically laid out on a grid between two rivers – the Kamo on the east and the Katsura on the west. Despite frequent fires, civil wars, and the passage of over 1200 years, today you still follow the original plan. Roads were laid out 120 meters apart both north-south and east-west.*

For a Capital of Peace, Kyoto has seen more warfare and destruction than any other Japanese city. There is an old story about a taxi driver telling a tourist that Kyoto has not been the same since the war. Knowing Kyoto was not bombed in World War II, the tourist questioned the driver and was really surprised when the driver said he meant the Onin War (1467-77). The driver has a point; at the end of the Onin War, Kyoto was in ashes; that decade was followed by another hundred years of warfare.

*In the late 16th century, Hideyoshi had a major role in rebuilding the city. He built roads 60 meters apart, the configuration that survives today. Tiny alleys called roji connect the small merchant houses to the road and to major thoroughfares. As far as we're concerned, it's a first-rate luxury to walk these alleys often discovering something unexpected – a sweet shop, a small restaurant serving traditional foods, a store selling crafts. Most **roji** are dead ends. Even if you think you're lost, you're not; just retrace your steps.*

Kyoto residents learn a nursery rhyme that tells them the order of the streets. The rest of us use a map and a compass to be on the safe side.

4. Central Higashiyama

Yasaka Shrine*, Gion* and Pontocho*, Chion-in, Shoren-in. Depending on much time you spend wandering around Gion, you can easily combine this area with Northern Higashiyama (5) or Southern Higashiyama (3) in one day.

Take bus no. 206 or 18 from Kyoto Station to Gion stop for Yasaka Jinja Shrine.

Yasaka Jinja Shrine. *Grounds always open. Admission free.* This Shinto shrine, known locally as Gion-san, is at the eastern end of Shijo Dori and mainly serves the merchant class. Kyoto's citizens go there to pray for business prosperity and protection from illness as have countless generations before them. When visiting, we feel we're witnessing a piece of every day life.

While Yasaka dates from the 9th century, most of the present structures were built in 1654 when the shogun ordered Yasaka rebuilt. The main building's architecture is called Gion style; it's one story and covered with thin wooden shingles. To the north is a building raised on stilts; it houses *ema*, literally horse pictures. Devotees used to make offerings of horses to shrines. When that became too expensive, they substituted pictures of horses on wood. Today, the paintings on the small wooden plaques are of many different things including signs of the Japanese zodiac and paintings of shrine buildings.

On New Year's Eve, the temple burns a special sacred fire, and enthusiasts take home an ember for good luck. Yasaka is the home of the famous Gion Matsuri Festival when the spirits of the deceased are welcomed to Yasaka Jinja.

Leaving by the front gate of Yasaka Shrine, you are at the top of Shijo Dori, a busy commercial street and the heart of the **Gion** district. Let's take a circular walk around Gion. Turn right on Higashi Oji Dori (the large road running north-south in front of the gate) and walk up several blocks until you reach **Shinmonzen**, a small street on the left that's filled with antique stores. Walk east until the road ends (you'll have to cross the canal) and turn south on Nawate Dori. Wander around this area; the streets by the canal are a preservation district. It's one of the prettiest walks in urban Kyoto. From Nawate Dori, we usually turn east on Shimbashi Dori and then return to Nawate Dori following the canal. Further south on Nawate Dori you'll go past Kappa, a boisterous restaurant where you might like to have dinner.

To see **Pontocho**, follow Nawate Dori to Shijo Dori. Turn right, cross the river and immediately turn right. There is only one building between the river and the small alley of Pontocho, once Kyoto's second largest pleasure quarters. There are still many teahouses and restaurants along this road, but every year more traditional buildings get knocked down and cement monstrosities rise in their place. If you come in the early evening, you may see *maiko* and *geisha* going to the teahouses.

Return to Shijo Dori. A right will take you to the heart of Kyoto's shopping districts with its large department stores and many small shops, but we will turn left and go across the Kamo River.

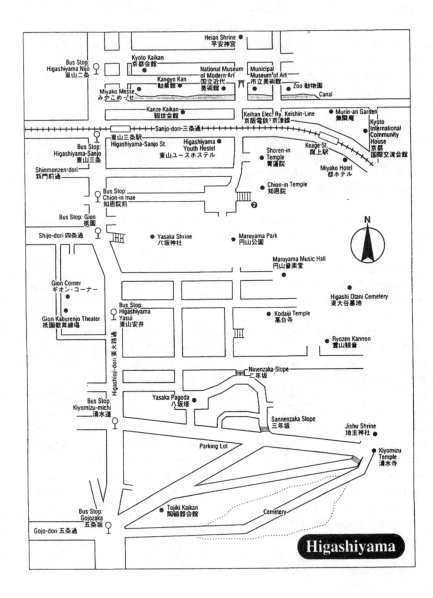

Higashiyama

On the right is **Minami-za Kabuki Theater**, the oldest *kabuki* theater in Japan, which dates back to the 17th century. The current building was built in 1929. *Kabuki* started on the banks of the Kamo River right in front of Minami-za. In 1603, a temple maiden from Izumo Shrine called **Okuni** began performing an avant-garde dance that developed into *kabuki*. Kitty-cornered from the theater, a small stone statue on the bank of the river marks the place. Performances are held daily for a month, but not every month. The matinee begins at 11am and goes until about 4pm; the evening performance begins at 4:30pm and runs until around 8pm. But it's okay to leave whenever you wish. *Tel. (075)561-1155.*

MAIKO & GEISHA

Gion is one of the pleasure quarters approved by the Tokugawa Shogunate during the Edo Period. Developed as the temple town (monzen-machi) of the major temples in the Eastern section of Kyoto such as Kiyomizu Temple and Yasaka Shrine, at its peak there were about 3000 geisha (or geiko, as they are known in Kyoto) and 700 teahouses in the area. During the time leading up to the Meiji Restoration in 1868, lots of ambitious men had secret meetings not only with their colleagues but also with their favorite geisha. These women are highly trained in music and dance and are living storehouses of traditional culture. In the old days training would begin at age 11 or so, but today it's more like age 18. The apprentice geisha, called maiko, wear extremely flamboyant kimono and high geta (sandals) and have their faces painted white. Once they graduate to geisha, they wear much simpler kimono. To enjoy teahouse entertainment you need an introduction and a limitless expense account. An alternative is to see geisha perform at a theater, which they do in the spring and autumn.

The schedule is:

• Miyako Odori (April 1-30): Gion Kaburenjo Theater, Tel. (075)541-3391

• Kitano Odori (mid-April): Kamishichiken Theater, Tel. (075)461-0148

• Kyo Odori (April 6-20): Geisha Miyagawa Kaburenjo, Tel. (075)561-1151

• Kamogawa Odori (May 1-24, October 15-November 7): Pontocho Kaburenjo, Tel. (075)221-2025

Continue down Shijo Dori towards Yasaka Shrine and, on the right you'll find a traditional building with dark rust-colored walls. This building is **Ichiriki**, a famous teahouse. Turn south at Ichiriki, on to Hanamikoji, and you'll reach the Gion Kaburenjo Theater where *geisha* dances are performed every April. Next to it is **Gion Corner** where every Japanese art from tea ceremony to *bunraku* is crammed into one hour.

Return to Shijo Dori and back to Yasaka Shrine. North of the Shrine is **Maruyama Park** where weeping cherry trees bloom in April. At the northern perimeter is a well-known restaurant, Hiranoya, that has been serving *imobo*, cod simmered with potatoes, for 300 years. Continue north until you reach the large gate of Chion-in.

Chion-in Temple. *Open 9am to 4:30pm; December through February until 4pm. ¥400.* When we are walking in this area, it's easy to get temple overload, but Chion-in is well worth a visit. The imposing **Sanmon Gate**, the world's largest wooden gate, will awe even the most jaded.

The priest **Honen**, who started the Jodo or Pure Land sect of Buddhism, founded Chion-in. Honen studied at Mt. Hiei. When he became disenchanted with the infighting between the established Buddhist sects, he founded a new teaching that said you can reach salvation by simply chanting a short prayer called the *nembutsu*. Suddenly Buddhism was accessible to the masses. Until the introduction of *nembutsu*, you had to meditate and undergo rigorous training. Jealous of his success, other temples banned Honen from Kyoto in 1207, but he was allowed to return four years later. The following year he fasted to death on the grounds of Chion-in.

It's truly impressive to walk through the massive Sanmon gate built in 1619. Behind the gate are two paths that lead uphill to the main compound: a very steep set of stone steps called the man's path and a more gentle woman's path. Your choice. The large Miei-do, built in 1639 and decorated with ornate golden objects, enshrines Honen although his statue is hidden. The main hall and small hall have sliding doors graced with Kano school paintings. The temple's bell, high on a hill, weighs 67 tons. On New Year's Eve, 17 monks ring the bell for the prescribed 108 times to erase the sins of the past year. This annual event is broadcast nationally from Chion-in.

Continue up the quiet street until you reach the giant camphor trees marking the entrance to Shoren-in.

Shoren-in Monseki Temple. *Open 9am to 5pm. ¥500.* Shoren-in is a charming place to visit. There are two, actually three, gardens that exist side by side; each completely different. Shoren-in's long history dates back to the 9th century when it was a retirement villa for emperors. In 1788 the Imperial Palace burned for about the 100th time, and Shoren-in became the actual residence of the imperial family, albeit temporarily. The Muromachi Period garden designed by **Soami**, a well-known 15th century artist, has a pond, a waterfall and lots of rocks. Adjacent to it is an azalea garden built 200 years later and attributed to **Kobori Enshu**, a 17th century landscape architect. It's breathtaking to view in early May when the azaleas are in bloom. The sound of the water cascading over boulders into the pond creates a meditative atmosphere. We love listening to it as we sit in the pavilion drinking tea, savoring our total environment.

On the other side is the building used as an imperial residence the simple garden it faces. The green leaves of a large, old camphor tree contrast with the white walls behind it, and the thick moss sets off the simple garden for an entirely pleasing effect. Best of all, you can walk through all three gardens.

Continuing on the road in front of Shoren-in, the serene area soon gives way to a busy commercial street. Cross Sanjo Dori and continue straight to be on the approach to the Heian Shrine.

5. Northern Higashiyama

Heian Shrine*, Okazaki Park: Kyoto National Museum of Modern Art, Kyoto Municipal Museum of Art, Museum of Traditional Crafts, and Kyoto Zoo; Murin-an Garden, Nanzen-ji*, Eikan-do, Philosopher's Path, Ginkaku-ji* and Haku Sonso Garden and Museum.

Take bus no. 5 from Kyoto Station to Heian Jingu-mae stop for Heian Shrine.

Approach the Heian Shrine from Jingu-michi, the road from the south with the giant *torii* gate. This road has a number of shops selling antiques and craft items.

Heian Shrine (Heian Jingu). *Grounds always open. Garden open 8:30am to 5:30pm, March through August; until 5pm September and October; and until 4:30pm November through February. ¥600.* To be honest, the Heian Shrine doesn't do a lot for us. The white and red buildings with the large white gravel grounds are so sterile. And difficult to navigate! Have you ever tried to roll a stroller over gravel? Yet the Heian Shrine is worth visiting to get a feeling for the original imperial buildings constructed at the time Kyoto was founded. And the garden behind the shrine is wonderful.

The Heian Shrine was built in 1895 to celebrate Kyoto's 1100th birthday. It's a two-thirds reproduction of the palace Emperor Kammu built in 794 and is in the Tang Chinese architectural style with brilliant vermilion pillars. It's quite a contrast with the subdued yet elegant imperial palaces of the later emperors. Emperor Kammu (Kyoto's founder) and Emperor Komei (the last emperor before the capital moved to Tokyo in 1868) are enshrined here.

The large central building is the Hall of the State (Daigokuden). The Tower of the Blue Dragon is its right and the Tower of the White Tiger is on the left. The orange tree and cherry tree in the courtyard are symbols always used in imperial gardens.

Behind these buildings is a large, beautiful garden that was popular during the Heian era; its entrance is to the left of the Hall of State. The garden has blossoms all year round but is especially popular in June when the irises bloom. There's a wooden bench on the graceful bridge over the pond where we love to sit and feed the colorful, fat carp. Obviously they don't need our offerings. Next to the large pond is the Pavilion of Peace; there's a phoenix on its roof.

Okazaki Park, south of the Heian Shrine, has a number of museums including the **National Museum of Modern Art** (Kyoto Kokuritsu Kindai Bijutsukan; *open 9:30am-5pm; closed Mondays; ¥420 for permanent exhibition*), the **Kyoto Municipal Museum of Art** (Kyoto-shi Bijutsukan; *open 9am-5pm; closed Mondays; admission fee varies*) and the **Kyoto Museum of Traditional Crafts** (Dento Sangyo Fureai-kan; *Miyaki Messe, B1 Floor; open 10am-6pm; closed Mondays*). Don't miss the museum of traditional crafts, but please note that we save the others for rainy days or when they have temporary exhibitions of interest.

Cross the canal south of the museums and follow the road along side it going east until you see a sign for **Murin-an**. *Open 9am to 4:30pm. ¥300.* Statesman Yamagata Aritomo built this garden in the late 19th century. The garden uses running water from the canal and borrows the hills of Higashiyama for background scenery. The residence is an eclectic blend of Japanese and Western architecture. You can have a cup of tea overlooking the garden.

Continue along the same road heading east. When the roads curves, turn left for the road leading to Nanzen-ji. Along this road, many restaurants serve *yu-dofu*, but we prefer to eat within the temple grounds at Okutan or Chosho-in although Yachiyo on the approach road is also pleasant. On the way, you'll find Utsuwa Akane, a nice pottery shop.

Nanzen-ji Temple. *Open 8:30am to 5pm; December through February until 4:30pm. ¥400 to see Hojo (Main Hall); ¥300 to climb up Sanmon.* Nanzen-ji, a serene oasis set in the hills of Higashiyama, is one of the temples we keep revisiting. This temple, the center of Rinzai Zen Buddhism, has had its share of ups and downs. Founded in 1291, it became one of the five great Zen temples of Kyoto. Jealous priests from Mt. Hiei's Enryaku-ji Temple burned it down in 1393. Two hundred years later, Hideyoshi supported Nanzen-ji, rebuilding it in the late 16th century.

The 22-meter high **Sanmon gate** is truly impressive. It's one of the few gates where you can climb to the second story. Spring for the ¥300 entrance fee because the steep steps lead to a veranda with a fabulous view of Kyoto and the hills of Higashiyama. The ceiling is painted with phoenixes and heavenly maidens who oversee the Buddha and his 16 Bodhisattvas. In front of the Buddha are the seated figures of Tokugawa Ieyasu and Todo Takatora, one of Hideyoshi's generals and the gate's rebuilder.

One of our favorite stories is about the notorious but popular outlaw, Ishikawa Goemon — a Robin Hood type character. On the lam, he was spotted and caught at the Sanmon Gate because he couldn't stop admiring the panoramic view. Poor Goemon was boiled alive, but at least he achieved immortality — he's even depicted in *kabuki*.

The main parts of Nanzen-ji are the **Dai Hojo** and **Sho Hojo**, the quarters of the greater and lesser abbots. The emperor donated his living quarters (Dai Hojo) to the temple in 1611. The Zen garden off the veranda of the Dai Hojo is a National Treasure. It is one of the few gardens that can prove its designer was Kobori Enshu. So many gardens are attributed to him, but usually there's no way of knowing whether or not he actually designed it or if it is merely in his style. Most of the garden is white, raked gravel with are rocks, moss, and a few impeccably pruned bushes and trees along the far wall. Some think the garden represents tigers and cubs; others say cranes and tortoises — the true answer is within the viewer. The proportions of the garden are perfect, and the tile-roofed perimeter wall harmonizes with the roofs on the buildings behind. We never tire of this garden.

Both the Dai Hojo and Sho Hojo have sliding door paintings by the Kano School. Moved from Hideyoshi's Fushimi castle, Sho Hojo provides a home for Kano Tanyu's famous painting, *Tiger Drinking Water*. Amazingly, the painters had never seen a live tiger: they had skins brought from Korea; they knew cats; and they had seen Chinese paintings. These charming paintings are the result.

Nanzen-in Temple. *Open 8:30am to 5pm; December through February until 4:30pm. ¥350.* Nanzen-in is a small subtemple of Nanzen-ji that has a famous Kamakura-era garden. Nanzen-in was the main part of Nanzen-ji when Emperor Kameyama founded it in 1291, but it's no longer the center of things. The garden has a pond with islands in the shape of the Chinese character for heart. **Muso Kokushi** is credited with designing this garden as well as the one at Tenryu-ji in Arashiyama, western Kyoto. They are considered the two best Kamakura Period strolling gardens in Kyoto.

As you walk from the center of Nanzen-ji south to Nanzen-in, you walk under a tall **aqueduct**. No, you are not in Rome. When Kyoto was stripped of its title of capital of Japan in 1868, it was a blow to the Kyoto economy as well as to its psyche. One way the governor revitalized the city was by building a canal to get fresh water from Lake Biwa to Kyoto. Kyoto had been dependent on wells, but after 1000 years, the water was brackish and the rivers were used by the textile industry rendering that water undrinkable. This public works project encompassing canals, tunnels and aqueducts was the largest the government had ever undertaken. Canal buffs may want to stop at the free museum on the canal just north of where Nanzen-ji's approach road meets the main road.

Courtesy of Japan National Tourist Organization

Konchi-in. *Tel. (075)771-3511. Open 8:30am to 5pm; until 4:30pm December through February. ¥400.*

Konchi-in is a subtemple of Nanzen-ji and is on the right just before you enter the gate to Nanzen-ji. We like its peaceful garden as well as its masterpieces of Japanese art. The temple dates to the late 14th century when it was founded in the northwest region of Kyoto. The powerful priest Suden revitalized it and moved it to its current site around 1600. Suden was known as the Black-robed Minister because of his close ties to the shogun Tokugawa Ieyasu.

The main building was moved from Hideyoshi's Fushimi castle and has door paintings by Kano Tanyu and his son, Naonobu. Off the veranda is a splendid dry-landscape garden. Yes, there are many wonderful dry-landscape gardens in Kyoto. But the scale of this garden gives you a sense of vastness and depth. We sat silently on the veranda enjoying the tranquillity. The gravel in the foreground gives way to moss, then rocks and small plants, then large bushes and finally large, thick trees in the background. The rock formation on the left is said to represent a tortoise while the a crane is on the right. Each is symbol of longevity, and it's an auspicious combination. The white sand is the ocean where you imagine a treasure boat.

The temple has some treasures that require an advance reservation to see. ¥700 admission. Ask the Tourist Information Office to arrange for a volunteer guide. It's worth the extra effort to see Hasegawa Tohaku's masterpiece painting of *The Monkey Catching the Moon* as well as the famed Hassoseki teahouse, an Important Cultural Property. Designed in the Furuta Oribe style of tea for the warrior class, this house is more open and cheerful than the rustic simplicity favored by the famous teamaster Sen-no-Rikyu. As you enter the waiting room to the Hassoseki, you'll see an unusual comb-shaped window. The guide opens the *shoji* covering about one foot of the lower portion of the window; it forms a natural art screen with the trees outside the subject matter. It's a fantastic photo opportunity, but unfortunately picture taking is prohibited.

Heading north from Nanzen-ji, you'll come to the **Nomura Museum** (Nomura Bijutsukan). Between Nanzen-ji and Eikan-do. *Tel. (075)751-0374. Open 10am to 4:30pm. Closed Monday. Open only mid-March until mid-June and September through early December. ¥600.* If you are in town during the brief times this museum is open, put it on your itinerary. This unassuming building houses a great collection of *noh* and tea ceremony items.

Just past the Nomura Museum is **Eikan-do** or Zenrin-ji Temple. *Tel. (075)761-0007. Open 9am to 4:30pm; November from 8:30am. ¥500; ¥1000 in November.* Eikan-do is famous for its autumn foliage. A favorite travel poster of ours has brilliant red maple leaves covering the entire mountain and is framed by an old wooden temple gate. This is Eikan-do. Yes, it's beautiful in autumn, but we prefer any other time so we can enjoy its beauty without hoards of people.

The large temple complex is located in a serene forest; you may not believe that Kyoto is just outside the temple's gates. The many buildings are connected by covered wooden walkways.

The temple was started in the late Heian Period. The temple's Amida Buddha is a beautiful and delicate statue that's unique; his head is turned to look behind himself. The legend goes that when the priest Eikan was walking around the Amida Buddha while chanting sutras, the Amida came down from the altar and walked in front of him. A dumbfounded Eikan froze; at that point, the Buddha turned around and said, "Eikan, don't be so slow!" Eikan had a statue made to commemorate this moment.

Turn right as you leave Eikan-do's gate and take the next right. Then take your first left, and you'll be on **Philosopher's Walk** (Tetsugaku no michi). The two-kilometer path runs along a small canal to Ginkaku-ji. Flanked by cherry trees, it's a pleasant walk any time of year and is very popular with the dating set. It has its unusual name because a philosophy professor at Kyoto University used to walk along this path daily. Stop at the Kano Shoju-an teahouse for tea ceremony tea. It's at the southern end of Philosopher's Walk. *Tel. (075)751-1077. Open 10am to 4pm. Closed Wednesday. Tea: ¥1040. Reservations not necessary.*

At the northern end of Philosopher's Walk is **Ginkaku-ji Temple** (Silver Pavilion). *Open 8:30am to 5pm; December through March 14: 9am to 4:30pm. ¥500.* Since the Golden Pavilion is covered with gold leaf, you're sure to expect the Silver Pavilion covered with silver leaf, perhaps slightly tarnished. Instead, you'll find simple wooden and plaster buildings in a fabulous garden setting. We love to come here in the morning before the tour buses arrive.

The eighth Ashikaga shogun, **Yoshimasa**, built Ginkaku-ji in 1480. He hated politics and wanted to retire but did not have an heir. He finally persuaded his brother to leave the religious world and become shogun. Within a year, Yoshimasa's wife produced a son and the battle for succession led to the Onin War, which destroyed most of Kyoto.

Yoshimasa was much more interested in the arts than the affairs of the day. He designed Ginkaku-ji to be his retreat from the outside world and busied himself with tea ceremony, painting and poetry, and was a central figure in Higashiyama culture. It is called the Silver Pavilion because Yoshimasa intended to cover it with silver leaf, but never did. As such, it contrasts with the Golden Pavilion, across town, built by Yoshimasa's grandfather. The Silver is more subdued and represents the aesthetics of *yugen* (subdued elegance), a hallmark of Higashiyama culture that's probably best displayed in *noh* theater.

Ginkaku-ji's garden is one of the Kyoto's most famous. Unlike most Zen temples that have impressive main gates facing south, Ginkaku-ji's gate is modest and tile roofed; it opens to a sandy path bound with hedges and bamboo fences. Although Yoshimasa designed it to be an isolated retreat, nowadays it is unlikely you will find it isolated. But as you stroll along around the large pond, you'll see moss, bushes, small trees and carefully positioned rocks bearing poetic names. Hopefully you will find some serenity, but it may be difficult among the tour groups.

The most controversial feature in the design of the garden is a weird sand mound that appeared in the 17th century. Some say the sand of the white sand cones reflects the moonlight thus illuminating the rest of the garden. Others say it was extra sand used for the walkways and the gardeners decided to pile into a mound. Some people complain it doesn't belong, but like it or not, the mound is now part of this famous garden.

Stop for tasty noodles at **Omen**, just south of Ginkaku-ji's parking lot.

Hakusa Sonso Garden. *Open 10am to 5pm. ¥800.* On the east-west road leading to Ginkaku-ji (Ginkaku-ji michi, east of Shirakawa Dori), you can escape the gaggle of bus groups and enter the quiet refuge of the Kyoto of another era — the Taisho era to be precise. The artist Hashimoto Kansetsu (1883-1945) lived and painted here for 30 years. We love sitting on the studio's veranda, drinking tea and absorbing the serenity of his large garden that's filled with stone sculptures. His house contains an eclectic collection of Persian miniatures, Greek pottery and Japanese pots.

KYOTO'S ONE-MINUTE HISTORY

Heian Period (794–1185). Capital moves to Kyoto. High aristocratic culture – an era of elegance and good taste.

Kamakura Period (1185–1333). The first shogunate: warrior class holds political power; the administrative center moves to Kamakura.

Muromachi Period (1333–1568). Political power returns to Kyoto and warrior class takes on aristocratic traits. The highly cultured Higashiyama and Kitayama cultures creates masterpieces like the Golden and Silver Pavilions.

Onin War (1467–77) and Sengoku Jidai (Warring States Period – 1467–1568). Military leaders fighting for supremacy leads to disintegration and destruction of large parts of Kyoto and Japan.

Momoyama Period (1568–1603). Reunification of country and warlord Hideyoshi rebuilds Kyoto. First encounter with Europe. Golden age of screen painting.

Edo or Tokugawa Period (1603–1868). Political power in Edo (Tokyo) extended period of peace; growth of merchant culture. Japan is closed – isolated from rest of the world. The arrival of Commodore Perry and his "black ships" adds turbulence to a tottering regime and the shogunate falls.

Meiji Period (1868–1912). Emperor restored to power by rebellion of young, low-ranking samurai. Big blow to Kyoto because capital and emperor move to Tokyo.

6. North-central Kyoto

Shimogamo Shrine, Shokoku-ji, Kitano Tenmangu Shrine*, Nishijin District*, Nishijin Textile Center, Orinasu-kan, Urasenke Chado Research Center, Raku Art Museum.

Take bus no. 4, 14 or 205 from Kyoto Station to Rakuhoku Koko-mae for Shimogamo Shrine.

Shimogamo Jinja Shrine. *Grounds always open. Admission free.* Shimogamo together with its sister, Kamigamo, make up a Shinto shrine devoted to the gods of thunder and rain. Shimogamo is located at the confluence of the Kamo and Takase Rivers. Shimogamo predates the founding of Kyoto in 794 and is one site of the Aoi Festival every May 15.

Shokoku-ji Temple. *Open 10am to 5pm. Jotenkaku Museum entrance fee ¥600*. This temple, nestled in a pine grove, is a pleasant get-away from the bustle of Kyoto. The temple dates to 1392; it was one of the Kyoto's main Zen temples in the early 15th century. The great Zen artists Josetsu, Shubun, Sesshu and Jakuchu worked here. Like most of Kyoto, Shokoku-ji was destroyed in the civil wars of the 15th century. Toyotomi Hideyori, Hideyoshi's son, rebuilt it in the early 1700s but most of those buildings also perished. We love to walk among the many pines and to go to the Jotenkaku Museum, which is worth a trip to see Zen masterpieces and Hasegawa Tohaku's famous screen, *Monkeys in a Bamboo Grove (open 10am to 5pm, ¥600)*.

Kitano Tenmangu Shrine. *Always open. Admission free.* Kitano Tenmangu Shrine is dedicated to Sugawara Michizane, a great scholar and poet of the 9th century. As a prominent court official, he rose to the high position of Minister of the Right, but the jealous Fujiwara faction had Michizane transferred to Kyushu, which essentially was exile. Michizane died in Kyushu in 903, a heartbroken man yearning for the capital and its plum blossoms.

But Michizane had the last laugh. After his death, Kyoto experienced many earthquakes and other natural disasters that were attributed to Michizane's unhappy spirit. In 942 a woman said Michizane appeared in her dream and told her he wanted to be enshrined at Kitano, a small shrine dedicated to the god of thunder. Five years later, the Fujiwara family built a large shrine dedicated to Michizane. Emperors would visit the shrine to try to appease Michizane's spirit, and the shrine became a popular place. Hideyoshi held his grand tea party on Kitano's grounds in 1687; he shocked Kyoto society by inviting the entire city.

Hideyori, Hideyoshi's son, constructed most of the present buildings in 1607. The shrine's 2000 tree plum garden plays host to a plum festival every February and March. Not only did Michizane love plum blossoms, but they were his family crest. There's also a large pine grove, the site of Hideyoshi's tea party.

Kitano is still the center of a cultural scene active with poetry readings, music performances, tea ceremony and other events. Michizane has become the benevolent god of learning so thousands of students come to pray for success in entrance exams. The thousands of *ema*, small wooden planks, are visible petitions. On the 25th of each month, the shrine also hosts a large flea market that you can attend if you're in Kyoto. Patrice still has a cotton yukata she bought here in the 1970s during her first trip to Japan.

One block east of Kitano Shrine is **Kami-shichi-ken**, an old *geisha* district where there are theatrical performances of *geisha* dances in the spring.

The **Nishijin District** is the center of Kyoto's silk weaving industry. The Hata family, who came from China brought silk with them and settled in Kyoto even before it became the capital. The city became a silk center, but the Onin War in the 15th century seriously disrupted production. They reestablished production on Nishijin (literally western camp), a field abandoned by the army. Today the production continues in a thousand tiny workshops behind the wooden lattice doors of traditional houses as well as in newer concrete buildings. The area is one of our favorite places to stroll among the many wooden buildings that mentally transport us to a Kyoto of an earlier age. And the clatter of the looms is a reminder that this traditional industry has not yet been relegated to museums.

One place where you can see it all come together is at the **Nishijin Textile Center** (Nishijin Kaikan). *Open daily 9am to 5pm. Closed December 29 through January 2. Admission free.* The center displays the weaving process and finished products. We have friends who always take their guests to the kimono show which changes with the seasons. You can dress in a *maiko's* (apprentice *geisha*) formal kimono for the large fee of ¥8800. Dressing in a simple kimono costs ¥1500 – ¥3000 if you want walk around Kyoto wearing it. Reservations required for kimono. *Tel. (075)451-9231.*

One block from Nishijin Textile Center is **Aizenkobo**, a shop selling indigo dyed goods.

The **Orinasu-kan** is another must for the textile enthusiast. The museum was redone several years ago and has weavers working as well as displays of sumptuous *noh* costumes, kimono and *obi. Open 9am to 12 noon; 1pm to 4pm. Closed Monday (no weavers on weekends). ¥500. Tel. (075)431-0020. One block east of Senbon Dori; 1 1/2 blocks north of Imadegawa Dori.*

Urasenke Foundation Chado Research Center (Chado Shiryokan). *Tel. (075)431-6474. Open 9:30am to 4:30pm. Closed Monday. ¥500.* Followers of tea master Sen-no-Rikyu divided into two groups: Urasenke and Omotesenke. Urasenke is active around the world spreading the tea ceremony culture. Despite its academic sounding name, the center's exhibitions are designed for the general public. The four exhibitions a year all center on tea ceremony and related crafts. All visitors are offered a cup of green tea and sweets.

Raku Art Museum. *Tel. (075)414-0304. Open 10am to 4:30pm. Closed Monday. ¥800.* Raku is a ceramic ware used in the tea ceremony. It got its start at the end of the 16th Century when the great tea master Sen-no-Rikyu fell in love with Raku Chojiro's works. Today the 15th generation master continues the tradition. *Raku* ware is handmade and fired in a special way.

The Raku Museum is on a quiet street in a traditional building. The first floor has a room filled with tea bowls; the second floor has exhibits showing how *raku* is made and displays other *raku* tea ceremony utensils. It's a wonderful museum for those interested in the tea ceremony.

7. Northeast Kyoto

Shugaku-in Imperial Villa*, Manshu-in*, Shisen-do*, Kimpuku-ji, Nobutoke-an Teahouse and the Kyoto Folk Art Hall.

Take bus no. 5 from Kyoto Station to Shugakuin Rikyu-mae stop for Shugakuin Imperial Villa.

Shugaku-in Imperial Villa (Shugaku-in Rikyu). *You must apply in advance at the Imperial Household Agency Office at the Imperial Palace (see Planning your Stay at the beginning of this chapter) for permission to join a tour (in Japanese) of Shugakuin. Tours are at 9am, 10am, 11am, 1:30pm and 3pm, Monday through Friday. People under 20 are not permitted.*

Since you need permission to view Shugaku-in, this exquisite villa is not overrun with bus loads of visitors. We find it a splendid get-away and understand why **Emperor Gomizuno**, one of the most powerful emperors in history, built Shugakuin as a retirement retreat when he abdicated in 1629. He also built the Sento Palace in central Kyoto — the Tokugawa shogun put lots of yen at his disposal. The large tract of land on the gently sloping hills of northeast Kyoto is a splendid setting for his villa. The buildings are called teahouses, emphasizing the rustic nature of the villa. The teahouses are built in the hills at three different levels and are connected by groves of pine trees.

The lower teahouse, **Jugetsu-kan**, has stepping stones on the pathway positioned in such a way that a different view of the building is revealed with each step. The middle teahouse consists of the **Rakushi-kan**, an elegant study room where you can enjoy the beauty of the pond and garden and the **Kyaku-den** (Guest House). The upper teahouse, **Rin'un-tei**, is deep within a pine grove. Looking out over this garden with its large pond, you have a superb view of the Kyoto hills. Shugaku-in has Japan's largest-scale, borrowed-landscape garden and uses distant mountains as part of its design.

Manshu-in Temple. *Open 9am to 5pm. ¥500.* We find Manshu-in to be one of the most graceful buildings in Kyoto. If you like the Katsura Villa, you are bound to love this temple which combines the elegance of the aristocracy with the austerity of the warrior class.

Yoshihisa, an imperial prince, built Manshu-in as a retirement villa in the early 17th century. Tokugawa Ieyasu adopted him in the late 16th century, but once the shogun consolidated power, he felt he no longer needed an imperial son and allowed Yoshihisa to retire. The graceful buildings set among maples, azaleas and evergreens include the **Daishoin**

(Large Study) and **Koshoin** (Small Study) that has sliding doors painted by Kano Tanyu, and a teahouse and garden attributed to Kobori Enshu. The dry-landscape garden, a National Treasure, uses rocks, moss, trees and gravel to create a splendid image of islands and waterfalls. Personally, we prefer seeing the garden from the Koshoin rather than from the Daishoin. It has more depth.

Outside the entrance to Manshu-in is a noodle shop called Benten Chaya.

Shisen-do Temple. *Open 9am to 5pm. ¥500.* We think this serene garden hermitage is one of Kyoto's best kept secrets. The warrior **Ishikawa Jozan** was an attendant to the first Tokugawa shogun, Ieyasu. Jozan was so overzealous in trying to please Tokugawa that at the Battle of Osaka in 1615, he participated in combat, a no-no for someone of his position. Disgraced by his actions, he renounced the military way of life and turned to studying the Chinese classics.

Ishikawa built Shisen-do in 1641. The unassuming hermitage is reached by walking through a simple bamboo gate and a small bamboo grove. Shisen-do's main attraction, the garden, features carefully pruned azalea bushes, white sand, beautiful red pine trees (we're convinced someone polishes the trunks) and maple trees. The natural plants of the hillside are part of the garden. We love to view the garden from the *tatami* mat rooms of the small hermitage at the top of steep stone steps. But, best of all, you're allowed to walk around this garden, even on the gravel, as long as you wear the special slippers that are provided. It's probably such fun because it feels as though we're breaking the rules.

Even today we feel the solitude and serenity that Jozan must have experienced. The place is so cold in winter, but in summer it's a delightful respite from Kyoto's heat. Surprisingly, Jozan lived to the ripe old age of 89; we thought he would have caught pneumonia much earlier.

Across from Shisen-do is **Nobutoke-an**, which has five tea arbors and is a delightful place to sit and drink tea in a splendid garden setting. The ¥500 admission includes tea and sweets as well as admission to the **Kyoto Folk Art Hall** (Kyoto Mingei-kan) next door. *Open 9:30am to 4pm. Closed December 30-31.*

Kimpuku-ji Temple. *Open 9am to 5pm. Closed January 16-31, August 5-20 and December 30-31. ¥300.* Originally founded in 11th century, Monk Tesshu rebuilt this tiny place as a Zen temple during the Edo Period. Kimpuku-ji has a small but well-kept garden and teahouse. We like to relax in the *tatami* mat room and enjoy the garden. Since not many people come here, we often enjoy it in solitary splendor.

Restaurant possibilities include Bistro Kimura, down the hill between Shisendo and Shirakawa Dori and ramen at Tenka Ippin on Shirakawa Dori.

8. Northern Kyoto

Kamigamo Shrine*, Entsu-ji*, Jisso-in, Kyoto Botanical Garden, Kyoto Garden of Fine Art, Daitoku-ji*, Koestsu-ji, Genko-an and Josho-ji.

This area is fairly spread out; many places are easily reached by short taxi rides. You can start at the Kitayama Subway Station, but if you wish to bypass the Botanical Garden and Garden of Fine Art, take take bus no. Kita 3 from the Kitaoji subway station to Kamigamo Jinja Mae stop.

Kyoto Botanical Garden. *Tel. (075)701-0141. Open 9am to 5pm (enter by 4pm); Conservatory open 10am to 4pm. Closed December 28 through January 1. Garden ¥200; Conservatory ¥200; combined ticket ¥250.* The Botanical Garden covers a large expanse; we don't recommend it for time-pinched travelers unless they have a special interest in plants.

Kyoto Garden of Fine Art. *Tel. (075)724-2188. Open daily 9am to 5pm. Closed at New Year's. ¥100.* At the Kitayama Subway stop, near Kyoto Botanical Garden. Designed by Ando Takao, this modernistic open air museum displays masterpieces of art reproduced on ceramics. Monet's *Water Lilies* is displayed under water. While it's fun to touch the art, it's the architecture that makes the museum worthwhile.

Kamigamo Shrine (Kamigamo Jinja). *Grounds always open. Admission free.* Kamigamo and Shimogamo Shrines are two halves of a shrine dedicated to the god of thunder. Founded in the 6th century, Kamigamo predates the establishment of Kyoto as a capital city and is home to one of Kyoto's best known festivals, the Aoi Festival. In the 6th century, a number of natural disasters led people to believe that the gods of the shrine were neglected. The emperor sent a messenger to placate them and harmony was restored. Thus began an annual parade on May 15 from the Imperial Palace to the Shimogamo and Kamigamo Shrines, a tradition that is carried on today. The participants dress in Heian costume and place *aoi* leaves (hollyhocks) in their hats to present to the shrines.

Kamigamo's buildings date only from the 17th to 19th centuries, but they are constructed in the original style. Surrounded by greenery, the gate has vermilion pillars and a huge roof. The Honden and Gonden buildings are National Treasures. In front of them is a white sand garden. The garden has white gravel raked into large cones that mark the place where the gods arrive. Kamigamo was designated a UNESCO World Heritage Site in 1994.

Across the street from the bus stop in front of the entrance to the shrine is **Shinmedo**, a small sweet shop selling *yakimochi* (grilled pounded rice cakes). They are filled with sweet bean paste but aren't sweet in a traditional Western way. Try them straight from the grill or at room temperature — they're good either way. ¥100 each.

The southern perimeter of the shrine is a historical preservation district called Shake-machi. Behind the plaster walls are the residences of the shrine's priests. The **Nishimura House** *is open to the public 9:30am to 4pm but is closed December 9th until March 15.* ¥*500.* Stop in to see how Shinto priests live. There's has a lovely teahouse and garden.

Nearby Kamigamo is **Azekura**, a 300-year old *sake* warehouse, that's now a *soba* noodle restaurant. We highly recommend a lunch stop here. From the Kamigamo area to Entsu-ji, it's easiest to take a taxi.

Entsu-ji Temple. *Open 10am to 4pm.* ¥*500.* Emperor Gomizuno built Entsu-ji as a small retirement villa in 1629. He was the emperor who called on the Tokugawa shogun at Nijo Castle in 1626. He was also the person who built Shugaku-in and Sento Palace and retirement villas — what a pension plan. The emperor designed the garden, the temple's most well-known feature, which is dry-landscape style and has three layers. The first layer uses rocks and moss and its unusual horizontal composition is emphasized by the second layer: low hedges of camellia and azalea bushes and tall, straight cedar trees. Between the trees you can view Mt. Hiei, the third layer. Borrowed scenery and three layers are two ingredients of many Japanese gardens. We try to visit on a clear day because Mt. Hiei in the background is an essential element of the design. After Emperor Gomizuno's death, Entsu-ji became a convent.

Reach Jisso-in by bus #4 North from Kitaoji Subway Station or by taxi from Entsu-ji.

Jisso-in Temple. *Open 9am to 5pm.* ¥*500.* Jisso-in is a subtemple of the Tendai sect of Buddhism and was powerful at the end of Momoyama and early Edo Periods. The temple has many sliding doors painted by the Kano school of artists, which isn't surprising since the Kano artists were at their peak during this time. Not many people visit the temple, but we love to admire the famous painting of Chinese Lions by Kano Tanyu in the entrance hall.

From Jisso-in, take bus #4 to Kitaoji and transfer to #204, 205 or 206 to Daitoku-ji mae.

Daitoku-ji Temple. *Open 9am to 4:30pm.* Daitoku-ji is one of Kyoto's most important Zen temples. Founded in 1319, the temple had the support of several emperors in the 14th century but fell into decline and was completely destroyed during the 15th century Onin War. The priest **Ikkyu** revived the temple in 1474, and Zen Buddhism became fashionable with the warrior set. Hideyoshi held Oda Nobunaga's funeral here in 1582. Trying to show their loyalty to Hideyoshi, many feudal lords built lots of subtemples. When the Meiji Government was established in 1868, the temple suffered in the purge against Buddhism. Today it's a mere shadow of its former self with only 22 subtemples remaining.

The main temple of Daitoku-ji is famous for its garden, paintings and Karamon gate that was moved from Hideyoshi's Kyoto residence, Jurakudai. It is not normally open to the public. You can see the garden only by taking the garden tour run by Keihan Bus (see Garden Tours at the beginning of this chapter); occasionally, at special times it's open. Most of the subtemples are not open to the public, but to get the sense of how impressive their power was, wander around the vast grounds and glimpse the well-kept gardens through the gates.

The following four subtemples are open:

• **Daisen-in Temple**. *Open 9am to 5pm; until 4:30pm December through February. ¥400.* Daisen-in is the most famous of all the subtemples. Probably constructed around the time of the temple's founding in 1509, its Zen dry-landscape garden on the east side of the Hon-do (Main Hall) is a masterpiece of the genre. The actual garden is quite small but the masterful placement of rocks, gravel, plants and trees achieves a sense of spaciousness. The Hon-do has paintings by Kano Motonobu and Soami. Tea is served.

• **Koto-in Temple**. *Open 9am to 4:30pm. ¥400.* Hosokawa Tadaoki, a general who was one of the leaders of Hideyoshi's Korean invasion, founded Koto-in in 1601. His wife, Gracia, converted to Christianity, becoming one of the highest ranking people to do so. Hosokawa Morihito, prime minister of Japan in the early 1990s, is a direct descendant of Tadaoki. One garden is simply composed of moss, trees and a stone lantern. Another garden, site of the Hosokawa tombs, is natural. A stone lantern, gift of the tea master Sen-no-Rikyu, marks Tadaoki's tomb.

• **Ryogen-in**. *Open 9am to 4:30pm. ¥350.* Ryogen-in's Muromachi rock garden is a powerful example of the genre.

• **Zuiho-in**. *Open 9am to 5pm. ¥300.* The temple of the Christian feudal lord, Otomo Sorin, the stones in one garden are in the shape of a cross. The Garden of the Blissful Mountain uses raked gravel and positions rocks to form a mountain.

Daitoku-ji is noted for its *shojin ryori*, Buddhist vegetarian fare. The subtemple Daiji-an runs the Izusen Restaurant; outside the East Gate, Daitoku-ji Ikkyu also serves elegant vegetarian food. Wakuden, a few buildings down from Ikkyu, serves Japanese food in a very contemporary setting.

From Daitoku-ji, walk to Horikawa Dori to board the #1 North bus to Genko-an mae.

Genko-an Hut. Located on the way to Koetsu-ji temple. *Open 9am to 5pm. ¥300.* Founded as a temple for the abbot of Daitoku-ji for his retirement in 1346, the Main Hall has a ceiling said to be moved from Fushimi Castle. Next to Genko-an is Josho-ji.

Josho-ji Temple. Josho-ji is a Nichiren-sect temple located next to Genko-an. *Open 8:30am to 5pm. ¥300.* Originally founded in 1616 by

Koetsu's son (see Koetsu-ji, above) as a seminary for Buddhist novices, it was once a huge temple. Remaining today are the red gate, the main hall, the kitchen and the teahouse; the red gate was donated by the famous courtesan Yoshino Tayu, who married a wealthy merchant.

Koetsu-ji Temple. *Open 8am to 5pm. ¥300.* The shogun Tokugawa Ieyasu gave the artist Hon-ami Koetsu a large grant of land in 1615. Koetsu built a home here and established an artists' colony. Sotatsu, Korin and Kenzan, a veritable *Who's Who* of 17th century art, resided at the colony. Koetsu was a renaissance man, well versed in calligraphy, painting, ceramics, lacquer and dyeing. After Koetsu's death, his residence became a temple. Look for the special kind of bamboo hedge called Koetsu-gaki designed by Koetsu; it's used all over Japan. The temple has several rustic teahouses.

A short walk from the entrance of Koetsu-ji is a lovely thatched-roof restaurant called **Zenrimbo** that serves a *bento* lunch in a woven willow box.

9. Northwestern Kyoto

Ryoan-ji*, Kinkaku-ji*, Ninna-ji, Koryu-ji, Myoshin-ji, Kyoto Studio Park. From Kyoto Station, take the #12 bus to Kinkaku-ji mae.

Kinkaku-ji Temple (Golden Pavilion). *Open 9am to 5pm. ¥400.* The Golden Pavilion has to be Kyoto's most famous site, and its photograph graces countless travel posters. Try to visit it when it opens to get a head start on the tour buses; even if you can't, usually you'll get some quiet moments between groups. Walking along the wooded paths of the temple precincts, the Golden Pavilion suddenly appears in front of you; its ethereal beauty makes it one of the great buildings of its time. When you see its reflection in the pond, its beauty is magnified.

Ashikaga Yoshimitsu, the greatest of the 15 Ashikaga shoguns (actually, they were a pretty undistinguished lot), took over an aristocrat's residence in 1397 where he built his retirement villa. Yoshimitsu presided over an age noted for its refinement in the arts, even among the warrior class. *Noh* plays were performed frequently and warriors wrote poetry. After retirement, Yoshimitsu became a monk but did not live a monk's life. He remained active in politics and tried to settle a crisis caused by two warring emperors, each with his own court.

The Golden Pavilion was Yoshimitsu's statement about harmony between heaven and earth. Built over a pond, it joins the temporal with the spiritual. Even the eclectic architecture of the pavilion has the same vision. The first floor of the three-storied structure is *shinden* style, like the residences of Heian aristocrats. The second floor, a study, is in the style of a Kamakura Period warrior's residence while the top floor, a prayer hall, is in the Zen Buddhist *shariden* style. A glittering gold phoenix sits atop the structure. The entire building is covered in gold leaf, a reflection of the wealth and power of the Ashikaga shogunate. In 1950, a deranged monk burned the original pavilion (a fictitious version is chronicled in the novel *The Temple of the Golden Pavilion* by Mishima Yukio). Built in 1955, the present structure is an exact replica.

In 1408 Emperor Gokomatsu honored Yoshimitsu with a twenty-day visit, an unprecedented event since the retired shogun was not a court noble. Can you imagine the preparations necessary for a twenty-day visit? Following his father's instructions, Yoshimitsu's son turned the villa into a Zen temple after his father's death. Yoshimitsu built other elegant buildings on the site but none survives.

Up the hill is a small tea arbor; the stone basin, seat and lantern came from Yoshimitsu's palace. The main temple building has images of Yoshimitsu and Muso Kokushi, who is credited with designing the garden. Outside, the pine, pruned in the shape of a boat, is some 500 years old.

When you leave Kinkaku-ji, turn right and follow Kitsuji-dori, the narrow road that hugs the temple grounds. Do not walk to the large street, Nishi Oji Dori. About two blocks down on the right, you'll find **Gontaro**, a small noodle shop in a traditional building. To top off a morning visit to Kinkaku-ji, we like to have lunch at this cozy restaurant seated either at the tables or on *tatami* mats overlooking the small garden. If you'd prefer Western food, **Hinadori** is a French bistro on the same side of the street. If you'd like to sandwich your visits to Kinkaku-ji and Ryoan-ji with a Zen culinary experience, go to **Wara** for *yu-dofu*, simmered tofu.

To Ryoan-ji, continue walking on Kutsuji Dori for about 20 minutes or take the #59 bus to Ryoan-ji mae.

For a temporary break in temple viewing, take a short detour to Ritsumeikan University's **Kyoto Museum for World Peace** (Kokusai Heiwa Museum). It is on the grounds of the university, on the left when Kutsuji-dori makes a major turn to the right. *Open 9:30am to 4:30pm. Closed Mondays.*

Ryoan-ji Temple. *Open 8am to 5pm; 8:30am to 4:30pm December through February. ¥400.* The temple's rock and sand garden is probably the most famous of the Zen minimalist genre. The bad news is it's on the itinerary of every tour bus in Kyoto so if you are expecting to have a meditative Zen experience, be there when it opens in the morning. The good news is there's more to Ryoan-ji than the one garden.

The feudal lord Hosokawa Katsumoto, one of the main warlords in the Onin War that basically destroyed Kyoto in the 15th century, built Ryoan-ji in 1450 as his villa. The war claimed the buildings, but Hosokawa's son rebuilt it in 1488; today's buildings date from the early 19th century, having been rebuilt after a fire that did not damage the garden. The garden's origins are vague, but it was probably built in the early 16th century; Soami, a well-known painter and landscape designer, is usually credited with its creation.

After you enter through the main gate, walk around a pond and garden that belonged to a Heian aristocrat. Spend some time in this lovely strolling garden either on your way in or out. Beyond the garden, you'll come to a wooden temple building; take off your shoes and go inside to the veranda to view the rock garden. The garden, breathtakingly simple and small, consists of 15 rocks arranged in three groups, surrounded by moss, and set on a bed of perfectly raked white sand. There isn't one vantage point where you can see all 15 rocks simultaneously. A tiled-roof mud wall encircles the garden isolating it from the outside world; the wall itself is a work of art.

Many people look at the garden and wonder what all the fuss in about. In Zen dry-landscape gardens, the garden only suggests a form; it is not meant to be an entire landscape. Ryoan-ji's minimalist work is the epitome of the Zen ideal of reducing everything to its simplest — the participant completes the picture. Only by destroying illusions about life can one achieve a higher level of consciousness after being discouraged by the destruction and chaos outside. It's no accident that Zen reached its peak during the Onin War.

It's unlikely that you'll be able to concentrate on such philosophical matters while tour groups are shuffling in and out with megaphones and loudspeakers blaring. Yes, they even have un-Zen-like recorded messages to make sure you get the message of the garden. It's still worth seeing, but don't count on reaching enlightenment.

Don't rush out of Ryoan-ji after you see the rock garden. The grounds contain a Burmese stupa (a Buddhist shrine) as well as a lovely strolling garden with a pavilion where you can eat *yu-dofu* (boiled bean curd) overlooking the garden. This garden is a good contrast to Ryoan-ji's stone garden.

As you exit Ryoan-ji, continue walking along Kitsuji-dori for another 10 minutes to reach Ninna-ji Temple.

Ninna-ji Temple. *Open 9am to 4:30pm. ¥400.* Ninna-ji dates to 886 when Emperor Koko built it as a retirement villa. His successor, Emperor Uda, turned it into a temple and became its chief priest after his own retirement. Until 1868, the temple always had a prince as its chief priest. The Miei-do was moved from the Imperial Palace and dates from the 16th century, and the five-storied pagoda was built in 1637. The temple's Omuro no sakura, a grove of cherry trees, is famous; the trees have short trunks and look dwarfed, and the flowers have many petals. The peak season is usually mid-April, later than traditional cherry blossoms.

We often stop at **Ippuku Chaya**, the teahouse on Ninna-ji's grounds. The owner is the eighth generation keeper of the temple's famed cherry trees. Regardless of the season, cherry ice cream, a delectable pale pink concoction, is available at ¥400. *Open 9am to 5pm. Closed Thursday.*

To reach Myoshin-ji, walk southeast down the large road at an angle from the southeast corner of Ninna-ji.

Myoshin-ji Temple. *Open 9am to 4pm. ¥400.* Emperor Hanazono's villa was turned into a temple in 1342 and is a main temple of the Zen Buddhist Rinzai sect. It has a huge compound that contains 47 subtemples, but most are not open to the public. The three that are open are **Taizo-in, Keishun-in** and **Daishin-in.** Their gardens are worth visiting if you're looking for inspiration for creating Japanese corners in your garden. The temple's bell, cast in 698, is Japan's oldest. The Sanmon Gate dates from 1599 and is a masterpiece of Momoyama architecture. We especially like Taizo-an's dry-landscape garden that contains rocks, gravel and beautifully pruned shrubs and trees. It skillfully depicts a waterfall and islands almost like a landscape painting. No wonder Kano Motonobu, a famous painter of the late 16th-early 17th century, lived in this subtemple for some time. For Buddhist vegetarian cuisine, try **Ajiro Honten** at the south entrance of Myoshin-ji.

About one kilometer southwest of Myoshin-ji are Koryu-ji and Kyoto Studio Park.

Koryu-ji Temple. *Open 9am to 5pm; until 4:30pm December through February. ¥600.* Koryu-ji dates to 622 when the Prince Shotoku, generally credited with the spread of Buddhism in Japan, gave a statue of Buddha to the Hata family. The main hall dates from 1165, but most of the statues are from the 7th and 8th centuries. The statue of the Buddha of Mercy, a National Treasure, is in the Kodo (Lecture Hall). The statue of the Future Buddha is housed in the Reiho-kan. This National Treasure shows the Buddha in meditation; the serene facial expression and delicate hands make it one of the masterpieces of its era. If you can only see one statue of the Buddha in Kyoto, choose this one.

Kyoto Studio Park. Also known as Toei Uzumasa Movie Land (Toei Eigamura Uzumasa). *Tel. (075)864-7716. Open 9am to 5pm; December through February 9:30am to 4pm. Closed December 21 through January 1. ¥2200.* Eight film studios were centered in this area in the 1930s. Today, television companies use Kyoto Studio Park sets everyday to film samurai dramas. The place is a theme park where you can see movies being filmed and also lots of demonstrations of special effects. It's a good place to take the kids. Yes, it is tacky, but then again, this is Hollywood, or at least Japan's version of it.

KYOTO OUTSKIRTS

10. Arashiyama & Sagano areas

Tenryu-ji*, Okochi Sanso Garden, Rakushisha, Nison-in, Gio-ji, Daikaku-ji*, Monkey Park, Boating on the Hozu River.

Arashiyama can be reached via the Keifu Electric Streetcar from Shijo Omiya Station to the terminus or Saga Station on the JR San-in Main Line from JR Kyoto Station. By bus from Kyoto Station: 71, 72 or 73 to Arashiyama.

Togetsu-kyo Bridge. This bridge, over the Oi River, owes its name (Moon Crossing Bridge) to Emperor Kameyama who was struck by its beauty while moon viewing. The bridge was reconstructed in the 1930s but is faithful to the original design.

Tenryu-ji Temple. *Open 8:30am to 5:30pm; until 5pm November through March. ¥500.* For a time in the 14th century, two courts with two emperors battled for control of the throne. The emperor of the Southern Court, Godaigo, died in 1338. A Zen priest warned the Northern Court that Godaigo's spirit had to be appeased or else it could wreak havoc on them. Tenryu-ji was built in 1340 and dedicated it to Godaigo. The temple's buildings date from the late 19th century, but the garden is one of the best known of the Muromachi Period. It features a pond with islands and a dry

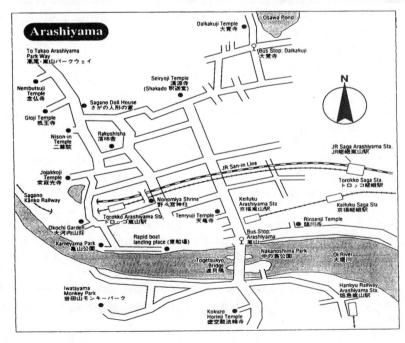

waterfall. In the upper grounds is a building based on Daigoji's palace in Yoshino. The cherry tree planted there is another reminder of Yoshino, an area famous for its blossoms.

Leave Tenryu-ji by its north gate and when the path ends, turn to the left walking uphill through a bamboo grove, a wonderfully peaceful stroll. At the top of the path and to the right is **Okochi Sanso Garden**. *Open daily 9am to 5pm. ¥900 includes tea.* Actor Okochi Denjiro (1898-1962) built this garden on a hill that offers great views of the Arashiyama Gorge, Mt. Hiei and Mt. Nyoigatake. Stop at the teahouse near the entrance for tea and sweets.

North of Okochi Garden is Ogura Pond; the Shinto shrine on the far side is **Mikami**, a place to pray for hair. It's a popular place with Kyoto's barbers, and perhaps with some men.

Rakushisha, a short walk from Mikami, is poet Mukai Kyorai's (1651-1704) country hut. The famous *haiku* poet, Basho, was his teacher and the two spent time here. Stones in the garden have poems inscribed on them, and it's a perfect place to compose poems. We've always planned to do it, but haven't made it so far. *Open 9am to 5pm; January and February until 4pm. ¥150.*

Nison-in Temple. *Open 9am to 4:30pm. ¥500.* Yakui Mon, Nison-in temple's main gate, was moved from Hideyoshi's Fushimi Castle. Its two guardian Buddhas were carved in the late Heian Period and are Important Cultural Properties. We love to come here at the time of autumn foliage.

Gio-ji Temple. *Open 9am to 5pm. ¥300.* In the midst of a bamboo grove, this small, rustic thatched-roof nunnery is well known to Japanese as the refuge for Taira no Kiyomori's (1118-1181) cast-off mistress. Gio was a dancer who so dazzled Kiyomori with her beauty that he took her as his mistress. She lived a life of privilege until Kiyomori fell for another dancer, Hotoke Gozen, and banished Gio. Before she left, Gio wrote a poem on the wall of her room: "The fresh or fading flowers of the same moor, In autumn meet with the same hapless fate." (translated by Arthur Waley). Hotoke Gozen became depressed by Gio's fate, and Kiyomori sent for Gio to cheer her up. Gio refused his invitation but her mother convinced her to go. At the palace she sang one song that reduced everyone to tears. The 21-year old Gio then left and became a Buddhist nun, spending the rest of her life in prayer at the small hut. Interestingly, Hotoke Gozen later joined Gio as a nun. The statues on the altar are of Gio, Gio's mother, Ginyo (Gio's sister), Taira no Kiyomori, and Hotoke Gozen.

Daikaku-ji Temple. *Open 9am to 4:30pm. ¥500.* Originally an imperial villa, Daikaku-ji became a temple in 876. The Shinden Hall, an Important Cultural Property, was moved from the Imperial Palace in the early 17th century. The epitome of Momoyama style paintings are Kano Sanraku's plum trees with their pink and white flowers that extend over eight sliding doors. We can't image how he managed to execute painting the branches, but they sure brighten up any room.

The buildings are connected by roofed corridors so you can imagine how you would have felt walking from one building to another in the old days. The temple is the center of the Saga Goryu School of flower arrangement and beautiful flower arrangements are everywhere. We enjoy stopping here to admire this classical flower style that is so different from more contemporary schools like Sogetsu. The garden, dating from the Heian Period, is one of Kyoto's oldest.

Near Togetsukyo Bridge is the Monkey Park.

Iwatayama Monkey Park. *Open 9am to 5:30pm; until 4pm December through February. ¥500.* Almost no one, with the exception of a few primatologists, associates Kyoto with monkeys. Yet on this Arashiyama hill, a steady climb on a gravel path leads you to a preserve that's home to about 300 Japanese macaques. This preserve isn't an amusement-type place like many monkey parks in Japan; the animals are fed twice a day to keep them out of the farmers' fields, otherwise they live a wild life. Don't feed or touch the monkeys. It's a fun diversion, especially if you are with kids. But make sure you eat your wheaties and don't wear spike heels because it's an uphill trek.

KYOTO WITH KIDS

Don't try to do too much. If the kids are young, one activity a day may be enough. Even older children can get pretty bored with templing so make sure you vary the itinerary. A couple tried and true favorites are:
- *Kyoto Zoo (near Heian Shrine)*
- *Riding the rapids down the Hozu River (north of Arashiyama)*
- *Iwatayama Monkey Park (in Arashiyama)*
- *Umekoji Steam Locomotive Preservation Hall (near Kyoto Station)*
- *Observation Deck on Kyoto Tower (near Kyoto Station)*
- *Kyoto Studio Park (near Uzumasa Station on Keifuku Arashiyama Line),*
- *Nijo Castle (kids love the squeaking floors) and*
- *Nijo Jinya (for older kids – unfortunately the under 15 set is not allowed)*

Boat ride down Hozu River (Hozu Gawa Kudari). A boat ride down the Hozu River is a welcome break from the usual sightseeing in Kyoto and is an agreeable diversion for kids. For a better view, sit on the right side of the train going up to Kameoka. JR Sagano line also goes from Arashiyama to Kameoka; the station is a 10-minute walk to the pier. At Kameoka, you board engineless boats for the 16-kilometer trip down river that takes 1 hour and 40 minutes. The mountain scenery is gorgeous, and the river is delightful, meandering at some places, and going through rapids in steep gorges in others. The boatmen use poles to paddle and steer. *Take the Torokko train from Arashiyama to Kameoka. There are nine trains a day, and the trip takes 25 minutes. ¥600 one way. Closed Wednesdays and in January and February. Between March and November, boats leave once an hour between 9am and 3:30pm, more frequently on weekends, national holidays and in the high season. December through early March, boats depart 10am, 11:30am, 1pm and 3pm. ¥3900. Tel. (0771)22-5846.*

11. Takao & Togano areas
Kozan-ji*, Jingo-ji and Saimyo-ji.
These temples are located deep in the mountains off Rt. 162. Take the JR bus from Kyoto Station to Ume no-o stop. 60 minutes. From there walk 10 minutes to Kozan-ji.

Kozan-ji Temple. *Open 9am to 5pm. ¥600.* Located on the far side of the Kiyotaki River dividing the worldly from the spiritual, the path to the temple has stones in rhomboid shape. The temple dates back to 774 but became important in the 13th century when the priest Myo'e, who incidentally kept records of his dreams long before Freud and Jung, reemphasized that it takes hard work to achieve enlightenment. Among the temple's treasures are scrolls with ink drawings of monkeys, frogs and other animals as caricatures of priests and other people. The original now lives at the Tokyo National Museum in Ueno.

The temple has a tea grove that is supposed to be the oldest in Japan. Monk Myo'e brought tea bushes from China as a special medicine for longevity. The temple is also well known as a good place to view fall foliage.

From Kozan-ji, it's a 20-minute walk to Saimyo-ji.

Saimyo-ji Temple. *Open 9am to 5am. ¥400.* We like to stop at this secluded temple when we're in the area. In the 8th century, Saimyo-ji was founded as a subtemple of Jingo-ji by Chisen, a disciple of Kukai. The statues of Shaka-nyorai Buddha and the 1000-handed Kannon are Important Cultural Properties. Even when the mountainside is in a blaze of red, this temple is still uncrowded. Saimyo-ji has a huge bell that you can ring for ¥100.

Saimyo-ji is a 20-minute walk to Jingo-ji.

Jingo-ji Temple. *Open 9am to 4pm. ¥400.* Visiting this secluded temple transports you back to the Heian Period when Esoteric Buddhism was strong. Cross the Kiyotaki River and go up a steep flight of stairs. The

Kiyotaki River is considered the divide between the secular and the divine worlds. Constructed in 1299, a red bridge at the temple welcomes you to the world of the sacred.

Founded in 781, Jingo-ji was one of the main temples for Esoteric Buddhism. The famous priest Kukai, also known as Kobo Daishi, spent some time at Jingo-ji. Despite illustrious beginnings, the temple fell into disrepair and would not exist today except for a flamboyant warrior and priest, Mongaku. He saw a woman, Kesa, on the street, and fell in love with her immediately. She was married, but Mongaku refused to take no for an answer. Finally, on the condition that he first kill her husband in his own bed, Kesa agreed to meet him. He readily accepted his assignment and did the dirty deed at the appointed hour. Much to Mongaku's horror, Kesa herself was in her husband's bed. Moral of the story: always identify your victim before it's too late. Deeply distraught, Mongaku became a priest.

Mongaku wanted to restore Jingo-ji but couldn't get an audience with Goshirakawa, the former emperor, to request assistance. Sword and all, he fought his way into the palace only to find himself exiled to the Izu Peninsula where he met another exile, Minamoto Yoritomo. Mongaku urged Yoritomo to destroy his family's enemy, the Taira clan; and in 1180, he convinced the emperor to order Yoritomo to do so. Once the Taira clan was defeated, Mongaku was rewarded by being allowed to reconstruct Jingo-ji.

Jingo-ji is deep in the mountains on the eastern side of Mt. Takao and is famous for its views of autumn foliage. The temple's copper bell was cast in 875 and is one of Japan's three most famous bells. The statues of the five Bodhisattvas in Godai-do Hall are masterpieces of Heian art. The temple's guardian Buddha, the Buddha of Healing, is carved from one block of cypress; only the eyes and lips are colored. This carving is one of the earliest examples of a more natural Japanese trend in sculpture. Prior to the mid-9th century, statues were strongly influenced by Chinese aesthetics and constructed of bronze, dry lacquer or clay.

12. Western Kyoto

Saiho-ji (Kokedera)* and Katsura Villa*. These two places are located fairly close to each other, but it's quite difficult to see them consecutively because you need reservations for both.

Take bus #73 from Kyoto Station to Saiho-ji (50 minutes).

Saiho-ji Temple (also known at Kokedera, the Moss Garden). *Application must be made by postcard to the temple from three months to at least five days in advance. See Planning your Stay at the beginning of this chapter for further information. Visitors must participate in calligraphy or attend a ceremony before visiting the garden. You need to plan ahead to visit Saiho-ji and give a* *minimum donation of ¥3000. 15-minute walk from Kami-Katsura Station on Hankyu Arashiyama Line.*

Yes, ¥3000 is a substantial amount but if you think of it as a fee that gives you the privilege of enjoying the garden in relative isolation, it's a bargain. Without tour groups with megaphones and classes of school children, you may be able to appreciate the garden the way priest Muso intended over 650 years ago. You'll have tranquillity to admire the thick moss covering the earth, the banks of the lake, the stones, the rocks, and the roots of the trees where sunlight filters down through the foliage canopy. We were tempted to lie down on the thick green carpet of moss, but stepping on the moss and taking photos are prohibited. Do you suppose the clicking of the camera upsets the moss?

A Zen master and one of the earliest landscape designers, Muso Kokushi, rebuilt the temple in 1339; it may go back to the 7th century but its history is obscure. Muso designed the temple's magnificent garden. The lower garden has a large pond with islands representing Buddhist heaven. The heavily wooded garden is covered with thick moss — over 100 varieties. Patrice first saw the garden on a cold December day when the contrast between the green moss and the gray trees was particularly striking.

Visit here even during the rainy season (mid-June to mid-July) when the brilliant colors of the moss are accentuated; for us, the rainy season is the most beautiful time to view it. On the upper level is a dry-waterfall landscape garden considered to be Japan's oldest.

Kokeno Chaya is a convenient lunch stop for noodles. (See *Where to Eat*).

Take bus #33 from Kyoto Station to Katsura Rikyu mae, about 25 minutes.

Katsura Imperial Villa (Katsura Rikyu). *Be sure to apply in advance at the Imperial Household Agency office at the Imperial Palace for permission to join a tour (in Japanese). Tours are at 10am, 11am, 2pm and 3pm, Monday through Friday. People under age 20 are not allowed. (See the Planning your Stay at the beginning of this chapter). 15-minute walk from Hankyu Dentetsu Line, Katsura Station or Bus 33 from Kyoto Station to Katsura-mae stop.*

Katsura, a masterpiece of Japanese architecture and gardens, is a must on the itinerary of anyone who has more than a day in Kyoto. From the moment we saw the bamboo hedge that borders Katsura's perimeter, we knew this would be a once-in-a-lifetime experience.

Prince Toshihito, an adopted son of the warlord Hideyoshi, began construction of Katsura in 1620. It continued for 35 years and was completed by Toshihito's son Toshitada. It's the epitome of elegantly rustic architecture and stands in stark contrast to the grand edifices constructed by the shoguns. The garden is built around a pond and is reminiscent of the aristocratic strolling gardens of the Heian Period, half a millennium earlier.

Built in 1620, the main building, the **Shoin**, is one of the finest examples of the *sukiya* form of architecture, an informal style of building often located in a garden. It also has the simplicity and lightness of teahouses. The sliding doors can be removed to open the traditionally closed teahouse to the garden. The effect is to blur the distinction between the inside and the outside thus making the viewer at one with nature. The Shoin is at a pond's edge and has three sections. The **Koshoin** has a veranda for viewing the reflected moon in the pond. The **Chushoin** is famous for its paintings: *Mountains and Rivers* by Kano Tanyu and *Seven Sages* by Kano Hisanobu. The **Shinshoin's** exquisite Ichi-no-ma room has a beautiful ceiling and shelves while the window in the Ni-no-ma is world famous.

The garden is an early example of the strolling type that became popular in the Edo Period. You'll be amazed how many varieties of stones, cobblestones and flat rocks make up the paths; their irregularity forces you to keep your eyes on the path. When you stop and look up, a new vista awaits you. We're really amazed that everything in the garden — the size and position of the rocks and stones, the bushes and trees were all calculated for the maximum effect.

Scattered around the garden are several teahouses, including **Shokin-tei**, a rustic retreat used as a summer villa. The bold sky-blue and white checkerboard pattern on the sliding doors gives the villa a very contemporary feel.

After Katsura, stop for a snack at **Nakamura-ken**. *61 Asamura-cho, Katsura, Saikyo-ku. Tel. (075) 381-2650. Open 8am to 6pm. Closed Tuesday and Wednesday.* The house specialty of this Japanese sweet shop is *mugite mochi*, pounded rice dough filled with sweet beans. It's surprisingly tasty. The family has been producing *mugite mochi* for more than hundred years. Cost is ¥280 a piece; eat it here or take it with you.

13. Fushimi Area

Fushimi Inari Shrine*, Fushimi sake breweries, Tofuku-ji*, Fushimi Momoyama Castle.

It is easy to continue on to Uji after seeing the Fushimi area. Just take the JR Nara Line to Obaku Station (for Mampuku-ji) and Uji (for Byodo-in).

Tofuku-ji Temple. *Open 9am to 4pm; November 8:30am to 4pm. Hojo teien ¥300; Tsutenbashi ¥300. From Kyoto Station, take JR Nara Line one stop to Tofukuji Station. You can also take the Keihan line, running parallel to the Kamo River in eastern Kyoto, to Tofukuji Station.* Tofuku-ji is off the main route for tourists, and we love to come here to escape the bustle of downtown Kyoto. But remember, if it's tranquillity you're seeking, avoid the autumn leaf-viewing time. Tofuku-ji is well known for its red maple leaves in November and although it's really beautiful, it's also crowded.

Tofuku-ji was started in 1236 by the aristocratic Kujo family; its name combines the To of Todai-ji with the Fuku of Kofuku-ji, the two most influential temples in Nara.

The **Sanmon Gate**, the largest and oldest of any Zen temple, is a Kamakura Period two-storied gate with a tile roof. It and the **lavatory**, a magnificent 14th century building with rows of latrines sitting idle today, and the **Zen Hall** all date from the 14th century. The **Hojo** (Head Priest's Quarters) has dry-landscape gardens on all sides; the largest one has gravel raked into wonderful swirls and majestic rock formations. Covered walkways connect the main temple buildings.

Tofuku-ji has 25 subtemples; four are open to the public. **Funda-in's** garden was designed by Sesshu, a 15th century painter. *Open 9am to 5pm. ¥300.*

Fushimi Inari Shrine. *Grounds always open. Admission free. JR Kyoto Station JR Nara Line to Inari Station, 5 minutes, or from Keihan Sanjo, the Keihan Line to Fushimi Inari Station.* The cute and clever-looking **fox** that welcomes you at the gate is the servant of the god of rice. The fox spends winters in the hills but comes down to the fields and villages in the spring about the time farmers plant rice. Foxes hang around during the summer because there's so much food, but about the time of harvest in the autumn, they return to the hills. Since they are around only during the growing season, farmers associate the animals with a good harvest and build shrines to them near the rice fields. This belief dates back at least to Heian times. There are over 30,000 Inari shrines all over Japan, but Fushimi is the main one. In time, Inari shrines have become the favored places to pray for a prosperous business.

The **main hall**, rebuilt in 1449, combines elements of Muromachi and Momoyama architecture. But the most engaging aspect of the shrine is the thousands of vermilion *torii* gates that line the paths behind the hall. Donated as requests for good luck, the tightly placed gates resemble a red tunnel. Apparently the *torii* gate is tax deductible. They're erected by companies such as local *sake* shops, supermarkets and cram schools as well as individuals who want to ensure prosperity. You can easily spend an hour or two following the innumerable *torii* gates lining trails in the mountains behind the main shrines.

Fushimi also has many small shrines where you can pray for good harvest and good business, and the temple is thronged with people at New Year's. While at the shrine area, buy some foxy sweets at Matsuya and some traditional Fushimi clay dolls at Tanka.

Tanka. *22-504 Hon-cho, Fushimi, Fushimi-ku. Tel. (075)561-1627. Open 9am to 6pm. Closed Sunday and holidays.* Fushimi used to have several shops making these brightly painted clay dolls, but Tanka is the only one left. Located in a traditional wooden building, the 250-year old shop has a charming display of the dolls. They are also available at some of the souvenir shops near Fushimi Shrine. Tanka is located on the road running parallel to the JR tracks, about a 7-minute walk from the shrine.

Matsuya. *27 Ichinotsubo-cho, Fukakusa, Fushimi-ku. Tel. (075)641-1906. Open 8am to 7pm.* A block from Fushimi Station, this little shop sells sweets nicknamed Kitsune-chan, cute little fox. Molded in the shape of a fox, the guardian god of Fushimi shrine, and filled with sweet white bean paste, they are good to munch on.

From the JR Inari Station, take the JR Nara Line to Momoyama Station.

Fushimi Momoyama Castle. *Open 9:30am to 5pm; winter until 4:30pm. ¥800. Momoyama Station on JR Nara Line and Tambabashi Station on Keihan Main Line.* Built in 1594, Hideyoshi's grand castle, his piece de resistance, was the epitome of Momoyama architecture; the period was named for the hill on which the castle stood. Hideyoshi died in 1598 and Tokugawa distributed the many buildings and gates to Kyoto temples. This 1964 reconstruction is part of a theme park and is best avoided.

HOW TO DISMANTLE FUSHIMI CASTLE IN ONE EASY LESSON

Before Hideyoshi died in 1598 and left a young son, he tried to make the succession as foolproof as possible by setting up a council of regents composed of his five strongest generals. Well, it didn't take long before Tokugawa Ieyasu took matters in his own hands and, with the Battle of Sekigahara in 1600, it was clear that he would become top dog.

Ieyasu didn't want the splendor of Fushimi Castle to remind him of Hideyoshi's crowning achievement, but he didn't want to alienate Hideyoshi's followers by destroying it for no good reason. He came up with the idea that he would move each part to different places. This way the receiver would feel permanently obligated, and he wouldn't have to look at the castle every time he was in Kyoto. How clever of him and how environmentally advanced. This major undertaking was possible only because Japanese wooden buildings were made without nails and could be dismantled and reassembled easily.

Our nonexhaustive list shows buildings, gates and teahouses ended up at the following places, all in Kyoto: Nijo Castle, Nishi Hongan-ji, Nanzen-ji, Konchi-in, Daigo-ji, Kodai-ji, Genko-an and Nison-in. A teahouse and guest house made it all the way to Sankei-en Garden in Yokohama.

Gekkeikan Sake Museum (Gekkeikan Okura Kinenkan). *Tel. (075)623-2056. Open 9am to 4:30pm. Closed Monday. ¥300 (includes sake tasting).* Opened in 1982 to celebrate Gekkeikan Brewery's 350th anniversary, the museum displays the history of *sake* making and manufacturing in an authentic Meiji-era building. Fushimi is famous for its *sake* because of its delicious water and access to good rice. If you give advance notice, they will try to arrange an English-speaking guide.

Terada-ya. *263 Minamihama-cho, Fushimi-ku. Tel. (075)611-1223.* From the end of the Edo Period, this very old, traditional inn is famous because young samurai involved in the Meiji revolution met here. It was the scene of a scuffle between the shogun's troops and the rebellious samurai. During the day, it's a museum and at night, an inn. Open for daytime visits 10am to 3:50pm. ¥400. You can stay at the inn for ¥6500 with breakfast. If you want to spend the night, arrive after 6pm and leave at 9am. The inn's large paper lanterns hang out front.

14. Uji

Byodo-in* and Mampuku-ji.

Mampuku-ji Obakusan Temple. *Open 9am to 4:30pm. ¥500. From Kyoto Station take the JR Nara Line to Obaku Station, then a 3-minute walk. From Keihan Sanjo Station take the Uji Line to Obaku Station, then a 3-minute walk.*

When you tire of visiting temples with dry-landscape gardens and subdued cedar shingled buildings, it's time to visit Mampuku. We like to visit Mampuku-ji because there's nothing else like it in Kyoto.

Founded by the Chinese priest Ingen in 1661, it's a relative newcomer to the ancient world of Kyoto temples. Ingen built the temple in the Ming Chinese style, one of the few in Japan. The temple serves *fucha ryori*, vegetarian Chinese fare, a splendid gastronomic experience. The *bento* lunch box costs ¥3000; courses are from ¥5000, but you need a minimum of four people to order it. Make reservations between 11am and 1pm. *Tel. (0774)32-3900.*

Byodo-in Temple. *Open 8:30am to 5:30pm; December through February 9am to 4:30pm. Phoenix Hall open 9am to 5pm; December through February until 4pm. ¥600. From Keihan Sanjo Station take Keihan Uji Line to Keihan Uji Station. Check out the new futuristic station building designed by architect Wakabayashi Hiroyuki. From Kyoto Station or Obaku Station, take JR Nara Line to Uji Station.*

Byodo-in is another must on the itinerary of every visitor to Kyoto; the majestic, dream-like structure is a masterpiece of Japanese architecture. Byodo-in was the villa and temple of the aristocratic Fujiwara family. They served emperors as high-ranking ministers and through a brilliant plan of marrying their daughters to emperors, gained nearly total control of the government for some 300 years.

Fujiwara Michinaga (966-1027), probably the greatest of the Fujiwara ministers, built Byodo-in as his summer villa. His son Yorimichi rebuilt it as a magnificent temple in 1052 encompassing 33 buildings that included seven pagodas. The **Phoenix Hall**, completed in 1053, is all that remains from the Heian Period. The graceful structure hovers over the pond like a bird in flight that's preparing to land. At one time the pond encircled the Phoenix Hall, probably protecting it from the fire that destroyed most of the temple's other buildings.

You may not know it, but you've probably already seen the Phoenix Hall — its image graces the ¥10 coin.

A Heian visitor to Byodo-in would take the Uji Bridge across the river, leaving behind the secular and entering the spiritual world. Heian aristocrats feared the world was coming to an end and began preparing for the afterlife. The temple represents the *Gokuraku*, Buddhist heaven. The soul must cross the Lotus Pond to enter heaven and the Phoenix Hall on the western shore is a representation of the Amida Buddha's Western Paradise. Amida is the Buddha who comes to earth to accompany the souls of the newly departed to heaven.

Inside the Phoenix Hall, the famous sculptor **Jocho** created the statue of the Amida Buddha in a meditating position. This serene Buddha sits on a 64-petal lotus flower; the backdrop contains representations of 13 Buddhas. On the wall, there are 52 heavenly musicians depicting the joy of being in paradise. Paintings on the walls show the nine levels of heaven; unfortunately, time has been unkind to the paintings. You can still make out some, but others have been reproduced and the best paintings have been moved to the Homotsu-kan that displays them only in spring and autumn (¥300). These paintings are early examples of the genre called Yamato-e that contrast with the Chinese landscape painting — they show the more gentle rolling hills of the Japanese landscape.

Near the pond is a bell tower with a graceful bell that is considered one of the three most beautiful in Japan; the bell is supposed to be from India.

A trip to Uji would not be complete without a taste of **Uji tea**, considered Japan's finest. Uji has been famous for tea for over 1000 years since the priest Eisai brought tea bushes back from China. The great ruler Hideyoshi loved Uji tea and once stopped on the Uji Bridge to have his servants draw water to make tea.

Nakamura Tokichi-ten is a well-known tea shop that sells only Uji tea. Started in the mid-19th century, the shop has had a teahouse dating back to the Edo Period. You can buy different kinds of Uji tea, and, with a reservation, you can enjoy *matcha* (green tea) with sweets in the teahouse for ¥2000. In their beautiful garden, you'll see the famous black pine tree considered to be one of most valuable trees in the Uji area. Nakamura is across from the JR Uji Station. *Tel. (0774)22-7800. Open daily 9am to 5pm; teahouse open 11am to 3pm.*

Taihoan is a teahouse supported by Uji City. Tea with sweets costs ¥500. *2 Uji Togawa, Uji-shi. Tel. (0774)23-3334. Open 10am to 4pm. Closed December 24 through January 14.*

15. Southeast

Daigo-ji*, Kanju-ji and Zuishin-in. Take the subway to Daigo Station, the end of the Tozai line, then a 10-minute walk.

Generally the south has fewer visitors than other areas, which is one reason why we love it; and it has some fabulous places to see. Being out of the center of town, some of the temples escaped the destruction of warfare and fires so you can find quite ancient buildings still standing.

Daigo-ji Temple. *Open 9am to 5pm; November through February until 4pm. Daigo ¥300, Sambo-in ¥500.* Daigo-ji is so appealing to us that we return again and again. Its setting, on a small mountain south of the Kyoto in an area of rice paddies and low buildings, is superb and is as we imagine old Japan. The vast temple consists of Kami (Upper) Daigo, Shimo (Lower) Daigo and Sambo-in.

Daigo-ji was started in 874 by the priest **Shobo** who was attracted to the mountain by a multicolored cloud. At the top, an old man showed Shobo a well of pure water and gave him the mountain. In 907 **Emperor Daigo**, who took his name from the temple, designated it as his temple and built several buildings at the top of the mountain, forming what is today called **Kami Daigo**.

In 926 Emperor Daigo began constructing **Shimo Daigo** as a temple to pray for his afterlife. His successor built the five-storied **pagoda** in 951 for Emperor Daigo. It still stands today, one of the oldest buildings in Kyoto. The area around the pagoda is not manicured. It's a peaceful place to go for a picnic and to get away from the bustle of the city. If you have two or three hours, climb up the mountain to the grounds of Kami Daigo. Up there among other buildings, you can see the well discovered by priest Shobo and the **Yakushi Hall**, which houses the Buddha of Healing, a National Treasure.

Most of Daigo's buildings were destroyed during the 15th century Onin War. **Hideyoshi** visited the temple to view the cherry blossoms and the abbot talked him into restoring the temple, which, at that point, wasn't much more than a pagoda.

Hideyoshi, of course, did everything big time. He restored the temple and then invited the entire population of Kyoto, high and low, to his famous **cherry-blossom party** on March 15, 1598. This date was in the old lunar calendar. Based on the current calendar, the flowers blossom in early April. You can go back every year on the second Sunday of April when the temple has a parade of citizens in Momoyama Period dress imitating Hideyoshi's tea party.

The **Kon-do** (Golden Hall) was moved from Wakayama by the order of Hideyoshi; dating to the end of the Heian Period, it's a National Treasure.

TOYOTOMI HIDEYOSHI (1536-1598)

*Larger than life, **Hideyoshi** is still Japan's most popular historical hero – rising from the lowly foot soldier to the highest rank of all. Events for the masses, like the Daigo cherry blossom party and the Kitano tea party, capture anyone's imagination. Obviously he loved to enjoy life and to show it off to others. Even today, TV dramas based on Hideyoshi's life are always enormously popular.*

The Idemitsu Museum in Tokyo has a screen painting depicting his famous cherry blossom party at Daigo. Under a red umbrella, a frail, old Hideyoshi admires the flowers. He died a few months after this event.

Hideyoshi set out to restore the subtemple of **Sambo-in** although recreate it might be a more appropriate term. Hideyoshi turned the subtemple into a secular monument, a place where he could host cherry blossom parties, have tea ceremony and entertain his guests in grand style. Ironically, set in a Buddhist temple, Sambo-in is the height of Momoyama residential architecture. He died before it was completed, but his plans were followed.

Sambo-in is on the left as you enter the grounds of Daigo-ji; it would be easy to walk past were it not for the ticket booth outside. To the right of the entrance gate is an elegant wooden gate called **Chokushi-mon**, moved from Hideyoshi's Fushimi Castle. The simple gate has two crests on it: the 16-petal chrysanthemum, the imperial symbol, and Hideyoshi's paulownia leaf crest.

The building you enter has two rooms with paintings by Kano Sanraku and a third has a painting of the Aoi Festival. The hall leads to the **Omote Shoin**, which has rooms looking out on to one of Japan's most famous gardens. Most of the Momoyama Period gardens were designed to be viewed from a veranda, but this one you could stroll through as well as admire from the buildings. Today you can't set foot in it; actually, you can't even point your camera at it. The opulent garden has 800 stones including the famed **Fujito** stone, which legend says was used in 1184 by the Minamoto general to cross a strait and win the battle. The garden incorporates just about every garden design device. The pond has islands representing a tortoise, a crane and Mt. Horai, a Chinese heaven. The pond's bridges are tall enough that a boat could pass under them. Near the Omote Shoin's veranda is a small dry-landscape garden containing three famous rocks representing (from left to right) rapids, a slow moving stream and the churning water of the Kamo River.

Junjo-kan, designed for entertaining, is the next building, and beyond it is the **Hon-do** (Main Hall), the only religious building on the premises. Kaikei, the 12-13th century master, carved the Buddha displayed here.

A 15-minute walk will take you to Zuishin-in.

Zuishin-in Temple. *Open 9am to 4:30pm. ¥300. 15-minute walk from Kanju-ji.* This temple is special because most of its buildings date from 1018; only the main hall is a 1599 reconstruction. Founded in 1018 by a priest from the powerful Fujiwara family, the temple is a good example of Heian architecture as well as the setting of a well-known story.

A famous beauty and poetess of the Heian Period, Ono-no-Komachi, lived at Zuishin-in. A suitor pursued her but Ono-no-Komachi agreed to meet him only if he came to her residence every day for 100 days. Faithfully he came, in good weather and bad, to prove his love and devotion. The luckless man breathed his last breath on the 100th day, never consummating their relationship. This tale has become the theme of *noh* plays: a distraught Ono-no-Komachi racked by guilt for what she had caused. One sample of her poetry: "Like a ripple that chases the slightest caress of the breeze — is that how you want me to follow you?" (from *The Ink Dark Moon*, translated by Jane Hirshfield with Mariko Aratani).

Plum trees abound on the grounds making Zuishin-in a popular place in February and early March. Just north of Zuishin-in is **Manjutei Tachibana**, a good lunch stop.

A 15-minute walk will take you to Kanju-ji.

Kanju-ji Temple (also called Kanshu-ji and Kaju-ji). *Open 9am to 4pm. ¥400.* Kanju-ji has a lovely strolling garden that dates back over 1000 years. Dedicated to his mother, the temple was established by Emperor Daigo in 900. It later became a residence for princesses. The Shinden and Shoin buildings are reconstructions but retain an aristocratic Heian feel. The temple was devastated during the 15th century Onin War, but in 1682, supported by the Tokugawa shoguns, regained its prominence.

The garden still has many Heian characteristics. There is an island representing heaven, and the garden is designed to be viewed from a boat in the pond. Since you're not allowed to take out a boat, enjoy strolling around the peaceful garden that is most beautiful in early summer when the irises and water lilies bloom.

Every year at New Year's during Heian times, the harvest time was predicted based on the thickness of the ice in the pond. The Shoin and

Main Halls are closed to the public. In front of the Shoin, there is a famous stone basin made for the 8th Tokugawa shogun and also a stone lantern with an open umbrella-like top that was donated by a Tokugawa.

16. Ohara

Sanzen-in* and Jakko-in*.
To get to Ohara, take Kyoto bus no. 16, 17 or 18.

Ohara is a small village on the western slope of Mt. Hiei. Women dress in colorful peasant costumes: blue *ikat* kimono tied up for mobility, pants, red apron, and a bamboo basket on the head to carry firewood. Every day these women came to Kyoto to sell wood. They don't sell wood anymore, but they still wear these costumes for the sake of local color. The area is very popular in the autumn when the maples turn bright red.

Sanzen-in Temple. *Open 8:30am to 4:30pm; until 4pm December through February. ¥550.* While meditating in the main hall of Sanzen-in in 965, the famous priest **Genshin** had a vision of Amida's paradise. He realized that the Amida Buddha, who accompanies you to the afterlife, is generous and accessible through sincerely chanting, "Namu Amida Butsu"(save me, Amida). This was a great step forward in making Buddhism popular with the masses. At the same time, Buddhist images came to play a bigger role in people's understanding of Buddha.

Originally built in 965 and reconstructed in 1143, the **Main Hall** (Hon-do), is a small, serene structure as befits a mountain temple. The Main Hall's ceiling, shaped like a boat's bottom, once had paintings of Amida and Bodhisattvas coming to earth to accompany the soul back to heaven. Fragments of paintings remain on the walls and pillars. The Amida statue was carved by Genshin in 985; its halo contains 13 Buddhas. In front of the Buddha are the two Bodhisattvas who accompany Amida when he takes a spirit to heaven. One Bodhisattva prays for the soul while the other transports it on a lotus flower.

Genshin's vision of Amida's heaven is illustrated in the **Ukiyo-en Garden** which has a pond, moss and maple trees. Three hundred hydrangeas are especially beautiful in the rainy season. The Shinden Hall has a statue of Fudo that many believe was carved by Genshin. The Kyaku-den Hall faces Juheki-en, a small garden, that has a pond in the shape of the Chinese character for heart.

Jakko-in Temple. *Open 9am to 5pm; until 4:30pm December through February. ¥500.* To Japanese, Jakko-in always conjures up images of the defeat of the military Taira clan by the rival Genji. **Kenrei Monin**, the daughter of the Taira leader Kiyomori and mother of the child emperor Antoku, spent the rest of her life at this secluded convent praying for the souls of her defeated family.

The Main Hall has a Jizo, the statue of the protector of children, to whom Kenrei Monin used to pray for her son. The pond in the garden is shaped like the Chinese character for heart. Jakko-in is a prime viewing place for autumn foliage.

17. Sakamoto Otsu

Mt. Hiei, Enryaku-ji*, Mii-dera.

Enryaku-ji has two approaches, but the one from Sakamoto is more spectacular. Take the JR Kosei Line from Kyoto Station to Eizan Station, then bus to Sakamoto Cable Car Station, then ride the Hiei-san Cable Railway to the top. An alternative is to take the Eizan Electric Railway from Demachiyanagi Station in northern Kyoto to Yase Yu-en Station and then board the Keifuku Cable Railway to Hiei. From here you will have to walk about a kilometer to the temple. Another alternative is to take the direct bus from Kyoto Station and Sanjo Keihan to the top of Mt. Hiei, but there are only about a half-dozen a day. We prefer to go up Mt. Hiei from the Sakamoto side and come down the western side.

Kyoto has thousands of temples, but few have a more illustrious history than **Enryaku-ji**. Emperor Kammu ordered the priest **Saicho** to establish a temple on Mt. Hiei to protect Kyoto from the evil spirits dwelling in the northeast. Saicho had studied in China and returned to Japan to establish the Tendai sect.

The priests of Enryaku-ji were ambitious and politically savvy. To gain the upper hand over the emperor, they co-opted Shinto gods, claiming them to be part of the Buddhist pantheon. Enryaku-ji formed an army that became very powerful and would attack other temples as well as take sides in political battles. Emperors were powerless against them. Then, in 1571, **Oda Nobunaga**, the first of the three unifiers of his era, attacked Enryaku-ji, destroyed nearly all of the thousand buildings and slaughtered the 3000 monk-warriors. Hideyoshi, Nobunaga's successor, rebuilt the temple but limited its size to try to keep it under control.

Enryaku-ji has three parts: the Eastern Precincts, the Western Precincts and Yokawa. In the eastern precincts, the **Kompon Chudo** is the main building of the temple, and the present building dates from 1642. The Buddhist image, the Buddha of medicine and healing, was carved by Priest Saicho. The original cannot be seen but a copy is on display. The shogun requested that the feudal lords give the flower panels that are on the ceiling. The temple claims Kompon Chudo's three large lanterns still burn a flame lit by Saicho over 1200 years ago. We don't want to be too cynical, but could this flame really have survived Nobunaga's onslaught?

Also in the this area are the **Monju-ro**, a gate that was once the entrance to the temple, and Kaidan-in, a small hall where priests are ordained.

Walking to the Western precinct will take you past the **Jodo-in**. The main hall houses a statue of the priest Saicho; the second is the Amida-do that contains a statue of the Amida Buddha carved by Saicho — the original can't be seen, but a copy is on view; and the third building is Saicho's tomb.

In the Western Precinct are the twin halls called **Jogyo-do** and **Hokke-do** that were built in 1595 and used for religious training. The Shaka-do is the oldest building of the temple. It dates from the Kamakura Period but was moved here from Mii-dera temple in the late 16th century.

The Yokawa area, about four kilometers away, is recommended only for those who want a long walk. Instead, take the path about 1 1/2 kilometers to the west side of the mountain where the Hiei-zan ropeway takes you to the peak. There you'll find kiddy rides and a revolving observation deck. You can safely miss this and instead take the Keifuku Cable Railway to Yase Yu-en at the bottom of Mt. Hiei. From there the Eizan Electric Railway will return you to Kyoto.

Mii-dera Temple. Located in a deeply wooded area, Mii-dera dates to 764. In the 10th century, a group of monks from Enryaku-ji broke off and made Mii-dera the center of the Tendai Jimon sect. They formed an army and had many battles against Enryaku-ji. When Oda Nobunaga destroyed Enryaku-ji in the mid-16th century, he supported Mii-dera — Nobunaga's motto could have been the enemy of my enemy is my friend. Nobunaga's assassination brought a quick end to this support because Hideyoshi, his successor, rebuilt Enryaku-ji. Today Mii-dera has only a fraction of the buildings it had in its heyday.

18. Side Trip to Miho Museum in Shigaraki

We highly recommend you spend a half day or more at the **Miho Museum** in Shigaraki. The beautiful museum, designed by I.M.Pei, is built deep in a mountain ravine. The design combines Japanese and Western architectural forms and is a triumph of form blending with nature. The $250 million structure was built by Shumi-kai, a religious group which worships deities of harmony and beauty.

The museum's outer pavilion houses a restaurant and admission desk. After obtaining your ticket you walk up to the museum and go through a long tunnel. As you exit the tunnel, the vista of the mountains and the entrance to the museum open up before you. The museum entrance, constructed of glass and steel, takes its form from a Shinto shrine. Much of the museum is built underground 80% according to the official statistics, but large windows and atriums bring lots of light and also unite the visitor with nature outside.

The collection on display is not overwhelmingly large. One wing houses Japanese art while the other an eclectic mix of objects from Egypt,

West Asia, Greece, Rome, South Asia, China and Persia. Each object is exquisitely displayed.

The museum is a little over a one-hour trip from Kyoto. From Kyoto Station, take the JR Biwako line at platform #2; get off at Ishiyama Station, about 15 minutes from Kyoto. Both the local and shin-kaisoku trains stop at Ishiyama. After going through the ticket barriers, turn right and go down the stairs to the bus area. The bus to the Miho Museum is marked in English and leaves from bus stop #2. There are only five buses a day on weekdays and seven on weekends so make sure you have the schedule before you go (available from the museum or Kyoto Tourist Information Office). The bus takes 50 minutes and costs ¥800. The bus does not run on days the museum is closed.

The museum is only open during certain periods of the year, approximately March 15 through June 10, July and August and September 1 through December 15. Call the museum before going or contact the Kyoto Tourist Information Office, Tel. (075)371-5649, to make sure it's open.

The museum operates two restaurants, one Japanese and one Western, both using food grown with organic gardening methods.

The Miho Museum is located at 300, Momodani, Shigaraki, Shiga-ken 529-1814. Tel. (0748)82-3411. www.miho.or.jp. Open 10am to 5pm, enter by 4pm. Saturdays open 10am to 8pm, enter by 7pm. Closed Monday. Open only certain periods of the year (see above).

NIGHTLIFE & ENTERTAINMENT

Kyoto's nightlife areas are not as wild as Tokyo's, Osaka's and Fukuoka's, keeping in line with its fairly subdued image. The Gion district, an entertainment quarter for several hundred years, is still the nightlife center with lots of restaurants, clubs and bars. If a place does not look inviting, don't go in. There are many small pub bars that are only open to people who have an introduction. If a place is brightly lit, has big windows and is otherwise enticing, give it a try. Just make sure you have some idea of the cost if you are on a budget.

BAR, ISN'T IT?, *from Sanjo Dori walk south on Kawaramachi Dori for two blocks and turn east. On south side of street.*

Bar, Isn't It? belongs to a chain of a half-dozen bars around the country. All food and drink cost ¥500. Vending machines sell beer, and there's bar service for the rest. Friday and Saturday it's open from 6pm until 5am; until midnight on other nights. It's a popular place with foreigners.

TAKU TAKU, *Tominokoji, south of Bukkoji. Tel. (075)351-1321. Open 6pm to 11pm.*

Taku Taku is the sort of blend that makes Kyoto such a neat place. It's a "live house" in a traditional warehouse and usually has blues, folk or country music. Prices vary with the performer.

CULTURAL EXPERIENCES

Seeing the sights is just one dimension of visiting Kyoto. Be sure to see a *kabuki* or *noh* performance, experience the serene tea ceremony, or practice *zazen* meditation. There are plenty of places willing to share their expertise with a novice, and there's no need to shave your head or join a monastery or nunnery.

Performing Arts

Check *Kyoto Visitor's Guide* for listing information.

Kabuki is performed at the Minami-za Theater in the Gion district, but not every month. Matinees run from 11am to 4pm; the evening show from 4:30pm until about 8pm. *Kabuki* performances are remarkably casual — you can come and go freely and eat and drink in the theater, probably because in Edo times it was entertainment for the common folk. Tickets cost ¥4000 to ¥14,000.

Noh. Unlike *kabuki* performances that run for a month, a *noh* play is performed only once. The Kanze Noh Theater has an active schedule usually hosting about 8 plays a month. The Kongo Noh Theater also has performances.

Geisha Dance. If you are in Kyoto in April, May, or early November, make sure you see the sumptuous performances by Kyoto's *geisha* at several theaters in different *geisha* districts around the city. Tickets cost about ¥3900 and often include tea and sweets.

Bunraku, a marvelous puppet theater, performs periodically in Osaka. Take the train (less than an hour). You won't be disappointed.

Gion Corner is a potpourri of Japanese performing arts. Within one hour you will be exposed to tea ceremony, flower arranging, *koto* music, *gagaku* dance, *kyogen* comic plays, Kyoto dance and *bunraku* puppet theater. It's the McDonalds of performance. All is done by professionals for the evening entertainment of busloads of tourists. Our preference is to put the money toward seeing one of these fine arts in depth. ¥2800. March through November, 7:40pm and 8:40pm.

Tea Ceremony

MIYAKO HOTEL, *on Sanjo Dori east of Higashi Oji Dori. Tel. (075)771-7111. Daily 10am to 7pm. ¥1155.*

No reservation required.

KANO SHOJU-AN, *On the southern part of Philosopher's Walk. Tel. (075)751-1077. Open 10am to 4:30pm. Closed Wednesday. ¥1050.*

Participants sit at table and chairs. No reservation required.

TAIHO-AN, a teahouse run by the city of Uji. *10 minutes from JR Uji Station. Tel. (0774)23-3334. Open daily 10am to 4pm. ¥500.*

No reservation required.

KYOTO INTERNATIONAL COMMUNITY HOUSE, *close to directly across from the entrance road to Nanzen-ji. Tel. (075)752-3511. Every Tuesday afternoon at 1:30pm. ¥1000.*

Run in English by the Urasenke Center. Make a reservation at the Community House by noon Tuesday at 9pm or at Urasenke Foreign Affairs Department by Monday at 4pm, *Tel. (075)451-8516.*

SHISHIGATANI SABIE, *Honenin-cho-15, Sakyo-ku. Tel. (075)762-3425. Bus #5 or Bus #17 from Kyoto Station to Kinrin Shako-mae stop.*

Shishigatani offers English-language tea ceremony in a traditional Japanese house on Friday from 10am to 12 noon. Reservations necessary, ¥2000. They also have tea ceremony at 3pm except on Monday, make reservations by the previous day, ¥3000.

SAIO-IN TEMPLE, *121 Kurodani-cho, Sakyo-ku. Tel. (075)752-0455. ¥500.*

Experience tea ceremony in a temple setting. Saturday from 1pm to 5pm. Reserve by the previous day.

Zazen

The best place for a non-Japanese to experience *zazen* (Zen meditation) is at the **Kyoto International Zen Center** in Kameoka, outside Kyoto. You need to stay overnight, and you can stay for longer periods if you so like. No, you do not need to shave your head. They teach Zen meditation and introduce people to Zen temple life.

The day begins with a 5am wake-up bell followed by sutra chanting, *zazen*, cleaning and breakfast, all before 8am. Then you participate in group work, have lunch and have the afternoon free. Dinner is a 5pm, *zazen* from 7 to 8:30pm and lights-out at 9pm. The fee is ¥3000 per night. Formal *zazen* is not done on Wednesday or Sunday nights.

To make a reservation, contact the center by mail, telephone (between 8-9am and 1-5pm), fax or email. All reservations are automatically accepted; confirmations are not sent. Contact the temple for directions. *Kyoto International Zen Center (Rinzai sect) Jotoku-ji, Inukai Sogabe-cho, Kameoka-shi, Kyoto, 621. Tel. (0771)24-0152, Fax (0771)24-0378. e-mail: kyotozen@zen.or.jp.*

Seitai-an Zenkai. Another good place for Westerners to experience Zazen is at Seitai-an where English-language zazen sessions are held on the second and fourth Saturdays of most months. For information contact Rev. Tom Wright at (075)752-0421. *Seitai-an is located at Omiya Gentaku, Kitamachi 35, Kita-ku. Tel. (075)491-2579. Take the subway to Kitaoka, board bus Kita 1 at gate E and get off at Gentaku. You can also take the #6 bus from Kyoto Station to Gentaku.*

The following temples conduct zazen in Japanese:

Ryozen-an (Rinzai sect). *54 Shimodaitokuji-cho, Kita-ku, Kyoto. Tel. (075)491-0543. 6:40am to 8am Wednesday to Sunday, except the 1st, 15th, and 22nd.* First timers should call ahead and attend a session at 6:30am.

Rinko-ji (Rinzai sect). *Shokokuji Monzen-cho, Kamigyo-ku, Kyoto. Tel. (075)231-3931. 9am to 11am, 2nd and 4th Sunday.*

Mugeko-in (Rinzai sect). *65 Takano Shimizu-cho, Sakyo-ku, Kyoto. Tel. (075)781-1227. 5pm to 6pm Saturday.*

Nanzen-in (Rinzai sect). *Nanzenji Fukuchi-cho, Sakyo-ku, Kyoto. Tel. (075)771-0365. 6am to 7am April to October. 6:30am to 7:30am November to March. 2nd and 4th Sunday.* A sub-temple of Nanzen-ji.

Textiles

Kodai Yuzen-en Museum allows you to paint your own *yuzen* handkerchief or necktie masterpiece. *Tel. (075)823-0500. Takasuji, west of Horikawa Dori. Open 9am to 5pm.* Handkerchief ¥1050, necktie ¥4200 plus ¥500 entrance fee. Reservations not necessary. It takes about one hour.

Orinasu-kan teaches you how to weave. ¥5000 plus ¥500 entrance fee. You'll need about three hours. *Tel. (075)431-0020. Open 10am to 4pm. Closed Monday.* Reservations necessary.

Kyoto Museum of Traditional Crafts (Furiai-kan) on B1 level of Miyako Messe, 9-1 Seishoji-cho, Okazaki (near Heian Shrine) offers yuzen dyeing on Saturday and Sunder between 10am and 5pm. No reservation necessary. Handkerchief ¥800; T-shirt ¥1500. *Tel. (075)762-2670.*

Nishijin Textile Center (Nishijin Ori Kaikan), *Horikawa-Imadegawa Minami-iru, Kamigyo-ku. Tel. (075)451-9231. Open 9am to 5pm. Closed December 29 through January 3 and August 13-15.* Try hand weaving at this center and bring home your handiwork. ¥1800. Reservations necessary.

Kyoto Yuzen Cultural Hall (Kyoto Yuzen Bunka Kaikan) offers instruction in stencil dyeing ¥450 and hand-painted dyeing ¥2100. *6 Mameda-cho, Nishikyogoku, Ukyo-ku. Tel. (075)311-0025. Open 9am to 5pm. Closed Sunday.*

Papermaking

Make your own Japanese *washi* paper at **Rakushi-kan** in the Museum of Kyoto. Papermaking on Thursday, Friday and Saturday afternoons. Cost is ¥700 to ¥900. Make reservations several days in advance: *Tel. (075)251-0078, Fax (075)231-0130.*

Handicrafts

The **Kyoto Handicraft Center** (on Marutamachi, north of Heian Shrine) has hour-long classes in English every afternoon for woodblock printing, cloisonné making and doll making. Cost ¥1500/per class. *Tel. (075)761-5080.*

Kimono

It's become very trendy to dress up in kimono like a maiko geisha, either to have your picture taken or to walk around town. While it's not inexpensive, it is a once-in-a-lifetime experience. Reservations are necessary.

Nishijin Textile Center, *Horikawa Imadegawa, Minami-iru, Kamigyo-ku, Tel. (075)451-9231. Open daily 9am to 3:30pm. ¥8,800 includes photograph.* Choose either maiko geisha or the 12-layered Heian period dress. While you can walk around inside the center, you aren't allowed outside.

Jidaiya, *2F Palace Jingu Bldg, 149-1 Nishimachi 2-chome, Sanjo-dori, Shirakawabashi, Higashi-iru, Higashiyama-ku. Tel. (075)771-1075. Open from 10am. Closed Monday.* ¥11,000 includes photo and 20-minute walk outside.

KYOTO'S FESTIVALS

Walking Kyoto's streets and alleys you unexpectedly encounter many small, charming temples and shrines tucked among the wooden merchant houses and modern buildings. Each temple and shrine, however small, seems to have its own festival.

We're not sure who does the counting but "they" say that in Kyoto, there are more than 1000 festivals annually. The most famous is the Gion Matsuri held in the summer and usually listed as happening on July 15, 16 and 17. The major festival activities occur on these three days, but the festival officially starts on July 1, climaxes in mid-July and ends on July 29. No wonder some people call Kyoto the city of festivals.

The Big Four

Aoi Festival. May 15. The Aoi Festival dates back to 6th century and is held to pray for a big harvest. During the Heian Period, it became a big deal. It's named *Aoi* (hollyhock) because the 600 participants clad in Heian Period costumes adorn their hats and the ox-drawn carriages with hollyhocks. Even at the end of the 20th century, these ox carts speed along at four kilometers per hour! In the old days, the houses were also decorated with *aoi* to get rid of disease. The parade begins at the Kyoto Imperial Palace at 10am and goes via Shimogamo Shrine to arrive at Kamigamo Shrine at 3:30 in the afternoon.

Gion Festival. July 1-29. Started in the 9th century, the festival originally began as an attempt to drive away the plague. Halberds were mounted on a portable shrine and dipped in the sacred pond of the Shinsen-en Garden. The plague ended, but the parade continues annually to appease the vengeful spirits. Even today the festival is not just spectacle. A ten-year old boy, seated on the first float, is the messenger to the Shinto gods and undergoes rigorous training to perform the rituals.

The festival is run by merchants. During the Yoiyama, the colorful evening festival on July 16, the floats are on display in neighborhoods that sponsor them; houses show off their art treasures. Musicians play festival music under brightly lit lanterns. And although there are lots of visitors, it still feels like a neighborhood festival.

The Yamaboko parade on July 17 is the highlight. The floats are pulled through Kyoto's streets starting from Shijo Karasuma at 9am and ending up at Oike Dori near Nijo Castle about 2 1/2 hours later. There are two kinds of floats: *yama*, tall floats carried on the shoulders of 10 to 20 men, and *hoko*, huge, 10-ton floats on wheels that 40 people pull by rope. The *hoko's* wheels cannot navigate corners; there's a fascinating ritual of putting down bamboo mats and manually turning the huge floats. To witness this difficult maneuver, make sure you watch the parade somewhere near a corner.

The *hoko* carry an ensemble of musicians playing flutes, gongs and drums. The music is energetic yet doleful. The floats themselves are ornately decorated, some with European tapestries procured from traders in the 16th century.

Daimonji Okuri. August 16th. During the Buddhist Obon Festival, August 13-16, the souls of one's ancestors return to the family. Even nowadays, many families observe the old ceremonies at home although it's more like Thanksgiving or Christmas in America when people go back to their hometowns to see family and friends. On the 16th, they want to make sure the souls travel back safely to wherever they come from. *Okuribi* is the fire that's lit for their journey back home.

The huge fires are in the shape of *kanji* (Chinese characters) on the five mountains of Kyoto. After these fires Kyoto-ites say they can feel the cool autumn breeze on their faces in the evening although daytime is still hot and sticky. You can see the fires from some hotels in Kyoto.

Jidai Festival. October 22. The Festival of the Ages, sponsored by the Heian Shrine, honors Emperor Kammu who established Kyoto as the capital. The parade's 1600 participants dress in costumes worn by courtiers, warriors and merchants, all who were instrumental in developing Kyoto's culture. The parade starts with people dressed in 19th century costumes and regresses through the major periods until it reaches the 8th century.

Not only is it fun, it's much more interesting than going to a costume museum. The parade begins at 12 noon at the Kyoto Imperial Palace and arrives at Heian Shrine at around 2:30pm.

SHOPPING

Shijo Dori is the main shopping area. There are three large department stores: Daimaru, Hankyu and Takashimaya and a million smaller shops. Takashimaya has a fabulous selection of Japanese ceramic ware and other traditional goods. Shijo has covered sidewalks making shopping more pleasant during inclement weather.

Teramachi Dori, a long stretch between Marutamachi Dori and Shijo Dori, is one of the most interesting streets to walk for shopping. Near the Marutamachi Dori intersection are a number of shops selling antiques, paper, tea, tea ceremony utensils and calligraphy supplies. Just north of Nijo Dori is the famous tea shop **Ippodo**, and further south is the paper shop **Kakimoto**. South of Oike Dori, Teramachi becomes a covered arcade. Make sure you stop in **Kyukyodo**, a shop selling paper, incense and tea ceremony items, and in **Daishodo**, a woodblock print shop. East of Teramachi Dori is another covered arcade called Shin-kyogoku filled with *pachinko* parlors and souvenir shops. In the early evening, visiting school groups come here to buy their souvenirs.

Nishiki Ichiba, Kyoto's food market, crosses Teramachi Dori one block north of Shijo Dori. The market is a riot of color and sensations with fish and seafood, vegetables, fruits, pickles, seaweed, sweets and more all spilling out onto the narrow pathway crowded with shoppers. Make sure you stop at venerable **Aritsugu**, a 400-year-old institution selling Japanese knives, hand-hammered copper and bronze pots and other kitchen utensils.

The **Kyoto Handicraft Center**, north of the Heian Shrine, advertises heavily to attract foreign tourists. There are some high quality goods but beware of their low quality tourist trinkets, such as polyester kimono. Unless your time is really limited, do your shopping in some of the more interesting shops listed below.

Flea Markets

If you are in Kyoto when there's a **flea market** held at a temple or shrine, make sure you go. Even if you have no intention of buying anything, it's a fun experience.

To-ji Temple, on the 21st of each month, the death anniversary of the priest who founded the temple. This wonderful market sells ceramics, textiles, kimono, furniture and anything else your heart desires. Recently, we've heard that a lot of Chinese antiques have shown up. Several of our friends time their trips to Kyoto to coincide with this market. *6am-4pm.* To-ji also holds a flea market with antiques only on the first Sunday of the month.

Kitano Tenmangu Shrine holds its flea market on the 25th of each month; it specializes more in textiles and old kimono. *8am-9pm.*

Chion-ji (not to be confused with Chion-in) has a craft fair on the 15th every month. *10am-5pm.*

Kyoto Antique Fair is held three times a year at Pulse Plaza near Fushimi — three days in March, June and October. 8am to 6pm.

Kyoto Station Area

Isetan Department Store, located in the Kyoto Station Building, features a good selection of Japanese handicrafts. The basement food floor provides a wide selection of foods, both Japanese and Western.

Porta, an underground shopping arcade at the Karasuma exit, has lots of shops that sell both traditional and contemporary goods. At the Hachijo exit, you'll find **Avanti**, another building filled with stores.

Tanji Renshodo. *On Shichijo Dori, southern perimeter of Higashi Hongan-ji. Kitagawa Nishiiru, Karasuma, Shichijo Dori, Shimogyo-ku. Tel. (075)361-0937. Open 8am to 7:30pm. Closed Sunday.*

This Japanese shop sells elegantly shaped candles made of pure plant wax in various colors. (Buddhism forbade the use of animal fat.) These unusually shaped candles make lovely presents.

Central Kyoto

Kurochiku. *On Shinmachi Dori, north of Shijo Dori. 380 Mukadeya-cho, Shinmachi Dori, Nishiki-koji agaru, Nakagyo-ku. Tel. (075)256-9393. Open daily 10am to 5:30pm.*

Located across from the restaurant Mukadeya, this charming gift shop specializes in small handmade items — small bags, *noren* curtains, luncheon mats — using Kyoto *yuzen* fabric. Small *furoshiki*, which incidentally make nice napkins, cost ¥500; *noren* from ¥10,000.

Wazahyakushu. *On Takoyakushi Street, west of Karasuma Street. Tel. (075)211-6710. Open 10am to 6pm. Closed Wednesday.*

This shop is a crafts cooperative and features a wide range of goods all made by Kyoto artisans. We find it stimulating to find traditional items interpreted to suit the modern world. Stop in to buy reasonably priced textiles, clothing, *washi* paper crafts and lots more. Japanese-style lamps from ¥5500, *noren* from ¥12,000, lacquer trays cost ¥2800.

Kikuya. *Manjuji, east of Sakaimachi, Shimogyo-ku. Tel. (075)351-0033. Open 9am to 7pm. Closed Sunday and holidays.*

Antique and used kimono and obi with an extensive selection of wedding kimonos. They run a branch near Okazaki Zoo.

Asakoji. *Senbon Higashi iru, Sanjo Dori, Nakagyo-ku. Tel. (075)841-0005. Open 10am to 6pm. Closed Monday.*

We bumped into this small shop on Oike Dori between Shinsen-en Garden and Horikawa Dori after having lunch at Shinsen-en. It's stocked with 100% linen, a hemp believed to get rid of illness and valued since ancient times. The owner has engaged in the wholesale linen business for ages but only recently decided to sell finished products as well. The subtly dyed fabric is available by the meter, but there is also a tasteful selection of products including *noren* curtains, table mats and dolls.

Ippodo Kissashitsu Kaboku. *On Teramachi Dori, north of Nijo Dori. Tel. (075)211-3421. Open 9am to 7pm. Closed Sunday and holidays.*

This green tea shop has to be the most famous in Japan. The family has been in the tea business for 280 years. You can learn how to make a nice pot of tea and then, at the cafe, test your newly acquired skill. Green tea with a sweet costs ¥280.

Kyukyodo. *On Teramachi Dori, at corner of Anenokoji. Anenokoji-kado, Teramachi, Nakagyo-ku. Tel. (075)231-0510. Open 10am to 6pm. Closed Sunday.*

This shop is the headquarters of a well-known Japanese stationery store; it's a delight to browse around admiring the range of goods. Items start at ¥60 for a silk-screen postcard and go as high as ¥50,000 for a calligraphy brush. Incense is also for sale. We never go home empty-handed.

Kakimoto. *On Teramachi Dori, north of Nijo Dori. Nijo agaru, Teramachi Dori, Nakagyo-ku. Tel. (075)211-3481.*

Established in 1845, Kakimoto has more than 2000 different kinds of Japanese *washi* paper as well as *washi*-like paper you can use in your computer printer. We've had some friends buy *washi* here to make their own lampshades.

Daikichi. *On Teramachi Dori at the intersection of Nijo Dori. Nijo sagaru, Teramachi, Nakagyo-ku. Tel. (075)231-2446. Open daily 11am to 7pm.*

Judging from the wooden lattice entrance door, you may surmise that Daikichi is a Japanese restaurant. Well, it was until the owner got tired of that business and turned it into an antique shop. The shelves are lined with old Imari ceramic ware. We love to browse here and sometimes find some lovely pieces for as low as ¥1000. We top off shopping with a delicious cup of coffee in the cafe corner.

Tachibana Shokai. *Takasegawa, south of Rokkaku, Kiyamachi, Nakagyo-ku. Tel. (075)221-0073. Open 12 noon to 8:30pm. Closed Wednesday.*

Tachibana Shokai specializes in Meiji/Taisho-era lamps and lights. The owner used to sell electric lamps but now only deals with antiques.

Yojiya-Pontocho. *211 Nabeya machi, Shijo-agaru, Kiyamachi, Nakagyo-ku. Tel. (075)221-4919. Open 12 noon to 8am. Closed Wednesday.*

If you are interested in the traditional makeup *maiko* (apprentice *geisha*) still use today, you'll enjoy exploring this shop. You'll find Kyoto's famous powder paper, safflower lipstick and eyeliner that have proved safe over the centuries. Prices are reasonable: lipstick paper ¥200, powder paper ¥320 and eyeliner and eyebrow pencils ¥800 each.

Museum of Kyoto. *On Takakura Dori, north of Sanjo Dori.*
The first floor of the museum has a several shops that sell Kyoto crafts. We stop here if we don't have time to shop: **Sanko**, *Tel. (075) 255-0054; Closed Monday;* sells paper, calligraphy brushes, ink, and other art supplies. **Rakushi Kan**, *Tel. (075)251-0078; Open 10am to 7pm; Closed 3rd Wednesday.* Rakushi Kan sells Japanese *washi* paper in sheets and crafts made from paper such as notebooks, dolls, stationery, etc.

Nishimura. *At the Corner of Sanjo Dori and Teramachi Dori. Tel. (075)211-2489.*
This classic shop sells *ukiyo-e* prints including Hiroshige, Utamaro and other greats. Don't be surprised when you don't see any stock —ask about the prints, and they'll bring them out to you on the *tatami* mats.

Nishimura Kissho-do. *On Sanjo Dori, east of Yanaginobamba Dori. Tel. (075)221-3955. Open 9am to 8pm.*
This reasonable and reputable shop sells lacquer ware from Kyoto as well as other Japanese lacquer. Go upstairs to the second floor gallery — you never know what will be on display.

Yamato Mingei-ten. *On Kawaramachi Dori, north of Takoyakushi Dori. Tel. (075)221-2641. Open 10am to 8:30pm. Closed Tuesday.*
Most Kyoto craft shops sell the refined works of the ancient capital, but Yamato sells folk art from all over Japan. It's a fun place to browse and pick up some unusual items.

Tachikichi. *At the Corner of Shijo Dori and Tominokoji Dori. Tel. (075)211-3143. Open 10am to 7pm. Closed Thursday.*
Shop here for an extensive selection of contemporary Kyoto ceramics in a wide range of prices.

Guild House Kyogashi. *On the west side of Karasuma Dori, north of the Imperial Palace. 3F, Tawaraya Yoshitomi Building, Tel. (075)432-3101. Open 10am to 5pm. Closed Wednesday.*
If you want to know how Japanese sweets are made, don't miss this museum. On display are old utensils used to make elaborately molded sweets that are traditionally served to celebrate weddings and festivals. What's really nice is that on the first and third floors, you can have tea and sweets while resting your tired feet.

Maruzen. *Kawaramachi-dori north of Takoyakushi-dori. Tel. (075)241-2169. Open 10am to 8pm. Closed 3rd Wednesday.*
Large bookstore with the best selection on English books. Also carries stationery items.

Kiyomizu & Gion Areas
Shichimitogarashi. *At the top of Sannenzaka where it meets Kiyomizu-zaka. 2-211 Kiyomizu, Higashiyama-ku. Tel. (075)551-0738. Open daily 9am to 6pm.*

This shop specializes in a seven spice mixture that is on the table of practically every noodle shop in Japan. Shichimitogarashi is the place where the blend was invented in the 17th century. In addition, small ceramic spice containers are for sale. They make great gifts and are ideal for storing your goldfish food.

Asahido. *1-280 Kiyomizu, Higashiyama-ku. Tel. (075)531-2181.*

As you go up Kiyomizu hill, Asahido is one of the last shops on the right before the entrance steps to Kiyomizu-dera Temple. Amid the souvenir shops, Asahido stands out. Asahido carries high quality Kiyomizu ceramics in a wide price range — you can get bowls for ¥400 or ¥400,000. We still treasure a plate purchased here 20 years ago.

Kyonaka. *Tel. (075)531-8031. Open 11am-5pm. Closed Mondays.*

Heading down the hill from Kiyomizu-dera, take the left fork just before the parking lot. This paper shop has a wide variety of attractive goods. In addition to sheets of *washi* paper, Kyonaka has woodblock print postcards.

Miura Shomei. *North side of Shijo Dori, just west of Yasaka Shrine. Tel. (075) 561-2816.*

The light outside says *Akari*, Japanese for lanterns. This shop is a treasure trove of Japanese-style lights from the portable *andon* lantern to hanging lamps. These works of art are pricey, but they have selection rarely seen elsewhere.

Kyoto Craft Center. *North of Shijo Dori, west of Yasaka Shrine. Open 10am to 6pm. Closed Wednesday. Tel. (075)561-9660.*

An excellent place to see contemporary craft work in Kyoto. Enjoy seeing how today's craftsmen combine the traditional with the contemporary. You'll see pottery, weaving, wood, bamboo, paper, baskets and more. It's also a good place to find small gifts.

Aikobo. *On Hanami-koji, south of Shijo Dori.*

This small shop carries natural indigo-dyed items including bags, clothing and accessories.

Tessaido. *On north side of Furumonzen Dori, near Nawate Dori. Yamato Daichi Higashi iru, Furumonzen, Higashiyama-ku. Tel. (075)531-2829. Open daily 10am to 6pm.*

Inside, Tessaido has the feel of a small *kura* (warehouse) that's filled with antique ceramic ware. The specialty is colorful Imari ware, one of the most popular of Japanese ceramics. Even if you have no intention of buying ceramics, this store is a must for anyone interested in the highly decorated Japanese pottery. Prices run from ¥1000 to over ¥100,000 per piece.

Shinmonzen Dori Street. *Located in the Gion area between Shijo and Sanjo Streets.*

Shinmonzen is the antique center of Kyoto. You can find shops specializing in old Imari and Kutani ceramic ware, *ukiyo-e* woodblock paintings, antique *tansu* (chests) from all over Japan, kimono and old textiles, lacquer ware, screens and even old utensils made for daily use. Some shops carry Chinese and Korean antiques. To the Japanese, anything made after 1868 is not really considered antique, but it doesn't necessarily mean that you won't find these items. When the price is rather inexpensive, chances are the item is not antique in the true sense of the word — but who cares if you like it?

Prices vary widely — you can pick up a small blue and white dish for ¥800 or an early Edo screen for ¥8 million. You can often bargain, but don't expect to get more than 10% off. Most shops welcome browsers and accept credit cards. Moreover, they are accustomed to shipping abroad. Generally, store hours are 9:30am to 6pm.

A couple of our favorite shops for woodblock prints are **Ezoshi**, *Tel. (075)551-9137* and **Yokota Garo**, *Tel. (075)752-9390*. **Kawasaki Bijutsu** (it used to be called Kyoto Screen), *Tel. (075)541-8785*, has outstanding screens and *tansu*. **Renkodo**, *Tel. (075)525-2121*, has Imari blue and white porcelain. At **Nakajima**, you'll find Buddhist art, tea ceremony objects and other stuff. **Tenpyodo**, *Tel. (075)561-5688*, has excellent quality Korean furniture.

Northern Higashiyama

Utsuwaya Akane. *Tel. (075)752-4560. Open 10:30am to 5:30pm. Closed Monday.*

Located on the right at the corner of the entrance road to Nanzen-ji, Utsuwaya is a tiny shop carrying tea bowls and dishes for daily use. The owner's father has an antique shop in Shinmonzen.

Heianden. *On Jingumichi, the approach road to Heian Shrine, south of the large torii gate. Sanjo agaru Jingu-michi, Higashiyama-ku. Tel. (075)761-3355. Closed Monday, but open daily March to May and September to November.*

Heianden is a traditional Japanese sweet shop that offers many different types. We often pick up something to eat after lunch. Usually they have a few free samples.

Heian Art. *On Jingumichi, the approach road to Heian Shrine, south of the large torii gate. Agaru Jingumichi, Sanjo, Higashiyama-ku. Tel. (075)751-0277.*

A lovely traditional shop specializing mainly in contemporary ceramics and textiles that you can coordinate with your Western interior decoration. The goods are beautifully displayed on antique Japanese and Western furniture, and prices are reasonable. They also sell old blue and white dishes.

Gallery Takano. *14 Honen-in machi, Shishigatani, Sakyo-ku. Tel. (075)771-0302. Open 10am to 5pm in spring and autumn; 12 noon to late afternoon at other times. Closed Tuesday.*

As you walk along Tetsugaku-no-michi (Philosopher's Path) toward Ginkaku-ji, turn right before you come to the Honen-in temple. It's really fun to browse in this small shop filled with woodblock prints and handmade postcards that you won't find at the shops catering to tourists.

Bon Kyoto. *38-1 Dohnomae-cho, Kita-shirakawa, Sakyo-ku. Tel. (075)711-7095. Open 10am to 6pm. Closed Sunday. Bus #3 or #5 to Kita-Shirakawa Betto-cho.*

Features a wide selection of antique and used kimono at reasonable prices.

Kikuya. *Near Okazaki Zoo, across from parking lot. Open 10am to 6pm Friday through Sunday and holidays. Closed Monday through Thursday.*

A branch of Kikuya located in central Kyoto. In addition to kimono and obi, this store carries ceramics and other antique items.

Western Kyoto

Gallery Gado. *On Kitsuji Dori, south of Kinkaku-ji Temple. 27 Miyashiko-cho, Hirano, Kita-ku. Tel. (075)464-1655.*

This gallery sells the works of Ido Masao, a contemporary woodblock print artist who delights in capturing Kyoto scenes. You can watch a video on the techniques of woodblock printing and you can make a postcard at no charge. In addition to Ido's prints, they also sell *noren* curtains and cloth printed with Ido's colorful designs.

Kamigamo

Raku-an. *47 Kamigamo Shobuen-machi, Kita-ku. Tel. (075)702-7273. Open 10am to 6pm. Closed Tuesday and August. Call the shop to ask them to fax you a map.*

Everytime we go there, we get lost. But it's worth it! Raku-an is one of our favorite lacquer shops in Kyoto. You're surrounded by a variety of beautifully displayed and sturdy lacquer ware — bowls, trays, dishes and much more. They are reasonably priced and meant to be used, not put on display. Raku-an also has indigo-dyed textiles made into wall hangings and luncheon mats as well as metal candlesticks designed by contemporary craftsmen. The owner and his assistant are friendly and speak some English. Ask to see the inner room where you'll find more expensive items such as red and black lacquered tables — they are simple but would fit into a contemporary home.

PRACTICAL INFORMATION

Bicycle Rental

Rental Cycle Yasumoto *on Kawabata north of Sanjo. Tel. (075)751-0595. Open 9am to 5pm. Closed 3rd Sunday. ¥200/hour; ¥1000/day.*

Rent Pia Service Cycle Center, *south of JR Nishioji Station. Tel. (075)672-0662. Open 8am to 8pm. ¥900/day.*

Eki Rent-a-Cycle at Saga. *Tel. (075)881-4899.*

Medical

Japan Baptist Hospital, *south of Kitaoji, between Shinmachi and Aburanokoji. Tel. (075)781-5191.*

Japan Helpline can assist with any sort of crisis 24 hours a day. *Toll free: 0120-461-997.*

Home Visit System

At least one day in advance, call the Kyoto City International Foundation to arrange a visit to a Japanese home. Please remember it's customary to take the family a small gift such as cookies, flowers or something from your home country. *Tel. (075)752-3511. Closed Mondays.*

Internet

Internet access is available at the **Kyoto Prefectural International Center**, *9F, Kyoto Station Building, Tel. (075)342-5000. Open 10am to 6pm. Closed 2nd and 4th Tuesdays. ¥250 for 30 minutes.*

Since Internet cafes open and close with alarming regularity, check with the Kyoto Tourist Information Office, *Tel. (075)371-5649*, for current internet access.

Listings Information

Pick up the monthly freebie *Kyoto Visitors Guide* for information on festivals, exhibitions, dining and shopping. It's available at hotels and the Tourist Information Office. Their website is *www.city.kyoto.jp/sankan/kankoshinko/visitor/index.html.* Kyoto City maintains a website at: *www.city.kyoto.jp.* Click on the English icon.

Kansai Time Out is a monthly magazine that covers happenings in Kyoto, Osaka and Kobe. It's available in bookstores selling English books and at hotels.

Maruzen Books is the best place in town to get English-language books. It's on Kawaramachi Dori north of Takoyakushi Dori. *Open 10am to 8pm. Closed 3rd Wednesday.*

Money Exchange

Exchange money at banks with "Authorized Foreign Exchange" sign in English at the entrance. Banks are open 9am to 3pm, Monday through Friday. You can also exchange money at the department stores, but the rate will not be as good.

The **All Card Plaza** on Teramachi Dori just north of Shijo Dori has cash machines where you can use major credit cards; you must have a PIN number to access. You can get advances using Visa at Mitsubishi-Tokyo Bank, Sumitomo Bank and Nanto Bank branches; MasterCard at Nanto Bank (Karasuma Oike, *Tel. (075)223-2200)* and Diners Club at JTB on Sanjo Dori.

Post Office

The **Central Post Office** is north of Kyoto Station and is open Monday through Friday 9am to 7pm, Saturday 9am to 5pm and Sunday 9am to 12:30pm. It has a 24-hour window.

Tours

For a personally arranged tour, contact **Joe Okada** at *1137 Amarube-shimo, Maizuru, Kyoto, 625. Tel. (0773)64-0033, Fax (0773)64-0066.* He knows Kyoto like the back of his hand and can tailor an itinerary to fit your interests.

Johnnie Hillwalker's Kyoto Walking. Johnnie Hillwalker, aka Hajime Hirooka, gives wonderful walking tours Monday through Thursday March through November. Meets at 10am the Sunken Garden area in front of the main entrance to Kyoto Station (Karasuma side). The four-hour tour covers about 3 kilometers and gives you a cross section of Kyoto experiences. ¥2000 for one person, ¥3000 for two. *Tel. (075)622-6803.*

MK Taxi has English-speaking drivers who can give guided tours. ¥18,800 for three hours. *Tel. (075)721-2237, Fax (075)721-3663.*

Goodwill Volunteer Guides. The Tourist Information Center can arrange volunteer guides. *Call (075)371-5649.* Remember, these people are not professional guides.

Virtual Tours

Armchair travelers and real travelers alike can experience Kyoto's major sights through a virtual reality tour on a series of CDs called **Explore Kyoto**. Contact **Discover History**, *PO Box 293, Clayton, New York, US 13624, Tel. 914/793-8166.*

21. NARA

Is your head spinning from Kyoto? Is the large modern city with its thousands of temples more than you can swallow? If so, get on a train and within an hour you'll be in **Nara**, Japan's 8th century capital, where many of the important sights are in a spacious and peaceful park. Among the tame deer and the trees, the world's largest bronze Buddha lives in the world's largest wooden building. At first glance, the temples look similar to their Kyoto cousins, but many have buildings eight centuries older. **Nara Park** offers one of the most unhurried touring experiences of any historic area in Japan.

Nara champions itself as the cradle of Japanese culture. Until 710 when Nara was established as the first "permanent" capital, the capital itself moved every time the emperor died. Nara remained the center of government for a mere 74 years, a blink of an eye in Japan's long history. But those seven decades saw a tremendous flowering of culture and the arts heavily influenced by Chinese culture. Nara was the far eastern end of the Silk Route that stretched across China and continued through Afghanistan and the Middle East.

During the Nara period Buddhism, firmly in center stage, was an impetus for innovation. But this power was also its undoing. To get away from the powerful monks who were devoting too much time to secular matters, the emperor moved the capital in 784. Some of Nara's temples remained powerful forces until the 16th century.

Even if your time is short, skip the third day in Kyoto and go to Nara. Better yet, make it an overnight for a less hurried stay.

Planning Your Stay

Most people make a day trip from Kyoto and see only Nara's top sights like Todai-ji and Kofuku-ji Temples. If you can swing it, try to stay overnight for a more complete exploration of this city's treasures.

• **One day trip**: Stay in the Nara Park area and make a large loop: Kofuku-ji Temple, Nara National Museum, Todai-ji Temple, Nigatsudo and

NARA HIGHLIGHTS

- *Daibutsu, the largest bronze Buddha in the world*
- *A superb collection of sculptures at Kokuhokan, Kofuku-ji temple*
- *Yakushi-ji and Horyu-ji for masterpieces of Buddhist sculpture*
- *Omizu-tori, an unusual ritual, at Nigatsudo in early March*
- *Buddha of the Future at Chugu-ji Temple*
- *Hase-dera and Muro-ji, two off-the-beaten-path temples*
- *Cherry blossom viewing at Yoshino*
- *A rare center of contemporary religion at Tenri*
- *Cycling around Asuka and Horyu-ji areas*
- *Warabi-mochi, cha gayu, and kakinoha zushi – local delicacies*

Kasuga Shrine. If you still have time and energy, wander around Nara Machi, the old merchant quarter.

- **Two day trip**: Day one is as above. Day two: Nishino-kyo area that includes Yakushi-ji Temple and Toshodai-ji Temple; Horyu-ji Temple.

For travelers with more time, you can go farther afield visiting Hase Dera Temple, Muro-ji Temple and the mountaintop village of Yoshino.

One warning: the standard Nara itinerary is not for those who already are on temple overload. If the thought of seeing another temple or shrine gives you vertigo, try these alternatives: wander around Nara Machi, the old merchant district, and stop in the contemporary Nara Museum of Photography; spend a half day in Tenri, a town created by a new Buddhist sect; go hiking in the hills above Nara Park.

Dates to Remember
- **January 15**: The grass of Mt. Wakakusa is set on fire at 6pm. Within minutes the mountain is wrapped in flames, an awesome spectacle. This practice began to avoid territorial claims among Kasuga Shrine, Todai-ji Temple and Kofuku-ji Temple, but it also had the practical effect of reducing the insect population.
- **February 3 and August 14–15**: 1800 stone lanterns leading to Kasuga Shrine and the 1000 hanging lanterns along the covered walkways are lit and *noh* is performed.
- **March 1–14**: *Omizu-tori* at Nigatsudo of Todai-ji Temple. These fire and water rituals date back to 752. In the evening 11 monks run up the covered walkways of Nigatsudo carrying huge torches on long bamboo poles. To purify the audience standing below, they wave and swirl the torches out over the edge of the balcony. These monks have

undergone special rituals and eat only one meal a day for the entire two-week period; they do not even drink water. In the early dawn of the last day, purified water is drawn from a special well. The monks, now numbering 12, spray water to purify everything to welcome spring.

• **October**: The *Shika no Tsuno Kiri*, cutting of the deer antlers, usually takes place on Sundays and holidays in October. The 1200 deer wandering around Nara Park are considered messengers of the Shinto god of Kasuga Shrine. But these sacred animals have a secular problem. Male deer naturally shed their antlers in March and begin growing new ones in May. In October, the mating season, the hard antlers are a danger, so a Shinto priest cuts them off. If you are in Nara during the October mating season, you'll also hear the male deer yelp the strange mating cry.

ARRIVALS & DEPARTURES

Trains provide convenient access from Kyoto and Osaka.

By Train

To/from Kyoto: The Kintetsu line runs nonstop limited express trains to Kintetsu Nara Station (33 minutes, ¥1110). The regular express trains take about 45 minutes; most necessitate a change at Saidaiji Station, ¥610.

For JR rail pass holders, take the JR Nara line to JR Nara Station (1 hour, ¥690).

To/from Osaka's Kintetsu Namba Station: Kintetsu line's limited express trains take 31 minutes and cost ¥1030. Regular expresses take 45 minutes and cost ¥540.

GETTING AROUND TOWN

Although Nara city is a fairly spread out, the sights are clustered around three main areas: Nara Park, Nishino-kyo and Horyu-ji. Kintetsu trains and buses provide excellent access.

Tourist Information

Nara doesn't lack tourist information centers, all have English-speaking staff and lots of English-language pamphlets and maps.

Kintetsu Nara Station City Tourist Information Office: Open daily 9am to 5pm. Closed December 29 through January 3. *Tel. (0742)24-4858.*

JR Nara Station City Information Office: Open daily 9am to 5pm. Closed December 30 through January 3. *Tel. (0742)22-9821.*

Nara City Information Office: Open 9am to 7pm (English speaker until 5pm). Closed December 30 through January 3. Halfway between JR Nara and Kintetsu Nara Stations. 23-4 Kamisanjo-cho. *Tel. (0742)22-3900*.

Nara Sarusawa Information: Sarusawa Pond. Open 9am to 5pm. Closed December 31 through January 3. *Tel. (0742)26-1991*.

Goodwill Guides

English speaking volunteers, who have taken a special course on guiding through Nara, are glad to show you around. Pay their admission fees and lunch. Arrange a guide at least one day in advance by phoning any of the above tourist information centers or call student guides at *Tel. (0742)26-4753* and YMCA guides at *Tel. (0742)45-5920, Fax (0742)49-6459*.

WHERE TO STAY

KASUGA HOTEL, *40 Nobori-oji, Nara, 630-8213. Tel. (0742)22-4031, Fax (0742)26-6966. From ¥18,000 per person with two meals. Credit cards.*

Conveniently located between Kintetsu train station and Nara Park, Kasuga is constructed in the *azekura* style, based on the famous Shoso-in treasure house just a few blocks away. This architecture uses huge tree trunks for the exterior walls. All the rooms are traditional Japanese style, and you may have *cha gayu*, rice porridge cooked in green tea, for breakfast.

KANKASO, *10 Kasugano-machi, Nara, 630-8212. Tel. (0742)26-1128, Fax (0742)26-1301. From ¥18,000 per person with two meals. Credit cards.*

Tucked between souvenir shops on the road leading to the Great Buddha, you can easily miss the small path that leads to Kankaso. An antique dealer who built the traditional Meiji-era house spared no expense acquiring antique transom panels, shelves, ceilings, pillars and even the handles on the sliding doors. The stones in the garden were once the base for pillars at Todai-ji Temple, a mere block away. Three communal baths overlook a small garden: one for women, one for men and a third for families. Kankaso is one of the few inns where hot food is actually served piping hot. The staff is very helpful and friendly.

EDO-SAN, *1167 Takabatake-machi, Nara, 630-8301. Tel. (0742)26-2662, Fax (0742)26-2663. From ¥18,000 per person with two meals. Located to the right of the gate to Kasuga Shrine. Credit cards.*

To experience Old Japan, stay at one of the 11 traditional Japanese cottages; arranged around a lovely garden, no two are alike. Edo-san began as a restaurant in 1907 and the cooking is still a strong point. *Wakakusa-nabe*, the winter specialty, is a rich seafood stew.

NARA HOTEL, *1096 Takabatake-cho, Nara, 630-8301. Tel. (0742)26-3300, Fax (0742)23-5252. Singles from ¥14,000. Twins from ¥22,000. Credit cards.*

This classic Western-style hotel opened in 1909 and remains one of the few grand Western hotels of that era. The rooms in the old wing feature high ceilings and old fashioned bathrooms. The newer wing resembles any modern hotel room. A real treat is eating breakfast in the wood- paneled restaurant.

KITA PENSION, *155-1 Nishino-kyo-machi, Nara, 630-8042. Tel. (0742)33-0268, Fax (0742)35-1840. From ¥7700 per person with two meals. No credit cards.*

A quiet pension, Kita is located close to Yakushi-ji Temple, away from the center of Nara. Built in the *azekura* style, the exterior resembles a traditional storehouse. But the eight rooms are Western style. The pension offers views of Yakushi-ji's two pagodas.

RYOKAN SEIKAN-SO, *29 Higashi Kitsuji-cho, Nara, 630-8327. Tel. and Fax: (0742)22-2670. Singles ¥4000. Twins ¥8000. Credit cards. Member of Japanese Inn Group and Welcome Inn Reservation Center.*

An excellent budget inn choice, Seikan-so offers Japanese-style rooms and a large garden. It's just minutes away from Kofuku-ji Temple and the other sights of Nara Park.

WHERE TO EAT

Nara Park area

YANAGI CHAYA *(Japanese, moderate to expensive). 48 Todaiji-machi, in Nara Park. Tel. (0742)22-7560. Lunch 11:30am-5pm; dinner 5pm-7pm. Closed Monday. Children not welcome. Reservations necessary for dinner.*

Located next to the main hall of Kofuku-ji Temple, Yanagi Chaya is famous for its *chameshi*, rice cooked in green tea with dried tofu, a temple vegetarian food first cooked by monks at Todai-ji and Kofuku-ji temples. Yanagi Chaya dates back to 1902. Try the *shokado bento* at lunch, ¥3200. *Kaiseki* set meals at dinner begin at ¥6000 and require reservations.

TONO CHAYA *(Japanese, moderate). 47 Todaiji-machi. Tel. (0742)22-4348. Open 11:30am to 7pm. Closed Tuesday.*

Tono, located to the east of Kofuku-ji's pagoda, specializes in *cha gayu*, a Nara specialty. The *cha gayu bento* for ¥3000 is a good lunchtime choice; Tono serves it until 4pm.

UMANO-ME *(Japanese, moderate to expensive). 1158 Takahata-cho. Located near the southern part of the Nara National Museum, inside Nara Park. Tel. (0742)23-7784. Open 11:30am-3pm; 5:30pm-9pm. Closed Thursday. Children not welcome.*

Umano-Me means "horse's eye;" developed during the Edo period, the design is on the restaurant's ceramic plates. Although Umano-me describes itself as serving family-style cooking, it's rather pricey. The *Okimari* set costs ¥3500 and includes four dishes featuring seasonal fresh ingredients. Reservations required for dinner; courses are ¥8000 and ¥13,000.

KAN *(Soba noodles, inexpensive). 731 Todaiji-machi. Tel. (0742)22-0602. Open 11:30am-3pm; 4pm-7:30pm. Closed Wednesday.*

A *soba* noodle shop in the southern part of Nara Park serves a delicious *Kan teishoku* set for ¥1500, which includes noodles, *tempura*, cooked vegetables, salad and even rice for carbo loaders.

MOMOYA *(Regional Japanese, inexpensive). Takabatake Fukui-machi. Tel. (0742)22-8797. Open 11am to 5pm. Closed Monday and Thursday.*

Taste one of Nara's signature dishes, *cha gayu*, rice gruel cooked in green tea. Before you turn up your nose at it, give it a try. People in Nara have been eating it for breakfast for generations. *Cha gayu* set costs ¥900 and includes nine tiny side dishes.

TODAIJI EMADO CHAYA *(Noodles, inexpensive). In front of Sangatsudo compound. Tel. (0742)27-6152. Open daily 10am to 5pm.*

This shop serves a variety of noodles but serves them in a broth made from kelp and mushrooms. For a change of pace, order the toasted French bread for ¥100.

YOSHIKAWA TEI *(French, inexpensive). 1F, San-Fukumura Building, 17 Hanashiba-cho. Tel. (0742)23-7675. Open 11:30am to 2pm; 5:30pm to 8pm; Sunday 5:30pm to 8pm. Closed Monday. From the plaza at Kintetsu Nara Station, cross the large street, Noborioji, and turn left into a narrow road with an arch at the entrance. The restaurant is about a five-minute walk down this street, on the right about one block before it dead ends.*

For a change from Japanese food, Yoshikawa offers inexpensive French bistro fare. The tiny restaurant has only about a half-dozen tables and the cooks work in a closet-sized kitchen. They offer two or three entrees a day; a three-course lunch costs ¥1200.

YUSUI CHATEI *(Japanese, inexpensive). 158 Kasugano-cho. Tel. (0742)22-4744. Open 9am to 5pm. If you make reservations, they will be happy to stay open for dinner. Located on the long stairway on the path between Nigatsudo and Kasuga Shrine; as you descend the steps, it's the last store on the right.*

This nondescript souvenir shop and teahouse serves surprisingly good *warabi mochi*, a sweet made from ground *kuzu* root and dusted with bean flour, a very healthy sweet, for ¥350.

TAKABATAKE SALON *(Tea, inexpensive). 1247 Takabatake Daido-machi. Tel. (0742)26-4082. Open 11am to 6pm. Closed Tuesday and 1st and 3rd Wednesdays.*

A comfortable teahouse where you can savor your English-style tea and enjoy the garden. We enjoyed the not-too-sweet cheese cake for ¥600.

KIKUYA SWEET SHOP *(Japanese sweets, inexpensive). Tel. (0742)23-4855. From the plaza next to Kintetsu Nara Station, cross the main street and turn left into a fairly narrow road with an archway at the entrance. The shop is several minutes walk on this street on the right.*

Stop here to try Kikuya's *shiro no kuchi mochi,* a Japanese sweet made with pounded sweet rice, filled with red bean paste and dusted with bean flour. Kikuya has been making sweets for 400 years. ¥60 each.

Nara-Machi Area

HARISHIN *(Japanese, moderate). 15 Nakashinya-machi. Tel (0742)22-2669. Open 11:30am to 2:30pm. Closed Monday.*

Slightly off the beaten track, Harishin is in a traditional 200-year-old building with a wooden lattice front. Sit on *tatami* mats at a table with a sunken hearth and have the only item on the menu, the *Kamitsumichi bento* (¥2700), basically a fancy lacquer box filled with a variety of seasonal delicacies. For instance, in autumn you can expect dishes prepared with mushrooms; in spring you get bamboo shoots.

MASAGOYA *(Sushi, moderate). 31 Fukuchi-in machi. Tel. (0742)22-3859. Open 11:30am to 2pm; 5pm to 8pm. Closed Wednesday.*

This wooden-lattice-front traditional building houses a *sushi* shop. Try the *kaze* set for ¥2500.

Nishino-Kyo Area

MANKYO *(Japanese, moderate). 410 Rokujo-machi. Located close to the parking lot of Yakushi-ji. Tel. (0742)33-8942. Open 11am to 8:30pm. Closed Monday.*

This restaurant, in a traditional Japanese building, serves interesting contemporary Japanese food — 50 different dishes. A healthy minicourse for those dieters costs ¥2800; it's basically vegetarian food. The *Otegaru* set meal costs ¥3800 and gives a sampling of the popular specialties.

DAINAGON *(Japanese, inexpensive). 9-44 Gojo-machi. Located between Yakushi-ji and Toshodai-ji Temples. Tel. (0742)33-3387. Open 10:30am to 5pm. Closed Tuesday.*

Dainagon serves a variety of Japanese food including *soba teishoku* for ¥700 and *tendon* for ¥900.

RYUO-AN *(Japanese tea, inexpensive). 16-13 Gojo-machi, close to Toshodai-ji. Tel. (0742)33-9676. Open 10am to 6pm.*

We like to stop here to have Japanese tea in the garden under a red umbrella. Green tea with sweets runs ¥500.

Saidaiji Area
TABENIKO (*Okonomiyaki, inexpensive*). *3F, Poporo Building. Tel. (0742)34-9016. Open 5pm to 10pm.*

Run by a friendly couple, Mr. and Mrs. Shimase, world travelers who enjoy meeting other travelers, they offer a special to foreigners: a large *okonomiyaki* and beer for $11 on Monday and Thursday evenings.

SEEING THE SIGHTS

Nara Park Area
We usually do a circular tour of the Nara Park area, beginning at the Nara Exhibition Hall of Japanese History, then Kofuku-ji Temple, the National Museum, Todai-ji Temple, Nigatsudo and Kasuga Shrine, all in all taking the better part of a day. If you are on a really tight schedule, limit yourself to Todai-ji, Kasuga and Kofuku-ji, about two hours.

A good place to start your exploration of Nara is right in the Kintetsu Nara Station building, at the **Nara Exhibition Hall of Japanese History** (Rekishi Kyoshitsu) where maps and models provide a good visual overview. The explanation panels of Nara history are only in Japanese, but an English pamphlet provides information. *Open daily 10am to 6pm. ¥300.*

From Kintetsu Station, pass through the small plaza and turn right to walk through a lively shopping arcade until you come out to a street. Turn left and you will come to Sarusawa Pond, famous for the reflection of Kofuku-ji's five-storied pagoda.

Walk up the steps north of the pond to enter the grounds of **Kofuku-ji Temple**. The temple was founded in 669 and moved from Asuka in 710 when Nara became the capital. Once encompassing over a hundred buildings, today only a handful remain including a five-storied pagoda built in 1426 as an exact copy of the original. The five stories symbolize the five elements — water, fire, earth, metal and wood — that constitute the universe. The **Kokuhokan** treasure house has a superb collection of Buddhist art. It's only a slight exaggeration to say that half the treasures you see in Japanese art history books are here. Even if you don't have time to go to the National Museum, don't miss the Kokuhokan. *Open 9am to 5pm. ¥500.*

Here are a few not-to-be-missed treasures: a huge bronze head of a Buddha expressing "sensual compassion" from Yamada-dera; the statue of Asura, a beautiful, youthful face with a tinge of melancholy; and dry lacquer figures of Buddha's ten disciples in vigorous poses showing threatening facial expressions.

Founded by the Fujiwara family, high-ranking court nobles, Kofuku-ji prospered and became one of Japan's most powerful temples. Like its rival Enryaku-ji outside of Kyoto, Kofuku-ji formed a monk-army and became embroiled in political confrontations. During the 11th century

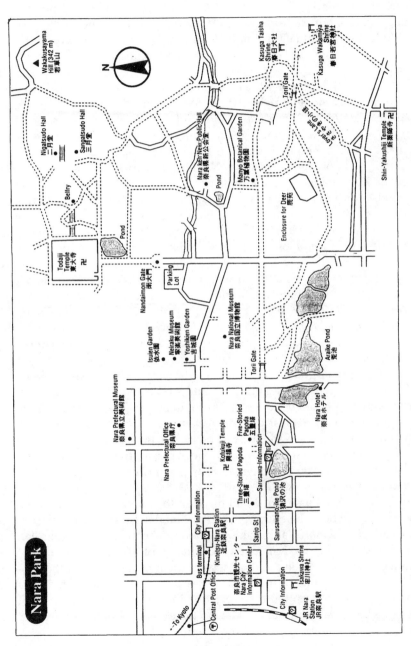

Nara Park

Wakakusayama Hill (342 m) 若草山

N

Nigatsudo Hall 二月堂

Sangatsudo Hall 三月堂

Belfry

Pond

Todaiji Temple 東大寺 卍

Nandaimon Gate 南大門

Parking Lot

Nara ken New Public Hall 奈良県新公会堂

Pond

Manyo Botanical Garden 万葉植物園

Kasuga Taisha Shrine 春日大社

Torii Gate

Kasuga Wakamiya Shrine 春日若宮神社

Shin-Yakushiji Temple 新薬師寺 卍

Love's Lane 恋のみち

Enclosure for Deer 鹿苑

Isuien Garden 依水園

Neiraku Museum 寧楽美術館

Yoshikien Garden 吉城園

Nara National Museum 奈良国立博物館

Torii Gate

Araike Pond 荒池

Nara Prefectural Museum 奈良県立美術館

Nara Prefectural Office 奈良県庁

City Information

Kofukuji Temple 興福寺 卍

Three-Storied Pagoda 三重塔

Five-Storied Pagoda 五重塔

Sarusawa-Information

Nara Hotel 奈良ホテル

Sarusawa-no-ike Pond 猿沢の池

Sanjo St.

Bus terminal

Kintetsu-Nara Station 近鉄奈良駅

Nara City Information Center 奈良市観光センター

Central Post Office

Isakawa Shrine 率川神社

City Information

JR Nara Station JR奈良駅

To Kyoto

struggle for power between the Taira and the Minamoto, Kofuku-ji supported the Minamoto and as a result was destroyed by the Taira. Since the Minamoto eventually triumphed, Kofuku-ji was rebuilt by its powerful patron; masterpieces of dynamic Kamakura-era sculpture come from this era.

Kofuku-ji is in **Nara Park**, a huge expanse of land encompassing some of Nara's most notable sights. Tame deer, some 1200 strong, rule the park. Make sure you keep paper and food out of sight. Friends visiting from New York were plotting out their route when suddenly a deer started munching on their map. Fortunately they had a spare.

The **Nara National Museum** (Nara Kokuritsu Hakubutsukan), just beyond Kofuku-ji Temple, concentrates on the art of the Nara and Heian periods, much of it from area temples. The collection of Buddhist art is one of the best in Japan. The museum consists of a Beaux Arts-style building constructed in 1898 and a 1970s expansion building, a modern rendition of *azekura* or storehouse architecture. Every year in late October and early November, the museum holds an exhibition of the treasures of the Shoso-in, the ancient storehouse of Todai-ji Temple that houses Emperor Shomu's collection as well as temple treasures. *Tel. (0742)22-7771. Open 9am to 4:30pm. ¥420, additional for special exhibitions. Closed Monday and December 26 through January 3.*

Garden aficionados may want to take a small detour to **Isui-en Garden**, off a small street north of the Nara National Museum. The front part of the garden goes back to 1670 and the back part was added in 1899. The tranquil garden uses the big gate of Todai-ji Temple and Mt. Wakakusa as borrowed scenery. ¥600. Sit in the tea villa overlooking the garden and enjoy a meal of the specialty, *mugitoro,* which is mashed mountain potato mixed with wheat and rice. In the old days it was known as poor man's food. Nowadays it is a type of rice for the health conscious. *Mugitoro* costs ¥1200. *Mugitoro-gozen,* which includes eel, costs ¥2400. *Open 11am to 3pm. Closed Tuesday. Call (0742)22-2173 for reservations.*

Return to the main road and turn left to continue further into the park. Turn right at the entrance path to **Todai-ji Temple**. You will pass through Nandaimon Gate; make sure you notice the fantastic guardian gods sculpted in the Kamakura era, the most striking examples of Kamakura-period wood sculptures. Note their vigor and strength.

Emperor Shomyo ordered the construction of Todai-ji, which was completed in 752, to house a great Buddha and to head the series of temples being built throughout Japan. The present building, constructed in 1692, is a mere two-thirds of the original.

The massive wooden building is surrounded by covered walkways. On the path to enter the **Daibutsuden**, the main hall, is a bronze lantern dating from the Nara era and designated a National Treasure. Enter the dimly lit interior of the Daibutsuden to make out the towering Buddha. The 15-meter statue is the world's largest bronze Buddha, an incredible achievement for its time, and a huge toll in money and labor. Walk around the back of the Buddha where a model displays Todai-ji in its heyday. One of the building's huge pillars has a hole bored in it near the floor. Legend has it that anyone able to pass through the hole will enter heaven. *Open 7:30am to 5:30pm April through September; 7:30am to 5pm October; 8am to 4:30pm November to March. ¥400.*

Walk around the back of Todai-ji to see the **Shoso-in** storehouse building. While the raised wooden edifice doesn't look like much, it has protected priceless treasures belonging to the emperor and Todai-ji since the 8th century.

SHOSO-IN TREASURE HOUSE

It's almost hard to believe that this simple wooden storehouse, looking a lot like an overgrown log cabin on stilts, could play such an important role in preserving 1300-year-old treasures.

*Emperor Shomu's widow constructed the **Shoso-in** in 756 to store the late emperor's treasures. Brilliantly built in an architectural style called **azekura zukuri**, the raised floor of the entirely wooden building deters rodents and keeps out moisture. In summer the wooden logs of the walls swell to keep out humidity while in winter they shrink to allow in the dry air. This system worked so well that today some of the 7th and 8th century objects stored there are the only remaining examples in the world.*

Shoso-in protected a treasure trove of 9000 articles, the collections of both Emperor Shomu and Todai-ji. In addition to Japanese art, there is a huge array of objects from the Asian continent: calligraphy, stationery, furniture, musical instruments, armor, everyday dishes, costumes. The articles from Central Asia and Persia show the high level of interaction between these areas and Nara, connected by the Silk Route.

Today Shoso-in's collection lives down the road at the Nara National Museum, rersting in modern, climate controlled storerooms. Every year the museum displays about 70 objects in late October and early November. If you are in Nara at this time, make sure you stop in for a fascinating glimpse of Nara's glorious past.

The **Kaidan-in** (Ordination Hall), located in a quiet forest west of the Daibutsuden, should not be missed. The construction of this building was crucial to the history of Japanese Buddhism. Until the Kaidan-in was built in 755, ordination of monks had to be done by Chinese authorities. The present building was rebuilt in 1732, but it is not the building that makes

Kaidan-in special. It houses four superb Tenpyo-style 8th century statues of Shitenno, the four heavenly guardian kings of the universe. Take time to look at each guardian god's expression; they are all slightly different. One favorite is Komokuten, the god who knows too much of the world; his face is tinged with sadness. *Open the same hours as Daibutsuden. ¥400.*

Go up the hill east of Todai-ji. Halfway up is a bell tower containing a seven hundred-year-old bell, a National Treasure. At the top of the hill is **Nigatsudo**, a subtemple of Todai-ji. The large front porch built out over the mountainside resembles Kyoto's Kiyomizu Dera Temple. Every March, the dramatic Omizu-tori festival takes place; monks run up the stairs onto the terrace carrying large torches on long bamboo sticks.

The unassuming **Sangatsudo** or Lotus Hall subtemple next door contains treasures of Nara art, including the towering central image, whose silver crown holds thousands of pearls. This statue is said to be sculpted by the same workmen who made the original Great Buddha in the Daibutsuden. *Sangatsudo is open the same hours as Todai-ji's Daibutsuden. ¥400.*

As you continue along the path that eventually leads to Kasuga Shrine, you'll walk along the perimeter of Mt. Wakakusa, a grassy hill that is the site of a giant blaze every January 15. Take the long stairway and go through the deep woods to reach **Kasuga Shrine** (Kasuga Taisha), one of Japan's most famous Shinto shrines. Like Kofuku-ji, the Fujiwara family founded the shrine way back in 710 as the guardian shrine for the new capital. Nearly 2000 stone lanterns, donated by individuals and groups of people, line the approach road. Another 1800 metal lanterns hang from every available space inside the walkways of the brilliant vermilion-colored shrine. The scene is so photogenic that a picture turns out well even if you use a point and shoot camera.

If you still have any energy to see more sights, continue on to Shin Yakushi-ji Temple. Otherwise, go down the hill through Nara Park, past Manyo Botanical Gardens, a large garden containing all the plants mentioned in the *Manyoshu*, the 8th century anthology of poetry compiled in the Nara period. *Open 9am to 4pm. ¥500.* The path through the park leads to Sarusawa Pond. The Nara Machi district (see below) is due south, and Kintetsu Nara Station is a few minutes walk.

A ten-minute walk south of Kasuga will bring you to **Shin Yakushi-ji Temple**, built by Empress Komyo as thanks for her husband, Emperor Shomu's recovery from an eye ailment. The main hall, the Hondo, dates from the 8th century and is one of only three buildings in Nara remaining from the Nara era. *Open 9am to 5pm. ¥500.*

Just west of Shin Yakushi-ji stands the **Nara Museum of Photography** (Nara-shi Shashin Bijutsukan). Housed in a stunning specimen of contemporary architecture, the building with its long sloping tile roof manages to retain the atmosphere of traditional Nara. The museum houses a superb collection of photographs of Nara taken by the late noted photographer, Irie Daikichi, a Nara native. *Open 9:30am to 5pm. Closed Monday, March 25 through April 1, June 24-28, September 24-28 and December 24 through January 4. ¥500.*

Nara Machi Area

For a change of pace from the seemingly endless temples and shrines, wander around the Nara Machi district, the merchant area during feudal times. A completely different atmosphere prevails. In place of temple buildings on large tracts of land, the merchant houses were placed side by side. Since taxation was based on the amount of frontage to the street, these houses were relatively narrow but very deep. Quite a few of the old buildings remain, but they are interspersed with newer structures.

Go into **Naramachi Koshi-no-ie** (Naramachi Lattice House) to view the interior of a traditional *machiya* merchant house. This excellent replica has different types of lattice used when glass windows were precious. The garden in the center of the narrow house gives maximum light and privacy. *Tel. (0742)23-4820. Open 9am to 5pm. Closed Monday and December 30 through January 3. Admission free.*

The **Nara Oriental Kan**, a few minutes walk from the Lattice House displays items from the Silk Route in an old merchant house. Nara was the end of the Silk Route. *Open 10am to 5pm. Closed Monday, August 13-16 and December 25 through January 3. ¥300.*

Jurin-in Temple's tiny main hall dates from the mid-Kamakura period; its elegant and graceful roof and latticework have earned it National Treasure designation. The hall houses an unusual stone crypt with Buddhist images that predate the hall by several hundred years. The outer gate, built in the mid-Kamakura period and designated an Important Cultural Property, still has its original cinnabar paint. You may have to ring the bell at the office to the left of the main hall to gain access. *Open 9am to 4:30pm. Closed August 22-23, December 28 through January 5 and January 28. ¥300.*

Imanishi Ke Shoin House is truly old for the house dates from the 14-16th century Muromachi period. Layers of paper form the interior walls and the beams have beveled edges. *Open 10am to 4pm. Closed Thursday, August 10-20 and December 20 through January 10. ¥350.*

Nishino-Kyo Area

To reach the Nishino-kyo area from Kintetsu Nara Station, take bus #52, 97 or 98 and get off at Toshodaiji Higashi-guchi, about 15 minutes. Alternatively, take the Kintetsu train two stops to Saidaiji and change to the Kintetsu Kashihara line going two stops to Nishino-kyo Station. From

Nishino-kyo Station, Toshodai-ji Temple is a 10-minute walk north and Yakushi-ji Temple is a 5-minute walk east.

Yakushi-ji Temple's masterpiece of Nara architecture is a graceful three-storied pagoda. Dedicated to the Buddha of Healing, Emperor Temmu founded Yakushi-ji in the 7th century at his capital Fujiwara-kyo as a prayer to cure the empress' eye ailment. In 718 Yakushi-ji moved to the new capital in Nara, to be in the heart of the action. Time has not been kind to the temple; the eastern pagoda is the only remaining original structure. In the last few decades, the temple has rebuilt the western pagoda and the main hall. Visitors can now get a better sense of the magnificence of this ancient temple.

Built in 730, the east pagoda seems to have six stories, but actually has three. Smaller fake roofs are sandwiched between the real roofs. This asymmetry sets the graceful pagoda apart from others in Japan. An American who was charmed by Japanese art in the late 19th century described the pagoda's roofs as "frozen music."

The main Buddha of the temple, called the Medicine Buddha or Buddha of Healing, is flanked by two guardian Bodhisattvas, Nikko (Sunlight) and Gakko (Moonlight). The graceful statues are swinging their upper bodies outward as though they are putting weight on one foot only, a clear indication that they were influenced by sculpture from India that was transmitted through China. *Yakushi-ji's treasure house is open only October 20 to November 10 and January 1-10. The temple itself is open daily 8:30am to 5pm. ¥500.*

Toshodai-ji Temple, a ten minute walk north of Yakushi-ji, contains some of the few remaining 8th century buildings in Nara, including the masterpiece **Kondo**, the Golden Hall. The Emperor Shomu desperately wanted a Chinese monk to come to Japan to establish monasteries and ordain monks. Monks hesitated to come to an undeveloped country across a treacherous sea, but after a ten-year search, the respected master Ganjin agreed. He had to endure five unsuccessful sea crossings over seven years, and he finally arrived in 754, blind and 67 years old. Ganjin immediately set about training monks. In 762 he ordained Japanese monks at Todai-ji in the presence of the emperor and the imperial court. Ganjin became disillusioned by the secular nature of the monks in Nara's existing temples. With the empress' assistance, he founded Toshodai-ji in 759. The temple's most famous treasure, the dry lacquer statue of Ganjin in the Mieido, is unfortunately shown only one day a year, June 6, the anniversary of Ganjin's death. His blind eyes closed, the Master Ganjin is in deep meditation yet his face still shows emotion.

The Kondo houses a 3.3 meter Buddha, sculpted by the Chinese artists who accompanied Ganjin. The large halo around the Buddha once held 1000 Buddhist images; 864 remain today.

The **Kodo**, lecture hall, sits behind the Kondo. This building from 710, more Japanese in style (note the horizontal nature of the roof lines), was once at the Heijo Imperial Castle and was a gift from the empress. *Toshodai-ji is open daily 8:30am to 4:30pm. ¥600.*

For a change from seeing temples, visit the nearby crafts center. Cross the train tracks at Nishino-kyo Station and turn right, walking north, parallel to the tracks for about a block. The **Ganko Ittetsu Nagaya** is a series of buildings that has artisans working on the 1000-year-old crafts Nara has been producing: ceramics, tea utensils, masks, wood sculpture, seal making and bamboo crafts. Their finished objects are for sale. Across the street is the **Sumi no Shiryokan** that is used for demonstrations of making the black-stick ink used in calligraphy and painting. Nara produces 90% of Japan's black ink. *Open 10am to 5pm. Closed Monday. ¥500 for admission to both places.*

About 10 minutes on foot north of Toshodai-ji is the **tomb mound of Emperor Suinin**. This tomb is believed to be the first to bury clay Haniwa figures as stand-ins for real people and animals. Other than a large mound covered with trees and surrounded by a moat, there's little to see. Imperial tomb mounds dot Nara's countryside but Suinin's has the distinction of being easy to reach. You can get a good view from the Kintetsu train right by Amagatsuji Station, between Nishino-kyo and Saidaiji Stations.

Horyu-ji Area

To reach the Horyu-ji area, you can take the JR Kansai Honsen line from JR Nara Station to Horyuji Station, about 15 minutes. Since the JR Nara Station is fairly inconvenient, you can also take bus # 52, 97 or 98 from Kintetsu Nara Station to Horyuji-mae stop, about 55 minutes. From the Nishino-kyo area, bus #52, 97 or 98 take about 35 minutes.

Horyu-ji is the granddaddy of Buddhist temples, the cradle of Japanese Buddhism. Prince Shotoku established the temple in 607 on the site of his residence. The prince was instrumental in establishing Buddhism as the underpinning of the state. He was the son of an emperor but never became emperor himself although he ruled Japan for 30 years as regent for his aunt, Empress Suiko. This ardent scholar of Buddhism is still revered by Japanese today.

Prince Shotoku's Horyu-ji Temple burned down in 670 and it took another 40 years to rebuild. Three buildings: the main hall, the pagoda and the Chumon Gate remain from this era, making them the oldest wooden buildings in Japan and some of the oldest in the world.

You will enter Horyu-ji through the **Nandai Mon gate**, constructed in the 15th century. Next you reach the ancient **Chumon gate**, a graceful two-storied structure with one black and one white guardian that symbolize light and darkness. These guardians have survived since 711.

Inside the walls of the inner compound are the **pagoda** to the west and the **Kondo** (Golden Hall) to the east, the **lecture hall** up front, and **sutra hall** and **bell tower** at the rear. Entering through the Chumon, you can see the three main buildings of the temple simultaneously — in most temples, the buildings are lined up behind one another. Blowing in the breeze, the *noren* curtains at the lecture hall add a graceful touch as does the half-opened east cloister. The five-storied pagoda towers over the area, and the tapering of the rooftops makes it look even taller. Horyu-ji's monochrome buildings photograph best in black and white.

The Kondo is an excellent example of Asuka period (552-645) architecture although it was built after the era ended. The Kondo's art treasures are some of Japan's most famous. The Shaka Triad in the center was made in 623 by Kuratsukuri no Tori, Japan's first bronze sculptor. To the right is the Yakushi Buddha, the Buddha of Healing, made in 607 by Tori. To the left is the Amida Buddha, a relative youngster, made in the 13th century. Fantastic murals painted in the 8th century once covered the interior walls of the Kondo but a fire in 1948 destroyed them. The reproductions now on the walls do little justice to the originals.

After you leave the inner courtyard, go into the **Daihozoden** (treasure hall), aptly named because the temple overflows with treasures. Among the most notable items are Gigaku masks used in religious dances; the 7th century Yumetagae Kannon, the dream-changing Bodhisattva who changes your nightmares into pleasant dreams; the Kudara Kannon that either came from Korea or was made by a Korean sculptor; the Tamamushi-no-zushi portable shrine from the mid 7th century, made of camphor and cypress woods, inlaid with the wings of tamamushi beetles, and painted with scenes from the Jataka tales (stories of the Buddha's previous lives that are not represented in later Japanese art); and reproductions of the destroyed Kondo murals.

You may think you have seen all of Horyu-ji, but follow the corridor to the **To-in**, Eastern Temple, which exists because of the tragic events that occurred at Horyu-ji. Prince Shotoku's son wished to become emperor, but court intrigue prevented him. He escaped to Horyu-ji but was attacked; and he and all his family committed suicide. The Eastern Temple was built to appease the spirits of Shotoku's family. The octagonal **Yumedono**, Hall of Dreams, is built at the place Prince Shotoku would sit and meditate, trying to understand difficult sutra passages. Among other images, the hall contains the Guze Kannon, a "secret image," which, historically, even the abbot did not see. This policy changed in the early Meiji period when the statue was unwrapped. Today it is on view annually from April 11 until May 15 and October 22 to November 20. *Horyu-ji is open daily 8am to 4:30pm. ¥1000.*

Just beyond Horyu-ji's To-in sits **Chugu-ji Temple**, the residence of Prince Shotoku's mother. After her death, it became a convent. The main hall houses an exquisite masterpiece, the meditating Miroku Buddha, the Buddha of the Future. While Buddhas can be female, most are depicted as male. This statue conveys maternal tenderness and has a profoundly serene expression. Her right hand is beneath her chin, her leg folded in a half-lotus position. The statue expresses sincere devotion and compassion and is quite moving. The Miroku Buddha is so famous it graces a postage stamp.

Also in the main hall are fragments of the Tenjukoku Mandala, woven by court ladies after Prince Shotoku's death. *Open 9am to 4pm. ¥400.*

If you think you can would like to see one more temple, walk about 15 minutes from the back of Chugu-ji to **Horin-ji Temple**. The temple was one of three built after Horyu-ji burned down in 670, but none of the buildings is original. The pagoda is a replica of the one struck by lightning in 1940. The main hall contains treasures from the Nara era.

. To return to central Nara, you can catch a bus at Chuguji-mae or Horyuji-mae.

Saidai-ji Area

While most first-time visitors to Japan may not have the time to explore this area, return visitors should make the effort.

Take the Kintetsu train from Kintetsu Nara Station two stops to Saidaiji Station, about 5 minutes.

Akishino Dera Temple, a 15-minute walk from Saidaiji Station or a short taxi ride, is the last temple built by the rulers during the Nara period. Constructed from 776 through 780, the main hall, designated a National Treasure, is noted for an array of Buddhist statues from the Heian and Kamakura periods. The most famous is the Buddha of Arts — the head from the Nara period and the body from Kamakura. We like the temple's quiet setting in the midst of a residential area. *Open 9:30am to 4:30pm. ¥400.*

Saidai-ji Temple, literally Great Western Temple, was the complement to Todai-ji, "Great Eastern Temple," but while Todai-ji has been able to retain at least some semblance of its former greatness, Saidai-ji has not. Ravaged by fire, the remaining halls are Edo period constructions. The four guardian hall contains an 11-headed Kannon and four guardian statues, all designated Important Cultural Properties. *Open 8:30am to 4:30pm. ¥400.*

Yamato Bunkakan. This museum housed in a modern building holds an excellent collection of Japanese and Asian art belonging to the founder of Kintetsu Railroad. Exhibits rotate at regular intervals. *1-11-6 Gakuen Minami. Tel. (0742)45-0544. Open 10am to 5pm, but enter by 4pm. Closed*

Monday and December 28 through January 4. ¥600. 10-minute walk from Gakuen Station on the Kintetsu train line.

Joruri-ji area

Joruri-ji Temple. Tucked away in a southeast corner of Kyoto Prefecture, Joruri-ji is actually easier to reach from Nara than Kyoto. The remote setting of this 11th century temple has protected it from the countless wars and fires that ravaged Kyoto and Nara. Joruri-ji is the only remaining example of an original Pure Land garden and pond and a Nine States of Amida Hall, both dating from 1150. The three-storied pagoda in the east and the Amida Hall in the west, both designated National Treasures, create an atmosphere more intimate and serene than Byodo-in at Uji, the other famous Pure Land garden. *Open 9am to 5pm March through November; 10am to 4pm December through February. Free admission to the garden, ¥300 to enter the main hall. 25 minutes from Kintetsu Nara Station by bus.*

SHOPPING

Nara has shopping arcades starting at the plaza at Kintetsu Nara Station. The myriad stores sell clothing, souvenirs, crafts, antiques and nearly anything else you may desire. You'll also find fast food and other restaurants here. The following are a few stores we like:

Nakagawa, *31-1 Genrin-in-machi. Tel. (0742)22-1322. Open 11am to 5pm. Closed Sunday.* The store put a stainless steel facade on an old merchant building. The blend of two completely different architectural styles works. The interior is traditional with exposed wooden beams and stucco walls. Nakagawa sells an attractive selection of ceramics and lacquer ware as well as textiles dyed with natural dyes.

Sanrakudo, *7 Tarui-cho. Tel (0742)22-2075. Open daily 9:30am to 10pm.* When the arcade from Kintetsu Nara Station ends, turn left and Sanrakudo is on the right, just before Sarusawa Pond. While the front of the store looks a lot like the other souvenir shops on the street, the interior has a good selection of Nara crafts including masks, dolls, stationery and other items. Go for after-dinner shopping.

EXCURSIONS & DAY TRIPS

You can make a side trip to Tenri, Imai-cho or Asuka in one day. But for Hase, Muro-ji Temple and Yoshino, plan to spend the night.

TENRI

Tenri Station is served by the Kintetsu train line. From the station, take a bus or taxi about 10 minutes or walk for about 20 minutes to reach the huge Tenri-kyo complex.

Seeing the Sights

A stop at Tenri will give you a glimpse into a contemporary Japanese religion. Although hundreds of temples dot the Nara area, most are historic relics. Tenri, the headquarters of **Tenri-kyo**, a "new" religion, is the exception. The entire city, the site of the birthplace of its founder, has grown up around the religion.

Tenri-kyo, founded in the 19th century, claims three million believers today. Originally Tenri-kyo was considered a Shinto religion but in 1880 became part of Buddhism. Huge *torii* gates mark the entrance to large plaza in front of the main hall. The immense central religious hall, with *tatami* mats on the floor, always has believers praying, chanting and performing hand gestures. The religion attracts young people as well as old.

Tenri-kyo tries to eliminate human suffering through medical treatment and spiritual guidance. They emphasize living a happy life and doing works of charity. The grounds are kept immaculate by believers for whom cleaning is a form of worship. The religion runs hospitals, a university, a library and a full range of social services. We were amazed to see so many dormitories in the town, each assigned to a Japanese prefecture or a region of the world. They gladly accommodate any believers.

IMAI-CHO

Use the Yagi Nishiguchi Station on the Kintetsu Kashihara line; if you are starting at Kintetsu Nara Station, you'll have to change trains at Saidaiji Station; it's about 30 minutes.

Where to Eat

SAMPO-AN *Tel. (0744)24-3030. Open from 11am to 2pm; 5pm to 9pm.*
Stop here for delicious original Japanese-style cooking. *Imai sushi* costs ¥300 and *shokado* sets run from ¥1000.

Seeing the Sights

This merchant village from the Tokugawa era is one of the best preserved in Japan. During the turmoil of the 16th century, the True Pure Land Sect, headquartered in Osaka, led a populist movement empowering common people. After they gained control of large sections of the Kanazawa area, they set their sights on greater Osaka. The group set up a temple town under the control of priests and common people and walled it off from the rest of the area, isolating themselves from the turbulence all around.

When Oda Nobunaga, the first of Japan's 16th century unifiers, was struggling to bring the area under his control, Imai-cho was on his enemies' list. Nimble bargaining on the part of the residents, however, spared the town in exchange for tearing down the outer walls and moat.

Under the long period of peace during the Tokugawa era, Imai-cho thrived as a merchant center. Today, over 500 traditional houses survive from the Edo and Meiji periods but because they are lived in, Imai-cho doesn't seem like a museum. But the concentration of houses is so great, you may feel you're on a samurai movie set.

A half-dozen houses have received the Important Cultural Property designation but are open irregularly. The oldest house, **Imanishi Residence**, dates from 1650. You can enter it only April 15 through May 14 and October 15 though November 14. Another noted building, the **Kawai Residence**, is still used as a *sake* brewery and private home. You can tour it for ¥300 but it's safest to have someone call ahead. *Tel. (0744)22-2154. ¥300.*

ASUKA

Asuka is reached by Kintetsu line. From Kyoto or Nara; take the Kintetsu Kashihara line to the terminus (from Kyoto about 70 minutes; 30 minutes from Saidaiji Station in Nara) and change to the Yoshino line (about 10 minutes) to Asuka Station. ¥1230 from Kyoto Station, ¥730 from Kintetsu Nara Station.

Bicycle Rentals

At the station, rent a bicycle for ¥900 a day on weekdays, ¥1000 on weekends; it's the best way to get around the area. For an additional ¥200, you can drop off your bicycle at a different shop. Rent-a-cycle shops are at Asuka station, Oka station and Asukaji-mae bus stop.

Where to Eat

ASUKANO *(Japanese, inexpensive). Close to Ishibutai Kofun. Tel. (074454)4466. Open daily 10am to 4pm.*

Catering to cyclists as well as happy walkers this restaurant is a good place to try *Asuka teishoku* for ¥900. It includes red rice *onigiri* rice balls, thin *somen* noodles and *sake* rice wine.

SAKANOCHAYA *(Japanese, inexpensive). Near Oka Dera Temple. Tel. (074454)3129. Open 11am to 4pm. Closed irregularly in winter.*

Order the set lunch *Sakanochaya teishoku,* which includes noodles, rice with mountain herbs and *warabi mochi,* a sweet made of pounded rice, ¥700.

Seeing the Sights

The quiet plains of Asuka are the cradle of Japanese civilization, the area where the early emperors held court. Asuka has no great cities because the site of the court changed every time an emperor died. Then, in the 7th century, upheaval in Asuka transformed Japanese society. Rival clans slugged it out for domination. The Soga clan gained supremacy for the first time placing Japan under a single rule. At the same time, Japanese rulers soaked up Chinese culture like sponges, adopting Buddhism, Confucianism, the written language and art.

YAMATO, THE SPIRIT OF JAPAN

*The Asuka area is also known as the **Yamato Plain**. The development of Japanese culture in the Asuka area, the heartland of Japan, gave rise to the word "Yamato" as a synonym for the nation of Japan. In modern times Yamato took on the nuance of extreme nationalism; the "Yamato spirit" was used to exhort World War II kamikaze pilots to fly off on their suicide missions and Yamato nadeshiko (a small summer carnation) was used to describe Japanese women: dainty, fragile, and obedient to father, son and husband.*

Asuka is the oldest part of Nara and most of the remains are stone structures, burial mounds and an occasional temple. From Asuka Station, head to the **Takamatsuzuka kofun**, a burial mound excavated in 1972. Bright murals, similar to ones found in Korean burial mounds, decorate the interior walls. The mound was resealed to preserve it, but the nearby **Hekigakan** (Fresco Hall) has an excellent reproduction. *Open 9am to 5pm. Closed Mondays except in April, May, October, and November. Closed February and December 28 through January 3. ¥210.*

Asuka Dera Temple, founded in the late 6th century, is Japan's first Buddhist temple. When Nara became the capital in 710, part of the temple moved and became known as Gango-ji. Asuka Dera, a part that didn't move, houses what is believed to be the oldest Buddhist statue made in Japan. *Open daily 9am to 5:30pm April through September; until 5pm October through March. Closed April 7-9. ¥250.*

Tachibana Dera Temple is on the site of Prince Shotoku's birthplace and **Oka Dera Temple** houses Japan's largest clay Buddhist statue. *Both open daily 8am to 5pm.*

The **Ishibutai Kofun**, probably from the 7th century, is an enormous stone tomb exposed to the elements that offers nothing more than huge rocks placed together. But it gives you a feeling for the structure of the crypts under the many burial mounds that dot the entire Nara area. *Open daily 8:30am to 5pm. ¥200.*

Asuka has many unusual carved stones; their purpose is a mystery to archaeologists. Among them are **Kame Ishi**, shaped like a turtle; **Saru**

Ishi, shaped like monkey men; **Nimen Seki**, a stone with faces carved on both sides; and **Sakabune Ishi**, a circular stone that may have been used to make *sake.*

HASE

The **Hase Dera Temple**, built high on a mountainside, has been attracting pilgrims for centuries. A small town has grown up around the temple.

Take the Kintetsu Kashihara line to Yagi (from Kintetsu Nara Station, take the Kintetsu train to Saidaiji Station and change trains) and at Yagi, change for the train going toward Haibara; get off at Hase Dera, the fifth station. From the station, it's about a kilometer to the temple; a 20-minute walk or you can also take a taxi.

Where to Stay

ITANIYA GRAND HOTEL, *Hase, Sakurai-shi, Nara, 633-0112. Tel. (07444)7-7012, Fax (07444)7-7272. From ¥13,000 per person with two meals. Credit cards.*

Itaniya proves our theory about Japanese hotels: avoid staying in places with "Grand" in the name. But then again, it is the best in town, so there isn't much choice. Itaniya is faded and overpriced. But it does offer hot spring baths so you can relax and soak your tired legs. If you plan to see Muro-ji as well as Hase Dera and need to overnight in one of the two, we recommend you head to Muro-ji.

Hase Dera

In addition to pilgrimages, Hase Dera conjures up visions of flowers to Japanese: cherry blossoms and peonies in spring, hydrangeas in summer, autumn foliage and winter peonies. But Hase offers much more than pretty flowers.

Originally founded by the monk Domyo in 686, Hase Dera heads of a network of 3000 subtemples all over Japan. The temple's most impressive feature is its covered wooden walkways or cloisters that include 399 steps up the mountain to reach the main hall. Lanterns hang every few meters and add to the atmosphere. Shuhozo, the treasure house located part way up, displays some of the temple's treasures but is open only in spring and autumn.

When you finally reach the top, the main hall rewards you with extraordinary views from the terrace that juts out over the mountainside. The third Tokugawa shogun, Iemitsu, rebuilt the hall in 1650. You can't help bumping into pilgrims circling the building again and again; walking around the building is equivalent to making a pilgrimage. *Open 8:30am to 5pm; 9am to 4:30pm October through March. ¥400.*

Close to the temple entrance, many shops sell *kusamochi*, the local sweet made of pounded rice filled with sweet been paste and rolled in steamed herbs.

A LONG TRADITION

*Today Westerners have a stereotyped view of Japanese in tour groups following their flag-toting guides. But traveling is nothing new to Japanese; going on a pilgrimage was a good excuse to hit the road. In the 11th century Hase was a popular pilgrimage for Kyotoites, both aristocrats and common-ers, and they didn't always get along. The court lady Sei Shonagon writes in her **Pillow Book**: "It is very annoying when one has visited Hase Temple and retired to one's enclosure, to be disturbed by a herd of common people who come and sit outside in a row, crowded so close together that the tails of their robes fall over each other in utter disarray." (Translated by Ivan Morris).*

MURO-JI TEMPLE

To reach Muro-ji take the Kintetsu line train to Murojiguchi-ono Station, two stops past Hase Dera Station. If you are traveling from Nara, it takes about 1 hour 15 minutes. From Muroguchi-ono Station, take a bus to Muro-ji, about 15 minutes.

Where to Stay

HASHIMOTOYA RYOKAN, *800 Muro, Muro-mura, Uda-gun, Nara, 633-0421. Tel. (0745)93-2056, Fax (0745)93-2755. From ¥15,000 per person with two meals. No credit cards.*

Located at the base of the wooden bridge leading to Muro-ji, many of the hotel's rooms overlook the river and the temple. The old wooden inn, with only ten rooms, has lots of character. Even if you don't stay there, stop for a delicious lunch on *tatami* mats overlooking the river. Mountain vegetables are the specialty. Have the *ajisai* (hydrangea) set (¥2000), which includes *tororo* (grated mountain potato), mountain vegetables prepared in a variety of ways, soup and rice. *Lunch served 11am to 4pm. Closed Monday and December through March.*

Where to Eat

SHIMAZU, *In front of Muro-ji bus stop. Tel. (0745)93-2700. Open 11am to 8pm. Closed Thursday.*

Shimazu offers good views of the mountains and tasty *kaiseki* fare. A *minikaiseki* meal costs ¥2500. To eat after 5pm, you must make a reservation; dinners run ¥8000 and up. In front is a sweet shop serving green tea ice cream for ¥200.

Seeing the Sights
From the bus stop, walk along the road until you come to the arched wooden bridge crossing the river. Cross the bridge and enter the temple's grounds.

Muro-ji Temple, deep in the mountains, is in an area revered as sacred since ancient times. A monk belonging to Nara's Kofuku-ji Temple built Muro-ji in 780 as thanks for the recovery of the ailing crown prince, who later became Emperor Kammu, the founder of Kyoto. Probably some sort of temple existed even earlier. Since 1694 Muro-ji has officially belonged to the esoteric Shingon sect.

Muro-ji is sometimes called the women's Koya because women, barred from Mt. Koya until the late 19th century, were always welcome. The temple is also known for its rhododendrons and the maple trees' red foliage in autumn.

Like Hase Dera Temple, Muro-ji is a mountain temple and, by necessity, its layout differs from the symmetry of lowland temples. Tall cryptomeria trees grow throughout the temple grounds. Muro-ji's setting, a heavily forested mountain behind it and a small village at its base, is unforgettable.

As you enter the temple you get to the **Mirokudo Hall**, a Kamakura-era structure moved from Kofuku-ji in Nara. The image inside is the Miroku Buddha, the Buddha of the Future, an early Heian period National Treasure, which stands gracefully with a lotus flower in his left hand. Beyond the Mirokudo Hall is the **Kondo**, Golden Hall, an early Heian-period building that dates from the late 8th century. This building, a contrast to the stately temples of Nara and Kyoto that were heavily influenced by Chinese architectural styles, has a delicately shingled roof made of thin sheets of cryptomeria bark. The National Treasure building houses some superb pieces of Heian sculpture including the 11-faced Kannon and the Shakamuni. Make a point of noticing how Shakamuni's clothing is draped, large waves alternate with pointed, shallower waves, an exquisite example of early Heian sculpture. The Taishakuten mandala occupies the wall behind the statues. Esoteric sects stress the use of mandalas; believers use them to meditate, trying to understand the essence of the universe.

Continuing up the stairs, you next reach the **Hondo**, main hall. The Kamakura-era edifice holds the Nyoirin Kannon, a beautiful sculpture depicting the Bodhisattva who eliminates human suffering. Past the Hondo is the **five-storied pagoda**, a dainty structure only 16 meters tall, the smallest pagoda in Japan, yet one of the most photogenic. You'll need to climb about 400 steep stone steps to reach the **Okuno-in**, inner temple, dedicated to Kobo Daishi, founder of the Shingon sect. *Muro-ji is open 8am to 5pm April 11 to September 30; 8am to 4:30pm October, November and March through April 10; 8am to 4pm December through February. ¥400.*

Ono Dera Temple, just a few minutes walk from Murojiguchi-ono train station, is famous for the large Buddha carved in the cliff and for its weeping cherry trees.

YOSHINO

Perched on a ridge of Mt. Yoshino, visitors pack the small village of **Yoshino** in the spring when the 100,000 cherry trees are in bloom. The rest of the year you pretty much have the place to yourself. Mt. Yoshino has four huge groves of cherries, each at a different elevation. The groves lowest on the mountain bloom before the upper ones, stretching the usually brief cherry viewing season to a month.

We like to go there for a quiet getaway. Although Yoshino feels remote, it is only about an hour and a half from Nara City.

Reach Yoshino by taking the Kintetsu Yoshino line to the last stop, Yoshino Station. From Saidaiji Station the trip takes about 1 1/2 hours: take the Kintetsu Kashihara line to its terminus, Kashihara Jingu-mae Station, and switch for the Yoshino line. Make sure you don't get off the train at Yoshino Guchi Station, nine stops before Yoshino Station. From Yoshino Station, take the cablecar for the three-minute ride up the mountain, ¥300. If you want to take a taxi, you must get off at Yoshino Jingu Station, one stop before the terminus (about ¥3000).

For **Tourist Information:** *Tel. (07463)2-8014.*

Where to Stay

YOSHINO HOTEL HO-UN KAN, *Yoshino-machi, Yoshino-gun, Nara, 639-3115. Tel. (07463)2-3001, Fax (07463)2-8633. ¥13,000 per person with two meals. Credit cards.*

The 32 rooms in this traditional Japanese hotel have panoramic views of the mountains and valleys. The interiors use Yoshino cedar and cherry wood. The evening meal emphasizes seasonal ingredients.

SAKO-YA, *Yoshino-machi, Yoshino-gun, Nara, 639-3115. Tel. (07463)2-5155, Fax (07463)2-3002. From ¥15,000 per person with two meals. Credit Cards.*

Located just beyond the Kuromon Gate, near the cable car station, Sako-ya is an attractive Japanese-style inn with an outdoor hot spring bath.

YAGIYA SUIZANSO, *Yoshino-machi, Yoshino-gun, Nara, 639-3115. Tel. (07463)2-3161, Fax (07463)2-8714. ¥12,000 per person with two meals. No credit cards.*

Located just north of Katte Jinja Shrine, the unpretentious inn provides warm hospitality and good local cooking.

NEVER A DULL MOMENT IN YOSHINO

The remote village of Yoshino has been the unlikely setting for dramatic events in Japanese history. The first goes back to the 12th century and involves Minamoto Yoritomo and his brother Yoshitsune. The two fought brilliantly to defeat their rival clan, and Yoritomo went on to establish the first shogunate. Intensely jealous of his younger brother's popularity, Yoritomo exiled Yoshitsune, who fled to Yoshino with his mistress, Shizuka Gozen, a woman famed for her dancing. Yoshitsune got away, but Shizuka Gozen was captured. She danced for her captors on the grounds of Katte Jinja shrine in the center of Yoshino. Yoshitsune ended up in remote Hiraizumi in Tohoku where he eventually committed suicide. Yoshitune's tragic tale is a favorite theme of kabuki and bunraku.

Yoshino next entered center stage in the 14th century. For 150 years, since the establishment of the Kamakura shogunate, Japan had been under a dual form of government. The warrior class called the shots while the emperor's court in Kyoto busied itself with matters of culture and religion. With the collapse of the shogunate in Kamakura, Emperor Godaigo tried to wrestle back power. He incurred the wrath of his strongest general, Ashikaga Takauji, by refusing to name him shogun. Takauji retaliated by putting another emperor on the throne. Godaigo fled to Yoshino and established a court in exile.

For sixty years Japan had two emperors, the Northern (Kyoto) and Southern (Yoshino) courts, until the Southern collapsed. The entire episode further weakened imperial power, the opposite of Godaigo's intentions.

But not every event in Yoshino was tragic. The great unifier Toyotomi Hideyoshi held a giant cherry viewing party here in 1594 inviting all citizens, high and low, young and old, to admire the blossoms and partake of tea. Screen paintings record the event for posterity. Yoshino couldn't have had a better public relations boost – since then it's been one of Japan's most popular cherry viewing places.

CHIKURIN-IN, *Yoshino-machi, Yoshino-gun, Nara, 639-3115. Tel. (07463)2-8081, Fax (07463)2-8088. From ¥15,000 per person with two meals. Credit cards.*

Chikurin-in is an inn at a temple. The Honkan (original building) has charming rooms overlooking the beautiful garden where your meals are served; the guests rooms are in the newer west and south wings. The traditional wooden foyer is like a private residence's entrance; painted screens line the walls.

Where to Eat

YOSHINOYA HONTEN *(Japanese, inexpensive). Located between the Kuromon Gate and the bronze torii gate. Tel. (07463)2-2989. Open 9am to 6pm.* Yoshinoya's specialty is *kakinoha sushi*, pressed *sushi* wrapped in a persimmon leaf — please don't eat the leaf. The leaf acts as a preservative, which explains why it's okay to eat *sushi* in the mountains.

YAKKO *(Japanese, inexpensive). Across from the back exit of Zao-do. Tel. (07463)2-3117.*

A good place for lunch, Yakko offers mountain views and serves *sansai udon* noodles for ¥550 and *zaru soba* with *kakinoha sushi* for ¥1100.

Seeing the Sights

A shuttle bus runs from the cable car station through town, but you are better to go on foot unless you have heavy luggage.

As you walk along Yoshino's main (and virtually only) street, you'll notice houses on the hillside that appear to have only one story. On closer examination, you'll see they have several lower floors built down the side of the mountain. This style is called Yoshino architecture (hillside ranch), built in such a way the entire house enjoys panoramic views.

Kuromon Gate is the first gate you reach as you get off the cable car and is followed by a bronze *torii* gate. The Kuromon is Buddhist, and the *torii* gate is Shinto, showing the close interaction between the two religions for the better part of Japan's history. Further down is the Niomon Gate with the guardian statues for **Kimpusen-ji Temple**. The Niomon, designated a National Treasure, faces north to greet the believers from Kyoto and Osaka. The bottom story of the gate was built in the Southern and Northern Court period while the upper part is from the Muromachi era.

Zao-do, Kimpusen-ji's main hall, claims to be the second largest wooden building in Japan. The temple is a center of Shugendo, a religious tradition combining Shinto, Buddhist and folk beliefs. The priests undergo rigorous training on sacred mountains. Kimpusen-ji has been around since the end of the 7th century; the current Zao-do Hall, a National Treasure, was built in 1455. The 68 pillars that support the building still have the natural shape of trees. *Open 8am to 5pm. ¥400.*

Just past Zao-do is a visitors center with some exhibits and an information booth. Unfortunately, the area prints little information in English.

After the Zao-do, turn to the left and walk down to **Yoshimizu Jinja Shrine**. Once a seminary for mountain priests, it turned into a Shinto shrine in the 19th century when Buddhism was persecuted. The shrine has seen a lot of action: in the late 12th century Yoshitsune bid sad farewell to his mistress Shizuka here; in the mid-14th century Emperor Godaigo designated Yoshimizu as the state shrine; in the late 16th century Toyotomi Hideyoshi admired and held his cherry viewing and tea party here. The beautiful shoin style architecture is the oldest remaining and offers superb views of the Yoshino mountains. *Open 8am to 5pm. To view the inside of the building ¥400.*

Back on the main road, **Katte Jinja Shrine** will be on the right. It's usually deserted except during cherry blossom season. Yoshitsune's mistress Shizuka danced at the shrine. A little walk uphill takes you to **Chikurin-in**, a Buddhist temple known for its beautiful strolling garden that uses the Yoshino mountains as borrowed scenery. The tea master Sen no Rikyu is supposed to have a hand in the garden's design. *Open 8am to 5pm. ¥300.*

After Chikurin-in, the road forks. Go to the left for about a 20-minute walk to **Nyoirin-ji**, a temple established in 901 and the burial place of Emperor Godaigo. *Open 8am to 5pm. ¥400 for Treasure House.*

Back at the fork in the road, you can take a bus up the mountain to **Okusenbon**, the inner grove of cherry trees — about 20 minutes. At the terminus, walk a few minutes up to reach Kimpu Jinja, a tiny, quiet Shinto shrine. Beyond Kimpu Jinja is the trail to the sacred mountain Omine, off limits to women.

You can either take the bus back down or take the hour-long walking trail, passing **Yoshino Mikumari Jinja Shrine**. A popular place to pray for fertility, you'll see cotton circles symbolizing women's breasts and baby clothes hanging as offerings. Toyotomi Hideyoshi came here to pray for an heir and, lo and behold, his favorite mistress produced a son not long after. In gratitude, Hideyoshi's son rebuilt the Momoyama-style shrine in the early 17th century.

22. OSAKA & KOBE

Two of Japan's largest cities bustle with activity from dawn to dusk. **Osaka**, a sprawling commercial city offers excellent museums, soaring postmodern architecture and, tucked away under the modern veneer, traditional culture. **Kobe**, a cosmopolitan port city with a long history of interaction with the outside world, features charming turn of the century Western-style buildings which lend an international flavor. Castle buffs can't miss the small city of **Himeji**, home of the greatest remaining Japanese castle.

Tired of city life? Escape to the 1200 year old Buddhist center atop a mountain — **Mt. Koya** — where you can stay at a Buddhist temple and eat vegetarian cuisine. Or pamper yourself in the hot spring resort of **Arima**.

OSAKA & KOBE AREA HIGHLIGHTS

- *World-class Kaiyukan Aquarium in Osaka*
- *Bunraku puppet theater in Osaka*
- *Temple lodging and cuisine on the sacred mountain, Koya-san*
- *Some of the world's most tender meat, Kobe beef*
- *Superb collection of Chinese ceramics at Museum of Oriental Ceramics*
- *Western-style turn-of-the-century residences on the bluff in Kobe*
- *Rustic hot spring baths in Arima, near Kobe*
- *Soaring, majestic castle at Himeji*

Planning Your Stay

You should spend at least two days in Osaka and one in Kobe. Make a day trip to Himeji (if you are heading to Hiroshima or Kyushu by *shinkansen* train, you can easily stop en route). Overnight at Mt. Koya for a unique temple experience.

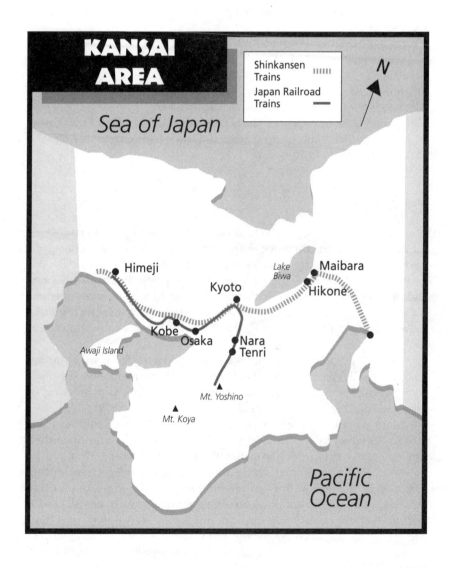

Customize your trip to fit your interests:
- **Museums**: Museum of Oriental Ceramics, Idemitsu Museum, Suntory Museum, National Ethnology Museum, Kobe City Museum
- **Folk Art**: Japan Craft Museum, Japan Folk Craft Museum
- **Traditional Gardens**: Nihon Teien
- **Aquarium**: Kaiyukan
- **Turn of the Century Western Architecture**: Bank of Japan, Nakanoshima Public Hall and Osaka Prefectural Library, Osaka; Kitano district in Kobe
- **Castles**: Himeji, Osaka (reconstruction)
- **Theater**: *Bunraku* puppets, *kabuki*, Takarazuka
- **Shopping**: Kuromon Food Market, Doguya Market, Den Den Town, America Mura and Europe Mura in Osaka; Motomachi in Kobe
- **Spiritual Center**: Koya-san

OSAKA

We want to get the word out: **Osaka** is now a great place to visit. Over the last two decades, the once drab industrial city has made a concerted effort to spruce itself up. And it has paid off. New developments like the **World Trade Center**, **Tempozan** and **Osaka Dome** boast postmodern architecture and have changed the city's skyline. Innovative museums and a state-of-the-art aquarium are prime attractions. Centuries old *bunraku* puppet theater still enchants young and old. And Osaka knows how to eat well.

As Japan's premier commercial city, Japanese from other areas, particularly Tokyo, poke fun at Osaka's merchant mentality. Having a more entrepreneurial spirit than their Tokyo cousins, a greeting in Osaka's dialect is, "Have you made money today?"

Many of Japan's largest trading companies such as Sumitomo and Itochu, founded by individuals, were formed in Osaka and flourished during Japan's rush to modernize in the late 19th century.

As an industrial center Osaka was a prime bombing target during World War II, and few prewar buildings survive. Rapid postwar reconstruction of utilitarian buildings turned Osaka into a pretty ugly place with little aesthetic appeal. Unlike its neighbors Kyoto, Nara and Kobe, Osaka was low on the list of places to visit. But Osaka has been working hard to change its image and attract visitors. To challenge Tokyo's Disneyland, Universal Studios will open there in 2001.

Osaka's history as a commercial center dates back several centuries. During the 1500s, the populist Buddhist sect Ikko established its temple fortress-center and controlled large areas of central Japan. The town grew up around the temple. Oda Nobunaga overthrew the Ikko in 1580 and in 1583, his successor, Hideyoshi, established his castle on the site of the temple. Hideyoshi rose from a common foot soldier to rule Japan, and merchants flourished under his rule. He commanded the merchants of Fushimi and Sakai to move to Osaka. He mandated that taxes were paid in rice, and centralized its collection. Osaka thrived as the distribution point for rice and other commodities.

The Tokugawa defeated Hideyoshi's son in 1615 and consolidated its power by ruling from Edo (Tokyo). The Tokugawa gave Osaka merchants a monopoly on the storage and distribution of rice collected as taxes. Great warehouses once lined Nakanoshima Island.

Osakans, under the fairly benign direct rule of the shogun, were able to run their city independently and never developed an allegiance to a feudal lord as most other places did. In the later part of the feudal era, Osakans opened themselves to Western ideas. Although merchants were on the lowest rung of the feudal social hierarchy, they prospered and loaned large sums of money to the cash-strapped samurai.

With the establishment of the Meiji Government in 1868, the government forgave the debts of the samurai to the merchants. Such a seemingly generous gesture on the part of the government — no cost to it — was a devastating blow to the city's merchants and to the city itself. But Osaka came back, industrializing very quickly.

Incidentally, Osaka is center of the *yakuza*, the Japanese Mafia; but visitors have no reason to fear for their personal safely.

Planning Your Stay

Most people spend a minimum of time in Osaka thinking the city is nothing more than a business center. Don't fall into this trap; the aquarium alone is worth a visit. The castle grounds are lovely but if you have been to Himeji Castle, 40 minutes west of Osaka by *shinkansen,* you will be disappointed by the castle's concrete interior. Osaka has scads of good museums, so they are bound to be at least a handful with exhibitions that pique your interest. If the *bunraku* puppet theater is performing, by all means go. When it comes to food, the many restaurants will keep you fed for several lifetimes.

Highlights of a trip to Osaka are the Osaka Aquarium, *bunraku* theater, the Museum of Oriental Ceramics, the Japan Folk Craft Museum and the Japan Ethnology Museum.

ARRIVALS & DEPARTURES

By Air

International and some domestic flights arrive and depart from the new Kansai International Airport located on a man-made island in Osaka

Bay. Known locally as Itami, Osaka International Airport handles domestic flights. Make sure you know which airport your plane is leaving from; don't be confused by the word "International" in Osaka International Airport. The airports are about 1 1/2 hours apart, so a mistake could be disastrous.

Kansai International Airport

Kansai International Airport handles a large volume of domestic flights in addition to international flights including service to the following cities: Akita, Aomori, Hakodate, Hanamaki, Kagoshima, Kochi, Kumamoto, Matsumoto, Matsuyama, Misawa, Miyazaki, Nagasaki, Niigata, Oita, Okinawa Sapporo, Sendai, Takamatsu, Toyama, Tokyo and Yamagata. Unless you have a connecting flight at Kansai International Airport or have business in the southern part of Osaka, you'll find Osaka International Airport (Itami) more convenient for domestic flights (see below).

For Ground Transportation:

You have a wide range of transportation choices including train, bus and boat. Call the airport's 24-hour information line (English is spoken) for questions on ground transportation as well as flight information. *Tel. (0724)55-2500.*

See information detailed in "Getting to Japan" in Chapter 6, *Planning Your Trip.*

Osaka International Airport (Itami)

Since the opening of Kansai International Airport, Osaka International Airport (Itami) handles only domestic flights; domestic flights also land at Kansai International Airport.

To/from Tokyo Haneda: 9 flights/day (ANA, JAL, JAS. ¥16,250)
To/from Sapporo Chitose: 3 flights/day (ANA, JAL, JAS. ¥30,850)
To/from Sendai: 6 flights/day (ANA, JAL. ¥22,800)
To/from Fukuoka: 5 flights/day (ANA, JAL. ¥15,800)
To/from Kumamoto: 6 flights/day (ANA, JAL. ¥16,850)
To/from Nagasaki: 6 flights/day (ANA, JAL, JAS. ¥18,950)
To/from Miyazaki: 8 flights/day (ANA, JAL, JAS. ¥17,350)
To/from Kagoshima: 9 flights/day (ANA, JAL, JAS. ¥19,650)
Service also to/from Akita, Aomori, Fukushima, Hanamaki, Iwami, Izumo, Kochi, Matsumoto, Matsuyama, Misawa, Niigata, Oita, Okinawa, Takamatsu, Tokushima, Yamagata and Yonago.

For Ground Transportation:
Bus: to Shin Osaka Station (25 minutes, ¥490)
To central Osaka: Abenobashi (Tennoji), 30 minutes; Kintetsu

Uehonmachi, 30 minutes; Kyobashi (OBP) 50 minutes; and Namba Station, 30 minutes; Osaka Station (Umeda), 30 minutes; (all cost ¥620). To Kansai International Airport (80 minutes ¥1700)

Taxi: to Osaka to Shin Osaka Station about ¥3500; to Namba Station about ¥4600

By Train

The JR shinkansen train stops at JR Shin Osaka Station, north of central Osaka but subway connects it to Osaka Station and Namba Station.

To/from Tokyo: by the super-fast *Nozomi* shinkansen takes 2 1/2 hours (¥14,720), the slightly slower *Hikari* takes about 3 hours (¥13,750). In the opposite direction, Osaka is about 2 1/2 hours (¥15,560) from Fukuoka (Hakata) by *Nozomi* and 3 1/2 hours by *Hikari* (¥14,590).

In the greater Osaka Area: Both JR and private train lines provide extensive service in the Osaka area. The JR Tokaido line connects Nagoya and Kyoto with Osaka. The JR Osaka Loop line circumnavigates the city. The Hanshin Main line runs from Kobe to Umeda Station. Hankyu has train lines connecting Umeda Station to Kobe, and Kyoto and Takarazuka. The Kintetsu lines go from Osaka's Namba Station to Nara and on to Kyoto. The Nankai lines head south and take you to Mt. Koya. Subways provide another transportation network within the city.

By Bus

Osaka, a major transportation center, has highway buses to many parts of Japan. The primary bus centers are at Abenobashi near Tennoji, Kintetsu Uehonmachi, O-CAT, and Namba Kaisoku Bus Terminal, and Osaka Station (Umeda). Many of the long-distance buses will stop at least two of these places.

Overnight buses service Beppu (9 hours, ¥9300), Fukuoka (9 hours, ¥10,000), Fukushima (12 hours, ¥12,130), Niigata (9 hours, ¥9450), Hagi (12 hours, ¥9480), Hiroshima (7 hours, ¥6630), Kagoshima (12 hours, ¥12,000), Kumamoto (9 hours, ¥10,300), Miyazaki (12 hours, ¥11,500), Nagano (8 hours, ¥6930), Nagasaki (10 hours, ¥11,000) and Sendai (12 hours, ¥12,230).

By Car

When you arrive in the city of Osaka, do yourself a favor and drop off your rental car as quickly as possible; you really won't want to drive there. Osaka is reached by the Meishin Expressway that runs from Nagoya to Kobe and the Hanshin Expressway Wangan Route that runs from Kansai International Airport following the Osaka Bay shore line to Kobe. The Hanwa Expressway is on the western side of Osaka and runs north-south.

ORIENTATION

Central Osaka divides easily into two areas — *kita* (north) and *minami* (south). The adjacent Umeda and Osaka Stations form the center of northern Osaka while Namba is the heart of the southern part. Subways provide excellent access and the JR Osaka Loop Line rings the city and leads to countless neighborhoods and districts, each with a distinct personality.

GETTING AROUND TOWN

Osaka is a large city connected by a fast and efficient subway, JR and private-train network. At your hotel or a tourist information office, make sure you pick up a transportation map in English.

You may transfer freely among Osaka's seven subway lines and one tram line. Find your destination on the English fare chart that's posted and buy a ticket from the machines for that amount. Children ages 6 through 11 pay half-fare rounded up to the next ¥10; children under six travel free. An adult is only entitled to take two children free of charge.

Don't be daunted by the look of the ticket machines; there's a button to press to get information in English. The machines take ¥1000 notes and some specially marked ones accept ¥5000 and ¥10,000 notes; they also accept coins. The top row of buttons is for one-day passes, rainbow cards and "No-My-Car Day" tickets. To the right of this row is a round button to press for children's fares. Use the buttons in the row below to buy tickets for more than one person at a time. The row below that one is for buying a transfer ticket to the bus or to other train lines such as JR or Hankyu — transfers within the subway system are included in the posted fare. The buttons in the bottom row list fares. Press the button for the fare you need, and remember to take your ticket and your change.

If you make a mistake and pay too much for your ticket, go to the station attendant for a refund. Just tell him *"machigai."* Once you enter the system using the incorrect ticket, you cannot get a refund. If you didn't pay enough, you can always pay the difference to the station attendant as you exit. Make sure you remember to take your ticket from the machine as you enter. Actually, it will remind you with a loud beep. Keep your ticket during the ride and surrender it when you exit. If you have a transfer that necessitates leaving the ticket barriers, show your ticket to the attendant rather than put it in the machine.

One-Day Pass: You can buy a one-day pass, *"ichi nichi joshaken,"* good on subways, local buses, and trams for ¥850 for adults and ¥430 for children ages 6 through 11. Buy it at the ticket machines in each station. The machine at the ticket barrier prints the date on the pass the first time you use it.

Rainbow Cards: stored-value cards in denominations of ¥1000, ¥2000, ¥3000 and ¥5000 for adults and ¥500 and ¥1000 for children. They save you the hassle of having to buy a ticket and figure out the fare every time you use the train. Simply insert the card in the machine at the ticket gate and the subtracted fare is noted on the back. In addition to subways, Rainbow Cards are good on municipal buses and private railways such as Hankyu, Hanshin, Kita Osaka Kyuko and Nose Dentetsu, but not on JR trains.

"No-My-Car Day" passes: Valid on Fridays and on the 20th of each month, this ungrammatically named pass is used on the day when Osaka's citizens are urged to leave their cars at home and take public transportation. If the 20th falls on a Sunday, use the pass on the 21st. The pass works just like a One-Day Pass, good on subways, buses and the tram, but is cheaper — ¥600 for adults.

Tourist Information

The Visitors' Information Centers have English information and English-speaking personnel and are located at the following sites:

JR Osaka Station: *Umeda*. It's a little difficult to locate at the Midosuji East Gate, across the street from the Hankyu Department Store, but the staff is very helpful. *Tel. (06)6345-2189*. Open daily 8am to 8pm.

JR Shin Osaka Station: *at the Central Gate. Tel. (06)6305-3311*. Open daily 8am to 8pm.

JR Tennoji Station: *inside the station. Tel. (06)6774-3077*. Open daily 8am to 8pm.

JR Namba Station. *O-CAT Building, B1. Tel. (06)6643-2125*. Open daily 8am to 8pm.

Home Visit System: Contact one of the Tourist Information Offices listed above to arrange a home visit.

Goodwill Guides: The Osaka Goodwill Guides Club provides volunteer guides. Contact them at the OCAT Satellite, *Tel. (06)635-3143,* or contact one of the Tourist Information Offices listed above.

WHERE TO STAY

Osaka Station, Umeda & Nakanoshima Area

OSAKA HILTON, *1-8-8 Umeda, Kita-ku, Osaka, 530-0001. Tel. (06)6347-7111, Fax (06)6347-7001. Singles from ¥26,000. Twins from ¥32,000. Credit cards.*

The attractively furnished guest rooms feature *shoji* screens and *fusuma* (traditional sliding doors) harmonizing with Western furniture. There is a nonsmoking floor and a business center. The hotel is connected to an upscale shopping mall called the Hilton Plaza that has restaurants on the B2 level and the 6th and 7th floors. We especially like Madonna, the *okonomiyaki* restaurant on B2.

IMPERIAL (TEIKOKU) HOTEL, *1 Tenmabashi, Kita-ku, Osaka, 530-0042. Tel. (06)6881-1111, Fax (06)6881-4111. Twins from ¥27,000. Credit cards.*

Located in Osaka's OAP Park (Osaka Amenity Park), which consists of office and residential buildings and hotels, the Imperial opened in 1996. Every room has fax and computer lines; the 18th floor is nonsmoking. With 12 restaurants, you can find a cuisine to suit your palate. A sports club and shopping mall also are under the same roof. For a change of pace, the hotel's Pata Pata cabaret features a salsa orchestra.

RIHGA ROYAL HOTEL, *5-3-68 Nakanoshima, Kita-ku, Osaka, 530-0005. Tel. (06)6448-1121, Fax (06)6448-4414. Singles from ¥14,000. Twins from ¥26,000. Credit cards.*

Located on the west side of Nakanoshima Island, the 30-storied Royal Hotel has many restaurants including a branch of the famous Japanese restaurant Kitcho. The soothing, soft beige decor provides a refuge from the city outside. An extensive shopping mall in the hotel complex sells everything you may want.

HOTEL GRANVIA OSAKA, *3-1-1 Umeda, Kita-ku, Osaka, 530-0001. Tel. (06)6344-1235, Fax (06)6344-1130. Singles from ¥13,500. Twins from ¥24,000. Credit cards.*

At the JR Osaka Station on the 21st to 26th floors of the Daimaru Building, Hotel Granvia boasts an excellent location at this transportation nexus. The rooms are high up and very quiet. Most of the guests are businessman, so they have a lot of single rooms. In addition to the hotel restaurants, the Daimaru Building is overflowing with restaurants, and you can go into the underground arcade of Umeda without going outside; actually it's a whole underground city.

Shin Osaka Station Area

HOTEL MIELPARQUE OSAKA, *4-2 Miyahara, Yodogawa-ku, Osaka, 532-0003. Tel. (06)6350-2111, Fax (06)6350-2117. Singles from ¥6800. Twins from ¥13,000. Credit cards (no Amex or MasterCard).*

This reasonably-priced hotel, which opened in 1990, features pastel colored rooms. The hotel also has some Japanese-style rooms.

Osaka Castle Area

HOTEL NEW OTANI, *1-4-1 Shiromi, Chuo-ku, Osaka, 540-8578. Tel. (06)6941-1111, Fax (06)6941-9769. Singles from ¥18,000. Twins from ¥29,000. Credit cards.*

The hotel is not in the center of the business district but offers spectacular views of Osaka Castle; if an expansive view is more important than a central location, the New Otani is for you. The 12th floor is nonsmoking. Windows in all the rooms open, albeit not very wide. The fitness room is well equipped as is the business center.

Shinsaibashi - Namba Area

HOLIDAY INN NANKAI OSAKA, *2-5-15 Shinsaibashi suji, Chuo-ku, Osaka, 542-0085. Tel. (06)6213-8281, Fax (06)6213-8640. Singles from ¥14,500. Doubles from ¥22,500. Credit cards.*

Located near Dotonbori, the Holiday Inn is very convenient for business and pleasure and yet still quiet. Even the single rooms have double-sized beds. The hotel has various restaurants, including a branch of Sanda-ya that serves Kobe beef. There's a swimming pool on the roof.

D-HOTEL, *2-5-15 Dotonbori, Chuo-ku, Osaka, 542-0071. Tel. (06)6212-2995, Fax (06)6212-7462. Doubles from ¥18,000. Credit cards.*

Very contemporary, D-Hotel is a pleasant change from the standard Western-style hotel. We love the stylishly minimalist rooms. D-Hotel's location in the active Dotonbori area puts tons of restaurants, bars and night spots at your doorstep.

RIHGA ROYAL HOTEL YOTSUBASHI, *1-10-12 Shinmachi, Nishi-ku, Osaka, 550-0013. Tel. (06)6534-1211, Fax (06)6534-6360. Singles from ¥8800. Twins from ¥15,000. Credit cards.*

Slightly north of the Shinsaibashi area, this comfortable hotel caters to business travelers. Each room comes equipped with a fax machine and a pants presser.

Kansai International Airport

HOTEL NIKKO KANSAI KUKO, *1 Kuko-kita, Izumisano, Osaka, 549-0001. Tel. (0724)55-1111, Fax (0724)55-1155. Singles from ¥19,000. Twins from ¥28,000. Credit cards.*

Located at Kansai International Airport, this hotel is a convenient place to spend the night when you have an early flight.

HOTEL SUN PLAZA, *3-3-4 Minato, Izumisano, Osaka, 598-0063. Tel. (0724)61-2911, Fax (0724)61-2921. Singles from ¥6200. Twins from ¥18,000. Credit cards.*

A less expensive alternative to the Nikko, this hotel is also convenient when you want to spend the night close to Kansai International Airport — about a 15 minute drive. The hotel has Western as well as Japanese rooms.

WHERE TO EAT

The Japanese have an expression: *"Kyoto kidaore; Osaka kuidaore,"* Kyoto-ites bankrupt themselves buying kimono and Osakans bankrupt themselves by eating out. There are countless restaurants in the city.

Underground and street-level arcades, restaurant buildings, shopping malls, small alleys and department stores all house restaurants to match every budget and taste. Here's a sampling of our favorites.

Osaka & Umeda Stations Area

The huge terminals have restaurants on the street level as well as in underground malls. Even Osaka people get lost in the maze, so pay attention to the signs. Even upscale restaurants are underground.

KITCHO (*Kaiseki, moderate to expensive*). *3-1-1 Umeda, Kita-ku. Tel. (06)6347-0380. Open 11am to 2pm; 4pm to 8pm.*

A branch of the famous Japanese restaurant, the chef received a cultural achievement award from the emperor. At the main shop, a meal can set you back ¥50,000. At this branch located on the 14th floor of Umeda Daimaru Department Store, the lunchtime *kisetsu tenshin* courses start at ¥4000. Taking into consideration the freshness of the ingredients, the beautiful ceramic plates and the excellent service, the price is quite reasonable. Kitcho's menu changes every month. *Kaiseki* dinner courses start at ¥12,000.

SHIRUHISA (*Kushikatsu, expensive*). *B1, Umeda OS Hotel, 2-11-5 Sonezaki, Kita-ku. Tel. (06)6312-2703. Open 5pm to 9:30pm. Closed Sunday, holidays and the 3rd Monday.*

At the entrance a *noren* (hanging curtain) welcomes you. Shiruhisa serves *kushikatsu*, deep fried morsels on a stick. Sit down at the counter, but don't worry about ordering because the staff automatically start bringing you sticks of food. Let them know when you've had enough. The average person eats about 20 sticks, but they have a repertoire of 40 including beef, shrimp, salmon, vegetables, and white fish wrapped in *shiso* leaves. With *sake* the average check is about ¥6000 per person.

ASHOKA (*Indian, inexpensive to moderate*). *B2, Osaka Maru Building, 1-9-20 Umeda, Kita-ku. (same building as Tower Records). Tel. (06)6346-0333. Open 11:30am to 2:30pm; 5pm to 9pm; Sunday and holidays open only in the evening. Closed 2nd Tuesday.*

Walk into Ashoka and the smell of the pungent spices transports you to India. The food is authentic Indian with few compromises for the Japanese palate. The full course Ashoka dinner costs ¥4800, but you can also order a la carte. Tandoori chicken is available and you can order take-out food for a picnic.

MADONNA (*Okonomiyaki, inexpensive*). *B2, Hilton Plaza, 1-8-16 Umeda, Kita-ku. Tel. (06)6347-7371. Open daily 11am to 9:30pm.*

This small eatery serves *okonomiyaki*, a decidedly down home dish. Sit at the counters or at a table and cook your pancake, vegetable and meat/fish concoction on the gleaming steel grill in front of you. *Okonomiyaki* costs ¥1000 to ¥1350, depending on the ingredients. *Yakisoba* (fried Japanese noodles) is also served.

OTOYA *(Okonomiyaki, inexpensive). 5F, Itoya Building, 1-6-21 Sonezaki Shinchi, Kita-ku. Tel. (06)6341-2891. Open 5pm to 11pm. Closes 9:30pm on Saturday. Closed Sunday and holidays.*

This *okonomiyaki* restaurant dates to 1937 and used to have a lot of *geisha* as customers when Sonezaki was a pleasure quarter. Don a bib to keep your clothes clean. The mixed *okonomiyaki* includes pork, octopus, shrimp and vegetables and costs ¥1080. The recipe for Itoya's special sauce is so closely guarded it might as well be a state secret. Cost depends on ingredients, but *yakisoba* (fried noodles) starts at ¥980.

MANDOLINO *(Italian, inexpensive). 1F, Daini Sanki Building, 1-6-28 Sonezaki Shinchi, Kita-ku. Tel. (06)6345-3007. Open 11:30am to 2pm; 5:30pm to 9:30pm. Closed Sunday.*

Large portions and reasonable prices for good Italian fare make this casual Italian restaurant popular. The signature dish is spaghetti *watarigani* (with crabs) for ¥1450. The emphasis is on Southern Italian cooking with lots of tomato and seafood sauces.

EATING YOUR WAY THROUGH OSAKA

Some of Osaka's favorite dishes follow:

Udon suki: udon noodles, seafood, vegetables and meat cooked in broth in a stew pot at your table.

Takoyaki — we call them octopus balls. A thin pancake-like batter is poured into a round iron mold and chunks of octopus is added. A special sauce tops off the cooked balls. Takoyaki is often sold from street stalls.

Okonomiyaki is sometimes called Japanese pizza, but frankly we don't see the connection other than it's round. You sit in front of a grill on which vegetables, seafood and meat cook; they're held together by thin pancake batter.

Oshizushi is Osaka's rendition of sushi. Fish and vinegared rice are put in a rectangular mold, pressed into a long block, and sliced into normal sushi-sized pieces.

Shin Osaka Station

Inside the station are many small restaurants. On the first floor are branches of Mimiu, famous for its *udon suki;* Kushitaro for *kushikatsu;* and Kawakyu for traditional Japanese food. Shikai Hanten, a Chinese restaurant, is on the second floor.

Nakanoshima-Yodoyabashi Area

MIMIU HONTEN *(Udon noodles, moderate).4-6-18 Hirano-cho, Chuo-ku. Tel. (06)6231-5770. Open 11:30am to 8:30pm. Closed Sunday.*

Try *udon suki,* one of Osaka's best known dishes, at the place that made it famous. *Udon* noodles, shrimp, chicken, clams and seasonal vegetables cook in a tasty broth at your table. The *udon* noodles are made with special flour so they won't fall apart when cooked. *Udon suki* costs ¥3300; an *udon suki* set meal runs ¥5500.

YOTARO HONTEN *(Japanese, moderate). 2-3-14 Koraibashi, Chuo-ku. Tel. (06)6231-5561. Open 11:30am to 8pm. Closed Sunday and holidays.*

Tai gohan (sea bream rice) is the specialty here. Rice is placed in a clay pot, and a whole grilled sea bream is cooked on top. The staff brings the pot to your table so you can see how it's cooked; and the fish is boned and mixed it into the rice. You need a minimum of two people to order *tai gohan* (¥2700 per person). Yotaro also serves *tempura* and *sashimi.*

Shinsaibashi-Namba Area

Dotonbori, a busy entertainment area along the canal, symbolizes the typical Osaka zest for eating. Colorful neon lights beckon you to the district where restaurants, bars, and *pachinko* and karaoke parlors all jam together. You can't miss the huge mechanical crab at **Kani Doraku restaurant**, the most famous landmark of the area. The alleys around Dotonbori are crammed with tiny bars, hole-in-the-wall restaurants and peep shows, but the area isn't unsavory. During the day shoppers come for inexpensive food, but you must come at night for the full neon effect.

ALONG THE OLD CANAL

Dotonbori dates from 1612 when a prominent merchant, Mr. Doton, financed the construction of a canal to serve as its main transportation route. Doton himself was killed in the Battle of Osaka in 1615, but his successors completed the canal in the 1620s. During the Edo Period, directly south of Dotonbori, five theaters bustled with activity from morning until late at night. Boats on the canal disgorged theater patrons. One of the five theaters was Naniwa-za, the birthplace of **bunraku** *puppet theater.*

TAKOUME *(Oden, moderate). 1-1-8 Dotonbori, Chuo-ku. Tel. (06)6211-0321. Open 5pm to 10pm. Closed Sunday. Entrance has a large blue and white noren curtain with "Takoume" written in Japanese.*

This traditional restaurant with a 150-year history looks out of place among its modern neighbors; upon entering you take a step back into old Osaka. The restaurant has only 20 seats at the counter. Takoume's specialty is *oden,* a large soup pot with a variety of ingredients boiling in it — fish cakes, eggs, fried *gobo* patty, *daikon* radish, squid, etc. You choose what you'd like to eat by pointing at it. The cost varies from ¥100 to ¥1450 depending on the food. An average bill runs about ¥3000 with *sake* or beer.

DAIKOKU *(Japanese, moderate). 2-2-7 Dotonbori, Chuo-ku. Tel. (06)6211-1101. Open 11:30am to 3pm; 5pm to 8pm. Closed Sunday and holidays.*

Paper lanterns hanging from the eaves mark this restaurant that has been in business since the turn of the century. For ¥450, Daikoku serves *kayaku gohan,* individually steamed bowls of rice with thinly fried tofu, vegetables, soy sauce and *sake.* Daikoku also serves grilled fish such as yellowtail *(buri)* and sea bream *(tai)* and homestyle cooked vegetables called *nitsuke.* You can order a la carte. This reasonably priced restaurant is popular among the young as well as their seniors. Since it's crowded at lunchtime, be prepared to share a table.

IMAI *(Japanese, inexpensive). 1-7-22 Dotonbori, Chuo-ku. Tel. (06)6211-0319. Open 11am to 9pm. Closed Wednesday.*

Imai serves a combination of Osaka *udon* noodles in broth and a bowl of rice cooked with seasonal favorites: peas in spring, fragrant *shiso* leaves in summer, chestnuts in autumn and oysters in winter. *Anago udon* has eel served on top of the *udon* noodles in broth and costs ¥1100. *Yonaki udon* with shredded fried tofu plus bonito flakes in the broth is ¥650.

NIWA-TORI *(Yakitori, inexpensive). 1-7-7 Dotonbori, Chuo-ku. Tel. (06)6211-1519. Open 5pm to 10pm. Closed Sunday.*

At this friendly *yakitori* shop, you can sit at the counter and watch the chef grilling the chicken. Since the cooking is done over a charcoal fire, don't come dressed in your best silk. A set of 13 sticks costs ¥3000; you can also order a la carte.

IL GEMELLO *(Italian, inexpensive). 2F, Daiki Building, 2-4-8 Nishi Shinsaibashi, Chuo-ku. Tel. (06)6211-9542. Open 5:30pm to 12 midnight. Lunch 11:30am to 2:30pm weekends only. Closed Monday.*

The chefs were all trained in Rome. This cheerful and bright restaurant has good Italian food at reasonable prices. The *buccatini* with Italian bacon in tomato sauce is delicious and costs ¥1300. The weekend lunch courses start at ¥800.

SEEING THE SIGHTS

Osaka Castle Area

Osaka Castle (Osaka-jo). *Open 9am to 5pm. Closed at New Year's. ¥600 entrance to the keep. 7-minute walk from JR Osaka-jo Koen Station or Tanimachi 4-chome subway station.* Osaka Castle, one of the city's most popular attractions, is beautiful from afar but a disappointment when you actually enter the reconstructed castle keep. Spend some time here only if you aren't able to get to Himeji or need to see some green open space.

Some of the buildings surviving from the Tokugawa era are noteworthy. After you enter through the massive Otemon main gate built in 1629, you'll come to the Tamon tower built about the same time. Both are designated Important Cultural Properties. Nishinomaru, the large area between the moats, contains two Tokugawa-era guard towers, the Sengan and Inui, as well as the Ensho-gura, an ammunition storehouse made of stone. The Japanese garden, the site of Hideyoshi's official wife's residence, has lots of blossoms including cherries, azaleas and chrysanthemums. *Garden open 9am to 4:30pm, closed Monday and rainy days, ¥200.*

From the Nishi-no-maru, go through the Sakuramon gate; note the 130-ton Octopus Stone, the castle's largest, that leads into the Honmaru, the inner section of the castle. Try to ignore the offensive souvenir stands and eateries and appreciate the beauty of the exterior of the reconstructed castle. Remember that no attempt was made to build the interior architecturally accurate, so don't be disappointed. Ride up the elevator (yes, elevator!) to the 8th floor for a magnificent panoramic view of Osaka; contemplate the power Hideyoshi must have felt when he surveyed his territory. The lower floors of the keep display armor, Hideyoshi's letters and other paraphernalia as well as photos and models relating to the castle and Osaka.

Osaka City Museum (Osaka Shiritsu Hakubutsukan) is also in the Honmaru, south of the castle keep. This Western-style building, vaguely based on German castles, was the regional headquarters for the Imperial Army but escaped bombing damage during World War II. Today the museum houses exhibits relating to Osaka including excavated objects from the 7th century Naniwa Palace. Check out the contents of a time capsule buried in front of the museum at the time of the Osaka Expo in 1970; a replica is on view in the museum. *Tel. (06)6941-7177. Open 9:30am to 5pm; closed Monday. ¥300.*

Aqua Liner. This low-lying, glass-topped boat cruises the Yodo River and is especially popular in cherry blossom season. The boat stops at Osaka Castle Pier, Tenmabashi Bridge, Yodoyabashi Bridge and OAP (Osaka Amenity Park) Pier at the Imperial Hotel. A tape in English provides a translation of the running Japanese commentary. *Boats depart once an hour between 10am and 5pm, until 7pm on weekends and in the warmer months. The cruise takes one hour. ¥1830.*

Osaka Business Park (OBP). Across the river from the castle, on the delta formed by the confluence of two rivers, a high-rise business development was built by some of Japan's corporate giants including Fujitsu, NEC and Matsushita (see Panasonic Square, below). With attractive plazas and public spaces, the contemporary office buildings make for a nice stroll of a corporate *Who's Who*.

Panasonic Square is a paean to high-tech development and is filled with interactive electronics equipment and school-age children. Visit to see the latest technology, but avoid weekends and holidays. *Tel. (06)6949-2122. 2F, Twin 21, National Tower. Open daily 10am to 6pm. ¥500.*

OSAKA CASTLE

Osaka Castle has a long and violent history. In 1532 Ikko, a Buddhist sect, built Ishiyama Hongan-ji Temple on the site. Ostensibly a religious center, the Ikko sect was actually a highly armed force that controlled large areas of central Japan. And the temple was really a fortress. It took Oda Nobunaga, first of Japan's three great unifiers, 10 years to subdue the temple and ultimately, in 1580, he did so only by negotiating a settlement.

Toyotomi Hideyoshi, the great unifier who succeeded Nobunaga, chose to build his main castle and residence on the Hongan-ji site between 1583 and 1587. Thousands of laborers worked to build the grandest castle in the land – at one point, feudal lords supplied 50,000 men; the site contained 48 large towers and 76 smaller ones, and the outer moat was 12 kilometers long. Over 10,000 boatloads of rock arrived each day during the peak of construction. The walls were the most extensive constructed in a Japanese castle; some were over 20 meters in height and featured musket loopholes at the top. The castle's keep rose eight stories and was topped by gold dolphins and gold-leaf roof tiles. Paintings of cranes and tigers adorned the exterior walls of the top floor.

Hideyori, Hideyoshi's son and heir, moved to Osaka Castle after his father's death in 1598. Tokugawa Ieyasu, regent to the young son, quickly usurped power. The control of Osaka Castle was the last impediment to his domination of Japan. In the winter of 1614, he laid siege to the castle, surrounding it with 200,000 men. Despite these overwhelming numbers, Ieyasu could not win and negotiated a settlement with Hideyori. As an act of good faith, Hideyori demolished the outer moat of the castle only to have Ieyasu renege and attack the castle in 1615. This time Ieyasu was victorious, the castle was left in ruins and Hideyori and his mother committed suicide. Ieyasu's control of the country was complete.

Tokugawa rebuilt the castle in the 1620s, albeit not on such a grand scale, and it remained under shogunate control until the end of the feudal period in 1868. A fire in 1660 destroyed the castle's keep, which was not rebuilt until the 1840s. In 1868 most of the castle's buildings were destroyed in the civil war that overthrew the feudal government. The present castle, a 1931 concrete reconstruction, is based on screen paintings of Hideyoshi's masterwork.

Fujita Museum (Fujita Bijutsukan). The art collection of Baron Fujita, a captain of industry during the Meiji period, is displayed in the store-houses that were once part of his residence. This outstanding collection of Japanese and Chinese art has 45 pieces designated either as a National Treasure or an Important Cultural Property. Only a small part of the collection is on display at any one time. The garden, complete with a pagoda from Mt. Koya and a teahouse, makes for a pleasant stroll. *Tel. (06)6351-0582. Open 10am to 4pm. Closed Monday and closed early June until mid-September and early December until mid-March. ¥700.*

Osaka Mint and Museum (Okura-sho Zohei Kyoku). When the first mint in Japan opened in 1871, the employees had samurai hair styles, complete with a topknot, but wore Western dress to show they were modern. The museum displays notes and coins from all over the world. To tour the mint and actually see yen created before your very eyes, you must make a reservation at least 10 days in advance: *Tel. (06)6351-5361. 9am to 2:30pm. The museum is open 9am to 3:30pm. Closed Saturday, Sunday and holidays. Admission free. 5-minute walk from Tenmabashi Station.*

Nakanoshima Area

Nakanoshima, an island in the Dojima River, sports a view that could have rivaled the Seine if it weren't for an expressway built along the river. The island has some attractive Meiji-era buildings and some top museums. It is within walking distance (10 minutes) of JR Osaka Station and Umeda Station and is served by the Midosuji subway (Yodoyabashi Station) and the Yotsubashi subway (Higobashi Station).

Museum of Oriental Ceramics (Toyo Toji Bijutsukan). This unassuming brick building contains a world-class collection of Chinese and Korean ceramics collected by Mr. Ataka, founder of one of the biggest trading companies in Japan. He got so involved in collecting ceramics that his company went bankrupt and was absorbed into Sumitomo. Fortunately Sumitomo donated his collection to Osaka City. The display includes a spectacular Southern Sung black tea bowl and a Yuan celadon vase. In addition to the permanent display, a small room has temporary shows. A tea room on the first floor serves a light lunch. *Tel. (06)6223-0055. Open 9:30am to 5pm. Closed Monday. ¥500. 5-minute walk from Yodoyabashi subway station on Midosuji Line.*

Nakanoshima Central Hall (Chuo Kokaido) is next to the Ceramics Museum. Built in 1918 by Western-trained architect Okada Shin-ichiro, the hall is Neo-Renaissance style. The building is open to the public and has a restaurant in the basement. Next door is the Roman Revival-style **Osaka Prefectural Library** designed by Noguchi Magoichi in 1904. Continue along the river, cross Midosuji Boulevard and you reach the **Bank of Japan**. The Western-style main building was built in 1903; behind it is a tasteful 1982 addition. In April, walk along by the river to enjoy some of Osaka's nicest cherry blossoms.

Science Museum of Osaka (Osaka Shiritsu Kagakukan). The oval glass and tile building was completed in 1989. Kids love the high-tech exhibits. The Science Theater doubles as a Planetarium and Omnimax theater, and both are well worth the price of admission. *Tel. (06)6444-5656. Open 9:30am to 4:45pm. Closed Monday and December 28 through January 4. ¥400 for exhibitions; Omnimax and Planetarium ¥600 each. Yotsubashi Subway to Higobashi Station.*

Teki-juku, a small wooden structure sandwiched between tall buildings, is one of the few traditional merchant houses that has survived. In 1838, Ogata Koan, a noted doctor, established his famous school in this building. He studied Western medicine in Nagasaki and, with his colleagues, translated Dutch medical books to provide the first insight into Western medicine. Many of his students went on to lead the movement to westernize Japan. The first floor was Ogata's residence while the second was the school and dormitory. *Tel. (06)6231-1970. Open 10am to 4pm. Closed Sunday, Monday, holidays and December 28 through January 3. ¥220. 5-minute walk from Yodoyabashi subway station.*

FOR A CHANGE OF PACE...

Looking for something different? Bored with Japanese screens, samurai armor and Chinese ceramics? Here are two that might be of interest:

Wine Museum: *This museum is devoted to the appreciation of fine wine. Exhibits include information about Osaka's sister cities' wine production and an historic survey of wine. Conveniently, a French restaurant and cafe are connected so you can indulge in some fine wines. B1, Fureai Minatokan. Tel. (06)6613-2411. Open 10am to 5pm. Closed 3rd Wednesday. ¥600. New Tram to Nakafuto Station.*

Daiwa Bank Money Museum *(Daiwa Ginko Kahei Shiryokan): Daiwa, one of Japan's largest banks, has seen a lot of money pass through its hands, but not everything that comes in goes out. The bank has a collection of some 10,000 pieces of currency from China and Japan; 3000 are attractively displayed to present the long history of currency in Japan. Dai-ni Nomura Building, 2-1-1 Bingo-cho. Sakaisuji Honmachi subway station. Tel. (06)6268-1770. Open 9:30am to 4:30pm. Closed weekends and holidays. Free admission.*

Umeda

The Floating Garden Observatory (Kuchu Teien Tenbodai). This futuristic building is not for the faint of heart. A glass elevator whisks you to the 39th floor where you ascend to the observatory by an escalator in a glass tube. Various diversions such as documentary films and high-tech displays vie for your attention, but the real attraction is the panorama of Osaka and its bay laid out before you. *Tel. (06)6440-3901. Open 10am to 10:30pm. ¥700. 10-minute walk from JR Osaka Station and Hankyu Umeda Station.*

Kids Plaza Osaka is a magnet for families. A children's museum occupies part of the complex, Kids Mall the other part. The Creative Floor has hands-on and computer activities, Adventure Floor sports a play area and Discovery Floor focuses the kids with workshops.

Shinsaibashi — Namba

Shinsaibashi and Namba are the center of the southern commercial district and are filled with restaurants, stores and office buildings. Until the Meiji period, the Sennichimae area was a graveyard, cremation site and execution ground for criminals. Today it's covered with stores, restaurants and bars. Tucked among all these are a few museum gems.

Idemitsu Museum of Arts, **Osaka** (Idemitsu Bijutsukan). Along with its sister museum in Tokyo, the Idemitsu displays the splendid collection of Japanese, Chinese and Korean art assembled by Mr. Idemitsu, the founder of an oil company bearing his name. The museum also has temporary exhibitions from other museums. *13F, Idemitsu Nagahori Building. Tel. (06)6245-8611. Open 10am to 5pm. Closed Monday and December 28 through January 3. ¥500. 3-minute walk from Shinsaibashi subway station.*

Manno Museum of Art (Manno Bijutsukan). The museum exhibits Oriental art including Chinese ceramics, Japanese handscrolls, screens and samurai armor. Enjoy green tea and a panoramic view of the city after you've viewed the art. *Tel. (06)6212-1517. Open 10am to 4:30pm. Closed Monday. Open only mid-March until early July and late September until late December. ¥700. On the 13th floor of Dai-san Shoho building on Midosuji. 3-minute walk from Shinsaibashi subway station.*

Japan Craft Museum (Nihon Kogeikan). The crafts museum displays traditional Japanese crafts made before Meiji Period and also contemporary renditions that include lacquer, *washi* paper, dyed textiles, pottery and traditional toys. *Tel. (06)6641-6309. 8-minute walk from Namba subway station. Open 10am to 5pm. Closed Monday and second Tuesday. ¥300.*

Tennoji

Shitenno-ji Temple. Founded by Prince Shotoku in 593, Shitenno-ji is the oldest Buddhist temple in Japan. None of the original buildings from that era exists; most are concrete reconstructions. The layout is still based on the original design. *Tel. (06)6771-0066. Open 8:30am to 4:30pm; until 4pm October through March. Treasure House closed Monday, ¥200. 5-minute walk from Shitennoji Station on Tanimachi Subway Line.*

Osaka Municipal Museum of Art (Osaka Shiritsu Bijutsukan). The museum has an excellent collection of Chinese art, ancient Japanese Jomon pottery and Japanese Edo-period art. *Tel. (06)6771-4874. Open 9:30am to 5pm. Closed Monday. ¥500. 5-minute walk from JR Tennoji Station on the JR Loop Line or from the Tennoji Station on the Tanimachi and Midosuji subways.*

Festivalgate, a new indoor/outdoor amusement complex based on the theme of a city at the bottom of the ocean, features amusements, shopping and dining under one roof. *Open daily 10am to 10pm. Admission free; purchase stored-value cards. Tel. (06)635-1000.* **Spa World** is a bathing theme park, 16 different baths from 11 countries. All bathing all the time — open 24 hours (except for cleaning 9am to 10am). ¥2400. *Tel. (06)631-0001. Dobutsuen-mae station on the Midosjui and Sakaisuji subway lines.*

Tempozan Harbor Village

Over the last few years, this waterfront area has been revitalized by the opening of an aquarium, a museum, a shopping mall, a boat pier, a huge ferris wheel and a hotel. While Tempozan is in an out-of-the-way place, access is easy enough on the Chuo Subway Line to Osaka-ko, the end of the line.

CREATING LAND

When you see Tempozan, you get the feeling that it is a recent land-reclamation project, but actually it dates to the 1830s, the Tempo era of the Edo Period. During this time of great famine, the Tokugawa shogunate felt it had to give people work to prevent massive starvation. So, as a kind of forerunner to the US's depression-era CCC – Civilian Conservation Corps – the river's mouth was dredged to create land that was turned it into a park.

Osaka Aquarium (Kaiyukan). You can't miss this innovative aquarium for two reasons: the structure has large blue and red cubes that command your attention, and inside the aquarium is one of the best we've seen. We were initially put off by the ¥2000 admission fee but, after exploring it for two hours, felt it was worth every yen. Even if you are not a fish person, the aquarium piques interest in the wonders of nature. The aquarium is called the "Ring of Fire" after the circle of volcanoes ringing the Pacific Ocean, a belt supporting a high-density of life, both in the sea and on land. The large tanks along the perimeter, each with a different ecological environment, flank a huge central tank that contains large sharks, manta rays and other sea life. Your route, which continues to go round and round while descending, enables you to see these tanks at a variety of depths. The aquarium is extremely popular so make sure you go early in the day on weekends and holidays. Our kids can't get enough of this place. *Tel. (06)6576-5501. Open 10am to 8pm (enter until 7pm). ¥2000.*

Suntory Museum. From land, the building's massive cylinder resembles New York's Guggenheim Museum, but from Osaka Bay, the cylinder's windows remind us of an overgrown airport control tower. The museum's collection centers on posters and glass art, but the gallery is only a part of this entertainment complex, which contains the world's largest Imax screen, a theater, a restaurant and a sky lounge. *Tel. (06)6577-0001. Open 10am to 8pm. Closed Monday. ¥1000 for gallery, ¥1000 for Imax theater.*

Tempozan Marketplace is an upscale eating and shopping center along the same lines as San Francisco's Ghiradelli Square. *Shops are open 11am to 8pm; restaurants until 10pm. Tel. (06)6576-5501.*

Santa Maria Tour of Osaka Bay leaves from the pier alongside the Kaiyukan Aquarium. The day cruise lasts 45 minutes and is a fascinating look at Osaka from the sea. Never mind that the cruise is taking place in a hokey replica of Columbus' ship — was he searching to find a new route to Osaka? *The day cruise departs every hour between 11am and 5pm. ¥1520. In the warmer months, a two-hour night cruise leaves at 7pm and costs ¥2800. Dinner costs an additional ¥8000. Tel. (06)6942-5511.*

Nanko & Cosmosquare

This landfill island, located at the terminal station of the Nanko Port Town Line (New Tram), has been developed as a business and exhibition hub. The high-rise Osaka World Trade Center, also called WTC Cosmotower, has an observation deck with panoramic views of the region. *Open 10am to 7:30pm; ¥800.* Its 47th-floor restaurants include a reasonably priced *sushi* shop called Otanko. The Asia and Pacific Trade Center (ATC) and Intex exhibition centers attract large numbers of visitors. You'll find the Hyatt Regency Hotel in this area.

Nanko Bird Sanctuary. From the New Tram Nakafuto station, walk along the promenade for about 20 minutes or borrow a bike free of charge. Incongruously placed at the end of a landfill island with the WTC Cosmotower and other high-rise buildings in the background, the sanctuary features fresh water ponds and tidal pools of sea water that attract a variety of birds. *Tel. (06)6613-5556. Observatory open 9am to 5pm. Closed Wednesday and December 28 through January 4. The park itself is open all year round. Admission free.*

Banpaku Commemorative Park (Banpaku Kinen Koen)

Take the Midosuji Subway line to Senri Chuo Station, the end of the line, and take the monorail two stops to Banpaku Kinen Koen (six minutes).

After the 1970 Osaka Exposition, the Osaka government decided to turn the area into a huge park containing several excellent museums, a large Japanese garden and lots of open space. *Admission to the park is ¥100. Don't come on Wednesday, the park and the museums in it are all closed.*

Japan Folk Craft Museum (Nihon Mingeikan). This low, understated building houses one of the best folk craft museums in Japan. The museum features baskets, fabrics, ceramics, toys and furniture and has contemporary as well as historic pieces. *Tel. (06)6877-1971. Open 10am to 5pm. Closed Wednesdays and end of December to early March. ¥450.*

National Ethnology Museum (Minzoku Hakubutsukan) has an excellent collection of ethnographic material from all over the world and uses high-tech displays in a dramatic, contemporary building. *Tel. (06)6876-2151. Open 10am to 5pm. Closed Wednesday. ¥420. Between March through November shuttle buses run from the monorail station to the museum, otherwise it's a 20-minute walk.*

National Museum of Art, **Osaka** (Kokuritsu Kokusai Bijutsukan) features a large collection of modern art including works by Picasso, Warhol, and Henry Moore as well as excellent traveling exhibitions. The stunning building of glass and steel was saved from destruction after the Expo. *Tel. (06)6867-2481. Open 10am to 5pm. Closed Wednesday. Admission ¥420.*

Japanese Garden (Nihon Teien), one of Japan's largest and nicest landscape gardens, is a quiet place to stroll. *Tel. (06)6877-1039. Open 9am to 5pm; enter by 4pm. Closed Wednesday. ¥310.*

NIGHTLIFE & ENTERTAINMENT

Osaka has a nightlife that can keep even the most devoted bar aficionado busy. Two of the prime nightlife areas are Sonezaki, between Osaka (Umeda) Station and the river, and Shinsaibashi/Dotonbori.

Osaka has an active jazz scene with a branch of the **Blue Note** presenting world-class performers. Cover usually ¥7000 to ¥10,000. *Tel. (06)6342-7722. Sonezaki-shinchi, 2-3-21.*

Royal Horse is another well-known club hosting international and Japanese artists. *Tel. (06)6312-8958; on Shin Midosuji north of the American Consulate. Cover ¥1000. Open 5pm-midnight.*

New Suntory 5 has New Orleans Jazz on Saturday nights, swing on Wednesday and a variety on other nights. Closed Sunday. *Tel. (06)6312-8912. 5F, Sonezaki Building, Sonezaki Dori, in the arcade east of Midosuji. Cover ¥1800. Open 5:30pm-11:30pm.*

Over Seas has be-bop most nights. *Tel. (06)6262-3940. Asia Building, Honmachi Dori. Cover ¥1000 to ¥1500.*

Club Quattro has a variety of jazz, rock and pop performers; cover charges vary with the act but usually run from ¥2500 to ¥7000. *Tel. (06)6281-8181.*

Hard Rock Cafe is for the hard-core Americans who want to round out their T-shirt collections. *Tel. (06)6646-1470. 2-8-110 Nanbanka, Naniwa-ku at Osaka Stadium, near Nankai Namba Station. Open 11am-11pm, until 3am Friday and Saturday.*

If you find yourself longing for Guinness on tap, head to **Pig and Whistle** in Shinsaibashi at *"ACROSS" Building, Tel. (06)6213-6911 and Umeda at Ohastu-tenjin Building, B1, 2-5 Sonezaki, Tel. (06)6361-3198. Both branches open from 4pm until midnight, and until 1am on Friday and Saturday.*

Murphys, in Shinsaibashi, serves enough beer to quench even the biggest thirst. *6F, Lead Plaza Building, Higashi Shinsaibashi. Tel. (06)6282-0677. Open 5pm until 1am; until 3am Friday and Saturday.*

PERFORMING ARTS

Osaka features traditional theaters for *noh*, *kabuki* and *bunraku* as well as concert halls.

National Bunraku Theater. Colorful banners hang outside the home of the fabulous *bunraku* puppet theater that you must see if there's a performance. This national theater was constructed specifically for *bunraku*. The excellent acoustics allow you to hear the narrators and music without use of microphones. Performances are held in January, April, June, August and November at 11am and 4pm; tickets are ¥5600 and ¥4400. Student discounts are available. Make sure you rent the English earphones for an explanation of the art form as well as the plot. *Tel. (06)6212-1122. 3-minute walk from exit 7 of the Nipponbashi Station of the Kintetsu line or Sakaisuji subway.*

Osaka Noh Hall. Several *noh* performances per month. *Tel. (06)6373-1726. 5-minute walk from Osaka or Umeda Station.*

Osaka Shochiku-za was Japan's first Western-style theater. It was recently renovated, actually reconstructed. While the Neo-Renaissance facade has been preserved, the interior is a new, 1000-seat traditional *kabuki* theater. *Tel. (06)6214-2211; tickets: (06)6214-2200. 1-minute walk from Namba Station, exit 14. Tickets range from ¥4200 to ¥16,000.* Unfortunately the theater does not sell one-act tickets. *Kabuki* performs here about six months each year.

Concert Halls

Check the *Meet Osaka Guide* for performance schedules.

• **Festival Hall**. *Tel. (06)6231-2221. 2-minute walk from exit 4 Higobashi Station on Yotsubashi Subway.*

PUPPET THEATER

Bunraku, *one of the three major forms of traditional Japanese theater, began in Osaka around the end of the 16th century. Its forerunner was* **joruri**, *ballads told by a narrator accompanied by* **shamisen** *music. Large puppets, manipulated by three people, were added to combine the three elements defining bunraku: puppets, narrated tales and shamisen music. Takemoto, a narrator who developed a unique style of telling ballads, established a company at Dotonbori in 1684. Collaboration between Takemoto and Chikamatsu Monzaemon, the Shakespeare of Japan, produced many famous works.*

One common theme is the dilemma faced by the hero and the heroine torn between their love for each other and their sense of obligation in the feudal society. One of the most famous love-suicide stories, "Sonezaki Shinju," was greeted enthusiastically by the Osaka people when the Takemoto-za performed it two weeks after the actual incident took place in the precincts of Sonezaki Shrine; today that area is a busy commercial and entertainment section of Osaka just south of Umeda Station. The son of a rich merchant family fell in love with a courtesan of the Sonezaki pleasure quarters, but his friend deceived him, took the money he saved to buy her freedom and bought the courtesan for himself. Dejected, his family advised him to forget her; but the two tragically committed suicide on the grounds of Sonezaki Shrine. Sonezaki Shinju is still performed today.

- **Symphony Hall**. *Tel. (06)6453-6000. 10-minute walk from Fukushima Station on the JR Loop Line.*
- **Izumi Hall**. *Tel. (06)6944-1188. 3-minute walk from Osaka-jo Koen Station on the JR Loop Line.*
- **Ishihara Hall**. *Tel. (06)6444-5875. 1-minute walk from Higobashi Station on the Yotsubashi subway, exit 5-B.*

Other Information

Kansai Time Out is a monthly magazine that lists events happening in the Osaka/Kobe/Kyoto area. You can find it at hotel bookstores.

Meet Osaka, published quarterly by the Osaka Tourist Federation, lists events and is available at hotels and tourist offices.

SPORTS & RECREATION

Sumo

Osaka hosts the 15-day, mid-March sumo tournament at the **Osaka-furitsu Taiikukan** — a 10-minute walk from Namba Station. Most tickets sell out quickly, but a small number of standing-room tickets go on sale at 9am each day for ¥1500, and there still might be some ¥3300 seats available. Usually you have to get there well before 9am to get a ticket, especially on weekends and toward the end of the tournament. Sumo begins at 10am and lasts until 6pm.

The lowest ranking wrestlers fight first, and the really good guys don't start until 4pm; most people don't show up until mid-afternoon. It's okay to sit in a lower seat until the ticket holder arrives and kicks you out. The hall is most convenient to exit 5 of Namba Station. Head toward the Hard Rock Cafe, turn right and walk one block.

Baseball
The **Kintetsu Buffaloes** have a new, futuristic-looking home in the **Osaka Dome**, Japan's largest covered stadium, which seats 48,000.

Soccer
Two professional soccer teams call Osaka home: **Gamba Osaka** and **Cerezo Osaka**. They play at Nagai Stadium and Banpaku Memorial Stadium (the Expo 70 grounds).

Theme Parks
Universal Studios Japan opens in Osaka in the spring of 2001.

SHOPPING
Wander through some of Osaka's specialized markets.

Kuromon Food Market sells fish and other food items. Visit for a glimpse of everyday life for Osaka's residents. *Open from 10am to 5pm. Most shops closed Sunday. 3-minute walk from exit 10, Nipponbashi Station of Sennichimae and Sakaisuji subways.*

Doguya, a street in Namba with shops selling kitchen and restaurant goods is a fun place to browse.

Osaka Chuo Wholesale Market. If you are up early in the morning with jet lag, this market is for you. Fish, seafood and produce are sold from 4am until about 6am. *Near Noda Station on Sennichimae Subway.*

Den Den Town is the electronics district, the Akihabara of Osaka, with nearly 300 shops selling every gadget imaginable. Foreign visitors can get tax-free purchases at shops with tax-free signs, but you need to show your passport. *Closed Wednesday. Most shops open from 10am to 7pm. Use exit 1 or 2 Ebisu-cho station on Sakaisuji Subway Line.*

America Mura and **Europe Mura** are two districts in the Namba area. America Mura is filled with Osaka's young shopping for inexpensive clothes while Europe Mura is a Japanese version of the old world.

Department Stores

Osaka's large department stores are grouped in three main areas:

- **Umeda - JR Osaka Station**: Hankyu, Hanshin, and Daimaru Department Stores plus Hankyu Ings, Umeda Loft and Navio Hankyu, among countless smaller stores.
- **Shinsaibashi**: Sogo and Daimaru Department Stores plus Crysta Nagahori (one of Japan's biggest underground malls), Shinsaibashi BAL, Shinsaibashi Vivre, Shinsaibashi Parco, Sony Tower, and Big Step.
- **Namba**: Takashimiya and Printemps Department Stores as well as Namba Walk and Namba City.

PRACTICAL INFORMATION

Consulates

- **Australia**, *Tel. (06)6941-9271*
- **Canada**, *Tel. (06)6212-4910*
- **United Kingdom**, *Tel. (06)6281-1616*
- **United States**, *Tel. (06)6315-5900*

Money Exchange

Exchange money at any of the banks that say, "Authorized Money Exchange." Bank hours are 9am to 3pm, Monday through Friday. We find Citibank usually is the most efficient; Osaka has two branches:

Citibank Shinsaibashi Branch. *1F, Midosuji Diamond Building, 2-1-2 Nishi Shinsaibashi, Chuo-ku. Exit 7, Shinsaibashi subway station, on Midosuji Street south of the station. Open 9am to 3pm weekdays and 10am to 2pm Saturdays. Tel. 0120-50-4189.* 24 hour ATM on premises.

Citibank Honmachi Branch. *1F, Kanese Building, 3-5-5 Honmachi, Chuo-ku. Honmachi subway station, exit C3, on Honmachi Dori. Open 9am to 3pm weekdays.* 24 hour ATM on premises.

Post Office

The **Central Post Office**, south of JR Osaka Station, is open 9am to 7pm weekdays, until 5pm Saturday and 9am to 12:30 Sunday and holidays.

Telephone Numbers

Osaka telephone numbers are now 8-digits (in addition to the 06 area code). If you have an old 7-digit number, bring it up to date by adding an additional "6" at the beginning of the number. For instance, the old number (06)123-4567 is now (06)6123-4567.

KOYA-SAN - MT. KOYA

If you try to visit only Japan's major sights, you'll end up skipping the best part of Japan — the small towns and special places outside the big cities. **Koya-san** is a town with 117 temples on one of Japan's most sacred mountains. Monks compose a quarter of the population, many of them studying Buddhism at Koya University. Temples are set up with their own small inns, and it's probably the easiest way to experience staying at a Buddhist temple. Best of all, this remote place is less than two hours by train from Osaka.

Koya-san has been a major religious center since 816, when the famous priest Kobo Daishi established a temple there. Far from population centers, the peaceful mountain filled the bill as a meditation center for his priests. Until the late 19th century, the mountain was off limits to women.

ARRIVALS & DEPARTURES

By Train

To/from Osaka: From Namba Station, take the Nankai Railway to Koya-san. Gokurakubashi Station is the terminus; you then take a cable car for the five minute ride to the top of the mountain. The all-reserved-seat Koya limited express trains whisk you to Koya-san in 90 minutes (¥1990 including cable car). The problem is only a few operate each day. If these don't fit your schedule, take the nonreserved express trains, 1 hour 40 minutes (¥850) to Gokurakubashi Station and five minutes on the cable car (¥380).

To/from Kyoto: the quickest way is to take either the shinkansen or JR Tokaido line to Osaka Station; then take the subway to Namba Station, and follow the above directions.

Planning Your Stay

If you get an early start from Osaka, you can take a (long) day trip to Koya-san, but we really don't recommend it. Staying overnight at a Buddhist temple is an essential part of the experience.

ORIENTATION

The cable car station is too far from the center of town to walk. The bus takes about 15 minutes to the center of town, ¥280; taxi about 10 minutes. A one-day bus pass costs ¥800. Bicycle is a good way to get around town; rent them at the Koya-san Tourist Association at ¥1200 for the day.

Tourist Information

A small booth at the Koya-san cable car station has English-language maps and will make reservations for temple accommodations. A larger **Tourist Information Center** is at the center of town. *Tel. (0736)56-2616.*

WHERE TO STAY

Fifty-three temples in Koya-san offer accommodation. You can make reservations directly with the temples, through the Koya-san Tourist Association or through major travel agencies.

Most temples have modern facilities with Japanese-style rooms similar to moderately priced Japanese inns, but don't expect a private bath or toilet. The food, *shojin ryori*, Buddhist vegetarian fare, is usually served on lacquer trays in your room. Temples have early morning prayer services but attendance is almost always optional.

RENGE-IN, *399 Koya-san, Koya-cho, Ito-gun, Wakayama, 648. Tel. (0736)56-2017, Fax (0736)56-3109. From ¥9000 per person with two meals. No credit cards.*

Centrally located, Renge-in is our hands-down favorite place to stay in Koya-san. The 1200-year-old temple had a special relationship with the Tokugawa family and includes a beautiful audience room decorated in black and gold lacquer, used by the Tokugawa family when they visited Koya-san. The current main building is several hundred years old. The guest rooms in a modern wing are comfortable and Japanese style. The personable head priest, Mr. Higashiyama, has attained the high position of *ajari* (similar to a cardinal in the Catholic Church), requiring 15 years of intense preparation. His wife is a superb cook; the delicious home-style Buddhist vegetarian fare was the best we've ever eaten.

Other centrally located temples, all with rates from ¥9000 per person with two meals, include:

FUDO-IN, *Tel. (0736)56-2414.*

A few blocks away from the main street, but it's a good location.

DAIEN-IN, *Tel. (0736)56-2009.*

On Koya-san's main street, convenient the Okuno-in area and the Garan.

SHOJOSHIN-IN, *Tel. (0736)56-2006.*

SEKISHO-IN, *Tel. (0736)56-2734. Member of Welcome Inn Reservation Center.*

Close to the Okuno-in area, Sekisho-in has a beautiful garden from the early 1700s.

WHERE TO EAT

Koya-san is famous for its Buddhist vegetarian cuisine, but you have to stay at a temple to try it. See the sidebar below for more information. The few restaurants in town are noodle shops.

BUDDHIST VEGETARIAN FARE

If you are picturing Buddhist vegetarian fare as boring and bland, guess again. A meal provides a variety of delicious foods, and you won't miss your meat or fish; you won't find onions or garlic either. Before the Meiji Period (1868) women were forbidden to enter Koya-san, so the monks did all the food preparation. These days, overseeing the kitchen is one of the tasks of the wife of each temple's head priest, although the young monks still spend a lot of time in the kitchen.

What can you expect to find on your plate? Vegetable tempura, sesame tofu, dengaku (skewered chunks of tofu), kon-nyaku gelatin, mountain potato or wheat gluten topped with a miso paste), seasonal vegetables and fruit. And, naturally, koya-dofu, a freeze-dried tofu. Apparently, one winter a long time ago, the tofu froze and the consistency changed; when soaked in water, it was an instant hit.

SEEING THE SIGHTS

Koya-san's sights are clustered around two main areas: the Okuno-in Cemetery and the Garan. You can buy a pass for ¥1000 that admits you to the major temples and halls.

Okuno-in Area

Start at Ichinohashi Bridge and enter **Okuno-in Cemetery**. For nearly two kilometers you'll walk through a deep cryptomeria forest with moss-covered tombstones under the tall trees. Kobo Daishi is buried at the end of the cemetery — devotees believe the great priest is deep in meditation. When he rises to meet the Buddha (Buddha of the Future), everyone buried near him will also attain salvation. So there are thousands and thousands of tombstones, grand ones for imperial family members, aristocrats and feudal lords and very modest ones for commoners. Even people who are not Shingon Buddhists want to be buried at Koya-san. You'll pass tombs for Oda Nobunaga and Toyotomi Hideyoshi.

Corporate Japan is also here with its tombs for the employees of UCC Coffee, Sharp, Nissan and many other companies both large and small. Most tombs contain only a portion of the deceased's ashes or a lock of hair, so a tomb may have the remains of hundreds of people.

A stone marker with five shapes tops many graves. Inscribed in Sanskrit, these symbolize (from the top down) air, wind, fire, water and earth. According to Buddhist thought, these five elements compose the universe. Many graves also have large flat wooden sticks bearing posthumous prayers stuck in the ground.

At the end of the cemetery, across a bridge, lies the **Okuno-in**, Kobo Daishi's burial place and Koya-san's holiest site. The bridge over the stream symbolizes crossing over from secular into sacred space. After you cross the bridge, you reach the Lantern Hall which is lit with thousands of lanterns donated by believers. Directly behind the Lantern Hall is Kobo Daishi's simple mausoleum.

JAPAN'S HOLIEST RENAISSANCE MAN

*The priest **Kukai** (774-836), known posthumously as **Kobo Daishi**, is Japan's most revered religious figure. Born in Shikoku, where he later established the famous 88 Temple Pilgrimage (see Inland Sea for details), Kukai became a priest at age 20. In 804, at 31 years old, he went to China and studied esoteric Buddhism in the Tang capital of Chang-an (present day Xian). Kukai returned to Japan two years later and founded Japan's Shingon sect of Buddhism.*

According to legend, on the boat returning from China, Kukai threw a religious implement. The place where it landed was to become the site of a new temple. As soon as he arrived in Japan he started his search. Wandering alone he encountered a hunter with a dog with two heads, one black and one white. The hunter gave Kukai the dog who accompanied him to the Koya-san area. There he met a woman who claimed to be the mother of the hunter. Deep in the mountains, Kukai found the Buddhist implement that he had thrown, and realized that he had found the place. He established Kongobu-ji Temple on Koya-san in 816; today you can see paintings of the two-headed dog.

Kukai's fame has spread beyond religious circles. He is credited with inventing kana, the syllabic writing system derived from Chinese characters, and was a noted calligrapher and painter. But he was still human. A well-known Japanese proverb says, "Even Kobo Daishi makes a mistake."

Garan Area

On the other side of town is **Kongobu-ji Temple**. Kobo Daishi called the mountain monastery Kongobu-ji, but now it specifically refers to this one temple. Toyotomi Hideyoshi built the temple in 1593 to pray for the soul of his mother. The edifice was rebuilt in 1863, but the Buddhist and secular art treasures including screen paintings by the famous Kano school painters date from the earlier time. Upon the order of his uncle, Hideyoshi's nephew committed suicide in Kongobu-ji's Willow Room. The Ohiroma, where religious ceremonies are held, is graced by wide Momoyama-style sliding doors decorated in gold.

Although you can't see the huge kitchen, the great chimney gives some idea of its size. Also don't miss the wooden containers on the roof that hold water for fire. After touring the temple, sit and have a cup of green tea overlooking Banryu-tei, the temple's large rock garden. *Open 8am to 5pm; 8:30am to 4:30pm November through March. ¥350.*

Just beyond Kongobu-ji is the **Garan**, Koya-san's central compound and home to a number of religious buildings. The most important buildings in the compound are **Daito**, or Great Stupa, a vermilion two-storied pagoda reconstructed in 1937 but still the symbol of Koya-san; **Fudo-do**, built in 1197, the oldest building on the mountain; **Mie-do**, the holiest next to Okuno-in, houses a portrait of Kobo Daishi; and **Kondo**, the main hall, rebuilt in 1937. *¥200.*

On the other side of the main road is the **Reihokan Museum**, exhibiting Shingon Buddhist treasures belonging to Koya-san temples. The museum has an excellent collection of Buddhist art, including many National Treasures. *Open 8am to 5pm; 8:30am to 4:30pm. Closed December 20 through January 4. November through March. ¥500.*

KOBE

A showcase of Japanese resiliency, **Kobe** is back in business after the 1995 earthquake flattened portions of it. The city functions extraordinarily well today considering the proportions of the disaster and transportation systems are back to normal.

Kobe, one of Japan's most international cities, was a center of trade with China and Korea as far back as the 8th century. One of the first Japanese ports opened to the outside world in 1868 after a 250-year period of isolation, foreigners gravitated to Kobe. The city still has large Chinese and Indian expatriate communities. Americans and Europeans built Western-style houses on the slopes of Kitano; many are open as museums today.

Japanese flock to Kobe (20 million visitors in 1996) for its exotic and cosmopolitan atmosphere. Foreign visitors won't find it quite as exotic but can still enjoy its cosmopolitan nature.

Planning Your Stay

Plan to spend one day in Kobe. Start in the Kitano district to get a feeling for cosmopolitan Kobe; then go to Motomachi and Nankin-machi for browsing and shopping. Visit the Kobe Museum and the museums at Meriken Park or Port Island. A cablecar whisks you up Mt. Rokko for a great panorama at night.

ARRIVALS & DEPARTURES

By Air

The two Kansai airports serve Kobe: Kansai International Airport, primarily for international flights, and Osaka Itami Airport for domestic flights. If you have a choice, Itami is closer.

For Ground Transportation:

From Kansai International Airport: bus to Sannomiya (70 minutes, ¥1800). By Jet Foil Boat: 27 minutes from Kobe City Air Terminal on Port Island (KCAT) plus 15 minutes from the pier to the terminal, ¥2200.

From Itami: bus to Sannomiya (40 minutes, ¥1020). Taxi takes about 35 minutes and costs around ¥8500.

By Train

The JR Shinkansen train, running from Kyushu to Tokyo, stops at JR Shin Kobe Station, a little more than one kilometer north of the main station, Sannomiya. From Shin Kobe Station, take the subway one stop to reach Sannomiya (¥200). Regular trains on the JR Tokaido line connect Kobe to Osaka (20–30 minutes), Kyoto (1 hour) and Himeji (1 hour). The Tokaido trains stop at Sannomiya, Motomachi and Kobe Stations; Sannomiya is usually the most convenient station.

The private Hanshin Railroad connects Kobe with Osaka's Umeda Station in 30 minutes (¥310). The Hanshin train stops at Sannomiya and Motomachi. The Hankyu Kobe line also runs between Umeda Station in Osaka and Sannomiya Station in about the same time (¥310).

By Bus

Overnight buses connect Kobe with Kagoshima (13 hours, ¥11,500), Kumamoto (10 hours, ¥9800), Nagasaki (10 hours, ¥10,500) and Tokyo (8 hours, ¥8690).

By Car

Kobe is on the Hanshin Expressway. You won't need a car in Kobe. We recommend arriving by train.

ORIENTATION

Kobe is a sliver of a city shoe-horned between the mountains and the sea. With no place to expand, Kobe has undertaken large land reclamation projects including Port and Rokko Islands.

GETTING AROUND TOWN

Sannomiya is the transportation hub of the city. A subway connects the city primarily east-west. From Sannomiya, the Port Liner, an unmanned monorail, circles Port Island. The City Loop Bus is a convenient way for tourists to get around town because it connects areas that are otherwise difficult to reach.

The route is Sannomiya Station – Kitano – Shin Kobe Station – Tor Road –Meriken Park – Harbor Land – parallel to Motomachi and Nankin-machi – Old Settlement area – Sannomiya. You can get on and off the bus at any stop. The fare is ¥250; a day pass (*Ichi-nichi Josha-ken*) is ¥650. Buy a day pass if you're going to be getting on and off a lot. The bus runs about three times an hour from 9:30am until 5:20pm; 6:30pm on weekends and holidays. Buy passes on the City Loop Bus and at the Tourist Information Office.

TRENDSETTING KOBE

Among the first ports open to the West after a long period of isolation, Kobe claims lots of Japan's firsts, including:

• First movie showing: to members of the Shinko Club at the Bunka Center in 1896.

• First golf course: designed by Englishman Arthur Gloom in 1903; female caddies wear kimono and straw sandals.

• First female office worker: Kansai Power Company employed a woman as an office worker in 1894. At the time everyone was shocked at the company and the woman.

• The first shop selling beef opened in 1871.

• The first aquarium opened in 1897.

• The first hair perm was given in 1923.

• The first soccer game was in 1871; rugby in 1876.

Tourist Information

Kobe City Tourist Information Center (Hello Station Kobe) in front of JR Sannomiya Station. English-language assistance open daily 9am to 5pm. *Tel. (078)322-0220.* A small tourist information desk is also at JR Shin Kobe Station, where the *shinkansen* trains arrive.

Home Visits

The **Kobe International Tourist Association**, in the Kobe International Exchange Hall on Port Island, arranges visits to Japanese homes; this arrangement is for a two or three hour visit, not an overnight. Call the Association at *Tel. (078)303-1010.* Open 9am to 5pm. Closed weekends.

Goodwill Guides: Three groups in Kobe provide volunteer Goodwill Guide services. Contact the Kobe Tourist Information Office for current contact numbers.

WHERE TO STAY

Kobe primarily has Western-style hotels.

SHINKOBE ORIENTAL HOTEL, *1 Kitano-cho, Chuo-ku, Kobe, 650-0002. Tel. (078)291-1121, Fax (078)291-1154. Singles from ¥13,000. Doubles from ¥23,000. Credit cards.*

Although the name Oriental Hotel conjures up images of the legendary service that put Bangkok's Oriental Hotel on the map, don't be misled. There are several Oriental Hotels in Kobe and they are attractive and efficient, but nothing memorable. The Shinkobe Oriental is at Shin Kobe JR Station so if you are arriving by *shinkansen* train, you don't waste any time getting from station to hotel — you don't even have to go outdoors. This new, high rise offers good mountain and sea views and has an airy modern decor. The rooms are average size. The complex includes a huge shopping plaza (called OPA) with a multitude of stores and restaurants and the subway station is conveniently in the third basement.

KOBE WASHINGTON HOTEL, *2-11-5 Shimo Yamate Dori, Chuo-ku, Kobe, 650-0011. Tel. (078)331-6111, Fax (078)371-6651. Singles from ¥9000. Doubles from ¥17,000. Credit cards.*

The Washington Hotel is a red brick structure conveniently located between Tor Road and Sannomiya and is close to shopping, dining and transportation. Rooms are typical business-class size and clean and bright.

HOTEL AMALIE, *2-2-28 Yamate-dori, Chuo-ku, Kobe, 650-0011. Tel. (078)334-0039, Fax (078)334-1778. Singles from ¥8800. Doubles from ¥19,000. Credit cards.*

Located across from Ikuta Jinja Shrine, Amalie is conveniently located in downtown Kobe. The hotel is small with a European atmosphere and serves good food. This spot is our favorite place to get away from the anonymity of a large hotel.

HOTEL ARCONS, *3-7-1 Kitano-cho, Chuo-ku, Kobe, 650-0002. Tel. (078)231-1538, Fax (078)231-7505. Singles from ¥6500. Doubles from ¥11,000.*

A "petit hotel" at the top of the hill of Kitano-cho, it's in the middle of the foreign district. The hotel has two restaurants, one serving Western food and the other *okonomiyaki*, one of the Kansai area's special dishes — a sort of glorified pancake.

WHERE TO EAT

Kobe's beef is famous but, in addition, a wide variety of international restaurants exist including Chinese and Indian. If you aren't sure what you want, go to one of the shopping arcade areas that have restaurant rows — there are tons of food to choose from and lots of plastic models to help you select. The basement arcade around Sannomiya's Sogo Department Store, Shumi-gai, and also in Sannomiya, the basement under Center-gai — all are chock full of restaurants.

At Shin Kobe Station, the OPA shopping center has 30 restaurants that provide variety, speed and something for every budget.

SANDA-YA *(Steak, inexpensive to moderate). Kitano-zaka. Tel. (078)222-0567. Open daily 11:30am to 8pm.*

Sanda-ya serves delicious Kobe beef steak with Japanese-style sauce and lots of sliced onions which, according to the owner, help digestion! Prices are reasonable: Lunch set menu (¥1200) includes 100 grams Kobe beef steak, vegetables, rice and *miso* soup. They also serve local beer. This restaurant has several branches.

LAS RAMBLAS *(Spanish, inexpensive to moderate). B1, KDD Kobe Building, 83 Kyomachi, Chuo-ku, across the street from the Kobe City Museum. Tel. (078)393-0730. Open 11:30am to 2pm; 6pm to 9pm. Closed Monday and the first Sunday.*

This casual Spanish restaurant serves a variety of *tapas* and *paella*. The Las Ramblas paella costs ¥3000 for two people.

OZEKI *(Japanese, inexpensive). On Higashimon Tsugi Street. 1-5-4 Shimo Yamato. Tel. (078)332-0091. Open daily 4pm to 11pm.*

Ozeki features robata-yaki, food grilled over charcoal. All the dishes at Ozeki cost ¥500 and the proprietor is great fun.

TOKEYA *(Japanese, moderate to expensive). On Kitano-zaka. 4-7-23 Kano-cho. Tel. (078)321-0555. Open 11am to 9pm.*

Try Kobe beef in the rustic atmosphere of Tokeya. Sukiyaki costs ¥4900, shabu-shabu ¥5900 and Kobe-beef steak ¥7000.

Chinese Food

Nankin-Machi (Chinatown) has a wide variety of restaurants, not all Chinese. Try **ROSYOKI**, near the central square for its *butaman* (steamed pork buns). You'll probably have to wait in line to buy them. **HAISHIN** has Chinese food at reasonable prices.

Indian Food

As a center for Indian residents in Japan, Kobe abounds with good Indian restaurants.

MAAYA *(Indian, inexpensive). ITC Building, Isobe Dori, Chuo-ku. Tel. (078)231-0703. Open 11:30am to 2:30pm; 5pm to 9:30pm. Closed Monday.*

Maaya serves a wide variety of curries in the ¥800 to ¥1000 price range as well as tandoori.

GANDHARA *(Indian, inexpensive to moderate). 4F, Nikaku Building, 1-2-3 Kitanagasa Dori, across from Hankyu Sannomiya Station. Tel. (078)391-4975. Open 11:30am to 3pm; 5pm to 9:30pm.*

Lunch costs from ¥700 to ¥2000 and dinner from ¥2200 to ¥5000.

RAJA *Tel. (078)332-5253. Open 11:30am to 2:30pm; 5pm to 9pm. Closed Monday.*

Located in Nankin-Machi, Raja serves delicious Indian food. Its ¥1500 lunch special is a good deal.

NISHIMURA COFFEE HOUSE *(Coffee, inexpensive). Near Sannomiya Station. Tel. (078)221-1872. Open 8:30am-10pm.*

Known among coffee connoisseurs, high quality coffee beans and Mt. Rokko's famous pure water combine to produce a great cup of coffee for ¥450.

WORLD'S MOST EXPENSIVE BEEF

Kobe beef is known worldwide for its tenderness and rich flavor. Don't picture animals roaming the streets of Kobe; they are actually raised in the countryside about an hour away from the city. Until the 1870s, Japanese didn't eat meat since Buddhism frowned upon the killing of animals. Apparently fish was not considered animal; hence, it was the major source of animal protein in the Japanese diet during the Edo period.

Kobe's steer must be the world's most spoiled – they are not allowed to exert themselves, lest their muscles grow strong and tough. These pampered beasts are massaged so their meat is finely marbled. They also drink beer although we don't know what brands; perhaps they now drink microbrews to fit their boutique image. Some farms play classical music to relax the cows. Poor things, with all this pampering, to end up at the slaughterhouse.

Quality, of course, has a price and prime Kobe beef can cost as much as ¥5000 for 100 grams (about ¥22,000 a pound) at a department store. Some of the meat is so well marbled, it is light pink. Talk about a low cholesterol special...

SEEING THE SIGHTS

Kitano District

Before the turn of the century, foreigners could only build weekend villas in this area; their main houses had to be in Kyu-kyoju-ku, the old residential area, which today is the commercial area around the Kobe City Museum. When you get up on the hill and see the sea views and feel the fresh air, you understand why they would build weekend retreats just a stone's throw away. From about 1900, the government eased restrictions and many foreigners built year-round residences.

Some twenty of the old Kitano houses, called *ijinkan*, are open to the public, but see just a sampling such as the Kazamidori (Weathercock) House, Uroko (Fish Scale) House, Moegi no Yakata, Kobe Kitano Museum (the former American Legation Building) and Catherine Swedish House. Most are furnished with period pieces. *These buildings are open 9am to 5pm; until 6pm in summer. Admission varies from ¥500 to ¥700 for each but some participate in a pass system: three buildings for ¥1300, four buildings for ¥2000; nine for ¥3500.* Kitano has many coffee houses and lots of shops; it's a pleasant way to while away an afternoon.

Ikuta Jinja, between Kitano and Sannomiya, is a Shinto shrine with a long history, but the current buildings date from after the war. Kobe literally means "God's door," but it's believed it originally meant "persons paying taxes to the shrine," and that shrine is Ikuta.

Motomachi Area

At the turn of the century, Motomachi was the most fashionable place in Japan to shop for Western clothing and accessories, books and sweets. Now a covered arcade, shoppers still throng to the area, patronizing the wide array of stores.

Nankin-machi, Kobe's Chinatown, is parallel to Motomachi. Four Chinese gates mark the district, the center for Kobe's 40,000 Chinese residents. Restaurants, take-out shops, grocery stores and trinket shops flank Nankin-machi's central plaza.

Downtown Kobe

Kobe City Museum (Kobe Shiritsu Bijutsukan). *Tel. (078)391-0035. Open 10am to 5pm. Closed Monday. ¥200. 10 minutes from Sannomiya or Motomachi stations.* The 1935 classical building, formerly a bank headquarters, is home to the Kobe City Museum. The Kobe City Museum houses the world's best collection of 16th century Nanban, Southern Barbarian, art (see sidebar on the next page). To protect the delicate works of art, they are only on display for a few months a year, usually in the winter. The museum's permanent display focuses on the archaeology of the area and Kobe's role as an international port. On the first floor, you'll find an extensive collection of bilingual videos ranging in subject from history and art to devastation by the earthquake.

Port Island

Work on the huge landfill island began in 1966 and took 15 years to complete; an addition is now underway. Convenient to Sannomiya Station by the Port Liner train, the island has a convention center and an international exhibition hall. It also is home to the **UCC Coffee Museum**

(Japan's only coffee museum) and **Tasaki Pearl Gallery**, which displays the culturing process.

Rokko Island

Rokko Island, another landfill island, an international area with many foreign companies, is home to the **Kobe Fashion Museum**, Japan's first museum devoted to the subject. On addition to the display of 20th century fashion, the museum displays world folk costumes. *Open 11am to 6pm, until 8pm on Friday. Closed Wednesday. ¥500. Use Rokko Liner Island Center Station.* Also on the island is the **River Mall** (Suiro Hiroba) filled with stores and restaurants.

SOUTHERN BARBARIAN ART

*The Portuguese and other Europeans, who first came to Japan in the second half of the 16th century, sailed in from the south, hence the unflattering name, **Nanban** or **Southern Barbarians**. Under the catch-all phrase, Nanban art encompasses several distinct forms: Europeans as the subject matter in Japanese art forms like screen paintings; Christian articles such as Bible stands rendered in lacquer and other traditional Japanese materials; and Japanese artists' first attempts to replicate the perspective of Western painting.*

Looking at the detail on a Nanban screen can easily enthrall you for a half-hour or so. Take in the European faces, all with large noses. Clergy have black or brown robes, depending on whether they are Jesuits or Franciscans. Nonclergy wear colorful costumes: pantaloons, ruffled collars and flowing capes. Ships, often in full sail, have sailors performing acrobatics on the high rigging. When the artists wanted to show the homeland of these Southern Barbarians, they drew Chinese-style buildings, the most exotic structures they could imagine.

Meriken Park

Does the name of this park have a familiar ring? At beginning of the Meiji period, Japanese didn't hear the "A" sound in American, thus the name of this waterfront park. From the water you cannot help but notice the distinctive soaring glass structure, the **Kobe Maritime Museum** (Kobe Kaiyo Hakubutsukan), whose exhibits focus on the sea, ships and Kobe's thousand-year role as a port. *Tel. (078)391-6751. Open 10am to 5pm. Closed Monday. ¥500. 10-minute walk from JR or Hanshin Motomachi Stations.*

Port Tower. This gangly observation tower offers views of the harbor and mountains. *Open 9am to 9pm. ¥500.*

The **Port of Kobe Earthquake Memorial Park** in Merikan Park features the half-sunken Merikan Pier, a graphic reminder of the force of the massive 1995 trembler.

Harborland

Kobe's major development on the water is located close to JR Kobe Station. Young people throng **Mosaic**, a complex with stores, movie theater, restaurants and amusement park. Lunch and dinner cruises leave from the Ferry and Cruise Terminal. The cruise to the Akashi Kaikyo Bridge, the world's longest suspension bridge (see below), makes a good fair-weather diversion.

Akashi Kaikyo Bridge

The world's longest suspension bridge connects Kobe with Awaji Island. Opened in 1998, the graceful, 3911-meter bridge is a technological marvel. Stop by the **Bridge Science Museum** at its Kobe base for all the technical details. The **Maiko Marine Promenade** is the only walkway on the bridge and is a thrilling stroll. For a view of the bridge from the sea, board a cruise ship on Harborland.

Other Areas

Sorakuen Garden. *Tel. (078)351-5155. Open 9am to 5pm. Closed Thursday. ¥150. 5-minute walk from Kencho-mae Subway station.* Sorakuen, Kobe's only Japanese garden, is a serene place except when azaleas and chrysanthemums flower (spring and autumn). Several historic buildings designated Important Cultural Properties were moved to the park, including the 1902 Hassan residence from Kitano and a boat house used by feudal lords.

Hakutsuru Fine Art Museum (Hakutsuru Bijutsukan). *Tel. (078)851-6001. Open 10am to 4:30pm. Closed Monday. JR Sumiyoshi Station take #38 bus, exit at Hakutsuru Bijutsukan-mae.* One of Japan's most well-known *sake* breweries invested profits in exceptional examples of ancient Chinese and Japanese art. The new wing displays Oriental carpets.

NIGHTLIFE & ENTERTAINMET

Jazz

Kobe has an active jazz scene.

Sone, *Kitano-zaka north of Nakayamate Dori. Tel. (078)342-5821. Music from 6:50pm. Cover ¥500.*

A Kobe institution for over a quarter of a century, Sone is a warm and friendly family-run jazz club that Japanese and international musicians frequent.

Satin Doll, *2nd Floor, Bacchus Building, Nakayamate Dori, west of Kitano-zaka. Tel. (078)242-0100. Music from 7pm. Cover ¥900 plus ¥600 order.*
Satin Doll moved to new and larger quarters and can now accommodate brass bands and swing combos in addition to piano trios. Satin Doll serves French food.

Breweries
Breweries in the **Nada** area have been making high-quality *sake* for 600 years, benefiting from the unbeatable combination of pure water and good rice. Visit a few to taste *sake* and observe the fermentation process.
Hamafukutsuru Ginjo Kobo. Observe the fermenting process and sample fresh *sake. Tel. (078)411-8339. Open 10am to 5pm. Closed Monday. 7 minute walk from Hanshin Uozaki Station.*
Kikumasamune Shuzo Kinenkan. The earthquake destroyed several storehouses, but the watermill cottage displays *sake* brewing items. They also have videos and *sake* tasting. *Tel. (078)854-1029. Open from 10am to 3pm. Closed weekends. Reservation required. 3-minute walk from Rokko Liner Minami Uozaki Station.*
Sakura Masamune. *Tel. (078)436-3030. Open 10am to 10pm. Closed Tuesday.*
Sawa no Tsuru. *Tel. (078)882-7788. Open 10am to 4pm. Closed Wednesday.*

SPORTS
Baseball: The **Orix Blue Wave** call Kobe home and play at Green Stadium Kobe.
Soccer: The home team **Vissel Kobe** plays at Universiade Memorial Stadium.

SHOPPING
Kobe has lots of shopping arcades, underground shopping areas and urban shopping malls. Some of the shops in **Motomachi** have been around since the turn of the century. **Santica** underground shopping area in Sannomiya and **Sannomiya Center-Gai Shopping Arcade** are popular with trendy young Japanese. For low-priced goods, try **Kokashita** under the JR tracks between Sannomiya to Kobe Stations.
Harbor Circus, a distinctive seven-storied building with cascading arches, houses a new shopping and entertainment complex. One section rents out small spaces at low prices to businesses that lost their premises during the earthquake. Other shops sell imported goods at reduced prices, including a Toys R Us. In the entertainment area, you will find the amusement arcade "Sega World," a 3-D theater, a miniature train and an

art village. Located just two minutes from JR Kobe Station, it's a stop our kids love.

Harborland on the water houses lots of stores, boutiques, and restaurants.

PRACTICAL INFORMATION
Money & Banking
Citibank, 1F, Recruit Kobe Building, 95 Edomachi, Chuo-ku, Kobe. *24-hour toll free Tel. 0120-50-4189*. Open weekdays 9am to 3pm. 24 hour ATM on premises.

ARIMA

Arima, Japan's oldest hot spring town, has been attracting visitors for over a thousand years. Nestled in the hills on the northern side of **Mt. Rokko**, Arima is a mere 30 minutes by train from Kobe. Despite it's proximity, Arima has a rural hot spring atmosphere — some large hotels and narrow streets lined with shops catering to visitors. Arima has two kinds of hot spring water, one transparent and the other red, rich in iron. Arima is most crowded in the autumn when we soak surrounded by mountains in a blaze of glorious color.

The great 16th century leader Hideyoshi loved this place and visited with his wife and with the famous tea ceremony master, Sen no Rikyu.

ARRIVALS & DEPARTURES
By Train
From Kobe, take the subway to Tanigami and change to the Kobe Dentetsu line to Arima Onsen Guchi where you change again to take the spur to Arima Onsen. A few trains from Tanigami run directly to Arima Onsen. ¥970. About 30 minutes from Sannomiya Station.

By Bus
Hankyu and Shintetsu buses run between Sannomiya and Arima via Shin Kobe (40 minutes. ¥680).

Tourist Information
For **Tourist Information Office**, *Tel. (078)904-0708.*

WHERE TO STAY
HYOE KOYOKAKU, *Arima-cho, Kita-ku, Kobe, 651-1401. Tel. (078)904-0501. Fax. (078)904-3838. From ¥24,000 per person with two meals. Credit cards.*

Apparently Hideyoshi named the inn that was his and his wife's favorite. The hotel completed a major renovation in December 1994, only to be destroyed by the Great Hanshin Earthquake one month later. It has again reopened, and we hope its luck improves.

KOSENKAKU, *1455-1 Arima-cho, Kita-ku, Kobe, 651-1401. Tel. (078)904-0731, Fax (078)904-3481. From ¥24,000 per person with two meals. Credit cards.*

Built on the top of the mountain, Kosenkaku has commanding views of the valley and surrounding hills. It is more isolated than hotels closer to the station, yet it is in easy walking distance. The inn offers friendly service and delicious dinners combining Buddhist vegetarian cooking with local fish and meat specialties. Ask for a room with a view of the valley.

WHERE TO EAT

KEIGETSU *(Japanese, moderate to expensive). 1455-1 Arima-machi. Tel. (078)904-0731. Open 11am-2pm; 5pm-7:30pm. Reservations necessary. 6-minute walk from Arima Onsen Station.*

The entrance gate has a thatched roof. Keigetsu, run by the Kosenkaku Inn, serves delicious vegetarian temple fare, a feast for the eyes as well as the belly. They offer three courses: *Hana* for ¥5000; *Yuki* for ¥6500 and *Toku* ¥9500. Even *Hana*, the simplest, has 16 different dishes.

SEEING THE SIGHTS

Arima Onsen Kaikan. *Tel. (078)904-0256. Open 8am to 9:30pm. Closed first and the third Tuesday. ¥520.* If you are not staying at a hotel or inn but would like to try the hot springs, take a bath at this public facility. They claim drinking the water is beneficial to your health and can improve digestive functions! Personally, we prefer *sake.*

Nembutsu-ji Temple was, in the 17th century, the villa of Hideyoshi's wife, Nene. The temple has a beautiful Japanese garden with a 250-year old bodhi tree. Japanese visit in late June to see the tree's delicate white blossoms falling on the moss garden.

SHOPPING

Arima produces Ningyo-fude, doll's brush, woven painting brushes with a little doll's head that bobs in and out, just as one dips in and out of the hot spring baths.

Arima's bamboo crafts are readily available. We especially like **Yoshitakaya,** a small shop across the street from the train station. It carries charming Japanese goods including bamboo baskets and lamp shades and items made from *washi* paper and ceramics. *Tel. (078)904-0154.*

TAKARAZUKA

A hot spring town not far from Osaka, its all-female revue theater has put **Takarazuka** on the map. The revue is an interesting contrast to *kabuki* theater where the actors are all male! The imaginative, entrepreneurial president of Hankyu Railways started the troupe in 1914 to increase traffic on his train line. The troupe performs in Tokyo and Takarazuka; if Tokyo isn't on your itinerary, stop in Takarazuka for a uniquely Japanese performance.

ARRIVALS & DEPARTURES

By Train

From Osaka's Umeda Station: Hankyu Takarazuka line to Takarazuka Station (40 minutes, ¥270).

From Kobe: Take Hanshin train to Imazu and transfer to Hankyu Imazu line to Takarazuka.

Tourist Information

The "i" Tourist Information Office is at **Hankyu Takarazuka Station**. Open daily 9:30am to 5:45pm. Closed December 29-31. *Tel. (0797)81-5344.*

WHERE TO STAY

TAKARAZUKA HOTEL, *1-46 Umeno-cho, Takarazuka, Hyogo, 665. Tel. (0797)87-1151, Fax (0797)86-1795. Singles from ¥9500. Twins from ¥15,000. Credit cards.*

A nicely maintained old-style hotel; its French restaurant serves excellent food.

SEEING THE SIGHTS

Takarazuka Grand Theater is where the Takarazuka Revue (Takarazuka Kagekidan) *performs at 1pm on weekdays and 11am and 3pm on Friday and weekends, closed some Wednesdays. The theater is a 10-minute walk from Takarazuka station. Tickets are ¥3500 to ¥7500. Tel. (0797)86-7777.* Your ticket to the Revue entitles you to enter Takarazuka Family Land on the same day, but we wouldn't bother.

Tezuka Osamu Manga Museum (Tezuka Osamu Kinenkan). This new museum is dedicated to the creator of Japan's *manga* comic books. This high-tech museum, with a massive stained glass window of Tezuka's characters, has a screening room and a workshop demonstrating the art of animation. *7-35 Mukogawa-cho, Takarazuka. Tel. (0797)81-2970. Open 9:30am to 5pm; until 8pm July 21 through August 31. Closed Wednesday and December 21-31. ¥500. 10-minute walk from the station.*

TAKARAZUKA REVUE

*Mix together the Rockettes and Las Vegas, throw in a healthy dose of old Japan and you have the recipe for Takarazuka. This unlikely combination has been going strong since 1914. The **Takarazuka All-Female Revue** invented the genre that combines drama, Broadway-type musicals and Japanese theater. Women play the male as well as female roles and some of these male impersonators, otoko-yaku, have achieved star status among their many devoted fans.*

Training begins at a two-year academy that accepts only 40 of the 1600 applicants annually. The women, on a strict regimen not unlike boot-camp – during the first year they clean for two hours from 6am to 8am, study Western and Japanese dance and singing. In their second year, they specialize and learn either male or female roles. The top stars go on to television and theater.

Takarazuka attracts some 2.5 million people each year, an overwhelmingly female audience. There are hundreds of fan clubs and the average member attends some 20 performances annually. In Japan where men tend to be self-centered and unromantic, women croon at the idea of a sensitive and fanciful male, even if it is a woman playing the role. For a long time, Takarazuka graduates were highly sought after as brides because they were trained to be "perfect wives" in the eyes of Japanese men.

HIMEJI

Himeji is Japan's grandest remaining castle. It fits every samurai movie you have ever seen and is a hit with young and old. More than that, it's also conveniently located as an easy stopover on the *shinkansen* between Kobe and Okayama. It's also a great day trip from Kyoto, Osaka or Kobe.

Also, take a little time to see the excellent **Hyogo Prefectural Museum of History**. If you are on the *shinkansen* train passing through Himeji but don't have time to stop, make sure you at least get a glimpse from the train.

Planning Your Stay

A half-day is enough time to see the castle and museum. We recommend a side-trip from Kyoto-Osaka-Kobe or a stopover when traveling between the Hiroshima and Osaka areas.

ARRIVALS & DEPARTURES

By Train

Himeji Station is on the JR shinkansen line between Kobe and Okayama; many but not all of the *Hikari* shinkansen trains stop. The super-express *Nozomi* does not stop. Himeji is 25 minutes from Shin Kobe Station, 45 minutes from Shin Osaka Station, 1 hour from Kyoto Station and 25 minutes from Okayama. Slower trains run on the Tokaido line connecting Kyoto, Osaka and Kobe with Himeji: the Shin Kaisoku express leaves Kyoto, Osaka and Kobe several times an hour and takes one hour from Osaka.

GETTING AROUND TOWN

From the station to the castle is about a 15 minute walk; it's a straight shot down Otemae Street. There are also buses and lots of taxis.

Tourist Information

Tourist information is available at the JR Himeji Station "i" Tourist Information Office. Open 9am to 5pm. Closed December 29-31. *Tel. (0792)85-3792.*

Goodwill Guides: Contact the Tourist Information Office to arrange a volunteer guide through the Volunteer Guide Association of Himeji Castle.

WHERE TO STAY

While most travelers don't overnight in Himeji, there are a number of business hotels.

HOTEL SUNGARDEN, *Minami Ekimae-cho, Himeji, Hyogo, 670-0962. Tel. (0792)22-2231, Fax (0792)24-3731. Singles from ¥10,300. Twins from ¥18,000. Credit cards.*

This hotel, located at the south exit of the station, has an open and inviting lobby with restaurants on the mezzanine. The 15th floor restaurant has a view of the castle. The rooms are warm and inviting and the staff goes out of its way to accommodate your needs.

HIMEJI WASHINGTON HOTEL, *98 Higashi Ekimae-cho, Himeji, Hyogo, 670-0926. Tel. (0792)25-0111, Fax (0792)25-0133. Singles from ¥7800. Twins from ¥14,600. Credit cards.*

Part of the business hotel chain, the Washington Hotel is a short walk from the station near the Omizusuji arcade. The rooms, while nothing special, are adequate for a comfortable stay.

WHERE TO EAT

KAWATOBI *(Japanese, moderate to expensive). 169 Kuriyama. Tel. (0792)22-2627. Open 11am to 2pm; 4pm to 9:30pm. Closed Wednesday.*

A typical Japanese restaurant serves fresh fish from the Inland Sea. At lunch the mini-*kaiseki*, a set meal of tiny bits of so many different dishes, costs ¥3000. The dinner courses starts from ¥6000.

SENJU *(Steak, moderate to expensive). 596 Chiyoda-cho. Tel. (0792)97-3907. Open daily 11am to 10pm.*

Located in a quiet residential area, Senju serves delicious Tajima (Kobe) beef steak. Lunch set meals start from ¥3000.

SEEING THE SIGHTS

Himeji Castle. *Open 9am to 4pm, until 5pm June through August. Closed December 29-31. ¥500.* Nicknamed Shirasagi (White Heron) Castle because it has the grace of a heron taking off, Himeji Castle is the grandest of Japan's remaining castles. Edo (Tokyo), Osaka and Kumamoto were more important, but none survives in its original form today. The handful of other original castles still around are more modest.

UNESCO designated Himeji Castle a World Heritage Site. The castle is all dressed up in early April when cherry trees blossom. While spring is a lovely time to visit, expect crowds. But remember, Himeji is good to visit any time of year.

Himeji's has been home to a castle since the 14th century. In 1577, Hideyoshi, one of the three great unifiers, who was a top general for Oda Nobunaga at that time, took control and enlarged the castle. After the Battle of Sekigahara in 1600, the Tokugawa gave the castle to the Ikeda family, who constructed the castle you now see. Ikeda Terumasa, the son-in-law of the first Tokugawa shogun, built Himeji on a grand scale (second only to Osaka's) to intimidate the feudal lords to the west who opposed Tokugawa power.

By the early 1600s, the Tokugawa were consolidating power; the grand and brutal wars were all but a thing of the past although the final battle was not until 1615. Castles took on new importance as administrative centers and tangible symbols of power as well as fortresses.

As you snake through the maze of high stone walls with sharp turns to trap the invading forces, you see how sophisticated castle design had become by the early 17th century. Two types of holes, one circular for musketeers and one rectangular for archers, are placed strategically to pick off invaders. Holes in the floor to drop stones, hot water and oil make you reflect on the fate of the poor souls trying to enter. This castle was never under siege, one big reason why we can see it today.

The five-storied keep actually has six stories and a basement. The roofs combine arching Chinese-style gables with triangular dormer gables for a very graceful effect. The fish tiles on the roof ridges, *shachi-gawara*, represent mythical animals that protect against fire. The logic is if fish are swimming, they must be underwater, so there can't be fire. Under the eaves, the feudal lord's crest is in imprinted on the roof tiles.

Inside, the wooden interior is quite dark and stark. There were armaments stored in the keep, and the interior wasn't ornately decorated like the residences. The keep was the residence for the feudal lord only when the castle was under siege; at other times, he lived in an eminently more pleasant abode in the Ninomaru, within the second moat.

The wooden stairs in the keep are slippery and steep. We wonder how the samurai used them while in full battle gear. Make sure you take care using them; we find it best not to wear the slippers proffered at the entrance; true to their name, they are slippery and can be dangerous. In winter, bring an extra pair of heavy socks to wear on the castle's cold floor. The rooms become smaller and smaller as you ascend until the penthouse is living-room size with panoramic views on all four sides.

English Guides: Several Goodwill Guides usually wait at the entrance and offer to take you around. They're volunteers who want to make sure that foreign visitors appreciate their landmark.

Koko-en Garden, located close to the castle, provides a pleasant stroll and includes a tea ceremony room. *Open 9am to 5pm. ¥300. You can buy a combination ticket for the castle and garden for ¥640.*

Hyogo Prefectural Museum of History. The Museum of History, located behind Himeji Castle, is well worth a visit. It has the usual archaeology and local relics that you seem to find in all prefectural history museums, but it also has extensive displays on Japanese castles, focusing, naturally, on Himeji. The museum exhibits parts of the castle replaced during the extensive renovation in the 1950–60s and models of the surviving castles in Japan. It also has some videos with English narration. The museum's floor-to-ceiling glass walls bring the castle inside the museum. *Tel. (0792)88-9011. Open 10am to 5pm. Closed Monday and at the end of the year. ¥200.*

23. INLAND SEA
- SANYO & SHIKOKU

The **Inland Sea** lies between the southeast coast of Honshu Island and the north coast of Shikoku, the smallest of Japan's four main islands. **Hiroshima**, in western Honshu, is the largest city in the area, and its place in modern history makes a visit worthwhile. But beyond the large cities are gems like **Kurashiki** — with its beautiful storehouses along a canal and **Miyajima**, an island with an ingenious ancient shrine that's built over the sea, just 40 minutes from Hiroshima.

INLAND SEA HIGHLIGHTS
- *The Peace Museum at Hiroshima*
- *Kurashiki's well-preserved storehouses*
- *Remote mountaintop castle at Bitchu Takahashi*
- *Imbe's thousand year old tradition of Bizen ceramics*
- *Japan's oldest hot spring resort at Matsuyama*
- *Feudal lord's hunting garden at Takamatsu*

Planning Your Stay

You will need one day to see each of the following places: Hiroshima (but overnight at Miyajima), Miyajima and Kurashiki, Okayama, Kibi Plains, Bitchu Takahashi, Takamatsu, and Matsuyama. If your time is short, limit yourself to Kurashiki and Hiroshima.

Customize your itinerary to suit your interests.
- **War and Peace**: Hiroshima
- **Gardens**: Koraku-en at Okayama, Raikyu-ji Temple at Takahashi, Ritsurin Park at Takamatsu
- **Castles**: Bitchu Matsuyama in Takahashi, Matsuyama, Okayama, Hiroshima

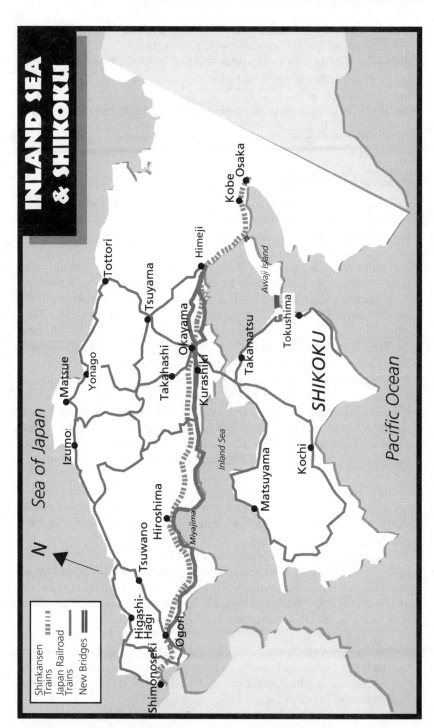

- **Shinto Shrine**: Itsukushima Jinja Shrine at Miyajima
- **Well-preserved historic storehouses**: Kurashiki
- **Museums**: Kurashiki — Ohara Museum and Folk Art Museum
- **Japanese craft shopping**: Kurashiki
- **Ceramics**: Bizen in Imbe
- **Unusual accommodations for foreign visitors**: Six International Villas in Okayama Prefecture

HIROSHIMA

Unfortunately, the city of **Hiroshima** entered the international lexicon with the atomic bombing on August 6, 1945. Visiting the museum and memorials at the Peace Park is a very moving experience and makes Hiroshima a must-see in western Japan.

Hiroshima is a clean, modern prefectural capital. Quaintly old-fashioned tram cars run on broad avenues. The large city boasts museums, a professional baseball team, a reconstructed castle and sophisticated department stores. It is a gateway to the scenic Inland Sea. The historic and hauntingly beautiful island of Miyajima is just 40 minutes away. Hiroshima's cuisine centers on seafood: oysters and *fugu* (blowfish) as well as *okonomiyaki*, a sort of Japanese pancake.

Historically, Hiroshima was the port used for Japan's colonial expansion in the 19th and 20th centuries. The dropping of the atomic bomb altered Hiroshima instantly. Since then the city has become the center of many peace movements. The mayor sends letters of protest to world leaders after every nuclear test. The annual peace gathering, marking the anniversary of the dropping of the bomb, attracts tens of thousands.

Planning Your Stay

Plan on spending one day in Hiroshima. If you are going to spend only one night, we recommend you stay at Miyajima, an island about 40 minutes from the city center.

Our recommended itinerary is as follows:

From JR Hiroshima Station, take the streetcar to Genbaku Dome Mae. See the A-Bomb dome, the monuments in Peace Park and the Peace Memorial Museum. Walk through the downtown area to Hiroshima Castle, then to Shukkei-en Garden and back to the station.

Dates to Remember

- **August 6**: Anniversary of the dropping of the atomic bomb. In addition to Peace Ceremonies, small lanterns are floated on rivers to comfort the souls of the deceased.

ARRIVALS & DEPARTURES

By Air

Two airports serve Hiroshima: **Hiroshima Airport** and **Hiroshima Nishi Airport**. Most flights arrive at Hiroshima Airport, but Nishi serves some smaller cities. Hiroshima Airport is inconveniently located about 50-minute drive from the city.

Make sure you know which airport you are flying from so you don't go to the wrong one. At the JR Hiroshima Station, buses to Hiroshima Airport leave from the shinkansen side of the station while buses to Hiroshima Nishi Airport leave from the main entrance of the station.

Hiroshima Airport

To/from Tokyo Haneda: 10 flights/day (ANA, JAL, JAS. ¥22,000)
To/from Sapporo: 2 flights/day (ANA, JAS. ¥33,700)
To/from Sendai: 2 flights/day (ANA. ¥27,300)
To/from Miyazaki: 1 flight/day (ANK. ¥17,200)
To/from Kagoshima: 2 flights/day (ANK. ¥18,300)
To/from Okinawa: 2 flights/day (ANA. ¥22,800)
Service to/from Hakodate (ANA), Aomori (ANA) and Matsumoto (JAS) several times a week.

Hiroshima also has international flights to Hong Kong, Seoul, Shanghai and Singapore.

For Ground Transportation:
Bus: to JR Hiroshima Station (shinkansen side) and to the Hiroshima Bus Center in central Hiroshima. Buses leave from platform B in front of the air terminal (50 minutes, ¥1300). Buy tickets from machines inside the airport terminal.
Taxi: to JR Hiroshima Station (45 minutes, ¥14,000)

Hiroshima Nishi Airport

Hiroshima Nishi Airport serves the following airports: Izumo, Kansai, Komatsu, Matsuyama, Niigata, Oita and Tottori.

For Ground Transportation:
Bus: to/from JR Hiroshima Station by Hiroden bus #3 or #13 from Platform #1 (30 minutes, ¥240)
Taxi: to/from JR Hiroshima Station (25 minutes, ¥2650)

By Train

Hiroshima is located on the shinkansen train line 4 1/2 hours from Tokyo (¥18,050); 2 hours from Kyoto (¥10,790); and 1 hour 20 minutes from Hakata in Kyushu (¥8700). It is also on the JR Sanyo line that connects Shimonoseki, the very western tip of Honshu Island, to Kurashiki, Okayama and other cities to the northeast.

By Bus

Overnight buses connect Hiroshima with Tokyo (12 hours, ¥12,060), Osaka (7 1/2 hours, ¥6630) and Kyoto (7 hours, ¥8070). Highway buses also serve Matsue (12 buses/day, 4 hours, ¥3950), Izumo (8 buses/day, 3 1/2 hours, ¥3950), Hagi (4 buses/day, 3 3/4 hours, ¥3300), and Nagasaki (1 bus/day, 7 hours, ¥6620).

GETTING AROUND TOWN

Hiroshima is fairly easy to navigate because basically, it is laid out on a grid system and many signs are bilingual. A series of streetcars emanates from the JR Hiroshima Station; a map in English is available. Many buses also leave from platforms near the streetcar terminal.

Tourist Information

Hiroshima City runs tourist information offices at the main entrance and the *shinkansen* entrance of JR Hiroshima Station. While you can pick up English maps and brochures there, staff members do not speak English. Open 9am to 5:30pm. The **Tourist Information Center** at the Peace Park has English-speaking staff members. Open 8:30am to 5pm; 9:30am to 6pm April through September. *Tel. (082)247-6738.*

Home Visit: Call the **Hiroshima International Exchange Lounge**. *Tel. (082)247-9715.*

Goodwill Guides: Call the **Hiroshima SGG Club**. *Tel. (082)842-3317* or contact the Tourist Information Center.

WHERE TO STAY

ANA HOTEL HIROSHIMA, *7-20 Nakamachi, Naka-ku, Hiroshima, 730-0037. Tel. (082)241-1111, Fax (082)241-9123. Singles from ¥9000. Twins from ¥17,500. Credit cards.*

This deluxe hotel near the Peace Park has a handful of restaurants.

HOTEL GRANVIA HIROSHIMA, *1-5 Matsubara-cho, Minami-ku, Hiroshima, 732-0822. Tel. (082)262-1111, Fax (082)262-4050. Singles from ¥9300. Twins from ¥15,500. Credit cards.*

Hotel Granvia, run by the JR Group, is conveniently located next to Hiroshima Station.

HOTEL NEW HIRODEN, *14-9 Osuga-cho, Minami-ku, Hiroshima, 732-0821. Tel. (082)263-3456, Fax (082)263-3784. Singles from ¥7400. Twins from ¥13,000. Credit cards. Member of Welcome Inn Reservation Center.*

Just a three-minute walk from Hiroshima Station, the hotel offers average business-hotel accommodations at a convenient location.

MINSHUKU IKEDAYA, *3-36 Dobashi-cho, Naka-ku, Hiroshima, 730-0854. Tel. (082)231-3329, Fax (082)231-7875. ¥4000 for one person without meals. ¥7000 for two people without meals. Credit cards. Member of Japanese Inn Group and Welcome Inn Reservation Center.*

A good choice for budget Japanese-style accommodations, Ikedaya is close to the Peace Park and just a two-minute walk from the Dobashi tram stop. There are 15 rooms; not one has a private bath.

WHERE TO EAT

KANAWA KAKI FUNE *(Oysters, moderate to expensive). Motoyasu River. Tel. (082)241-3493. Open 11am to 2pm; 5pm to 10pm. Closed 1st and 3rd Sundays.*

Moored on the Motoyasu River near the grounds of the Peace Park, step aboard this boat where you can enjoy oysters. Seated on *tatami* mats, you can eat oysters raw, fried and stewed with a mild *miso* sauce *(kaki dotenabe)*. Set lunches start at ¥2800 and dinners from ¥7000. You can also order a la carte, making your selections from the extensive English menu. If you don't have time to eat a meal, stop at their shop in the mall at the *shinkansen* side of Hiroshima Station.

OKONOMI MURA *(Okonomiyaki, inexpensive). 5-13 Shin Tenchi, near Hondori Arcade. Tel. (082)241-8758. Open 11am to 9pm or later.*

This run-down building is a great place to try Hiroshima's specialty, *okonomiyaki,* a pancake-like dish containing vegetables, seafood and meat. The more-than-twenty stalls are crowded with Hiroshima's residents gobbling them up.

SEEING THE SIGHTS

From JR Hiroshima Station take the tram to Genbaku Domu-mae. One of only a handful of Japanese cities still using trams, Hiroshima uses cars from the dismantled systems of Osaka, Kobe, Kyoto and Germany. Yes, Germany.

A-Bomb Dome (Genbaku Domu). The Industry Promotion Hall had the misfortune of being close to ground zero of the atomic bomb — all the occupants died instantly. But, the hall was one of the few structures within two kilometers of the blast to remain standing. The city decided to preserve that building only, no matter what the expense, because the dome's twisted metal girders are a moving testament to the horrors of war. UNESCO has designated the A-Bomb Dome a World Heritage Site.

Walk a few minutes from the A-Bomb Dome to the **Hiroshima Peace Memorial Museum** (Heiwa Kinenkan) in the Peace Park. *Tel. (082)241-4004. Open daily 9am to 5:30pm, until 4:30pm December through April. Closed December 29 through January 2. ¥50.* Housed in a simple contemporary stone building designed by noted architect Tange Kenzo, the museum has two sections, east and west. The East Building's displays set the stage for the dropping of the bomb by documenting Hiroshima's role as a military shipbuilding center and seaport before and during World War II. This more recent addition is an answer to the criticism that the museum concentrated on the horrors of the atomic bomb without putting it into perspective.

The West Building shows the bomb's awesome destructive power: all that remains of a person is the shadow on the stone steps of the Sumitomo Bank Building; watches and clocks with their hands permanently frozen on the minute of the explosion; a mangled tricycle whose three year old driver died instantly.

The museum is a moving statement for peace. Even the most hardened hawk can't help but be affected by the horrors the bomb inflicted. The museum has fairly good English explanations, and you can rent portable earphone guides.

In the Peace Park is the **Cenotaph** for the A-bomb victims that is inscribed, "Rest in peace. We will never repeat the error." The flame that burns in commemoration of the victims will be extinguished when all nuclear weapons are eliminated from the globe.

Other monuments also dot the park. Many are draped with strings of *origami* (folded paper) cranes, a practice begun by a young A-bomb victim who, before she died, pledged to fold 10,000 cranes to encourage world peace. Many school groups make strings of cranes and offer them at the monuments.

You can take a boat ride along Hiroshima's rivers; board it near the A-Bomb Dome. While not quite like cruising on the Seine, it's pleasant if you have some extra time.

While the atomic bomb tends to dominate the city's sights, there are a few other sights:

Shukkei-en Garden, a 15-minute walk from Hiroshima Station. The Asano feudal lord founded this strolling garden, which is detached from the castle. Azaleas and cherry blossoms make a special springtime walk. *Open 9am to 6pm; until 5pm October through March. ¥250.*

Hiroshima Castle is a 7-minute walk from Kamiya-cho tram stop. The powerful Mori feudal lords founded the castle in 1589; the atomic bomb destroyed the keep. The 1958 reconstruction houses a display of local history. *Tel. (082)221-7512. Open daily 9am to 5:30pm; until 4:30pm October through March. Closed December 29 through January 2. ¥320.*

Hiroshima Art Museum (Hiroshima Bijutsukan) near Hiroshima Castle, exhibits mainly works by European artists with a heavy emphasis on the Impressionists. *Tel. (082)223-2530. Open daily 9am to 5pm. Closed at New Year's. ¥1000.*

Hiroshima City Museum of Contemporary Art is in the outskirts of the city in Hijiyama Koen Park, which has a fantastic view of the city and is a good place to admire cherry blossoms. The museum exhibits post-World War II contemporary art. *Open 10am to 4:30pm; until 6:30pm mid-July through August. Closed December 29 through January 3. ¥320.*

SHOPPING

The main shopping area in Hiroshima is along **Aioi Dori** from JR Hiroshima Station going toward the A-Bomb Dome. You'll find Mitsukoshi, Sogo, Tenmaya and Fukuya department stores and specialty stores like Tokyu Hands.

SPORTS & RECREATION

Baseball: In the heart of downtown, Hiroshima Municipal Baseball Stadium has to be one of the world's most centrally located baseball fields and home to the professional league **Hiroshima Toyo Carp**.

Soccer: The professional team **Sanfrecce Hiroshima** plays at Hiroshima Big Anchor and Hiroshima Stadium.

MIYAJIMA

The island of **Miyajima** has been considered the sacred haunt of the Goddess of the Sea for more than a thousand years. **Itsukushima Jinja Shrine** was built in the 12th century and dedicated to the Goddess of the Sea to protect fishermen. The red *torii* gate in the water was the entrance gate to the family shrine of the Taira (Heike) clan.

The Japanese call the Itsukushima Jinja, which appears to float on water during high tide, one of the three most beautiful spots in the country. This honor, however, might be more of a curse than a blessing because many tawdry souvenir stands and other shops have sprung up catering to the bus loads of tourists arriving daily. The good news is serenity returns by dinnertime since most people do not overnight on the island.

ARRIVALS & DEPARTURES

By Train

To/from Hiroshima: JR Sanyo Honsen line to Miyajima Guchi (35 minutes, ¥400). From the station, it's an easy 5-minute walk to the JR ferry. Boats leave frequently and the crossing takes only ten minutes, ¥170. (JR Rail Passes are accepted).

The private Hiroshima Electric Railway *(Hiroden)* from Hiroshima Station to *Hiroden* Miyajima-guchi Station (60 minutes, ¥250).

ORIENTATION

The island is so small you can cover the main sights on foot. A cable car whisks you to the top of Mt. Misen,

Plan to spend a half-day on Miyajima, longer if you climb up Mt. Misen. Consider spending the night here rather than in Hiroshima. Not only is the air fresh, but when the tourists leave, you have the island practically to yourself.

Tourist Information

A tourist information counter is in the ferry terminal building at Miyajima Island. They also rent bicycles.

WHERE TO STAY

IWASO RYOKAN, *Miyajima, Saeki-gun, Hiroshima, 739-0500. Tel. (0829)44-2233, Fax (0829)44-2230. From ¥18,000 per person with two meals. Credit cards.*

The oldest of the 23 inns in Miyajima, Iwaso is a pleasant Japanese inn above Itsukushima Shrine, heading to Momiji Dani Park. Some of the rooms face the river gorge; the rooms in the older wing have more character than the rooms in the newer addition. An elegant *kaiseki* dinner is served in your room but breakfast is in the communal dining room. You have a choice of either a Japanese or a Western breakfast.

MIYAJIMA KOKUMIN-SHUKUSHA, *Miyajima, Saeki-gun, Hiroshima, 739-0500. Tel. (0829)44-0430, Fax (0829)44-2248. Rates from ¥8400 per person with two meals. ¥5000 per person without meals. No credit cards.*

Slightly out of the way, this public lodge offers comfortable rooms at a reasonable price. More than 70% of the rooms are Western style with twin beds. Take a bus towards Suizokukan-mae and get off at the last stop, which is the third stop. The inn is located in front of the bus stop. On foot, it's about 20 minutes from the ferry pier.

WHERE TO EAT

Nearly every shop in Miyajima sells *momiji manju*, a confection shaped like a maple leaf and filled with sweetened bean paste.

TACHIBANA, *Along the path between the ferry terminal and Itsukushima Jinja. Tel. (0829)44-0240. Open 10am to 5:30pm. Closed irregularly.*

Tachibana serves delicious *anago* sea eel, which is caught in the sea rather than raised in eel farms like most eel eaten in Japan. *Anago donburi* costs ¥800.

SEEING THE SIGHTS

As you get off the ferry you'll be greeted by some of Miyajima's 550 sacred (and tame) deer. Just make sure you keep any food and paper tucked away.

Itsukushima Jinja Shrine is a 10-minute walk from the ferry pier beside the water. Taira no Kiyomori, the powerful head of the Taira clan, built the Shinto shrine in the 11th century and dedicated it to the Goddess of the Sea. The vermilion *torii* gate, standing at the mouth of the small cove, is the formal entrance to the shrine buildings. In the old days, all the ships going to Itsukushima Island had to pass through this gate. This gate has to be one of Japan's most photographed structures — no easy feat in the land of Nikons and Canons.

The temple itself is situated on stilts on the shore; when the tide comes in, the water floods the area and the buildings appear to float on the water although they are actually connected by covered walkways. When the tide is out, the buildings look firmly anchored to land. The halls, connected by the corridors, resemble Heian-period *shinden* architecture. A *noh* stage sits in front of the buildings. Imagine the elegant and mysterious atmosphere of a *noh* performance in such a glorious setting.

With luck, some worshipper will have donated money to light the shrine's many stone lanterns; this nighttime sight is truly splendid.

The **Homotsukan Treasure Hall** holds the Heike Sutras, given by the clan to the shrine in the 12th century. While the fragile originals are rarely displayed, you'll see good reproductions. *The shrine is open daily 6:30am to 7pm. ¥300.*

Up in the hills above the shrine is a wonderful park called **Momiji Dani**, maple leaf valley. True to its name, the peaceful natural setting turns crimson every November. Beyond the park is the ropeway that will take you to the top of Mt. Misen; its slopes have virgin forest because the island is sacred; i.e., cutting down trees is still forbidden. The mountaintop offers great views of Hiroshima and the Inland Sea. Be sure you keep any food away from the many roaming monkeys.

Egami Historical and Folk Art Museum (Egami Rekishi Minzoku Shiryokan). This wealthy merchant's house has been converted into a museum displaying everyday utensils and furniture used by the family. The beautiful lattice windows and garden make a stop worthwhile. *Open 8:30am to 5pm.*

KURASHIKI

The small city of **Kurashiki** is guaranteed to enchant and delight even the most jaded visitor. The "town of storehouses" is home to one of

Japan's best preserved districts. Whitewashed, black-tiled rice store-houses flank a quiet canal that's lined with graceful willow trees. Kurashiki seems so Japanese, but it is the unlikely venue of Japan's first major collection of Western art. Today, it has some half-dozen museums, all within a few minutes walk of each other.

Tourism is Kurashiki's mainstay but unlike many places in Japan, the town has established strict building controls to preserve the character of its Bikan Historic District.

During the Edo period (1603–1868), Kurashiki was one of only a handful of areas under the direct control of the Tokugawa shogunate centered in far away Edo (Tokyo). Kurashiki became a major rice-storing area. The sturdy plaster buildings, called *kura*, hence the name of the city, protected the valuable commodity from fire and theft. The merchants acquired great wealth as the economy developed, and they were pretty much left alone.

Following the end of the Edo era, Kurashiki joined the frenzied race to modernize. The city's water sources and good transportation routes made textile manufacturing a natural. In 1920, Ohara Magosaburo, a wealthy industrialist, sent a young art student, Kojima Torajiro, to Europe to study and purchase European art. His purchases formed the first collection of Western art in Japan, and the collection is the basis for the Ohara Museum built in 1930.

ARRIVALS & DEPARTURES

By Air
Okayama is the closest airport. (See Okayama for flight information). A bus from the airport goes to Kurashiki Station Bus Center (45 minutes, ¥1000). A return bus leaves Kurashiki Station Bus Center 90 minutes before Tokyo flight departures.

By Train
JR Shin Kurashiki Station is on the shinkansen line, but not all shinkansen trains stop here. If the one you are on does not, get off at Okayama and take the local train on the JR Sanyo line to JR Kurashiki Station (15 minutes). Even if your shinkansen train does stop at JR Shin Kurashiki Station, consider changing at Okayama because JR Kurashiki Station is much more convenient than JR Shin Kurashiki Station.

To/from Tokyo: JR shinkansen train to JR Shin Kurashiki Station (4 hours 20 minutes, ¥16,360)

To/from Kyoto: JR shinkansen train to JR Shin Kurashiki Station (1 1/2 hours, ¥8070)

To/from Okayama: JR shinkansen train to JR Shin Kurashiki Station (12 minutes, ¥1310); JR Sanyo line to JR Kurashiki Station (14 minutes by local, ¥480)

To/from Hiroshima: JR shinkansen train to JR Shin Kurashiki Station (1 hour, ¥5130)

By Bus

Overnight bus runs from Tokyo's Shinagawa Station (11 hours, ¥10,400). Day bus from Osaka: 3 buses/day (5 hours, ¥3360).

GETTING AROUND TOWN

While Kurashiki is a sprawling city, the historic district is near the JR Kurashiki Station and reached easily on foot.

Tourist Information

JR Kurashiki Station. *Tel. (086)426-8681*. Open daily 9am to 5:30pm. Closed around New Year's.

Another tourist information office is in the Bikan Historic District at the bend in the canal: **Kurashiki-kan Tourist Information Office**, *Tel. (086)422-0542*. Open daily 9am to 5:30pm; 8:30am to 5pm November through March. Closed around New Year's. The wooden, Western-style building was originally a ward office. Inside you'll find coin lockers and vending machines, both prohibited on the streets of the preservation district.

Both are "i" Tourist Information Offices.

Home Visits: The Kurashiki Association of International Friendship will arrange a home visit. *Tel. (086)424-3593.*

Goodwill Guides: Arrange a volunteer Goodwill Guide from the Association of Kurashiki Goodwill Guides by calling *Tel. (086)424-7774* after 6pm.

WHERE TO STAY

Kurashiki has wonderful traditional Japanese inns in the center of the historic district. If Kurashiki's hotels and inns are filled, consider staying at neighboring Okayama, just a 15-minute train ride away.

RYOKAN KURASHIKI, *4-1 Honmachi, Kurashiki, 710-0054. Tel. (086)422-0730, Fax (086)422-0990. From ¥20,000 per person with two meals. Credit cards.*

This lovely Japanese inn has 20 rooms, each with a different decor and views of the garden, and features both Japanese and Western antiques. Enjoy English tea or coffee in the cozy tea room overlooking the lovely garden and open to nonresident guests. The owner was in the sugar wholesale business until the end of World War II. Supported by Ohara and others who loved Kurashiki's charming streets, the owner, now in her eighties, decided to preserve the beauty of the old merchant house by converting it to an inn. She still arranges flowers every day for each room and serves green tea to her guests.

TSURUGATA RYOKAN, *1-3-5 Chuo, Kurashiki, 710-0046. Tel. (086)424-1635, Fax (086)424-1650. From ¥15,000 per person with two meals. Credit cards.*

Located centrally in the Bikan Historic District, this authentic Japanese inn was a seafood wholesaler's residence in 1774. The interior has modern amenities but still maintains classic details such as lovely wooden beams. A small restaurant on the first floor serves delicious food, but as a guest of the inn, you are served in your room.

KURASHIKI KOKUSAI HOTEL, *1-1-44 Chuo, Kurashiki, 710-0046. Tel. (086)422-5141, Fax (086)422-5192. Singles from ¥8000. Twins from ¥14,000. Credit cards.*

Despite being a large Western-style hotel (106 rooms) and part of the JAL group, Kurashiki Kokusai Hotel maintains a real sense of individuality. Folk art decorates the average sized rooms. A huge mural painting by Munakata Shiko greets you in the lobby. For a Western-style hotel just around the corner from the historic district, it's a good choice.

KURASHIKI IVY SQUARE HOTEL, *7-2 Honmachi, Kurashiki, 710-0054. Tel. (086)422-0011, Fax (086)424-0515. Singles from ¥7000. Twins from ¥11,500. Credit cards.*

In the Ivy Square complex, a former textile factory has been converted into a shopping, restaurant, museum and hotel center. The low-lying brick buildings lend themselves to an attractive compound. Some of the rooms are quite small considering the price, but they are neat and tidy.

MINSHUKU KAMOI, *1-24 Honmachi, Kurashiki, 710-0054. Tel. (086)422-4898, Fax (086)487-7615. ¥6000 per person with two meals. No credit cards.*

Next to the *torii* gate on the approach to Achi Shrine, Kamoi is a comfortable inn run by the friendly family who owns the *sushi* shop with the same name is located in the heart of the historic district. The 15-room inn has no private baths.

EL PASO INN, *1-9-4 Chuo, Kurashiki, 710-0046. Tel. (086)421-8282, Fax (086)426-6030. Singles from ¥5500. Twins from ¥10,000. Credit cards.*

Located behind the Ohara Museum, El Paso's building looks like a traditional *kura* storehouse but the rooms are all Western style. The bathrooms are minuscule, but at least each room has a private one.

KURASHIKI STATION HOTEL, *2-8-1 Achi, Kurashiki, 710-0055. Tel. (086)425-2525, Fax (086)426-6702. Singles from ¥6000. Twins from ¥11,000. Credit cards. Member of the Welcome Inn Reservation Center.*

Across the street from Kurashiki station, this business hotel offers inexpensive accommodations.

WHERE TO EAT

KIYUTEI *(Steak, inexpensive to moderate). 1-3-20 Chuo. Tel. (086)422-5140. Open 11am to 8pm. Closed Monday.*

Kiyutei is around the corner from the Kurashiki Kokusai Hotel. The restaurant is run by the hotel and is in a converted traditional building located across from the Ohara Museum. This casual restaurant serves steak, but you can also order other Western food such as salmon and stews. Steak dinners start at ¥2000; a la carte is also available.

KAMOI *(Sushi, inexpensive). 1-3-17 Chuo. Tel. (086)422-0606. Open 9am to 5:30pm. Closed Monday.*

In the center of the Bikan Historic District, across from the Ohara Museum, you'll find this long-time *sushi* shop. Kamoi's most popular is *daikan-zushi*, a kind of *sushi* with lots of ingredients buried under the rice. In the Edo period, commoners were not allowed to enjoy any luxuries no matter how wealthy they were (what a life!). They were smart enough to come up with this *sushi* that appeared to have only a few vegetables on top. But marinated fish and other delicacies were hidden under the rice. Plastic models out front make ordering easy.

EL GRECO, *To the right of the entrance to the Ohara Museum. Open 10am to 5pm. Closed Monday.*

Look for the red canopy on the ivy-covered stucco building to the right of the Ohara Museum. El Greco is a great place for a delicious cup of coffee.

SEEING THE SIGHTS

From JR Kurashiki Station, walk down Motomachi Dori. Turn left before the Kurashiki Kokusai Hotel to enter the Bikan Historic District.

On the right, behind a typical Kurashiki wall, but in a building resembling a Greek temple, is the **Ohara Museum** (Ohara Bijutsukan). Established in 1930 by industrialist Ohara Magosaburo, the museum houses Japan's first collection of Western art. The artist Kojima Torajiro, who was also Ohara's agent, collected the works in Europe in the 1920s by selecting art that he felt would have educational value for art students in Japan. While the museum does have some masterpieces such as El Greco's *Annunciation,* Monet's *Water Lilies* and Matisse's *Cliffs Downstream on the Etorta,* the entire collection is not up to these standards.

But there is more to the museum than its Western paintings. The annex houses works by other contemporary artists such as Alexander Calder and Henry Moore. But the most interesting to us is the **Kogeikan**, a building in the traditional storehouse style, where works of Japan's folk craft movement are on display. It's fascinating to compare the ceramic works of Hamada Shoji, Tomimoto Kenkichi and Kawai Kanjiro with

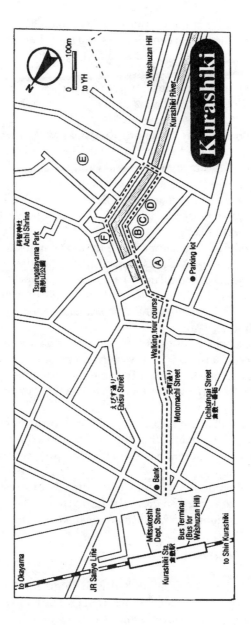

Kurashiki

A. Ohara Museum
B. Kurashiki Ninagawa Museum
C. Kurashiki Folkcraft Museum
D. Japan Folk Toy Museum
E. Ivy Square
F. Kurashiki Archaeological Museum

Courtesy of Japan National Tourist Organization

British potter Bernard Leach's work as each developed his own style. An entire room contains Munakata Shiko's marvelous paintings on wood. *Ohara Museum is open 9am to 5pm. Closed Monday and December 28 through January 1. ¥1000.*

Across the canal from the entrance to the Ohara Museum are two impressive houses, one with green roof tiles and the other Japanese style; both belong to the Ohara family. Unfortunately they are not open to the public.

Kurashiki has many other museums, although none on the same scale as the Ohara. Two of our favorites are the Folk Art Museum and the Toy Museum.

The **Kurashiki Folk Art Museum** (Kurashiki Mingeikan) occupies several storehouses near the bend in the canal. The complex displays folk crafts including baskets, furniture, ceramics and textiles from Japan and other parts of the world. The ambiance of the storehouses' interiors adds to the pleasure of viewing the charming collection. *Open 9am to 5pm; until 4:15pm December through February. Closed Monday. Closed December 29 through January 1. ¥700.*

The **Japan Folk Toy Museum** (Nihon Kyodo Gangu-kan), in an old storehouse near the Folk Art Museum, displays traditional toys from Japan and other countries. You'll notice many of the Japanese toys are red because it was believed that wearing the color red could prevent smallpox. The attached shop sells traditional toys. *Open daily 8:30am to 5pm. Shop open until 6:30pm. Closed January 1. ¥500.*

The only merchant house open to the public as a museum is the **Ohashi Residence** (Ohashi-tei). This wealthy family was allowed to build a gate, which was usually restricted to samurai. The house dates from 1796. *Open 9am to 5pm. Closed Monday and December 28 through January 1. ¥500.*

A few minutes walk from the canal, you'll find **Kurashiki Ivy Square**, the former Kurabo Textile Mill that is currently turned into museums, shops, restaurants and a hotel. In the summer the large courtyard sports a popular beer garden.

And now for something completely different...**Kurashiki Tivoli Gardens,** a theme park based on the real thing in Denmark. Just the other side of JR Kurashiki Station. *Open 9am to 6pm, until 8pm weekends and holidays. ¥2000.*

SHOPPING

The **Bikan Historic District** is filled with shops for fun browsing. Some sell traditional crafts, others Bizen ceramics. The good news is there isn't the plethora of junky souvenir shops that seem to take over most popular tourist areas. Young artsy vendors along the streets sell their own handicrafts as well as items they picked up overseas. This combination seems to symbolize Kurashiki — the traditional and the Western have co-existed for decades here.

Here are a few shops we especially enjoyed:

Ueshima Shoten, *10-5 Honmachi. Tel. (086)422-3183.* Master lanternmaker Ueshima has been making Japanese lanterns for over 50 years. Watch him form them in his tiny six-mat workshop located within the historic district. His wife helps to shape the lanterns.

Kaze no Yakata, *Tel. (086)425-1502. Open daily 9am to 6:30pm.* This shop is on the road that leads to Ivy Square, one block over and parallel to the canal, and specializes in reasonably priced mobiles and other items made of Japanese *washi* paper, which make good gifts.

Dotemori Sake Shop, *Tel. (086)423-1221.* In a traditional building across from the canal, this quaint *sake* shop sells locally-made *sake*, some bottled in unusual containers. Samples are offered.

OKAYAMA

Once the center of the domain run by the Ikeda feudal lords, **Okayama** is a modern city that is the home of Koraku-en, one of Japan's best gardens, and a reconstructed castle. Although we don't recommend you detour to Okayama, you can easily spend a half-day visiting the garden and castle if you are passing through the area.

Japanese arrive in droves to marvel over the Seto Ohashi Bridge connecting Okayama with the island of Shikoku, previously an hour-long ferry ride. Today trains whisk you across the engineering wonder in about 15 minutes.

ARRIVALS & DEPARTURES

By Air

Okayama Airport is about 30 minutes outside of the city.

To/from Tokyo Haneda: 4 flights/day (ANA. ¥21,750)
To/from Sapporo Chitose: 1 flight/day (ANA. ¥32,200)
To/from Sendai: 4 flights/week (JAS. ¥25,700)
To/from Kagoshima: 3 flights/day (JAC. ¥21,350)

For Ground Transportation:
Bus: to Okayama Station (32 minutes, ¥680)
Taxi: to Okayama Station (25 minutes, ¥4500)

By Train

Okayama Station is on the JR shinkansen line.

To/from Tokyo: shinkansen train (4 hours, ¥16,670)
To/from Kyoto: shinkansen train (1 1/4 hours, ¥7330)
To/from Hiroshima: shinkansen train (1 hour, ¥5860)

By Bus

To/from Tokyo: Overnight bus from Shinagawa and Shinjuku Stations. (11 hours, ¥10,200)

To/from Fukuoka: Overnight bus (9 hours, ¥7200)

Service to/from Osaka (2 buses/day, 4 1/4 hours, ¥3060), **Matsue** (4 buses/day, 3 1/2 hours, ¥3400) and **Matsuyama** (6 buses/day, 3 hours, ¥4300)

GETTING AROUND TOWN

The tram system and buses are the best way to get around Okayama.

Tourist Information

The "i" Tourist Information Office is located in Okayama Station. *Tel. (086)222-2912*. Open daily 9am to 6pm.

WHERE TO STAY

OKAYAMA WASHINGTON HOTEL, *2-6-201 Honmachi, Okayama City, 700-0901. Tel. (086)231-9111, Fax (086)221-0048. Singles from ¥8000. Twins from ¥15,000. Credit cards.*

Just a few minutes walk from JR Okayama Station, this business hotel has Western, Chinese and *kushiage* restaurants and even an oldies "live house."

HOTEL GRANVIA, *1-5 Ekimoto-cho, Okayama City. 700-8515. Tel. (086)234-7000. Fax (086)234-7099. Singles from ¥9500. Twins from ¥22,000. Credit cards.*

A member of the chain of JR hotels, Hotel Granvia provides comfortable rooms at a convenient station location.

CHISAN HOTEL OKAYAMA, *1-1-13 Marunouchi, Okayama City, 700-0823. Tel. (086)225-1212, Fax (086)225-1322. Singles from ¥6600. Twins from ¥11,500. Credit cards.*

Part of a moderately priced chain, Chisan is a business hotel located close to the garden and museums. It's a 10-minute walk from the JR Okayama station, but if you take a tram car heading toward the castle, get off at the third stop and the 10-storied building will be in front of you.

Okayama International Villas

Okayama's gift to foreign travelers is the group of **International Villas**, the brainchild of a governor of the prefecture who was an exchange student in America. He wanted to do something to repay the kindness he received. The result: six architecturally distinctive villas in different locations around Okayama Prefecture and available only to foreigners and Japanese who accompany them.

The fee is only ¥3000 per person in a twin room and an additional ¥500 for single occupancy. Membership, which costs ¥500, entitles you to a ¥500 discount per night. No meals are served, but all the villas have kitchens equipped with dishes and pots. The villas also have lists of nearby restaurants.

While it sounds too good to be true, we have to warn you of one drawback – most of the villas are in fairly remote areas that can be time consuming to reach, especially if you are using mass transportation. While staying at them gives you the opportunity to see some rural areas, they can be troublesome to reach if you are on a tight schedule. However, if you can travel at a leisurely pace, staying at the villas gives you a good excuse to see areas of rural Japan.

The six villas, each with a completely different architectural style, are located in:

Ushimado. A contemporary building on a hillside with sweeping views of the Inland Sea, Ushimado is the most dramatic of the villas. It's also the most convenient to major sightseeing spots like Bizen and Okayama City.

Shiraishi is on an island about a half-hour ferry ride from Kasaoka City, located between Hiroshima and Kurashiki. The quiet fishing island makes a good getaway. The outside terrace has a barbecue grill and good views of the sea. But bring your food from the mainland because there aren't many shops nearby. This fact itself makes the stay a treat, but you'll need to be prepared.

Fukiya is in a quiet, charming village famous for its traditional wooden buildings decorated with red ocher mined in the district. The villa, a replica of a soy warehouse, has a lot of character.

Takebe, about one hour due north of Okayama City, sports a hot spring bath. Other than that, there's not much to the town. A local architect designed this contemporary structure.

Hattoji, on the eastern border of Okayama Prefecture, features a villa in a 120-year old, thatched-roof farmhouse. The village itself is a quiet farming community with many thatched-roof buildings.

Koshihata, the most remote of the villas, stands near the northern border of the prefecture. The 19th century thatched-roof farmhouse has only two guest rooms.

To make reservations at any of the villas, contact the Okayama International Villa Group, *Okayama International Center, 2-2-1 Hokancho, Okayama, 700-0026. Tel. (086)256-2535, Fax (086)256-2576; www.harenet.ne.jp/villa. Closed Monday.* They can give you detailed directions. You can also book the villas through the Welcome Group Reservation Center.

WHERE TO EAT

AZUMAZUSHI *(Regional sushi, inexpensive). 3-1-48 Omote-machi. Tel. (086)231-0158. Open 11am to 2pm; 4:30pm to 9pm. Closed Wednesday.*

Facing the Inland Sea, Okayama is noted for its delicious fresh fish. Order *barazushi* for ¥1500, Okayama's special dish mixes seafood and vegetables with vinegared rice. Try the *Azuma teishoku* at lunch time for ¥2000 for a sampling of fresh fish and local delicacies.

MAGANEDO *(Soba, inexpensive). 1-8-2 Uchisange. Tel. (086)222-6116. Open 11am to 7pm. Closed 1st and 4th Sunday and national holidays.*

The chef's father opened this shop as a confectionery store in the late 1920s, but he was more interested in making perfect *soba*. He goes to great lengths to select the best ingredients. Try the *inaka soba* for ¥600.

SEEING THE SIGHTS

From JR Okayama Station, board a bus at platform #2 that's heading to Fujiwara Danchi or Takeda and get off at Koraku-en-mae — about 10 minutes. Alternatively, take the tram to the Shiroshita stop and walk about 10 minutes.

Koraku-en Garden is Okayama's pride and joy. The 300-year old garden was completed in 1700 and is considered one of the three most beautiful in Japan along with Kenroku-en in Kanazawa and Kairaku-en in Mito. It is an obligatory stop for every tour bus in the area. Don't let that put you off because the beautiful garden is still worth a stop and, fortunately, it doesn't attract anywhere near as many visitors as Kenroku-en.

The feudal lord Ikeda took 14 years to build the strolling garden, the first in Japan to use broad expanses of lawn extensively. Divided into sections, the garden features groves of plum, cherry and bamboo trees and tea bushes. The small island, connected by a pretty bridge, has a rustic teahouse. The adjacent castle is used as borrowed scenery, a design device often used in Japanese gardens. *Open daily 7:30am to 6pm; 8am to 5pm October through March. ¥350.*

The **Okayama Prefectural Museum** (Okayama Kenritsu Hakubutsukan), near the entrance to Koraku-en Garden, displays the area's archaeological finds, pottery and folk craft objects. *Open 9am to 6pm; 9:30am to 5pm October through March. Closed Monday and December 28 through January 4. ¥200.*

The black walls of **Okayama Castle** (Okayama-jo) tower over the adjacent garden. Built in the 16th century and destroyed in World War II, the 1966 reconstruction duplicates the exterior of the original. The interior is another story; you can ride to the top of the four-storied castle keep in an elevator. We wondered what the samurai would think. The black walls have earned it the nickname "crow's castle." *Open daily 9am to 5pm. Closed December 29-31. ¥300.*

Adjacent to the castle, on the site of the castle's Audience Chamber, is the **Hayashibara Museum** (Hayashibara Bijutsukan). The museum displays a wealthy entrepreneur's collections – the Ikeda feudal lords' *noh* costumes, *tansu* chests, armor and other artifacts. *Open daily 9am to 5pm. Closed December 25 through January 2. ¥300, additional for special exhibits.*

Okayama Prefectural Museum of Art (Okayama Ken Bijutsukan) is about a 10-minute walk from the castle area. The contemporary building, built with granite and ceramic tiles from Arita in Kyushu, displays mostly Japanese, 20th-century paintings plus temporary exhibitions; there are also works by the 15th-century master painter Sesshu. The architect drew inspiration from Okayama castle – one window offers castle views. *Open 9am to 5pm. Closed Monday and December 28 through January 4. ¥300, additional for special exhibitions.*

THE KIBI ROAD - KIBI-JI

Between Okayama and Kurashiki is **Kibi**, an area rich in folklore and legend that was settled as long ago as the 4th century A.D. Today cycling and hiking trails connect the area's sights. If you are so inclined, plan on spending about four hours to cover the mostly flat area on bicycle or about seven hours on foot. If you have a car, you can cover the main sights in two to three hours.

We will start from Okayama, but you can also easily start at Kurashiki and do everything in reverse.

ARRIVALS & DEPARTURES

From Okayama, take the JR Kibi line to Bizen Ichinomiya Station (12 minutes). Rent a bicycle at the station – it can be returned at Higashi Soja Station or Soja Station. The bike and hiking trails begin at the station.

SEEING THE SIGHTS

Near the station is **Kibitsuhiko Jinja Shrine**, a quiet place built in Kamakura's architectural style. The shrine's huge stone lantern is Japan's largest.

About two kilometers away is **Kibitsu Jinja Shrine**, which dates back to the 4th century A.D. The main building has beautiful twin gables and a wooden, 300-meter covered walkway that's on a slight incline – it's one of the most graceful structures we have ever seen. The shrine is dedicated

MOMOTARO, THE PEACH BOY

For a long, long time, Okayama has been associated with peaches. Mention the word peach to a Japanese and the first reaction is, "You must try Okayama peaches." The famous legend of Momotaro, the Peach Boy, is one of Japan's most beloved children's tales.

An elderly farmer and his wife didn't have any children. One day when the farmer's wife went to the river to wash, she saw a big peach floating down the river. Carefully, she picked it up and took it home. When the couple opened it, lo and behold, out came a beautiful boy! They named him Momotaro, Peach Boy.

The boy grew to be a strong but gentle young man. At the time, a rumor was circulating about a wicked goblin from the sea who had attacked people in the neighboring area. Without hesitation, Momotaro decided to go on a mission to conquer the goblin, who lived on an island off Shikoku. His old mother made him Kibi-dango, a special Kibi-area dumpling, and off he went. As he walked along, Momotaro met a pheasant who asked if he could taste the special Kibi-dango. In exchange, he offered to accompany Momotaro on his mission. The same thing happened twice more and Momotaro and the pheasant were joined by a dog and a monkey.

Full of energy from eating the Kibi dumplings, the foursome reached the goblin's island, fought valiantly and slew the enemy. Triumphantly, they returned home with the goblin's treasures and lived happily ever after.

to Kibihitsuko no Mikoto, a god sent by the court of Yamato to subdue the area.

After several more kilometers, you'll reach **Tsukuriyama Burial Mound**, a huge (350-meters long and 30-meters high) keyhole-shaped mound built for the 5th century rulers of the area.

A little further along is **Bitchu Kokubun-ji Temple**, originally built in the 8th century. The 17th century five-storied pagoda that today lords over the green fields is pretty much all that remains of the once extensive complex. A Kibi Road Tourist Information office is on the grounds of the temple. At Soja you can catch the train for the short hop to Kurashiki or Okayama.

BITCHU TAKAHASHI

This small castle town features Japan's highest mountaintop castle and a small but well-preserved samurai district. It's definitely off-the-beaten path, which adds to its appeal. You can make a one-day side trip from Kurashiki or Okayama or combine it with a trip to the charming village of Fukiya.

ARRIVALS & DEPARTURES

By Train

JR Hakubi line from Okayama (50 minutes) and Kurashiki (35 minutes).

GETTING AROUND TOWN

The Ishibiya samurai district and Raikyu-ji temple are easily reached on foot or by taxi from the station. The castle is about an hour's walk uphill, so unless you are really hearty, take a taxi up and walk back down.

Tourist Information

Across from Bitchu Takahashi Station. *Tel. (0866)22-6789.* Open 7:15am to 6:45pm. There is also a rent-a-cycle shop at the station.

SEEING THE SIGHTS

Raikyu-ji Temple's claim to fame is that Kobori Enshu, the lord of the area and one of Japan's greatest garden designers, made its garden in 1609. It is one of the few existing gardens confirmed to be designed by Kobori. View it from the veranda of the temple; it's the dry-landscape style rather than a strolling garden. The masterful placement of gravel, rocks and bushes and the "borrowed scenery" of Mt. Atago makes it look larger than it is. Gravel in front of the well-pruned azalea bushes symbolizes the ocean; in front you see two islands. *Open 9am to 4:30pm. ¥300.*

The **Ishibiya Samurai District** has some traditional houses and lovely walls that retain the atmosphere of bygone days. One fairly modest house has been turned into the Samurai House Museum. *Open 9am to 4pm. Open daily March through November and open only on weekends December through February. ¥300.*

Bitchu Matsuyama Castle (Bitchu Matsuyama-jo) is Japan's highest mountaintop castle. During the 15th century Warring States Period, castles were built on top of mountains. But with the change of warfare techniques brought about by the introduction of firearms, the first great unifier, Oda Nobunaga, built his castle on a small hill rather than on a remote mountaintop; others followed his example. Bitchu Matsuyama Castle is one of the few to survive from that earlier era.

From the small parking lot, it's still about a 20-minute walk up to the castle's keep. The tiny keep, the castle's oldest building, was rebuilt in 1683. Recently the prefecture has been building an exact replica of its walls and gates based on historical documents. *Open 9am to 4pm. ¥300. Closed December 28 through January 4.*

FUKIYA

Deep in the mountains lies the charming hamlet of **Fukiya**, once a center of copper and red ocher mining. The mines are long closed, but the houses built by the once-wealthy merchants remain. Red ocher colors the lattice windows and doors, adding a very distinctive touch. Wander around the quaint village and make sure you stop in the **Local History Museum** (Kyodokan), the former residence of a family involved in red ocher production. Overnight in Fukiya at the Okayama International Villa that's built like a traditional warehouse.

ARRIVALS & DEPARTURES

Fukiya is about one hour from Bitchu Takahashi by Bihoku bus but there are only a few buses a day, so check the schedule.

WHERE TO STAY

FUKIYA INTERNATIONAL VILLA, *836 Fukiya, Nariwa-cho, Okayama, 719-2341. Tel. (0866)29-2222. For reservations contact Okayama International Villa Group, Okayama International Center, 2-2-1 Hokancho, Okayama, 700-0026. Tel. (086)256-2535, Fax (086)256-2576. ¥3000 per person with no meals. ¥500 additional for single room. ¥2500 for members (membership ¥500). No credit cards. Member of the Welcome Inn Reservation Center.*

A member of the Okayama International Villas, the inn is open only to foreigners and to Japanese who may be traveling with them. The villa is a replica of a soy sauce warehouse that was once on the site; its exterior has the typical charred black walls, ocher windows and latticework for which the town is known. Four rooms are Western and one is Japanese style, but all have Japanese touches like *shoji* screens and light-colored wood.

IMBE

Fans of Japanese ceramics should put **Imbe**, home of Bizen ceramics, on their list of must-sees. The small town is filled with kilns and shops making and selling the rustic ceramics long prized by tea connoisseurs.

Bizen, one of the oldest kilns in Japan, has a thousand-year history of making everyday utensils. Bizen pottery is set apart from other Japanese ceramics because it has to be fired at a temperature of 1300°C. The firing takes nearly two weeks and then another ten days to cool down the kiln enough to remove the work.

The earthy, unglazed pottery caught the eye of tea masters in the 16th century, giving a major boost to production and assuring Bizen a place in the sun.

Since Bizen is unglazed, designs are achieved through a number of effects that occur in the kiln. Some designs rely on ash from burning pine wood landing on the piece, and others on tying rice straw around the pot or by adding salt or charcoal. Today much of the work on sale in town is mass produced although some artists still create individual pieces that, of course, come at a hefty price.

Plan to stay in Okayama (see *Where to Stay* in Okayama above).

ARRIVALS & DEPARTURES

From the JR Okayama Station, take the Akoo line to Imbe Station, about 45 minutes.

GETTING AROUND TOWN

The kilns and shops are clustered near the train station.

Tourist Information

The **tourist information counter** is inside Imbe Station. *Tel. (0869)64-1100.* Closed Tuesday; when closed, pick up maps at the JAL ticket counter.

WHERE TO EAT

KOKORO-ZUSHI *(Japanese cuisine, inexpensive). Ekimae, Imbe. Tel. (0869)64-0288. Open 10:30am to 7:30pm. Closed Wednesday.*

Kokoro serves all its food on Bizen plates, elevating even the most plebeian food to an art form. After seeing Kokoro's innovative presentation, we looked at Bizen plates in the shops with new inspiration. Despite its name, Kokoro serves much more than *sushi;* you can have *tempura,* cooked eel and other Japanese delicacies. A set of *sushi* starts from ¥800.

FUTABA SHOKUDO *(Japanese, inexpensive). Next to the Bizen Traditional and Contemporary Art Museum, facing toward the busy street in front of the station. Tel. (0869)64-2723. Open 11am to 11pm.*

This conveniently located restaurant offers lots of different types of Japanese food including home-style cooking; it's a good place for a quick lunch.

SEEING THE SIGHTS

Your first stop should be the **Bizen Traditional and Contemporary Art Museum** (Okayama Bizen Togei Bijutsukan), next to Imbe Station, for an excellent overview of Bizen ware. True to its name, both historic and contemporary pieces are on display. Our only fear is after we see the good stuff, we have a difficult time settling for a piece in a reasonable price range. *Tel. (0869)64-1400. Open 9:30am to 5pm. Closed Monday except in*

April, May, October, November and December. Closed December 29 through January 3. ¥500.

Fujiwara Kei Commemorative Museum (Fujiwara Kei Kinenkan) displays the works of Fujiwara Kei, a Living National Treasure who died in 1970. Enjoy his dynamic tea bowls and vases that epitomize postwar Japanese ceramics. *Tel. (0869)67-0638. Open 10am to 4:30pm. Closed Monday and December 20 through January 10. ¥500.*

SHOPPING

Bizen Kilns and Shopping. Wander along the short road perpendicular to the main entrance of the station, and along the road into which it dead ends. You'll see lots of kilns and shops with Bizen ceramics in all price ranges — some will permit you to enter their studios.

SHIKOKU ISLAND - TAKAMATSU

Across the Inland Sea lies **Shikoku Island**, the smallest of Japan's four main islands. **Takamatsu City**, located at the north coast of Shikoku facing the busy and narrow Inland Sea, is much closer to Honshu Island since the 1988 opening of the Seto Ohashi Bridge, the longest two-tiered bridge system in the world. Ten years in the making, this massive construction project strings together a number of bridges over five islands to make the island of Shikoku just a 15-minute train ride from Honshu. Both train and cars use the 10-kilometer bridge, which itself has become quite a popular sightseeing spot for Japanese. The bridge now makes Takamatsu an easy day trip from anywhere on the Kyoto-Hiroshima *shinkansen* corridor.

The old name for the Takamatsu area is Sanuki.

ARRIVALS & DEPARTURES

By Air

Takamatsu Airport serves the city.

To/from Tokyo Haneda: 5 flights/day (ANA, JAS. ¥21,650)
To/from Osaka Itami: 1 flight/day (ANK. ¥10,850)
To/from Osaka Kansai: 2 flights/day (ANK. ¥10,850)
To/from Fukuoka: 2 flights/day (JAC. ¥17,700)
Service to/from Sapporo's Chitose (ANA. ¥32,750), Sendai (JAS. ¥26,100) and Kagoshima (JAC. ¥21,300).

For Ground Transportation:
Bus: to JR Takamatsu Station (35 minutes, ¥740)
Taxi: to JR Takamatsu (30 minutes, about ¥3800)

By Train

From JR Okayama Station, take the JR Marine Liner across the Seto Ohashi Bridge to JR Takamatsu Station (about 1 hour). To Okayama by shinkansen train from Tokyo (about 4 hours) and from Kyoto (1 hour 20 minutes).

By Bus

Overnight service connects Takamatsu with Tokyo (10 1/2 hours, ¥10,500), Yokohama (11 hours, ¥9990) and Nagoya (7 1/4 hours, ¥7130).

Highways buses between Takamatsu and Osaka (4 buses/day, 4 hours, ¥4590) and Matsuyama (12 buses/day, 2 1/2 hours, ¥4000).

GETTING AROUND TOWN

A fairly compact city laid out in a grid pattern, use buses and trams to get around.

Tourist Information

The "i" Tourist Information Office is at JR Takamatsu Station. *Tel. (087)851-2009.* Open 9am to 5pm. Closed December 30 through January 3.

Goodwill Guides: Arrange for a Goodwill Guide by contacting the Takamatsu Tourist Information Office.

Kagawa Welcome Card

Kagawa Prefecture has instituted a Welcome Card for foreigners entitling them to discounts at hotels, restaurants, shops and sights. You can obtain the card free of charge at JNTO offices or at the Tourist Information offices at Takamatsu Airport and Takamatsu Station. To be eligible, you must bring your passport and have a visa for a period less than one year.

WHERE TO STAY

ROYAL PARK HOTEL TAKAMATSU, *1-11-3 Kawara-machi, Takamatsu, 760-0052. Tel. (087)823-2222, Fax (087)823-2233. Singles from ¥10,000. Twins from ¥20,000. Credit cards.*

Opened in 1989, this art deco hotel offers sleek designs and larger-than-average rooms. It's a five-minute taxi ride from JR Takamatsu Station.

TAKAMATSU GRAND HOTEL, *1-15-10 Kotobukicho, Takamatsu, 760-0023. Tel. (087)851-5757, Fax (087)821-9422. Singles from ¥7000. Twins from ¥12,500. Credit cards.*

Just a few minutes from JR Takamatsu Station and Tamamo Park, the reasonably priced 136-room hotel is popular with businessmen and tour groups. For great panoramic views of the park and harbor, eat or have a drink in the 7th floor Yashima Restaurant.

WHERE TO EAT

KAISENDONYA NAKAMISE *(Seafood, inexpensive to moderate). 15-2 Furubaba-cho. Tel. (087)851-8100. Open daily 11am to 11pm.*

This restaurant in central Takamatsu seems like a cross between a country inn and a fish market. Fish tanks are everywhere, keeping your meal alive until you order it. You can order set menus or a la carte. The *osusume* set meals run from ¥1500 to ¥4000 and feature the daily specials. You can also order *nabe* stews or *sashimi*. We love the very friendly atmosphere.

WARAYA *(Udon noodles, inexpensive). 91 Yashima Nakamachi. Tel. (087)843-3115. Open daily 10am to 6:30pm.*

This thatched-roof farmhouse restaurant at the entrance to Shikoku Farmhouse Museum is one of the best places to eat Takamatsu's special Sanuki *udon* noodles. In good weather, you can eat outdoors on long tables. Order the *kazoku udon* and for ¥2300 you will get a wooden tub with enough noodles to feed three or four people. The dipping sauce is served in a large *sake* bottle. Pour the sauce into the small stoneware bowl and dig in.

SEEING THE SIGHTS

The city of Takamatsu was once a castle town, but only the walls and a few outer buildings remain in **Tamamo Park** near the train station. One of the few castles built by the sea, the sea water fills the moats.

About three kilometers from the JR Takamatsu Station is **Ritsurin Park** (Ritsurin Koen), the playground of the feudal lords who once ruled the district. Divided into Southern and Northern gardens, the Southern garden is a traditional Japanese strolling garden with ponds, curved bridges and teahouses where you can easily spend more than a half-day. Once the feudal lord's hunting grounds, the Northern one underwent a transformation to a modern garden early in this century. Wild ducks still visit the ponds but no longer fear for their lives. The Northern garden also has the excellent **Sanuki Folk Craft Museum** (Sanuki Mingeikan) on its grounds. *Open 9am to 4:30pm.* Ritsurin Park is about 20 minutes by bus from JR Takamatsu Station to Ritsurin Koen-mae. *The park is open from sunrise to sunset, at a minimum from 7am to 5pm. ¥310.*

About twenty minutes out of town is **Shikoku Farmhouse Museum** (Shikoku Mura), featuring farmhouses moved there from all over Shikoku Island. The spacious open air museum, set on a lovely wooded hillside, is a good retreat from the city. The water flowing downstream from pool to pool enhances the rustic atmosphere. One of our favorites is a sugar pressing shed with a conical thatched-roof. Another striking building is a theater from Shodojima Islands where amateur *kabuki* is staged every May 5th. Try the delicious *udon* noodle restaurant, Waraya, at the entrance to the museum (see Where to Eat). *Tel. (087)843-3111. Open daily 8:30am to 5pm; until 4:30pm November through March. ¥800. 10-minute walk from JR Yashima Station or Kotoden Tram Yashima Station.*

MATSUYAMA

Castles and hot springs are Matsuyama's claim to fame. The castle keep was reconstructed in 1854, making it one of the last authentic ones built in the feudal period. Matsuyama's Dogo hot spring is one of the oldest spas in Japan.

ARRIVALS & DEPARTURES

By Air

Matsuyama Airport serves the city.

To/from Sapporo Chitose: 1 flight/day (ANK. ¥36,150)

To/from Tokyo Haneda: 8 flights/day (ANA, JAL. ¥22,650)

To/from Nagoya: 3 flights/day (ANA. ¥17,100)

To/from Osaka Itami: 4 flights/day; **from Kansai**: 3 flights/day (ANA, JAL. ¥12,150)

To/from Fukuoka: 2 flights/day (JAS. ¥15,000)

To/from Hiroshima Nishi (JAIR. ¥7160), Kagoshima (JAC. ¥18,850), Miyazaki (JAC. ¥17,300), Okinawa (JTA. ¥22,200) and Sendai (ANA. ¥36,150)

For Ground Transportation:

Bus: to Matsuyama-shi Station (35 minutes, ¥400); it stops en route at the JR Matsuyama Station.

Taxi: to Matsuyama-shi Station (20 minutes, ¥1900)

Bus: to Dogo Onsen (45 minutes, ¥450)

Taxi: to Dogo Onsen (40 minutes, ¥2800)

By Train

To/from Takamatsu: the JR *Ishizuchi* limited express train (2 1/2 hours, ¥6010). The JR *Shiokaze* limited express train between Okayama and Matsuyama (2 hours 45 minutes, ¥6630).

By Bus

Overnight service to/from Tokyo (12 1/2 hours, ¥12,000), and Osaka (7 hours, ¥6700).

Express service to/from Okayama (6 buses/day, 3 hours, ¥4300) and Takamatsu (12 buses/day, 2 1/2 hours, ¥4000).

GETTING AROUND TOWN

Matsuyama is a fairly compact city with trams offering convenient access.

Tourist Information

Matsuyama City Tourist Information, an "i" Tourist Information Center, is in JR Matsuyama Station. *Tel. (089)931-3914.*

Ehime Prefectural International Center, *Tel. (089)943-6688.* Open 8:30am to 5pm. Closed Sunday, holidays and December 28 through January 4. *8 Horinouchi, Matsuyama.*

Goodwill Guides: Contact the Ehime Prefectural International Center, *Tel. (089)943-6688,* to arrange a volunteer guide.

O-HENRO: BUDDHIST PILGRIMAGE IN SHIKOKU

*The island of Shikoku is famous for its pilgrimage to **88 Buddhist temples**, the greatest pilgrimage in Japan. Since the Heian period (8th–12th century) Japanese from all walks of life made pilgrimages to temples and shrines to ask for divine favor and to repent for their sins. During the Edo period (17th–19th century), pilgrimages became one of the few legitimate ways commoners could travel so they became fun trips to escape from the monotony of everyday life.*

What makes Shikoku's pilgrimage so special? Kobo Daishi, the great priest who founded Shingon Buddhism, was born in Shikoku in 774. His followers were sent out to preach and they, along with the lay people, visited the temples where Kobo Daishi had some association. Before long, people were following Kobo Daishi's path in Shikoku.

In the old days, local people were requested to give food and shelter to these pilgrims at any time. Today, you see the efficient pilgrims in air-conditioned buses while the more traditional pilgrims wear o-henro attire (white robe, huge umbrella-like straw hat, prayer beads and a banner marked with the stamp of each temple), all visiting the 88 temples to earn merit. Bus pilgrims can complete the circle of 88 in two to three days while it takes about two weeks on foot.

Regarding the amount of merit you receive for such an endeavor – you'll just have to wait for the afterlife to find out.

WHERE TO STAY

ANA (ZENNIKKU) HOTEL MATSUYAMA, *3-2-1 Ichiban-cho, Matsuyama, 790-8520. Tel. (089)933-5511, Fax (089)921-6053. Singles from ¥6500. Twins from ¥15,000. Credit cards.*

Matsuyama's finest hotel features a central location near Matsuyama Castle, shopping and on the tram tracks to Dogo Onsen. During the warmer months, relax at the rooftop beer garden.

UMENOYA, *2-8-9 Kamiichi, Matsuyama, 790-0845. Tel. (089)941-2570, Fax (089)941-1025. ¥20,000 per person with two meals. Credit cards.*

An anomaly among the many charmless concrete hotels and inns in Dogo Onsen, Umenoya has retained traditional architecture. There are only ten rooms, each different. Enjoy a relaxing soak in the outdoor and indoor hot spring baths.

HOTEL PATIO DOGO. *20-12 Yunomachi, Dogo, Matsuyama. Tel. (089)491-4128, Fax (089)941-4129. Singles from ¥7000. Doubles from ¥12,000.*

A business hotel in the Dogo Onsen district, Hotel Patio Dogo is a great budget choice in the area, with a friendly staff and spotless rooms and amenities usually not found in this price range.

WHERE TO EAT

GOSHIKI-SOMEN *(Noodles, inexpensive). 3-5-4 Sanbancho. Tel. (089)933-3838. Open daily 11am to 9pm.*

Somen, the thinnest of Japan's many noodles, is a Shikoku specialty. Usually eaten cold in summer, *somen* also tastes great warm in winter. Goshiki's *somen* costs ¥650. The *taimeshi* set, ¥1300, combines *somen* and rice cooked with red snapper, another local delicacy. Located next to the Central Post Office at Matsuyama City.

KAWASEMI *(Kaiseki, inexpensive to moderate). 2-5-18 Nibancho. Open daily 12 noon to 2pm, 5pm to 9:30pm.*

Kawasemi serves delicious *kaiseki* cuisine. At lunchtime course starts from ¥1500, dinner from ¥3500. The ingredients come only from local areas. Reservation recommended.

SEEING THE SIGHTS

From JR Matsuyama Station, take the tram towards Dogo Onsen and get off at Okaido; walk along the perimeter of the castle grounds until you reach the ropeway and lift. Round-trip on the ropeway costs ¥400 and in just three minutes, you'll be whisked to the top of the hill where **Matsuyama Castle** sits. The castle keep dates back to 1628 and was built by the Kato feudal lords. Before long it was under the control of the Matsudaira, relatives of the Tokugawa shoguns. The castle keep displays armor and other belongings of the Matsudaira. *Open 9am to 5pm; until 4:30pm in December and January and until 5:30pm in August. ¥350.*

Matsuyama's other famous attraction, **Dogo Onsen**, dates back 3000 years and is one of the three oldest hot springs in Japan; the others are Arima Onsen near Kobe and Shirahama Onsen in Wakayama Prefecture. The area is filled with Japanese inns catering to hot water lovers, but even if you stay at one of those inns, don't miss **Dogo Onsen Honkan**. The traditional wooden building dates from 1894 and houses a number of baths. The adjacent **Yushinden**, built in 1988 as a bath reserved for the imperial family, offers tours for ¥210. Admission to Dogo Onsen Honkan ranges from ¥300 to ¥1240 depending on if you want to take only a bath or if you want to have a private lounging room and eat Japanese sweets as well. *Open daily 6:30am to 10pm. From JR Matsuyama Station, take the tram heading toward Dogo Onsen and get off at the last stop (about 20 minutes).*

While you are in the neighborhood, take a walk over to **Ishite Temple**, one of the 88 temples of Shikoku's famous pilgrimage. Ishite dates back to 1318. You can't help noticing the sandals on the gate, placed there by people praying to strengthen their legs.

Textile lovers should make time to go to **Mingei Iyo Kasuri Kaikan**, to see *kasuri* (ikat) fabric made. The hall demonstrates the complex process from dyeing to weaving. A shop sells the fabric. Dye a handkerchief for ¥1000. *Open daily from 8:10am to 4:50pm. ¥50. Take the 61 or 62 bus from JR Matsuyama Station to Kumanodai stop.*

Tobe Ceramics: About a half-hour from Matsuyama City is the town of Tobe, a center for Tobe ceramics, a blue and white stoneware. From Matsuyama Station, take the #13 or 14. At Dento-sangyo-kan mae stop is an exhibition hall of the ware. At the **Umeno Seitosho Workshop** you can make your own ceramic masterpiece. The workshop is a 25-minute walk from the Dento-sangyo-kan-mae bus stop. *Tel. (089)962-2311. Closed Monday and second Sunday.* At **Baizan Kiln**, a 10-minute walk from the same bus stop, you can see the workshop, climbing kiln and museum. *Closed Monday.* The **Tobe Ceramics Hall** displays and sells the local ware. *Tel. (089)962-3900. Open daily 8am to 6pm. Near Toritaniguchi bus stop.*

SHOPPING

Go to the covered **Okaido arcade** next to Mitsukoshi Department Store and near the Ichibancho tram stop. You'll find more shops and restaurants than you can possibly imagine.

Ehime Prefectural Products Association (Ehime-ken Bussan Kyokai) displays and sells Tobe ceramics, Iyo-kasuri fabric, lacquer ware and other local products. *Open 9am to 6pm. From Matsuyama Station take the bus for Mistuport (departs every 20 minutes) and get off at the Aitemu Ehime bus stop. Tel. (089)951-5711.*

24. SAN'IN

San'in means "the shadow side of the mountain," but don't let that deter you from visiting this isolated, beautiful area. To see off-the-beaten-path Japan, be sure to put on your itinerary **Matsue**, **Hagi** and **Tsuwano**, all former castle towns, and **Izumo**, home to one of Japan's most sacred Shinto shrines.

San'in, the westernmost part of Honshu, faces the Japan Sea. The **Chugoku Mountain range** runs through the center of the island, dividing the west from the more populous eastern part. It's called the shadow or gloomy side because San'in is in the long shadow of the mountains. Detached from the rest of the country, the area has retained aspects of a traditional way of life that's lost in less secluded areas.

Winter gets pretty wicked. Winds from Siberia blow across the cold Japan Sea and slam into the San'in region. While the coastal areas don't get a lot of snow, the weather is very cold and damp. Spring, summer and autumn are better times to visit.

SAN'IN HIGHLIGHTS

- *Climb to the top of Matsue Castle*
- *Eat noodles in a former samurai residence looking out over a garden in Matsue*
- *Stand in awe at Izumo Shrine, one of Japan's most sacred Shinto shrines*
- *Watch the thousands of carp swim in the tiny stream in Tsuwano's historic quarter*
- *Browse among the many kilns making Hagi's distinctive pottery*
- *Bicycling through Hagi's quiet streets*

Planning Your Stay

Matsue, Izumo, Tsuwano and Hagi are the places to see. You can either start in Hagi and work your way up the Japan Sea coast or start in

Matsue and work your way down. Plan on spending at least one full day in each place and if, you can spare it, two days in Matsue.

Plan your trip to suit your interests:
- **Shinto shrines**: Izumo Grand Shrine, Kamosu Shrine, Yaegaki Shrine
- **Well-preserved former castle towns**: Hagi, Matsue, Tsuwano
- **Good eats**: Duck stew at Yakumo Honjin between Matsue and Izumo
- **Japanese Washi Paper**: Abe Eishiro Memorial Hall, outside of Matsue
- **Ikat Textiles**: Hirose, outside of Matsue
- **Art Museums**: Adachi Museum of Art
- **Good cycling towns**: Hagi, Tsuwano.
- **Castles**: Matsue
- **Ceramics**: Hagi

MATSUE

Matsue, a city of 140,000 on the shores of **Lake Shinji**, would be just another small Japanese city except for a towering early 17th century castle, a well-preserved samurai district and archaeological sites on the outskirts of town. Horio Yoshiharu, a feudal lord who served under Toyotomi Hideyoshi, selected the sleepy little fishing village as the site of his castle, from where he ruled the entire Izumo region. As in most castle towns, the city was divided into sections for samurai and merchants.

Matsue has been immortalized by Lafcadio Hearn, a Western journalist who spent only 15 months there in 1890–91. His writings put Matsue on the map. Hearn married into a samurai family but then left for a teaching position in Kyushu because he could not take the bitterly cold winters. Matsue, so proud of its adopted son, actually posts signs with his descriptions of local sights at the sights themselves.

ARRIVALS & DEPARTURES

Matsue's isolation from major metropolitan areas is its saving grace, but it means getting here is time consuming or expensive.

By Air

Matsue is served by two airports, Yonago and Izumo. If you plan to visit Izumo first, fly into Izumo Airport. Izumo Airport is closer, but airline schedules may make it more convenient to fly in to Yonago.

Izumo Airport

To/from Tokyo Haneda: 5 flights/day (JAS. ¥22,750)
To/from Osaka Itami: 4 flights/day (JAS, JAC. ¥14,600)
To/from Fukuoka: 1 flight/day (JAC. ¥19,650)

To/from Nagoya: 1 flight/day (JAS. ¥19,900)

For Ground Transportation:
Bus: to JR Matsue Station (35 minutes, ¥890)
Taxi: to JR Matsue Station (30 minutes, ¥6700)
Bus: to Dentetsu Izumo City Station (25 minutes, ¥670)
Taxi: to Dentetsu Izumo City Station (25 minutes, ¥4200)

Yonago Airport:
To/from Tokyo Haneda: 4 flights/day (ANK. ¥22,650)

For Ground Transportation:
Bus: to JR Yonago Station (30 minutes, ¥570)
Taxi: to JR Yonago Station (25 minutes, ¥3700). JR Matsue Station is 30 minutes from JR Yonago Station.

By Train
   To/from Tokyo: JR *Izumo* overnight train takes 13 hours to Matsue, ¥14,180. To take a day train, take the shinkansen to Okayama (about 4 hours) and change for the *Yakumo* limited express train to Matsue (2 1/2 hours, ¥20,640).
   To/from Osaka: Shinkansen to Okayama, *Super Yakumo* limited express to Matsue (4 hours, ¥10,310).
   To/from Okayama: *Yakumo* limited express train (2 1/2 hours, ¥5870).

By Bus
   To/from Tokyo: overnight bus from Tokyo's Shibuya Station (11 hours, ¥12,070)
   To/from Osaka: from Shin Osaka Station 5 buses/day (6 hours, ¥5650)

ORIENTATION
   Matsue is pretty easy to get around. Many of the sights are near the castle, about a 15-minute walk from the train station.

GETTING AROUND TOWN
   Matsue's bus network is extensive. The town operates a trolley bus called the Lake Line, which runs every 30 minutes — once an hour December through March. Departing from JR Matsue Station, it goes to the castle, then over to Matsue Onsen and around Lake Shinji. It is definitely not the fastest way to get back to the station from the castle area, but it gives you a good view of the town. ¥200/ride or ¥500 all-day pass *(ichi nichi joshaken)*.

Bicycles are a good way to get around this fairly compact city. Rent them at the train station.

Tourist Information

The **Tourist Information Office** is at JR Matsue Station. *Tel. (0852)21-4034.* Open 9am to 6pm. English-speaking staff can assist you and they have excellent maps and brochures.

Goodwill Guide: You can arrange a volunteer goodwill guide to escort you around Matsue or Izumo. Apply at least one day in advance at the Matsue tourist office.

WHERE TO STAY

Matsue has business-type hotels near the station and a built up hot spring area along the city's shores of Lake Shinji. Our preference is to by-pass them and stay in the area between Matsue and Izumo, a 10- to 20-minute train ride, either at Yakumo Honjin or at Tamatsukuri Onsen hot spring area.

CHORAKUEN, *Tamayu-machi, Yatsuka-gun, Shimane, 699-0201. Tel. (0852)62-0111, Fax (0852)62-0115. ¥18,000 per person with two meals. Credit cards.*

Chorakuen's claim to fame is that it has Japan's largest outdoor hot spring bath. While it's large enough to swim across, the heat of the water definitely discourages any swimming. The rooms overlook the large Japanese garden. The inn serves crab and other regional specialties.

YAKUMO HONJIN, *1335 Shinji, Shinji-cho, Yatsuka-gun, Shimane, 699-0406. Tel. (0852)66-0136, Fax (0852)66-0137. From ¥15,000 per person with two meals. Credit cards. Just a few minutes walk from Shinji Station on JR San'in Honsen line, about 20 minutes from Matsue Station going towards Izumo.*

This charming inn is our favorite place to stay in the area. Yakumo Honjin dates from the Edo period when it was a stopping place for feudal lords on their way to Edo (Tokyo). The building, designated an Important Cultural Property, is an excellent example of a commoner's building from the Edo period. Of course, this one is fit for a feudal lord. In the entrance way, there is an area where the feudal lord's palanquin was placed – his guards stood watch from the mezzanine. The inn's specialty is *kamo no kaiyaki*, a duck stew cooked at your table in a large abalone shell.

MINAMI-KAN, *14 Suetsugu Honmachi, Matsue, 690-0843. Tel. (0852)21-5131, Fax (0852)26-0351. From ¥20,000 per person with two meals. Credit cards.*

The 11 rooms at this small and elegant inn have views of Lake Shinji. The inn, which also runs a restaurant, excels in the kitchen.

MATSUE WASHINGTON HOTEL, *2-22 Higashi-honmachi, Matsue, 690-0842. Tel. (0852)22-4111, Fax (0852)22-4120. Singles from ¥7770. Doubles ¥13,650. Credit cards. 5-minute taxi ride or 12-minute walk north of station.*

The rooms at this business hotel are simple, but adequate. It's about a 10-minute walk from JR Matsue Station.

MATSUE URBAN HOTEL, *590-3 Asahi-machi, Matsue, 690-0003. Tel. (0852)22-0002, Fax (0852)26-3833. Singles from ¥5500. Doubles from ¥9200. Credit cards.*

The hotel is conveniently located at the north exit of JR Matsue Station. Basic business-hotel accommodations are available in the hotel and its newer annex next door. The annex also has a few double rooms while the main hotel has singles and twins.

WHERE TO EAT

KURAUDO *(Kushiage, moderate). 19 Suetsugu-honmachi. Tel. (0852)27-7869. Open 5pm to 10pm. Closed Sunday.*

The chef goes to market every day to search out fresh ingredients that inspire him to create Japanese nouvelle cuisine. The *kushiyaki* set meal costs ¥5000 and consists of four different types of *kushiage, oden* (stewed fish and vegetables) served with the shop's special sauce, Shimane beef fillet steaks, salad and dessert.

YAKUMO-AN *(Regional noodles, inexpensive). 308 Kitabori-cho. Tel. (0852)25-0587. Open daily 9am to 4:30pm.*

This restaurant is a great place to have lunch while sightseeing. Located in a former samurai residence next to Buke Yashiki Samurai House, the specialty is *wariko soba*, noodles served in small round dishes stacked on top of each other. Each dish is seasoned with a different condiment. Afterwards, you'll be given the cooking water from the *soba* noodles. Pour it into your dipping sauce to make a soup. Opt to sit on *tatami* mats for a view of the well-sculpted garden with a 250-year old pine tree.

NANIWA HONTEN *(Eel and other Japanese cuisine, inexpensive to moderate). Tel. (0852)21-2835. Open 11am to 2pm; 5pm to 8:30pm. Closed Monday.*

Located at the big bridge on Lake Shinji, you can enjoy lovely views while eating their delicious eel. At lunch order *ounameshi*, eel and mushroom soup, that you pour over rice. *Ounameshi* sets cost ¥1800, ¥2500, and ¥4000.

SEEING THE SIGHTS
Central Matsue

Most of Matsue's sights are clustered around Matsue Castle, about a 15-minute walk from the JR Matsue Station. You can purchase a "universal pass" for ¥720. Contrary to its name, it's not universal but good for admission to Matsue Castle, the Lafcadio Hearn Memorial Museum and Buke Yashiki Samurai House and offers discounts at another dozen sights. The pass is good for three days although we doubt you would spend that much time in Matsue.

One of only a handful of original castles left in Japan, **Matsue Castle** stands on a hill in the center of the city. The castle was built between 1607 and 1611 by Horio Yoshiharu. The elegant Momoyama-style structure was as much an assertion of authority as it was a fortress because by this time, the Tokugawa shogun was firmly in control. The castle keep was once surrounded by residential and administrative buildings, but these were torn down at the end of the Tokugawa period (1868). The lobbying of citizens' groups saved the keep from demolition.

Since Horio had no heirs, the castle passed to the Kyogoku family for a brief time and then to Matsudaira Naomasu, Tokugawa Ieyasu's grandson. The shogun wanted trusted feudal lords to supervise the large and powerful clan, the Mori, who ruled the Hagi region to the west. The Matsudaira ruled Izumo, the old name for the entire region until the end of the feudal era.

Extensive renovations were carried out on the castle keep in the 1950s. Displayed in the basement are objects too damaged to repair including the *shachi,* the dolphins that adorn the roof. The idea is to con the fire gods into believing the castle is under water and thus immune to fire.

You'll find samurai armor and other articles from the feudal era on display. Notice the small windows at the floor line. These windows were used for dropping stones, hot oil and other wonderful surprises on invading armies. The top floor offers great panoramic views of Matsue.

One tip: don't use the slippers offered at the entrance. The steep wooden stairs are safer climbed barefoot.

On the castle grounds are hundreds of cherry trees, and the city celebrates a cherry blossom festival every April 1–15. *Castle is open daily 9:30am to 5pm. ¥500.*

South of the castle is a compact shrine, **Matsue Jinja**, dedicated to Tokugawa Ieyasu and several of the Matsudaira lords. Next to the shrine is a Western-style building that would look more at home in New Orleans than next to a medieval castle. The **Matsue Museum of Local History** (Matsue Kyodo-kan), built in 1903 in anticipation of a visit by the Meiji

Emperor that never happened, houses folk arts and regional artifacts. *Open daily 8:30am to 5pm.*

The street northeast of the moat is Shiomi Nawate, the heart of the old samurai quarter. Walk along the castle moat that's lined with pine trees; on the other side of the street, wood and stucco walls hide many historic residences. This district is the heart of Matsue's traditional section; the area that Lafcadio Hearn fell in love with when he arrived to teach English in the 1890s.

Buke Yashiki Samurai House is the well-preserved residence of the Shiomi family, chief retainers to the Matsudaira. Two large paper lanterns, bearing the family crest, hang at the entrance gate. The house is very simple and not very large; even though the Matsudaira were relatives to the Tokugawa, the domain wasn't wealthy. Take off your shoes and walk on the *tatami* mats; look out on the well-tended garden and get a feel for the austere life of the warrior class. We like the display of furniture and household objects because it shows how people actually lived. Stop and have green tea and sweets in the pavilion to the left. *Open daily 8:30am to 5pm; until 6pm April through September. ¥250.*

As you exit, the next building on the right is Yakumo-an, which we highly recommend for noodles (See Where to Eat).

Further along Shiomi Nawate is the **Tanabe Art Museum**, home of an excellent collection of tea bowls and other tea ceremony objects. *Open 9am to 5pm. Closed Monday and December 29 through January 1. ¥500.*

Next door is **Lafcadio Hearn's Residence** (Koizumi Yakumo Kyukyo). Hearn lived here from May 1890 through November 1891 when he taught at the Shimane Prefecture Normal Middle School. Hearn fell in love with Japan figuratively and literally; he married the daughter of a Matsue samurai family and adopted a Japanese name. His sentimental writings introduced many Westerners to the country. He based his treatise, "In a Japanese Garden," published in *Glimpses of an Unfamiliar Japan* on the garden in this house. *Open 9am to 5pm; until 4:40pm December through February. Closed December 16-29, January 1. ¥200.*

On the corner is the **Lafcadio Hearn Memorial Museum** (Koizumi Yakumo Kinen-kan). Photos, manuscripts, furniture and other paraphernalia of his life are on display. *Open daily 8:30am to 5pm; until 6pm April through September. ¥250.*

On a hill above Shiomi Nawate Street is **Meimei-an Teahouse**, which was built in 1779 by Matsudaira Fumai and moved to this site in 1966. Fumai, the 7th generation feudal lord, was a great tea connoisseur and perfected the Fumai or aristocratic style of tea. *Open 9am to 5pm. ¥200. You can be served green tea for ¥300.*

Tea aficionados may also like to see **Kanden-an**, the villa where Fumai sought retreat. The teahouse built in 1792 is an Important Cultural

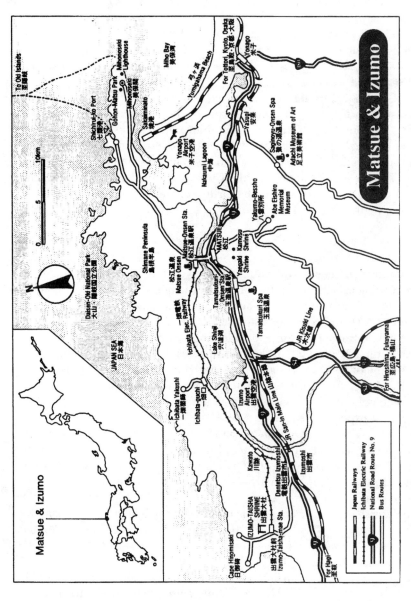

Matsue & Izumo

Property. The bright and open Kogetsu-tei, built by Fumai's brother, is also on the grounds. *Open 9am to 4pm. Closed Thursday. ¥700. Take Shiei bus towards Daigaku Kawatsu and get off at Kanden-an Iriguchi; 10-minute walk. Tel. (0852)21-4288. Phone ahead before going.*

The **Prefectural Museum** (Kenritsu Bijutsukan) houses works of *ukiyo-e* woodblock masters Hiroshige and Hokusai, as well as folk art. *Open 9am to 5pm. Closed Monday, holidays and around New Year's. ¥300; additional for special exhibitions.*

Gessho-ji Temple in the western part of the city, serves as the mausoleum for the Matsudaira lords. All nine generations are buried here. The Buddhist temple has many Shinto *torii* gates as the two religions once blended freely. In the late 1800s, with the resurgence of State Shinto, the main building was destroyed and never rebuilt. Near the 6th Matsudaira lord's grave is a statue of a turtle with a stone obelisk on its back. The obelisk was placed to prevent the turtle from taking nocturnal walks and terrifying the local residents.

South of Matsue

Central Matsue has lots of monuments and mementos of the feudal era. A five-kilometer trip south will take you further back in time to an archaeological era famed for ancient settlements and mystical legends. Digs have found remains of major population centers as early as the 4th century A.D. and of even earlier Yayoi (300 B.C.– A.D. 300) remains.

Public transportation is a little troublesome in this area. You can reach some, but not all, of the sights by bus. Driving is surprisingly easy as the major routes and sights are marked in English. You can rent cars at JR Matsue Station. Bike rentals are also available for the hearty; it's probably about a 45-minute ride from the station. A third alternative, and the most expensive, is to take a taxi.

Fudoki no Oka Archaeological Hill is designated a National Preservation District. This area has large funeral burial mounds and a reconstruction of a primitive hut. The park houses a museum called Fudoki no Oka Shiryokan. Unfortunately, there's no English commentary and also some objects that date to the first century A.D. are displayed in a rather amateurish way. *Open 9am to 5pm. Closed Monday, holidays and December 29 through January 4. ¥150. From JR Matsue Station, take the Oba bus to Oba stop or buses for Kumano or Akiyoshi and get off at Fudoki no Oka stop.*

A few minutes walk from Fudoki no Oka is a beautiful old shrine, **Kamosu Shrine**. The small raised main building dates from 1346 and is Japan's oldest extant Taisha-style shrine. Taisha-style shrines are made of simple undecorated wood and pillars raise the buildings off the ground. Surrounded by a fence, the shrine itself is off limits to visitors. The towering cryptomeria trees and tall stone lanterns around Kamosu add to the sacred and serene atmosphere. The shrine honors Izanami, who with her brother-husband Izanagi, descended from heaven and gave birth to the islands of Japan.

Nearby is **Izumo Kanbe no Sato**, a center with visual reenactments of legends and folklore. In another section, craftsmen demonstrate basketmaking, woodworking, weaving, pottery and paper-covered *temari* balls. Make a reservation to try your hand at these crafts; costs range from ¥1000 to ¥4000. *Tel. (0852)28-0040. Open 9am to 5pm. Closed Monday and New Year's. ¥400.*

Yaegaki Jinja Shrine, is dedicated to Susano-o and his wife Kushi Inada. Susano-o is the son of the gods who created the islands of Japan and brother of Amaterasu, the Sun Goddess. He saved his wife by slaying a serpent demon. Dedicated to love, the shrine is popular for weddings and sells amulets for marriage and fertility. A concrete treasure hall houses a 12th century mural painting of the gods – the oldest shrine mural in Japan. *Open daily 9am to 5:30pm; until 5pm December through March. ¥200.*

Buy a special piece of paper at the office and follow the path to the back of the shrine, cross the street and continue on the path into the woods until you reach a pond. Put a coin on your paper and place it in the pond. The faster it sinks, the faster you will find happiness in the pursuit of love.

A short drive down the road is **Washi no Sato** (paper village), a collection of thatched-roof buildings well known for the production of handmade Japanese paper. The home of Abe Eishiro, a National Living Treasure who died in 1982, has been turned into the **Abe Eishiro Memorial Museum** (Abe Eishiro Kinen-kan). You can make your own paper for ¥500. *Open 9:30am to 4:30pm. Closed Tuesday. ¥500. From JR Matsue Station or Fudoki no Oka bus stop take the bus to Yakumo Bessho and get off at the last stop.*

EXCURSIONS & DAY TRIPS

Adachi Museum of Art (Adachi Bijutsukan) is a splendid museum exhibiting modern Japanese art. An extensive traditional Japanese garden looks like a work of art itself when you see it framed by the museum's many windows. In addition to paintings, works by the famous potters Kitaoji Rosanjin and Kawai Kanjiro are displayed. *From JR Matsue Station, take the train to JR Yasugi Station and take the bus heading to Hirose. Get off at the Saginoyu bus stop (20 minutes). A taxi from JR Yasugi Station takes about 15 minutes. Open daily 9am to 5:30pm; until 5pm October through March. ¥2200 but foreigners showing a passport pay half price.*

The town of Hirose is about a five-minute drive from the Adachi Museum — continue on the same bus from JR Yasugi Station. The **Hirose Kasuri Center** has demonstrations of weaving of *kasuri*, a blue and white ikat, a fabric woven with dyed threads. There's a good selection for sale. *Tel. (0854)32-2575. Open 10am to 5pm. Closed Wednesday from mid-April through mid-March; also closed around New Year's. Admission free.*

IZUMO

The legends of ancient Japan dominate **Izumo**, a small city of 65,000. During the month of October, all the gods of the Shinto pantheon visit Izumo Grand Shrine, Japan's oldest Shinto shrine. Elsewhere in Japan, October is known as the "godless month;" Izumo boasts October is the "month of the gods."

ARRIVALS & DEPARTURES

See Matsue for additional travel information to the area.

By Air
Ground Transportation
From **Izumo Airport**, the bus takes 25 minutes and costs ¥670 to JR Izumo-shi Station. Taxi takes 25 minutes and runs about ¥4200.

By Train
To/from Matsue: to JR Izumo-shi Station take JR San'in Honsen line local (45 minutes, ¥570), the limited express (30 minutes, ¥1810).

To/from Izumo Shrine area: The private Ichibata Railway has direct service from Matsue-onsen Station (not the JR Matsue Station) to Izumo Taisha-mae (about 55 minutes, ¥790). Change trains at Kawato.

GETTING AROUND TOWN

JR Izumo-shi Station is about a 25 minute bus or train ride from Izumo Shrine. Take the Ichibata bus from the station to Taisha-mae bus stop (about 25 minutes). You can also take the Ichibata Railway, but the station is a little difficult to locate — it is tucked away behind the department store on the right as you exit JR Izumo-shi station.

Tourist Office
A **tourist office** is on the main approach road to Izumo Shrine on the right. *Tel. (0853)53-2298. Open 9am to 5pm.*

WHERE TO STAY

TAKENOYA, *Izumo taisha Seimon-mae, Shimane, 699-0711. Tel. (0853)53-3131, Fax (0853)53-3134. From ¥12,000 per person with two meals. Credit cards.*

This quaint old wooden inn has the distinction of being right across the street from the entrance to Izumo Shrine. Take advantage of the proximity by taking leisurely walks on the shrine grounds. During the off season, the proprietor will upgrade your room for the same rate.

SEEING THE SIGHTS

Izumo Taisha Shrine is Japan's oldest Shinto shrine and is ranked second only to Ise Grand Shrine near Nagoya. In our minds Izumo is the one to see. Ise is rebuilt every twenty years and looks so pristine; Izumo's weathered buildings are several hundred years old.

The shrine is nestled into the base of the mountains and feels sacred even to people who are not believers in Shinto. Izumo is dedicated to Okuninushi-no-Mikoto, the god known for marriage, agriculture and medicine. Legend has it that Amaterasu, the Sun Goddess, constructed the shrine to thank Okuninushi for turning over his lands to her grandson. The buildings have been rebuilt many times; the current **Honden** (main hall) is the 25th and was last built in 1744. The architectural style, called *taisha-zukuri*, apparently developed in Izumo; earlier structures were nearly four times as tall. The Honden is enclosed by two fences, and the casual visitor cannot enter the inner one. Pilgrims who offer donations can enter the enclosure but only the head priest can enter the Honden.

Three million people visit the shrine annually, but we found it a tranquil and spiritual place. Eleven *torii* gates line the approach to the shrine, dividing the secular world from the spiritual. One of the gates is Japan's largest.

Dwarfed by tall cryptomeria trees, the weather-beaten simple wooden structures exude a quiet dignity. Izumo is used by everyday people — unlike Ise that is reserved for the emperor and priests. Izumo is especially popular for weddings. If you are at Izumo on an auspicious day, you are bound to see happy couples surrounded by family and friends. Weddings take place in the **Kaguraden**, the large building west of the main courtyard. You can't help noticing the imposing *shimenawa* (huge rope of twisted rice straw) at the entrance. This *shimenawa*, weighing an incredible 6000 kilograms, symbolizes purity and fertility.

The shrine's treasures are displayed on the second floor of the **Shinko-den**, *open daily 8am to 4:30pm. ¥150.*

To the east of the shrine is a row of **Shake houses** belonging to the priests of the shrine. The houses have lovely clay and stone walls.

A little past Izumo Shrine on Route 431 heading toward the sea is the grave and monument to **Izumo-no-Okuni**, the shrine maiden who went to Kyoto to collect money to support the shrine and started an avant-garde dance that developed into *kabuki*.

A little beyond the monument is **Inasa-no-Hama** beach, the place where the gods land during their annual visit to Izumo in October. There's a *torii* gate and a large rock on the beach. In summer, lots of swimmers and sunseekers come.

If you have a little extra time, there is a beautiful cliff drive along the water to **Cape Hinomisaki**. The bus from Izumo Shrine takes about 25 minutes to reach **Hinomisaki Shrine**, a shrine built at the command of shogun Tokugawa Ieyasu. The buildings date from 1644. The vermilion upper building is dedicated to Susano-o and the lower one to Amaterasu, his sister.

From Hinomisaki shrine, it's about a 10-minute walk to the tip of the cape where you'll find the tallest lighthouse in Asia, built in 1903.

While in Izumo, go to the **Izumo Folk Craft Museum** (Izumo Mingeikan) for an excellent collection of folk art including ceramics, *tansu* chests, folk toys and textiles in a wealthy farmer's house that's been converted into a museum. It's a little out of the way but worth it. The small shop has an excellent assortment of local folk arts. *From JR Izumo-shi Station, take the train one stop on the JR San'in line to Nishi Izumo or about 20 minutes by bus from JR Izumo-shi Station. Open 8:30am to 5pm. Closed Monday.*

TSUWANO

The small former castle town located along a narrow river ravine deep in the mountains dates back to 1295. Its well-preserved samurai district enchants visitors. Thousands of colorful carp live in the small stream running between the road and the walls of the samurai houses. The stream served both as a source of water for putting out fires and for irrigation.

Quick quiz: what significance are the numbers 7800, 80,000 and 1.6 million? The number of residents, carp and visitors, in that order.

ARRIVALS & DEPARTURES
By Air

Iwami Airport serves Tsuwano. See Hagi for flight details.

For Ground Transportation:
Bus: to Tsuwano (75 minutes, ¥1150)
Taxi: to Tsuwano (50 minutes, ¥10,000)

By Train

To/from Matsue and Izumo: *Oki* limited express train (3 1/2 hours from Matsue, ¥5870, and 3 hours from Izumo, ¥5550). Check the schedule because there are only a few a day. An alternative is to change trains at Masuda.

To/from Hagi: limited express train to Masuda (55 minutes); limited express from Masuda to Tsuwano (30 minutes, ¥3820); by local train (45 minutes, ¥1620).

To/from Ogori (shinkansen stop): *Oki* limited express train (1 hour, ¥2770); local train (1 1/2 hours). A vintage steam locomotive "SL Yamaguchi" runs on weekends and national holidays March through November (about 2 hours). Seat reservations essential.

GETTING AROUND TOWN

Tsuwano is small enough for you to walk or bicycle. Rent bicycles near the station.

Tourist Information

The **tourist information office** is at Tsuwano Station. *Tel. (08567)2-1771.*

WHERE TO STAY

RYOKAN MEIGETSU, *Tsuwano-cho, Kanoashi-gun, Shimane, 699-5605. Tel. (08567)2-0685, Fax (08567)2-0637. From ¥10,000 per person with two meals. Credit cards.*

This rustic, country-style inn has been in business for over 100 years. The food served at dinner changes with the season; some diehard guests make a point of returning each season to try the new fare. The beautiful wooden bathtubs made of cypress can lure you into a leisurely soak. Special Japanese *washi* paper decorates the ceiling and walls of some of the rooms; this handiwork was done by the late Abe Eishiro, who was a National Living Treasure.

MINSHUKU WAKASAGI NO YADO, *Tsuwano-cho, Kanoashi-gun, Shimane, 699-5600. Tel and Fax: (08567)2-1146. From ¥7000 per person with two meals. No credit cards.*

A simple family inn, the accommodations are comfortable, the home-cooked food delicious and the staff friendly.

WHERE TO EAT

YOUUKI *(Regional cuisine, inexpensive). Ushiroda. Tel. (08567)2-0162. Open 10am to 5pm. Closed Thursday. Close to Post Office, five minutes from JR Tsuwano Station.*

Youuki excels at local fare; try the *Tsuwano teishoku* (¥2000) for a sampling of the best the area has to offer.

FURUSATO *(Regional cuisine, inexpensive). Gion-machi. Tel. (08567)2-0403. Open 11am to 3pm. Closed irregularly. Across from the Post Office.*
Furusato's claim to fame is *uzume-meshi* — literally "buried under the rice dish." Chopped mushrooms, tofu and vegetables are buried under the rice; spice the concoction with *wasabi* horseradish and *yuzu*, a fragrant citrus. ¥1000.

SEEING THE SIGHTS

On Sundays, get an early start with a visit to the morning market held in front of the station from 5am to 7am. The main street, **Tono Machi Dori**, is a picturesque road with its white clay and black tile walls; multicolored carp swim in the small stream that runs alongside the walls. Small patches of irises add color.

Yorokan Museum (Yorokan Bijutsukan), the school for samurai built in 1786, now displays local artifacts. *Open daily 8:30am to 5pm. Closed around New Year's. ¥200.*

Tsuwano Local History Museum (Tsuwano Kyodo-kan) contains information and documents relating to the men who have made Hagi famous; the area's crafts; and information about the Yorokan, the feudal school that taught Western science before Japan opened to the West in the 1850s. *Open daily 8:30am to 5pm. Closed around New Year's. ¥350.*

Katsushika Hokusai Museum (Katsushika Hokusai Bijutsukan) houses an excellent collection of Hokusai, the early 19th century master *ukiyo-e* woodblock artist and painter. *Tel. (08567)2-1850. Open 9:30am to 5pm. Closed when exhibitions change and around New Year's. ¥450.*

Taikodani Inari Shrine was founded in 1773 by Tsuwano's feudal lord. A tunnel, formed by 1197 vermilion *torii* gates, lines the approach to this Shinto shrine. Believers who prayed at the shrine donated the money to build these gates after their wishes were fulfilled.

St. Maria Chapel (Otome Toge Maria Seido) is dedicated to the 153 Christians who were rounded up in 1868 by the new Meiji government; they were tortured until they renounced their religion. This incident caused such a stir from foreign countries that in 1874, the Japanese government relented and lifted the ban on Christianity, but not before 39 people died. In 1948 the church was built to commemorate the martyrs. *Open 7:30am to 5pm. ¥100 to enter the exhibition hall.*

Tsuwano is famous among the Japanese as the hometown of **Mori Ogai**, a writer and surgeon born in 1862, and **Nishi Amane**, a statesman and scholar born in 1829. Unless you are particularly interested in them, we recommend that you skip their houses now converted into museums. Mori, the recipient of numerous awards (although he refused to receive medals from the emperor), requested this simple epitaph: "A Man of Iwami" (Iwami is the name of this area).

Next to Mori's house is **Sekishukan**, a museum of handmade paper. *Open 8:30am to 5pm. Admission free.*

If you feel like climbing, take the tram and then scamper up the ruins of **Tsuwano Castle** on the outskirts of town. The castle no longer remains, but the rambling walls on the hill afford great views of Tsuwano.

UNREQUITED LOVE

Here's a great idea for a great soap opera. Tokugawa Ieyasu married one of his favorite granddaughters, Senhime, to Toyotomi Hideyori, the son of Hideyoshi, his archenemy. In 1615, Ieyasu laid siege to Hideyori's Osaka Castle and Senhime, holed up in the castle with her husband's family, was clearly going to perish. Sakazaki, Tsuwano's feudal lord, told Ieyasu that he would rescue Senhime if he could have her hand in marriage. Ieyasu agreed and Sakazaki, the dummy, took Ieyasu at his word. He risked his life and entered the burning castle to save Senhime. Miraculously, he brought her out alive, carrying her on his back, only to have Ieyasu break the promise and marry her to someone else. Hideyori, Senhime's original husband, perished in the siege.

HAGI

Hagi reeks of history. The small town on the Japan Sea, seat of the powerful Mori feudal lords, has a marvelous samurai district and a thriving pottery tradition, a favorite for tea ceremony. Low-ranking samurai from this area were instrumental in bringing down the Tokugawa shogunate in 1868 so, for Japanese, a visit here is like going to Philadelphia to see where the Declaration of Independence was signed. Ironically, visitors flock to Hagi today for its old time feeling, the very thing Hagi's revolutionaries devoted their lives to ending.

ARRIVALS & DEPARTURES

By Air

Iwami Airport is a perfect example of what happens when every prefecture feels it must have an airport regardless of passenger load. Built during the height of the 1980s bubble economy, a mere three flights a day fly into the pristine — and nearly deserted — airport.

To/from Tokyo Haneda: 2 flights/day (ANA. ¥26,350)

To/from Osaka Itami: 1 flight/day (ANA. ¥18,700)

For Ground Transportation:
Bus: to JR Higashi Hagi Station (75 minutes, ¥1560)
Taxi: to JR Higashi Hagi Station (70 minutes, ¥12,000)

By Train

The main train station for Hagi is JR Higashi Hagi Station, served by only a few limited express trains a day.

To/from Matsue and Izumo: *Isokaze* limited express train from JR Matsue Station to JR Higashi Hagi Station (3 hours 45 minutes, ¥6710); from JR Izumo-shi Station (3 hours, ¥5870).

To/from Tsuwano: by limited express to Masuda Station (55 minutes, ¥3820); then to Tsuwano (30 to 45 minutes, ¥1620).

To/from Shimonoseki: by *Isokaze* limited express to JR Higashi Hagi Station (2 hours, ¥4180).

By Bus

To/from Tokyo: Overnight bus from Shinagawa Station (14 hours, ¥14,250).

To/from Osaka: Overnight bus from Namba Station (9 hours, ¥9480).

GETTING AROUND TOWN

The best way to get around Hagi is by bicycle. And rentals are everywhere: at the station, at shops and at hotels.

Buses can take you to the main areas or you may opt to take taxis since the town is fairly compact.

Tourist Information

The **tourist information office** is on the ground floor of the Rainbow Building, to the left as you exit the station. The office has maps and brochures in English, and the staff speaks a little English. *Tel. (0838)25-3145.*

WHERE TO STAY

HOKUMON YASHIKI, *210 Horiuchi, Hagi, Yamaguchi, 758-0057. Tel. (0838)22-7521, Fax (0838)25-8144. From ¥28,000 per person with two meals. JCB and UC credit cards only.*

This inn, in the center of the old samurai district, has a wonderful traditional gate at the entrance. Then you enter an incongruous English-style building surrounded by English gardens. You enter Japan again when you reach the traditional Japanese guest rooms. The inn's superb food and pampering service combine to make a stay here worth the splurge.

RYOKAN TOMOE, *Koboji Tsuchihara, Hagi, Yamaguchi, 758-0025. Tel. (0838)22-0150, Fax (0838)22-0152. From ¥25,000 per person with two meals. Credit cards.*

The inn has a long history but recently moved to a new location where it built a traditional-style building just a few minutes walk across the river from the JR Higashi Hagi Station. The wide corridors provide a strong feeling of spaciousness and the large rooms are more like suites with a main room, a side room and a dressing area, all with *tatami* mats. The traditional service means a maid assigned to serve you brings one by one the more than 10 courses, bowing politely between each. Tomoe serves regional specialties, heavy on fish and seafood, placed on beautiful ceramic plates. We have to admit that even though we have adventurous palates, we could not bring ourselves to eat the whitebait fish that arrived still merrily swimming in water and *sake*.

FUJITA RYOKAN, *Shin Kawa, Nishi-ku, Hagi, Yamaguchi, 758-0011. Tel. (0838)22-0603, Fax (0838)26-1240. From ¥10,000 per person with two meals. No credit cards.*

This small inn, with only 13 Japanese-style rooms, is only a few minutes walk from the JR Higashi Hagi Station.

HOTEL ROYAL, *3000-5 Chintoo, Hagi, Yamaguchi, 758-0011. Tel. (0838)25-9595, Fax (0838)25-8434. Singles from ¥9000. Twins from ¥14,000. Credit cards.*

Locating the hotel is never an issue; it's at the JR Higashi Hagi Station in the Rainbow Building. This business hotel's popularity extends to tourists. Rooms are small, but the staff is friendly.

KOKUMIN SHUKUSHA JOEN, *Horiuchi, Hagi, Yamaguchi, 758-0057. Tel. (0838)22-3939, Fax (0838)26-0471. From ¥8000 per person with two meals. No credit cards.*

This no-frills public lodge offers reasonable Japanese-style accommodations in an excellent location near the castle grounds.

WHERE TO EAT

HOSOKAWA *(French, inexpensive to moderate). Tel. (0838)22-6606. Open 11:30am to 2pm; 5:30pm to 8pm. Closed Monday and 3rd Sunday.*

Hosokawa is a cozy French bistro located in the center of Hagi, a great place for a leisurely meal. It looks like a private house from the outside. Lunchtime sets start at ¥2000, dinner ¥3000. Seafood is the specialty.

MIRAKUTEI *(Japanese, inexpensive). Kikugahama, Horiuchi. Tel. (0838)22-0326. Open daily 11am to 8pm.*

Overlooking the peaceful Kikugahama beach, Mirakutei is convenient for a quick Japanese lunch. The *tempura* lunch costs ¥2000.

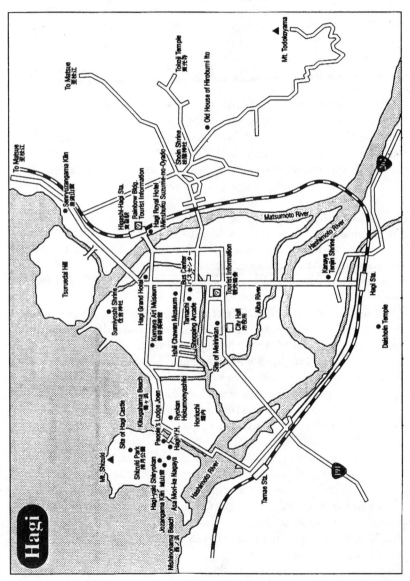

Hagi

Mt. Todokoyama
To Matsue 萩松江
Tokoji Temple 東光寺
Old House of Hirobumi Ito
Shoin Shrine 松陰神社
To Matsue 萩松江
To Matsue 萩松江
Senryuzanama Kiln 笹山窯
Higashi-Hagi Sta. 東萩駅
Rainbow Bldg. Tourist Information
Hagi Royal Hotel
Minshuku Suzume-no-Oyado
Matsumoto River
Hashimoto River
Tsuruedai Hill
Sumiyoshi Shrine 住吉神社
Hagi Grand Hotel
Kumaya Art Museum 熊谷美術館
Bus Center バスセンター
Tamachi
Tourist Information 観光協会
Kanaya Tenjin Shrine 金谷天満宮
Hagi Sta.
Ishii Chawan Museum 石井茶碗美術館
Shopping Arcade
City Hall 市役所
Aiba River
Site of Meirinkan
Daishoin Temple
Site of Hagi Castle 萩城跡
Kikugahama Beach 菊ヶ浜
People's Lodge Joen
Ryokan Hokumonyashiki 北門
Horiuchi 堀内
Mt. Shizuki
Shizuki Park 指月公園
Hagi-yaki Shiryokan 萩焼資料館
Hagi Y.H.
Jozanzama Kiln 城山窯
Asa Mori-ke Nagaya
Nishinohama Beach 西之浜
Heshimoto River
Tamae Sta.

SEEING THE SIGHTS

If the weather is good, tour Hagi by bicycle. The town is fairly flat so the standard one-speed bicycles are okay.

Start out at the Tamamachi Shopping Arcade, Hagi's main shopping street. **The Ishii Chawan Museum** (Ishii Chawan Bijutsukan) displays antique Hagi tea bowls. *Open daily 9am to 5pm. Closed Tuesday and January 6-31. In December open only on weekends and holidays. ¥1000.* Along the arcade are two good places to see Hagi pottery, the shops **Harada Chojuen** and **Miwa Seigado**.

Another good museum is the **Kumaya Art Museum** (Kumaya Bijutsukan). Located in storehouses belonging to the Kumaya, a wealthy merchant family, the museum displays its collection of Hagi tea bowls, famous Kano school screen paintings, other art and the oldest piano in Japan, which the famous German physician Von Siebolt gave to the Kumaya family in the early 19th century. *Open daily 9am to 5pm. Closed January 1. ¥700.*

Kikuya Residence (Kikuya-ke Jutaku) is the estate of a wealthy merchant family. But they were more than merchants. The Mori sided with the losing faction at the Battle of Sekigahara in 1600 and needed money to get back to their domain. The Kikuya sent them the money. The lavish house shows how well they lived. *Open daily 9am to 5pm. Closed December 31. ¥500.*

Next go to the **Horiuchi** district where the samurai lived. Many beautiful clay walls and wooden gates remain from those days. Notice all the summer orange trees for which Hagi is famous.

Take the bridge over to the **Shizuki Park** (Shizuki Koen) area. The park is on the site of Hagi castle. The castle itself was dismantled after the feudal era ended in 1868 as a statement that Japan was entering a modern era. The inner walls and moat still remain. Inside the park is the **Hananoe Teahouse**, a thatched-roof rustic hut in a quiet park. You can have tea for ¥500. *Open 8am to 6:30; 8:30am to 4:30pm November through February. ¥210.*

Admission fee also includes the **Mori House**, the long house where the foot soldiers stayed.

Near the park are a number of kilns including **Shogetsu Kiln**, **Kagijo Kiln**, **Jozangama Kiln** and the **Hagi-yaki Shiryokan**. They should more than satisfy your thirst for pottery. Also in this area is the **Hagi Local History Museum** (Hagi Shiryokan). *Open daily 9am to 5pm; 9am to 4:30pm December through February. ¥500.*

Two temples located on the outskirts of town, **Daishoin** and **Toko-ji**, are well worth visiting. If you don't have time to see both, Toko-ji is easier to reach.

Daishoin is near Hagi Station, the next stop after the main Higashi Hagi Station. Half the Mori clan is buried here, the first and second feudal lords and then the even-numbered generations. The feudal lords' wives are buried next to them, a rare custom. The temple also has hundreds of lanterns. When the first feudal lord died, a number of his retainers committed suicide. This practice was outlawed and the retainers donated lanterns instead. Daishoin has 603 lanterns. *Open 8am to 5pm. ¥200.*

Toko-ji is east of the Matsumoto Bashi Bridge on the same side of the river as Higashi Hagi Station. The Zen temple serves as the mausoleum for the other half of the Mori lords, the odd-numbered generations. As at Daishoin, there are hundreds of stone lanterns as well as graves of wives of feudal lords. *Open 8:30am to 5pm. ¥200.*

REVOLUTIONARY HAGI

One of Japan's strongest clans, the Mori, lost against Tokugawa Ieyasu at the decisive Battle of Sekigahara in 1600. Tokugawa assigned them the Hagi area to rule and always kept an eye on them. The domain was fairly prosperous and the Mori behaved themselves. It may have taken 260 years, but the Mori had the last laugh.

The movement to overthrow the Tokugawa shogunate was started by a group of revolutionary, lower-ranking samurai. **Yoshida Shoin** *(1830-59), headmaster of the samurai school in Hagi, believed passionately that the emperor, as symbol of unity, could be used to bring down the shogun, and that the only way to counter the threat from Western countries was to learn from them. Yoshida tried to get passage to the West on one of Commodore Perry's black ships, but was turned down. He then plotted to assassinate a shogunate official but before he carried it out he was arrested and executed.*

His students carried on his beliefs. They allied with Satsuma, the southern Kyushu domain, and began learning Western military techniques. England assisted with arms. They took on the domain's army and then the shogun's army. In 1867, they marched to Kyoto where they took the palace and proclaimed the emperor as ruler of the land.

Some of Hagi's native sons became the new government's leaders. **Ito Hirobumi** *succeeded where Yoshida failed and smuggled himself to England to study. In 1886, Ito became Japan's first prime minister.* **Yamagata Aritomo** *built up a new army based on his experience of establishing a local army. He, too, became a prime minister, in 1889.*

Japanese visit Hagi much the same way Americans go to Philadelphia to see the birthplace of their revolution. Yoshida's school is now a museum as are the homes of Ito and Kido Koin, another revolutionary.

25. KYUSHU

Kyushu is a microcosm of Japan. It has large cities, agricultural areas, high mountains that offer skiing in winter and hiking in summer, volcanoes, hot springs, forests, ceramics, textiles, festivals, shrines and temples, varied cuisines and archaeological sites. Who could ask for anything more? It's less crowded than Honshu, the main island, and travel between places takes less time. Although first time visitors to Japan may have trouble fitting Kyushu into a one or two week stay, returnees should put it on their itinerary. And Kyushu is a must-see for all ceramics aficionados.

The southernmost of Japan's four main islands, **Kyushu** has one tenth of Japan's land and one tenth of its population — 12 million. In winter northern Kyushu is quite cold, actually colder than Tokyo because the chilly Siberian winds blow straight in while the mountains in central Japan protect Tokyo. Southern Kyushu boasts milder weather, especially on the eastern coast.

Kyushu-ites, living far away from the nation's capital, have a reputation for being rebellious. Although in the vanguard to overthrow the Tokugawa shogun in 1868, less than ten years later they rose up against the new Meiji government. Maybe it's because they have been around so long — Kyushu was an active population center in the Jomon Period (10,000 B.C. to 300 B.C.).

Of all the areas of Japan, Kyushu also has had the most interaction with foreigners including Chinese, Southeast Asians and Europeans. Recently, the island, which was considered a backwater, has been developing high-tech and other industries hoping to leapfrog into the 21st century. Exploiting its proximity to Korea, China and Taiwan (which are closer by air than Tokyo), corporations are investing heavily, especially in the more densely populated north.

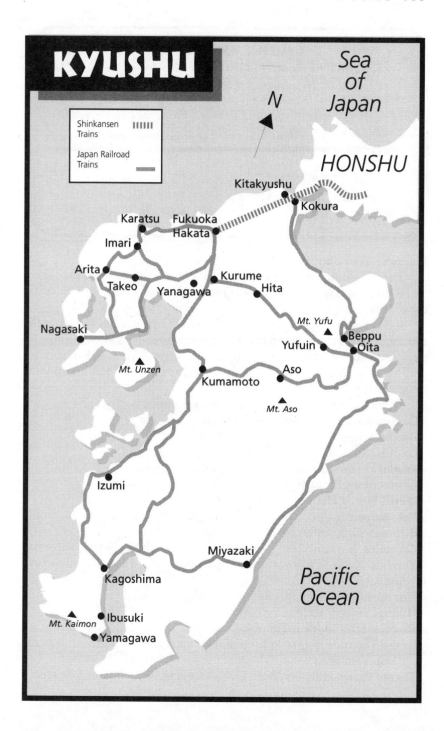

KYUSHU HIGHLIGHTS

- *Sand baths on the beach of Ibusuki or Beppu*
- *Graceful cranes wintering at Izumi*
- *Volcanic Mt. Sakurajima viewed from Iso Garden in Kagoshima*
- *Arita, Karatsu, Onta and Satsuma's distinctive ceramic traditions*
- *Postmodern buildings of Fukuoka*
- *Eclectic shippoku cuisine of Nagasaki*
- *Towering cedar trees on Yakushima*
- *Miyazaki's giant indoor re-creation of the sea at Seagaia*
- *Steep stone walls of Kumamoto's castle*
- *Attractive gardens of samurai houses in Chiran*

Planning Your Stay

There's so much to see in Kyushu that unless you have unlimited time you'll have to select your itinerary with care. There is no one right itinerary for Kyushu.

It takes about two weeks to tour the main areas in a not too leisurely fashion: Use these suggested times as a rough guideline: Fukuoka area, 2 days; Karatsu, 1 day; Arita area, 1 to 2 days; Nagasaki, 2 days; Kumamoto and Mt. Aso, 2 days; Kagoshima and environs, 2 days; Yufuin and/or Beppu, 2 days.

Tailor your trip to fit your interests as follows:

- **Contemporary Architecture**: Fukuoka
- **Gardens**: Kagoshima, Kumamoto, Chiran
- **Castles**: Kumamoto, Shimabara
- **Feudal History**: Kumamoto, Kagoshima, Fukuoka
- **Interaction with Europeans**: Nagasaki
- **World War II History**: Nagasaki, Chiran
- **Volcanoes**: Mt. Aso, Sakurajima (Kagoshima)
- **Bird-watching**: Izumi for cranes (winter only)
- **Ceramics**: Karatsu, Arita, Kagoshima, Okawachiyama, Onta, Satsuma
- **Textiles**: Kurume (cotton ikat), Kagoshima (silk), Fukuoka (silk weaving)
- **Hot Springs**: Yufuin, Mt. Aso, Takeo, Beppu, Ibusuki
- **Hiking**: Yufuin, Mt. Aso
- **Shrines**: Dazaifu (near Fukuoka)
- **Grand Festivals**: Nagasaki Kunchi, Fukuoka: Hakata Dontaku, Hakata Gion Yamagasa
- **Theme Parks**: Huis Ten Bois, Holland Village, Space World, Seagaia

FUKUOKA - HAKATA

The city's name is **Fukuoka**, but the train station is called **Hakata** so people are always confused about what is where. This schizophrenia came about in 1889 when a vote decided the name of the prefectural capital. Fukuoka was the castle and samurai district while Hakata was the merchant area. Rank won, but the consolation prize was naming the train station Hakata, today the terminus of the Tokyo–Kyushu *shinkansen* train. The name Hakata is far from forgotten; today in Fukuoka you can buy Hakata *ori* (silk) and Hakata dolls and participate in the Hakata Dontaku and Hakata Gion Yamagasa festivals.

At first glance, Fukuoka's only saving grace appears to be its conveniently located airport. Actually,it's a colorful modern city, and we think it has some of the best food in Japan. With the decline of heavy industry, Fukuoka was forced to restructure, and it's now prospering as the regional center for Kyushu. Trade is booming with Korea, China and Russia's eastern ports. While little of old Fukuoka remains, the city has made a determined effort to construct the boldest, most colorful new buildings in Japan. There are dozens of striking new buildings, including many postmodern structures; more are either under construction or in the planning stage. A stop in Fukuoka is a must for anyone seriously interested in postmodern architecture. Unlike most Japanese cities, Fukuoka has exuberantly embraced its waterfront, so much so that Momochi Seaside Park features a 2.5 kilometer landfilll beach.

Planning Your Stay

Plan on spending one day in Fukuoka. From the city you can make side trips to Dazaifu, Yanagawa, Yoshinogari and Space World, so you can easily spend several days in the area.

While Fukuoka has its share of museums and gardens, to best experience the city wander its many new urban centers like Canal City and Bayside Place. Head to Saibu Museum for art made by burning natural gas. A stop in Fukuoka is a must for anyone seriously interested in postmodern architecture.

Dates to Remember

• **May 3–4: Hakata Dontaku Festival**: Dontaku comes from the Dutch word *zontag* meaning holiday. 25,000 people parade dressed in period costume.

• **July 1–15: Hakata Gion Yamagasa Festival**: Floats decorated with Hakata dolls are placed throughout the city. The festival climaxes on July 15 with the Oiyama race; at dawn, seven floats pulled by hundreds of men dressed in *happi* coats and loin cloths race through the streets and are doused with water by spectators.

• **November for two weeks**: A **sumo** tournament is held at Kyushu Kokusai Center.

ARRIVALS & DEPARTURES

By Air
Fukuoka Airport is the major airport in the region and is the most conveniently located to a large city in Japan.

To/from Tokyo Haneda: Over 20 flights/day; **Narita**: 1 flight/day (ANA, JAL, JAS. ¥27,050)

To/from Nagoya: 9 flights/day (ANA, JAL, JAS. ¥18,600).

To/from Osaka Itami: 5 flights/day. **Kansai**: 6 flights/day (ANA, JAL, JAS. ¥15,800).

To/from Sapporo: 4 flights/day (ANA, JAL, JAS. ¥38,400)

There is also service to/from Akita, Aomori, Fukushima, Hakodate, Hanamaki (Morioka), Izumo, Kagoshima, Kochi, Komatsu, Matsumoto, Matsuyama, Miyazaki, Niigata, Sendai, Takamatsu, Tokushima, Toyama, Yamagata and Yonago.

For Ground Transportation:
Train: from Fukuoka Airport to Hakata Station in Fukuoka (10 minutes, ¥250; 11 minutes to Tenjin, ¥250).

Taxi: 15 minutes to Hakata Station, ¥1200. Didn't we say this airport is was a convenient airport?

By Train
Hakata Station is the western terminus of the shinkansen train that runs from Tokyo. The fastest train, the *Nozomi*, takes 5 hours to Tokyo and 2 1/2 hours to Kyoto while the *Hikari* takes about 6 1/2 hours to Tokyo and 3 1/2 hours to Kyoto. Hakata is the transportation hub for Kyushu; there are convenient trains to Nagasaki, Kumamoto, Kagoshima, Miyazaki and Beppu. The shinkansen station is in the Hakata district right in the middle of the city.

By Bus
There are overnight buses from Tokyo (14 1/2 hours, ¥15,000), Nagoya (10 1/2 hours, ¥10,500), Kyoto (9 1/2 hours, ¥10,500), Osaka (9 hours, ¥10,000), Okayama (9 hours, ¥7200), Kanazawa (12 hours, ¥12,000). There is express bus service with frequent departures to Imari (2 hours, ¥2150), Nagasaki (2 1/2 hours, ¥2900), Kumamoto (2 hours, ¥2400), Beppu (2 hours, ¥3100), Miyazaki (4 1/2 hours, ¥6000), Kagoshima (4 hours, ¥5300).

GETTING AROUND TOWN

The large city of Fukuoka is well-served by subway, train, bus and ferry. Both Hakata, the main JR train station, and Tenjin, the largest downtown district, have bus centers. The Nishitetsu Station, terminus for this private rail line, is in Tenjin. Ferries, both long distance and commuter, leave from the Bayside Place Hakata Futo. The Fukuoka subway has two lines that connect at Nakasu–Kawabata station. Both Hakata and Tenjin have bus terminals: Hakata-eki Kotsu Center and Tenjin Bus Center respectively. They handle local as well as long distance service.

Tourist Information

Fukuoka City Tourist Information, an "i" information office, is in Hakata Station. *Tel. (092)431-3003*. **Rainbow Plaza**, on the 8th floor of the IMS Building in Tenjin, has lots of information on Fukuoka in English. IMS is the large building in front of Nishitetsu Station. 1-7-11 Tenjin, Chuo-ku, Fukuoka. *Tel. (092)733-2220*. Open 10am to 8pm daily.

Home Visits: To meet a Japanese family; contact the **Fukuoka International Association** at Rainbow Plaza, 8F, IMS Building, 1-7-11 Tenjin, Chuo-ku, Fukuoka, 810-0001. *Tel. (092)733-2220, Fax (092)733-2215*. Open 10am to 8pm daily.

Goodwill Guides: To arrange a volunteer Goodwill Guide, contact the ACROS Fukuoka Tourist Information Center, *Tel. (092)725-9100* between 10am and 4pm.

WHERE TO STAY

GRAND HYATT FUKUOKA, *1-2-82 Sumiyoshi, Hakata-ku, Fukuoka, 812-0018. Tel. (092)282-1234, Fax (092)262-1175. Singles from ¥12,000. Doubles and twins from ¥23,000. Credit cards.*

This ultramodern hotel is located in the Canal City complex and has an excellent food court at the mall level.

HOTEL IL PALAZZO, *3-13-1 Haruyoshi, Chuo-ku, Fukuoka, 810-0003. Tel. (092)716-3333, Fax (092)724-3330. Singles from ¥13,000. Doubles from ¥22,000. Credit cards.*

Il Palazzo is such a wonderful change from the big international hotels that we've included it in our selection of Best Places To Stay in Japan (see Chapter 11 for a full description). It's a five-minute walk from Canal City on a side road across the canal (in the middle of a love hotel district) and is the ultimate in postmodern, high-Milan style. If you don't stay here, be sure to come and check out the decor, especially in the restaurants and bars.

CLIO COURT HOTEL, *5-3 Hakata-eki, Chuo-gai, Hakata-ku, Fukuoka, 812-0012. Tel. (092)472-1111, Fax (092)474-3222. Singles from ¥9900 without and ¥11,000 with windows. Doubles from ¥14,300. Credit cards.*

This newish, midpriced hotel, on the *shinkansen* side of Hakata Sstation, boasts a convenient location. The lobby, on the third floor of the contemporary building, is a study in marble and chrome. The rooms are art deco, a welcome change from the dreary decor of most midrange hotels, but beware — the cheapest rooms are windowless. The basement houses a restaurant–bar complex called Clio Seven.

SEA HAWK HOTEL AND RESORT, *2-2-3 Jigyohama, Chuo-ku, Fukuoka, 810-8650. Tel. (092)844-8111, Fax (092)844-7887. Singles from ¥9000. Doubles from ¥18,000. Credit cards.*

A high-rise, ship-shaped hotel on the waterfront; different floors have different motifs such as African, European, early American, Asian and Oceania. The rooms on the "bow" of the ship have baths with spectacular views. One floor is Japanese style complete with a garden and inn service. The restaurant area has a 40-meter glass-domed atrium. Not surprisingly, the hotel is especially popular with honeymooners and baseball fans attending the games next door at the Fukuoka Dome.

HAKATA GREEN HOTEL, *3-11 Hakata-eki, Chuo-gai, Hakata-ku, Fukuoka, 812-0012. Tel. (092)451-4111, Fax (092)451-4508. Singles from ¥6500. Doubles from ¥8800. Twins from ¥9400. Credit cards. Member of the Welcome Inn Reservation Center.*

This hotel offers basic accommodations at a very convenient location — Hakata Station — and is popular with foreign tourists.

WHERE TO EAT

There are so many shopping–restaurant centers that it's easy to find any type of food. Just try Marizon, Bayside Wharf or Canal City. The Nakasu area, an island in the river between Hakata and Tenjin, is home to a zillion restaurants, bars, *yatai* (night stalls) and cabarets. The Tenjin area has lots of restaurants and tends to be cheaper, especially on Oyafuko Dori, a popular place for young people.

AMIMOTO *(Fugu, expensive). 2-3-8 Nakasu, close to the Haruyoshi Bridge. Tel. (092)271-2222. Open 11:30am until 1am the next morning.*

Amimoto specializes in *fugu*, the delicately flavored Japanese blowfish. The *Chiri Genkai* course includes *fugu sashimi, fugu nabe*, stew, fried *fugu* and *fugu* soup; the cost is ¥6500. More expensive courses have more dishes; for ¥14,000 they even include some of the poisonous liver, but we recommend you don't take a chance.

WHAT'S COOKING IN FUKUOKA?

The three meals in Fukuoka that we recommend are **mizutaki** *(a kind of* **nabe** *or stew with chicken), a good ramen (Chinese noodles) and fish.*

Mizutaki is a one-pot stew containing chicken, vegetables, and rice cakes that cooks at your table. Try the tasty dish as a change from the fish and yakitori diet of many visitors to Japan.

Fukuoka prides itself on having the best fish of any big city in Japan – the claim is debatable, but the fish is very good, very fresh (often live) and plentiful. Try **fugu**, *the famous (or is it infamous?) Japanese blowfish, in season September through March. While the liver is poisonous, the chefs go through rigorous training on how to remove the liver and make sure the toxins are gone, so eating fugu is quite safe. Slices are cut so thin, you can see the plate's pattern through the fish.*

Ramen, *a Fukuoka specialty, is freshly made in dozens of spots around town. The broth is not as salty as elsewhere in Japan. Try ramen at the yatai (food stalls).*

SHIN MIURA *(Japanese, moderate to expensive). 21-12 Sekijo-machi at the foot of Chidoribashi, a 10-minute taxi ride from Hakata Station. Tel. (092)291-0821. A branch is on the B1 floor of the Tenjin building. Tel. (092)721-3272. Open 12 noon to 8pm. Reservation necessary.*

Shin Miura is one of the best places to eat *mizutaki*. The modern Japanese gate at the entrance to the main store belies its 90-year history. The Tenjin branch is decorated in Japanese country style, and the service is very friendly – its owner is a proud graduate of Waseda University, one of Japan's top universities. A *mizutaki* course starts off with chicken *sashimi*, slightly braised slices of chicken with a vinegar, soy and scallion dipping sauce. For those of you worried about nearly raw chicken, the shop states that its chickens are raised especially for this purpose and, after several trips, we haven't had a problem. Chicken *sashimi* tastes mild and sweet and is less an acquired taste than even the easiest of the fish *sashimi*! The main course is a soup containing chicken, cabbage, *shiitake* mushrooms, scallions and *mochi* (rice cake) cooked and served in a clay pot at your table. The broth is slightly sweet and has very little salt. The meal finishes with noodles cooked in the broth. Courses start at ¥10,000; at the Tenjin branch, you can get just *mizutaki* for ¥5000.

ANCHOR *(Bar, moderate). 4F, Iwata Building, Nakasu-san (3)-chome. Tel. (092)291-1657.*

Patrice's husband's favorite place is this small drinking establishment, pronounced Ankaa – a World War II Navy bar – around the corner from the police station. As you enter, the bartenders rings the ship's bell in welcome and gives you a souvenir, a small Navy cap, to wear. The atmosphere is incredible. The walls are covered with pictures of the famous — a former US ambassador — and the not-so-famous in military uniforms; a video of Japanese World War II songs runs constantly. Order *biru* (beer), *whiskey & water (mizuwari)* or Japanese *shochu* (a clear vodka-like drink) served here with warm water and a sour plum.

After a couple drinks, a bartender encourages you to dress in a Japanese Navy tunic or *kamikaze* flyer jumpsuit; don a hat, have a mustache painted on your face, and pose for a Polaroid photo in front of the mural of a Japanese battleship or a Zero fighter. There is a 1950s video of Japanese and English versions of the Tennessee Waltz so just clap along or volunteer to sing one of the English songs. At least once a night, the bartender usually comments in Japanese that the Japan of those days had more confidence — personally we prefer a nervous Japan! A bottle of beer costs about ¥2500; it's pricey, but what an experience!

Yatai

Yatai are found in the Nakasu district along the river and other areas around town. They open around 6pm and many don't close until the wee hours of the morning. Unlike Tokyo where the *yatai* are covered with blue tarpaulins and seem grungy, the night stalls in Fukuoka are bright, well - kept and many are surrounded by Japanese wood and paper *shoji* screens. Apparently some stalls have mob connections; friends paid the outrageous sum of ¥7000 for a bowl of *tendon* (rice and fried shrimp). To make sure you don't go to a place like that, pick a stall where young women are eating.

Hakuryu, in front of the Mitsubishi Bank in Tenjin, is famous for its *gyoza* (dumplings), *ramen* and *yakitori*. **Umatsura** is a *yatai* near the Kego Branch of the Fukuoka Bank on Keyaki Dori, has great *okonomiyaki* (a pancake with meat and vegetables). **Sanyu**, another *yatai*, has good Hakata *ramen* for ¥600; it's in Nakasu, directly across the Haruyoshi Bridge. **Ippei** is noted for its seafood *tempura*, ¥2500 for seven to eight different pieces; it's also located in Nakasu — turn left immediately after crossing the Haruyoshi Bridge; it's on the left.

SEEING THE SIGHTS

Rather than seeing a lot of historic sites, Fukuoka is city to which you should experience — a great place for people watching. Visit the new shopping–eating–entertainment centers like **Bayside Place**, **Canal City** or **Marizon** and while away an afternoon. **Tenjin** is a business and shopping district of Fukuoka. Don't miss the large underground arcade filled with shops or **Oyafuko Dori**, a street crowded filled with discos and young people buying trendy clothes and cheap food.

In the afternoon, take a quick look at the Canal City complex, eat dinner and stroll through the Nakasu ward afterwards. If you prefer, spend all your time in Canal City, a large, striking combination shopping mall–theater–arena and hotel complex right in center city. It houses 13 cinemas, a Sega amusement center complete with virtual reality games, the Grand Hyatt and Washington Hotels, and more stores and restaurants than you can count. Canal City is covered in orange, red, green and blue tiles and stands about 12 stories high on the main canal in Nakasu ward.

The mall is open to a fountain and protected from street noise by the new Grand Hyatt hotel. The city has installed a long brick promenade that runs for several kilometers along the canal and is bustling with strollers and food stalls at night.

A short walk away, on the opposite side of the canal, is the equally stunning Il Palazzo Hotel. See our Best Places to Stay in Chapter 11. The hotel is located in a district of small upscale (and love) hotels. Both are a short walk away from one of the wildest, most upscale nightlife-districts in Japan, near the Nakasukawabata police station. Besides having glitzy skin shows, the energy of the place is overwhelming and it makes for a great after-dinner stroll.

Central Fukuoka

Bayside Place–Hakata Futo. Originally the Hakata Wharf, the area has been rebuilt and features a new glass and steel harbor-side shopping complex. The New Orleans feel to the place is completed with an actual Cafe du Monde, the perfect spotplace to while away an hour on a rainy day. From the pier, you can catch ferries to outlying islands as well as take short hops across the bay to Uminonakamichi.

Kushida Shrine, located halfway between Tenjin and Hakata, has been the Shinto guardian shrine for the area since the Heian period. Dedicated to commerce and longevity, the shrine has thrived in the center of the Hakata merchant district. A gigantic red paper lantern greets you at its entrance. On the precincts is a small Hakata *Rekishikan* (History Hall) where festival floats are on display. *Tel. (092)291-2951. Open daily 10am to 4:30pm. ¥200.* The **Hakata Gion Yamagasa Festival race** begins at Kushida Shrine on July 15.

Hakata

Hakata Machiya Folk Museum. *Tel. (092)281-7761. Open daily from 10am to 5:30pm. ¥200.* Stop in at this reproduction of an old merchant residence for demonstrations of Hakata silk weaving.

Uminonakamichi

Uminonakamichi, literally "the road in the center of the sea," is a long spit of land with parks, an aquarium, beaches, hotels and an amusement park. It is reached by ferry from Hakata Futo and Marizon and by train on the JR Kashii line. The Marine World Uminonakamichi is a large aquarium featuring dolphin and sea lion shows. *Tel. (092)603-1111. Open 9:30am to 5:30pm; until 5pm November through February. Closed December 31, January 1 and the first Monday and Tuesday in February and September. ¥2100.*

Western Area

Hawks Town is home to the **Fukuoka Dome** and the Sea Hawk Hotel. The Daiei Hawks baseball team plays at the 52,000-seat dome, the only stadium in Japan with a retractable roof. A popular backstage stage tour shows you the inner workings of the high-tech roof *(Tel. (092)847-1539 for tour reservations).* In addition to baseball games, the dome hosts concerts and other events, and outside the stadium, bronze-cast hands of stars such as Michael Jackson and Paul McCartney commemorate their performances.

Marizon, a marina filled with shops, restaurants and young people, is on the man-made beach at **Momoichi Seaside Park**. *Shops are open from 11am to 9pm;, restaurants from 11am to 11pm. Closed on the second Tuesday January through March.* Catch a hydrofoil every 30 minutes for the 15-minute trip across the bay to **Uminonakamichi**.

Next to Marizon is the **Fukuoka Tower**. A huge mirrored tower with two observation floors offers great views on clear days. *Open 9:30am to 10pm; November through March until 9pm; until 11pm in August. ¥800.*

South of the Fukuoka Tower is the **Saibu Gas Museum**, a futuristic building housing the Gallery of Flame — art created by natural gas. It's a surreal experience. *Open 10am to 5pm. Closed Monday. Admission free.*

Just south of the Saibu Gas Museum is the **Fukuoka City Museum** (Fukuoka-shi Hakubutsukan). *Tel. (092)845-5011. Open 9:30am to 5pm; until 7pm in July and August. Closed Monday and December 28 through January 4. ¥200.* In addition to displaying Fukuoka's history and way of life, the museum has exhibits on Fukuoka's relationship with Southeast Asia. A gold seal, sent by the Chinese emperor to the empress of Japan in the 3rd century, is the museum's proudest possession. This National Treasure was found on Shikanoshima Island across the bay.

Heading east toward Tenjin (take taxi or subway to Ohori Koen stop) you'll find the **Fukuoka Art Museum** (Fukuoka Shiritsu Bijutsukan). *Tel. (092)714-6051. Open 9:30am to 5:30pm. Closed Monday and December 28 through January 4. ¥200.* Located in Ohori Park, the museum has temporary exhibits as well as Asian contemporary art, modern Japanese painters and some works by Western artists including Chagall and Miro.

East of Ohori Park is Maizuri Park containing **Fukuoka Castle's Walls** (Fukuoka-jo Ato). All that remains of the castle are Otemon gate, some walls and a guard tower, but they are reminders of the time when Fukuoka was a castle town. Lots of Fukuoka-ites visit here in cherry blossom season.

Fukuoka Outskirts

Yusentai Garden. *Tel. (092)711-0415. Open 9am to 5pm. ¥200.* Now a park owned by the city, Yusentai was the site of a villa built by one of the feudal lords of Fukuoka. The lovely garden has a pond and pavilion and is a great retreat from the city.

SHOPPING

The whole city is one big shopping center. Apart from Hakata silk and Hakata dolls, stores concentrate on the modern and trendy. Arcades at Tenjin and Hikata compete with centers like Canal City and Bayside Place.

EXCURSIONS & DAY TRIPS

DAZAIFU

Dazaifu was one of the most important places in Kyushu during the Heian period, but today little remains of its glory. Still, it is a pleasant day trip from Fukuoka and a place where you can bike leisurely around the town.

By train, it's 40 minutes by Nishitetsu train from Nishitetsu Fukuoka Station in Tenjin to Nishitetsu Daizaifu Station (¥360). Sometimes you have to transfer at Futsuka-ichi.

Tourist Information

At the tourist information office, located inside the train station, you can rent a bicycle for ¥200/hour. Bilingual signs make navigating easy.

Where to Eat

YASUTAKE *(Noodles, inexpensive). Sando Dazaifu. Tel. (092)922-5079. Open daily 10am to 6pm.*

Located on the right side at the main road leading to Dazaifu Tenmangu Shrine, near the first big *torii* gate. Homemade noodle shop features *kama age* (noodles in hot water), *tempura* ¥1400 and *tori nanban* (noodles in broth with chicken or duck) ¥750.

Seeing the Sights

Dazaifu Tenmangu Shrine. *Tel. (092)922-8225. Open daily. Treasure House is open 9am to 4pm. Closed Monday. ¥300. 5-minute walk from Dazaifu*

Station. Sugawara Michizane, a scholar and poet, was unjustly exiled from Kyoto in the 9th century and died here, pining to return to Kyoto. After his death, natural disasters befell Kyoto and it was determined these were caused by Michizane's vengeful spirit. To atone for the error, Michizane was deified as the god of scholarly achievement. Around the country there are many Tenmangu Shrines, all dedicated to Michizane, but this is the top one. The present vermilion-colored shrine, built in 1590, is a pilgrimage site for students praying to pass high school or college entrance exams. People write their wishes on hundreds of *ema* (small wooden boards) that hang in the compound.

The shrine's treasure house is on the grounds *(¥300, closed Monday)* as is a museum which shows Michizane's life illustrated in Hakata dolls *(¥200, closed Tuesday).* The shrine also has thousands of plum trees which have become a symbol of Michizane's life.

At the **Tourist Information Center** at the shrine's entrance, rent earphones for a 30-minute explanation of the shrine in English. It's well worth the ¥300 fee.

Komyozen-ji Temple. *Tel. (092)922-4053. Open daily 8am to 5pm.* *¥200.* Founded during the Kamakura period, Komyozen-ji has strong ties to Tenmangu Shrine and has a beautiful stone and moss garden.

Kyushu History Museum (Kyushu Rekishi Shiryokan). *Tel. (092)923-0404. Open 9:30am to 4pm. Closed Monday. Admission free. 10-minute walk from Tenmangu Shrine.* This pleasant museum displays items excavated at Dazaifu from the Jomon, Yayoi and Kofun periods.

SPACE WORLD

From Fukuoka: 55 minutes by JR Kagoshima Honsen Line from Hakata Station. Get off at Edamitsu, then a 5-minute walk. Tel. (093)672-3600. Open daily 9:30am to 5pm. 1-day ticket ¥4300; entrance without rides, ¥2400.

Always wanted to be an astronaut but didn't have the right stuff? Well, **Space World**, a theme park, was made for you. In addition to the usual amusement park rides (of course, with a space spin to them), you can experience some of the training that astronauts go through at NASA. Kids love it here.

YANAGAWA

Yanagawa is a pleasant getaway from the big cities in Kyushu. This lovely former castle town is famous for its canals bordered with willow trees. Although the castle is gone, the maze of moats remains an idyllic place for a sleepy boat trip. Since there is no current on the canals, the boatmen, wearing straw hats and *happi* coats, propel the small wooden boats with long poles. To keep you warm in winter, the boats have quilts with heaters underneath. The narrow canals take you past historic samurai houses and warehouses.

Yanagawa is nearly as famous for its eels as for its canals. The trademark dish is *unagi no seiro mushi* (rice topped with thinly sliced omelet topped with eel all steamed together). The rice is delicious having absorbed the flavorful juices; steaming makes the eel less fatty. Don't miss a chance to try it.

By train, take the private Nishitetsu Omuta train line, 55 minutes from Fukuoka, ¥830.

Where to Stay

OHANA SHOTO-KAN, *1 Shinhoka-machi, Yanagawa, Fukuoka, 832-0069. Tel. (0944)73-2189. Rates from ¥15,000 with two meals. Credit cards.*

This traditional Japanese inn, with rooms overlooking the garden, is famous for its *unagi* (eel) cuisine and duck during the winter season.

Where to Eat

MOTOYOSHIYA *(Eel cuisine, inexpensive to moderate). 69 Asahi-machi. Tel. (0944)72-6155. Open 11am to 8:30pm. Closed 2nd and 4th Monday.*

One of the oldest eel cuisine restaurants, a set of steamed *unagi no seiro mushi* costs ¥2700.

FUKURYU *(Eel cuisine, inexpensive). 29-1 Okihata-cho. Tel. (0944)72-2404. Open 11am to 7pm. Closed Thursday.*

A restaurant popular among the locals serves *unagi no seiro mushi* (steamed eels with rice and shredded omelet) for ¥1600 and *Yanagawa nabe* (stew with small river eels and vegetables) for ¥1300.

Seeing the Sights

Canal Boat Trip (Kawa Kudari). The boat trip on the sleepy canals is the highlight of a trip here. The pier is a 5-minute walk from the Nishitetsu Station. The hour-long trip costs ¥1500.

Ohana Mansion. *Tel. (0944)73-2189. Open daily 9am to 6pm. ¥400 for garden, ¥500 for mansion.* A villa of Yanagawa's feudal lords, the Tachibana residence is half-Japanese and half-Western style, and displays family treasures. Along the pond 280 pine trees evoke the memory of the beautiful islands of Matsushima near Sendai in northern Japan.

YOSHINOGARI

If you have wondered what the Japanese lived in before wooden houses with *shoji* screens and *tatami* mats, find out at **Yoshinogari**, the excavated site of a Yayoi Period village (300 B.C. to AD 300). Some scholars speculate that Yoshinogari could be the home of Queen Himiko whose kingdom is recorded in 3rd century Chinese journals. Even if it isn't, the area gives insight into that era with its reconstructed homes and watch towers. Rice cultivation began in that period and as irrigation became increasingly sophisticated, so did social patterns, molding Japanese society to the present day. Archaeologists have unearthed hundreds of burial urns. A display hall houses some of the excavated artifacts. *Tel. (0952)52-4130. Open daily 9am to 4:30. Admission free.*

From Fukuoka (Hakata Station): take the JR limited express train to Tosu (20 minutes) and change for the local train; 3 stops to Yoshinogari Koen park (12 minutes). ¥820.

KARATSU

Karatsu, a seaside town with a long beach and a reconstructed castle, is well known for colored earthenware brought by Korean potters after Japan's invasions in the 1590s. A hotly debated topic is whether they were kidnapped or came of their own free will. Their works were immediately admired and the feudal lord gave the potters official positions. Their understated, rustic creations fit the aesthetic of the tea ceremony masters of the early 17th century.

Even today, Karatsu is considered one of the three that tea ceremony connoisseurs want to own and admire. "Raku first, Hagi second, Karatsu third" is a familiar mantra.

Planning Your Stay

From Fukuoka, an outing to Karatsu can be either a day trip or an overnight. We urge you to make an overnight trip to give yourself an opportunity to stay at Yoyokaku, a charming inn that we thoroughly enjoy.

In Karatsu, see the castle, the float exhibition hall and some of the many kilns dotting the town.

Dates to Remember

• **November 2-4, Karatsu Kunchi Festival**: At the Autumn Festival of Karatsu Jinja Shrine, 14 floats parade through the streets of Karatsu. Many of the floats shows the Chinese influence in the area: great lion heads, phoenix, dragons and dolphins. Others are helmets of famous Japanese warriors. On the second day of the festival, the floats are dragged across the dunes of Nishi-no-Hama as tests of strength for the men pulling them. During the rest of the year, the Hikiyama Tenjijo, near Karatsu Jinja Shrine, displays the floats (see *Seeing the Sights*).

ARRIVALS & DEPARTURES

By Train

From Fukuoka: take the subway to Meinohama, (¥290, 25 minutes), the end of the line (19 minutes, ¥290), and change to the JR Chikuhi Line to Karatsu (1 hour, ¥820).

By Bus

To/from Fukuoka: Tenjin Bus Center (8 buses/day, 1 hour 10 minutes, ¥1050).

By Car

Take Route 202 along the coast from Fukuoka.

GETTING AROUND TOWN

The main sights in Karatsu are fairly spread out. Bicycle rental is available in front of Karatsu Station.

Tourist Information

At Karatsu Station. *Tel. (0955)72-4963.*

WHERE TO STAY

YOYOKAKU, *Higashi Karatsu, Karatsu, 847-0017. Tel. (0955)72-7181, Fax (0955)73-0604. Rates from ¥15,000 per person with two meals. Credit cards.*

Our stay at this wonderfully old-fashioned Japanese inn was so enjoyable that we've included it in our Best Places to Stay (see Chapter 11). The entrance hall, dimly lit with a hanging lantern, leads to a quiet reception area. The rooms open onto a Japanese garden filled with more than 100 delicately pruned old pine trees. Karatsu ware by Nakazato Takashi is on display and for sale in a small gallery near the front desk.

KARATSU CITY HOTEL. *2942-1 Shin Ko-machi, Karatsu, 847-0816. Tel. (0955)72-1100. Fax (0955)73-8417. Singles ¥7000. Doubles ¥12,000. Credit cards.*

A new hotel at the Minami (south) exit of Karatsu Station, the Karatsu City Hotel combines attractive accommodations with a very central location. The hotel includes a rooftop spa with outdoor bath.

KOKUMIN SHUKUSHA NIJI NO MATSUBARA HOTEL, *4 Higashi Karatsu, Karatsu, 847-0017. Tel. (0955)73-9111. Singles from ¥6000. Twins from ¥10,000 without meals. Credit cards.*

Located in the midst of a pine tree grove of pine trees near a long sandy beach, this public lodge offers excellent value. While the hotel is a no-frills operation, it's in a great location, and the rooms are clean.

Avoid the **Karatsu Seaside Hotel** — a moldy, run-down dump.

WHERE TO EAT

TAKEYA UNAGI (*Eel cuisine, inexpensive*). *1884-2 Nakamachi. Tel. (0955)73-3244. Open 11:30am to 7:30pm. (6:30pm on Sundays and holidays).* This restaurant is very proud of its special sauce used in cooking fresh eel. *Unagi teishoku* (set meal of eel, rice, soup and pickles) costs ¥1700; *unagi donburi* (eel on top of the rice) costs ¥1500.

SEEING THE SIGHTS

Karatsu Castle. *Tel. (0955)72-5697. Open 9am to 5pm. Closed December 29–31. ¥310.* Located on a promontory, the castle has a fantastic view of the sea. In fine weather, you can see as far as the Iki Islands, 30 kilometers offshore. Originally built in 1602, the present keep is a modern reconstruction and houses displays of old Karatsu ceramics and materials concerning Karatsu's history. The castle was the staging ground for Hideyoshi's invasion of Korea in 1592.

Float Exhibition Hall (Hikiyama Tenjijo). *Tel. (0955)72-2264. Open 9am to 5pm. Closed December 29–31. ¥200.* Karatsu comes alive for its November 2–4 Kunchi Festival, which is the Autumn festival for the nearby Karatsu Jinja Shrine. Stop by here at other times to see these spectacular floats.

Kinsho-ji Temple. The entrance gate to this Buddhist temple was moved from Nagoya Castle.

Kilns

Karatsu has lots of kilns. A couple of our favorites follow:

Nakazato Taroemon Kiln. *Tel. (0955)72-8171. Open daily 8:30am to 5:30pm.* The Nakazato family were among the first Korean potters to come to Karatsu. The kiln's traditions are carried on by the 13th generation master. He is the eldest son of Nakazato Muan, designated a National Living Treasure for reviving Karatsu pottery. The kiln's gallery displays both contemporary and historic pieces. Architecturally, the building is interesting – two buildings connected over a fish pond.

Nakano Kiln. *Tel. (0955)73-8881. Close to Nakazato Kiln.* We like to come here to see its contemporary ware.

Ryuta Gama Kiln. *Tel. (0955)74-3503). Open 9am to 12 noon, 2 to 4pm. Closed Saturday afternoons and Sunday. 20-minute drive from Karatsu.* Phone for a map. Ryuta Gama, the kiln of Nakazato Takashi, the fifth son of the 12th generation Nakazato master, is set in the hills in a rural area outside of Karatsu. The attractive complex has a showroom, working areas, kilns and a private residence set on several acres of land. After mastering Karatsu techniques, Takashi went to Tanegashima, an island south of Kyushu, where he developed the Karatsu Nanban style. Nanban means "Southern Barbarians," the lovely name given to Portuguese and by extension all other Europeans because they reached Japan from the south. The unglazed ware from Southeast Asia came to be called Nanban pottery since Portuguese ships carried it to Japan. The kiln combines traditional Karatsu ware with individualistic elements. Nakazato Takashi's works are also for sale at a gallery in the Yoyokaku Inn in Karatsu City.

IMARI

This city's name has become synonymous with Japanese porcelain. Although it wasn't an actual production center, porcelain was shipped from the port of Imari. The city itself has little to interest visitors, but on the outskirts is **Okawachiyama**, a small pottery village that is a must for anyone seriously interested in ceramics.

Planning Your Stay
Ceramic enthusiasts can easily spend the better part of a day in Okawachiyama.

Dates to Remember
• **April 1-5** and **November 1-5**: **Okawachiyama Pottery Fair**. You are sure to find some bargains amongst all the pottery.

ARRIVALS & DEPARTURES
By Train
　　To/from Karatsu: JR train on Chikuhi line (50 minutes, ¥630)
　　To/from Arita: Matsu-ura Tetsudo private line (25 minutes, ¥400)

By Bus
　　To/from Fukuoka: 9 buses/day, 2 hours, ¥2150.

By Car
　　To/from Fukuoka and Karatsu: Route 202
　　To/from Arita: Route 202

Tourist Information
The "i" Tourist Information Office is located at Imari Stataion, *Tel. (0955)22-6820.*

WHERE TO STAY
IMARI HOTEL. *115 Hasuike-cho, Imari, Saga-ken, 848-0042. Tel. (0955)22-3118, Fax (0955)22-3119. Singles from ¥5300. Doubles from ¥9800.*
This centrally-located business hotel has Japanese and Western rooms.

SEEING THE SIGHTS
Okawachiyama

From the Imari Bus Center, take the Saihi bus to Okawachiyama. 8 buses/ day (¥270, 18 minutes); Taxi ¥1500 one way.

If you are really interested in ceramics, don't miss this secluded village. From the mid-17th century until the mid-19th century, in this small village nestled deep in the mountains, Lord Nabeshima kept his potters as virtual prisoners in order to keep special production techniques a secret. A barrier gate prevented the artisans free access, and potters who disclosed secrets were executed.

Thirty kilns are tucked into a gorgeous mountain setting reminiscent of a brush painting landscape. At the entrance to the village, there's a bridge decorated with colorful ceramic tiles. Make sure you stop in the public toilets, even they show the mark of the town. Don't worry about which is which — a ceramic queen hangs on one door and a king is on the other. Although scattered, all the kiln shops are within walking distance.

Near where you get off the bus is the **Imari Arita Traditional Arts Museum** (Imari Arita-yaki Dento Sangyo Kaikan). *Tel. (0955)22-6333. Open from 9am to 5pm. Closed Monday. Free admission.* This museum displays masterpieces of old Imari and Nabeshima ware and shows how they are hand painted. Stop here to get an orientation before browsing around the village.

Akira Kurosawa Memorial Museum

Imari is the master filmmaker's hometown and a large complex including a hotel is planned. The main museum is slated to open in 2001. Open now is the **Satellite Studio**, containing film memorabilia, props and costumes, an Oscar, scripts, his paintings and film clips on video. *358 Imari-cho. 8-minute walk from JR/MR Imari Station. Open 9am to 5pm, until 7pm on Saturday. Closed the 2nd and 4th Mondays. ¥500.*

ARITA

Pottery lovers must stop in **Arita**, a small town that has been a center of Japan's porcelain for 400 years. Despite its size, it's crammed with museums, kilns and shops. Pottery has been so central to this town that even the bridges have ceramic decorations. The shopping is excellent.

Planning Your Stay

Spend a full day in Arita.

From the train station, go to the **Kyushu Ceramic Museum** for a good overview of Imari ware. From there, go to **Akae-machi**, in central Arita, the ceramic painting district in the Edo period which is crowded with kilns and shops. Go to the **Arita Post Office** to see its their gate and displays and then browse along the main road. Stop at **Imaemon** and **Tozan Jinja** and if you turn to the left, you'll come to the **Arita Ceramic Museum** and the **Tombai walls**. You can continue on to the **Arita Museum of History** and the **quarry**. If you haven't had your fill of ceramics, go via taxi to **Gen'emon** and **Kakiemon** at the other end of town. Serious shoppers should go to the wholesale district, **Oroshi Danchi**.

Dates to Remember
• **April 29-May 5: Pottery Festival**. During Golden Week, Arita turns into a giant bazaar and offers great bargains. Don't expect to shop in solitary splendor; over one million make the pilgrimage.

ARRIVALS & DEPARTURES
By Train
Arita is an express stop on the JR Sasebo Line; from Fukuoka's Hakata Station, the limited express takes 90 minutes. ¥2990.

From Imari, take the Matsu-ura Tetsudo private line (25 minutes, ¥400).

By Car
From Imari: take Route 202 south to Route 35.

GETTING AROUND TOWN
Although Arita isn't a large town, the sights are fairly spread out. Plan to walk a lot or take taxis from area to area.

Bus Tour
There's a tour in Japanese that begins in Sasebo, but you can pick it up in Arita. It departs Arita Bus Station at 1:25pm and visits the Kyushu Ceramic Museum, Kakiemon, Gen'emon, Imaemon Kiln and the Kaolin Quarry. The tour goes on to Sankawauchi Dento Sangyo-kaikan and then back to Sasebo, but these are out of town, so you want to finish at the quarry. ¥1830.

Tourist Information
The "i" Tourist Information Center is at Arita Station. *Tel. (0955)42-4052.*

WHERE TO STAY

Arita itself has very little in the way of accommodations. **Takeo Onsen**, a hot spring town that has many hotels and inns, is a short train stop away. See Takeo Onsen, *Where to Stay*, below.

WHERE TO EAT

RYUSUI-TEI *(Japanese, moderate). Ryumon-kyo. Tel. (0955)46-2155. Open 11am to 7:30pm. Closed the first and third Wednesday. Reservations necessary.*

About a 15-minute taxi drive from Arita, it's in the mountains near the Arita dam. Arita ceramics painters went to this area to learn how to paint the rocky mountains that resemble mountains in Chinese landscape paintings. Ryusui-tei is a lovely traditional restaurant overlooking a pond where fish happily swim, ignorant of the possibility that their turn could be next. The restaurant specializes in river fish, carp *sashimi* and duck *nabe* in winter. The Arita set costs ¥2900; Ryumon set costs ¥3700.

KURINTO, CHINA ON THE PARK *(Western, inexpensive to expensive). Genmyo, Arita-machi. Tel. (0955)46-5000. Open from 11:30am to 2:30pm; 5pm to 8pm. Closed Tuesday.*

A spacious, modern restaurant that serves Western-style food on Arita ceramic ware. Steak lunch costs ¥1800; chef's dinner is ¥2500.

SEEING THE SIGHTS

Kyushu Ceramic Museum. *Tel. (0955)43-3681. Open from 9am to 4:30pm, closed Monday. No fee for permanent exhibition, admission fee for temporary exhibitions.* Thise museum offers an excellent display of ceramic ware from all over Kyushu, representing the Edo period to the present. A problem might arise after you see museum-quality ceramics: what you find for sale in the stores just may not measure up. The museum's coffee shop is a good place for a light lunch of sandwiches and fast foods served on elegant Arita ware. What a way to whet your appetite to acquire some plates — not extra sandwiches — for your dining pleasure at home.

Arita Ceramic Museum (Arita Toji Bijutsukan). *Tel. (0955)42-3372. Open from 9am to 4:30pm. Closed on Monday. ¥100.* Housed in a former storehouse, the museum displays an array of Iro-Nabeshima (colorful Nabeshima) as well as Imari wares dating back to the early 17th century.

Tombai Walls are made of bricks that were once used for kilns; glaze still remains on some bricks. Check out these walls near the Arita Ceramic Museum.

Arita Post Office. Stop by to see the ceramic pieces on display in the lobby; they were unearthed during construction of the post office.

Tozan Jinja Shrine. Built high on a hill, the Shinto shrine is dedicated to the potters of Arita. It is especially interesting because the *torii* gate is made of porcelain as are many of the amulets on sale.

Imaemon Kiln. *Tel. (0955)42-3101. Open 9am to 5pm. Closed on 1st Sunday.* The Imaemon kiln descends from one of the families that made the prized Iro-Nabeshima porcelain. The tradition of perfection continues to this day. The delicately painted ware uses both blue underglaze and an overglaze (usually red, green and blue) on a white surface.

Koransha Museum. *Tel. (0955)43-2131. Open 8:30am to 4:30pm. Sundays and holidays open 9:30am to 4:30pm. Closed on 1st Sunday.* This museum is run by Koransha, a large ceramics company, which seems to supply the wedding-present trade. Next to the museum is a workshop where artisans paint. Today goods sold by Koransha today have a mass-produced look.

ARITA & IMARI PORCELAIN

When Hideyoshi invaded Korea towards the end of 16th century, he commanded some of his feudal lords, mostly from Kyushu and western Honshu, to send troops. Among these feudal lords was Lord Nabeshima who ruled the Saga area, which includes Arita. While in Korea, Nabeshima decided to take a Korean master potter and his group back to Japan (whether against his will or willingly is a hotly debated topic). This potter, Ri Sampei, is credited with discovering a large kaolin deposit in the Izumiyama mountains in the Arita area where white porcelain is said to have originated in Japan. In 1648, Nabeshima imposed strict rules to protect and encourage porcelain manufacture. Imari was the only port from which Arita wares could leave the domain. Thus, another name for old Arita porcelain is Imari ware.

The Nabeshima made special gifts for the shogun and other feudal lords; this production was tightly controlled and any piece less than perfect was destroyed . They also made goods for the export market. Europe had developed a taste for Ming Chinese porcelain, but at this time, the Ming Dynasty was in decline and production suffered. The Japanese were pleased to take up the slack. Sounds familiar, doesn't it? With the introduction of sakoku (the policy of national isolation) in 1639, Arita porcelains were shipped through Imari to Nagasaki, and then to Europe by the Dutch East India Company. Did you ever wonder how those huge, ornate Imari plates, basins and vases as tall as a person managed to survive the long trip to the European courts and manor houses?. Before bubble wrap, everything was carefully packed in many layers of straw and carefully placed in barrels. Arita porcelains were in such demand in Europe that ounce-for-ounce, they were worth more than gold.

Kakiemon Kiln. *Tel. (0955)43-2267. Open daily 9am to 5pm.* The founder of the kiln, Sakaida Kakiemon, perfected the overglaze technique with a *kaki* (persimmon) red color in the 1640s, and the ware became very popular in Europe in the 17th and 18th centuries. The showroom is located in a complex of traditional buildings away from the center of town.

Gen'emon Kiln. *Tel. (0955)42-4164. Open 8am to 5:30pm weekdays;, 9am to 5pm Sundays and holidays.* The kiln has sophisticated handpainted designs, primarily blue and white, with a contemporary look. Gen'emon has successfully applied its ceramic floral patterns to fabric items such as handkerchiefs and luncheon mats while Kakiemon and Imaemon seem more bound by tradition. A museum on the premises displays the impressive collection of Tatebayashi Gen'emon, a scholar as well as master of the kiln.

Arita Museum of History and Archaeological Pottery Museum. *Tel. (0955)43-2678. Open 9am to 4:30pm. Closed Monday and December 29 through January 3. ¥100.* This new museum displays shards as well as some very interesting exhibits on how pottery was packed and transported. Its location on the outskirts of town is near the Izumiyama Kaolin Quarry, where clay used for porcelain ware is still excavated today.

Izumiyama Kaolin Quarry. Located near the Arita Museum of History, kaolin was discovered here in early 1600s, establishing Arita as a porcelain production center.

Arita Porcelain Park. *Tel. (0955)42-6100. Open 9am to 5pm; December through February 9:30am to 4:30pm. Closed Tuesdays. ¥2300.* This is a theme park on the outskirts of Arita cashing in on the town's ceramics tradition. A replica of the Zwinger Palace, home of Augustus I in Dresden, houses a collection of porcelain from around the world. It is only fitting to pay homage to Augustus because he was so fond of Arita porcelain that he imprisoned European artisans who mastered the techniques of copying Arita ware into what became known as Meissen wares. In addition to the wide variety of Arita wares and ceramics from all over the world, the park offers restaurants, tea rooms, street performers, workshops where you can paint your own Arita wares, other amusements such as trains and games and, of course, huge souvenir shops. *From JR Arita Station, it's a 10-minute taxi ride.*

SHOPPING

There real question is where not to shop. All the main kilns (Kakiemon, Imaemon, Gen'emon, Koransha, Fukagawa) sell their products. Arita's main streets are lined with shops selling ceramics, and you might find some good buys. Away from the center of town, but only a 5-minute taxi ride, is the **Arita Oroshi Danchi**, *Tel. (0955)43-2288,* a wholesale district where some 20 shops offer a wide range of ceramics at reduced prices. Although we vowed we'd only browse, we couldn't leave empty handed.

Tip: If you don't want to carry your purchases, ask the shop to ship them by *takkyubin* (domestic shipping service) to your final hotel destination in Japan. You can also arrange to ship overseas.

TAKEO ONSEN

A hot spring town just four local stops from Arita on the JR train, **Takeo Onsen** is a good place to overnight in the area. In the center of town is a large Chinese-style gate called Ryugumon that leads to the town's public bath, a grand building designed by the architect of Tokyo Station. **Keishu-en**, Kyushu's largest landscape garden, is on the outskirts of Takeo near the Takeo Century Hotel. It's especially lovely in spring when the azaleas are in blossom.

Tourist Information

The "i" Tourist Information Center is at Takeo Onsen Station. *Tel. (0954)22-2542.*

WHERE TO STAY

TAKEO CENTURY HOTEL, *Takeo-machi, Takeo, Saga, 843-0022. Tel. (0954)22-2200, Fax (0954)22-3058. Twins from ¥18,900, without meals. Credit cards.*

This large spa resort hotel on the outskirts of town offers Western- and Japanese-style rooms as well as a disco, lounges and an indoor swimming pool.

TOYOKAN, *Takeo Onsen Dori, Takeo-machi, Takeo, Saga, 843-0022. Tel. (0954)22-2191, Fax (0954)23-3967. From ¥15,000 per person with two meals. Credit cards.*

A small inn with friendly service located next to the Ryugumon gate.

SHUNKEIYA. *Takeo Onsen Dori, Takeo-machi, Takeo, Saga, 843-0022. Tel. (0954)22-2101, Fax (0954)23-9625. From ¥15,000 per person with two meals. Credit cards.*

The Showa Emperor stayed here in 1949, and we don't think anything has changed since then. Although a bit rundown, it's certainly charming and the staff is friendly.

NAGASAKI

Situated on a beautiful bay surrounded by low mountains, **Nagasaki** must have once been naturally picturesque. Today, modern industry dominates the bay and undistinguished buildings climb up the mountains. Despite this, we feel that Nagasaki's history, interaction with Europe, eclecticism and good food make a stop here a must.

Nagasaki has a long history of interaction with foreigners. Even today as you stroll around the city, you'll definitely get the sense that Nagasaki is more "exotic" than other Japanese cities. The first Portuguese trading ship arrived in 1571. Along with guns, the Portuguese brought Catholicism and her missionaries had some success converting Japanese. As an omen of troubled times for Christianity in Japan, the first persecutions took place in Nagasaki in 1597 at the great leader Hideyoshi's order. The Portuguese were expelled from Japan in 1638; the Dutch were the only Europeans allowed to remain although virtually held prisoner on the tiny island of Dejima. Nagasaki was the only Japanese city open to Chinese and Dutch traders during the the period of isolation from 1641 until 1854.

After foreigners were once again allowed in the country in 1854, Nagasaki became a center for Westerners and Western culture. Some of their houses survived. Imagine Madame Butterfly in one of these Western-style houses, overlooking a peaceful Nagasaki Bay, waiting for her beloved fiancé, Pinkerton, to come back on a big American ship. Nagasaki is one of the few places in Japan where a Gothic cathedral and a Chinese Confucian temple are in the same neighborhood.

Situated on a protected bay, Nagasaki became a shipbuilding center, making it the unfortunate recipient of the second atomic bomb dropped in World War II on August 9, 1945. The bomb missed the shipyards by a few kilometers and, ironically, struck an area heavily populated by Japanese Christians.

Planning Your Stay

Spend at least one full day in Nagasaki; two is better.

Start your day at the Shrine to the 26 Martyred Saints, close to the JR Nagasaki Station. Next, take the #1 or #3 streetcar to Matsuyama-machi to see the Atomic Bomb Museum, Peace Park and Urakami Cathedral (about 1 1/2 hours). Then take the #1 streetcar (transfer at Tsuki-machi to #5) or #3 (transfer at Kokaido-mae to #5) to the Oura Tenshudo-mae stop to see Glover Garden, the Hong Kong Bank Building, Oura Cathedral and the Confucian temple (2 1/2 hours). From there it's a short walk to the Holland Slopes, Dejima, and Shinchi, the Chinese district.

Dates to Remember

• **August 9**: anniversary of the dropping of the atomic bomb in 1945; Nagasaki holds large peace festivities.

• **October 7–9 Nagasaki Kunchi Festival**: large autumn festival with floats, firecrackers and dancing, inspired by the Chinese and Dutch.

ARRIVALS & DEPARTURES

By Air

Nagasaki Airport is located about one hour north of the city on a reclaimed island.

To/from Tokyo Haneda: 7 flights/day (ANA, JAL, JAS. ¥29,100)

To/from Nagoya: 4 flights/day (ANA, JAS. ¥23,200)

To/from Osaka Itami: 6 flights/day. **Kansai**: 1 flight/day (ANA, JAL, JAS. ¥18,950)

Service to/from the Goto Islands, Kagoshima, Miyazaki, Okinawa and Sapporo.

International service to Shanghai on China Eastern Airlines; to Seoul on Korean Airlines.

For Ground Transportation:

Bus to/from Nagasaki Station takes 1 hour and costs ¥1200.

Taxi: 50-minute ride to Nagasaki Station averages ¥9000.

By Train

Nagasaki Station is the terminal stop for the JR Nagasaki line which goes to Hakata Station in Fukuoka. It takes two hours from Nagasaki to Fukuoka on the *Kamome* limited express, ¥4710. Travelers wishing to go to Kumamoto or Kagoshima have to change trains at JR Tosu Station. Overnight train enthusiasts please note: there is service from Nagasaki to Tokyo and from Nagasaki to Kyoto.

By Bus

Express buses depart from Nagasaki Kanei Bus Terminal in front of Nagasaki Station. Express buses connect Nagasaki with Kumamoto. 10 buses/day, fare ¥3600. 3 hours.

Nagasaki to Beppu: 7 buses/day, 3 1/2 hours, ¥4500.

Nagasaki to Fukuoka: 28 buses/day, 2 1/2 hours, ¥2900.

There is overnight bus service from Nagasaki to: Osaka (10 hours, ¥11,000), Kyoto (11 hours, ¥11,310), and Nagoya (12 hours, ¥12,230).

By Car

The Nagasaki Expressway connects the city to the Kyushu Expressway that runs from Fukuoka to Kagoshima.

GETTING AROUND TOWN

The sites in Nagasaki are rather scattered and best accessed by street car. The fare is ¥100 or ¥500 for a one-day unlimited pass *(ichi nichi joshaken)* available at the **Tourist Information Office** and at some hotels. The pass is not available on the streetcar. You probably wouldn't take more than five tram trips in a day, so buying the pass makes sense only as a matter of convenience. If you need to transfer from one line to another, and are not using a pass, tell the driver *norikae* and he will give you a transfer ticket that you use in lieu of payment on the second streetcar.

Nagasaki signs are well-marked in English, making it easy to tour on your own.

Tourist Information

The **Tourist Information Office** is to the left as you exit the JR Nagasaki Station. *Tel. (095)823-3631.* Open 8am to 7pm, until 5:30pm mid-November through February.

The **Prefectural Tourist Office** is on the second floor of the bus station, located across the pedestrian walkway from the train station.

Both are "i" Tourist Information Offices.

Bus Tours

There are bus tours of Nagasaki in Japanese, but the city is so easy to navigate on your own that we recommend tours only if you need to fit in the main sights in a half-day. A 3-hour, 15-minute tour departs from in front of the Tourist Information Office at Nagasaki Station daily at 8am, 11am and 1pm; it takes you to Oura Catholic Church, Glover Garden, Juroku-ban Mansion, Confucian Shrine, Peace Park and the Atomic Bomb Museum. Fare ¥1450. *Tel. (095)826-6221.*

Harbor Tour

Nagasaki was one of the world's most beautiful natural harbors, but today it's pretty ugly. However, if you would like to explore it from the water side, there are harbor cruises leaving from the Nagasaki Port Terminal daily at 11:10am, 11:30am, and 3:15pm. The hour-long tour costs ¥1980.

WHERE TO STAY

Nagasaki has mostly Western hotels.

NAGASAKI PRINCE HOTEL, *2-26 Takara-machi, Nagasaki, 850-0045. Tel. (095)821-1111, Fax (095)823-4309. Singles ¥15,000. Twins from ¥23,000. Credit cards.*

Located about a 5-minute walk north of Nagasaki Station, the Prince is considered one of the best hotels in town. The upper floors and the 15th floor Sky Lounge have good views of Nagasaki harbor. We like to have an evening drink at the lounge and take in the views.

NAGASAKI PARKSIDE HOTEL, *14-1 Heiwa-machi, Nagasaki, 852-8116. Tel. (095)845-3191, Fax (095)846-5550. Singles ¥12,000. Twins from ¥18,000. Credit cards.*

This modern and bright hotel is in a quiet location next to the Peace Park. While it's away from the center of Nagasaki, the streetcar stop is convenient.

NAGASAKI TOKYU HOTEL, *1-18 Minami Yamate-cho, Nagasaki, 850-0931. Tel. (095)825-1501, Fax (095)823-5167. Singles from ¥9800. Twins from ¥18,000. Credit cards.*

The hotel, located close to Glover Garden and Oura Church, has an excellent location. Its ground floor restaurant specializes in *shippoku* cuisine, a Nagasaki specialty.

HOLIDAY INN NAGASAKI. *6-24 Doza-machi, Nagasaki, 850-0841. Tel. (095)828-1234, Fax (095)828-0178. Singles from ¥9500. Doubles from ¥15,000. Credit cards.*

The Holiday Inn is situated in the center of the shopping district but is off the main road so it's very quiet. The only drawback is the rooms don't have views. The lobby has the ambiance of an intimate European hotel — Oriental rugs on the floor and exposed wooden beams; check-in is at a low desk. The rooms are average size. There's no charge for children under 12 if they occupy the same room as their parents — a nice benefit for families.

TREDIA HOTEL DEJIMA. *1-25 Dejima-machi, Nagasaki, 850-0862. Tel. (095)826-4176, Fax (095)825-0081. Singles from ¥6400. Twins from ¥12,000. Credit cards.*

A business hotel, but the best in its class, conveniently located near the main shopping district and lots of sights. It's an excellent choice for the economy-minded traveler.

WHERE TO EAT

ICHIRIKI *(Regional Japanese, inexpensive to expensive). 8-20 Suwa-machi, on Teramachi Dori. Tel. (095)824-0226. Open 12 noon to 2pm; 5pm until 7:30pm. Reservations recommended.*

Nagasaki's most popular *shippoku* restaurant serves you on genuine red lacquered tables. The lunchtime *Himeju shippoku* course for ¥2500 offers a wide array of dishes. The evening course combines *shippoku* and *kaiseki*.

HAMAKATSU *(Regional Japanese, moderate). 6-50 Kajiya-machi. Tel. (095)826-8321. Open from 11:30am to 8:30pm.*

Burabura shippoku is a huge meal including soup, something from the sea, fields and mountains, stewed pork, steamed *soba* and *sashimi*. ¥2800.

EATING YOUR WAY THROUGH NAGASAKI

Castella is a cake introduced to Japan by the Portuguese. Originating in the Castella Kingdom (present-day Spain), it's made with eggs, sugar and flour. Today it's thoroughly Japanized and is a soft, steamed sponge cake. You'll see shops on the street leading to Glover Garden displaying castella in large glass cases; it's available all over the city as well as all over Japan. Castella comes in a variety of flavors including green tea, honey, chocolate and cheese – the 16th century Portuguese would turn over in their graves if they knew.

According to one theory, **champon** (simple meal in Fukien dialect) was invented in 1899 by the chef at Shikairyo, a Chinese restaurant, for Chinese students in Japan needing to eat something nutritious and cheap. Ingredients include pork, shrimp, squid, fish cake, octopus, bean sprouts and cabbage served over noodles in soup.

In **sara udon**, a sibling to champon, noodles are fried crispy and the topping poured over them.

Shippoku (red-lacquer round table) is a blend of three different cuisines. Influenced heavily by Chinese cooking and by Western cooking at Dejima, shippoku is a blend of these two cuisines with a healthy dose of Japanese thrown in. Food is served family style: you serve yourself from large platters, Chinese-style. The meal includes soup, sashimi, a stewed pork so tender it's soft, grilled fish, tempura with a sweet crust and more. Shiruko (a sweet bean paste with plums) and coffee complete the meal.

IKEDAYA (*Coffee and light meals, inexpensive*). *6-29 Kajiya-machi. Tel. (095)820-3751. Open 11:30am-2:30pm; 5pm-11pm.*

This coffee shop and pub, decorated with antique English furniture, serves food and drinks on Japanese antique ceramic ware.

KOUZANROU (*Chinese, inexpensive to moderate*). *12-2 Shinchi. Tel. (095)824-5000. Open daily 11:30am to 8:30pm.*

There are several branches around Nagasaki including three in the Shinchi Chinatown area. We prefer the main branch in Chinatown. The food is good and the setting is modern. Noodle dishes including *champon* begin at ¥800. Set courses run from ¥1500 to ¥10,000 — so there is something for every pocketbook.

YOSSO, *8-9 Hamacho. Tel. (095)821-0001. Open 11am to 8pm. Closed 2nd and 4th Tuesdays.*

This Japanese restaurant, started in 1866, specializes in *chawan mushi* (warm egg custard), which costs ¥700. They also serve *mushi zushi* set for ¥1200, consisting of vegetables, eel and shrimp steamed over rice. *Chawan mushi teishoku* (set) costs ¥1700.

SEEING THE SIGHTS

Shrine to 26 Martyrs. (Niju Roku Seijin Junkyochi). *Open daily 9am to 5pm except December 31 through January 2. ¥250. 5-minute walk from Nagasaki Station.* When they refused to abandon their faith, six Western priests and 20 Japanese Catholics, including a 12-year-old boy, marched from Kyoto and, under Hideyoshi's order, were hung on the cross in 1597. Thus began the tragic history of Japanese Christians. In 1862 the Catholic Church declared them saints. A chapel and small museum on this hill are dedicated to the martyrs.

Fukusai-ji Temple. *5-minute walk from 26 Martyrs Site.* This temple used to have a beautiful bright red-tile roof, but the atomic bomb destroyed everything except the bell tower. The temple was built in 1628 by a Chinese monk. At that time, the persecution of Christians was so severe that the Chinese built the temple to prove they were not Christians.

Suwa Jinja Shrine. Built at the top of a hill, climb 277 stone steps to reach the shrine and good views of Nagasaki Bay. This Shinto shrine is responsible for all of Nagasaki's Shinto gods. The original buildings (some built in the mid-16th century) burned down in 1857 but were rebuilt several years later. Suwa offers fortunes written in English, so this is a good place to check out what your future holds. Suwa is the home of the large Nagasaki Kunchi Festival *(kunchi* means "autumn festival" in northern Kyushu dialect) which climaxes October 7–9 with a procession of floats, dragon dancing and fireworks, displaying the Chinese influence. There is also dancing inspired by the Dutch. The festival flourished during the Edo period because the government wanted to make it very clear they favored Shinto over Christianity; people participated to prove they were not Christian.

Kofuku-ji Temple. *Tel. (095)822-1076. Open daily 8am to 5pm. ¥200. 5-minute walk from Kokaido-mae streetcar stop.* Located in the center of Teramachi and built in 1620, Kofuku-ji is the oldest temple in the area. Popular with Chinese from Nanking, Kofuku-ji is also known as the Nanking Temple. The Buddha Hall and other buildings are built in the Chinese style.

Spectacles Bridge (Megane Bashi). Down the hill from Kofuku-ji is Spectacles Bridge, so named because when you view its reflection in the river, the two-arched bridge looks like a pair of glasses. The stone bridge, built in 1634, is the oldest in Japan.

Sofuku-ji Temple. *Tel. (095)823-2645. Open daily from 8am to 5:30pm; until 5pm November through March. ¥300. 5-minute walk from Shianbashi streetcar stop.* One of the big three Chinese temples in Nagasaki, Sofuku-ji was founded by a Chinese monk from Fukien province in 1629. The colorful entrance gate is based on the gate you see in the paradise under the sea. The next gate is a National Treasure from the late Ming period.

The Treasure Hall is also a National Treasure. On the grounds is a huge pot that was used to make gruel for 3000 people daily in 1682, a year of great famine.

FIRSTS IN NAGASAKI

Coffee: Coffee supposedly reached Japan in the early 1600s. Brought by a Portuguese ship, coffee was called nanban cha (Southern Barbarian tea). The first record of a Japanese drinking coffee dates to 1804. Mr. Ota said he was served coffee brought by a red-haired captain and couldn't stand the roasted smell.

Bowling: After allowing Westerners into the port, the first international bowling alley opened in Nagasaki in 1861.

Spectacles: Mr. Hamada went to the Philippines, learned how to make spectacles and in 1624 opened Japan's first spectacle shop in 1624. During the Edo Period, Nagasaki was the place to come to have good glasses made.

Beer: During the Edo period, the Dutch at Dejima enjoyed drinking beer. Beer production in Japan began in the 1880s by a company started by Thomas Glover. Later it became known as Kirin.

Ham: In 1873 Mr. Kataoka learned how to cook ham from an American. Could the first ham and potato salad sandwich have been far behind?

Ruins of Dejima Island (Dejima Oranda Shokan Ato). *3-minute walk from Dejima streetcar stop.* When we see Dejima Island, we are amazed that such a small spot could have played such a large role in history. For almost 200 years, Dejima was the only place where Japan could access the Western world, the only source for European trade and Western learning, including medicine and science.

In 1639, the Edo government banned the Portuguese from Japan and allowed the Dutch to live in this secluded area. The Dutch would usually come to Dejima in July or August and sail away in November or December. The fan-shaped island was surrounded by earthen walls and only one gate connected it to the mainland, holding the Dutch virtual prisoners. Landfill means Dejima is no longer an island, but stone markers designate its borders. On the grounds is a scale model of Dejima as the Dutch outpost.

Nagasaki Museum of History and Folklore (Dejima Shiryokan). *Tel. (095)821-5117. Open from 9am to 5pm. Closed Monday and December 29 through January 4. Free admission.* Housed in an 1898 building, the museum shows Nagasaki when Dejima was a Dutch trading outpost.

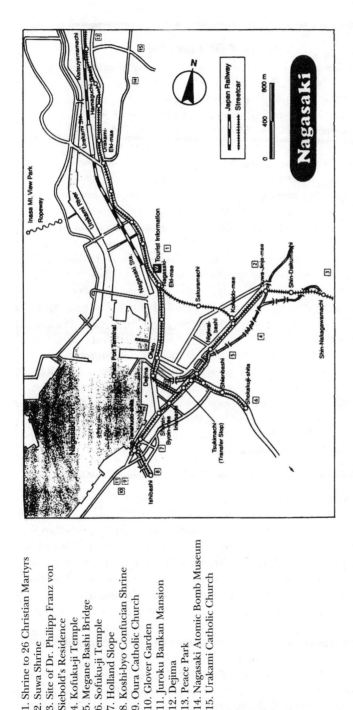

1. Shrine to 26 Christian Martyrs
2. Suwa Shrine
3. Site of Dr. Philipp Franz von
   Siebold's Residence
4. Kofukuji Temple
5. Megane Bashi Bridge
6. Sofukuji Temple
7. Holland Slope
8. Koshi-byo Confucian Shrine
9. Oura Catholic Church
10. Glover Garden
11. Juroku Bankan Mansion
12. Dejima
13. Peace Park
14. Nagasaki Atomic Bomb Museum
15. Urakami Catholic Church

THE DUTCH ENCLAVE

Dejima, a small, fan-shaped island, was the Dutch outpost in Japan for 210 years. In 1641, the captain of a Dutch ship asked civil servants in Nagasaki to remodel two Japanese houses with Western interiors. Since 1609, the Dutch had been living in Hirado, further north in Kyushu, and they had the freedom to move about freely and to marry Japanese. Once they moved to Nagasaki they were not allowed one step off the island without permission. Japanese were watched by guards and not allowed to get in touch with Dutch. Eminently practical, the Japanese authorities allowed women from the pleasure quarters and monks begging for alms to enter Dejima. European women, forbidden to come, decided one year to accompany their husbands; they were expelled as soon as they were discovered.

The Dutch put up with these prison-like conditions because trade was so lucrative. Japanese trade was the most profitable for the Dutch East India Company. The Tokugawa shogunate prohibited its citizens from going overseas, and the Dutch were the only Europeans allowed to sail into Japan. They acted as middlemen, bringing silk from China and India, as well as sugar, leather and European woolen carpets. Japan exported gold bullion and items made of gold, silver, lacquer ware and ceramics. Just to show that things haven't changed, Japan exported more than it imported.

Periodically, Dutch officials would travel to Edo (Tokyo) to have an audience with the shogun. They were treated like feudal lords and traveled in style. During their two to three-week stays in Edo, they were the subjects of great curiosity; the shogun and his entourage spied upon the visitors in almost voyeur-like ways. On special occasions, the Dutch were asked to sing or dance, just like present-day karaoke.

Oura Catholic Church (Oura Tenshudo). *Tel. (095)823-2628. Open 8am to 5:45pm; December through March until 5pm. ¥250. 5-minute walk from Oura Tenshudo Shita streetcar stop.* The oldest wooden Gothic church in Japan, Oura is designated a National Treasure. Completed in 1864 under the direction of a French priest, Bernard Petitjean, the first Bishop of Nagasaki, the church was built for Westerners who flocked to Nagasaki after the trade treaty. Shortly after the church was constructed, a group of Japanese women from Urakami asked to see the Santa Maria statue; they were hidden Christians whose families had kept their beliefs through the 200 years of persecution. Next to the church is a wooden building that displays objects relating to the persecution of Christians.

Glover Garden (Glover-en). *Tel. (095)822-8223. Open daily 8am to 6pm; 8:30am to 5pm December through February; July 20 through October 31 open until 9:30pm. ¥600. 5-minute walk from Oura Tenshudo Shita Streetcar* *stop*. Glover Garden is a hillside open air museum of 19th century European-style houses overlooking Nagasaki harbor. Some of the houses were originally built here while others were moved from other locations in Nagasaki. **Glover House**, the former residence of Scottish trader Thomas Glover, was completed in 1863. The colonial building, designated an Important Cultural Property, has a splendid view of the bay and is the setting for the fictitious story of *Madame Butterfly*. The **Alt House**, residence of a tea trader, was built in 1865 and has big stone pillars on the terrace. Decoration of the entrance doors is the same as the Oura Cathedral.

Ringer House is wooden with foundation stones from Vladivostok. Ringer was an Englishman who came to Japan as a servant to Mr. Glover in 1865. The **Walker House** was built by Englishman Robert Walker who lived in Nagasaki from the early 1880s for 70 years. After retiring as a ship's captain, he founded the Walker Co., which sold soft drinks including Banzai Lemonade and Banzai Cider. The tour of Glover Garden ends at a modern hall displaying Kunchi festival floats and showing a film of the festival.

THOMAS GLOVER

Thomas Glover (1837–1911) was a Scot who came from Aberdeen; of seven siblings, three came to Nagasaki to start businesses. Glover landed in Nagasaki in 1859 at age 21 and became involved in the tea trade. He became a major player in the Meiji Restoration by supplying arms to Choshu and Satsuma, areas that led the movement to unseat the shogun. He married a Japanese woman, Tsuru, in 1866, and had two children. After the Meiji Restoration, he turned to coal mining; his company went bankrupt in 1871. In the early 1880s, he managed to rebuild the coal mining company and also began a beer company, the forerunner of Kirin. To this day, Kirin uses a Chinese mythical beast as its logo. Next time you have a Kirin, look closely; you will see the creature is bearded because Thomas Glover sported a beard.

Old Hong Kong Shanghai Bank Building (Kyu Honkon Shanhai Ginko). *Tel. (095)827-8746. Open 9am to 5pm. Closed Monday and December 29 through January 3. ¥100. 3-minute walk from Oura Tenshudo-shita streetcar stop.* Designed by Shimoda in 1904, this building was the largest Western stone building in Nagasaki. Beautifully restored, it opened to the public in October 1996. The first floor shows the original bank layout while the upper floors have meeting rooms and displays relating to Nagasaki's extensive contact with the West.

Juroku Bankan. *Tel. (095)827-6111. Open daily 8:30am to 5:30pm; 8am to 5pm December through March. ¥400. Near the exit of Glover Garden.* Originally located at the eastern side of the hill as a women's college, Juroku Bankan displays a potpourri of objects related to the West including furniture, Mr. Glover's collection of furniture, hidden Christian items and Dejima trade related things.

Confucian Shrine and National Museum of Chinese History (Koshi-Byo Chugoku Rekishi Hakubutsukan). *Tel. (095)824-4022. Open daily 8:30am to 5pm. ¥525.* The vermilion walls and the bright yellow roof tiles immediately tell you this building is not Japanese. The Chinese in Nagasaki built this Confucian Shrine in 1893. The buildings were badly damaged by the atomic bomb, and in 1982 received an extensive facelift that included building the National Museum of Chinese History behind the shrine. This museum houses antiquities on loan from the Chinese National Museum of History and the Palace Museum in Beijing.

Holland Slope (Oranda-zaka) is the cobblestone area that was a center for foreigners living in Nagasaki. The Japanese called all Westerners "Hollanders," no matter what their nationality. On the slope is **Junibankan**, a building dating from 1868, originally the Prussian Legation.

Shinchi Chinatown. In 1698 a large fire destroyed the cargo of Chinese ships docked at the pier. The Tokugawa administration decided to reclaim some land to make an artificial island where the Chinese could live. After the Meiji Restoration, the island was connected to the mainland and, since then, has developed as Chinatown. A small district with four ornate gates, Shinchi has mostly Chinese restaurants and shops with Chinese goods, similar to many Chinatowns.

Heiwa Koen (Peace Park) is the area near ground zero of the atomic blast. There are many monuments and statues dedicated to victims of the bomb.

Nagasaki Atomic Bomb Museum (Nagasaki Genbaku Shiryokan). *Tel. (095)844-1231. Open 8:30 to 5:30pm. Closed December 29-31. ¥200.* This new museum, opened in April 1996, commemorates the dropping of the atomic bomb on Nagasaki on August 9, 1945, three days after Hiroshima. In the contemporary building, you walk down a circular space to reach the exhibition hall; the dome you are under is reminiscent of the mushroom cloud of an atomic bomb explosion. In a darkened room downstairs, the reconstructed facade of Urakami Cathedral and other objects display the destructive power of the bomb. On a wall, you see the shadow of a ladder and a workman vaporized by the blast. The museum has areas explaining the history of the war, the aftermath of the bombing and the history of nuclear weapons. All the panels are translated into English.

The museum has been strongly criticized by Japanese conservatives who wanted it to focus solely on the destruction of Nagasaki. But the former mayor of Nagasaki, Motoshima Hitoshi, a strong foe of nuclear arms, fought hard to make sure the museum shows the link between Japan's belligerent actions and the dropping of the bomb.

Urakami Catholic Church (Urakami Tenshudo). *5-minute walk from Heiwa Koen (Peace Park)*. In 1873, the Japanese government allowed Japanese to be Christians. In Nagasaki in 1880, they started their own church, converting an old manor house into a church. After 43 years, in 1923, they managed to build their own church, which was destroyed by the atomic bomb in 1945. The current church was rebuilt in 1959.

SHOPPING

Nagasaki's crafts include tortoise shell jewelry, pearls, decorative glassware, pottery and "Koga" clay dolls of old Nagasaki characters. Across the street from the train station, on the second floor of the Kanei Bus Terminal, is the Nagasaki-ken Bussan-kan (Prefectural Products Hall). The display, although uninspired, offers a good selection of locally produced goods.

The downtown shopping district is the area around **Kanko Dori**. Several covered arcades house a myriad of shops and restaurants; it's fun and interesting to stroll through the area even on cold, rainy days.

A short walk from the Hamaguchi-machi streetcar stop and in the same general area as the Peace Park is a new, touristy complex of shops and restaurants called the **Nagasaki Seiyokan**.

EXCURSIONS & DAY TRIPS

About an hour outside Nagasaki are two theme parks celebrating Nagasaki's ties with Holland: **Huis Ten Bois** and **Nagasaki Holland Village**. These major attractions draw Japanese from all over the country. We don't think they're of much interest to an international visitor who has limited time in Japan, but visit them if you want to see Japanese theme parks or what happens when the 17th century meets high tech.

HUIS TEN BOIS

Tel. (0956)58-0080. Open 9am to 9pm, December through February closes at 7pm weekdays; 8pm holidays and weekends. Admission from ¥4200 to ¥5800; more expensive tickets give you points to see attractions with additional fees.

Huis Ten Bois is a mecca for Japanese on package tours in much the same way people go to Disneyland. We aren't sure about its of the appeal, but it's easier and safer than going to Holland although maybe not necessarily not cheaper. And besides, you don't have to worry about your passport, speaking a foreign language or jet lag.

This huge theme has half-a-dozen European style hotels, including the Dutch-renaissance style ANA Hotel; museums; Dejima Rankan — a life size replica of part of Dejima Island complete with a robot guide; lots of restaurants; amusements including simulations of a flood ravaging a 17th century Dutch town and the tale of Noah's ark — is there any connection?; auctions; and even rent-a-cycle or one built for two. You could spend several days seeing it all.

Getting to Huis Ten Bois
To/from Nagasaki Station by train: JR Seaside Liner (15 trains/day, 1 hour 8 minutes, ¥1430).
To/from the Nagasaki Kanei Bus Terminal: Express bus across from the station (16 buses/day, 1 hour 15 minutes, ¥1300).

NAGASAKI HOLLAND VILLAGE
Tel. (0959)27-0080. Open 9am to 6pm March through November but later at the height of summer; 9am to 5pm in December through February. ¥2500 for adults.

Nagasaki Holland Village (Nagasaki Oranda-mura) is another theme park cashing in on Nagasaki's relationship with the Dutch. It is a re-creation of a 17th century Dutch village built on Omura Bay. On the water is a reproduction of the *Prince Willem*, a 17th century ship. The park includes folk craft museums; craft demonstrations, including cheese making and diamond cutting; a film of the sea voyage from Holland to Japan complete with a moving platform for the total experience; and, of course, lots of shops and restaurants.

Getting To Nagasaki Holland Village
To/from Nagasaki by bus: departs from in front of the train station (52 minutes, ¥720).
A few **ferries** go daily from Nagasaki Airport (50 minutes, ¥1520).

SHIMABARA
Shimabara is famous for the ill-fated uprising against the anti-Christian persecution in 1637. The area had been ruled by the Christian lord Arima, but in 1616, the Tokugawa shogunate replaced him with Matsukura, an anti-Christian *daimyo* (feudal lord). Some 37,000 Christians and sympathizers, many who supported Hideyoshi's defeated clan, rose up against the shogunate, taking their last stand in the ruins of **Hara Castle**, 30 kilometers down the road. Shimabara Castle was the center for the government forces that eventually defeated the rag tag group, but not

until the rebels repulsed the first attacks and held out for 88 days. The surviving Christians were marched off Hara's high cliffs to their death.

The failure of this rebellion marked the end of Christian protest, and the remaining Christians went underground until 1864 when they presented themselves to a French priest who founded Oura Church in Nagasaki.

ARRIVALS & DEPARTURES

Shimabara offers ferry service to Kumamoto. Try it as a picturesque way of traveling from Nagasaki to Kumamoto.

By Train

Take the **JR Nagasaki Line to Isahaya**: Limited express is 18 minutes; regular train, (30 minutes, ¥450); change for the private Shimabara Tetsudo line to Shimabara Station (1 hour 10 minutes, ¥1330).

By Ferry

To/from Kumamoto Port: to Shimabara Port, 12 ferries/day. 1 hour, ¥590.

SEEING THE SIGHTS

Shimabara Castle. *Open 9am to 5pm. ¥510. 5-minute walk from Shimabara Station.* Once the center of the domain ruled by Lord Matsukura, the castle built in 1618 was destroyed in 1874. Recently rebuilt, the keep holds a museum of Christian history.

Samurai District. *5-five minute walk on the far side of the castle.* A well-preserved area for lower-ranking samurai, including original walls. A stream, once used for drinking water, runs down the middle of the pathway.

KURUME

The only reason to stop in **Kurume** is to see its *ikat* style weaving called *kasuri*. The town is a large, sprawling commercial center but has a hall dedicated to *kasuri* weaving.

In 1800, a young woman, Inoue Den, noticed the white spots that form when indigo-dyed cotton wears out. This inspired her to develop the *kasuri* technique of bundling cotton thread, tying sections so they remain white when dyed and then weaving the dyed threads. Japanese *kasuri* differs from Southeast Asian weaves because both the warp and weft have patterns, resulting in more complex designs. There are 3000 different kinds of *kasuri* patterns! The tying of the threads, the most essential part of *kasuri*, is still done by hand. Recently, most *ikat* is machine woven, a procedure that doesn't diminish its beauty.

ARRIVALS & DEPARTURES

By Train

Kurume is on the JR Kagoshima Hon-sen line.

To/from Kumamoto: about 1 one hour on the JR limited express *Ariake*, ¥2830.

To/from Hakata Station in Fukuoka: 40 minutes, ¥720.

To/from Nagasaki Station: *Kamome* limited express, change trains at JR Tosu Station, ¥4090.

SEEING THE SIGHTS

Kurume Exhibition Hall (Kurume Kasuri Shiryokan) *is located on the second floor of the Jibasan Kurume Center. Tel (0942)44-3701. Open 9am to 5pm. Closed Sunday. Admission free. 10-minute taxi from the train station.* In a non-descript, industrial building next to the expressway, this surprisingly attractive exhibition space shows the history of *kasuri* weaving and representative samples made by masters. All the explanations are in Japanese, but you can still appreciate the textiles and weaving technique. Across the hall is an excellent shop run by the weaver's association that has clothing and other household items as well as *kasuri* material by the bolt. We became so inspired we bought a roll of *kasuri*.

Gi'emon-kan. *12-12 Hiyoshi-machi. Tel. (0942)33-7233. Open from 8:30am to 5:30pm. Closed Sunday.* This attractive shop has a wide variety of *kasuri* fabric and clothing.

Visit a Workshop: If you speak Japanese or have a companion who does, call Mr. Nomura and go see his workshop in **Hirokawa**, a village south of Kurume. Mr. Nomura is a gracious host and an energetic proponent of continuing Kurume's *kasuri* production. His products are sold all over Japan, but you can also buy them on the spot. *Tel. (0943)32-0018, Fax (0943)32-1098.*

ONTA

Attention pottery enthusiasts! Take a side trip to **Onta**, a small mountain village where folk pottery has been produced since 1705 when a local leader invited Korean potters to settle there. Today, ten families produce simple ware intended for everyday use — plates, urns for pickles and soy bean paste, large platters and bowls. Most have more decorative uses — soybean paste jars make great umbrella stands; bowls are wonderful for flowers, and there are lots of tea pots and cups, *sake* cups, and pitchers. Glazes are usually earthen colors like mustard yellow, brown and black, but some bright green glazes sneak in.

The kilns are built into the hillside, and river water still powers the large wooden mortars that pound the clay. Onta is the last place in Japan still using this system. The dull thump of the mortar hitting the clay resounds through the air. At the top of the hill, a small museum displays Onta ware. Admission is free.

Onta has blue-chip folk art credentials. In 1931, Yanagi Soetsu, a father of the folk craft movement, recommended Onta ware as a first-class folk craft. Bernard Leach stayed in the village in 1954, and in 1970, the national government declared it an Intangible Cultural Property.

ARRIVALS & DEPARTURES

Access is relatively limited.

By Car

From the Hita interchange of the Kyushu Expressway, take Route 212 to Route 107, about 40 minutes to Onta.

By Bus

To/from the downtown Hita Bus Center, there are only a few buses a day; the trip takes about 40 minutes. Check the schedule before you go to make sure you don't get stuck.

By Train

Hita is located on the JR Kyudai Honsen line that connects Kurume to Oita.

SEEING THE SIGHTS

It's easy to walk from house to house, for the residences double as studios and all have showrooms offering free entry. Onta potters do not take apprentices; they hand down their skills down only within the family.

The annual pottery festival is the second weekend in October.

YUFUIN

Located at the foot of **Mt. Yufudake** (1584 meters), **Yufuin** is a spa town known for its beautiful morning mist. We like it because Yufuin is quieter and has a more serene atmosphere than bustling Beppu. And it has a wonderful, elegant country inn, **Tamanoyu**, one of Japan's finest.

Earlier this century, when the town leaders wanted to develop Yufuin into a tourist center, they traveled through Western Europe and were especially influenced by the way traditional German villages have become tourist attractions because of their careful preservation. Realizing that in the long run drastic development of any sort would destroy the environment, they decided to develop Yufuin in harmony with nature.

A visit today shows that the town fathers were not completely successful (witness the glaring neon of the downtown *pachinko* parlors), but more so than other Japanese resorts. Many of the buildings were constructed to blend in with nature; some are very traditional and others not at all what we think of as Japanese. Even if you are not interested in hot springs, it is still worthwhile to visit.

Planning Your Stay

Make sure you overnight at Yufuin. Both the upscale Japanese inns Tamanoyu and Kamenoi Besso and the less pricey pensions offer good accommodations.

While Yufuin has hosts of museums, we recommend you limit yourself to the Kyushu Yufuin Folk Art Village and spend the rest of your time enjoying quiet mountain walks and browsing through the town.

ARRIVALS & DEPARTURES

By Train

Yufuin is on the Kyudai Hon-sen line which runs between Kurume (90 minutes on the *Yufuinno-mori* limited express, ¥3290) and Oita (40 minutes, ¥1810).

To/from Hakata-Fukuoka: Limited express *Yufu*, 2 hours 20 minutes, ¥4400.·

To/from Beppu: Limited express, 55 minutes, ¥2300.

To/from Kumamoto: Kagoshima Hon-sen line to Kurume then change to the Kyudai line, ¥3570.

By Bus

To/from Beppu: 1 hour, ¥1050

To/from Kumamoto via Mt. Aso: A sightseeing bus travels along the Yamanami Highway for a beautiful trip through the mountains and around the volcanic Mt. Aso. Several buses leave each day, and the price varies from ¥3850 to ¥8000 depending on whether it stops at Mt. Aso and whether lunch is included.

By Car

The town of Yufuin is a short drive from the Yufuin interchange of the Oita Expressway.

GETTING AROUND TOWN

The town is fairly small and is best toured on bicycle, if the weather is good.

Tourist Information

The **Tourist Information Office** is inside the JR Yufuin Station. *Tel. (0977)84-2446.* Open 9am to 7pm; until 8pm, July through September.

WHERE TO STAY

TAMANOYU, *Yufuin Onsen, Oita-gun, Oita, 879-5197. Tel. (0977)84-2158, Fax (0977)85-3541. From ¥35,000 per person with two meals. Credit cards.*

Tamanoyu is one of our favorite inns in Japan and is included in Chapter 11, Best Places to Stay. At first glance from the street, we immediately realized that this hotel is different. Instead of a front wall and an immaculately manicured garden, we encountered a stand of trees with — horrors — leaves on the ground, just like a real live woods. In amongst the trees lies a low building with a long, sloping tile roof, a successful mixture of California and Japanese architecture. Behind it are cottages connected by a wooden covered walkway. Japanese folk art is used extensively throughout the inn, resulting in a very sophisticated and modern look.

KAMENOI BESSO, *2663-1 Kawakami, Yufuin, Oita-gun, Oita, 879-5198. Tel. (0977)84-3166, Fax (0977)84-2356. From ¥30,000 per person with two meals. Credit cards.*

Formerly a private villa, Kamenoi features 15 cottages and 6 Western-style rooms, all set in a tranquil wooded area. The inn has maintained an air of rustic simplicity, from its entrance through a thatched-roof gate to the cypress bathtub in each room. The inn's large hot spring baths, housed under a wooden roof, has glass doors to commune with nature.

PENSION MOMOTARO, *839-1 Kawakami, Yufuin, Oita-gun, Oita, 879-5100. Tel. (0977)85-2187. ¥8500 per person with two meals. Credit cards.*

Tucked away in the woods with an unpretentious country atmosphere, this small pension has four A-frame cottages with glass walls. The main building is a rustic wooden house. There are several hot spring baths indoors plus an outdoor spa.

SANSO YAMASHIGE, *Kawakami Takemoto, Yufuin, Oita-gun, Oita, 879-51. Tel. (0977)84-3650. From ¥11,000 per person with two meals. No credit cards.*

A tiny, eccentric thatched-roof inn run by an eccentric elderly couple.

PENSION YUFUGOKI, *2760 Kawakami, Yufuin, Oita-gun, Oita, 879-5102. Tel. (0977)84-3766, Fax (0977)84-2143. ¥8900 per person with two meals. American Express only.*

Staying in this pension is like being a guest in a friend's house. The triangular wooden building is modern but rustic with very simple country interiors; a wonderful smell of fresh wood permeates the air. A hot spring bath is in a separate building.

WHERE TO EAT

BUDOYA *(Japanese, moderate to expensive). 2731-1 Kawakami. Tel. (0977)84-4918. Open 11am to 3pm; 5:30pm to 8pm.*

This restaurant, located in the Tamanoyu Inn, is open to the public. Large glass doors overlook a wooded garden outside the contemporary Japanese building. *Sumiyaki* (grilled local beef with mountain vegetables) and *jidori* set (grilled chicken), ¥4500, are served on local ceramic plates and bowls.

YUNOTAKE-AN *(Japanese, moderate). 2633-1 Kawakami. Tel. (0977)84-2970. Open 11am to 8pm.*

Yunotake-an is the dining room of Kamenoi Besso Inn. Its popular meal, *yamaga bento*, features regional specialties and costs ¥2000.

IBIZA *(Spanish, inexpensive to moderate). 108-5 Kawa Minami. Tel. (0977)85-2294. Open 11am to 2:30pm; 6pm to 8:30pm.*

A few minutes south of the station, you can't miss the Mediterranean whitewashed walls of Ibiza. The house specialty is *paella*, cooked in huge pans big enough to serve 40 or 50 people. Lunch costs from ¥1500; dinner courses from ¥3500. A plate of the mouth-watering *paella* is ¥2800.

YUFUIN BEER HALL *(Beer hall, inexpensive). Kawa Minami. Tel. (0977)84-2101. Open 11am to 4pm (lunch until 2:30); 5:30pm to 9:30pm. Located close to Ibiza, south of the station.*

You can sample nine different kinds of local beer and, for ¥1500, have an all-you-can-eat buffet.

SEEING THE SIGHTS

The small **JR Yufuin Station**, designed by Isozaki Arata, one of Japan's internationally known architects, and completed in 1990, is constructed of local *sugi* (cedar). The exterior is stained black to remind you of a locomotive engine, and the interior is a soothing gray and white. Isozaki was inspired by visiting a small chapel in northern Italy. Even the ticket machines and coin lockers were specially designed to harmonize with the architecture. Under the flooring, pipes fed by natural hot springs heat the station. The lobby is quite small but the high vaulted ceilings give you a feeling of space. In the station is an exhibition hall with changing displays.

Yufuin is a popular destination for young Japanese working women who have a good bit of disposable income. The unfortunate result is there are attractions that are more gimmick than substance, designed to relieve them of their cash. One is touring Yufuin by horse-drawn carriage, leaving from the train station at 30 minutes after the hour between 9:30am and 2:30pm. The 50-minute tour costs ¥1200. The ride is canceled on rainy days from December through February.

Shitan-yu. A thatched-roof outdoor bath on Lake Kinrin. *Open 8am to 8pm. ¥100 (place in the box outside the entrance)*. The bath is on the shore of a hot spring lake and is not for those who cherish privacy; it's mixed-sex bathing and hedges aren't thick.

Lake Kinrin. Kinrin means "golden fish scales" and is named after the glittering scales of a jumping fish. The mist produced by the warm water on cool mornings has made Yufuin famous. There is a bicycle trail that goes around the lake and through the woods.

Kyushu Yufuin Folk Art Village (Kyushu Yufuin Mingei Mura). *Open 8:10am to 5:30pm. ¥610*. Located along a stream where even the water's warm. Traditional thatched-roofed and samurai houses have been turned into small galleries displaying folk crafts of the area. In addition to watching craftsmen work, you can try your hand at making Japanese *washi* paper and blowing glass.

Originally, Yufuin was only a spa area, but as the number of tourists increased, so did the number of activities to pass time. Yufuin has some dozen **museums** displaying folk art to automobiles, including the Art Deco Glass Museum, Yufuin Stained Glass Museum, Kindai Bijutsukan (Modern Art Museum), Herb Garden and Kyushu Jidosha Rekishikan (cars). The Yufuin Bijutsukan (Art Museum) and Sueda Art Museum are interesting architectural statements well worth a visit to those interested in contemporary buildings.

Many of the other places are good excuses for visitors to part with their yen (some of the admission fees are ridiculously high), so choose what really interests you. Otherwise rent bikes, take hot baths, go hiking up Mt. Yufu or along lower trails, browse in the many shops and enjoy Yufuin's relaxed pace.

BEPPU

Beppu has been a hot spring resort for a long time and has developed into a pretty hideous city. We much prefer the serenity of Yufuin, just an hour away. But if you are looking for sand and mud baths, boiling "hells," large resort-like hotels or sleazy nightlife, you can be one of the 12 million annual visitors to Beppu. Beppu sports over 3,750 hot springs and more than 168 public bath houses. Steam escapes from vents all over the city, giving it an eerie look. The hot water is even used to fuel ovens.

Planning Your Stay
Visitors to Beppu should spend a day. Visit Suginoi Palace for a bathing theme park or the quieter baths of the Kannawa or Myoban areas. The Takegawara bath house is not to be missed.

ARRIVALS & DEPARTURES

By Air
Oita Airport serves the Beppu area.
To/from Tokyo Haneda: 8 flights/day (ANA, JAL, JAS. ¥25,200).
To/from Osaka Itami: 5 flights/day; **Kansai:** 2 flights/day (ANA, JAL. ¥13,700).
Also service to/from Kagoshima, Nagoya, Okinawa and Sapporo.

For Ground Transportation:
Bus from the airport to Beppu Kitahama (35 minutes, ¥1450).

By Train
Beppu is on the JR Nippo Hon-sen line.
To/from Oita City: 14 minutes, ¥270.
To/from Yufuin: *Yufuinno-mori* limited express, 54 minutes, ¥2300.
To/from Hakata-Fukuoka: Limited express. 2 hours, ¥5550.
To/from Miyazaki: *Nichiren* limited express. 3 hours 40 minutes, ¥6070.

By Bus
To/from Nagasaki: 7 buses/day, 3 hours 40 minutes, ¥4500.
To/from Fukuoka: 20 buses/day, 2 hours 10 minutes, ¥3100.
To/from Nagoya: Overnight bus. 11 hours 30 minutes, ¥11,000.

By Ferry
To/from Osaka and Kobe: 2 overnight ferries in each direction; one stops at Matsuyama en route. ¥7030 to ¥14,070.

By Car
Beppu is on the Oita Expressway.

Tourist Information
The **tourist information center**, an "i" information center, at JR Beppu Station. *Tel. (0977)24-2838.* Open 9am to 5pm.

The **Foreign Tourist Information Service** is located at 3F Kitahama Center Building, 2-9-23 Kitahama, Beppu. *Tel. (0977)23-1119.* It's well equipped to assist foreign tourists.

Goodwill Guides: Contact the Foreign Tourist Information Service, *Tel. (0977)23-1119,* between 9:30am and 6pm to arrange a volunteer guide.

WHERE TO STAY

KANNAWA-EN, *Miyuki Rokkumi, Kannawa, Beppu, Oita, 874-0045. Tel. (0977)66-2111, Fax (0977)66-2113. From ¥20,000 per person with two meals. No credit cards.*

This lovely traditional Japanese inn has a large garden and its *rotemburo* is rated one of the top three in Kyushu. It's cherry blossoms bloom in January, Japan's earliest after Okinawa.

SUGINOI, *1 Kankaiji, Beppu, Oita, 874. Tel. (0977)24-1141, Fax (0977)21-0010. From ¥15,000 per person with two meals. Credit cards.*

A huge spa resort hotel located at the top of the hill overlooking Beppu Bay. Most of the rooms are Western-style. The hotel is only one part of a huge spa entertainment complex (see *Seeing the Sights*). Stay here if you want to see how well-heeled Japanese play.

KANKAISO, *Kankaiji, Beppu, Oita, 874-0822. Tel. (0977)23-1221, Fax (0977)21-6285. From ¥16,000 per person with two meals. Credit cards.*

Located in the highest hills of Beppu so all the rooms have views of Beppu Bay. Kankaiso has a variety of baths open 24 hours so you can even enjoy sunrise in a bath.

ONSEN HOYOLAND, *Kon-ya Jigoku, Beppu, Oita, 874-0843. Tel. (0977)66-2221, Fax (0977)22-1358. ¥7500 per person with two meals. No credit cards.*

This small hostel-type inn is located at the Hoyoland complex and has many baths. It's located in the Myoban Onsen area, which is about 50 minutes by bus from Beppu Station.

MINSHUKU KOKAGE, *8-9 Ekimae-cho, Beppu, Oita. 874-0935. Singles ¥4000. Doubles ¥7000. Credit cards. Member of the Japanese Inn Group and Welcome Inn Reservation Center.*

The wooden clapboard building looks very Western from the outside but most of the rooms are Japanese style. The very central location means the area is congested, but the rooms are quiet. You are also close to the many restaurants and bars in the area and can easily catch buses at the train station to get to the other areas of Beppu.

WHERE TO EAT

FUGUMATSU *(Fugu, expensive). 3-6-14 Kitahama. Tel. (0977)21-1717. Open 11am to 9pm.*

A great place to taste blowfish so fresh that the claim is it was swimming in the nearby Bungo Straits until shortly before it's served. A set course starts from ¥7000.

ISHIKAWA *(French, inexpensive to moderate). 2 Kumi Shin-Beppu. Tel. (0977)23-2910. Open 10am to 6pm. Closed Monday. Reservations necessary.*

French bistro in the Kannawa spa area serves inventive French cuisine prepared by owner-chef Madame Ishikawa. Set dinner courses from ¥2800. The coffee shop, open all day, serves coffee and light meals.

SHINANOYA *(Japanese, inexpensive). 6-32 Nishinoguchi. Tel. (0977)21-1395. Open daily 10am to 10pm.*

The building was originally built as a private villa in the late 1920s. *Shinanoya teishoku* (set menu) consists of soup with dumplings, grilled beef, rice and pickles and costs ¥1300. Good for lunch and supper!

SEEING THE SIGHTS

Nearly everything to do in Beppu is related to the hot spring water that percolates up from the ground.

The most famous sites in Beppu are the boiling hells, open pits of colorful boiling water and mud. There is a **Jigoku-meguri** or "circuit of hells." The *Umi Jigoku* or Sea Hell is bright sea green; *Chinoike Jigoku* or Blood Pond Hell is as you would expect, blood red. *Hon Bozu Jigoku* or Monk's Hell, has gray mud; when it bubbles up it resembles a monk's head. You can take a 2 1/2 hour tour from Beppu Kitahama costing ¥1540 or do it on your own. Seven of the hells are within walking distance of each other while the other two, *Chinoike* and *Tatsumaki*, are a 5-minute bus ride away.

Sand baths: Takegawara Bathhouse. *Tel. (0977)23-1585. Open 6:30am to 10:30pm. ¥60 for a regular bath and ¥630 for sand bath. 5-minute walk from Beppu Station, towards the bay.* Takegawara was built in 1879 and is one of Beppu's oldest public baths and has an indoor sand bath. Today the roof is tiled but when built it was made of bamboo; Takegawara means bamboo tiles. The building is essentially a Meiji-era gymnasium. The sand bath is divided into men's and women's sections; you remove your clothes and lie down on the sand. A small towel covers your private parts and the staff shovels hot sand over you. The sand isn't unbearably hot and after about 10 minutes, when you're comfortably warm, you get up and jump into the hot bath. It's a fun experience, so don't miss it.

Beppu Beach also offers hot sand baths, al fresco; here you wear a cotton *yukata* robe while the hot sand warms your body. *Tel. (0977)66-5737. Open 9am to 4pm. ¥610.*

Myoban Onsen area has mud baths called *doro-yu*. Although the idea of submerging your body in mud like a human hippo may not appeal to you, it has incredible health benefits. Mud baths are supposed to lower blood pressure and are especially good for rheumatism and for mitigating the side effects of cortisone. But you do not need to be ailing to try a mud bath. The water is about one-third mud so it is difficult to walk through even though the mud makes your body float. Myoban, up in the hills past the boiling hells, is much quieter than central Beppu. Japanese have been coming here for over 1000 years — an 8th century anthology mentioned the mud baths of this area.

Myoban also has a lot of thatched-roof huts that collect the sulfur and other solids in the hot spring water. These solids are sold as *yu-no-hana*, (literally flower of hot water). Buy some packets to take home and turn your bath into a hot spring. They also make great gifts and are available not only in Beppu but in any drug store in Japan. Myoban is about a 30-minute drive from central Beppu or a 50-minute bus ride by bus 41, 43, 51 or 53 departing from the West Exit of the station.

Head to **Hoyoland** for your mud bath. This bathing center in Myoban Onsen also has several outdoor baths and large indoor baths. You can overnight at their hostel (see *Where to Stay*). *Tel. (0977)66-2221. Open daily 8:30am to 8pm. ¥1050.*

Another mud bath is at **Kodei**, located on the left side of the parking lot for the Bozu Jigoku Hell. *Open 8am to 12 noon, ¥840. Open year round except during typhoons or wild weather. Tel. (0977)66-0863.*

Suginoi Palace, **U Zone** and **Aquabeat**. *1 Kankaiji, Beppu, Oita, 874. Tel. (0977)24-1141. Open 9am to 9pm. ¥2000 until 5pm; ¥1000 after 5pm.* Although run by the Suginoi Hotel next door, the palace is open to the public. Suginoi Palace is a convenient and fun place to experience hot springs in a Disneyland-like fantasy land. The palace features two large areas resembling overgrown greenhouses called Dream Bath and Flower Bath. They are filled with a multitude of pools of every size, depth and design, including slides for the kids, and decorated with tropical plants, *torii* gates and revolving Buddhas. What more could you want for your soaking pleasure? Aquabeat is an amusement park with water including a wave pool. When you get tired of the water, head to U Zone for a game center, a fake ice-skating rink, roller-blade rink, and karaoke rooms. There is more than enough to keep you busy for days.

Museum of Japanese Bamboo (Nihon Take no Hakubutsukan). *Tel. (0977)25-7776. Open from 8:30am to 5pm. ¥400. 5 minutes from Kotsu Center.* The museum displays a whole range of crafts made from the versatile bamboo. The second floor features craftsmen at work. Make a reservation to construct your own bamboo masterpiece; the charge for a small bamboo vase is ¥700.

SHOPPING

Oita Prefectural Products Hall (Oita-ken Kanko Bussan-kan). *Tel. (0977)23-0201. Open 8:30am to 5pm. Close to the Kotsu Center.* The hall carries the full range of Oita products from local *sake* to wooden folk toys and *yu-no-hana*, powdered minerals you can bring home to turn your bath into an instant hot spring.

Bamboo Crafts (Takezaiku Dento Sangyo Kaikan). *8-3 Higashi Soen. Tel. (0977)23-1072. Open 8:30am to 5pm. 15-20 minute taxi ride from Beppu Station.* Anything and everything to do with bamboo is on display; with advance reservations you can make your own.

KUMAMOTO

Kumamoto has much more character than your average midsize Japanese city. Yes, at first glance the sprawling city seems charmless, but the large castle surrounded by greenery in the center of town gives Kumamoto an open and spacious feeling. South of the castle is an area where the merchants and craftsmen had their shops attached to small, simple houses during the Edo Period; the ambiance of that era still remains.

Kumamoto boasts one of the largest populations of residents over age 100 in Japan; this is attributed to healthy diets and *mokkosu* (a local word meaning feisty). Kumamoto-ites have a reputation for being stubborn and moody, swinging from warm to cold, but we found people quite pleasant and friendly. Kumamoto is known as *Hi-no-Kuni*, (land of fire). Is it named for the volcano Mt. Aso, or could it be its citizens have a fiery reputation?

Kumamoto also has an interesting history. The imposing **castle**, one of the largest in Japan, was built between 1600 and 1607 by Kato Kiyomasa, a powerful feudal lord who sided with Tokugawa Ieyasu at the decisive Battle of Sekigahara in 1600. In 1632, the domain changed hands and the Hosokawa took over, ruling until the end of the feudal era in 1868. To show how much politics has changed, Hosokawa Morihiro, who headed the government in 1994, is the only Prime Minister in the postwar era to have descended from feudal lords.

The castle was destroyed in 1877 when Saigo Takamori, one of the leaders of the Meiji Restoration, rebelled when he became disillusioned with the new Meiji government. He attacked the castle where government troops were garrisoned, and the battle raged for two months. Saigo was defeated, but the castle was left in ruins. The keep was re-constructed in 1960 on the original, spectacularly steep walls.

Planning Your Stay

Plan to spend one day in Kumamoto. Start your day at Kumamoto Castle, the Prefectural Art Museum, the Prefectural Crafts Center and then take the streetcar to Suizenji Park.

ARRIVALS & DEPARTURES

By Air

Kumamoto Airport is located east of the city.

To/from Tokyo Haneda: 8 flights/day (ANA, JAL, JAS. ¥27,250).

To/from Osaka Itami: 6 flights/day; **Kansai**: 2 flights/day (ANA, JAL. ¥16,850).

Also flights to/from Okinawa, Nagoya and Sapporo.

For Ground Transportation:

Bus: to JR Kumamoto Station: 50 minutes, ¥670.

Taxi: about 45 minutes to JR Kumamoto Station, ¥4500.

By Train

Kumamoto is on the JR Kagoshima Honsen line connecting Kagoshima with Fukuoka-Hakata.

To/from Fukuoka-Hakata: Limited express. 1 hour 20 minutes, ¥3740.

To/from Kagoshima: Limited express. 2 hours 10 minutes, ¥5860.

To/from Nagasaki: Change trains at Tosu Station, ¥6770.

By Bus

Overnight bus service from: Nagoya (11 hours, ¥11,500), Kyoto (10 1/2 hours, ¥10,800), and Osaka (9 3/4 hours, ¥10,300).

Express bus service to: Fukuoka (3 buses/hour, 2 hours, ¥2400), Nagasaki (10 buses/day, 3 hours, ¥3600), Miyazaki (10 buses/day, 3 1/2 hours, ¥4500), and Kagoshima (10 buses/day, 3 1/2 hours, ¥3600).

By Car

Kumamoto is on the **Kyushu Expressway** that runs north-south from Fukuoka to Kagoshima.

GETTING AROUND TOWN

The train station is several kilometers away from the business and entertainment center, near the castle; streetcars conveniently link the two. At the Kumamoto Station tourist information desk and on the streetcars, you can buy a ¥500 one-day pass *(ichi nichi joshaken)* good on streetcars and buses. Tourist sites are clustered around the castle with the exception of Suizenji, which is several kilometers away but linked by streetcar.

Tourist Information

The **tourist information counter**, an "i" information office, is in Kumamoto Station which, incidentally, is one of the more attractive JR stations in Japan. *Tel. (096)352-3743.*

Home Visits: To visit a Japanese family, contact the **Kumamoto International Foundation** at least one day in advance. 4-8 Hanabada-cho, Kumamoto-shi, Kumamoto 860. *Tel. (096)359-2121, Fax (096)359-5112.* Open 9am to 7pm.

Goodwill Guides: Contact either the Tourist Information Office or the Kumamoto International Foundation (above) for the current contact number for a volunteer goodwill guide.

City Tours

Tours in Japanese leave from the Kumamoto Bus Center and Kumamoto Station daily except December 29-31. The 3 1/2 hour Ginnan course covers the Hosokawa Residence, Kumamoto Castle and Suizenji Park. Departs 1:15pm. No afternoon tours on Monday. ¥3860. Take the tour only if you want to practice Japanese or make sociological observations of Japanese tourists. With the *ichi nichi joshaken* and a good map, try it on your own. We think you're better off.

WHERE TO STAY

NEW SKY HOTEL, *20 Higashi Amidaji-cho, Kumamoto, 860-0034. Tel. (096)354-2111, Fax (096)354-8973. West Wing: Singles from ¥8000. Doubles from ¥17,000. East Wing: Singles ¥12,000. Doubles from ¥15,000. Credit cards.*

The New Sky Hotel, part of the ANA group, is fairly close to the train station, but not very conveniently located. Fortunately, a streetcar stop is right next to it so you can easily get around Kumamoto. The West Wing is older and 11 stories tall while the East Wing rises 25 floors, giving good panoramic views of Kumamoto. The daily lunch special at the Chinese restaurant, Rihaku, costs only ¥800.

KUMAMOTO HOTEL CASTLE, *4-2 Joto-machi, Kumamoto, 850-8565. Tel. (096)326-3311, Fax (096)326-3324. Singles from ¥8900. Twins from ¥16,000. Credit cards.*

The hotel is a large red-brick Western style hotel built in 1960 and has nice views of Kumamoto Castle. There are three restaurants: Western, Chinese and Japanese. At the Japanese restaurant, you can eat like a feudal lord at a princely price. They serve food similar to what was once served to the Hosokawa family: *Ko ryori* is ¥10,000. Reservations are needed three days in advance.

HOTEL NEW OTANI KUMAMOTO, *1-1-13 Kasuga-cho, Kumamoto, 860-0047. Tel. (096)326-1111, Fax (096)326-0800. Singles from ¥11,000. Doubles from ¥18,000. Credit cards.*

Part of the New Otani chain of luxury hotels, the staff goes out of its way to welcome foreign guests and even offers non-smoking rooms. Located next to Kumamoto Station, the station streetcar stop there provides convenient access to the city.

MARUKO HOTEL, *11-10 Kamitori-machi. Kumamoto, 860-1217. Tel. (096)353-1241, Fax (096)353-1217. Singles ¥6500. Doubles ¥12,000. Credit cards. Member of Welcome Inn Reservation Center.*

Located between the station and the castle, the Toricho-suji streetcar stop is the most convenient. Meals are optional, but if you do choose to eat there, you are served in your room, unusual for an inexpensive inn. Most of the rooms are Japanese style.

WHERE TO EAT

The main restaurant and entertainment district is in the area around the castle on two covered streets, **Sunroad Shingai** and **Shimotori**.

OKUMURA *(Japanese, moderate to expensive). 1-8-8 Shin-machi. Tel. (096)352-8101. Open from 11:30am to 2pm; 5pm to 9:30pm. Reservations necessary.*

A beautifully kept entrance with elegantly arranged flowers welcomes you. The ambiance makes you want to don a kimono to enjoy the atmosphere. Their lunchtime *kaiseki* course costs ¥5000; some of the low Japanese tables have pits so you can stretch your legs.

GORYOHACHI *(Regional Japanese, moderate). 1F, 12-8 Icho Kaikan, Hanabatake-Machi. Tel. (096)352-5751. Open from 5pm to 11pm. Closed Sunday.*

Goryohachi strives to use the freshest ingredients at the lowest prices. The menu consists only of local delicacies such as fresh *sashimi*, *ba sashi* and *karashi renkon*. They claim they serve the world's best *ba sashi* for ¥2500 and *nigiri uma zushi* (horse *sushi*) for ¥800. Goryohachi also stocks a variety of local *sake*, including Taito, a well-known brand named Taito. Courses run ¥3000, ¥4000 and ¥5000.

SANDO *(Steak, inexpensive to expensive). 1-9 Sutorimu Choanji, Suido-machi. Tel. (096)324-3571. Open 11:30am to 1:30pm: 5pm to 9pm. Closed on 1st, 2nd and 3rd Tuesday.*

This steak house serves abalone and locally raised beef. The lunchtime steak course is a good deal for ¥2000; the dinner course runs ¥8500.

DANJURO *(Japanese, inexpensive). 1-10-6 Shimo Dori. Tel. (096)326-5681. Open 6pm to 1:30am. Closed Sunday.*

As you enter, barrels filled with the catch of the day greet you. Choose your own fish (the price is listed on the barrel) and order it prepared as *sushi, sashimi* or stewed in a *nabe*. Another specialty is *Seiro meshi* (rice steamed with fish and vegetables) for ¥780.

AOYAGI *(Kamameshi, inexpensive to moderate). Shimo-dori near the Daiei Store. Tel. (096)353-0311. Open 11:30am to 9:30pm.*

The number one specialty here is *kamameshi* (rice cooked with vegetables, meat and seafood in a small individual pot). A *kamameshi* set costs ¥2500. Aoyagi also serves unique local specialties such as horse meat *sashimi* (from ¥2000).

KOTSU CENTER HOTEL BEER GARDEN *(Beer garden, inexpensive). 3-10 Sakura-machi. Tel. (096)354-1111. Open 5pm to 9pm.*

Open only April through August, this roof "garden" on the roof of the hotel is a good place to drink beer, eat an inexpensive meal such as *yakitori* or sausages, and enjoy splendid views of the castle and city.

WHAT'S COOKING IN KUMAMOTO?

*Or maybe we should say what's not cooking? A popular local dish is **ba sashi** (raw horse meat). Before you turn away in disgust, try it! It tastes a lot like tuna and is not as strong as raw beef. Very thin slices of meat are dipped in a vinegar sauce and served on top of lettuce. Some restaurants also serve horse meat sushi, slices of meat on a cake of rice.*

__Karashi renkon__ (deep-deep fried lotus root stuffed with a mustard miso) is a popular dish in Kumamoto. Back in the early 1600s a Kumamoto monk, Gentaku, discovered that lotus root grown in the local sandy volcanic soil helped people regain their vitality. He developed the dish for the frail feudal lord, Hosokawa Tadatoshi. Best of all, when the lotus root is sliced, the holes resemble the Hosokawa's family crest, nine dots around a circle.

*Kumamoto is also known for its **sake**; the water is supposed to be very pure because of the volcanic soil. One of the most famous brands is Bishonen, literally "Beautiful Boy." Try it with some ba-sashi.*

SEEING THE SIGHTS

Kumamoto's sights are centered around Kumamoto Castle with the exception of Suizenji Koen Garden.

Kumamoto Castle. *Open 8:30am to 5:30pm. Closes at 4:30pm November through March. Closed December 29--31. ¥500 to enter grounds and keep, ¥200 for grounds only. English audio tape tour, ¥200.* Kumamoto Castle dominates central Kumamoto. Begun in 1600 during a time of great political instability, the castle has a very masculine and martial look. Castles built only a dozen years later, such as Himeji, have more decorative flourishes. In those ensuing years, peace had become much more of a certainty.

Built on an imposing hill by Kato Kiyomasa, Kumamoto Castle has massive stone walls with a distinctive slope. These walls are called *musha-gaeshi; nezumi-gaeshi* (samurai return, mice return) because both warriors and mice alike were unable to scale them and and found themselves back on the ground before they knew it.

The castle originally had 49 watchtowers and 29 gates and the circumference of its outermost walls was 12 kilometers. In 1632, fearing the feudal lord Kato Tadahiro was involved in an intrigue to replace the shogun, the Tokugawa shogunate dispossessed the Kato family and replaced them with the Hosokawa.

Kumamoto Castle was the site of the major battle of the Seinan War in 1877. Saigo Takamori, a samurai from Kagoshima and a major player in the Meiji Restoration 10 years earlier, became disillusioned with the new Meiji Government, raised an army in Kagoshima and marched north to lay siege to Kumamoto. Greatly outnumbered, Saigo retreated, but not before Kagoshima Castle was in ashes. Only one original guard tower remains, the Uta-Yagura, which is open to the public.

The keep was rebuilt in 1960 and houses a good museum that gives the history of the castle and Kumamoto City armor and other objects belonging to the Kato and Hosokawa clans and, best of all, a wonderful small ship that the Hosokawa used to travel to and from Edo (Tokyo) to fulfill the *sankin kotai* (system of forced alternate attendance) required by the shogun. No attempt was made to make the interior of the castle keep architecturally accurate, but the wide stairs make access much easier than in original castle.

THE DEVIL GENERAL

Kato Kiyomasa (1562-1611), lord of Kumamoto from 1588 until his death in 1611 (a contemporary of Sir Francis Drake), was one of the great generals of the era. As co-leader of the military invasion of Korea in 1592, Kato's victories earned him the name "Devil General" from the enemy. He opposed a peaceful settlement in Korea and was recalled by Hideyoshi but was sent there again in 1597 when war erupted. Kato became interested in Korean culture and imported exotica, including stone lanterns, as gifts to Hideyoshi. After Hideyoshi's death in 1598, Kato returned to Japan and sided with Tokugawa Ieyasu at the decisive Battle of Sekigahara in 1600. Tokugawa rewarded Kato by doubling the size of his territory. Kato died in 1611; some suspect that Tokugawa Ieyasu had a role in his death for he feared Kato might support Hideyori, the son of Hideyoshi and the last major obstacle to Ieyasu's total control of Japan.

Near the castle is the **Kumamoto Prefectural Art Museum** (Kumamoto Kenritsu Bijutsukan), which displays fine arts including Kato and Hosokawa family belongings and replicas of archaeological finds from the prefecture. We find the architecturally distinctive building is also a pleasant place to take a tea break. *Tel. (096)352-2111. Open 9:30am to 5pm. Closed Monday and December 25 through January 4. ¥260.*

Kumamoto Municipal Museum (Kumamoto Shiritsu Hakubutsukan). A good place to take the kids who are loath to visit another temple — lots of natural science displays and a planetarium. *Tel. (096)324-3500. Open 9am to 5pm. Closed Monday, national holidays, July 11-15 and December 26 through January 5. Planetarium ¥300.*

Hosokawa Residence (Hosokawa Kyobu-tei). This residence, belonging to a branch of the Hosokawa family, is a house typical of a high-ranking samurai family. *Tel. (096)352-6522. Open 9am to 4:30pm. Closed Monday. ¥300.*

Kumamoto Prefectural Traditional Crafts Center (Kumamoto Kenritsu Dento Kogeikan). Located just north of the castle or a 5-minute walk from the streetcar Shiyakusho-mae stop. The center attractively exhibits and sells crafts of the area including furniture and other objects fashioned from wood, baskets, paper, ceramics and folk toys. There is even a woodworking room. *Tel. (096)324-4930. Open 9am to 5pm. Closed Monday and December 28 through January 4. ¥190 admission to the second floor gallery.*

You have to take a taxi or streetcar to get from the castle to **Suizenji Koen Garden**. Founded in 1632 by Hosokawa Tadatoshi, the first in his line to move into Kumamoto Castle. It is a strolling garden with a lake at its center. Mounds are supposed to represent the 53 stages of the Tokaido, the historic road between Kyoto and Tokyo. Unfortunately, nothing is marked so you have no idea what is what. Only Mt. Fuji, the tallest mountain, is recognizable. The park is disappointingly commercial with many tawdry souvenir shops lining its perimeter. *Open 7am to 6pm; December through February 8:30am to 5pm. ¥400.*

Next to the garden is the Jones residence, the oldest Western building extant in Kumamoto.

SHOPPING

Near the castle and the bus center are two shopping arcades, **Sunroad Shingai** and **Shimotori**.

What to Buy

Local crafts include gold and silver inlaid work, *yamaga* lanterns (gold colored paper-cut lanterns); colorful toys like *kijiuma* (brightly painted pheasant on wheels) and *kinta* dolls (a head with eyes that roll and a tongue that sticks out when you pull its string) — named after a guard at Kumamoto Castle who was always joking.

In addition to the **Prefectural Crafts Center** (see *Seeing the Sights*), a wide range of goods is available in the **Kumamoto Products Display Hall** on the 3rd floor of the Sangyo Bunka Kaikan (Industrial and Cultural Hall) near the Kumamoto Kotsu (Bus) Center.

MT. ASO

Mt. Aso, the world's largest volcano, symbolizes Kumamoto prefecture, giving it the name *hi-no-kuni* (country of fire). The caldera is huge with a circumference of 128 kilometers. Actually Mt. Aso consists of five mountains; Daikanbo is the highest at 936 meters. Nakadake is still active and spews out smoke daily. The area is attractive at any time but literally comes alive with the bright green of new leaves in May. Ski here from mid-December through early March.

Mt. Aso is an easy trip from Kumamoto.

ARRIVALS & DEPARTURES

By Train

To/from Kumamoto: JR Hohi Line: 90 minutes by regular train, ¥1080; 1 hour by infrequent limited express, ¥1980. On weekends and peak travel times, JR runs a steam locomotive, "Aso Boy," that takes 2 1/2 hours to Aso. Buy seat reservation tickets at any JR Green Window one month in advance.

To/from Beppu: JR Hohi line: Infrequent limited express trains take about 2 hours, ¥3740.

By Bus

From Kumamoto to Asozan Nishi: 2 buses/day, 90 minutes, ¥1630.

Tour Bus

The **Trans Kyushu Sightseeing Bus** links Kumamoto and Beppu. The Japanese tour buses take the Yamanami Highway across Kyushu and stop at Mt. Aso for about 30 minutes. The entire trip takes about 8 hours and costs from ¥3850 to ¥8000, depending on whether lunch is included.

By Car

From Kumamoto, take Route 57.

ORIENTATION

Mt. Aso is a large area; trains and buses can take you to the larger towns, but you have to drive to get to the more secluded spots. The northern section of the mountain is the most developed and devoid of any charm. It is magnificent to see the craters and meadows, but avoid the larger towns and big hotels.

WHERE TO STAY

We find the northern perimeter of Mt. Aso overdeveloped and lacking in character. To the south, the following places have the rustic charm that we look for in mountainous areas.

SEIFU-SO, *Kawayo, Choyo-son, Aso-gun, Kumamoto, 869-0014. Tel. (09676)7-0005, Fax (09676)7-1678. From ¥9000 per person with two meals. No credit cards. Twenty minutes by infrequent bus from Aso Shimoda Station of the Minami Aso Railway; about ¥1600 by taxi.*

Seifu-so is the only inn at Jigoku Onsen. The rooms are quite simple, and meals are served in a separate building where you sit around an *irori* (open hearth) and cook your own meal. You have a choice of menus with pictures to help in your selection. There are a number of different hot spring baths, including Revenge Bath — the women's is higher on the hillside than the men's.

YAMAGUCHI RYOKAN, *Kawayo, Choyo-son, Aso-gun, Kumamoto, 869-1404. Tel. (09676)7-0006, Fax (09676)7-1694. ¥9000 per person with two meals without bath; ¥14,000 with bath. Credit cards. Twenty minutes by infrequent bus from the Aso Shimoda Station of the Minami Aso Railway; about ¥1600 by taxi.*

Yamaguchi is the only inn at Tarutama Onsen and offers outdoor hot spring baths at the foot of a waterfall and under a thatched roof hut. If you are looking for a rustic setting, it's a great getaway.

PENSION MORI ATELIER, *1810 Shirakawa, Hakusui-mura, Aso-gun, Kumamoto, 869-1502. Tel. (09676)2-3006, Fax (09676)2-2079. From ¥7300 per person with breakfast. Dinner ¥2500 to ¥5000. No credit cards. Five minutes by taxi from Takamori Station on the Minami Aso Railway.*

This wooden pension is farmhouse style with open rafters. Built next to an observatory, the pension has skylights for star gazing.

KYUKAMURA MINAMI ASO, *3219 Nakajima, Takamori-machi, Aso-gun, Kumamoto, 869-1602. Tel. (09676)2-2111, Fax (09676)2-2100. Rates from ¥8000 per person with two meals.*

This public Vacation Village has great views of Mt. Aso and is a popular and relaxing place to stay. Like most vacation villages, the building is not fancy but offers clean and comfortable accommodations as well as tennis and other activities.

SEEING THE SIGHTS

Daikanbo is one of Mt. Aso's peaks. To reach the viewing point at the top of Daikanbo, take a bus from Aso Station and get off at Daikanbo Toge (30 minutes, ¥480). Walk for about 20 minutes to find a truly spectacular view of the whole area.

Nakadake is the only active volcano among Aso's five peaks. You can take a cable car to the top to look into the smoky crater. If you're lucky, you'll get a glimpse of the putrid green lake far below. *From Aso Station, take the bus heading to Asozan Nishi-eki station and get off at the last stop (40 minutes, ¥620). Take the Asozan ropeway to the top (4 minutes, ¥820 round trip).*

IZUMI

Calling all crane lovers — **Izumi** is a must! In the winter, Izumi is home to some 10,000 Siberian cranes, the largest gathering of cranes in the world. Even if you aren't a birder, stop here to see these magnificently graceful and elegant birds. The cranes come to Izumi in November and stay until mid-March. They set off on the long trek home to Eastern Siberia, via Korea and China, where they hang out for the summer months. Winter in Izumi seems pretty chilly to us but, compared to Siberia, it must be positively balmy. The birds mate in Siberia; both male and female cranes take turns sitting on the eggs.

A document dated 1705 recorded the visit of cranes in the area, so they have been coming to Izumi for a long time. Lord Shimazu of Kagoshima, always in search of arable land to feed his minions, started to reclaim the land towards the end of the 17th century. The new marshy land was perfect for the cranes.

In the 1950s, the cranes were eating farmers' crops, so they tried unsuccessfully to get rid of them. Eventually the farmers changed their approach and began to feed the cranes in the hope of keeping them in a certain area and out of their fields. Now, each morning and evening, the farmers put out 500 kilograms of wheat for the birds. The district is a Wildlife Protected Area — the government reimburses the farmers for winter use of the land and pays for the food. The land is still owned by farmers, so there is a continuing tension between conservation and agriculture.

The best times to view the birds are sunrise and sunset when they fly to the **Arasaki fields** to eat. They are so graceful in the air, flying in formations of 5 to 50 birds. They eat wheat, sweet potatoes, *dojo* (small eels) and small fish. After their morning meal, the crane families spend their day together resting and eating in the surrounding area. You can always find some birds in the eating area because they return to it knowing it's a safe place. Cranes are extremely cautious; one family member stands guard while the others eat.

Planning Your Stay

The morning and evening feeding times are the best times to see the cranes at the Crane Viewing area at the Arasaki field, so it's best to stay overnight.

ARRIVALS & DEPARTURES

By Train

JR Izumi Station is on the Kagoshima Honsen line and is convenient to both Kagoshima and Kumamoto. *Tsubame* limited express trains take 2 hours 15 minutes from Kumamoto to Izumi, ¥3740, and 1 hour 40 minutes from Kagoshima to Izumi, ¥3290.

JR has a special discount ticket to travel from Kagoshima or Kumamoto to see the cranes and return to the same city. Called a *Tsuru Kanko Waribiki Kippu*, it includes round-trip, nonreserved train fare on a limited express train and admission to the Crane Museum and the Crane Viewing Hall. The cost from Kagoshima is ¥4900; from Kumamoto, ¥5900. This package is available from early December until mid-March. You must pay an additional ¥1200 in Izumi to use the shuttle bus.

By Car

From Kumamoto: Route 3 runs from Kumamoto to Izumi. To save a little time, you can take the expressway for part of the way.

GETTING AROUND TOWN

Arasaki, the feeding site of the cranes, is about a 20-minute drive from JR Izumi Station. There is a bus that runs from the train station to Crane Park, site of the Museum of the Crane, to the feeding area at Arasaki, to the samurai district, and then back to the train station. The bus departs from the station four times a day at 9:55am, 10:55am, 11:55am and 12:55pm. The last bus leaves Arasaki to return to the station at 4:45pm.

Taxi from the JR Izumi Station to Arasaki will cost about ¥4000 one way, or you can rent a car at the station from JR's Eki Rent-a-Car: about ¥8000 for 6 hours for an average-sized car and about ¥6000 for a tiny car.

WHERE TO STAY

You have a choice: stay at a *minshuku* adjacent to the cranes' feeding ground where the accommodations are basic, or stay in **Izumi City**, a 20-minute drive away. We prefer to stay in Izumi and commute.

IZUMIYA RYOKAN, *3-16 Showa-machi. Izumi, Kagoshima, 899-0202. Tel. (0996)62-0464, Fax (0996)62-0465. ¥6500 per person with private bath and two meals. No credit cards.*

Izumiya is our first choice for accommodations in the area. This small Japanese inn is close to the JR Izumi Station, just a two-minute walk down the road perpendicular to the station. The accommodations are modest but very clean. You'll even find a fresh flower arrangement in your tiny alcove, and the food is good home-cooked fare. The manager was even flexible enough to accommodate our request to hold our breakfast until after we saw the cranes eat theirs at Arasaki.

HOTEL WING INTERNATIONAL, *1-1 Showa-machi, Izumi, Kagoshima, 899-0202. Tel. (0996)63-8111, Fax (0996)62-7575. Singles from ¥6300. Doubles from ¥11,000. Credit cards.*

Hotel Wing is a business hotel directly across the street from the JR Izumi Station. You don't have to worry about the noise because the hotel is a few blocks from the main street and JR Izumi is hardly Grand Central Station. Rooms are average business hotel size (not large), and each room has a small bath. There's a cheerful restaurant on the 1st floor.

MINSHUKU TSURU MITEI, *Arasaki, Izumi, Kagoshima, 899-0135. Tel. (0996)83-3944. No fax. ¥6800 per person with two meals. No credit cards.*

These accommodations are quite basic but clean, and cater to birders. It's the best place to stay if you want to see, hear and feel the cranes very close by. But the biggest drawback is the limited heating; an English friend says she has never been so cold in her life (and English homes are known for being cold!).

SEEING THE SIGHTS

Izumi City Crane Viewing Center (Izumi-shi Tsuru Kansatsu Senta). *Tel. (0996)85-5151. ¥200.* The watch tower has an indoor viewing room overlooking the feeding fields so you can keep warm while you see the birds. The only drawback is it keeps bankers hours, 9am to 5pm, which aren't the best time for bird watching. The roof is available for crane watching 24 hours a day, but make sure you dress warmly. Remember your flashlight; it gets dark by 4:30pm in December and January.

Crane Park, which is not the feeding site, contains the **Museum of the Crane** (Tsuru Hakubutsukan), a modernistic tribute to the bird. All the descriptions are in Japanese, which limits its appeal to foreigners, but a domed theater shows a film on cranes. *Open 9am to 5pm. Closed Monday April through October. ¥300. Tel. (0996)63-8915.*

KAGOSHIMA

Kagoshima has one of the most spectacular settings of any city in the world. Across the bay is the smoking silhouette of **Sakurajima**, an active volcano. Actually Sakurajima is both a blessing and a curse. Depending upon how the wind blows, it gives Kagoshima-ites beautiful views or blankets them in thick volcanic fog. And, unfortunately, the city hasn't even tried to match its awesome natural surroundings; the haphazard postwar development gives little consideration to aesthetics.

Then why would you go? Kagoshima's close association with the **Ryukyu Islands** makes the area different from other parts of Japan. The Ryukyu Islands, now Japan's southernmost Okinawa Prefecture, were once an independent country. In the Edo era they became a tributary of Satsuma (the name of the old feudal domain of today's Kagoshima). Okinawa had close contact with China and Southeast Asia and brought aspects of these cultures to Kagoshima.

The uniqueness is seen in craft traditions like silk brocade and Satsuma ceramics; in the popularity of *shochu*, a liquor made from sweet potatoes; and in a cuisine that uses a lot of pork and sweet potatoes. Rice doesn't grow well in the volcanic soil of Kagoshima.

Iso Teien, the feudal lord Shimazu's garden and villa on the sea overlooking Mt. Sakurajima, ranks among Japan's finest. **Chiran**, about an hour from Kagoshima, features well-preserved samurai quarters with excellent gardens.

Where there are volcanoes, there are hot springs; the Kagoshima area has lots of them. The most famous is **Ibusuki** where you can indulge yourself in a sand bath. Kagoshima is also the jumping-off point to see the island of **Yakushima**, a UNESCO World Heritage Site, famous for its giant ancient cedar trees and wildlife.

So, there's more than enough to keep you happily occupied for at least several days. But when you arrive at Kagoshima, don't say we didn't warn you — the city is ugly. Remember to look beyond it for some gems.

Planning Your Stay

Spend one full day in Kagoshima, more if you are into local crafts or want to spend time hiking around Mt. Sakurajima. Our favored itinerary is to begin at Iso Garden and also see the Shoko Shuseikan next door and Ijinkan down the road. If you are interested in ceramics, stop at Tanoura-gama Kiln and then go over to the central part of the city to see the Reimeikan. Volcano lovers should spend a half-day at Mt. Sakurajima.

ARRIVALS & DEPARTURES

By Air

Kagoshima Airport is located north of the city.

To/from Tokyo Haneda: 10 flights/day (ANA, JAL, JAS. ¥28,600).

To/from Nagoya: 5 flights/day (ANA, JAL. ¥23,300).

To/from Osaka Itami: 9 flights/day; **Kansai**: 3 flights/day (ANA, JAL, JAS. ¥19,650).

Also flights to/from Beppu, Fukuoka, Hiroshima, Komatsu, Matsuyama, Nagasaki, Okayama, Okinawa, Sapporo, Sendai and Takamatsu.

For Ground Transportation:

Bus: to Nishi Kagoshima Station. 60 minutes, ¥1200.

Taxi: 50 minutes to Nishi Kagoshima Station, about ¥11,200.

By Train

JR Nishi Kagoshima Station is the city's main station, but note that there is also a Kagoshima Station.

To/from Kumamoto: JR limited express *Tsubame* on the Kagoshima Honsen line takes 2 hours 45 minutes, ¥5550.

To/from Hakata (Fukuoka) 3 hours 50 minutes on the JR *Tsubame* limited express train, ¥8070.

To/from Miyazaki: 2 hours on the JR Nippo Line *Kirishima* limited express, ¥4090.

By Bus

Kagoshima is connected with other Kyushu cities by a series of express buses to Miyazaki (10 buses/day, 2 hours 40 minutes, ¥2700), Kumamoto (10 buses/day, 3 1/2 hours, ¥3600), Fukuoka (16 buses/day, 4 hours, ¥5300).

Overnight bus service is available from Osaka (11 1/2 hours, ¥12,000).

By Car

Kagoshima is the southernmost exit of the Kyushu Expressway which runs north through Fukuoka and on to Honshu Island. The expressway connects with the Miyazaki Expressway for easy access to Kyushu's eastern coast.

GETTING AROUND TOWN

JR Nishi Kagoshima Station is a new, postmodern structure with a red triangularly shaped entrance with bright aluminum steps leading up to the second floor entrance. The rear of the building is bright blue, a pleasing piece of contemporary architecture but compared to the dingy buildings surrounding it, you would think it came from Mars.

Streetcars, buses and the airport limo bus leave from outside the front of the station. The station has many individual shops that sell local specialties and offer lots of samples. If you don't fill yourself up on samples, there is a mini food mall on the second floor, and Kentucky Fried Chicken (KFC) on the first. The bus station is across the large plaza.

Kagoshima has a castle town layout, which means the streets are not parallel and are quite difficult to navigate. Streetcars offer the best access because they do not get stuck in traffic. Streetcars cost ¥160 and a ¥500 **one-day pass** (ichi nichi joshaken) is sold at the tourist offices. The Kagoshima City View is a bus that looks like a trolley that covers the main tourist sites. Fare is ¥170 or ¥600 for a one-day unlimited pass and operates every 30 minutes between 9:30am and 5pm.

Tourist Information

The **Tourist Information Office** is at Nishi Kagoshima Station to the left as you exit. *Tel. (099)253-2500.* Open 8:30am to 6pm. There's another one at Kagoshima Station, *Tel. (099)222-2500,* and a third is on the 3rd floor of the Kagoshima-ken Sangyo Kaikan Building, 9-1 Meizan-cho, *Tel. (099)223-5771.*

The Nishi Kagoshima Station Office and the Kagoshima-ken Sangyo Kaikan office have English-speaking staff.

Goodwill Guides: Contact the International Desk Foreign Language Institute, *Tel. (099)224-3451,* or the Tourist Information Office to arrange a volunteer guide.

City Tours

Japanese language bus tours operate daily leaving Nishi Kagoshima Station at 9:05am and 1:45pm. Cost is ¥2500 for the 3 1/2 hour tour. We recommend that you skip the tour; strike out on your own.

WHERE TO STAY

SHIGETOMI-SO, *31-7 Shimazu-machi, Kagoshima, 890-0802. Tel. (099)247-3155, Fax (099)247-0960. From ¥25,000 per person with two meals. Credit cards.*

This lovely old mansion was formerly the villa of Lord Shimazu. It has a spectacular view overlooking the bay and Sakurajima. The spacious garden is picture perfect: the lawn, stone lantern and palm trees give a tropical feeling. Azaleas flank the waterfalls and streams. The building itself is a one-storied wooden structure in "geese flying style," i.e., the rooms are staggered in a "V" formation so each one has a view, but still maintains privacy. Shigetomi-so serves mouthwatering Satsuma dishes such as *sakezushi*, *tonkotsu*, Satsuma style soup and deep fried vegetables. There are only 20 guest rooms, so personal attention is assured.

KAGOSHIMA HAYASHIDA HOTEL, *12-22 Higasahi Sengoku, Kagoshima, 892-0842. Tel. (099)224-4111, Fax (099)224-4553. Singles from ¥8000. Doubles from ¥11,000. Credit cards.*

A very conveniently located Western-style hotel in the center of town, Hayashida has an atrium from the 3rd to 8th floor. It is located across from Takashimaya Plaza.

HOTEL NEW CENTRAL, *12-16 Yamanokuchi-machi, Kagoshima, 892-0844. Tel. (099) 224-5551, Fax (099)26-5610. Singles from ¥6200. Twins from ¥9500. Credit cards.*

As its name implies, the hotel is located centrally in the shopping area of Tenmonkan Tensha Dori, convenient for business as well as for touring. It's a 7-minute taxi ride from Nishi Kagoshima Station.

HOTEL MIKASA, *5-12 Higashi Sengoku-cho, Kagoshima, 892-0842. Tel. (099)225-5111, Fax (099)225-5112. Singles from ¥5000. Twins from ¥8000. Credit cards. Member of the Welcome Inn Reservation Center.*

Located at the gate of Terukuni Shrine. This no-frills hotel is convenient for business and entertainment.

FURUSATO KANKO HOTEL, *1076-1 Furusato-machi, Kagoshima, 891-1592. Tel. (099)221-3111. Closed Thursday. From ¥13,000 per person with two meals. No credit cards.*

Furusato is on Sakurajima, across the bay from Kagoshima, and features an outdoor hot spring bath overlooking the bay. Next to the bath is a tree believed to be inhabited by the dragon god. To avoid provoking the god, when using the outdoor bath, patrons must don white *yukata* (robes) provided by the hotel. The rooms are Japanese style. This hotel, in the shadow of the volcano, is a respite from the city. The bath is open to the public from 8am to 8pm; 3pm to 8pm Monday. ¥500 plus ¥200 *yukata* (white robe) charge.

WHERE TO EAT

KUMA SO TEI *(Regional Japanese, moderate). 6-10 Higashi Sengoku-cho, in the Tenmonkan arcade. Tel. (099)222-6356. Open daily 11am to 2:30pm; 5pm to 10pm.*

Authentic Satsuma-style cooking features *sakezushi*, *kibinago sashimi*, *Satsuma age* and *tonkotsu*. Dinner courses start at ¥4000.

SATSUMA *(Regional Japanese, inexpensive to moderate). 27-30 Chuo-machi. Tel. (099)252-2661. Open 11am to 3pm; 5pm to 11pm. Closed Monday.*

The restaurant's big red paper lantern out front makes it easy to spot. The specialty is *tonkotsu* cooked in their brown sugar, *miso* and *shochu* sauce. Satsuma prides itself on having kept the same pot of sauce going for over 20 years. Prices begin at ¥700.

WHAT'S COOKING IN KAGOSHIMA?

Sakezushi: fish, seafood and vegetables are marinated in vinegar and sake, then mixed with sushi rice.

Kibinago: small fish available in the Kagoshima region eaten as tempura, sashimi or marinated in vinegar.

Tonkotsu: not to be confused with tonkatsu (deep fried pork cutlets). Satsuma's specialty is pork slowly stewed with shochu and bean paste for at least for three hours and served with vegetables cooked in the same broth. The meat is so soft you can cut it with a spoon.

Satsuma age: brown patties found in nearly every food shop in Kagoshima. The meat of white fish is ground, formed into a patty and deep fried until golden brown. Sometimes minced mushrooms, carrots, burdock root, yams and other vegetables are added. Satsuma age is best eaten piping hot.

Satsuma jiru: a soup made with bean paste but differs from the normal miso soup because it contains pork and mountain potatoes.

Karukan: one of Kagoshima's many sweets made from sweet potatoes. Attention calorie counters: it contains no butter or fat. Don't ask about sugar.

GONBE-E *(Japanese, inexpensive to moderate). 8-12 Higashi Sengoku-machi. Tel. (099)222-3867. Open 5pm to 11pm. Closed Sunday.*

Gonbe-e is a cozy restaurant with a wooden folk art decor; the matron of the shop is very friendly. Tofu is the main menu item and Gonbe's is homemade, as is its *yuzu*-flavored dipping sauce. *Yu-dofu*, tofu cooked in front of you, costs ¥1500.

KUROBUTA *(Tonkatsu, inexpensive). 6-17 Higashi Sengoku-cho. Tel. (099)224-8729. Open from 11:30am to 2:30pm; 5:30pm to 9:30pm. Closed Monday. 5-minute walk from Tenmonkan Dori streetcar stop.*

Kurobuta serves *tonkatsu* (deep-fried pork cutlet). Only Kagoshima pork, prized by gourmets, is used. The crust is crispy and the meat inside is tender and juicy. *Tonkatsu* is always served with shredded cabbage; at Kurobuta the cabbage is especially delicious because it's shredded with *shiso* (a tasty mint). Fillet cutlet costs ¥1300. At lunch you can eat unlimited quantities of rice and cabbage.

SHOCHU TENGOKU *(Drinking establishment, inexpensive). 1F, Edo Yoshi Building, 9-33 Yamanokuchi-machi. Tel. (099)224-9750.*

Shochu Tengoku means Shochu Heaven and is aptly named. The walls of this bar are lined with bottles of 150 different kinds of *shochu* collected from all over Kyushu. A cup costs ¥100 and up. They also serve delicious side dishes that go with drinking *shochu*.

SHOCHU

Shochu, a strong liquor made from sweet potatoes, is more than just the preferred drink in Kagoshima, it is a way of life. When Kagoshima residents say sake (rice wine in the rest of Japan), they mean shochu. The drink is used to mark important occasions like weddings and New Year's. Kagoshima is not a rice producing center; it is the only Japanese prefecture that does not have a sake brewery. But it makes up with shochu: 127 distilleries make over 900 brands of shochu.

No one knows for sure how shochu made its way to Japan. Most likely, it came through Okinawa, which paid tribute to Kagoshima in the Edo period, but it could have come through Korea or China. Sweet potatoes grow extremely well in Kagoshima soil. It is usually served mixed with hot water or on the rocks. Shochu has become a popular drink for young people all over Japan because it's much cheaper than other alcoholic drinks because of low taxes. But that is about to change. Bowing to pressure from the World Trade Organization, Japan has agreed to bring its liquor taxes in line. Currently the tax for a liter of shochu is ¥102, while whiskey's is ¥982.

SEEING THE SIGHTS

Iso Garden Area

Iso Garden (Iso Teien). *Tel. (099)247-1551. Open 8:30am to 5:30pm; until 5pm November through March. Combined admission with Shoko Shuseikan ¥1000.* The garden is a highlight of Kagoshima. The feudal lord of Satsuma constructed the residence and garden in 1659-61 as a detached villa. The vast strolling garden overlooks the bay and Sakurajima. The current one-storied residence, built in 1884, became the abode of the Shimazu family after the feudal period ended. You'll note it's fairly austere, which was considered appropriate for a warrior. You pay an additional charge of ¥400 to tour the residence, but it's worth it.

Since Kagoshima's climate is quite mild, the garden has a tropical air. It goes up and down hills and has different areas such as a bamboo garden, a plum garden and heavily wooded areas. A gazebo-like structure with Chinese-style tiles was a gift from Okinawa. Tasteful buildings in harmony with the environment house stores and restaurants scattered throughout the garden. Unfortunately, the noise of truck traffic from a busy road nearby somewhat mars the serenity of the garden.

Shoko Shuseikan. *Next to Iso Garden; combined admission with Iso Garden ¥1000.* A machinery factory built by Lord Shimazu in 1865, it's now a museum housing belongings of the Shimazu family as well as products once manufactured there.

Ijinkan. *Tel. (099)237-3401. 9am to 5pm. Closed Wednesday and December 29 through January 4. Admission free.* A short walk from Iso Garden. A late 19th century Western-style house, Ijinkan was the residence of the British invited by Lord Shimazu to come to Japan to build the country's first spinning mill.

At the foot of Togo Hill, as you head back from Iso Garden, is **Tanoura-kiln**. *Tel. (099)248-0795.* The oldest Satsuma ceramics kiln still operating in Kagoshima, Tanoura makes white Satsuma, the ivory colored, crackle pottery decorated with colorful painting. You can watch the clay being thrown.

KAGOSHIMA HISTORY

*Historically, Shimazu clan ruled the area around Kagoshima, called **Satsuma**, from the late 1200s until 1868. During the Edo period, Satsuma enjoyed more independence than most domains because of the great distance from the capital, Edo. A unique system of protection developed: instead of relying on one large castle, the samurai were disbursed to 120 areas of Satsuma. To the Shimazu lords, the warriors were their walls. The main castle in Kagoshima was small and not heavily fortified by large walls or deep moats. It served more as an administrative and residential center than a military stronghold. It never even had a keep. With this strategy, there were more samurai than in most domains; feeding them was a burden, so the Satsuma domain was always in a precarious financial state.*

Satsuma's geographic position, at the southern part of Kyushu, led Satsuma to look outward. The Shimazu ruled Okinawa from 1608 until 1879 (and taxed it heavily). St. Francis Xavier landed at Kagoshima in 1549 and the Shimazu lord allowed him to proselytize during the year he spent in Japan. This wasn't out of altruism: the Portuguese had guns so the Satsuma lords were interested in trade.

Satsuma was one of the areas that led the revolt resulting in the Meiji Restoration in 1868, toppling nearly 300 years of Tokugawa control and ushering Japan into the modern era. Their relationship with Europe (in the modern era) began in 1854 when British ships bombarded Kagoshima in retaliation for refusing to pay compensation for the death of a British citizen in Yokohama. Realizing the British had far superior weapons, Kagoshima quickly capitulated and then enlisted British assistance in building up the Satsuma navy, which later became the basis for the national navy, and helping with industrialization. Although the shogun prohibited Japanese from traveling overseas, Shimazu secretly sent several young men to study in England.

Central Area

Tsurumaru Castle stood in a district now called a culture zone, which is the location of Reimeikan and the Kagoshima City Museum of Art. All that remains of the castle are some stone walls and a small moat. Tsurumaru Castle was unusual; most feudal lords built forbidding fortresses on hills, but the Shimazu clan believed that their people were their best protection and clustered the samurai in over one hundred areas around the domain. The modest central castle, located on the flatlands, never had a keep.

Reimeikan. *Tel. (099)222-5100. Open 9am to 5pm. Closed Monday, the 25th of each month and December 28 through January 4. ¥300.* Built on the site of the castle, the museum displays the history of the area from samurai times through Kagoshima's role in the Meiji Restoration and the Seinan War. It's a good place to get an overview of the area's history.

Kagoshima Municipal Art Museum (Kagoshima-shiritsu Bijutsukan). *Tel. (099)224-3400. Open 9am to 5pm. Closed Monday and December 29 through January 3. ¥200.* The museum houses works by artists born in Kagoshima, an extensive collection of Satsuma ceramics and works by modern Western artists.

St. Francis Xavier Church and Memorial are about a 10-minute walk from the museum area. The church was built in 1949 to mark the 400th anniversary of Xavier's landing.

Museum of Meiji Restoration. *Tel. (099)239-7700. Open daily 9am to 5pm. ¥300.* This new, high-tech museum devotes itself to Kagoshima's role in the Meiji Restoration. It's of interest only to the real diehard Japanese history buffs.

Kagoshima Outskirts

Oshima Tsumugi no Sato. *Tel. (099)268-0331. Streetcar to Taniyama. Open daily 9am to 5pm. ¥412.* This silk is woven in the Oshima Islands, an 11-hour boat ride from Kagoshima. Stop in to watch the intricate dyeing and weaving processes in an attractive setting. Their *tsumugi* (handmade woven silk) kimono sell starting at a reasonable price — ¥350,000; reasonable, that is for an Oshima *tsumugi* kimono. Why not buy several? Ties and change purses are affordable starting at ¥5500 and ¥1500 respectively.

Honbu Shochu Brewery. *Tel. (099)68-1431. Open daily 9am to 4:30pm. Closed January 1. Near Oshima Tsumugi no Sato.* Stop in here to tour the facility and to see how *shochu* is manufactured.

Sakurajima

Locals call **Sakurajima**, literally cherry island, the island of fire. Smoke pours from it on a daily basis — an awesome sight. Having erupted

KASEDA'S SAND-CRAFT FESTIVAL

A small city of 25,000 on the Satsuma Peninsula facing the East China Sea, **Kaseda** *comes alive for a few days in July for its annual* **sand-craft** *festival. Located on Fukiage-hama Beach (47 kilometers in length), Kaseda discovered its sand is perfect for sculpting. As a way to revive a dying city that had lost 70 percent of its population to the large cities, the festival began in 1987. It attracts over 200,000 visitors to see some 40 gigantic sculptures crafted by international teams. The festival is held for five days in late July.*

Telephone the Kagoshima Tourist Federation at (099)223-9171 for the exact dates. Take a JR train to Ijuin Station (12 minutes from Nishi Kagoshima Station) where you catch a bus to Kaseda (8 buses/day, 1 hour, ¥800).

30 times since 708, most recently in 1946, it's unlikely that Sakurajima is ready to call it quits yet. In 1914 an eruption of this active volcano poured lava into the small strait behind the mountain and connected it to the peninsula. Board a ferry at Sakurajima Pier, several minutes walk from Kagoshima Station and a 15-minute bus ride from Nishi Kagoshima, the main station. Frequent ferries take 15 minutes and cost ¥150.

On the island, a bus ride away from the Sakurajima ferry pier, lies the **Arimura Lava Observatory**. Go for great views of the volcano and the bay. Enjoy a walk along a lava path (more than a kilometer long) that stands as a tangible reminder of the power of the earth.

Kurokami Buried Torii Gate was a stone gate to a Shinto shrine that was buried in the 1914 eruption. Only the curved lintel of the gate remains visible.

SHOPPING

Two morning markets, one near Nishi Kagoshima Station and one near Kagoshima Station, are good places to witness everyday life. The markets sell primarily local produce and seafood and are open from early morning until noon.

Tenmonkan, the downtown shopping area is home to Mitsukoshi, Yamagataya and Takashimaya Department Stores as well as shopping arcades with loads of small shops.

Prefectural products are on sale on the 3rd floor of **Sangyo Kaikan**, 9-1 Meizan-cho.

SATSUMA CERAMICS

In 1598, Lord Shimazu brought several craftsmen from Korea and ordered them to start producing ceramic ware. White Satsuma and black Satsuma ware are the result. White, a connoisseur ware made for the upper class, features an ivory-colored crackle surface with designs painted in gold and bright colors. Artisans specialize in either making the pots or painting, but don't do both.

In the late 1800s, white Satsuma became popular with Westerners – huge quantities were exported, so you may find some pieces in your grandmother's attic. If you buy white Satsuma tea cups, be sure to soak them in water before using or the tea will discolor the fragile, crackle surface – it isn't intended for everyday use.

Black Satsuma, glazed with dark colors and unpainted, is more of a folk craft and is suitable for daily use. Kagoshima's department stores have good selections of both white and black Satsuma.

Fun items are shochu servers, which look like squashed tea pots, conical cups and cups with a hole in the side. Since drinkers of shochu are too busy imbibing to put down their cups, there is no reason to have a flat bottom.

EXCURSIONS & DAY TRIPS
CHIRAN

Located on the Satsuma Peninsula between Kagoshima and Ibusuki, **Chiran** was one of the 120 samurai districts the Satsuma feudal lord established to protect Satsuma. The Tokugawa shogunate prohibited more than one castle in a domain. Satsuma's way of defense was to disperse the samurai to local centers. They could then defend the main castle if attacked.

It takes the better part of one day to make a side trip from Kagoshima to Chiran. Chiran is a convenient stop en route to Ibusuki if you are traveling by car. Spend about an hour or so in the gardens and then go to the Peace Museum a short distance away.

Getting to Chiran

Buses depart from Kagoshima's **Yamakataya Bus Center**. It's one hour from Kagoshima.

By car, take the Ibusuki Skyline to Chiran interchange; it's a 15-minute drive from the interchange. One hour from Kagoshima.

Note: there's no train service to Chiran.

Where to Eat

TAKIAN (*Regional Japanese, inexpensive*). *Tel. (0993)83-3186. Located in the center of the samurai district. Open daily 10:30am to 4pm.* Set in a samurai house, Takian is a restaurant serving local specialties. You sit on *tatami* mats and overlook the wonderful garden. Try the *sakezushi teishoku* set for ¥1200 or the Takian set for ¥2000.

Seeing the Sights

Samurai Houses and Gardens. Chiran contains some well-preserved samurai houses with gardens reflecting the taste of their owners. To confuse would-be attackers, the district has attractive twisting, narrow streets with low stone walls topped by hedges. The retainers at Chiran had opportunities to travel to Edo (Tokyo) and Kyoto with their feudal lord and saw the gardens in these two centers. They then set about creating their own gardens.

The resulting gardens are quite small and most use a lot of rocks, a fashion among the warrior class. Seven gardens are open to the public including **Hirayama**, a hedge-style garden, unusual because it doesn't use rocks; **Sata Garden**, a dry landscape-style using mountains as borrowed scenery and stone walls for defense; and **Morishige Garden**, the only strolling garden and the only one with a pond. Sit here and enjoy the complimentary tea. A pass admitting you to all the gardens costs ¥310.

Peace Museum for Kamikaze Pilots (Tokko Heiwa Kaikan). *Tel. (0993)83-2525. Open daily 9am to 4:30pm. ¥500.* At the top of a hill, a few kilometers from the samurai houses, is the site of the training grounds for the Imperial Air Force. For a few months in 1945 during the waning days of World War II, an increasingly desperate Japan launched young *kamikaze* pilots on their one-way trips. Their small planes, filled to the brim with explosives, carried little fuel.

Today, cherry trees abound on the crest of the hill. Cherry trees have always been a favorite of the Japanese military. The brief glorious blossoming of the trees recalls the brief lives of the pilots, snuffing out so prematurely. The Peace Park is dedicated to the memory of the 1026 *kamikaze* pilots who flew from Chiran.

IBUSUKI

About one hour south of Kagoshima lies **Ibusuki**, a popular spa and resort town on the sea that's particularly well known for its hot sand baths. Ibusuki's mild, almost semitropical climate features temperatures averaging 18.3°C (about 65°F). Many palm trees add to the tropical feel, and you can swim in the sea from May. There are 804 sources of hot spring water — the city is sitting on one great big pot of boiling water.

Ibusuki has a slightly rundown feel as if the better times have passed. And they probably have. These days Japanese tourists, especially honeymooners, often choose Hawaii or Australia over Japanese resorts like Ibusuki.

Not only a hot spring center, Ibusuki has lots of kilns with artisans making mostly black Satsuma ware because the local clay has a high iron content.

Planning Your Stay

Allow yourself one full day in Ibusuki to experience a hot spring bath, wander through the kilns and enjoy the seaside ambiance.

ARRIVALS & DEPARTURES

By Train

From Nishi Kagoshima Station: Frequent train service on the JR Ibusuki Makurazaki Line; 50 minutes by *kaisoku* express; 1 hour 20 minutes by local train, ¥970.

By Bus

To/from from Kagoshima Airport: Express bus (11 buses/day, 1 hour 50 minutes, ¥2300).

To/from Kagoshima Bus Center and Nishi Kagoshima Station: (8 buses/day, 1 hour 40 minutes, ¥850).

By Car

For magnificent views of the mountains and sea, take the **Ibusuki Toll Road**. High on a ridge in the center of the Satsuma Peninsula, you'll see some of the best scenery in Japan. On one side are unobstructed views of Sakurajima volcano while on the other side is Mt. Kaimon, an extinct volcano with an almost perfect conical shape. The trip from Kagoshima takes a little over an hour and tolls total ¥930. The alternative is Route 226 along the coastline; but near Kagoshima City, the road is enmeshed in suburban sprawl and can be quite slow going.

GETTING AROUND TOWN

The city hugs the coast, is relatively compact and the streets are more or less on a grid system. The main roads parallel the sea. Since Ibusuki is flat, cycling is an excellent way to get around town. Bike rentals are available at the station and the Ibusuki Kanko Hotel.

Tourist Information

The **Ibusuki tourist office** is at the train station. *Tel. (0993)22-3252.*

WHERE TO STAY

There are lots of hotels; some are huge resort complexes like the mammoth Ibusuki Kanko Hotel. Many hotels are quite rundown.

SHUSUIEN, *5-27-27 Yunohama, Ibusuki. Kagoshima, 891-0406. Tel. (0993)23-4141, Fax (0993)24-4992. From ¥25,000 per person with two meals. Credit cards.*

This is our hands down choice in Ibusuki. In some pricey Japanese inns, you're never quite sure why it costs so much. This isn't true in Shusuien. The number of staff is overwhelming: several valets to park cars; ten women lined up at the entrance, bowing to welcome you and whisking out slippers and *geta*; desk staff; and more. The hotel has only 45 rooms and, as we would hope, offers exceptional service. There is a lovely garden off the lobby. They offer a *shabu-shabu* dinner if you don't want their *kaiseki*, but *kaiseki* is so good, with lots of regional dishes. The only drawback is the high-rise Ginsho Hotel across the street partially obstructs Shusuien's view of the sea.

HOTEL GINSHO, *5-26-29 Yunohama, Ibusuki, Kagoshima, 891-0406. Tel. (0993)22-3231, Fax (0993)22-2219. From ¥18,000 per person with two meals. Credit cards.*

Located right on the sea, Hotel Ginsho's rooms have great sea views. The outside of the high-rise building looks very Western, but the interior is pure Japanese, down to *tatami* mats in the foyer.

HAKU-SUIKAN, *Chirin no sato, Higashi Kata, Ibusuki, Kagoshima, 891-0404. Tel. (0993)22-3131, Fax (0993)23-3860. From ¥19,000 per person with two meals. Credit cards.*

Haku-Suikan is a combination of Western-style hotel and Japanese inn, located in the midst of pine groves. The large modern inn, located on the sea, features a beautiful garden with lots of flowers. The resort-type establishment has an outdoor pool for swimming in summer and a beer garden.

KYUKA MURA IBUSUKI, *(National Vacation Village Ibusuki). Higashi Kata, Shiomi-cho, Ibusuki, Kagoshima, 891-0491. Tel. (0993)22-3211. Fax (0993)22-3213. From ¥7200 per person with two meals. Credit cards.*

The waterfront vacation village offers modest but comfortable accommodations at a reasonable rate. It could use a facelift but has tennis courts and bike rentals in addition to hot springs. The staff is very friendly.

WHERE TO EAT

TOSENKYU (*Somen noodles, inexpensive*). *5967 Jitcho Kaimon-cho, Jumachi. Tel. (0993)32-2143. Open 8:30am to 5:30pm.*

About 30 minutes by bus from Ibusuki, it's an original and fun place to eat noodles. The spring water stays a constant 13° C year round and is the perfect temperature to cool *somen* (a very thin noodle). Each table has a basin of swirling water in the center where you put your hot noodles. Fish them out and eat with a dipping sauce. Noodles cost ¥500.

SEEING THE SIGHTS

Sand Bath Center (Sunamushi Kaikan Saraku). *Tel. (0993)23-3900. Open daily 8:30am to 9pm. ¥900 including yukata use.* Everyone must try sand bathing at the new municipal facility on Surigahama Beach (bring a small hand towel that most Japanese inns give away): Go up the escalator to the second floor, pay the fee and receive a *yukata* cotton robe, a big bath towel and locker key. Go downstairs, undress and slip on the *yukata*, put your clothes in the locker and head outside to the sand beach. Cover your head and the back of your neck with your small towel and lie down in the shallow "grave" that workers dig. They will then cover everything but your head with the warm sand. Relax and enjoy the sound of the waves and the view of the sea.

The sand isn't unbearably hot; it warms you up slowly. The weight and heat of the sand stimulate your system, increase blood circulation and are supposedly especially effective for helping back and muscle pains. Even if you don't have any pains, it's an experience not to be missed. After about 15 or 20 minutes, you'll probably have had enough and can get up, go back into the hall, shower and then indulge in a relaxing hot spring bath. Make sure you bring some pocket change so you can enjoy a cold drink from the vending machine.

COCCO Archaeological Museum (Jiyukan COCCO Hashimure). *Tel. (0993)23-5100. Open 9am to 5pm. Closed Monday. ¥500.* A new, modern structure in central Ibusuki houses artifacts from Hashimure, Kagoshima's Pompeii. The village was buried by volcanic ash from an eruption of Mt. Kaimon in 874. The museum is a friendly, hands-on place that includes life-size reconstructions of primitive houses.

Kilns. There are half a dozen kilns in Ibusuki; most produce black Satsuma. They are fairly spread out but can be easily visited by bicycle. We especially enjoyed:

Ginsho Gama, close to the Ibusuki Royal Hotel. The female potter, Arimura-san, produces attractive black Satsuma ware. *Tel. (0993)23-2752. Open 8:30am to 6pm.*

Shugetsu Kiln, near the station, produces white Satsuma. Come and watch Mr. Nishida paint delicate patterns on the ivory-colored crackle ware. *Tel. (0993)24-2427. Open 10am to 7pm.*

Chotaro Kiln has received awards for contemporary interpretations of black Satsuma. While we didn't find anything we wanted to take home, his work is unusual. *Tel. (0993)22-3927. Open 9am to 6pm. Closed Sunday afternoons.*

EXCURSIONS & DAY TRIPS

Mt. Kaimon is an almost perfectly shaped conical volcano. You can hike up or just appreciate its beauty from a distance. The mountain is about a 40-minute bus ride from Ibusuki.

For a more off-the-beaten-track alternative to Ibusuki, head to the town of **Yamagawa** about 10 kilometers south. It's the next station after Ibusuki on the Ibusuki Makurazaki line. Yamagawa has its own sand bath, and you'll find you have the beach (in some places with steam escaping) practically to yourself. Nearby **UNAGI ONSEN** has a small *minshuku*, Unagi Kohan, with an outdoor mixed bath. *Tel. (0993)34-1954. ¥8000 per person with two meals.*

YAKUSHIMA

The ancient cedar trees and unique fauna have earned **Yakushima**, an island 60 kilometers south of Kyushu, a UNESCO World Heritage Site designation. Adventurers can hike for days through rain forests and over mountainous peaks under the towering canopy of the gnarled cedar trees. The granite cliffs are popular with rock climbers. The more sedentary traveler can head to Yakusugi Land outside Ambo which boasts short hiking courses among the cedars.

Don't be deceived by Yakushima's semitropical location. The coastal areas average 20°C (about 70°F) but snow covers the interior mountains in winter and spring. At 1935 meters, **Mt. Miyanoura** is the highest peak in Kyushu.

Planning Your Stay

You need to spend at least one night on Yakushima, more if you wish to hike extensively.

ARRIVALS & DEPARTURES

By Air

To/from Kagoshima: 5 flights/day (JAC. ¥10,620).

For Ground Transportation:
Bus to Miyanoura: 20 minutes, ¥450; taxi 15 minutes, ¥2500.
Bus to Ambo: 15 minutes, ¥410; taxi 13 minutes, ¥2200.

By Ferry
From **Kagoshima**: 2 1/2 hours by hydrofoil, ¥6000. 4 hours by ferry, ¥3970 and ¥7130.
From **Ibusuki**: 1 hour 15 minutes by hydrofoil, ¥6000.

GETTING AROUND TOWN

Other than hiking, car is the most convenient way to get around the island; rentals are at Miyanoura Port and the airport.

Don't forget your umbrella; Yakushima has the highest precipitation in all of Japan: 1000 centimeters inland (only 400 centimeters on the coast).

Tourist Information
Yakushima Kanko Renraku Kai. *Tel. (09974)6-3221.*

WHERE TO STAY & EAT

Most of the facilities in Yakushima are modest; there are over 50 pensions and *minshuku*. The only hotel is Seaside Hotel Yakushima.

SEASIDE HOTEL YAKUSHIMA, *208-9 Miyanoura, Yakushima, 891-4205. Tel. (09974)2-0175. From ¥14,000 per person with two meals. Credit cards. 5-minute walk from Miyanoura Port.*

This 77-room hotel has nice views of the sea. It opened a few years ago and is the only upscale hotel on the island. Dinner is heavy on seafood, naturally. The hotel is popular with young Japanese women on vacation.

PENSION FUYO SANSO, *Tel. (09974)8-2665. ¥8500 per person with two meals. No credit cards. 45-minute drive from the airport at the southern side of the island.*

The owners moved from Osaka to enjoy the natural beauty of Yakushima island. The pension's interior uses lots of cedar so it exudes a wonderful woody scent. The rooms overlook the ocean. The proprietress is a good cook — her peanut tofu is legendary, and she serves copious quantities of food.

SEEING THE SIGHTS

Adventurers can hike for days through rain forests and over mountainous peaks among the ancient cedar trees. There are basic mountain huts along the trails.

Yakusugi Land. *Tel. (09974)6-3221. Open 9am to 5pm; until 4:30pm in December through January. ¥300. 50-minute drive from the airport.* This park, located at 1000 meters above sea level, offers access to the cedar forests for those who don't want to hike long distances. The cedar forests have been untouched for centuries and one tree, Kigensugi, is 3000 years old. Four different trails, ranging from 30 minutes to 2 1/2 hours, take you through this awesome forest where you can't help being overwhelmed by its antiquity and grandeur.

Kaicho Onsen. On the beach on the southern side of the island, these hot springs become baths only during low tide. *No admission fee. 45-minute drive from the airport.*

MIYAZAKI

Miyazaki has one of the mildest climates of the four main Japanese islands. The city roads are lined with phoenix palm trees that emphasize the tropical atmosphere. Almost completely destroyed during the war, today Miyazaki is a modern city. Once a mecca for honeymooners, Miyazaki still is one of the most popular places for newlyweds if they decide to stay in Japan. But more than half go abroad.

You have to visit **Seagaia**, a re-creation of the sea, by the sea. Japanese technology, in the form of a retractable roof, ensures perfect weather. We find Seagaia fascinating to visit as a sociological study of the vacation habits of Japanese.

Planning Your Stay

One day in Miyazaki is sufficient for most people, unless you want an extended vacation at the Seagaia resort.

ARRIVALS & DEPARTURES
By Air
To/From Tokyo Haneda: 8 flights/day (ANA, JAL, JAS. ¥27,000)
To/From Nagoya: 4 flights/day (ANA. ¥21,700)

To/From Osaka Itami: 8 flights/day; **Kansai:** 1 flight/day (ANA, JAL, JAS. ¥17,350)
Also flights to/from Fukuoka, Hiroshima, Kochi, Matsuyama, Nagasaki, Okinawa and Sapporo.

For Ground Transportation:
Bus to Miyazaki, Kotsu City Bus Center: 11 minutes, ¥250.
Bus from Airport: to JR Miyazaki Station, 12 minutes, ¥360.
Taxi: 15 minutes to JR Miyazaki Station, ¥1600.

By Train

Miyazaki is on the Nippo Honsen line running down the east coast of Kyushu to Kagoshima.

Kagoshima is 2 hours from Miyazaki by limited express.

By Bus

There are two bus terminals: Miyako City Terminal located close to Minami Miyazaki Station, and Miyazaki Eigyosho near JR Miyazaki Station. Most long distance buses stop at both.

To/from Kagoshima: 10 buses/day, 2 1/2 hours, ¥2700.

To/from Fukuoka: 14 buses/day, 4 1/2 hours, ¥6000.

To/from Kumamoto: 8 buses/day, 3 1/2 hours, ¥4500.

By Car

The Miyazaki Expressway runs east-west from Miyazaki to Ebino where it joins the north-south Kyushu Expressway.

ORIENTATION

The sites in Miyazaki are fairly spread out. The main shopping and entertainment district is around Tachibana Dori. The Seagaia resort complex is about 20 minutes away by bus or taxi.

Tourist Information

The "i" Tourist Information Office is at JR Miyazaki Station. *Tel. (0985)22-6469.* Open 9am to 7pm. Closed January 1-2.

Home Visit: Contact the Miyazaki International Foundation, *Tel. (0985)32-8457,* to arrange a visit with a Japanese family.

WHERE TO STAY

HOTEL OCEAN 45, *Seagaia, Miyazaki, 880-8545. Tel. (0985)21-1133, Fax (0985)21-1134. Singles from ¥19,000. Twins from ¥30,000. Credit cards.*

Located at the Seagaia complex, this hotel is one of the reasons why Miyazaki has once again become a tourist mecca for Japanese. The 45-storied tower dominates the area and the triangular floor plan ensures all rooms have panoramic ocean views. The hotel features seven restaurants and seven bar lounges. An atrium to the 11th floor lends a very airy and spacious atmosphere.

COTTAGES HIMUKA, *3083 Hamayama Shioji, Miyazaki, 880-8545. Tel. (0985)32-5131. Reservations: Tel. (0985)21-1113, Seagaia Group. ¥5000 per person in a room for four. Credit cards.*

If the prices of Hotel Ocean 45 put you off, try Cottages Himuka. It's the perfect choice for the budget-minded or for families. On the same spacious grounds as Seagaia and Hotel Ocean 45, these bright apartments have cooking facilities.

HOTEL MERIDIAN, *3-1-11 Tachibana Dori, Miyazaki, 880-0805. Tel. (0985)26-6666, Fax (0985)26-6111. Singles from ¥8000. Twins from ¥15,500. Credit cards.*

Located in the central part of Miyazaki city, the hotel has a business salon equipped with fax, copy machine, and word processor. The rooms are fairly spacious.

WHERE TO EAT

Miyazaki is known for producing good *shiitake* mushrooms and *kabocha* pumpkins.

SUGINOKO *(Regional Japanese, moderate to expensive). 2-1-4 Tachibana Dori. Tel. (0985)22-5798. Open 11:30am to 2pm; 4pm to 11pm. Closed Sunday.*

Suginoko specializes in Miyazaki cuisine. You can sit at tables, at the counter or in *tatami* mat rooms. *Imogara bokuto* course ¥4000; *hiuga kabocha* course ¥6000.

GYOSSANTEI *(Regional Japanese, moderate). 1-8-11 Shoko Kaikan B1, Tachibana Dori. Tel. (0985)24-7070. Open 11:30am to 1:30pm; 5pm to 9pm. Closed Sunday.*

This is a good place to try Miyazaki cuisine which is a combination of *sashimi* and Chinese dim sum. Himuka-zen is popular course and costs ¥4000. Gyossantei also serves a wide range of *shochu*.

TORI NO SATO *(Japanese, inexpensive). 4-18 Kawahara-machi. Tel. (0985)28-5550. Open 5pm to 12 midnight.*

Satsuma free-range chicken is renowned all over Japan. The full course for ¥2000 won't leave you hungry: it includes chicken *sashimi*, grilled chicken thigh and *tataki* (barely cooked chicken).

SEEING THE SIGHTS

Seagaia. *Tel. (0985)21-1177. Open 9am to 10pm; 9:30am to 9pm November through April. ¥4200. Special admission for foreigners: ¥2000. 20 minutes by bus from Miyazaki Station.* Seagaia has to be seen to be believed; you can't come to Miyazaki without stopping by. Too poor or too timid to go to Hawaii? Seagaia is the place for you. Its owners call it a theme park, but we think it is more like a complete vacation village with golf course, zoo, hotels and ocean dome: a water park with a retractable roof. Tom Watson designed the golf course. The entire complex is surrounded by groves of pine trees.

The Ocean Dome maintains the water temperature at 28°C, and the air temperature at 30°C. The retractable roof opens to let in the real sun on nice days. The pool has artificial waves and one side of the building has a re-created Bali Hai mountain, complete with eruptions. Ironically, the real sea is close by. An array of restaurants are on the second and third floors. Rent a cycle, either a regular or mountain bike, for ¥500 for two hours. Taking a cue from Club Med, you can buy a wrist band, a prepaid card, so you don't have to carry cash: ¥3000, ¥5000 and ¥10,000.

Miyazaki Jingu Shrine. *Tel. (0985)27-4004. Near from JR Miyazaki Jingu Station.* A wooden Shinto shrine, dedicated to Emperor Jimmu, goes back at least to the 9th century although the present building dates from 1907. On the grounds of the shrine is the Miyazaki Prefectural Museum, which has archaeological displays and local crafts.

Miyazaki Science Center. (Miyazaki Kagaku Gijutsukan). *Tel. (0985)23-2700. Open 9am to 4pm. Closed Monday and December 28 through January 1. Exhibitions: ¥510; ¥710 with planetarium. Near to JR Miyazaki Station.* Enter and be guided through the displays by Mr. Robot Cosmo. The center features the world's largest planetarium.

Heiwadai Koen Park. *From Miyazaki Station take Heiwadai Koen bus to and get off at the last stop.* In the northern part of this large park is a replica of a tomb decorated with Haniwa clay figures. The Miyazaki area has many of these tombs. This park also has a large peace tower of peace that almost reminds you of a Southeast Asian temple. The tower, constructed with stones from all over the world, was built in 1940; maybe it was wishful thinking.

Aya, a village 50 minutes by bus from Miyazaki Station, features contemporary Japanese crafts. More than 20 craftsmen display their works that include grass dyeing, weaving, pottery and bamboo work. It's well worth a side trip for anyone seriously interested in crafts.

SHOPPING

Miyazaki Prefectural Products Center. (Miyazaki-ken Bussan Tenjijo). *Tel. (085)22-7389. Open 8:30am to 6pm. Closed Saturday, Sunday and national holidays. 10-minute walk from JR Miyazaki Station.* Spacious halls displays products made in the prefecture including Miyazaki lacquer ware strongly influenced by Chinese and Okinawan patterns, textile weaving and *shochu* liquor.

Kami Fusen. *2-1-1 Tachibana Dori. Tel. (0985)28-1662. Open 9am to 9pm.* This wonderful little shop is stuffed with Japanese traditional hand-crafted toys made from bamboo, *washi* paper and pottery. Browse here to find inexpensive and unusual presents to bring bring home.

26. JAPANESE LANGUAGE GLOSSARY

COMMON JAPANESE TERMS

Bento: Lunch box – when ordered at a restaurant, can be an extensive meal

Daimyo: Feudal lord

Dori: Street or avenue

Futon: Thin mattress put on tatami mats

Geisha: Female entertainer

Haiku: Seventeen syllable poem

Happi: Short jacket worn at festivals

Honmaru: The central area of a castle where the keep stands

Irori: Open hearth

Jinja: Shinto shrine

Kaiseki: Formal Japanese cuisine

Kimono: Traditional Japanese garment

Koen: Public park

Mikoshi: Portable Shinto shrines used in festivals

Minshuku: Small family-run inns

Ninja: An Edo-period spy

Noren: Short curtain hung in doorways

Onsen: Hot springs

Oshibori: Wet towel offered at restaurants

Origami: Folding paper craft

Otemon: Main gate of a castle

Pachinko: Pinball-like game

Post town: Towns which served as stopping points for Edo period travelers

Rotemburo: Outdoor bath, spa

Ryokan: Japanese inn

Shiatsu massage: Traditional Japanese massage using acupressure

Shogun: Military governors who ruled Japan from late 12th century until 1868

Shogunate: The government of the shogun

Shoji: Sliding doors with translucent paper panels

Tabi: One-toed socks

Tatami: Woven rice straw mats placed on the floor in traditional Japanese rooms

Teishoku: Set meal

Tokonoma: Alcove in traditional Japanese room where art and a flower arrangement are placed

Ukiyo-e: Edo period woodblock prints

Washi: Hand-made Japanese paper

Yukata: Casual cotton kimono

COMMON JAPANESE SUFFIXES

-san: Mountain (Mt. Fuji is Fuji-san)

-san: Mr., Mrs., or Ms. (Mr. Yamada is Yamada-san)

-dera: Buddhist temple (Kiyomizu Temple is Kiyomizu-dera)

-ji: Buddhist temple (Nanzen Temple is Nanzen-ji)

-jo: Castle (Himeji Castle is Himeji-jo)

-bashi: Bridge (Nihon Bridge is Nihonbashi)

-ko: Lake (Lake Biwa is Biwako)

INDEX

THINGS CHANGE!

*If you come across any new information, drop us an email note at: Jopenroad@aol.com, or write us at: **Japan Guide**, Open Road Publishing, P.O. Box 284, Cold Spring Harbor, NY 11724.*